The Greenwood
Encyclopedia of Daily Life

6 THE MODERN WORLD

The Greenwood Encyclopedia of Daily Life

A Tour through History from Ancient Times to the Present

Joyce E. Salisbury
GENERAL EDITOR

Andrew E. Kersten
VOLUME EDITOR

GREENWOOD PRESS
Westport, Connecticut • London

Library of Congress Cataloging-in-Publication Data

The Greenwood encyclopedia of daily life : a tour through history from ancient times to the
  present / Joyce E. Salisbury, general editor.
       p. cm.
     Includes bibliographical references and index.
     Contents: v. 1. The ancient world / Gregory S. Aldrete, volume editor; v. 2. The medieval
world / Joyce E. Salisbury, volume editor; v. 3. 15th and 16th centuries / Lawrence Morris,
volume editor; v. 4. 17th and 18th centuries / Peter Seelig, volume editor; v. 5. 19th
century / Andrew E. Kersten, volume editor; v. 6. The modern world / Andrew E. Kersten,
volume editor.
     ISBN 0–313–32541–3 (set: alk. paper) — ISBN 0–313–32542–1 (v. 1: alk. paper)
— ISBN 0–313–32543–X (v. 2: alk. paper) — ISBN 0–313–32544–8 (v. 3: alk. paper)
— ISBN 0–313–32545–6 (v. 4: alk. paper) — ISBN 0–313–32546–4 (v. 5: alk. paper)
— ISBN 0–313–32547–2 (v. 6: alk. paper)
     1. Manners and customs—History—Encyclopedias. I. Salisbury, Joyce E.
  GT31.G74   2004
  390—dc21   2003054724

British Library Cataloguing in Publication Data is available.

An online version of *The Greenwood Encyclopedia of Daily Life* is available from
Greenwood Press, an imprint of Greenwood Publishing Group, Inc. at:
http://dailylife.greenwood.com (ISBN 0–313–01311–X).

Library of Congress Catalog Card Number: 2003054724
ISBN: 0–313–32541–3 (set)
       0–313–32542–1 (vol. 1)
       0–313–32543–X (vol. 2)
       0–313–32544–8 (vol. 3)
       0–313–32545–6 (vol. 4)
       0–313–32546–4 (vol. 5)
       0–313–32547–2 (vol. 6)

First published in 2004

Greenwood Press, 88 Post Road West, Westport, CT 06881
An imprint of Greenwood Publishing Group, Inc.
www.greenwood.com

Printed in the United States of America

∞™

The paper used in this book complies with the
Permanent Paper Standard issued by the National
Information Standards Organization (Z39.48–1984).

10 9 8 7 6 5 4 3 2 1

Copyright Acknowledgments

The editors and publisher gratefully acknowledge permission for use of the following material: excerpts
from *Doctor Zhivago* by Boris Pasternak, translated by Max Hayward and Manya Harari, copyright ©
1958 by William Collins Sons and Co. Ltd. Copyright 1958 by Pantheon Books Inc. Used by permission
of Pantheon Books, a division of Random House, Inc.

Every reasonable effort has been made to trace the owners of copyright materials in this book, but in
some instances this has proven impossible. The editors and publisher will be glad to receive information
leading to more complete acknowledgments in subsequent printings of the book and in the meantime
extend their apologies for any omissions.

Everyday life consists of the little things one hardly notices in time and space. . . . Through the details, a society stands revealed. The ways people eat, dress, or lodge at the different levels of that society are never a matter of indifference.

~Fernand Braudel, *The Structures of Everyday Life*
(New York: Harper and Row, 1979), 29.

CONTENTS

Contents

TOUR GUIDE: A PREFACE FOR USERS

What did people, from the most ancient times to the most recent, eat, wear, and use? What did they hope, invent, and sing? What did they love, fear, or hate? These are the kinds of questions that anyone interested in history has to ask. We spend our lives preoccupied with food, shelter, families, neighbors, work, and play. Our activities rarely make the headlines. But it is by looking at people's everyday lives that we can truly understand history and how people lived. *The Greenwood Encyclopedia of Daily Life* brings into focus the vast majority of human beings whose existence is neglected by the standard reference works. Here you will meet the anonymous men and women of the past going about their everyday tasks and in the process creating the world that we know.

Organization and Content

The Greenwood Encyclopedia of Daily Life is designed for general readers without a background in the subject. Articles are accessible, engaging, and filled with information yet short enough to be read at one sitting. Each volume provides a general historical introduction and a chronology to give background to the articles. This is a reference work for the 21st century. Rather than taking a mechanical alphabetical approach, the encyclopedia tries something rather more elegant: it arranges material thematically, cascading from broad surveys down to narrower slices of information. Users are guided through this enormous amount of information not just by running heads on every page but also by "concept compasses" that appear in the margins: these are adapted from "concept mapping," a technique borrowed from online research methods. Readers can focus on a subject in depth, study it comparatively through time or across the globe, or find it synthesized in a way that provides an overarching viewpoint that draws connections among related areas—and they can do so in any order they choose. School curricula have been organizing research materials in this fashion for some time, so this encyclopedia will fit neatly into a modern pedagogical framework. We believe that this approach breaks new ground in the structuring of reference material. Here's how it works.

Level 1. The six volumes of the encyclopedia are, naturally, arranged by time period: the ancient world, the medieval world, 15th and 16th centuries, 17th and 18th centuries, the 19th century, and the modern world.

Level 2. Within each volume, information is arranged in seven broad categories, as shown in this concept compass:

DAILY LIFE

|

DOMESTIC LIFE

ECONOMIC LIFE

INTELLECTUAL LIFE

MATERIAL LIFE

POLITICAL LIFE

RECREATIONAL LIFE

RELIGIOUS LIFE

Level 3. Each of the introductory essays is followed by shorter articles on components of the subject. For example, "Material Life" includes sections on everything from the food we eat to the clothes we wear to the homes in which we live. Once again, each category is mapped conceptually so that readers can see the full range of items that make up "Material Life" and choose which ones they want to explore at any time. Each volume has slightly different categories at this level to reflect the period under discussion. For example, "eunuchs" appear under "Domestic Life" in volume 2 because they served a central role in many cultures at that time, but they disappear in subsequent volumes as they no longer served an important role in some households. Here is one example of the arrangement of the concepts at this level (drawn from the "Domestic Life" section of volume 1):

DOMESTIC LIFE

|

FAMILY LIFE

WOMEN

MARRIAGE

CHILDREN

SEXUALITY

Level 4. These conceptual categories are further subdivided into articles focusing on a variety of representative cultures around the world. For example, here users can read about "Children" in Egypt, Greece, medieval Europe, and 16th-century Latin America. Here is an example of a concept compass representing the entry on money in Ancient India:

ECONOMIC LIFE
|
MONEY
|
Mesopotamia

Egypt

Greece

Rome

India

The articles at each level can stand alone, but they all also offer integrated information. For example, readers interested in food in ancient Rome can focus right in on that information. If curious, they can look at the next conceptual level and learn how Roman food compares with that of other cultures at the same time, or they can see how food fits into material life in general by looking at the highest conceptual level. Readers may also decide to compare ancient Roman food with menus in Italy during the Renaissance; they need only follow the same process in another volume. Readers can begin at any of the levels and follow their interests in all directions: knowledge is linked conceptually in these volumes, as it is in life. The idea is to make it easy and fun to travel through time and across cultures.

This organization offers a number of advantages. Many reference works provide disparate bits of information, leaving it to the reader to make connections among them. More advanced reference tools assume that readers already have the details and include articles only on larger conceptual issues. *The Greenwood Encyclopedia of Daily Life* assumes no previous knowledge but recognizes that readers at all stages benefit from integrated analysis. The concept-mapping organization allows users to see both the details of the trees and the overall shape of the forest. To make finding information even easier, a cumulative subject index to the entire encyclopedia appears at the end of each volume. With the help of detailed running heads, concept compasses, and an index, anyone taking this "Tour through History" will find it almost impossible to get lost.

This encyclopedia is the work of many contributors. With the help of advisory boards, specialists in daily life around the world wrote the detailed articles in the "level 4" concept category. Many of these experts have published books in Greenwood's award-winning "Daily Life through History" series, and their contributions were crafted from those books. Each volume's editor wrote all of the many higher-level conceptual articles that draw connections across the topics, thus providing a consistent voice and analysis throughout the volume.

Coverage

The chronological coverage of this encyclopedia is consistent with the traditional organization of history as it is taught: the six volumes each take on one of the standard periods. But in reality, history is messy, and any strictly chronological or-ganization has flaws. Some societies span centuries with little change, whereas others change rapidly (usually because of cross-cultural interactions). We have addressed these questions of change and continuity in two ways. Sometimes, we introduce cultures in one volume, such as the Australian Aborigines in volume 1, and then we do not mention them again until they were transformed by colonial contact in volume 4. In these entries, readers are led by cross-references to follow the story of the Australian indigenous peoples from one volume to another. At other times, cultures have experienced enough change for us to introduce many new entries. For example, volume 5, devoted to the 19th century, includes many entries on Muslim lands. But some aspects of the 19th-century Muslim world (e.g., education) had long remained largely unchanged, and in these instances readers are led by cross-references to entries in earlier volumes. This network of cross-references highlights connections and introduces users to the complexities of change and continuity that form the pattern of the social fabric.

We also depart from the chronological constraints of each volume when describing cultures that left few written records. Borrowing from anthropological methods, we sometimes (cautiously) use evidence from later periods to fill in our understanding of earlier lives. For example, colonial observers have at times informed our descrip-tion of earlier indigenous cultures in many parts of the world.

The geographic scope of this encyclopedia reflects the relatively recent recogni-tion that culture has always operated in a global context. In the Stone Age, blood-stone from Rhum, an inaccessible island off the stormy coast of Scotland, was traded throughout Europe. Domesticated plants and animals from Mesopotamia spread to Africa through Nubia in the third millennium B.C.E., and throughout the ancient world the trade between China and the Mediterranean was an essential part of life. Global history is woven throughout these volumes.

We do not attempt to document every one of the thousands of societies that have arisen throughout history and around the world. Our aim—to provide a general reference source on everyday life—has led to a careful focus on the most studied and representative cultures of each period. For example, ancient India is introduced in volume 1 and then reappears in the complexities of a global society in volumes 5 and 6. Nubia, the path from Egypt to sub-Saharan Africa, is introduced in volume 1, but the range of African cultures is addressed in depth in volume 4 and again in volume 6. Muslim cultures are introduced in volume 2 with the birth of the Prophet, reappearing in volume 3 with the invigorated society of the Turks and then again in volumes 5 and 6 with modern Muslim states. This approach draws from archae-ological methods: we are taking deep samples of cultures at various points in time. The overall picture derived from these samples offers a global perspective that is rich and comprehensive. We have covered every area of the world from Australia and the South Pacific to Viking Scandinavia, from indigenous cultures to colonial ones, from age-old Chinese civilization to the modern United States.

Another issue is that of diversity within some dizzyingly complex regions. Africa, China, Polynesia, and India, for example, all contain many cultures and peoples whose daily life is strikingly diverse. Rather than attempt exhaustiveness, we indicate the range of diversity within each entry itself. For instance, the many entries on Africa in volume 4 recognize that each society—Yoruba, Swahili, Shona, and all the others—is unique, and each entry focuses on the cultures that best represent trends in the region as a whole.

The United States is yet another complex region. It grew from its inception with a mingling of European, Native American, African, and other cultural groups. Instead of treating each individually, we combine them all within the entries on the United States. For example, as volume 4 discusses Colonial New England, it weaves a description of Native American life within the entries showing the full range of social interaction between native peoples and colonists. This organization recognizes the reality that all these groups grew together to become the United States.

Features

This work has been designed by educators, and pedagogical tools help readers get the most out of the material. In addition to the reader-friendly organization already described, we have added the following special features:

- *Concept compasses*. Each section of each volume contains a concept compass that visually details the contents of that section. Readers are immediately able to see what topics are covered and can decide which ones they want to explore.
- *Illustrations*. The illustrations drawn from primary sources are in themselves historical evidence and are not mere ornament. Each shows some aspect of daily life discussed in the text, and the captions tell what the picture illuminates and what readers can see in it.
- *Maps*. Maps give readers the necessary geographic orientation for the text. They have been chosen to reinforce the global perspective of the encyclopedia, and readers are consistently offered the view of the parts of the world under discussion.
- *Chronologies*. In addition to geography, students can quickly lose track of the chronology of events. Each volume offers a list of the major events of the periods and of the cultures covered in the volumes. These chronologies serve as a quick reference that supplements the historical introduction.
- *Snapshots*. The fascinating details of the past engage our curiosity. Each volume is scattered with boxed features that highlight such evidence of past life as a recipe, a song, a prayer, an anecdote, or a statistic. These bits of information enhance the main entries; readers can begin with the snapshot and move to more in-depth knowledge or end with the details that are often designed to bring a smile or a shocked insight.
- *Cross-references*. Traditional brief references point readers to related entries in other volumes, highlighting the changes in daily life over time. Other "See" references replace entries and show readers where to find the information they seek within the volume.
- *Primary documents*. The encyclopedia entries are written to engage readers, but nothing brings the past to life like a primary source. Each volume offers a selection of documents that illustrate the kinds of information that historians use to re-create daily life. Sources range widely, from the unforgettable description of Vikings blowing their noses in a water basin before they wash their faces in it to a ration book issued by the United States government during World War II.

- *Bibliography.* Most entries are followed by a section called "For More Information." These sections include recommended readings, as one might expect in a bibliographic attachment, but they often provide much more. For this media age, the authors recommend Web sites, films, educational videos, and other resources.
- *Index.* Even in the 21st century, a comprehensive index is essential. Concept compasses lead readers from one topic to the next, but an index draws connections among more disparate entries: for example, the history of the use of wine or cotton can be traced across many volumes and cultures. A cumulative index appears in each volume to allow fast and easy navigation.

The Greenwood Encyclopedia of Daily Life: A Tour through History from Ancient Times to the Present has been a labor of love. At the end of the day, we hope that readers will be informed and entertained. But we also hope that they will come to a renewed appreciation of an often-spoken but seldom-felt reality: at the most basic level all humans, across time and space, share concerns, pleasures, and aspirations, but the ways these are expressed are infinite in their range. The six volumes of this encyclopedia reveal both the deep similarities and the fascinating differences among people all over the world. We can participate in our global village more intelligently the more we understand each other's lives. We have also learned that people are shown at their best (and sometimes their worst) in the day-to-day activities that reveal our humanity. We hope readers enjoy taking this tour of people's lives as much as we have enjoyed presenting it.

~*Joyce E. Salisbury*

1

HISTORICAL OVERVIEW

Europe, 1910–20

In eight days, stretching from the close of July to the start of August 1914, the major powers of Europe—Austria-Hungary, Germany, Russia, France, and Great Britain—entered the conflict we know as World War I. The war's eventual scope and cost came to astonish and dramatically impact many Europeans, but few of the Continent's statesmen or informed members of its various populations were completely surprised at the outbreak of hostilities.

The conflicts among these large and powerful states had deep roots. Many tensions stemmed from the emergence of a powerful nation at the center of the Continent. The victory of the German states, led by Otto von Bismarck's Prussia, over France in the Franco-Prussian War of 1870–71 produced a united Germany. It also created lasting tension between a suddenly humbled France and its newly potent neighbor. France's humiliation was sealed by the successful German demand for strategic border regions: the entire province of Alsace and a portion of Lorraine.

Germany's quick emergence as the leading power on the Continent also cast a shadow over British interests. The Germans took a leading role in international trade and colonial questions, bedrock issues for British statesmen. Especially when Germany intruded into the British sphere of interest in South Africa—Berlin openly sided with Britain's Boer opponents before and during the Boer War of 1899–1902—relations deteriorated sharply. Above other factors, Germany's construction of a world-class navy based upon battleships put the government in Berlin at loggerheads with its counterpart in London. Such a fleet containing the most powerful vessels of the era seemed destined to meet Britain's Grand Fleet in the North Sea. The possibility that Germany might dominate the sea lanes around Britain, and thus imperil the island nation's food supply, made hostilities likely, if not actually inevitable.

The dangers caused by German ambitions were matched by intractable conflicts elsewhere. Austria-Hungary faced a hostile Russia as Ottoman Turkish power collapsed in the Balkans, creating a power vacuum that sucked in both countries. Austria-Hungary had compelling reasons to intervene here, fearing for its very existence as Balkan states like the Kingdom of Serbia grew larger at Turkey's expense. Populated by a dozen nationalities including Serbs, Austria-Hungary feared it might collapse if its Serb population and the southern territories they inhabited broke away to join the Kingdom of Serbia. A nightmare scenario in Vienna pictured other discontented ethnic groups in Austria-Hungary emboldened to break away as well.

Russia stood equally ready to intervene in Balkan affairs. The giant Slavic power in eastern Europe had assumed the role of Serbia's patron and ally. Russia desired to assert its standing as a Great Power, and contesting Austria for influence in the Balkans was the most likely way in which to do so. Russia's religious and cultural ties to the Serbs, with whom they shared a devotion to Eastern Orthodox Christianity, augmented St. Petersburg's political interest in the region. Thus, no Austrian move could take place without risking a serious Russian response.

Crises in one area of Europe threatened to spread. The alliance systems developed in the prewar decades made localized conflict unlikely. So too did informal understandings that tied the security of one country to another. Thus, Austria-Hungary had a formal treaty tying it to Germany. France and Russia were similarly linked. But the rising German threat had made Great Britain a probable—if not yet a formal—ally for France and Russia.

And specific events in the decade prior to 1914 saw the tensions become harder and harder to manage. A bumptious Germany precipitated two crises—one in 1905, a second in 1911—over France's efforts to tighten its control of Morocco. The area was generally seen to be a French sphere of influence, but the Germans hoped to obstruct French policy and thus to assert their own role in international affairs. More specifically, the Germans were trying to sever the tie between Britain and France, isolating their hostile neighbor to the west. In both cases the effort backfired. In the earlier crisis, Britain provided diplomatic backing to France in the face of German pressure. The crisis begun in 1911 was the more dangerous of the two. By dispatching a gunboat to a Moroccan port, the Germans provoked an official British pledge to stand by France even in the face of war. A humiliated Germany found itself compelled to back away.

Starting in 1907, Balkan crises threatened to bring Russia and Austria-Hungary into direct confrontation. Initiatives by Russian diplomats helped set off the two Balkan Wars of 1912–13, removing Turkey's control from all but a sliver of the Balkans. A series of international conferences worked out new borders for the states in the region. But a perilous instability persisted. The enmity of many Serbs toward Austria-Hungary was matched by the determination of a "war party" in Vienna to wipe the Kingdom of Serbia off the map.

The British and Germans made an effort to negotiate a limit to their naval arms race when Britain's Secretary of State for War, Richard Haldane, visited Berlin in 1912. Educated in Germany and fluent in the language, Haldane hoped to lessen tensions. Limiting naval construction might improve Anglo-German relations as well as lighten the crushing financial burden the naval arms race put on both countries. The mission failed, the naval race went on, and mutual suspicions deepened.

In this volatile atmosphere, a single unfortunate incident had the potential to set off a European war. The assassination of Archduke Franz Ferdinand, the heir to the throne of Austria-Hungary, at the hands of Serb nationalists on June 28, 1914, was the lighted match that set off the explosion. Austria-Hungary's ensuing determination to go to war with Serbia received German backing. Russia moved to defend Serbia. Vienna's ultimatum to the Kingdom of Serbia on July 23—an ultimatum the Austrians saw no reason to think the Serbs could accept—set off one declaration of war after another: Austria-Hungary against Serbia on July 28, Germany against Russia on August 1, Germany against France on August 3, Britain against Germany on August 4.

And what were the prospects for the war's participants who soon found themselves in deadly struggle on the western front and elsewhere? Decades of steady—often frenzied—industrial growth had equipped Germany, France, and Britain with the capability of waging war on an unprecedented scale. These countries could raise armies numbering millions of men. They could equip those men with almost limitless quantities of deadly weapons ranging from rifles and machine guns to artillery of unprecedented size and lethality. The scientists and technicians in all of these nations could be enlisted to conjure up new tools of destruction.

The war began in August 1914 with a massive German offensive on the western front. Kaiser Wilhelm's armies smashed through Belgium and northeastern France, and penetrated almost within sight of Paris. Like the commanders of Napoleon's armies in the previous century, the Germans hoped to destroy their opponent's armed forces in a single, gigantic campaign; to seize his capital; and to watch him sue for peace. They were not alone. The French also began the war with an offensive against German territory, portions of Lorraine the Germans had seized from France in 1871.

Neither plan worked. The French assault ended in bloody failure. A successful French and British counterattack halted the German advance. The rival armies raced northward to outflank the other side and to regain the initiative, but neither the Anglo-French nor the German forces could move fast enough to unhinge their enemy's defenses. By the close of 1914, the war on the western front had settled down to a confrontation between millions of soldiers, soon to be reinforced by millions more.

The conflict raged in eastern Europe as well and eventually spread to the coast of China, the islands of the Pacific, the Middle East, and Africa. Germany had to fight a sizable conflict on the eastern front against Russia. Nonetheless, all three of the principal antagonists from central and western Europe—Britain, France, and Germany—gathered the bulk of their armed strength on the western front. Initially, the war at sea also ranged far from Europe, but it soon came to focus on the waters of the North Sea and the eastern Atlantic. As the combatants took to the air, the skies over northwestern Europe saw the greatest combat in this dimension too.

By the start of 1915, French offensives to expel the Germans from territory they had taken the previous autumn gave the western front its grisly character. The pattern became ominously clear. Huge infantry assaults, prepared by as much artillery fire as the attacker could muster, hurtled against the opponent's defensive line. Artillery fire presumably weakened the enemy's defenses—in this case German defenses—but it also attracted his attention and his reserves to the point of the attack. With defensive lines consisting of trenches protected by barbed wire and held by soldiers with quick-firing rifles and machine guns, attacks failed. They produced little more than a grim list of casualties.

New weapons came into play as both sides grew impatient with the stalemate. Both sides employed poison gas starting in 1915, and the first tanks appeared on the battlefield in 1916. The airplane was transformed from a fragile reconnaissance tool to a part of a large aerial armada. Those squadrons began to contest the skies over the battlefield with an equally strong enemy air force. The Germans employed airships (zeppelins) in 1915, then bomber planes starting the next year to strike at their enemies' homelands. The Allies responded in kind.

The French experienced their greatest losses of the war in the futile infantry attacks of 1915. The year 1916 saw Germany and Britain suffer in a comparable way. The German high command under Field Marshal Erich von Falkenhayn put aside hopes for a breakthrough. In February 1916, its forces attacked the French salient (an exposed bulge in the battle line) at the historic city of Verdun. The Germans hoped to destroy France's armed forces and the nation's will to fight by inflicting intolerable losses on French forces compelled for political reasons to hold Verdun. Following eight months of combat on a titanic scale, both sides suffered comparably painful losses.

During that same year, the new British armies, formed by volunteers in the first part of the war, took the field at the Battle of the Somme in France. British leaders such as Field Marshal Douglas Haig clung to the hope that enough artillery combined with an aggressive infantry assault could penetrate the enemy lines. Victory would come, Haig assumed, when his troops plunged into the enemy rear and began an unstoppable advance into Germany. Instead, the battle began with a massacre of British infantry by German machine-gun fire unprecedented even on the western front. Continuing the attack to wear down the enemy by attrition, Haig spilled even more British blood. The Germans died in huge numbers as well, but the front remained solid.

The year 1916 saw the admirals on both sides of the North Sea abandon the caution they had shown since the war's beginning. The British waited in vain for the German High Seas Fleet to sail out of port and set the stage for a new Trafalgar, the decisive naval victory on the high seas that the British inflicted on the French navy in October 1805. The Germans were equally disappointed that the British Grand Fleet conducted its blockade of German ports from a safe distance. Skirmishing in the North Sea produced only a frustrated stalemate, with the admirals showing a healthy respect for the potential of weapons like modern minefields and submarine-launched torpedoes. The clash of the two great battle fleets at Jutland at the close of May brought heavier British than German losses. But it was a singular event, unmatched at any later point in the war, and it left command of the ocean's surface in British hands.

Desperation for both sides became even more evident in 1917. The French began an offensive against the Germans in Champagne, spurred on by the optimism of their new army commander, General Georges Nivelle. The collapse of the Nivelle offensive in the face of skilled and determined German resistance plunged much of the French army into mutiny. French forces became the first—but not the last—on the western front to see discipline and fighting spirit collapse. A new commander, General Philippe Pétain, restored order to the army, but at the cost of suspending the bloody offensives that had been the sole hope for a quick victory.

The Germans also took desperate measures in the hope of quick success. The submarine, a novel weapon used for the first time in World War I, seemed to be the tool for victory at sea. By cutting Britain's food supply, most of which was imported, the submarines of the German navy could, it was hoped, produce the national victory the army had failed to attain. The submarine assault continued in ominous fashion throughout the war, but by the close of 1917 it showed it would not succeed. Allied losses remained manageable, and the vital supply ships continued to cross the Atlantic. A variety of novel or distasteful measures—using naval convoys despite the opposition of aggressively minded naval commanders, rationing food despite the hardship it levied on much of the population—defeated the German lunge. The cost of the German effort was to bring the United States into the war. Woodrow Wilson's government had declared two years earlier that it would not tolerate an unlimited submarine war by the Germans.

Meanwhile, the British continued their hopeful offensives to break the German line and thereby to open the road to victory. A new offensive—this time around the northwestern Belgian city of Ypres—began in the dry weather of summer, and continued into the rains of fall. With the low-lying terrain transformed into a sea of mud, the British suffered some of their worst losses of the war in the Third Battle of Ypres (also known as Passchendaele)—and for negligible scraps of territory.

The final year of the war began with a massive German offensive. Hoping to defeat the French and British before large American forces could arrive, the German command team of Paul von Hindenburg and Erich Ludendorff struck a series of powerful blows from one end of the western front to the other. The Germans surged forward, crippling an entire British field army in the process. But ultimately the Allied lines held. By late summer, the morale of the German army began to crack. The huge but untrained American army ground forward in the Meuse-Argonne sector around Verdun in northeastern France, while the French and especially the British conducted sweeping offensives that drove the Germans back toward their own border.

As Allied forces approached the German frontier, German desperation produced momentous military and political consequences. Ludendorff, the key figure in the German high command, called upon the political leaders of Germany to obtain an armistice. Under the pressure of America's president, Woodrow Wilson, before the armistice the Germans moved to create a parliamentary system akin to that of Great Britain. But events outran anyone's intention. German admirals, seeking a final sea battle in the North Sea, ordered their High Seas Fleet to prepare for a final offensive, but long-abused seamen rebelled against their officers and spread the message of revolt into Germany's civilian population.

As Germany's delegation to the armistice talks traveled to meet Allied representatives at Compiègne in the first week of November, Germany plunged into revolution. Kaiser Wilhelm II reluctantly abdicated, a provisional republic was formed, and radical leaders such as Karl Liebknecht prepared to move the revolution into a more sweeping phase. They envisioned a change that would not halt at the stage of a middle-class republic; instead, it would move on into a revolutionary workers' government akin to the one Russia had accepted in November of the previous year (Heyman, 1–8).

FOR MORE INFORMATION

Bessell, R. *Germany after the First World War*. Oxford: Clarendon Press, 1993.

Brittain, V. *Testament of Youth: An Autobiographical Study of the Years, 1900–1925*. New York: Macmillan, 1933.

Coffman, E. M., *The War to End All Wars: The American Military Experience in World War I*. New York: Oxford University Press, 1968.

Heyman, N. M., *Daily Life during World War I*. Westport, Conn.: Greenwood Press, 2002.

Holocaust

The Holocaust is the name given to the period of persecution and extermination of European Jews by members of Germany's National Socialist Party. The Nazis rose to power in 1933 with the "election" of Adolf Hitler as chancellor. Hitler's hatred for Jews was no surprise to anyone who had read his book or had listened to his speeches. Once in power, the Nazis quickly moved to terrorize, disenfranchise, and destroy Germany's Jewish population. The Nazis built a system of concentration camps and forced thousands into them. After the start of World War II, Hitler embarked on what he termed the "final solution to the Jewish question." Concentration camps became extermination camps virtually overnight. Moreover, death squads were sent to the fronts, where they killed all Jews that they encountered. In one such operation in Babi Yar (a town outside Kief, Russia), 10,000 Jews were murdered by these paramilitary troops. By the end of the war, over six million European Jews had been killed.

Although the Allies knew of the Holocaust, they did little to prevent or stop it. True enough, late in the war the Roosevelt administration brought about 1,000 Jews to a relocation camp in upstate New York. And the Russians did bomb Dachau in 1945. Nevertheless, by 1941, the vast population of Jews was doomed to a terrible fate. The time to do something was the late 1930s, and very little had been done. The horrifying fate of the steamliner *St. Louis* perhaps stands as an allegory for the entire period. In 1939, the *St. Louis* left Hamburg, Germany, and steamed to Cuba, where its captain, Gustav Schroeder, expected its 950 Jewish passengers to disembark, thus escaping the encircling noose of the Nazis. However, Cuban officials refused entry to the passengers. Captain Schroeder then tried to dock at Miami, but the U.S. Coast Guard did not allow the ship into American waters. Thus the boat was forced to return to Europe. Fewer than half of the passengers survived the Holocaust. Clearly the Cubans and Americans had abandoned these Jews to an awful fate. Like nearly all the Allied powers, they had failed the basic test of humanity and stood by while the Nazis sought to destroy all Jews.

The Nazi persecution of European Jews, homosexuals, Gypsies, and others deemed "undesirable" left an indelible mark upon the history of the 20th century. It transformed international law and politics. It recast relations among religious groups in Europe and the United States. It led to a new state, Israel, and thus altered the course of international politics. And, perhaps most importantly, it led to the creation of standards of human rights, which became embodied by the United Nation's Universal Declaration of Human Rights in 1948. The Holocaust remains one of those great touchstones and watershed events that will continue to define not only the history of the 20th century but the history of humanity as well.

Latin America

The term Latin America refers to a culturally lined geographic region that stretched from North America to the southern cone of South America. Beginning in 1492, Spain began a process of conquest and colonization. The conquistadors not only pillaged and plundered but also created a system of economics and governance. These colonial governments were overthrown in the 19th century. However, the new leaders of the independent Latin American nations from Mexico to Chile did not replace colonial officials and bureaucrats with representative democracies. Rather, strongmen or caudillos ruled until the 20th century, when a series of major political upheavals and revolutions dramatically reshaped the political landscape of Latin America. Many hoped that these political events would impact daily economic and social life for those toward the bottom of the social ladder. Unfortunately, this did not happen.

The first major revolution of the period happened in Mexico. In 1910, a group of radicals rose up to oppose the dictatorship of Porfirio Díaz. The Mexican Revolution inspired many Mexicans (as well as others, including the Bolsheviks in Russia) to envision a future in which average citizens would have the same opportunities as the rich. The successes of this revolution encouraged other Latin Americans to fight for more democracy. Not all political changes were as violent. In the 1930s, as a result of the Great Depression, many new leaders took center stage in Latin American nations. Such politicians as Brazil's Getulio Vargas (1930–45) and Argentina's Juan Perón (1946–55) came to power offering promises of a better day.

Unfortunately for many Latin Americans, the democratic dreams of their politicians were left unfulfilled and in some cases became nightmares. The political system continued to function for the rich. The poor increasingly faced desperate conditions.

Regardless of whether they lived in urban or rural areas, poverty existed in exceedingly high rates. Perhaps the worst situation was faced by urban dwellers who were packed into shantytowns in hyperurbanized regions of millions. Rural farmers struggled to get ahead within a system of land tenancy where the rich held most of the arable farm plots. In these hard economic and social conditions, ideas such as compulsory education were untenable because children had to work to help support their families.

In this milieu of misery, some Latin Americans sought more radical solutions. In Cuba, the radical left finally won and took power. Fidel Castro's revolution spooked the rich not only in Latin America but in the United States as well. As a result, the United States supported politicians and political groups who opposed the radical left. This support led to many civil wars in Argentina, Chile, El Salvador, Honduras, and several other countries. It also fostered right-wing coups by Latin American military generals. Once in power, the generals waged "dirty" wars on their own people, killing thousands of young men and women without trial or due process. Eventually owing to international pressure and to the ceaseless actions of the mothers of the "disappeared," these dictatorships were brought down by the 1990s.

In the aftermath, Latin American countries struggled to maintain political legitimacy and economic stability. In Mexico, the solution was to invite foreign corporations to build large factories that paid low wages to largely uneducated and nonunionized workers. The ruin, disorder, and hardships of the 20th century had taken their toll on the daily lives of Latin American men, women, and children who continue to hope for a brighter future where opportunities exist, poverty is an exception, and food is plentiful.

India

India in the 20th century underwent a series of challenges to its prosperity, stability, and secular ideology. Despite suffering some serious setbacks, India in the late 20th century represented a state that promised to emerge as a world power in the 21st century.

India's historical roots begin about 2500 b.c.e. near the Indus River Valley. Over the next 2,000 years, the center of Indian culture, which included the Hindu religion, shifted eastward to the Gangetic plain. During the reign of Bimbisara (540–490 b.c.e.) India developed two of its most important cultural belief systems: Jainism and Buddhism. Over the subsequent centuries, India's political and cultural influence grew, as did its military might. In 325 b.c.e., Chandragupta, founder of the Mauryan Empire, repelled Greek armies led by Alexander the Great. India's golden age came in the 4th and 5th centuries c.e., when Indian art, literature, and science reached high levels. Five centuries later India was invaded by Muslims, who eventually took control. Throughout Muslim rule, Hindus struggled to maintain their culture and political power. Despite the Islamic influences, Muslims never constituted a majority of the Indian population.

Another significant influence on India's historical development was the arrival of European traders in the late 15th century. In 1498, the Portuguese sailor Vasco da Gama landed at Calicut. Soon the British, Dutch, and French followed the Portuguese. Initially, foreign trade was conducted in a few special stations at Surat, Bombay, and Calcutta. However, by the 18th century, India's ruling elite had become weakened by both invasions from Afghans and internal revolts led by Hindus, and India slowly came under the direct control of European powers. By the middle of the 18th century, England and France were fighting each other for the sole right to control India. In 1763, the British defeated the French in India (and in North America) and became the main colonial force on the subcontinent.

Supported by the British colonial administration and backed by a well-armed regular army, the British East India Company helped to exploit India's markets and agricultural resources. The British believed, of course, their rule to be benevolent. They developed India's exports, including cotton and tea; improved transportation routes; and built irrigation systems. When asked, the British also pointed out their cultural impacts, such as the spread of Christianity and educational reforms. Yet, not all Indians appreciated British colonial rule. In 1857, there were two revolts against British rule. These movements were crushed, and the British took steps to reform colonial rule. Nevertheless, Indians kept the pressure on the colonial government by forming nationalist organizations such as the Indian National Congress (1885). These groups became critical for the independence movement in the 20th century.

From 1900 to 1947, India slowly built momentum toward freeing itself from British colonial rule. The key person in the Indian independence movement was Mohandas K. Gandhi, who began to organize against the British in 1919. Not only did he tap into the long-standing resentment of colonialism, but he also drew on the discontent that had arisen from World War I. Additionally the movement was given a jump start after the Amritsar Massacre of 1919, when British troops killed hundreds of Indian nationalists. Shortly thereafter, the colonial government slowly—and nationalists said way too slowly—began to include Indians. One of the critical fights about governance concerned the increasingly large split between the Hindu and Muslim communities in India. This animosity, as well as the legacy of colonialism, greatly influenced India in the 20th century.

By the mid-1940s, the idea of a secular democratic India began to be challenged. Jawaharlal Nehru and Gandhi championed the secular idea whereas Muhammad Ali Jinnah sought a separate homeland where Muslims would be the majority. In 1942, the British government announced that it planned to establish self-rule for India following the war. In 1947, the British withdrew from the former crown jewel of their empire. They left, however, a political, economic, and social mess. Despite years of western rule, India's economic infrastructure was inadequate. Staggering overpopulation, economic underdevelopment, and a lack of social services created widespread poverty. A more serious threat related to the social and political order.

In 1947, to settle the growing tensions between Hindus and Muslims and meet Jinnah's demand for a separate Muslim state, the British helped form Muslim Pakistan out of northeastern India. However, the border between India and Pakistan, particularly as it concerned possession of the princely state of Kashmir, was not resolved. As a result, several wars were fought over Kashmir, in 1948, 1964, 1972, and 1998, and the region remains a flash point between the two countries today.

Within India itself, politics were volatile in the 20th century. Conflict among Hindus, Sikhs, and Muslims led to many massacres. Nehru, head of the Congress Party, became the first prime minister of independent India in 1947. At his death in 1964, Nehru was briefly succeeded by Lal Bahadur Shastri, who was in turn succeeded by Nehru's daughter, Indira Gandhi, in 1966. By 1975, her electoral victory had come under scrutiny; to avoid losing power, she declared an emergency that suspended the constitution and allowed for draconian social "improvement" projects to be carried out. Gandhi and Congress lost power in 1977, and the former prime minister was thereafter briefly imprisoned for alleged abuses of power while in office. Gandhi was reelected prime minister in 1980.

By the 1980s, the central government began to mix politics with communal identities. Indira Gandhi catered to the Sikh community of Punjab, eventually paying with her life for her meddling. In 1984, after ordering an attack on the Golden Temple of Amritsar in response to Sikh demands for an autonomous state, Gandhi was assassinated by Sikh extremists among her own bodyguards. Indira Gandhi's eldest son, Rajiv, succeeded her as prime minister, serving until a series of scandals brought about his electoral defeat in 1989. Rajiv Gandhi courted India's Muslims by allowing separate Islamic law to be followed instead of a uniform civil code. He also intervened in Sri Lanka's civil war, paying for this with his life. Gandhi was killed by a bomb while he was campaigning in southern India in 1991.

The 1990s saw the blossoming of communal politics in full form. To challenge the Congress Party and fill the political void, the Hindu nationalist Bharatiya Janata Party (BJP) made significant electoral gains campaigning as "protectors" of India's Hindus. On December 6, 1992, the BJP stood by as their militant underlings tore down a mosque, thus threatening the continuance of India's secular government. The late 1990s saw India continuing on a path of economic liberalization and recurring communal violence. The BJP cobbled together a coalition government, thwarted terrorist attacks, and has continued (albeit shakily) to keep India on a path to becoming both a political and economic giant in the new millennium.

Islamic World

Literally speaking, Islam is an Arabic word meaning "submission to God." Founded by the Prophet Muhammad in the 7th century, Islam is one of the most influential world religions. A majority of the people in the Middle East and significant groups in Africa, Asia, and Europe practice Islam. During the 19th century, Muslims were largely concentrated in the Middle East and Asia. During the 20th century, a majority continued to live in that area, but the Muslim communities in the United States and Europe grew significantly.

The core of the Islamic faith is the Qur'an, which contains the final revelations from Allah (Arabic for "the God") to Muhammad. Muslims believe in the five pillars of faith: *shahadah* (the affirmation that there is only one God and Muhammad is the Messenger), *salah* (the ritual of five daily prayers), *zakat* (giving alms to the poor), *sawm* (the dawn-to-sunset fast during the lunar month of Ramadan), and *hajj* (the pilgrimage to Mecca). Another important aspect to Islam is that it acknowledges its relationship to Judaism and Christianity. And it recognizes Old Testament and New Testament figures such as Adam, Noah, Abraham, Moses, and David. Although Muslims disagree with various aspects of Islam, there is enough flexibility within the religion to accommodate various ethnic traditions. This ability helps to account for Islam's success.

For Muslims in the 19th century, their world was dominated by larger geopolitical developments. European powers, particularly Portugal and Great Britain, had been pushing into the Middle East since 1498. In the 18th century, Great Britain managed to make major advances as the old Ottoman Empire began its descent, opening the way for others to take control of Turkey and other Middle Eastern areas. In 1801, British forces pushed the French out of Egypt. In 1805, Mohammed Ali, an Albanian soldier in the Ottoman army, took control of the Ottoman Empire and began to modernize it along European lines.

As European influences spread through the Middle East and northern Africa, the clash between Islam and Christianity flared up again. But in the 19th century, Muslims infused their religious battle with the Europeans with a sense of nationalism. Islam became a way of reclaiming Muslim identity in the midst of European domination. During the 20th century, this conflict between the Middle East and the West grew precipitously. Moreover, military conflict inside the region was also an aspect of daily life. Predominantly Muslim states were integrally involved in World Wars I and II. During the Cold War, several conflicts were waged, including the Iranian Revolution, the Iran-Iraq War, the Soviet-Afghanistan War, the Israeli-Palestinian wars, and the Gulf War, that had greater geopolitical significance. In the decades following the end of World War II, American and European diplomats sought to find peaceful resolutions to the conflicts in the Middle East, without much result. The region remained war-torn and highly volatile. Throughout the end of the century and into the 21st century, the Middle East existed as a powder keg waiting for a match. This was true not merely because of the battles with the West, but because of the brewing social upheavals within Muslims countries as well. Islamic states such as Afghanistan, Iran, and Saudi Arabia maintained legitimacy through social regimentation and oppression. Democracy, freedom of speech, and civil rights were not parts of Muslim daily life. Hence, although conflicts with the West and with Israel made headlines and drew the most attention, underneath, the social conditions remained ripe for transformations in daily life in terms of economics, politics, and domestic relations.

United States, 1920–39

Although historians usually concentrate on important political, diplomatic, military, and economic developments of a past era, some acknowledge that such an approach presents an incomplete picture. A few find themselves drawn to examine the unusual occurrences, the eccentricities and frivolities, the human failings, and the pain and suffering of any era. The very first history of the 1920s to appear, Frederick Lewis Allen's *Only Yesterday*, published in 1931, did exactly that, forging a picture of the 1920s as a "lost weekend" of irresponsible excess by a cast of distinctive characters that left the Great Depression in its wake. Odd events are, of course, as much aspects of the human experience as are great depressions and world wars, but neither individually nor in combination do they represent the full story.

A comprehensive history of an era must go beyond the momentous and the distinctive to include the story of the unspectacular and routine everyday lives of ordinary people. Daily life for the mass of people in a society tends to get lost in the focus on rulers, religious and business leaders, generals, and other notable or flamboyant individuals. To grasp the full reality of any era, however, an investigator of the past must attempt the difficult task of understanding the routines of daily life for the many. Not only does such an undertaking illuminate the reality of most lives, it also clarifies what makes so extraordinary the lives of the few who receive the lion's share of attention.

The decades between the two world wars of the first half of the 20th century were both an important period for an evolving American nation and a time in which it was easy for historians to lose sight of the routines of life for the majority of people. At the outset, Frederick Lewis Allen and other historians of the era were drawn to focus on a relative handful of "jazz babies," stock market plungers, religious zealots, cultural celebrities, fallible politicians, and notorious bootleggers to create an image of "the Roaring Twenties." With the economic collapse that immediately followed, historians found it equally easy to construct a picture of unrelieved desperation during the Great Depression. Both portraits were, of course, too simple and one-sided, but historical myths, once created, are hard to dispel.

Serious historians, those not content to retell old stories but committed instead to digging deeper into the many surviving records of the 1920s and 1930s, have been gradually constructing a more well-rounded picture of the interwar years.

The dramatic developments in the United States during the so-called New Era of the 1920s and the Great Depression of the 1930s, about which so much has been written, occurred in the midst of a society that carried on its affairs day by day and year by year without much notice or comment. Those daily life aspects of the times are the focus of this book. In the pages that follow, the reader will discover not only that significant innovations were taking place in the way ordinary people handled their everyday affairs, but also that change was uneven and sometimes slow to be embraced. Readers need to appreciate differences between the experience of urban and rural life, among various regions of the country, among economic groups, and among races. Above all, the reader needs to recognize that daily life was lived by individuals and that their experiences varied considerably, not always fitting neatly into the common pattern of the group of which they were a part.

An excellent way to understand clearly what common circumstances prevailed for the mass of Americans is to make use of the information gathered by the U.S. Bureau of the Census in the Fourteenth Census (1920), the Fifteenth Census (1930), and the Sixteenth Census (1940). The census data compiled each decade on a wide variety of American characteristics provide a highly reliable picture of what the American people as a whole faced at any one moment as well as a useful index of the extent to which conditions changed from time to time. The alterations in daily life were not merely observable, but also quantifiable to those on the scene. The measures of progress in turn raised tangible prospects of further advancement. Census data may not at first seem as engaging to read as colorful individual stories, but they provide a realistic measure that an isolated example, however vivid, may not fully capture. Readers should be able to use census data to obtain a firm sense of the overall reality of the United States in the 1920s and 1930s. Census statistics will enable readers to perceive a story of change from decade to decade. The information will also allow those who wish to do so to make useful comparisons between a period a full lifetime ago and the contemporary realities of American life.

The articles that concern this period attempt to stress that American daily life was carried out in communities of disparate character. People lived in a variety of circumstances in 1920. All were affected by some national developments, notably the arrival of national prohibition of alcoholic beverages and a federal declaration of women's right to vote, but factors of locality, ethnicity, and economic circumstances helped shape their lives in different ways. The variations in local condition were not erased by the changes of the next 20 years—the impact of automobiles, electricity, radio, and cinema; the evolving character of diet, fashion, health care, consumerism, courtship, family relations, education, religion, and leisure; the consequences of crime and disorder; the standardizing influences of culture; and the consequences of the economic collapse of the early 1930s. At the end of the era, Americans still lived in distinctive communities, six of which are examined in some detail. The appearance of conditions that raised the promise of a better life together with pain that beset people when those conditions were beyond reach generally characterized the United States in the 1920s and 1930s. It is important to remember, however, that the patterns of promise and pain were arranged in many different ways on the vast patchwork quilt of America. Differential experiences emerge as a central theme of this book as well as a source of fascination for anyone who tries to understand what daily life was like in the third and fourth decades of the 20th century, decades when many of the structures, practices, and problems the nation still confronts began to emerge (Kyvig, xi–xiv).

FOR MORE INFORMATION

Allen, F. L. *Only Yesterday: An Informal History of the Nineteen Twenties*. New York: Harper, 1931.

Grossman, J. R. *Land of Hope: Chicago, Black Southerners, and the Great Migration*. Chicago: University of Chicago Press, 1989.

Kyvig, D. E. *Daily Life in the United States, 1920–1939: Decades of Promise and Pain*. Westport, Conn.: Greenwood Press, 2002.

Leuchtenberg, W. E. *The Perils of Prosperity, 1914–1932*. Chicago: University of Chicago Press, 1955.

United States, 1940–59

Growing up in the 1930s and early 1940s, children not only confronted the maimed veterans of World War I begging on street corners, but they also saw a new jobless class, hawking apples or carrying suitcases of shoelaces and dishrags from door to door, desperate for even small amounts of money. Newspaper want ads for real jobs—then divided by gender—frequently disappeared altogether during the Depression. Instead, networks of church kitchens and organized soup societies emerged to help the homeless and jobless willing to wait in long lines to relieve their hunger. "Brother, Can You Spare a Dime?" was a catchy popular song many young people may have heard without understanding its economic implications. A dime in the 1930s bought a cup of coffee and a doughnut.

When President Franklin Roosevelt acknowledged in his 1937 second inaugural address that one-third of the nation were ill-housed, ill-fed, and ill-clothed, his promise to take aggressive action against the failures of the system was welcomed by most Americans eager for a "new deal" in their own lives—even if changes meant more government control. FDR's New Deal was designed to regulate money policy and generate jobs. The new administration set up a vast range of government agencies: the Works Projects Administration, the National Recovery Act, the Civilian Conservation Corps, the National Youth Administration, and writers' and artists' organizations like the Federal Theater Project that created jobs for talented citizens who could not find work. In the 1930s unskilled laborers built roads and housing projects; engineers designed new bridges and dams as well as scenic waterways like Riverwalk, the famous tourist attraction in San Antonio, Texas, and the mountain road to Sabino Canyon in Tucson, Arizona. Artists painted historic murals on post office walls and in public buildings, writers prepared useful state guidebooks, and scholars of folkways catalogued the cultural resources of rural and Native Americans with subsidies from the government. Although some complained of too much bureaucracy and of government interference in the realm of art—a topic still debated—there can be little doubt that much of the work supported at this time enabled many serious artists and writers to survive. And at the turn into the 21st century the American people continue to enjoy post office murals and make use of music archives and public facilities created by New Deal expenditures. That the United States in the early 1940s had a government concerned with both the documentation and the creation of local culture—as well as with the people whose contributions to America enriched the quality of life—remains something to be proud of. The New Deal valued dimensions of America related not just to the successes of capitalism but also to the greater range of human possibilities in American life.

As World War II pulled the economy back into action, the need to generate jobs disappeared. By then the country needed many new workers to replace the young men going off to war. Yet the fact that FDR was elected president three times, and then for a fourth term to lead the nation through the war, suggests how strong the New Deal's "approval rating" was. Most Americans welcomed the concerned roles both Franklin and his wife Eleanor played in defining what their country could be. Children reaching adolescence in the 1940s had known no other leaders. The sense of security and stability that such an American royal couple created is now hard to imagine. Even people who came to hate the Roosevelts could not deny their vitality and their commitment to their ideals.

FDR's presence was a part of daily life. What the New Deal accomplished most successfully was the restoration of faith in the power of government to help individuals—those forgotten men and women who worked hard but could not manage to support their families. No manuscript collection is more moving than the file of letters collected in Eleanor Roosevelt's archives in the Roosevelt Library at Hyde Park from needy people asking for small loans of money until they could get on their feet again. Eleanor Roosevelt acted as Franklin's eyes and ears as she traveled all over the country to help the New Deal become synonymous with concern for human dignity. The creation of Social Security, workers' compensation, and higher income taxes for the rich, along with guarantees that workers could strike for fair wages, demonstrated respect for the American worker, even if a number of political promises fell short of fulfillment. Called a "traitor to his class," FDR made his commitments the source of loyalty for many blue-collar workers. The 31 "fireside chats" he gave on the radio made him a father figure to many who thought of the Roosevelts not as politicians but as moral leaders. Although people never saw pictures of Roosevelt in a wheelchair at the time or realized just how physically helpless he was (no one talked about disabilities), everyone knew about his bravery in reentering politics after surviving polio. His overpowering smile and his sense of humor won him admirers all over the world, while his aristocratic self-assurance—enriched by Eleanor's great social awareness—proved to be exactly what the country needed to inspire a national turn from provincial isolationism to global power.

The paternalism of the New Deal made it easier for many to accept the new constraints on freedom that preparation for war demanded. Price controls and gasoline and food rationing, blackouts and air raid drills, limits on travel, censorship, and security clearances were all part of the war world that took over the New Deal in 1941. "Loose lips sink ships" declared a poster plastered in coastal towns, reminding ordinary people that everyone was involved in winning a war. Along both the East and West Coasts citizens prepared for attacks from enemy submarines or bombers. Communities set up first-aid stations, and even middle school children trained with Red Cross manuals to learn simple survival techniques. Air raid drills in schools were conducted with buddy systems so that older children became responsible for smaller ones in reaching makeshift shelters or simply hiding under designated tables. Looking back on these moments as Dr. New Deal was replaced by Dr. Win the War, those who lived through that time find it hard today to reconstruct that reality of fear. More often they cherish the orderliness of the daily tasks that made them feel useful to the country as a whole. The New Deal raised America's self-confidence.

Major problems remained in America, however. Racism remained alive even during the war years. In 1943 alone over 200 racial battles took place in more than 45 different cities. The clashes involved not just African Americans but also Hispanics. The famous zoot suit riots in Los Angeles in 1943 targeted Mexican Americans simply for wearing extreme baggy styles that were supposedly a threat to men in neat uniforms—just as long hair was considered a threat to established society during the Vietnam War.

Eleanor Roosevelt worked behind the scenes to arrange the escape of European Jews, especially children. Yet except for Secretary of the Treasury Henry Morganthau, the only Jewish member of the Cabinet, she could not get the government to support her efforts to expedite their rescue. The State Department's record in this regard is embarrassing. To America's credit as a country committed to human rights, the United States Holocaust Memorial Museum, which opened in Washington, D.C., in 1993 to educate visitors about the reality of Nazi atrocities, does not hide the reluctance of the American foreign service to allow greater numbers of refugees to come here. Although a number of distinguished artists and intellectuals were aided in their escape, including the scientists who would help build the atomic bomb, the official State Department policy toward ordinary European Jews was not hospitable. A study of the contributions to American life made by the children who did manage to get into America during the war years would be a valuable undertaking. Students too easily forget that immigrants—and their children—often represent exceptional vitality in their pursuit of the American dream.

Reluctance to put aside long-standing prejudice against Asians must also account in some degree for the humiliating experiences heaped on many worthy Japanese Americans at this time. Fear that connections in Japan might turn some Americans of Japanese ancestry into efficient spies precipitated the confiscation of many good citizens' properties and their incarceration in what amounted to American concentration camps. Such remote places as Rivers, Arizona; Heart Mountain, Wyoming; Topaz, Utah; and Manzanar, California contained small prison worlds where children still pledged allegiance to the American flag and wrote letters to family members in the armed forces fighting for the United States—even as their parents wondered about who was watering their cherry trees. That the United States would much later make monetary amends to these Japanese American families must be noted, but the humiliation of loyal Americans over a period of years cannot be measured in dollars. Of the 110,000 "persons of Japanese ancestry" incarcerated, 72,000 were U.S. citizens by birth.

The decade of the 1950s also had its ugly prejudices and fears. McCarthyism so defined the extremism of its times that the decade's achievements are too often diminished. Because women during this paradoxical decade were offered few alternative career roles outside of mothering, much pity has been heaped upon them. But World War II had helped women recognize their rights, and they continued to work outside the home in growing numbers. Although denied access to many professions and high-paying careers, the women of the 1950s did more than raise children. Too little has been written on *how* women managed to lead fulfilling lives—both as mothers and as part-time workers and volunteers—at a time when good jobs for women were scarce. Much still needs to be written on the varieties of voluntarism during this period. Social, political, and educational activities emerged not only to enhance many women's definitions of the good life, but also to improve the quality of American life for everyone.

The racism that has defined American history from the French and Indian War through the Civil War to the murders during the 1960s civil rights movement also existed in the 1950s in many forms of harassment, segregation, and job discrimination. But the 1954 *Brown* decision on school desegregation and the integration of the army brought hope for modest progress. The presence during the decade of an astounding range of black talent—tennis player Althea Gibson, baseball great Hank Aaron, singer Billie Holiday, musician Louis Armstrong, writers Ralph Ellison and Lorraine Hansberry, jurists Thurgood Marshall and Constance Baker Motley—inspired many to hope that the American dream—not of money, but of the fulfillment of the self—might actually be possible. As the GI Bill extended education and society prospered, concern for equality of opportunity fell into place as part of the definition of the good life everyone was looking for. But it would be the next decade that would focus its attention militantly on "rights" as the means to self-fulfillment.

Few politicians cared about the natural environment during the 1950s—or, worse, they continued to permit the destruction of valuable natural resources. Yet out of a world of indifference rose one of America's most important nature writers, Rachel Carson. Her writing was of such scientific clarity and literary grace that the whole world wanted to read her books. *The Sea Around Us* not only won the National Book Award in 1951 but remained on the best-seller list for 86 weeks. It was translated into 32 languages. Although her masterpiece on the effects of pesticides, *Silent Spring* (1962), brought the wrath of chemical manufacturers down upon her, it would later be declared a classic in the tradition of *Uncle Tom's Cabin* or *The Rights of Man*. The impact this book had on the 20th century's careless attitudes toward the environment was, at the time, enormous. Like Edward Steichen, Carson made an effort to communicate with all levels of humanity in every part of the world—to underline the sense of beauty and wonder essential to the definition of a good life. She used her talents and knowledge not simply for personal success in the world of men but also to make the earth a better place for everyone to live in.

In 1956 Rachel Carson published an article on the importance of the education of children, not in a journal of science but in a women's magazine. "Help Your Child to Wonder" emphasized the importance of training children's intuitive sense to recognize that we are all part of the natural world. The good life of the 1950s had to contain a complex vision of the broadest human possibilities.

Emerging from over two decades of material deprivation and international strife, the Americans of the 1950s struggled to define themselves in an entirely different world. In spite of the fear of Communism, theirs was one of the most creative decades of the century in terms of critical intelligence as well as in all the arts and literature. To see the Americans of the 1950s solely in terms of their anxieties and their consumerism, or to define them solely as conformists, diminishes the importance of their broad and complicated contributions to the search for what really matters in life (Kaledin, 3–12, 181–82).

FOR MORE INFORMATION

Kaledin, E. *Daily Life in the United States, 1940–1959: Shifting Worlds*. Westport, Conn.: Greenwood Press, 2000.

Leuchtenberg, W. E. *A Troubled Feast: American Society Since 1945*. Boston: Little Brown, 1979.

Miller, D. T., and M. Nowak. *The Fifties: The Way We Really Were*. Garden City, N.Y.: Doubleday, 1977.

United States, 1960–90

In 1960, things taken for granted in 1990 were unheard of—cable television, VCRs, and microwaves, for instance. Stereophonic sound and LP records had grown in popularity since the 1940s, but audiocassette tapes did not arrive until 1966 and compact disks until 1983.

Huge, cumbersome computers entered the business world in the early 1950s; but not until the Apple II appeared in 1977 with 16K of memory did personal computers capture attention. Used in schools, they replaced clumsy mechanical gadgets called learning machines.

Medical practices seemed advanced in 1960, but yet to come were coronary bypass procedures and organ transplants. Gone or drastically reduced were many infectious diseases, but the incidence of sexually transmitted diseases increased on a per capita basis by 50 percent. By 1990, a new and deadly disease known as AIDS afflicted nearly 200,000 persons.

In 1960, earnings of women across all occupational classes averaged less than half the earnings of men. By 1990 they had risen to above 70 percent. In three decades, the percentage of women employed outside the home increased from 31.9 to 58.4 percent.

In 1960, the middle class mused on economist John Kenneth Galbraith's provocative book *The Affluent Society,* published two years earlier. As he saw it, affluence was not a vision for the future but a reality of the present. By 1990, middle-class Americans wondered where the affluence had gone, and growing numbers of have-nots in America wondered why affluence had eluded them.

Not that change was something new. In the three preceding decades, the nation battled the Great Depression, fought and won history's greatest war, and waged a "police action" in Korea. The population grew from 123,202,624 in 1930 to 179,323,175 in 1960, a result of the "baby boom" that began in 1946.

Between 1930 and 1960, polio vaccines defeated a terrible scourge and widespread use of antibiotics put bacterial infections on the defensive. Television, room air conditioners, and automatic washers and dryers changed the way people lived. So did the arrival of jet aircraft, detergents, supermarkets, transistors, synthetic fabrics, and small imported cars. For new homeowners, something as ordinary in today's world as latex-based paint was a welcome innovation.

Although changes in the three decades before 1960–1990, and in earlier trios of decades, were notable too, something about the character of the changes in more recent times captures our attention. The positions set forth in two sharply contrasting books published in 1970 reflect the uncertainties of the times treated in this book. At one extreme was Charles Reich's naive but wildly popular *The Greening of America.* Bemoaning America's plight, Reich described with dismay the destruction of the environment, the artificiality of work and culture, and the absence of community in America. Submission to uncontrolled technology and reliance on a hypocritical "establishment" had made things worse. These forces were not evil by design, Reich said, but represented logic and science gone awry. In his view, the "counterculture," comprised largely of youth raised by "permissive" parents, would evolve naturally into a nonviolent, loving culture. "Consciousness III," as he called it, would reign in America as the corporate state and the surrounding evils crumbled and fell. Ugliness, competitiveness, and meanness would disappear from daily life. A new moral code stressing love, consideration, and the greening of the landscape would prevail. *The Greening of America* proved to be a romantic, mystical footnote on the 1960s rather than a forecast of things to come, but for a fleeting, sensational moment it captured the imagination of one segment of the population as much as it terrified another.

At the other extreme, but with far less immediate impact, political scientist Andrew Hacker raised concerns that anyone studying the decades treated in this book must take into account. In *The End of the American Era,* he contended that Americans in the coming decades would soon "no longer possess that spirit which transforms a people into a citizenry and turns a territory into a nation." We were at a point, he said, when "a preoccupation with private concerns deflects a population from public obligations" and when "the share of energy devoted to common concerns gradually diminishes."

America, Hacker continued, consisted of two classes. In the majority were "productive citizens who have attained respectable incomes and an honorable position in the social scheme of things." The minority were "superfluous people without steady employment or means of support, and looked upon with no small fear and disdain by those who have attained superior status." The majority would see their private lives get better and better, but they would never seem to have enough money for the enjoyments that enticed them. Meanwhile, the public lives of all would decline in quality as things decayed at an accelerating rate. "The list of discomforts," Hacker wrote, "is too familiar to warrant elaboration: overcrowded schools and understaffed hospitals, clogged highways leading to jammed recreation areas, growing slums producing a rising crime rate. When Americans set foot from their homes, they enter an environment that is physically dangerous, aesthetically repellent, and morally disquieting."

Although critics at the time generally dismissed Hacker's thesis as overstated, it helps define this book's purpose. Its purpose is not to treat with unwarranted pessimism the evolution of society in these decades, nor to celebrate with false optimism the promise of times to come. Rather, it tries to make sense of these years by examining changes in the daily lives of the American people and the part the people played in causing these changes.

Given the differences of age, gender, race, education, social class, economic status, and geographical location of the people it treats, every generalization in this period has self-evident exceptions. Nonetheless, it is possible to strike four broad themes. These themes will be treated in each of the four parts in this book, although not necessarily in the same sequence.

The first theme deals with the dailiness of life in such things as family relationships, making a living, spending money, attending school, staying fit and fashionable, attending to daily routines, and being a member of various communities.

The second theme concerns changing patterns and relationships in the American population. In earlier times, despite occasional testings, rising resentments, and growing restlessness, dominant groups kept others in their place and ensured their own "domestic tranquility." By the early 1960s, however, the civil rights movement assumed a new intensity. Court decisions and legislation enabled African Americans to claim rights long denied them, but they were not alone in getting "out of their place." Women, Native Americans, Hispanics, Asian Americans, members of white ethnic groups, senior citizens, students, homosexuals, persons with disabilities, and members of other groups engaged in activities designed to ensure their rights. Their struggles reflected discord in American society but also showed that discord can promote positive change.

The third theme considers changes wrought by technology in communication, transportation, medicine, food, schools, space exploration, business, and many other aspects of human concern. Technology affected livelihoods, personal routines, family life, politics, and the general shape of American society.

The fourth theme examines cultural transitions in the 1960s, 1970s, and 1980s. These resulted in a gradual displacement of the "modern" standards, temperaments, and behaviors prevailing at midcentury by new ones reflecting conditions gathered together loosely under the term postmodern. In modern times, the emphasis was on progress achieved through rational, coherent, single-minded processes. Commitment, predictability, and stability contributed to the progress that was sought and valued. In modern times, organizational structures tended to be centralized and hierarchical, and boundaries within them were clearly drawn. Government was seen as a positive force for change (Marty, xv–xix).

FOR MORE INFORMATION

Boyer, P. *Promises to Keep: The United States since World War II*. Lexington, Mass.: D.C. Heath, 1995.

Chafe, W. H. *The Unfinished Journey: America since World War II*. New York: Oxford University Press, 1995.

Marty, M. A. *Daily Life in the United States, 1960–1990: Decades of Discord*. Westport, Conn.: Greenwood Press, 1997.

Soviet Union

"Russian Empire" refers to a place and a time—the nearly two centuries from 1721, when Peter the Great was awarded the title "Emperor of All Russia" by his Senate, to the end of Emperor Nicholas II's reign in 1917. However, the process of empire building was already well advanced in Russia by the reign of Peter, though he raised the empire to the status of world power, and did not end following the abdication of Nicholas, who ushered in the cruelest chapter of its history (1914–53), a generation of wars, revolutions, famines, and political terror. One of the striking things about Soviet history is that near the end of this cataclysmic time, Russian/Soviet imperialism reached farthest, achieved its fullest power, and exhibited its greatest influence on world affairs. Dozens of formerly independent states or peoples who had suffered under the heel of the imperial government in St. Petersburg were now dominated by the Soviet government in Moscow. The lives of Soviet peoples were more or less transformed and brought into a general cultural mainstream by central planners and Party bosses. There were benefits in this arrangement, especially for those at the very bottom of the social order. However, when the empire began to crumble in the late 1980s people in the satellite countries and Soviet republics clearly showed their nonallegiance to Moscow by running for the exits.

The collapse of the USSR meant independence for six satellites controlled by Moscow since the late 1940s (Poland, Czechoslovakia, East Germany, Hungary, Romania, and Bulgaria) and independence for the 15 Soviet republics. These republics, which together made up the USSR, were as follows: Russia or the RSFSR (Russian Soviet Federated Socialist Republic, also referred to as the Russian Federation), larger than all the other union republics together; the Baltic states, annexed by

Russia in the 18th century (Estonia and Latvia in 1721, Lithuania in 1795), freed as a result of the revolutionary upheavals of 1917–20, but annexed by Stalin in the summer of 1940, a move sanctioned by a secret "sphere of interest" division of East Central Europe made at the time of the Molotov–Ribbentrop Pact of August 23, 1939; Moldova (or Bessarabia), taken by Russia in 1812, granted to Romania in 1918, and grabbed by the USSR in June 1940 in accordance with the same 1939 Soviet–Nazi secret agreement; the two East Slavic nations that share much the same historical and cultural heritage as Russia—Ukraine and Belorussia; the three Caucasian republics—Georgia and Armenia, whose histories as states go back to pre-Christian times, and neighboring Azerbaijan; and finally, five Central Asian republics: Kazakhstan, Uzbekistan, Turkmenistan, Kyrgyzstan, and Tajikistan, comprising a territory most of which was conquered by Russia in the latter half of the 19th century.

Each former satellite and Soviet republic is populated by several or dozens of different ethnic groups, and these are further separated by various circumstances into subethnic populations; the Russian Federation alone has hundreds of such groupings. To write even briefly about each one would require volumes.

In some parts of the Russian/Soviet empire indigenous peoples became minorities as Russians moved in. In a few places Russians came to far outnumber local peoples, for example, accounting for about 70 percent of the populations in the Buryat and Karelia Autonomous Republics (ARs) according to the 1979 census. Some groups have been uprooted and transplanted. This was true especially during the Stalin dictatorship (1928–53), when hundreds of thousands of people were driven from their home territories to distant places, such as the Crimean Tatars and Volga Germans who were deported en masse and scattered into western Siberia and Central Asia. The intrusion of Russians, Ukrainians, and Belorussians into non-Slavic cultures and the rooting out and scattering of peoples tended to homogenize Soviet society, but nothing was more important in creating a general sameness than the great leap forward that transformed the USSR from a predominantly farming into a largely industrial and urban society. The most far-flung groups, from arctic hunters to Central Asian herders, shared, more or less, in these changes, and their lives came to exhibit common features, making possible a general study of Soviet culture. On the other hand, not all human activities and beliefs were pressed into the same mold. Much as some ideologues wanted a secular and socialist uniformity, the Soviet Union remained a community of many contrasts.

The great ethnic diversity of the USSR is quite noticeable in the large populations of Slavs and Turks. But even small Siberian populations, like the Even or Yukagir, who numbered only several thousand each, were separated into subethnic tribes or clans. The two main ethnic populations—East Slavs (Russians, Ukrainians, Belorussians) and Turkic Muslims—together made up about 80 percent of the empire's population in 1897 and nearly 90 percent in 1959. These figures reveal a noticeable increase in both the number and the relative strength of Russians. At the same time, Ukrainian and Turkic Muslim populations grew sufficiently in number to hold steady as a percentage of the whole.

After 1959, however, the census records present quite a different picture, a reversal of some important trends. In the 1960s the death rate among East Slavs, which had been falling, began to rise (for reasons noted in the section on health care), while birthrates continued to go down. For the two major Slavic republics (RSFSR and Ukraine) this meant a sharp decline between 1960 and 1980 in natural growth: 15.8 to 4.9 per thousand for the RSFSR and 13.6 to 3.4 per thousand for Ukraine. In Muslim republics the trends were similar but much less pronounced so that they remained far ahead of Slavic republics in rates of natural growth. These figures for the republics do not reveal, however, just how striking the differences were between the two ethnic populations. A great many Russians lived and still live in the Kazakh Republic (outnumbering Kazakhs 4 to 2.8 million in 1959 and 6 to 5.3 million in 1979). The census data for the republic naturally represent this mixture—more Russian than Kazakh. In fact, the birthrate for Kazakhs by themselves in the 1960s was about 41.2 per thousand and for the Central Asian Turkic Muslim population generally about 45.0 per thousand during that decade, pointing toward an even greater natural growth rate than that shown by census numbers for the republics.

Clearly the Soviet Muslim population exhibited a substantial growth in number and relative strength from the 1960s. In addition it was becoming a much more youthful population than the East Slavs, and this had every appearance of being a long-term trend. Thus, during the last three decades of the Soviet Union the three major Slavic peoples grew in number and continued to represent well over half the total population of USSR, but their relative numerical strength was declining. Thus, in 1989 Russians, Ukrainians, and Belorussians made up the largest language-related family (East Slavs) in the Soviet empire—199.4 million, 69.8 percent of the whole population. Turkic speakers, representing many different dialects (Uzbek, Kazakh, Tatar, Azerbaijan, Turkmen, Tajik, Bashkir, Kirghiz, etc.), Central Asian and Muslim, for the most part, were the next largest: more than 52 million and about 19 percent of the total. As mentioned before, compared to the East Slavs, the Muslim population, though smaller in number, was younger and growing much more rapidly. Regarding Russian/Soviet Jews, western regions of the empire were, for a time, home to the largest population of Jews in the world. The decline in their number began with an emigration movement in the late 19th century, spurred by waves of violent anti-Jewish persecution that followed the assassination of Tsar Alexander II in 1881. Then, during World War II, hundreds of thousands of Soviet Jews were destroyed by the Nazis and their Romanian allies. Between 1897 and 1959 their number was reduced by more than half, from about 5 to 2.3 million. The further decline in their population in the 1970s and 1980s was the result of emigration, mostly to the new state of Israel.

Though it is possible to talk about the different peoples of the Soviet Union (Russians, Jews, Uzbeks, etc.) as if each was a single community, tied together by a more or less common history and culture, it is unlikely that any of them were ever ethnically uniform. During the Soviet era each was composed of some or many groups, clearly distinguished one from another by important aspect(s) of their lives: linguistic, religious, social, economic, and so on (Eaton).

FOR MORE INFORMATION

Eaton, K. B. *Daily Life in the Soviet Union*. Westport, Conn.: Greenwood Press. Forthcoming.

Japan

The 20th century has been a roller-coaster ride for Japan. It began very near the top when Japan was allowed pride of place in the victory parade celebrating the end of the Boxer Rebellion in China in the summer of 1900. Japan led the parade because it had been the only army not to commit atrocities against the civilian population. Half a century later Japan suffered the ignominy of occupation by a conquering army, and then watched as its military and civilian leaders were tried, convicted, and executed for crimes against humanity in World War II.

Japan's economy had concomitant ups and downs. Resurfacing in the international economy in the 1850s after two centuries of near isolation, Japan had built robust industrial and commercial sectors on the strength of four decades of modernization and reform. It had emerged as a world economic power in the middle of World War I when it had supplanted the European powers in East Asian trade. Yet within a decade it had sunk into the world economic depression. The 15 years of what Japan calls the Great Pacific War (1931–45) taxed the domestic industrial engines, which were consumed by atomic and conventional bombing in 1944–45.

Yet Japan emerged from the horrific 1940s to become an economic giant. Its Mutual Defense Treaty with the United States brought untold riches in the form of manufacturing orders to supply American and United Nations forces in Korea and Vietnam. By the 1970s journalists were trumpeting "Japan As Number One," and one of its own right-wing politicians penned a best-selling diatribe called *The Japan That Can Say No*, implying that Japan no longer had to cooperate blindly with its American partner.

As a society, Japan managed to survive "the slings and arrows of outrageous fortune." At the beginning of the century it was quaint and exotic to Westerners, who grudgingly admired the "plucky" Japanese for their recent successes. Japan had surpassed China and the Middle East as the darling of Western artists, philosophers, and historians. The Zen arts brought thousands of foreign visitors to its shores in search of enlightenment and salvation.

By virtue of its alliances with the victorious World War I allies, Japan had sat at the victory table at the Treaty of Versailles in 1919 and was one of the founders of the League of Nations. It became a pariah in the late 1930s and remained so until 1952, when the Allied Occupation ended.

Issues of peace and war cloud the Japanese horizon. America would prefer Japan become more active as fellow international peacekeepers; the Japanese themselves collectively shudder at the thought of armed Japanese troops marching once again on foreign soil. Japan's victims in World War II recoil in horror as well.

The Japanese would prefer to enjoy the fruits of their labors. Few would trade their stable and comfortable political system in a quixotic search for world éclat.

~*Louis G. Perez*

Africa

For Africa, the 20th century was filled with exploitation and oppression, promises and hopes. At the start of the century, almost the entire continent was under the control of European powers, particularly Great Britain and France. This state of affairs continued for most of the first half of the century, while the last four decades saw the advent of self-rule throughout most of Africa, but also further economic disparity and inequality.

Each colony reported to and served its respective European power. Arbitrary borders, irrespective of African ethnic groups, were created and maintained. Many ethnic groups became divided, and thus many groups had sizable populations in multiple colonies. The Somali, for example, were divided among four colonies. Colonialism robbed Africans of their freedom. European colonial governments were self-serving and ignored the needs and wants of their African populations. When they could be manipulated, indigenous rulers, like chiefs and sultans, were maintained to serve European interests. The overwhelming majority of Africans received low wages, and poverty rapidly spread throughout the continent. Consequently, the continent's wealth was not spread among the African people but was extracted for the benefit of external powers. The military and police forces were authoritarian and brutal, and they served colonial interest, not the native population.

Ironically, World War II ushered in a period of change for Africa. European powers demanded more from their African colonies to fund their war campaigns. African soldiers were conscripted and sent to fight in the war. Soldiers who returned home were bitter and demanded compensation for their participation. The colonial economies during this period were poor, and many Africans, in particular young men, migrated to cities in search of employment and better wages. At the same time, an educated African elite began to emerge throughout the continent. Members of this elite began to petition for independence, and urban populations soon joined them in the struggle for independence.

Ultimately, colonization bred widespread anticolonial sentiment and eventually African nationalism. African discontent began to emerge in the 1950s, and by the 1960s, most African nations had achieved or were in the process of achieving their independence. Independence ushered in a brief period of optimism among the African population. Many Africans believed that political independence would create economic opportunities that would result in the betterment of life on the continent.

Unfortunately, these expectations were not met. Independence did not result in a complete transfer of power. Many African leaders and governments indirectly served European interests. Colonial infrastructures were often maintained, and African nations remained dependent on their former colonial rulers in many ways, such as through humanitarian aid and loans. Therefore, independence did not lead to rapid improvements in everyday life for the majority of Africans.

The main aims of the postindependence governments have been to foster a cohesive national unity while promoting development. Most governments have failed miserably in both regards. The legacy of colonial rule is simply too strong, and the high expectations are left unmet. This condition leads to discontent among the people, and martial law is often imposed to maintain governmental power. Thus, the challenge for Africa in the 21st century is to discover a way to compete in a global economy while promoting development and maintaining legitimate governments. This goal is easier described than achieved, and poverty remains rampant, with diseases such as HIV/AIDS reaching epic proportions. To improve conditions, African governments have begun competing with each other for foreign investments.

~Tyler Fleming

FOR MORE INFORMATION

Davidson, B. *Modern Africa*. London: Longman, 1983.

Falola, T., ed. *Africa*. Vols. 3, 4, and 5. Durham, N.C.: Carolina Academic Press, 2002–2003.

Inuit

The Inuit are one of the indigenous peoples of the Circumpolar North and are closely related to the Yupik of Southwest Alaska, Chukotka, and St. Lawrence Island. Archeological data suggest that the ancestors of contemporary Inuit and Yupik were part of the last wave of human migration across the Bering Strait from Asia to North America. Unlike earlier migrants, who may have walked across the Bering Sea land bridge, these last migrants traveled after the end of the Pleistocene and probably reached Alaska by boat. By 500 C.E. these migrants were well established on Alaska's Bering Sea coast and had begun spreading out. The ancestors of the people who we know as the Inuit moved north, settling for several centuries in what is now North Alaska. Around 1000 C.E. some moved east across North America, settling at coastal sites in Northern Canada, Greenland, and Labrador.

These Thule peoples, as they are known, were not the first inhabitants of the North American Arctic. A Paleoeskimo people, called Dorset by archeologists, had lived in the region for several millennia but disappear from the archeological record around the time that the Thule Inuit appear. Inuit oral histories also describe a group of earlier inhabitants.

Inuit means "the people" in Inuktitut, the Inuit language, and is the collective self-designation of the indigenous peoples of North Alaska, Canada, and Greenland. Inuit and Yupik together are sometimes labeled Eskimos, but except in Alaska or when referring to archeologically known populations, many Inuit now consider this term pejorative. Contemporary Inuit also use regionally specific ethnonyms, referring to themselves by terms such as Inupiat (North Alaskans), Inughuit (Northwest Greenlanders), and Kalaallit (West Greenlanders).

~Pamela Stern

Chronology of the 20th Century

1898	United States engages in a war against Spain in Cuba and the Philippines.
1901	French troops occupy Morocco.
1904	Morocco becomes a French protectorate.
1914	Austrian Archduke Franz Ferdinand is assassinated in Sarajevo in June; Germany declares war on Russia on August 1, thus beginning World War I.
1917	United States enters war in Europe in April; American soldiers arrive in May under command of General John Pershing; Russian Revolution begins.
1918	Syria and Damascus become French protectorates.
1918–19	Millions succumb to worldwide influenza epidemic.
1919	Participants in World War I sign Versailles Treaty; United States refuses to sign treaty.
1920	American women receive right to vote in all elections; national prohibition begins.
1921	United States and Germany sign separate peace treaty.
1922	USSR is founded.
1924	Soviet leader Lenin dies.
1928	Turkey is declared a secular state.
1929	American stock market collapses, signaling start of worldwide economic downturn.
1931	Japan invades Manchuria (northern China), thus beginning World War II in Asia.
1932	League of Nations declares Iraq an independent nation.
1933	Adolf Hitler becomes chancellor of Germany and begins official persecution of Jews; Dachau concentration camp is built; President Franklin D. Roosevelt initiates his New Deal program for economic recovery.
1933–45	President Roosevelt initiates his "Good Neighbor Policy" to establish broad cooperation between the United States and Latin America.
1936–38	Soviet leader Josef Stalin conducts his purges of the Communist Party; millions are tortured and executed within the Soviet Union.
1937	Buchenwald concentration camp opens in Germany.
1938	On November 9 and 10, in what became known as *Kristallnacht*, Nazis and others attack German Jews, destroying synagogues, houses, and businesses; thousands of Jews are arrested and sent to concentration camps.

1939	Germany invades Poland and World War II begins in Europe.
1940	President Roosevelt establishes the first peacetime draft.
1940–45	Millions of Jews, Gypsies, and others are systematically killed by the German Nazis.
1941	British and Russian forces invade Iran; surprise Japanese attack on Pearl Harbor in Hawaii brings the United States into World War II.
1945	Germany surrenders in May; Japan surrenders in September after two atomic bombs are dropped on the Japanese cities of Hiroshima and Nagasaki.
1947	President Harry S Truman institutes a system of loyalty oaths to weed out suspected Communists from government employment; Pakistan is created from a Muslim majority area of northwestern India.
1948	Jewish state of Israel is created.
1950–53	United States and North Korea, the latter aided by Communist China, fight to a stalemate on the Korean peninsula; fighting ends in 1953 without the signing of a formal peace treaty.
1951	Libya becomes an independent state.
1954	United States Supreme Court hands down its decision in *Brown v. Board of Education of Topeka, et al.*, ordering nationwide school desegregation; Senator Joseph McCarthy, a Republican from Wisconsin, is censured by the United States Senate, effectively ending McCarthy's crusade against the Left; United States stages a coup in Guatemala.
1955	Reverend Martin Luther King Jr., leads the Montgomery (Alabama) bus boycott.
1956	Morocco becomes independent.
1959	Fidel Castro ousts Cuban dictator Fulgencio Batista.
1960	John F. Kennedy, a Democrat, is elected president of the United States.
1960s–80s	Much of Latin America is engulfed in civil wars (otherwise known as "dirty wars") between right-wing and left-wing political groups.
1961	Cuban ex-patriots unsuccessfully invade Cuba with backing from the United States.
1962	United States and Soviet Union nearly go to war over the placement of Russian missiles in Cuba.
1963	President Kennedy assassinated in Dallas.
1964	Landmark Omnibus Civil Rights Bill is passed by the United States Congress.
1964–69	President Lyndon B. Johnson wages a war in Vietnam as well as a self-styled war against poverty in the United States; both wars are considered failures by the late 1960s.
1969	Colonel Gadhafi stages a coup and takes control of Libya.
1972	Republican President Richard M. Nixon is reelected; during the campaign, his Committee to Reelect the President (CREEP) engages in several illegal acts, including a break-in at the Democratic Party national headquarters in the Watergate Hotel in Washington, D.C.

1973	United States reaches a cease-fire agreement with North Vietnam and begins to pull troops out of Southeast Asia.
1979	Soviet Union invades Afghanistan; Shah of Iran is forced from office and the country; left-wing Sandinistas take over Nicaragua.
1980–89	Iraq-Iran war.
1982	Great Britain and Argentina fight over the Falkland Islands.
1983	Argentina's brutal military dictatorship ends; United States invades Grenada.
1984	Indian prime minister Indira Gandhi is assassinated.
1985	Mikhail Gorbachev becomes general secretary of the Communist Party and leader of the USSR; Gorbachev advances his *glasnost* (openness), *perestroika* (reconstruction), and political democratic reforms.
1989	United States invades Panama; Berlin Wall falls.
1990	Russia withdraws from the Union of Soviet Socialist Republics, thus leading to collapse of the USSR.
1990–91	First Gulf War ends with ejection of Iraqi forces from Kuwait.
1991	Soviet Union is formally dissolved; Indian prime minister Rajiv Gandhi is assassinated.
2001	Members of Osama bin Laden's al-Queda terrorist network attack targets in the United States, destroying the World Trade Center in New York and damaging the Pentagon.
2003–	Second Gulf War overthrows regime of Saddam Hussein.

HISTORICAL OVERVIEW: WEB SITES

http://arcticcircle.uconn.edu/
http://www.cbc.ca/stories/2003/03/05/arctic_toxins030305
http://www.auschwitz.dk/
http://www.courses.rochester.edu/homerin/REL247/Class/india/noframes/20thc.html
http://www.geocities.com/Athens/1818/overview.htm
http://www.hinduonnet.com/thehindu/mp/2002/09/26/stories/2002092600660200.htm
http://www.fordham.edu/halsall/mod/modsbook55.html
http://www.teacheroz.com/20thcent.htm
http://www.paynesvillearea.com/News/HeadlinesArticles/archives/010301/centurydates.html
http://www.timelines.info/history/conflict_and_war/20th_century_conflicts/world_war_one/
http://lcweb.loc.gov/exhibits/archives/intro.html
http://www.geographia.com/russia/rushis07.htm
http://fcit.coedu.usf.edu/holocaust/resource/website.htm

2

DOMESTIC LIFE

DOMESTIC LIFE
|
FAMILY LIFE
MEN
WOMEN
CHILDREN

The center of daily life is the home and, more importantly, the people who inhabit our domestic space. Domestic life here is defined as the humans who share our private spaces rather than our friends and acquaintances with whom we interact in the public worlds of work, politics, and recreation. However, even this definition of domestic life is a little slippery, because we include family members within our private sphere even if they live in separate homes and join us in the holidays and celebrations that mark our domestic life. Over time the definitions of those who are our intimates have changed. Who are the people who might share our domestic life?

The first ties are a married couple with their children. But even these relationships defy clear definition: Throughout history children have often depended upon the kindness of strangers to raise them, whether they were orphaned or fostered or fed by wet nurses. All these people share the domestic intimacy of home life. In the 20th century, the daily lives of children were transformed by several developments. War, of course, impacted kids. But other things, such as television, redefined their lives. By the end of the century, both parents and their sons and daughters shared a sense of powerlessness against the intrusive forces of the media as well as politics and war.

Twentieth-century families also included unmarried partners or even roommates who combined living space for convenience or necessity, or concubines who shared the private life of rulers. The relationships that make up domestic life are impossible to define perfectly, but (like art) we recognize them when we see them. Still, during the latter part of the century, many reformers and politicians debated whether a single woman or man could lead a successful family. This social contest about the proper makeup of the family had significant political consequences, particularly in the United States. When reading the entries in this section, pay attention to the ways in which the family itself becomes a part of politics.

This study of domestic life also focuses on the roles family members play—including at times the emotional functions they fill. In the domestic life societies define the roles of men, women, children, and everyone else who shares this space. It is here that we learn early on who we are and how we are to act and feel. Compared with the 19th century, fathers of the 20th century were expected to be more active and supportive in their families. Mothers' role remained to nurture the family, but increasingly they were expected (and in fact needed) to enter the labor force, thus transforming their traditional role.

During the 20th century, daily life in the family went under steady transformation. Some of the changes were technological. In the United States, the television and later the computer changed children's lives. Some changes were economic. During the Great Depression, families across the world suffered in poverty conditions. Unfortunately, these entries also indicate that too many families continued to struggle economically throughout the century. Making matters worse were wars. The 20th century was one of the bloodiest hundred years in human existence. Moreover, military leaders specifically targeted noncombatants. The results, of course, were tragic. Finally, families were changed by political and social movements such as the civil rights and feminist movements.

Given the changes in familial daily life, it is important to see that one aspect of life did not change much. Each society one studies was trifurcated by class and caste. The lives of the rich differed from middle-class lives, which were quite separate from those of the working class. It was not just a matter of relative wealth, although that certainly played a major part. In comparing families across cultures (and in fact across time), try to pull out major similarities and differences such as class and caste. Also, keep in the back of your mind certain categories like gender and life cycle to help guide your analysis. Above all, in making comparisons, be sure to keep your ideas rooted in place and time.

FOR MORE INFORMATION

Veyne, P., ed. A *History of Private Life*. Vols. 1 & 2. Cambridge, Mass.: Harvard University Press, 1987.

DOMESTIC LIFE
|
FAMILY LIFE
|
United States,
1920-1939

United States,
1940-1959

United States,
1960-1990

Latin America

India

Japan

Inuit

Family Life

During the 20th century, one of the major transformations in families concerned courtship. Before World War I, not only in the United States but also in other places such as Latin American countries and India, families controlled the ways boys met girls. We might view the rules that used to govern relationships with a wry smile. In the United States, young men and women, generally from the same class, engaged in a formal, public, and family-sponsored encounter known as the call. A man would stop by a woman's house and if he was lucky he would venture into the parlor to meet her parents and siblings. Time alone was rare until after marriage. Parents controlled the developing relationships. Of course, in India, this parental power was dramatic as marriages were often arranged. This pattern of control shifted significantly after the 1920s.

In part, the power that parents had possessed diminished because of the changes in daily life. Parental control was easily subverted through the use of such technological advances as automobiles. In other words, escaping the watchful eye of one's mother and father was no longer a problem. Additionally, family rules began to shift, because society began to alter its values. In India, for instance, the proscriptions on intercaste marriages began to fade. In the United States, in the 1920s, for another example, social commentators began to emphasize the compassionate marriage in which mutual devotion, sexual attraction, and spousal equality were seen as extremely important. Thus, spending time alone before marriage was crucial for a couple. Dating became the subject of several influential intellectual investigations that revealed that young people were more sexually active than previously realized. Most Americans believed that couples who successfully dated often created successful marriages. Of course, sometimes dating led to disasters. Hence, the 20th century was also known for an increase in the divorce rate, particularly in the United States.

Given the changing structure of courtship, dating, and premarital sex, it is not surprising to note that single-parent households also were on the rise in the 20th century. This was true for the United States as well as other nations, including those in Latin America, albeit for different reasons. Certainly divorce and separation played an important role in creating the large numbers of single-parent households in Central and South America. Another reason was war, particularly the "dirty wars" in South and Central America in which tens of thousands of men and women disappeared.

In Japan and the Inuit North, areas that experienced extensive social change because of increased contact with foreign cultures, the family remained the main instrument for the transmission of culture and for the formation of individual personality. Although outside pressures brought changes to the rules of courtship, sex, and marriage, the family was where one learned those rules and where one learned how to function in one's own society and to interact with people of other societies.

When reading the following entries, pay close attention to the ways in which families changed and the ways in which they remained the same.

UNITED STATES, 1920–39

As recently as the first decade of the century, families, particularly parents, controlled the ways in which boys met girls. Much courtship had taken place in the home according to well-defined customs. A young man would be encouraged to call on a young woman. In doing so, he would meet her parents, talk to her in the family parlor, perhaps be offered refreshments, possibly be entertained by her piano playing or singing, and ultimately be encouraged to call again or discouraged from doing so. This social ritual, originating with the upper class, common within the middle class, and copied insofar as possible by families of more modest means, gave eligible women and watchful parents some power over the courtship process. Men could, of course, decline to call, but if they did proceed, they ventured into the woman's environment. If the courtship progressed, the couple might move from the parlor to the still highly visible front porch or attend a public function together, but only well along in the

DOMESTIC LIFE

FAMILY LIFE

process could a young lady properly consent to the privacy involved in going for a buggy ride alone with her suitor.

The automobile further extended the range of possibilities for dating couples.

Dating began to replace calling early in the 20th century. Homes in the urban environment, in which more and more people found themselves, provided, especially for those of lower income, less space for receiving and entertaining guests. At the same time, cities offered greater possibilities outside the home. Gradually, courting couples began going on dates, pre-arranged excursions to soda and coffee shops, movie theaters, restaurants, and other places where, even in the midst of a crowd, they experienced less supervision and greater privacy than in the parlor. The automobile further extended the range of possibilities for dating couples, not only as transportation to entertainment but as a place for private intimacy as well. As the possibilities of a nonmoving automobile began to be appreciated, the term "lover's lane" entered the vocabulary.

Because dates cost money and males were far more likely to be able to earn cash for such purposes, dating tended to give men greater control over courtship. Since they were now the hosts, men gained control over their choice of partner and the entire process; indeed, it was considered improper for a woman to propose a date, though she might hint that she would welcome a man's invitation. As costs mounted, so too did the female sense of obligation and the male expectation of appreciation.

In the 1920s, dating became common practice among the nation's youth. It prevailed not only in the cities where it started but in suburbs and smaller communities as well. Young urban men and women who had left school but had not married or acquired a steady companion found that they could meet at dance halls, speakeasies and bars, skating rinks, and other public places. Only in rural areas and especially in the South, where there was little surplus income, access to automobiles, or commercial entertainment, did dating fail to develop and older social patterns persist.

Dating soon ceased to be just a search for a mate. It became a primary means for casual social entertainment for adolescents and postadolescents. Robert and Helen Lynd observed that in Middletown, Indiana, frequent dates using the family automobile had become one of the most common sources of tension between teenagers and their parents. At colleges, and also at high schools as the practice spread, dating came to be regarded as a means of demonstrating popularity. The more numerous and varied the dates and the higher the standing of the persons dated, the higher one's status. Thus, continual and diverse dating became an ideal, and often a practice. For many young people, dating served as general recreation and social self-affirmation, not necessarily courtship of a potential life companion.

The shift from calling to dating encouraged greater sexual exploration and intimacy. Long before the rise of the dating system, young people regularly experimented with kissing games. Engaged couples often enjoyed what was coming to be called "heavy petting," and enough people engaged in premarital intercourse that nearly 1 in 10 late-19th-century brides went to the altar pregnant. Dating, however, brought with it freer attitudes about sexuality and more freedom to explore them. Movies provided "how to do it" guides for the inexperienced, and the culture of high schools and colleges, which more were attending, encouraged young people to try things for themselves. Prolonged kissing and embraces became accepted aspects of romantic relationships. Necking and petting (the distinction depended on whether the contact was above or below the shoulders) were customary if not universal practices; evidence compiled later pointed to a sharp rise in premarital sexual intercourse after World War I with over four-fifths of males and nearly half of females acknowledging participation. These gender differences reflected the persistence of the "double standard," the widespread attitude that sexually active males were just "sowing wild oats" and couldn't be expected to be faithful to a single mate, whereas women who behaved in the same fashion abandoned their virtue. Although gender distinctions and sexual attitudes in general were beginning to change, most of the sexual activity that did take place was with only a single partner whom the individual expected to marry.

As courtship practices evolved and dating exposed many young people to a greater variety of potential partners, the decision to marry was cast in a new light. Marriage had traditionally been regarded as a partnership for economic, educational, and welfare purposes as much as a social relationship. The most common justification offered in court for the few divorces of the 1880s was that "he wasn't an adequate (or reliable) provider" or "she didn't carry out her duties at home." By the 1920s, however, fewer persons participated in family economies such as farming, other institutions were taking over educational and welfare responsibilities, and more people were involved in work settings where cash wages allowed individuals to purchase daily necessities. The mutual dependency in dealing with various basic life functions that had hitherto held couples together began to diminish. A mate's lack of attention, consideration, or romantic appeal came to be mentioned far more often in divorce petitions as a reason for marital dissatisfaction.

A new notion emerged, popularized by psychologists, social service professionals, and educators, that a successful marriage was based primarily on affection and companionship. Denver judge Ben Lindsay, in a 1925 book, wrote that "companionate marriage" succeeded because of mutual devotion, sexual attraction, and respect for spousal equality. Pressure from society, church, or state to stay together could not produce a happy marriage in the absence of personal emotional fulfillment, he continued, and in fact could prove harmful to a couple and any children they might have. Marriage could not be expected to be free of tension or conflict, but husbands and wives who were loving companions could communicate and resolve difficulties. Couples unable or unwilling to do so, Lindsay concluded, were better off separating.

Some but not all states eased divorce requirements, their legislators saying that marital happiness was more important for couples (and their children) than family economic security (and the risk of adults and children having to be supported by the state). Divorce skyrocketed, increasing from 1 per 18 marriages in the 1880s to 1 per 6 in the 1920s, but remarriage likewise became common. In 1930, census takers found only slightly more than 1 percent of adults listing their current status as divorced, far fewer than at one time had been divorced. The figures had grown fractionally since 1920 and would rise minimally further by 1940, but overall the percentage of the population that divorced and did not remarry remained quite low.

People were not turning against marriage, as some concerned observers grimly suggested. Instead they had come to desire a happy and fulfilling family life and, if disappointed in an attempt to achieve it, proved increasingly willing and able to start over rather than accept less. Simply put, emotional and sexual satisfaction was replacing economic security as the standard of marital choice and contentment.

A steelworker's family having dinner in Aliquippa, Pennsylvania, ca. 1920. © Library of Congress.

A few states, most notably New York, maintained highly restrictive divorce laws, while South Carolina refused to allow divorce at all. In many locales the Roman Catholic Church and other influential conservative voices opposed easier divorce as a threat to family stability. Residents of such places did not forego divorce but often had to resort to exaggerated claims of spousal misconduct to satisfy legal requirements. Others traveled out of state to dissolve their marriages.

Nevada, which permitted anyone who had resided in the state for six months to divorce easily even a spouse who had never set foot in the state, became the most popular destination for migratory divorce. Realizing that divorce seekers were spending millions of dollars in the state's hotels, restaurants, and gambling parlors and that other poor rural states—Arkansas, Idaho, Oklahoma, and the Dakotas in particular—were competing for this business, Nevada reduced its residence requirement to three months in 1927 and then slashed it further to six weeks in 1931. By far the least populous state, with only 77,000 residents in 1920 and 110,000 in 1940, Nevada granted 1,000 divorces in 1926 and five times that many in 1931, and continued to have the highest divorce rate of any state. Even with relaxed rules, however, a migratory divorce remained inconvenient and expensive, and only a small fraction of divorce seekers, mainly the wealthy, pursued this route (Kyvig, 114–19).

To read about family life in the United States in the 19th century, see the United States entries in the section "Family Life" in chapter 2 ("Domestic Life") in volume 5 of this series.

FOR MORE INFORMATION

Kyvig, D. E. *Daily Life in the United States, 1920–1939: Decades of Promise and Pain.* Westport, Conn.: Greenwood Press, 2002.

Lynd, R. S., and H. M. Lynd. *Middletown: A Study in Modern American Culture.* New York: Harcourt, Brace, and World, 1929.

Mintz, S., and S. Kellogg. *Domestic Revolutions: A Social History of American Family Life.* New York: Free Press, 1988.

UNITED STATES, 1940–59

In terms of family members and family behavior, no greater revolution took place during the 1950s than the shift in attitudes toward sex. By the end of the decade all institutional control over individual sexual behavior seemed to melt away. Beginning with the two gigantic Kinsey reports, *Sexual Behavior in the Human Male* in 1948 and *Sexual Behavior in the Human Female* in 1953, and ending with the government's approval of the birth control pill in 1960, the nation's mores were turned upside down within two decades. But it was still not possible to get a legal abortion during the 1950s, when Massachusetts and Connecticut even made prescriptions mandatory for birth control devices.

Alfred Kinsey, a distinguished entomologist from the University of Indiana, identified his sudden interest in sexuality with his discovery of playwright Tennessee Williams's fascination with façades. Kinsey had come to appreciate the contrasts Williams presented between "social front and reality." His research into sex patterns funded by the Rockefeller Foundation, his books marketed by Saunders, a respected publisher of medical texts, Kinsey represented himself as a crew-cut, bow-tied, middle-American square. He saw himself as a serious if somewhat quirky professor who remained stunned when his scientific sexual surveys became best sellers.

What Kinsey revealed, as David Halberstam neatly summarized in his survey of the 1950s, was that "there was more extramarital sex on the part of both men and women than Americans wanted to admit," and that "premarital sex tended to produce better marriages." Kinsey documented that masturbation also was a normal part of sexual development. Perhaps his most controversial discovery was that more homosexuality existed in the United States than Americans wanted to acknowledge. Scholars continued to question the sources of his homosexual statistics because he interviewed prison populations.

People were outraged at Kinsey's refusal to make moral judgments. His materials were delivered as pure statistics without emotional or moral contexts. Yet few scientists were willing to come forward to support his work. And although he poured his book royalties back into the Institute for Sex Research of Indiana University, his funding grew insufficient when the Rockefeller Foundation withdrew support after the book on female

A father and his two sons salvage steel for the war effort, 1942, East Montpelier, Vermont. © Library of Congress.

sexuality received hostile reviews. Following the spirit of the times, the Rockefellers shifted their money to Union Theological Seminary. On the defensive from then on, Kinsey saw his health deteriorate. In 1956, at the relatively young age of 62, he died.

Even if the age of the "feminine mystique" was not any more eager to sanction women's sexuality than their need for serious education, all such social debate was liberating for women. Institutions began to change. By the end of the decade *Playboy* magazine was thriving, and the mail censorship of classics like Henry Miller's *Tropic of Cancer* and *Tropic of Capricorn* and D. H. Lawrence's *Lady Chatterley's Lover*, which contained sexually explicit material, would be a memory. Admitted to the United States after protests, Vladimir Nabokov's distinguished novel *Lolita*, about an adolescent and her older lover, published in 1958, sold more than 3 million copies. And the big-time best seller of the 1950s, Grace Metalious's *Peyton Place*, about secret lives in a quaint New Hampshire town—far from Thornton Wilder's Grover's Corners—sold 6 million copies in 1958. It would go on to become the best-selling novel ever, surpassing 10 million copies.

Even Hollywood modified its restrictive sexual codes by the end of the decade in which *Baby Doll*, a 1956 Tennessee Williams story about a child bride, had been condemned by the Legion of Decency as an evil film. Compassion for alienated, vulnerable heroes like the young men James Dean and Sal Mineo played in *Rebel without a Cause* was as real as the ongoing cult of the cowboy John Wayne. The Mattachine Society appeared in California in 1951 to promote better understanding of homosexuality as well as to prevent individual harassment. One of the most popular films of the decade, *Some Like It Hot* (1959), featured Jack Lemmon and Tony Curtis in drag. With the Food and Drug Administration's marketing approval of the birth control pill in 1960, Claire Boothe Luce declared modern woman had become as "free as a man is free to dispose of her own body."

Until the mid-1960s the early marriage boom and the baby boom continued to define preferences in American life. As long as women were willing to subordinate their ambitions to their husbands', marriages remained stable. But the family did not fully absorb most women's energies for long. The proportion of married women in the workforce rose from 36 percent in 1940 to 52 percent in 1950. At the same time, the divorce rate went back to its steady rise. By the mid-1960s the American family—always more complex than portrayed by media myths like *Leave It to Beaver* or *Ozzie and Harriet*—found different representations in movies. In *East of Eden* (1955) James Dean's role as a misunderstood son became the actor's best performance, and *All that Heaven Allows* (1956) described an older woman who shocked people by loving her gardener. American women, who were now living longer, imagined richer lives outside their families. A useful book on changing images of women in the movies during the 1950s, *On the Verge of Revolt*, suggested that even in the world of media myths a new awareness was taking shape. The seed of rebellion described in Molly Haskell's critical classic *From Reverence to Rape: The Treatment of Women in the Movies* (1973) germinated in the kitchen (Kaledin, 109–11).

To read about family life in the United States in the 19th century, see the United States entries in the section "Family Life" in chapter 2 ("Domestic Life") in volume 5 of this series.

FOR MORE INFORMATION

American Memory. <http://lcweb2.loc.gov/ammem>.
Kaledin, E. *Daily Life in the United States, 1940–1959: Shifting Worlds*. Westport, Conn.: Greenwood Press, 2000.

May, E. T. *Homeward Bound: American Families in the Cold War Era*. New York: Basic Books, 1988.

Mintz, S., and S. Kellogg. *Domestic Revolutions: A Social History of American Family Life*. New York: Free Press, 1988.

UNITED STATES, 1960–90

Hoping and dreaming came naturally for young couples in 1960. They had begun their families in the "golden age of the American family," as historians call the 1950s. Historian Steven Mintz and anthropologist Susan Kellogg, in *Domestic Revolutions*, treat this decade as a reference point for measuring changes in family life. Young adults married in unprecedented numbers and at younger ages than had earlier generations. By 1960, 70 percent of all women were married by the age of 24, compared with 42 percent 20 years earlier and around 50 percent 30 years later. They bore more children at a faster rate. Between 1940 and 1957, the birthrate for third children in a family doubled and for fourth children tripled.

Perhaps the start-early pattern of young families was a reaction to tales told by their parents, whose marriages may have been delayed or childbearing limited by separations caused by war or the hardships of the Great Depression. By the 1950s, Elaine Tyler May notes in *Homeward Bound*, "childlessness was considered deviant, selfish, and pitiable." Large families, on the other hand, were an indication of a man's potency and ability to provide and a woman's success as a professional homemaker. Popular magazines extolled the virtues of marriage and family life, and movies and television programs portrayed them as romantic ideals. Psychologists, educators, journalists, and religious leaders reinforced the idea that marriage was necessary for personal well-being. Failure to marry suggested some sort of personal deficiency. In the prevailing view, according to Mintz and Kellogg, women's primary responsibility was to "manage the house and care for children."

These circumstances, along with state laws limiting the grounds for divorce, explain why families in the baby-boom era stayed together to an extraordinary degree. The divorce rate between 1955 and 1963 fluctuated between 2.1 and 2.3 per 1,000 population. Not since 1940 had it been so low. It rose to 2.5 in 1966 and continued upward until reaching a peak of around 5.3 in 1981 before declining gradually.

For many young couples, bringing a child into the world in 1960 was largely a matter of letting nature take its course. Family planning like that done in later years, when two-career marriages demanded it, was not commonly practiced—at least not until several children had already arrived. Besides, reliable means for preventing pregnancies were limited. In 1960, however, the Food and Drug Administration approved the use of the birth control pill—known simply as "the pill." The next year an intrauterine plastic contraceptive device known as the IUD came on the market, providing an alternative method for those wary of the medical side effects of the pill. Also in 1961, the National Council of Churches of Christ, a coalition of mainstream Protestant denominations, gave its blessing to the practice of birth control. Not coincidentally, these events occurred when the number of births had reached an all-time high: The 4,258,000 births in 1960 represented an increase of 80 percent over the 2,360,000 births in 1940.

If young couples *had* given their situation and the world around them an informed look, they could well have judged 1960 to be a good time to add to their families. The father's monthly paycheck may have been on the meager side, but his fringe benefits were probably good and his job was most likely secure. Both unemployment and the rate of inflation were relatively low.

Economist John Kenneth Galbraith was partly right in calling the America in which young families lived the "affluent society." Even with relatively low incomes, many of them managed to scrape together the down payment on a home. Sometimes that required a little help from parents and such things as loans drawn against life insurance policies.

For many families, adding another child in their modest home would leave them physically crowded for a while, but that was also the case for their friends and acquaintances. The typical family, according to the 1960 census, consisted of the father, mother, and three children. Many such families purchased homes in suburban developments, continuing the great migration of the 1950s. Suburbanites outnumbered city dwellers for the first time in 1960, and during the 1960s the margin of difference widened. "Starter" homes for many families were nearly identical to the other homes in their suburban neighborhoods, standing on small treeless lots and having one-car detached garages, but they were a sign of better things ahead.

Nonetheless, had young parents chosen to be uneasy about their families' prospects, they could have found reasons for being so. Unreserved optimism about the future of the American economy was unwarranted, for the United States was on the brink of a transition to times in which a growing percentage of jobs would be in lower-paying service sectors. Labor unions, which claimed 35 percent of nonagricultural workers as members at the end of World War II, saw that figure drop to 28.4 percent in 1965 and to 17.5 percent in 1986. Although the number of work stoppages by unions attempting to enforce their demands for increased pay, improved fringe benefits, and better working conditions increased gradually throughout the 1960s, unions were slowly losing their power.

Another concern had to do with threats of nuclear war with Russia, portrayed by some political leaders as a real possibility if not a virtual certainty. Black and yellow signs in public buildings identifying fallout shelters—places to go during a nuclear attack—were reminders of the Soviet threat. So were articles like one in *Life* magazine showing how a family of five could survive in an 8 1/2- by 12-foot room equipped with food, a TV set, and exercise equipment. If war never came, the article explained, the children could use the shelter as a hideaway, the father for poker games, and the mother as a guest room. Despite a "bunker mentality," however, most people lived as though prospects that the "cold war"—the term used to characterize the hostile but peaceful relations between the United States and the Soviet Union—would turn hot were slight. Indeed, the Civil Defense Agency, troubled by the difficulty of stirring interest in building backyard shelters, distributed a pamphlet entitled *Family Fallout Shelter* to some 22 million homes, but most families ignored it. Even when a crisis with the Soviet Union occurred in 1962 over placement of missiles in Cuba, the scare was short-lived. There is evidence, however, of underlying fears in children, who may have taken seriously the concerns their parents brushed aside. In *Baby Boomers*, for example, political scientist Paul C. Light cites a 1961 survey of 3,000 elementary school children that showed that "even the youngest baby boomers worried about the fate of the family and friends in the event of a nuclear war." Although fears subsided in subsequent years, Light notes that in a 1979 survey, 50 percent of the sample reported that "advances in nuclear weaponry affected their thoughts about marriage and the future, and the majority said they were even affected in their daily thoughts and feelings." This sense of "futurelessness," he muses, "may haunt the baby boom through life, and may well be the most intense of the generation's shared experiences."

By 1967, many parents who had begun raising families in the 1950s could say that their hopes and expectations were being realized. Not that they had struck it rich, but they had managed to buy larger homes in suburban neighborhoods. The future looked promising, perhaps because of pay increases and promotions for the fathers. The mothers' willingness to find part-time jobs made a difference, too.

As families' prosperity inched upward, they enjoyed such things as genuine summer vacations. In earlier times vacation travels may have taken them to visit grandparents, aunts, uncles, cousins, and friends. Now, perhaps with borrowed camping gear loaded into low-powered, non-air-conditioned sedans, they traveled to such events as Expo '67 in Montreal. The innumerable technological wonders displayed at this world's fair dazzled even the most sophisticated visitors.

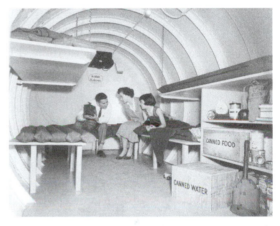

An American family tests their new bomb shelter, which was supposed to protect them from a nuclear attack. © Library of Congress.

For the children, each year in school meant a new grade, a new teacher, and, in larger schools, new friends. Studies, music lessons, sports, church activities, friendships, playtime, visits to doctors and dentists, camping trips, other family outings—all these claimed a place in their crowded lives. With the children all in school, mothers had greater freedom to take occasional jobs, such as substitute teaching or trying their hand in retail sales. Some found full-time jobs, although they preferred seasonal ones that allowed them to be at home in the summer with the kids.

Such families no doubt regarded their way of life as normal, although they did not think too much about what *normal* meant. They did not strive to live up to some fantasy of an ideal family. Yet their composition—mother, father, and three or four children—represented a large portion of the American population. So did their everyday activities. Children and parents, occasionally joined by grandparents, worked together around the house. Mowing the lawn, raking leaves, and in other ways maintaining their homes as do-it-yourself suburbanites provided all family members with creative diversions from workday and school-day worlds.

Countless families of the late 1960s, however, would have considered this depiction as atypical. Single-parent families facing lives of hardship and discrimination in urban ghettos, for example, would surely have thought so. Rural families in the South and Jewish families in New York would have had little in common with the social circumstances of these suburban families. Asian immigrants in California and Hispanic families in the Southwest or Harlem would have seen their own lives as much different. Indeed, all generalizations about families have exceptions. Yet despite differences in their daily lives, it is possible to consider matters that touched most of them.

Tensions existed in all families, even in ones regarded as rock solid. Placing sunrise-to-sunset child-rearing responsibilities on mothers caused some tensions. So did missed career and personal opportunities resulting from demands at home. Issues faced by families show more possibilities for tension: If both mothers and fathers pursued careers outside the home, how were they and their children affected by placing the children in the care of others during the workday? How did the division of labor in child rearing and home management affect relations between husbands and wives? In single-parent homes, what did placing all the responsibilities of child rearing and home management on one person do to that person's relationship with her or his child? What kind of social lives were possible outside the home?

In most two-parent families, the commitments of husbands and wives to stability for their children and to faithful, lifelong marriages made the division of domestic and wage-earning responsibilities acceptable, at least temporarily. Their family relationships seemed part of the natural order of things. Not that these relationships would necessarily continue in future generations, but for them they worked.

The natural order soon changed, resulting in different patterns of family life. As increasing numbers of women found employment outside the home, time for tasks inside the home diminished sharply. In some families the husbands and children pitched in, but a survey in the late 1980s showed that housework was still almost exclusively women's work. One observer wrote that "men recognize the essential fact of housework right from the beginning. Which is that it stinks."

Two trends established during the 1960s, rising divorce rates and declining birthrates, continued throughout the next three decades. Between 1960 and 1967 the divorce rate increased from 2.2 per 1,000 population to 2.7, but this gradual increase began to accelerate rapidly, so that by 1974 it stood at 4.6 per 1,000. The birthrate per 1,000 population declined annually: from 23.7 in 1960, to 17.8 in 1967, to 14.9 in 1974.

Another trend that accelerated in later years was the increase in single-parent families. In 1970, 87.1 percent of households with children included both a father and a mother; by 1980, the number had dropped to 78.5 percent, and by 1990, to 71.9 percent. The numbers for white households in each year were slightly higher, but for black households dramatically lower: 64.3 percent of households with children had two parents in 1970, 48.1 percent in 1980, and 39.4 percent in 1990. In the earlier years, men in white families were the single parent in about one in seven instances, although the number gradually increased. In black families, women were the single parent more than 13 times as often as were men (Marty, 3–10, 79–85).

📷 Snapshot

U.S. Single-Parent Households in the Late 20th Century

The percentage of married couples with children fell from 50 percent to 37 percent of all families between 1970 and 1990. It has dropped only 1 percentage point (to 36 percent) since then. (U.S. Census Bureau, 1998)

To read about family life in the United States in the 19th century, see the United States entries in the section "Family Life" in chapter 2 ("Domestic Life") in volume 5 of this series.

FOR MORE INFORMATION

American Memory. <http://lcweb2.loc.gov/ammem>.

Marty, M. A. *Daily Life in the United States, 1960–1990: Decades of Discord.* Westport, Conn.: Greenwood Press, 1997.

May, E. T. *Homeward Bound: American Families in the Cold War Era.* New York: Basic Books, 1988.

Mintz, S., and S. Kellogg. *Domestic Revolutions: A Social History of American Family Life.* New York: Free Press, 1988.

U.S. Census Bureau. <http://www.census.gov/Press-Release/cb98–88.html>.

LATIN AMERICA

In Latin America, as elsewhere, the traditional ideal conception of family was a legally or religiously married, coresident unit of husband and wife with their young children. In reality, however, alternative structures prevailed throughout much of Latin America. Although legal and social discrimination continued toward common-law and nonresidential unions, in the latter part of the century, people increasingly came to understand such unions as culturally appropriate solutions to the problems of living in socio-economic circumstances of deprivation and uncertainty. Thus, the 20th century brought about a partial reevaluation of the definitions of family.

For much of the century, the cohabiting married couple was the standard by which society judged all relationships. Dominant cultures deemed any other kind of union immoral or promiscuous and children from such a union illegitimate. The Catholic Church, an extremely influential organization in Latin American society, excluded common-law couples. Although so-called illegitimate children could be baptized, such ceremonies often occurred only weekdays; the Church reserved Sundays for babies born in wedlock.

For the more traditional families, gender determined the balance of power and the division of responsibilities within the household. Men worked outside the home, providing financial support, while women typically worked at home, taking care of the house and children. Such gendered standards shifted through the century as women's roles expanded. Economic crises, as well as broader societal changes, brought many women into the labor force and into social and political spotlights.

Unless economics or education demanded otherwise, Latin American children typically remained at home with their parents until they married. Indeed, it was not uncommon to see children in their twenties or thirties residing at home, contributing their incomes to the upkeep of the family and house.

Yet, in much of Latin America, marriage was not a true measure of family. Informal, consensual unions prevailed. In rural areas of Central America, for example,

DOMESTIC LIFE

FAMILY LIFE

United States,
1920-1939

United States,
1940-1959

United States,
1960-1990

Latin America

India

Japan

Inuit

most couples lived and raised children together, but never officially married. In the Caribbean, visiting, extraresidential unions were common. In one rural Caribbean community, legally married partners constituted fewer than one-third of the households. In such cases, alternative patterns of parenting developed, including owning (accepting paternity), minding (financially supporting), and caring (rearing). These obligations fell not only to biological parents, but also to those considered social or adoptive parents, to extended family members, and to the community as a whole.

Reasons for such alternative unions are many, including that civil and religious formalization of unions was often selective, leaving out those who were not in the middle or upper ranks of society. Formalization was particularly difficult for sectors that had not been fully integrated into the social and legal structures of society, such as communities of indigenous and African descent. In addition, the costs of marriage ceremonies and licenses were prohibitive for many people.

In much of Latin America, extended families were of extreme importance—for financial as well as emotional reasons. Several generations often lived together under one roof. As the 20th century progressed, extended families became networks that often extended across national borders and oceans. Mothers typically remained at home while husbands, children, siblings, and extended family members sent remittances of cash and materials from their positions in the city or abroad.

Another kinship tie of great importance in Latin America was *compadrazgo*, or godparentage. Upon a baby's birth or baptism, new parents carefully chose *un padrino* (godfather) and *una madrina* (godmother). The godparents were often of a higher socioeconomic position and therefore able to more adequately attend to the young child's needs. Godparents routinely covered educational expenses and assured that the child had proper clothing and shoes.

Female-headed households constituted another trend in 20th-century Latin America. Although such families always existed, their numbers increased through the century; by the early 1980s, women were de facto heads of one out of every five homes. In some places, such as Nicaragua and various Caribbean nations, women headed more than half of all homes.

In addition to separation and divorce, one reason for this trend was that men often needed to travel great distances to find work. Rural dwellers with little or no land of their own were particularly susceptible to this need. Many male laborers migrated with the seasons and agricultural harvests, or they traveled to urban centers to work in factories or construction. As the century progressed, more men migrated internationally—many to the United States—seeking higher wages.

Another reason for the high number of female-headed households was war. During the 20th century, Latin America witnessed many revolutions and civil wars, leading to millions of deaths. The Mexican Revolution (1910–17), for example, resulted in two million dead. In Guatemala, some 200,000 lost their lives during more than three decades of unstable political conditions and civil war. And the "dirty wars" in many South American countries during the 1970s and 1980s led to tens of thousands of disappearances. Not all of the dead and disappeared in these countries were men, of course. The violence, however, did tend to target men more than women because they were most often visible on the front lines, either as true revolutionary fighters or suspected subversives. In any case, such violence tore families apart and often left women to fend for themselves and their children.

Women were at a disadvantage as heads of households, being responsible not only for family income, but also for the upkeep of home and children. Furthermore, in many countries, basic institutional support—such as social services and credit—was available only for traditional families and, thus, distributed solely to male heads of household. Some governments, moreover, recognized women's rights only for women who were legally married.

Given the politics, economics, and other specifics of Latin American history, many nations reassessed the definitions of family through the course of the 20th century. Churches and governments increasingly acknowledged the prevalence of a variety of family patterns; some even moved to end legal discrimination against nontraditional unions. By the 1980s, some Caribbean countries had passed family law reforms, abolishing legal distinctions between illegitimate and legitimate offspring and extending rights of inheritance to common-law wives and illegitimate children.

In short, in 20th-century Latin America, despite decades and even centuries of preaching and legal discrimination, marriage rates continued to be low and illegitimate births high. Though some governments made advances, in terms of making family law more inclusive of alternative family structures, the true and lived meanings given to "family" in Latin America were as diverse as the population itself.

~Molly Todd

FOR MORE INFORMATION

Barrow, C. *Family in the Caribbean: Themes and Perspectives*. Kingston, Jamaica: Ian Randle, 1996.

Bethell, L., ed. *The Cambridge History of Latin America*. Vol. VI, Part I. Cambridge, U.K.: Cambridge University Press, 1994.

Burns, E. B. *Latin America: A Concise Interpretive History*. 5th ed. Englewood Cliffs, N.J.: Prentice Hall, 1990.

Winn, P. *Americas: The Changing Face of Latin America and the Caribbean*. New York: Pantheon Books, 1992.

INDIA

The roles of kinship and family connections were important components in everyday life in India. Families in India were generally large. There were two reasons for this. First, a husband and wife in a rural area might have had several children to help with the family occupation. Second, sadly, many couples that had daughters first kept trying until a son was born. Boys, especially in rural areas, were considered more desirable than girls. A boy would carry on the family name and did not require an expensive dowry at the time of his wedding, whereas a girl, in most of the families, in general, would have to be married with dowry given either in kind, in cash, or both. Finally, in many regions, the infant mortality rate was high, so couples might

DOMESTIC LIFE

FAMILY LIFE

United States, 1920-1939

United States, 1940-1959

United States, 1960-1990

Latin America

India

Japan

Inuit

have expected some children to perish in childhood, more particularly their female children.

Parents and families expected children to get married when they reached a suitable age. Sometimes the family performed a marriage while the boy and girl were still children, that is, before puberty. Most marriages, however, were performed when the bride was in her late teens and the groom either of the same age or older. In some cases, young girls were married to men (usually widowers) who were much older.

Marriages within families were important events. The parents of the bride and groom would arrange the marriage. Families arranged matches based on shared characteristics such as caste, language, and shared customs. Marriage alliances took place within caste bounds, and usually within subcaste-specific occupational groups. Marriages between members of different castes were rare; the exception being the occasional marriage between a high-caste man and a lower-caste woman. Hindu custom forbade a woman to marry a man of a lower caste than she. In addition, marriages between Hindus and other faiths (Muslims, Buddhists, Christians, etc.) were not common. However, since India's independence in 1947, mixed marriages have become more common and socially accepted, especially among the educated urban population. Families sometimes arranged marriage alliances within the same extended family. For example, these marriages might have occurred between distant cousins, or occasionally between an uncle and a niece. Recently, this practice has been much less in use.

Family life within India required different living situations. A husband and wife with children might have lived in the husband's family home, along with his parents. At the marriage time, the groom's new wife was "given" to him. She would move into his home with her new in-laws. For the new bride, leaving her own home and moving in with her new husband and his family was often a difficult and traumatic event. The relationship between the new bride and her mother-in-law was frequently acrimonious, and the subject of many proverbs and movie plots. The new bride was expected to prove herself by excellence in cooking and other chores relegated to her. However, her main goal was to produce a child, preferably a son. When her pregnancy advanced, she returned to her own parents' home for the birth and until she recovered from her postnatal debility.

Several rites marked a child's life. First, generally on the 12th day after birth, there was a name-giving ceremony. The baby wore new clothes and the ceremony might have included a priest, singing, prayer, and the pronunciation by the priest of the child's name. The event would conclude with a celebratory meal.

For boys of higher castes, especially those under 10 years of age in Brahman communities, the family performed a thread-tying ceremony. This marked his belonging to the higher caste. The ceremony entailed the tying of several banded threads around the boy's neck and chest. The boy repeated several lines from sacred texts. The boy's father and a priest, as well as friends and other family members, would attend the ceremony. The next rite for parents and children was the fixing of a marriage mate and the engagement ceremony. When a young man was ready for marriage, "His father makes the boy's eligibility known to kinsmen, friends, and office colleagues, and is soon contacted by men engaged in the even more urgent task of trying to marry off a daughter" (Vatuk, 81). This ceremony, like most within Hinduism, might have included a priest, parents, sacred texts, gifts, friends, and a lavish meal.

Newlyweds or new parents could expect more than just the husband's parents to be in the same house. Within joint families, grandparents, especially if widowed, were frequently afforded a place of honor within the home— the greatest respect being given to elders. Also, brothers and their wives and children might have also lived under the same roof. A pecking order generally developed whereby the oldest son had the highest rank. His wife was highest among the other wives in the home. Add to this mix any unmarried sisters, aunts, and uncles, and the family unit was quite large. To help lessen any confusion, within many Indian languages specific kinship terms developed to identify each relative. For example, within Telugu, a language spoken by 75 million Indians in the southern part of the country, there were not only specific words for older brother (*anna*) and younger brother (*tamudu*), but also terms for each of their wives.

> *Family life in India focused on a large core family and its extended members.*

The central importance in Indian life of the family unit and kinship ties has given rise to several prominent family dynasties over the last decades. In the last 50 years, none has captured India's attention more than the Nehru dynasty. Motilal Nehru was a prominent Indian politician during the beginning of the 20th century. His son, Jawaharlal Nehru, became a leader in India's independence movement and went on to become the country's first prime minister. He had no sons, but his daughter, Indira Gandhi, followed in her father's footsteps. She was elected prime minister twice, from 1966 to 1977 and from 1980 to 1984. She had two sons, Sanjay and Rajiv. After his older brother Sanjay's unexpected death and his mother's assassination, Rajiv stepped into the political spotlight. He was elected prime minister from 1984 to 1989. Rajiv was himself assassinated in 1991, and since then his Italian-born wife, Sonia, and their two children, Priyanka and Rahul, have been at the forefront of Indian politics and gossip. At the regional level in different states, several family dynasties have emerged in the postindependence India.

Family life in India focused on a large core family and its extended members. Many lived in joint families under one roof, and their lives were punctuated by marriages, births, and other important life events. More recently, due to the impact of modernization and social mobility to cities and urban centers, the educated and the elites have adopted a nuclear family system.

To read about family life in 19-century India, see the India entry in the section "Family Life" in chapter 2 ("Domestic Life") in volume 5 of this series.

~Benjamin Cohen

FOR MORE INFORMATION

DuBois, A. J. *Character, Manners, and Customs of the People of India and of Other Institutions Religious and Civil.* 3d ed. Translated by Rev. G. U. Pope. New Delhi: Asian Educational Services, 1992.

Frank, K. *Indira: The Life of Indira Nehru Gandhi*. Boston: Houghton Mifflin, 2002.

Vatuk, S. *Kinship and Urbanization*. Berkeley: University of California Press, 1972.

JAPAN

The family has long been thought to be one of the most important components of Japanese society. For example, the reason for Japan's success during the country's 1990s economic boom was said to be the strong family values—such as loyalty, selflessness, discipline, and hard work—that were fostered in the Japanese home. Though such claims are no doubt simplifications, the Japanese family is indeed an important part of Japanese culture; this is the place where the individual's personality is formed, and where people become enculturated, or absorbed, into the larger society. And because many Japanese and western sociologists believe that the structure of Japanese society is hierarchical—and, thus, it is especially important that a person learn his or her place in the social order—the Japanese family has received much attention in the academic literature and the popular media.

Traditional Japanese families were what anthropologists call patrilineages (*ie*), which consisted of a long line of male blood relatives often living together in close quarters and sometimes sharing an occupation. The *ie* was self-perpetuating; its maintenance took precedence over any individual. The oldest living male head of the household was the nominal authority figure, though often his oldest son, who would later inherit his position, carried out his day-to-day responsibilities. Though the other, younger sons (and their male children) were also members of the *ie*, the eldest son was the owner of the property and had responsibility to insure the economic success of the lineage and to care for the ancestors' tombs and altars. This last obligation was particularly important, as the deceased relatives were thought to be as much a part of the *ie* as the living and theoretically were included in all important activities and decisions. Because all interactions with the ancestors involved Buddhist and Shintō ceremonies, the formalized *ie* family in traditional Japanese society was a place where social structure met religion.

In the traditional *ie* system, women usually had a secondary role. Daughters married outside the lineage, with the wife (and her subsequent children) becoming members of her husband's *ie*. At the same time, a needed hardworking hired hand or loyal servant might also be incorporated into the line as a fictive son (with the requisite filial obligations and benefits).

Ambitious younger sons might establish their own branches of the family, which, along with the main house, were called *dôzoku*. The branches always held allegiance to the main house. Because the *ie-dôzoku* system was codified into law in prewar Japan, this pattern of a special relationship between the main and branch houses became manifested in various ways from business to politics. Even personal friendships or relationships took on this character, with the older or established (*sempai*) taking the new or younger (*kôhai*) under their protection and guidance.

During the Allied occupation of Japan (1945–51), American advisors felt that the *ie* system contributed to the rise of prewar militarism and abolished it as a legal entity. The nuclear family of parents and their children is now the legally recognized social unit. Individual rights—as opposed to familial obligations—are now emphasized. However, in spite of these official proscriptions, vestiges of the old system still remain. For example, many Japanese young adults will still live at home until marriage, and eldest sons are expected to care for aging parents, still frequently inheriting much, if not all, of the parent's property.

Nevertheless, the contemporary Japanese family is very different from that of even a half-century ago. Part of the reason for this is modernization and industrialization, which make Japanese families today on the surface look very much like those found in North America and western Europe. Another reason is the remarkable demographic shifts that have occurred in Japan in recent decades. Simply put, Japanese today are living longer, marrying later, divorcing more often, and having fewer children than at any time in their history. Almost 18 percent of the Japanese population was over the age of 65 in 2001, compared to just 7 percent in 1970; there were 1.25 persons over the age of 65 for every one person 14 or younger. The average number of children per household was only 0.5 children (versus 1.41 in 1970). From 1970 to 2000, the average age of marriage increased by almost three years for males and four years for females; the divorce rate doubled and the birth rate halved.

In the past, under the auspices of the traditional *ie-dôzoku* system, an individual's marriage was very much a family matter, and these concerns overrode any single couple's wants or desires. Marriages, therefore, were strictly arranged. Although formally arranged marriages (*miai-kekkon*) are now on the decline, the custom still persists in somewhat looser form. So-called love marriages (*renai-kekkon*) are common—and perhaps are even the theoretical norm—but it is often difficult to determine if a marriage was actually instigated by the individuals themselves or resulted from the influence of friends, relatives, or coworkers—who may have acted as official or unofficial go-betweens (*nakôdo*). Dating as practiced in the United States and Europe is still somewhat uncommon, as Japanese young adults most often socialize in groups. Thus, the idea of an outsider taking an interest in one's love life is seen not so much as interference as concern or participation.

The stereotype of the modern Japanese family is one where the workaholic salaryman stumbles off to the office before dawn, leaving his wife to tend to the children and their schoolwork in a crowded apartment all day, returning home after 8:00 or 9:00 P.M. for supper and bed. Though perhaps applicable 20 or 30 years ago, today 40 percent of the Japanese workforce is female, and half the women of working age are employed outside the home. Better pay, higher education, and smaller families have changed gender roles substantially in recent years.

Finally, Japanese families are somewhat more extended than those found in North America or Europe. About 5 percent of Japanese families consist of households of three or more generations, and about a fifth to a quarter have a person 65 or older living with them. These numbers have remained fairly constant since the 1970s.

To read about marriage and family life in early modern Japan, see the Japan entry in the section "Marriage" in chapter 2 ("Domestic Life") in volume 4 of this series.

~*James Stanlaw*

FOR MORE INFORMATION

Fukutake, T. *The Japanese Social Structure*. Tokyo: University of Tokyo Press, 1989.

Hendry, J. *Understanding Japanese Society*. London: Routledge, 1995.

Hsu, F. *Iemoto: The Heart of Japan*. New York: John Wiley & Sons, 1975.

INUIT

At the end of the 20th century, kinship continued to be one of the most important social institutions in many communities in the Inuit North, and kin relations continued to overshadow the kinds of relationships, such as those between coworkers, church congregants, or neighbors, that dominated social interactions in the modern nation-states of which Inuit were a part. Additionally, despite superficial similarities, Inuit families in the late 20th century were not identical to Euro-American and Euro-Canadian family forms.

In the era preceding European colonization of the North and the construction of government-supported towns and villages, the Inuit had few institutions that were not based in kinship. The composition of social groups, usually referred to in the ethnographic literature as camps, changed throughout the year, but camps were almost always organized on the basis of kinship. Even in North Alaska, where the Inupiat maintained relatively large and permanent settlements, membership in whaling crews and *qalgit* (ceremonial houses) tended to be according to patrilineage.

One of the distinctive aspects of Inuit social life concerns the way that newborn babies are understood as part of the web of relations connecting all past and present members of a social group. According to Inuit cosmology, a person's name is associated with his or her soul. Upon a person's death, this name soul, or *atiq,* chooses to return to the social group as a new baby. Parents or other relatives may discover the "true identity" of a baby through a dream. The living relatives of the infant's namesake frequently have a special relationship with the baby and may call it by the kinship referent of their late relative. For example, a widow may call a child, either male or female, whose name is that of her late spouse "my little husband" and will treat the child with special affection. Likewise, the dead man's children may call the child "my little father." Contemporary Inuit maintain that while the child is not the exact reincarnation of his or her namesake, they can often recognize similarities in the actions or personality of the child and his or her deceased namesake.

Perhaps related to this understanding of a child as an already formed person, Inuit tend to regard a child as capable of independent thought and desire rather than as a personality to be shaped and molded by careful parenting. In the recent past, children, and especially teenagers, were permitted to make many of their own decisions about such things as when and where to eat and sleep, whether to go to school, or even which household to live in. Although children were never totally without adult guidance and supervision, they learned to make important choices and to be responsible for those choices. The Inuit believed that children would make correct choices as they grew and developed wisdom. At the same time, children had a relatively wide kin network providing emotional and material support.

Not surprisingly, the seemingly permissive Inuit style of child rearing conflicted with Euro-Canadian and Euro-American understandings about the capabilities of children. Non-Inuit teachers, social workers, and government officials often attempted to enforce different norms of child rearing, and Inuit child-rearing practices have changed, in part due to those pressures. More importantly, however, the Inuit have discovered that the child-rearing methods that were effective in small, kin-based communities are not suitable in contemporary towns and villages where adults can no longer supervise children discreetly or offer guidance modestly. One result has been a narrowing of the family circle to incorporate fewer categories of people and to make parents more directly accountable for the development of their children.

The increased incorporation of the Inuit into the economic and political life of nation-states during the last few decades of the 20th century has also affected Inuit family life in other ways. Various modern institutions and practices, such as wage labor, welfare payments, and government-sponsored programs, have tended to treat the family and the household as coterminous. Whereas the Inuit historically shared food and other resources among a fairly wide kin group, many current programs assume that Inuit social and financial obligations do not extend beyond the immediate household. For example, much of the housing in the Canadian North is public rental housing for which households are charged rent according to their income. Thus, households with higher incomes from wage labor jobs are generally charged higher rents than households with less cash income. On the surface, this policy seems fair, but it fails to consider financial obligations to and demands made by members of the extended family. Almost of necessity, wage-earning households are forced to withdraw from these kin-based sharing and support networks. Other programs encourage the elderly to live in old-age homes rather than with kin, young adults to seek independent living arrangements, and the young to pursue schooling and employment that take them away from their natal communities. One result is that while kin relations continue to be extremely important in the Inuit North in the 21st century, the understandings of who are kin and of one's obligations to kin are being redefined.

~*Pamela Stern*

FOR MORE INFORMATION

Briggs, J. L. *Never in Anger*. Cambridge, Mass.: Harvard University Press, 1970.
———. *Inuit Morality Play*. New Haven, Conn.: Yale University Press, 1998.
Condon, R. G. *Inuit Youth: Growth and Change in the Canadian Arctic*. New Brunswick, N.J.: Rutgers University Press, 1997.
Nuttall, M. *Arctic Homeland: Kinship, Community, and Development in Northwest Greenland*. Toronto: University of Toronto Press, 1992.
Sprott, J. W. *Raising Young Children in an Alaskan Iñupiaq Village*. Westport, Conn.: Bergin and Garvey, 2002.

ISLAMIC WORLD

From its inception in the Arabian Peninsula, Islam gave a central role to the family, and any modern understanding of Islamic life must recognize the deep attachment of Muslims to family. See the Islamic World entry in the section "Kinship" in chapter 2 ("Domestic Life") in volume 2 of this series. See the Islamic World entry in the section "Family Life" in chapter 2 ("Domestic Life") in volume 5 of this series for a description of family life in Islam in the 19th century.

DOMESTIC LIFE
|
MEN
|
United States

Latin America

India

Japan

Men

Given the wealth of scholarship on women and gender written in the last few decades, it is somewhat surprising that there are not more studies of men in the 20th century. Cynics might say that this is because written history typically focuses on men: their achievements, their failures, their thoughts, and their aspirations. Be that as it may, sophisticated gender analysis of men in the United States and elsewhere in the world is still a topic open for research. The entries in this section represent some of the current understanding of the daily lives of men in the 20th century.

As in earlier periods, patriarchy remained the central concept for understanding men's lives. Throughout the century, in India, Latin America, Japan, and the United States, men reaped the benefits of a social system that provided them with a dominant position in the family, in politics, and in the economy. This position did not go unchallenged. In India, Latin America, Japan, and the United States, women gained social, economic, and political power. But such things as the 19th Amendment to the U.S. Constitution, the increase in the numbers of female factory workers, and new laws giving women the power to divorce and claim full custody of children did not eliminate men's overriding power. Thus, although feminist groups made inroads against the system, patriarchy remained largely intact. One can see this in terms of wages. Regardless of education, qualifications, and experience, men made more money than women for the same work, though this gender gap was closing at the end of the century. One can also see patriarchy at work in general social preferences. In India, for example, the birth of a boy was seen as preferable to the birth of a girl. In Japan, men received better education than women and in Latin America the *machismo* ideal taught that women should be submissive to and supportive of men.

Although one might expect men to revel in their power, this was not always the case. In the United States, for example, there is a long tradition of men rebelling against the social expectations for them. In particular, some felt discomfort with the idea of having to become a self-made man. To deal with the pressures, some sought to control themselves and their environment whereas others sought escape and escapism. These notions did not appear for the first time with figures like James Dean. Rather, these two coping mechanisms were rooted in 19-century experiences.

In the 20th century, they gave rise to several movements, including those that advocated temperance of alcohol and those that encouraged males to join sex-segregated organizations such as the Boy Scouts and Men for Tomorrow. A confluence of these groups and ideas eventually produced the men's liberation movement of the 1970s and 1980s. Despite the growth of all-male organizations and the popularity of male-centered entertainment and support groups, the notion of the self-made man, like patriarchy itself, remained virtually unaltered.

UNITED STATES

The roots of American masculinity in the 20th century are found in the 18th and 19th centuries. The cadre of male revolutionaries that committed political patricide and broke the colonies from their king also established the general ideal of manhood in the United States. In a democratic society, men were to be strong individuals who regardless of birth made their own economic and political careers. They were to be, in a phrase first coined by the statesman Henry Clay in 1832, "self-made men." Despite the opportunities open to men, particularly white men, in the United States, the expectations of self-made manhood were high and were by definition in need of constant proof. One could not merely say that he single-handedly created his fortune. Rather, it had to be obvious and easily explained. Moreover, getting ahead was not easy for American men. The rich, both then and now, controlled the lion's share of economic and political resources. In 1774, the richest 10 percent of the population owned 50 percent of the nation's wealth. In 1860, the top 10 percent held 73 percent of the nation's riches. Such a situation caused men deep anxiety. In a nation of limited wealth, how were they to find the individual path to success? Since the nation's founding, American men have struggled with the tension that the ideal of self-made men has created, and by the late 20th century many men had rejected the notion completely.

At first, when faced with the difficulties of achieving self-made manhood, American men sought two solutions: self-control and escape. These two coping mechanisms developed in the 19th century had a strong influence in the 20th. In the Victorian era, self-control centered around alcohol and sex. The successful man was one who refrained from drink, an idea that made a lot of sense at the dawn of the industrial age in America. (Even today sobriety is a highly valued attribute in working men.) Though the prohibition movement had some striking achievements, such as the 18th Amendment to the U.S. Constitution, attempts to curb male sexuality were largely a failure. Reformers thought that

African American and white men work together in a Chrysler-Dodge factory during World War II. © Library of Congress.

controlling the male sex drive was the key to manhood. Specifically, they worried that masturbation would lead to sexual depravity and ultimately to madness, thus denying a young man opportunities to forge his economic and political future.

African-American and white workers vote in a union election at Ford's River Rouge plant; 80,000 workers voted in this wartime election. © Library of Congress.

To some concerned about curbing male libido, medical devices provided the cure. To others, such as J. H. Kellogg, the way to avoid sexual urges was to alter diet, and of course to eat Kellogg's invention designed for that purpose, corn flakes. Some men opted to control their passions for neither drink nor sex and chose instead to escape the struggles of attaining proven manhood. Joining the tradition set by Henry David Thoreau, many men went west to the frontier to avoid the rat race.

In the twentieth century, American men continued to struggle with the self-made man ideal. Indeed, the struggle grew more intense and divisive. Many men, particularly white men, believed that their path to manhood was being blocked by African Americans, immigrants, and women. Some men even formed single-sex organizations such as the Ku Klux Klan to regain their manhood at the expense of those they believed were in their path. The conflict grew more widespread in the early decades of the twentieth century as American women and African Americans fashioned their own civil rights movement to break down discrimination in family, political, and economic life.

White men relied on their old solutions to the anxieties relating to self-made manhood: they sought escape and self-control. The icon of male escape was (and still is) Theodore Roosevelt. His transformation from a sickly, effeminate boy to a rugged conqueror of the wilds made him an exemplar of manhood. For men at the turn of the century, it was also important to show self-control and display the proper male values, which included trust, loyalty, bravery, among others. Avoiding any hint of femininity or homosexuality were major aspects of the code of masculinity. To achieve this, men formed more all male clubs, both for adults and children, like the Men of Tomorrow, the Boone and Crockett Club, and the Boy Scouts of America.

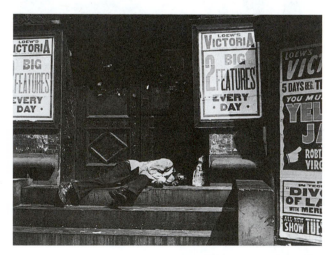

The Great Depression was a challenge to the ideal of the self-made man. Many men struggled to find their place in society. © Library of Congress.

World War II seemed to provide a temporary respite for American men. Achieving manhood in the economy was easy as high-paying jobs were plentiful and the war itself gave men and boys a chance to prove their mettle. However, in the decades following the war, men again struggled with achieving the ideal manhood. As had been the case before the war, white men saw the civil rights movements as a threat. African American men carried slogans such as "I Am a Man," which to white men was a direct challenge. So was the feminist movement. Solutions to this old dilemma changed somewhat by the end of the century. Escape was still a popular way to deal with the tensions arising from becoming the ideal man. In fact, by the turn of the millennium, extreme escape had become quite popular. Men would travel to locales and do sports that had significant dangers attached to them, all in an attempt to prove their manhood.

In the 1970s and 1980s a more popular way to deal with the inability to achieve self-made manhood was to join the "men's liberation movement," a group of loosely affiliated organizations that fought what they saw was the emasculation of men. For instance, men's lib groups wanted to end sexual harassment laws. Supporters of such an idea, such as Warren Farrell, believe that consensual sex between employees is courtship when it works and harassment when it does not. In addition to men's liberation, others decided that to achieve the masculine ideal one had to become hypersexual or hypermale, that is, sexually agressive or physically fit to an extreme.

The popularity of overmuscled superheroes like Rambo, professional wrestling, and for-male-only television programs such as *The Man Show* attest to this. Finally, for those men who worried about masculinity, there was a small movement to "get in touch with one's feminine side." In other words, some men opted out of the self-made man ideal completely. To put it in the popular terms of the day, it was the choice to become more like Dustin Hoffman in *Tootsie* than like Sylvester Stallone in *Rambo*.

To read about men in the United States in the 19th century, see the United States entries in the section "Men" in chapter 2 ("Domestic Life") in volume 5 of this series.

~*Andrew E. Kersten*

FOR MORE INFORMATION

Farrell, W. *Why Men Are the Way They Are*. New York: McGraw-Hill, 1986.
Kimmel, M. *Manhood in America: A Cultural History*. New York: Free Press, 1996.
Kotcheff, T., dir. *Rambo: First Blood*. 1982.
Pollack, S., dir. *Tootsie*. 1982.

LATIN AMERICA

DOMESTIC LIFE
|
MEN
|
United States

Latin America

India

Japan

Since the time of the European colonization of the Americas, Latin American men's roles have been heavily influenced by the gendered myths of male *machismo* and female *marianismo*. Machismo, a coterie of masculine superiority, celebrated male sexual–social power and often served as justification for aggressive and assertive behavior. Its counterpart, marianismo, glorified women's docility and subservience. As gender roles shifted in response to societal changes in the 20th century, the myth of machismo lost much of its potency, though it continued to exist.

In the early 20th century, men generally continued to dominate their families and households. Men demonstrated their familial authority in two basic ways: physical and financial. Their wages provided for their own needs as well as the needs of their wives and children. When deemed necessary, men resorted to physical means to assert their control and maintain order in their houses.

Men also found backing from the government, such as through a legal code—a holdover from previous centuries—known as *patria potestas*. This code designated men as legal custodians of all family members. Such laws supported the long-standing tradition that men work outside of the house while women remain at home.

Accordingly, the reputations of both men and women rested on gendered prescriptions. Whereas a wife's reputation depended upon her ability to rear children who would be an asset to her husband and herself, a man's reputation depended on his own virility. In other words, of utmost importance was a man's ability to simply procreate, or have multiple children. For the most part, the proper raising and educating of those children fell outside his purview, meaning the wife-mother often took sole responsibility for these tasks.

In the Caribbean, a slightly different pattern predominated. In large part due to the legacies of slavery, nonresidential conjugal unions were most common. Families were matrifocal; in most homes, women dominated—physically and financially. Accordingly, men were often considered marginal. The expectations associated with fatherhood were minimal. Fatherhood did not require a man's presence at home on a regular basis. Indeed, his responsibility was primarily financial; whenever possible, he provided his children with food, clothing, and school necessities. Often, a father's relationship with his children was rather formal and distant. In some cases, a father was responsible for disciplining his children, especially sons. This sometimes meant a physical punishment, strong enough for the child to remember it well into the adult years.

Throughout the century, men typically labored in the public sphere. If from a high racial or ethnic and economic standing, they entered politics or became lawyers or businessmen. Middle-ranking men often took jobs as teachers, or in the government bureaucracy. The vast majority of men—those of lower socioeconomic standing—were relegated to hard labor. Many worked in agriculture, on the *haciendas* (large landholdings dedicated to agriculture) and ranches of wealthy upper-class men. Others labored in the many mines of Latin America: copper in Chile, gold and diamonds in Brazil, tin in Bolivia. Still others migrated to large urban areas in search of work. As the century progressed, an increasing number of men found employment in factories, where they made shoes, assembled cars and electronics, or packed meat.

The middle and late 20th century brought major changes that seriously affected men: women gained many civil rights and entered the labor force in increasing numbers. By midcentury, as women won voting rights in most Latin American nations, they became more involved in the public sphere. Women entered politics and became the recognized leaders of social organizations and movements. In response to societal changes as well as economic necessity, more women entered the labor force. By the final decades of the century, many industries preferred female workers over their male counterparts. For example, along the U.S.–Mexico border and in numerous urban free-trade zones, many *maquilas* (export-focused factories) often exclusively hired women. For garment and electronics factories in particular, management preferred women for their dexterity and supposed docility, as well as the fact that they often received far less pay than men.

Whereas women generally perceived their expanded roles in a positive light, men typically did not. When men had a difficult time finding work, they might blame women for stealing their jobs. And their own wives who left the confines of the home became increasingly independent of their husbands, both socially and financially. As such, men felt their traditional authority threatened. In many cases, men vented their frustration through physical violence—in the latter part of the century, reports of domestic abuse dramatically increased.

As men's and women's roles shifted during the twentieth century, a certain "de-gendering" of Latin American society occurred. In other words, certain activities and beliefs became less associated with particular gender identities and more with other social groups such as adolescents, truck drivers, mestizos (an ethnic and racial mix of Spanish and Indian), or the rich. Yet, while practices on the ground may have changed, stereotypes continued to assert themselves. Traditional patriarchal relations, based largely on machismo, continued to prevail in much of Latin America. Many practices continued to be male dominated, such as alcohol consumption, domestic abuse, and hard labor, whereas housework and child rearing continued to be female dominated.

~Molly Todd

FOR MORE INFORMATION

Barrow, C. *Family in the Caribbean: Themes and Perspectives*. Kingston, Jamaica: Ian Randle, 1996.

Gutmann, M. C. *The Meanings of Macho: Being a Man in Mexico City*. Berkeley: University of California Press, 1996.

Klubock, T. M. *Contested Communities : Class, Gender, and Politics in Chile's El Teniente Copper Mine, 1904–1951*. Durham, N.C.: Duke University Press, 1998.

Paz, O. *El Laberinto de la Soledad* (The Labyrinth of Solitude). Mexico: Cuadernos Americanos, 1950.

INDIA

Within Hinduism in India, men have played the dominant role both socially and economically. The social ordering of the caste system generally afforded men a place of prominence. The caste system has had four idealized and broad divisions with which most Hindus associate themselves, and these were dominated by the men within each. At the top were the priests, a position filled by men. Next were the warriors, often royal and male. Third were the merchants, restricted mostly to men. Finally there were the laborers. Thus, the caste system that supported Hinduism was undergirded by a patriarchy. Even though the caste system of today has shed some of its rigidity, still it is a male-dominated society.

At the household level, men were at the head of each home, the oldest (fathers or grandfathers) at the pinnacle of power. In some cases, a matriarchy could be found, but generally, women were relegated to household upkeep while men were both the income earners and guards of the family's honor. Another link between being male

DOMESTIC LIFE

|

MEN

|

United States

Latin America

India

Japan

and the Hindu faith was that at the death of a man the eldest or surviving son, not daughter, of the deceased was to perform certain ceremonies, both for establishing himself as the universal heir and for the soul of the deceased to achieve eternal peace, or nirvana. Thus, the family name was passed from father to son along with rights and property. In many cases, one or all of the sons would continue not only the family line, but also the family occupation. For example, if a farmer died, his eldest son would be called upon to perform the funeral rites, and he might inherit the family property as well as the responsibilities of running the farm. In this way, having sons and being male often assured continuity within one's caste and occupation over generations.

For a Hindu, there were four symbolic stages of life. Though these were once closer to reality, they have now faded from common practice during the past 50 years. The first stage of life was *brahmacharya*, or youth and premarriage age. During these early years, a boy began to become educated and to develop physically. The second stage, *grihastha*, was that of the householder. During this time, a man was to be married and produce children, as well as become established in his occupation to provide for his wife and family. The third stage of life was one of spiritual retirement and contemplation. This was called *vanaprastha*. Having raised his children, a man retreated to worship and meditation. He might read and memorize spiritual texts and spend time at a temple or an ashram. The final stage of life, leading to death, was that of renunciation. This was called *sannyasa*. During this twilight of life, a man would leave or renounce his home and spend his days wandering in search of further spiritual fulfillment. He wore only a simple waistcloth and carried nothing other than a begging bowl and walking stick. A man might have wandered to spiritual centers or places of worship—mountaintops or river confluences. In his last days, he might have made his way to the holy city of Benares (also called Kashi) that he might die there. This was considered among the most auspicious places to die in India. To this day, it is possible to see men who have renounced their earlier lives and spend their time wandering and begging, only to find their way to Benares to spend their last days.

Generally, Hindu society considered producing a male child highly desirable, and thus the birth of a daughter resulted in mixed feelings. For example, in the early 20th century, a nobleman from Rajasthan (an area in northwest India) heard that his wife had borne him a daughter. The nobleman, Amar Singh, casually noted in his diary, "I do not much care whether the child is a male or a female" (Rudolph 317). He himself was indifferent, but he felt badly for his father and his patron, who would be disappointed at the failure to produce a male heir.

Yet the birth of a son would frequently elevate the position of the mother within the family hierarchy. Having sons guaranteed the perpetuation of the family line, and a common blessing for new brides continues to be "May you be the mother of a hundred sons."

Within much of Hindu India and among people who profess different faiths, namely, Islam, Christianity, Buddhism, Jainism, and Sikkhism, among others, men have dominated society. Reaffirmed by tradition, family, and caste, men have remained much at the center of everyday life. However, some changes have occurred as women's education and concepts of equality between the sexes have made their way into the male psyche. Still, after thousands of years of patriarchy, it will require more time before greater changes can be seen.

To read about men in 19th-century India, see the India entry in the section "Men" in chapter 2 ("Domestic Life") in volume 5 of this series.

~Benjamin Cohen

FOR MORE INFORMATION

Bumiller, E. *May You Be the Mother of a Hundred Sons*. New York: Random House, 1990.

Rudolph, S. H., L. I. Rudolph, and M. S. Kanota. *Reversing the Gaze*. Boulder, Colo.: Westview, 2002.

JAPAN

DOMESTIC LIFE

|

MEN

|

United States

Latin America

India

Japan

Because it is general knowledge that Japan continues to labor under a misogynistic social tradition, the popular misconception is that the country must be ideal for men. There is an element of truth to this, of course. Men are the beneficiaries of a double moral standard that allows them to philander with significant social license. Men commonly receive better educations and are treated preferentially in employment, in promotion, and in leadership roles.

But one must consider that men in Japan live six years less than women (75.86 years vs. 81.81 in 2002). Part of this disparity is attributed to overwork. In addition to complying with the standard 46-hour workweek, men are often coerced into staying on the job longer without additional pay to demonstrate "earnestness and sincerity." Government statistics claim that men work 1,800 hours per year; most labor unions report that the number is probably closer to 2,400. Coupled with a national average of a daily 90-minute round-trip commute to work (114 minutes in Tokyo) in packed commuter trains, and an all-too-common round of after-work drinks encouraged by management, men are simply tied to the office for too long.

Recently a survey showed that 65 percent of men considered themselves overworked and 79 percent of women considered that their husbands were. This has become a serious issue because 317 men died of what has been called "death by overwork" *(karoshi)* in 2002. Japanese medical associations show that in recent years the average blood pressure reading in men has increased by 17 percent. The National Police Agency reported a shocking 62 percent increase in work-related suicides between 1997 and 1998, with the number skyrocketing from 4,786 to 7,935.

Women complain that their husbands rarely spend more than two hours per week with their children. Men leave for the office before their children awaken and return long after they have gone to sleep. Until recently most businesses worked a half-day on Saturday. On Saturday afternoons and Sunday mornings men felt obliged to go golfing with their bosses.

Workplace pressures are exacerbated by other social expectations. Good citizens were expected to "volunteer" for neighborhood committees, and trade unions and religious organizations make similar demands. Also, financial pressures land squarely on the shoulders of men. No wonder that the suicide rate is so high among unemployed middle-aged men and those who retire (average age 55) only to discover that their savings are not enough to support their families.

Recently some younger men have rebelled against the traditional salaryman life. Many are shifting professions in midcareer, and many more are refusing to work overtime without pay or to accept transfers docilely. A substantial number have chosen to work for foreign companies that do not make as many demands on their time. The government has made some half-hearted public relations efforts as well.

To read about men in early modern Japan, see the Japan entry in the section "Men and Women" in chapter 2 ("Domestic Life") in volume 4 of this series.

~*Louis G. Perez*

FOR MORE INFORMATION

Ikuya, S. *Kamikaze Biker: Parody and Anomy in Affluent Japan*. Chicago: University of Chicago Press, 1998.

McCormack, G. *The Emptiness of Japanese Affluence*. Armonk, N.Y.: M. E. Sharpe, 2001.

DOMESTIC LIFE
|
WOMEN
|
Europe, 1914-1918

United States,
1920-1939

United States,
1940-1959

United States,
1960-1990

Latin America

India

Soviet Union

Japan

Africa

Islamic World

Women

Around the globe, 20th-century women struggled with and fought against patriarchy. In the Western world, improvements in women's social, economic, and political positions did appear, albeit slowly. Women pushed consistently and concertedly for political rights. In the United States, the women's suffrage movement began in the 19th century. Only in 1920, however, did American women finally achieve national voting rights. When reading these entries, be sure to compare the American political experience with women's political experiences in other nations. In Latin America, women also achieved some political goals and even became a major force in places such as Argentina and Chile. Even in Japan, women made gains in the second half of the century. But in other areas, such as India, Africa, and the Islamic World, the changes were less dramatic. In fact, notice the limits of Western feminism as well as the reasons that it did not spread further, especially in the case of Islamic societies in Asia, Africa, and the Middle East.

Also, when reading the entries, pay careful attention to how women's lives have been shaped by broader world events. World War I greatly influenced women in Europe and in Russia. Women served in the military and fashioned new roles on the home fronts. In particular, they entered industrial work in large numbers. Although women's labor participation rates fell immediately following the war, over the course of the century, women's place in the economies of many Western nations increased dramatically. During World War II, women in the United States, the Soviet Union, and many other countries again took on a range of traditional male jobs, maintaining military and industrial production at home and even sometimes fighting alongside men at the front in regular or partisan units. By the 1960s several nations, most notably the United States, passed legislation to insure that women and men were paid equally for equal work. Although in practice this did not happen consistently, in principle, these fairness laws were a significant advance.

Finally, women made some social gains as well. In terms of reproductive rights, the 20th century was quite important. In the United States, women slowly achieved rights to control their own bodies. In some countries, such as Argentina and Chile, women achieved social change in a different way. During the 1960s and 1970s, many Latin American nations engaged in what were termed *dirty wars*, in which national governments abducted, tortured, and murdered countless thousands of young men and women. When their individual protests fell on deaf ears, the mothers of these children banded together. Las Madres (the mothers) organized peaceful protests to learn about the fate of their children. Eventually, they became a mighty social force that helped to overturn many Latin American right-wing governments. Yet, as in politics and economics, there were limits to women's social advancement. In India, Africa, Japan, Latin America, the Soviet Union/Russia, and the United States, notions of women's "proper" social place kept women from making further gains. In the Islamic World, many women considered the religious and social restrictions of their culture liberating, even though those restrictions were often bitterly attacked by Western feminists. The destruction of patriarchy and of the ancient attitudes that supported it remained an elusive goal of many 20th-century feminist groups around the world.

Female employees at Oscar Schindler's enamelware factory in Krakow, Poland. Courtesy of the USHMM Photo Archives.

EUROPE, 1914–18

Women in all the belligerent countries entered the war bound by a range of peacetime social restrictions. Women of the middle and upper classes rarely worked, and their opportunities for higher education, especially professional study, were limited. Travel for young women took place only under the watchful eyes of their parents or other responsible adults. But many young women wanted to play a role in the war, and the intense and expanding nature of the conflict forced governments to listen to their wishes. Shortages of manpower opened the way, but so did the view that women could bring valued talents to the war effort.

Any consideration of women and the armed forces begins with the military nurse. She and her auxiliaries played the most predictable role, and the one all societies found most acceptable. Countries such as Britain and France had brought female nurses into their military systems around the start of the century and now recruited many more for wartime service. With the nurse's well-defined position as subordinate and helper to the physician, she did not overtly challenge what the era thought a

woman's work should be. Nonetheless, the circumstances of war gave skilled and experienced female nurses far greater responsibilities than were available to them in peacetime, and nurses had the best chance of any women to approach the fighting line and share the experiences of the combat soldier.

> *Nurses had the best chance of any women to share the experiences of the combat soldier.*

All the principal belligerents on the western front assigned large numbers of nurses to serve in military hospitals, sometimes well behind the front, sometimes in closer proximity to the fighting. Nurses had been an official part of the British army since the formation of Queen Alexandra's Imperial Military Nursing Service during the Boer War (1899–1902). As war approached in 1914, the service had 300 experienced professionals on its rolls, while nearly 3,000 nurses were enrolled with the Territorial Army, the British equivalent of the American National Guard. By 1918, approximately 23,000 women had served as nurses for the British military. Another 15,000 nurses' aides—known as VADs from their association with the Volunteer Aid Detachments formed before the war to help care for wounded members of the Territorial Army—were trained by organizations like the Red Cross to work alongside Britain's professional nurses.

The United States formed the Army Nurse Corps (ANC) in 1901 and the Navy Nurse Corps in 1908. The ANC expanded from 400 nurses in 1914 to more than 21,000 by 1918, with about half serving with the military in Europe. The expansion in the ANC was paralleled by the growth of the Navy Nurse Corps, which grew from 160 to 1,400 members. The French army began using Red Cross volunteer nurses in Morocco in 1907 and began training small numbers of military nurses in the years following. By 1918, more than 63,000 nurses had served in the French military. Germany enlisted female nurses for the first time in 1914, and by 1918 had employed 92,000 nurses and nursing assistants.

Intensive training courses accounted for these dramatic wartime increases in all countries. In France, thousands of women took hastily organized classes that concentrated on how to dress wounds. In Britain, service in the VADs attracted many enthusiastic amateurs, especially women from affluent families, such as the future feminist writer Vera Brittain, who soon found herself putting in 13-hour shifts in wards full of mutilated soldiers of all classes. VADs like Brittain took on more of the responsibilities of nursing professionals as the war went on.

Women volunteered for war service for a variety of reasons. Some were personal; as one French nurse put it, "A young girl, in ordinary life, is nothing or next to nothing. For the first time I was going to be someone. . . . I would count in the world." The call of patriotism was also strong. German nurses spoke vehemently of their desire to be "off to the field" to serve the fatherland, but also wrote in diaries and memoirs of how serving near the front allowed them to escape the stultifying and oppressive routine of peacetime nursing.

The influenza epidemic that swept through the military ranks in the closing months of the war created an additional burden for nurses. They were already straining to care for masses of wounded men, and now they were confronted with masses of disease victims. There was little to be done for those infected except to keep them warm and provide them with fluids. Some nurses had the opportunity to serve in a casualty clearing station close to the actual fighting. Considered to be a "plum" assignment by American nurses, these rare openings attracted 10 volunteers for every slot. Two hundred American nurses received decorations for bravery under fire from the American, British, and French authorities.

Nurses sometimes shared the danger of the battle zone. By 1917, German, British, and French nurses served close to the front where they risked being struck by enemy artillery fire. British and French nurses in rear areas perished from enemy air attacks. British nurses ran substantial risks because their duties often took them on sea voyages where submarines were a threat. A total of 195 British nurses perished during the conflict, 36 as a result of enemy action. Although no American nurses died of combat wounds, three were wounded by aerial bombs or shellfire.

The perils of wartime extended beyond the danger of combat. Proximity to the sick and wounded combined with physical exhaustion to expose nurses to a variety of diseases. Treating septic wounds meant that the slightest cut in a caregiver's hand could infect her as well. American medical authorities in France set up two hospitals to care specifically for nurses who had fallen seriously ill. Approximately 120 American nurses died overseas and about 180 at home, with most felled by influenza or typhus. German nurses frequently found themselves transferred from the western front to the Russian front, where diseases like malaria and typhus killed both soldiers and noncombatants.

By the end of the war, women were filling many other war service roles besides that of nurse. The first women to attach themselves to the military services were determined volunteers. From the first days of the war, women's organizations sprang up in Britain, France, and Germany to offer direct assistance to the fighting forces. Affluent women dominated the membership rolls of such organizations because they could serve without pay. Working-class women were unable even to afford the uniforms these formations adopted.

Prominent individuals founded hospitals and put them at the disposal of military authorities. Groups like Britain's First Aid Nursing Yeomanry, for example, took on a variety of tasks. As the war went on, Allied governments accepted the services of civilian women from a variety of backgrounds to work near the fighting front as clerks, cooks, ambulance drivers, canteen workers, and, in particularly large numbers, telephone operators.

No country moved quickly to put women into formal military service. By 1917, manpower shortages pushed Britain into leading the way. Auxiliaries to the army, then the navy, and finally the air force came into existence during the last two years of hostilities. Women from the upper and middle classes were welcomed into the WRNS (Women's Royal Naval Service, or the Wrens) to augment the navy and into the WRAF (Women's Royal Air Force) to free men in the air force for combat duties. The army equivalent, the WAAC (Women's Army Auxiliary Corps), soon got a reputation as the one auxiliary that opened the door to women from the working class. By the war's close, more than 100,000 women were serving in these adjuncts to the army, navy, and air forces.

British women volunteered in numbers that far outstripped the places available. A typical aspirant for a slot in the WAAC submitted an application accompanied by personal recommendations and went before a medical board composed of female physicians. A recruit who had reached the age of 18 was eligible for service in Britain; at the age of 20, she could be sent abroad. She received about a month's military training before being sent to a rear-area assignment in France. In Britain, some WAACs were permitted to live at home. WAACs were enrolled starting in March 1917, and the following month the first of them arrived for duty in France. WAACs mainly served as clerks, cooks, and telephone operators, but some took on such "unladylike" work as servicing army vehicles.

The United States responded more reluctantly to the wartime employment of women. The army refused to enlist women, but Secretary of the Navy Josephus Daniels saw no reason that enlisted clerks (yeomen) in the navy's ranks had to be male. Because so few men had the requisite skills in taking dictation, women could fill a pressing need. In March 1917, on the eve of American participation in the war, the American navy began to enlist "yeomanettes," whose numbers eventually reached 11,000. A bureaucratic dilemma arose because navy regulations barred women from serving at sea while those same regulations dictated that all yeomen had to be assigned to a ship. The navy's yeomanettes were assigned, at least on paper, to tugs that had sunk in the Potomac River.

With the onset of heavy fighting in the summer of 1918, the United States Marine Corps found itself short of trained men and followed the navy in calling for women volunteers. In New York City alone, 2,000 volunteers appeared. In the end, the Marines enrolled about 300 women, selecting only a tiny percentage of those who applied. Marine recruiters eliminated most applicants with a ferocious test of their secretarial skills. Female service members had to pass a physical examination as well as a test of their office skills. Unlike male recruits, women received no basic training. Many of them reported to their office assignments the day after they were sworn into service. Similarly, the military had no living accommodations for women, and they had to use their own energies, helped by a military housing allowance, to find a roof over their heads. The typical woman sailor or Marine filled a clerical position in the United States, although some women worked as messengers. Although barred from serving on ships at sea, females in the Marine Corps and navy held ranks equal to those of men in the same military specialties, and in the navy some rose to become senior petty officers. At the close of the war, all became eligible for veterans' benefits.

The Germans proved almost totally unwilling to place women in uniform. Only in the closing months of the war did they consider a female auxiliary to the Signal Corps. The conflict ended before the plan could be put into operation. The French government and military were no more flexible.

Civilian women involved themselves with the military forces from the start of the war. French women set up canteens at railroad stations to provide some comforts to the troops leaving for the front and the wounded making their way to hospitals in the rear. Individual women, often of prominent social background, set up hospitals and other organizations, then offered them to the armed forces. When the British armed forces refused the services of female physicians, several went to the western front anyway to treat French and Belgian patients. Individual Americans set up canteens behind the lines and volunteered to drive ambulances.

Women's organizations that offered the chance to wear a military-style uniform appealed to many in Britain. The first two years of the war produced, among others, the Women's Legion, the Women's Emergency Corps, and the Women's Volunteer Force. The Women's Volunteer Force, formed in September 1914, was intended to protect noncombatants in the event of a German invasion. The Women's Legion, founded in 1915, served a more practical purpose; its military cookery and motor transport sections performed many useful tasks. However, the sight of women in uniform stirred furious opposition to this blurring of gender lines. Letters to British newspapers advised these ladies to instead "put on sunbonnets and print frocks and go and make hay or pick fruit or make jam, . . . the thousand and one things that women can do to help."

Some French women served as war godmothers (marraines de guerre), becoming pen pals for soldiers at the front, especially those from French territory occupied by the Germans. The godmothers offered French soldiers moral support through the mail and often invited their "godsons" to visit them while on leave.

As early as 1915, the pinch of military losses raised the question of having French women provide direct assistance to the armed forces. By 1917, some spokesmen for public opinion, pointing to the British precedent, even called for women in uniform; however, such a campaign had no impact on official policy. The typical woman in the service of the military remained firmly identified as a civilian. She swore no oath to the country; she could leave her position at any time. Placed in kitchens and clothing shops, such women undertook work that differed little from their peacetime occupations.

The sight of women in uniform stirred furious opposition.

Only in 1917 did the situation change. The French government needed to place women in remote locales and to keep their services even though it could not pay them competitive wages. Policy now required a woman willing to work for the military to sign a three-month contract that forbade her from leaving her job. Even more of a departure was the government's willingness to let a small number of women, other than nurses, enter the combat zone. These were the drivers of the Woman's Transport Corps, who served as chauffeurs for army officers, as motorcycle messengers, and as ambulance drivers.

After the United States entered the war, large numbers of civilian women came to the front. Recruited by such organizations as the Red Cross, American Telephone and Telegraph Company, and the YMCA, thousands served as canteen hostesses, clerks, translators, and most frequently as telephone operators (the "Hello Girls"). All these women wore uniforms. Telephone operators had formally been sworn into service. Like soldiers, Hello Girls were expected to obey military authorities. Nonetheless, the uncertainty and hesitation of army authorities kept them from being formal members of the American Expeditionary Force. Unlike their sisters in the navy, they received no veterans' benefits after the war.

The role of canteen hostess brought only a small departure from a woman's role at home in peacetime. American YMCA hostesses were intended to maintain the soldier's tie with the world he had left across the Atlantic. These women were expected to provide a comfortable resting place for soldiers and to give them refreshments and a friendly female partner with whom to talk. Implicitly, they were to keep soldiers away from sordid sexual encounters with French women and the accompanying threat of venereal disease. Their own social lives and free time were closely supervised, and almost all found themselves serving under a hierarchy of male officials. No special skills were required for a canteen worker, who spent much of her time washing dishes and handing out doughnuts. Often educated and affluent, the majority of canteen workers were grossly overqualified for the tasks they carried out.

In marked contrast, hundreds of clerks and telephone operators brought to France by the United States Army in 1918 had crucial talents that the military needed. Although many army officers had doubts about bringing American women across the Atlantic to help run a complex communications network, General John Pershing, the commander of the AEF, decided that the need was pressing, especially for telephone operators. The inefficient French system brought intolerable delays to the transmission of important military messages, and bilingual American operators, under the control of the AEF, offered a solution.

The need to house and supervise female clerks and female telephone operators created a novel problem for the leaders of the AEF. They solved it by placing these women under the control of the YWCA, which set up residence halls for American women and provided chaperones and rules that resembled those in a college sorority (Heyman, 119–33).

FOR MORE INFORMATION

Heyman, N. M. *Daily Life During World War I*. Westport, Conn.: Greenwood Press, 2002.
Macdonald, L. *Roses of No Man's Land*. London: Michael Joseph, 1980.
Summers, A. *Angels and Citizens: British Women as Military Nurses, 1854–1914*. London: Routledge and Kegan Paul, 1988.

DOMESTIC LIFE

WOMEN

Europe, 1914-1918

United States, 1920-1939

United States, 1940-1959

United States, 1960-1990

Latin America

India

Soviet Union

Japan

Africa

Islamic World

UNITED STATES, 1920–39

The political position of women changed dramatically during the 1920s. Only seven months after national prohibition took effect, women's lives were transformed again by a constitutional amendment. On August 18, 1920, a tumultuous special session of the Tennessee legislature completed ratification of an amendment guaranteeing women the right to vote. Though in recent years a number of states had granted suffrage to women, that fact scarcely reduced the 19th Amendment's importance. The amendment not only gave the country's 30 million voting-age women a new political status, but it also conferred upon every female in the land the opportunity to claim enhanced social standing and greater independence.

Eager to respond to women's new voting power, Congress moved quickly to improve conditions in the risky, fearsome, and uniquely female activity of childbearing. An appalling 250,000 infant deaths occurred in the United States each year. In the poorest families, one child in six died within a year of birth; though the rate stood at 1 in 16 for wealthier families, it remained well above the rate in countries with maternal health care programs. The Sheppard-Towner Maternity- and Infancy-Protection Act of 1921 established the first modest federal health care program, administered through small grants to states for maternity education. Social and political conservatives complained, however, that the Sheppard-Towner Act invaded family and state responsibilities. As Congress came to realize that women's votes would divide much as did men's, its enthusiasm for maternal health benefits faded, and it terminated the Sheppard-Towner Act in 1929. Yet despite its brief existence, this progressive reform underscored the potential of legal change and federal government action to influence daily life. Thanks no doubt to increased prosperity, improved diet, and the new widespread availability of pasteurized milk together with the Sheppard-Towner innovations, the U.S. infant death rate fell 17 percent during the 1920s (Kyvig, 2–3).

To read about women in the United States in the 19th century, see the United States entries in the section "Women" in chapter 2 ("Domestic Life") in volume 5 of this series.

FOR MORE INFORMATION

Chafe, W. H. *The Paradox of Change: American Women in the 20th Century*. New York: Oxford University Press, 1991.

Cott, N. *Grounding of Modern Feminism*. New Haven: Yale University Press, 1987.

Kyvig, D. E. *Daily Life in the United States, 1920–1939: Decades of Promise and Pain*. Westport, Conn.: Greenwood Press, 2002.

Women and Social Movements in the United States. <http://womhist.binghamton.edu/index.html/>.

UNITED STATES, 1940–59

Although race had emerged from World War II as a clear category, gender was not used in the 1950s to help women define their rights. But the experiences of American women from the end of World War II through the 1960s also reflected the underlying social upheaval. The high marriage and birth rates and the low divorce rate intertwined naturally with the "feminine mystique"—the idea that woman's fulfillment was in the home and nowhere else. Yet women were already questioning domesticity as a consuming and permanent role. Like many blacks, they needed to make invisible selves visible and valued. They came slowly to realize that sex discrimination could be subtle as well as overt—even as they played the roles of wife and mother that society demanded. Most women were content for a time to make the most of these old-fashioned roles. Yet although many middle-class 1950s women are identified in women's magazines with suburban homes and large families,

the truth is that many others kept working after the war—not just to help pay the mortgage, but because work outside the home was satisfying. In 1955 that stalwart feminist Eleanor Roosevelt published an article titled "What Are the Motives for a Woman Working When She Does Not Have to for Income?" Self-esteem was Roosevelt's conclusion. She made readers recognize women's right to fulfill all their potential.

In *Personal Politics: The Roots of Women's Liberation in the Civil Rights Movement and the New Left*, a documentary book on radicalism, Sara Evans asserts that throughout the 1950s, "[W]omen from middle income families entered the labor force faster than any other group in the population." By 1956, 70 percent of all families in the $7,000 to $15,000 annual income range had two wage earners. Although women usually took the duller jobs offered them and suppressed the higher aspirations provided by better educations, they often saw such jobs as temporary. Instead of regarding themselves as victims—as later feminists often saw them—they just put their lives on hold while their children were very young. By no means did they accept domesticity, as their mothers might have, as their only choice—any more than they believed the television commercials that made "ring around the collar" the reason for their husbands' failures. American women have never been as gullible as Madison Avenue advertising writers—or as historians—see them. Tupperware may have made life in the kitchen easier for some women, but it also made jobs for the many women who sold it.

This mother in Buffalo, New York, picks up her children from daycare after work in 1943. © Library of Congress.

Nor were women obsessed with the appliances that Ronald Reagan and Miss America displayed on television. Large refrigerators with freezers allowed people to shop less often. And middle-class women with families made good use of washing machines without wringers and dryers that did away with clotheslines. Some still liked the smell of clothes dried in the wind, and others enjoyed baking as a kind of escape therapy. Prepared foods like soup mixes and cake mixes—and even instant coffee—entered the kitchen slowly. Whether most housewives felt guilty—as supposed—for making their chores simpler is worth examining in oral history interviews. When labor-saving devices like dishwashers appeared, homemakers of childbearing age often took advantage of freed time to explore new opportunities to do volunteer work.

In the 1950s, to be sure, women were denied access, as blacks were, to equal professional education and equal salaries. They were not readily welcomed back into competition with men. Betty Friedan, a Smith College summa cum laude graduate, published *The Feminine Mystique,* which, based on questionnaires sent to Smith College graduates in 1957, explored the glorification of homemaking. Though the book sold three million copies and made her famous, Friedan was labeled "too old" at age 42 to master statistics for a Ph.D. at Columbia. Most medical schools at the time had quotas to admit fewer than 5 percent women. And a number of prestigious law schools, and some graduate schools, often denied all women admission, asserting that they would be taking places away from more serious men. Too many women grew depressed at being locked out of professions and high-paying jobs. Psychotherapy flourished. But other women found ways to escape confinement. As Friedan discovered even as she decried the feminine mystique, American women often became ingenious at creating lives that enabled them to be useful citizens outside the home. In the 1950s, however, women put family needs first. Although women struggled to redefine their roles, they came through the 1950s with the same egalitarian sense of possibilities African Americans experienced.

A belief in Cold War victimization that shed light on some women's lives at this time by no means captured the energies of vast numbers who defined themselves beyond the narrow confines of one decade. Historians need to adapt interpretive time frames to women's biological roles to value women's achievements more precisely as opposed to those of men. The magazine articles usually cited to describe women's lives during the 1950s suggest little about their vision of society in any depth, or about their future goals for themselves. And such articles do little to assert the significance of the many important older women on the scene. The same magazines that celebrated domesticity offered lively journalism by Martha Gellhorn, Dorothy Thompson, Marguerite Higgins, and others. Betty Friedan suggested at one point that mothers be given the GI Bill to compensate for child-rearing years, as men were rewarded for a different kind of social service. Of those women who had been in the armed forces, fewer than 3 percent were able to take advantage of the GI Bill.

A good number of women did not envy the lives of middle-income "organization men," advertising executives in gray flannel suits, or even well-paid factory workers creating appliances for the new world of consumers. At a time when there was no organized child care, few families had relatives nearby to help with babysitting, and the jobs offered to women—still advertised in separate sections of the newspapers—were dull and ill-paid, many women willingly stayed home with their children if they could afford to do so. At that time it was still possible for many families to live on just one income. People seemed to have fewer needs.

Even if they did not see themselves fighting the Cold War in the kitchen, many middle-class college grads seemed to take Adlai Stevenson seriously when he urged the young women at Smith College's 1955 graduation to value the role of nurturing the "uniqueness of each individual human being." Yet new patterns of domesticity were emerging that were more deeply connected with the human rights of the nurturers. When Dr. Benjamin Spock rewrote his bestseller *Baby and Child Care* (originally published in 1945) for the third time, it was to eliminate sexist biases that perpetuated discrimination against girls and women. Spock acknowledged that his use of the male pronoun and his early childhood gender differentiation might well begin "the discriminatory sex stereotyping that ends in women so often getting the humdrum, subordinate, poorly paid jobs in most industries and professions; and being treated as the second-class sex."

In 1957, when Betty Friedan read the responses to questionnaires sent to her college classmates as the basis of her research on what was happening to women, she discovered a deep restlessness among the respondents. But she also found an attitude different from those of earlier decades that saw having children as limiting access to other roles. The "either/or" dilemma—children or career—that had characterized women's lot before the war was changing. Although Friedan herself acknowledged never having known a woman who had both a good job and children, the 1950s brought about a decided change. All the women she interviewed were planning ahead for freedom to be themselves. Postwar actuarial statistics revealed that women lived longer than men and would often have as many as 40 years ahead of them to lead creative lives after their children left the nest. Most women entering the workforce in the 1950s were older. The number of women over age 35 in the labor force had jumped from 8.5 million in 1947 to almost 13 million by 1956. As the median age of women workers rose to 41, the proportion of married women who worked outside the home also doubled between 1940 and 1960.

When she later became a founding member of the National Organization for Women (NOW), Betty Friedan spoke to the needs she had discovered in the lives of 1950s women. NOW's statement of purpose proclaimed, "Above all, we reject the assumption that women's problems are the unique responsibility of each individual woman rather than a basic social dilemma which society must solve."

Bringing about social change is never fast or easy. The self-consciousness of the 1950s became essential preparation for the decades of action ahead. Consensus and containment describe much of the postwar era, but history demands that more serious attention be given those—like Betty Friedan—who also worked hard to define and improve the moral quality of American life (Kaledin, 99–106).

To read about women in the United States in the 19th century, see the United States entries in the section "Women" in chapter 2 ("Domestic Life") in volume 5 of this series.

FOR MORE INFORMATION

Chafe, W. H. *The Paradox of Change: American Women in the 20th Century.* New York: Oxford University Press, 1991.

Friedan, B. *The Feminine Mystique.* New York: Norton, 1963.

Harrison, C. *On Account of Sex: The Politics of Women's Issues, 1945–1968.* Berkeley: University of California Press, 1988.

Kaledin, E. *Daily Life in the United States, 1940–1959: Shifting Worlds.* Westport, Conn.: Greenwood Press, 2000.

Women and Social Movements in the United States. <http://womhist.binghamton.edu/index.html/>.

DOMESTIC LIFE
|
WOMEN
|
Europe, 1914-1918

United States, 1920-1939

United States, 1940-1959

United States, 1960-1990

Latin America

India

Soviet Union

Japan

Africa

Islamic World

UNITED STATES, 1960–90

Women in the 1960s seeking to claim certain rights could trace the origins of their efforts as far back as the 1848 convention at Seneca Falls, New York, led by Elizabeth Cady Stanton. That convention had adopted a Declaration of Sentiments and Resolutions modeled on the nation's Declaration of Independence. "We hold these truths to be self-evident," they asserted, "that all men and women are created equal." It took more than 70 years for the sentiments to be translated into the right to vote, accomplished in 1920 with the adoption of the 19th Amendment.

If women expected their votes to bring swift changes into their lives, they had few reasons to cheer. They benefited from employment opportunities created by the impact of World War II, but most of those opportunities evaporated in the postwar years. After the war women were expected to step aside for returning veterans who wished to reclaim jobs; as a result, most women assumed roles that were just as restricted as before the war.

Two events in 1963 demonstrated women's plight and frustration. First, a report on sex discrimination by the Presidential Commission on Women, appointed by President Kennedy in 1961, documented inequities women experienced in the workplace and showed these inequities to be similar to those suffered by minority groups. The commission's findings revealed, among other things, that only 7 percent of the nation's doctors and fewer than 4 percent of its lawyers were women. Though acknowledging the larger role married women played in the economy than they had previously, the commission nonetheless asserted that a woman's primary role was as mother and wife, and it recommended special training of young women for marriage and motherhood. It also expressed opposition to an equal rights amendment, maintaining that the 14th Amendment sufficiently protected women's equality of opportunity. This amendment provides that states may not "deprive any person of life, liberty, or property, without due process of law; nor deny any person within its jurisdiction the equal protection of the laws."

From today's perspective the commission's recommendations seem unaccountably misdirected, but at least the federal government was looking more closely than before at the place of women in society. So were state governments. By 1967, all 50 states had set up commissions on the status of women. One tangible consequence of the commission's recommendations was the enactment of the Equal Pay Act in 1963, prescribing that women must receive pay equal to that of men when they performed comparable work—the first federal legislation in American history to prohibit discrimination based on sex. Changes were slow in coming, however, for in 1995 the average pay of women remained 31 percent below that of men.

A major boost to the women's movement occurred in a quirky way. Shortly before the bill leading to enactment of the 1964 Civil Rights Act went to the floor of the House of Representatives, Howard Smith, the 80-year-old chairman of the powerful Rules Committee, surprised everyone: he proposed inserting the word *sex* into the list of grounds on which discrimination would be prohibited by the act, thus making its provisions applicable to women. He thought this would kill the bill by making it unpalatable to a majority in the House. Emmanuel Celler, the 75-year-old chairman of the Judiciary Committee, reacted with outrage. He feared that granting women equal rights would deprive them of health and safety protections provided by other laws. He also believed the amendment would kill the bill. But pressure from women's groups and spirited work by a bipartisan coalition of congresswomen—three Republicans and two Democrats—caught Smith in his own trap. President Johnson had no choice but to offer his support for the amendment, and the kill-the-bill ploy failed. The result was a law that became the single most important force in guaranteeing women equal rights: the 1964 Civil Rights Act.

Despite new laws and new activism on behalf of women from such groups as the National Organization for Women, the place of women in families remained much the same in the 1960s. The majority of married, middle-class women were full-time homemakers, and those who by necessity or choice were employed outside the home arranged their lives around their duties in the home. Women generally entered the workforce at later ages than men, after fulfilling their primary child-rearing roles, and fewer than half of those who worked outside the home held full-time, year-round jobs. Thus their jobs, often taken simply as a way of adding to their families' income, did little to increase their sense of autonomy within the family, and their opportunities for advancing in the workplace were limited.

In the 1970s, however, the women's movement struggled to improve women's employment opportunities and working conditions and to help women better understand themselves and the surrounding society. Publications played an important role in accomplishing these purposes. For example, in 1973 a women's health collective—a discussion group of 11 women, itself a sign of the times—published *Our Bodies, Ourselves*, encouraging women to understand and control their own bodies. By 1976 the book had sold 850,000 copies. *Ms.* magazine, founded in 1972 by Gloria Steinem, sold 300,000 copies of its preview issue in eight days and had 250,000 subscribers by the end of its first year of publication. *Ms.* dealt with sexuality, employment, discrimination, and other feminist issues, whereas the traditional women's magazines such as *Ladies Home Journal* and *Good Housekeeping* continued to focus on domestic interests, celebrities, and romantic fantasies. Use of the term *Ms.* in place of *Miss* and *Mrs.* was controversial for a number of years, and only gradually did it gain acceptance. The *New York Times* began to use it in 1986.

In addition to encouraging women to assume new roles, the National Organization for Women pressed for such things as equal employment opportunities, child care centers, and reform of abortion laws. The word *for* in the organization's name showed that these were the causes that mattered and that men were welcome to help pursue them. NOW also led the quest for congressional passage and ratification of the Equal Rights Amendment (ERA), which stated: "Equality of rights under the law shall not be denied or abridged by the United States or by any state on account of sex."

Some in the women's rights movement wanted more radical changes in understandings of women's sexual identity and a swift end to male domination and social exploitation. Even though the pursuit of radical goals failed to win widespread support, and even though the ERA eventually failed to be ratified (despite approval in 35 states and polls showing support by 60 percent of both men and women), changes in both attitudes and practice revealed by several surveys in the early 1970s are worth noting. One showed that in a two-year period the number of college students who believed that women were oppressed doubled. Others showed that women interested in entering such fields as business, medicine, engineering, and law were outnumbered by men in 1970 by a ratio of 8 to 1; by 1975 the ratio stood at 3 to 1. The number of women entering law schools between 1969 and 1973 increased four-fold.

Women styling themselves as traditionalists played a big part in the defeat of the ERA. Believing that the women's movement had dealt mainly with the concerns of professional women, most of them with college degrees, these traditionalist women found a spokesperson in Marabel Morgan. Her book *The Total Woman*, published in 1975, urged women to scorn the feminists' concerns and "cater to her man's special needs." In other words, traditional roles of men and women should be perfected rather than changed or condemned. Although there were no formal affiliations between those who shared Morgan's views and Jerry Falwell's Moral Majority, their general purposes had much in common.

The traditionalists' most outspoken and influential leader was Phyllis Schlafly, an attorney, writer, and political activist who was anything but a stay-at-home mom. She and her followers charged that feminists' criticisms of traditional roles for women were an attack on ways of life that had brought them fulfillment and respect. Schlafly claimed in *The Power of the Positive Woman* (1977) that women who had been good wives and homemakers for decades would be "turned out to pasture with impunity" by what she called "a new, militant breed of women's liberationists." Her foes, she asserted, were willing to sacrifice justice for equality. The next year, when 20,000 women at the National Women's Conference in Houston celebrated the successes of the women's movement, Schlafly rallied a force of about 8,000 antifeminists. She drew cheers by denouncing the ERA, "lesbian privileges," child care funded by the government, and abortion.

Abortions were not illegal in the United States until after the Civil War, but legislation enacted at that time made those performing them and their patients criminally liable. However, prohibitions against advertising availability of abortions, convictions of persons who performed them, and rising public sentiment stirred by medical and moral concerns did not end women's desire to terminate unwanted pregnancies. According to informed estimates, a million or more abortions were performed annually in the 1960s, many of them exposing pregnant women to physical dangers. The fact that abortions could be done in ways that reduced the risk, along with fears of overpopulation, sensitivity to economic difficulties faced by large families, and growing acceptance of abortion as an alternative birth control method, led legislatures in about one-third of the states to make abortion laws less restrictive.

Abortions were not illegal in the United States until after the Civil War.

On January 22, 1973, the Supreme Court handed down a decision that would standardize abortion policies across the nation. In *Roe v. Wade*, the Court ruled by a 7 to 2 vote that all restrictions on a woman's right to an abortion during the first trimester of pregnancy were unconstitutional. In the second trimester, before a fetus could survive outside the womb, the Court ruled that a woman's right to privacy required a decision for an abortion to be made only by the woman herself and her physician. This provision grew out of the Court's determination that persons trained in medicine, philosophy, and theology could not agree on when a fetus becomes a person. In the third trimester—the last three months of a pregnancy—abortion was restricted to cases in which it was necessary to save the life of the mother. Following the Court's decision, the number of abortions performed increased dramatically. In 1977 doctors performed 1.3 million legal abortions. Every 10 live births were matched by three abortions.

Opponents of abortion rights reacted with horror to the Supreme Court's decision and its consequences. They began almost instantly to mobilize forces seeking its reversal. Annual rallies on January 22, the anniversary of the *Roe v. Wade* decision, were signs of what was to come in the 1980s, as those opposed to abortions organized a "pro-life" movement. Before long courts and legislatures were involved. In a highly publicized 1975 case, Dr. Kenneth C. Edelin, a physician in Boston, was convicted of manslaughter in the death of a fetus in a therapeutic second-trimester abortion. The Massachusetts Supreme Court overturned the verdict in December 1976 on the grounds that there was insufficient evidence to find him guilty.

The first legislative effort to neutralize the effects of the decision was the Hyde Amendment to the Health, Education, and Welfare appropriations bill in 1976. Named for its sponsor, Representative Henry Hyde of Illinois, the amendment barred the use of federal funds to pay for abortions "except where the life of the mother would be endangered if the fetus were brought to term." In 1980 the Supreme Court upheld the provisions of the Hyde Amendment. By then, Medicaid-funded abortions had declined from nearly 300,000 annually before the Hyde Amendment went into effect to under 4,000.

In response to restrictions imposed by the Hyde Amendment and the attacks on rights legally guaranteed by *Roe v. Wade*, those who believed that abortion decisions should be the prerogative of women in consultation with their physicians organized what came to be called the "pro-choice" movement. As the two sides squared off, middle ground disappeared and abortion became a central issue in the cultural stand-offs of the 1980s.

By the 1980s, a number of highly visible events provided evidence of a changing place for women in American life. In 1981, President Reagan appointed Sandra Day O'Connor, a state appellate court judge and former state legislator from Arizona, to the Supreme Court. As the first woman on the Court, she followed in the path-breaking roles of Justice Louis Brandeis and Thurgood Marshall, respectively the first Jewish and the first African American members of the Court. The following year Congresswoman Geraldine Ferraro was chosen by Democratic presidential candidate Walter Mondale as the first woman to run for vice president. The first woman to travel in space was physicist Sally Ride, and the first to work in space outside a spacecraft was Kathryn Sullivan.

In material terms, women gained from a 1983 ruling by the Supreme Court that differentiating between men and women in determining rates or benefits for group retirement plans was improper. Almost immediately, pension and annuity plans were required to offer equal rates and benefits. Members of Congress then began a move to require a comparable provision in life, health, and automobile insurance policies. Insurance companies, arguing that statistical criteria showing differences in longevity between men and women should be used in determining rates, spent millions of dollars to bring about its defeat.

In 1987 the Supreme Court ruled in a case involving the promotion of a woman by a city transportation system to create a more balanced workforce. Employers were permitted to take gender into account in promotion decisions even if a history of sex discrimination was not proven. Next came a unanimous decision by the Court upholding a New York City law that prohibited private clubs from denying membership to women and minorities. Because many cities had similar ordinances, this decision had a broad impact—although there was no rush by women and minorities to join clubs formerly closed to them, and when they did join there was little disruption.

Less visible but having greater effect on the daily lives of ordinary women was their growing importance in the workforce. The numbers of women employed in all kinds of regular, full-time jobs grew steadily, and more women found their way into executive, managerial, and professional positions. They still encountered extraordinary barriers, many of them rooted in stereotypical notions concerning their capabilities and proper roles, but many women managed to overcome them (Marty, 16–20, 93–94, 234–35, 260–61).

To read about women in the United States in the 19th century, see the United States entries in the section "Women" in chapter 2 ("Domestic Life") in volume 5 of this series.

FOR MORE INFORMATION

Chafe, W. H. *The Paradox of Change: American Women in the 20th Century*. New York: Oxford University Press, 1991.

Evans, S. *Personal Politics: The Roots of Women's Liberation in the Civil Rights Movement and the New Left*. New York: Vintage Books, 1980.

Marty, M. A. *Daily Life in the United States, 1960–1990: Decades of Discord*. Westport, Conn.: Greenwood Press, 1997.

Women and Social Movements in the United States. <http://womhist.binghamton.edu/index.html/>.

LATIN AMERICA

Since the European conquest of the Americas, women's roles in Latin America have been heavily influenced by marianismo. This myth, named after the Virgin Mary, exalted the ideal feminine virtues of propriety, humility, and sacrifice. Along with its male counterpart of machismo, marianismo designated women as docile, at all times subordinate to men.

Twentieth-century events challenged these myths and the stereotypes that accompanied them. Through the century, in response to political, social, and economic changes, women created new organizations and developed new ways of thinking. As women expanded their roles, they altered not only their own lives and families, but their societies as well.

Positive change came gradually for women. In the early part of the century, many Latin American countries continued to host an outdated civil code, known as patria potestas, which placed the male in charge of the household and all family members. Accordingly, most women (and particularly those from the middle and upper classes) found themselves confined to the private sphere, honored as the bearers of legitimate children, the keepers of familial and cultural traditions. There were few roles outside the home for these women; they could not enter universities or professions, only convents. For women of the lower classes—many of whom were heads of household—a broader spectrum of "public sphere" options existed, including factory work and prostitution.

In the 1920s, a wave of feminism rolled into Latin America. Women organized and pressed for expanded political roles. Due to pressure from women's groups like Chile's Movement for the Emancipation of Chilean Women (MEMCH), many national governments granted women the right to vote in the late 1930s and 1940s. (Suffrage dates ranged from 1929 in Ecuador to 1960 in Paraguay.)

Although women had long been an important part of Latin America's labor force, their contributions were often considered supplementary. Midcentury, however, as many countries underwent rapid industrialization and urbanization, women poured into the labor force as never before—from 1950 to 1980, women wage laborers increased from 18 percent to 26 percent of the workforce. Many women abandoned the sugar plantations and sheep ranches of rural areas to seek employment in urban industries, such as meat and fruit packing and cigar and shoe production. Some industries even favored female labor. This was particularly true for the garment and apparel industries in the Caribbean, in Central America, and along Mexico's border with the United States.

Although women increasingly filled the employment ranks, they continued to suffer from occupational segregation. In other words, they often received less-skilled and lower-paying jobs than their male counterparts. This was in large part due to the myth of marianismo and its accompanying stereotypes. Indeed, the management of Puerto Rico's garment industry and Mexico's *maquiladoras* (assembly plants for export products) evoked marianismo to explain why they preferred female employees and paid them less than men. To employers, women were more docile and tolerant than men and less likely to ask questions or complain.

Such beliefs and continued discrimination often led women and their organizations to focus on female-specific rights. For example, the Federation of Cuban Women (FMC) influenced government education programs. Beginning in the 1960s, technical schools in Cuba established quotas for female students, which allowed women better access to skilled trades and technical professions. Perhaps the most celebrated of the FMC's successes, however, was the 1975 passage of an egalitarian family code, which held men legally responsible for one-half of all household chores. In Brazil, an active women's movement shared similar successes, as the government created councils to address women's rights and opened new police stations specializing in cases of violence against women.

The political and economic crises of the 1970s and 1980s pushed many Latin American women further into prominence as revolutionary leaders (as in El Salvador, Nicaragua, and Peru) and pioneers of grassroots organizations. In the shantytowns around Lima, Peru, and Santiago, Chile, women confronted poverty by first establishing communal soup kitchens. Then, with leaders such as Peru's María Elena Moyano, they struggled against government neglect. In time, they won small victories for their lower-class communities such as teachers and schools, medical clinics, and basic services like electricity and running water.

One of the most well-known organizations of modern Latin America is Argentina's Madres de Plaza de Mayo, or Mothers of the Plaza de Mayo. Las Madres emerged in the late 1970s, when a repressive military regime ruled the country. Despite the fact that the government had forbidden public protest, the ever-growing group of mothers gathered every week before government buildings in Buenos Aires and demanded to know the whereabouts of their children who had been detained by the regime and had disappeared. They carried pictures of their missing children and on their heads wore white kerchiefs embroidered with their children's names and dates of disappearance. Even after Argentina's return to a civilian government, Las Madres continued its work, leading marches and protests and joining forces with other human rights groups to publicize the plight of *los desaparecidos*, or the disappeared, on national and international levels.

Chilean women protesting the abduction and possible murder of their children. © Neal Preston/CORBIS.

Similar organizations of mothers, grandmothers, and family members of the detained-disappeared emerged in other countries, including Guatemala, El Salvador, and Chile. During the Pinochet dictatorship in Chile (1973–89), women who lost relatives in the repression gathered to weave *arpilleras*, burlap and cloth appliqué landscapes that expressed important messages—of tortures, disappearances, and broken families. In a time when the military had banned traditional politics, the *arpilleras* became a new form of political action and protest.

Like the *arpilleras* makers, many of Latin America's most famous women artists integrated politics with art. Chilean writer Gabriela Mistral, the region's first Nobel laureate (1945), was also a diplomat. Other writers, like Elena Poniatowska (Mexico), Clarice Lispector (Brazil), and Isabel Allende (Chile), addressed politically charged themes in their books and essays. And the compositions of Chile's Violeta Parra inspired *nueva canción* (new song), a continentwide movement of protest through music.

Despite women's prominence in 20th-century Latin America, the twin myths of marianismo and machismo survived. Although there have been female presidents and prime ministers in many countries (including Argentina, Bolivia, Dominica, Nicaragua, and Panama), in the mid-1990s, women held only 10 percent of legislative and ministerial positions. Some sectors of society simply refused to let go of their antiquated opinions about women. Nubia Becker, a former political prisoner in Chile, explained that military officials of the Pinochet regime "rejected the fact that women were involved in politics, because women should be at home . . . looking after the family." Contrary to such beliefs in Chile and elsewhere, many women's experiences with war, repression, and poverty encouraged them to become strong feminists, as well as political and social activists. As women expanded and enlarged their own roles, they altered the political, economic, and social realities of Latin America.

To read about women in 19th-century Latin America, see the Latin America entry in the section "Women" in chapter 2 ("Domestic Life") in volume 5 of this series.

~*Molly Todd*

FOR MORE INFORMATION

Agosín, M. *Tapestries of Hope, Threads of Love: The Arpillera Movement in Chile, 1974–1994.* Albuquerque: University of New Mexico Press, 1996.

Skidmore, T. E., and P. H. Smith. *Modern Latin America.* 5th ed. New York: Oxford University Press, 2001.

Winn, P. *Americas: The Changing Face of Latin America and the Caribbean.* New York: Pantheon Books, 1992.

INDIA

Women have played a vital role in Hindu India, both within the domestic sphere and increasingly outside of the home in business and politics. Since time immemorial, women have been associated with spiritual power and the realm of the divine in the form of goddesses. More recently, women have risen to the forefront of politics (becoming prime ministers in India, Pakistan, Bangladesh, and Sri Lanka, which were under the British Empire) and have begun to amend many of the injustices and inequalities they have long suffered. Until the last century, though in theory considered to be powerful, in practice women were often mistreated. Women (and men) have been at the forefront of reforms that have begun to resolve certain inequities between the sexes.

Patriarchic practices have dominated India, yet some matriarchal societies did exist. They included the communities of the Garo, the Khasi, and the Nayar. However, they have been the exception and not the rule. Women in India have had a binary existence. On the one hand, they have been the mothers of children and the keepers of the domestic sphere. On the other hand, they have been revered as the holders of the *shakti*, or divine power. Some have capitalized on this role, leading troops into battle or commanding at the helm of national politics.

From birth, women have struggled to survive. Within a male-dominated society, the birth of a daughter was not always celebrated; infanticide has plagued Indian society. Mothers often put daughters to work as soon as they were able, helping in the field, in the home, or both. Cleaning, cooking, tending animals, and other tasks were all passed down from mother to daughter. In many cases, schooling for girls was not an option. At a young age, families arranged the engagement of girls to their future husbands. On some occasions, young girls would be married to much older men, who would accept them for a lesser dowry. The girl's family gave a dowry—a material gift that accompanied the bride—to her new husband and his family. At one time, it was to insure that the new bride would have adequate resources in her new home, but it has recently become a price that was paid to "sell off" a daughter to an appropriate husband. Dowries frequently exceeded the means of the bride's family. Further, many a groom and his family have demanded greater dowries after the marriage occurred. More recently, new brides have died under suspicious circumstances. Their husbands or in-laws have been suspected of murder but rarely prosecuted, and sons again remarried. For women, widow remarriage has not been accepted until recently and remains somewhat rare.

When a woman's husband died before her, there was the practice of *sati*, where the widow threw herself (or was pushed) onto her husband's funeral pyre, thereby joining him in death. Though outlawed, this practice has occurred in remote villages where law enforcement and education have been less stringent. Laws protecting women against rape and prostitution have also been lax and difficult to enforce. As women entered the workforce, they were less organized than male workers and thus have been exploited as laborers. These situations have led to the formation of both Indian and non-Indian women's groups. The social reform and feminist movements that have arisen from the plight of women in India have not been easily adapted within the subcontinent. In short, the types of feminism that have developed in Europe and North America cannot always easily be applied in India.

Although women in India have had a difficult role in society, there is no shortage of famous women from whom to draw inspiration. Within Hinduism mythical women have served as ideals for women of modern times. The epic tale *Ramayana* portrays Sita as the loving wife of Lord Rama. She was beautiful, devoted, and the perfect companion to her husband. Even today, women echo the virtues of Sita when asked what qualities form an ideal wife. These include "giving service," "bearing children to continue the family line," and "meeting a husband's sexual needs" (Poffenberger, 28).

Modern India has produced many remarkable women, including social workers, politicians, academics, writers, and scientists. Perhaps first among them in recent decades was Indira Gandhi, the daughter of Jawaharlal Nehru, India's first prime minister. At the time Indira was born, perhaps allaying disappointment in the birth of a girl, Nehru's father, Motilal Nehru, commented that the daughter might "prove better than a thousand sons." Indira was an only child and grew up in a somewhat lonely environment. Her mother was obscured by her father's participation in India's freedom struggle. Indira married and had two sons, Sanjay and Rajiv. She was among her father's closest confidants during his years as prime minister, and she herself was elected to the position in 1966. She oversaw tumultuous years, climaxing in the political "emergency" of 1977 where her party lost the election and she lost her position as prime minister. She was defeated after its withdrawal but staged a masterful political comeback in 1980. Indira Gandhi again served as prime minister from 1980 to 1984. However, after she ordered an attack on the Golden Temple of the Sikh community, two of her Sikh bodyguards assassinated her on October 31, 1984.

Another well-known woman in India was Phoolan Devi, who was born in 1959. At a young age she was attacked and raped by a group of high-caste men. After this, she fled her village and began a life of dacoity. After many years of marauding, during which she became known as the Bandit Queen, she was arrested and jailed for the murder of 20 high-caste men but was later released and went on to successfully run for a seat in India's parliament. She served from 1996 to 1998 and again from 1999 to 2001. In 2001 she was murdered in front of her home in New Delhi.

Women in India continue to play a role of ever-increasing prominence in society. Traditionally bound to the home, they have begun to enter the workforce and political sphere. Yet, for many women in rural areas, life continues much the same as it has gone on for centuries, and their uplift from countless difficulties cannot come too soon.

To read about women in ancient India, see the India entry in the section "Women" in chapter 2 ("Domestic Life") in volume 1 of this series; for 19th-century India, see the India entry in the section "Women" in chapter 2 ("Domestic Life") in volume 5 of this series.

~*Benjamin Cohen*

FOR MORE INFORMATION

Devi, P. I, *Phoolan Devi: The Autobiography of India's Bandit Queen*. London: Little Brown, 1996.

Poffenberger, T. *Fertility and Family Life in an Indian Village*. Ann Arbor: University of Michigan Press, 1975.

SOVIET UNION

The revolution in Russia changed women's roles in that country. According to the Soviet constitution, men and women were equally required to defend their country. During World War I, the provisional government formed women's battalions to shame the many male deserters into returning to the fight. During the civil war, tens of thousands of women volunteers (2% of the force), many of them soldiers' wives or sweethearts, joined the Red Army. Most were nurses or administrators, but some fought alongside male soldiers. For many, these women warriors signaled the beginning of a new era of gender equality. In his civil war diary, Isaac Babel described the female cavalry he saw in 1920:

The squadrons go into battle, dust, din, bared sabers, furious cursing, and they gallop forward with their skirts tucked up, covered in dust, with their big breasts, all whores, but comrades, whores because they're comrades, that's what matters, they're there to serve everybody, in any way they can, heroines, at the same time, despised, they water the horses, tote hay, mend harness, steal from the churches and from the civilian population. (Eaton)

During World War II, huge casualties caused a drastic shortage of able-bodied men, so the military recruited women as volunteers and also drafted them, although policies for drafting and promoting women were not consistent. Approximately 800,000 women served in combat and noncombat roles of every kind—besides being fighters and snipers, they were clerks; doctors; nurses; paramedics; cooks; postal workers; construction workers; military truck drivers; train engineers and crews on dangerous frontline routes; and radio, telegraph, and telephone operators. Many women who worked behind the lines were called on to fight at critical moments.

The government apparently never kept hard statistics on the age, nationality, or rank of women in the military in World War II, but, in general, most were probably teenagers and low in rank. Few were trained as noncommissioned officers (NCOs) or admitted to officer training. Of those who did become officers, most were political workers, attached to brigades and divisions, who served as Party organizers, Komsomol leaders, newsletter and newspaper editors, and political indoctrinators. Like male political officers, women commissars were expected to, and did, fight in frontline combat and often lost their lives. As the war continued, the line between combat and noncombat duties faded—nurses often carried and used guns while rescuing soldiers on the battlefield. Beginning in mid-1942, women began showing up on the front lines as regular army soldiers, sometimes fighting in all-female units and sometimes in mixed combat units. Altogether over a million Soviet women served in army units and partisan bands.

Partisans were guerrilla fighters who carried out sabotage operations in enemy-held territory by shooting; sniping; burning buildings; and blowing up bridges, trains, and railroad tracks. If caught, they were tortured and executed. Like their regular army sisters, Soviet women partisans in World War II fulfilled a range of overlapping roles, from medics to machine gunners, cooks, washerwomen, and lovers. The extent to which women were treated as equals by male partisans varied widely, depending on the group. Some bands preferred to keep females "in the kitchen," as one would-be woman fighter complained. Nina Kosterina was allowed to be a partisan even though her father and other close relatives had been arrested as "enemies of the people." In 1941, before departing her Moscow home to parachute behind enemy lines, Nina wrote in her diary, "I have a single thought: perhaps my action will save father?" Many male soldiers resented women fighters, and sexual rivalries and jealousies were common in mixed partisan bands and army units.

Few women served in the Soviet navy in World War II, but they made a significant contribution to the air force. During the 1930s, Soviet women pilots achieved more world flight records than women pilots in any other country and represented almost a third of all pilots trained in the Soviet Union. When war came, women made up 24 percent of air force personnel. There were three all-female air force regiments; their assignments, whether as flight crews or ground crews, were no less dangerous or difficult than those given to male colleagues. Yet, as in civilian life, women military personnel were not allowed to escape working double shifts. They might risk their lives on the battlefield and still be expected to cook and launder for the men and be the first on hand with medical care for wounded comrades. Female or male, those serving in the air force during World War II probably had a more fulfilling experience than infantry soldiers.

As soon as Germany was defeated, most women were immediately discharged from service, and their contributions were largely ignored. Although they received many thousands of military decorations and suffered proportionately higher losses than their male colleagues, Soviet women veterans were not allowed to participate in the massive postwar Moscow victory parade (June 24, 1945). Instead, they came home to official policies demanding their fast return to a steady, full-time civilian job, as well as to childbearing and nurturing, shopping, cooking, laundering, and cleaning. In a speech to a group of recently discharged female veterans, President Kalinin praised them for having "won equality for women . . . in the defense of your country, weapons in hand." Then he counseled them: "Do not give yourself airs in your future practical work. Do not speak of the services you rendered, let others do it for you. That will be better." Except for celebrations of Victory Day on May 9, when women veterans traditionally emerged, medal-bedecked, most official histories and commemorations bypassed them. Not until the 1960s did the military once again recruit large numbers of women specialists. In the late 1980s several thousand women were in the armed forces, in medical, communications, and administrative jobs, most with the low rank of warrant officer. Women served in the Afghan war in the 1980s in a much more limited role than they had in World War II; they were not sent in to fight, but served in medical and other support roles. Nevertheless, female medics were frequently in danger, especially when they worked under fire to remove the wounded. At least 12 servicewomen died in Afghanistan. Females were never admitted to military academies, the main route to promotion in the officer corps.

In the world of work, the equality proclaimed by the Russian Revolution meant that women were rapidly included in all parts of the workforce. Official Soviet philosophy proclaimed women's right to work outside the home; even without that encouragement, low salaries made it imperative for most wives to contribute income, although for many the "double shift" of work inside and outside the home was exhausting. In I. Grekova's novella *The Hotel Manager,* the heroine, Vera, is a colonel's full-time housewife. When she enters the hospital to get an abortion, she has to endure the contempt and envy of her fellow patients in the abortion ward, all of whom are working women: drivers, stockroom attendants, librarians, guards, and even a woman judge.

At home and at work, men were the privileged class. A working woman might spend as long as two hours a day, every day, searching for goods and standing in lines, and then return home to do the household chores. On a typical weekday evening, laden with heavy shopping bags, women rushed home (by overcrowded subway and bus) to their Moscow apartments, anxious about whether their husbands had remembered to feed the children—which they often hadn't. The exhausted mother (who had been going nonstop since 6 A.M.) then lit the stove and put on potatoes, water, milk, and cutlets, the first meal of the day for her since she did not have time to eat breakfast or lunch. After supper the woman bathed the children and put them to bed. By 9 P.M, she was ready to wash dishes and then her children's clothing and handkerchiefs. She might close her day by mending some clothes and getting the children's clothing and supplies ready for the next morning.

A popular joke illustrated Soviet women's second-class citizenship. A shipwrecked Russian couple are cast away on a desert island. When after many months rescuers finally arrive, only the man is found, snoozing in the sun. "Where is your wife?" the rescuers ask him. "The masses are working in the fields," he replies. To their credit, Russian husbands were often the family fixers, repairing household items, including the car and plumbing (for families that had those items) (Eaton).

FOR MORE INFORMATION

Eaton, K. B. *Daily Life in the Soviet Union*. Westport, Conn.: Greenwood Press. Forthcoming.

Noggle, A., ed. *A Dance with Death: Soviet Airwomen in World War II*. College Station: Texas A&M University Press, 1994.

Thurston, R. W., and B. Bonwetsch, eds. *The People's War: Responses to World War II in the Soviet Union*. Urbana: University of Illinois Press, 2000.

JAPAN

In June 2003 the Japanese Cabinet released a white paper on equal gender participation that castigated Japan for remaining a "developing country" in gender equality. The implication is that although Japan was of the First World in terms of economic development, it was more like a Third World nation in its treatment of women. This stunning admission of gender inequality comes as no surprise to most social scientists, who have for years criticized the country for the pervasive discrimination of women in the workplace and in society in general.

Despite the equivalent of an equal rights amendment embodied in the 1947 constitution and in spite the 1986 equal employment opportunity law, Japan continues to lag far behind the rest of the developed world in its treatment of women. The statistics are woeful indeed.

Only 20.2 percent of all civil servants are female, the lowest rate among all nations surveyed. Japan trails the Philippines (53%), the United States (49.3%), and Great Britain (49.1%). Among new employees in all public sectors only 37 percent received some college education and only 50 percent of all women over the age of 15 years of age were in the paid labor force. A shockingly low 3.7 percent of all middle managers in public companies and less than 1 percent of all CEOs are women. About 40 percent of the total workforce are women, but they are relegated to the lower levels of service industries, receiving less than 60 percent of male wages.

Worse, women are often categorized as temporary part-time workers despite the fact that they work as many hours and often have held their jobs for as long as men. Their second-class employment status denies them full employment benefits including health insurance, retirement packages, seniority, and promotion schemes. Members of the "permanent" and "regular" male workforce derisively refer to women as "helpers" and "office ladies" (OLs), demanding that women serve tea and tidy up the office. Even women who are college graduates and hired as regular employees are pressured to marry and to take long maternity leaves. Those who do so lose seniority; those who do not are treated with scorn.

Sexual harassment has long been tolerated in male-dominated workplaces. Few men are punished or even reprimanded for such behavior. Women are rarely invited to join their male peers in after-hours drinking and bonding. These social gatherings become "old boy networks" that predominate in all major hiring and promotion schemes.

Part of the reason for this sorry show is that Japan continues to labor under traditional misogynistic social mores. For centuries women were little more than

chattel in a feudal neo-Confucian social system. During the feudal centuries (1192–1868) women were relegated to servant status and were considered little more than rented wombs for the perpetuation of a patriarchal society.

The Meiji constitution (1890) and the civil code (1898) denied women all civil and political roles and made them wards of the "three obediences" (to father, to husband, and, if widowed, to son). Women received all civil rights in the 1947 constitution, but an increasingly conservative "reverse course" of the government after that period relegated women to inferior status.

A small but very vocal feminist movement has tried to ameliorate the worst aspects of discrimination, but it has made little real progress in that uphill struggle. The most progress has been in the green movement, where women have led the fight for environmental protection; safety laws; and the peace movement. The leftist parties have long championed the cause of women. The peripatetic president of the Japan Socialist Party has been a woman (Doi Takako). Even the dominant Liberal Democratic Party pays some lip service to women, though mostly in the Cabinet Secretariat. Recently, two women have risen to serve in one of the most important cabinet posts, minister of foreign affairs. One, Tanaka Makiko, is the scion of a former prime minister (Tanaka Kakuei); the other, Kawaguchi Yoriko, succeeded Tanaka in large part to counter the argument that Tanaka had been ousted from the position because of misogyny. There are rarely more than two female cabinet ministers (of some twenty).

Some Japanese argue that Japanese feminism should not be compared with its Western counterparts. Women in Japan, they argue, have tremendous anonymous power in that they control family budgets and determine the futures of their children without much help from their husbands. While men are off at work for up to 18 hours a day (including long commutes and obligatory company socializing), women control the house and the neighborhoods. Women lead neighborhood PTAs, co-ops, and recycling and neighborhood development committees with virtually no male membership. Also, women have made great strides recently in terms of university faculty as well as in the leadership of many foreign-owned companies. A number of influential women have risen to important positions within various United Nations agencies.

The counter-argument is that these caveats are the exceptions that prove the rule of institutionalized misogyny in Japan. Men make the important and national decisions; women are important in the affective and the international spheres of influence.

A full two-thirds of Japanese women surveyed in the previously mentioned Cabinet white paper on equal gender participation stated that they believe that men are given preferential treatment. Only 57.3 percent of women surveyed opposed the traditional idea that women should stay at home and take care of the home and children. In comparison, 93.2 percent of Swedish women opposed that idea. Japanese women reported that their husbands averaged about 48 minutes per week helping out with housework. In Europe, women reported that the average was three hours.

Without substantial change, women will continue to be tied to traditional home and family responsibilities and will lag behind men in virtually every public and political role.

To read about women in early modern Japan, see the Japan entry in the section "Men and Women" in chapter 2 ("Domestic Life") in volume 4 of this series.

~Louis G. Perez

FOR MORE INFORMATION

Bernstein, G. L. *Recreating Japanese Women, 1600–1945*. Berkeley: University of California Press, 1991.

Imanura, A. E., ed. *Re-Imaging Japanese Women*. Berkeley: University of California Press, 1996.

Sievers, S. L. *Flowers in Salt: The Beginnings of Feminist Consciousness in Modern Japan*. Stanford: Stanford University Press, 1983.

AFRICA

Throughout the 20th century, it has become increasingly difficult to provide a general, all-encompassing account of the lives and experiences of African women. Variations in region, religion, culture, lifestyle, ethnicity, race, educational background, and class have all produced diverse and inherently different experiences for the African woman. Consequently, one must be careful when attempting to compile such an analysis, as the experience of a Yoruba market woman in Lagos, Nigeria, is certainly different from that of her cattle-herding Maasai counterpart in rural Kenya.

For most of Africa, precolonial societies were male dominated. Men dominated politics, wars, economies, food production, trade, and even the family unit. In general, the precolonial African woman's responsibilities were tending the fields, food preparation, and child rearing. Women were vital members of their societies but were certainly secondary to their male counterparts in terms of power, independence, and affluence.

Colonial rule only accentuated these gender differences. European colonization claimed that one of its aims was to liberate the oppressed African woman from a chauvinist society, but these claims were superficial at best. Colonization served to perpetuate and worsen the oppression of African women. Colonial rule aimed to profit from African labor, goods, and raw materials. Most forms of employment (i.e., mining and commercial farming) were for African men. African men flocked to these jobs in order to pay colonial taxes, but they earned meager wages and only a small amount of money was ever sent back home to wives and families. Therefore African women were forced to adapt, stretching tight budgets to compensate for the loss of male family members in the fields.

World War II increased migration to the cities and mines and thus gravely altered the lives of African women. The war and an economic depression created dire conditions throughout the continent. During this time many men enlisted in military regiments and many others migrated to urban areas in search of better wages. As a result, the responsibilities of most women increased dramatically. Many women were forced to maintain subsistence farms, raise the children, and even look for wage employment to supplement their husbands' meager wages.

The majority of African women still live in rural areas and work in agriculture. Cash crop and subsistence farming are both practiced, but cash crop production has become dominated by men. As African economies have become dysfunctional, subsistence farming has been increasingly abandoned for cash crops.

Poor economies and economic inadequacies have forced both married and single women to migrate into cities. For most of the 20th century, Africa experienced unprecedented levels of migration to urban areas, a trend that has yet to cease. African cities are seen as having steady employment and economic opportunity, and thus more Africans are abandoning their traditional rural lifestyle in hopes of improving their economic status in the cities. These hopes, however, have not translated into reality. Employment opportunities for urban women have been inadequate and few. Middle-class government jobs and the formal economy have been dominated by men, both through colonial rule and even after independence. Colonial governments often allowed only men to attain such jobs, and this trend has yet to be altered in the postindependence period. Therefore urban women had to find employment as domestic servants, prostitutes, and eventually schoolteachers. They also found work in the informal economy.

The informal economy is petty trading that is not taxed and has not been incorporated into a global economy. This is one area where African women have flourished and even grown to dominate in some areas. These women trade fruit, cloth, foodstuffs, handicrafts, and other basic necessities. This trading offered women an avenue to provide for their families. In western Nigeria, Yoruba women have come to dominate this area in comparison to their male counterparts, and the trend has continued throughout the continent. Today, African women continue to dominate these informal economies in cities such as Dakar, Johannesburg, Lagos, Accra, Brazzaville, and Nairobi.

Educational opportunities for African women have traditionally been inadequate. For much of the century, European and African officials viewed women's education as being only marginally important. For the majority of colonial rule, European authorities sought to instill Victorian ideals of femininity through education. In the early 1900s, schooling often aimed to teach African women the benefits of "civilized" behavior and Christianity. Consequently, women's education served only to reinforce and cement their status as second-class citizens to men. Only toward the end of colonial rule (the 1940s and 1950s) and during independence was women's schooling reformed to provide women a more adequate education.

In general, educated African women have found few economic advantages. Professions such as teaching were offered to women only in the later phases of colonial rule. This lack of employment opportunities for educated women has translated into a low percentage of African women attaining university degrees or even finishing secondary education. Families have often felt that boys have the best chance of using their education for economic gain, so many girls withdraw from schools before completing primary school. Many girls choose to withdraw in order to pursue employment, help with child rearing, or find apprenticeships in the informal economy.

Even today, education for women has not necessarily translated into the betterment of African women. The nations of Lesotho and Swaziland have relatively high levels of female literacy, but both continue to have two of Africa's most desolate economies.

In sum, it is impossible to state whether the positions and lives of African women have been improved throughout the 20th century. It is possible, however, to state that the experience of the African woman has been inherently altered since colonial rule. Certainly, life has not been easy for the overwhelming majority of African women as they have been both oppressed and neglected by foreign powers as well as their neighbors and husbands. African women have shown a tremendous amount of strength and perseverance in surviving and adapting to the changing landscape of this past century.

To read about the roles of women in Africa in the 17th and 18th centuries, see the Africa entry in the section "Men and Women" in chapter 2 ("Domestic Life") in volume 4 of this series.

~*Tyler Fleming*

FOR MORE INFORMATION

Allman, J., S. Geiger, and N. Musisi, eds. *Women in African Colonial Histories*. Bloomington: Indiana University Press, 2002.

Bay, E. G., ed. *Women and Work in Africa*. Boulder, Colo.: Westview Press, 1982.

Berger, I., and E. F. White. *Women in Sub-Saharan Africa: Restoring Women to History*. Bloomington: Indiana University Press, 1999.

Coquery-Vidrovitch, C. *African Women: A Modern History*. Boulder, Colo.: Westwood Press, 1997.

ISLAMIC WORLD

Muslim women in the 20th century found themselves in a dramatic confrontation between their traditional roles and the increasing globalization that marks the modern world. In some countries, such as Tunisia, Muslim women worked outside the home in occupations as varied as traffic police officers and travel agents. In other countries, however, such as Saudi Arabia, women were expected to remain covered and enclosed.

Perhaps the most striking example of the challenges to modern Muslim women's roles may be seen in the creation of an Islamic counterpart to the American Barbie doll, which is popular all over the world. In 1996, Iran began selling the Sara doll, which was intended to compete with Barbie dolls. Sara is dressed in long, flowing robes and head coverings and is intended to promote traditional Muslim values of modesty and family obligations. In the future, Muslim women will forge new roles that will no doubt differ from those of both their traditional past and those of Western women. See the Islamic World entries in the section "Women" in chapter 2 ("Domestic Life") in volume 2 of this series for the traditional beginnings of women's roles; to see the endurance of this traditional role for women, see the

DOMESTIC LIFE

WOMEN

Europe, 1914-1918

United States, 1920-1939

United States, 1940-1959

United States, 1960-1990

Latin America

India

Soviet Union

Japan

Africa

Islamic World

Ottoman Empire entry in the section "Women's Roles" in chapter 2 ("Domestic Life") in volume 3 of this series.

Children

Perhaps in no other century did the daily lives of children change as much as they did in the 20th century. In 1900, children around the world shared a common existence. Generally speaking, the birth of a child was considered a blessing. And yet, for most children, life was exceedingly hard, and for too many it was short. This was true in the United States, in Latin America, in Europe, and in India and Japan. And yet, by the middle of the century, there was a significant difference between children in the so-called First World and children in the so-called developing world.

Take the entries on the United States as examples of daily life for children in the First World. Following the Great Depression and World War II, families became better off and more able to afford nice clothes, good food, toys, and adequate health care for their children. At the same time, American culture became intensely focused on the upbringing of children. Parents and politicians alike considered education a top priority. Dr. Spock's baby care books were best sellers. Milton Berle, one of the most popular television figures, called himself Uncle Miltie because his show was so popular with children. He actually helped put the kids to bed at night. Though many parents welcomed television into their homes, some feared its impact on their sons and daughters. Sure, *Ding Dong School* and *Sesame Street* were fun and educational, but they did expose children to new ideas, ones of which their parents may or may not have approved.

Japanese culture is also heavily focused on raising children. But a Japanese childhood is short and the pressure to achieve and conform according to societal expectations has proved to be the greatest danger to the health of Japanese children and young people.

Daily existence was quite different in Latin America and India. Despite having compulsory education systems, Latin American countries lagged behind in primary schooling. In India, only the higher-caste kids had access to education. Most Indian and Latin American children were needed to work in the fields, the factories, and the home. Working conditions for children were exceedingly poor and dangerous. It was not uncommon in some Latin American countries for children to labor more than 50 hours a week. As the entry on India indicates, work for children there typically began before dawn. The pressures, hardships, and monotony of these children's lives was broken only by books and games, particularly football (soccer).

It is important to note that at times in the 20th century the children of the developed world also lived joyless lives. During World War II in particular, children in Europe and Japan were at risk to experience the horrors of man's hatred for man. Despite the opportunities and possibilities for children in the 20th century, they remained among the most powerless and the most at risk.

EUROPE, 1914–18

European children saw their lives change during World War I. Many of their male teachers left for military service. With one out of every three German schoolteachers gone, children attended school only a few days a week and sat in combined classes that held as many as 80 students. The army regularly requisitioned German schoolhouses, and a child was likely to attend classes in an uncomfortable makeshift location provided by local government or religious authorities. School curricula everywhere included topics connected to the war, and children became the objects of official propaganda. German schoolchildren received lessons in the vital area of food conservation. History and geography were obvious areas for patriotic wartime themes. But with a little imagination, a teacher could use a mathematics lesson as well—for example, asking a class to convert the 200 marks a German prisoner of war in England received from his family into English pounds.

Starting in 1917, war study courses appeared in American schools. Elementary school students learned that the United States was at war with Germany to protect the victims of German aggression in Europe. A more emotional theme certain to make an impression on a young child also appeared in the syllabus: American soldiers were fighting "to keep the German soldiers from coming to our country and treating us the same way." High school students received much the same message in a short book for them prepared by Samuel B. Harding, a professor of history at Indiana University. David Kennedy has summarized Harding's message as declaring "that Germany alone had caused the war, that German soldiers fought cruelly without regard to the laws of God or Man . . . and that the Allies sincerely wished peace, which the Germans callously scorned." In 1915, German schoolchildren were asked to draw their impressions of the war for an exhibit in Berlin. Whereas many elementary school girls sketched an absent father, male students of that age produced detailed and accurate drawings of submarines, guns, and zeppelins. Children in the 10- to 14-year range showed their awareness of the gritty side of the war with violent combat scenes and images of battlefield casualties. By early 1917, teachers were dazzling schoolchildren with stories of heroic U-boat commanders and their promising efforts to win the war for Germany.

French children were presented with a curriculum that integrated the war into every subject. Essays made up a large part of the school routine, and they offered a chance for children to hail French heroes like General Joseph Joffre; to express pride in the fighting men at the front; and, most striking, to articulate their hatred for the Germans. One French schoolboy in 1916 wrote of that hatred that "will always exist between the French nation and the German nation, for what they have done is unforgivable and unforgettable." On the other hand, a youngster's willing immersion in wartime feelings did not always last. By the final year of the war, French schoolteachers reported that many children were indifferent to the conflict's events. Some even expressed pacifist sentiments.

The strains on the school system combined with a wealth of job openings to pull older children into the factories. Meanwhile, the departure of fathers and schoolteachers, along with the general disruption of peacetime routines, led to a surge in juvenile crime. In Germany, unexcused absences from school became common, and the number of adolescents convicted of crime in 1918 stood at twice the prewar figures. Adolescent boys found their labor in high demand in wartime industry. The resulting high wages gave them a freedom the authorities found dangerous and disturbing. Such young men were much in evidence in Germany's bars, tobacco shops, and movie theaters. They were reputedly frequent clients of the country's prostitutes.

German authorities approached the problem with a variety of measures. An employed teenage boy was likely to encounter one of the growing number of youth-welfare workers, and he also faced recruitment into an officially sponsored paramilitary organization, the "youth army," designed to prepare him for life in uniform at a later age. He faced a curfew in many areas and often found himself forbidden to smoke in public. His freedom to visit bars after nine o'clock in the evening and even to attend the movies without an adult was also subject to official restrictions. Starting in 1916, many workers younger than 19 saw the bulk of their wages placed in bank accounts that they could tap only with official permission.

In Britain, the delinquency of young females stirred concern, especially during the early part of the war. The sudden expansion of the army meant that military camps were springing up all over the country. The dislocation of the nation's young men was matched by blows to the routine lives of young working-class women, many of whom lost their jobs as the war disrupted civilian industry. Alarmed middle-class observers saw many of these young women turn into so-called "khaki girls," who clustered around military camps and sought relationships with new army recruits.

The fear of khaki girls reflected a mixture of concerns: the spread of venereal disease, the new social freedoms being seized by lower-class women and girls, and especially the possibility that these practices would move up the social ladder to provoke similar behavior from young females in "better" families. An image of wild girls corrupting innocent young men in uniform appeared in some commentaries. One writer described a group of soldiers pursued by young girls like "tigresses at their heels." An even more alarmed observer worried that "impressionable, undisciplined girls, hardly more than children, . . . have often ended by entangling themselves and their soldier friends in actually vicious conduct." Creating British women's police patrols became one remedy for the problem. Once established, these enforced middle-class moral standards in public places. Some women's police organizations eventually became integrated into regular police forces. During the war, their stated aim, as one spokeswoman put it, "was to act as a steadying influence on girls and young women, and in general to look after their interests." The danger faded as the conflict continued. The growing war effort provided abundant places for potential khaki girls in war industries, health services, and eventually in women's auxiliaries to the armed forces. The Girl Guides, founded before the war as a sister organization to the Boy Scouts, seemed to offer a healthy outlet for young women's exuberance and energy. Their numbers almost doubled during the course of the war—from 40,000 to 70,000 members—and observers saw them turning potential khaki girls into upstanding junior citizens (Heyman, 171–73).

FOR MORE INFORMATION

Harding, S. B. *The Study of the Great War: A Topical Outline, with Extensive Quotations and Reading References*. New York: U.S. Committee on Public Information, 1918.

Heyman, N. M. *Daily Life During World War I*. Westport, Conn.: Greenwood Press, 2002.

Kennedy, D. *Over Here: The First World War and American Society*. New York: Oxford University Press, 1980.

Williams, J. *The Other Battleground: The Home Fronts: Britain, France and Germany, 1914–1918*. Chicago: Henry Regnery, 1972.

HOLOCAUST

The tragedy upon the tragedy in the Holocaust related to the children who had no means whatsoever to defend themselves or escape Nazi-occupied Europe. Few Europeans or Americans answered the call for help. The World Movement for the Care of Children from Germany was the response of the British people to *Kristallnacht*. It was the umbrella organization for many groups, including the Jewish Refugees Committee, the Quakers, the churches, and countless individuals. What was missing was the necessary emergency legislation to give the operation legal status. A Quaker, Bertha Bracey, on behalf of the Quakers, accompanied Lord Samuel, the Liberal statesman, to meet with Sir Samuel Hoare, then home secretary, who secured Parliament's urgent consent.

On November 21, 1938, only 10 days after *Kristallnacht*, the House of Commons debated the refugee issue, and on the same day the government announced its decision to permit "an unspecified number of children up to age seventeen from German-occupied lands to enter the United Kingdom as 'transmigrants.' " A £50 bond had to be posted for each child. On December 8, former prime minister Stanley Earl Baldwin issued a radio appeal: "I ask you to come to the aid of victims not of any catastrophe in the natural world, nor of flood, nor of famine but of an explosion of man's inhumanity of man."

The English responded. Within a short time, more than £500,000 had been contributed. Great Britain permitted the largest number of refugees to enter the country. The *Kindertransport* (children transport) program in part sponsored by the World Movement for the Care of Children from Germany permitted 10,000 refugee children to go to England.

The news of the *Kindertransport* spread, and all parents tried to save their children. The committees in charge of rescuing the children tried to identify those in dire need, such as orphans, to give them priority. In some cases, German Quakers helped in the identifying process.

Of course, not all children were fortunate enough to escape to England. Ernest Gelb was a teenager when he was taken to the camps. He was born in Czechoslovakia, in a 150-year-old house that had been in his family since it was built. At one point his family had been fairly wealthy, but they had suffered a setback during the Depression. Still, he and his large family, which included three sisters and several young aunts and uncles, were happy. Their dining table seated 18 and was often full

DOMESTIC LIFE
|
CHILDREN
|
Europe, 1914-1918

Holocaust

United States, 1940-1959

United States, 1960-1990

Latin America

India

Japan

of family and guests, especially on the Sabbath, when his mother, after cooking all day, would ceremoniously collapse before dinner.

When the war began, Ernest's family was aware of what was happening in the rest of Europe. Although there was only one radio in the town, newspapers were available and everybody followed the progress of the war. In 1941 the Russians had allowed some Polish soldiers to stay in the town, and Ernest had heard them talk about what was happening to the Jews. The soldiers taunted the listeners, claiming that the same thing was going to happen to them.

In addition, foreign Jews living in Czechoslovakia had been deported to Poland, and some had escaped and made their way back home and told stories of what they had seen. Ernest's aunt had been arrested and his mother had managed to rescue her by "paying bribes to anyone who asked." She too came back with stories. Despite all of this information, no one was willing to believe how much danger they were in.

Child victims of the Holocaust. Courtesy of the USHMM Photo Archives.

On Passover in 1944, as he rode the train home from school, Ernest saw German soldiers at every stop. On April 21, a horse and wagon and two border police stopped at the Gelbs' house. In a recent interview Ernest recalled, "we had a half hour to pack. We were being taken 'for our own protection.' That we didn't want to be protected did not much matter (and why didn't the non-Jews have to be transported for safety?)."

Ernest's family had known this was coming for several days, and Ernest had buried valuables in the yard with a note in a flask telling where everything was hidden. Nobody in the village thought to run—they had nowhere to run to—and no one asked to hide: "I don't think anybody could possibly believe that anything really bad was going to happen."

His mother had spent three days baking, while Ernest delivered to his relatives things that they had to leave behind. His father had already been taken by the Hungarians to serve in a forced-labor battalion, and his mother was exhausted from trying to keep the family safe and fed.

The family was taken to a ghetto about three miles from home, where they stayed for about a week, and then, "again for our protection," to a camp where some 50,000 Jews were being held prisoner. After three weeks, his mother was frantically worried about her children's future, and about her parents, whom she believed were in the camp, though she was not allowed to look for them. Ernest's uncle had been beaten by a guard and his shoulder was broken. (His injury healed just in time for him to be deported to Auschwitz.)

Finally, the time for deportation arrived. As always, the Nazis lied: "We were told we were going to the promised land, families would not be separated, nothing is going to happen to anybody, this place isn't so bad, the next won't be either."

Ernest and his family, along with 95 others, their luggage, and their packages of food, were loaded into a cattle car.

There was one huge can in the center for going to the bathroom and another one for water. You sat down and spread your legs and the next person sat in the space. Once we were in there and the doors were locked there was instant panic, people with claustrophobia, and children, were frightened. There was one little window which was barred. . . . The train started moving. We didn't know where we were going. We realized there was a guard at the sides of each wagon. When there was too much noise there was hitting and yelling. At each station, the children were held up [to the window to identify where they were]. We went through Cracow and then we didn't think we were going in the right direction because Poland was not our favorite place.

They were taken to Auschwitz, where Ernest, his older sister, and his uncle were selected for work. Happily, he and his uncle were assigned to the same barracks. "We were greeted by a person with a name tag *schreiger* [boss]." They were given a "welcoming" lecture. " 'You are no longer people, you are prisoners. What you are wearing on your head is called a "mitzer," a cap. When I say "mitzer up" you obey.' As he was talking to us he pointed to the chimney. 'By the way, those are your relatives over there.' " Ernest was horrified. "And you know what, I don't know how a heart attack feels, but I had a rush of something and I knew that I believed him and I made up my mind that I did not want to be here. The next day they asked for volunteers to go somewhere, and I told my uncle I was going."

He was taken to Buchenwald and from there to a series of labor camps. At Buchenwald he was assigned a number, 2562, and learned that during the previous winter 30,000 inmates had perished. This was the best of the camps to which he was taken. "You went through the gates and walked ten minutes to work. The biggest factory I ever saw. Two huge tunnels that the trains went through, forty-six halls 200–300 feet long."

Along with prisoners from France, Poland, and Russia, he was put to work building the scaffolding used to construct the walls of the camp. Although the food was good and the work was bearable, the 17-year-old boy still lived in constant fear.

At Auschwitz, when he was told to leave his clothes and shoes behind, he had managed to keep his shoes, his first pair of handmade shoes, a special present for his 13th birthday. They were the only piece of home he had. One day, during lunch, while doing his best to remain invisible, he was accosted by a "seven-foot giant," a Gypsy capo.

Without even looking at me he says, "Take off your shoes." I think, should I give him my shoes? He's not even my Kapo. I had tried to keep my shoes dirty, covered them with dust. He was not yet forceful, so I asked my Kapo—"Do I have to give him my shoes? Who is he?" My Kapo just nodded. And that was the end of my shoes.

I want you to know, in the seventeen-year-old's mind in the concentration camp, I think I lamented the shoes as much as when I heard about my family. Seventeen is supposed to be quite aware, but this really punished me. The shoes were like a connection. There was still something. Now you're on your own.

As winter approached, life became even more precarious. The 15-minute walk to the tunnel, in cotton pajamas, and the roll calls were increasingly harder to bear. Some prisoners used the inner shell of cement bags to line their pajamas, but even these had to be accounted for, and stealing them was very dangerous. "One day there was an inspection. On the way back, unfortunately, they started hanging people. For the next week or so, almost daily, there were two or three corpses. Right there when we got back there was a reception for us. So, I stopped [taking the bags]. I guess I wanted to live."

In November, Ernest was shipped to a "bad camp." The grounds were muddy all the time and walking was very difficult. The work was hard, and they had to be up at 4:00 A.M., washed, dressed, and in line. "The roll call was really punishment, almost a competition of endurance, whether the weather would outlast us or we would. Counting and looking and looking and counting. It was a game and there was no way out."

The work was out-of-doors, building bridges, putting up telephone poles. The food was mostly water and a little piece of bread for supper.

In February, some Russian prisoners of war (POWs) entered the camp:

They were fiercely independent and had a special spirit. One would go near the SS kitchen every day and bring a full set of potatoes and cook them and share them. Nobody asked where they came from. He was caught and killed—immediately sentenced and hung right in front of all of us. . . . You felt terrible, you felt bad, and then you went on immediately. We had to go back to work. You couldn't say because of this I can cop out. You couldn't.

Anne Frank, October 10, 1942. © Getty Images.

Ernest tried hard to get a job in the kitchen. "You had to pass a test peeling potatoes [quickly] with only a few eyes left." He flunked the test, but a friend who passed it brought him a carrot, a beet, and a couple of potatoes.

One day he felt so sick he had to do something to get some rest. He had a bad foot and was suffering from a gangrenelike vitamin deficiency.

I kept washing it, but it did no good. The cloth stuck to it, and it smelled terrible, and I decided I must take a vacation. So I lost my pants on purpose, in February. It was cold and I was standing outside with no pants. The guard says, "Where are your pants?" "I don't know, I lost them." "Twenty-five lashes." He started beating [me] and I passed out and the vacation started.

Ernest was sent to the infirmary. A kind French-Jewish doctor helped him for a week, but he was in a tuberculosis ward and had to leave. The doctor put him in the typhoid ward—a huge barracks of naked men, allowed only blankets so they couldn't escape and infect others. "It was warm, corpses with eyes open in the beds. That's me and the whole bunch."

He was given no treatment for his leg. Nonetheless, he survived for three weeks—just long enough to be ordered out. The inmates were being marched west. Unable to walk, even with help, Ernest was put in an open wagon. It was March and they were all freezing.

For nine days they traveled on bombed-out roads, in snow and rain. He was numb. There were continual requests for dead bodies to be thrown from the cart, but he kept some to keep himself warm. For five days there was food. For the next four there was none. There was constant shooting. When they arrived at their destination, another camp, of the 80 men in the wagon, only nine were carried out. The rest were dead.

Ernest was still alive. He was served soup, "[t]he best I ever ate in my life." It was April 1945. Finally the shooting had stopped. "The Germans were out—the Russians were in."

There was plenty of food. Everybody was running around with food, but Ernest remembered the lessons he had learned from the Talmud, and he proceeded to tell his friends a story:

Once, before the destruction of the Temple, one man, Reb Tzadek, fasted for forty years. He ate only at night, and only a small amount. His stomach was as thin as parchment. When the doctor went to feed him, he gave him only a little soup, a spoonful of flour. Slowly. If we eat now we will die. (Soumerai and Schulz, 214)

They boiled some potatoes and ate just a little. It was May 1, 1945. For Ernest, the war was over.

When he was feeling a little better he made friends with a young Russian soldier. The soldier decided to celebrate the end of the war by killing a German. So they went to a nearby village and walked into a house. The Russian demanded rice, thinking the family would have none and he would then have an excuse to kill them. Astonishingly, he was given rice. The family cooked it; they chatted and had a little meal, and the Russian thanked them. Then the father asked them to sign a little book, to show to other soldiers so they would be safe. That the Russian would not do, but he did spare their lives.

Ernest spent the next two months in a Russian hospital, where he was operated on and recuperated from his wounds. Then he went home. His father, an old man at 44, and one sister were alive and waiting for him. Ernest's sister, who was with their mother when she died, later told him of those last days:

In February 1945, after weeks of marching, my mother in the bitter winter weather became ill with typhus and severe frostbite. She did manage not to fall, because whosoever fell was summarily shot. They arrived at Proust near Gdansk, Poland, and found shelter in some barracks next to a makeshift air terminal. They considered themselves fortunate. There were about 1,000 women there—all waiting to die. There were no medications but a lot of kindness. Two days before my mother passed on, a friend from a previous labor camp was able to procure a bowl of hot oatmeal cereal with cinnamon which my sister fed her gently. A week later my mother died a peaceful death. The Russian liberators arrived three weeks later. By then, most of the women had died.

(Soumerai and Schulz, 64–65, 210–15).

FOR MORE INFORMATION

Holliday, L. *Children in the Holocaust and World War II: Their Secret Diaries*. New York: Pocket Books, 1995.

Klein, G. W. *A Memoir: All But My Life*. New York: Hill and Wang, 1995.

Soumerai, E. N., and C. D. Schulz. *Daily Life during the Holocaust*. Westport, Conn.: Greenwood Press, 1998.

Spielberg, S., dir. *Schindler's List*. 1993.

DOMESTIC LIFE

|

CHILDREN

|

Europe, 1914-1918

Holocaust

United States,
1940-1959

United States,
1960-1990

Latin America

India

Japan

UNITED STATES, 1940–59

During the early years of World War II, when day care was socially acceptable and wages were high, the birthrate surged. In 1939 American women earned 62 percent of men's wages, but by 1953 they would earn only 53 percent of what men earned. Although the war did much to demonstrate that women could do men's work, it did little to provide women with long-lasting competitive moneymaking careers. Because "family life" had been defined as an important value worth dying for during the war, as the wartime economy soared, the birthrate did, too. The low birthrate of the Depression years disappeared. Many women chose to give full attention to families of three or four children. As more people learned about birth control and family spacing, both very large families and only children became associated with the past. The Census Bureau proclaimed the 1943 birthrate the highest in U.S. history.

Babies also became a consolation for the great number of young women offered no training in career alternatives. The war had weakened general standards of education in the 1940s. A poll of high school students in 1942 revealed that 44 percent had no idea what the war was about. Yet in 1943 Congress killed a bill to raise teachers' salaries to attract more stimulating people to the profession. Some politicians were afraid of hot rods and comic books and the youthful hysteria for pop stars like Frank Sinatra—new and different interests that represented a separate teenage culture. Sociologists speculated that the easy money of wartime may have distorted the values of many teenagers who could not see how learning related to earning—and how work led to a better life.

These two wartime patterns—an increase in the birthrate and worries about childhood upbringing—continued after the war. The idea of personal sacrifice that characterized the world of the Great Depression and World War II might have disappeared altogether had it not been for the baby boom that suddenly anchored many young people to new and larger families. In 1946 an all-time record of 3.4 million babies were born—26 percent more than in 1945. Into the next decade babies poured onto the American scene in record numbers. Indeed, by 1964 two-fifths of America's population had been born since 1946. Having developed a strong sense of their capabilities during the war, women transferred many of their skills to raising large families. It was no longer just religious opponents to birth control or the poor who had large families. The greatest jump in fertility occurred among well-educated white women with medium to high incomes. And just as the war

Not all children led "typical" lives. This Japanese-American child is bound for an internment camp. © Library of Congress.

created new jobs and prosperity, so did the baby boom. Diaper services, baby food, educational toys and playgrounds, and special furniture for children became big business. Dr. Spock's book on "commonsense" child care became an all-time best seller. For a brief period—for a vast middle class—the sense of prosperity and family solidarity was real. Before the next decade was over the divorce rate would continue to climb again—as it had done before the war—and the family would begin to lose power as a source of community stability in American life.

One source of instability in family life was the introduction of television and worries about its effect on children. Many parents tried to limit young children's programs to cartoons and educational shows. In the norms adults were trying to establish for their own lives, many struggled to provide sensible entertainment for the boom generation of children. Milton Berle even called himself Uncle Miltie because so many children enjoyed his slapstick show that their parents asked for his help in putting them to bed.

In the beginning gentle programs for preschoolers like *Kukla, Fran, and Ollie*, *Ding Dong School*, and *Captain Kangaroo* counteracted the violence of Saturday morning cartoons. These programs often dealt sensitively with specific problems children experienced, emphasizing rational approaches to conflicts rather than fighting. And there were educational programs for older children about zoo animals and space travel. But the amount of airtime given over to shows that would enhance the lives of America's children was meager. From the beginning there was more interest in the buying power of little people than in their minds. By the end of the 1950s the extreme violence that characterized American television at the end of the century would be available to everyone who switched on a station for news or sitcoms at almost any hour. One waggish critic remarked that more people were killed on television in 1954 than in the entire Korean War. Whether excessive exposure to murder, rape, and bizarre horrors of all sorts could create generations of criminals became an ongoing debate. Statistics proved beyond doubt that the jail population was increasing, and a

Children play in the steel town of Aliquippa, Pennsylvania, ca. 1942. © Library of Congress.

few sociopaths credited television with ideas they used for particularly horrible crimes. Children could see almost anything when they turned on the set. The TV spectacle of so much blood and cruelty, many feared, might produce generations of youthful viewers who would grow up completely callous to human suffering. In one of her best reviews on how television seemed to be depriving the young of their childhood, Marya Mannes introduced a Danish scholar who challenged America: "If fifty million children see terrible things like this every day," he said, "do you not think they will feel less about shooting and murder and rape? They will be so used to violence that it does not seem like violence anymore."

Mannes characterized the Westerns that flourished for a short time as plays that "concerned good men and bad men who rode horses over magnificent country and decided issues by shooting each other." In clarifying how little educational value there was in such programs, she noted that they "were all very much alike in that they bore no resemblance to what used to be the pioneer West of the United States except in the matter of clothes and horses." What these Westerns did most successfully, she perceived, was "to sell a great amount of goods." As children became the most promising group of consumers for televised products, Hopalong Cassidy items boomed. The grandfatherly cowboy became a children's idol, inspiring a line of toys that grossed $100 million in 1950. Howdy Doody, a freckled clown, also inspired quantities of consumer toys at the time. And Davy Crockett seemed capable of putting coonskin caps on every small head in America before overproduction led to warehouse surpluses. Such toys often provided a source of community for kids of different backgrounds. Just as adults found a source of identity in discussing their cars or their hi-fi music equipment with each other, children came together with their collections of televised loot designed for young people.

Davy Crockett, a one-hour prime-time Western series sponsored by Walt Disney, garnered the highest ratings of the decade. Not only did the show make children

"World's Highest Standard of Living," West Virginia, 1937. Even in 1937, the national unemployment rate was dramatically high, although one does not get that impression from this street sign. © Library of Congress.

eager for coonskin caps, but it also inspired some parents to turn to the simplicity of the old West for housing and furnishing styles. Log cabins and wagon wheels were easy to copy even in suburbia. By the end of the decade the ranch house would become the most popular style among the choices at Levittown. The West brought back echoes of a simpler life and easier living. Dungarees became the classic weekend wear for suburbanites.

The television show *Disneyland* appeared in the early 1950s, testing on air all the American themes that would be incorporated during the next decade into the sparkling California amusement park. At the time few realized that Walt Disney's construction of this utopian vision would come to represent a worldwide dream of American possibility. In 1954 when *Disneyland* first appeared regularly on TV, it was a source of publicity for the Disneyland theme park Disney was building to represent his dreams. Some critics called the show an hourlong commercial. Fantasyland, Frontierland, Adventureland, and Tomorrowland, with all the star-studded glitz that attended the grand opening of the park, quickly became as real to the American imagination as America itself—perhaps more real. Child viewers eager to participate in the televised adventures Disney conjured up might indeed learn something from the details of the displays, but many reviewers criticized the brash commercialism. One described the theme park as "a giant cash register, clicking and clanging as creatures of Disney magic came tumbling down." Television previews had prepared visitors to Disneyland for necessary compromises, but it was the tension between perfection and reality, Karal Ann Marling suggests, "between the real and the more or less real," that really delighted so many visitors.

On New Year's Eve in 1957, attendance at Disneyland reached 10 million. The kind of entertainment the theme park offered fit perfectly with the togetherness of the car-centered suburban family. On one admission Walt Disney's TV dream worlds conducted everyone from an imperfect present into an idealized past or a thrilling future. And Main Street, USA, like an exhibit at a world's fair, suggested that utopia was already possible in middle-class America. Some children may have been inspired to pursue a study of Disney's themes even if many more were seduced into buying Mickey Mouse Club paraphernalia and other trademarked toys and T-shirts. Eager children often found both pleasure and instruction in Disney's optimistic distortions. In a world of chaotic diversity, Marling points out, "Disney motifs constituted a common culture, a kind of civil religion of happy endings, worry-free consumption, technological optimism and nostalgia for the good old days." Such dreams could define survival.

If parents monitored the hours small children sat before their television sets, they need not have been concerned. And adults did not have to worry about the disc jockeys shaping teenage taste at the time; Dick Clark's decency charmed everyone. Jukeboxes in popular hangouts still offered songs with inoffensive lyrics in the decade that was still by all contemporary standards quite innocent (Kaledin, 21–22, 69–70, 143–44).

To read about children in the United States in the 19th century, see the United States entries in the section "Children" in chapter 2 ("Domestic Life") in volume 5 of this series.

FOR MORE INFORMATION

American Memory. <http://memory.loc.gov/ammem/amhome.html/>.

Hayes, C. D., J. L. Palmer, and M. J. Zaslow, eds. *Families that Work: Children in a Changing World*. Washington, D.C.: National Academy Press, 1982.

Kaledin, E. *Daily Life in the United States, 1940–1959: Shifting Worlds*. Westport, Conn.: Greenwood Press, 2000.

Tuttle, W. M. Jr. *"Daddy's Gone to War": The Second World War in the Lives of America's Children*. New York: Oxford University Press, 1993.

UNITED STATES, 1960–90

Between the early 1970s and the end of the 1980s, the proportion of women with children under the age of 6 who were employed outside the home nearly doubled, reaching almost 60 percent. That meant that more than 10 million children under age 6, about two-thirds of them under age 3, had working mothers. The majority of these mothers were part of two-parent families, allowing for sharing of parental duties. In most instances, however, these families also had to find ways to care for their preschool children as well as for those in school (nearly 20 million of them between the ages of 5 and 14) during nonschool hours. For everyone—regardless of

DOMESTIC LIFE
|
CHILDREN
|
Europe, 1914-1918

Holocaust

United States,
1940-1959

United States,
1960-1990

Latin America

India

Japan

income, marital status, or race—questions of accessibility and affordability of child-care arrangements were ongoing concerns. Reports of sexual abuse in child-care situations made parents particularly attentive to matters of safety, and having to cope with the children's illnesses and emergencies was a constant worry.

Ways of meeting the challenges varied as widely as the circumstances of the families facing them. A 1987 survey showed that about one-fourth of the primary child-care arrangements involved group facilities, typically called day-care centers. In almost as many instances, children were placed in "family day care," usually in the caregivers' homes. Roughly one child in six was cared for in the home by the father and an almost equal number by a relative or nonrelative; about the same proportion stayed with a relative outside the home. In almost all the remaining instances the mother took the child to work with her. Parents who faced the challenge of finding caregivers for their children during these years knew that although these numbers might represent an accurate picture at a given time, there was considerable movement of the children from one arrangement to another. It was not uncommon for parents to try as many as four or five different arrangements within a single year.

Because employment of women outside the home had become so common, instances of women quitting their jobs to become "stay-at-home moms" were treated as newsworthy. However, stay-at-home moms who found it necessary to return to work were merely statistics, not news.

By the end of the 1980s it seemed certain that the proportion of children cared for by persons other than their parents, and for more hours of the day, would continue to increase, so debates about their care continued. A critical question concerned the short-term and long-term effects on children of being cared for day after day by persons other than their parents. The answers given by scholars who studied the questions were mixed. Other questions usually indicated the need for government involvement: What standards should be required of day-care centers and family-care providers? How much insurance should be required, and how could the insurance be kept at affordable levels? What should be the policies of businesses concerning grants of parental leave to enable mothers and fathers to attend to their newborns or to children who become ill? What should be the government's policies with respect to tax credits for working parents and parental leave?

Addressing the last of these questions, in 1990 Congress passed legislation granting $22 billion in tax credits, mostly for parents in low-income families. It also passed a bill requiring employers to provide up to 12 weeks of unpaid leave to allow employees to care for a newborn or adopted child or for a seriously ill person in their families. President George Bush vetoed the bill, contending that it dealt with matters that should be worked out by employers and employees, not by the government. Attempts to override the veto failed (Marty, 250–53).

To read about children in the United States in the 19th century, see the United States entries in the section "Children" in chapter 2 ("Domestic Life") in volume 5 of this series.

FOR MORE INFORMATION

American Memory. <http://memory.loc.gov/ammem/collections/finder.html>.

Lynd, R. S., and H. M. Lynd. *Middletown: A Study in Modern American Culture*. New York: Harcourt, Brace, and World, 1929.

Marty, M. A. *Daily Life in the United States, 1960–1990: Decades of Discord*. Westport, Conn.: Greenwood Press, 1997.

May, E. T. *Homeward Bound: American Families in the Cold War Era*. New York: Basic Books, 1988.

LATIN AMERICA

Children in Latin America juggled multiple responsibilities during the 20th century. Though Latin Americans valued education, often it was simply not feasible for children to attend school for more than one or two years. Instead, the main preoccupations for many young people were family and work—both in and out of the home.

Although Latin American educational systems expanded remarkably after 1950, and particularly since the 1970s, the goals of universal education continued unmet. Many children fell through the cracks, as the provision of education continued to be closely related to the social and economic status of parents.

By midcentury, most Latin American countries had compulsory education systems ranging from 5 to 12 years in length. In Honduras, for example, public education was free and obligatory from 7 through 14 years of age; likewise, in Chile, children were required to attend 8 years of primary school. In many Caribbean countries, schooling began at age 5 and continued through age 14 or 15.

In reality, however, attendance rates were low throughout Latin America. At preschools in Haiti, Guatemala, Nicaragua, and El Salvador, attendance often fell below 80 percent, and even lower for the populations of indigenous and African descent. In Paraguay, as late as 1980 nearly two-thirds of registered students dropped out of primary school.

There were multiple reasons for such low school attendance. First, educational systems offered limited coverage. In Central America, just 7 percent of the population had access to preschools, and in some nations of the Caribbean, 32 percent had access. Even where schools did exist, students often had to travel great distances on foot, over very rough terrain. Such was the case for rural youths in particular. These access issues accounted for very different rates of enrollment between urban and rural students. In Guatemala in 1982, for example, 56 percent of urban seven-year-olds were enrolled in primary school, compared with just 25 percent of their rural counterparts. Children in rural areas generally averaged three years fewer of formal schooling than children from urban areas.

In various countries of Latin America, language and cultural issues caused additional access problems. In Paraguay, many children spoke Guaraní at home; in Ecuador, they spoke Quechua or Shuar; and Guatemalan children spoke a variety of different Mayan languages. Many other indigenous languages survived in Mexico, Central America, the Andes, and Brazil. It often proved difficult, if not impossible, for many children with a different first language to adjust to Spanish-language instruction (or Portuguese, in Brazil) and the dominant cultural mores that accompanied it.

Insufficient resources were also to blame for low attendance rates at schools. Many families were simply unable to afford the costs of uniforms and materials. Schools provided few materials, if any. Indeed, through the 1980s, public spending on primary education in Latin America dropped from US$164 to $18 per student per year. Furthermore, many regions suffered from a lack of school buildings and teachers, with shortages especially acute in rural areas. Teachers often taught some 80 students, at all levels, and received very low pay and few training opportunities. In rural El Salvador during the 1980s, it was common to see young people teaching other youths in "classrooms" under the trees. The teachers of these *escuelas populares* (popular schools) often had just a few years of schooling themselves before they began teaching their peers.

Another prominent reason for low school attendance rates was the need to contribute to a family's survival. Indeed, most Latin American children began working at a very early age. Parents expected children as young as five or six to do certain chores, like tend to small animals such as chickens and pigs. As children grew older, the gender distinctions of their work became more clearly defined. Boys worked primarily outside of the house, collecting water and wood, tending crops and livestock. Girls worked primarily inside the home, cleaning and taking care of younger siblings.

Beyond helping their parents at home, many children worked outside the home. According to one 1990s statistic, there were 17 million child workers in Latin America (Salazar 1998, 3). Such statistics, however, often do not recognize the many children who worked in the informal sector, at extremely low wages, for example, as ragpickers or vendors on the street; in industrial workshops; or, especially for females, as domestic servants.

Costa Rican Alexander Monger, 10, works pulling weeds from a lettuce field outside Cartago, Costa Rica, some 25 kilometers east of the capital of San Jose, Friday, November 16, 2001. © AP/Wide World Photos.

A great number of child laborers worked in agriculture—some on fields related to family subsistence, others at commercial and export-oriented fields where crops including coffee, fruits, flowers, and sugarcane were grown. In the latter part of the century, 65 percent of child laborers in Guatemala, and nearly half of those in Ecuador and Peru, worked in agriculture.

Labor outside the home also divided along gender lines. This was quite apparent in agriculture, as in Colombia, where 82 percent of all male child laborers worked in the fields, compared with just 36 percent of female laborers. Many statistics repeatedly noted that more young men than women joined the labor forces. For example, in Guatemala, 84 percent of workers between 7 and 17 years old were male, and in Ecuador, 64 percent of workers between 10 and 17 years were male. Such numbers, however, often did not consider the domestic labor done by females. Indeed, like many adult women, girls often had a double workload: in addition to laboring outside the home, they also had to do chores in their own households, such as cooking and caring for siblings.

Many child laborers in Latin America worked long hours under terrible conditions. Children worked in the dangerous coal and gold mines of Colombia and Peru. Others manufactured fireworks for companies in Guatemala and Colombia. Also in Colombia, female domestic servants under 15 years of age often worked 50 hours a week or more.

In many cases, children themselves never received payment for their labor. Rather, their efforts contributed to a family endeavor, as when the head of a family (typically male) received payment per bushel of potatoes collected or per bag of coffee beans picked. When children did receive payment, they often earned half the income of adults.

Even at such low wages, the monetary contributions of child laborers to their families' budgets were considerable. Among poor families in Lima, Peru, for example, children's wages accounted for 10 percent of the total income. In Guatemala, they contributed some 15 percent of the total family income.

Generally speaking, Latin American and Caribbean children found little time to play in the 20th century. Though boys enjoyed their *futbol* (soccer) games and girls their jump ropes or softball, toys, books, and free time were scarce in many parts of the region. When not in school—by either necessity or choice—the children and youth of Latin America worked steadily, both for their parents at home and for bosses outside the home.

~Molly Todd

FOR MORE INFORMATION

Jermyn, L. *Paraguay*. New York: Marshall Cavendish, 2000.

Morrison, M. *Ecuador: Guide to the People, Politics and Culture*. Brooklyn, N.Y.: Interlink Books, 1997.

Salazar, M. C. "Child Work and Education in Latin America." In *Child Work and Education: Five Case Studies from Latin America*, edited by María Cristina Salazar. Aldershot, England: Ashgate, 1998.

INDIA

Children in every culture are special, and Hindu families are no exception. Though children were warmly regarded within their immediate and extended family, so too were they bound by caste and rituals marking their development throughout childhood.

To begin, in the same way that families arranged most marriages, families expected those couples to produce a child soon after marriage. For many couples, a

DOMESTIC LIFE
|
CHILDREN
|
Europe, 1914-1918

Holocaust

United States,
1940-1959

United States,
1960-1990

Latin America

India

Japan

male child was most desirable in that males within India were needed not only to perpetuate the family name and perform certain rites, but also because they could add to the family's income. Female children were also welcomed into the world, but often with less enthusiasm. At the time of her marriage, a girl would require an expensive dowry (a gift of money or material goods) to be given to her groom's family. Further, most new brides left their home to live with the groom's family, thus resulting in the loss of that child to help within the family.

For many families, children were assets that could add to the family income. Thus, the larger the family, the greater the income potential. However, the negative side of this was that because families needed children to work, the children were frequently not able to attend school, or were taken out of school at a young age. Children performed a variety of tasks: helping with household chores, tending livestock or crops, or working in industry such as in carpet or match factories where production required small hands. Children also worked on tea plantations picking leaves, and some were used in the sex trade as well.

A child's life begins with hope and promise. Certain rites marked the first years. On the 12th day after a child's birth, the family performed a naming ceremony. This ceremony included the parents and extended family as well as friends and a priest. The priest recited lines from a spiritual text and, after consulting the *Hindu Almanac* or *Panchangam*, pronounced the name of the child as chosen by the parents.

From birth to about age five, children were allowed great freedom by their parents and families to play and grow as children. In earlier times, many did not survive past this age due to sickness and disease. After the age of five, children began to be shown how to help within the family and were increasingly incorporated into their respective gender groups: boys went with the men and girls went with the women. Within these groups, children began to learn more about their respective roles.

The next rite of childhood was for boys of the higher-caste groups. In a ceremony known as *upanayana*, which took place when the boy reached his early teens and is meticulously observed by the Brahman communities even today, a boy's father and a priest tied a sacred thread around the boy's neck and shoulder. The ritual marked the rebirth or "twice born" status of the boy and was deeply linked to Hindu notions of birth and reincarnation.

Until the time of his marriage, a boy was in the first of four stages of his life. He was free of marital bonds and was expected to either learn a trade or become educated so that at the time of his marriage, he would be able to adequately provide for his new wife.

For girls, the onset of menstruation was a rite of sorts. This event signified that the girl had become a woman, capable of conceiving, and in some cases ready for marriage. Yet, the first menstrual cycle itself was not often celebrated, and young women were sometimes isolated during this time. Within many families, a woman who was menstruating was considered to be "polluting."

Children in India, depending on their family's position, may have had different daily experiences. Children of middle- and upper-class families had lives that were not dissimilar to those of their European or American counterparts. They awoke early in the morning and bathed. Some might have made a small prayer to the deity worshipped in their home. They ate their breakfast and left for school. Most schools required a uniform. The school might have been nearby or far away, a modern building or simply the shade under a tree. In the afternoon the children returned home, changed out of their uniforms, and had time to either play or start their homework. Many attended supplementary after-school tutoring to help them master their school subjects. In the evening they would have their dinner and sleep.

Not all children attended school, and for those who did not, daily life was much different. These children might have risen before dawn and immediately begun work. Preparing meals, tending animals, washing clothes, or helping with other siblings all might have demanded a child's first few hours of the day. Then, depending on their occupation, children began work. Children worked at home, in the fields, or in factories or industry. The hours were long and their treatment by employers was often poor. At night, there might be more work to do at home before sleeping. Many children subsisted on one meal per day.

Some children were able to rise above adversity. Mahatma Gandhi, the leader of India's nonviolent independence movement, was the youngest child of a large family. Following custom, he was married in his early teens, to Kastur Bhai. However, his family invested in young Gandhi to provide for them. His parents sent him to school, and at the age of 19 he was sent to England for further schooling. This broke with custom in that many Hindus considered crossing the ocean, or "black water" (*kala pani*), to be polluting. Gandhi, despite his unremarkable experience of growing up, went on to become one of the world's great leaders.

Children in India were a vital part of the family. They held the promise of both earning income and perpetuating the family name. Yet, depending on social position, childhood could be a difficult and joyless time, a fight for survival. For others, childhood was a carefree and happy phase of life.

To read about children in 19th-century India, see the India entry in the section "Children" in chapter 2 ("Domestic Life") in volume 5 of this series.

~*Benjamin Cohen*

FOR MORE INFORMATION

Brown, J. *Gandhi: Prisoner of Hope*. New Haven: Yale University Press, 1989.

Weiner, M. *The Child and the State in India: Child Labor and Education Policy in Comparative Perspective*. Princeton: Princeton University Press, 1991.

JAPAN

Most foreigners consider Japan to be a children's utopia. Children in Japan have a very short but almost idyllic childhood. Westerners note how happy and carefree young children seem to be. They are well attended by doting parents and grand-

parents who seem to cater to their every need. Children are seldom seen without adults hovering around to protect them. There are nearly as many mothers and grandmothers as children in any park or playground.

Thousands of toys abound in virtually every shop. Amusement parks teem with young parents following their toddlers around. One has to make reservations days in advance at the major ones such as Tokyo Disneyland. Virtually every department store of any size has a huge toy area as well as a playground on the roof.

Plentiful day care is available in almost every neighborhood. Adult to child (1:3) ratios at these centers is nearly ideal. Mothers are required to "volunteer" several hours per week to help tend the children.

Child abuse is very rare. Children seem to be safe wherever they go. It is not unusual to see them traveling on public transportation unaccompanied starting at about age seven.

Yet, at about that age children are swallowed into a rigorous academic machine that allows them little time to play except in tightly managed learning activities. The school system is very serious about education. Long hours of homework are assigned every day, with special weekend packages foisted on the tots midday Fridays. Most children wear hard leather backpacks that are usually crammed with books. Recently a study showed that the average weight of a backpack is nearly nine pounds!

Fairly early on, children are enrolled in after-hours private cram schools (*juku*), where they receive additional instruction aimed at helping them pass various stringent qualification exams. The high school entrance exams require many hours of study. The standard joke is that children "succeed with four (hours of sleep per night); fail with five." Children must endure hours of moral training per week and must help in school tasks such as cleaning the classrooms and helping to serve snacks and meals.

Conformity and regimentation are expected to result in group harmony. Children who are different in any way are often harassed and hazed. This bullying (*ijime*) has become such a great problem in the middle schools that physical attacks result in serious injuries, and some hazed children have committed suicide.

Despite this seemingly grim picture, drugs and juvenile crime is much less a problem in Japan than in any other industrialized urban society. Most children are polite and cheerful. Petty theft, graffiti, and other such misbehavior is practically unknown in Japan. Despite a ready access to dreadful pornography in coin machines, rape and other sexual crimes are rare. Beer and *sake* are sold in corner machines like soft drinks, yet juvenile drunkenness is practically unknown.

To read about children in early modern Japan, see the Japan entry in the section "Children" in chapter 2 ("Domestic Life") in volume 4 of this series.

~*Louis G. Perez*

FOR MORE INFORMATION

Kuklin, S. *Kodomo: Children of Japan.* New York: G. P. Putnam's Sons, 1995.

Shwalb, D. W., and B. J. Shwalb. *Japanese Childrearing: Two Generations of Scholarship.* New York: Guilford Press, 1996.

INUIT

Traditional Inuit child-rearing practices differed greatly from American and Canadian practices but began changing in the 20th century under pressure from the national governments under which modern Inuit live. To read about the changing patterns of Inuit child rearing in the late 20th century, see the Inuit entry in the section "Family Life" in this chapter.

DOMESTIC LIFE: WEB SITES

http://web.uccs.edu/~history/index/women20th.htm
http://www.mcaonline.ca/healthmanual/hinduism_familydynamics.html
http://womenshistory.about.com/library/ency/blwh_chile_gender_family.htm
http://www.bu.edu/wcp/Papers/Gend/GendVoro.htm
http://nationalhistoryday.org/03_educators/2001–2002curbook/new_page_16.htm

3

ECONOMIC LIFE

People work. The basic principle of economic life is that men and women must work to provide for themselves. Of course, throughout history some have always had to work harder than others, but this does not violate the basic importance of work; it only reveals the complexities of economic life that includes everything from the production of income to trade to the unequal distribution throughout society.

At the basic level, people work on the land to produce their food and other items they need. Even at this simplest level, however, people trade goods among themselves. Thus, economic life moves from the work that we do to the exchange of the products of our labor. This diversification contributes to increasing variety in society as some work on the land living in villages and farms whereas others move to urban areas that grow ever larger throughout history. The patterns of farm, village, and urban life exist all over the world and help define the lives of the people who work within them.

Commerce, or the exchange of goods, is as central to human economic life as the production of goods. From the beginning of town life in Mesopotamia, the excitement generated within shops lining a street is palpable in the sources. Merchants hawking their wares and shoppers looking for the exotic as well as the ordinary form a core of human life. Merchants (and merchandise) have always ranged far beyond local markets as people moved their goods across large areas. Even during the prehistoric late Stone Age, domestic animals native to the Middle East moved down the Nile valley to sub-Saharan Africa, and plants native to the Euphrates valley moved as far east as China. Our global marketplace is only the logical extension of the constant movement of people and things that goes on as people engage in their economic lives.

All societies have been defined in part by people at work. Societies have been built with divisions of labor, of city and country, and of class as some people grow richer than others. To study daily life through history is in large part to understand people at work. And in the 20th century, the working world changed significantly. The entries in the following section reveal two major transformations: the introduction of women industrial workers and the assembly line. In the Western world, women entered the factories en masse during World War I. Although they were largely kicked out after the war, their labor force participation rates increased during the century. By 2000, women were a statistically significant part of the wage labor force in Europe and the Americas. The other change affected how people worked. Perfected by such famous (or infamous) industrial luminaries as Henry Ford and Frederick Winslow Taylor, the assembly line made artisans into factory workers. In other words, factory work required not knowledge of manufacturing but merely time on the line. The upside of this kind of labor was money. Ford paid his employees a decent wage. And yet, in another hallmark of the 20th century, class lines never disappeared. In some nations such as Chile, Argentina, and Peru, class lines actually intensified, particularly in cities. Even in the United States, class remained an extremely important category for understanding economic life. Still, 20th-century Americans needed constant reminders that the poor existed. In some ways, the "discovery" of poverty by such investigators as Michael Harrington was as important as the problem itself. Another struggle over the structures of economic life in the 20th century concerned discrimination. Particularly in the United States, reformers sought to eliminate the hardships that the accident of birth caused. In the United States, the federal government passed laws to forbid discrimination against minority and women workers. Similar legislation was passed in India. The history of the 20th century illustrates that positive government action did indeed work to remedy the daily hardships that prejudice and bigotry caused. Yet much prejudice remained, as the entry on the Soviet Union describes. Thus, by the same token, the century's history also showed that when government failed to act or fostered hate, terrible things happened to workers and their families.

FOR MORE INFORMATION

Braudel, F. *The Wheels of Commerce*. New York: Harper and Row, 1979.
Wallerstein, I. M. *Historical Capitalism*. London: Verso, 1983.

ECONOMIC LIFE

| WORK |

Europe

United States, 1920-1939

United States, 1940-1959

United States, 1960-1990

Japan

Africa

Work

As one can glean from these entries, there were three major transformations in the nature of work in the 20th century. First, women made great advances into paid industrial work. World War I provided the impetus for this change. Millions of British, French, and German men left their daily labors for their respective armies. Women filled the void in the factories making weapons, uniforms, and all sorts of goods for the home fronts. Although women workers in both Europe and the United States were treated as a reserve working force that was called out only in times of crisis, their participation rates in the labor market increased dramatically during the century. By 2000, many middle-class families were two-career families. In other words, both the mother and the father had to work. Paid work for women was not merely a political and feminist statement. It was a reaction to the reality that keeping and housing a family required two incomes.

The second major change, also evident in the entries, was the rise of organized labor. As in no previous century, unions gained ascendancy in the workplace. Organized workers waged a bitter fight over control of the shop floor. Employers in Europe and the United States did their best to stop unions from creating better conditions for their members. Concerted battles began during World War I. German, French, American, and British workers all went on strike. The most serious labor conflict happened in Russia when factory workers along with soldiers and sailors joined forces to overturn the economic and political order, illustrating, among other things, the ability of laborers to reshape their daily lives.

The final change apparent in these entries is the transformation of work itself. In 1900, many daily items, from tools to carriages, were handmade. The rapid rise of modern factories, however, altered this. Increasingly, workers labored not to fashion a finished product but to do a specific task along an assembly line. In essence, the knowledge of how to build and manufacture goods was taken from under the worker's cap and placed into a machine. By World War II, it was quite common for workers to spend their days tightening bolts on automobiles or filling forms or stamping metal. It was rare for a worker to see a product through from beginning to end. The mass introduction of assembly-line work alienated workers from work and turned over control of work to employers and managers. The manager or foreman, not the worker, controlled the pace of work. Even white-collar work was not immune to this change. By the end of the century, office and even retail workers were stuck in highly specialized positions. Moreover, as the number of tasks that average workers performed decreased, so did their pay. As economist John Kenneth Galbraith and socialist Michael Harrington pointed out in the 1950s and 1960s, industrial nations like the United States that had modern, assembly-line factories did not create enough wealth that their working class could quickly and easily join the middle class.

In Japan and the countries of Africa, the rise of industrialized societies during the 20th century had a profound impact on how and where people worked. Japan was a largely agrarian society until the advent of the 20th century and most of Africa was rural and agrarian until well into the century. The shifting of large numbers of workers from fields to factory and, in Japan, to office buildings affected every aspect of society. As in other centuries, work dominated most people's lives, and it was not always as profitable as one might have hoped.

EUROPE

The busy factory with workers laboring long hours in harsh conditions became a hallmark of working life during World War I. Prewar labor restrictions faded with the onset of the conflict and the desperate need to produce arms and ammunition. The demand for workers to meet the needs of the military brought boom times to many regions from the war's beginning. Boot orders for the expanding British army overwhelmed factories in Leicester, where the industry was centered. By the close of 1914, a report from the local labor union indicated the dimensions of the demand

ECONOMIC LIFE

WORK

Europe

United States,
1920-1939

United States,
1940-1959

United States,
1960-1990

Japan

Africa

for workers: For the first time ever, not one of its members needed to apply for unemployment benefits. Factories in various countries were filled with men who had been released from military service—or excused from it—to take valuable roles in industry. Women in large numbers entered the labor force producing war matériel.

In late 1916, Germany attempted an extreme example of expanding the factory workforce. The Patriotic Auxiliary Service Law, otherwise known as the Hindenburg program, required all males from ages 17 to 60 to work in war plants. But the difficulties of enforcing such a measure soon emerged, and the government exempted large categories of men, such as students and civil servants. At the same time, it established boards to consider claims of extreme hardship from those men who remained affected. Many men avoided registering or else sought an exemption on medical grounds. Others falsely claimed they were farmers and hence not subject to the law's grasp.

Women in large numbers entered the labor force producing war material.

Britain, France, and Germany all felt the jolt of factory workers laying down their tools to go on strike. The essential role of miners, workers in munitions factories, and those running the transport system in a wartime economy gave them enormous leverage. During the early portion of the war, patriotism was a powerful adhesive holding such workers to key jobs, and the workers held back from seeking major concessions. In Britain 10 million working days were lost due to industrial unrest in 1913; in 1915, the total fell to 3 million, and it declined further in the following years. In the Isère district of southern France, there were 15 strikes in the first seven months of 1914, and only 10 strikes in the 30 wartime months that followed. As the conflict continued, labor militancy revived in both France and Britain. The spectacle of entrepreneurs reaping wartime profits as well as the inflation that pinched workers' families combined to produce bitterness throughout the Allied home front. Labor unrest broke out in some of Britain's Welsh coal mines and Scottish shipyards as early as the first months of 1915.

In March 1917, Russian factory workers (along with mutinous soldiers and sailors) overturned the existing political order. Many workers in the other belligerent countries took this revolution as a signal to present their grievances. The year saw labor unrest in Britain over issues ranging from the employment of Chinese workers to the disparity between the earnings of munitions workers and the lesser pay given miners. In late September, there were 75 strikes within the space of a week. By the year's end, strikes over food prices—which sometimes escalated into attacks on food stores—took place in Coventry and Birmingham.

But the central core of patriotic devotion held steady. The Germans imposed a harsh peace on the Russians at Brest-Litovsk in March 1918, which helped block the spread of workers' discontent in western Europe. As one British labor leader wrote, even the German socialists representing the workers of that country had allowed this painful settlement to be forced on a workers' government in Russia. The Russians' willingness to stop fighting, he noted, just allowed the Germans "to carry out their annexationist programme to the letter." That year, the threat posed by the dangerous German spring offensive on the western front reinforced British workers' willingness to support the war effort. Even in areas of South Wales famous for their opposition to the war, young miners rushed to enlist. Occasional strikes continued, such as the walkout of London policemen in late August 1918, but nothing took place to block the flow of men and arms to the front.

In France, too, the spring of 1917 saw a wave of labor unrest sparked in part by rising prices. If popular slogans were an indication, the walkouts also showed some workers' desire to end the war. A year later, even in the face of the German spring offensive, a more dangerous outbreak of labor unrest appeared in the crucial metals industry. The Russian Revolution of November 1917 inspired revolutionary syndicalists to call for an end to the war and for revolution in France.

Such ambitions soon faded. The government of Premier Georges Clemenceau resorted to harsh repression, arresting some strike leaders, tightening the censorship system, and even sending a number of strike leaders off to the front. But Clemenceau's success was also due to the commitment of most workers to see the war through to victory. The visibility of American troops, now landing at the rate of 250,000 a month, supported hopes that the war could be won. As one historian put it, "The reservoir of patriotism among the least privileged citizens of the Republic is perhaps the key to understanding why the French nation was able to go [to the bitter end]." In Germany striking workers also threatened the war effort. As early as May 1916, a walkout in Berlin involved thousands. Their slogan of "bread, peace, and freedom" had an ominous ring for German authorities, because it combined political with economic demands. Later strikes, whatever their immediate cause, were accompanied with even more overtly political goals. A cut in the bread ration in the spring of 1917 led to massive walkouts from war factories, first in Berlin and Leipzig, then across much of the country. In all, more than 600,000 workers struck in 1917; that was five times the number who had abandoned their workplaces the previous year. In January 1918, massive strikes, organized by left-wing political parties, broke out at the munitions plants in Berlin. The strikers' demands again included nonpolitical items such as a call for better food supplies. But the workers also called emphatically for a quick end to the war. Neither hordes of mounted police nor the government's cry that such strikes imperiled German soldiers at the front stopped the walkouts from growing. By the last day of the month, the other major cities in Germany witnessed similar strikes, and the total number of workers who lay down their tools reached one million. The authorities seized the strikes' leaders, put them into uniform, and sent them off to the western front. Along with the government's threat to militarize the plants—making all workers subject to military courts and paying them the same meager wages soldiers earned—this harsh response brought a period of uneasy calm.

Although unions may not have reaped all the rewards of wartime work, women certainly did. Women made up a substantial part of the prewar workforce in all four key countries that fought on the western front. But women's roles had been restricted in a variety of ways. About 32 percent of British women worked outside their homes. The most common women wage earners were domestic servants and workers in the textile industry. Most were single. The poorly paid and overworked domestic servant was likely to be a young woman, who would leave this dreary form of employment if she managed to marry. The textile worker tended to be older and better paid, a married woman helping to support her family. But her prospects of obtaining highly skilled positions, even in the industry where she was heavily represented, remained slim. In France, 39 percent of the nation's women and girls claimed a working occupation. Only 10 percent called themselves domestic servants, and the majority worked in some kind of industry or, more likely, in agriculture. The employment pattern for German women was similar, and some 25 percent of all German women worked for wages. In rural regions like Bavaria, the figure climbed to 35 percent. In all the belligerent countries that fought on the western front, women found that the war opened vast new opportunities for employment. In no instance did the total female workforce grow dramatically. But many women found it possible for the first time to move from poorly paid positions such as domestic servants to more lucrative work. Novel opportunities such as openings in armaments factories appeared only after some delay. British, French, and German working women often had a spell of unemployment as peacetime jobs disappeared when their societies entered the war (Heyman, 156–59).

FOR MORE INFORMATION

Braybon, G. *Women Workers in the First World War: The British Experience*. London: Croom Helm, 1981.

Greenwald, M. W. *Women, War, and Work: The Impact of World War I on Women Workers in the United States*. Westport, Conn.: Greenwood Press, 1980.

Heyman, N. M. *Daily Life During World War I*. Westport, Conn.: Greenwood Press, 2002.

Williams, J. *The Other Battleground: The Home Fronts: Britain, France, and Germany, 1914–1918*. Chicago: Henry Regnery, 1972.

ECONOMIC LIFE

WORK

Europe

United States,
1920-1939

United States,
1940-1959

United States,
1960-1990

Japan

Africa

UNITED STATES, 1920–39

The spreading use of new mass market commodities such as the automobile and the techniques developed for their production and distribution altered the country's economic life. The means by which Americans earned their daily bread shifted perceptibly during the 1920s. Though the overall labor force grew from 41.6 to 48.9 million workers during the decade, the number of workers engaged in the traditional pursuits of agriculture, forestry, fishing, and mining fell slightly (from 12.6 to 11.9 million). Meanwhile, even as the methods of production changed and output per worker grew, the number of persons engaged in manufacturing held steady (10.988 to 10.99 million). A huge increase in so-called white-collar work contrasted sharply to the stable number of workers producing food and commodities. The segment of the workforce engaged in sales (from 2.1 to 3.1 million), service (1.9 to 2.8 million), clerical (3.4 to 4.3 million), managerial (2.8 to 3.6 million), and professional and technical work (2.3 to 3.3 million) grew rapidly, for the most part a direct reflection of opportunities and needs presented by new commodities.

Automobiles in particular transformed patterns of work for millions of Americans. The use of automobiles, together with that of their close relatives, tractors and trucks, created or markedly changed many jobs. The nature of work was perhaps most nontraditional for those who came to be employed in the auto industry itself. In addition, however, the auto industry set the pattern for other manufacturing enterprises that mass-produced consumer goods based on new technologies. One of Billy Durant's acquisitions for General Motors, for instance, had been a little company that at the time had only 42 customers for its electric refrigerators. Durant, deciding that refrigerators could be built like automobiles because both consisted of cases containing motors, renamed the company Frigidaire and put it in a position to adopt the GM system of advertising, credit sales, and production. Whereas established industries such as steel and textiles, food processing, mining, and lumbering changed but little, lessons learned in automobile and other manufacturing influenced still other large-scale employment, such as office work. The fruits of mass production also altered farm labor and housework.

This 1939 farm machinery exhibit in Marshalltown, Iowa, demonstrates advanced tools of the trade. © Library of Congress.

Henry Ford led the way in the creation of vast factories, but he soon had many imitators. Beginning in 1910, Ford gathered the previously scattered and subcontracted manufacture of parts for the Model T into one huge plant at Highland Park, Michigan. He brought together thousands of machine tools to fabricate the myriad parts required for even as simple a car as the Model T. The machines, closely spaced on the factory floor, functioned at set speeds and set the pace for the workers who tended them. Ford's metal-cutting machines made possible what few manufacturers had previously achieved: the production of parts so nearly alike that they could be used interchangeably. Then, without the need to adjust each part to fit, a much more rapid process of assembly became possible.

Within three years of moving into his Highland Park plant, Ford discovered that, whereas one worker at a bench took 20 minutes to build a magneto, a team of workers each doing a single task and then handing the unit along could assemble the same devices at a much faster rate. By moving each unit along with a chain-driven line and refining the process still further, Ford soon had magnetos being produced at the rate of one per worker every five minutes. The use of the same techniques reduced the time required to assemble an engine from 10 hours to 6.

Operating a constantly recycling metal-stamping machine or working on a steadily moving assembly line did not require great strength, skill, or even training. In fact, Ford workers were themselves very much interchangeable parts. Most jobs did, however, involve constant, rapid, repetitive labor, performed hour after hour with only a 15-minute lunch and bathroom break in the middle of a shift while the line was briefly stopped. Such work was tedious and boring, yet, as processes were refined and the pace of production speeded up, increasingly stress filled. Workers used to a less feverish pace and a greater sense of individual accomplishment found it difficult to take and at first often quit.

To secure dependable workers to operate his machines and staff his assembly lines, Henry Ford found it necessary to depart from conventional hiring practices. He offered jobs to those most likely to appreciate them, those whom most employers avoided: African Americans, Mexicans, ex-convicts, and people with disabilities. He also challenged the standard practice of paying wages so low that industrial workers and their families could barely subsist. To attract capable workers and avoid the high cost of frequent turnover, Ford began in 1914 to offer wages of $5 a day for a work week of 40 hours after six months of probationary employment. Compared to the prevailing standards of $2 to $3 a day and a 48-hour or longer workweek, the offer drew workers to Ford's assembly line and kept them there despite the strain.

The wife of one Highland Park worker revealed some of the costs and benefits of the Ford labor system to the average worker in a 1914 letter to her husband's employer:

The chain system you have is a slave driver! My God! Mr. Ford. My husband has come home and thrown himself down and won't eat his supper—so done out! Can't it be remedied? . . . That $5 a day is a blessing—a bigger one than you know but oh they earn it.

The Ford labor system forced other employers to boost wages as well to compete successfully for workers. In 1919 Ford upped the ante further by raising wages to $6 a day. Even at that level, Ford wages fell below the auto industry average during the 1920s. The increase in industrial wages put funds for the purchase of cars and other consumer goods in the pockets of a larger population. Not coincidentally, beginning in the mid-1910s, the sales of automobiles, Model Ts especially, grew at a faster rate.

The manufacturing of other new large-volume consumer goods—vacuum cleaners, washing machines, radios, and low-pressure balloon automobile tires, to name only the most common—employed fabrication and assembly-line innovations similar to those of the automobile industry. Likewise, attention was constantly paid to ways in which the production process could be made more rapid, more efficient, and less expensive. In all varieties of manufacturing, a premium was placed on quick, nimble movements done over and over. Young men under 35 years of age were therefore the most highly sought industrial workers. Once they began slowing down, however, their days were numbered. In Muncie, Indiana, where auto parts manufacturing was a large source of employment, few factory workers held onto their positions far into their 40s; and once laid off, they found it very difficult, if not impossible, to find another factory job.

Not all factory work was unskilled labor. Even in the mass-production auto plants, roughly 30 percent of the workforce practiced skilled trades. Painters, upholsterers, carpenters, welders, and mechanics were all needed, and, especially with the advent of the annual model change, tool and die makers were in constant demand. Skilled workers usually enjoyed more varied tasks, normally received higher wages, and almost always held their jobs longer. They, too, however, labored under the unrelenting pressure to work quickly and efficiently that characterized the industrial system.

The volume of white-collar work expanded dramatically as the manufacturing, distribution, sales, and service of consumer goods increased. The evolution of the retail store and business office paralleled, indeed, in some respects even preceded, the transformation of the factory. Both experienced the mass employment of interchangeable low-skilled workers carrying out subdivided tasks. Not coincidentally, the time clocks used to monitor the arrival and departure of masses of employees that became increasingly common in factories began to appear as well in large offices and retail stores.

Retail sales work had begun to change in the late 19th century as large department stores began to dominate the urban commercial scene. Department stores relied on volume sales stirred by lower prices as well as greater selection of goods and services to compete successfully with specialty stores. By the early 20th century, chain stores, multiple retail emporiums under centralized management, brought the same economies of scale to smaller cities and towns. Determined to cut costs, department and chain stores relied far more on the eye-catching display of goods than on the sales staff's knowledge of products and customer needs. Sales work came to require few substantial skills; instead it became primarily a matter of gracious treatment and gentle encouragement of customers who examined products for themselves and then the processing of sales transactions. Except in the case of male-oriented markets, such as the automobile business, sales work was increasingly dominated by women. Supervision, however, remained overwhelmingly in male hands. Men were assumed to be full-time workers in the wage economy who could be depended upon, whereas women were thought of as temporary workers likely to depart for home and family when they had earned a little "pin money." These gender stereotypes reinforced a preference for hiring men, a custom of paying women less, and a casualness about dismissing women first when business declined.

> *Women were seen as temporary workers likely to leave when they had earned a little "pin money."*

The management of larger numbers of workers, the production and distribution of an increasing volume of goods, and the provision of a wider range of services required a notable expansion of office work. Much like mass-production manufacturing, office work came to be organized and subdivided in the interest of efficiency. Old-style rolltop desks with many drawers and pigeonholes for storing various items were replaced in most larger, more modern offices by flat-top desks and centralized files. The introduction of the typewriter in the 1870s, its gradual improvement, and its widespread adoption after pools of trained female typists became available (male clerks aspiring to advance could not be expected to learn such a dead-end skill as typing) led to the adoption of standardized forms and a growing concern with the flow of paperwork. Office work was subdivided, and employees came to do one job only, whether it was typing, operating the telephone switchboard, maintaining personnel records, processing accounts receivable or payable, or distributing the office mail. These changes presumably improved paperwork management and cut costs. They definitely increased the monotony of office work and reduced each worker's sense of privacy and individuality (Kyvig, 27–37).

To read about work in the United States in the 19th century, see the United States entries in the section "Work" in chapter 3 ("Economic Life") in volume 5 of this series.

FOR MORE INFORMATION

Coal Mining in the Gilded Age and Progressive Era. <http://history.osu.edu/Projects/Gilded_Age/default.htm>.

Kyvig, D. E. *Daily Life in the United States, 1920–1939: Decades of Promise and Pain.* Westport, Conn.: Greenwood Press, 2002.

Parrish, M. E. *Anxious Decades: America in Prosperity and Depression, 1920–1941.* New York: W. W. Norton, 1992.

Williams, R. C. *Fordson, Farmall, Popin' Johnny: A History of the Farm Tractor and Its Impact on America.* Urbana: University of Illinois Press, 1987.

ECONOMIC LIFE
|
WORK
|
Europe

United States,
1920-1939

United States,
1940-1959

United States,
1960-1990

Japan

Africa

UNITED STATES, 1940–59

American workers experienced an unprecedented period of economic prosperity after World War II. As people settled down to domesticity to compensate for the uprootedness of the war years and the fear of the Cold War, it became a paradox that materialism provided comfort. Americans saw themselves in close-knit nuclear families rather than as a lonely crowd. What is called "the culture of the Cold War" not only had an impact on the growing birthrate—in 1955 as great as India's—but also influenced the increased production of material goods. By the mid-1950s, with only 6 percent of the world's population, the United States was producing and consuming over one-third of all the world's goods and services. The gross national product, considered by many the most important index of economic success, leaped from $206 billion in 1940 to over $500 billion in 1960.

In place for defense reasons at the end of the Korean War, the military budget continued to provide economic stimulus for research and development in fields like electronics and aviation. Easily available credit for installment buying encouraged Americans to purchase "consumer durables" on budget terms, while the booming public relations industry took note that people spent 35 percent more using plastic credit cards than they would using money.

In 1950 "plastic" entered the vocabulary of the American financial world with the creation of the Diners' Club card. American Express and credit cards from oil and phone companies and car rental services followed by the mid-1950s. Such installment purchases caused consumer indebtedness to soar during the decade, from $73 billion to $196 billion. Madison Avenue writers preached immediate personal gratification as a way of life, and manufacturers complied by building "planned obsolescence" into many new products. Along with new lives people were encouraged to refurbish their personal worlds. The Model T car that still drove and the turreted GE refrigerator still running when given away were treasures from the past. So many additional appliances appeared in new households that the use of electricity nearly tripled during the decade.

As the country's population increased by one-third between 1940 and 1960—in the Pacific states it rose by 110 percent—people needed more basic material goods. Half of the population in the Far West now lived in a state different from the one in which they were born. And one-fifth of the nation's new population had settled in California, which surpassed New York by 1963 as the most populous state. From 1946 to 1958 venture capitalists invested huge amounts of money in mechanization and power. Air-conditioning helped open new territories along with more available water. And the electronics industry also began to thrive. Industry experienced a great rise in output per man-hour as automation intensified postwar scientific management.

If many unskilled workers did indeed lose their jobs to machines, economists argued that technology would create many new ones. The first giant computer, built around the time of the invention of the transistor during World War II, was marketed in 1950. IBM, the industry leader, could not turn computers out fast enough to satisfy demand. In 1954 the company produced only 20; by 1957 it produced 1,250; only a decade later it managed to turn out 35,000. Factory sales increased from $25 million in 1953 to $1 billion by the end of the decade, bringing all sorts of new jobs into the marketplace.

The huge spending on research and development still used as much as 50 percent government funding to support the Cold War's defense needs. Long after World War II the electronics industry continued to sell costly weapons systems. In 1956 military items amounted to $3 billion—40 times the amount spent in 1947.

With the new interstate highway system demanding construction workers, the government remained one of the decade's largest employers. Jobs in the public sector doubled between 1950 and 1970. And incomes rose enough to create an expanded middle class. The proportion of the population enjoying an income of $10,000 or more increased from 9 percent in 1947 to 19 percent by 1968. The proportion of those earning below $3,000 also fell, from 34 percent to 19 percent. As late as 1940 fewer than two million Americans had any education beyond high school, but the GI Bill enabled many ex-soldiers to become professionals. By 1960 college enrollment reached 3.6 million, creating a range of skilled graduates with higher salaries to spend.

Some believed America had experienced a bloodless revolution. But the statistics about personal wealth did not document great changes. In 1953 just 1.6 percent of the population, for example, held 90 percent of the corporate bonds. By 1968 only 153 Americans possessed nine-digit fortunes, while millions still lived in want. The gap between rich and poor actually increased during the 1950s, when 0.5 percent of the population owned 25 percent of all personal wealth. In 1957 a University of Wisconsin sociologist, Robert Lampman, produced research revealing that 32.2 million Americans (nearly one-quarter of the population) had incomes below the poverty level. And many people still lacked minimal comforts like indoor toilets and hot water and heating systems. Because there was so much visible well-being it remained easy to ignore "the other America."

Along with all the new homeowners, but not living beside them, grew a varied culture of poverty that included old people, Puerto Ricans, Mexican Americans, and residents of Appalachia as well as many rural citizens who wanted to remain on farms. From 1948 to 1956 the American farmers' share of the wealth fell from 9 percent to scarcely 4 percent. Small farmers could not profit from the mechanization that was creating agribusiness to make the wealthy wealthier. Even during this period of baby boom, the farm population declined by nine million from 1940 to 1960. By the end of the 1960s only 5 percent of the American population remained on farms.

Yet, paradoxically, many unlikely people seemed to have more material goods. In a place as poor as Harlan County, Kentucky, a depressed coal mining community, 40 percent owned homes; 59 percent had cars, 42 percent telephones, 67 percent TV sets, and 88 percent washing machines. Michael Harrington noted that in the most powerful and richest society the world has ever known the poor remained "the strangest in the history of mankind." An American prophet, Harrington wrote a number of essays during the decade passionately reminding readers that the misery of the poor "has continued while the majority of the nation talked of itself as being 'affluent' and worried about neuroses in the suburbs."

César Chávez, the head of the United Farm Workers, was a champion of the farm laborer and of working-class people everywhere. © Library of Congress.

It was true that more Americans owned their homes in the 1950s than at any other time in the country's history. The 1949 National Housing Act had promised to build 810,000 low-cost homes so that every American family could have "a decent home and a suitable living environment." But by 1964 only 550 units had been built. The Federal Housing Authority made matters worse by refusing to allow integration in public housing projects. Michael Harrington insisted that it would take an effort of the intellect and will even to see the poor.

Many Americans later learned much from Harrington's book *The Other America*, the collection of his research on the poor. But almost everyone knew about John Kenneth Galbraith's 1958 best seller on the American economy, *The Affluent Society*. Not just concerned with examining America's newly defined wealth, Galbraith also seriously considered the remaining poverty. He attempted to shatter the myth that increased production would destroy poverty. Better distribution of wealth did not eliminate the poor. Although by 1960 per capita income in the United States was 35 percent higher than in the war boom year 1945, the very poor were still with us.

And public spaces deteriorated as surely as transportation systems decayed. The cities became impoverished as money set aside for low-income housing remained unused or was spent inappropriately on soon-to-be-destroyed high-rise buildings. Not until the social and environmental movements of the 1960s formed would many Americans begin to recognize that public spaces were as important to a democracy as personal consumer goods. The appeal of a simpler life had always been a powerful force in America's spiritual heritage, but the abundance of the 1950s made it hard to escape the materialism that defined the times.

A famous passage from *The Affluent Society* epitomizes the dilemma of this period. Americans still need to think seriously about the implications of the story John Kenneth Galbraith tells:

The family which takes its mauve and cerise, air-conditioned, power-steered and power-braked automobile out for a tour passes through cities that are badly paved, made hideous by litter, blighted buildings, billboards and posts for wires that should long since have been put underground. They pass on into a countryside that has been rendered largely invisible by commercial art. . . . They picnic on exquisitely packaged food from a portable icebox by a polluted stream and go on to spend the night at a park which is a menace to public health and morals. Just before dozing off on an air mattress, beneath a nylon tent amid stench of decaying refuse, they may vaguely reflect on the curious unevenness of their blessings.

By the end of the decade the hazards of successful free enterprise had become as real as the Cold War anxieties that Communism had provoked (Kaledin, 127–30).

To read about work in the United States in the 19th century, see the United States entries in the section "Work" in chapter 3 ("Economic Life") in volume 5 of this series.

FOR MORE INFORMATION

Galbraith, J. K. *The Affluent Society*. Boston: Little Brown, 1958.

Kaledin, E. *Daily Life in the United States, 1940–1959: Shifting Worlds*. Westport, Conn.: Greenwood Press, 2000.

Winkler, A. *Home Front U.S.A.: America During World War II*. 2d ed. Wheeling, Ill.: Harlan Davidson, 2000.

Women and Social Movements in the United States. <http://womhist.binghamton.edu/index.html/>.

📷 *Snapshot*

Most Popular Halloween Costumes in the U.S., 1995, 1998, 2001

Since the attacks of September 11, 2001, there has been a general increase in the amount of respect that average Americans have for service workers such as firefighters, police officers, and health care workers. One way to gauge this increase is to look at the changes in the kinds of Halloween costumes people have been wearing. The year 2001 saw a change from previous years. It will be interesting to see how long this newfound admiration for working-class heroes continues.

1995

O. J. Simpson
Judge Ito
Pocahontas

(CNN, 1995)

1998

Bill Clinton
Monica Lewinsky
Teletubbies

(CNN, 1998)

2001

Firefighters
Police officers
Uncle Sam
Statue of Liberty
Harry Potter

(http://www.kovr13.com/09sep01/vo092701b.htm)

UNITED STATES, 1960–90

ECONOMIC LIFE

WORK

Europe

United States, 1920-1939

United States, 1940-1959

United States, 1960-1990

Japan

Africa

The transformation of work during the 1980s had both encouraging and discouraging features. By the end of the decade, more than 35 million persons did part-time or full-time income-producing work at home. Increasing most rapidly among them, to a total of more than five million, were telecommuters, that is, employees of companies who did part of their work at home during business hours, most typically involving the use of computers. The trend toward telecommuting was so strong that it seemed likely that it would soon be regarded as unexceptional. Telecommuting served the needs of dual-career families particularly well, in that it reduced the need for child care outside the home. Twice as large a number as telecommuters were those who worked at home as freelancers, earning extra income during hours away from their regular jobs—if they had regular jobs.

Yet another change of the 1980s was the growing resistance of employees to management-dictated relocations. Dual-career families found uprooting particularly difficult, even when it involved promotions or pay increases. The costs involved in buying and selling homes also accounted for the reluctance, as did the sense that accepting a move in the new economic times would not necessarily guarantee job security. Employers had increasingly come to regard their employees as a contingent workforce, to be retained or dismissed depending on immediate circumstances. Employees responded by regarding themselves as entrepreneurs seeking advancement where it best served their interests (Marty, 272–73).

To read about work in the United States in the 19th century, see the United States entries the section "Work" in chapter 3 ("Economic Life") in volume 5 of this series.

FOR MORE INFORMATION

CNN. <www.cnn.com/STYLE/9510/halloween>.

Downsizing of America. New York Times.

Ehrenreich, B. *The Worst Years of Our Lives: Irreverent Notes from a Decade of Greed.* New York: Pantheon Books, 1990.

Marty, M. A. *Daily Life in the United States, 1960–1990: Decades of Discord.* Westport, Conn.: Greenwood Press, 1997.

Moore, M., dir. *Roger and Me.* 1989.

ECONOMIC LIFE
|
WORK
|
Europe

United States,
1920-1939

United States,
1940-1959

United States,
1960-1990

Japan

Africa

JAPAN

Work has for centuries taken on a mystical importance in Japan similar to that of the Protestant Christian work ethic in the West. Confucianism ruled Japanese society for nearly 12 centuries. The fundamental premise is that humans are inextricably bound to their social profession. The literati-bureaucratic class ruled society because it provided order and harmony to a society of working folk. Those who did not produce were anathema.

Propriety within social class was determined by what one did in society. Buddhism also evolved to reward devotion to vocation. Even the most renunciatory of its meditation schools argued that humans could achieve enlightenment by proper devotion to avocation.

In modern Japan great attention is paid to what one does. Great shame is ascribed to those who shirk their duties or repay workplace loyalty with indifference. All citizens contribute to society by fulfilling their obligations. The ritualized exchange of name cards (*meishi*) incorporates the idea that ascribed worth of the individual is to be appreciated. It is believed that people are promoted according to their abilities, and therefore a manager, a foreman, or a CEO deserves respect. Wealth and family lineage are important, of course, but one may achieve respect by devotion to one's job.

Despite this pride in one's vocation, Japan is not very efficient in its work. The harmony of society and of the workplace is more important than its productivity. Japan therefore does not put much stock in downsizing or streamlining the workforce. It is considered to be heartless and un-Japanese. It is akin to forcing a needy relative from one's home in times of financial exigency. It is more important to *be* at work than actually to do anything. People often spend 10 to 12 hours at the office doing 6 hours of work. To see people chatting and reading the newspaper during long tea breaks is not at all unusual.

The practice of lifetime employment is not as widespread as it used to be, but Japanese routinely hire more people and keep them employed far longer than absolutely necessary. In return, employees report a much higher level of loyalty to their employers than in the West.

Unemployment is very low in Japan, but then so are the public financial benefits for being unemployed. The idea is that it is somehow shameful not to be employed. Little thought is given to reeducation of the workforce when economic downturns occur. It is up to the unemployed to quickly find something to do. Middle-aged men who have lost their jobs go to great lengths to find employment of any kind rather than suffer the humiliation of unemployment insurance. Unfortunately, many men commit suicide when they cannot find work.

Hard work on the farm is, of course, a very different thing. One contributes to one's family by working hard. Shirking there is highly discouraged.

To read about work and professions in early modern Japan, see the Japan entries in the section "Industry" in chapter 3 ("Economic Life") in volume 4 of this series.

~*Louis G. Perez*

FOR MORE INFORMATION

Hendry, J. *Understanding Japanese Society.* London: Routledge, 1995.
Waswo, A. *Modern Japanese Society, 1868–1994.* Oxford: Oxford University Press, 1996.

AFRICA

Throughout the 20th century, the concept of employment and work in Africa has changed radically. Cities have expanded and agriculture has shifted from self-sufficient to commercialized fields while industry and standards of living have failed to progress.

Before colonial rule, the overwhelming majority of Africans either raised food crops or herded cattle. These occupations were aimed at feeding one's family while using surpluses for trade or storing them. Due to this emphasis on agriculture and herding, the majority of Africans lived in rural areas. These rural communities produced plenty of food and few went hungry.

Africans who did not rely on farming or herding usually specialized in trade. These Africans tended to live in urban areas, and these areas often served as major centers of commerce for the region. Swahili and West African trading networks were quite complex and even traded goods from Europe, Asia, and the Middle East as well as other parts of Africa. However, as colonial rule came into effect throughout the late 1800s and early 1900s, these systems were forever altered.

ECONOMIC LIFE

WORK

Europe

United States,
1920-1939

United States,
1940-1959

United States,
1960-1990

Japan

Africa

The main aim of colonial rule was to profit from the continent's natural resources. Europeans soon realized that the Gambia could produce large amounts of peanuts, rubber trees were plentiful in the Congo, and there were huge diamond reserves in South Africa. To profit from these resources, colonial governments had to find ways to produce a domestic workforce that was willing to work cheaply. It was unfeasible for European governments to import massive amounts of European workers, so they had to find a way to force Africans out of subsistence living and into wage labor. Colonial governments began taxing African populations in order to force them into the workforce. Taxes on housing, imported goods (alcohol and tobacco), schools, and the like were implemented to force Africans to find paying jobs and thus join the colonial economy. Instead of working on fields or tending their herds, many Africans found jobs on cash crop plantations, in the mines, or building colonial infrastructure like railroads.

This shift to wage labor profoundly altered the continent. Men and teenage boys often joined labor pools to earn money while women and children tended to fields and livestock. Also, as land became more valuable, many Africans were forced off their land by colonial governments. Family agriculture in Africa is often labor intensive, and production was deeply impeded as these family members were lost to wage labor. This caused fields to be less productive and further exacerbated a family's meager economic situation.

Today most African nations focus agriculture on only one or two certain crops. Colonial rule used African colonies to produce crops for European consumers. These governments often forced or convinced farmers to specialize in one cash crop to sell for export. Cash crops such as cashews, peanuts, kola nuts, coffee, tobacco, and cocoa came to dominate various African economies. The effects of this specialization have been profound and unfortunate. Many African farmers stopped growing foodstuffs, requiring governments to import food from Western powers. Second, crop specialization often causes problems for African economies in that a country's economy hinges on the year's harvest. If there is a good harvest, then the market is flooded, resulting in lower prices and lower profits for farmers. During times of flooding or drought when harvests are poor, many farmers produce a small crop and earn very little. Thus, while crop specialization benefited colonial governments, it has marred African nations since independence.

State-run and state-owned facilities were vital to colonial rule. These governments owned and controlled the universities, banks, ports, and utilities, among other institutions. Consequently, the government was usually a colony's largest employer, and this did not change at the end of colonial rule. For many Africans, the point of attending a university was to obtain a government job. Therefore government and civic service was viewed by many as a way to acquire wealth rather than an opportunity to serve one's nation and represent its people.

At the end of the 20th century much of Africa was not industrialized. Most manufactured goods were imported from Europe, North America, or Asia. Only basic industries such as shoe companies and breweries met with some success. Most African industries did not manufacture cars, airplanes, heavy machinery, or other complex manufactured goods. Thus, African economies failed to develop, and few

Africans worked in mills or factories. This further weakened African economies, as they exported cheap raw materials only to purchase manufactured goods, which Western countries sold for a profit. To further compound the situation, oil and mining companies often brought specialists from Europe and America to fill upper-level positions. Thus, Africans were stuck in lower levels of employment.

For the greater part of the 20th century, Africa underwent a massive migration from the countryside to urban areas, and the trend continues now. Rural areas often lack decent jobs and have weak local economies; many people in these areas struggle to survive. These migrants move to the cities with the belief that they will be able to find a sufficient job and live a decent life. Cities are the hubs of industry, government, and commerce for most nations, and thus many migrants pin their hopes of better living on moving to urban areas. These hopes are often crushed because African cities also have weak economies, high unemployment, and rampant poverty. This situation further hinders the ability of governments to promote development, strengthen their economies, and increase employment.

As this entry has illustrated, work in Africa was drastically altered throughout the 20th century. Colonization and the implementation of a global economy led the African continent to rampant poverty, high levels of unemployment, and even starvation in many nations. At the end of the 20th century, it became clear that Africans were worse off than they were before colonization and globalization.

~Tyler Fleming

FOR MORE INFORMATION

Bay, E. G., ed. *Women and Work in Africa*. Boulder, Colo.: Westview Press, 1982.

Freund, B. *The African Worker*. New York: Cambridge University Press, 1988.

Fry, J. *Employment and Income Distribution in the African Economy*. London: Croom Helm, 1979.

Swindell, K. *Farm Labour*. New York: Cambridge University Press, 1985.

LATIN AMERICA

The values and patterns of work in Latin America in the 20th century grew directly from the traditions established in the 19th century. See the Latin America entry in the section "Work" in chapter 3 ("Economic Life") in volume 5 of this series for a discussion of the labor traditions that emerged in the region after the end of Spanish colonial rule.

Class and Caste Experience

Class and caste are often difficult concepts to grasp. On one level they deal with birthright, money, wealth, and power. The upper classes clearly are richer and more influential than the middle and working classes. Yet a rich person like Donald Trump

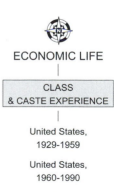

ECONOMIC LIFE
|
CLASS
& CASTE EXPERIENCE
|
United States,
1929-1959

United States,
1960-1990

Latin America

India

Soviet Union

remains among the elite even though he has declared bankruptcy at various times. Similarly, in the heady days of the 1990s, many factory workers became paper millionaires as their pension plans increased astronomically during the stock market boom. But no one would mistake these line workers for the upper class. Nor would anyone mistake a Brahman for an untouchable in the Indian caste system, which in some ways has historically been more rigid than economic class. Still, class and caste have shifted over the centuries. In other words, class has other changing and sometimes hard-to-define qualities.

In the 20th century, class and caste still influenced daily life, but people struggled to challenge their social position and the barriers to social and economic advancement. Take India as an example. In the years following World War II, reformers and activists such as Mahatma Gandhi fought to change the caste system. The battle was partially successful. In 1947, the newly independent India created a constitution that outlawed untouchability. Although the caste system did remain, equality was closer to becoming a reality. Meanwhile in the Soviet Union and other communist states, class was officially eliminated although in practice the members of the Communist Party formed the new elite.

People in the Western hemisphere also struggled to overcome the accident of birth. Being born into a lower class in places such as Chile or Cuba or the United States relegated many to lives of desperation and poverty. Those living in the United States liked to think that the situation was worse in Latin America. Indeed, there was some truth to that assumption. Late in the 20th century in Brazil, less than 6 percent of the population held nearly three-quarters of all the arable land. Despite the efforts of Latin American reformers and revolutionaries, high rates of poverty and inequality were common class experiences. Yet in the United States, poverty remained all too common. The lower classes tended to live quiet lives of despair. At various points during the century, writers such as Michael Harrington and John Kenneth Galbraith had to point out to the affluent classes that the poor existed and struggled to make their way. American presidents from Franklin Roosevelt to Lyndon Johnson to Richard Nixon sought to eliminate poverty, with varying success. Nonetheless, by the end of the century, homelessness, hunger, and high unemployment remained a part of lower-class daily life. This situation was not just a random product of a volatile economy. The concerted effort by politicians and employers to dismantle the industrial economy and to destroy labor unions fostered the growing numbers of working poor. As it was sometimes said, the 20th century was an era in which the rich got richer and the poor got poorer.

ECONOMIC LIFE

CLASS
& CASTE EXPERIENCE

United States,
1929-1959

United States,
1960-1990

Latin America

India

Soviet Union

UNITED STATES, 1929–59

The two decades following the Great Depression were characterized by economic growth. The prosperity was real, and people did not complain about the federal taxes that were also subsidizing so much. In 1939 only 3.9 million people paid federal income taxes; in 1949, 35.6 million paid personal income taxes. Just as higher education shifted from being an upper-class privilege, so taxation shifted from being the

Chicago soup kitchen line, 1931. Although few people starved in the United States during the Great Depression, many out-of-work middle- and working-class Americans had to get help to feed themselves and their families. © National Archives.

burden of the very rich. As the country prospered, more workers contributed to the national coffers. In the late 1940s the United States, with only 7 percent of the world's population, accounted for half of the entire world's manufacturing output. At that time Americans possessed 42 percent of the world's income. Per capita income in the United States in 1949 was $1,450—much higher than that of other prosperous nations. In Canada, Great Britain, New Zealand, Switzerland, and Sweden, the average was between $700 and $900. And in 1945 unemployment was only 1.9 percent in America; it remained under 4 percent from 1946 to 1948.

Controlled immigration eliminated the fear of job loss from invasions of cheap workers, and the small cohort of young men born during the Depression contributed to making most American cities safe places. From the 1930s to 1945 the murder rate in the United States had been cut in half. Such statistics do indeed suggest a kind of momentary postwar utopia. Yet millions of people—not defined by the more formal poverty level—still did not share what would be defined by the middle class in the 1990s as the good life.

The Great Depression devastated not only the economy but American workers as well. This jobless man illustrates well the common phrase of the times, "down and out." © Library of Congress.

The material changes in America from World War II to the 21st century have been so overwhelming that students may find it hard to believe that in 1947, 40 million people (30 percent of all Americans) were poor—even by the standards of the time. One-third of American homes had no running water, two-fifths had no flush toilets, three-fifths lacked central heat, and four-fifths were heated by coal or wood. And in spite of the miracle of Levittowns, most people still lived in rented housing. Many workers continued to labor at demanding physical jobs on farms or in mines, in factories, or in construction.

Pete Seeger, working-class folk hero and musician, plays for a crowd of servicemen and women as well as Eleanor Roosevelt. © Library of Congress.

In 1945, 17.5 percent of the population still made its living from the soil, but by the late 1940s the exodus from the land represented one of the greatest demographic shifts in contemporary history. The number of family farms would fall from 5.9 million at the close of World War II to only three million 25 years later. The shift to agribusiness, the control of gigantic farms created from the consolidation of small farms—with the help of government subsidies—did little to improve the quality of life for most farmworkers, many of whom were black or Hispanic (Kaledin 69).

To read about class and caste in the United States in the 19th century, see the United States entries in the section "Class and Caste Experience" in chapter 3 ("Economic Life") in volume 5 of this series.

FOR MORE INFORMATION

Dubofsky, M. *The State and Labor in Modern America.* Chapel Hill: University of North Carolina Press, 1994.

Kaledin, E. *Daily Life in the United States, 1940–1959: Shifting Worlds.* Westport, Conn.: Greenwood Press, 2000.

Lichtenstein, N. *Labor's War at Home: The CIO in World War II.* Cambridge: Cambridge University Press, 1982.

ECONOMIC LIFE
|
CLASS
& CASTE EXPERIENCE
|
United States,
1929-1959

United States,
1960-1990

Latin America

India

Soviet Union

UNITED STATES, 1960–90

Like the period 1940 to 1959, from the 1960s to the 1990s, a general prosperity enjoyed throughout America reached into nearly all homes and families. But if migration to suburbs was a sign of affluence, the city neighborhoods and the people left behind soon showed the many faces of poverty. Poverty was abundantly evident in rural America as well, particularly in Appalachian regions of West Virginia, Kentucky, Tennessee, and North Carolina. Although industries had moved from the North to the South, particularly in textile and furniture manufacturing, it was the prospect of paying lower wages that lured them, so increases in living standards were slow in coming. Most African Americans who earlier had migrated from the South to what they saw as the promised land in northern cities found poverty rather than promise there. Slums and derelict housing projects populated almost exclusively by blacks became common in major cities, and racial discrimination posed barriers as formidable as those existing in the South.

Some economists and social activists who had kept an eye on the conditions faced daily by America's poor proposed strategies for economic development to ameliorate them, but action did not come quickly. President Kennedy's slight margin of victory in 1960 would have hobbled any major reform efforts he might have proposed, and his conservative instincts probably discouraged him from recommending ambitious plans anyway. His measures to stimulate the economy had some positive effects; as the gross national product (GNP) grew at an average annual rate of 5.3 percent between 1961 and 1964, compared to the 3.2 percent annual average of the 1950s. But problems of unequal distribution of wealth—indeed, of outright poverty—persisted.

Just as *Silent Spring* and *Unsafe at Any Speed* had stimulated interest in environmental and product safety concerns, Michael Harrington's passionate book *The Other America* (1962) changed what many people thought about problems of poverty. Although Harrington sprinkled statistics throughout the book, it was his description of the "invisible poor," particularly the elderly, the young, and minorities, that gave the book its power. "In a sense," he wrote, "one might define the contemporary poor in the United States as those who, for reasons beyond their control, cannot help themselves. All the most decisive factors making for opportunity and advance are against them. They are born going downward, and most of them stay down. They are victims whose lives are endlessly blown round and round the other America." There were 40 to 50 million of them, he estimated. Harrington asked his readers "to respond critically to every assertion, but not to allow statistical quibbling to obscure the huge, enormous, and intolerable fact of poverty in America. For, when all is said and done, that fact is unmistakable, whatever its exact dimensions, and the truly human reaction can only be outrage."

Although Harrington chose not to use statistics to dramatize the condition of the "other Americans," one can see in the numbers of the early 1960s that daily life differed dramatically according to where one stood on the nation's economic ladder. The 20 percent of Americans on the top rungs of the ladder owned more than 75 percent of the nation's wealth; the 20 percent on the bottom rungs owned only 0.05 percent. Those on the bottom rungs received 23 percent of the total money income; those on the top, 77 percent.

In 1968, 13 percent of the American population still lived below the poverty line as defined by the federal government. This compared with 20 percent at the beginning of the decade. Twenty percent of African Americans remained below the poverty line, down from 40 percent eight years earlier. These improvements meant that the Great Society's War on Poverty could claim only a partial victory.

When Richard Nixon became president in 1969, he supported modest growth in the size and cost of a few Great Society programs, went along with legislation that increased Social Security benefits, and approved construction of subsidized housing and expansion of the Job Corps. More significant, he offered a bold and ambitious plan for welfare reform. The Family Assistance Plan (FAP) would have ended piecemeal allowances and guaranteed every family of four an annual income of $2,400, with a maximum of $3,600 for a family of eight or more. The FAP passed the House of Representatives but died in the Senate, caught between liberals who thought it too conservative and conservatives who thought it too liberal.

Mostly left out of the political debates of the 1970s, the American poor suffered even more in the 1980s. Hit especially hard by economic circumstances and policy decisions in the mid-1980s were those Americans affected by the reductions in various welfare programs. President Reagan's inaugural address dramatically revealed his intentions: "Government is not the solution to our problem," he asserted, as he had throughout his campaign; "government *is* the problem." Government generosity and good intentions, he believed, were out of control; he called for "new federalism," a plan to make the down-and-out in society a local and state responsibility. Reductions in federal welfare programs caused worries about whether there would be a "safety net" to catch those losing government assistance.

In 1984, the percentage of children living in poverty was higher than that of adults.

Statistics on poverty in 1984 reveal the plight of many Americans. More than 33 million people, about one-seventh of the nation's population, lived below the poverty level, reversing trends set in motion by the Great Society. The percentage of children living in poverty was higher than that of adults. Among both blacks and persons living in female-headed households, the ratio was one in three. Monthly payments to the 3.7 million families covered by the Aid to Families with Dependent Children (AFDC) program averaged $338. About 21.5 million persons received services funded by Medicaid, with average annual costs of $1,569 per person. Nearly 20 million people were eligible for food stamps, a four-year low resulting from more stringent eligibility requirements.

From time to time Congress attempted to reform the welfare system, with specific measures aimed at giving the poor the job training or education needed to get off welfare. In 1988 Congress passed a law requiring parents on welfare whose children were past the age of three to enroll in appropriate education, training, job search, or work programs. The new law, which had an estimated cost of more than $3 billion over five years, allowed for a long lead-in time, reflecting awareness of the difficulty of moving welfare recipients into independence: By 1995, 20 percent of those eligible for welfare would be required to enroll in an appropriate program.

At the very bottom of society were those who lived with no place called home. Estimates of homeless Americans reached a record high in 1986, but the numbers were still rising. New York counted 10,000 single people and 5,500 families as homeless. In Chicago the number of homeless was somewhere between 9,000 and 22,000; in Newark, New Jersey, 4,000–7,000; in Atlanta, 5,000; in Philadelphia, 13,000; and in Los Angeles, 40,000. Included in the tallies were higher proportions of women, children, and younger men than in previous decades.

More than a sluggish economy and a tight employment market accounted for the increased numbers of homeless persons. As noted earlier, in the 1960s and 1970s state and local governments had released mentally ill people from medical facilities. As a result of these deinstitutionalization policies, the population in state mental hospitals dropped from more than 550,000 in the 1950s to fewer than 150,000 three decades later. Community-based programs were intended to help these former patients, but the programs were never sufficiently funded. Those who lacked the mental, physical, financial, and familial resources to cope with life in the outside world, and particularly the ability to find and keep jobs, ended up on the streets. Cities grappled in various ways with the problem of caring for them, none with notable success.

Compounding government failures to handle poverty was the decline in the labor movement that in the early 20th century had helped poor working-class people emerge from poverty. From the mid-1930s until the 1960s labor unions had played an important part in improving the economic security of many working-class Americans. By 1970, however, the unions' influence had begun to erode, not only in the workplace but in politics too. The unions had built their strength in earlier years by taking an aggressive approach to organizing and bargaining, but now their implicit partnership with the Democratic party tempered their actions.

In only two respects did unions maintain or increase the strength they had enjoyed in the 1950s and early 1960s. First, as women entered the workplace they formed two organizations—the National Association of Working Women (known as Nine to Five) and the Coalition of Labor Union Women. Recognizing the potential power of women in the labor movement, the AFL-CIO, labor's largest organization, endorsed the Equal Rights Amendment in 1973. In subsequent years unions provided support on what came to be called women's issues, such as affirmative action, child care, and pay equity.

Second, unions representing government workers at all levels gained power and influence. By 1970 membership in public employees' unions exceeded four million, making it 10 times larger than it had been 15 years earlier. Particularly powerful were the American Federation of State, County, and Municipal Employees; the American Federation of Teachers; and the National Education Association, along with unions of police officers, firefighters, nurses, and postal workers. Yet their power was limited by the fact that work stoppages—some legal, some illegal—by public servants directly affected the lives of those whom they served, thereby arousing resentment.

The recruitment of women and the growth of government workers' unions were insufficient to offset the decline of industrial unions. That decline reflected many changes in economic processes that attracted little attention until their consequences were widely felt. One was the increased automation of manufacturing processes, making assembly-line workers dispensable. Another involved the rising aspirations of families that had moved to the suburbs and worked their way into white-collar jobs. They sent their children to college with expectations that the children could reach even higher rungs on the employment ladder through individual rather than collective effort.

More significant was the process known as deindustrialization. In the 1970s the United States became an exporter of raw materials and an importer of more cars and steel as well as electrical, electronic, and other manufactured goods. The U.S. share of global manufactured exports declined significantly and trade deficits ballooned. Large corporations invested their money in mergers, so much so that in 1968 the Federal Trade Commission launched a sweeping investigation of the causes and consequences of runaway conglomerate mergers. The chairman of the commission referred to these conglomerates—the joining of companies engaged in unrelated or remotely related businesses—as a virus threatening the health of the American economy. Corporations also acquired related business enterprises and invested in overseas operations. Consequently, workers found themselves competing more strenuously against one another for jobs in the United States and against poorly paid workers in other countries. This competition allowed businesses to call for concessions, or "givebacks," as they were known. These included reductions in pay, elimination of formerly protected jobs, and the scaling back of such fringe benefits as medical insurance.

Also affecting unions' effectiveness was something unseen by most Americans, that is, the development of more than a thousand consulting firms that specialized in advising corporations on how to keep union organizers and sympathizers out of the workplace. These firms also showed how to defeat a union when elections could not be avoided and helped employers find ways to decertify unions that had won elections.

The 1980s got off to a bad start for labor unions when President Reagan fired 12,000 members of the Professional Air Traffic Controllers Organization (PATCO) on August 5, 1981. PATCO had rejected the final bargaining offer made by the Federal Aviation Authority (FAA), and the traffic controllers had gone on strike a week earlier. Because the strike violated federal law, the firings were legal. "Dammit, the law is the law," Reagan said to his aides, "and the law says they can't strike. By striking they've quit their jobs." With the firing of the professional controllers, the FAA had to use military controllers, nonstrikers, and supervisors to keep the nation's planes in the air. The immediate results included a cutback in services; loss of business from people who were reluctant to fly in uncertain skies; and, according to the International Air Transport Association, a $200 million loss by the airlines in the month of August alone.

The symbolic effects of the firings lasted longer. Unions could not expect cordial or deferential treatment from the new administration, particularly the increasingly restive unions of government employees. These effects, along with the changing nature of workplaces across the nation, made it natural for the decline in union membership to continue. Fear of company shutdowns or permanent layoffs weakened individual union members' readiness to support aggressive tactics by unions in dealing with employers. For ordinary workers, union membership had once symbolized a mutual commitment between themselves and their employers, even in times of difficult negotiations. That sense of commitment gave way to anger and humiliation in the 1980s when unions were compelled to accept distasteful provisions in bargaining agreements. These included such things as lump-sum payments based on company profits rather than permanent wage increases; givebacks of benefits and wage increases that were won in earlier bargaining; and systems of pay with two tiers, allowing for lower wages for new employees.

In the early 1980s, organized labor represented about one worker in four; by the end of the decade it represented one in six. With the decline in membership and the disadvantaged positions in which union workers found themselves, the use of work stoppages in disputes with management declined. In 1988, according to the Bureau of Labor Statistics, the 40 stoppages involving 1,000 or more workers was the lowest number since it began keeping records 40 years earlier (Marty, 43–44, 100–103, 268–69, 271–72).

To read about class and caste in the United States in the 19th century, see the United States entries in the section "Class and Caste Experience" in chapter 3 ("Economic Life") in volume 5 of this series.

FOR MORE INFORMATION

Harrington, M. *The Other America: Poverty in the United States*. Baltimore: Penguin, 1963.

Marty, M. A. *Daily Life in the United States, 1960–1990: Decades of Discord*. Westport, Conn.: Greenwood Press, 1997.

Moore, M., dir. *The Big One*. 1998.

Newman, K. *Falling from Grace: The Experience of Downward Mobility in the American Middle Class*. New York: Free Press, 1988.

LATIN AMERICA

ECONOMIC LIFE

CLASS
& CASTE EXPERIENCE

United States,
1929-1959

United States,
1960-1990

Latin America

India

Soviet Union

Though Latin American nations share a hemisphere, and all countries share histories of European conquest and domination, in reality the region is diverse in terms of race and ethnicity, politics and culture, and economics. In the 20th century, Latin Americans spoke many languages, including Spanish, Portuguese, English, French, Japanese, German, and hundreds of indigenous languages. They followed many different religions: Catholicism, Protestantism, and many forms of spiritualism. And they opted for many distinct forms of political leadership, including democracy, socialism, and military rule. Despite this diversity, one trend was common throughout 20th-century Latin America: class structures remained remarkably unequal.

A legacy of conquest and slavery, racial and class hierarchies existed in the region for hundreds of years. In the 20th century, race relations continued to be tense, yet attitudes were much more tolerant than in previous centuries. Four major racial and ethnic groups existed in Latin America: indigenous, African, Creole, and immigrants (particularly from Europe and Asia). Following European conquest and colonization in the 16th and 17th centuries, some populations indigenous to the Americas became extinct. Others survived, in drastically reduced numbers. By the 20th century, their numbers had grown considerably. In the 1970s, indigenous groups accounted for some 60 percent of the populations of Guatemala and Bolivia, nearly 50 percent in Peru, 30 percent in Ecuador, and around 15 percent in Mexico.

During the 16th through 19th centuries, many Latin American countries imported African slaves. More than three million arrived in Spanish America, and some five million were sold into Brazil. By the 20th century, populations of African descent were particularly prevalent in the Caribbean and Brazil. In the Brazilian censuses of 1950 and 1980, approximately 40 percent of the population identified as black or *parda* (mixed). Approximately 30 percent of Cubans identified as black or mixed in that nation's 1953 census. The Dominican Republic and Haiti were home to large populations of blacks as well.

Immigrants have also played an important role in the racial and ethnic makeup of Latin America. Of primary importance were the Spanish and Portuguese *conquistadores* and their Americas-born offspring, known as *criollos*, or Creoles. Through the years, often due to labor demands, Latin American governments actively recruited other immigrants. Foreign-born populations were quite large in some locations, such as Costa Rica and the Southern Cone countries of Chile and Argentina. Indeed, some 2.4 million immigrants from Europe and Asia arrived to Argentina by 1950, accounting for 15 percent of the total population.

A social hierarchy based largely on race existed in Latin America since the times of conquest and colonization. The small number of white Spanish, Portuguese, and Creoles controlled the top of this hierarchy, and the masses of indigenous, blacks, and mixed races populated the bottom ranks.

In large part because of efforts of members of movements such as the Black Consciousness and Pan-Indigenous movements, people on the lower rungs of society gained many freedoms and rights during the 20th century. Some governments granted voting rights to the predominantly nonwhite illiterate populations. Others recognized indigenous communities' legal rights to own property.

A gap continued to exist, however, between the written word and peoples' lived realities. Discrimination continued, in overt and covert forms. Thus, although Brazil's constitution of 1946 officially barred racial discrimination, and legislation passed in 1951 imposed penalties for discrimination in public places, Brazil's nonwhites continued to be relegated to society's lower rungs.

Just as one's race and ethnicity determined to a large extent one's position within Latin American society, so too did one's socioeconomic class. Indeed, the discriminatory aspects of race and class were tightly interconnected.

A major element in Latin America's social and economic class structures was land tenure. Even in the 20th century, landholding was extremely uneven, with few people controlling most of this precious resource. A typical pattern was visible in 1975 in northeastern Brazil: a full 70 percent of the population held less than 6 percent of national territory in parcels of between 1 and 10 hectares, whereas just 6 percent of the population controlled 65.4 percent of the land in giant parcels of between 100 and 10,000 hectares. A similar imbalance existed in some Caribbean nations, such as Jamaica, where 1 percent of landowners occupied 56 percent of total acreage. Such imbalances existed not only in agricultural societies, but also where mining prevailed, as in Bolivia, where, until the 1952 revolution, a few families dominated the industry as well as all of its related resources, including land.

Latin American inequalities were also clearly visible in the distribution of income. In four of the largest countries of the region—Argentina, Brazil, Chile, and Mexico—the wealthiest fifth of the population received over half of national incomes in the 1960s, compared with the poorest fifth of the population's less than 5 percent.

Two decades later, little had changed, as exemplified by statistics from Brazil: in 1983, the wealthiest fifth received 62.6 percent of income, compared to the poorest fifth's 2.4 percent.

The distribution of resources in Latin America also demonstrated vast inequalities. Differences were particularly evident between urban and rural settings. To be from a rural area often indicated poverty, which meant not only a lack of money and material goods, but also blocked access to health care, education, and government services. The lack of access to schools was evident in the fact that illiteracy rates were often two to six times higher in rural regions than in urban areas. Rural populations, furthermore, often lacked access to roads, potable water, and electricity.

Through the 20th century, many social movements emerged that pressured for greater social and economic rights for the majority of Latin Americans. Some revolutionary governments—in Cuba, Nicaragua, and Mexico, for example—made serious efforts to redistribute their nations' wealth. Yet old habits die hard. Latin America's connections to international markets, along with its heavy dependence on export, made the region particularly vulnerable to swings in world economic health. In addition, the massive debts accrued by Latin American governments through the years led to a reliance on international lending agencies such as the World Bank for financial support. Such dependence removed much of local governments' abilities to adopt creative responses to national problems.

Thus, though many of the social and economic underclasses gained rights, Latin America continued at the end of the 20th century to be highly unequal. A small portion of the population controlled national economies and politics, while the masses often lacked even the most basic necessities.

To read about class and caste in 19th-century Latin America, see the Latin America entry in the section "Class and Caste Experience" in chapter 3 ("Economic Life") in volume 5 of this series.

~Molly Todd

FOR MORE INFORMATION

Bethell, L., ed. *The Cambridge History of Latin America*. Vol. 6, Part 1. Cambridge: Cambridge University Press, 1994.

Burns, E. B. *Latin America: A Concise Interpretive History*. 5th ed. Englewood Cliffs, N.J.: Prentice Hall, 1990.

Henderson, J. D., H. Delpar, M. P. Grungardt, and R. Weldon, eds. *A Reference Guide to Latin American History*. Armonk, N.Y.: M. E. Sharpe, 2000.

Salazar, M. C. "Child Work and Education in Latin America." In *Child Work and Education: Five Case Studies from Latin America*, edited by María Cristina Salazar. Aldershot, England: Ashgate, 1998.

INDIA

The caste system in India was unique to the region. In no other part of the world was there such an intricate and developed system of social identification. The caste

ECONOMIC LIFE

CLASS
& CASTE EXPERIENCE

United States,
1929-1959

United States,
1960-1990

Latin America

India

Soviet Union

system has survived in India for centuries and continues to do so today. In short, caste was a way for people to identify themselves with a larger group. A person might identify himself or herself by religion or region, but also by caste affiliation. The term *caste* comes from the Portuguese word *casta*, which relates to the "purity" of one's blood. The Portuguese mistakenly applied the term to the Indian situation. During British rule, the term changed from *casta* to the current *caste*.

An individual attained caste identity largely through birth. Parents arranged marriages between children who were of the same caste group, and their children in turn retained the same caste identity. One's birth determines caste identity but does not necessarily determine occupation.

Castes generally fell into four idealized and broad divisions of Indian society. At the top were *brahmans*, who served as priests and scholars. Next were *kshtryas*, who were the kings and warriors. Third were *kshatriyas*, the merchants. Finally, there were *shudras*, who were servants. Beyond these four groups were the "untouchables," "unseeables," and "unapproachables," who were outside the system. They performed the most polluting tasks (animal skinning, removing night soil, etc.) and were often mistreated. Within each division were different castes, and ideally a person performed the occupation of his or her caste group. However, this idealized system, though still recounted in myth, probably was never the daily practice in India.

Being a member of a certain caste was not necessarily a lifelong role. Over time, members of caste groups sometimes changed their caste identity to attain some benefit. A group belonging to one caste might relocate to another region and take up a more prestigious occupation. Sometimes this included changing their caste name as well. In addition, relationships between caste groups were not always the same. For example, a caste of weavers might have been able to advance their position by moving to a region where weavers were more highly regarded. In the same way, all members of a particular caste group were not related to each other or descended from a common ancestor. Members of the same caste may live at opposite ends of the subcontinent and share nothing more than a common caste name. However, it was common and even preferred to arrange marriages for children with members of the same caste, sometimes even from far afield. Caste distinctions also existed within India among other religious groups including Christians, Jews, Sikhs, Buddhists, and even Muslims. Caste within these groups functioned much as it did within Hinduism.

Throughout the existence of the caste system, movements have arisen and individuals have spoken out against it. For example, the Hindu devotional movements (*bhakti*) of the Shivites, Vaishnavites, and Lingayats, and individuals such as Mahatma Jyothi Rao Phule, Periyar E. V. Ramaswamy, Dr. B. R. Ambedkar, and Mahatma Gandhi, have challenged the caste system. Despite challenges to its existence, the caste system continues today. The Indian constitution has outlawed untouchability and any discrimination based on untouchability but does not outlaw caste itself.

When India gained its independence from the British on August 14, 1947, its founding members crafted a constitution that would shape the country's future and uphold its values. The preamble of the constitution outlined the basic tenets that, in some ways, stood in contradiction to the caste system. The republic of India secured for its citizens "justice, social, economic and politic; liberty of thought, expression, belief, faith and worship; equality of status and of opportunity; and to promote among them all fraternity assuring the dignity of the individual and the unity of the Nation . . . " The Indian constitution came into force on January 26, 1950.

A major force in shaping the constitution and in helping the plight of untouchables was Dr. Bhimrao Ramji Ambedkar (1891–1956). Ambedkar was born into the untouchable *mahar* caste, in the northern state of Maharashtra. With the aid of the maharaja of Baroda, Ambedkar traveled to the United States. There, he earned MA and Ph.D. degrees from Columbia University in New York. He later studied law in London, where he also earned an MA and a doctorate from London University. Upon returning to India, Ambedkar faced discrimination for being from an untouchable background. He devoted his life to the uplift of this group. India's first prime minister, Jawaharlal Nehru, appointed Ambedkar to be the country's first law minister. It was Ambedkar who helped shape India's constitution and the criminality of untouchability. The constitution states, " 'Untouchability' was abolished and its practice in any form is forbidden. The enforcement of any disability arising out of 'Untouchability' shall be an offence punishable in accordance with the law" (Part III, Fundamental Rights, Article 17).

The caste system in India was an ancient institution that still finds sustenance in today's social order. A person's caste identity was one more way for people to arrange and group themselves within society. Within the system, inequalities have been perpetuated against those considered to be of a lower caste, or outside the system and considered untouchable. Among equal caste groups, the system has provided for marriage matches and other social needs. Modern India still occasionally reels from violence along caste lines, and much work has yet to be done to fulfill the noble aspirations laid down in the constitution.

To read about class and social structure in ancient India, see the India entry in the section "Social Structure" in chapter 6 ("Political Life") in volume 1 of this series.

~Benjamin Cohen

FOR MORE INFORMATION

Elder, J. "India's Caste System: Enduring Stereotypes about Asia." *Education about ASIA* (Fall 1996): 20–22.

Indian constitution. <http://www.constitution.org/cons/india/const.html>.

SOVIET UNION

When it was founded, the Soviet Union intended to abolish the class structure that had so oppressed the Russian people for centuries before. The Marxist ideology of the Soviet Union also intended to eliminate a class system based on wealth as exemplified in the United States and increasingly in postwar western Europe. How-

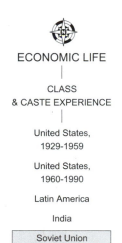

ECONOMIC LIFE

CLASS
& CASTE EXPERIENCE

United States,
1929-1959

United States,
1960-1990

Latin America

India

Soviet Union

ever, this never happened; the Soviet Union was stratified by class just as everywhere else, but this was a class system based within the communist structure.

Anyone who was ambitious knew that the main prerequisites for social climbing were Party membership; education; Russian nationality or language ability; and residence in an important Soviet city, preferably Moscow or Leningrad. Full-time Party workers were guaranteed special benefits and social status. The tip of the social pyramid consisted of the highest Party bosses (the First Secretary and members of the Politburo); then government ministers; the most senior military commanders; top officers in the secret police and militia; diplomats; directors of large enterprises; and top-ranking academics, artists, performers, and scientists.

Perks available to the internationally known painter Ilya Glazunov, a "People's Artist of the USSR," show the kind of luxuries available at the top: spacious penthouse apartment, expensive Western furniture, valuable paintings and carpets, fine food and drink, a white Mercedes sedan (few ordinary citizens owned cars, let alone pricey foreign models). Top Party officers had the use of state-owned cars with drivers, private apartments, summer homes, servants, and foreign travel, the most luxury at the least cost to themselves. Retired officers jumped the line for private apartments wherever they wanted to live within the USSR and could select a well-paid second career, especially in security-related fields.

Beneath the military elite were the ambitious middle classes—middle- and lower-level Party officials, white-collar workers, managers, professors and other academics, teachers, doctors, and hardworking black marketeers, for example. These people lived very well in comparison to the classes below them and their parents' and grandparents' generations, and they knew it. They were also conscious of the special privileges accorded to the classes above them and aimed for a piece of that pie, if not for themselves then for their children. However, a middle class standard of living in the Soviet Union was much lower than that in other developed countries. Lower-level urban workers were the class below the middle class. Except for prisoners, peasants—agricultural workers on collective farms—were the lowest social class. Farmworkers on state farms were regarded as workers rather than peasants, which placed them a cut above peasants on the social ladder.

Although the Bolsheviks had declared the Soviet Union a state by and for workers and peasants, in reality, if you had a grandmother or a grandfather who came from a village, you didn't talk about it. The situation had been quite different in the 1920s and 1930s, when (the world having been turned upside down) being a member of the nobility, a businessperson, an officer of the czar's armed forces, a wealthy peasant, or a priest could cost a person liberty or even life itself. Such people often fled into the lower classes. Their children took factory jobs to qualify for higher education, to rebel against their parents, or simply because they were proud to be known as proletarians.

The government's system of distributing food, clothing, and other goods and services, from education to transportation to health care and anything else, largely ignored the countryside and small towns, so big-city residency was an important status symbol for people of all classes. Moscow conferred the biggest bragging rights. Because it was the seat of government and center of power, it received more and better consumer goods than other cities and had the best educational and cultural opportunities. As a result, Muscovites as a group were a privileged class: wealthier, more sophisticated, better clothed, fed, and educated than residents of any other city, including Leningrad. In the early 1980s about a million visitors came to Moscow every day for shopping. As a crude measure, the larger the Soviet city, the greater its range of amenities.

The upper classes lived in clean, well-maintained apartment buildings, in contrast to littered working-class buildings with their smelly stairwells. It was usual for a building in an upper-class area to have a vigilant retiree sitting in a glassed-in booth just inside the entrance. These elderly gatekeepers recognized all the residents and kept track of everyone's comings and goings. Kiril, whose mother was a cleaning lady and father a night watchman and who passed the entrance exam to an elite Moscow "special" high school, quickly discovered the social gulf separating him from his wealthy classmates. Unlike his family, his friends had VCRs, color TVs, imported furniture, fashionably faded jeans, and other imported clothing and ate foods not available to the general public, much less cleaning ladies.

The top elite, including leaders in the arts, had special restaurants open only to members and their families and guests. These restaurants, unlike public ones, provided well-prepared luxury foods (e.g., steak, caviar, and shellfish); attentive, friendly service complete with clean tablecloths; and also carry-out privileges; members could walk into the kitchen and buy nicely prewrapped raw meat or could telephone ahead to have such items ready for pickup. The top elite, such as KGB officers with the rank of captain and above, had their phone orders boxed and delivered weekly to their homes or desks by an unmarked van. The higher the social class, the easier it was to get good food at bargain prices.

~*Joyce E. Salisbury*

FOR MORE INFORMATION

Eaton, K. B. *Daily Life in the Soviet Union*. Westport, Conn.: Greenwood Press. Forthcoming.

Discrimination

The famous Swedish sociologist Gunnar Myrdal called it the American dilemma. How can a nation founded on liberty allow discrimination to be so pervasive in society? Far too frequently discrimination was a daily rigor of life in the United States. Taking our cue from Myrdal, perhaps we can call discrimination the 20th-century dilemma. How can a world seemingly committed to human rights allow discrimination to continue. Indeed, much of the 20th century was spent struggling to eliminate caste, racial, and gender bias, with varying degrees of success. The entries in this section not only provide an excellent summary of the civil rights movements in the United States, but also allow for some comparative analysis of discrimination with the European, Indian, Japanese, and Soviet experiences.

ECONOMIC LIFE
|
DISCRIMINATION
|
Europe—
Anti-Semitism

United States,
1920–1939

United States,
1940–1959

United States,
1960–1990

India

Soviet Union—
Anti-Semitism

Japan

As one will see, the 20th-century American civil rights movement is broken into two historical periods, pre–World War II and post–World War II. Before the war, anti–civil rights organizations such as the Ku Klux Klan reached their height of influence. Although inspired by southerners such as Thomas Dixon, the KKK was a national phenomenon with its strongholds in Midwestern states such as Indiana. The Klan and groups like it strove to maintain social bias against various people including African Americans, Jews, and Catholics. They did so by enacting laws, holding public demonstrations, and participating in violence. Lynching was not uncommon. Moreover, during the 1920s, there were several race riots in which whites attacked blacks.

In the 1940s, the United States proclaimed itself to be the world's greatest defender of democracy. As such, the daily humiliations that discrimination brought became an embarrassment to the Roosevelt administration. As a result, President Franklin Roosevelt acted to improve economic conditions for minority groups in the United States. There were limits to this justice movement. During the war, President Roosevelt caved into those in his administration who desired to put Japanese Americans in concentration camps. He also did little to aid European Jews who were trying to flee Nazi-controlled Europe.

After the war, however, the United States committed itself even more strongly to improving the conditions for minorities and women. Although the American dilemma has not been resolved, progress against discrimination has been significant.

It is also important to note that other nations have struggled with discrimination. During the 20th century, Indians had to contend with the traditional caste system as well as the biased views of the British. Additionally, Indian women faced another layer of discrimination, gender prejudice. Japanese women also faced discrimination, as did the *Burakumin*, an ethnically Japanese people whose ancestors did jobs that were considered ritually impure and who have been victims of discrimination throughout Japanese history.

Given the situation in India, Japan, and the United States, nothing can quite compare with Europe and the Soviet Union. What Jews faced there is almost unimaginable. Building upon hundreds of years of discrimination and violence, the Nazis carried discrimination to its full extension. In doing so, European racism and discrimination has become a powerful cautionary tale that some have still refused to understand. It remains to be seen if nations in the 21st century will learn from the lessons of hate and bigotry of the 20th century.

EUROPE—ANTI-SEMITISM

Anti-Semitism is a term used to refer to the hostile attitude of non-Jews toward the Jewish people. Although the term itself is fairly new, the hatred of Jews is possibly as old as Jewish history itself, about 4,000 years. In the 20th century, anti-Semitism, a key ingredient in the Holocaust, resulted in the unimaginable suffering of millions of Jews. Millions died in the gas chambers; millions more were shot to death or worked to death, or died of disease as a result of mass starvation. Approximately six

ECONOMIC LIFE

DISCRIMINATION

Europe—
Anti-Semitism

United States,
1920-1939

United States,
1940-1959

United States,
1960-1990

India

Soviet Union—
Anti-Semitism

Japan

million Jews ended their lives in the crematoria or in mass graves, frequently dug with their own hands.

Before the beginning of Jewish history, people worshipped a multiplicity of gods. They believed that these gods controlled natural occurrences, human events in the life cycle, and tribal or community life. Some believed that these gods warred with one another to prove which were the strongest, and some of the worshippers fought as well. Most people, however, acknowledged and tolerated the existence of a different god, or gods, in the cultures of the other societies around them.

Then, according to the Bible, Abraham, the first Hebrew patriarch, began to espouse a new idea: There is only one God, who is omnipotent and omniscient, just and merciful. No other nation at that time had denied the gods of its neighbors. This one Hebrew God, the creator of the universe and of humankind, demanded of Abraham that he organize his people and keep God's covenant to spread among all the people of the world the knowledge of the one true God and to formalize the ritual and ethical requirements of His law. In return, God promised that the Hebrew (Jewish) people would be a blessing to all mankind and a "light unto the nations."

Many Jewish practices offended the values of those around them. "The Jews regard it as crime to kill any newborn infant," wrote the Roman historian Tacitus. The Romans, and earlier the Greeks, believed in killing mentally and physically handicapped infants because they served no useful purpose. Greek and Roman leaders even accused the Jews of slaughtering and eating non-Jews in religious rituals.

Anti-Semitic cartoon, 1938. Notice how Jews are made to seem threatening to Germany and the world. © Library of Congress. Courtesy of the USHMM Photo Archive.

Monotheism, the notion of one God, was later espoused by Christians as well as Muslims, and the Judeo-Christian tradition became an integral part of Western civilization. The Jewish "gift" of ethical monotheism, however, neither pleased the worshippers of the many gods nor endeared the Jews to those who integrated ethical monotheism into their own religions because the Jews would convert neither to Christianity nor to Islam. Massive anti-Jewish resentment resulted.

Furthermore, various customs of the Jews also set them apart. The laws regarding food preparation and consumption made sharing meals with non-Jews impossible. Special requirements for prayer and the observance of holy days, festivals, and the weekly Sabbath, as well as their strict laws against intermarriage, also separated Jews from their neighbors. These customs were interpreted by non-Jews as Jewish hostility to others, not simply the Jewish desire to obey the dictates of their own religion.

For whatever reasons—anger, fear, jealousy, envy, or hurt feelings—anti-Semitism developed. Those who abandoned their Jewish practices were accepted by the non-Jewish community, but those who did not were persecuted.

By the fourth century, Christianity had spread throughout the Roman Empire, and, although Christianity was considered the "daughter" of Judaism, Christian hostility to the Jews had spread as well. Because they refused to accept their fellow Jew

Jesus as the son of God, Jews were regarded as a threat to the power of the Church fathers. If the Jews rejected Jesus as the Messiah, they reasoned, so might others.

Even so, the numbers of those who joined the Church grew. Catholicism preached that Jewish laws were unnecessary as long as people had faith. Thus Catholicism became an easier route to salvation than Judaism. In a world filled with hardship and pain, this was a welcome development for pagans, but a growing Catholic population made life for the Jewish people even more precarious and miserable. The Jews were not just accused of rejecting Jesus' preachings, but were often accused of murdering God himself, an idea that caused the torture and death of Jews for the next 2,000 years.

During the Middle Ages, if life for the average European peasant (peasants made up 98% of the population) was, as Thomas Hobbes later wrote, "solitary, brutish and short," life for the Jew was almost unbearable. Forbidden to own property, to farm even as serfs, to join guilds and work as craftsmen or merchants, or to deal in new products of any kind, Jews were reduced to a handful of occupations: selling used goods, safeguarding the money of traveling merchants, working for each other as teachers or butchers, and raising a few animals for food.

Despite the myth that the Jews were wealthy, as a group they were extremely poor. In one thousand years, from C.E. 500 to 1500, only a handful became even modestly comfortable. Barred from living in the countryside as serfs or freemen, they lived within the walled cities and towns, confined to ghettos, a "dwarfed, walled-off collection of alleys and creaking ancient buildings, its ugliness and loneliness in marked contrast to the warmth and charm" of their surroundings. After nightfall on Sundays and on Christian holidays, the gates of the ghettos were locked by city officials to prevent anyone from leaving.

As late as the 19th century, one ghetto was described by an Italian writer as "a formless heap of hovels and dirty cottages, ill-kept, in which a population of nearly four thousand souls vegetates, when half that number could with difficulty live there. The conglomeration of human beings, wretched for the most part, render this hideous dwelling place nauseous and deadly."

Inside the ghetto, the Jews continued to practice their religious customs, to study the Torah, to run their own schools and hospitals, and to try to support themselves. Bad drinking water and little room to exercise caused most children to look drawn and sallow. Fires were frequent, and sanitary facilities were nonexistent. Plagues and epidemics were common. The Jews of Prussia were strictly limited in the number of children they were allowed, and restrictions were also placed on who could marry. In Hamburg, Jews were forbidden to worship in numbers greater than 10, to walk past church grounds during a service, or to appear in public on any occasion at which crowds of people assembled.

Even when traveling from one region to the next, allowed for business purposes only, Jews were subjected to "head" taxes not levied on the general population. "The duties levied by the customs officials of Mainz, for example, were classified under the following headings: Honey, Hops, Wood, Jews, Chalk, Cheese, Charcoal."

Once European political leaders had exhausted the resources of the Jewish communities through taxes and mandatory "loans," the Jews were expelled from their homelands: from England in 1290, France in 1306, Germany in the 14th century, and Spain in 1492 during the time of the Inquisition. They were not allowed to return to England until the mid-17th century, nor could they go back to France until the time of the French Revolution. Most Jews migrated to Poland, and their descendants remained there until the Holocaust.

In addition to the political attacks on the Jews, the Church of the Middle Ages carried out a continual campaign against the Jewish community, basing their persecution on a whole set of fabricated accusations. Between the 12th and the 20th centuries, Jews and often entire Jewish communities were put on trial on over 150 occasions for engaging in ritual murder. In almost every instance Jews were tortured and put to death . . . despite the nonexistence of any supporting evidence except for confessions exacted under torture.

Jewish physicians were constantly accused of killing their patients. In his letters, Martin Luther wrote, "They know all that is known about medicine in Germany, they can give poison to a man of which he will die in an hour, or in 10 or 20 years."

Jews were repeatedly blamed for, and subsequently murdered for, other imaginary plots against Christians. Although they were the first religious community to outlaw human sacrifice and were forbidden by their own faith to consume even animal blood (the laws of *kashruth* require that animals be slaughtered following specially designed humanitarian methods and that the meat be soaked in salt before cooking to remove all traces of blood), the Jews were routinely accused of drinking the blood of their fellow humans.

During the 14th century, Jews were even blamed for the existence and spread of the black death, despite the fact that they, too, perished in large numbers. In September 1348, in Switzerland, Jews were tortured to confess to their spreading of the plague; then all those over the age of seven were murdered. The orphans were baptized and raised as Christians. Throughout Europe, even as recently as the 19th century, whole communities of Jews were burned alive for supposedly "torturing the host," the wafer used during the Mass.

Anti-Semitic cartoon, 1939. Notice how the Nazis justify their anti-Semitism on the grounds of protecting women. © National Archives. Courtesy of the USHMM Photo Archives.

In the years leading up to World War II, life for Jews in Europe varied dramatically from region to region. The lingering presence of anti-Semitism was negligible in such western European countries as France and Great Britain and even in Austria and Germany at the time of World War I. In Poland, Russia, and other eastern European countries, people vacillated between tolerating Jews and subjecting them to violent pogroms, or organized massacres.

By the early 20th century, most western European and German Jews had successfully assimilated into society, without having to convert to Christianity. Over the centuries, Jews had gradually gained most of the rights enjoyed by the Christians. Although most countries (including the United States) still maintained quota systems that limited Jewish immigration, Jews were allowed to attend universities, hold local offices, travel freely, own businesses, and serve in the military. In Germany, as in France, Italy, and England, there was a rising educated middle class into which the Jews could fit comfortably.

On the other hand, the typical eastern European Jew fared quite differently. In Germany there was a rising middle class comprising both Jews and non-Jews; in eastern Europe, there was no significant middle class for either group. Therefore, city-dwelling Jews had no group within which to assimilate. When compared with their fellow Polish countrymen, most Polish Jews were better educated, looked different (especially their hairstyles), dressed differently, and often spoke a different language. Even more significant is the fact that their religion was much more important to the Jews of Poland, Romania, and Russia than to the Jews of Germany and France. Participation in the social, economic, and political life of their country was much less important to these more pious Jews.

Thus, Jews were found mostly in villages, towns, and cities living surrounded by, but apart from, Christians. Few Jewish boys were allowed to attend universities, and when they did go, it was usually to schools in western Europe or even in the United States. By 1936, in Poland, for example, there was an unofficial *numerus clausus* (quota) against Jewish students, and by 1937 "ghetto benches" had been established at all Polish universities. The left side of the classroom was set aside for Jewish students—a policy that was implemented by "clubbing Jewish classmates, wrecking lecture halls, insulting and hooting down liberal professors."

Joseph Korzenik, a Holocaust survivor who grew up in Poland, recalls vividly his impression of these laws. "It was a mocking, ridiculing way of segregating the student within a learning facility . . . this was extremely cruel." In addition, "signs, like graffiti, on sidewalks, on fences, on the walls of houses, saying 'Jew get out,' 'Jew go to Palestine,' 'Jew you are not wanted,' appeared often."

Just before the rise of Nazism, Franz Kafka, a world-famous author and philosopher, and a Jewish-German resident of Czechoslovakia, wrote to his friend Milena:

I've spent all afternoon in the streets, wallowing in the Jew-baiting. "*Prasive plemeno*"—"Filthy rabble" I heard someone call the Jews the other day. Isn't it the natural thing to leave the place where one is hated so much? . . . The heroism which consists of staying on in spite of all is that of cockroaches which also can't be exterminated from the bathroom. (Soumerai and Schulz, 11)

The image of the cockroach reappeared later in his most famous work, *The Metamorphosis*, in which extreme alienation was a major theme. Hated by the Czechs for being an intellectual German and for being Jewish, Kafka experienced a great deal more anti-Semitism than the Jews in Germany before the Nazi era.

Although the Communist Party did not, for the most part, subject Jews in the Soviet Union to the pogroms common under the czars, popular anti-Semitism still existed, especially in the Ukraine. In addition, as were members of other religious groups, Jews were forbidden by the Communists to practice religious customs of any kind.

Eastern European Jews who wished to become full citizens, Poles or Russians rather than Polish Jews or Russian Jews, had to convert to Christianity and separate themselves from their families, their friends, their culture, and their histories. The only way to escape persecution and still remain Jewish was to emigrate, which many Jews did during the three centuries prior to the Holocaust. Not everyone, however, had the desire to leave home and family; the health to survive the journey; and the money needed to pay for the bureaucratic red tape, the cost of the trip, and the establishment of a new life elsewhere far from home.

By 1932, 75 percent of the Polish people were still uneducated peasant farmers who had been "weaned on anti-Jewish folk legends" by their government and their Church. In fact, it would not have been at all surprising for the Holocaust to have begun in Poland. Most of the concentration camps and all of the death camps were situated not in western Europe, not even in Germany, but in Poland, where the Nazi government expected the population to be far less sensitive to their presence.

The Holocaust, however, began in Germany, and although it was not caused by Christianity (Hitler and his followers were decidedly anti-Christian in their beliefs and philosophy), 1,600 years of Christian anti-Semitism made the Holocaust possible. Its tremendous success in creating a world without Jews was directly related to the manner in which the Christian population had historically viewed their Jewish compatriots.

In one significant way Nazism and historical anti-Semitism differed. Although both the Catholic and Protestant churches had often encouraged Jew-hatred, once a Jew converted and was no longer a Jew, the persecution stopped. To the Nazis, however, a Jew was a Jew no matter what. Medieval European rulers had forced the Jews to convert or to leave their lands; Nazi rulers called for the extermination of all Jews in all lands. In Germany and most of eastern Europe, nearly 90 percent of the Jews perished. In the countries of western Europe, fewer than 50 percent were murdered. In some countries the Christian population found a way to save most of their Jews.

Hitler had once complained to a friend, Hermann Rauschning, that it was the Jews who brought their "tyrannical God, and his life-denying Ten Commandments" into the world. Only if he murdered every Jew in the world, Hitler believed, would he fully eliminate the idea of one God and His one moral imperative (Soumerai and Schulz, 6–12).

FOR MORE INFORMATION

Dawidowicz, L. *The War Against the Jews, 1933–1945*. New York: Holt, Reinhart, and Winston, 1975.

Hilbert, P. *The Destruction of the European Jewry*. Chicago: Quandrangle Books, 1967.

The Holocaust History Project. <http://www.holocaust-history.org/>.

Pakula, Alan J., dir. *Sophie's Choice*. 1982.

Soumerai, E. N., and C. D. Schulz. *Daily Life during the Holocaust*. Westport, Conn.: Greenwood Press, 1998.

UNITED STATES, 1920–39

In the early 1920s, no outgrowth of the tensions within American society gained more visibility than the widespread popularity of the Ku Klux Klan (KKK). With national membership estimates ranging from three to six million or beyond and with

sizable ranks in such places as New Jersey, Ohio, Indiana, Illinois, Colorado, California, and the Pacific Northwest, the Klan in the 1920s was not the limited Southern phenomenon of Reconstruction or the post–World War II civil rights era. Nor was it simply a racist organization. The Klan reflected many of the fundamental tensions that divided Americans at the time, and it made it difficult for many minorities to make a living and raise their families.

Originally a creation of white Southerners seeking to resist post–Civil War federal policy by intimidating blacks and conciliatory whites while preserving their own anonymity, the robed and hooded Ku Klux Klan had faded as Reconstruction ended. An exaggerated image of the masked Klan's effectiveness in preserving white authority arose with the publication of Thomas Dixon Jr.'s popular novels, *The Leopard's Spots* (1902) and *The Clansman* (1905). The Klan myth increased in 1915 when D. W. Griffith based the first feature-length motion picture, *The Birth of a Nation*, on *The Clansman*. William Simmons, an Atlanta-based salesman of fraternal organization memberships and a former circuit-riding Methodist preacher, seized the opportunity presented by the film's appearance to create a new Klan in which he could sell memberships, costumes, and life insurance. Simmons's Klan grew to several thousand members by mid-1920. It expanded rapidly once he enlisted a pair of effective recruiters, Edward Clarke and Elizabeth Tyler, by offering them $8 of the initial $10 dues paid by every initiate they brought in. Clarke and Tyler in turn used most of their recruitment fee to motivate and assist an aggressive commission-based sales force.

"We Cater to White Trade Only," 1938. This sign posted in Lancaster, Ohio, provides evidence that racial discrimination was as entrenched in the North as it was in the South. © Library of Congress.

The marketing of Klan memberships became a hugely profitable commercial enterprise for Clarke and Tyler as they struck a sympathetic chord with millions of Americans. Simmons's initial appeal to fraternity, secrecy, and white supremacy was supplanted by a message that broadly identified the Klan with any "one-hundred-percent American" who was a morally and legally upright white Protestant patriot. To defend such qualities meant to oppose and suppress their alternatives, the Klan insisted. Therefore not only did the KKK remain antiblack, it became anti-Jewish, anti-Asian, and especially anti–Roman Catholic. It expressed hostility to any group or individual, recent immigrants in particular but old stock as well, that did not embrace what the Klan regarded as dominant American traits and practices. Klansmen vocally disapproved of prohibition violation, labor union membership, inflated retail prices, Sabbath breaking, political graft, immodest dress, bobbed hair, and all forms of unconventional sexuality. They often actively forced minority workers from their jobs and from their homes. With fiery crosses, tar and feathers, and other means, they warned individuals and groups not meeting Klan standards to conform or leave. Joining the Klan was a means of asserting personal opposition to various changes taking place in American society. Those who enrolled thought of themselves not as bigots but rather as defenders of traditional standards in a battle with proponents of change.

Though the membership of a secretive organization is difficult to assess, enough Klan records have survived to make possible some conclusions. Klan members came from large and medium-sized cities as well as small towns and the countryside. They were, in the words of Leonard Moore, a careful investigator of the Indiana Klan, from the mainstream of white Protestant society. Not disproportionately rural, fundamentalist, or lower class as is the stereotype, the Hoosier Klan represented a broad spectrum of Indiana's native-born population. Its ranks included many solidly middle-class individuals, white-collar and skilled workers, and farmers. A female counterpart organization, Women of the Ku Klux Klan, enrolled over a million women nationally. The only conspicuous absentees were the business and social elite who were adjusting to and benefiting from changes in American commerce and culture.

The average citizens who enlisted in the Klan seemed to share a concern that their communities were threatened by forces that ignored their traditions and upset their customs. The Klan's picnics, occasional acts of charity, and involvement in local politics and school administration sought to maintain traditional community culture. Its public parades and rallies attempted to both celebrate that culture and intimidate those who might seek to alter it. Cross burnings at the homes of suspected prohibition violators, union organizers, bankers or businessmen charging more than a "fair" price, or persons of questionable sexual morals served as a Klan warning not to violate approved standards. If flaming crosses failed to achieve the desired effect, floggings and tar and featherings sometimes followed.

The KKK prospered until the mid-1920s. Its pronouncements attracted support, and its local political endorsements often proved effective, especially in the Midwest. The Klan staged mass rallies and parades in Washington, D.C., as well as elsewhere. Its frightening outbursts of nighttime vigilantism, however, began to alarm bystanders as well as targets. In 1924, the Democratic Party's national convention divided evenly over whether to condemn the Klan by name. The northern urban wing of the party saw the KKK as threatening its large Catholic, Jewish, and immigrant following but lost a censure motion by a single vote to the southern and western delegates who either embraced the Klan or at least did not wish to offend its members. Democrats did poorly in the 1924 national elections, but in some areas Klan-endorsed candidates won local political office.

Soon thereafter Klan support declined sharply. Some of the Klan's followers became discouraged over its ineffectiveness in blocking change, obtaining prohibition enforcement, or preventing the evolution of morality and behavior. Episodes of brutality alienated others. Inept or corrupt leadership, financial mismanagement, and exposure of political bribery were recurring problems. Most damaging of all was the revelation of a spectacular crime in which the Grand Dragon of the Indiana Klan, David C. Stephenson, sexually assaulted a secre-

After years of Civil Rights abuses perpetuated by the government and groups like the KKK, African Americans in the 1950s found new and effective ways to fight the status quo. Here, Rosa Parks is arrested for protesting discrimination. © Library of Congress.

tary on a train ride to Chicago and then, after the disconsolate young woman attempted suicide, kept her from obtaining medical attention so that she died painfully a month later from the aftereffects of poison and infected wounds. This gruesome story, and Stephenson's subsequent attempt to use his political connections to avoid punishment, offended thousands who had joined the Klan thinking that they were taking a stand against such behavior. Before the decade's end, the Klan was a tiny remnant of what it was at its 1924 peak.

Although large crowds attended many lynchings, almost no one was ever punished.

The Ku Klux Klan did not hold an exclusive franchise on racial hostility in the 1920s and 1930s. Southern white society felt free to do spontaneously whatever it chose to keep African Americans, and occasionally others, in what it thought was their proper place. Throughout the South (where 90 percent of the African American population resided prior to World War I), whites had resorted to lynching more than a hundred times a year between 1885 and 1900 and between 50 and 75 times a year from then until 1920. Lynching of whites, briefly more numerous in the mid-1880s, thereafter fell to a tiny fraction of what blacks experienced. Occasional lynchings outside the South followed a similar pattern. Local authorities usually did little to restrain white mobs from seizing African Americans accused of crimes, especially those against white women. Dissatisfied with the state's ability to deliver sufficient punishment, such mobs would torture and mutilate their African American prisoners, sometimes set them on fire, and almost always hang them from trees. Although large crowds attended many lynchings, took bits of the victim's clothing as souvenirs, and posed for photographs, almost no one was ever punished. Law enforcement officers stepped aside, and coroners' reports usually indicated that death was the responsibility of "persons unknown."

Lynchings represented more than just the denial of the right to a fair trial and civil punishment. Even as they declined in number during the 1920s before rebounding in the early 1930s, lynchings sent a stark warning to the black community not to challenge white supremacy. The message was clear: crimes by blacks against whites, whether murder or rape or even trivial behavior deemed "uppity," would be punished swiftly and brutally. Many lynchings had no initiating crime at all. As Ida B. Wells had demonstrated in her newspaper articles, many lynchings were the result of economic rivalry between whites and blacks. African Americans carried the knowledge that, despite their every effort to be law-abiding, cautious, and polite, they could be the target of a lynch mob incited by false charges. In the late 1930s, singer Billie Holiday started singing "Strange Fruit," a blues song that stunned audiences with the shocking image of an African American being lynched. The song's powerful lyrics characterized black bodies swinging in the wind as the "strange fruit" of Southern trees (Kyvig, 145).

The National Association for the Advancement of Colored People began campaigning during World War I for a federal law against lynching. Antilynching bills passed the House of Representatives in 1922 and 1938 but failed to overcome Senate filibusters by Southern opponents who talked of the need to limit the excessive power of the federal government and preserve the sanctity of states' rights. The specter of lynching thus persisted throughout the 1920s and 1930s and for another three decades.

White antagonism toward African Americans took other forms as well. Vivid memories remained of the 1919 flurry of race riots that produced extensive property damage, serious injury, and over 100 deaths. Violence against African Americans in 1919 had been by far most destructive and murderous in Chicago, but thereafter its focus shifted to the South. On May 31, 1921, the *Tulsa* (Oklahoma) *Tribune* published an inflammatory report of a young white woman's unproven and improbable claim of a midafternoon sexual attack by a black man in a downtown elevator. A white lynch mob formed, blacks armed themselves to resist, and shots were exchanged. Whites then rampaged through the black neighborhood of segregated Tulsa, setting fire to the Greenwood Avenue business district and more than 1,000 homes. By the time the mob's fury was spent, black Tulsa smoldered in ruins. At least 75 residents, perhaps as many as 250, lay dead. Though the Tulsa riot was the last large-scale outburst of racial violence during the 1920s, its grim message of continuing racial tension lingered.

Perhaps even more devastating to African Americans' sense of security than the brutality of lynching or mob violence was their realization that they could not count on the Southern legal system for protection. One highly publicized case drove this point home with particular force. In March 1931 near Scottsboro, Alabama, police arrested nine black teenagers hitching a ride on a slow-moving freight train. The two white women accompanying them, both prostitutes, immediately claimed to be victims of rape. Quickly indicted, the boys were provided no real legal representation, convicted in a one-day trial, and sentenced to death. The Scottsboro case attracted national attention, largely because American Communists made it a symbol of American racism. Convinced that the women were lying (one admitted so within a year), the original judge ordered a retrial that produced more convictions and death sentences. This verdict was overturned by the U.S. Supreme Court. In *Powell v. Alabama* (1932) the Court said, for the first time, that states must provide an attorney to indigent defendants in death penalty cases to assure them the due process of law guaranteed by the 14th Amendment. However, a third all-white Alabama jury again convicted the Scottsboro boys and sentenced them to prison. Eventually these verdicts were also overturned. The defendants finally all went free, but not until after spending, collectively, over a hundred years in jail (Kyvig, 141–46).

FOR MORE INFORMATION

Documenting the American South. <http://docsouth.unc.edu/>.

Jackson, K. T. *Ku Klux Klan in the City, 1915–1930.* New York: Oxford University Press, 1967.

Kyvig, D. E. *Daily Life in the United States, 1920–1939: Decades of Promise and Pain.* Westport, Conn.: Greenwood Press, 2002.

Singleton, J., dir. *Rosewood.* 1996.

UNITED STATES, 1940–59

During World War II—another war for democracy—racism remained alive in the United States. Aside from the daily discrimination in factories, hundred of fights took place between whites and blacks. Although Americans saw themselves as democracy's standard bearers, racism and discrimination were significant aspects of daily life during the Second World War. Still, there were those who battled against prejudice.

Eleanor Roosevelt worked behind the scenes to arrange the escape of European Jews, especially children. Yet except for Secretary of the Treasury Henry Morganthau, the only Jewish member of the Cabinet, she could not get the government to support her efforts to expedite their rescue. The State Department's record in this regard is embarrassing. To America's credit as a country committed to human rights, the United States Holocaust Memorial Museum, which opened in Washington, D.C., in 1993 to educate visitors about the reality of Nazi atrocities, does not hide the reluctance of the American foreign service to allow greater numbers of refugees to come here. Although a number of distinguished artists and intellectuals were aided in their escape, including the scientists who would help build the atomic bomb, the official State Department policy toward ordinary European Jews was not hospitable. A study of the contributions to American life made by the children who did manage to get into America during the war years would be a valuable undertaking. Students too easily forget that immigrants—and their children—often represent exceptional vitality in their pursuit of the American dream.

Reluctance to put aside long-standing prejudice against Asians must also account in some degree for the humiliating experiences heaped on many worthy Japanese Americans at this time. Fear that connections in Japan might turn some Americans of Japanese ancestry into efficient spies precipitated the confiscation of many good citizens' properties and their incarceration in what amounted to American concentration camps. Such remote places as Rivers, Arizona; Heart Mountain, Wyoming; Topaz, Utah; and Manzanar, California contained small prison worlds where children still pledged allegiance to the American flag and wrote letters to family members in the armed forces fighting for the United States—even as their parents wondered about who was watering their cherry trees. That the United States would much later make monetary amends to these Japanese American families must be noted, but the humiliation of loyal Americans over a period of years cannot be measured in dollars. Of the 110,000 "persons of Japanese ancestry" incarcerated, 72,000 were U.S. citizens by birth.

Despite the prejudice and discrimination minorities experienced, there was a movement in the 1940s and 1950s to build a better, more tolerant United States. Throughout the 1940s the idea of racial harmony—one of our most valued myths— was pursued by extensions of rules and laws, both in the services and on the labor front. The number of African Americans in the army leaped from 5,000 to 920,000, the number of black officers from just 5 to more than 7,000. And many new jobs for blacks opened up in both the army and the navy between 1941 and 1945. When Harry Truman issued Executive Order 9981 in 1948, ending segregation in the armed forces, he made such changes a matter of legal rights. Doris Kearns Goodwin noted that one historian, Carey McWilliams, saw more improvement in race relations during the 1940s than had occurred in the entire span of years from the Civil War to 1940.

The need for workers also extended opportunities to Asian Americans long denied the rights of naturalization. Filipinos, Indians, Koreans, and Chinese, previously limited to "ethnic jobs" such as work in laundries and restaurants, found new opportunities just as women had. Allowed in the army for the first time, and allowed to buy some of the farms confiscated from Japanese Americans, Filipino Americans felt especially grateful and eager to fight to free the Philippines from Japanese occupation. But Filipino soldiers in uniform were still refused service in mainstream American restaurants. And like Chinese and Korean Americans, they often chose to wear big badges so that people would realize that they were not the hated Japanese. On December 22, 1941, *Time* magazine published an anthropologically questionable article on how to distinguish your Chinese friend from your Japanese enemy by physical traits.

In 1941 Roosevelt also signed Executive Order 8802, asking that both employers and labor unions "provide for the full and equitable participation of all workers in defense industries without discrimination because of race, creed, color or national origin." A commission was established at the same time to investigate grievances. Many Americans might have agreed with lawyers who saw this moment as the most significant government action on behalf of equal opportunity since the Emancipation Proclamation. But good laws do not always bring about immediate results. Overwhelming numbers of workers had crowded into small areas where war production flourished. And many people did not want to share jobs or housing with migrants—black or white. Detroit, with $11 billion worth of war contracts, extended its boundaries to include Willow Run, a subsidiary town that grew from 15,000 people to 47,000 during the war years, bringing in what one native in a Studs Terkel interview saw as an influx of riffraff (Kaledin, 11–12, 22–23).

FOR MORE INFORMATION

Daniels, R. *Prisoners Without Trial: Japanese Americans in World War II*. New York: Hill and Wang, 1993.

Hilbert, P. *The Destruction of the European Jewry*. Chicago: Quandrangle Books, 1967.

Kaledin, E. *Daily Life in the United States, 1940–1959: Shifting Worlds*. Westport, Conn.: Greenwood Press, 2000.

Kersten, A. E. *Race, Jobs, and the War: The FEPC in the Midwest, 1941–1946*. Urbana: University of Illinois Press, 2000.

UNITED STATES, 1960–90

By the late 1960s it was obvious that if enacting civil rights laws was difficult, changing practices was going to be even harder. Still harder was changing attitudes. For example, despite the passage of antidiscrimination laws, job bias was still all too

ECONOMIC LIFE
|
DISCRIMINATION
|
Europe—
Anti-Semitism

United States,
1920-1939

United States,
1940-1959

United States,
1960-1990

India

Soviet Union—
Anti-Semitism

Japan

common. Growing impatience by blacks was understandable. A year after his speech at the Lincoln Memorial in 1963, when he spoke hopefully of his dream that "someday" freedom would ring in America, Martin Luther King Jr. published a book titled *Why We Can't Wait*. Challenges to his leadership by more radical figures— Malcolm X, Stokely Carmichael, and the Black Panthers, among others—and changing circumstances in 1967 compelled him to become more radical too.

Television networks that year brought the nation live coverage of riots in Detroit. Scenes of looting, fires, injuries, and deaths reminded viewers of the riots in Watts two years earlier. The next year a commission appointed by President Johnson to investigate the causes of civil disorders formally reported that the United States was moving toward two societies, "one black, one white—separate and unequal."

Did it have to be that way? In the year that Martin Luther King Jr. spoke passionately of his dream for America, novelist James Baldwin acknowledged that creating one nation had proved to be "a hideously difficult task." The past that blacks had endured, a past "of rope, fire, torture, castration, infanticide, rape; death and humiliation; fear by day and night, fear as deep as the marrow of the bone," had forced them each day to "snatch their manhood, their identity, out of the fire of human cruelty that rages to destroy it." In so doing, Baldwin wrote in *The Fire Next Time*, they achieved their own unshakable authority. Blacks had the advantage, he claimed, of never having believed the myths to which white Americans cling about the heroism of freedom-loving ancestors, about American invincibility, about the virility of white men and purity of white women. They were free to take on the problems they faced. But they could not do it alone:

If we—and now I mean the relatively conscious whites and the relatively conscious blacks, who must, like lovers, insist on, or create, the consciousness of the others—do not falter in our duty now, we may be able, handful that we are, to end the racial nightmare, and achieve our country, and change the history of the world. If we do not now dare everything, the fulfillment of that prophecy, re-created from the Bible in song by a slave, is upon us: "*God gave Noah the rainbow sign, No more water, the fire next time!*" (Marty, 88)

By 1968 it looked as though the fire was coming. The assassination of Martin Luther King Jr. on April 4 led to more urban riots. Before the decade was over, riots occurred in more than 100 cities and resulted in at least 77 deaths. Thousands suffered injuries, and property destruction was incalculable. The well-publicized purpose of a civil rights law passed one week after King's death was to prohibit racial discrimination in housing policies and practices. However, a provision insisted on by Senator Strom Thurmond of South Carolina showed the ambivalence of white politicians toward militant blacks. This provision made it a crime to use the facilities of interstate commerce "to organize, promote, encourage, participate in, or carry on a riot; or to commit any act of violence in furtherance of a riot." Robert Weisbrot, a historian of the civil rights movement, has observed that the bill's priorities were clear: "modest federal involvement in black efforts to flee the ghetto, but overwhelming force to curb all restiveness within it."

Before his death, Martin Luther King Jr., had planned a "poor people's march on Washington" to shift the focus of the civil rights movement from racial to economic issues, believing that this might attract broader support. Leadership of the campaign fell to his successor in the Southern Christian Leadership Conference, Ralph David Abernathy. Even under ideal conditions, the prospects of success were limited, but the weather in Washington at the time of the march was miserable. The political climate the campaigners faced was even worse, and their well-intentioned efforts seemed only to call attention to the powerlessness of poor blacks and their isolation from poor whites.

The death of King, the riots, and exhaustion took much of the impetus out of the civil rights movement. The election of Richard Nixon in November 1968 dealt it an additional blow. Nixon's "Southern strategy" played on the resentments of whites. At the same time, supporters of civil rights turned to Congress for laws calling for affirmative action policies in hiring and protective measures of other kinds. The notion of establishing race-conscious policies and preferential treatment for blacks to remedy past injustices caused strains among supporters, both black and white. Some contended that the struggle should be for a color-blind society, with neither advantages nor disadvantages resulting from the color of one's skin. Race-conscious policies also intensified the backlash by those who thought the movement had already gone too far too fast. Pursuit of civil rights goals in the courts also encouraged the backlash, particularly on the matter of busing to achieve school desegregation. A period that had begun on a note of gloom ended on an even gloomier one.

Hoping to serve the interests of African Americans more effectively, black leaders sought to increase their representation in executive positions at the local level and in state legislatures and the Congress of the United States. By 1971, 12 African Americans held seats in the House of Representatives, and a number of cities had African American mayors, but this did not have much effect on the daily lives of African Americans. Policy changes to achieve success would require that they hold more political power.

> *The death of Dr. King, the riots, and exhaustion slowed the civil rights movement.*

With that in mind, the Congressional Black Caucus, formed in 1971, cooperated tactically with the more militant blacks in planning the National Black Political Assembly in Gary, Indiana, in March 1972. The assembly was the largest black political convention in U.S. history; about 3,000 official delegates attended, representing almost every faction and viewpoint. An additional 9,000 persons attended as observers. Historian Manning Marable refers to the assembly as a marriage of convenience between the aspiring and somewhat radicalized black petty bourgeoisie and the black nationalist movement. The collective vision of the convention, he says, "represented a desire to seize electoral control of America's major cities, to move the black masses from the politics of desegregation to the politics of real empowerment, ultimately to create their own independent black political party."

The fiscal, social, and demographic problems urban blacks faced were awesome, for as the affluent populations of cities had fled to the suburbs, the tax base declined sharply. Racial conflicts over dwindling job opportunities were common. Civil service laws protected the jobs of insensitive or racist city bureaucrats. States and the federal government were losing interest in coming to the cities' rescue. At the national level, President Nixon made no moves to increase the voting power of African Americans. He supported only voluntary efforts to integrate schools, did little to push integration of federal housing programs, and failed to provide adequate funding for black entrepreneurs seeking to start businesses.

The laws passed in the 1960s with the intention of making things better, or at least of offering hope that things would change, instead magnified African Americans' sense of hopelessness. Ending discrimination in the workplace provided one major test for the federal government's new commitment to civil rights.

In 1965 President Johnson, applying the principles of the 1964 Civil Rights Act, issued an executive order requiring federal contractors "to take affirmative action to ensure that applicants are employed . . . without regard to their race, creed, color, or national origin." A series of court cases followed that dealt with the barriers to affirmative action principles. In a 1971 decision involving a standard written examination for employment, *Griggs v. Duke Power Co.*, the U.S. Supreme Court ruled that so-called objective criteria for hiring employees could in fact be discriminatory. Specifically, the Court said that the aptitude tests being challenged were illegal because they resulted in a relative disadvantage to minorities without at the same time having a "compelling business interest." To be permissible, the knowledge and skills they evaluated had to be directly applicable to the jobs for which the employers used them. The Court later extended the principles of this ruling to recruitment practices, job placement, transfers, and promotions. The Court rulings made it possible for women and minorities to get jobs from which they had previously been excluded, but unequal pay remained a problem (Marty, 88–91, 101–2).

FOR MORE INFORMATION

Documenting the American South. <http://docsouth.unc.edu/>.

Lemann, N. *The Promised Land: The Great Black Migration and How it Changed America.* New York: Vintage Books/Knopf, 1991.

Marty, M. A. *Daily Life in the United States, 1960–1990: Decades of Discord.* Westport, Conn.: Greenwood Press, 1997.

Williamson, J. *The Crucible of Race: Black-White Relations in the American South Since Emancipation.* New York: Oxford University Press, 1984.

ECONOMIC LIFE
|
DISCRIMINATION
|

Europe—
Anti-Semitism

United States,
1920-1939

United States,
1940-1959

United States,
1960-1990

India

Soviet Union—
Anti-Semitism

Japan

INDIA

Discrimination was not unique to India; it occurred throughout the world and in every culture. However, because of some of India's unique cultural conditions, certain forms of discrimination have persisted. Discrimination here means treatment based on difference and inequitable for one or another party involved.

Early in India's history, and persisting through much of the 20th century, rulers held sway over their subjects. Rulers held power—the ability to collect tax, wage war, or decide matters of the law. Their subjects generally had little or none of this power and thus faced a basic kind of discrimination. Some mechanisms were in place for subjects to address their ruler, a *raja* or king. Most rulers held regular—even daily—meetings of their top administrators, as well as opening a portion of the meeting to their subjects. This type of meeting was called a *durbar*. At the *durbar*, the ruler heard complaints or problems raised by his or her subjects and made a decision to redress the issue. Not all rulers were judicious, nor did all hold *durbars*, and many subjects of ancient and recent India suffered under this monarchic form of rule.

Another form of discrimination occurred when the Indian subcontinent met with the advent of European colonial powers. The Portuguese, the Dutch, the French, and the English all vied for increased power within the subcontinent. By the 20th century, the British were triumphant. India became part of the British Empire and was the "jewel in the crown" of Queen Victoria's reign. Indians within the empire faced certain challenges and discrimination. Part of the structure of the empire rested on ideas of race and racial superiority. Some British officials believed that they were racially superior to Indians. These ideas led to discrimination against Indians in different ways. For example, British officers did not allow Indians into officers' clubs; Indians were not allowed to command British troops; and they were not allowed to serve as judges in cases with European litigants. Indians also did not have basic rights in choosing or electing leaders and officials. The British governor generals of India were picked in London, and they in turn chose other officials to serve under them. Indians participated in this process in a limited form.

Though many of these discriminatory practices continued, at the same time the British established schools, colleges, and universities as well as hospitals, police forces, and courts for their Indian empire. Many within the British Empire felt that Indians could be Indian in color but British in habit and custom. This idea was clearly voiced in a "minute" written by Thomas Macaulay. Macaulay was a council member in Calcutta who argued that education in India should produce "a class of persons, Indian in blood and colour, but English in taste, in opinion, in morals, and in intellect" (Clive and Pinney, 237–51).

Yet another way discrimination found root in India was through the caste system. The caste system, in short, was a way in which people identified themselves with certain groups, each of which was in a hierarchical relation to the others. The caste system led to a wide variety of discriminatory practices. For example, members of a certain caste group might not allow a person from outside that group to join them in marriage, or even share a meal. A brahman priest (at the pinnacle of religious hierarchy) did not tolerate a lower caste member attempting to perform similar services. Members of different caste groups also felt that contact with a lower caste group was in some way polluting. An upper-caste person might have refused to share a meal with someone of a lower caste in the belief that, through sharing utensils and possibly saliva, the meal would be polluted.

More recently, caste has been used to both discriminate against as well as uplift certain members of society. The Indian government provided for the protection of certain caste and tribal groups, known as the scheduled castes (SCs) and scheduled tribes (STs). Members of these protected groups received special reservations in schools and were awarded government jobs. The idea was that by reserving a position for these traditionally oppressed groups, over time they would advance within society. In 1990, India's prime minister, V. P. Singh, put into law the Mandal Commission Report, which suggested further reservations for lower-caste groups. The report incited a violent reaction, mostly by upper-caste Hindus who felt that their position in society was being threatened by a wave of lower-caste reservations and advancements.

Another area of Indian society where discrimination persisted was between the sexes. Women in India, while worshipped on the one hand, have been oppressed on the other. Women have generally been confined to the domestic sphere—they maintained the household and raised the children. Until recently, women were not encouraged to join the workforce in large numbers. Before India's independence, women were sometimes forced into oppressive and sometimes fatal situations. It was not uncommon for parents to arrange for a young girl to be married to an older man from whom she had no hope of escaping. Further, in some regions, should the husband die, his widow was expected to jump on her husband's funeral pyre and die with him. This practice of *sati* was long ago outlawed, but even in recent times it has occasionally been practiced. Wives of India's princes were expected to jump to their deaths because "the number of women burned on the funeral pyre was often considered an index of success" (Liddle and Joshi, 27).

~Benjamin Cohen

FOR MORE INFORMATION

Clive, J., and T. Pinney, eds. *Selected Writings of Thomas Babington Macaulay.* Chicago: University of Chicago Press, 1972 (originally published 1898).

Galanter, M. *Competing Equalities: Law and the Backward Classes in India.* Berkeley: University of California Press, 1984.

Liddle, J., and R. Joshi. *Daughters of Independence.* New Brunswick, N.J.: Rutgers University Press, 1986.

SOVIET UNION—ANTI-SEMITISM

The status of Soviet Jews was complicated by official ambiguity about whether Judaism was primarily a religion or a nationality. On the one hand, the Soviet government, as well as the general population, regarded Judaism as a particular nationality, and in the space for "nationality" on internal passports and other official papers, a believing or nonbelieving person of Jewish heritage would have "Jewish" inscribed, whereas non-Jews were recorded as being from a certain geographical area: "Estonian" or "Azerbaijani," and so forth. Jews of mixed parentage could choose for themselves at age 16 how they wanted to be listed on their passports, and very many, with their parents' encouragement, chose to put themselves down as belonging to a geographic area. Being labeled Jewish could be a formidable handicap for young people trying to make their way in the Soviet world. Because nationality was the fifth point (or item) on internal passports, people often derogatorily referred to Jews as "fifth pointers."

Until the early 1970s, the Jewish population of the USSR was larger than that of Israel and was second only to that of the United States. By 1980, because of emigration (starting in the late 1960s) and assimilation, the USSR's Jewish population had dropped to third place. In 1989 most of the Soviet Union's 1.4 million Jews lived in the Russian, Ukrainian, and Belorussian republics. Jews were also a large minority in the Moldavian Republic and Central Asia (mainly in Uzbekistan and in Tajikistan, where they spoke a dialect of the Tajik language). There was a unique community of Georgian Jews, whose first language was Georgian and whose ancestors may have settled there in the first centuries of the Christian era. For some reason, there was relatively less repression of Georgian Jews' religious activities. In 1979 almost half of the synagogues in the USSR were in Georgia, and they were more successful in preserving their customs and religious rites than were other Soviet Jewish communities. A community called Mountain Jews lived mainly in Dagestan and Azerbaijan, where they speak Tat, a Persian dialect. Although Mountain Jews maintained religious beliefs identical with those of mainstream Orthodox Judaism, they assimilated some customs from the Islamic majority around them, such as covering their synagogue floors with carpets. For traditional Mountain Jews, life revolved around the demands of religious observance, the patriarchal family, and clan.

Violence against Jews was a regular feature of life under the czars, a feature that did not disappear after the revolution even though the Bolsheviks offered Jews equal opportunity to join the mainstream of Russian life and banned anti-Semitism in all its forms. At the same time Bolsheviks were as hostile toward Judaism as they were to other religions. In 1919 the state swept away Jewish councils that had traditionally maintained synagogues and supervised social and spiritual good works within Jewish communities. Newly established Jewish sections within the Party had, among other responsibilities, the job of producing propaganda against Judaism and rabbis. After the revolution, hundreds of thousands of Jews eagerly grasped the opportunities offered them to integrate into and contribute to Russian/Soviet life. Many achieved important, even key positions in higher education, art, and science. In government, Jews such as Leon Trotsky, Grigory Zinoviev, Lev Kamenev, Lazar Kaganovich, and Maxim Litvinov held some of the highest Party positions. Yiddish, the first language of most eastern European Jews, was allowed to have a renaissance, with, by the 1930s, more than 1,200 Yiddish schools and university departments of Jewish studies. There were also a number of Yiddish newspapers and several artistically important Yiddish theaters. Stalin's 1930s purges of top Party leaders, however, severely and permanently limited Jewish participation in high levels of government. Jews remained prominent in the arts to the end of the USSR, but by the mid-1930s cultural life was crippled by the state's meddling with and even terrorizing of artists and art critics. Although Lenin detested anti-Semitism, Stalin, Khrushchev, and other Party leaders had no such qualms. As Stalin aged, his hatred for Jews seemed to grow ever more virulent. During the 1920s and into the late 1940s, aspects of Jewish culture, such as a few Yiddish publications, were allowed to continue and even (as in the case of Yiddish theater in the 1920s and 1930s) to flourish. But overall the regime systematically destroyed Jewish religious observance and culture, eventually suppressing written and spoken use of Yiddish and Hebrew. Most of the 5,000 synagogues in existence at the time of the revolution were closed under Stalin; by 1964, synagogues were down from about 400 at the beginning of Khrushchev's antireligious campaign to 60 or fewer. But the greatest suffering of Soviet Jews came during the first several months of World War II, when invading Germans murdered about 2.5 million of them, often with help from other Soviet ethnic groups and Romanians who were Germany's allies.

The threat to Jewish lives did not end with the German defeat. Official persecution of Jews and other groups waxed and waned according to shifting policies. Hitler's surprise attack in 1941 meant a cooling off of persecution of Jews, whose international connections were useful for the war effort. But when the German forces besieging Stalingrad were vanquished in February 1943, Stalin smelled victory and began going after the Jews in his domain. Many suddenly lost their jobs, no matter how devotedly they had labored for state and Party. Shortly after the Stalingrad victory a newspaper editor was ordered to fire the Jews on his staff. The editor, David Ortenberg, replied, "It has already happened," and proceeded to list nine war correspondents who had been killed at the front. "I can add one more . . . myself," Ortenberg said as he walked out the door. Toward the end of his life Stalin began a vendetta against prominent Jews. In 1948 Solomon Mikhoels, a prestigious actor-director and leader of the Soviet Jewish community's support for the war effort, was murdered in a staged automobile crash. Two weeks later, his murderer was secretly given a high government award (the Order of Lenin) "for exemplary execution of a special assignment from the government." That was just phase one. Arrests of Yiddish-language writers, other prominent Jews, and in some cases their close relatives began in 1948. The actor Benjamin Zuskin was snatched, heavily sedated, straight out of his hospital bed and deposited in prison. When he awakened the next day he was still in his hospital gown. Coerced confessions led to more arrests. Most of the arrested Jewish cultural leaders were executed; others, including hundreds not well known, were also murdered outright or perished in prisons and labor camps. The arrests occurred at about the same time that Yiddish writers' organizations, theaters, and journals were being closed down across the country.

In 1952, in what came to be known as the Doctors' Plot, several prestigious Jewish doctors were arrested, among them the chief physician of the Red Army during the war, and a pediatrician who tended to the offspring of high officials. Perhaps to deflect foreign charges of an anti-Semitic campaign, Stalin's personal physician, who was not Jewish, was also arrested. These doctors were charged with conspiring with Zionist organizations and the United States to murder Kremlin officials and their children. Stalin's death in March 1953 saved the doctors and may have saved Soviet Jews from large-scale trials, executions, and massive deportations to Soviet Asia.

With a few exceptions, by the later Soviet period most Jews were unofficially barred from careers in diplomacy, political journalism, the military, and high Party posts. There were quotas in publishing (only so many Jewish authors allowed per year) and science (highly qualified scientists were rejected for research positions on the grounds that "we already have enough Jews"). Khrushchev insisted that such discrimination was for the Jews' own good, so as not to engender resentment in the hearts of others. It became increasingly difficult for Jews to be accepted to prestigious universities. Yelena Mandel, a Jewish woman brought up as an atheist, had been an A student all her life but was "warned against ever trying to get into [Moscow State University], but I told myself, I should at least try, I would never forgive myself if I don't." In the 1970s, when she was 18, she applied to the university's history department.

The examination commission was clearly and explicitly trying to knock me down. They had to work hard, because I did know a lot. . . . They asked me question after question, until finally they asked me something I couldn't answer; then, triumphantly, they gave me a grade of B. I was not accepted to the university. This was the kind of thing that happened to all the Jews. . . . Of course, it felt bad not to be accepted—especially because the Department of History that year had accepted one of the worst students in my high school class. (Eaton)

Nevertheless, Soviet Jews tended to be high achievers despite the obstacles, and, compared to Russians, for example, they were more likely to have higher education. Jews also had special prominence in arts and sciences.

Anti-Jewish policies, along with the wish, by some, to live in a homeland of their own or just to escape the hardships of Soviet life, impelled Jewish dissidents to demand that the government actually enforce the human rights promised in the Soviet constitution, including the right to leave. Although worldwide publicity, diplomatic considerations, and support groups helped Jewish emigration go forward, there were, beginning in the 1970s, harsh crackdowns on selected Jewish would-be emigrants and their relatives, as well as on Armenians, Lithuanians, Ukrainians, and others who tried to get exit visas.

Envy of Jews' ability to emigrate intensified Russian anti-Semitism, but it also motivated people to acknowledge Jewish roots and relationships. People joked about a man named Abramovich who applied to emigrate and was called to the Office of Visas and Registration for questioning by a KGB officer. The officer asks Abramovich why, as a professor with all the benefits of Soviet privilege—a private apartment, summer cottage, and a car—he would want to leave. Abramovich protests that he does not wish to leave, but his wife, children, mother-in-law, aunts, and cousins want to go, and he is his family's only Jew.

"Refuseniks," Jews who had applied to emigrate but were refused exit visas, were in a bad situation. Having applied to leave, they were fired from their jobs and thereafter remained jobless or stuck in low-level work (Eaton).

FOR MORE INFORMATION

Eaton, K. B. *Daily Life in the Soviet Union*. Westport, Conn.: Greenwood Press. Forthcoming.
Veidlinger, J. *The Moscow State Yiddish Theater: Jewish Culture on the Soviet Stage*. Bloomington: Indiana University Press, 2000.
Wolfson, E. *Stalin's Secret Pogrom: The Postwar Inquisition of the Jewish Anti-Fascist Committee*. New Haven: Yale University Press, 2001.

JAPAN

The *Hisabetsu Burakumin*, more commonly known as the *Burakumin* (people of the hamlet), are an ethnically Japanese people who have been victims of discrimi-

ECONOMIC LIFE
|
DISCRIMINATION
|
Europe—
Anti-Semitism

United States,
1920-1939

United States,
1940-1959

United States,
1960-1990

India

Soviet Union—
Anti-Semitism

Japan

nation throughout most of Japanese history. Because they are not distinguishable from the rest of Japanese society, they have been referred to as the invisible minority. As part of the *sabetsubito* (discriminated people) during early Japanese history, the *Burakumin* were among the general populace and performed vital functions dealing with the removal of impurities.

Traditionally found in Japan *Shintōism* abhors impurity and pollution caused by impurity. Thus the *Burakumin* performed vital functions for the society such as dredging mud from ditches and ponds, handling the dead, taking care of the cemeteries, disposing of dead animals, skinning and tanning animal hides, and so on.

With the creation of the Japanese state, *Burakumin* were marginalized and faced institutionalized discrimination. Although regional differences were a factor, the root causes for this discrimination were religion and occupation; their occupations were considered to be religiously taboo. It was believed that by coming in contact with impurity, the *Burakumin* became the source of pollution.

During the Edo period (1600–1868), the state clearly defined the social stratification. The samurai were the elites, followed by peasants, artisans and craftsmen, and merchants. The *Burakumin* were not considered part of this social structure, and therefore they were segregated from the rest of society. Referred to as the outcasts, the *Burakumin* were forced to live in hamlets or villages distant from others, with strict regulations imposed on them, including what they could wear and the size of their dwellings.

Called *eta* (abundant filth) during the Edo period, the *Burakumin* were expected to avoid contact with others to prevent pollution. As in the past, the *Burakumin* were able to work only in those areas that were exclusively reserved for them, meaning those occupations that were considered impure. The *Burakumin* continued to perform functions that were vital to the society, such as cleaning the city streets and taking care of the dead, but they would never be allowed to occupy the same space as the rest of Edo society.

Although Edo Japan was dominated by the samurai class, the *Buraku* skinners and tanners who produced the leather that was an integral material in samurai armament would never be viewed as important members of society. During the period, discrimination against the *Burakumin* took three forms: (1) hierarchical/vertical discrimination, whereby the *Burakumin* occupied the lowest social level; (2) spatial/horizontal discrimination, whereby their villages and hamlets were physically located outside other Japanese communities; and (3) temporal discrimination, whereby the *Burakumin* were excluded from festivals and other social functions that were open to the rest of society.

With the rise of the Meiji government in 1868, various reforms were instituted to meet the global challenges of the 19th-century world. Social reforms came about in 1871 when the social structure of the Edo period was abolished and people were given the right to choose an occupation. Legally, the *Burakumin* as a social group was abolished, but this did not signal the end of discrimination. The civil rights of *Burakumin* would be violated, and the social discrimination raged on. Many *Burakumin* continued to live in segregated areas and marry among themselves.

With the introduction of the military conscription system, Burakumin men would be drafted into the military alongside other Japanese men. But even within the military, Burakumin soldiers faced harsh discrimination. Clearly, discrimination was incorporated into the emerging industrialized society. To combat discrimination, the first *Burakumin* organization, called the *Suiheisha* (Leveling Association), was established in 1921. Aimed at identifying violators of Burakumin rights, the *Suiheisha* grew to national prominence and began to address the state's responsibility to protect the social and economic rights of the *Burakumin*. The *Suiheisha* no longer exists, but various organizations, including the Buraku Liberation and Human Rights Research Institute, continue its goal and mission.

There are about three million *Burakumin* and approximately six thousand *Buraku* communities in Japan today. Although the situation regarding the *Burakumin* has improved, they still face discrimination in many areas, including education, employment, and marriage.

~*Roy S. Hanashiro*

FOR MORE INFORMATION

De Vos, G., and H. Wagatsuma, eds. *Japan's Invisible Race: Caste in Culture and Personality.* Berkeley: University of California Press, 1972.

Keiji, N. "The Medieval Origins of the Eta-Hinin." *Journal of Japanese Studies* 5, part 2 (1979): 385–403.

Neary, I. *Political Protest and Social Control in Pre-war Japan: The Origins of Buraku Liberation.* Atlantic Highlands, N.J.: Humanities Press International, 1989.

Nobuo, S. *Burakumin: A Japanese Minority and Education.* The Hague: Martinus Nighoff, 1971.

Shigeaki, N. "An Enquiry Concerning the Development and Present Situation of the Eta in Relation to the History of the Social Classes in Japan." *Transactions of the Asiatic Society of Japan* 10 (1933): 47–154.

Weiner, M., ed. *Japan's Minorities: The Illusion of Homogeneity.* London: Routledge, 1997.

INUIT

To read about the problem of discrimination among the Inuit in the 20th century, see the Inuit entries in the sections "Education" and "Health and Medicine" in chapter 4 ("Intellectual Life") in this volume.

Urban and Rural Experience

Rural peoples' lives were vitally important to all major transformations in the 20th century. For example, in many ways, peasants dictated the outcome of the Russian Revolution and the subsequent development of the Soviet Union. That said, however, in the 20th century, many countries across Europe and in the Western Hemisphere became urban nations. People had moved to cities to take advantage

ECONOMIC LIFE

URBAN
& RURAL EXPERIENCE

United States,
1920-1939

United States,
1940-1959

United States,
1960-1990

Latin America

Soviet Union

Japan

Africa

of booming industrial economies. In Chile, Peru, and the United States, for example, major manufacturers such as Ford Motor Company and Proctor and Gamble provided well-paying jobs to thousands of workers. In good times, urban life afforded a comfortable standard of living and access to the nascent but dynamic urban culture that included shopping malls, professional sports, and a vibrant nightlife. In bad times, however, life was far more difficult. During the Great Depression in the United States and elsewhere, the urban workforce bore the brunt of the economic disaster. Thousands were thrown out of work without means of support. Even those who kept their jobs found their paychecks and hours cut. Workers in rural areas suffered from the Great Depression but not to the extent that urban workers did. On the farm, during economic downturns, one could always eat the crop or the pigs. In the cities, one had to rely on organized assistance. For example, in one Ohio city, the Fraternal Order of the Eagles opened a free soup kitchen to feed the hungry in February 1930. At first it served 200 people a day. Twelve months later the Eagles were feeding 700 people a day and preparing daily 130 gallons of soup, 200 loaves of bread, 100 gallons of milk, and 175 pounds of cheese. Things got so bad in Detroit that the city decided it could no longer justify feeding the animals in its zoo, which were slaughtered for meat to feed hungry people.

Men farming with mules in a typical farming scene in rural Georgia during the 1920s. © National Archives.

Despite the hardships and horrors of urban daily life during the Great Depression, the size of cities increased during World War II and into the postwar period. In the United States, the growth was largely due to the increase in manufacturing and construction jobs in the 1940s. Also, the federal government pumped billions of dollars into cities for the construction of new homes. The Federal Housing Authority helped fulfill the mandate of federal policy and laws such as the GI Bill by creating thousands of new single-family dwellings. The ultimate goal was, to paraphrase President Franklin D. Roosevelt, to build a nation of city homeowners. The most famous of the postwar urban construction projects was the city built by William and Alfred Levitt. Shortly after the war, the Levitts purchased 4,000 acres of old potato farms and began to build a small town. After four years, 17,447 houses were on that Long Island potato field. The houses were small but affordable, perfectly designed for the returning GI and his family.

In Japan, conflict between rural areas and the growing cities was muffled after World War II by the policies of the Liberal Democratic Party (LDP), which provided subsidies to farmers to keep prices high for their produce while also providing better health care and educational opportunities to urban workers and white-collar city dwellers. Thus, both urban and rural voters have kept the LDP in power for most of the post-war period.

The growth of cities in Latin America and Africa was not as triumphal. Cities were a place to escape revolution and violence in the rural areas. Yet Latin American and African cities had a difficult time accommodating newcomers, and large slum areas developed. These shantytowns in Brazil, Peru, Argentina, Chile, and in some of the large cities of southern Africa, where growth has been particularly explosive, are very primitive and lack basic necessities of daily life such as running water and electricity. These urban problems were not uncommon in the United States. From the 1960s to the 1990s, American cities continued to grow, but so did urban problems such as blight. As cities appeared to get meaner, many sought to move to the sub-urban areas. In turn this movement created another problem: urban sprawl. Thus at the end of the 20th century, cities were bigger, as were the daily urban problems confronting all Americans regardless of country.

UNITED STATES, 1920–39

The early 1920s witnessed a growth in cities. This movement of Americans had accelerated in the mid-1920s but then slackened in the 1930s. Between 1920 and 1930, the percentage of people living in urban places (as defined by the modest standards of the Census Bureau) increased from 50.8 percent to 56 percent. By 1940, no doubt as a result of the Depression and the difficulties of city life, the urban population rose only to 56.3 percent. Overall, however, this meant that 20 million more people, 74.4 million in 1940 compared to 54.1 million in 1920, resided in urban places. During the same period the rural population also grew, but only from 51.6 to 57.2 million.

The largest cities encompassed much of the era's urban growth, particularly during the 1920s. Cities with more than 500,000 residents swelled from 12 with 16.4 million people in 1920 to 13 with 20.8 million in 1930 to 14 with 22.4 million by 1940. Cities of 100,000 to 500,000 increased over the same 20-year period from 56 to 78 in number and from 11.1 million to 15.6 million in population. In the 1930s, communities of 10,000 to 100,000 grew the most and at the end of the decade totaled 984 with 24.7 million residents, in contrast to 684 with 16.3 million people in 1920 and 889 with 22 million in 1930. Over the same 20-year span, towns of 2,500 to 10,000 enlarged in number from 1,970 to 2,387 with combined population growth from 9.4 million to 11.7 million. Villages under 2,500 expanded from 12,855 with 6 million residents to 13,288 with 9.3 million. Rural dwellers completely outside of settled communities had aggregated 42.6 million in 1920, and by 1940 totaled 47.9 million. Thus, while the 24 percent population growth of the era was concentrated in urban areas, it was distributed across the country.

During the Great Depression, the urban work-force that had been growing dramatically in the 1920s was, not surprisingly, disproportionately affected by the industrial collapse. Those in the largest cities were hit the hardest. For example, in Ohio, a large state with an economy divided be-

ECONOMIC LIFE

URBAN
& RURAL EXPERIENCE

United States,
1920-1939

United States,
1940-1959

United States,
1960-1990

Latin America

Soviet Union

Japan

Africa

Main Street on Saturday afternoon, Harmony, Georgia, ca. 1925. © National Archives.

tween industry and agriculture, unemployment figures told the tale. In 1937, after some recovery had been achieved, a survey reported that joblessness in rural areas and small towns in Ohio stood at around 12 percent. In cities of 10,000 to 100,000 it was 13.5 percent, but in the eight major cities it averaged 20.5 percent. Big-city unemployment ranged from 14.7 percent in relatively small Dayton to 23.7 percent in the largest urban center, Cleveland. The 1930s Depression should be remembered as being most severe in America's great cities.

Even at its worst, complete joblessness faced only a minority of the overall American workforce. Most American workers held onto their positions. But they too were affected. Rather than dismiss workers with experience and skills, many businesses tried to keep them at reduced hours and wages. The rubber industry experimented with 6-hour daily shifts and 30-hour weeks as a substitute for the 8-hour shift and 40-hour workweek. Rubber workers held onto their jobs, but with no hourly wage increase, paychecks shrunk by 25 percent. Steel foundries went to a four-day workweek, then three days, then less. By 1932, the average for all U.S. factory workers who could claim to have jobs was less than 35 hours per week at a time when most still considered normal a five-and-a-half-day workweek of 44 hours. Coal miners in 1932 averaged only 27 hours a week.

In previous periods of industrial distress in the United States, some workers had returned to the countryside while farmers, knowing that they could at least feed themselves, stayed put. By the 1930s, however, far fewer urban residents had rural roots to which they could return, and farmers were facing a severe crisis of their own. The post–World War I agricultural depression continued throughout the 1920s and into the next decade. The mechanization of farming with tractors and other equipment reduced the need for hired labor and put small farmers out of business. Another blow was the drought beginning in 1930 that made growing crops or feeding livestock extremely difficult. Seventeen million farm people, half the nation's total, from Maryland and Virginia to Missouri and Arkansas, from the Dakotas to Montana and the states of the southern Great Plains, were affected by drought conditions.

Farmers gathered to protest the sale of family farms in Williston, North Dakota, to large corporations, 1942. © Library of Congress.

The agricultural areas to be hit the hardest and longest were the southern plains of Kansas, Colorado, New Mexico, Oklahoma, and Texas, which turned into what was called the Dust Bowl. Extreme heat accompanied by the lack of rain throughout much of the decade caused dry soil literally to blow away in great dust storms. Most farmers struggled on through a bleak decade, but especially in the Dust Bowl many left, unable to pay even the interest on their mortgaged land or forced to give up unproductive tenant farming. An estimated 3.5 million people left their farms during the 1930s, many of them taking along only what could be packed into the Model T, farm truck, or pushcart. They headed west to California, where agricultural jobs were rumored still to be available.

In the 1920s, temporarily unemployed workers could usually obtain assistance from community institutions, churches, mutual aid societies, philanthropic agencies, and local government. As urban unemployment and agricultural displacement mounted in the early 1930s, these resources were soon overmatched. One civic-minded Ohio Fraternal Order of Eagles lodge opened a free lunchroom for the needy in February 1930. At first it served 200 people a day, but 10 months later the number had doubled, and by early 1931, the Eagles were serving 130 gallons of soup, 200 loaves of bread, 100 gallons of milk, and 175 pounds of cheese to 600 or 700 people each day. By April, the Eagles, along with other groups such as parents and teachers associations, the Salvation Army, and Volunteers of America who also tried to feed the hungry, had exhausted their resources. The city of Akron, which had provided small relief checks, could not take up the slack. Its debt had already passed the legal limit; it had been forced to slash the number of municipal workers and the salaries of those who remained, and it was facing a 25 percent decline in tax receipts. The dimensions of the Depression stretched city as well as private generosity past the breaking point.

Community self-help, the traditional American response to economic distress, was swamped by the tide of unemployment. Bank failures deprived many people of what little savings they had. Philanthropy did not cease, but its providers found themselves with less to give just as the need was soaring. The magnitude of the Depression, together with inherent flaws in a system of private, voluntary, selective, and localized assistance, exhausted the system's capacity to provide relief. By 1932, most private charities were able to offer only food relief, and even that was limited. Soup kitchens, often using past-its-prime surplus produce, and breadlines did not offer the destitute a sufficient or balanced diet but represented the best that churches and charities could do.

Even when banks did not fail, and the vast majority did not, communities found themselves with far too few resources to care for the number of people in need. With tax revenues shrinking, even paying the modest wages of municipal workers and schoolteachers proved difficult. Public employees who knew that their positions paid less than private-sector jobs but thought that they were more secure found themselves laid off. For those fortunate enough to retain their posts, salaries were cut, then cut again. Some government units borrowed in anticipation of tax payments that then did not appear. By 1933, 1,300 cities, towns, counties, and school districts, together with the states of Arkansas, Louisiana, and South Carolina, had defaulted on obligatory payments, in essence declaring bankruptcy. Maintaining routine services proved hard, especially if they could not be justified as essential (Kyvig, 187–88, 219–20).

To read about urban rural experiences in the United States in the 19th century, see the United States entry in the section "Urban and Rural Environments" in chapter 3 ("Economic Life") in volume 5 of this series.

FOR MORE INFORMATION

Kyvig, D. E. *Daily Life in the United States, 1920–1939: Decades of Promise and Pain*. Westport, Conn.: Greenwood Press, 2002.

Miller, Z. L. *The Urbanization of Modern America: A Brief History.* New York: Harcourt Brace, 1973.

New Deal Network. <http://newdeal.feri.org>.

Sternsher, B. *Hope Restored: How the New Deal Worked in Town and Country.* Chicago: Ivan R. Dee, 1999.

UNITED STATES, 1940–59

Decent housing was a most pressing need in the 1940s and 1950s. In 1947, six million families were doubling up with relatives or friends; another 500,000 occupied wartime temporary housing or Quonset huts. In Atlanta the city bought 100 trailers for veterans' homes; in Chicago, 250 trolley cars were sold as homes. Responding to desperation, the federal government underwrote a new construction program for five million homes, adding billions to Federal Housing Administration (FHA) funding, which, along with the GI Bill, minimized down payments and guaranteed mortgages. Such government insurance promoted new single-family homes on the edges of cities. Hence, by 1960, the United States was actively building suburbia. Construction grew from 114,000 homes in 1944 to 1,692,000 by 1950, as down payments for prospective homeowners diminished and long-term mortgages made it easier for owners to keep their homes. The rate of mortgage foreclosures dropped from 250,000 nonfarm units in 1932 to only 18,000 by 1951. Reinforced by President Roosevelt's belief that "a nation of homeowners, of people who own a real share in their own land is unconquerable," Congress continued to approve government backing for the vast building operations that flourished right after the war.

The most famous housing developments to appear in response to ongoing federal support were the result of the enterprise of Abraham Levitt and his sons, William and Alfred. Like Ford, the name Levitt would become identified with a mass-produced consumer need. Before the war the Levitts had built expensive houses, but government contracts for temporary shelters and work with the Navy Seabees had given them the skills of assembly-line production associated with winning the war. Immediately after the fighting stopped, the Levitts bought up 4,000 acres of potato farms in Hempstead, Long Island, where they initiated the biggest private housing project in American history. At the height of their house production their assembly-line technique created one home every 16 minutes to become a unit in the first famous Levittown.

Trucks dropped off building materials on cellarless concrete slabs every 60 feet. The invention of new power tools added to the increased productivity when freight cars loaded with lumber went directly into a cutting yard where one man could cut parts for 10 houses in only one day. Construction was divided into 27 efficient steps performed by crews who did only one job. Not only did the Levitts own their own forests and make their own concrete, but they paid their workers above-average wages to avoid unionization and flouted standard union rules—such as those against spray painting—to finish the homes faster. Yet their employees never worked more than a five-day week. At its building peak, onlookers at Levittown often saw more than 30 houses a day going up. In four years 17,447 houses appeared on the Long Island potato field.

Originally designed for rental to veterans at $60 a month with an option to buy, the houses became a steal starting at $6,990 because long-term government mortgage guarantees made buying even cheaper than renting. People lined up, the way they would for tickets to rock concerts or sporting events in the future, to put $90 down payments on the original models. And although these homes were $1,500 cheaper than any comparable housing at the time, the Levitts still averaged a profit of $1,000 on each one. With the basic Cape Cod–style home—which soon developed into choices of four other models—the purchasers not only got homes with windows placed so that mothers could watch their children at play, but they also got an array of built-in appliances. Washing machines and later even television sets came with the houses.

Levitt took care to provide a larger social environment as well, including "nine swimming pools, sixty playgrounds, ten baseball diamonds and seven village greens." He also set aside land for churches, schools, and libraries. All over the country builders imitated the Levitts with differing community scales to take advantage of the government subsidies that made it possible for builders to risk little and gain much. In Park Forest, Illinois, the FHA insured 8,000 houses; in Henry J. Kaiser's Panorama City in California, 3,000. The entitlements extended to veterans by Congress continued to provide incentives to the entire building industry. Moreover, at a moment when the fear of Communism was once again rising, it was easy for everyone to agree with William Levitt that no man who owned his own house could be a Communist because he had too much to do. (Few at the time would have imagined a woman in the position to buy her own house.) Nor did anyone suggest how "communistic" were the enormous government subsidies that enabled Americans to own these properties. Indeed, when Frank Magruder suggested in a classic 1940 text, *American Government*, that the postal system, power projects, public free education, and old age assistance were examples of communism, many educators wanted his book censored. Harry Truman's astonishing reelection in 1948 also suggested to many historians a national enthusiasm for active government involvement in the private economy. He had campaigned vigorously against a do-nothing Republican Congress.

Sociologists at the end of the decade struggled to understand the meaning of living in such homogeneous communities. Architectural historians, admitting that the Levitt homes were a good value, deplored the possible rise of acres of suburban slums of ticky-tacky. People wondered if being surrounded by conformity would lead to intellectual stultification or to dangerous mass thinking. But owning a house by putting just $90 down gave many GIs a stake in the society they had been defending, just as FDR predicted. At the beginning the people who lived in Levittown were more interested in preserving prewar family values than in any politics. They did put their energy and their extra money into their homes. Far from turning into shambles or diminishing in value, by 1996 the classiest Levittown models were selling for as much as $180,000.

It would take a while for Americans to notice that the impoverishment of such communities lay—as predicted—in their social and cultural homogeneity. The predominance of young families, the exclusion of people of color—not challengeable legally at the time—and the scarcity of elderly inhabitants seemed to more sophisticated critics to make for a dull society. Even as late as 1960, after the original restrictions had been removed, not one of Long Island's Levittown's 82,000 residents was African American. Levitt insisted that economic reality, not prejudice, determined his policies on race. He had wanted black leaders to guarantee resales after African American purchases. Nor was the paternalism of Levitt's policies forbidding clotheslines and fences questioned. Some people might have been glad to get monthly bills for having the agency do the mandatory lawn cutting they had ignored. Just out of the army, many ex-GIs may also have found such community restrictions a source of order rather than an impediment to freedom.

Among the many valuable sociology texts that appeared after the war to help Americans understand who they were and where they were going was *The Levittowners: Ways of Life and Politics in a New Suburban Community* by Herbert J. Gans. Like an anthropologist living among natives as a participant-observer, Gans himself lived in a second Levittown community in New Jersey during the first two years of its existence. Believing in sociology as a democratic method of inquiry, he wrote of the experience from the perspective of his neighbors, not from preconceived academic ideas. Gans asserted that people had the right to be what they are. He found much more cultural diversity among his neighbors than many housing experts predicted. When he conducted a poll asking if people considered the community dull, only 20 percent responded yes. A former Philadelphian replied, "If Levittown is compared to city living [we will see that] there are no taverns or teenage hangout places, then it is dull. . . . We are perfectly content here." Another wrote, "We like quiet things . . . visiting, sitting out front in summer, having people dropping by." Gans found that they also took satisfaction in the more than 100 voluntary organizations that soon sprang up; 73 percent of those polled belonged to at least one. Of course their children—unlike the parents, who had grown up during the Depression—found fewer satisfactions in a home-centered life, but such restlessness might have been found among adolescents in any community in America. Many young people identified with James Dean's notorious character in the film *Rebel without a Cause* (1955). Intellectual stimulation became more certain when a branch of New York State's university system also soon appeared on different potato fields at nearby Stonybrook, offering educational opportunities to many whose families had not had any college graduates in the past.

Using class to define American differences remains a problem for sociologists, but Gans did not hesitate to assert that the criterion for vitality in Levittown was "home centered and private"—characteristic of lower-middle-class values as opposed to the more visible demands of professional-class visitors and critics, who like himself might live there only temporarily as they pursued upward social mobility. Yet he concluded without hesitation that Levittown was a good place to live. Creating more such communities, he believed, was a way to offer the benefits of uncrowded suburban life without high prices to the many poor people and nonwhites trapped in growing urban ghettoes.

The government spending on housing that was focused on single-family homes on the fringes of cities instead of on urban development and the rehabilitation of good older housing produced great social inequity. Many families would have been glad to remain within city limits and have more access to public transportation, but federal funds were shaping a different America. Herbert Gans helped Americans see that social planning as well as physical planning would be essential to optimize both social compatibility and individual liberty in a realistic future. Just as the freedoms we fought for could be achieved only by community effort and federal controls, so the response to postwar needs continued to involve the government. No piece of legislation would ever have more impact on the entire texture of American life than the GI Bill, not simply in terms of the creation of housing but, even more significantly, also in terms of the great new access to higher education reaching across America (Kaledin, 61–64).

To read about urban and rural experiences in the United States in the 19th century, see the United States entry in the section "Urban and Rural Environments" in chapter 3 ("Economic Life") in volume 5 of this series.

FOR MORE INFORMATION

Gans, H. J. *The Levittowners: Ways of Life and Politics in a New Suburban Community*. New York: Pantheon Books, 1987.

Jackson, K. T. *Crabgrass Frontier: The Suburbanization of the United States*. New York: Oxford University Press, 1985.

Kaledin, E. *Daily Life in the United States, 1940–1959: Shifting Worlds*. Westport, Conn.: Greenwood Press, 2000.

Miller, Z. L. *The Urbanization of Modern America: A Brief History*. New York: Harcourt Brace, 1973.

UNITED STATES, 1960–90

One of the major urban developments from the 1960s was the building of thousands of city shopping centers or malls to attract consumers (and their dollars) to urban and suburban areas. Before shopping centers, discount stores, and specialty mail-order houses became plentiful, most consumers shopped in locally owned stores. Even big department stores were owned by hometowners, or at least by local businesspeople from nearby towns. One study reported that in each decade after 1950, more than three-fourths of the towns with populations under 2,500 suffered net losses of such retail and service businesses as gas stations, farm implement dealers, and lumberyards as well as grocery, hardware, and furniture stores. Population decline accounted for some of the losses, but the readiness of small-town residents to drive 50 miles or more for the variety and savings offered in shopping malls and discount stores made a bigger difference.

In cities, stores on main thoroughfares served people in their neighborhoods while big department stores lured them downtown. Competition from malls and grocery supermarkets put many neighborhood stores out of business and emptied the downtowns. Ironically, mall developers eventually discovered that the vacant spaces they had helped create in America's downtowns might be ideal for malls, so that is where, in the 1970s and 1980s, they began to build them (Marty, 134–35).

To read about urban and rural experiences in the United States in the 19th century, see the United States entry in the section "Urban and Rural Environments" in chapter 3 ("Economic Life") in volume 5 of this series.

FOR MORE INFORMATION

Jackson, K. T. *Crabgrass Frontier: The Suburbanization of the United States*. New York: Oxford University Press, 1985.

Marty, M. A. *Daily Life in the United States, 1960–1990: Decades of Discord*. Westport, Conn.: Greenwood Press, 1997.

Miller, Z. L. *The Urbanization of Modern America: A Brief History*. New York: Harcourt Brace, 1973.

ECONOMIC LIFE

URBAN & RURAL EXPERIENCE

United States, 1920-1939

United States, 1940-1959

United States, 1960-1990

Latin America

Soviet Union

Japan

Africa

LATIN AMERICA

The 20th century witnessed major shifts in the rural-urban balance in Latin America. As late as the 1930s, the majority of Latin Americans continued to make their living off of the earth, and land ownership was key to economic and political power. By the 1980s, however, the urban sphere dominated: two-thirds of the region's population lived in cities, and agricultural labor accounted for only one-fourth of the total workforce.

One of the main factors in these changes was the consolidation of export economies throughout Latin America. In the late 19th and early 20th centuries, subsistence agriculture gave way to plantation agriculture; sugar crops expanded in Puerto Rico and Cuba, coffee in Brazil, and bananas through Central America. Vast tracts of land in Uruguay and Argentina became home to herds of grazing cattle, and mining activity expanded in Chile (copper) and Bolivia (tin). The majority of these products ultimately appeared in marketplaces in Europe and the United States.

As large-scale commercial ventures grew, companies and oligarchs squeezed subsistence agriculturists off their land. Many rural people lost their traditional livelihoods, and thus migration became a central feature of rural life. Some people followed seasonal harvests from coasts to highlands and back, always in search of work. Others chose to leave rural areas altogether, seeking a better life in the cities.

A second factor in the rural-urban shift was industrialization. The first industrial push of the century occurred in light of the Great Depression, which devastated Latin America's export-dependent economies—between 1929 and 1934, exports dropped by nearly half. Many governments responded to the crisis by further industrializing the cities, to produce manufactured goods formerly imported from abroad.

Industrial expansion continued through World War II, contributing to a strong urban bias in terms of state investments in infrastructure and public services. During this period, more than 100 million people moved to places like São Paulo and Mexico City.

Human-induced calamities also factored into the 20th-century changes. Violence in particular prompted many people to leave the countryside, as struggles over land fired the Mexican Revolution (1910–17) and civil wars in Central America and Peru (1970s–1990s). Meanwhile, environmental conditions worsened as chemical warfare (particularly in the Central American and Andean regions), deforestation, and overuse aggravated problems of soil erosion.

Massive urban migration throughout the century drastically altered both urban and rural landscapes. By 1980, 65 percent of Latin America's population was urban, whereas in 1930, 83 percent lived in rural zones. Mexico City, which had a population of just 3.1 million in 1950, grew to nearly 14 million by 1980.

Such hyperurbanization, combined with limited government ability or willingness to address social welfare issues, highlighted already stark contrasts between wealth and squalor. While rich sections of cities boasted mansions and theaters to rival any found elsewhere in the world, squatter settlements appeared on the outskirts and in the centers of cities. These shantytowns in Brazil, Peru, Argentina, and Chile were very primitive and lacked basic necessities for daily life such as running water and electricity.

One positive result of urbanization was the development of new social groups. A middle class emerged out of the growing numbers of professionals, shopkeepers, and government bureaucrats. An active working class also appeared. By the 1930s, trade unions operated in most Latin American cities.

The face of rural Latin America also changed during the century. The plight of *campesinos* (small farmers) became particularly precarious as access to land became more difficult. In 1961, for example, 700 *hacendados* (large landowners) owned one-third of Peru's productive land, whereas 40 percent of the population had access to less than one-quarter of the country's productive land. When *campesinos* did acquire land, it was often too little, or of poor quality. Also frustrating was the lack of access to government aid. Again in Peru, between 1948 and 1953, small farmers received only 24 percent of the available credit and aid, despite the fact that they made up 80 percent of the agricultural workforce. State favoritism toward export-oriented operations, combined with the isolation of *campesinos* from markets and their dependence on rudimentary production techniques, made farming for the majority of Latin Americans an increasingly difficult proposition.

Inequalities in distribution of land and access to government goods and services contributed to rising tensions between urban and rural spheres. In fact, many of the wars waged during the century had roots in such issues. On many occasions—often following wars, or in an effort to curtail pending violence—Latin American governments attempted to address the issues through land reform. Guatemalan president Jacobo Arbenz began a massive land reform program in 1952. His plans were cut short, however, when he expropriated land (with compensation) from the U.S.-based United Fruit Company (UFCO), which controlled some 42 percent of Guatemala's land. UFCO officials pressured their Washington connections until, in 1954, the United States Central Intelligence Agency sponsored a coup d'état that deposed Arbenz and installed a government more amenable to U.S. business interests. A more successful case of land reform was that of the Dominican Republic's Rafael Trujillo, known by many small farmers as the protector of agriculture. By 1955, Trujillo's government had distributed nearly 225,000 hectares of land, accounting for 10 percent of the nation's occupied land and 31 percent of rural production. Perhaps the most celebrated land reform program was that of Mexico's Lázaro Cárdenas, who, after the Mexican Revolution, distributed some 18 million hectares, primarily to landless peasants.

Despite the limited successes of some land reform programs and industrialization efforts, poverty and inequalities continued to plague Latin America throughout the century. In Central America in 1980, 70 percent of the population lived in poverty, with unemployment and underemployment ranging from 46.7 percent in Guatemala to 86 percent in Honduras. In the early 1990s, one-tenth of Latin American households received 40 percent of total income, whereas the bottom two-tenths of society received less than 4 percent of total income. The situation in rural areas was especially dire.

The 20th century clearly altered both rural and urban environments in Latin America. Despite the best efforts of governments, profound inequalities continued to provoke sharp tensions between social sectors and sometimes erupted in violence. Citing political, social, and economic reasons, people continued to leave their rural roots, seeking better opportunities in Latin America's cities.

~Molly Todd

FOR MORE INFORMATION

Skidmore, T. E., and P. H. Smith. *Modern Latin America.* 5th ed. New York: Oxford University Press, 2001.

Winn, P. *Americas: The Changing Face of Latin America and the Caribbean.* New York: Pantheon Books, 1992.

ECONOMIC LIFE
|
URBAN
& RURAL EXPERIENCE
|
United States,
1920-1939

United States,
1940-1959

United States,
1960-1990

Latin America

Soviet Union

Japan

Africa

SOVIET UNION

Rural life in the Soviet Union was hard. The seasonal rhythm of farmwork was, of course, interrupted by good times and joyous occasions, but the peasant (*krest'ianin* or *muzhik*) was among the hardest-working and least rewarded of citizens and was especially vulnerable to natural and human-made disasters. In the perilous so-called Thirty Years' War of the 20th century (1914–45), peasants of the Russian Empire and Soviet Union suffered great calamities. After World War II peasants were no longer victimized by such great misfortunes but continued to be treated as second-class citizens. Soviet leaders talked about the immense importance of agriculture and the need to increase food production, but industry and defense were always first in line for state support. Large investments, when they came, were sometimes poured into ill-conceived giant projects, like the creation of agro-cities or plowing up vast tracts of arid grassland. Meanwhile, the life and work of peasants continued to be characterized, as they had in the past, by low productivity and a poor standard of living.

The late czarist and early Soviet years brought extraordinary changes to village life. But much remained the same. Emancipation of the serfs (1861 and 1864) did not entirely lift peasants from servile status, nor did economic growth prevent famines. Though emancipation freed former serfs from the reign of their landlords, they were still tied to the village commune (*mir*) and collectively responsible for its debts and taxes and subject to its often outmoded methods, especially the farming of multiple strips of land. Because emancipation allotments were inadequate for, or barely met, their needs, freedmen sometimes had to work the fields of their former masters as well as their own. Peasants did manage to purchase additional land, but this was largely offset by two circumstances: rapid growth in the number of peasants and their continued use of inefficient ways of farming.

During the relatively prosperous years between the Revolution of 1905 and World War I, Peter Stolypin (prime minister, 1906–11) began a program to change rural life fundamentally, vigorously promoting private individual ownership of farmland at the expense of the commune. As a result, nearly half the heads of peasant households owned their land by 1916. However, the Stolypin reforms were interrupted and largely undone by war and revolution. In 1917–18 what remained of the old

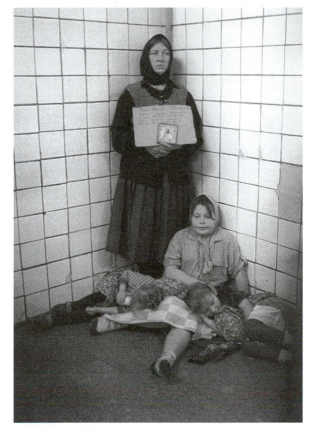

Commuters are a blur as they pass a woman and her three children begging in a Moscow subway, Friday, September 11, 1998. © AP/Wide World Photos.

estates, much public land, and many of the recently enlarged private holdings of better-off peasants was taken over, often violently, by the mass of mainly poor peasants. The result was a substantial increase in peasant land and a leveling of peasant wealth in terms of livestock and acreage per household. There were substantially fewer peasants who had no land or animals and fewer peasants with large farms. Various types of farms took shape, ranging from the private family farm (*khutor*) to the completely socialized collective (*kommuna*) in which peasants were housed and ate together and land, animals, tools, crops, and buildings were held in common. Most numerous by far were farms joined together in the old traditional commune where the village community periodically reallocated land so as to maintain an even distribution based on the number and size of households.

The gains made by peasants in the tumultuous months following the overthrow of monarchy (March 1917) represent a short-lived acquaintance with good fortune, followed as these gains were by the grinding civil war of 1918–21 and great famine of 1921–22. In the civil war both Reds (Bolsheviks) and Whites (anti-Bolsheviks) expropriated grain from peasants, but the Reds devised an especially systematic and brutal method that set poor and better-off peasants (*kulaks*) against each other and included armed expropriation teams of Party-led workers. In the Red- and White-controlled zones peasants sharply reduced their production of grain because it was likely to be taken with little or no payment. Sometimes all the peasant's grain was taken, even seed for the next year's planting. Forced requisitions, reduced planting, and drought resulted in poor harvests for 1920 and widespread starvation during the next two years. "War Communism," the Red slogan for the ruthless, all-out effort to defeat the Whites, succeeded. But just as victory appeared secure, peasant resentment toward War Communism exploded into violent opposition against the Bolshevik expropriators. The revolt of Kronstadt sailors in March 1921, in part a sympathetic response to the peasant movement, was a clear indication that anti-Bolshevik resentment ran deep

> *Soviet collectivization of agriculture was one of the great disasters of the 20th century.*

and went beyond the village. So serious was this threat to the Communists that Lenin decided to make a dramatic tactical and ideological retreat by introducing the New Economic Policy (NEP). At its heart NEP restored to peasants their incentive to produce: to cultivate the land as their own and sell or otherwise dispose of their produce as they determined, paying a reasonable tax in kind or money. Forced requisitions were abolished. Details remained to be worked out, but the plan called for a significant shift in the direction of a market economy. In the history of Soviet peasants NEP (1921–28) was a rare episode of relative peace and prosperity.

For Bolsheviks, however, an economy dominated by industrial workers was politically imperative, so it is not surprising that many in the Party had misgivings about NEP favoritism toward peasants and private enterprise and were eager to harness agriculture to the building of industry. Stalin answered their concerns, beginning in the late 1920s, by pushing industrialization at a blistering pace and at the same time ruthlessly collectivizing Soviet agriculture, turning it into the servant of industry and cities.

Collectivization of agriculture in the 1930s meant that private farming was replaced by large state-controlled agrarian enterprises. Most farms were joined together into large collectives (*kolkhozy*; singular, *kolkhoz*) and the former peasant proprietors into the collective worker-members (*kolkhozniks*, Russian, *kolkhozniki*). A smaller area of farmland was turned into agricultural factories or state farms (*sovkhozy*; singular, *sovkhoz*) and former proprietors were here employed as wage earners. Stalin and his government met the peasants' considerable resistance to these changes with ruthless and uncompromising force. Most unfortunate, more so even than the *kolkhozniks* and their counterparts, the state farm workers (*sovkhozniks*, Russian, *sovkhozniki*), were the *kulaks*, the more industrious and prosperous peasants, ones who stood to be the greatest losers and who, as a group, most strongly opposed collectivization. Millions of them, including women and children, were executed outright, or died as a result of imprisonment in camps or other brutal treatment. "They mostly kicked out those [*kulaks*] who had lots of kids," one witness recalled.

Then they'd bundle them into a cart, and there'd be no room for any belongings. All the poor wretches could carry were little cases for a change of clothes. . . . Off the family went, and where to? . . . They spent the winter living in tents, the whole winter. They all caught colds, some died. (Eaton)

Collectivization of agriculture in the USSR was one of the great disasters of the 20th century. Besides the massive destruction of humans, tens of millions of farm animals were destroyed by peasants who did not want to see them taken away and collectivized with the livestock of others. The result of this slaughter was to make even more serious the scarcity of meat and other animal products and also to drastically reduce animal draft power and natural fertilizer. Composition of the peasant farming community was also radically altered. Of the more enterprising and hardworking peasants who were not killed or sent to labor camps, many left the countryside, if they could, to seek work in industry. The largest group among these migrants to cities and factories were younger males. Thus, in the beginning the new Soviet agriculture was born in crisis and, in part because industry always took first place in the Party's economic plans, was never wholly raised from its depressed circumstances.

In exchange for their labor *kolkhozniki* were promised a lifetime stake in a member owned and governed large farm and cradle-to-grave benefits. Except for the lifetime commitment, the reality turned out to be much different from the promises: central planning rather than local self-government, marked inequalities in wages, little if any time off or time for hobbies or cultural pursuits, and few of the amenities of city life. Before 1976 *kolkhozniks* did not receive internal passports, so they had difficulty traveling away from their farms. Most collective farmers' pay and benefits were quite meager. Andrei Amalrik, a Russian dissident writer sentenced in 1965 to exile and labor on the Kalinin *kolkhoz* in western Siberia, compared collective farming to a sentence of lifelong slave labor.

Forced to choose, peasants usually opted for the collective. Party leaders, on the other hand, saw state farms as the ideal way to organize socialist agriculture and at first gave them preferential treatment. In fact, the two types of farms were quite similar, and in the post-Stalin decades what differences existed were further minimized. In a major readjustment of Soviet agriculture, beginning in the 1950s and 1960s Party central planners began to narrow the most obvious inequalities—wage differentials, for example—between collective and state farms, among various classes of farmworkers, and between them and industrial workers. Heavy state investments in agriculture were made to increase production and raise the quality of life on collective farms closer to that on state farms.

Another event that narrowed the differences between the two types of farms was the decommissioning in 1958 of machine tractor stations. These had served groups of neighboring *kolkhozes* for 30 years, spreading around the resources of mechanized power but also serving central planners as a means of controlling farm operations. Beginning in 1949, however, the state set out to amalgamate *kolkhozes* into many fewer but much larger units, and as a result it became convenient to require them to have and operate their own machines. At the same time collective farms were being amalgamated the government was substantially increasing the number of state farms so that by the 1980s they came to resemble each other in size and number also (Eaton).

FOR MORE INFORMATION

Eaton, K. B. *Daily Life in the Soviet Union*. Westport, Conn.: Greenwood Press. Forthcoming.

Lewin, M. *Russian Peasants and Soviet Power: A Study of Collectivization*. New York: W. W. Norton, 1975.

Volin, L. *A Century of Russian Agriculture: From Alexander II to* Khrushchev. Cambridge, Mass.: Harvard University Press, 1970.

ECONOMIC LIFE

URBAN
& RURAL EXPERIENCE

JAPAN

In most nations, the deep divide between the traditional rural and modern urban economies festers and threatens to create political disruption. In Japan, the divide is sharp, but not in terms of economic and political inequities. The reasons for this anomaly can be found in two places: externally imposed reform and domestic realpolitik.

Post–World War II Allied Occupation reformers subscribed to the Roosevelt New Deal liberal interpretation that disparity between town and farm had contributed to the rise of fascism and communism. The best panacea was to create the yeoman farmer, who, once landed, would fight to retain political voice. "Landowning farmers make good citizens" was their argument. Prewar absentee landlords were therefore dispossessed of any surplus land that the nuclear family could not farm, which was sold at rock-bottom prices to tenant farmers.

The two major postwar political parties merged in 1955 to form the Liberal Democratic Party (LDP), whose platform was to cater to the needs of rural farmers as well as the rank-and-file urban worker. Together with Japan's civil service workers, the LDP managed to keep this tripartite coalition in control of Japan's political economy.

So although the rural areas of Japan (making up less than 15% of the population) lag behind in economic amenities, the lag is neither serious nor substantial. High agricultural price supports and protective tariffs keep the farmer well paid and well fed in comparison to the rest of the world. These price supports and generous tax shelters make keeping the tiny farms in the individual patrimony very attractive.

Most farms would barely qualify as large gardens in America and can be managed on a part-time basis using ingenious new mechanized tools. Indeed, most male farmers actually work in regional industries and only occasionally work the farms, usually during their vacations. Women, children, and the older generation do most of the farmwork.

Urban residents do not benefit from price supports and tax shelters, but medical care, police, sanitation, and other excellent city services keep them voting for the LDP as well. Both sectors benefit from excellent schools and transportation systems. Most rural areas are linked to the cities by clean and dependable bus and train networks. Telephone service, electricity, and Internet access are modern and reliable in even the most remote areas.

Cities benefit from numerous clean and attractive department stores in city centers, but people continue to buy their daily necessities in small boutique neighborhood stores that provide excellent service. Fresh produce and protein, though not particularly inexpensive, is reliable and found in adequate supply and selection.

Durable goods such as refrigerators, stoves, washers, air conditioners, televisions, and the like are available to virtually everyone. Prices for these and other consumer goods are somewhat high to encourage export exchange, but virtually everyone, whether in town or on farms, can afford them.

~Louis G. Perez

FOR MORE INFORMATION

Buckley, R. *Japan Today*. 3d ed. Cambridge: Cambridge University Press, 1999.
McCargo, D. *Contemporary Japan*. New York: St. Martin's Press, 2000.

AFRICA

African cities and towns grew exponentially during the 20th century. Although the majority of the continent's people live in rural areas, urban areas throughout the continent continue to grow and expand. Some scholars have even predicted that the urban African population will soon outnumber those dwelling in rural areas. Cities such as Dakar, Accra, Nairobi, Johannesburg, Lagos, and Kinshasa are now large metropolises and are comparable to other cities throughout the world.

Cities, however, are nothing new to the African continent, nor are they creations born out of European colonial rule. Still, precolonial cities were significantly different from their modern equivalents. Precolonial cities were usually founded as either centers of empires or kingdoms or centers of commerce. They were places where various people interacted and traded goods. Cities like Timbuktu became great places of cultural interaction and eventually centers of knowledge and religion.

Colonial rule forever altered the meaning and significance of the African city. African cities became not only centers of commerce but also hubs of governmental administration and industry. The largest cities served as a country's capitals of commerce, industry, and government. Colonial regimes were often not interested in expanding precolonial cities; rather, they often built cities that best suited the interests of the colonial government. Consequently, these cities were concentrated around large mining areas, centers of agriculture, or seaports. Only precolonial cities that met this criterion remained big or influential. Postcolonial governments usually retained colonial contacts and governmental systems, and these colonial cities have remained the major urban areas of the postindependence period.

African cities and towns remained rather small until World War II, which ushered in a new phase for urban areas in Africa. Economic conditions in Africa during the war were poor, and European governments used colonial industries and products to fund their war campaigns. Cities and towns soon became areas where one could find employment and best provide for families. Many Africans, predominantly men, flocked to the cities in hopes of finding a better life and providing for their families back home. As a result, the populations of these cities ballooned.

Throughout the continent, cities and towns were and still are seen as having many more opportunities (e.g., economic, educational, professional) than the rural countryside. Images of Mercedes-Benz automobiles, skyscrapers, large houses, and wealthy elites dominate the popular opinion of urban life. Migrants flock to the

ECONOMIC LIFE

URBAN
& RURAL EXPERIENCE

United States,
1920-1939

United States,
1940-1959

United States,
1960-1990

Latin America

Soviet Union

Japan

Africa

cities in hopes of escaping poverty and in search of better wages; better schools; running water; electricity; political contacts; and a modern, cosmopolitan lifestyle. It is important to note, however, that although cities and towns offer more opportunities, that certainly does not mean they can accommodate all their residents. Often unemployment rates in urban areas are remarkably high, living conditions are poor, and poverty is rampant. Those who do find work frequently earn meager wages and live in relative squalor. Consequently, the dreams of success and wealth that are associated with city life rarely materialize. In other words, for most Africans living in urban areas, life is filled with despair and struggle for survival rather than wealthy government jobs and expensive tastes.

In general, kinship ties are vital components in African cultures, but their importance is lessened in urban areas. Many who move to the cities leave families and friends behind. To cope and survive in a very new and different society, these migrants often find ways to band together and form new ties once in the city. Neighborhood pubs, gangs, soccer clubs, religious groups, social clubs, and various other networks take the place of kinship ties found in the rural areas.

Many scholars have remarked that these urban areas produce "detribalized" Africans, in that the urban African undergoes a very different experience than his or her rural counterpart. Urban Africans are more likely to dress in Western attire, eat European dishes, drink imported liquor, have an education, and be willing to look past ethnicity. In other words, their actions, tastes, opinion, thoughts, and so forth have a distinctly Western influence, and thus they are classified as detribalized. As these ethnic and regional ties weaken, some urban Africans have come to associate themselves with their hometowns or cities. The effects of this association are profound; it has created the initial stages of national identities rather than the maintenance or bolstering of ethnic or regional identity.

African cities and towns are bastions of diversity. These cities draw in people from different parts of the country and often have sizable populations of foreigners from Asia, Europe, and various other African nations. Consequently, many, many languages are spoken throughout each city—up to 20 in the largest African cities—and European languages like French or English are often the only common languages. With so many Africans from various cultures, areas, ethnic groups, class, religions, and educational backgrounds, cities and towns are places where new ideas, opinions, and movements are formed. This was particularly true in the 1940s, 1950s, and 1960s, as these areas were usually where anticolonial and nationalist movements began to take shape. Consequently, many of the most influential anticolonial and political movements arose from these urban areas during the latter half of the past century.

Political gains were not the only positive product from this urban explosion of the 20th century. Urban areas brought together musicians from various backgrounds, and many new forms of music emerged from the cities and towns. Throughout the past century, music forms such as Ghana's highlife, Nigeria's juju, and South Africa's kwaito all had their roots in urban areas.

Overall, urban areas have been extremely important throughout the past century. They have been the hubs of commerce, industry, politics, government, and culture as well as despair and hardship. As these cities continue to expand and begin to increase in population, they will continue to gain significance in Africa throughout the 21st century.

~Tyler Fleming

FOR MORE INFORMATION

Anderson, D. M., and R. Rathbone, eds. *Africa's Urban Past*. Portsmouth, N.H.: Heinemann, 2000.

O'Connor, A. *The African City*. New York: Africana, 1983.

Salm, S. "Cities and Urban Life." In *Africa*, Vol. 4, edited by Toyin Falola. Durham, N.C.: Carolina Academic Press, 1982.

ISLAMIC WORLD

From its beginnings, the culture of Islam was centered in cities. The Arabian cities of Mecca and Medina formed the heartland of Muhammad's religious life, and Jerusalem, Damascus, and Baghdad soon followed as major sites of religion, culture, and trade. See the Islamic World entries in the section "Urban Economic Life" in chapter 3 ("Economic Life") in volume 2 of this series for the important beginnings of Islamic city life. See the Baghdad entry in the section "Great Cities" in chapter 2 ("Economic Life") in volume 2 of this series for a description of one of the greatest cities in the early Islamic world. Finally, follow the continuity of Muslim Islamic life in the Ottoman Empire entry in the section "City Life" in chapter 3 ("Economic Life") in volume 3 of this series. Muslim cities continue to be hubs of economics, culture, and politics in the modern world.

ECONOMIC LIFE: WEB SITES

http://www.hinduonnet.com/thehindu/2001/06/20/stories/05202525.htm
http://www.ahrchk.net/hrsolid/mainfile.php/1999vol09no04/910/
http://fatty.law.cornell.edu/topics/civil_rights.html
http://www.med.harvard.edu/chge/qrfall/engelfull.htm
http://lucy.ukc.ac.uk/csacpub/russian/radaev.html

4

INTELLECTUAL LIFE

The human mind is an amazing thing that allows people to reflect on ideas so abstract that we can imagine things we could never see or touch. We can think about things as complex as philosophical considerations of ethics, justice, and even thought itself. The study of ideas is called intellectual history, and it includes science, philosophy, medicine, technology, literature, and even the languages used to record the ideas.

At the basic level, the capacity for abstraction permits people to impose order (or to see order) in the astonishingly complex universe that surrounds us. As Stone Age people looked at the dark night sky dotted by millions of stars, they organized the view in patterns of constellations that allowed them to map and predict the movement of the heavens. They then echoed the heavenly order in such earthly monuments as Stonehenge in Britain and the Maya pyramids in Mexico. Through time, this capacity to order extended from the heavens to the submicroscopic particles that dominate 21st-century physics, and the development of mathematics as the language to express these abstractions. An important part of intellectual life throughout history has been the growing evolution of science, but this is only one aspect of the accomplishments of the mind.

Some people have applied their creative capacity for abstract thought to technology, finding ways to make our lives easier. Technological innovations have spread more rapidly throughout the world than even abstract scientific explanations. Horse collars from China, windmills from Persia, and Muslim medical advances transformed medieval western Europe, whereas the Internet dominates world culture in the 21st century.

What makes these escalating advances possible is not an increase in human intelligence. Instead, the ability to record abstract ideas in writing and preserve past accomplishments in education have allowed human knowledge to progress. As a medieval thinker (John of Salisbury) noted, if we can see farther than the ancients, it is only because we build on their knowledge. We are as dwarfs on the shoulders of giants, and through our intellectual life, we can look forward to even greater vision.

If for most of recorded history, we were dwarfs on the shoulders of giants, during the 20th century we became giants on the shoulders of giants. The intellectual advances of the century are truly amazing. At a basic level, education became much improved. Although caste, class, gender, and race limited one's ability to receive an education, the century still witnessed a boom in the number of educated people. Literacy and access to information increased dramatically. Along with advances in education came improvements in communications. Whereas in 1900 most of the world was isolated, by 2000 no corner of the planet was beyond reach. The world was smaller due to several technological advances such as cellular telephones and the Internet. In fact, communications was not the only aspect of daily life reorganized by new technologies. The list of advances is staggering: the airplane, the computer, the television, the Saturn V rocket with its lunar modules, and many more. It was a hallmark of the 20th century that these developments brought out not only the best in human intellectual ability but the worst as well. Take, for example, the field of medical science. Advances here such as antibiotics and the polio and smallpox vaccines revolutionized life, making it healthier and more predictable. At the same time, the science that furthered medicine also created horrible new weapons. Even the atom, whose power was harnessed during the century, also became weaponized, placing the world under the mushroom-clouded specter of doom.

At the dawn of the 21st century, it is difficult to weigh the pros and cons of intellectual developments. In some areas such as education and literature, there is very little question. But as for science and technology, the final analysis is more difficult. Certainly, the development of atomic science and genetic medicine have created beneficial technologies that have aided millions. But, to paraphrase the first nuclear generation, did the scientists and inventors of that century let the genie out of the bottle? Did the ability to advance science and technology outstrip the ability to philosophically and morally deal with the machines that they created? These are the central questions for the current generation.

FOR MORE INFORMATION

Tarnas, R. *The Passion of the Western Mind: Understanding the Ideas that Have Shaped our World View.* New York: Ballantine Books, 1991.

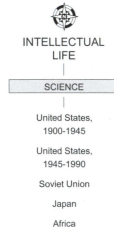

INTELLECTUAL
LIFE
|
SCIENCE
|
United States,
1900-1945

United States,
1945-1990

Soviet Union

Japan

Africa

Science

As much as the 19th century was the Victorian era for science and related technology, the twentieth century was the American. At the turn of the century, American inventors dominated the scene. People like Thomas Edison and Orville and Wilber Wright were not professional scientists. And yet, they used scientific methods and theories and relied on scientists to get their work done. Where they differed from the scientific community was in their relentless experimenting. Scientists did not generally pursue the kind of technological breakthroughs that inventors were seeking. Therefore, they were less likely to continue the search when success seemed so far off.

Advances such as the light bulb or the internal combustion engine airplane bred not only material profits but political gains as well. By World War I, American inventors had developed a close relationship with the U.S. government, particularly the military. When the relationship with the quixotic inventors did not pan out, the federal government turned to scientists to develop its weapons of mass destruction. American scientists and their European counterparts who had come to the United States in the 1930s worked together on the most expensive and expansive program in the history of the world. From the late 1930s through the 1940s, the federal government spent billions of dollars to produce an atomic weapon. Although many nuclear scientists eventually joined together to admonish the United States not to use the bomb, there is no underestimating the historical impact of the weapon. The atomic bomb and its more horrific cousin, the hydrogen bomb, had a dramatic influence over world politics in the 20th century.

In the 20th century, science was also highly valued in other nations such as the Soviet Union, which after World War II strove to keep pace with the United States and Japan, where the government invested billions of dollars in scientific research and education. In Africa, Western science brought many benefits especially in terms of technology and medicine but economic difficulties have prevented the independent states of modern Africa from developing their own scientific institutions or communities and the continent is still, at the start of the 21st century, largely dependent on Western technology and scientific knowledge.

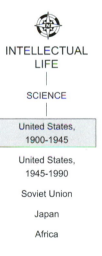

INTELLECTUAL
LIFE
|
SCIENCE
|
United States,
1900-1945

United States,
1945-1990

Soviet Union

Japan

Africa

UNITED STATES, 1900–45

During the first half of the 20th century, American scientists and inventors battled for supremacy. Each group jockeyed for the same public and private patrons. Initially inventors advanced their interests over those of the scientific community. But by the end of World War II, the country's main technological and scientific patron, the U.S. government, had thrown most of its money and support behind scientists. The relationship between inventors, scientists, and the military helped the United States become a dominant world power. Thus American inventors and scientists together were critically involved in making the 20th century the "American century."

The age of the inventor began at the end of the 19th century. The list of American luminaries is literally a who's who in the world of major technological breakthroughs: Hiram Stevens Maxim (the machine gun), Alexander Graham Bell (the telephone), Thomas Edison (the light bulb and motion picture system), Wilbur and Orville Wright (the internal combustion engine airplane), Elmer Sperry (gyrocompass), and Reginald Fessenden, Lee de Forest, and Edwin Armstrong (wireless telegraphy and telephony). All of these men had a close relationship with contemporary scientists and science. In fact, when asked, these professional and nonprofessional inventors maintained that they used scientific approaches and methods in their workshops. But when science failed them, they adopted more experimental techniques that in turn led to major breakthroughs. For example, Edison struggled to find the right type of filament for his light bulb largely because the state of chemical science drove him to a trial-and-error methodology. But more than this, the inventors needed scientists. Edison and Sperry both employed scientists on their teams. Scientists were never quite happy working with empiricists, and yet they were the ones who provided the inventors with the theoretical models that made their work possible. Still, it was a truism in America before World War II that invention led science, not the other way around.

During much of the 20th century, scientific invention and technological advancement in the United States were integrally tied to the nation's intense entrepreneurial spirit. Perhaps like all great scientists and experimenters in the past, Americans like Edison sought to move science and technology forward to (among other things) make money. By the time of World War I, the easiest way to make money was to sell one's scientifically sound, technologically advanced device to the U.S. military. The history of the Wright brothers demonstrates this clearly. We all know about Orville and Wilbur's accomplishments at Kitty Hawk, North Carolina. Few know about their attempts to create what amounted to the first cruise missile. The aerial torpedo was an unmanned flying bomb, a prototype for a later, more sophisticated age. But even the Wright airplane generated considerable interest from military leaders. Although the combination of airplanes and heavy bombs waited until World War II, the Wrights still garnered considerable profit from their relationship with the military. Even Edison participated in the system that would later be labeled the military-industrial complex. Immediately prior to American involvement in World War I, he was tapped to head the Naval Consulting Board to develop, examine, and select the best technology for the new navy. Edison consciously omitted adding members of the scientific community to the board, which failed to produce many advanced weapons. In fact, by the end of the war, Edison's stature had diminished somewhat, largely because he had not delivered the "terrible weapons of destruction" that he had promised (Hughes, 123).

During World War II, the federal government turned to scientists and not inventors to develop weapons that they hoped would quickly end the war. In particular, the Roosevelt administration relied upon physicists to build the ultimate weapon, the atomic bomb. Partly at the urging of atomic scientists including Albert Einstein, President Franklin D. Roosevelt began to invest large amounts of money into what became the Manhattan Engineer District, otherwise known as the Manhattan Project. The program was decentralized in terms of the science. Several teams operated both dependently and independently. The main facilities were at Oak Ridge, Tennessee, close to the newly established Tennessee Valley Authority with its gigantic capability to produce electricity. Brigadier General Leslie Groves administered the Manhattan Project while J. Robert Oppenheimer was the lead scientist. The American efforts to make an atomic bomb benefited from the Nazis, who had forced Europe's top scientific investigators to come to England and the United States. Although the scientists believed that they had some control and autonomy, in reality they did not. When the federal government felt that there was not enough progress, they brought in new project leadership from the Du Pont Company. The completion of the first two bombs occurred after the scientists were removed from direct project control. Nothing illustrated the scientists' political impotence more clearly than when the United States was ready to use the bombs. In the summer of 1945, several atomic scientists wrote to President Harry Truman expressing their wish that the weapons not be used. Simply, they were ignored. Thus the atomic scientists finally learned what the great American inventors had learned. The patronage of the federal government came at a price. To get the money and access to facilities, scientists learned to swallow their pride and give up control of the technology that they helped to create. They were mere tools for an ultimate end, nothing more and nothing less.

To read about science in the United States in the 19th century, see the United States entry in the section "Science" in chapter 4 ("Intellectual Life") in volume 5 of this series.

~Andrew E. Kersten

FOR MORE INFORMATION

Hughes, T. P. *American Genesis: A Century of Invention and Technological Enthusiasm, 1870–1970*. New York: Viking, 1989.

Kelly, F. C. *The Wright Brothers*. New York: Ballantine Books, 1975.

Rhodes, R. *The Making of the Atomic Bomb*. New York: Simon & Schuster, 1986.

UNITED STATES, 1945–90

After World War II, science and scientists became closely related to the federal government, especially with the development of nuclear science and space exploration. Not only did hundreds of scientists devote their careers to advancing the scientific goals of the federal government, but they also became the subject of government investigation. Anyone involved with specialized military knowledge had always had to be scrutinized. In the decade after the war the case that embarrassed the entire country was that of J. Robert Oppenheimer, former director of the Manhattan Project to build the atomic bomb. After his success at Los Alamos, America valued Oppenheimer as the man whose energies created the bomb that ended the war. He became a national hero and in 1948 was on the cover of *Time* magazine. And a new professional journal, *Physics Today*, also displayed his picture on its first issue—in spite of Oppenheimer's having put aside his career as a research physicist to build the bomb. As head of the Manhattan Project he experienced no doubts about his status, but the intellectual depth that made him question future atomic wars and oppose the development of the devastating hydrogen bomb turned Oppenheimer, in many eyes, into a security risk.

Edward Teller, a physicist enthusiastic about building the "Super"—as the new hydrogen bomb was called—blamed Oppenheimer for alienating the best scientists from working on the project. Because of the witch-hunting atmosphere the tensions among scientists and government officials in 1954 were extreme. When Oppenheimer had gone before the House Un-American Activities Committee (HUAC) in 1949, the young Nixon had praised him for his candor. But in 1954, the government moved to strip Oppenheimer of his security clearance. Always naive about politics,

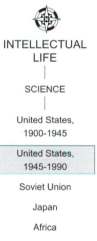

INTELLECTUAL
LIFE
|
SCIENCE
|
United States,
1900-1945

United States,
1945-1990

Soviet Union

Japan

Africa

the great physicist had confessed to past left-wing beliefs and Communist associates. But these had not been held against him as director of the Manhattan Project. Suddenly his opposition to the H-bomb made Oppenheimer a target for spy hunters who wanted to define all disagreement as treason. The trial of J. Robert Oppenheimer, a series of hearings before the Atomic Energy Commission, remains a scar on the history of American justice. With abundant personal detail David Halberstam captures its intensity in *The Fifties:* "There hadn't been a proceeding like this since the Spanish inquisition," declared David Lilienthal, former head of the Atomic Energy Commission.

The H-bomb in action. © Library of Congress.

The hearings against him left Oppenheimer stunned. Although the most distinguished scientists in America testified on his behalf, the government's judges paid no heed. After a lifetime of eloquence, Oppenheimer wilted. He could no longer be "the powerful witness for freedom of scientific opinion" his friends had expected him to be. At this moment, as one journalist reported, the great scientist appeared sadly as a man "diminished by tiny misdeeds from the past." Edward Teller's calculated praise of Oppenheimer's patriotism ended with implications that he was no longer fit to protect the vital interests of the country. In April 1954 the AEC voted two to one to deny security clearance to the man who had enabled the United States to build the atomic bomb.

Meanwhile Harry Truman had already gone ahead with the construction of the hydrogen bomb. He had never shared Oppenheimer's doubts about using the atom bomb. He knew he had done the right thing.

Moreover, Truman listened to political advisors, not to scientists. In March 1954 the United States made a series of hydrogen bomb tests at Bikini Atoll, spreading radioactive ash over 7,000 square miles and incidentally harming a boatful of Japanese fishermen 80 miles away, who were labeled, in this era of paranoia, as possible Communist spies (Kaledin, 81–82).

The other major postwar scientific development related to the Cold War as well. In the United States, space exploration reflected not only the close relationship between scientists and the government but also the strong desire to beat the Communists in the space race.

American scientific technology propelled the United States into space. Computer technology, in particular, played an essential role in America's first flights into space. In 1961, navy commander Alan Shepard and air force captain Virgil Grissom each piloted space capsules in suborbital flights of just over 300 miles, preparing the nation for the big moment to come the following winter. At 9:47 A.M. on February 20, 1962, with schoolchildren bunched around television sets in their classrooms and their parents interrupting tasks at work and at home, an Atlas missile at Cape Canaveral, Florida, launched the space capsule *Friendship 7* into orbit around the earth, with Colonel John Glenn aboard. Minutes short of four hours later, CBS newsman Walter Cronkite narrated Glenn's reentry into the atmosphere and his splashdown in the Caribbean Sea. In orbit, the capsule had reached a velocity of 17,500 miles per hour, and in the four hours between launch and recovery from the water Glenn had seen three sunrises. Viewers cheered what they saw and buzzed with excitement as they talked about it. Still, the way it was carried out was so precise that it looked routine, matter-of-fact, predictable. It had all the marks of a choreographed theatrical production. Surely this was American progress, the success of modern times.

There was more to come: Three months later, astronaut Scott Carpenter repeated John Glenn's feat, this time taking control of functions done by computerized instrumentation in the first flight. The follow-ing October, navy commander Walter Schirra completed a nearly perfect flight of more than nine hours, circling the earth six times and making a pinpoint landing in the Pacific Ocean. Television viewers began to take success for granted, but even bigger things were yet to come.

Based on the counsel of the National Aero-nautics and Space Administration (NASA) and his advisors, and at the urging of Vice Pres-ident Lyndon Johnson, President Kennedy de-clared in a speech before Congress on May 25, 1961: "This nation should commit itself to achieving the goal, before this decade is out, of landing a man on the moon and returning him safely to earth. No single project . . . will be

> ### 📷 *Snapshot*
>
> **Nations with Stockpiles of Nuclear Weapons, 2002**
>
> China*
> France*
> India*
> Iran
> Iraq
> Israel
> Libya
> North Korea*
> Pakistan*
> Russia*
> United Kingdom*
> United States*
>
> *Indicates declared nuclear weapon states
> (Nuclearfiles.org, 2002)

more exciting, or more impressive to mankind, or more important for the long-range exploration of space; and none will be so expensive to accomplish." The cost? Likely to be $30 to $40 billion, with those dollars contributing little to economic growth. The Cold War explains why American taxpayers were willing to pick up the tab. Johnson was correct in saying he did not believe "that this generation of Americans is willing to resign itself to going to bed each night by the light of a Communist moon." Anyone doubting that the Soviet Union saw the contest in the same terms should remember that every day thousands of Russians pass a statue of Yuri Gagarin mounted on a pedestal 40 meters tall on a main thoroughfare in Moscow. Gagarin was the Russian hero whose single-orbit flight on April 12, 1961, three weeks before Alan Shepard's suborbital flight, showed America that the Soviet Union could beat the United States in launching a man into spatial orbit.

The only immediate benefit of the space flights for the American people seemed to be bolstered pride in the nation's technology. The flights had been accomplished in full view of the American people, via television. So what if comparable feats had occurred earlier in the Soviet Union? They had been done in secret. How could we know, Americans asked, how many failures had preceded the Russians' successes?

More tangible benefits were to come, space scientists claimed, as by-products of space exploration reached into many quarters of daily life. One such benefit became apparent by mid-1962, with the placement in orbit of AT&T's Telstar communi-cations satellite. The satellite permitted transmission of the straight-line waves of television, unhampered by mountains or oceans. When more orbiting stations were launched later, continuous transmission via satellites became possible. Television networks and weather forecasters soon came to rely on satellite transmissions, and eventually homeowners willing and able to mount a "dish" in their yards or on their roofs enjoyed the benefits too. Meanwhile, the American people maintained their interest in space flights, particularly those with two men tucked tightly into the Gemini capsules. In a period of 20 months, 20 astronauts in Project Gemini conducted a variety of experiments in space. Despite scary moments, NASA called each one of them an unqualified success.

As the Gemini space capsules scored successes in the mid-1960s it became only a matter of time before a moon landing would be attempted. In May 1969, *Apollo 10* astronauts took their lunar module into orbit within nine miles of the moon before reconnecting with the command module. On July 20, hundreds of millions of Americans listened to communications preceding the landing on the moon of "the Eagle," *Apollo 11*'s lunar module, by astronauts Neil Armstrong and Edwin Aldrin. When it touched down, their television sets enabled them to watch events as they occurred. Speaking the first words on lunar soil, Armstrong called the venture "one small step for a man, one giant leap for mankind." The astronauts conducted experiments on the lunar surface, collected about 45 pounds of rock and soil samples, and returned safely to the command module for the journey back to earth.

The prototype of video cameras was developed for space missions.

"After centuries of dreams and prophecies," wrote *Time* magazine, "the moment had come. Man had broken his terrestrial shackles and set foot on another world. Standing on the lifeless, rock-studded surface he could see the earth, a lovely blue and white hemisphere suspended in the velvety black sky." One of the six remaining missions, *Apollo 13*, survived a near-disaster without a moon landing, but the other five were successful, the last one in December 1972. In that year NASA began a space shuttle program to provide means for further scientific exploration, and possibly future colonization and commercial activities. In the meantime, though, NASA faced deep budget cuts. Some were caused by the costs of waging war in Vietnam, others apparently by the belief that the big goal, reaching the moon, had been accomplished. By 1970, NASA's employment force of about 136,000 was roughly half of what it had been five years earlier.

What were the dividends of the space program for the American people, the payoff on the $25 billion it cost them? Photographs of the lunar surface. Rock samples of great geological interest but no known practical significance. Considerable knowledge concerning how to maneuver vehicles in space. Improved technological bases for telecommunication via satellites and weather surveillance worldwide. Information that would prove useful in advances in medicine. Most important, perhaps, was the restoration of American morale that had been damaged when the Russians sent *Sputnik* into orbit 12 years before the moon landing. Never mind that the Soviet Union used unmanned moon landings to accomplish many of the same results as the manned landings of NASA. Of the tangible benefits of space technology, one cited frequently, sometimes sarcastically, is Velcro. This material had been designed to help space travelers keep track of pencils and other handheld objects in the zero gravity of space. The prototype of video cameras that later came into common usage was developed for space missions, as were electronic stethoscopes, fire-resistant fabrics, lightweight insulation materials, dehydrated foods, computer technology for automated control of highly sophisticated equipment, and many other things.

Early fascination with television spectaculars featuring the accomplishments of the space program had seduced viewers into ignoring its cost. So what, they seemed to say, if with each launching a $200 million Saturn rocket sank into the ocean? As the consecutive launchings and returns blurred together, however, viewers' interest waned. The technical and political milestone represented by the linking of an *Apollo* spacecraft and the Russian *Soyuz* on July 17, 1975, attracted only passing attention. Television showed the exchange of visits by the American astronauts and Russian cosmonauts during the nearly 44 hours their spacecrafts were linked, but viewers seemed to take this historic occurrence for granted. The same was true when two *Viking* spacecraft landed on the planet Mars in 1976 and sent back spectacular pictures.

The 1980s saw more technological feats in space. The decade began on a promising note for the space program when the *Columbia*, the first reusable spacecraft, touched down at Edwards Air Force Base in April 1981. Its landing in the Mojave Desert concluded a flight begun more than 54 hours earlier when the spaceship launched as a rocket. In 36 orbits of the earth it operated like a typical spacecraft, and it landed like an airplane on a runway. An amazingly successful mission, it gave Americans a renewed sense of pride and raised the prestige of the nation worldwide.

The goals of the space program, though, went beyond pride and prestige. NASA hoped to make orbiting in space a profitable venture. The communications industry was its early client, but NASA wanted to encourage advancements in medicine and other technologies. It faced competition from other nations as well as from private companies trying to break into space travel.

The American people took success in space exploration for granted until January 28, 1986. On that day the space shuttle *Challenger* exploded 73 seconds after liftoff from Cape Canaveral, Florida. Six astronauts died, along with a teacher on board, Christa McAuliffe. Her presence had attracted special attention to the flight, and millions of schoolchildren saw the explosion on television. News reporters could say nothing to set the children at ease, and the entire nation was stunned.

Failures of other spacecraft occurred in subsequent months, but none so dramatically as the *Challenger*. Almost three years passed before the launching of *Discovery* again put a shuttle in space. Things went well for a while, but an event in 1990 that should have been a spectacular achievement turned out to be tarnished. The space shuttle *Discovery* launched the $1.5 billion Hubble space telescope into orbit, only to find very soon thereafter that an incorrectly made mirror blurred the images it was to transmit back to earth. Another shuttle disaster, again resulting in the loss of the seven-person crew, occurred on February 1, 2003, when the *Columbia* broke up upon reentry. The new tragedy again resulted in the grounding of the shuttle fleet. Nevertheless, despite the disasters and mistakes, the scientific-government complex, as one might call it, remained firmly intact and hard at work developing more scientific and technological breakthroughs that helped to advance humanity in general and the U.S. government and people in particular (Marty, 60–61, 153–54, 222–23, 305–6).

To read about science in the United States in the 19th century, see the United States entry in the section "Science" in chapter 4 ("Intellectual Life") in volume 5 of this series.

FOR MORE INFORMATION

American Experience: Race for the Superbomb [film]. <http://www.pbs.org/wgbh/pages/amex/bomb/>.

Boyer, P. S. *By the Bomb's Early Light: American Thought and Culture at the Dawn of the Atomic Age.* Chapel Hill: University of North Carolina Press, 1994.

Halberstam, D. *The Fifties.* New York: Ballantine Books, 1994.

Kaledin, E. *Daily Life in the United States, 1940–1959: Shifting Worlds.* Westport, Conn.: Greenwood Press, 2000.

Kubrick, S., dir. *Dr. Strangelove.* Tristar Home Video, 1964.

Marty, M. A. *Daily Life in the United States, 1960–1990: Decades of Discord.* Westport, Conn.: Greenwood Press, 1997.

Nuclearfiles.org. <http://www.nuclearfiles.org>.

Williams, T. I., ed. *Science: A History of Discovery in the Twentieth Century.* New York: Oxford University Press, 1990.

INTELLECTUAL
LIFE
|
SCIENCE
|
United States,
1900-1945

United States,
1945-1990

Soviet Union

Japan

Africa

SOVIET UNION

In the late 1950s and early 1960s, an impressive series of Soviet firsts, including the launch of the first artificial earth satellite, *Sputnik* (October 1957); the first man in space (1961); the first woman in space (1963); and the first cosmonaut to "walk" in space (1965), spurred the American government to embark on a space race with the USSR. Although it relinquished its plan to be first on the moon, the Soviet space program made steady progress in the 1970s and 1980s, including deployment of the first true modular space station (1986). These and other accomplishments resulted from the work of some brilliant scientists who had strong government backing. Beyond the space program, USSR researchers received six Nobel Prizes in physics and one in chemistry, although none in physiology or medicine.

Paradoxically, the six Soviet physics Nobel Prizes were awarded for work done in the 1930s and 1940s, a period of intense terror against Soviet citizens, including some of the very scientists who carried out the prize-winning research. In addition, Sergei Korolev, who pioneered the Soviet space program, and Andrei Tupolev, who designed the USSR's finest aircraft, also did their most striking work during that period, after their release from prison. In the late 1940s and early 1950s, while Josef Stalin's terror still raged, Andrei Sakharov, a brilliant physicist and a father of the Soviet hydrogen bomb, achieved his groundbreaking accomplishments and was highly rewarded for them. His banishment to the city of Gorky, followed by intermittent imprisonment and torture, did not occur until 1980.

Despite its attainments, Soviet science suffered the same problems and conditions that afflicted the rest of Soviet society. Besides government-sponsored terror, there was war; famines; censorship; cultural and professional isolation; lack of both basic and sophisticated equipment; a stifling, centralized economy and bureaucracy; and political interference. Under Stalin, thousands in the scientific community disappeared, including some of the best and brightest. Those researchers who survived were often sentenced to work on projects in special prison laboratories (*sharashki*). In the upside-down arena of Soviet science, the world-respected geneticist Nikolai Vavilov was sentenced to death and classic genetics research was crushed, whereas Stalin's favorite, Trofim Lysenko, commanded the biological sciences. In the Lysenkoist universe, winter wheat morphed into spring wheat, rutabagas became cabbages, hornbeam trees spontaneously developed hazelnut branches, and warblers spawned cuckoos.

More benevolent conditions in the United States account for the far greater number of Nobel Prizes in science awarded to Americans during the Soviet period. From 1917 to 1991, U.S. citizens—many of them foreign-born—won 54 Nobels in physics, 35 in chemistry, and 66 in physiology or medicine. Although some of the American prize-winning research was applied to space exploration and nuclear weapons, Western researchers who pursued the breakthroughs in these areas also found applications that improved the lives of ordinary people and enriched the consumer economy. Soviet research, in contrast, rarely had a trickle-down effect. The hardships of their day-to-day lives motivated many Soviet citizens to protest the costly space program when, under Mikhail Gorbachev in the 1980s, they were finally allowed a voice.

~Katherine B. Eaton

FOR MORE INFORMATION

Birstein, V. J. *The Perversion of Knowledge: The True Story of Soviet Science*. Boulder, Colo.: Westview Press, 2001.

Graham, L. R. *Science in Russia and the Soviet Union*. Cambridge, U.K.: Cambridge University Press, 1993.

Kaiser, R. G. *Russia: The People and the Power*. New York: Pocket Books, 1977.

Lourie, R. *Sakharov: A Biography*. Hanover, N.H.: Brandeis University Press/University Press of New England, 2002.

Medvedev, Z. A. *Soviet Science*. New York: W. W. Norton, 1978.

Rezun, M. *Science, Technology, and Ecopolitics in the USSR*. Westport, Conn.: Praeger, 1996.

Soyfer, V. N. *Lysenko and the Tragedy of Soviet Science*. Translated by Leo Gruliow and Rebecca Gruliow. New Brunswick, N.J.: Rutgers University Press, 1994.

JAPAN

The realm of science in Japan has long been denigrated on the basis of anecdotal and incomplete information. It became the stereotype that Japan was not strong

INTELLECTUAL LIFE

SCIENCE

United States, 1900-1945

United States, 1945-1990

Soviet Union

Japan

Africa

in sciences because it devoted its resources to technology and the applied sciences rather than purely scientific research. It was common knowledge that Japanese companies spent very little on scientific research, relying on their Western counterparts to provide it with the intellectual property at relatively low cost. To further the argument, critics pointed to the relatively low number of Japanese Nobel Prize winners in the sciences (seven), and that most (six) of that number received their prizes as collaborators in American scientific projects.

Nevertheless, science is highly valued in Japan. The government spends billions to improve science instruction in the public schools. As a clear indication of its success, Japanese students annually score two or three grades above their Western counterparts in science and four or five in mathematics. Education specialists suggest that Japanese middle-school students receive better education in those subjects than Americans do in high school and even the first two years of college. Japan has created a giant "science city" centered around Tsukuba University to facilitate the free exchange of scientific research.

Billions more are spent on individual research grants, almost equaling the total of American governmental spending (excluding private industry spending) for the sciences. The result is astounding by anyone's calculations. Japanese authors produced nearly 10 percent of all the scientific papers published in the world from 1998 to 2002 and the percentage was even higher in physics (14%), pharmacology (13%), chemistry (12%), and biology and biochemistry (11%). In comparison, Japanese authors published only 1 percent of the papers on the social sciences.

In the realm of astrophysics and nuclear science, Japan is in the vanguard even though very little of the research in these disciplines is accomplished with the benefit of the huge expenditures from what Dwight Eisenhower called the military-industrial complex. Japan's burgeoning space industry has very little support from its Self-Defense Forces, at least compared to what NASA receives from the American military or what China, Russia, France, Great Britain, India, and Pakistan receive from theirs. Japan's nuclear generators supply nearly a quarter of its domestic electricity. No one doubts that the Japanese could produce (or may already have produced in secret) atomic bombs virtually overnight if it wished to do so. The bombing of Hiroshima and Nagasaki during World War II, however, has given Japan what one wag has called "nuclear allergy."

To read about science and technology in early modern Japan, see the Japan entry in the section "Science and Technology" in chapter 4 ("Intellectual Life") in volume 4 of this series.

~*Louis G. Perez*

FOR MORE INFORMATION

Bartholomew, J. R. *The Formation of Science in Japan: Building a Research Tradition*. New Haven: Yale University Press, 1999.

Coleman, S. *Japanese Science: From the Inside*. London: Routledge, 1999.

AFRICA

The development of science in 20th-century Africa has been both a blessing and a curse to Africans and African lifestyles. On the one hand, Western science has brought new forms of technology and medicine to Africa, which have significantly improved the standard of living of many Africans. On the other hand, these same scientific processes and technologies have often served to undermine efforts on the part of Africa to achieve independence and equality in the global scene.

For the first half of the 20th century, European colonial governments controlled almost the entire African continent. With European control came the introduction of Western scientific institutions and processes. Europeans brought new technologies to Africa, notably transportation systems and Western biomedicine. These scientific systems came with limited benefits to African populations, but they also brought considerable detriment to the continent. Western science in the early 20th century expounded a theory of scientific, biologically based racism. Under this belief system, European scientists placed the world's races in a hierarchy, with white Europeans at the top, representing the most civilized and developed race. Black Africans were placed near the bottom of this hierarchy, characterized as uncivilized, barbaric, and a relic of humanity's forgotten past. This system of biological racism has since been completely debunked, but during the colonial period in the early 20th century, it was accepted as science.

Colonial governments used this system of biological racism to justify colonial rule in Africa. According to these governments, Europeans, as the most advanced race, had a duty to bring civilization and progress to the less developed races of the world, which were incapable of self-rule in their present state. Through the colonial process, Africans would presumably achieve "civilization" and gain the right to self-government. Thus, Western science was used to deny Africans self-rule throughout the early 20th century.

Part of the so-called civilizing process that the colonial governments brought involved the introduction of scientific technologies and knowledge. Colonial governments brought transportation systems and natural sciences such as medicine and ecology to Africa under the auspices of promoting civilization. These institutions did little to develop the continent or improve the lives of many Africans, however. Colonial governments used transportation science to figure out the fastest and cheapest way to ship such African resources as cash crops and metals from the interior of the continent back to Europe where they could be turned into a profit for European corporations. Likewise, medical establishments originally were designed to ensure the health of the white populations in Africa, with the exception of missionary medical establishments, which nonetheless never managed sufficient funding or manpower to reach a large percentage of the African population. Thus, when African countries gained political independence, mostly in the 1950s and 1960s, they had been offered a taste of Western science but could not boast well-developed, efficient, or pervasive scientific institutions.

With this being the case, upon independence most African countries began to build facilities for the research and dissemination of scientific knowledge. African countries promoted scientific degrees and original research in newly founded universities. They expanded education and medical facilities, building hundreds of schools and hospitals in the decade after independence in an effort to make their new countries both self-sufficient and respectable in the eyes of the developed world.

Unfortunately, these goals have not been fully recognized. By the 1980s, most African countries had fallen on extremely hard economic times and could not afford to devote the necessary funds to scientific research and development, focusing instead on meeting the more immediate fiscal needs of the countries. As a result, Africa has not become self-sufficient in terms of developing technologies and producing a local scientific community. African countries rely heavily on Europe and the United States for imports of technology items like electronics and automobiles, while at the same time many of the few scientists that African universities do produce are fleeing their countries in search of more prosperous livelihoods in Europe and the United States. This situation has put many African countries in a conundrum about the future of their scientific programs. As the World Bank has put it, "No African nation can afford to have [high-quality scientific research] programs in the short run, yet none can afford not to have them in the long run . . . " (Ahmad, 81). Indeed, it appears that African countries will continue to rely on Europe and the United States to meet their limited scientific and technological needs, and the necessary requirements to ameliorate this situation in the future are not being met.

The unfortunate state of affairs outlined here should not provoke the notion that Africa or Africans are deficient in scientific know-how or ingenuity. In fact, due to the lack of technological niceties and scientific professionalism on a local level, many Africans have developed unique and locally appropriate methods of scientific development. Indigenous medical practices continue much as they have for centuries past, with the notable exception that now some indigenous medical practitioners will refer patients to medical doctors or hospitals on occasion. In many African countries, young children, lacking video games and other electronic devices, build cars out of scrap metal and rubber, constantly updating them to achieve greater speed and control. In Kenya, because so few people have access to electricity, let alone the financial means to afford it, many people rely on charcoal burners to heat their homes and cook their food. For this reason, the production of charcoal burners has become a scientific process. Newer models are lined with ceramic to conserve heat, thereby making charcoal use more economical. This kind of scientific innovation has occurred in Kenya despite the fact that charcoal is by and large an outdated heating fuel in industrially developed countries. Nonetheless, these charcoal burners meet the immediate needs of most Kenyans and as such have been actively promoted by the Kenyan government. Thus, Africans use science daily, even if not in the same fast-paced, industrialized manner as more economically prosperous countries in other parts of the world.

~Matthew Heaton

FOR MORE INFORMATION

Ahmad, A., ed. *Science and Technology Policy for Economic Development in Africa.* Leiden, The Netherlands: E. J. Brill, 1993.

Dubow, S., ed. *Science and Society in Southern Africa.* New York: St. Martin's Press, 1995.

Swiderski, R. M. *Eldoret: An African Poetics of Technology.* Tucson: University of Arizona Press, 1995.

Education

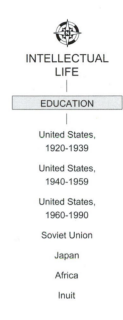

INTELLECTUAL LIFE

EDUCATION

United States, 1920-1939

United States, 1940-1959

United States, 1960-1990

Soviet Union

Japan

Africa

Inuit

Both the leaders of the American Revolution and the leaders of the Russian Revolution believed seriously that educating the young was a social and political priority. And yet, during the 20th century, there was little agreement about how to educate children. Both the United States and the Soviet Union established elaborate educational systems. And, for most of the century, American and Russian schools languished in an awful state. Americans first began to realize the dire condition of the nation's education system during World War I. The military conducted tests on its new draftees and discovered that two out of every five soldiers had below-average scholastic skills. The 1920s saw an influential movement to improve public schools, colleges, and universities. Thousands of new teachers and professors were hired. Curricula and textbooks were rewritten and emphasized the latest thinking about mathematics, science, history, politics, and economics. Soviet schools began a program of improvement following the death of Joseph Stalin in 1953.

There were significant limits, however, to educational reform in the early 20th century. In the United States, despite the improvements, African Americans were left out in the cold. By the 1920s, every state, except those states that had belonged to the Confederacy, had mandatory school attendance. Southerners refused to enact such a measure because it would have guaranteed a modicum of learning for blacks. In both the North and the South, school systems were segregated along racial lines. Simply put, the American educational system was separate and unequal. Furthermore, the sad fact was that African Americans were not the only group denied a basic education. American women of all races and ethnicities were deprived a decent education. Women, it was thought, were created for a life in the home. Therefore, their education emphasized home economics and not hard science, mathematics, politics, or history.

In America, change came in the 1950s. African Americans benefited from a U.S. Supreme Court ruling that declared segregated education unconstitutional. Likewise, women gained new access to education institutions because in 1964 Congress passed a law mandating equal educational opportunity for all Americans regardless of race, sex, color, or religion. Finally, educational improvement came as the federal government began to spend millions and then billions of dollars on schools and pupils. From Roosevelt's GI Bill to Eisenhower's National Defense Education Act to Johnson's Elementary and Secondary Education Act, the federal government became the primary supporter of education reform and funding. And yet, the challenges to provide a quality education with equality of access doggedly remained through the end of the century. Rather than solving the educational crises of the 20th century, reformers and politicians merely left them for the future to fix.

Education in the Soviet Union remained uneven despite attempts at reform. The disastrous results of World War II, the repression of the Soviet government, and the serious financial crises limited educational growth and opportunities.

In Japan, Africa, and the Inuit North, the struggle was to integrate traditional methods of education with Western educational ideas. After World War II, Japan largely emulated the American educational system and by the 1970s Japanese students were regularly outperforming their American and European counterparts. Nonetheless, critics of the Japanese system claimed that its emphasis on grades stifled creativity and imagination. The new nations of Africa sought to replace the educational systems left by the colonial powers, which tended to educate Africans only in ways that served colonial interests, with modern systems that promoted full political and economic advancement for the African people. By the end of the century, economic difficulties left this reform only partially complete. In the Inuit North, language was a major issue as the Inuit community tried to combine the continued transmission of Inuit culture with the educational mandates of the Canadian government.

INTELLECTUAL
LIFE

EDUCATION

United States,
1920-1939

United States,
1940-1959

United States,
1960-1990

Soviet Union

Japan

Africa

Inuit

UNITED STATES, 1920–39

Educating the younger generation was a task that parents and other elders confronted in every era. Once viewed as a family responsibility, by the start of the 20th century education had come increasingly to be seen as a matter in which the whole society had a stake to insure that young people became capable workers and good citizens. Mandatory school attendance laws intended to insure at least a minimum of literacy among a state's citizens appeared as early as the 1840s in New England. By 1900 compulsory attendance at public or private school was almost universal outside the states of the old Confederacy but nonexistent there—in large part because of white opposition to spending on black schools. Only in the era of World War I did states such as South Carolina, Georgia, and Mississippi adopt even weak school-attendance requirements. By 1920, 85.7 percent of 5- to 17-year-olds were in public or private schools, a proportion that would rise steadily over the next two decades to 95.5 percent by 1940. Nonpublic, mainly parochial schools accounted for 10 percent of total enrollment by 1940.

Although most young people during the 1920s and 1930s had at least some experience with school, the nature of that experience depended on who they were and where they lived. About 10 percent more nonwhite than white children did not attend school at all, due mainly to the woeful state of schools for African Americans in the segregated South. With schools funded predominantly from local resources, the length of the school year varied widely. In the poorest rural districts, the school year was as short as three months. At the same time the national average school year lengthened from 32 to 35 weeks, and student average attendance went from 25 to 30 weeks per year.

Segregation of schools was not unique to the South. Residential segregation together with the custom of neighborhood-based schools and carefully drawn school district lines meant that most children saw only other students of their own race. And although African Americans were graduating from teacher-training colleges, the racism of parents and school officials meant that white schools would not accept African American teachers. Therefore only African American students had the experience of teacher role models and authority figures who were African American.

Desire or need to enter the world of work as well as a sense of having gained all that one could from school led many students to make what from a later perspective seems like an early departure from school. Males left school a year earlier than females on average, and nonwhites left three years earlier than whites. As of 1920, only 17 percent of the population had graduated from high school, though that was nearly three times the percentage that had graduated at the start of the century.

A one-room schoolhouse in Grundy County, Iowa, 1939. The teacher is at the blackboard with the only second grader in class. © Library of Congress.

World War I sent shock waves through the United States regarding the inadequacy of its schools. In the midst of a severe manpower shortage, the country discovered that many young men were unfit for military duty because of inadequate education. Two of five recruits scored below average on the Yerkes Alpha Test designed to identify potential officers and weed out those unsuited for service. Often referred to as an intelligence test and used to argue that immigrants, blacks, and people from lower economic classes in general were incapable of higher reasoning and unworthy to participate in a democracy, the test was in fact a measure of the individual's education, particularly his schooling in English and mathematical reasoning. The need to improve American education became evident.

Nearly one in four students in 1920 attended a school in which there was only one teacher. Two hundred thousand such schools were spread across rural America, most notably in the South, where racial segregation further reduced the number of students gathered in any one school. Students often had to walk a mile or more to reach these schools. When they arrived, they were greeted by a teacher who had to provide instruction in all subjects at all grade levels. Many of these rural teachers had only a high school education, or less, themselves. The stock of schoolbooks and equipment was equally meager.

The 1920s saw a great movement toward school consolidation. The advent of the school bus made it possible to bring together in a central location students from a wide area. A consolidated school allowed teachers to concentrate on particular subjects or age groups. Busing permitted students to attend classes with others of the same age and ability. With enough students in one place to justify it, high schools in particular could offer a wider range of courses. The school bus became a symbol of significant educational improvement. By the end of the 1920s the number of one-teacher schools had fallen by a quarter and within another decade by almost half. Only Southern schools for African Americans, stifled by segregation and neglect, failed to share in the progress.

Consolidation raised expectations and rewards for teachers as their numbers grew from 700,000 to 912,000. At least a two-year course at a state teachers' college or normal school became standard, and, especially at the high school level, a four-year college degree became commonplace. Teachers began thinking of themselves as professionals. At the end of World War I only 1 in 70 teachers belonged to the National Education Association; on the eve of World War II nearly 1 in 4 did so. Salaries, never high in the predominately female profession, did nevertheless improve considerably, from an average of $871 annually in 1920 to $1,441 by 1940.

For students, the typical school day included a combination of study periods for reading textbooks, writing, and solving math problems and recitation periods. During recitation sessions students told their teacher what the book had said or how the problem should be worked out. Some progressive school systems were beginning to shift from a common, lockstep curriculum for every student to more individual instruction. Projects, in which a range of subjects such as mathematics, vocabulary, science, geography, and history might all be taught in combination as a part of a special inquiry into some topic such as ships, frogs, or Italy, began replacing recitation, especially at the elementary level. Most schools, however, either did not change their basic approach or went no further than the intermediate step of dividing students into slow, average, and rapid learner sections. Parochial schools changed more slowly than public ones. Textbooks became more colorful and attractive, more up-to-date, and more often supplemented by flash cards, workbooks, and filmstrips in schools that could afford them. However, all schools, as they grew in size, acquired administrative bureaucracies, adopted common practices, and became increasingly impersonal.

Larger urban or consolidated rural schools gave their expanding population of students with differing abilities and goals a more diverse range of courses from which to choose. English, history, math, and science remained at the core of the curriculum. The most notable expansion occurred in the area of vocational education. Agriculture, typing, home economics, and mechanical arts, such as woodworking and metalworking, received particular attention. Physical education, art, and music also increased.

Foreign language instruction, on the other hand, decreased, hard hit by the World War I concern that English become the universal American language. As late as the early 1920s, more than a quarter of all students learned Latin, 15 percent took French, and 11 percent studied Spanish, but those figures fell sharply over the next dozen years, and no other languages received much attention. With the foreign-born population decreasing as well, the United States had turned a corner on the path to becoming a society that overwhelmingly comprehended only English (Kyvig, 122–28).

To read about education in the United States in the 19th century, see the United States entries in the section "Education" in chapter 4 ("Intellectual Life") in volume 5 of this series.

FOR MORE INFORMATION

Cremin, L. *American Education, 1876–1980: The Metropolitan Experience*. New York: Harper and Row, 1988.

Kyvig, D. E. *Daily Life in the United States, 1920–1939: Decades of Promise and Pain*. Westport, Conn.: Greenwood Press, 2000.

Spring, J. *The American School, 1642–1993*. 3d edition. New York: McGraw Hill, 1994.

UNITED STATES, 1940–59

"No other idea has seemed more typically American," wrote Diane Ravitch, a historian of education, "than the belief that schooling could cure society's ills." In *The Troubled Crusade: American Education, 1945–1980*, she made a list of all the problems—from crime rates to unemployment, to ethnic differences, to health standards, to traffic accidents, to general morality—that most Americans placed at the door of public education. In a society that continued to pay teachers low salaries and to reward athletes and media stars with much more money than scientists and scholars earned, the government began to take greater responsibility for better education. Between 1944 and 1965, the United States was willing to spend $14.5 billion to educate its people.

The disparity between the elementary education offered the middle classes and that offered the poor emerged sharply during the war. Community differences in income meant sharp differences in the quality of education, determining whether children had books and paper to write on—or even chairs to sit on. When defense jobs offered new opportunities for better pay, many teachers in poverty-stricken communities simply quit. In the three years following Pearl Harbor, 11,000 out of 20,000 teachers in Alabama left their jobs. In Iowa 800 rural schools had no teachers at all. In 1947 the *New York Times* reported that 350,000 teachers had quit teaching for better jobs. Those who remained worked at salaries lower than those of garbage collectors. Twelve major teacher strikes took place after 1946, calling attention to the fact that both Russia and Great Britain spent more on education than Americans did.

Federal aid to education began to be considered essential to bringing about equality of opportunity for American children. By the mid-1940s even "Mr. Republican," Robert Taft, congressman from Ohio, would agree that "children were entitled not as a matter of privilege but as a matter of right to a decent roof, decent meals, decent medical care and a decent place in which to go to school." Astonishing to many was his conclusion—"Education is socialistic anyway."

After the war a variety of new schools—with some experimental programs—grew up in the midst of all the freshly built communities. Although the relaxed ideas of John Dewey's "progressive education" extended in many directions, debates were ongoing on the need for rote learning versus more imaginative programs. The same debates would continue into the 1990s—not only in Walt Disney's utopian town of Celebration, Florida, but in every community where parents became involved in what children needed to be taught to be civilized and productive members of society.

Funding for religious education came under renewed discussion. Because the GI Bill was sending people to all sorts of religiously oriented schools, and because lunches at every elementary school were also subsidized in the mid-1940s, it was hard to argue then that the separation of church and state was clear-cut. A 1947 Supreme Court decision even allowed public funds to be used for transporting children to parochial schools. But a strong anti-Catholic movement arose to limit such funding. Fear of church influence was ongoing. A book by Paul Blanshard attacking the intrusion of the Catholic hierarchy into public education went into 26 printings and remained on the national best-seller list for six months. Even Eleanor Roosevelt wrote in her "My Day" column in June 1949, "I do not want to see public education connected with religious control of the schools which are paid for by taxpayers' money." The issue of federal funding for education relating to the separation of church and state remains alive. The only federal money freely given at the time would be for local schools near military installations because such bases contributed no real estate taxes to subsidize the education of youngsters on base.

The postwar commitment to educating all the children in a democracy used the vocabulary of John Dewey's progressive education movement to define its goals. Such education stressed training in problem solving more than memorizing historical facts and arithmetic. Modern pedagogy favored projects, field trips, life experiences, and group learning instead of rote and drill to acquire knowledge. Although high school attendance went up by over 50 percent by 1950, such education was broadly attacked for lowering standards. The progressive faith, as Lawrence Cremin, another historian of education, described it, believed that "culture could be democratized without being vulgarized, and everyone could share not only in benefits of the new sciences but in pursuit of the arts as well." Yet narrow professionalism and anti-intellectualism often impeded such ideal goals. One of the most unfortunate results was a shift to "life adjustment" courses that taught little of substance and kept many young people—especially women and working-class students—in social grooves.

In 1947 the National Commission of Life Adjustment for Youth created state commissions to respond to a general demand for vocational or functional education. Simultaneously the study of foreign languages and the serious study of the history of past civilizations were considered less significant for everyone. Later decades would call this "dumbing-down" education. By the mid-1950s only 20.6 percent of American high school students would study a second language. And multiple-choice exam questions began to replace essay writing in tests that measured the critical-thinking skills students had mastered. Conservatives began to blame progressive education for all that was vacuous and anti-intellectual in postwar America. Before the decade was over strong debates would take place all over the country about what students should be taught. It must be an ironic comment on Americans' refusal to study the details of their history that the same intellectual debates recur at different times and people continue to argue about what is essential for everyone to know.

Even *Time* magazine ridiculed the frenzy for "life adjustment education" that seemed to absolve teachers from teaching and students from learning. A famous elite educator, Robert Hutchins, president of the University of Chicago, tried to define the direction general education in America should take: "Our mission here on earth is to change our environment, not to adjust ourselves to it." More specifically, Hutchins questioned how minds were to be trained. "Perhaps the greatest idea that America has given the world is the idea of education for all," he wrote. "The world is entitled to know whether this idea means that everybody can be educated or only that everybody must go to school."

After World War II, when liberal education—once available only to a privileged few—became available to everyone, educators had to consider attitude changes related to who was being educated, not just to what was being taught. The social texture of postwar America no longer resembled Thornton Wilder's small town, Grover's Corners. "Our Town" might be a trailer camp or a Levittown more often than a community of elm-lined streets.

Many vets chose more education over the immediate possibility of earning a living.

The most significant development in higher education related to the GI Bill. Specific entitlements offered returning soldiers the choice of a year of monetary benefits while job hunting or—more important for fulfilling the dream of human potential—a chance for paid higher education or additional training in skills that postwar America needed. As the gross national product expanded from $91.1 billion in 1939 to $213.6 billion in 1945 to $300 billion in 1950, 17 million new jobs had been created. Between 1944 and 1946 also, the six million working women who had done so well during the war were pressured to give up their lucrative jobs; four million either were fired or left voluntarily, offering returning vets a vast array of work opportunities. But many vets still chose more education over the immediate possibility of earning a living.

Instead of going to work, almost eight million veterans took advantage of the GI Bill to pursue the higher education they would not otherwise have been able to afford. The creation of a new educated class meant extending professional status to all sorts of ethnic newcomers in law and medicine and in the university. For the first time on a broad scale, colleges and universities became multicultural. Unfortunately, elitist admissions policies continued to work against blacks and women. But there can be no doubt that the expansion of all higher education in terms of huge enrollments and new buildings and new kinds of community colleges also opened doors wider for everyone, preparing the way for a more meritocratic society. Many people going to college after the war would become that first person in the family to get a higher degree. The government gave each veteran $65 a month ($90 to those with families) and $500 a year to cover tuition and books—adequate at most colleges at the time. State institutions felt a special mandate to meet the great need, expanding at new campuses—like Stonybrook in New York—and offering new courses of intellectual pursuits.

Conservative educators predicted the end of quality education in the great tides of mediocrity flowing into America's most famous institutions. They began to give attention to creating more complex entrance exams for the best universities. But after only a few years of experience with GIs in the classroom, many had to concede that maturity, motivation, and hard work often produced scholarship as competent as that of young people trained at prep schools. Instead of lowering standards, these older students forced educators to reassess their vision of America's potential. By the 1990s the State University of New York at Stonybrook, built only 40 years before, was ranked the third best public research university in the country.

The creation of more possibilities to get an education grew out of the great sense of need that was discovered during the war. A 1940 census revealed that only 2 out of 5 people in America had gone beyond the eighth grade; only 1 in 4 had graduated from high school; and only 1 in 20 went on to complete college. During World War II the government was so concerned about the low level of American education that it set up all sorts of additional training programs for soldiers: to help make illiterates literate, to teach foreign languages, and to train mechanics and builders in new electronics skills. The United States Armed Forces Institute set up courses in which more than 6,000 students enrolled during its peak. Many poor young men joined the army as a way to achieve the upward mobility that education promised. Indeed, the U.S. government spent $321 billion on education between 1941 and 1945, twice as much as in the entire preceding 150 years of its existence. Investing in education represented an ongoing belief in America's citizens—an affirmation of faith in the future.

When the army was officially integrated in 1948 such training was clearly extended also to African Americans. As early as 1944, Wendell Willkie, the Republican who ran against FDR in 1940, asserted that the war should make us conscious of the "contradiction between our treatment of the Negro minority and the ideals for which we are fighting." With the congressional establishment of the Women's Armed Services Act, also in 1948, the country acknowledged that women too were entitled to the same educational rewards offered men. Yet Americans learned slowly

> *Most institutions would not let women with families attend college part-time.*

that legalization may be just the first step toward achieving broader social goals. Fewer than 3 percent of the women eligible took advantage of this opportunity to educate themselves, and too many African Americans coming out of segregated schools did not have adequate preparation for higher education. Nevertheless, the GI Bill provided education for 50 percent of all the people who served in the armed forces. By 1956, when it ended, 7.8 million vets had taken advantage of its entitlements: 2.2 million (97% men) had gone on to college, 3.5 million to technical schools, and 700,000 to agricultural programs. In the academic year 1949–50, 497,000 Americans got university degrees—over twice as many as in 1940. No longer would higher education be seen simply as the proprietary right of the upper middle class. The quality of cultural experience had begun to change for everyone.

Even women began to see changes in their educational opportunities. Although larger numbers of women had begun to go to college in the 1950s, only 37 percent stayed to graduate, and the number going on for higher degrees was smaller than in the 1920s and 1930s. Yet women glad to sacrifice careers for family at the beginning of the decade were eager to get back to school by its end, even though most institutions would not let women with families attend college part-time. One brilliant Wellesley dropout, divorced with four children, was told that to return to college she would have to attend full-time and take gym.

Betty Friedan praised the few enlightened institutions that modified their degree programs to accommodate women with children. In 1955 the New School for Social Research set up a human relations workshop to help the homebound pursue broader goals. In 1959 the University of Minnesota set up a revolutionary program to encourage older women to get degrees. By 1962, when Sarah Lawrence College announced a grant to help mature women finish their education or get graduate degrees, the number of eager inquirers put their switchboards out of commission. Most adult education programs during this decade gave no credits and led nowhere—except in fields like nursing and teaching, where there were labor shortages. In these fields a few programs also met women's needs by scheduling classes during the daytime when children were in school. And some schools tried to make good use of women who already had bachelor's degrees by setting up master of arts programs in teaching.

"Unless we get more women equal education we can't get them equal pay and opportunity," declared the president of the Federation of Business and Professional Women in the *New York Times* in 1952, anticipating the idea of equal rights embodied in the *Brown* decision in 1954. Keeping women undereducated in the 1950s by maintaining quotas for the young and denying older women—often in their early 30s—admission to professional schools was also a way to keep establishment power in the hands of white men. When the Educational Testing Service at Princeton went on to design college-level equivalency exams to enable women students who had followed their husbands' jobs to write off credits, such exams were often not accepted by schools that relied heavily on Scholastic Aptitude Tests—produced by the same company—to evaluate the young. No one wanted to make it easy for women who were also mothers to do anything more with their lives. In 1956 the *New York Times* described a mother and daughter who were both getting degrees at Rutgers. The mother—also still taking care of her house and family and commuting—was "permitted" to take six courses to catch up. Another mother commuting from New Jersey to Brooklyn College three nights a week so she would not have to leave her children alone managed to graduate with Phi Beta Kappa honors. With a tone of amazement, the *Times* completed this story with her future plans for law school. Such "superwomen" stories made people pay attention to general concerns about what was happening to other bright women with complicated lives.

Perhaps just as embarrassing as the quota systems of the 1950s that kept women out of competition with men for professional jobs was what was called sex-directed, gender-focused education. Mills College in California, trying to compensate for the indifference of Eastern establishment schools to talented women faculty, defined gender education that would cater to women's needs. Unfortunately, like the high schools that fostered functional education, these colleges often ended up emphasizing "life adjustment" rather than intellectual achievement. Categories of experts—sociologists, psychologists, and psychoanalysts—banded together to persuade women to believe they were better off in the role of housewife. As noted sociologist Talcott Parsons described the American woman, her life was as "her husband's wife, the mother of his children." At a time when the Cold War made Americans critical of progressive education designed to foster good judgment and problem-solving skills rather than rote learning, women were urged back into functional feminine molds, not developed as critical thinkers.

Although progressive education, expressing the ideas of the great pragmatic philosopher John Dewey, reached back to the 1930s, it became another target for the paranoia of the 1950s. All sorts of local groups thought such education responsible for Marxist ideas and juvenile delinquency. In 1951 in Pasadena Willard E. Goslin, a creative progressive educator and president of the American Association of School Administrators, was pressured by organized right-wing groups to resign. In the same year the American Association of School Administrators chose to devote its entire annual meeting to examining widespread assaults on public education. Anxiety produced best sellers like *Educational Wastelands* (1953) and *Why Johnny Can't Read and What You Can Do About It* (1955). But few new programs emerged. Successful schools long influenced by progressive ideas continued to produce well-trained, creative students. And Dr. Spock, whose child-rearing classic was in almost every home with children during this era, did not hesitate to label his book a "commonsense" guide to child care. "Trust yourself," he urged new mothers.

In 1957, when the Russians sent two *Sputnik* satellites to circle the globe, a huge outcry went up for more serious education that would improve standards for everyone. Americans confronted the reality that in Russia 69 percent of the medical students and 39 percent of the engineers were women, whereas in the United States in 1956 three out of five women in coeducational colleges took secretarial, home economics, nursing, or education courses. Only 20 percent of all science and math majors in American colleges were women. A 1957 book, *Signs for the Future*, prepared by a varied group of educators, urged greater flexibility in admissions and scheduling and use of educational television, adult education, and refresher courses to enable more women with children to come back into a more high powered career stream. The Cold War concern that we had fallen behind the Russians inspired Congress to pass the National Defense Education Act in 1958, allotting over $900 million for scholarships and loans to encourage the study of science, math, and foreign languages. This act also provided 12,000 counselors for secondary schools. Although the pendulum seemed to be swinging back to conservative education, with the subsequent creation of a huge number of community colleges (one every two weeks by the mid-1960s), many child-free women as well as young men were given the chance to begin entirely different lives. The flexibility of our institutions was helping us turn away from what Betty Friedan had labeled a culture that educates its most capable women to make careers out of raising their families. Again the government was helping the individual find human fulfillment.

The importance of the GI Bill in enriching institutions and changing old-fashioned educational environments cannot be overestimated. Not only did the army of new learners not diminish academic standards, as feared, but the presence on campus of older students able to make mature judgments also worked to erode sophomoric customs like fraternity hazings and wearing freshman beanies. Older students were presumed to be wiser. The idea that college discipline replaced the parent—strong before World War II—began to erode by the 1960s, when parietal rules and dress codes became quaint memories. Who could even imagine that women at Radcliffe College, going to classes at Harvard, were not permitted to wear pants on the streets of Cambridge, Massachusetts? Wellesley students had to leave their dormitory doors open while entertaining men. Because so many men everywhere also returned to college with wives, married women were slowly tolerated as part of the learning environment (Kaledin, 64–68, 106–9).

To read about education in the United States in the 19th century, see the United States entries in the section "Education" in chapter 4 ("Intellectual Life") in volume 5 of this series.

FOR MORE INFORMATION

Cremin, L. *American Education, 1876–1980: The Metropolitan Experience*. New York: Harper and Row, 1988.

Kaledin, E. *Daily Life in the United States, 1940–1959: Shifting Worlds*. Westport, Conn.: Greenwood Press, 2000.

Ravitch, D. *The Troubled Crusade: American Education, 1945–1980*. New York: Basic Books, 1983.

Spring, J. *The American School, 1642–1993*. 3d ed. New York: McGraw Hill, 1994.

UNITED STATES, 1960–90

The most striking changes in education in the early 1960s affected adults, who enjoyed new opportunities in higher and continuing education. A burst of enrollment in higher education had followed the GI Bill in the years after World War II. Of 14 million persons eligible, 2.2 million veterans jumped at the chance to have their college tuition paid as partial compensation for their military service. Eventually, nearly 8 million took advantage of the Bill's educational benefits. This set the stage for continued growth of colleges and universities in the 1960s. In states with rapid population growth the expansion was breathtaking. In Florida, for example, where in the early 1940s there had been one university for men, one for women, and one for blacks, along with one public junior college, by 1972 there were nine public coeducational universities and 28 community colleges.

The demand for such institutions increased in part because of the enrollment of women. Nationwide, the proportion of women in college populations grew from around 33 percent in 1960 to more than 40 percent a decade later. The increased enrollment of both women and men was served mainly by the establishment and enlargement of public institutions. In 1940 about 47 percent of the 1,494,000 students enrolled in colleges and universities were in private, denominational, or sectarian institutions. By 1970 the enrollment reached 7,136,000, with nonpublic institutions serving only 28 percent of the total.

The establishment of community colleges—160 between 1960 and 1966—opened doors for many young people and brought back to school adults seeking to acquire new knowledge and skills. In the five years preceding 1968, enrollment of full-time students in community colleges increased from 914,000 to 1,909,000, and part-time enrollment rose from 489,000 to 888,000. Priding themselves on the comprehen-

siveness of their offerings, community colleges enabled students to lay the ground-work for transferring to four-year institutions or to equip themselves for better jobs by enrolling in two-year vocational programs. Community colleges also provided credit and noncredit continuing education courses of almost limitless variety, some of them designed to improve job opportunities, some for intellectual and artistic growth.

Mario Savio, a founder of the Free Speech Movement, leads a campus protest at the University of California, Berkeley, 1966. © Bettmann/CORBIS.

In those same years of educational growth, school admin-istrators, board members, and teachers wrestled with such issues as minimum competency testing, community advisory councils, programs in "values clarification," bilingual edu-cation, and questions about textbooks. In their student pop-ulations were some judged to be at-risk, others gifted and talented, and still others learning disabled (a term used ini-tially in 1963). For those judged to be learning disabled, that designation most likely meant separate classrooms, in that mainstreaming was not yet a part of schools' responses or vocabularies.

Moreover, until the 20 years of enrollment growth ended in 1970, school administrators faced overcrowded schools and classrooms. Predictably, but with seeming suddenness, enrollment problems shifted into reverse in 1971, as a long downward spiral began. Soon decisions over which schools to close became battles between neighborhoods within school districts. Convenience of location was one issue. The perception that an empty school building signaled neighborhood decline was another.

School administrators as well as teachers, students, and parents had to deal with schools' perennial scarcity of funds. A snapshot of the budget picture of schools in 1970–71 reveals their plight. In that year, about 52 percent of the $39.5 billion spent to operate public elementary and secondary schools was raised by local taxes, typi-cally on property; 41 percent came from state taxes on sales, income, and property; and 7 percent came from the federal government under a variety of programs. A report on school finance showed that in 1970 voters approved only 48 percent of school bond issues, compared with 81 percent a decade earlier. In other words, as the public increased its demands on schools it also became more reluctant to foot the bill. Unequal distribution of dollars among schools and school districts caused another budgetary problem: where the tax base was low, so was tax revenue, and the schools suffered. Poor children attended inferior schools. Court decisions over the next several years achieved only limited success in equalizing the resources of school districts.

The other major issue educators, parents, and students dealt with was school desegregation. In some parts of the country, school districts with racially segregated schools had for more than a decade defied the Supreme Court's 1954 ruling in *Brown v. Board of Education* that such schools had to be eliminated. They changed school boundaries, redrew bus routes, and offered "voluntary choice" programs to perpetuate segregation. A series of Supreme Court rulings, however, particularly one in 1968, declared that the federal courts would insist on proof of racial integration in areas that formerly had segregated their schools by law. In 1971 the Court upheld busing of schoolchildren as a means to achieve racial balance where segregation still had official local sanction and where school authorities had not offered acceptable alternatives to busing. By 1976, as a result of court orders, 77 percent of black schoolchildren in the South attended schools that had at least 10 percent white students.

In 1972 the Court ruled that segregated schools resulting from residential segregation must be treated as the result of deliberate public policies, just as if they had been segregated by law. Such schools were judged to be in violation of the Constitution, and remedies to eliminate segregation were required. Busing and the creation of magnet schools—schools offering special programs in the arts or the sciences, for example—were the most common remedies. "Pairing" schools was another remedy, with a portion of black students bused to a predominantly white school and vice versa. School desegregation proceeded slowly, partly because many families moved to avoid sending their children to newly desegregated schools. So-called white flight meant that neighborhood populations changed swiftly and dramatically, and desegregation plans had to be updated almost yearly. Thoughtful persons wondered aloud why the task of desegregating society was being given mainly to children, but where they were given a chance, the children showed they were capable of making desegregation work.

Desegregation posed many challenges. Children of both races found themselves in classrooms with other children from whom they had been taught, or even required, to keep their distance. Teachers encountered children who had been denied solid educational opportunities and who therefore had difficulty meeting their expectations. Administrators were compelled, often against their personal wishes, to design desegregation plans and make them work. Parents worried about the effects of desegregation on their children and often resisted it passionately. In Charlotte, North Carolina, for example, the Parents Concerned Association vowed to boycott schools if busing plans were implemented. "I'm willing to go to jail if I have to," one parent said. Even if board members and community leaders supported school desegregation, they had to cope with the resistance of citizens who did not.

But the simple and obvious truth was that the only way to eliminate schools attended solely by black children was to enroll those children in schools with whites. Controversies over school policies, court decisions, and legislative and executive actions at both state and federal levels aimed at desegregation continued throughout the 1970s. Some of them became violent. A much larger effect of the Supreme Court's decisions, as well as of decisions by lower courts, was that color consciousness and sensitivity to group identities came to permeate virtually all decisions in schools, particularly in urban districts.

By the 1980s, conservatives had found a way to challenge school desegregation plans that required children to attend schools in neighborhoods other than their own. Since the Brown decision in 1954, some Americans saw desegregation as a threat to a seemingly sacred neighborhood-school concept. By the 1980s, however, some parents wanted to choose their children's school with less regard for its location. *School choice* became a popular phrase. For some, this meant giving parents tax monies to send their children to private schools. Others simply wanted to send their children to schools across district boundaries. The practice of allowing students to attend out-of-district schools gained acceptance, but using tax funds for sending children to private schools was tried on a very limited basis and almost always challenged in the courts.

Conservatives also challenged school textbooks. In a number of school districts, particularly in Southern states, parents identifying themselves as Christian and conservative found certain textbooks objectionable. In Hawkins County, Tennessee, for example, a number of parents removed their children from public school reading classes because the textbooks offended their religious beliefs. A lower court ruled in their favor, but an appeals court asserted in 1987 that neither the books nor the classes violated religious freedom guaranteed by the First Amendment. A district court in Alabama allowed the banning of 44 history, social studies, and home economics textbooks on the grounds that they promoted "the religion of secular humanism." Promoting moral behavior without reference to God, claimed the lower-court judge, made humanism a religion, and using books that lacked information on Christianity and other religions advanced godless principles that also amounted to a religion. The judge's rulings were reversed by a court of appeals, also in 1987, but that did not change the sentiments of the 600 fundamentalist parents, students, and teachers (or those of Alabama's former governor, George Wallace) who had initiated or supported the lawsuit that brought the case to trial (Marty, 51–52, 159–67, 309–13).

To read about education in the United States in the 19th century, see the United States entries in the section "Education" in chapter 4 ("Intellectual Life") in volume 5 of this series.

FOR MORE INFORMATION

Cremin, L. *American Education, 1876–1980: The Metropolitan Experience*. New York: Harper and Row, 1988.

Marty, M. A. *Daily Life in the United States, 1960–1990: Decades of Discord*. Westport, Conn.: Greenwood Press, 1997.

Ravitch, D. *The Troubled Crusade: American Education, 1945–1980*. New York: Basic Books, 1983.

Spring, J. *The American School, 1642–1993*. 3d ed. New York: McGraw Hill, 1994.

INTELLECTUAL
LIFE

|

EDUCATION

|

United States,
1920-1939

United States,
1940-1959

United States,
1960-1990

Soviet Union

Japan

Africa

Inuit

SOVIET UNION

From the start, the Bolsheviks' educational vision was very ambitious. The new government's Commissariat (ministry) of Education, from 1917 to 1929 under the direction of Anatolii Lunacharskii, quickly laid plans to provide the huge, mostly dirt-poor and illiterate population with education that was free, universal, coeducational, and compulsory (from ages 7 to 17), with equal opportunity for higher education. The dream was not realized in Lunacharskii's lifetime, however. Set back by the devastating consequences of war and revolution, the Commissar's efforts were stymied by extreme shortages of schoolroom space, books, and equipment. Children used pieces of coal or chalk to write on cooking pans, boards, their desks, the school's stove, or pages ripped from old journals. Teachers, always on pitifully low salaries, were expected to devote many unpaid hours per week to social work. In rural areas, a single teacher might well have to teach all grade levels in a one-room schoolhouse without heat or plumbing. Throughout the 1920s, the pupil absentee and dropout rate was very high: in 1926 the average schoolchild finished with only 2.77 years of education. Nevertheless, by that same year the literacy rate was up to about 51 percent of those age nine and older.

At the start of the 1920s, Lunacharskii oversaw the creation of remedial schools for workers (rabfaki). Located in or near factories, rabfaki gave basic instruction in reading, writing, and arithmetic and usually had an affiliation with a university or some other institution of higher education. Nikita Khrushchev was among the millions of workers who attended the rabfaki. The last such school closed in October 1941. For peasants, who tended to have even less book learning than urban workers, the government established schools called likbezy, or circles for the elimination of illiteracy.

From its beginnings in 1917 into the early 1920s the Commissariat of Education experimented with and encouraged a variety of progressive educational methods aimed at developing and educating the whole child. Lunacharskii envisioned an educational environment in which children worked cooperatively in groups without the constraints of tests, grades, or textbooks. Academic subjects such as literature, math, and science would be studied not as separate disciplines, but in the context of themes such as farming and other national and local concerns. These liberal ideas included generous amounts of time devoted to creative arts and class discussions rather than lectures. Children were to venture frequently outside the schoolroom walls into their communities as observers and helpers. Corporal punishment was prohibited, and parents and children were to have a strong voice in running their schools.

At the university level, the Commissariat mandated similar experiments: there were orders to abolish the traditional lecture method of presenting information; all classes were to become laboratories of political discussion; anyone (except members of exploiting classes) could go to college without having to show a high school diploma or even registering, and students could graduate without having to take finals. Doctors, construction engineers, and other so-called professionals without real qualifications were loosed upon the country while established universities and other higher-education institutions were deluged with academically unqualified students. New institutions of higher education with questionable credentials sprang up around the country. Then, in response to educational chaos and public resentment, the pendulum began to swing back. In 1922 the government ordered all college-level students to officially register; those without a high school certificate could register only at rabfaki, not at universities; exams were restored for those preparing for professions; graduates once again received diplomas; many newly created universities closed down.

At the primary and secondary school levels, Lunacharskii's reforms were not widely or systematically carried out by teachers and principals who far preferred a traditional approach with regular classroom hours, schoolbooks, lectures, dictation, memorization, and homework. Parents were also hostile to the unfamiliar methods of progressive education. Under Stalin, school management, teaching methods, and curricula were hauled back under central authority and educational experiments were officially squelched. Teaching returned to the traditional European system: formal exams; strict, regimented classroom atmosphere; authoritarian teachers; centrally prescribed courses of study; lectures; much memorizing; compulsory homework; a five-point grading scale; and school uniforms. The uniforms were bus driver–gray pants and jacket, white shirt, and peaked cap for younger boys and dark dresses, dark pinafores (white pinafores for special occasions), white collars, and big white hair bows for primary school girls. Older boys and girls wore blue uniforms with white shirts and the red neckerchiefs of the Young Pioneers youth club.

The constitution of 1937 guaranteed everyone the right to an education, but for many that entitlement ended after fourth grade, when children had to pass rigorous exams to continue. But it wasn't just the exams that forced children, especially rural children, out of school. Many factors worked against them and their teachers. During the famines of the 1930s, rural children and teachers suffered from hunger and starvation. Children's farm labor was needed and exploited. After Stalin's death in 1953, the government abolished the fourth-grade winnowing exams and raised the number of compulsory school years to eight. Especially in the countryside, however, school administrators often allowed their charges to drop out before eighth grade.

In the mid-1930s Stalin decreed that children of "alien social elements" (the former priesthood, nobility, the bourgeoisie, prosperous peasants, and political arrestees) should be admitted to schools, but severe discrimination against them continued. At about the same time, thousands of teachers were among those arrested, deported, or killed during the Great Terror of the 1930s. During World War II, an untold number of teachers died and some 82,000 schools were destroyed. Despite the catastrophes, by 1939 the literacy rate was 81 percent, up from 51 percent in 1926, and by the mid-1960s, illiteracy was probably at most 5 to 10 percent (many classified as literate had completed four years or less of school). In 1940 low tuition fees—discontinued in 1956—were introduced for students in the upper grades of secondary school and university-level students (Eaton).

FOR MORE INFORMATION

Eaton, K. B. *Daily Life in the Soviet Union.* Westport, Conn.: Greenwood Press. Forthcoming.
Grant, N. *Soviet Education.* Harmondsworth, England: Penguin Books, 1964.
Jacoby, S. *Inside Soviet Schools.* New York: Hill and Wang, 1974.

JAPAN

The Japanese educational system has recently been the topic of heated debate. In the 1970s it was praised because Japanese students routinely test higher in mathematics and natural science than their American and European counterparts. An astounding 95 percent of students graduate from high school and the nation enjoys 98 percent adult literacy in a very difficult written language. More recently, however, domestic reformers have suggested that the system stifles student creativity, imagination, and critical thinking.

The system is similar to Western educational systems. In the Meiji era (1868–1912) and again during the Allied Occupation (1945–52) Japan emulated the American system of six grades of elementary school and six of secondary school. What is different is that after the first nine years, about 20 percent of Japanese students are tracked into vocational and industrial training. The remainder must pass difficult entrance exams to enter high school and then college. Most attend after-hours private cram (*juku*) schools where they prepare for those exams. Critics argue that this extra study leaves little time for children to mature socially and point to a serious bullying (*ijime*) problem in middle school as a symptom of social pressure. Also, many contend that the exams themselves are too stressful and can lead to psychological problems such as social withdrawal and even suicide.

Japanese children attend school for nearly six weeks longer each year than their American and European counterparts and must endure long hours of moral education in an attempt to inculcate good character traits. Almost all students receive at least five years of English-language instruction, but the curriculum emphasizes grammar and vocabulary, which is part of the strenuous English section of high school and college entrance exams at the expense of aural and oral skills, which are not tested.

Japanese schoolchildren listen to Colombia's Hector Sierra, creator of Artists Without Borders. © AP/Wide World Photos.

Until recently students attended school for half-day instruction on Saturday. That has been phased out, but cram schools have absorbed that time so students do not benefit from the reprieve.

Attempts at reform have been stifled by powerful teachers' unions and by the more conservative political parties. They argue that Japanese society is justly proud of and content with the education of its citizens. A few private schools have mushroomed, notably those that employ the Montessori method; these schools cater to the needs of children who have lived abroad.

Virtually everyone graduates from college once they have gained entry because very little is required of them by their instructors. Only about 7 percent go on to graduate school (compared to 13 percent of the American cohort). Entrance into one of these graduate schools virtually guarantees good employment. The five or six top universities supply the bulk of employees for the most important companies and government ministries. In some ways, students mature socially in college because it is here that they create lifelong networks that benefit them throughout their social and professional careers.

To read about education in early modern Japan, see the Japan entry in the section "Education" in chapter 4 ("Intellectual Life") in volume 4 of this series.

~*Louis G. Perez*

FOR MORE INFORMATION

Dore, R., and S. Mari. *How the Japanese Learn to Work*. New York: Routledge, 1989.

Schoppa, L. J. *Education Reform in Japan: A Case of Immobilist Politics*. London: Routledge, 1991.

AFRICA

For untold centuries, African societies have relied on traditional methods of education, using such community-based methods as tribal proverbs, initiations, and transfer of wisdom from one generation to the next to explain the laws and customs of their society as well as pass on agricultural and trade skills. Although traditional African education did not take place in a classroom, African children learned the culture and heritage of their society and their place within that society, allowing them to grow up and fulfill their required roles responsibly and effectively.

Islam had also penetrated parts of Africa from the 8th century C.E. and continued to spread across the continent over time. Along with the acceptance of Islam came Qur'anic schools, in which pupils would memorize the Islamic holy text and gain an understanding of the social requirements of the religion.

Christian missionaries brought yet another form of education to Africa. Missionary schools have existed in Africa since at least the 17th century and until the early 20th century were the only institutions of Western education in Africa, as European governments had made little effort to provide education to the African masses, even after the onset of colonial rule around the turn of the 20th century.

These forms of education, with their roots in precolonial Africa, have persisted throughout the 20th century and into the present day. However, during the 20th century, a competing model of education complicated the social makeup of Africa, and consequently the goals and aspirations of African education.

After World War I, European colonial governments began to take some initiative in providing Western education directly to Africans. Although each colonial power, be it Great Britain, France, Belgium, Portugal, Germany, or Italy, instituted its own specific form of Western education, many characteristics were held by all. The colonial education system focused on standard European education practices, largely disregarding the function of traditional African education. For instance, colonial schools focused heavily on teaching European languages to Africans rather than their own indigenous languages. Likewise, African students were taught European literature and history, which did little to help socialize African children into African society.

European colonial governments cared very little about this, because preservation of African heritage was not the goal of providing Western education to Africans. Quite the contrary, the ultimate goal of colonial education in 20th-century Africa was to create a small class of educated Africans who would serve the colonial machine, helping the European countries to rule the African population. Thus, Western education was essentially an attempt to socialize a small number of Africans into a European lifestyle.

The colonial education system was by no means interested in educating the majority of Africans. Primarily, Africans were needed to maintain unskilled positions in agriculture, mining, and the like, thereby perpetuating the colonial system of economic exploitation. As a result, the colonial education system was highly underdeveloped. Primary schools were the most prevalent educational facilities in Africa, and these focused mainly on educating the population in the language of the European occupier. Higher-learning facilities were very scarce. For instance, in Nigeria in 1952, enrollments in secondary schools were 2.9 percent that of enrollments in primary schools. In Kenya, the corresponding figure was 2.1 percent (Datta, 18). As of 1945, Fourah Bay College in Sierra Leone was the only university in sub-Saharan Africa (South Africa excepted) that offered a degree program recognized in European countries (Scanlon, 12).

Even though colonial powers attempted to keep the African population under-educated, these plans eventually backfired. Many Africans came to recognize that the only way to become successful in the colonial system was to receive a Western education and enter the colonial bureaucracy. As a result, a larger portion of the population began clamoring for the expansion of education facilities in the years after World War II. The Western-educated elite class often led these activists. Recognizing the poverty in which most of their people lived, and also understanding the limitations of their own professional advancement in the inherently racist colonial system, Western-educated Africans began to rally for increased educational opportunities and the extension of other social services.

Colonial administrations responded by expanding educational facilities. For instance, the number of recognized colleges in sub-Saharan Africa rose from 1 in 1945 to 18 by 1962 (Scanlon, 12), but the writing was on the wall. African peoples, particularly the Western-educated elite, were not going to settle for anything less than full independence, including the control of their own education systems.

From the late 1950s through the 1960s, most African countries achieved their independence. The new African administrations recognized the need to Africanize the outdated colonial education system. First, this meant rapid expansion of facilities, because it was believed that a better-educated African population would help the newly independent nations thrive politically, economically, and culturally. Second, education officials instituted Africanization of the curriculum. This meant moving away from courses in European history and literature to focus more on the history and culture of Africa itself, as well as a revitalization of indigenous African languages, instilling a sense of pride in African youth about their heritage that had been neglected and suppressed during the colonial era.

These first years after independence marked the golden age of African education. However, it would not last. Due to economic hardships caused by conditions in international markets, lingering European control of African resources, and often rampant corruption within African governments themselves, many African countries have fallen on hard times since the 1980s. As a result, educational facilities cannot be maintained and are falling into disrepair. International nonprofit organizations have offered some relief for this situation, but overall the 20th century in African education ended much like it began, with inadequate attention given to state-run institutions of Western education, although a larger percentage certainly attend public schools than did so in the past. Along with Islamic and Christian missionary schools, there also remains a continued reliance on traditional methods of education, meant to prepare African children to live in a uniquely African society.

To read about education in Africa in the 17th and 18th centuries, see the Africa entry in the section "Education" in chapter 4 ("Intellectual Life") in volume 4 of this series.

~Matthew Heaton

FOR MORE INFORMATION

Datta, A. *Education and Society: A Sociology of African Education*. New York: St. Martin's Press, 1984.

Falola, T. *Nationalism and African Intellectuals*. Rochester, N.Y.: University of Rochester Press, 2001.

Scanlon, D. G., ed. *Traditions of African Education*, New York: Bureau of Publications, Teachers College, Columbia University, 1964.

INUIT

Formal education was an issue of deep concern to contemporary Inuit and a place where differences in cultural values were exposed. Eben Hopson (1922–80), the first mayor of Alaska's North Slope Borough, fought to establish the borough in large part so that North Slope Inuit would have control over their children's educations. Not only did many Inuit feel that schooling offered for Native children was inadequate and often inappropriate given the social and economic environment, but until that time most Alaska Native villages had only grade schools. Children who wanted to attend high school were required to attend a boarding school. Hopson himself had been denied the opportunity to attend high school by Bureau of Indian Affairs officials after Hopson had protested the mistreatment of Inuit students on the North Slope.

Most Alaska Native villages obtained high schools only after 1976 following a class action lawsuit claiming that the lack of high schools in Native villages, but not in similarly sized non-Native communities, constituted discrimination. The discrimination case, which is known as the Molly Hootch case, was settled without trial, with the state of Alaska agreeing to establish a high school in every rural village that requested one. A state-operated boarding school remains as an option for Alaska's rural students.

Boarding schools were more widely used in Canadian North, where the federal government was very late in establishing day schools for Inuit children. During the 1950s and early 1960s Canadian Inuit as young as seven or eight were sent to government boarding schools for nine months of the year. There, as well as at earlier church-run boarding schools, children were punished for speaking Inuktitut, the Inuit language, and as a result, children sometimes returned home unable to speak their own language.

Language remains a contentious issue in northern schooling. Although today there are bilingual education programs in parts of Alaska and Canada, only in Greenland and in Labrador was schooling in Inuktitut provided to Inuit from the start. Northern Quebec provides an extreme example. There, the Canadian federal government rather than the province provided schools for Inuit until the mid-1970s, when Francophone nationalists won provincial elections. As part of their mandate, they determined that French rather than English should be the language of instruction for Inuit and other Native Canadians. When Inuit parents protested the imposition of French language, the provincial government responded with riot police. Eventually, as part of their land claims settlement, Inuit in northern Quebec won the right to form an independent school board, which established Inuktitut as the language of instruction in the earliest grades. In Nunavut, also, the first years of schooling are now conducted in Inuktitut.

The situation in Greenland is somewhat different. There schooling has always been in Inuktitut, or Kalaallisut, as the language is called in Greenland. Fluency in Danish, and sometimes English, is required for students who want to pursue university degrees or technical training. Although Danish is provided as a second language, many parents feel that their children's opportunities will be better if they learn Danish and have sought improved Danish instruction for their children. Others, fearing that Inuktitut will become a second-class language, have opposed moves to strengthen Danish instruction.

In Canada few Inuit have had the opportunity to pursue university degrees, and there are no true universities in the Canadian north. A teachers' training college has been in Greenland since the middle of the 19th century, but only in 1983 was the Inuit Institute, a precursor to the University of Greenland, established as a degree-granting institution. The University of Alaska operates branch campuses in a number of Native communities and has pioneered distance delivery for university instruction. Ilisagvik College, operated by the North Slope Borough, offers both technical and university courses. Since the late 1990s, the international Arctic Council has worked to establish the University of the Arctic, a sort of university without walls to meet the needs of northern populations.

~Pamela Stern

FOR MORE INFORMATION

Alaskool. <http://www.Alaskool.org/default.htm>.
Vick-Westgate, A. *Nunavik: Inuit-Controlled Education in Arctic Quebec*. Calgary: University of Calgary Press, 2002.

Literature

The emergence of the United States as a world power coincides with the rise of American literature. Perhaps this is coincidental. For the preceding two centuries, writers living in the United States had worked in the shadows of others. Indeed, the

INTELLECTUAL LIFE

LITERATURE

Europe
United States, 1940-1959
United States, 1960-1990
India
Islamic World
Soviet Union
Japan
Inuit

215

19th century had been the era of Victorian writers such as Charlotte Brontë, Charles Dickens, George Eliot, Elizabeth Gaskell, Thomas Hardy, and Anthony Trollope. But following World War II, American writers ran out from backstage and into the limelight. And, although other authors, such as Solzhenitsyn, have shaped many currents in 20th-century literature, many American authors, such as J. D. Salinger, Betty Friedan, and Jack Kerouac, remain internationally known and even household names today.

In the 20th century, American literature developed several main themes. First, writers struggled to find their place in the world. Authors such as Salinger, Kerouac, and their fellow Beat writers described the alienation that they felt living inside such a materialistic society. Another related theme was self-realization. Jewish and African American writers focused on what it meant to be a minority in the world's most powerful and often most flawed democracy. Key among the group of Jewish writers were Saul Bellow, Bernard Malamud, Delmore Schwartz, Philip Roth, and Isaac Bashevis Singer. African American luminaries such as Ralph Ellison and James Baldwin continue to be the touchstone for investigations into modern black identity. It is critically important to note that though all of these authors discuss what it meant to be a minority in the United States, their writings also dealt with what it meant to be an American generally. The third theme that emerged from postwar American literature was the emphasis on other times and other worlds (i.e., science fiction and fantasy). By staging their novels and short stories in places other than the 20th-century United States, people like Ray Bradbury were able to talk about the rise of far-right-wing politics and the effects of repressive governments.

Another hallmark of the 20th century was a decline in the numbers of Americans reading books, magazines, and newspapers. In part, one can attribute this historical development to the rise in other types of media such as television and the Internet. But no matter how distracted Americans became by other media, there was no denying the impact of this decline. Newspapers and magazines around the nation went bankrupt and disappeared. The newspapers that survived often emphasized style over content, like *USA Today*. Moreover, another reason for the decline in reading could be a general increase in anti-intellectualism. One of the best-selling books of 1988 was Robert Fulghum's *All I Really Need to Know I Learned in Kindergarten*. As the century came to a close, there were signs that the nadir in reading had been reached and the trend was reversing, particularly among children. Yet television, especially TV-based video games, and the Internet strongly competed for their time too.

Despite the prominence of American literature, by the end of the century many other countries were developing vibrant literary traditions. Indian literature flowered in the late 20th century producing important works in many languages and many forms. Islamic literature, which has a long and glorious history, also had a rebirth in the 20th century producing many well-received novels and dramatic works especially on political topics tied to the Arab-Israeli conflict. Japanese literature also achieved international standing during the century especially for novels and poetry, while the story of Soviet literature is a tale of overcoming ongoing repression and censorship.

EUROPE

Twentieth-century European literature was significantly affected by the numerous political, cultural, and economic upheavals of the period, including two world wars, widespread depression, and dramatic shifts in government from imperialist empires to republics, totalitarian dictatorships, and democracies. Already suspect in Victorian times, traditional Western values were seriously challenged by modern writers, who were also confronted with changing religious norms and the evolving social constructs of class, race, and gender. European consumers in this era were presented with a diversity of popular new venues—variety theaters, cabarets, cafés, salons, cinemas, television, and radio—and new narrative forms—literary periodicals, pulp fiction, and paperbacks mass distributed by major publishing houses. Modern writers, disillusioned with older literary conventions, pursued fresh means of expressing these varied social experiences, which coalesced in a variety of literary movements, so numerous and rapid in their evolutions that, though often discussed in terms of discrete trends, are best understood as inextricably intertwined and interdependent.

Although aspects of 19th-century Realism were to persist in European literature after 1900, notably in the poetry of Arno Holz (1863–1929) and Detlev von Liliencron (1844–1909), in war stories of authors such as Erich Maria Remarque (1898–1970, *All Quiet on the Western Front*) and much later in the *tremendismo* novels of Spain, for the most part the century can be characterized by its antinaturalistic modern trends. The Spanish peninsular Generation of 1898 poets, including Antonio Machado (1875–1939), and the French Impressionist poets, such as Charles Baudelaire (1821–67), wrote of nature as a key to the world of sensation rather than as a determining force. This significant break with Naturalism is echoed in the work of the German Symbolists, Stefan George (1868–1933), Hugo von Hofmannsthal (1874–1929), and Rainer Maria Rilke (1875–1926), who, like the sculptor Auguste Rodin and the painter Paul Cézanne, attempted to reveal not visible naturalistic phenomena but rather the invisible longings of the human spirit and soul. The work of Italy's great Symbolist poet, Giovanni Pascoli, and the pure sentimental poetry of the French Symbolists, Stéphane Mallarmé (1842–98), Arthur Rimbaud (1854–91), and Paul Verlaine (1844–96), are reminiscent of the lyrics of Paul Valéry (1871–1945) and Paul Claudel (1868–1955), who attempted a kind of *synaesthesia*, a style that combined the sound of music with the symbolic language of poetry, which they believed revealed an almost religious relationship between things and ourselves.

Guillaume Apollinaire (1880–1918), while approving of the magical aspect of literature, protested against the Symbolists' *l'art pour l'art* detachment and their highly self-conscious use of language with the literary style of Surrealism. The Surrealist movement, so indebted to Freud's exploration of dreams and the unconscious, was rooted in the conviction, upheld by such authors as André Breton (1896–1966) and Paul Eluard (1895–1952), that the real domain of the poet is outside reason, probing the incomprehensibility of the ordinary world. During the closing years of World War I several Surrealists, such as the Romanian-born Tristan Tzara (1896–1963), broke away from others to form a group of young poets and painters in Zürich, the Dadaists, which included Hugo Ball (1886–1927) and the visual artists Georg Grosz (1893–1959), Hans Arp (1887–1966), and Kurt Schwitters (1887–1948). Like the Italian Futurists under Filippo Marinetti, the Dadaists used the technology of sound and linguistic fragments to rebel against conventional forms of art and constructed meaning itself.

The Symbolists, Surrealists, and Dadaists all resisted what they felt were the crude voices of the cities audible in the concrete language of the Expressionists. This new Expressionist vision, pervading the apocalyptic urban images of Jacob van Hoddis (1887–1942), Georg Trakl (1887–1914), Georg Heym (1887–1912), and Gottfried Benn and the extreme dramas of Frank Wedekind (1864–1918) and August Strindberg (1849–1912), revealed repressed emotions and the unseen horrors of the war experience. The outstanding talents of poets such as William Butler Yeats (1865–39), born in Ireland, and the younger poet T. S. Eliot (*The Wasteland*, 1922), born in the United States, joined these testimonies of the World War I experience in expressing the despair and alienation of modern life, a theme reflected later in Federico García Lorca's (1899–1936) anguished poems of urban dehumanization and the loss of myth. This period also witnessed the evolution of the modern novel, heralded by the intellectual novels of Thomas Mann (1875–1955) and Ramón Pérez de Ayala (1880–1962); the Surrealist novels of Benjamín Jarnés and Franz Kafka (1883–1924); the picaresque novels of Juan Antonio de Zunzunegui (1901–82); the proletarian novels of Alfred Döblin (1878–1957); the sensuous novels of D. H. Lawrence (1885–1930) and Gabriele D'Annunzio (1863–1958); and the social novels of Vilhelm Moberg, Ivar Lo-Johansson, and Cesare Pavese. While Marguerite Duras (1914–96) and Alain Robbe-Grillet (b. 1922) perfected the antipsychological *nouveau roman*, the Bloomsbury Group, which included the Irishman James Joyce (1882–1941, *Ulysses*) and Virginia Woolf (1882–1941, *Mrs. Dalloway*), mastered the psychological novel and the technique of interior narration, a modernist style Marcel Proust was already practicing in his semiautobiographical cyclic novel, *Remembrance of Things Past* (1913–27). Controversial in both its stream-of-consciousness style and explicit language, the modern novel constituted a revolution in narrative prose.

> *The modern novel constituted a revolution in narrative prose.*

The experience of World War II, as with World War I, indeed shocked the literary and artistic world and shook Europe, which lost many great writers. Writing itself became a dangerous act under the repressive fascist regimes of the 1930s and 1940s, which were intent on censoring all forms of dissension and avant-garde content. Although some attempted resistance during wartime occupation, most serious authors who were to survive did so either by going into exile or by undergoing an "inner emigration," by taking their creativity underground. By the end of World War II, the so-called zero hour, countless works had been destroyed in public book burnings, and numerous authors, such as Spain's Jorge Guillén (1893–1984) in the Spanish Civil War, opposed their dictators and fled their homelands. After Hitler's defeat, German writers such as Wolfgang Borchert (1921–47), Heinrich Böll (1917–85), and Günter Grass (b. 1927) and Austrians in the Vienna Circle related the sense of dislocation and the psychological alienation of the returning soldier, whereas other poets, Primo Levi (1919–87), Günter Eich (1907–72), and Paul Celan (1920–70), probed the depths of the death camp experience. Ingeborg Bachmann (1926–73), Magnus Enzensberger, and Nelly Sachs also rejected the more popular turn toward escapist consumerism prevalent in the 1950s with a similar commitment to confront the events of Germany's recent past.

Postwar Europe was dominated by a sense of fragility and angst epitomized by the Existentialist writings of Jean-Paul Sartre (1905–80, *Nausea*), Albert Camus (1913–60, *The Stranger*), Spain's Fernando Arrabal (b. 1932) and Ireland's Samuel Beckett (*Waiting for Godot*), long considered, along with the Romanian Eugene Ionesco (1909–94) and Czech-born Tom Stoppard (b. 1937), to be the greatest and perhaps bleakest dramatists of Existentialism and the Theater of the Absurd. With sensitive compassion and deft sense of humor, Existentialist writers highlighted the simultaneous anxiety and sense of freedom and self-determination inherent in all acts. The works of the Swiss dramatists Friedrich Dürrenmatt (1921–90) and Max Frisch (1911–91) and Dámaso Alonso, who initiated Spain's Existentialist movement in the 1940s, explore such existential moments facing all human beings. Writers as diverse as Simone de Beauvoir (1908–86), Miguel de Unamuno (1864–1936), José Ortega y Gassett (1883–1956), Iris Murdoch (1919–99), and John Fowles are also counted among the Existentialists. With the exception of poets such as Francis Ponge, Jacques Prévert, and to some extent the Welsh poet Dylan Thomas, Existentialism remained best known as a movement of drama and prose rather than of poetry.

W. H. Auden and Christopher Isherwood, less taken with notions of nothingness and the absurdity of human existence, believed instead in the revolutionary potential of literature and its ability to effectuate political change. The epic theater of Bertolt Brecht (1898–1956), with its reliance on alienation, used parables and ballads to bring the social reality of those lacking a cultural voice, the soldier, the worker, and the unemployed, into sharper relief. Brecht later inspired the documentary style of Peter Weiss (1916–82), Erich Fried (1921–88), and Wolf Biermann (b. 1936), among many. Eastern European writers, such as Christa Wolf (b. 1929), Anna Seghers (1900–83), Sarah Kirsch (b. 1935), and Bernd Jentzsch (b. 1940), were positioning themselves vis-à-vis the dictates of Socialist Realism, the only literary style accepted by the State throughout the Eastern Bloc until the late 1980s, excepting occasional periods of "thaw," such as the short-lived "Prague Spring" (1968), notable for the popularity of Milan Kundera's (b. 1929) novels and the antigovernment plays of Václav Havel (b. 1936), later elected president of the Czech Republic in 1993. Soviet-based governments in the East considered Western cultural influences as "formalist" and "decadent" and not suitable to the building of a strong Socialist state. The Frankfurt School, notorious for its influential aesthetic theories critical of capitalist culture, included the philosophers and sociologists Theodor W. Adorno (1903–69), Herbert Marcuse (1889–1979), Max Horkheimer (1895–1973), and Jürgen Habermas (b. 1929) and the essayist and literary critic Walter Benjamin (1892–1940). Having moved into exile for most of the war, the Frankfurt critics returned to Europe afterward with a renewed commitment to demonstrate the contemporary relevance of Marx's historical materialism, which was rooted in the belief that all cultural institutions and ideas are structured foremost by economic forces. Though they dominated literary studies for many decades, their impact on literary criticism began to wane with the fall of Communism in the early 1990s.

The traditional heavy industrial base of European society in the last decades of the 20th century yielded to a more consumer-oriented society in which computer and communication technologies extended the reach of marketers and barraged readers with a tremendous influx of information. One effect of this ubiquitous electronic and nuclear age was to force authors to radically rethink the fundamental assumptions of Modernism. Poststructuralists and Deconstructionists, such as Roland Barthes (1915–80), Jacques Lacan (1901–81), Michel Foucault (1926–84), and Jacques Derrida (b. 1924), declared the very notions of meaning and self to be not stable, intentional constructs, but rather merely unstable fluid linguistic structures. For Postmodernists, ascribing to deconstruction, there is no grounded knowledge, no knowable self, no essence, no universal truth, no national boundaries, only a loose assemblage defined by a privileged spectator's gaze. Language is a labyrinth, as Jorge Luis Borges and to some extent Peter Handke (b. 1942), Italo Calvino (1923–85), and Vladimir Nabokov (1899–1977) would suggest. Although Postmodernists have abandoned the Modernist faith in literature's depth and its ability to save us from effacement by the cold institutions of modern life, their belief in the absence of true boundaries has also resulted in the expansion of interdisciplinary approaches to literature and the inclusion in the literary canon of a much wider range of multicultural and postcolonial texts both from within and beyond the continent. Contemporary European authors, writing in the tensions of a newly formed European Union (EU), amid the superabundance of images, styles, fragmentary sensations and simulacra (to use Jean Baudrillard's term), continue to renew the essentially utopian impulses on which literature ultimately relies—its depth, authenticity, and originality.

~Jennifer Ham

INTELLECTUAL
LIFE
|
LITERATURE
|
Europe

FOR MORE INFORMATION

Bede, A., and W. B. Edgerton, eds. *Columbia Dictionary of Modern European Literature*. New York: Columbia University Press, 1980.

Travers, M. *An Introduction to Modern European Literature: From Romanticism to Postmodernism*. New York: St. Martin's Press, 1998.

UNITED STATES, 1940–59

Two classical war novels, James Jones's *From Here to Eternity* (1951) and Norman Mailer's *The Naked and the Dead* (1948), remain testimonies to the fighting men of the time as well as skeptical statements about the nature and necessity of war. After *From Here to Eternity* became a movie in 1953, Frank Sinatra, who had been blacklisted for using an allegedly Communist songwriter, won an Academy Award, which allowed him to make his comeback as a singer. Norman Mailer believed the writer's role was adversarial. As one of America's most gifted authors, he would go on to record a panorama of his country's social dilemmas before shifting to a more allegorical style. Of special interest in connection with the 1950s view of war are the stories of Kay Boyle, whose short fiction documents the rarely articulated lives of members of the Occupation Army and their army wives.

If Mortimer Adler thought his series of the Western world's great books would continue to determine the best tastes, he was mistaken. Educated readers began to heed a richer variety of viewpoints. The self-consciousness that emerged from the postwar search for identity no longer neglected the writing of women and people of color—even as talent remained the 1950s criterion for judgment. After the war a great curtain lifted on the literary scene, revealing a tremendous operatic chorus of new and gifted performers.

The most common generalization about postwar fiction, connecting it with social criticism, is that it is a literature of alienation. Fifties writers depicted individuals who no longer feel part of any community. J. D. Salinger's *Catcher in the Rye* and Jack Kerouac's *On the Road* describe wayward lives seeking release from the material goals of civilization. Whether American teenagers—or all teenagers—have often felt such alienation is worth discussion. Herman Melville's Redburn and Mark Twain's Huckleberry Finn, and even Louisa May Alcott's Jo March, were not comfortable members of their own societies. In 1996, some 40 years after its initial publication, *On the Road* sold 110,000 copies, demonstrating that it was clearly not a book for just one decade. In the 1950s young women writers Carson McCullers, Flannery O'Connor, and Jean Stafford used a growing awareness of independent womanhood to express individual skepticism about social institutions.

Jean Stafford, Eudora Welty, Elizabeth Spencer, and Flannery O'Connor—all proud 1950s writers—made much of place in shaping their characters. During this period many powerful Southern writers emerged, following the earlier examples of Allen Tate and William Faulkner, to demonstrate that regional consciousness could teach much about the broader human condition. The plays of Tennessee Williams and Lillian Hellman; the stories of Truman Capote, Gore Vidal, William Styron, Walker Percy, Shelby Foote, and Shirley Anne Grau; and the poetry of Randall Jarrell and Robert Penn Warren helped keep the South a source of creativity. The only defeated section of the United States continued to offer the country impressive talent, adding to the national awareness of class as well as alienation. Searching for different levels of personal identity, the decade's literature offered a rich variety of complex individual worlds rather than established political contexts. The "dissidence from within," as the critic Richard Chase described it, may be "our most useful tradition." "In what other mood," he asked, "has the American mind ever been creative, fresh or promissory of the future?" Like Norman Mailer, Chase believed that American writers often worked best in opposition to the mainstream culture.

Women writers distinguished by their work in other decades—Edna Ferber, Gertrude Stein, Fannie Hurst, Pearl Buck, Katherine Anne Porter, Elizabeth Bishop, and Marianne Moore—produced some of their best writing during this period. Mari Sandoz's classic biography *Crazy Horse: The Strange Man of the Oglalas* was recognized as one of the best serious books on the West in 1954. Although few women would have labeled themselves feminists during the 1950s, they nevertheless found writing a source of power. Shirley Jackson became a popular writer who managed to capture both the humor and the anxiety involved in domesticity. As her 1947 classic story "The Lottery" was suggestive of the danger of modern witch hunts, so her 1950s stories explored the deep anxieties of homebound women.

A ladies' literary club in Irwin, Iowa. © National Archives.

In his celebration of the next decade, *Gates of Eden: American Culture in the Sixties* (1977), Morris Dickstein attacked the writers of the 1950s for being too concerned with the "elusive mysteries of personality" and too involved with "craft, psychology, and moral allegory"; yet readers must question whether these qualities do not continue to fortify the human spirit in ways that political attitudes may not. The three-volume unabridged collection of Emily Dickinson's poetry appeared in 1955, suggesting how profound a writer could be without needing to mention the Civil War she lived through. In 1955 another elusive novel of American adventure on the road, Vladimir Nabokov's allegorical classic *Lolita*, was published in Paris. After rejection by five American publishers and much public protest, the story of the older man's obsession with a young girl would be in bookstores in the United States by 1958, on its way to the best-seller list. By the 1990s *Lolita* would be accepted as a classic. Students of the 1950s fantasizing about what books to take to a desert island or what to read during a long stay in outer space could find a huge variety of satisfying choices to deepen every level of consciousness.

Many of the women writers of the 1950s tackled the social and political issues of the day—even as they delved into personal domestic lives for material. Grace Paley, Tillie Olsen, Hortense Calisher, Harriette Arnow, and Mary McCarthy offered outright challenges to the current definitions of women's roles. The great angry poets of the next decade—Sylvia Plath, Anne Sexton, Adrienne Rich, and Denise Levertov—were all writing away in the 1950s as they took care of their babies. Rich and Levertov would write their roles more specifically as political voices. Craft surely need not exclude awareness of the importance of social change.

Grace Paley and Harriette Arnow made social involvement part of the definition of being human. Gwendolyn Brooks, Ann Petry, Paule Marshall, and Lorraine Hansberry emphasized the distinguished tradition of black women, using their own culture to write about feminism and humanism. Hansberry could imagine a black heroine going to medical school at a time when the idea seemed preposterous. Brooks could write a poem about a journalist witnessing the horrors of Little Rock. In 1950 she won the Pulitzer Prize for poetry. Later Gwendolyn Brooks would be named poetry consultant to the Library of Congress, a job more recently redefined as poet laureate.

Strong writers from prewar days were still writing for a large audience. John Steinbeck, John Dos Passos, Eugene O'Neill, and Ernest Hemingway made their opinions heard. In 1952 Steinbeck wrote Adlai Stevenson, the defeated Democratic candidate, "If I wanted to destroy a nation I would give it too much." In 1954, two years after he published *The Old Man and the Sea*, Hemingway won the Nobel Prize for a lifetime of carefully crafted writing about human courage.

Two of the decade's great men of letters were African Americans. Ralph Ellison and James Baldwin emerged during the 1950s as writers of special evocative skills—not as polemicists. The intensity of their articulation of experiences as black Americans expanded the consciousness of many white readers and inspired a growing tradition of 20th-century black writing. Playwright Lou Peterson's *Take a Giant Step* opened in 1953 to warm reviews, remaining off-Broadway for 264 performances. These black artists did not write solely to help African Americans recover their identity. They were well aware of the distinguished writers still on the scene in the 1950s—Richard Wright, Langston Hughes, W. E. B. Du Bois, Zora Neale Hurston, and Jean Toomer. To be sure, many of their insights into the human condition cannot be separated from their color. But as black culture extended into the next decades, black writers spoke to more Americans of every color about the quality of American life. "You are white," Langston Hughes had written, "yet a part of me as I am part of you."

On Broadway a bowdlerized version of Anne Frank's diary helped remind audiences of why they had fought World War II. The 1950s became a liberating period for a new generation of American Jewish writers. Saul Bellow, Bernard Malamud, Delmore Schwartz, Philip Roth, and even Isaac Bashevis Singer, who wrote in Yiddish and whose novels were translated into English, spoke to many kinds of Americans in much the same way that Jewish American filmmakers had done at an earlier time. At this moment, when Jews and Catholics were beginning to be accepted on the faculties of elite colleges, gifted Jewish culture critics also emerged to explore their own roles in American civilization. Thinkers like Philip Rahv, Irving Howe, Lionel Trilling, Alfred Kazin, Norman Podhoretz, Diana Trilling, and Leslie Fiedler not only contributed original interpretations of American culture but also celebrated their personal—often ambivalent—success as they became more American than Jew. They too questioned the good life.

By the 1950s earlier immigrant consciousness was melting into everyone's postwar identity dilemmas. Heroes of contemporary novels, with a sense of ambivalence about all their choices in life, belonged as much to John Updike and John Cheever as to Bellow, Roth, and Malamud. J. D. Salinger's character Seymour Glass is more Buddhist than Jewish. And Kerouac's Catholics also turn to the Zen religions of the East. Norman Mailer would not have been placed with other Jewish writers at the time, nor would Adrienne Rich. Finding out who you were remained one of the exciting mind games of the 1950s, a period when complexity was cherished. The 1947 Broadway musical *South Pacific*, enormously popular throughout the decade and adapted as a movie in 1958, made identity dilemmas seem easy to resolve as *Abie's Irish Rose*, a mixed-culture drama, had done during the vaudeville era. Assimilation remained an attainable ideal in many of James Michener's successful 1950s novels. *Sayonara* (1957) and *The Bridges of Toko-Ri* (1954) also spread Michener's commitment to tolerance to the movies.

A few talented writers opted to drop out of society by becoming part of a drug culture that rejected connections with conventional communities. William Burroughs published *Naked Lunch* in Paris in 1959; Nelson Algren, *The Man with the Golden Arm* in 1947 and *A Walk on the Wild Side* in 1956.

Science fiction writers captured some of the most real social dilemmas of the time in books—as they were doing in original television dramas. Ray Bradbury published his classic on book burning, *Fahrenheit 451*, in 1953—the year before Joseph McCarthy was censured by the Senate. Andre Norton used intergalactic conflict to highlight human values, while Ursula Le Guin and Madeleine L'Engle began writing science fiction that appealed to both children and adults. In 1957 four of the best science fiction writers of the decade—Cyril Kornbluth, Robert A. Heinlein, Alfred Bester, and Robert Bloch—gained respect by lecturing at the University of Chicago.

Writing for young people has been another way for talented individuals to express ideas in a broader context. Helping children adapt to a new postwar world as they developed strong egos and an understanding of democratic choice were a number of distinguished writers who should be honored by the entire society—not just by the readers who award medals to writing for children.

Books for young people such as Jean Latham's on the doctor Elizabeth Blackwell and the biologist Rachel Carson not only described women who played roles outside the home but also stressed how they dealt with setbacks. In the 1950s Ann Petry and Dorothy Sterling both wrote about Harriet Tubman, the fugitive slave who helped many other slaves escape, making the point that black children had too long been deprived of knowledge of the bravery of their own forebears. And Elizabeth Yates wrote about Prudence Crandall as a pioneer in school integration at a time when many people, ignorant of the American past, believed such dilemmas began with the *Brown* decision in 1954.

Ann Nolan Clark's long experience in the Bureau of Indian Affairs enabled her to remind 1950s young people of the dignity of the Native Americans' nontechnological civilizations. Rachel Carson introduced children to the wonders of nature by educating their parents in elementary terms about the wilderness resources that many ignored at the time. "When I have something important to say," Madeleine L'Engle wrote, "I write it in a book for children." The 1950s baby boom may have made children especially visible, but it remains important for historians to be aware of the range of American myths—and realities—in books created for the young. Libraries have long played an underrated role in children's education, even as they have had to compete with schools for resources and with television for attention. During the 1950s special library rooms for children appeared in many places where mothers worked as library volunteers. And many children discovered E. B. White. *Stuart Little* had been a reading pleasure since 1947 and *Charlotte's Web* appeared in 1952 to the delight of Americans of all ages.

The poetry of the 1950s flowered in the midst of consumer delights. Not only did new poetry reflect the expanding consciousness of specific social groups, but a variety of experimentalists appeared, evoking America on many other levels.

Older poets basked in their honors. Robert Frost continued to give readings that celebrated New England as a metaphor for the human soul. T. S. Eliot continued to manicure his British conscience. Marianne Moore, Louise Bogan, and Elizabeth Bishop published collections of distinguished work during the 1950s. And William Carlos Williams continued to produce volumes of *Paterson*. Wallace Stevens, vice president of a Hartford insurance company, managed to offer the decade several magical volumes, and the hospitalized fascist sympathizer Ezra Pound continued to write *Cantos* of distinction. e. e. cummings also gathered together a summary of his life and work. And John Berryman began to celebrate sonnets.

Gifted young poets emerging at the time included Donald Hall, Richard Wilbur, John Ashbery, Randall Jarrell, Delmore Schwartz, Charles Olson, James Merrill, May Swenson, Denise Levertov, Sylvia Plath, and Adrienne Rich. Frank O'Hara helped shape a school of poets in New York City, and the Poets' Theatre flourished in Cambridge, Massachusetts. Yale University continued to offer gifted unpublished poets the opportunity to see their words in print. Perhaps the general prosperity made it possible for the great variety of new talents to take chances as poets. Visitors to America—chosen home of another great poet, W. H. Auden—could easily assume that this was a country that took poetry seriously. Too often historians who do not read poetry tend to neglect the cultural vitality of these times.

> *Poet Allen Ginsberg preached love to stunned audiences while taking off his clothes.*

Indeed, Robert Lowell, the best-known new American poet during the 1950s, quickly made his way into the academic canon, even as he extended his self-awareness into the confessional mode that would characterize much of the next decade's writing. With his solid New England ancestors and obvious talent, Robert Lowell sought a more complex identity in the 1950s. As he exposed his manic depression and his family's quirks in his poetry, Lowell gave permission to a new generation of younger poets to set aside traditions and be themselves.

The most outrageous poet of the decade, Allen Ginsberg would remain identified with the Beat community and their hostility to law and order. As he shocked his listeners Ginsberg insisted on being the heir to Walt Whitman. A poem called "Supermarket in California" addresses Whitman as "lonely old courage teacher" and asks the great poet to tell us where we are going. When Ginsberg read his famous long poem "Howl" in 1955 in a converted auto repair shop, the San Francisco City Lights Bookstore crowd greeted him with foot-stomping enthusiasm. By 1992 the City Lights quarto edition of Ginsberg's *Howl and Other Poems* would be in its 40th edition, with 725,000 copies in print.

The Beats insisted that they stood for more than rebellion against the world of comfort and conformity. They too were trying to define the good life as they expanded America's consciousness. During the 1950s and 1960s Allen Ginsberg preached love to stunned audiences while taking off his clothes or playing finger cymbals for interminable amounts of time. Identifying with Buddhism even though one of his most famous poems, "Kaddish," was a Jewish prayer for his dead mother, Ginsberg joined Salinger in the long American tradition of looking East for philosophical wisdom. In the dedication to "Howl" he called Jack Kerouac the "new Buddha of American prose" and asserted that Neal Cassady's biography enlightened Buddha. A distant neighbor in Paterson, New Jersey, William Carlos Williams, wrote a brief introduction to the text, recognizing that "this poet sees through and all around the horrors he partakes of."

Writing of America, wondering if his country would ever be angelic, Ginsberg wanted his love to show. Yet his disappointments spoke to many of his followers even as his gentle spirit transcended the vocabulary that shocked. By the early 1980s Allen Ginsberg had become so respected as a representative of America's counterculture that the State Department sent him all over the world as an ambassador of freedom.

When Ginsberg died in 1997 his poetic vigor and personal kindness were honored in every community where poetry mattered. Harvard professor Helen Vendler noted that Ginsberg was a liberator. For many young people, Vendler suggested, Ginsberg offered "the first truthful words ever heard." "How beautiful is candor," his American ancestor Walt Whitman had written—allowing Allen Ginsberg to continue a legacy of free expression touching every social and erotic experience.

"The real question"—asked by a dying friend of writer Grace Paley and included in the dedication to her collected stories—"How are we to live our lives?" was asked many times during this decade. The 1950s offered up no easy answers. Levittowners, black urban migrants, atomic scientists, victims of blacklists, and victims of quotas in professional schools—all struggled to define themselves in an affluent world that offered many the freedom Allen Ginsberg represented. Artists in other media also found that this moment offered time to explore new ideas and individual talents (Kaledin, 155–62).

To read about literature in the United States in the 19th century, see the United States entries in the section "Literature" in chapter 4 ("Intellectual Life") in volume 5 of this series.

FOR MORE INFORMATION

Chase, R. "Our Country and Our Culture (Part 3)." *Partisan Review* (Sept./Oct., 1952): 567–69.

Hart, J. D. *The Oxford Companion to American Literature*, 6th edition. New York: Oxford University Press, 1995.

Kaledin, E. *Daily Life in the United States, 1940–1959: Shifting Worlds*. Westport, Conn.: Greenwood Press, 2000.

Literature and Culture of the American 1950s. <http://Dept.English.upenn.edu/~afilreis/50s/home.html/>.

Patterson, J. T. *Grand Expectations: The United States, 1945–1974*. New York: Oxford University Press, 1996.

Rybczynski, W. *Waiting for the Weekend*. New York: Viking, 1991.

UNITED STATES, 1960–90

Newspapers had difficulty competing with television for readers' time. The *Washington Star* shut down in 1981 and the *Philadelphia Bulletin* in 1982; also in 1982 nine newspapers located in all parts of the country merged their morning and evening papers into single morning or all-day publications, resulting in the loss of one kind of coverage or another. In 1985 the 131-year-old *St. Louis Globe-Democrat* folded when a new owner could not rescue it from bankruptcy. At the end of the decade the *Los Angeles Herald Examiner* and the *Raleigh Times* (North Carolina) ceased publication, and the evening *Kansas City Star* was absorbed by the morning *Kansas City Times*.

Perhaps the biggest change in the newspaper business occurred in 1982 when the Gannett Company, owner of a chain of dailies, launched *USA Today*. This national newspaper made explicit attempts to compete with television as a primary source of news. Boxes dispensing it on street corners displayed the front page in windows that looked like television screens. News reports and features were brief and crisply written, and pictures, often in color, were more plentiful than in other newspapers. The fast-glimpse qualities of *USA Today* inspired critics to compare its fare with that offered in fast-food restaurants. McNews, they called it. Within the next several years Gannett also acquired a number of major newspapers, including the *Detroit News*, the *Des Moines Register*, and the *Louisville Courier-Journal* and *Louisville Times*. Although Gannett-owned newspapers maintained individual identities, they also reflected traits displayed most prominently by *USA Today*, such as the shortened news reports, and readers detected a loss of local flavor in the papers' coverage.

Following *USA Today*'s lead, other newspapers printed more pictures in color and abbreviated their reporting. Perhaps this enabled them to remain a staple in the life of the two-thirds of American adults who read them daily. Only one in five of the readers spent more than 30 minutes with the daily paper, and they tended to be older and better educated. Meanwhile television continued to grow as the main source of news for the American people, partly because the network anchors seemed like authoritative guests in many homes, and partly because of the news coverage of CNN.

Big-circulation magazines intended for general audiences saw their sales slump as their traditional readership was aging and dying. Smaller, more precisely targeted magazines fared better, as did some fashion magazines. The wide range of choices, symbolic of postmodern conditions, no doubt encouraged browsing rather than selecting one magazine and staying with it. Reflecting the get-rich climate of the times, *Forbes*, one of the nation's leading business magazines, saw its circulation grow and the median age of its readers move downward.

By the end of the 1980s total book sales approached $15 billion, double the amount recorded at the beginning of the decade. Much of publishers' revenue came from the works of best-selling authors. Stephen King landed 10 horror novels on best-seller lists during the decade, and Danielle Steele eight romances. Sometimes outstanding works like Umberto Eco's *The Name of the Rose* and Toni Morrison's *Beloved* also became best sellers, promising to become classics.

In 1982, readers of established classics by American writers welcomed the appearance of eight handsome, sturdy, meant-to-last volumes in the new Library of America series. Published in the first year were works by Walt Whitman, Herman Melville, Harriet Beecher Stowe, Nathaniel Hawthorne, Jack London, Mark Twain, and William Dean Howells. Admirers of such best sellers as Robert Fulghum's *All I Really Need to Know I Learned in Kindergarten* (1988) would contend that these were classics, too. The very fact that there were such best sellers alleviated fears that books would be crowded out of people's lives by television and computers. So did the continued popularity of children's books—longtime favorite writer Theodore Geisel published two more Dr. Seuss best sellers—since children who grow up with books are more likely to be serious readers as adults (Marty, 280–81).

To read about literature in the United States in the 19th century, see the United States entries in the section "Literature" in chapter 4 ("Intellectual Life") in volume 5 of this series.

FOR MORE INFORMATION

Hart, J. D. *The Oxford Companion to American Literature,* 6th edition. New York: Oxford University Press, 1995.

Marty, M. A. *Daily Life in the United States, 1960–1990: Decades of Discord.* Westport, Conn.: Greenwood Press, 1997.

Patterson, J. T. *Grand Expectations: The United States, 1945–1974.* New York: Oxford University Press, 1996.

Rybczynski, W. *Waiting for the Weekend.* New York: Viking, 1991.

INDIA

Literature in India dates back to the Vedic period (1500 to 500 B.C.E.). During this time priests memorized and orally transmitted different prayers, chants, formulas, and stories that were for the first time written down. These early works are the Vedas. The language used was Sanskrit, which literally means perfected. The oldest of the Vedas is the Rig Veda. It depicts war scenes, chariot racing, and consuming a magical drink called Soma that gave a pleasing sensation.

Near the turn of the millennium, India's two great epics came into existence, the *Mahabharata* and the *Ramayana.* In the latter, Rama (an incarnation of the deity Vishnu) is deprived of his royal throne and forced into exile in the forest. There he spends his time with his wife, Sita, the model Indian woman. A demon captures Sita, and Rama engages him in an epic battle on the island of Sri Lanka. Eventually, Sita is rescued and Rama is returned to his throne. These stories depict great battles, heroic figures, gods, and demons. To this day, parents and politicians alike use these widely read epics to teach morals and values. In the early 1990s, the *Ramayana* was aired on television, and during that hour each week, much of India came to a standstill as people flocked to watch the latest episode.

By the early 4th century, a poet named Vatsyana composed the famous manual on pleasure, the *Kama Sutra. Kama* means pleasure and *sutra* literally means thread, but *Kama Sutra* was also a short, easily memorized couplet or phrase that provided the learner with some instruction. At the same time, in the deep south of India, other literary works were being composed in Tamil, one of India's many indigenous languages.

When Islam came to the Indian subcontinent in the early 8th century, Persian became the language of government, and different Islamic rulers (sultans) patronized Persian poetry. In the military camps of this time, a new language was being born.

Persian speakers mixed with indigenous Indian language speakers, and Urdu was born. *Urdu* means camp. Since that time, many writers and poets used Urdu as their medium, and the language continues to thrive both within India and as the national language of Pakistan.

In 1498, the Portuguese sailor and trader Vasco da Gama rounded Africa's Cape of Good Hope, and after securing assistance from a Muslim navigator, he made his way across the Arabian Sea to India. Da Gama ushered in a new era in India's literary history as other Europeans followed him.

By the 18th century, the British East India Company installed itself in Calcutta. With the company came the use of English, and the printing press. The dissemination of English gave rise to a group of young Bengalis who became fluent and were the first generation of Indians to write in English. Among these were Raja Rammohun Roy (1772–1833), who was fluent in not only English, but Bengali, Persian, and Sanskrit as well.

The printing press allowed for drastic changes in India's literary history. First, it allowed for newspapers, pamphlets, and books to be printed in volume and their message to be understood by many. Frequently, one person read a newspaper or book aloud and many others gathered to listen. Early nationalists such as Roy, and later Bankim Chandra Chatterjee (1838–1894,) made use of print technology. Whereas Roy was a proponent of ending *sati* (widow immolation), Chatterjee used his pen to depict India as a motherland and call for an end to British rule.

At the same time, printing presses were developed to use local Indian languages. This allowed for works in Tamil, Telugu, Bengali, Urdu, and Hindi to be printed. Writers in those languages found new audiences and newfound success with the spread of print technology. Printing also allowed reference works such as dictionaries to be compiled. British officials used these as they struggled to learn and master local Indian languages.

Further, as English and print technology spread, so too did different forms of literary expression. English medium schools helped introduce the novel, the sonnet, and the poem. In 1913, Rabindranath Tagore won the Nobel Prize for literature. Tagore was from Bengal and had had a wide exposure to different literary forms. With Tagore were other famous literary figures including Muhammad Iqbal (1877–1938), whose works in Urdu and Persian focused on nationalistic themes as well as devotion to God and self-improvement. Both Tagore and Iqbal are still widely read.

Many literary works about India come from authors who have not called India home. For example, Paul Scott's quartet, *The Jewel in the Crown*, and its coda, *Staying On*, depict India at the height of the British Empire, and later follow up with those few who stayed on after the end of the raj.

The latter half of the 20th century saw a flourishing of literary figures in India. Raja Rao won international acclaim for his novel *The Serpent and the Rope*. A parade of well-known Indian authors writing in English have followed him. Rohinton Mistry (*A Fine Balance*, *Such a Long Journey*) and Gita Mehta (*Raj*) continue to produce fiction while Vikram Seth enthralled the literary world with his mammoth work, *A Suitable Boy*. In 1998 Arundhati Roy's *The God of Small Things* became an international best seller and catapulted Roy into a career blending literature, activism, and politics.

Bookshops and bookstalls are part of every town and city market. Students read the epics, works from India's colonial period, and more recent fiction. A high school student might read the *Ramayana* one semester and Shakespeare's *Hamlet* the next. Presses throughout the country continue to publish important literary works in local languages. Thus, India's literary history and practice continue to be rich and diverse, supported by a variety of forms, languages, and experiences and kept alive by a wide variety of authors and poets alike.

To read about literature in ancient India, see the India entry in the section "Literature" in chapter 4 ("Intellectual Life") in volume 1 of this series.

~*Benjamin Cohen*

FOR MORE INFORMATION

Chaudhuri, A., ed. *The Picador Book of Modern Indian Literature*. London: Picador, 2001.

ISLAMIC WORLD

INTELLECTUAL LIFE
|
LITERATURE
|
Europe

United States, 1940–1959

United States, 1960–1990

India

Islamic World

Soviet Union

Japan

Inuit

The colonial period in the Arab world—the region stretching from the Persian Gulf to the Atlantic Ocean, most of which had been part of the Ottoman Empire since the 17th century—began with the French invasion of Egypt in 1798. The French occupation of Egypt lasted only three years, but in 1830 France annexed Algeria, then occupied Tunisia and Morocco in 1912. Spain occupied parts of Morocco in 1886, and Italy occupied Libya in 1911. In 1882, Britain occupied Egypt, and then the Sudan in 1898. In the aftermath of World War I, the remaining parts of the Arab world—Greater Syria (which the colonists divided into what is now Syria, Lebanon, Jordan, and Palestine), Iraq, and the Persian Gulf—were divided into British and French colonies and protectorates, except for parts of the Arabian peninsula that remained relatively independent.

Both directly and indirectly, much of modern Arabic literature addresses the issues arising from Arab societies' experience under European colonialism. Yet it must also be noted that during the preceding three centuries, Arabic literature languished in decadence and stagnation within the stifling cultural milieu of the Ottoman Empire. In the mid-19th century, however, the new colonial threat led to a movement of revival (*Nahda*) that first aimed at borrowing European science and technology, but eventually exposed Arab intellectuals to European culture, thought, and literature. *Nahda* intellectuals saw their task as one of selective borrowing from Europe while at the same time striving for authenticity with regard to Arab cultural identity. Together with the rediscovery of classical Arabic literature, which came to be seen as the repository of Arab cultural identity, the exposure to European literary styles, genres, and movements revitalized Arabic literature. Much of modern Arabic literature is, therefore, the product of both anti-Ottoman and anticolonialist liberatory impulses, some of which paradoxically aimed at achieving their goal through the selective adoption of Western modernity while at the same time resisting Western cultural imperialism. Thus in a broad sense, a great deal of modern Arabic literature negotiates this complex response to the West that encompasses many themes, such as the problematic relationship between the Arab Islamic cultural tradition and Western modernity; the need for social, political, and religious reform; the status of women; resistance to colonialism and imperialism; the challenges of nation-statehood and of pan-Arab nationalism; and the Palestinian problem, among others.

These themes are not always explicitly or directly tied to colonialism, but they arise out of a social milieu that has been affected in innumerable ways by the multiple forms of political and cultural domination in the Arab world. In the late 19th and early 20th centuries, for example, the renewed interest in classical Arabic literature was to a great extent an attempt to revive a cultural identity associated with Arabic civilization at the height of its power. Not surprisingly, therefore, poetry, which Arabs have always considered to be one of their greatest cultural achievements, reclaimed its function as the expression of social values and aspirations, as well as an important organ of social and political mobilization. The classical poet was first and foremost a public figure and spokesman for the community, adopting the stance of a sage who formulated maxims and gave memorable poetic expression to prized moral values. This role was revived in the mid-19th century, and since then, with a few rare exceptions, political commitment has always infused modern Arabic poetry, from neoclassical (late 19th and early 20th centuries), to Romantic (between the two World Wars), to Modernist (since the early 1950s).

Drama also participated in the revival of the classical heritage and the assertion of a cultural identity in the face of colonialism. Drama was a newly imported genre with no roots or stylistic models in classical Arabic literature, but its treatment of subjects drawn from ancient Egyptian and Arab history served to raise awareness of Arab cultural identity. Here too Arab writers were again appropriating European forms to serve the cause of anticolonial resistance. In the postcolonial period, Arab dramatists in Egypt and elsewhere in the Arab world, where drama gradually took roots, turned their attention to social and political criticism. The popularity of drama is rivaled only by cinema and television miniseries (in fact, recordings of theatrical productions are routinely televised). Among the most important Arab dramatists are Tawfiq al-Hakim, Mahmud Taymur, Nu'man 'Ashur, Alfred Farag, and Ali Salem.

Like drama, the novel was imported from Europe, although the abundance of other narrative genres in the Arabic literary tradition informed and facilitated the appropriation of the novel. Examples of prenovelistic narrative forms in classical Arabic literature include the genres of Qur'anic narrative, *qissa, hikaya, riwaya, us-tura, khruafa, muwashah,* and *maqama,* as well as the famous tales of *The Thousand and One Nights.* The novel as such, however, began with loose translations and adaptations of European novels, notably by Jurji Zaidan, who also displayed a strong interest in classical Arabic literature. These early beginnings eventually resulted in the birth of the Arabic novel in 1913, with the publication of the Egyptian Mu-hammad Husayn Haykal's *Zaynab.* Significantly, the novel's explicit focus on Egyp-tian peasants was presented, in the words of the author, as part of the rising tide of nationalism that led to the 1919 revolution against the British occupation.

Over the next three decades, the genre of the novel would reach maturity in the hands of Naguib Mahfouz, and eventually achieve great popularity throughout the Arab world. Mahfouz's early novels thematized ancient Egyptian history, before depicting, in a series of novels culminating in the famous Cairo Trilogy, the conditions of life in Egypt during the British occupation and World War II. Since the 1950s, scores of other novelists from Lebanon (Tawfiq Yusuf Awwad, Layla Ba'albaki, Layla 'Usayran, Emily Nasrallah, Hannan al-Shaykh, Ilyas Khury), Syria (Hanna Mina, Muti' Safadi, Halim Barakat), Iraq (Gha'ib Ti'ma Firman, Isma'il Fahd Isma'il), Saudi Arabia ('Abd al-Rahman Munif), Egypt (Mahfouz, Nawal al-Sadaawi, 'Abd al-Rahman al-Sharqawi, Latifa al-Zayyat, Yusuf Idris, Fathi Ghanim), Sudan (Tayeb Salih), Tunisia (Mahmoud al-Mas'adi, Bashir al-Khurayyif), Algeria (al-Tahir Wattar), and Morocco ('Abd al-Karim Ghallab, 'Abdallah al-'Arawi [Laroui], 'Abd al-Majid Ben Jalloun, Muhammad Barradah, Muhammad Zafzaf) have written about the struggle for independence, nationalism and nationhood, the status of women, the failures of postcolonial Arab regimes, the Arab-Israeli conflict, the Lebanese Civil War, and the ongoing concern with Arab identity vis-à-vis Western culture and imperialism. Also noteworthy are Tunisian, Algerian, and Moroccan novelists writing in French, such as Albert Memmi, Katib Yassin, Assia Djebar, Muhammad Dib, Tahar Ben Jalloun, and Driss Chraïbi. Arab novelists, including Arab Americans, also write in English. Among them are Diana Abu-Jaber, Kathryn Abdul-Baki, Rabih Alameddine, Fadia Faqir, Waguih Ghali, Anouar Majid, Nabil Salih, Ahdaf Soueif, and Samia Serageldin.

One of the most persistent themes of Arabic literature since World War II has been the Arab-Israeli conflict following the dispossession of the Palestinians in 1948, then in 1967, by Israeli settler colonialism. The year 1948 is referred to in Arabic historiography as the year of *Nakbah*, or disaster, a term that hints at not only the scope of the plight of the Palestinians but also the magnitude of the historical dislocation felt throughout the Arab world, and that was reflected in the literature produced by Palestinians and non-Palestinian Arab writers alike. The fiction of Ghassan Kanafani, Tawfiq Fayyad, Rashad Abu Shawir, Emile Habibi, and Sahar Khalifa; the poetry of Ibrhim Tuqan, Fadwa Tuqan, Tawfiq Sayigh, Jabra Ibrahim Jabra, Tawfiq Zayyad, Salma Khadra Jayyusi, Samih al-Qasim, and Mahmoud Darwish; and the plays of Mu'in Basisu and Samih al-Qasim depict the conditions of Palestinians both in exile and inside Israel and the Occupied Territories.

To read about literature in the early Islamic World, see the Islamic World entry in the section "Language and Literature" in chapter 4 ("Intellectual Life") in volume 2 of this series.

~*Wail S. Hassan*

FOR MORE INFORMATION

Allen, R. *The Arabic Literary Heritage*. Cambridge: Cambridge University Press, 1998.
———. *The Arabic Novel: An Historical and Critical Introduction*. 2d ed. Syracuse, N.Y.: Syracuse University Press, 1995.

Badawi, M. M. *A Short History of Modern Arabic Literature*. Oxford: Oxford University Press, 1993.

Hassan, W. S. *Tayeb Salih: Ideology and the Craft of Fiction*. Syracuse, N.Y.: Syracuse University Press, 2003. Forthcoming.

Jayyusi, S. K. *Trends and Movements in Modern Arabic Poetry*. 2 vols. Leiden: E. J. Brill, 1977.

SOVIET UNION

The history of the arts in the Soviet Union is a history of lethal repressions that extended and refined the censorship apparatus of the czars. Lenin's 1905 article "Party Organization and Party Literature," the Bible of Soviet arts policy, spelled out the idea that literature

cannot be at all an individual affair independent of the proletariat as a whole. Down with non-party writers! . . . Literature must necessarily and inevitably become an inextricable part of the work of the Social-Democratic Party. Newspapers must become the organs of the various Party organizations. Publishing houses and storerooms, bookshops and reading rooms, libraries and book concerns of all sorts—must all become Party enterprises subject to its control.

After the October Revolution, the Bolsheviks moved quickly to control the arts. On November 9, 1917, Lenin issued a decree giving supervision of all arts activities to the newly formed Commissariat (later Ministry) of Education (*Narkompros*), headed by Anatolii Lunacharskii. In January 1918, perhaps the first instance of censorship in the Soviet era occurred with the shutdown of a Yiddish newspaper, *Togblat*; the seizure of its equipment; and the arrest of its publisher and editor.

Aside from newspaper editors, poets also recorded persecution. Before her arrest in 1934, Anna Barkova wrote poems that commented sardonically on the artistic-political situation and complained about the so-called poets who fawningly created lines to rhyme with Stalin. She also noted how poets struggled to find rhymes for "tractor." Her criticism of Soviet reality was implicit in such strategies as rhyming "bad" (*plokho*) with "epoch" (*epokha*), or "tears" (*slezy*) with "*kolkhozy*" (collective farms). In other poems she openly announced her disillusionment with the revolution she once supported, reproached herself and other idealists for their naïveté, and called her century "sick" because "It betrayed our hopes / It mocked our love / It promised us victories and gave us new despots." Her lyrics pointed out that perpetrators and victims were often one and the same.

Writers who seemed to have quit writing were as much an object of suspicion as those who produced the "wrong" kind of work. Besides, most artists and writers crave an audience. The poet Osip Mandelshtam attempted to harmonize his public silence and his private beliefs by reading his satirical poem about Stalin to a small group of friends. However, one member of the group was an informer. Mandelshtam perished in a prison transit camp in 1938, thereby merging his fate with other "enemies of the people" who were arrested by the millions. The last group of people from the arts community to be executed at Stalin's personal command, in 1952, had links to the Jewish Anti-Fascist Committee. The dictator's campaign against "people and the intellect" took various forms—physical, economic, psychological—but even during the worst times, some creative art continued, albeit secretively, and some unusual poetry written during the Stalin years was published abroad.

Censorship liberalization followed almost immediately after Stalin's demise in March 1953. Olga Berggolts declared her right to record her inner life without regard to the social usefulness of her writing. A newspaper critic attacked the heavy-handed chauvinism of Soviet film. The composer Aram Khachaturian publicly condemned the government's meddling with music. A literary journal, *Novyi mir* (New World), under its editor, Alexander Tvardovsky, published stories that ignored the easy patriotism and hopefulness of Socialist Realism to focus on some harsh realities of Soviet life. Other early "thaw" works attacked Stalinism and self-aggrandizing bureaucrats. In February 1956, First Secretary Nikita Khrushchev made a (well reported) "secret speech" to the 20th Party Congress in which he denounced Stalin's crimes. In 1961, after the 22nd Party Congress, Khrushchev led a "de-Stalinization" campaign that made it possible for Soviets to speak and write more freely. Many writers killed in Stalin's terror campaigns were "rehabilitated" beginning in the late 1950s. Their works were published, and others were allowed to write positively about them. But tolerance was turned on and off at the government's will, and crackdowns on artists, writers, and other intellectuals continued.

> *Censorship liberalization in the USSR followed almost immediately after Stalin's death.*

Prison and torture remained a government option, but physical terror against creative intellectuals took second place to other means, the main one being ejection from one's union or academic institution and the resulting loss of privileges. Celebrities might be forced out of the country and not allowed to return, as happened with the Nobel laureate Aleksandr Solzhenitsyn, who in 1975 was arrested and put on a specially chartered plane to West Germany. In other instances the government simply waited until troublesome artists went abroad before snatching away their citizenship and right to return.

In the 1960s and 1970s, Andrey Voznesensky, Bella Akhmadulina, Yevgeny Yevtushenko, Vladimir Voinovich, and Solzhenitsyn were among the brightest lights of the younger generation of writers. Sometimes poetry readings were held in soccer stadiums to accommodate all the fans. Solzhenitsyn's novel, *One Day in the Life of Ivan Denisovich*, a portrayal of prison camp life, which Khrushchev in 1962 had personally approved for publication, quickly sold out, but copies were shared about. In the same year, however, Khrushchev visited a small Moscow abstract art exhibit, pronounced the works to be "dog shit," and warned the artists, "Gentlemen, we are declaring war on you." Two weeks later, meeting with artists and writers, Khrushchev announced that the Party would decide what forms of artistic expression were permissible. According to Voznesensky, most writers and other artists ignored these warning signals, believing Khrushchev was dedicated to liberalization "in his heart." "We continued to have faith in Khrushchev," Voznesensky recalled, "and we continued to look to him for protection." They were in for a shock.

In March 1963, Khrushchev spoke at a Kremlin meeting devoted to a new official policy on the arts. Though Khrushchev's watershed "secret" 1956 speech seemed to open the door to a freer society, his public outburst at the 1963 meeting slammed the door shut. In the course of the meeting, Khrushchev made ominous references to traitors in the audience, singling out Voznesensky as the main target of his fierce abuse, and in closing spoke well of Stalin. Voznesensky fled Moscow to hide in the countryside. A fellow poet publicly demanded that Voznesensky and certain other writers be sentenced to death as traitors, even though producing illegal art had been downgraded from "counter-revolutionary activity," a capital offense, to "anti-Soviet agitation and propaganda," which carried sentences of long prison terms, forced exile abroad or within the USSR, or both.

After Khrushchev's fall in 1964, there was yet another official tightening up, beginning with the arrest (for "parasitism") and trial of the poet Joseph Brodsky, whose work, though not political, did not conform to official requirements. The year 1966 saw the trials of the writers Yuly Daniel (pen name Nikolay Arzhak) and Andrey Sinyavsky (pen name Abram Terts) for publishing anti-Soviet material abroad. Brodsky, Daniel, and Sinyavsky all served time in prison camps; the latter two also had to endure internal exile. And the art itself was punished: in 1974, in a Moscow suburb, the government used bulldozers to crush an outdoor exhibition of Modernist art, but at least the painters survived.

Throughout the Soviet period, the censorship apparatus had many bureaucratic levels, each of which had to judge a submitted work and then, if approved at that level, pass it on up to the next office. Although the procedures changed in their details over time, the basic process remained the same. For example, a playwright who hoped to have a play staged first submitted the script to *Glavlit* (the Soviet Union's official censorship organ established in 1922 as the Main Administration for Literary and Publishing Affairs), then waited for a later interview with a censor, at which time the writer would be told what revisions were necessary; submit the revisions in triplicate; wait for approval; then have the script returned, pages sealed in wax, with the number of authorized pages written on it by hand, along with a note stipulating the maximum number of copies allowed. These copies could be made only at a special office designated for that purpose. Then the author had to submit the play to *Glavrepertkom* (the Soviet Union's Main Committee for Control of Entertainment and Repertory; the governmental organization that directed theatrical, film, and other cultural productions and sanctioned their release for public viewing) censors. If the play was approved by *Glavrepertkom*, the playwright brought copies to the literary directors of various theaters. A literary director interested in the script would probably ask the writer for more revisions. If the play cleared the literary director and had the approval of a theater's chief director (often a genuine artist rather than a mere Party functionary), the playwright would be required to give a reading for the theater's artistic council. At this point, the council could refuse the play, accept it as it was, or order revisions. If the council approved the play, *Glavrepertkom* still had to be petitioned for permission to allow rehearsals. If permission was granted, that still was not the end of the vetting process, which continued until the very eve of public performance, and often beyond. The (theoretically) final hurdle was the closed dress rehearsal for members of *Glavrepertkom*, the artistic council, the author, the director, and the designer. If a show was banned at dress rehearsal, great expenditures of time, money, and energy were down the drain. If the council gave the thumbs-up at the dress rehearsal, a nervous bureaucrat or censorship committee could pull the play from the repertory at any time after its opening. Indeed, the more popular the play, the greater the likelihood this would happen. The Taganka's tremendously successful *The Poet Vladimir Vysotsky* (1981), for example, was finally given permission to be staged, but only twice a year; nevertheless, it was banned after a few performances (Eaton, *Daily Life*).

FOR MORE INFORMATION

Eaton, K. B. *Daily Life in the Soviet Union*. Westport, Conn.: Greenwood Press. Forthcoming.
Eaton, K. B., ed. *Enemies of the People: The Destruction of Literacy, Theater, and Film Arts in the Soviet Union in the 1930s*. Evanston, Ill.: Northwestern University Press, 2002.
Garrard, J. G., and C. Garrard. *Inside the Soviet Writers' Union*. New York: Free Press, 1990.

JAPAN

Japanese fiction shed its image of frivolity and was recognized as an intellectually legitimate pursuit only on the eve of the 20th century. Following the efforts of pioneering 19th-century writers, influential literary circles formed around such novelists as Ozaki Kouyou (1868–1903), whose *The Golden Demon* (*Konjiki yasha*, 1902) was the most popular novel of the Meiji period, and Kouda Rohan (1867–1947), noted for the realism and objectivity of his work. Many important Meiji writers, including most notably Mori Ougai (1862–1922) and Izumi Kyouka (1873–1939), had begun their careers under the influence of European Romanticism, imported in the 1890s.

The first decade of the 20th century witnessed the rise of another import: Naturalism, with its focus on human beings as products of heredity and environment rather than volition. Representative is Shimzaki Touson's (1872–1943) *The Broken Commandment* (*Hakai*, 1906), which describes the anguish of the outcast class.

No 20th-century writer has enjoyed more enduring fame than Natsume Souseki (1867–1916), whose popularity continues among Japanese of various age groups. Unaligned with any coterie, Souseki wrote in a variety of styles, ranging from the lighthearted *Botchan* (1906), a humorous account of a young man's first teaching position in a country school, to *The Three-Cornered World* (*Kusamakura*, 1906), a haiku-like story of a painter's quest for his aesthetic ideal. Men displaced by Japan's modernization are perennial figures in Souseki's fiction. Other literary mavericks include Nagai Kafuu (1879–1959), who demonstrated both nostalgia for old Japan and fascination with foreign literature, and Akutagawa Ryounosuke (1892–1933), many of whose stories effectively combined medieval themes and settings with modern sensibilities.

The literary scene in the second decade of the century also saw the rise of the White Birch (*Shirakaba*) School. With diverse styles and themes, its members shared a humanistic inclination and often also a pronounced social consciousness. Mushakouji Saneatsu (1885–1976), one of the group's founders, established a Tolstoyan utopian commune. Another noteworthy *Shirakaba* writer was Shiga Naoya (1883–1971), whose autobiographical *A Dark Night's Passing* (*An'ya kouro*, 1921–37) is widely appreciated as one of the great works of 20th-century fiction.

As a result of the censorship of the war years, many of Japan's best writers retired from activity. One who continued to write—though not to publish—was Tanizaki Jun'ichirou (1886–1964), much of whose masterpiece *The Makioka Sisters* (*Sasameyuki*, 1948) was created during the war years. Though the themes he treated underwent transformations, his idolization of womanhood remained constant. Though the war produced little memorable literature, the years following produced much poignant reflection. Its horrors are recalled in Ibuse Masuji's (1898–1993) *Black Rain* (*Kuroi ame*, 1966), which is set in Hiroshima at the time of the atomic bomb, and Ouka Shouhei (1909–88), whose *Fires on the Plain* (*Nobi*, 1952) describes the conditions of a Japanese soldier remaining in the jungles of the Philippines, trying to avoid capture. Noma Hiroshi's (b. 1915) *Zone of Emptiness* (*Shinkuu chitai*, 1952) recounted the harshness of military life. The postwar years also saw the rise of a libertine *(Burai)* school, whose authors often assumed a satirical tone and whose best-known representative is Dazai Osamu (1909–48). Dazai's *The Setting Sun* (*Shayou*, 1947) traces the fortunes of an aristocratic family following the war.

Japan's first Nobel Prize winner for literature (1968) was Kawabata Yasunari (1899–1972), whose best-known works include *The Izu Dancer* (*Izu no odoriko*, 1926), *Snow Country* (*Yukiguni*, 1937), and *The Sound of the Mountain* (*Yama no oto*, 1952). Kawabata shared with Tanizaki a reverence of the feminine, his male characters often serving to introduce major female characters.

Until at least the wartime generation, women's literature was regarded as a separate category of writing. Noteworthy women whose careers date from before the war and who were instrumental in rebuilding literary culture thereafter included Nogami Yaeko (1885–1985), whose novel *The Maze* (*Meiro*) is a scathing critique of the militaristic age through which she lived; Hayashi Fumiko (1903–51), whose *Journal of a Vagabond* (*Hourouki*) reflects the harsh conditions in which she grew up; and Enchi Fumiko (1905–86), whose *The Waiting Years* (*Onnazaka*) is based on her grandmother's experience of finding a concubine for her husband.

Of Japan's postwar writers, the most frequently translated and best-known abroad is Mishima Yukio (1925–70), whose treatment of homosexuality in his *Confessions of a Mask* (*Kamen no kokuhaku*, 1949) created a sensation. Other novels explore obsession with beauty, as in *The Temple of the Golden Pavilion* (*Kinkakuji*, 1956), adolescent psychology in *The Sailor Who Fell from Grace with the Sea* (*Gogo no eikou*, 1963), and death and reincarnation in his tetralogy *The Sea of Fertility* (*Houjou no umi*, 1965–70). Mishima's death by ritual suicide in 1970 made news around the world.

Fiction in the latter part of the 20th century revolved around individuals rather than schools and shows greater diversity. Some prominent writers included Endou

Shuusaku (1923–96), a Catholic writer who articulated a Japanese perspective on Christianity in *Silence* (*Chinmoku*, 1966); Abe Koubou (1924–93), who explored alienation in modern society with such works as *The Face of Another* (*Tanin no kao*, 1964); Oe Kenzaburou (b. 1935), winner of the 1994 Nobel Prize for literature, whose *A Personal Matter* (*Kojinteki na taiken*, 1968) was based on the author's struggle to come to terms with having a handicapped child; Murakami Haruki (b. 1949), the humor of whose works appeals to young people; and Yoshimoto Banana (b. 1964), whose works have been extremely popular both in Japan and abroad.

The most widely practiced forms of poetry in modern Japan continue to be the traditional *tanka* and *haiku*. A verse of tanka consists of five lines with five-seven-five-seven-seven syllables, respectively. For centuries associated primarily with the aristocracy, by the 20th century it had long been widely practiced among commoners. The poetic ideals of the modern tanka were articulated very differently by two poets, Masaoka Shiki (1867–1902) and Yosano Tekkan (1873–1935). Shiki repudiated the lyricism of the classical tradition, insisting on realism. Tekkan was noted for his advocacy of manliness rather than traditional delicate imagery. His lover, and later his wife—Yosano Akiko (1876–1942)—exceeded his fame with one of the most popular tanka collections of modern times, *Tangled Hair* (*Midaregami*, 1901), which celebrated her own beauty and womanliness and established a style distinct from Tekkan's. The compact imagery of Ishikawa Takuboku's (1886–1912) verses evocatively captures momentary thoughts and impressions. One of the most important tanka poets of the 20th century was Saitou Mokichi (1882–1953), whose first collection, *Red Light* (*Shakkou*, 1913), combined archaic diction with modern sensibilities. Tanka poetry was revitalized late in the 20th century by Tawara Machi (b. 1962), a high school teacher whose style was noted for its colloquial flavor. Machi's collection entitled *Salad Anniversary* (*Sarada kinenbi*, 1987) remained a best seller for several years.

Haiku, probably the world's shortest verse form, is written in three lines of five-seven-five syllables, respectively. Many modern haiku poets trace their artistic lineage to Masaoka Shiki, who is credited with revolutionizing that form as well as tanka. Shiki's literary progeny defies both enumeration and description, but Yamaguchi Seishi's (b. 1901) unsentimental treatment of unusual topics is noteworthy. One other haiku poet whose work has appealed to many Japanese is Nakamura Kusatao (1901–83), whose verses, unlike Seishi's, exalt ordinary human sentiments.

Modern poetry in nontraditional forms, generally referred to as *shi*, grew out of efforts in the late 19th century to translate Western poetry. The traditional metrical practice of alternating lines of five and seven syllables eventually gave way to blank verse. Most poetry continued to be written in classical language until such poets as Kitahara Hakushuu (1885–1942) and Takamura Koutarou (1883–1956) introduced colloquial diction. One of the best-known modern poets to write in a nontraditional form was Hagiwara Sakutarou (1886–1942), whose collection *Howling at the Moon* (*Tsuki ni hoeru*, 1917) remains widely read despite the difficult symbolism of many of its verses. Without doubt, the verses best known not only to the intelligentsia but to every schoolchild were penned by Miyazawa Kenji (1896–1933), whose Buddhist piety, advocacy of simple living, and humanity are summed up in his famous poem "Undaunted by the rain" (*Ame ni mo makezu*, 1931), which nearly every Japanese could recite by heart. The somber tone of much postwar poetry was broken by Tanikawa Shuntarou (b. 1931), who restored an oral quality to modern verse, and Ouoka Makoto (b. 1931), who brought an intellectual lyricism to modern poetry.

To read about literature in early modern Japan, see the Japan entry in the section "Language and Literature" in chapter 4 ("Intellectual Life") in volume 4 of this series.

~*Roger K. Thomas*

FOR MORE INFORMATION

Keene, D. *Dawn to the West: Japanese Literature of the Modern Era: Fiction.* New York: Holt, 1984.

———. *Dawn to the West: Japanese Literature of the Modern Era: Poetry, Drama, Criticism.* New York: Holt, 1984.

INUIT

Before the arrival of Christian missionaries in the Arctic all Inuit literature was oral and consisted primarily of stories told by one generation to the next. Poetry, which was often satirical, was also prominent. Some, but not all, of the traditional stories occurred throughout the Inuit region and were known by many groups of Inuit. Undoubtedly the first and primary purpose of the stories was entertainment. Nonetheless, many traditional stories were morality tales that helped reinforce Inuit values and cautioned children, especially, about the dangers of such things as disobeying elders or selfishness or wandering alone on the tundra. The morality or cautionary tale continues in contemporary Inuit fiction.

Inuit written literature dates to the mid- to late 19th century. Beginning in the 18th century in Greenland and Labrador and in the mid-19th century in Canada and North Alaska, missionaries created writing systems for Inuktitut, the Inuit language, in order to translate the Bible. Greenlandic Inuit, in particular, produced Christian-themed poetry and hymns, but once Inuit became literate in their own language they also created a secular literature in Inuktitut.

Although Inuktitut is a single language with regional dialects, there is no single standard orthography for the language. Rather there are standard orthographies for each geographic region of the Inuit North, and Inuit in one part of the Arctic cannot read literature produced elsewhere. Since the late 1970s, various Inuit groups have proposed the creation of a single writing system as a way to encourage the continued use of Inuktitut in daily life and literature. Regional chauvinism, however, seems to have made it impossible for Inuit in Canada, Greenland, and Alaska to reach agreement about which orthography to adopt as the standard. In recent years, most Inuit literature in Canada and Alaska has been in English rather than Inuktitut.

In Canada, a syllabic writing system based on Pittman shorthand, though introduced by missionaries, spread rapidly even in advance of Christianity. Inuit in the

INTELLECTUAL
LIFE
|
LITERATURE
|
Europe

United States,
1940-1959

United States,
1960-1990

India

Islamic World

Soviet Union

Japan

Inuit

eastern Canadian Arctic used the syllabic writing systems to write letters and to keep other kinds of records. The simplicity of syllabics enabled parents to teach their children to read before they started school. In early years of formal schooling, when Canadian Inuit children were sent to church or government boarding schools, the ability to write in syllabics meant that parents and children could continue to communicate during the long separations. Syllabics permitted Inuit without formal education to commit their ideas to paper, and several self-taught Canadian writers produced their own reference works using syllabics. Examples include Peter Pitseolak (1902–73), who kept voluminous records of the people and events of the Cape Dorset region of Southern Baffin Island; Taamusi Qumaq (1914–93), who created both a 30,000-word Inuktitut language dictionary and an encyclopedia of Inuit culture; and Mitiarjuk Attasie Nappaaluk (b. 1931), who wrote both fiction and non-fiction.

Some of the earliest writings by Inuit appeared in the Greenlandic newspaper *Atuagagdliutit*, first published in 1861. Early editions of the paper contained hunters' descriptions of settlements, weather reports, and travelers' tales. Hans Hendrik (1834–89), a West Greenland Inuk (singular of Inuit) famous for his travels with European explorers, wrote of his adventures and of his experiences living among the Inuit of northwest Greenland. *Atuagagdliutit* and other periodicals were also forums where Greenland Inuit could debate the importance of traditional occupations such as seal hunting to the developing Greenlandic identity.

Journalism remains an important outlet for the expression of Inuit ideas and concerns. The *Tundra Times*, the first statewide Native newspaper in Alaska, was edited for many years by Alaskan Inuk Howard Rock (1911–76). Under Rock's leadership, the paper was nominated for Pulitzer Prizes for coverage of the 1971 Alaska Native Claims Settlement Act and for investigative reports about the near slavery conditions suffered by Pribilof Islanders at the hands of the U.S. government. A set of letters to the editor discussing the Alaska Native Claims Settlement Act written by Frederick Seaguyak Bigjim and non-Native James Ito-Adler were republished as the book *Letters to Howard* (1974). Several Canadian Inuit are regular columnists in northern periodicals.

Memoirs and traditional stories are the most common genres of Inuit literature today and are produced throughout the Inuit North. In some cases early anthropologists, missionaries, and other non-Natives encouraged this type of writing. For example, Henrik Rink, who was the colonial administrator of South Greenland, encouraged Greenlanders to send him traditional stories. Rink was also responsible for arranging publication of Hans Hendrik's memoir of his travels and of various traditional stories with woodcut illustrations produced by Greenlandic hunter Aron of Kangeq (1822–69).

Among Inuit memoirs *Life among the Qallunaat* (1978) by Minnie Aodla Freeman (b. 1936) stands out. It diverges from most Inuit autobiographies that are reflections on past or passing traditional Inuit camp life. Instead, Freeman wrote of her first experiences living and working in southern Canada without her tight-knit family.

Novels are a relatively small proportion of the corpus of Inuit literature. Greenlander Mathias Storch (1883–1957) published the first novel in Inukitut in 1914.

The book, *Sinnattugaq (The Dream)*, is a morality tale in which the protagonist dreams of a future when Greenlanders are in more direct control of their lives and their country. The next Inuktitut novel, *Ukiut 300-nngornerat (The 300th Anniversary)*, written by another Greenlander, Augo Lynge (1899–1959) and published in 1931, was also set in the future. Like Storch, Lynge used the futuristic setting as a foil to critique the social issues of the day. Hans Anthon Lynge (b. 1945) also uses the novel for social criticism. His 1976 work *Seqajuk (The Useless One)* dealt with a perceived lack of purpose in the lives of young Greenlanders. Alaskan Fred Bigjim published *Plants* (1999), a science fiction mystery involving space aliens, a Native American shaman, and a government cover-up.

Other novelists have addressed personal issues. Canadian Markoosie Patsuaq's (b. 1942) novella *Harpoon of the Hunter* (1970) is a coming-of-age story. He drew on his experience as a pilot in his later work, *Wings of Mercy* (1972), published in serial form in *Inuktitut Magazine*. Personal tragedy is the subject of Maaliaarqq Vebaek's (b. 1917) *Bussimi nuupinneq (The Meeting on the Bus)*, published in 1981.

Other genres include poetry, drama, and children's literature. Perhaps the most widely read Inuit author is Michael Arvaaluk Kusugak (b. 1948), who produced the children's classics *A Promise Is a Promise* (1988) and *Baseball Bats for Christmas* (1990)

~Pamela Stern

FOR MORE INFORMATION

Geldof, R., ed. *Paper Stays Put: A Collection of Inuit Writing.* Edmonton: Hurtiq, 1980.

Lowenstein, T., ed. *Eskimo Poems from Canada and Greenland.* London: Anchor Press, 1970.

McGrath, R. *Canadian Inuit Literature: The Development of a Tradition.* Ottawa: National Museum of Man, 1984.

Petrone, P., ed. *Northern Voices: Inuit Writing in English.* Toronto: University of Toronto Press, 1988.

Communication

During the 20th century, there was a revolution in communications. In 1900, the world was beyond most people's reach. Simply put, it was quite difficult to deliver and receive information. People stayed in touch via personal letters and newspapers, but there was a significant time delay between communiqués. To paraphrase one historian, the world was organized into island communities. Even within nations such as the United States, not much communication took place between cities and rural towns. Twentieth-century technological advances changed all this.

The first major development was the radio. In 1896 the Italian inventor Guglielmo Marconi discovered how to transmit telegraphic codes through air. Americans quickly adapted the radio for their needs. By 1910, the first primitive radio station was operating in San Jose, California. Wireless communication soon became important to ship travel, but in the American setting radio communication was even

INTELLECTUAL LIFE
|
COMMUNICATION
|
United States, 1920-1939

United States, 1940-1959

United States, 1960-1990

India

Soviet Union

Japan

more critical as a central part of the capitalist economy. In 1916, a young radio developer, David Sarnoff, proposed making the radio a household utility that would deliver news, entertainment, and advertising. Three years later, Sarnoff's company, the Radio Corporation of America (RCA), cornered the market and began broadcasting sports, news, and music. The radio itself was a staple in the home by 1930. Even in rural areas, radios, particularly battery-operated ones, were popular. No other invention, not even the telephone, connected more Americans in the era before television.

By the 1950s, the television had replaced the radio as the premiere communications device in the United States. For the latter half of the 20th century, the television occupied the same niche as the radio. It delivered news, entertainment, and advertising. Furthermore, it created a truly national culture with national icons such as Lucille Ball and Elvis Presley. By the 1970s, television had replaced newspapers as the main source of national and world events. But the reign was short-lived. By the end of the century, radio had made a comeback. Additionally, television was challenged by more interactive forms of communication such as the new satellite telephone and computer networks.

The technological advances at the end of the century created a different problem with communications. Whereas one hundred years earlier there was a dearth of information as well as machines to provide communication, by 2000 there was perhaps too much information. Radio, television, telephone systems, and computer networks supplied 24 hours of news, entertainment, and advertising. In some ways, people were better informed and ideas were more democratically broadcasted. Thus the world became smaller and communication improved to all parts of the world as the entries on Japan, India, and the Soviet Union/Russia will show. Although the technology of communication may not be as readily available in, say, India, as it is in the United States, Japan, or Europe, very future areas are as isolated as they were at the start of the century. Nonetheless, within this cacophony of voices, ideas, and ideologies, it has also became harder to understand what is being said.

INTELLECTUAL
LIFE
|
COMMUNICATION
|

UNITED STATES, 1920–39

One new electrically powered communications technology with perhaps the greatest impact on the daily life of ordinary Americans in the 1920s and 1930s was the radio. Interestingly enough, it represented an instance in which the presence or absence of electrical wiring did not force a wedge between city and countryside. Battery-operated radios made it possible for rural and small-town Americans to experience the same striking sounds and, occasionally, sights as city dwellers. Town and country could share experiences impossible to obtain in their own immediate cultural environments. Thus, far more than any previous system of communication, the radio drew Americans together into a new and common culture.

Radio became enormously popular in a very short time. It soon linked rural and urban America together in a common listening experience. In the two decades after the first commercial radio broadcast in November 1920, nearly 41 million radios were manufactured in the United States, considerably more than one for every household in the nation. For the first time in the nation's history, one could realistically talk of a national audience for a political, sports, or other event. People across the country could simultaneously hear exactly the same thing, whether it was a presidential speech, a musical performance, an advertisement for a commercial product, or an eyewitness description of a World Series baseball game. A nationwide community of people sharing the same experience at the same moment was first formed.

Italian Guglielmo Marconi had discovered how to transmit telegraphic code through the air in 1896, initiating a scientific scramble to advance wireless communication. Marconi first demonstrated his wireless telegraph in the United States in October 1899, sending to shore reports on the America's Cup yacht races in New York Harbor. With a variety of inventors working on aspects of the problem, less than a decade later Americans achieved wireless transmission of voices and music, the first crude radio. In 1909, a primitive radio station began broadcasting every Wednesday evening from the San Jose, California, College of Engineering. Messages sent and received in the dots and dashes of Morse telegraph code remained the common medium, however, having quickly become commercially important.

Wireless messages from the sinking *S.S. Titanic* in 1912 underscored the value of ship-to-shore communication and increased enthusiasm for Marconi's invention. By 1913 advances in vacuum tube technology effectively amplified wireless telegraph and radio signals, marking a great improvement over existing transmitters and widely used crystal receivers. Soon several thousand amateur radio operators began demonstrating that interest in this new medium of communication existed beyond naval, military, journalistic, and business circles. They talked, sang, made speeches, gave time signals and weather reports, played phonograph records, and read poetry for other amateurs. In 1915 a voice message transmitted from Arlington, Virginia, was picked up in both Paris and Pearl Harbor, Hawaii. In 1916 a network of amateur operators was able to relay a message from Davenport, Iowa, to New York City in only two-and-a-half hours, using a series of intermediate receivers and transmitters. A year later they

The telephone was one of the most important communicative advances in the 20th century. Here a woman in Birney, Montana, makes a call in 1939. © Library of Congress.

sent a message from Los Angeles to New York and obtained a reply in less than two hours.

In 1915, Lee De Forest, using the vacuum tube equipment he had developed during the previous decade, began broadcasting phonograph music and lectures in New York. By regularly replicating a feat he had first accomplished in 1910 with a very limited broadcast of tenor Enrico Caruso from the Metropolitan Opera, he hoped to expand the market for the devices his company produced. In 1916 De Forest broadcast the Harvard-Yale football game and even presidential election results. De Forest's broadcasts (including the incorrect report that President Woodrow Wilson had been defeated for reelection) could be picked up within a 200-mile radius of New York by listeners using vacuum tube sets or homemade crystal sets and earphones.

In late 1916 a young visionary at the Marconi Wireless Telegraph Company in New York, David Sarnoff, proposed as "entirely feasible" a rethinking of uses for the rapidly developing technology. Rather than focus on sending private messages from point to point to compete with the telegraph and telephone, he urged the broadcast transmission of music, lectures, news, and sports over several channels to "radio music boxes" that combined receivers and loudspeakers. Sarnoff envisioned a "household utility" for urban and, perhaps most usefully, rural homes.

David Sarnoff urged the transmission of music, news, and sports to "radio music boxes."

World War I, however, redirected radio development for the time being by centralizing control and development in government hands. Speedy and secure military and diplomatic communication took priority for the moment. The war shaped the evolution of radio by, among other things, standardizing the many competing technological systems. Also, wartime desire to intercept German communications inspired Edwin Armstrong's 1918 invention of the superheterodyne circuit, an effective tuning device for electromagnetic signals that remains to this day the central element in radio and television transmission at precise and differentiated frequencies.

In the fall of 1919, the Radio Corporation of America (RCA) was formed with government encouragement and the support of the General Electric Corporation (the outgrowth of Thomas Edison's early enterprise) to take over the interests of the American Marconi Wireless Telegraph Company and avoid continued postwar government control of wireless communication. Although focused at first on ship-to-shore and international wireless telegraphy, the new company's leaders did allow Sarnoff to explore his idea of broadcasting to radio music boxes. By July 1920, the potential for conflict with the American Telephone and Telegraph Company (AT&T) over patent rights and competing systems for transmitting signals to American homes was resolved. RCA simply gave a million shares of its stock (about 10%) to AT&T, and the two firms agreed, with government approval, to cooperate rather than compete. RCA found itself in a powerful position to determine the nature of broadcasting.

Meanwhile, General Electric's principal rival, Westinghouse, shut out of international wireless telegraphy but holding the superheterodyne patent, among others, decided to compete with RCA in the field of domestic broadcasting. In Pittsburgh, Westinghouse engineer Robert Conrad began transmitting primitive programs. Amateur operators, of whom there were more than 6,000 nationally by 1920, were delighted to pick up vocal and musical broadcasts instead of just Morse code and encouraged his efforts. By May 1920, Pittsburgh newspapers were reporting on his regular Saturday evening concerts; in September a local department store began advertising $10 receivers capable of picking up Conrad's concerts; and at 8 P.M. on

November 2, 1920, Westinghouse station KDKA, which had just obtained the first U.S. government license to operate a general broadcasting service, began regular transmissions from the roof of the company's factory.

KDKA's first broadcast, which went on until after midnight, reported the results of that day's presidential election won by Republicans Warren Harding and Calvin Coolidge over Democrats James Cox and Franklin Roosevelt. The broadcast was heard by people throughout the Pittsburgh area, many of them Westinghouse employees who had been given receivers for the occasion. Broadcasts continued, at first for an hour each evening but soon for longer periods, and Westinghouse quickly established stations at its properties in Newark, New Jersey; East Springfield, Massachusetts; and Chicago, Illinois. The company's plan was simple: use broadcasts to create demand for radio equipment, then profit through the sale of sets.

The Westinghouse effort prompted a quick reaction from RCA. Seeking to retain control of the domestic radio market, RCA offered Westinghouse a million shares of its stock and a 40 percent share of the radio equipment market (the rest would belong to General Electric) in return for Westinghouse's radio patents and operations. Westinghouse accepted in March 1921, and RCA gained a dominant position in the newborn industry.

Americans quickly seized the opportunity provided by radio to participate in public events and enjoy entertainments without having to leave their own homes. Elections, heavyweight fights, and World Series did not occur frequently enough, however, to begin to occupy the hours available for radio broadcasting. The question of what to put on the air confronted the new radio industry from the start. Regular news coverage, as opposed to reports on a few special events, was beyond the capacity of early radio and would remain so until the 1930s. Music, live performances as well as phonograph recordings, quickly became the most popular way of filling the airwaves. Children's bedtime stories, educational programs, and weather reports also became standard fare.

From the outset, music filled much of radio's available broadcast time. Live performances of the parlor piano and vocal music of recent decades were most common at first, but classical music, especially opera and orchestral performances, enjoyed frequent broadcast. Though many Americans had joined in or at least heard the former sort of music at home, in saloons and vaudeville theaters or elsewhere, few had attended an opera or symphony concert. The audience that heard classical music with the low sound quality of early radio was soon eager for live performance. Between 1928 and 1939 the number of major professional symphony orchestras increased from 10 to 17; the total number of orchestras, including part-time, less professional ones in smaller cities, grew from 60 to 286. Perhaps more significant, whereas musical instruction in public schools was almost unheard of in 1920, two decades later it was widespread. Thirty thousand school orchestras and twenty thousand bands had sprung up.

Radio was much more effective than the earlier technological innovation, the phonograph, in building an audience for classical music. Until the long-playing record was developed in 1948, phonograph records could hold only about five minutes of music per side, creating difficulties in the presentation of all but the shortest classical works. Furthermore, by 1924, superheterodyne radios were producing better-quality sound than phonographs. Radio therefore took the lead in presenting classical music. The phonograph industry went into a radio-induced slump that lasted through the 1930s.

Radio also promoted the popularity of other forms of music. Both jazz and country music reached beyond the audiences they had known and evolved significantly as a result. Music that could be and often had been performed at home in the parlor included sentimental songs, ballads, vaudeville and musical comedy tunes, and less-challenging operatic pieces. Such parlor music was familiar and traditional and remained widely enjoyed by early radio audiences. The limitations of radio, however, reshaped this sort of music. Intense voices, especially high sopranos, had a tendency to blow out the tubes on radio transmitters. As a result, a number of singers developed a new, soft, gentle style that came across well and soon became known as "crooning." Female singers such as Vaughn De Leath and Kate Smith as well as males such as Rudy Vallee and Bing Crosby built large and loyal audiences as they perfected the crooning style (Kyvig, 59–68).

FOR MORE INFORMATION

Allen, Woody, dir. *Radio Days*. 1987.

Douglas, G. H. *The Early Days of Radio Broadcasting*. Jefferson, N.C.: McFarland, 1987.

Kyvig, D. E. *Daily Life in the United States, 1920–1939: Decades of Promise and Pain*. Westport, Conn.: Greenwood Press, 2002.

Patterson, J. T. *Grand Expectations: The United States, 1945–1974*. New York: Oxford University Press, 1996.

UNITED STATES, 1940–59

In the present world of instant telecommunication with excesses of information in every space, it is hard even to imagine the 1930s, when not every American family owned a radio. When Franklin Roosevelt gave his fireside chats, often more than one household joined together to listen. During this period rural electrification had just begun to extend airwaves to allow farmers to hear stand-up comedians like Jack Benny and Fred Allen and sitcoms like *Fibber McGee and Molly* and *Amos 'n Andy* (stories of blacks played by whites—not heard as racist at the time). Daytime soap operas (which really advertised laundry soap) like *Ma Perkins*, *My Gal Sunday*, and *Pepper Young's Family* enabled the homebound to imagine that other families' problems could be worse than their own.

A popular radio demagogue and Catholic priest, Father Charles Coughlin, used *The Golden Hour of the Little Flower* to attract as many as 40 million listeners. His original belief in the New Deal turned into hatred for FDR and support for European fascism, causing his audience to drop away before he left the airwaves in 1940. And one sensational reporter, Walter Winchell, broadcast gossipy versions of news like the items printed in the *National Enquirer*—even as a few serious journalists, like

Edward R. Murrow and H. V. Kaltenborn, felt free to express personal liberal opinions. Lowell Thomas, a daily newscaster, used broadcasting to help isolated families visit remote places like Arabia and Tibet, making more convincing the "One World" advocated by Wendell Willkie, FDR's 1940 Republican opponent, in a best-selling book. In trying to solidify new ideals, Americans have often found it difficult to imagine the vast range of cultural experiences others have had to put aside to become citizens of the United States. More than books or magazines, the radio became a source of "public relations" for unifying a frequently fractured society. Just as talking pictures took over from the silent films of the 1920s, movies replaced radio as a means of communication and entertainment, becoming one of the few American businesses that flourished in the 1930s.

After World War II, television began to replace movies and the radio as the main means of communication. By the end of the 1950s visual images taught Americans who they were. Although an advertising slogan of the decade boasted that movies were better than ever, and the introduction of drive-in theaters tried to accommodate both car culture and family—many had playgrounds, diaper services, and special foods for kids—the truth was that television was taking over as the main medium of communication. Gimmicks like three-dimensional films and aroma-ramas that puffed scents through the theaters' ventilation systems failed to bring in necessary crowds. Cinerama appeared in 1952, using overlapping cameras for a gigantic screen effect to extend the possibilities of adventure films. Pictorial innovations such as the famous chase across the face of Mount Rushmore in Alfred Hitchcock's *North by Northwest* (1959) suggested that the excitement of the big screen was far from over—but by then many movies were being created just for the living room viewer. Weekly movie attendance dropped from 90 million to 47 million in the 10 years after 1946. By 1952, 19 million Americans had television sets and a thousand new TV appliance stores were opening each month. When Lucille Ball bought the unused RKO film lot in 1955 to film *I Love Lucy*, the most popular sitcom of the decade, she became a pioneer producer in the new industry of making movies specifically for TV.

Critical feminists may attack *I Love Lucy* as another example of a ditzy housewife manipulating a loyal husband because Lucy's character's attempts at earning her own living remained dreams. In fact, however, the show reflected different levels of media liberation. For one thing, Desi Arnaz played himself on the show—Lucy's Cuban bandleader husband, Ricky Ricardo. Far from the suburban organization man, Desi offered a vast audience the chance to appreciate Latino culture. He used his accent and charm to introduce viewers who knew nothing about Cuba to a different kind of civilization, while audiences enjoyed the tensions of the mixed-culture marriage. Everyone knew that the slapstick character Lucy Ricardo played by Ball on-screen was far removed from the brilliant businesswoman producing the most popular show on television. Lucille Ball's business skills established a tradition that made it easier for later talented women such as Oprah Winfrey to succeed in different roles.

Always torn between trying to please her husband and dreaming of being a star, Lucy Ricardo responded to everywoman's fantasies while coping with the social mandate of the stay-at-home '50s. Ball insisted on playing the role as a housewife, not as a star. Desi and Lucy represented caricatures that helped many—in this most married of decades—laugh at the disasters and peculiarities of marital stress. There was never any suggestion that divorce and extramarital love affairs were realities. Both characters emerged as sympathetic and vulnerable, far from sure of their social status. Their on-screen dealings with their neighbors' points of view offered some exposure to the world of compromise many Americans experienced in new housing arrangements everywhere.

The Monday evening show was such a success that Marshall Field's, the Chicago department store, changed its weekly Monday night clearance sale to Thursday. As early as 1952, 10.6 million households were tuning in to *I Love Lucy*, the largest audience thus far in history. By 1954 as many as 50 million Americans watched. The show allowed CBS-TV to make a net profit for the first time in 1953. No problems emerged with Desi's being Latino—except behind the scenes when one producer argued that Americans would not accept Desi as a suitable TV husband for Lucy.

In 1947 Lucille Ball had been among the Hollywood stars who protested the activities of the House Un-American Activities Committee. On a radio show called *Hollywood Fights Back* she had read excerpts from the Bill of Rights. When the tabloid journalist Walter Winchell accused her of being a Communist in 1953, she acknowledged that she had joined the party to please her grandfather. But her television ratings were so high that Philip Morris cigarettes, Lucy's sponsor, refused to withdraw, demonstrating that in a capitalist society the bottom line frequently shapes ideals. Desi had left Cuba when Fidel Castro, the Communist leader, was just six years old. He insisted that both he and Lucy were 100 percent American. The only thing red about Lucy, Desi claimed, was her hair—and even that was dyed.

Sexist as Lucy's TV dilemmas appeared because she acted stupid, the situations described often challenged audiences to think more about marriage, especially when Lucy's pregnancy took center screen. The on-TV baby was another example of Lucille Ball's power to challenge network stereotypes. Before Lucy's baby all pregnancies had been hidden. CBS wanted her to stand behind chairs. Even the word "pregnant" was not to be used; she agreed to call herself an "expectant mother." By the time Desi, too busy on-screen to notice the change in his wife, acknowledged the great event, CBS had lined up a rabbi, a priest, and a minister to make sure the script was in good taste. But at the hospital it was Lucy who pushed Ricky in the wheelchair. When the baby emerged in January 1953, 68 percent of the television sets in the country were tuned in as 44 million people watched—twice as many as watched the inauguration of Dwight Eisenhower the next day. As time went on Lucy and Desi followed their fellow Americans into suburbia, but their domestic adventures ended at the close of the decade when their real marriage, sympathetic as it seemed, collapsed. Lucille Ball kept financial control of ongoing programs she made by herself. She remains a perfect paradoxical feminist of the 1950s in terms of the vast power she exercised and the limits of her political and social world (Kaledin, 30–31, 133–42).

FOR MORE INFORMATION

Barnouw, E. *Tube of Plenty: The Evolution of American Television.* 2d ed. New York: Oxford University Press, 1990.

Kaledin, E. *Daily Life in the United States, 1940–1959: Shifting Worlds.* Westport, Conn.: Greenwood Press, 2000.

Marling, K. A. *As Seen on TV: The Visual Culture of Everyday Life in the 1950s.* Cambridge: Harvard University Press, 1994.

Patterson, J. T. *Grand Expectations: The United States, 1945–1974.* New York: Oxford University Press, 1996.

UNITED STATES, 1960–90

There were two major themes in the history of communication during the period 1960 to 1990. The first was the continued dominance of television and the second was the rise of the computing age. The 1960s was the second decade of television's dominance of home life. The average number of hours of viewing per home per day increased from just over five in 1960 to almost six in 1970, nearly 18 percent. With more channels, there were more programs to watch. Although virtually no homes were hooked to a cable television system in 1960, the increase to 8 percent in 1970 was the beginning of an accelerating trend. The 2,350 cable systems, up from 640 a decade earlier, principally served isolated areas; but when the Federal Communications Commission allowed cable channels to enter major markets, they began to increase program options for viewers in urban areas, too.

Television did not become, as some had expected, a theater in the home with featured attractions being the center of attention. Although a set might be on most of the time, it did not interfere with the activities of people in the room. One study showed that about one-fifth of the time it played to an empty room. For another fifth, those in the room did not look at it at all. This study reported that children "eat, drink, dress and undress, play [and] fight . . . in front of the set," and that is where adults "eat, drink, sleep, play, argue, fight, and occasionally make love." Almost always the viewing was discontinuous. Hours spent in front of television sets were greater among persons of lower income and lesser education than among the wealthier and better educated, for whom other activities were within reach and within budgets.

By the mid-1970s, the affordability of televisions increased, and about half of the American households had two or more television sets. The sets had become, in historian Cecelia Tichi's words, the home's "electronic hearth," the focal point in a room. Viewers absorbed their radiating warmth and flickering images. They were also a home's window to the world, as the programs and commercials shaped viewers' needs, interests, habits, and values. Television's manipulated portrayals of reality became indistinguishable from reality itself. "As seen on TV" validated claims and opinions.

INTELLECTUAL
LIFE
|
COMMUNICATION
|
United States,
1920-1939

United States,
1940-1959

United States,
1960-1990

India

Soviet Union

Japan

Given television's dominant role in American life, it is not surprising that its images altered viewers' ways of apprehending the world. In contrast to the way one reads—from left to right across a line, top of the page to the bottom, page after page—television follows no predictable or essential lines. Viewers move quickly, not necessarily randomly but seemingly so, from one scene to another with subtle transitions or no transitions at all. Reading is another matter: one *learns* to read books, magazines, and newspapers, typically going through "reading-readiness" exercises and then moving from elementary to more complex material.

No one *learns* to watch television. Many programs, and particularly commercials, are designed to simultaneously hold the attention of 6-year-olds, 16-year-olds, and 60-year-olds. As television holds viewers' attention hour after hour it becomes what Marie Winn has labeled "the plug-in drug." Viewers may not be in a perpetual state of stupor—perhaps they cheer about what they see or talk back to those they hear—but they are addicted to viewing nonetheless. In her book *The Plug-In Drug* (1977) Winn described how the addiction changes viewers' ways of learning, thinking, and being, as well as their relationships with others and their environment. She focused particularly on television's narcotic effects on children, but adults suffered from them as well. These effects were by now widespread.

Television communication was changed significantly in 1975 with Sony's video-recording system known as Betamax. At first the system could be purchased only in a console package containing a videocassette recorder (VCR) and color TV that cost as much as $2,295. Even though the price soon dropped almost by half, JVC's Video Home System (VHS) soon displaced Betamax. The systems were incompatible, and VHS eventually won out (partly because of its longer recording time and lower cost), leaving Betamax owners with technology that was almost instantly obsolete.

But VCRs quickly overcame consumers' misgivings, and by the end of the 1980s about two-thirds of American households with television sets owned at least one unit. With a VCR connected to their set, viewers could for the first time arrange to watch whatever they chose, whenever they chose. Television schedules no longer controlled mealtimes and evening activities. Appreciated just as much was the ability to fast-forward through commercials as viewers watched programs they had recorded, although knowing how to program VCRs for recording was always a challenge. VCRs were used most frequently for watching rented VHS videocassettes. Within a decade, consumers were spending almost $2 billion on rentals and purchasing about 50 million videocassettes.

In addition to television, another important technological and communication development in the 1960s was the advent of computers. The first electronic digital computers, built in the 1940s, were huge machines that were usually dedicated to a single purpose. The development of the transistor in the early 1950s made possible integrated circuits, and old vacuum tubes swiftly became obsolete. The patenting by Texas Instruments in 1961 of a silicon wafer, known as a chip, opened the way for further changes in computer technology. No bigger than a postage stamp, the silicon chip eliminated the miles of wires required in earlier machines.

Although personal computers did not become common in American households until several decades later, IBM's production of a primitive word processor in 1964 was a first step in that direction. However, IBM failed to anticipate what was to come as far as personal computers were concerned. Not until 1981 did it market its first one.

As computer technology came to play a larger role in American life, it was not limited to such obvious processes as financial record management, credit card accounting, airline reservation systems, and word processing. In 1966 it took a small first step into the daily lives of users who were unaware of how it worked and even of its existence, as British technologists developed the first computer-controlled, fuel-injection automobile engine. Such advances, while making life easier in some respects, also made it more confusing—as backyard mechanics would soon discover.

In 1971, when Intel introduced the microprocessor, a whole new industry opened up.

The computerization of America accelerated rapidly in the late 1960s and early 1970s, with each step affecting more directly the lives of Americans. Until the mid-1960s, most computer applications were found in large businesses and the military, but they spread quickly to smaller settings. Office secretaries who had learned to use the IBM Selectric typewriter when it was introduced in 1961 were struggling with electronic typewriters by the end of the decade. Soon they faced the intricacies of primitive word processors.

In 1971, when Intel of California introduced the microprocessor—essentially a computer on a silicon chip—a whole new industry opened up. That meant new jobs in the production of both hardware and software. Boom times came to places like Silicon Valley, the 25-mile strip in California between Palo Alto and San Jose.

As computers entered the workplace, those who used them did not need to understand how they worked. Previously, processors of data worried about stacking and storing the punch cards or magnetic tapes carrying the data they worked with. Now they simply used hard drives and floppy disks to enter, manipulate, store, and retrieve data, all in unprecedented amounts and with impressive speed. But the picture was not all rosy for computer users. The repetitive nature of their work, as they sat in the same position hour after hour with their eyes focused on a screen with moving images, made them vulnerable to new physical maladies, particularly something called repetitive strain injury or cumulative trauma disorder.

As computer users became more adept and productive, they unwittingly caused the underemployment and unemployment of other employees who were displaced. Their work also unwittingly increased the prospects that confidential financial, legal, medical, military, and other records would be vulnerable to invasion by persons who had no right or reason to see them. Another worry was that records would be improperly transferred, scrambled, destroyed, or simply lost in the system. A problem that has persisted results from the perpetual introduction of new generations of hardware and software. Data generated and stored in obsolete generations cannot be retrieved in the next and are forever lost. This might not affect the immediate operations of an organization, but it is a concern to those who attempt years later to come back to original records.

Aside from affecting business life, the computer by the 1970s was changing personal and home life. A technological device with a large impact had small beginnings in 1976, when Steven Jobs and Stephen Wozniak, college dropouts, founded the Apple computer company. They designed the Apple I, a crude personal computer (PC) most notable for paving the way for Apple II. The Apple II, introduced in 1977, caught on quickly in both homes and schools and set in motion four important processes. The first led to the development of personal computers by IBM, the big company in the computer business. Before long many companies were manufacturing machines more important for the description "IBM-compatible" than for the name of the manufacturer.

The second came side-by-side with the first: the rapid expansion of Microsoft, founded in 1975 by software whiz Bill Gates, a 19-year-old Harvard dropout (who had scored a perfect 800 on his math SAT), and his 22-year-old partner, Paul Allen. Before long, Microsoft dominated the software market and Gates was on his way to becoming the richest man in America. Third, costly, complicated mainframe systems gradually came to play a different role in computer operations in businesses, as they accommodated increasingly flexible workstations connected through telephone networks. Fourth, the miniaturization of personal computers led to the development in the 1980s of battery-powered laptop models.

Home computers like Apple's IIg revolutionized communications among Americans. Here, Apple Computer founder Steven Wozniak demonstrates a new Apple IIg in Cupertino, California, September 16, 1986. © AP/Wide World Photos.

In anticipation of the PC's arrival, a scarcely noticed event occurred in 1976 when the German manufacturer of the slide rule presented the last one it produced to the Smithsonian Institution in Washington. For 350 years this venerable device had been the handheld calculator of mathematicians, scientists, and engineers and a mystery to the many in the general public who never mastered it.

The development of personal computers and desktop workstations accompanied other trends begun earlier. By 1980 computer technology had established itself in manufacturing and business processes and touched the daily lives of producers and consumers in many ways, from automated assembly lines to banking and credit-card operations, for example, as well as in the operating systems of automobiles and the most intricate surgical devices.

Personal computers had been manufactured since 1977, but the market for them did not come of age until 1981, when IBM produced its first one. IBM's size enabled it to market its PCs aggressively, and sales climbed in three years from 25,000 to 3 million, although its experiment with a low-cost model, the PCjr., failed. The Apple Corporation, famous for development of the Apple II, introduced the Macintosh in 1984. By 1987 its Macintosh II and SE models were the most powerful personal computers on the market. The Mac was also regarded as more user-friendly than personal computers with "disk operating systems," and debates over Mac versus DOS continued for years. The Mac's "mouse" for moving the cursor on the screen made it even more user-friendly, and eventually other lines of computers also made the mouse a standard feature.

Sales of personal computers stood at 1.4 million in 1981. Sales doubled in 1982, on their way to 10 million in 1988, at a cost then of $22 billion. A number of other computer developments made news that year. One was the "virus," a mischievous small program planted in an operating system with the intent of altering or deleting data throughout the network as the virus spreads. Another was the expanded capacity and speed of laptop computers, with sales exceeding $1 million. A third concerned possible health hazards posed by computer monitors, known as video display terminals. Studies showed that many people who worked at monitors for six hours or more each day developed difficulties in focusing their eyes. Long hours spent at keyboards also caused injuries to hands and arms, sometimes to a disabling extent (Marty, 59–60, 115–18, 151–53, 205–9, 221–22, 303–4).

FOR MORE INFORMATION

Barnouw, E. *Tube of Plenty: The Evolution of American Television*. 2d ed. New York: Oxford University Press, 1990.

History of Computing. <http://ei.cs.vt.edu/~history/>.

Marty, M. A. *Daily Life in the United States, 1960–1990: Decades of Discord*. Westport, Conn.: Greenwood Press, 1997.

Patterson, J. T. *Grand Expectations: The United States, 1945–1974*. New York: Oxford University Press, 1996.

Tichi, C. *Electronic Hearth: Creating an American Television Culture*. New York: Oxford University Press, 1991.

Winn, M. *The Plug-In Drug*. New York: Viking Press, 1977.

INDIA

Communication has always been important to rulers and governments in India. During the ancient period, kings considered information an important part of their survival strategies. Frequently they employed spies who lived and worked among the populace but reported to the king on matters of state security. From *The Laws of Manu* advice is given to a king: "When he has performed his twilight rituals, he should arm himself, and in the inner chamber he should hear about the movements of his spies and those who report secrets" (Donniger, 151). This practice has continued throughout India's history, and its modern incarnation is India's RAW (Research and Analysis Wing), responsible for gathering sensitive information for the government.

During India's medieval period, India's kings devised a number of ways to communicate with each other and with their subordinates. For short distances, messengers would go by foot or horseback. As empires grew, new strategies for communication were needed. A system of messengers, horses, and way stations developed. A messenger rode from one station to the next, switched horses, and

INTELLECTUAL LIFE
|
COMMUNICATION
|
United States, 1920-1939

United States, 1940-1959

United States, 1960-1990

India

Soviet Union

Japan

continued on. These switching stations were called *dak chaukis* (post stages). In this way, hundreds of miles could be covered in a short time.

Paths between locations became well worn and eventually became roads where animals and carts could travel. Under the Mughal Emperor Shah Jahan, one of the world's great roads was established: the Grand Trunk Road running from Agra to Lahore. Roads frequently were lined with trees so that travelers were shaded at all times, and water wells were dug at intervals to make the journey easier. Further, state-sponsored guest homes were constructed where travelers could spend the evening and find fresh supplies. Many of these developed into villages, towns, and cities.

India in its colonial period saw a boom in information technology. Not only were roads improved, facilitating trade and communication, but the British also helped to install telegraph lines, build railways, revamp the postal system, create phone lines, and stitch much of India together with the railway.

Shortly after India's independence in 1947, the first prime minister, Jawaharlal Nehru, established a series of technology schools called the Indian Institutes of Technology (IITs). These institutes were free of government bureaucracy and thus attracted and retained some of India's best instructors. At the same time, they implemented strict admission exams and were able to select India's brightest students. As one journalist said, combine Harvard, MIT, and Princeton, and you begin to have an idea of the prestige and quality of IITs. Initially, IITs were designed to train (and retain) technologically oriented students. By the 1980s, however, as jobs and corruption made finding work in India difficult, many IIT graduates sought further degrees and employment in Europe and North America. As such, when the computer and Internet booms occurred, Indians were among the leaders in the field. Although this might be seen as a "brain drain," it has in fact been the opposite. As labor prices increased in the United States, many companies, seeing a talented workforce from India among them already, opted to invest and outsource in India itself. This has directly affected two Indian cities.

In recent decades, the southern Indian cities of Bangalore and Hyderabad have become major centers for information technology development. Bangalore is located in the state of Karnataka, and Hyderabad is in the state of Andhra Pradesh. In the 1980s several high-tech companies, both Indian and foreign, established headquarters and branches in Bangalore. With an investor-friendly government and well-trained workforce, Bangalore quickly became India's leading high-tech center, earning the title of "the Silicon Valley of India."

By the early 1990s, Hyderabad also began to attract Indian and foreign technology companies. Like Bangalore, it has been supported by an investment-friendly state government. The chief minister (akin to an American governor) has been dubbed "the CEO of Andhra Pradesh" for his tireless promotion and campaigning to attract investors in the state. Many refer to Hyderabad as "Cyberabad."

By the late 1990s, with much of the world in fear of a Y2K disaster, Indian computer programmers were granted visas to come to the United States, England, and Australia in record numbers. Out of the 100,000 Indians granted visas, 90 percent were connected with the high-tech industry. Further, annual Indo-U.S. software trade topped the $5 billion mark. With advances in infrastructure and technology, it is possible for many software firms to operate on a 24-hour schedule. Programmers work in the United States during the day, and at day's end shift the work to India, where a new day is just beginning, and for the next 12 hours, work continues in India before being again transferred back to the United States.

After the turn of the millennium and the ensuing downturn in the high-tech industry, India found yet another way to participate in the global technology market. Because of its contact with the British Empire, the English language has been taught, studied, and mastered in India for nearly two centuries. Thus, when foreign firms have sought large numbers of English-speaking workers for call-answering and telemarketing centers, India was a prime choice. Both in the capital, New Delhi, and in the south in Hyderabad and Bangalore, call-answering centers have sprung up in rapid numbers. Coca-Cola, General Electric, Nestle, Motorola, and American Express are among hundreds of the top Fortune 1000 companies to open call-answering centers in India. Workers are given training not only in their company's products, but also in how to sound American. They are encouraged to watch and mimic American television shows and accents. Many adopt American names when on the job; thus Ramu living in New Delhi might answer an 800 help line as Roger.

Though India continues to be a major player in the high-tech world, it still faces significant problems. Much of the country's infrastructure is controlled by the government, which is itself bloated and frequently corrupt. For example, the railway reservation system is computerized, but to access that technology, one must navigate a bureaucratic jungle. The problems are best summarized by Guruchand Das: "Every time I ate in a roadside café or dhaba [roadside restaurant], my rice plate would arrive in three minutes flat. If I wanted an extra roti [bread], it would arrive in thirty seconds . . . In contrast, when I went to buy a railway ticket, pay my telephone bill, or withdraw money from my nationalized bank, I was mistreated or regarded as a nuisance, and made to wait in a long queue . . . There was no competition in the railways, telephones, or banks, and their employees could never place the customer in the center" (Das, 112). Yet, with continued liberalization of government-controlled services and an entrepreneurial spirit cultivated by contact via high-tech ventures, India stands poised to be a world information technology leader.

~Benjamin Cohen

FOR MORE INFORMATION

Bayly, C. A. *Empire and Information*. Cambridge: Cambridge University Press. 1996.
Das, G. *India Unbound*. New York: Anchor Books. 2000.
Donniger, W., and B. K. Smith, trans. *The Laws of Manu*. New York: Penguin Books. 1991.

SOVIET UNION

Communication in western Europe mirrored the developments in the United States. Information spread rapidly through radio, newspapers, and television. The rapid spread of communication formed an integral part of European events in the

20th century. What is perhaps not as obvious to Westerners was the role mass communication played in the Soviet Union and the Communist Bloc of eastern Europe.

There had been severe controls on the press since the time of Peter the Great, who personally founded the first Russian newspaper, *Vedomosti* (Official Reports). The last 10 years prior to the 1917 revolution saw a loosening of press censorship restrictions: some expression of differing political opinions was allowed, and there were occasional exposures of corruption in high places. A brief "thaw" occurred in 1917, under the short-lived Provisional Government, but following the wishes of Lenin, who advocated total control of the press, press freedom was quickly killed off after the October/November revolution. By the early 1920s Bolshevik authorities had eliminated all non-Bolshevik newspapers, nationalized printing presses, and radically tightened press censorship. From then until the fall of Soviet Communism, media were managed by a government bureaucracy that included the special censorship office, *Glavlit*. Everything that appeared in any of the media anywhere in the USSR had to be first approved by *Glavlit*'s censors, who were part of the staff in all editorial offices. Like all writers, journalists were expected to save time and trouble by censoring themselves before submitting material.

The government and Party published newspapers in about 60 languages, and most appeared six days a week. The two most important and prestigious national papers, *Pravda* (Truth), newspaper of the Central Committee of the Communist Party of the Soviet Union, and *Izvestiya* (News), newspaper of the Soviet government, were issued every day. Readers bored with their dry, predictable reporting would only get more of the same if they turned to other Soviet papers. Like all other Soviet periodicals, *Pravda* and *Izvestiya* were inexpensive and could be bought at newsstands or by subscription. In addition, these two national papers were posted in sidewalk displays and at workplaces so that anyone could read them for free.

The state did not publish periodicals devoted to crime and crime detection, sex, pornography, religion, or the occult. Of course, forbidden subjects could be found in foreign print media, but no foreign publications were sold except in a few foreigners-only hotels. To borrow foreign publications from libraries, people had to show they needed the material for officially approved research projects. Some news did circulate out and then back in. Foreign journalists stationed in the USSR fed news not only to their own countrymen, but also to radio broadcasters such as Voice of America and the BBC, which in turn beamed information into the USSR, thus keeping Soviets up-to-date about certain events in their own country and the outside world.

The danger to human life posed by the lack of a free press was horrifyingly demonstrated in 1986 with the Chernobyl, Ukraine, nuclear power plant explosion of April 26. Though Swedish instruments picked up the increased airborne radiation and Swedish news media reported on it, the Soviet government and its news media for three weeks suppressed, denied, or minimized what could have been lifesaving information for thousands of victims. In the meantime millions continued to live in the area, breathing deadly air, drinking toxic water and milk, while children continued to play in contaminated soil. Censorship of information from Chernobyl showed that despite Gorbachev's glasnost campaign, the government's habit of suppressing bad news had not gone away.

Soviet journalists were not encouraged to be objective in their reporting; their jobs depended on presenting the official point of view, and on following Party policies. All reporters, editors, and broadcasters were government employees who belonged to the Union of Soviet Journalists and were expected to join the Party or *Komsomol* (Communist youth organization). They were well paid by Soviet standards. A lucky few were appointed foreign correspondents with one of the two government news agencies—TASS (Telegraph Agency of the Soviet Union) and *Novosti* (News), which had correspondents around the world. Some of the information they collected was for government use only, some for the Soviet reading public.

By law, most buildings in most of the USSR had to be wired for government radio.

Soviet newspapers had few pages and a small number of advertisements and want ads. There were no comic strips, but there were political cartoons, at least one per issue. Besides the government-approved news (good things happening in the USSR vs. bad things happening in the United States and other capitalist countries), there were sometimes also short poems.

Radio was also strictly regulated. In July 1918 the Bolsheviks monopolized the fledgling radio stations and in 1922 built Comintern (short for Communist International), a powerful station that beamed revolutionary messages around the world. Inside the USSR broadcasts were a means for the government to extend its messages to millions of people, many illiterate, across a vast empire There were programs on a variety of subjects, aimed toward different audiences, including children, in over 70 languages. In the 1920s and early 1930s most people got their programming through radios wired directly into broadcasting stations.

By law almost every building in Russia and much of the USSR had to be wired for government radio. Until the 1960s there was only one station, offering a mixture "of stupefying ideology and world-class theater, interviews with tractor workers and gripping hockey games." Under Brezhnev listeners were offered a choice of two or three stations, including eventually a station (Radio Mayak or Lighthouse) teenagers loved because it broadcast foreign pop music.

As more people acquired radios that could receive foreign stations over the airwaves, and as those stations broadened their appeal, broadcasting in more and more of the USSR's many languages, the more the government tried to prevent people from listening. Authorities threatened to arrest listeners, jammed broadcasts, confiscated radios, prohibited the manufacture of short-wave radios inside the USSR, and tried to pressure foreign governments to stop broadcasting to its citizens. Nevertheless, programs from Radio Free Europe/Radio Liberty, the Voice of America, England's BBC, and West Germany's *Deutsche Welle* continued. Foreign broadcasters estimated they had two to three million regular listeners, plus more who listened now and then.

Television, too, became an increasingly influential force in the Soviet Union. There were 10,000 sets in 1950, almost 3,000,000 in 1958. In the 1960s factories began mass-producing TVs priced in a range most people could afford. In Russia in the late 1950s TV stations broadcast for about four hours a day and more than half the shows were live. Movies, then about 40 percent of the programming, were quickly moved from film theaters to TV. Programming ranged from exercise programs, music, and news to drama and children's programs. For most of the Soviet period there were few commercials; when they appeared they were stodgy promotions of consumer goods not necessarily available to viewers. By the mid-1980s, when most households owned at least one TV and state factories began producing VCRs, only two TV channels were broadcasting across the whole country from Vladivostok to Kaliningrad.

Before glasnost, anchors read heavily censored, predictable news in a formal style punctuated by film clips of bountiful harvests, productive factories, and government officials at public functions. Images of Soviet happiness and success contrasted with films of a troubled capitalism (horrors of the Vietnam war, strikes, unemployed workers, homeless people, race riots, etc.). Besides news, Soviet TV aired children's programs, sports, concerts, and ballet, but without the sophisticated camera work Western viewers were used to. Sex and violence were not depicted.

During glasnost Gorbachev kept the government's monopoly on broadcasting, and much of the old dullness persisted. But there were changes, including glitzier news programs that began to embrace Western-style "infotainment" along with some real news and investigations of previously taboo subjects. There were also rock music; MTV; talk, game, and fashion shows; and beauty contests. In addition, the fierce Cold War stereotypes of the evil capitalist West were softened as viewers were allowed a wider, more balanced range of pictures and stories of American and western European politics and everyday life. Even some portentous events of 1989—the collapse of Soviet satellite countries' governments and demolition of the Berlin Wall—were covered honestly and quickly. At the same time news programs were reined in when it came to broadcasting stories about social and political upheavals at home, such as when the Soviet military violently suppressed peaceful demonstrators in Georgia in April 1989, the occupation of Azerbaijan in 1990, and the Lithuanian secession movement later that year.

Despite constraints, TV journalists at the end of the Communist era felt excited and energized; at last they could begin to do their jobs. Though still shadowed by censorship, greater freedom for media journalists made it possible for striking workers and others to bring their grievances and demands to the attention of the general public as well as to bureaucrats high and low. It became more difficult for the government to quash strikes and other rebellions and dispose of troublemakers secretly. Still, even in its last months the government resorted to repression; Communism remained incompatible with a free press to the end.

~Joyce E. Salisbury

FOR MORE INFORMATION

Eaton, K. B. *Daily Life in the Soviet Union*. Westport, Conn.: Greenwood Press. Forthcoming.

JAPAN

Until recently Japan's communications were divided into four distinct sectors: telephone and telegraph, posts, press, and radio and television. The first was dominated by a government-owned monopoly named Nippon Telephone and Telegraph (NTT), which was regulated by the byzantine networks within the national parliament, known as the Diet.

With the advent of American Telephone and Telegraph (AT&T) deregulation in the 1980s, Japan's NTT came under severe attack both at home and abroad. In 1985 it was announced that NTT would be broken up as AT&T had been. But NTT managed to drag its feet for over a decade thanks to powerful friends in the Diet. Threatened with divestiture, NTT finally split up into regional versions, and a number of domestic telecommunications competitors sprang up.

The Ministry of Posts and Telecommunication regulated the national postal system, which, like its American analog, had come under attack by private mail carriers such as FedEx and UPS. The issue was further complicated by the fact that Japan's postal service controlled the largest savings system in the nation.

Television and radio were openly competitive for decades. Private television networks such as the industry giant Fuji have challenged the national network, NHK. NHK maintains a radio network as well, but local private systems have long ago eclipsed the total control it had in the early postwar period.

Cable television (and radio) has exploded on the market in the last decade. The wired networks spread throughout the country but are now threatened by satellite and wireless cable systems. The Internet has also loosened the control of industry giants. Recently a number of upstart entrepreneurial Internet providers have divided up market share. The old powerhouses like CompuServe and AOL have been undercut by the newcomers' competitive market strategies.

A similar explosion has occurred in the mobile telephone market. Virtually every urban teenager sports a colorful mobile phone clipped to his or her belt or backpack.

Japan's press has long been among the liveliest in the world. Independent newspaper systems such as Asahi, Yomiuri, and Mainichi compete with perhaps two hundred independent private newspapers in Japan. Indeed, the daily publication of newspapers exceeds the total population. Many households subscribe to a morning as well as an afternoon paper, and most companies subscribe to dozens. The Japanese boast that there are more daily English-language newspapers in Tokyo (five) than in New York City (four).

Telegraphy has dwindled in importance as it has in most of the developed world. Internet online banking has eclipsed the need for cabled fund transfers. One has great difficulty in even locating a telegraph office in most Japanese cities now. There are more Internet chat rooms in Tokyo alone than there are telegraph offices in the entire country.

~*Louis G. Perez*

FOR MORE INFORMATION

Krauss, E., and S. Pharr, eds. *Politics and Media in Japan*. Honolulu: University of Hawaii Press, 1996.

Ministry of Posts and Telecommunications. *White Paper on Telecommunications*, 2000. <http://www.soumu.go.jp/english/whitepaper/index.html>.

Health and Medicine

Staying healthy has been a challenge for all people at all times. Recent investigations show that even early humans struggled with this. Archaeologists have recovered many skeletons of early humans who apparently died of a wide range of ailments, from broken bones most likely caused by animal attacks to various diseases. During the 20th century, people continued to fight illness with some innovative methods. For example, in the Soviet Union, the government instituted free basic medical care for its citizens. Although politicians, bureaucrats, scientists, and doctors made clearly great strides during the century, medical hardship remained a common daily experience for many people. Moreover, wars and violent behavior increased human suffering. In other words, the world's belligerents often negated the great advances made by medical professionals.

Truth be told, the relationship between war and medicine has been more complicated. During World War I, medical knowledge and proficiency were expanded. The war produced casualties in unprecedented numbers. New and terrible machines of war produced legions of maimed and walking wounded. Doctors and surgeons learned how to treat these people. Success rates, however, were staggeringly low. Because of infections, by the middle of the war, wartime mortality figures had crept back to levels not seen since the American Civil War. But by the end of the war, new methods and systems were in place not only for those suffering from physical wounds but those with mental wounds as well.

More medical advances came during World War II. President Franklin D. Roosevelt's administration spent millions of dollars on the development of new drugs. Among the most important discoveries were the new antibiotics. By the end of the war, nearly all bacterial illness seemed to be under control. Other advancements included the mass production of penicillin, the manufacture of synthetic quinine, and the production of insecticides that combated disease-carrying insects. The influence of these drugs and medical innovations cannot be overstated. They not only helped American soldiers, but they also increased life expectancy in the United States and greatly improved medical care around the world including such countries as Japan, India, and the Soviet Union.

Thus, 20th-century medical science and health care received a jump start from the most horrific of all human activities. But one might speculate that even without the wars of the 20th century medical knowledge would have advanced. Moreover, it is clear that war did far more damage than it helped. Take the example of the Holocaust. Because of the Nazi war against the Jews, thousands of Europeans (not just Jews) became sick. After destroying the medical infrastructure of Jewish communities, epidemics appeared that affected Jews and non-Jews alike. Indeed, one of the tragedies of the 20th century is that so much unnecessary disease and illness could have been prevented. At the end of the century, new diseases such as AIDS, which was particularly devastating in Africa, ravished the world's population in part because of government neglect and unwillingness to implement policy and procedures to provide medical attention and to stop epidemics. In the Inuit North, pollution of traditional food supplies has caused severe health problems. Thus in terms of health and medicine, the 20th century was a period of terrific progress and terrible frustrations about what might have been done.

EUROPE

The carnage of World War I produced casualties in unprecedented numbers. The war also provided new challenges to the medical profession. The weaponry of the war was so potent that when it did not kill outright, it wounded men's bodies with violent force. Beyond that, the terrain in which much of the fighting took place—fields cultivated over centuries with animal droppings—helped create infectious wounds foreign to recent medical experience. Doctors on both sides of the fighting lines came to grips with the problem of reconstructing or, if need be, replacing the aftereffects of combat such as torn faces and crippled limbs. Finally, the shock to men's minds was often as calamitous as a physical injury, and medical science moved to treat this problem as well.

Doctors had to adjust to unprecedented numbers of patients in the wake of the great battles on the western front. All too often they themselves were under enemy fire. Sometimes they faced death at dressing stations near to the front, where they were in the same danger combat soldiers faced. Sometimes they were imperiled in rear-area medical centers that, deliberately or fortuitously, became the targets of enemy air or long-range artillery attack.

The number of men wounded during the war can only be estimated, and sources vary—sometimes wildly. Standard figures for Germany give a total of approximately 4.3 million military men who were wounded and survived their wounds. The German army typically lost 2.4 percent of its field army strength each month due to wounds. Almost 75 percent of that number returned to some kind of further service. The official British figure counts approximately 2.3 million wounded. In both instances, but especially for Germany, some of those counted received their wounds in areas other than the western front. French and American figures point in a different direction. For one thing, both countries saw their fighting men wounded primarily on the western front. Another characteristic is the smaller set of numbers than for Britain or Germany. French figures vary wildly. Official estimates place that country on the same level of the other major belligerents: a postwar French parliamentary study came up with a figure of nearly 3 million, with many of those wounded on more than one occasion. But several authorities give the startlingly low figure of approximately 400,000 wounded; this estimate indicates that many wounded French soldiers did not survive and were counted among the 1.4 million dead. The French experience at Verdun suggests what occurred in a poorly organized and overwhelmed medical system. Thirty-two officers were wounded during a surge of fighting in April 1916; 19 died of their wounds as gas gangrene set in. Overall, the French forces at Verdun suffered 23,000 fatalities among men who had been hospitalized in the first four months of the battle. An American ambulance driver described the chaotic

scene at a major hospital four miles south of Verdun: "Pasty-faced, tired attendants unloaded mud, cloth, bandages and blood that turned out to be human beings; an overwrought doctor-in-chief screamed contradictory orders at everybody, and flared into cries of hysterical rage." American losses were conditioned by the relatively brief length of time in which American soldiers participated in the fighting. Nonetheless, approximately 190,000 men in the AEF (American Expeditionary Force) were wounded.

A wounded soldier often remembered the suddenness of the sensation and the sense of helplessness. A British private at the Battle of the Somme recalled getting ready to jump over the front line "when I was hit in the shoulder with a bullet which penetrated my spine causing temporary paralysis." Vomiting blood, he fell into the trench with his body swept by nausea. "Afraid of losing consciousness I dug my nails in the earth . . . as I realized that in my position I could be trampled on and regarded as dead." Fighting in the Argonne Forest in the fall of 1918, Colonel William Donovan of the American 42d Infantry Division recalled a "smash, I felt as if somebody had hit me on the back of the leg with a spiked club." He later learned he had been shot in the right knee. H. Hale, a British artillery corporal, recalled what it was like being the victim of a mustard gas attack that had lasted for several hours. "After about six hours, the masks were no good. . . . By morning everyone was round the shell holes vomiting." It took two men to guide each of the injured back for treatment, and, as his comrades began to panic while unable to breathe, Hale kept telling himself, "Hold tight and take no notice." His stomach cramped from repeated vomiting, and by the time a wagon had carried his group to the rear, "we were blind, we couldn't see anything." When treated at the 4th Canadian General Hospital, he found "the worst part was when they opened your eyes to put droplets in them—it was just like boiling water dropping in!" In the fall of 1918, an American officer survived an artillery attack on a small building where he was standing. He recalled a terrific blast that blotted out everything, a sense of being stunned, and "a feeling one would experience after a violent fall to the ground." Pains in his face and left hand told him he had been struck there, and when he touched his face with his right hand, "my fingers came in contact with a mass of warm sticky matter, which I knew at once was blood and lacerated flesh." He saw pieces of bodies scattered around including "a severed foot" standing upright. For a moment he thought mistakenly it was his own. Equally vivid were the recollections of a British victim of an earlier artillery attack, Lieutenant John Bagot Glubb. On a road near Arras in 1917, he felt himself lifted by a "tremendous explosion almost on top of me," which then set him down. Running in "a kind of dazed panic," he felt that "the floodgates in my neck seemed to burst, and the blood poured out in torrents." While sitting in the dressing station, he noted, "I could feel something lying loosely in my left cheek, as though I had a chicken bone in my mouth. It was in reality half my jaw, which had been broken off, teeth and all, and was floating about in my mouth."

The intense concentration of heavy weaponry on the battlefields of World War I presented surgeons with cases they had never seen before. Soldiers wounded by machine-gun fire rarely had a single injury; rather, they were likely riddled with bullets. The extensive use of artillery, both before and during attacks, meant soldiers

During World War I, there were not enough hospitals to meet the needs of wounded soldiers. Here, Americans set up a makeshift medical facility in a ruined French church. © National Archives.

were brought to aid stations with metal fragments that had done grievous damage to their bodies. Large chunks of metal could decapitate a man or sever one half of his torso from the other. But even slivers of metal moving at great speed could penetrate the body with traumatic effect. The American surgeon Harvey Cushing noticed that an artillery shell exploding near the sandbags ostensibly protecting troops could propel grains of sand outward with a velocity that penetrated a man's eyelids and threatened his sight.

Another American doctor, William L. Peple, treated one soldier who had been wounded by a high-explosive shell. The man eventually lived, although he had more than 10 wounds from his right thigh down through his leg. As Peple recalled, "The shaft of the thigh was shattered just above the knee. Gas gangrene had developed. . . . A big piece of metal had torn through the left ankle joint and lay buried in the tissues of the leg." The soldier had also lost the sight in his left eye due to another shell fragment that had struck him in the temple. A French military doctor, working at a casualty clearing station, described the mutilated bodies he encountered: "[T]hey reminded us of disabled ships letting in water at every seam." Artillery caused most of the wounds suffered by soldiers on the western front. Bullet wounds followed, with injuries from gas attacks making up a relatively small number. Despite the emphasis on using the bayonet during military training, military doctors recorded only a tiny number of bayonet wounds. Troops seldom closed with the enemy in a way that permitted extensive combat with the bayonet. And men penetrated by a bayonet probably died quickly without receiving medical care.

Harvey Cushing saw the damage to human bodies and the future prospects of their owners in a visit to a British amputee ward in March 1918. Here he encountered a former stable worker who had lost both legs at the knee and a brass polisher who had to return home without his right arm. A 20-year-old ploughboy from the Orkney Islands had to face a future without one of his legs; so too did a Yorkshire housepainter. The ward also contained an apprentice butcher whom the war had left with a single arm.

By the late 19th century, doctors customarily performed operations using aseptic techniques, which blocked the danger of infection, and antiseptic techniques, which killed bacteria that had not penetrated deeply into the body. Even infected wounds were susceptible to antiseptic drugs applied to tissues close to the body's surface, and antisepsis had worked in the Franco-Prussian and Boer wars. As Europe approached World War I, standard practice for physicians called for standing aside and permitting wounds in portions of the body like the head, chest, lungs, and abdomen to heal largely on their own. In a future war, doctors expected to dress wounds, to amputate shattered limbs, and to set fractures.

The most experienced military physicians on the western front in 1914, British doctors who had served in the Boer War, were acquainted with injuries that struck vital organs and killed. They had also met wounds that penetrated the body without deadly harm. Belgium and France presented another possibility: wounds contaminated by dirt from fields that had been manured for centuries. Physicians were unprepared for the deadly infections that accompanied even the smallest wound, especially when men were hit by shell fragments. High explosives produced wounds in which shards of metal, shreds of soiled clothing, and mud invaded the body.

Antiseptics were useless against infections that thrived deep in the body's tissues or found their way into the bloodstream. In 1914, physicians on all sides encountered untold numbers of patients struck by an infection they labeled "gas gangrene." Bacteria that required no oxygen developed inside wounds that had been treated and closed. A swelling emerging within a few days indicated an infection that no tool available to the doctors of the day could treat. Medical science seemingly marched backward. All wounds became infected, and serious ones, like compound fractures of the femur, killed 8 out of every 10 men who bore them. Mortality figures climbed back to the level of the American Civil War.

As early as October 1914, a German surgeon described how even small shell fragments could lead to immense damage as they rapidly penetrated a body. Larger chunks of metal did even greater violence to bones and flesh. The worst consequence, however, was infection. "Healing these irregular, jagged wounds is complicated by the fact they are frequently dirty, and . . . most are penetration-wounds, which means that a large area of the wound is deprived of blood and hence subject to gangrene." Such a gangrenous wound meant "substantial wound discharge, infection, bleeding, and putrefaction." A young German military physician described his first clinical encounters with this deadly phenomenon. "Quite often the temperature of a soldier with an innocent-looking wound rose rapidly, and then I found the dreaded gas-gangrene had set in." Only new techniques could cope with such a threat. Doctors learned to cut away damaged tissues (the process called debridement) and, against conventional medical practice, left the wound open. In that state it had to be bathed constantly in a special cleansing fluid designed by Alexis Carrel, a physician, and Henry Dakin, a chemist. After debridement, rubber tubes were placed in all parts of the wound, which was flushed with Dakin-Carrel fluid every few hours. In conditions closer to the front, such a technique was not feasible. Instead, dressings were soaked in the fluid, applied to the wound, then removed and replaced every four hours. Provided it could be applied in time, the treatment proved effective. But it also meant that even minor wounds required doctors to slice away large amounts of flesh or even amputate. Similarly, doctors learned the necessity of treating all wounds with tetanus antitoxin.

> *The nature of trench warfare put some parts of the body at special risk.*

The difficulties of applying Dakin-Carrel fluid to wounded American soldiers being shipped home by a long sea voyage encouraged American doctors to develop a different technique to combat infection. After removing diseased tissue, doctors covered the wound with one or more layers of vaseline gauze, then surrounded the dressing with a plaster of paris cast.

But gas gangrene left tragically maimed men in its wake. In September 1917, one of Harvey Cushing's colleagues amputated both legs of a young soldier only to find that "fulminating gas-bacillus infection" had developed. The following day "a double thigh amputation, high up" took place, offering the young victim a hope of keeping his life.

The nature of trench warfare put some parts of the body at special risk. Anyone peering over the top of a trench was likely to draw the attention of one or more enemy snipers. The helmets adopted by 1916 protected only the skull while leaving the face exposed. A bullet passing through the face—especially if it spun after being deflected en route to its target—could damage most of the soft tissue of that part of the body. Severe disfigurement and blindness were the likely outcomes.

Patients with wounds to the face presented both standard and novel problems. Like all wounded, these men required treatment for shock. It could kill someone immediately or at any time throughout his journey back to a hospital. The infections that threatened all wounds, especially gas gangrene, needed to be countered by keeping the wound open and washed, and by aggressively and rapidly removing diseased tissue. But special lessons also emerged. For example, unless the patient with a facial wound was made to travel sitting forward, he would likely choke and die of asphyxiation.

All four of the major countries that fought on the western front made an effort to deal with such casualties, if only to return as many of them as possible to combat. British soldiers received a sophisticated form of treatment at the hands of special teams. Surgeons, dentists, anesthetists, and—most novel of all—sculptors and artists combined their skills to treat men with smashed faces or sometimes no faces at all. By the time of the Battle of the Somme in 1916, British facilities for treating facial wounds were able to deal with a sudden influx of 2,000 cases. In the closing years of the war, American and Canadian physicians trained at the British hospital at Sidcup, Kent, the center for the treatment of such wounds.

The leading reconstructive surgeon and the director at Sidcup was former ear, nose, and throat specialist Harold Gillies. Inspired first by German textbooks recounting treatment techniques and then by a visit to Hippolyte Morestin, the era's leading French plastic surgeon, Gillies determined to establish a center in Britain where facial injuries could be repaired. German military surgeons acquired a reputation for doing only enough to send men back to the front. Their French counterparts had no striking rehabilitative successes to which to point. In this framework, Gillies became a renowned and sympathetic figure within British society.

Hospital authorities forbade soldiers with facial wounds to have mirrors.

Colorful if exaggerated stories circulated in London about young officers with unmarked faces whom people met at social occasions. Ensuing conversations with these apparently unwounded men allegedly revealed that they had been Gillies's patients. Reality was far less romantic. The course of treatment stretched for months or even years, because Gillies preferred to repair injuries in deliberate stages. One soldier injured toward the close of the war was still being offered surgery four years later.

The psychological impact of disfigurement affected both the wounded and those around them. Sculptor Derwent Wood worked as an orderly in a hospital. That experience impelled him to create facial masks for the hopelessly maimed and disfigured. Working from prewar photographs of a wounded man, he molded, painted, and fitted a mask that would last for several years and permit him to go out in public once again.

Hospital authorities forbade those with facial wounds to have mirrors, but some men discovered enough of their disfigurement to go into hopeless depressions. A number found a way to kill themselves. Doctors, nurses, orderlies, and all others involved in treating these men had to learn to look at their patients without revealing the horror severe facial wounds evoked. As one orderly put it, he had never thought how normal it was to look someone directly in the face and how difficult it was to do so when the face before him was hideous. To have a face from which children would flee, he noted, "must be a heavy cross for some souls to bear." A number of men whose gargoyle-like faces prevented them from appearing comfortably in public devoted their lives to caring for similarly wounded men at military hospitals.

In April 1915, German forces used a chlorine gas attack against the Allied defenses at Ypres. Terrified Algerian troops in the French army first felt the impact of this novel weapon. The gas assault had the frightening feature of shutting off a man's breath and affecting him even as he fled the battlefield. From the spring of 1915 onward, both sides began to employ this weapon, and medical personnel had the standard task of treating the victims of poison gas attacks. In reality, there was often little a doctor or nurse could do either to prevent death or to ease the soldier's passage from life. Serious lesions on the lungs and other parts of the respiratory system meant that a gassed soldier's system would inevitably fill with fluid.

Ironically, more than a month before the gas attack at Ypres, three Germans had died and 50 were injured by the weapon. Carrying gas cylinders, 200 pounds each, to the front lines had been a noisy affair that attracted Allied shellfire on several occasions. One bombardment smashed some cylinders and made the Germans the western front's first gas casualties. It also showed the perilous nature of this weapon.

Witnesses recalled watching terrified casualties from the first gas attacks—their disorientation compounded by the blindness that often accompanied such injuries—drowning in their own fluids. In May 1915, a sergeant in the Northumberland Fusiliers passed a dressing station with a dozen gassed men. He described how "their colour was black, green & blue, tongues hanging out & eyes staring . . . some were coughing up green froth from their lungs." A German lieutenant suffered a severe gas wound at the Battle of Loos in September 1915 when he fell into a shell hole filled with chlorine. He described his injury as a feeling of soap bubbles in his chest, and, despite extensive treatment, had to be discharged. He could no longer breathe deeply enough to remain on active duty.

The growing use of more deadly phosgene gas in 1916 overshadowed chlorine, and 1917 saw the introduction of mustard gas. Both sides sought ways to protect soldiers exposed to such attacks. Gas masks were useful in defending against attacks of chlorine and phosgene. But surprise assaults might find soldiers unready to put them on, and gas attacks with artillery shells spread gas with deadly speed.

The quality of gas masks differed, putting the Germans at a disadvantage. German masks protected their wearers for only four hours, and facing prolonged Allied gas bombardments in the second half of the war put German troops in serious peril. In the summer and fall of 1917, German units faced harrowing British gas attacks by the powerful Livens projector. This device was a type of mortar that could put massive amounts of gas on a position across the battle line without warning. Officers of Germany's 54th Division, which had been assaulted with the Livens projector, calculated that they would incur 100 to 200 casualties from each such attack, of whom 10 percent would be fatally injured. As the war proceeded, treatment for gas wounds of all types improved. The number of gas casualties remained low compared to those produced by artillery fire and machine guns. Fresh air, rapid removal from the strains of the battle zone, and good nursing care aided recovery. Medical personnel learned to bathe gas victims as soon as possible and to spray their eyes, noses, and throats with bicarbonate of soda. Other treatments included the use of oxygen bottles to aid in breathing.

Spasms of coughing and retching induced by some gases put a strain on the heart, and doctors resorted to the hoary technique of bleeding patients to reduce the volume of the blood and the consequent strain of pumping it. Olive or castor oil helped protect the digestive systems of soldiers who had swallowed food or water contaminated by gas. More than 70,000 Americans had to be hospitalized following gas attacks, but only 1,221 of these died while under treatment. An additional 200 probably died on the battlefield. The total number of gas casualties on the western front remains impossible to calculate. Different armies began to list those killed and injured by gas at different points in the war; the French did not do so until the start of 1918. The chaos of the battlefield bred uncertainty of causes of death, and many men's bodies were never recovered. One authority gives an apparently impressive total of half a million. This figure, however, amounts to only 3 or 3.5 percent of a total of 15 million casualties on the western front throughout the war.

With the onset of trench warfare, the armies began to produce large numbers of men who, though unfit for combat, had no visible physical injury. Their disability took such forms as uncontrollable shaking, blindness, and deafness. To puzzled medical officers and angry combat commanders, such a "shell shock" casualty fit the model of a malingerer rather than a conventional patient.

Patients suffering psychological disabilities resulting from exposure to combat challenged deeply held elements in European culture. The 19th century had promoted an image of the calm, brave, and stoic patriot-soldier willing to sacrifice his life for his country. Such psychological disabilities fit more closely the maladies associated with females.

One view that emerged during the war held that the disability came literally from a nearby shell explosion. Alternatively, doctors blamed the passage of machine-gun bullets nearby for disrupting the functioning of a man's body. Rest, quiet, massage, and a bland diet were considered to be appropriate therapies. But many of the psychologically disabled turned out to be soldiers who had never been exposed to direct artillery or gunfire. Their malady came simply from the experience of trench life.

Another theory attributed psychological injury to a man's prewar disposition, not the strains of combat. It remained influential in the British army down to the end of the war despite the fact that many officers, representing the best families of the nation, appeared on the rolls of the stricken. In a postwar study, Lieutenant Colonel Lord Gort, a renowned infantry commander and future field marshal, proclaimed that elite units were immune to shell shock; such behavior "must be looked upon as a form of disgrace to the soldier." Even well-drilled troops in less distinguished formations, Gort insisted, could fend off the condition. The pre-1914 debate over the cause of psychological maladies had taken sharp form in Germany. There it was a practical issue, because it involved government-paid disability benefits for those injured in industrial accidents. At least some medical authorities had pointed to the trauma of having an accident to explain the psychological disabilities of the victims. Such a viewpoint had failed to persuade the government bureaucrats. Now, in wartime, most German doctors assumed that soldiers' psychological difficulties stemmed from character flaws.

In a conference held in Germany in 1916, the character flaw approach was formally adopted. It followed that a victim of shell shock had to be disciplined or subjected to painful medical therapies, and doctors in Britain, Germany, and France often applied painful electroshock treatments. One British medical officer made lines of shell-shocked patients watch while he applied electroshock (faradization) to the throat of a mute soldier. When the tormented patient finally screamed, he was told that he had been cured. The onlookers presumably took notice. In France, the forced use of electroshock (torpillage) produced a scandal when a soldier was court-martialed for refusing to submit to the treatment.

In Germany, too, treatment centered around a punitive regime that transformed the hospital into a barracks. A soldier being treated for shell shock first confronted a sympathetic and benevolent psychiatrist who tried to convince him that the subsequent treatment was necessary. This therapy, pioneered by Dr. Fritz Kaufmann and eventually adopted widely in the German military system, relied on excruciating electrical shocks. Accompanying these were military-style commands and physical exercises designed to shake the patient from his paralysis, muteness, or other disability. All the while, the therapist urged the patient to throw off his disability as quickly as possible. The therapist also insisted that recovery would occur rapidly and even a single agonizing session would bring progress. In England, Dr. Lewis Yealland at the Queen Square Hospital in London used a comparably harsh disciplinary therapy.

A minority of German doctors attempted to use other concepts. Some turned to a regime of rest, quiet, and good food, but the results seemed disappointing, and the punitive method reigned supreme. Others attempted a form of "talk therapy" in which the patient was encouraged to remember his traumatic experiences, to ventilate his feelings about them, and thereby to regain the ability to return to duty.

> *Doctors assumed that soldiers' psychological difficulties stemmed from character flaws.*

By 1917, doctors in several of Britain's 20 special hospitals for shell-shock treatment tried an alternative. They abandoned the use of pain and discipline for patients suffering from this allegedly deficient personality. Instead, they presumed that the patient was a normal individual who had undergone a traumatic experience. Thus, psychotherapy became the treatment of choice for some medical men. Many of them had had little interest in or knowledge of psychological maladies before 1914, but they later took this form of treatment into their postwar practices.

A famous figure who used these methods was Dr. William Rivers, who practiced at the officers' hospital at Craiglockhart, Scotland. There he persuaded traumatized officers like Wilfred Owen to return to the front lines. His most famous patient, Siegfried Sassoon, had more the character of a rebel against the military system— he had published a letter calling for a negotiated peace—than a victim of shell shock. Sassoon had been an aggressive and successful officer in trench warfare. Army authorities sent him to Rivers to avoid the embarrassment of court-martialing this distinguished but outspoken officer. After therapeutic meetings with Rivers, Sassoon also returned to combat; unlike Owen, who was killed shortly before the armistice, he survived his new period in the trenches and lived to old age (Heyman, 96–105).

FOR MORE INFORMATION

Babington, A. *Shell-shock: A History of Changing Attitudes to War Neurosis.* London: Leo Copper, 1997.

Cushing, H. *From a Surgeon's Journal, 1915–1918.* Boston: Little, Brown, and Company, 1936.

Heyman, N. M. *Daily Life During World War I.* Westport, Conn.: Greenwood Press, 2002.

Whalen, R. *Bitter Wounds: German Victims of the Great War, 1914–1939*. Ithaca, N.Y.: Cornell University Press, 1984.

HOLOCAUST

Many physicians and other medical personnel lived in the Polish ghettos. In Lodz, the second-largest ghetto in Poland, in 1939, there lived 92 doctors, including specialists in gynecology, urology, surgery, otolaryngology, ophthalmology, internal medicine, dermatology, neurology, psychiatry, and venereology. There were three ambulances, free insulin, and free care for tuberculosis patients. Still, the mortality rate was high. In Warsaw, in March 1942, the death to birth ratio was 45:1.

Medicine was nearly impossible to procure. In the winter of 1941–42, when sewer pipes froze, toilets became useless and excrement was dumped in the streets along with the garbage, causing widespread typhus epidemics, but "a single tube of anti-typhus medicine cost several thousand zloty." By contrast, by May 1942, the price of a kilogram of bread was 15 zlotys, and an average wage was 22 zlotys per day.

In a recent interview, Holocaust survivor Bernice Sobotka recalled that her father was diabetic. For a time, before the ghetto was completely sealed off, her sister was able to smuggle in insulin, but it was not enough. Even before the doors were locked, their father died. "The hospitals tried their best, but they had nothing to work with."

Epidemics frequently began in synagogues, where thousands were forced to live in cramped quarters with grossly inadequate sanitary facilities. The councils organized disinfection brigades, steaming actions, and quarantine stations, but by the end of March 1942, people were collapsing at work and in the streets, dying at the rate of 5,000 per month. Beggars, desperate for food, snatched it from the hands of shoppers. Corpses were left lying on sidewalks, covered with newspapers, for cemetery carts to pick up.

The earliest epidemic, and the most common, was characterized by severe diarrhea and a fever, resulting in death. Its cause was never identified. An epidemic of abdominal typhus was caused by the destruction of the water-filtering station during the German bombing. This affected both Jews and non-Jews until the plant was fixed.

A worse problem was the outbreak of exanthematic typhus, which spread unchecked from December 1939 until the end of 1940 and infected 1,727. Until the ghettos were sealed, however, even these conditions were bearable, and few people died.

Once the ghettos were sealed, the uncontrollable spread of typhus became a major problem. Some estimate that every family in the Warsaw ghetto experienced a case of exanthematic typhus, and the disease affected from one-quarter to one-third of the population. Most of these cases were not reported to the authorities but were treated at home. The penalty for having a typhoid victim in one's family was severe. All residents of the house were isolated for two weeks; the house was locked and guarded by the police; and no one was allowed to bring in any food, thus condemning the rest of the family to starvation (although the mortality rate of the disease itself was only 15%). In addition, all the residents of the house, and those in the two neighboring houses, were taken to the bathhouses, where conditions were so inhumane that many healthy people became ill after their baths and older, sicker people died.

By not reporting cases of typhus, families could avoid this treatment. Despite the fact that doctors and nurses who treated patients risked deportation to the Auschwitz death camp, many participated in this form of passive resistance. The Nazis sent out mobile teams to make surprise visits to houses in an effort to catch lawbreakers.

Other diseases were prevalent as well. Tuberculosis left patients emaciated and feverish, with weak cardiac activity. Colitis, a painful inflammation of the large intestine, had a mortality rate of 60 percent. Its most probable cause was the filthiness of the carts used to transport foodstuffs. These carts were frequently used for carting dung as well as food.

Deaths from starvation occurred with increasing frequency. Before hunger kills, it manifests other signs of malnutrition: weight loss (one woman, aged 30, 4 feet 10 inches tall, weighed 24 kilograms, or about 50 pounds), low body temperature, cataracts in young people, low blood pressure, slow pulse, dysentery, anemia, fatigue, dizziness, nausea, and diarrhea. The lack of food affected people's ability to do physical labor and think clearly. Tempers flared, manners disappeared, and incidents of greed and dishonesty increased tremendously, particularly with regard to the theft and black marketing of food.

Thirty percent of all deaths in Lodz were caused by heart disease, the result of the tension and stress of ghetto life. The worst off were the very old and the very young, who were least able to stave off hunger and disease. One other group, Jewish German and western European refugees, forced to live in a hostile environment, away from home and family, housed in public buildings unsuited for such purposes, died in far greater numbers than the Poles. Their presence in the ghetto was greatly resented because it added to the overcrowding and lessened the food supply. Some of these refugees even resorted to suicide.

In addition to disease and starvation was one other cause of death: being shot for attempting to escape or merely for being in the wrong place at the wrong time. The following excerpt is from a citation sent to an 18-year-old auxiliary policeman of the Protective Police Department for acting "resolutely to frustrate the escape of five Jews from the ghetto":

[The Jews] ducked out in a drainage canal which was strongly secured by barbed wire and, without the alertness and determination of the guard, would have disappeared in the dense terrain. The pursuit was extended over a distance of more than 1500 yards with the result that the 5 Jews were shot to death. "Because of the vigilance, resolution, and good shooting of auxiliary policeman Schulz, the great danger of a spread of spotted fever and other epidemics to the German population was removed."

(Soumerai and Schulz, 99–101).

FOR MORE INFORMATION

Dawidowicz, L. *The War Against the Jews, 1933–1945*. New York: Holt, Reinhart, and Winston, 1975.

Esh, S. *Yad Vashem Studies on the European Jewish Catastrophe and Resistance*. Jerusalem: Yad Vashem Martyrs' and Heroes' Remembrance Authority, 1959.

Hilbert, P. *The Destruction of the European Jewry*. Chicago: Quandrangle Books, 1967.

The Holocaust History Project. <http://www.holocaust-history.org/>.

Soumerai, E. N., and C. D. Schulz. *Daily Life During the Holocaust*. Westport, Conn.: Greenwood Press, 1998.

UNITED STATES, 1920–39

To resemble the examples of beauty and fashion presented in poster art, movies, newspapers, and magazines, Americans who could afford to do so quickly embraced the new standards of diet and dress. In particular, one historian observed, film and fashion encouraged the "unveiling of the female body, baring arms and legs and putting the body on display as never before." Altered expectations of appearance in turn encouraged new approaches to personal hygiene in the 1920s, particularly among the middle class.

Ever since the Civil War, a belief in the importance of keeping clean had been spreading in the United States as a result of new theories that diseases were carried by dirt, decayed food, and sewage. The increasing availability of piped water and indoor plumbing made frequent washing more convenient and common. Setting aside an entire room in the house for a separate toilet and bath, a practice that began appearing in middle-class home design in the early 20th century, provided one important measure of a growing commitment to cleanliness.

World War I stirred further concerns about personal hygiene. The shocking rejection as physically unfit of nearly one-third of all World War I draftees drew attention to deficiencies in American hygiene. Further anxiety was aroused by the influenza epidemic of 1918–19. This worldwide scourge cost perhaps 500,000 American lives, most of them in urban areas. An alarmed society began devoting more attention to matters of health and hygiene.

Public schools began instructing all children to bathe regularly, wash their hands before meals, and brush their teeth twice a day. Immigrants thought to present problems to themselves and dangers to others because of a lack of cleanliness became particular targets. Adult education programs for immigrants focused on English, civics, and hygiene. Elementary school texts dealing with hygiene and biology shifted from devoting 65 percent of their content to anatomy and physiology and 4 percent to sanitation in the 1890s to 5 percent on anatomy and physiology and 40 percent on sanitation by 1925. In New York City, public high school physical education classes with a component of personal hygienic instruction did not exist before 1922 but enrolled over 50 percent of all students by 1934.

Commercial advertising gave new prominence to cleanliness and introduced the new social diseases of body odor and bad breath. Lifebuoy soap ads featured a man with "b.o." who luckily discovered "what they're saying behind my back!" before losing friends and a job promotion. The ads also showed a young woman with underarm odor whom men avoided until she was rescued by the proper (you guessed it! Lifebuoy) soap. Toothpaste was also heavily promoted. Colgate was the early leader, but Pepsodent sales skyrocketed when it began sponsoring the *Amos 'n Andy* radio show. Expectations of a fragrant aroma as a measure of personal cleanliness quickly took hold.

The war against filth was also fought on the urban battlefield with the new weapons of electric vacuum cleaners and washing machines. In cities and electrified towns, standards of household and apparel cleanliness reached new heights in the 1920s. In rural America such change came more slowly. With dirt roads, coal and wood stoves, and farm animals, rural houses were hard to keep clean. The lack of electric appliances made the situation more difficult. Laundry was the farm woman's most time-consuming and backbreaking chore. The lack of running water and the sheer bulk of farm dirt in clothing rendered the task of cleaning clothes, bedding, other fabrics, and kitchen equipment daunting, if not impossible. The distinction between urban and rural America in this respect was, quite literally, a clean break.

Changes in diet, dress, and social attitudes regarding cleanliness converged in the post–World War I period in one particular case: feminine hygiene. Historian Joan Brumberg has observed that understanding their bodies and sexuality was quite limited but increasing rapidly for early-20th-century boys and girls. Inferior nutrition and health standards caused 19th-century adolescents to mature later, with a middle-class girl of the 1890s likely to reach menarche (age of first menstruation) at 15 or 16 and a working-class girl even later. As menarche declined and menstruation became less erratic and more frequent as a result of improved diet and health, parents and physicians struggled to understand what was happening as well as how to deal with their daughters' and patients' onset of reproductive capacity. Girls normally received little or no sex education because adults thought it best to protect them from sexuality as long as possible and, frankly, because their own knowledge was limited. Other than as a signal of fertility, menstruation was not well understood before the 1920s, when hormonal stimulation of the menstrual cycle was discovered, incidentally eroding the Victorian notion that a woman's life was defined by her ovaries—not her brain.

This recruiting poster underscores the importance of nurses during the First World War. © Library of Congress.

Dealing with menstruation as a practical matter changed according to individual circumstance. Traditionally, menstruating females used and reused washable rags to capture the blood flow. By the 1890s, upper-middle-class women, stirred by new ideas about germs and the spread of disease, began purchasing gauze and cheesecloth to make their own sanitary napkins or bought the first mass-produced napkins from the Sears & Roebuck catalogue. By World War I, disposing of, rather than reusing, napkins had become the standard middle-class routine; this practice soon came to be thought of as a measure of refinement and success, often one out of the economic reach of working-class and especially immigrant girls. In the 1920s, when the Kimberly-Clark Company began advertising a mass-produced disposable sanitary napkin it called Kotex in *Ladies Home Journal* and *Good Housekeeping*, it started taking over what was often an uncomfortable discussion for mothers with their daughters. Like earlier, not so widely circulated advice pamphlets, ads stressing the need to avoid fatigue, strenuous exercise, and exposure to disease during "that special time of the month" carried a subtle message of female disability and weakness.

The feminine hygiene products industry grew rapidly in the 1920s and 1930s. In 1936, the first commercial internal tampons were marketed under the brand name Tampax. Because of early perceptions that they might be either dangerous or immoral, tampons were slower than sanitary napkins to win acceptance, especially among not-yet-married women. Only after World War II transformed women's social and economic circumstances would the use of mass-produced feminine hygiene products of one sort or another become nearly universal (Kyvig, 109–12).

To read about health and medicine in the United States in the 19th century, see the United States entries in the section "Health and Medicine" in chapter 4 ("Intellectual Life") in volume 5 of this series.

FOR MORE INFORMATION

Brumberg, J. J. *The Body Project: An Intimate History of American Girls.* New York: Random House, 1997.

Kyvig, D. E. *Daily Life in the United States, 1920–1939: Decades of Promise and Pain.* Westport, Conn.: Greenwood Press, 2002.

Patterson, J. T. *Grand Expectations: The United States, 1945–1974.* New York: Oxford University Press, 1996.

Shorter, E. *The Health Century.* New York: Doubleday, 1987.

INTELLECTUAL
LIFE

HEALTH & MEDICINE

Europe

Holocaust

United States,
1920-1939

United States,
1940-1959

United States,
1960-1990

India

Soviet Union

Japan

Africa

Inuit

UNITED STATES, 1940–59

During World War II, the huge budget allotted for war—$321 billion from 1941 to 1943—was not solely focused on the creation of weapons. Americans' payroll deductions and defense bonds also went into research that would eventually contribute to the better health of humankind. First in this research was the massive production of antibiotics. Although Sir Alexander Fleming had discovered penicillin in 1928, it was hardly available until a number of scientists and facilities pooled their energies to meet the needs of war. The federal government, using the Department of Agriculture's regional laboratory in Peoria, Illinois, combined the talents of more than 21 companies to produce more than 650 billion units of penicillin a month by 1945—enough to include even some civilian needs. The discovery of streptomycin by Selman Waksman in 1943, subsequently produced by private pharmaceutical companies, demonstrated that industry and government cooperation remained important during this period, as it had been before in the history of American science.

Because private laboratories rarely had adequate money for complex research, government funding given to university laboratories enabled rapid and important discoveries to take place. One historian of medicine commented that the cooperation among university researchers, government support groups, and private industry seemed to be a unique American phenomenon leading to extraordinary productivity. Other antibiotics produced during this decade included bacitracin, chloramphenicol, polymyxin B, chlortetracycline, and neomycin. By the end of the 1940s almost all bacterial illness appeared to be under control. By 1950 John Enders had also succeeded in isolating viruses in tissue culture that would lead to the successful creation of vaccines against polio and other dread viral childhood diseases.

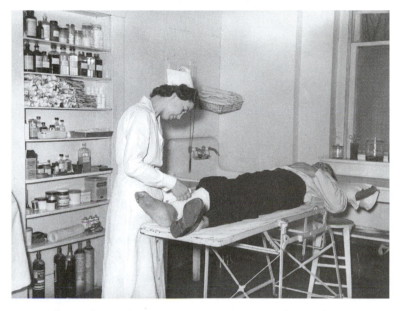

Herrin, Illinois, hospital emergency room, 1939. © Library of Congress.

Another concentrated wartime effort, the search for synthetic quinine to combat malaria—essential because the Japanese had cut off areas of natural production—also proved successful. Many American troops taking part in the Pacific war were completely disabled by the mosquito-borne illness. One survey from Guadalcanal reported three entire divisions inoperative with malaria. The discovery of the synthetics atabrine and chloroquine alleviated much physical suffering in the South Pacific. Just as important at the time was the mass production of insecticides such as DDT and insect repellents for personal use that wiped out the plague-carrying mosquitoes and body lice. A typhus epidemic was said to have been averted by these new vermin destroyers. No one thought about disturbing the balanced life cycle involving the other creatures who survived on such insects. Nor was there any awareness of other illnesses that human beings could develop from pesticides. What mattered most was saving the lives of soldiers and making their national service as comfortable as possible. Perhaps one of the most important areas of study to emerge from World War II has been the examination of secondary effects of goal-oriented knowledge. The realization that unforeseen results often arose from the pursuit of narrow purposes would become a challenging and legitimate field of study, as well as a source of popular fear—a favorite theme of science fiction.

Along with the antibacterial drugs that for a time ended pneumonia and tuberculosis came the extensive use and production of blood plasma. Death from infection became so rare that between 1945 and 1951 mortality from flu and pneumonia fell by 47 percent. Mortality from diphtheria dropped 92 percent and that from syphilis 78 percent. During World War II, research on steroids to relieve arthritic pain was also intensified. The discovery of cortisone led to the production of the most complex drug yet manufactured on a large scale. A detailed study of postwar science and technology could document how extensively wartime managerial and production skills became part of the nation's overall approach to health. Along with the 1948 expansion of the National Institutes of Health came the establishment of smaller foundations dedicated to research on specific problems. Only a few days after the bombing of Nagasaki, for example, General Motors—in the names of its directors, Alfred P. Sloan and Charles Kettering—gave $4 million to set up a cancer research center in New York City. Certain kinds of childhood leukemia would be eradicated before the end of the 1950s. Elsewhere new drugs were being discovered to alleviate severe allergies and anxieties and, most important, to combat certain forms of acute mental illness. Chlorpromazine, produced in quantity after the war by Smith, Kline and French, liberated many individuals who might have spent years in custodial care in mental hospitals.

The rapidity of change can be imagined in the assertion of historian James Patterson that by 1956, 80 percent of all the drugs being prescribed had reached the market only within the past 15 years. These "miracle drugs" had an immediate impact on the longevity of Americans. Life expectancy reached an average of 69.7 years by 1960, in contrast with 62.9 years in 1940. Women would continue to live longer than men, and whites to live longer than blacks, but wartime medical research unquestionably produced healthier lives for most Americans (Kaledin, 52–54).

To read about health and medicine in the United States in the 19th century, see the United States entries in the section "Health and Medicine" in chapter 4 ("Intellectual Life") in volume 5 of this series.

FOR MORE INFORMATION

Kaledin, E. *Daily Life in the United States, 1940–1959: Shifting Worlds*. Westport, Conn.: Greenwood Press, 2000.
Salk, J. <http://www.achievement.org/autodoc/page/sal0bio-1>.
Shorter, E. *The Health Century*. New York: Doubleday, 1987.

UNITED STATES, 1960–90

Technology has always been the essential link between science and the practice of medicine, and between 1960 and 1966 technological innovations were many. A list of these innovations is truly impressive, but the items in it take on particular meaning for the countless individuals and families who benefited from them at the time and the many more who have since been affected by the further medical progress those innovations made possible. In these years, among many other things,

- lasers were used for the first time in eye surgery;
- the first liver and lung transplants occurred, made possible in large part as a result of improvements in anesthesia;
- a prominent cardiac surgeon used an artificial heart to sustain his patient during surgery;
- pacemakers allowed persons with heart conditions to live normal lives;
- home kidney dialysis became possible;
- vaccines proved to be effective against German measles and rubella (which, if contracted during pregnancy, could injure the fetus);

- methods were perfected for dealing with the Rh factor, a blood condition that threatened the survival of babies at birth;
- an improved polio vaccine led to virtual eradication of the disease;
- the key antigen for development of a hepatitis B vaccine was discovered;
- development of antibiotics continued;
- radioactive isotopes were used widely in the diagnosis and treatment of diseases; and
- more sophisticated forms of chemotherapy for cancer treatment showed improved effectiveness.

Meanwhile, scientists engaged in basic research were laying the groundwork for technological innovations that would arrive in later years.

During these years the technological developments in medicine of the preceding decades were refined, but stunning new medical procedures captured the headlines. Although they were initially rare, just as organ transplants had been at first, new procedures offered hope to victims of various conditions. Perhaps the best example is the test-tube baby as an answer to problems of infertility. The first test-tube baby was born in London in 1978. She had been conceived when an egg extracted from her mother was fertilized in a laboratory by her father's sperm. The fertilized egg remained in a petri dish until it had developed into an eight-celled embryo; it was then implanted in the mother's uterus, where it developed as a fetus until delivered as a healthy five-pound, 12-ounce baby. Other such conceptions and births followed as use of the procedure spread.

Technological advancements in medicine and science ranged from those that seemed distant and exotic to those that affected the daily lives of millions of people. Sometimes the speed with which a rarity became commonplace was stunning. Within a decade of the first implantation of pacemakers to control irregular heartbeats, these devices enabled thousands of men and women to enjoy longer and happier lives. The same was true of coronary bypass surgery. Sometimes medical miracles captured worldwide attention, as when Christiaan Barnard, a South African surgeon, transplanted the first human heart on December 3, 1967. That it could be done was amazing; whether it was worth the time and expense required to extend one life for 18 days, as happened in this instance, was debatable. Four days later, the first transplant patient in the United States lived only a few hours.

Though there was no shortage of patients waiting to receive transplanted hearts, the number of hearts available for transplant was always very low. However, the shortage of organs available for transplants—of hearts, livers, lungs, kidneys, and corneas—was not the main obstacle to making transplants routine. Nor was it a lack of surgeons with technical skills for performing transplants. Rather, it was the limitations of drugs to prevent rejection of the implanted organs. In the seven years after Dr. Barnard's feat, more than 250 patients received transplanted hearts, but only about 20 percent lived more than a year after the surgery. For them, life each day was a reminder that the medical miracle performed by their surgeon was worth it, but general questions about transplant surgeries continued to raise ethical, medical, and financial questions.

Many changes in health care that made headlines during these years resulted from these technological advances. Less newsworthy than changes in technology, but undoubtedly more significant in the daily lives of the American people, were the dramatic reductions in infectious diseases occurring between 1960 and 1970, continuing a trend that had begun in the postwar years. Reported cases of measles, for example, which had increased from 319,124 in 1950 to more than 440,000 in 1960, dropped to 47,351 in 1970. Between 1960 and 1990, cases of diphtheria declined from 918 to 4, and poliomyelitis from 3,190 to 7. On the other hand, while deaths per 100,000 population from infectious diseases continued to decline, the decade-to-decade increases in deaths caused by cancer also continued to rise, as they would further in subsequent decades. Deaths from cardiovascular and kidney-related causes began to decline for the first time in the 1960s, although they remained 10 times as high as deaths caused by infectious diseases and 3 times as high as those caused by cancer.

Technological advances still did not solve some of the basic problems of the medical profession such as a shortage of doctors and the rising costs of health care. The federal government took steps to deal with shortages of physicians caused partly by the broadened availability of health care resulting from the instant popularity of Medicare and Medicaid. In 1971, Congress enacted legislation offering government funding for medical schools that increased their enrollments. Two years later it passed a law encouraging the development of health maintenance organizations (HMOs). These HMOs, consisting of groups of physicians and other medical providers, offered comprehensive health care to members of groups who paid fixed monthly premiums.

Decades earlier, physicians had stopped making house calls. Now the medical profession made other changes affecting doctor-patient relationships. Patients with acute illnesses and serious injuries were more likely to be referred by their primary doctors—family practitioners, pediatricians, obstetricians/gynecologists, and internists—to persons in specialized fields. Hospitals preferred having only board-certified physicians on their staffs, and health insurers paid higher fees to board-certified specialists, so the American Medical Association and other medical societies began to insist that every physician be certified in a specialty. Family practitioners, the primary care physicians who gradually replaced those known as general practitioners, also required certification. After 1970, therefore, almost all physicians-in-training served multiple-year residencies to be certified.

As medical specialization increased, physicians were more inclined to form group practices. Some groups included physicians with the same specialty, such as orthopedics or obstetrics/gynecology. Some included individuals or groups from a broad range of specialties, making it possible for them to provide comprehensive medical care through in-group referrals.

In 1970 more than 93 percent of the nation's physicians were men. By 1990 women physicians were beginning to claim a larger place in the profession, as the percentage of male physicians declined to below 83 percent.

In the period 1960 to 1990, there were several health issues that doctors struggled to solve. Among the biggest were the illnesses caused by smoking. Most aspects of health care depend on the willingness of individual Americans to exercise responsibility for their own health. The most persistent preventable health problems were caused by smoking. By 1967 the surgeon general's warning on the hazards of smoking had induced many smokers to tackle the difficult challenge of quitting, and smoking-withdrawal clinics appeared across America.

It is difficult to estimate the numbers of persons whose attempts to quit smoking succeeded. Many quit for short periods, but their addiction to nicotine was so powerful that they ultimately returned to their old habits. Nevertheless, it appears that between 1966 and 1970, 13 million Americans gave up smoking. The percentage of adult men who smoked dropped from 52 to 42, and of women from 34 to 31, although smoking among teenagers increased. The decreases and increases seem to have evened out the per capita consumption of cigarettes, for the figures for 1960 and 1970 were almost identical. By 1980, however, there had again been a slight increase in total consumption. The National Association of Broadcasters announced a plan in 1969 to phase out cigarette advertising on radio and television over a three-year period beginning on January 1, 1970. Publicity accompanying this announcement may have influenced some smokers to quit.

Smoking came to be regarded as a more serious threat to health and a greater social stigma after the surgeon general issued a warning in 1972 that secondhand smoke—that is, other people's cigarette smoke—may pose health hazards for non-smokers. Gradually thereafter restaurants began to provide nonsmoking areas, and hotels sometimes honored requests by hotel guests for rooms in which smoking was not permitted. Meetings and social gatherings that would once have been held in smoke-filled rooms began to be free of smoke. Laws calling for smoke-free workplaces and lawsuits demanding them carried restrictions against smoking even further. Tobacco companies fought the laws and challenged the evidence on the damaging effects of smoking, but they could only slow the imposition of restrictions.

Surgeon General of the United States Julius B. Richmond continued the efforts of his predecessors to publicize findings about the relationship between smoking and health. In 1979 he called smoking the "most important environmental factor contributing to early death." In 1980 he reported that cases of lung cancer in women were increasing rapidly and that lung cancer soon would lead to more deaths than breast cancer. In March of the same year came reports on research at the University of California at San Diego that produced the first scientific evidence that breathing secondhand smoke is harmful for nonsmokers. This report and others boosted efforts to limit smoking in public places.

The surgeon general's reports caused some smokers to fight their addiction and sometimes to win. Between 1970 and 1980 smoking dropped 28 percent among men age 20 and older, 13 percent among adult women, and 20 percent among teenage boys. Among teenage girls, however, it increased 51 percent in the dozen years preceding 1980.

Revenues generated from the 1998 voter-approved anti-smoking Proposition 10, which added a 50-cent tax on tobacco products, helped fund antismoking programs such as the billboard displayed. © AP/World Wide Photos.

Whether from eating too much, or eating the wrong foods, or failing to adequately exercise, many American men and women also jeopardized their health and appearance by being overweight. Diet plans promoted on television, in books, and through programs like Weight Watchers all attracted believers and followers. Some nutritionists placed the emphasis on healthful, balanced diets. Others called for drinking nutritious concoctions in place of solid foods. The range of gimmicks for losing weight was impressive, but then, as later, most who managed to lose weight by following one plan or another quickly regained it when they returned to their predieting habits.

During these years a number of psychophysiological eating disorders began to receive greater attention. The most common were anorexia nervosa and bulimarexia, or simply bulimia, whose victims were typically women. The symptoms of anorexia include an abnormal fear of being fat; a distorted image of one's appearance; aversion to food; and, consequently, extreme loss of weight. Victims of bulimia go on eating binges followed by periods of depression and guilt. To deal with their insatiable appetites, they try extreme diets, fasting, and self-induced vomiting and diarrhea. For persons suffering from these disorders, the problem is not unavailability of food but inability to cope with its presence.

> *Mental patients were often simply put out on the streets to become homeless.*

More and more people, faced with increasing complexity in their lives, sought counseling from psychologists and psychiatrists. Many received effective treatment through counseling and medication. At the same time, there was an increase in so-called pop psychology, that is, do-it-yourself approaches to coping with stress, depression, and other troubling conditions. Doctors and counselors on radio programs provided ready-made answers for questioners seeking help, but probably more significant were books promoting self-help. The first best seller in what was to become a self-help industry was *I'm OK, You're OK* (1969), a popular rendition of the principles of a field of treatment known as transactional analysis, by Thomas Harris, M.D. Transactional analysis was used widely by psychiatrists, though not without controversy, and it became something of a game, a means for people to discover much about themselves and others. One practitioner remarked, "Tom Harris has done for psychotherapy the same thing Henry Ford did for the automobile: made it available to the average person."

Reliance on medication by persons suffering from stress and physical pain had grown rapidly in the 1960s and early 1970s, so much so that drug manufacturers began to worry about dependence on it. They endorsed warnings to physicians by the Food and Drug Administration that tranquilizers not be prescribed for the stress of everyday life. Perhaps in response to such warnings, legally filled prescriptions for tranquilizers (the most widely used of which was Valium) dropped from 88.3 million to 62.3 million between 1975 and 1979.

Treatment of mentally ill persons changed in other ways as well, the most notable being that fewer of them were confined in institutions. In earlier times persons judged to suffer from mental illness could be institutionalized without their consent. To gain their release, they had to prove their sanity and ability to handle freedom. In

1975 the Supreme Court ruled that mental patients could not be confined against their will unless they were a danger to others or could not care for themselves. As a result, and also in reaction to worries inspired by reports of mistreatment in mental institutions (as depicted in Ken Kesey's 1962 novel *One Flew over the Cuckoo's Nest*, made into a film in 1975), mental wards were emptied. Mental patients, in many cases, were simply put out on the streets to become homeless.

Through the 1980s and into the 1990s, mental health remained a concern for millions of Americans. Such illnesses as schizophrenia were the subject of ongoing research, as were depressive illnesses that prevented their victims from functioning well in daily life. Antidepressant medications, along with electroconvulsive therapy, had been used for a number of years to bring about recovery from bouts of manic depression, but the quest continued to find something that would prevent recurrences. In 1970 lithium carbonate was made available by prescription for treatment of acute depression and maintenance of relatively normal lives by manic-depressive patients. This required close monitoring of side effects. Lithium is regarded as the first successful preventive medication in the treatment of psychiatric patients.

People in the 1980s complained frequently about pressures of time, family responsibilities, earning a living, and adjusting to change, among other things. The fact that many were indeed affected by stressful conditions could be documented by psychologists and psychiatrists. Moreover, a survey conducted by the National Institute of Mental Health in 1984 concluded that almost 20 percent of adults in the United States suffer mental disorders. Women were shown to be more prone to depression and phobias and men to drug and alcohol abuse and antisocial behavior.

Decades earlier the quest for relief from mental conditions often involved psychoanalysis. Patients poured out tales of their past to persons trained to listen and, by asking questions, help them understand themselves and deal with their problems. By the 1980s neither the pace of life nor the terms of medical insurance allowed for protracted psychoanalytical treatment, and psychoanalysts had few patients. Nonetheless, counseling—both individual and in group therapy sessions—remained important in dealing with mental and emotional problems.

At the same time, the growing belief that mental disorders were often caused by such physical problems as chemical imbalances led psychiatrists increasingly to prescribe medications. This may explain the popularity of Prozac, introduced in 1988 as an apparently effective treatment for depression. Before long it was also used to treat problems associated with obesity, gambling, and anxiety over public speaking. Although many benefited from it and its side effects were few, some physicians and psychologists were concerned that Prozac and similar drugs were substitutes for dealing directly with what was wrong in the lives of their users. There were reasons to wonder, too, whether medications might inhibit creative powers in those who were dependent on them.

Another mental condition that received considerable attention in the 1980s is attention deficit disorder (ADD); sometimes the term *hyperactive* also describes an aspect of the condition known as ADHD. Although physicians and psychologists made many of the diagnoses of ADD and ADHD, many other cases were self-diagnosed. In fact, most people could see in themselves varying degrees of ADD's most common symptoms: a tendency to be easily distracted from tasks at hand, a low tolerance for frustration or boredom, an inclination to act impulsively, and a fondness for situations of high intensity. When diagnoses were made by professionals, they were followed by counseling and sometimes by medication, such as Ritalin. Indeed, overuse of Ritalin for children suffering from attention deficit and hyperactive disorder worried parents and teachers. Persons who diagnosed their own condition apparently compensated for it by doing such things as establishing demanding schedules or setting goals that required them to work obsessively.

If there was in fact an ADD epidemic in the United States, it was probably related to the hyperactive nature of society. Edward Hallowell and John J. Ratey, both psychiatrists, wrote in *Driven to Distraction* that "American society tends to create ADD-like symptoms in us all. We live in an ADD-ogenic culture." They identified some of the hallmarks of American culture that are typical of ADD as well as of postmodern times:

The fast pace. The sound bite. The bottom line. Short takes, quick cuts. The TV remote-control clicker. High stimulation. Restlessness. Violence. Anxiety. Ingenuity. Creativity. Speed. Present-centered, no future, no past. Disorganization. Mavericks. A mistrust of authority. Video. Going for the gusto. Making it on the run. The fast track. Whatever works. Hollywood. The stock exchange. Fads. High stim.

It is important to keep this in mind or you may start thinking that everybody you know has ADD. The disorder is culturally syntonic—that is to say, it fits right in.

Americans in the 1980s also witnessed two major epidemics. First, in March 1981 the Centers for Disease Control (CDC) determined that cases of the sexually transmitted disease known as genital herpes had reached epidemic proportions in the United States. Victims suffered painful, recurring sores on their genital organs. Between unpredictable outbreaks the virus withdraws into nerve cells, where it remains out of the reach of the body's immune system. A medication existed to relieve the symptoms when initial outbreaks occurred, but there was no means as yet to prevent or relieve the symptoms in subsequent recurrences, making this the first incurable sexually transmitted disease since the introduction of antibiotics. Research continued for medications to prevent outbreaks for those afflicted with the disease and for vaccines to protect others from contracting it.

At the same time a more deadly disease, usually transmitted sexually, leaped into the nation's consciousness. In June 1981 the CDC reported five cases of a strain of pneumonia among previously healthy homosexual men in Los Angeles hospitals. This strain, *pneumocystis carinii*, usually occurs in infants or in adults receiving immunosuppressive drugs, as in the chemotherapy treatment of cancer patients. Reports of other cases of strange illnesses appeared elsewhere, most commonly among homosexual men. Initially labeled GRID (for gay-related immunodeficiency), the name was changed when the victims included recipients of blood transfusions, female prostitutes, intravenous drug users, and heterosexual Africans and Haitians. The disease was then named AIDS (acquired immunodeficiency syndrome).

By the end of 1982, 750 AIDS cases had been reported in the United States and almost 1,600 worldwide. A year later the number of reported cases reached about

3,000. With the number of cases growing daily, the AIDS crisis became one of the big stories of the decade. Other factors also made it so, such as movie star Rock Hudson's revelation in 1985 that he was battling AIDS and his death later that year. The dedication of an AIDS hospice in New York by Mother Teresa, a nun renowned for her work with the poor and suffering, also increased public awareness. Close-to-home reminders of the dangers posed by AIDS came in 1987 and 1988, when patients began to see their doctors and dentists slip their hands into latex gloves before treating them.

When the CDC reported the first cases of AIDS in June 1981, it opened one of the decade's big stories. At first awareness of AIDS spread slowly, but within five years just about everyone knew that scientists, physicians, hospitals, and the victims and their friends and families faced dreadful challenges. In 1986 the Department of Health and Human Services (HHS) estimated that the number of cases and deaths would increase tenfold in the next five years. In 1991, predicted HHS, some 50,000 Americans would die of AIDS—more than the number killed in most years in automobile accidents. That prediction may have been too grim. In 1990 there were 29,781 deaths, bringing the total since the center began keeping records in 1981 to 98,350. With about 140,000 cases known, however, the CDC made another grim prediction: that the AIDS death total could reach 340,000 by 1993.

Reporting on the spread of AIDS in 1986, HHS noted that about 70 percent of the victims of AIDS were homosexual or bisexual men. This prompted those who regarded homosexuality and bisexuality as sinful to call AIDS God's punishment. They judged the 25 percent of the victims who were intravenous drug users infected by contaminated needles in much the same way. The fact that more than one-third of the known cases were in New York and San Francisco gave those hostile to homosexuality an opportunity to condemn these cities as centers of wickedness.

Wherever cases appeared, AIDS victims were kept at arm's length, even though it was well established that the virus that caused AIDS could not be spread by casual contact. In well-publicized instances that caused controversy across the nation, even children who had been infected through blood transfusions were kept out of the schools they had been attending. The gravity of the AIDS epidemic, lack of information about the disease, and attitudes about it compelled the federal government to educate the American public about its nature and consequences. In May 1988 the government took the unprecedented step of mailing an explicit eight-page booklet, *Understanding AIDS*, to 106 million households.

Heather Magnus, center, explains the facts of HIV and AIDS to a group of children during a rally to boost awareness in the black community. © AP/Wide World Photos.

An often-controversial search continued for vaccines to prevent the further spread of AIDS and cure existing cases. In 1989, two studies showed that the drug AZT offered hope as a treatment for AIDS. Initially AZT had been used to treat severely ill patients, but the studies indicated that it could delay the onset of symptoms if it was administered when early signs of damage to the immune system appeared. But

AZT was not without side effects. The National Cancer Institute reported in 1990 that persons with AIDS who received it stood a nearly 50 percent chance of developing lymphoma after three years on the drug. The cost of $7,000 to $8,000 per year for those being treated with AZT also inhibited its widespread use. Although other therapies were beginning to be developed, it was too early to determine their effectiveness. Understandably, the slow progress in AIDS research coupled with homosexuality as a culturally divisive issue made this a hot political subject.

Technological advances in developing treatments for diseases such as AIDS played a part in pushing health-care costs upward. So did the increased longevity of the population. Another contributor, medical malpractice insurance, had grown in significance for a decade and reached crisis levels in the mid-1970s. Doctors and hospitals purchased malpractice insurance as protection against justified and unjustified claims of mistakes or negligence. Insurance funds were used to investigate the claims, provide legal defenses against them, and pay damages to patient-victims in court judgments or out-of-court settlements. Between 1969 and 1975, according to authoritative estimates, claims had increased by about 180 percent. One doctor in 10, on average, was sued, and the size of awards by juries rose during these years.

A number of factors played a part in the increase, including sharply rising doctors' fees; patients' beliefs that they were not given personal attention; lack of personal relationships between specialists and patients; and, apparently, the belief that greater sophistication in medical techniques should make doctors and hospitals infallible. The popularity of the television program *Marcus Welby, M.D.* seems to have encouraged notions of medical infallibility. The fact that awards in court cases and settlements were reaching into the millions of dollars also encouraged avaricious patients and lawyers to file claims. Even though the plaintiffs lost about 80 percent of the cases that went to trial, the cost of defending them was often so high that insurers frequently agreed to pretrial settlements. In the decade prior to the mid-1970s, insurance premiums for neurosurgeons and orthopedic surgeons increased more than tenfold, and practitioners in less-risky specialties also saw sharp increases. Where state insurance commissions refused to approve rate increases, insurance companies withdrew coverage. In such instances, some doctors declined to perform anything but emergency procedures. Even as solutions to the insurance problems proved elusive, most states tried to find them. Meanwhile, patients covered the cost of increased premiums when they paid the larger fees charged by their doctors.

In the 1980s the portion of the gross national product devoted to health care increased from 9.1 percent to 12.2 percent, on its way to more than 14 percent by the mid-1990s. The rate of increase in the total health bill for the nation was double the inflation rate. Not only did the annual increases have implications for state and federal budgets, but they also had significant effects on family budgets. Insurance premiums and payments made directly to doctors and hospitals multiplied several times between the late 1970s and 1990. Employers felt the squeeze, too, as the cost of providing health care insurance for their employees skyrocketed.

In the absence of a national plan guaranteeing health insurance for all Americans, some simply accepted the spiraling costs of individual and group coverage, some did without coverage and hoped that hospitals' emergency rooms or charity policies would meet their needs, and some tried to control costs by joining health maintenance organizations (HMOs). Although the relatively lower costs of HMO coverage made them popular, to compete with other forms of coverage they had to relax their initial limits on patients' rights to choose their doctors. Even so, the less-restricted choices left many of their members unsatisfied.

That dissatisfaction no doubt reflected a cynicism about providers of health care in general. One survey reported that only 29 percent of its respondents believed that physicians performed important services. Another 27 percent said that few physicians perform such services. In another survey, respondents expressed much greater confidence in pharmacists than in physicians and were more satisfied with their services. The changing health care scene prompted changes in the education of pharmacists, who were taught to counsel persons about their prescriptions. Their pill-counting role was being taken over by more accurate and efficient technological devices.

Despite the superior training of doctors and the breakthroughs in research, health problems were far from solved. The National Cancer Institute reported that cancer deaths continued to rise. Between 1973 and 1987, for example, occurrences of cancer increased by 14 percent. Melanoma (skin cancer) showed the greatest increase (83%), followed by prostate cancer (46%), lung cancer (31%), and breast cancer in women over age 50 (30%) and under age 50 (20%). Incidents of stomach, uterine, and cervical cancer declined. Heart disease also remained a major cause of death, with coronary disease or heart attacks accounting for more than 25 percent of the deaths occurring annually (Marty, 62, 135–38, 155–57, 217–19, 295–99, 321).

To read about health and medicine in the United States in the 19th century, see the United States entries in the section "Health and Medicine" in chapter 4 ("Intellectual Life") in volume 5 of this series.

FOR MORE INFORMATION

Brumberg, J. J. *The Body Project: An Intimate History of American Girls*. New York: Random House, 1997.

Grmek, M. D. *History of AIDS: Emergence and Origin of a Modern Pandemic*. Princeton: Princeton University Press, 1990.

Hallowell, E. M., and J. J. Ratey. *Driven to Distraction*. New York: Pantheon Books, 1994.

Marty, M. A. *Daily Life in the United States, 1960–1990: Decades of Discord*. Westport, Conn.: Greenwood Press, 1997.

Shorter, E. *The Health Century*. New York: Doubleday, 1987.

INDIA

Health and medicine in India arose from the subcontinent's rich historical background. Walking through India's cities, towns, and villages, one can find modern Western medical practices commingling with much older ayurvedic and yunani practices.

INTELLECTUAL
LIFE
|
HEALTH & MEDICINE
|
Europe

Holocaust

United States,
1920-1939

United States,
1940-1959

United States,
1960-1990

India

Soviet Union

Japan

Africa

Inuit

Ayurvedic medicine comes from India's early medieval period. Medical practice in India, and the treatment of health, has been and continues to be a combination of treating both the patient's illness and addressing his or her surroundings or spiritual well-being. Ayurveda, from Sanskrit, means the knowledge of science and has come to mean that which is connected with health and the body. Within the ayurvedic tradition, two early works survive that detail medicine and surgery: the *Charaka Samhita* and the *Sushruta Samhita*, dating from about 200 B.C.E. and A.D. 200, respectively. The *Charaka Samhita* gives extensive ingredients lists for making different compounds and drugs. The *Sushruta Samhita* outlines surgical practices for treating different ailments. Further, it is likely that the different bodily humors described by the Greeks actually came from India.

> The Islamic world has long had a rich tradition of medical practice.

The Islamic world has long had a rich tradition of medical practice. When Muslims came to the Indian subcontinent in 711, they brought with them their own practices that commingled with ayurvedic ones. The Islamic medical system was called yunani, which in Arabic means Greek. A Muslim doctor who used yunani medicine was called a *hakim*. Thus, in India and in the Islamic world and ancient Greece, medical practices and knowledge were shared among different practitioners. Within India today, there are hundreds of recognized yunani doctors, and thousands of dispensaries. Both yunani and ayurvedic practice depend on a holistic worldview that combines ideas about the body's temperature and moisture.

When Europeans came to India in the 15th century, they brought their own medical knowledge. By the time of Britain's supremacy over India in the 19th and early 20th centuries, Western advances in medicine were exported to India. Indians traveled to London and elsewhere to become trained in Western-style medicine. Yet old practices were never abandoned. India's founding father, Mahatma Gandhi, was an advocate of home remedies for illness. Gandhi also regularly fasted for spiritual, medicinal, and political reasons. Later, India's prime minister Morarji Desai, who followed Indira Gandhi in the 1970s, was known for his yogic practice of urine therapy. He drank his own urine each morning (called the "water of life" in ayurvedic circles).

One common medicinal tool in India was the neem tree, a fast-growing relative of the mahogany. Its botanical name was *azadirachta indica*, Persian for "India's free tree." Thriving in the semiarid climate, the neem tree was found throughout South Asia. It was popular because of the broad shade it provided from India's hot sun. The tree was also known to have powerful medicinal properties. Its bark, fruit, oil, seed, wood, and roots were used for a variety of purposes. For example, a few neem leaves dropped in water and gargled helped bad breath, its twigs were used as a toothbrush, and it was known to act as a mosquito repellant and excellent fertilizer as well. Both ayurvedic and yunani medical practices took advantage of the neem tree's properties, and recently it has become fashionable among Western naturalists. The tree was also endowed with spiritual good fortune, and many families planted at least one neem tree in their home gardens.

The medical world in India today reflects the nation's diverse backgrounds. Within India's villages, a sick person might visit a local doctor who works out of his or her home, or a small office. The patient rarely makes an appointment and pays in cash at the end of the visit. The doctor makes some diagnosis and prescribes treatment. In addition, within most village communities are ayurvedic and yunani practitioners whom the patient might call upon, depending on the patient's beliefs. Some people visit both. In larger towns and cities, the same triumvirate of medical practice can be found, only on a larger scale. India's cities such as Delhi, Bombay, Calcutta, and Hyderabad boast very modern hospitals that compete with any in the world. Indian doctors established many of these hospitals after receiving their training outside of India. With a prescription in hand, patients visit chemist shops (pharmacies) or yunani or ayurvedic dispensaries. Sometimes it is possible to go directly to the chemist shop and, having described one's symptoms, purchase a few pills without a prescription. Because of the less formal doctor-prescription-patient system in India, and because of the poverty, it is common to purchase only one or two pills, for example, just a few aspirins to cure a headache, and not an entire (costly) bottle.

India faces an array of health issues. With a population of over one billion, and continuing to grow, it is simply not possible for every person to receive adequate medical treatment. The population has put tremendous strains on the drinking water supply. In cities and villages alike, those who cannot afford better water frequently must drink from polluted sources. This leads to intestinal disease such as common diarrhea, which, although preventable and curable, still takes lives every day. Another medical challenge to India is malaria. This disease kills thousands each day throughout the world, yet many remain untouched by simple preventive measures such as mosquito nets, draining pooled water, and basic education. Finally, India is among the world's leaders in the growing AIDS epidemic. This sexually transmitted disease is frequently passed among prostitutes and truck drivers, the latter returning home and passing it to their spouses.

Health and medicine in India combine a variety of practices. From ancient Sanskrit and ayurvedic practice to the *hakims* of yunani to Western doctors, all these systems work together and are used in conjunction with each other. India faces daunting health problems in the new millennium, but at the same time is equipped with the knowledge and power to face such challenges.

To read about health and medicine in ancient India, see the India entry in the section "Health and Medicine" in chapter 5 ("Material Life") in volume 1 of this series; for 19th-century India, see the India entry in the section "Health and Medicine" in chapter 4 ("Intellectual Life") in volume 5 of this series.

~*Benjamin Cohen*

FOR MORE INFORMATION

Arnold, D. *Science, Technology, and Medicine in Colonial India.* <http://www.sscnet.ucla.edu/southasia/culture/cuisine/vegetar.html>.

Connor, L. H., and G. Samuel, eds. *Healing Powers and Modernity: Traditional Medicine, Shamanism, and Science in Asian Societies.* Westport, Conn.: Bergin & Garvey, 2001.

Harrison, M. *Climates and Constitutions: Health, Race, Environment and British Imperialism in India, 1600–1850*. Oxford: Oxford University Press, 1999.

SOVIET UNION

The Soviet government pioneered the concept of a national health service with free medical care for all citizens, a right proclaimed in their constitution. On July 18, 1918, Lenin created the People's Commissariat of Health of the Russian Republic. Nikolai Semashko, the first commissar of health, had his work cut out for him. Revolution, civil war, famine, mass migrations, and incursions of soldiers combined with long-standing, widespread conditions of poor hygiene, poverty, illiteracy, and primitive living conditions to produce raging epidemics. Scabies (a contagious itchy skin disease), malaria, syphilis, smallpox, cholera, typhus, and tuberculosis were common contagious diseases. Cholera and typhus epidemics erupted in 1918; between 1918 and 1920 there were more than six million cases of lice-spread typhus, a situation that prompted Lenin to remark, in his address to the Seventh Congress of Soviets, "Either lice will defeat socialism or socialism will defeat lice." In these early days of Bolshevik power the average life expectancy in Russia was 30 years, a statistic that put Russia about 150 years behind England and America. From its founding the Ministry of Health focused on preventive medicine through vaccination, personal hygiene education, and easy access to free basic health care. The government in the 1920s published eye-catching cartoon posters exhorting citizens to get vaccinated; bathe often; use soap; avoid alcoholic drinks; quit smoking; and be alert for their small children's safety, particularly during spring housecleaning when industrious housewives left windows wide open. However, there was always much greater emphasis on delivering medical care and education to urban workers than to peasants, and Moscow gave the Central Asian republics especially short shrift in medical services. Even at the end of the Soviet era most Central Asian hospitals did not have heat, running water, or indoor plumbing.

During the years immediately following the October Revolution, large numbers of physicians died from epidemic diseases and many others fled the country. Thousands of new doctors were needed, and fast, so the government turned to a source of plentiful cheap labor: women. Before the 1917 revolutions medical schools had been all but closed to women, but now on government orders the medical schools opened welcoming doors to them. Because many of these women were poorly educated, academic standards were compromised so that students could pass their courses and quickly get to work as low-level government employees. Professors who protested the changes were likely to be brutally silenced, as the medical-educational machinery continued to grind out legions of doctors (1,255,600 in 1988, compared with 612,000 that year in the United States). Most of these foot soldiers were female.

In 1946, 8 out of 10 medical students were women. In the 1970s, 72 percent of doctors were women, and they earned on average about two-thirds of the average factory worker's salary. In the 1980s a general practitioner was paid about 130 rubles a month, 40 rubles more than a hospital orderly, and less than a bus driver's salary of 200. A doctor without a wage-earning husband would likely have hard times, especially if she had children. With or without a co-breadwinner, women doctors shouldered all the same household responsibilities as other working women, in that it was not customary for men to help carry out these chores. Such "double shifts" made life particularly exhausting for women doctors, especially those who struggled to keep up with the latest developments in their field. In his novel *Cancer Ward*, Aleksandr Solzhenitsyn captured the Soviet doctor's dilemma in the character of Dr. Liudmila Dontsova. As she travels home from work after a long day, Dontsova, a highly respected radiologist, slowly and with great difficulty tears her thoughts away from her patients and tries to focus on the time-consuming tasks of a wife and mother:

Home was her responsibility, and hers alone, because what can you expect from men? Her husband and son, whenever she went to Moscow for a conference, would leave the dishes unwashed for a whole week. It wasn't that they wanted to keep them for her to do, they just saw no sense in this repetitive, endlessly self-renewing work.

In social prestige Soviets apparently ranked doctors on the same level with schoolteachers (rather than above them as in the United States and other Western countries). If women were the infantry troops of Soviet medicine, men were the officers. By the mid-1960s, however, the proportion of male to female doctors was beginning to change; more men than women were entering medical schools, and these men were intent on having a lifestyle closer to their western European and American counterparts. To achieve that standard, male students took advanced classes and training (beyond the six years required for an ordinary doctor) in order to become specialists and professors of medicine, and to land important posts in large city hospitals, research institutes, and medical schools. That sort of position guaranteed higher salaries, city residence, and respect. Besides being male, possessing a Party card and having excellent connections greatly improved one's chances of being admitted for advanced training and for reaching the higher echelons of medicine.

Feldshers and nurses were on the lowest rung of trained medical personnel. Feldshers, 75 percent of whom were women, were paramedics with two-and-a-half years' training, sometimes with a specialization in such fields as emergency care, midwifery, or public health (monitoring conditions in factories, giving first aid). After the revolution there was an attempt to eliminate feldshers because of their brief preparation, but that initiative quickly vanished, and instead the number of feldshers steadily increased. In the late 1970s, there were 500,000 such medical assistants in the Soviet Union. A feldsher could continue her medical education; Solzhenitsyn's Dr. Dontsova began her career as a feldsher-midwife. Perhaps feldshers could take comfort in the fact that they also were not at the very bottom of the health care profession. That space was reserved for nurses, virtually all of whom were women. Nursing was not respected, and like other Soviets who toiled in low-paying service jobs, nurses tended to be bossy and rude to those they were supposed to be helping. They often seemed more interested in making sure patients observed hospital rules than in providing professional care and comfort. For some women nursing was a stepping-stone to becoming feldshers.

Whether people were counseled or treated by specialists, general practitioners, feldshers, or nurses, the care was, according to the law, free of charge. Furthermore, all citizens were legally entitled to free medical care whether in a hospital or out-patient clinic or at home being visited by a medical professional. Nevertheless, it was customary to bribe doctors and other medical personnel with money, gifts, or services to get better care, a more qualified doctor, or "private" medical services (e.g., services provided off the books in the doctor's or patient's home, or in a clinic after regular hours). Many doctors felt it was more dignified to receive noncash gifts from their patients. Such bribes covered a range of scarce or expensive consumer items, including but not limited to food—especially meat—and clothing. A doctor in Riga, the Latvian capital city, helped a young stationery clerk get a private medical abortion for the bargain price of 10 rubles in exchange for two hard-to-find typewriter ribbons. The doctor's wife regularly received free meat at a collective farmers' market in exchange for her husband's ongoing treatment of the butcher's chronic endocrinological condition. In the 1970s it was customary to tip a doctor who made a house call 4 rubles, plus the cost of her round-trip taxi ride. In case of emergencies, however, payment was not expected. Hospital nurses and orderlies had to be bribed to perform such basic tasks of patient care as changing sheets, providing (and promptly emptying) a bedpan, or dispensing painkillers, especially if they knew the patient could pay. Even meals might not be available without a bribe. Soviet patients understood this and generally came into a hospital with plenty of rubles to distribute among hospital personnel. The amount patients paid unskilled and semiskilled hospital personnel under the table (na levo; literally, "on the left") was not much—a few rubles per day—and affordable for most. Sometimes, however, when lower-income patients or relatives wanted to assure the services of a highly regarded surgeon (200 to 400 rubles) plus extra tips for amenities such as antibiotics, a private or semiprivate room, and more intensive caregiving than was usual in a Soviet hospital ward, they could feel a financial pinch. One infant taken to a Moscow children's hospital in 1988 at first shared a room with 12 other children, but because his grandmother knew "how to talk to people the right way," a private room materialized (Eaton).

FOR MORE INFORMATION

Eaton, K. B. *Daily Life in the Soviet Union*. Westport, Conn.: Greenwood Press. Forthcoming.
Kaser, M. *Health Care in the Soviet Union and Eastern Europe*. Boulder, Colo.: Westview Press, 1976.
Knaus, W. A. *Inside Russian Medicine*. New York: Everest House, 1981.

JAPAN

The vast social, economic, and political changes in 20th-century Japan have been accompanied by dramatic changes in the health of the population and in medical care systems. At the beginning of the century, life expectancies at birth were 42.8 years for males and 44.3 years for females and remained under 50 years until after World War II. By 2000 the figures were 77.72 and 84.6 years, respectively. Infant mortality rates fell from 155 deaths per 1,000 live births in 1900 to 3.6 in 1999.

These dramatic changes can be attributed to vastly improved nutrition and sanitation, and to the control of infectious diseases. At midcentury the three most common causes of death were still infectious diseases: tuberculosis, pneumonia or bronchitis, and gastroenteritis. By the end of the century, the most common causes of death were those characteristic of advanced industrialized societies: cancer, heart disease, and cerebrovascular disease. Illness and death have been medicalized. During the 1960s and 1970s, the pharmaceutical industry was among the fastest-growing in the rapidly expanding Japanese economy. At the end of the 20th century, Japan spent approximately 8 percent of its GDP on health care, the seventh-highest national expenditure.

Affluence has provided a high level of health in the population but has also contributed to the increased risk of problems such as diabetes and heart disease, as well as those associated with smoking and stressful, sedentary work. Health topics are widely reported and discussed in print and broadcast media. In general, people are socialized to be aware of bodily states, and to make adjustments in lifestyle and to seek treatment for conditions deemed abnormal for themselves. Emotional difficulties are often somatized.

The establishment of mandatory, universal education from the 19th century has led to a highly literate population familiar with scientific theories of illness, although a variety of complementary and folk explanations and treatments exist alongside them. By the beginning of the 20th century the Japanese government had made biomedicine the country's official medicine system. Physicians wishing to practice traditional East Asian medicine had first to be licensed to practice biomedicine. Specialists in some East Asian treatments such as massage, acupuncture, and moxibustion were given paraprofessional status in the new medical system and must be formally educated and licensed by the state.

The government has excellent public health programs for maternal and child health and conducts regular screenings for a variety of diseases such as hypertension and cancers. The 20th century saw the development of biomedical hospitals for the treatment of illness. In the late 19th century, following the German model, the government established public hospitals for treatment of the poor, but soon high-quality doctors and facilities attracted middle- and upper-class patients as well. Now university and large public hospitals continue to have more prestige than small private hospitals and clinics, based on their reputations for having the latest knowledge and equipment. On the other hand, local private doctors' offices are considered more convenient and cleaner, have less waiting time, and offer more personalized care. Private practitioners do not have admitting privileges to the larger hospitals, which employ their own staff physicians. Under the insurance system, patients have their choice of physician and facility, public or private, although the government is moving toward a referral system for tertiary and specialty hospitals.

High-quality biomedical care is available to all through a universal medical insurance system. Japan's first health insurance law was enacted in 1927, covering only a small portion of the population but laying the groundwork for the later expansion of the system. At that point, the government was interested in "catching up with the West," but also wished to assure a healthy workforce to power industry. Over time, additional workers were added to the system, as were dependents. In 1958, the national legislature passed the National Health Insurance Law, which established universal, compulsory insurance to begin in 1960. The system relies on a mix of public and private insurers, but with a common fee schedule. In 1973, a system of free health care for the elderly was established, subsequently modified to include a small co-payment and a system of cost-sharing among various insurers for the more expensive elderly population.

Cost control became a major focus of health care policy by the 1990s. Long hospital stays, averaging 38 days for general hospital beds in 1990, was one target. By 1999 the average length of stay had decreased to 30.8 days. Another response has been to distinguish between acute and chronic illness. For chronic diseases, the government established a new category of "certified long-term-care beds." Hospice and palliative care units, which provide end-of-life care for cancer patients, introduced to Japan in the 1970s, increased rapidly in the last decade of the 20th century.

As a result of increasing life expectancies and declining birthrates, society has aged rapidly, with increasing probability for frailty or illness in the oldest age groups. In 1950, only 5 percent of the population was 65 years or older; by 1999, 17 percent were elderly. To relieve the fiscal burden of an aging population on the health insurance system and the emotional and physical burden on family caregivers, a new public long-term-care insurance program began operating in 2000. This program encouraged the development of home care services, medical equipment and supply industries, and construction of new facilities for elder care.

Recently, health policy also faced the challenges of integrating the newest genetics and high-tech medicine into society. From the 1960s, lively discussions and social movements formed around issues such as informed consent, brain death, AIDS, access to medical records, genetic testing, environmental pollution, and genetically modified food.

Although less well known than their Nazi counterparts, Japanese physicians engaged in medical atrocities during the Pacific War in the name of medical research. With that background and contemporary values of privacy and autonomy, medical ethics concerns have been increasingly expressed as human rights issues and tensions between such rights and the new technologies recognized and debated. Japan's brain death law of 1997, which recognizes brain death only for the purpose of organ donation, is an example of political compromise reached after decades of public discourse on the definition of death, the proper role of physicians, and the need for organ transplantation to save lives.

To read about health and medicine in early modern Japan, see the Japan entry in the section "Health and Medicine" in chapter 4 ("Intellectual Life") in volume 4 of this series.

~Susan Orpett Long

FOR MORE INFORMATION

Ikegami, N., and J. C. Campbell, eds. *Containing Health Care Costs in Japan*. Ann Arbor: University of Michigan Press, 1996.

Ministry of Health, Labor, and Welfare. <http://www1.mhlw.go.jp/english/database/index.html>.

Powell, M., and M. Anesaki. *Health Care in Japan*. London: Routledge, 1990.

AFRICA

African health and medicine in the 20th century must be discussed in terms of two separate systems of medical knowledge and practice. European missions and colonial rulers introduced Western biomedicine to the continent in the late 19th century and promulgated its expansion throughout the 20th century. Indigenous African groups also had their own traditional understanding of causes of and treatments for illnesses, which most Africans have continued to practice to the present day. Naturally, there have been tensions and conflicts between these two systems of medicine; however, there have also been many instances of similarity and cooperation.

Traditional African medical systems vary across communities and regions, with each exhibiting unique characteristics. Nonetheless, most traditional systems exhibit broad similarities. African traditional medical systems recognize several different ways that people can contract diseases. First, and as in Western biomedicine, diseases can be transferred through air, bad food or water, contact with other ill people, or habitual uncleanliness. Second, and unlike in Western biomedicine, many African traditional medical systems believe that some diseases can be spread through witchcraft or by violating certain social taboos.

Most traditional medical systems recognize the authority of a traditional medical practitioner (TMP), referred to frequently as a witch doctor, to administer treatment to an afflicted patient. The term witch doctor is a misnomer, however, in that the responsibilities of TMPs usually involve much more than combating witchcraft. Aside from performing antiwitchcraft rituals, TMPs also have a voluminous understanding of local plant life, often prescribing medications based on combinations of herbs and other medicinal plants.

In general, traditional African medicine focuses on a holistic approach to disease treatment. Most African traditional medical systems recognize disease as a disruption in the normal social order. This social order must be restored to vanquish the illness and prevent its spread to other members of the society. In this way, prescribing medicines often is not enough to safeguard the individual or the community from the ravages of disease. Purifying rituals are also commonly performed to realign the supernatural and psychological realms of the community, restoring the normal social order and thereby curing the disease. This is particularly true in cases deemed caused by witchcraft, in which a person is afflicted with an illness as a result of malicious curses placed upon him or her by another individual. In these cases, TMPs must perform curative rituals designed to counteract those of the witch. In the cases where

taboos have been broken, rituals often must be performed to realign the social order, which has been disrupted by the individual's transgression of social norms.

Traditional medical systems based on these kinds of concepts existed long before European missionaries and colonial rulers introduced Western biomedicine in the 19th and 20th centuries. With the introduction of colonial rule, however, Europeans attempted to force European ideologies and infrastructures on African peoples. This occurred in the realms of politics, education, and religion. Medicine was no exception. European colonial authorities saw African traditional medicine as superstitious and unscientific, in direct contrast to Western biomedicine, which was based on scientific understanding of the causes of illnesses and their appropriate curative treatments. As a result of this construction of African and European medical systems as polar opposites, colonial authorities continually tried to demean and diminish the role of traditional medicine in African societies in favor of Western biomedicine.

A Dinka elder drinks water from a gourd near Turalei in southwestern Sudan's famine-stricken Bahrel-Ghazal province, Sunday, April 5, 1998. There is no clean drinking water in most of the provinces, and aid workers fear the spread of diseases through the little water that is available, which is shared by human beings and livestock. © AP/ Wide World Photos.

These efforts on the part of European colonizers mostly failed, for several reasons. First, although Europeans desired to replace traditional medicine with Western biomedicine, colonial authorities did not develop the medical infrastructure of African colonies to nearly the level necessary to provide adequate health care to a majority of the indigenous population. Thus, in order to get quick, local care, most Africans continued to rely on nearby traditional medical practitioners. Second, as with most other colonially imposed institutions, many Africans distrusted the methods and motivations of Western medicine. Indeed, one of the main motivations of colonial authorities for extending Western medicine into Africa was to ensure that the colony could maintain a stable, healthy labor force in order to maintain levels of production and export of raw materials. Therefore, many Africans chose to avoid Western medical facilities in the belief that these facilities did not or could not substantially benefit Africans.

Despite the distrust exhibited by many Africans, after African countries achieved their independence in the 1950s and 1960s, the colonial medical system endured. Newly independent African countries focused primarily on extending Western medical services to greater percentages of their populations, while continuing to undermine traditional practices. However, since the late 20th century, some African countries have begun to cooperate more closely with traditional medical practitioners, recognizing their ability to examine and treat an illness holistically and inexpensively. Several African countries have even recognized the possible efficacy of many traditional medicinal plants and herbs and have begun cooperating with TMPs to develop these treatments into modern medicines.

Unfortunately, much of this increased cooperation between Western medical institutions and TMPs has been due to the catastrophic explosion of AIDS in Africa in the late 20th century. Some African countries now report that well over 25 percent of their entire populations may be HIV positive. Western medical facilities (e.g., hospitals, pediatricians, pharmacies) cannot even begin to deal with such large numbers. Thus, TMPs are increasingly being called upon to help treat the patients that hospitals cannot accommodate. Furthermore, although European and American pharmaceutical companies have developed medicinal treatments for HIV and AIDS that can significantly extend a patient's life, these medicines remain far too expensive for the average African patient. As a result, some biomedical institutions in Africa, with the help of TMPs, have begun to look for possible medicinal treatments in the plants and herbs prescribed by TMPs to their suffering communities. Though such cooperation between Western biomedicine and TMPs is good and must continue, unfortunately no cure has yet been found, and millions of Africans will die of AIDS in the years to come.

To read about health and medicine in Africa in the 17th and 18th centuries, see the Africa entry in the section "Health and Medicine" in chapter 4 ("Intellectual Life") in volume 4 of this series.

~*Matthew Heaton*

FOR MORE INFORMATION

Falola, T., and D. Ityavyar, eds. *The Political Economy of Health in Africa.* Athens, OH: Ohio University Center for International Studies, 1992.

Green, E. C. *Indigenous Theories of Contagious Disease.* Walnut Creek, Calif.: AltaMira Press, 1999.

Sindiga, I., C. Nyaigotti-Chacha, and M. P. Kanunah, eds. *Traditional Medicine in Africa.* Nairobi: East African, 1995.

United Nations AIDS Organization. <www.unaids.org>.

INUIT

European colonialism had a devastating effect on the health of the Inuit. Before the arrival of Europeans in the 18th and 19th centuries, the North American Arctic was relatively free of infectious diseases. Thus, Inuit had not developed immunities to the diseases that were common among Europeans and their North American descendants. Epidemics of smallpox, measles, influenza, polio, and even the common cold caused adult and infant mortality to soar. It is believed that by 1900 the Inuit aboriginal population had declined to half its precontact level as a result of the introduced diseases. Even when the diseases did not kill, the social disruption caused by illness was tremendous. During the early decades of the 20th century Inuit came to expect illness, sometimes referred to as "boat colds," to follow the arrival of every ship bearing trade goods and supplies.

Traditionally, medicine was the responsibility of shamans who diagnosed causes and effected cures through séances. Often illness or other misfortune was taken to be the result of a violation of one or more taboos. Shamanic methods were generally ineffective against the new diseases, and this may have encouraged Inuit to convert to Christianity. There is also evidence to suggest that poor health caused many Inuit to alter their subsistence activities and to settle near missions and trading posts where Western medical care was available.

INTELLECTUAL
LIFE
|
HEALTH & MEDICINE
|
Europe

Holocaust

United States,
1920-1939

United States,
1940-1959

United States,
1960-1990

India

Soviet Union

Japan

Africa

Inuit

Tuberculosis, because it both is highly infectious and has an extremely long incubation period, was one of the most serious health problems faced by Inuit throughout the North. No effective treatments existed until the 1950s, and even then Inuit diagnosed with the disease were often required to remain in hospitals and away from their homes and families, sometimes for many years.

Improvements in medicine and health care delivery in most parts of the Inuit North in the 1960s and 1970s reduced the prevalence of most infectious diseases, but like other North Americans, Inuit now suffer from a variety of chronic diseases such as obesity, heart disease, and cancer. Young Inuit adults, in particular, experience disproportionately high rates of mortality and morbidity from substance abuse, accidents, and suicide attempts.

In Alaska and Arctic Canada, health care is now under the supervision of regional health boards. In Greenland, the Home Rule Government has managed health care since 1992. At present, primary health care is available in most Inuit villages; however, diagnostic services, trauma, and hospital care often require patients to travel to distant centers where they are often separated from their families and support networks. Since the mid-1980s, Inuit women in Canada have been required to give birth in hospitals attended by physicians rather than in their home communities attended by lay or professional midwives. This requirement means that most near-term pregnant women must spend several weeks away from their homes and other children while waiting to give birth.

Pollution may also contribute to health problems experienced by Arctic populations. The Arctic ecosystem contains a disproportionate share of globally produced environmental contaminants, many of which arrive in the North as airborne particles. Several studies have indicated that Inuit in several parts of the North have extremely high levels of environmental pollutants in their bloodstreams. Contaminants, including heavy metals, radioactive fallout, pesticides, and other industrial chemicals, enter the Inuit food chain through game animals that remain an important source of nutrition for many Inuit. These are then often passed on to infants through breast milk. Unfortunately, although the contaminants are known to produce neurological, reproductive, and other health problems, it is difficult to assess the exact nature of the risk or to provide guidance on how to avoid exposure. Furthermore, for both social and economic reasons there are few ready replacements for the traditional foods.

~Pamela Stern

FOR MORE INFORMATION

Arctic Council, Human Health. <http://www.amap.no/>.

ArcticHealth. <http://www.arctichealth.org/>.

Fortuine, R. *Chills and Fever: Health and Disease in the Early History of Alaska.* Fairbanks: University of Alaska Press, 1989.

Lee, B. *Lutiapik: The Story of a Young Woman's Year of Isolation and Service in the Arctic.* Toronto: McClelland & Stewart, 1975.

National Film Board of Canada. *Coppermine* [Documentary], 1992.

INTELLECTUAL LIFE: WEB SITES

http://www.lib.virginia.edu/wess/etexts.html
http://www.esa.int/export/esatls/
http://inventors.about.com/library/inventors/blsatellite.htm
http://library.thinkquest.org/26451/contents/timeline/time9.htm
http://regentsprep.org/Regents/global/themes/science/wws.cfm
http://www.nasa.gov/
http://www.waytorussia.net/WhatIsRussia/Literature/20thCentury.html

5

MATERIAL LIFE

Material life describes all the things we use, from the houses that give us shelter to the food that sustains us, the clothes that protect us, and the items that amuse us. It also includes the luxury items that set us apart from others less fortunate than we. Studying material life is fascinating in its details: We learn that handkerchiefs were a luxury in 16th-century Europe designed to set the wealthy apart from the peasant who used a hat or sleeve, or that underwear was widely adopted in Europe only in the 18th century.

Aside from the delicious details that bring the past to life, the study of material life reveals much about society as a whole. For example, cultures that rely on rice as a major staple have to invest a great deal of labor into its cultivation, whereas societies that thrive on corn (maize), which is not labor-intensive, have ample spare time. People who had access to raw materials, such as iron ore, developed in ways different from those that did not, and groups that had domesticated animals or large plows had different organizing principles from others. If we know what a culture uses, we know a great deal about those people's lives.

As we study material life, it is also important to remember that humans want much more than the bare necessities of life. Indeed, we are creatures of desire rather than need, and this longing has fueled much of the progress in the world. We want spices to flavor our food, not just nourishment; we want gold to adorn us as much as we want clothing to cover us. Cultures (like those in the West) who have acquired a taste for change in fashion transform themselves (not necessarily for the better) in all areas much more rapidly than those (like those in Asia) who have preferred a more conservative approach to clothing. All in all, the details of our daily life matter. From the Stone Age, when humans adorned themselves with cowrie shells as they wielded stone tools, to the modern world shaped by high technology, humans are defined by the things we use. Our material life reveals and shapes who we are.

Material life in the 20th century changed rapidly for many and particularly for those living in the United States. The major transformations were sparked by technological advances. For instance, the electrification of the United States caused Americans to reshape the ways that they built and lived in their homes. By mid-century, nearly all Americans had access to safe, inexpensive electricity. From toast-

MATERIAL LIFE

FOOD

DRINK

HOUSING

TECHNOLOGY

ers to house lights to refrigeration, the effects were significant. Other innovations such as the mass-produced and mass-consumed automobile had similar far-reaching influences. The car not only enabled Americans to move around more freely but also created a significant economic boom as people needed to fuel, fix, and finance their new purchases. It is important to note, however, that not all people benefited from the technological advances of the 20th century. In India and Latin America, people did not have (and still do not have) the same easy access to electricity. In fact, these areas were left behind in many of the improvements in material life. With some notable exceptions, American housing improved significantly over the hundred years. Houses became well insulated, safe, and wired for every electric and electronic appliance imaginable. But in India and in Latin America, houses retained their traditional style. In many areas, they were still made out of mud or other low-tech building materials. In urban areas, where apartment living dominated, there was overcrowding and unsanitary conditions.

In part, spreading the benefits of the advances in material life for all people worldwide has been a political and economic problem. For instance, automobiles require highways, and highways are expensive. Similarly, the material effects of a space-exploration program (inventions such as Velcro, new foods like Tang, and new medicines) also demand sizable investments. During the 20th century, the United States was prepared to spend that money, whereas other nations such as Argentina and Peru were not. Furthermore, these material changes needed the political backing of politicians and citizens. Perhaps nothing illustrated this more than the fights in the United States over prohibition. In 1919, Congress added the 18th Amendment to the Constitution, thus paving the way for the criminalization of the manufacture and sale of alcoholic beverages. The repeal of Prohibition came in 1933 because the experiment had been a failure and because American voters demanded it. Thus there has always been a relationship between material life and political life. Your neighbor's gas-guzzling sport utility vehicle is not merely an addition to his net worth and a display of wealth, but it is also a political choice about the use of material resources as well as the reduction of pollution. At the end of the 20th century, these fights over material life appeared within countries like the United States as well as between nations around the world.

MATERIAL LIFE

FOOD

Europe, 1914-1918

United States, 1920-1939

United States, 1960-1990

Latin America

India

Soviet Union

Japan

Inuit

FOR MORE INFORMATION

Braudel, F. *The Structures of Everyday Life*. New York: Harper and Row, 1979.
Diamond, J. *Guns, Germs, and Steel*. New York: Norton, 1997.

Food

Among the necessities of daily life, food is at the top of the list. Even in a land of plenty, there is no underestimating the impacts that food brings to life. Sure, it is the fuel of our existence. But food is much more than that. It has cultural, political, and economic meaning. In the entries that follow, take special note of how food influences other aspects of daily life. Of course, the best way to experience this is to go out to eat at various restaurants. Take a notepad and analyze the class, cultural, and political implications of the foods that you eat.

During the 20th century, there were significant struggles over food. One culinary contest developed between regional and national foods. At the beginning

Thanks to the hard work of civilians back home, the average American soldier was much better fed than his counterparts from other nations. Here women learn food preservation techniques in an industrial kitchen. © Library of Congress.

of the century, in the United States and other countries such as India, regional cuisine was dominant. In the United States, for instance, one would find certain kinds of food in the South but not in the North. Moreover, different groups ate differently. African Americans and whites in the South not only consumed meals in separate locations but their diet was based on separate traditions. In India, this regional diversity also held true. In the north, near the Himalayas, wheat was the basic staple of life, whereas in the south rice was the choice at meals. Similarly, tea was a popular drink in the north and coffee was grown and consumed in the south. The British sought to unify the Indian national diet, even inventing "Indian curry" as a national food additive. In the United States, the national diet was created not by the federal government but by national corporations whose vast production capabilities and massive advertising budgets pushed sliced bread and canned foods (such as spaghetti) into everyone's household.

Another food fight occurred during World War I. The nations hardest hit by the war were, of course, in Europe. Initially, the war enhanced people's diets. The rise in high-paying factory jobs and the increase in the food supply (particularly for soldiers) meant that people had access to more and better foods. Yet this dietary boon in England, France, and Germany quickly dissipated as the war began to ravage the continent. Allied and Central Power armies targeted food production sites, including farms and factories. Shortages were a result of this and the war's long stalemate. Rationing food was the only solution to maintain a semblance of order. And yet, as supplies dwindled, people in Europe became desperate and began to riot. In fact, the turmoil in Germany and Russia can be directly linked to those governments' inability to feed their citizens. By 1919, even soldiers were going hungry. Thus food, as well as guns and tanks, was one of the main factors in deciding the outcome of the war. And food shortages were an important factor in the start of the Russian Revolution and the rise of the Soviet Union.

Globalization in the 20th century has made a significant impact on the foods people eat. We can see this in the varied diets from as far away as the United States, Japan, and India. Even societies that adhere to traditional menus have to confront the fact that they live in a global village. For example, Inuits eating a traditional diet of fish are slowly poisoned by mercury produced in industrial countries that gets into their food supply. American fast food can be found in Japan, India, Latin America, and even in the former Soviet Union. Likewise, foods from many of these countries have, in Americanized forms, become popular and common in the United States.

The final food battle represented in the entries is what some have called the battle of the bulge. At the end of the 20th century, many people, Americans in particular, struggled with creating a proper diet. Unlike the situation in many nations, particularly Latin America, food supply in the United States was no longer a primary issue; rather, eating the correct foods was. Among the countries in the world, America ranked near the top in daily caloric intake of its citizens. However, as the entry on the United States explains, well fed did not necessarily mean well nourished. Heart disease and other ailments were a direct result of poor dietary decisions. Moreover, American culture emphasized the idea that thin was beautiful, pushing many to take dietary supplements to lose weight. Americans wanted to eat whatever they pleased and still remain thin. In the end, the cost of the fast-food nation's diet was obesity, low self-esteem, and a myriad of health problems. Increasingly at the end of the 20th century, Americans looked to their government for assistance in making food safer, healthier, and more cost-effective.

MATERIAL LIFE

FOOD

Europe, 1914-1918

United States, 1920-1939

United States, 1960-1990

Latin America

India

Soviet Union

Japan

Inuit

EUROPE, 1914–18

By the 20th century, Europe's food supply had become linked to a world market, and many countries depended on trade to feed their citizens. Consequently, the great wars of the 20th century had a profound effect on what most of the population ate. The need to apportion national resources, the strains of the war effort, and even the direct assault of the enemy on the food supply reached into kitchens and dining rooms everywhere. In food more than in any other area of daily life, individuals in Britain, France, Germany, and the Soviet Union felt the new role of government in regulating personal behavior.

At the same time, the science of nutrition was developing rapidly. Some of its advocates preached the virtues of a simpler rather than a richer diet. The new knowledge of food values suggested that it was possible to replace one food for another in several categories. The shortages and food crises of the war gave the nutritionists an opportunity to win governments over to their program.

The diet of many Germans had changed with the decades of affluence prior to 1914. The domestically grown potato remained a staple food for most of Kaiser Wilhelm II's subjects. Nonetheless, consuming large amounts of animal products, especially pork and butter, was becoming a mealtime habit for much of the population. Another sharp change occurred in the bread supply. Bread made from rye—a domestic crop—had increasingly given way to white bread containing wheat from abroad.

In Great Britain as well, a shift away from starches symbolized rising national wealth. For many, change was only gradual. The staples for working-class families remained potatoes and especially bread. The average working-class Briton consumed far less meat, fats, and milk than the national norm. The working-class diet had only a limited place for fruit, eggs, and vegetables. Nonetheless, more Britons than ever, including the upper levels of the working class, had access to a diet with significant amounts of meat, milk, cheese, and butter. The nation's supply of meat had grown with the spread of refrigeration. This allowed frozen meat to be transported from distant locations such as Argentina and Australia to British dining rooms.

A decline in British agriculture meant that by 1914, fully 60 percent of the calories Britons consumed were imported. Most of the fruits and vegetables in the national diet had to be imported, and 80 percent of the wheat that went into British bread came from abroad. So too did Britain's crucial supply of sugar; the average Briton consumed almost two pounds a week, and working families bought as much as they could. As Margaret Barnett put it, "It was commonly believed by the working classes that children would die unless they ate a pound of sugar a week."

France had gone through the most gradual change in its food habits in the years prior to 1914. Much of its population remained tied to a diet in which the daily loaves of bread were the centerpiece. The average French citizen still ate only about four ounces of meat per day. But the wheat for his bread came from within the country; so too did most other products—including fruits and vegetables—the population consumed. France did not export large amounts of food, but France alone among the major European powers produced most of what was needed for the nation's stomachs—at least in peacetime.

Germany soon showed its vulnerability to food shortages. German domestic production depended on large quantities of foreign fertilizers for its fields; the country also required fodder from abroad to maintain its farm animals. Calling millions of able-bodied men into the military drained farm labor and caused diminished production. So too did the absence of hundreds of thousands of farmworkers from Russian Poland, who came in peacetime years to bring in the grain harvest in eastern Germany.

Britain's vulnerabilities in food supply became evident more slowly. Nonetheless, an early crisis emerged over sugar. In early 1917, the Germans used submarines to cut the British off from foreign food supplies, and a national crisis soon developed as the grains and meats upon which the country depended came under enemy attack. The Germans began to sink one out of every four merchant ships sailing from a

British port, and Britain's wheat reserves fell far below normal. Official government statistics had to be censored to prevent public knowledge of the decline in wheat imports.

Despite France's rich agricultural resources, that country found itself facing an increasing food deficit. One out of every four of France's 5.2 million farmers and farmworkers was mobilized in 1914; the military requisitioned many of the horses that provided motive power on French farms, and the jammed railroads were unable to deliver the usual supply of fertilizer. By 1917, the decline in French agriculture had become a national crisis. The women, children, and old men of the community had found it impossible to meet the physical demands of tilling the fields, and French wheat production fell to only 40 percent of its prewar level. Like Britain, France faced starvation without massive help from abroad.

When the weather's vagaries wrecked the potato crop, Germans felt the impact with particular force in the first months of 1917. Animals as well as humans depended on the potato, and the precipitous fall in potato production—almost half of the winter potato crop perished—overturned German eating habits. The turnip, an unappetizing vegetable and a meager source of nutrition, became the keystone of the German diet in the "turnip winter" of 1916–17. The resulting food crisis was massive and jarring, the worst to date for any of the major belligerent countries on the western front. But other nations faced difficulties that were comparable in kind if not in intensity. The wheat crop in Argentina also failed, and the government halted all exports. Britain and France, who depended on this source, now faced a deteriorating bread supply.

German authorities took the first steps among the major belligerents to regulate the wartime food supply. A system of price controls for bread, milk, and potatoes went into effect almost at once. By the start of 1915, the national government began to ration bread. But such measures soon appeared ineffective to much of the population. Although the practice was forbidden by law, many city dwellers spent spare hours or days traveling into the countryside to find food. Wealth and connections dictated diet in German life. Chain stores, for example, diverted food items to outlets in wealthier neighborhoods where the management could demand higher prices.

French troops eating in the field during World War I. Courtesy of the Hoover Institution Archives.

One device German society developed to deal with the growing food pinch was a set of artificial (or ersatz) goods. Ersatz coffee might be a beverage made from burned barley or tree bark, ersatz butter a combination of artificial fats and water. During the turnip winter of 1916–17, a vast range of foods, which most Germans found unpalatable, grew out of the one available staple, turnips—turnip jam being one example.

In contrast to the decentralized—and consequently unsuccessful—system in Germany, Britain created a rationing system under central control. The office of Food Controller, occupied starting in June 1917 by the energetic and effective Lord Rhondda, took increasingly tight charge of the nation's diet. The government also sponsored a program designed to increase farm production, thereby reversing a trend in

British agriculture that had gone on for decades. The production of grains instead of livestock became a mainstay of the program; it was more efficient to use farmland to grow crops such as wheat than to graze animals.

Compulsory rationing of key items began under the auspices of local authorities at the close of 1917. At that time, food lines were forming outside grocery stores by five o'clock in the morning. This indicated how shortages of bacon, margarine, and cheese—customary elements in the working-class diet—were beginning to pinch. By July 1918, the government put in place a centralized system that directly controlled the price and distribution of much of the nation's food supply. Everyone in the country received a ration book controlling the individual's purchases of sugar, butter and margarine, lard, and meat.

In France, the first effort to regulate the food supply came at the local level. In Isère, for example, the prefects and mayors dealt successfully with surging food costs at the war's start. They appealed to local merchants not to raise their prices, publicized the names of violators, and threatened to use powers under the penal code to seize food from the shops. In Paris, fear of disastrous popular unrest over the price of bread led the authorities at once to invoke a law dating from 1791. With it they were able to maintain the 1914 price almost unchanged until the close of the war.

French consumers encountered serious shortages and price increases in 1916. In response, the national government stepped in to set maximum prices for key goods. The authorities targeted, among other items, sugar, potatoes, milk, and coffee. Sugar rationing began in early 1917. As the nation's food situation slipped into crisis, the government placed more restrictions on the consumption and sale of meat, cheese, and bread.

In Germany, the strain on the food supply eventually became intolerable. By the closing year of the war, most of the population was malnourished. Food riots began in Berlin in October 1915. By the following summer, they were taking place from one end of the country to the other. The danger of such outbursts led the police to devote increasingly large resources to control them.

Extreme and prolonged hunger along with the other hardships of the war may have poisoned German life for decades. Peter Loewenberg has contended that the food shortages contributed to an emotional trauma that scarred German children of the wartime generation. Wartime deprivation had a causal relationship to the willingness of these individuals as adults to turn to radical figures such as Adolf Hitler in times of crisis. In Britain and France, effective food control from above helped maintain a high level of national unity. Government competence in this crucial area promoted political loyalty and social cohesion that lasted to the end of the war. By distributing food efficiently and fairly, the authorities gave the poorer groups in British society, in particular, a better, more healthful diet during the final stages of the war than they had in peacetime.

Food and eating on the battlefronts was quite different than on the home fronts. All the armies on the western front tried to provide their soldiers with regular meals even at the cost of limiting the food available on the home front. In addition, soldiers carried a basic or "iron" ration of foods like hardtack (a hard, crackerlike bread) and preserved meat. These items would not spoil, required no cooking, and remained available to be used in emergencies. Normally, a soldier had to await orders from a superior before opening this emergency ration. For troops engaged in battle, the emergency ration was commonly the only food available.

When the general officer commanding a British sector unit agreed, the soldiers also received a daily rum ration. In the hours before the attack on the Somme on July 1, one commander famously denied his men the rum ration, saying that they should be prepared to meet their Maker cold sober. French troops got alcohol on a regular basis. They received a daily ration (le pinard) of plain red wine along with a ration of brandy.

As representatives of the wealthiest society in the world, American soldiers ate predictably well—a daily diet of almost 5,000 calories. Troops in the trenches received a main meal consisting invariably of bread and butter, stew ("slum"), coffee with sugar, white bread, and jam. Many men put corn syrup ("Karo") on bread as dessert. Both officers and, more important, enlisted men commented that the quantity of the food, at least when troops were in a stationary position, was more than sufficient. Mainstays of the American diet in combat or on the march were cold canned corned beef ("corned willie") and canned salmon ("gold fish") with crackers. Unlike the other combatants, American forces got no alcohol ration. The fighting ability of the German army showed a fatal decline as the quality of food deteriorated.

After the devastating war, Europe struggled to bring agricultural production back to prewar levels and to restore the international trade that had fed Europeans in the previous century (Heyman, 35–38, 195–209).

FOR MORE INFORMATION

Augé-Laribé, M., and P. Pinot. *Agriculture and Food Supply in France during the War.* New Haven: Yale University Press, 1927.

Barnett, M. *British Food Policy during the First World War.* Boston: Allen and Unwin, 1985.

Chickering, R. *Imperial Germany and the Great War, 1914–1918.* Cambridge: Cambridge University Press, 1998.

Hallas, J. H. *Doughboy War: The American Expeditionary Force in World War I.* Boulder, Colo.: Lynne Rienner, 2000.

Heyman, N. M. *Daily Life During World War I.* Westport, Conn.: Greenwood Press, 2002.

Levenstein, H. A. *Revolution at the Table: The Transformation of the American Diet.* New York: Oxford University Press, 1988.

MATERIAL LIFE
|
FOOD
|
Europe, 1914-1918

United States,
1920-1939

United States,
1960-1990

Latin America

India

Soviet Union

Japan

Inuit

UNITED STATES, 1920–39

During and after World War I, Americans experienced what historian Harvey Levenstein has properly called a "revolution at the table," the peak stages of a dietary transformation that had been slowly accelerating for several decades. From the colonial era until past the middle of the 19th century, Americans had eaten a heavy British-style diet based primarily on roasted or fried meat, boiled potatoes and cabbage, grain-flour breads and baked goods, and sugar, foods easy to acquire, preserve, and prepare as well as capable of addressing the energy needs of strenuous agricultural labor. Americans consumed a great deal of meat, starches, fat, and sugar but few fruits and vegetables. Cooks used salt liberally but employed few other seasonings and hardly any spices. Until the 1830s, fermented cider and beer and distilled grain spirits were more common beverages than comparatively expensive coffee and tea. Thereafter, as its price fell, coffee in particular gained in popularity, especially with urban workers. Milk, considered unsafe in the days before pasteurization, was used primarily by infants and small children. Altogether, American food was heavy; bland; monotonous; and, especially for poorer people with the most restricted range of choices, nutritionally inadequate. The American diet produced a variety of dietary deficiency diseases and made constipation the most common, although not so deadly, national affliction.

In any age, 10 cents for a bowl of chili is a deal! Angelo's Lunch was located in Columbus, Ohio. This picture is dated 1938. © Library of Congress.

In the later decades of the 19th century, the eating patterns of urban dwellers began to change. Well-to-do Americans made French cuisine fashionable. With its elaborate entrées and sauces, soups, salads, and desserts, French food required servants for the preparation and service of meals. Thus, to choose a French diet served to proclaim one's economic success. The American middle class, seeking to copy society's elite with less domestic help, found it possible to do so by simplifying the menu and making use of a rapidly developing variety of commercially processed foods. Meat packers developed disassembly lines to turn livestock into table-ready cuts of meat. Professional bakers, breakfast cereal manufacturers, and brewers converted grain into edible forms. Other food processors refined sugar, created condensed soups, and canned or pickled fruits and vegetables. As railroads conveyed fresh as well as processed foods quickly and cheaply to distant markets, urban diets became more varied as well as more nutritious.

The rural diet lagged far behind because of economics and isolation. In the South, the most economically disadvantaged area, a black or white tenant farmer's normal diet consisted of little more than ground cornmeal made into mush or bread; fried salted pork; molasses; and, in season, some local greens. Pellagra, a serious disease resulting from a deficiency in niacin and protein, was widespread. In the more prosperous Midwest, most farmers ate a considerably better diet. Even there, however, farmers depended largely on what they could raise themselves and what was in season. Only the "summer diet" included much in the way of fruits and vegetables. These foods were consumed while they were fresh rather than preserved. The "winter diet," as a result, centered around pork and grains (mainly wheat or corn), supplemented by some potatoes, beans, and a little dried fruit. On the farm and elsewhere, getting enough to eat was far more of a concern than what was eaten.

New ideas about proper diet began emerging in the decades on either side of 1900. Detection of the presence of bacteria, discovery of pasteurization, and formulation of a germ theory of disease occurred during the latter decades of the 19th century. Only in the 1910s and 1920s, however, did dietary problems resulting from the absence of vitamins and minerals come into view and become a concern. At the end of the 19th century, the first generation of scientific nutritionists began to perceive a need for better dietary balance, but not until World War I created a food shortage did the idea spread that Americans could afford to eat less as long as they ate wisely.

Before World War I, eating a lot was thought to be sensible and being plump was regarded as a sign of good health as well as prosperity. Early nutritionists suggested that an adult male ought to consume 3,000 to 3,500 calories each day. Faced with an army and allies to feed as well as a reduced agricultural labor force, the U.S. government in 1917 began telling people they could remain healthy if they ate less as long as they consumed the proper proteins, carbohydrates, minerals, and vitamins. Claims that fewer calories sufficed for working adults were reinforced by rationing programs and campaigns for voluntary "wheatless" and "meatless" meals each day and entire days each week. During and after U.S. participation in the European war, a fundamental shift began taking place in American eating habits, especially among the middle and upper classes. Southern and immigrant soldiers who had been exposed to much more varied meals while in the military contributed to the change as well. By the end of the 1920s Americans were better fed, yet consumed 5 percent fewer calories per capita than they had on the eve of the war, a very significant overall drop during a period of general prosperity.

A clerk stocks shelves in a typical grocery store in San Antonio, Texas, 1939. © Library of Congress.

Commercial food processing companies consolidated, expanded capital investment and operations, and persuaded consumers to try new products to such an extent that by the end of the 1920s, the food industry was the largest sector of American manufacturing. Large-scale dairies and bakeries rapidly emerged to drive out of business or at least place at a severe competitive disadvantage many smaller milk and baked-goods producers. Improved production methods helped to increase sharply the sales of canned fruits and vegetables, not to mention condensed soups, beans with pork, sugar, and tomato sauce, and spaghetti in tomato sauce. The C. W. Post cereal company acquired over a dozen other companies, including the Jello Company, and used management and advertising skills to enlarge the market for the products of its new conglomerate, General Foods. Another expanding food processor, this one started by Minneapolis flour millers, called itself General Mills. It became very successful in encouraging the use of its products by creating a fictional housewife, Betty Crocker, who offered recipe recommendations in magazine and radio advertisements. Agricultural producers formed trade associations, some of them pooling and marketing their produce under common labels such as Sunkist oranges and Sun-Maid raisins. In these and countless other cases, the intent was to get the public to eat unfamiliar foods.

In 1925, Clarence Birdseye discovered how to quick-freeze fresh foods in cellophane packages (cellophane itself a new product developed by the DuPont chemical company). Birdseye was not the first to freeze food, of course, but he developed the means of doing it rapidly on a large scale. Quick-freezing avoided bursting cells and causing the food to turn to mush when thawed as had been the case with earlier, slower methods. Within three years, restaurants and the few Americans with home freezers were starting to purchase frozen foods in significant quantities. By 1934, they were buying 39 million pounds a year. It was not until after World War II, however, with the spread of electric home refrigerators and the sudden success of frozen concentrated orange juice, that the frozen-food industry would become a major aspect of commercial food processing (Kyvig, 92–114).

To read about food in the United States in the 19th century, see the United States entries in the section "Food" in chapter 5 ("Material Life") in volume 5 of this series.

FOR MORE INFORMATION

Farb, P., and G. Armelagos. *Consuming Passions: The Anthropology of Eating*. Boston: Houghton-Mifflin, 1980.

Kyvig, D. E. *Daily Life in the United States, 1920–1939: Decades of Promise and Pain*. Westport, Conn.: Greenwood Press, 2002.

Levenstein, H. *Revolution at the Table: The Transformation of the American Diet*. New York: Oxford University Press, 1988.

Patterson, J. T. *Grand Expectations: The United States, 1945–1974*. New York: Oxford University Press, 1996.

UNITED STATES, 1960–90

Since World War II, eating and drinking has amounted to more than meeting bodily needs. In *Eating in America*, published in 1976, Waverly Root and Richard de Rochemont summarized their observations on practices that were well under way by the early 1960s:

Americans are consuming, along with unheard-of amounts of valuable proteins in their meats and cereals, and along with vast quantities of fruits and vegetables full of good nutrients and vitamins, tens of billions of dollars' worth of packaging, additives, and advertising, as part of their total estimated two hundred and fifty billion dollar contribution to the food industry, agribusiness, and the conglomerate corporations that decide what we will be allowed to eat.

What was new in this "great glob," as the writers called it, that made up the American diet? By the early 1960s, what nutritionists called junk food had claimed a big place in the fare American people consumed. This included sugared breakfast foods and synthetic "fruit" drinks containing little fruit juice promoted by Saturday-morning cartoons, along with much of the fatty, salty, and sugary goods passed over the counter at fast-food restaurants. If Americans were improperly nourished, they were at least not underfed.

Just as important as the quantity and quality of what the young and old in America ate is when and where they ate it. In 1965 one meal in four was eaten outside the home, with that number on the rise. When meals *were* eaten at home, they were less likely to be occasions for families to come together. This is not surprising, given the many commitments to jobs, school, and leisure and cultural activities of all generations in the typical family.

Fashion consciousness, particularly that inspired by the super-thin "Twiggy" look that came into vogue in the 1960s, and health concerns made many Americans sensitive to being overweight, so it is not surprising that dieting became something of a national pastime. The most prominent organization in the weight-loss industry was Weight Watchers, begun in 1961 and incorporated for granting franchises in 1963. It gained adherents by using a combination of group therapy in weekly meetings and menus that prescribed foods low in fat and high in protein; the diet prohibited foods not fitting this description. Although Weight Watchers changed its prescriptions and prohibitions through the years and the character of its approach evolved with the times, Weight Watchers continued to attract followers. Other diet formulas and plans have enjoyed bursts of popularity and then faded away as new ones took their place.

Dieters had more than mere weight loss as their concern. Reports on relationships between nutrition and health appeared regularly. For example, the Food and Nutrition Board of the National Academy of Sciences published a calorie table showing dietary allowances based on one's age and desired weight. The American Heart Association recommended that people reduce the amount of fat they eat and begin "reasonable substitution" of vegetable oils and polyunsaturated fats for animal fats. Previously the association had suggested dietary changes for persons judged to be vulnerable to heart attacks. Now, for the first time, it called for changes in the eating habits of the general public. Sharp controversy followed, with representatives of the dairy industry leading the attacks on the recommendations.

Despite dieting fads, the American people were, in the words of historian David Potter, "people of plenty." Even so, many were distressed by the high prices of foods— so much so that in 1966 and again in 1970 and 1973 consumers in various parts of the nation organized boycotts of supermarkets. A Gallup poll showed that the 1973 boycott involved 50 million people, or 25 percent of all consumers. Boycott participants acknowledged that the increases in per capita spending on food resulted in part from their demand for more meat, bakery products, delicacies, and easy-to-prepare foods, but these were matters within their control. Beyond their control were such things as the amount of money producers and retailers spent on advertising, promotions, and trading stamps. Buyers "earned" trading stamps with their purchases, placed them in savings books, and exchanged them for such premiums as

---

▣ Snapshot

Fast Food Facts from Eric Schlosser, Author of *Fast Food Nation* (2001)

"The McDonald's Corp. has become a powerful symbol of America's service economy, the sector now responsible for ninety percent of the country's new jobs. In 1968, McDonald's operated about 1,000 restaurants. Today it has about 23,000 restaurants worldwide and opens roughly 2,000 new ones each year. An estimated one of every eight Americans has worked at McDonald's. The company annually trains more new workers than the U.S. Army. McDonald's is the nation's largest purchaser of beef and potatoes. It is the second-largest purchaser of poultry. A whole new breed of chicken was developed to facilitate the production of McNuggets. The McDonald's Corp. is the largest owner of retail property in the world.

"A survey of American schoolchildren found that ninety-six percent could identify Ronald McDonald. The only fictional character with a higher degree of recognition was Santa Claus. The impact of McDonald's on the nation's culture, economy and diet is hard to overstate. Its corporate symbol—the Golden Arches—is now more widely recognized than the Christian cross.

"Americans now spend more money on fast food than they do on higher education, personal computers, software or new cars. They spend more on fast food than on movies, books, magazines, newspapers, videos and recorded music— combined."

(http://www.mcspotlight.org/media/press/rollingstone1.html)

toasters, can openers, and electric blankets. Enthusiasm for stamps peaked in the early 1960s, and by the end of the decade most consumers regarded them as a nuisance. Some consumers, however, remained passionate stamp collectors who would shop anywhere to get them.

In the midst of plenty, well fed does not always mean well nourished. In recent decades consumers have gained more knowledge about nutrition than in earlier times, but increased knowledge has not always led them to better eating habits. Appealing advertisements aimed especially at children, catchy promotional jingles, and attractive packaging have often had more to do with choice of food than has its nutritional content.

The Fair Packaging and Labeling Act passed in 1966 was intended to assure consumers that packages and labels told the truth. So powerful was the lobby opposed to this act, however, that it required only that manufacturers print their name and address on the label, display the net weight prominently, state the size of servings, and stop using terms like *giant* and *jumbo*. Several packaging mandates came later, one requiring that a label list all the ingredients in a packaged product and another that package sizes be standardized. These requirements were poorly enforced, however, and by the end of 1969 the commissioner of the Food and Drug Administration (FDA) could only guess that 70 percent of the packages were in line with the law.

Had the labels been required to list all of a package's ingredients, what might have caught the consumer's eye? Artificial flavoring and sweeteners and such natural flavorings as salt and sugar to change food's taste. Food colorings to change its appearance; chemical preservatives to lengthen its shelf or refrigerator life; thickeners and thinners to change its texture; such ingredients as caffeine to change its effects. Revelations about the effects of some 3,000 food additives, many of them poorly tested, gradually led to new labeling requirements. In 1973 the FDA required standardized nutrition information on food labels and began to require the listing of such things as calories and grams of protein, fat, and carbohydrates per serving. As the printing of this information on labels became more widespread,

Readily available electricity radically changed the American kitchen and its appliances. This kitchen had the most advanced cooking tools of the day. © National Archives.

competition induced some marketers to include information that the regulations may not have explicitly required.

Just as important in changing the nutritional qualities of foods with additives were practices that removed important ingredients. Refining processes often removed fiber, now known to be important in preventing certain diseases. Canning, freezing, heating, and dehydrating destroyed at least part of such water-soluble nutrients as thiamin and various vitamins, enzymes, and proteins. Here, too, consumers heard wake-up calls and began to change their eating habits. Perhaps these changes reflected a change in the character of the American people, for, as anthropologists contend, to know what, where, how, when, and with whom people eat is to know the character of that society.

Advertising for foods thrived on ambiguities. Foods were called "natural" without particular attention given to what that meant. Restaurants served "shakes" containing no dairy products. Producers of imitation "chocolate" bars synthesized from various agricultural products, made tasty with an artificial flavor, mixed with bulking agents, and given the appearance of chocolate, could describe them as "all natural." Such developments, along with the profusion of foods to which chemical fertilization and pesticides had given a misleading appearance of wholesomeness, encouraged interest in "organically grown" foods. In their growth and processing, these foods were not touched by chemical fertilizers, pesticides, or additives.

Despite quickened lifestyles and changes in family structures, much good cooking continued to be done at home. Would-be gourmet cooks used high-tech food processors and cookbooks filled with nutritious and tasty recipes. Newspapers and women's magazines had long contained recipes, but now, as more and more men helped out with home cooking, sometimes taking over completely, food sections in newspapers moved from women's sections to lifestyles pages, and special magazines devoted to cooking began to appear. Television programs also featured cooking ideas, examples, and recipes.

According to estimates in 1973, one meal in three was eaten outside the home—many of them hastily at fast-food restaurants, the number of which doubled between 1967 and 1974. McDonald's, described by *Time* magazine as "the burger that conquered the country," had fewer than 1,000 restaurants in 1967 and more than 3,000 in 1974. New ones opened at the rate of one every day. In 1972 McDonald's passed the U.S. army as the biggest dispenser of meals; by then it had served more than 12 billion burgers. Numbers like this are only part of the story. McDonald's managers' greatest achievement, according to *Time*, was "taking a familiar American institution, the greasy-spoon hamburger joint, and transforming it into a totally different though no less quintessential American operation: a computerized, standardized, premeasured, superclean production machine." The fact that its menu items were loaded with fats and calories—almost 1,100 in a meal consisting of a Big Mac, a chocolate shake, and a small order of fries—did not keep customers away.

It was difficult in 1969 to avoid news reports of possible hazards in food, even in the milk of breast-fed children. The Sierra Club reported that mother's milk contained four times the amount of the pesticide DDT than was permitted in cows' milk sold in stores. High concentrations of DDT in coho salmon in Michigan lakes and streams led the state to restrict the spraying of crops with DDT. Baby-food producers discontinued use of monosodium glutamate (MSG), a flavor enhancer, when tests showed that mice fed large amounts suffered brain damage. Test rats given excessive amounts of artificial sweeteners known as cyclamates developed cancer in their bladders. The FDA then removed cyclamates from its "generally recognized as safe" list and revealed plans to remove products sweetened with it from stores. Later, however, serious doubts were raised about the validity of the tests. The next year the FDA ordered the recall of large quantities of canned tuna because the mercury levels were thought to be too high. Despite the scare, it turned out that only 3 percent of canned tuna exceeded the FDA-prescribed limit.

It seems somewhat ironic that in the midst of plenty, hunger was as serious a problem in the United States as it was in this period. Throughout the nation's history there have been people who have gone hungry, particularly in times of depression.

A 1968 CBS documentary, *Hunger in America,* revealed how serious the problems of hunger could be, even in relatively prosperous times. In the same year, a nutrition investigator claimed that malnutrition in some parts of the United States was as grim as any he had seen in India or any other country. At one school, he reported, children had vitamin A deficiencies worse than those who had gone blind as a result of this deficiency.

Buying food stretched the budgets of many beyond their limits. To help such persons, the government established a program to provide food stamps to purchase certain items in grocery stores. By Thanksgiving 1967, three years after this Great Society program was launched, 2.7 million Americans received food stamp assistance. That was just the beginning. By 1969 the number of participants climbed to 7 million, on the way to 19.6 million in mid-1975. Between 1969 and 1974, funding for the program increased from $4 million to $3 billion. Urban food stamp recipients typically had to pay more for food than more affluent suburbanites, because their parts of town had no supermarkets and prices in the small stores located there were higher. When government programs provided free or reduced-cost meals for schoolchildren in areas where feeding a family was difficult, these meals were often the best, if not the only, meals some children ate. The programs also benefited farmers and helped reduce government-financed food surpluses (Marty, 37–38, 127–30).

To read about food in the United States in the 19th century, see the United States entries in the section "Food" in chapter 5 ("Material Life") in volume 5 of this series.

FOR MORE INFORMATION

Farb, P., and G. Armelagos. *Consuming Passions: The Anthropology of Eating.* Boston: Houghton-Mifflin, 1980.

Levenstein, H. *Revolution at the Table: The Transformation of the American Diet.* New York: Oxford University Press, 1988.

Marty, M. A. *Daily Life in the United States, 1960–1990: Decades of Discord.* Westport, Conn.: Greenwood Press, 1997.

Schlosser, E. *Fast Food Nation: The Dark Side of the All-American Meal.* New York: Houghton-Mifflin, 2001.

Waverly, L. R. *Eating in America: A History.* New York: Morrow, 1976.

LATIN AMERICA

Despite the fact that Latin America is home to some 20 percent of the world's cultivable lands, many of the region's populations were unable to feed themselves in the 20th century. Exclusionary political and social systems—holdovers of the colonial era—contributed significantly to mass poverty and hunger.

Land distribution practices in many Latin American societies have long been unequal. Into the 20th century, land continued to be a source of wealth and prestige, even if owners allowed the land to lie fallow. In El Salvador in 1977, for example, a full half of land on farms larger than 100 acres lay fallow or served as pastureland (Burns 1990, 320). And in midcentury Bolivia, 6 percent of landowners possessed

MATERIAL LIFE
|
FOOD
|
Europe, 1914–1918

United States, 1920–1939

United States, 1960–1990

Latin America

India

Soviet Union

Japan

Inuit

90 percent of the nation's arable land, in estates averaging more than 2,000 acres. At the same time, 60 percent of landowners possessed just 0.2 percent of the land, and many families eked out their subsistence with fewer than 10 acres (Winn, 250).

Like land tenure, agricultural production was often skewed. Most farms, in fact, produced for international markets rather than domestic consumption. Modernization through the first part of the 20th century increased attention paid to export-oriented agriculture, and many countries came to depend on one crop. By the 1950s, for instance, several countries depended heavily on coffee exports to Europe and the United States. Coffee made up close to 70 percent of Colombia's exports and between 30 percent and 45 percent of exports in Brazil, Costa Rica, El Salvador, Guatemala, and Haiti. Similar dependence on sugar occurred in the Caribbean, and on bananas in areas of Central America. Other significant export crops included grains, cocoa, and soybeans.

Many countries also came to depend on food-based exports such as meats and grain alcohol. Thus, landowners reserved huge tracts of land not only for grazing cattle, but also for producing grains for cattle feed. By the mid-1970s, Latin America used nearly one-half of its cereal grains to feed cattle (Burns 1990, 320). In Brazil during the 1970s and 1980s, an increased amount of land produced grains for an alcohol petroleum substitute, for use in the automobiles of the middle and upper classes.

Nations focused on export agriculture to the detriment of native populations. Because they exported much of what they produced, they also had to increase imports of basic foodstuffs. By the mid-1950s, agricultural goods accounted for 25 percent of Chile's imports, as the government spent 18 percent of the national budget on importing foods that the nation could produce itself. By 1965, Latin America as a whole purchased some 20 percent of its foodstuffs from abroad. In the 1970s, acute food shortages struck several countries; between 1971 and 1979, shipments to El Salvador, Guatemala, Guyana, and Honduras quadrupled. By 1989, Haiti imported a full 75 percent of its food from abroad (Burns 1990, 229–30).

Brazilians shop in an American-style supermarket in Sao Paulo, Brazil, Thursday, January 28, 1999. © AP/Wide World Photos.

The skewed systems of land tenure and agricultural production had harsh human consequences. By the mid-1980s, two-thirds of the Latin American population was undernourished. Between one-quarter and one-half of children under four years old in Brazil, Guatemala, Peru, and elsewhere suffered from protein-energy deficiency and other diseases associated with malnutrition. Significant numbers died from such diseases. For example, in Honduras, 50 percent of all children died before their fifth birthday (Burns 1990, 230).

That malnutrition ran rampant in Latin America is understandable, given a person's typical daily intake. In southern Brazil, half of the urban population consumed fewer than 2,250 calories a day, and in rural areas, calorie intake was even lower (Burns 1990, 230). A typical day's meals in rural El Salvador included *el desayuno* (breakfast) of hot coffee and a tortilla, sometimes diced and soaked in warm milk. *El almuerzo* (lunch), the largest meal of the day, was soup, tortillas, beans, and sometimes corn or rice. *La cena* (dinner) was much lighter, consisting of a tortilla and perhaps some beans. In highland Andes, diets were similarly inadequate, with potatoes, rather than corn, as a basic staple.

In short, the historical structures of Latin America perpetuated mass hunger. Through the 20th century, many nations were unable to sufficiently provide for their populations due to systemic choices. Tillable lands lay fallow, cultivated lands were inefficiently exploited, and most production focused on export rather than staples for domestic consumption.

~Molly Todd

FOR MORE INFORMATION

Albyn, C. L., and L. S. Webb. *The Multicultural Cookbook for Students*. Phoenix, Ariz.: Oryx Press, 1993.

Burns, E. B. *Latin America: A Concise Interpretive History*. 5th ed. Englewood Cliffs, N.J.: Prentice Hall, 1990.

Foley, E. *El Salvador*. New York: Marshall Cavendish, 1995.

Lepthien, E. *Peru*. Chicago: Children's Press, 1992.

McGaffey, L. *Honduras*. New York: Marshall Cavendish, 1999.

Pateman, R. *Bolivia*. New York: Marshall Cavendish, 1995.

Winn, P. *Americas: The Changing Face of Latin America and the Caribbean*. New York: Pantheon Books, 1992.

Zaslavsky, N. *A Cook's Tour of Mexico*. New York: St. Martin's Press, 1995.

> **📷 Snapshot**
>
> **Recipe for *Salsa di Mali***
>
> *Salsa di mali* is traditionally served with potato patties. In Peru, it is made with fresh peanuts, but peanut butter can be used for a smoother, quicker sauce.
>
> 2 tablespoons vegetable oil
> 1 onion, finely chopped
> 1 clove garlic, finely chopped, or 1/2 teaspoon garlic granules
> 2 tomatoes, peeled and chopped, or 1 cup canned whole tomatoes (and juice)
> 1/2 cup chunky peanut butter
>
> *Equipment:* Medium-size skillet, mixing spoon
> Heat oil in skillet over medium-high heat, add onion, salt, and pepper to taste, and fry until soft (about 3 minutes). Add garlic, tomatoes, peanut butter, mix well to blend, and cook until heated through. Yields about 2 1/2 cups. Serve warm over potato patties. (Albyn and Webb, 236–37)

INDIA

MATERIAL LIFE

FOOD

Europe, 1914-1918

United States, 1920-1939

United States, 1960-1990

Latin America

India

Soviet Union

Japan

Inuit

Food and the customs surrounding its preparation and consumption in India have followed an extremely diverse pattern of practice. There is no "typical" Indian food. From the peaks of the Himalayas in the north to the tropical coasts of the south, every region, city, and village has had its own unique foods and customs. This diversity has made food culture in India unique.

At the broadest levels, we can distinguish some general food patterns between the north and the south. Throughout the subcontinent, rice was (and still is) the major grain staple. In the south it was the dominant choice at meals, whereas in the north, wheat barley, maize, and millet were also common. Rice was served either cooked or ground and shaped (with black gram added) into small cakes that were then steamed. These were called *iddly* and served with a variety of spicy sauces or chutneys. Wheat and other grains were made into flat, unleavened bread called *roti*, *chapatti*, or *nan*.

Another visible distinction between the north and south was the consumption of coffee versus tea. Coffee was grown and consumed in the south, whereas tea was grown and consumed in the north. Tea boiled with milk, sugar, and sometimes cardamom or ginger was called *chai*. It tasted different from the popular beverage of the same name now served in coffee shops. Traveling north or south in India by train, one would hear the station vendors call out "Chai! Chai!" Moving south, one might—for a few stations—hear both: "Chai! Coffee! Chai! Coffee!" Then, reaching the deep south, the vendors would call out only "Coffee!" Nowadays, with European and American influence, espresso bars can be found in many of India's major cities.

Many people in India followed strict dietary practices. Among Hindus, vegetarianism was common. If a Hindu consumed meat, he or she avoided beef because the cow was considered sacred. Some Muslims were also vegetarian, but most ate meat, including beef but not pork, which Muslims considered unclean. Nonvegetarian Hindus and Muslims sharing a meal could choose chicken or lamb—acceptable to both groups. Generally, peoples of southern India practiced vegetarianism more than their peers in the north, although meat dishes were not uncommon at restaurants and hotels.

Though eating out was becoming more common in urban areas throughout the subcontinent, most people still preferred to dine at home. Wives cooked for their husbands and mothers for their children. Some households employed cooks for preparing their food. From an early age, daughters received training in the kitchen from their mothers. The women of the home generally kept track of rituals and holidays when special foods were required. At celebrations—such as a wedding or a birth— great feasts were prepared and relatives and friends invited. Those attending brought boxes of sweets or other gifts for the host. At other occasions, such as New Year's or religious holidays, special foods were prepared to celebrate the event. For example, in the Indian state of Andhra Pradesh, a special punch, called *ugadi pachari*, was made for the New Year. If it tasted sweet, the coming year would be good, but if it tasted sour or bitter, the coming year would be more difficult. During somber events, food was not consumed at all. A death in the family might be reason to fast, or fasting might be invoked as a process of spiritual cleansing.

For many Hindus, food was linked with worship. It was common within Hinduism for people to make a food offering to a deity. This offering, in the home, might be very small—a pinch of rice or spice, or a piece of fruit. Outside of the home at a temple, the offering might be a coconut or other fruit. After it has been symbolically accepted by the deity, this food was then redistributed to those who were visiting the temple. It was very common upon leaving a temple to be given a small parcel of coconut or rice that came from the deity as a form of blessing.

The caste system that underlies much of Hinduism has affected food and food customs. Generally, members of the same caste prepared and consumed their own food. For example, a brahman family would employ a brahman cook to prepare their meals. It was also acceptable to have a cook of a higher caste preparing one's food, but generally not a cook of a lower caste, as this would be polluting. In addition, it was a display of rank for people to give away food to those who were of lower caste or rank than themselves. Thus, on an auspicious occasion, a Brahman might prepare food to be given away to members of the community.

Generally, it was more desirable to give food than to accept it. As such, it was not uncommon to see Indians bringing food with them when traveling away from home. For example, a businessman on a long train journey might have carried a packed meal that was prepared at his home. Travelers with home-cooked meals frequently offer to share their portion with others, and acceptance of such offers reflects changing and liberalizing trends in Indian food culture.

Food, its preparation, its consumption, and the rituals involved with it were as diverse as the subcontinent itself. Food was integral to daily life in India, as it was anywhere, and was much relished. Families prided themselves on "secret" recipes, and flattering a cook was among the highest praises that could be given. Indian cuisine has traveled around the globe; in the United Kingdom, chicken *tikka masala* is now consumed in greater quantities than fish and chips. Ironically, the "Indian curry" sold in North America and Europe was not found at all in India but was a European invention.

To read about food in ancient India, see the India entry in the section "Food" in chapter 5 ("Material Life") in volume 1 of this series; for 19th-century India, see the India entry in the section "Food" in chapter 5 ("Material Life") in volume 5 of this series.

~Benjamin Cohen

FOR MORE INFORMATION

Achaya, K. T. *Indian Food: A Historical Companion.* Delhi: Oxford University Press, 1994.

SOVIET UNION

Food shortages in Russia during World War I helped fuel the Russian Revolution, and the Soviet Union was born in times of famine and scarcity. When the Russian Civil War ended in 1921, Lenin introduced the New Economic Policy (NEP) to save his Party and rescue the economy by permitting the existence of small private businesses and farming. According to the policy, small private enterprises were to coexist inside the main socialist economy of government-owned businesses, industries, and public services such as banks, utilities, schools, transportation, communications, and heavy industry. However, the NEP and free agriculture did not long survive Lenin's death in 1924.

The central planning that had emerged in many European states during the war years came most vividly to the fore in the Soviet Union, where Stalin, Lenin's successor as leader of the state and the Communist Party, tried to feed the Soviet people through dramatic changes in agricultural production. Stalin's regime swept aside NEP enterprises and private farming quickly and ruthlessly and forced peasants

MATERIAL LIFE
|
FOOD
|
Europe, 1914–1918
United States, 1920–1939
United States, 1960–1990
Latin America
India
Soviet Union
Japan
Inuit

into state owned or supervised collective farms, smashing the considerable opposition without mercy.

The system of collectivization led to untold misery as some peasants killed their animals and destroyed their crops in protest. Hunger and long food lines marked the government stores. The *rynok*, or peasant market, was one alternative to state outlets. A *rynok* might be outdoors or inside long, low buildings that could be closed up in winter. Peasants, sometimes entire collective farms, rented stalls for selling their produce. Unlike the fixed low prices at state stores, peasants could set their own prices. Produce from the *rynok* tended to be smaller, less uniform, less glossy but more flavorful than American produce.

Given that convenience foods common in the West, such as mixes and prepared frozen and canned food, were scarce or unavailable in the Soviet Union, home cooks made meals from scratch. Their quality and quantity depended on availability of ingredients, personal connections, and amount of time the housewife could spare for cooking. For special occasions, Russians were fond of long-drawn-out feasting and drinking at home or in one of the few decent public restaurants. At a home party, guests arrived in the late afternoon or early evening, sat around the table dipping into the many courses, and celebrated late into the night and often into the next day or days. A typical multicourse feast would usually start with appetizers (*zakuski*), which might include red and black caviar on dense brown bread, smoked salmon, pickled or marinated mushrooms, salted herring, herring salad with pickled beets, salami, pickled cucumbers, or beet salad; and then proceed to soups, perhaps clear red beet borscht or cabbage *shchi*; perhaps another course; and then on to the main meal and dessert. For drinks there would be freely flowing vodka along with other alcoholic drinks such as cognac, wine, and Soviet champagne (which was sweet rather than dry), with sweetened hot tea accompanying the dessert course. Much time and money were spent hunting and gathering ingredients and then preparing such feasts. People with little money or few or no shopping connections hosted suppers as lavish as they could manage—saving up rubles and food and depending on friends and relatives to contribute to the meal.

The top elite, including leaders in the arts, had special restaurants open only to members and their families and guests. These restaurants, unlike public ones, provided well-prepared luxury foods (e.g., steak, caviar, and shellfish); attentive, friendly service complete with clean tablecloths; and carryout privileges—members could walk into the kitchen and buy nicely prewrapped raw meat or telephone ahead to have such items ready for pickup.

The lower urban social classes—office and factory workers—often had access to workplace canteens, from which they could order groceries weekly. The quality of canteen food depended on how valued the particular workplace was. For example, employees who manufactured computers or military weapons had better-stocked canteens than workers in the legal system or agriculture bureaucracy. A common way for workers at a large enterprise to order food through their workplace was for small groups of employees each to appoint a woman member who took orders and then transmitted them to the enterprise's purchasing officer, who in turn had access to food stocks not available to public grocery stores. Each week notices were posted listing what foods were available for that week, but employees could not simply pick and choose what they wanted. Instead, they had to buy according to prearranged lists. Generally each list contained at least one scarce item plus several less-enticing ones. People chose lists that contained something they desired, resigning themselves to buying the unwanted add-ons. In this way, some workers enjoyed a slight privilege over those who depended entirely on street shopping, and the government got rid of its surplus merchandise. As the century progressed the size and nature of the food supply became more widely divergent between eastern and western Europe. The West, freed from wartime regulation, flourished in food production and distribution. In the Soviet Union and later in its eastern European satellites, finding food seemed, by contrast, a perpetual battle with regulation and scarcity.

~Joyce E. Salisbury

FOR MORE INFORMATION

Eaton, K. B. *Daily Life in the Soviet Union.* Westport, Conn.: Greenwood Press. Forthcoming.

JAPAN

If nothing else is known about Japan, it can be certain that Westerners will be familiar with something about Japanese food and drink. One would have to be a hermit not to have heard about sushi and sake. They have become part of the world's cuisine.

The most salient point about Japanese food is that subtle shapes, colors, and aromas are nearly as important as the taste and nutrition. Even the most humble Japanese cook must pay close attention to the aesthetic palette of the mind in the preparation of food.

The staple of life was rice, from the simple mound of steamed "sticky" white rice that accompanied virtually every entrée to the vinegared thumb-sized base of sushi, and indeed to the nutty-flavored rice wine, sake. Rice crackers abounded in many flavors, and clear rice flour noodles swam in the ubiquitous soup that rounded out virtually every lunch platter. Rice was so important to the Japanese diet that the language teems with hundreds of tropes, metaphors, and similes linked with rice.

Because Japan had been predominately Buddhist for nearly 15 centuries, the standard diet contained very little meat. Not surprisingly, the Japanese made religious compromises to allow for the consumption of fish and other sea products in much the same manner that medieval European Roman Catholics abstained from meat but ate fish on Fridays. The traditional meal was "three dishes and a soup" (*issan issui*). Typically, the three dishes were served separately in small ceramic plates or bowls and consisted of rice or noodles, a plate of vegetables (often pickled), and some kind of protein (including soy tofu). The soup was very often a clear broth flavored with a bit of miso (fermented soybean paste).

In the north, where fuel was scarce during the winter, one-pot stews (*nabe*) warmed the belly as well as the house when cooked and eaten. In the humid south, pickled vegetables (*tsukemono*) were a cool comfort to the soul because they required no heat to prepare.

Salt has always been a staple of Japanese food, but not the granulated variety used in Western cooking. Food was preserved with sea salt, and virtually any edible (and a few otherwise virtually inedible) piece of vegetation could be pickled in salt brine. Even fruits were salt preserved. Candy and other sweet confections were very rare until the late 19th century.

Virtually nothing (except fish) was eaten raw until the Japanese began to emulate Westerners who popularized eating raw fruit. Some historians of nutrition suggest that the Japanese suffered fewer epidemics because they cooked or pickled almost everything they consumed. Steaming, broiling, and boiling were the traditional methods of cooking. Stir-fry sauté methods came from the Asian continent, and much later baking and deep-frying (*tempura*) came with the Europeans in the 16th century. Bread, pies, cakes, and tarts became popular in the late 19th century and remain so today. Virtually every neighborhood boasts two or three small "French" bakeries, though some of the fillings for tarts and dumplings would astound any Parisian. Sweet bean paste, curry, pickled vegetables, and even tiny hot dogs are stuffed into these small delicacies.

The standard fare in modern Japan can be divided into the following categories: noodle soups generically called *menrui*; steamed rice dishes (*donburi*) topped with scrambled egg, vegetables, or bits of meat; stir-fried rice (*chahan*); deep-fried battered vegetables or shrimp (*tempura*); raw fish accompanied by vinegared (sushi) rice and sheets of seaweed (the raw fish alone is called *sashimi*); portable lunches of rice, pickles, and some bits of meat served in lacquered lunch boxes (*bento*), which some argue was the world's first fast food; and the previously mentioned stews (*nabe*). Scores of other types of cooking abound, including the almost ubiquitous Western fast food stores (McDonald's, Pizza Hut, Kentucky Fried Chicken, Dunkin' Donuts, etc.); formal restaurants of all kinds; and tiny snack shops that serve late-night grilled skewers (*yakitori*), tortes (*oconomiyaki*), and the like.

To read about food in early modern Japan, see the Japan entry in the section "Food" in chapter 5 ("Material Life") in volume 4 of this series.

~*Louis G. Perez*

FOR MORE INFORMATION

Booth, S. *Food of Japan*. New York: Interlink Publishing Group, 2001.

Homma, G. *The Folk Art of Japanese Country Cooking: A Traditional Diet for Today's World*. Denver, Colo.: North Atlantic Books, 1991.

Ishige, N. *The History and Culture of Japanese Food*. New York: Paul Kegan, 2001.

Toynbee, A. *Introducing Japan: History, Way of Life, Creative World, Seen and Heard, Food and Wine*. New York: St. Martin's Press, 1978.

INUIT

Living in the vast expanses of the Arctic, which are not hospitable to agriculture of any kind, the Inuit traditionally have subsisted on many forms of animal protein from land and sea, including caribou, walrus, arctic char (and other fish), seabirds (and their eggs), rabbit, walrus, polar bear, and seal. Iqaluit (pronounced "Eehal-ooeet"), the largest town in Nunavut and capital of the semisovereign Nunavut Territory (population roughly 7,000), means "fishing place," an indication of the importance of sustenance from the sea in the traditional diet.

During the late 20th century, the traditional Inuit diet began to change swiftly as a result of the encroachment of industrialized society from the south. This encroachment took two forms. First, expansion of the money economy and urbanization has drawn many Inuit who once lived off the land to towns and urban employment. Iqaluit hosts a large supermarket as large as stores in larger urban areas, except that the prices (mainly because of air-freight charges) are three to four times higher than in Ottawa or Omaha. If one can afford the bill, mango-grapefruit juice and ready-cooked buffalo wings (as well as many other items of standard "southern" fare) are readily available. The village of Pangnirtung, north of Iqaluit, is home to a Kentucky Fried Chicken franchise.

Second, traditional Inuit food sources also have been threatened by widespread pollution that has made many traditional food sources unsafe. Toxicity in some cases extends even to mother's milk. Warming temperatures and erratic weather patterns (including out-of-season ice storms and thaws, causing thinning ice) also have made hunting riskier to human health. Despite urbanization, pollution, and warming temperatures, many Inuit still hunt "country food" for a portion of their sustenance, citing its spiritual connection to tradition as well as nutritional benefits.

A warming climate has made polar bears, a traditional Inuit food source, scarcer and skinnier. The bears usually obtain their food (seals, for example) from the ice. Canadian Wildlife Service scientists reported during December 1998 that polar bears around Hudson Bay were 90 to 220 pounds lighter than 30 years earlier, apparently because earlier ice melting has given them less time to feed on seal pups. When the ice melts, the polar bears can no longer use it to hunt for ring seals, many of which also have died.

Several manufactured toxins (among them mercury, dioxins, and polychlorinated biphenyls, or PCBs) are conducted into the Arctic via prevailing air and ocean circulation, making the area a toxic "sink." Many of these chemicals concentrate in the body fat of animals that comprise much of the Inuits' traditional diet. The degree of toxicity increases many times up the food chain and with each succeeding generation via biomagnification (also called bioaccumulation).

Geographically, the Arctic could not be in a worse position for toxic pollution, as a ring of industry in Russia, Europe, and North America pours pollutants northward. "As we put our babies to our breasts we are feeding them a noxious, toxic cocktail," said Sheila Watt-Cloutier, a grandmother who also is president of the Inuit Circumpolar Conference. "When women have to think twice about breastfeeding their babies, surely that must be a wake-up call to the world" (Johansen, 2000, 27). The three most common contaminants that researchers have found in Inuit mothers' breast milk are three pesticides (dieldrin; mirex; and DDE, a derivative of DDT) and two industrial chemicals—PCBs and hexachlorobenzene.

Persistent organic pollutants (POPs) have been linked to cancer; birth defects; and other neurological, reproductive, and immune-system damage in people and animals. At high levels, these chemicals also damage the central nervous system. Many of them also act as endocrine disrupters, causing deformities in sex organs as well as long-term dysfunction of reproductive systems. POPs also can interfere with the function of the brain and endocrine system by penetrating the placental barrier and scrambling the instructions of the naturally produced chemical messengers.

Inuit infants have provided "a living test tube for immunologists" (Cone 1996, A-1). Due to their diet of contaminated sea animals and fish, Inuit women's breast milk contains six to seven times the PCB level of women in urban Quebec, according to Quebec government statistics. Born with depleted white blood cells, Inuit children suffer excessive bouts of diseases, including a 20-fold increase in life-threatening meningitis compared to other Canadian children. Their babies have experienced strikingly high rates of bronchitis, pneumonia, and other infections compared with other Canadians. One Inuit child out of every four has chronic hearing loss due to infections.

"The last thing we need at this time is worry about the very country food that nourishes us, spiritually and emotionally, poisoning us," Watt-Cloutier said. "This is not just about contaminants on our plate. This is a whole way of being, a whole cultural heritage that is at stake here for us" (Mofina, A-12). "The process of hunting and fishing, followed by the sharing of food—the communal partaking of animals—is a time-honored ritual that binds us together and links us with our ancestors," she said (PCB Working group).

~Bruce E. Johansen

FOR MORE INFORMATION

Cone, M. "Human Immune Systems May be Pollution Victims." Los Angeles *Times*, May 13, 1996, A-1.

Johansen, B. E. "Pristine No More: The Arctic, Where Mother's Milk is Toxic." *The Progressive*, December 2000, 27–29.

Mofina, R. "Study Pinpoints Dioxin Origins: Cancer-causing Agents in Arctic Aboriginals' Breast Milk Comes from U.S. and Quebec." Montreal *Gazette*, October 4, 2000, A-12.

PCB Working Group, IPEN. "Communities Respond to PCB Contamination." No date. <http://ipen.ecn.cz/>.

ISLAMIC WORLD

The Ottoman Empire dominated the Islamic world throughout the 19th century, and the empire's rich culinary tradition represented a cultural continuation from an earlier period. See the Ottoman Turks entry in the section "Food and Drink" in chapter 5 ("Material Life") in volume 3 of this series for a description of what remains of this cuisine for travelers to modern Turkey.

Drink

Akin to eating food, drinking is one of those simple but all-important daily activities. As we consume water, soft drinks, or even alcoholic beverages, we probably do not realize the larger social, economic, and political ramifications of this quotidian and mundane activity. Nevertheless, as social activists of the 1960s continually pointed out, the personal is political. What we do in our daily lives does indeed have a larger significance. And in the 20th century, this has been particularly true about drinking. Although one could focus on a myriad of issues such as clean water or fluoridation, the entries that follow center on the issue of alcohol. Perhaps no other drink has been more politically and socially controversial.

The movement to restrict and to eliminate the sale and consumption of alcoholic beverages was over a hundred years old when the U.S. Congress finally enacted the 18th Amendment, which outlawed the sale and distribution of alcohol. Many Americans hailed this constitutional addition, along with its enforcing legislation, the Volstead Act, as a jewel in the crown of progressive reform. It aimed to improve the standard of living for working people while simultaneously making life better for women and children. By 1933, President Franklin D. Roosevelt ended the experiment in prohibition. Whether it was a success or a failure is a matter of interpretation. It seems clear that Americans drank less after prohibition. However, the criminalization of the sale and distribution of alcohol also put profit into illicit activity, thus fostering the growth of gangs, which survived prohibition's ups and downs.

Although the prohibition movement did not return in the 20th century, concern about alcohol remained. By the 1960s, major national studies had examined the causes and consequences of alcoholism. One of the startling discoveries was that children of alcoholics became alcoholics too. Thus a cycle of disease became apparent. Moreover, these reports made clear to the public that hundreds of traffic fatalities each year were directly related to drunk driving. Groups such as Mothers Against Drunk Driving (MADD) and Students Against Drunk Driving (SADD) did have an impact. By the late 1980s, their message of abstinence and moderate consumption had reduced the number of alcohol-related accidents. Correspondingly the quantity of soft drinks Americans consumed increased rather dramatically. This too created health-related issues, in that the drinking of large amounts of bubbly sugar water contributed to obesity. Thus, one might argue that Americans were slow to realize the larger significance of their central daily activity, quenching their thirst.

In Africa, the consumption of alcohol is viewed from every perspective. Many Africans enjoy alcohol while others abhor it with the decisive factor often being the local predominance of Western or Islamic influence. In Japan, the consumption of alcohol has increased and Japanese-made beer and scotch have found growing world markets.

UNITED STATES, 1920–39

In 1920 residents of the United States found themselves surrounded by easily observable signs that they were entering a new era in their everyday lives. Less than three weeks into the new year, a constitutional amendment took effect that prohibited the manufacture, transportation, and sale of alcoholic beverages. Temperance enthusiasts staged mock funerals for "King Alcohol" while opponents offered a few sad eulogies for "John Barleycorn." The days when alcohol remained a normal, or at least legal, part of most American diets ended on January 16, presumably forever.

The 18th Amendment brought the federal government into people's daily lives in a fashion never before experienced in peacetime. Significantly, national prohibition made it a crime to sell but not to purchase or use alcoholic beverages, leaving many people with conflicting feelings about personal decisions as to whether to drink. The resentment that many Americans felt toward national prohibition and the unhappiness of many others with its ineffective enforcement would provoke debate about the dry law all across the country in the years to come. By decade's end, prohibition violators accounted for over one-third of the 12,000 inmates of federal prisons while a glut of prohibition cases overloaded the courts. Despite the turmoil over prohibition in practice, the new law seemed to be an unavoidable permanent reality of daily life in America. As one proud sponsor boasted, "There is as much chance of repealing the Eighteenth Amendment as there is for a hummingbird to fly to the planet Mars with the Washington Monument tied to its tail!"

Rural America viewed alcohol as primarily a problem of urban life, where drinking took place in saloons. There, rural dwellers believed, saloon keepers encouraged drinking to excess; workers spent wages that should have been going to support their families; political machines influenced voters; prostitutes and gamblers plied their trades; and immigrants gathered to discuss the homeland, speak their native languages, and carry on old customs that slowed their progress toward becoming good Americans. These negative images help explain why the largest, most influential prohibitionist organization called itself the Anti-Saloon League of America.

The Volstead Act encouraged rural dwellers to view their own continued drinking as legal and harmless. The law prohibited manufactured beverages containing more than .5 percent alcohol, a standard that outlawed not only distilled spirits but even low-powered beer, the staples of working-class saloons. At the same time, the Volstead Act outlawed naturally fermented cider and wine only if proven intoxicating, which was in fact a much higher standard and one rarely if ever policed. Indeed, California grape juice or concentrate was shipped legally with U.S. Department of Agriculture labels indicating that, if allowed to sit and ferment for 60 days, it would become wine of 12 percent alcohol content. As a result, the California wine grape industry grew by 400 percent during the 1920s, reinforcing the rural view that the government did not consider homemade fruit-based beverages to violate prohibition.

Inhabitants of villages, towns, and smaller cities across the country generally observed alcoholic beverage prohibition, though, as elsewhere, there were exceptions, especially as the decade wore on. These middle-sized communities contained the bulk of Women's Christian Temperance Union and Anti-Saloon League members. Also concentrated there were many of the one-third to two-fifths of American adults who had not used alcohol before prohibition and a substantial number of those who gave up drinking when liquor became illegal. A nationwide survey by social workers in 1926 reported that, outside of a few large metropolitan areas, prohibition was largely effective. In Lima, Ohio; Sioux Falls, South Dakota; Boise, Idaho; and Tacoma, Washington, little evidence of drinking was to be seen. Community opinion, the subtle social pressure in places where individual behavior was easy to observe, appeared to be a stronger influence in achieving this result than police enforcement of the law.

In somewhat larger cities prohibition violation reportedly occurred more frequently, although the law met with general compliance. In Middletown (a hypothetical location), the Lynds noted, the example and influence of a core of industrial and civic leaders discouraged drinking by the business class, while the closing of legal saloons reduced it among the working class. Sinclair Lewis, whose *Main Street* (1920) appeared too early in the decade to address prohibition, subsequently turned his attention from Gopher Prairie to the fictional middle-sized Midwestern city of Zenith, the setting for both *Babbitt* (1922) and *Elmer Gantry* (1927). In Zenith, respectable middle-class people occasionally drank. Businessman George Babbitt regarded prohibition as good for the working class but surreptitiously bought gin from a bootlegger in the poorer section of town to fix cocktails for his dinner guests. Lewis showed some sympathy for Babbitt's mixed feelings and his awkward, infrequent transgression of the dry law, but none whatsoever for Protestant evangelist Gantry, an active prohibitionist characterized as a complete moral hypocrite.

Prohibition violation occurred most frequently in large cities from San Francisco to New Orleans to New York. In big cities, the native-born middle classes tended to drink less than either the wealthy or the working class. Among the reasons for this pattern was the high cost of alcoholic beverages during prohibition. Whiskey or beer could be, and often was, obtained legally with a physician's prescription declaring it necessary for medicinal purposes, but that required a visit to the doctor as well as the pharmacy where it was sold. The alternatives were to buy illegally manufactured or smuggled liquor or make your own. At $.80 for a quart of beer (up 600% since 1916) or $5.90 for a quart of gin (up 520%) by 1928, the cost of domestically produced beverages was more than the average family income of $2,600 per year could frequently absorb. Imported liquor, such as Canadian or Scotch whiskey or French wine, was better quality but much more expensive. Those who were wealthy or could produce their own liquor were best able to afford it. Thus, not surprisingly, drinking was most common among the upper classes and immigrant groups.

Immigrant communities did not generally consider drinking a crime, regardless of what U.S. law declared. Most came from cultures that took alcoholic beverages for granted as a normal part of everyday life. Home brewing and wine making were common traditions. Distilling any form of sugar into neutral spirits and then adding flavoring agents required less skill and soon spread in popularity. Hardware stores did a brisk business legally selling small inexpensive home stills. The most common and simple practice was to fill a bottle halfway with neutral spirits, add a few drops of glycerin and juniper berry juice, and top up with water. Because the preferred style of bottle was too tall to fill under a sink tap, the process was usually carried out in a bathtub, hence the term "bathtub gin."

White southerners supported prohibition to take liquor away from African Americans.

Those who made alcoholic beverages at home found it difficult to accept that what was allowable for personal use became illegal when collected and sold. State and local officials and the small force of federal prohibition agents found it impossible with the available resources to police small-scale but widespread alcoholic beverage production. Instead they concentrated their attention on commercial bootleggers and outlaw saloons, variously referred to as blind pigs, gin joints, or speakeasies.

Bootlegging, the business of obtaining, transporting, and selling illegal liquor, was a perilous but lucrative business in the 1920s given that a substantial number of people, especially in big cities, were prepared to ignore the prohibition law. Young, ambitious men, who because of their immigrant backgrounds found it difficult to obtain jobs or advancement in legal occupations, saw opportunity, profit, and no disgrace in bootlegging. Italian, Polish, and Jewish men in their 20s dominated bootlegging, often establishing and managing large and complex organizations to carry on the business. Competition among bootleggers was fierce and often violent, not surprising considering that the lucrative trade completely lacked the government regulation or protection enjoyed by legitimate enterprises. Whereas bootleggers fought and sometimes even killed each other, customers remained almost entirely untouched. They received the care and consideration essential to any successful retail business, particularly one dependent on repeat purchasers. As the most successful of the bootleggers, Chicago's Al Capone (the New York–born son of Italian immigrants who was only 32 years old when finally sent to prison in 1931 for income tax evasion after a decade in the business) observed, "I'm a public benefactor. . . . You can't cure thirst by law. . . . Some call it bootlegging. Some call it racketeering. I call it a business. They say I violate the prohibition law. Who doesn't?"

Although African Americans in urban areas shared the prohibition experience of other city dwellers, the large number situated in the rural South confronted different circumstances. White southerners, including those with little desire to give up drinking themselves, supported prohibition to take liquor away from African Americans. The social control whites exercised over blacks in all respects, together with the pervasive poverty of the African American community, insured that prohibition effectively reduced access to alcohol for at least this one segment of the population.

Consumption of alcohol in the United States during the years of national prohibition, 1920 through 1933, remains difficult to determine. Any illegal activity is hard to measure, and prohibition violation was no exception. The evidence is strong, however, that more Americans observed the law than did not and that total alcohol consumption fell by more than 60 percent. Per capita consumption in 1911–15, the last years before state and federal laws began significantly to affect drinking, amounted to 2.56 gallons of pure alcohol for every American above the age of 15, though obviously some drank nothing at all and others drank much more. This was actually consumed as 2.09 gallons of distilled spirits (45% alcohol), 0.79 gallons of wine (18% alcohol), and 29.53 gallons of beer (5% alcohol) per capita. In 1934, the year after prohibition ended, per capita consumption measured 0.97 gallons of alcohol consumed as 0.64 gallons of spirits, 0.36 gallons of wine, and 13.58 gallons of beer, suggesting that drinking alcohol had become a much less widespread practice during prohibition. During the same years, milk and Coca-Cola consumption almost tripled. Although alcoholic beverage consumption increased during the 1930s, three more decades would pass before liquor consumption again reached pre–World War I levels. Clearly national prohibition influenced the drinking patterns of a generation of Americans.

Despite the actual decline in alcohol consumption, an image of widespread drinking prevailed during the 1920s. The substantial amount that did continue was concentrated in cities where it was most visible. Bootleggers and speakeasies had to advertise, carefully to be sure, to attract customers. Bootlegging violence, not to mention police arrests of bootleggers and confiscation of liquor, gained a lot of media attention. Magazines and movies implied that a great deal of drinking was taking place, especially within the upper classes of society. As an overall impression emerged by the early 1930s that prohibition had not worked well, it became increasingly unpopular. Congress modified the Volstead Act in April 1933 to allow the manufacture and sale of weak beer. By December, despite the difficulty of changing the Constitution and the predictions of prohibitionists, the 18th Amendment was repealed and, except in several states that retained state prohibition, Americans resumed legal drinking.

The end of national prohibition in 1933 left a mixed legacy. On the one hand, public confidence in the law and the necessity of unquestioning observance of it had been shaken. On the other hand, the dry crusade accustomed Americans for the first time to the federal government's enforcement of laws bearing on individual conduct using customs officials; Coast Guard agents; postal inspectors; national park rangers; and a new federal police force, the agents of the Bureau of Prohibition. In the aftermath of prohibition, as concern about narcotics increased, federal policing of drug traffic was accepted as appropriate with little question. At the same time and perhaps most important, judicial sensitivity to the treatment of individuals in the criminal justice system began to increase. The Supreme Court was much more sympathetic to the Scottsboro boys than it had been to Sacco and Vanzetti. By the end of the 1930s, the Court was starting to show the concern for fair and equal legal treatment that would characterize its efforts in the decades that followed (Kyvig, 1–2, 15–18, 154).

To read about drink in the United States in the 19th century, see the United States entries in the section "Drink" in chapter 5 ("Material Life") in volume 5 of this series.

FOR MORE INFORMATION

American Temperance and Prohibition. <http://prohibition.history.ohio-state.edu/>.

Clark, W. B., and M. E. Hilton, eds. *Alcohol in America: Drinking Practices and Problems*. Albany: State University of New York Press, 1991.

Kyvig, D. E. *Daily Life in the United States, 1920–1939: Decades of Promise and Pain*. Westport, Conn.: Greenwood Press, 2002.

Lynd, R. S., and H. M. Lynd. *Middletown: A Study in Modern American Culture*. New York: Harcourt, Brace, and World, 1929.

Martin, J. K. *Drinking in America: A History*. New York: Free Press, 1982.

MATERIAL LIFE

DRINK

United States, 1920-1939

United States, 1960-1990

Japan

Africa

UNITED STATES, 1960–90

Champagne to toast newlyweds, a martini at a cocktail party, wine with dinner, a bottle of beer at a picnic, a gin and tonic at a bar—such customs came to America with immigrants from early times and have never disappeared. Drinking establishments, from the corner tavern to the bar in exclusive clubs, have long been fixtures in the American social landscape. With the drinking go friendly conversations, political arguments, television watching, and hanging out.

The other side of the story is also part of daily lives: poor schoolwork done during repeated hangovers, tragedies caused by drunk drivers, families ruined by alcohol-related conflicts, jobs lost because of excessive absences caused by drinking binges, homeless men and women clutching bottles barely concealed in giveaway brown bags, and illness and death caused by excessive drinking.

Although the effects of excessive drinking are well known, knowledge alone does not restrain those who are tempted to drink too much. By the mid-1960s the National Institute of Mental Health began to encourage research into causes and consequences of alcoholism, and in 1966 two federal appeals court decisions supported contentions that alcoholism was a disease. Two years later the Supreme Court took note of these decisions, observing that experts were divided on the matter; the Court then ruled that arrests for public intoxication were permissible. The next logical step was for Congress to establish an agency to direct federal efforts to deal with alcohol-related problems. The National Institute on Alcohol Abuse and Alcoholism made it possible for treatment, research, and educational activities to be conducted at new levels. One result was a recommendation that states remove many alcohol-related legal infractions from the criminal justice system, substituting medical treatment for punishment.

Researchers at the University of Iowa confirmed the increasingly popular theory that a tendency toward alcoholism might be inherited. Children of alcoholics had a high incidence of alcoholism even when they had been adopted and raised by nonalcoholics. Theories aside, the reality of the 1960s and 1970s was clear: Between 1960 and 1975, the annual per capita consumption of alcoholic beverages increased by one-third. Was this a return to earlier times? Not quite, given that the average consumption remained at a level half as high as in 1830. The increase came in part from the fact that teenagers began drinking at earlier ages and in larger numbers. Further, with liberation of women from old constraints, their drinking levels approached those of men. As far as consumption of hard liquor (distilled spirits) was concerned, 1978 was the peak year in recent times. Then came a steady decline, continuing to the mid-1990s.

Excessive drinking harmed the health of the drinkers, of course, but it also did damage to others—particularly when accidents resulted from drunk driving. Drunk drivers were involved in half of the 45,000 fatalities caused annually by automobile accidents between World War II and 1980. Mothers Against Drunk Driving (MADD), founded in 1980, became the most powerful organization striving to reduce drunk driving, particularly among the young.

Health and drunk-driving concerns contributed to a slight decline in consumption of alcoholic beverages in the later 1980s. At the same time, the consumption of soft drinks increased by almost 20 percent. Diet drinks got a boost in 1983 when the Food and Drug Administration approved the use of aspartame, an artificial sweetener. Although critics warned that aspartame's effects on certain chemicals in the brain could cause behavioral changes, diet-conscious consumers ignored the warnings and the sweetener quickly became popular. Much sweeter than sugar, aspartame has the advantage of not causing tooth decay. Consumption of bottled water doubled in the latter half of the 1980s.

Consumers of soft drinks were ready for a new sweetener, but millions let the Coca-Cola Company know they were not ready for a new taste. In 1985, a year before its 100th birthday, Coca-Cola decided to change its formula for Coke, the world's most popular soft drink, by making it sweeter. A $100 million advertising campaign promoting the new Coke attracted overwhelming attention. A survey by the company claimed that 81 percent of Americans heard about the change within 24 hours of its announcement—higher than the percentage who were aware in the same length of time of the 1969 moon landing. But the campaign failed to persuade angry protesters that the new formula was better than the old, so within three months the company brought back the original formula, now labeled Coca-Cola Classic. Some preferred the new taste, however, so the company produced both the old and the new. The controversy gave the Coca-Cola Company valuable free publicity, boosting sales of both old Coke and new and arousing suspicions (that the company denied) that creating controversy had been the plan all along. The episode provided a dramatic demonstration of corporate America's responsiveness to consumers (Marty, 130, 216, 291–92).

To read about drink in the United States in the 19th century, see the United States entries in the section "Drink" in chapter 5 ("Material Life") in volume 5 of this series.

FOR MORE INFORMATION

American Temperance and Prohibition. <http://prohibition.history.ohio-state.edu/>.

Clark, W. B., and M. E. Hilton, eds. *Alcohol in America: Drinking Practices and Problems*. Albany: State University of New York Press, 1991.

Martin, J. K. *Drinking in America: A History*. New York: Free Press, 1982.

Marty, M. A. *Daily Life in the United States, 1960–1990: Decades of Discord*. Westport, Conn.: Greenwood Press, 1997.

MATERIAL LIFE

|

DRINK

|

United States, 1920-1939

United States, 1960-1990

Japan

Africa

JAPAN

Japanese drink extends far beyond the clear rice wine, sake. Japanese are connoisseurs of a plethora of teas that divide by color into green (*ocha*) and black (*kocha*); tea-flavored foods abound as well. A barley-flavored cold drink (*mugi-cha*) is similar to Western iced tea. Japanese beers have become very popular, though imported American and European beers are very popular as well. Whiskeys of all types have been produced in Japan for over a century, but scotch is the most prestigious and most widely consumed.

One would be remiss not to mention the popularity of "energy" drinks produced and consumed in huge quantities during the last three decades. Tiny bottles of curiously named concoctions (*Calpis, Sweat*) are sold in vending machines at virtually every urban street corner and train station kiosk. Many are herb-based or laced with secret formulas containing caffeine or ginseng. Others contain iced sweet coffee or chocolate flavoring. Millions of busy businessmen gulp down a bottle or two of these energy drinks in hopes of coping with another mind-numbing hourlong commute to work.

The younger set consume American-style carbonated soft drinks (Coca-Cola, Pepsi, Fanta, Nehi, etc.), but bottled water has become increasingly popular with teenagers on the go.

Finally, food and drink have been important to the creation of Japan's notorious nightlife. Virtually all Japanese male (and, increasingly, female as well) employees gang together to drink themselves into a stupor in the thousands of tiny little bars throughout the large cities. The beer and whiskey consumed there is thought to give release to workplace tensions and contribute to bonding. It is generally believed that no one is promoted who does not indulge. Until recently, managers were given generous expense accounts to treat their employees to these binges.

Many bars provide female companionship in the form of bar hostesses who are not prostitutes but earn their living by inducing salarymen to drink more by flirting with them and laughing at their jokes. Many of these clubs are theme bars, specializing in adventurous décors or particular types of music.

The sing-along karaoke (which literally means open orchestra) bars still prosper throughout the country. Obviously, it is far easier to belt out or croon a tune when inebriated than when stone-cold sober. Young unmarried professionals often rent a tiny "studio" where sing-along videos are played and friends take turns singing and drinking. Obviously much alcohol is consumed. Small salty snacks are served in attractive ways to encourage patrons to consume more alcohol. Small snack-food sheds catering to late-night customers abound around bars and theaters.

To read about drink in early modern Japan, see the Japan entry in the section "Drink" in chapter 5 ("Material Life") in volume 4 of this series.

~*Louis G. Perez*

FOR MORE INFORMATION

Booth, S. *Food of Japan*. New York: Interlink Publishing Group, 2001.

Morris, V. *The Japanese Way of Tea: From its Origins in China to Sen Rikyu*. Honolulu: University of Hawaii Press, 1998.

Toynbee, A. *Introducing Japan: History, Way of Life, Creative World, Seen and Heard, Food and Wine*. New York: St. Martin's Press, 1978.

MATERIAL LIFE

|

DRINK

|

United States,
1920-1939

United States,
1960-1990

Japan

Africa

AFRICA

Opinions on the topic of alcohol in Africa are as varied as the continent's diverse cultures. There is certainly no single "African" opinion on alcohol and its consumption. Some Africans enjoy drinking beer, some profit from the sales of it, some view it as a plague on society, and some have come to abuse it. Regardless, alcohol has been and continues to be a major component of African societies.

Alcoholic beverages were popular throughout the continent before colonial rule of the 20th century. In precolonial African societies, alcohol was used in religious ceremonies such as weddings, funerals, and teenage initiation rites. Many of these societies had a strong sense of community, and alcohol was often used to promote communal ties. The traditional beers and wines used for this purpose had a brief shelf life and thus were usually consumed only on special occasions or by elites.

Traditional beverages were usually fermented and rarely distilled and thus tended to have a low percentage of alcohol (fermentation produces lower alcohol content than distillation). Beer and wines are examples of fermented beverages whereas gin, rum, and brandy are distilled beverages. Traditional beers were usually fermented from sorghum and millet, and wines were made from palm and honey. The beverages with the lowest percentages of alcohol often had high amounts of nutrients and were very important in fighting off malnutrition. Some of these nutritious brews were served to children and the elderly.

During the slave trade, European liquors began to make their way through the African continent. Liquors such as brandy and gin were major items bartered throughout the slave trade. As European involvement in the African continent developed, African interests in European products (e.g., tobacco and alcohol) intensified. European liquors offered a much more potent and condensed version of alcohol as compared to the domestic beverages already available throughout the continent.

Colonial governments took a somewhat hypocritical stance toward alcohol and African consumption. Although imperial rule was portrayed as a positive way to introduce Africans to civility and Christianity, European nations wanted colonies to pay for themselves. The rulers initially avoided direct taxation, as it tended to anger the colonial subjects. Taxation of European goods, however, was encouraged, because it was more discreet. Such taxes were a viable way to finance colonial governments, and the European nations eventually decided that monetary gains outweighed the moral ramifications of allowing the sales and importation of alcohol in the African colonies.

As they profited from taxes on alcohol, colonial authorities had to strike some sort of balance in regulating African alcohol consumption. Authorities felt that alcohol use could easily hurt these economies and governments just as much as it helped them. Alcohol was deemed as promoting laziness, crime, and disorder. Therefore colonial officials attempted to limit alcohol consumption and illegal brewing.

Imperial rule also introduced a variety of crops to Africa. As a result, African brewers experimented and came up with various beverages made from these crops. Bananas, grain, sugar, and other materials were introduced to various areas, and brewers consequently experimented with them as alcoholic products. These new ingredients often led to cheaper and more potent brews (some were even potentially deadly).

For those in cities and towns, alcohol was a way to adapt and socialize in a foreign environment. These areas were typically populated by men who had left their families and friends behind in rural areas and migrated in hopes of getting employment. In these unfamiliar surroundings, alcohol facilitated and cemented new bonds. Strangers and coworkers would gather in beer halls and socialize. For these migrants, drinking eased their transition into urban areas and lessened the pain of being away from their families.

Throughout Africa, alcohol has been associated with wealth and power. Precolonial kings, chiefs, and rulers were known to consume large amounts of alcohol. As European rule spread inland, European liquors began to be associated with wealth and power. Large numbers of Africans began to prefer European beverages over their traditional counterparts, because they were seen as the drink of the rich and powerful. As a result, instead of sorghum beer and palm wine, Africans began substituting bottles of Guinness and Heineken beer and the finest European liqueurs. These imported beverages soon were associated with modernization and thus came to represent elitism and the embracing of progress.

Though consumption of alcohol in Africa has been dominated by men, brewing has traditionally been the domain of African women. For many, homebrews have been quite profitable. Often the funds they earn from producing alcohol are used to supplement their husbands' meager wages or pay for their children's schooling. Whether in Nigeria, Kenya, Swaziland, or the Congo, female brewers were and still are operating throughout the continent. In this regard, alcohol has made an indelibly positive mark on African societies.

Over the 20th century, African alcohol consumption became a multibillion-dollar business, and these home brewers account for only a minute part of the continent's alcohol production. South African Breweries (SAB) became one of the world's largest brewing companies and expanded throughout the continent and into other areas of the world (most notably with its recent purchase of the Miller Brewing Company). Many postcolonial governments attempted to promote and capitalize on domestic beer production, in particular beverages that may promote or strengthen nationalist identities.

In places with sizable followings of Christian or Islamic fundamentalism, alcohol has increasingly been demonized. These groups realize the negative toll that alcohol has taken on the African people and thus have incorporated antialcohol sentiment into their preaching.

Since independence, African economies have been poor. Employment opportunities and decent wages are rare. These economic conditions, in combination with health problems such as starvation, HIV/AIDS, and malaria, have made alcohol consumption more popular and thus its abuse much more rampant. Consequently, as the 20th century progressed, African consumption, in general, shifted from ceremonial and communal celebrations to providing escape from an ever-worsening bleak reality.

~Tyler Fleming

FOR MORE INFORMATION

Akyeampong, E. *Drink, Power, and Cultural Change: A Social History of Alcohol in Ghana, c. 1800 to Recent Times*. Portsmouth, N.H.: Heinemann, 1996.

Bryceson, D. F. *Alcohol in Africa: Mixing Business, Pleasure and Politics*. Portsmouth, N.H.: Heinemann, 2002.

La Hausse, P. *Brewers, Beerhalls and Boycotts: History of Liquor in South Africa*. Johannesburg: Ravan Press, 1988.

Willis, J. *Potent Brews: A Social History of Alcohol in East Africa 1850–1999*. Athens: Ohio University Press, 2002.

Housing

MATERIAL LIFE
|
HOUSING
|
United States,
1920-1939

United States,
1940-1959

United States,
1960-1990

India

Japan

Inuit

A few years ago, a family friend who happens to be a Tibetan monk came to visit me in the United States. Dutifully, I showed her my new family home, which had been recently built and had many modern amenities. She seemed mortified by the tour. When I took her to my home office, a five-by-nine-foot room, she said it was as large as her house in Tibet. Clearly she and I live in two distinct worlds. Mine is a world of plenty and hers is not. Perhaps few aspects of daily life illuminate the differences in culture, class, economics, and politics as markedly as housing.

A housing revolution took place at the beginning of the 20th century, particularly in the United States. By the 1920s, American cities, and many cities in other places such as India, were being wired for electricity. It became easy to light houses at night. The old gas lamps were not only dirty but exceedingly dangerous. The incandescent light bulb was relatively safe and inexpensive. Additionally, electricity in the home led to other changes. Household chores dramatically changed. More and more electric appliances found their places in the kitchen and other workrooms. At first, these devices did not save much time. Electric sewing and washing machines still required a lot of work. For example, the first washing machines required the user to insert wet items into the wringer by hand. Additionally, not all of this new technology was reliable. The first electric refrigerators were notoriously unpredictable. But by the 1940s, often at the urging of large power companies, much of urban America had been wired. Moreover, as a direct result of President Franklin D. Roosevelt's New Deal, by 1945 most rural areas from small towns to farms also had direct access to electricity.

In fact, the World War II era was a transitional time for housing, particularly in the United States. As a result of wartime conditions and federal funding, vast new developments of single-family homes appeared. This trend was reinforced in the 1950s when the U.S. government invested millions of dollars in new housing especially for returning veterans. Manufactured by large construction firms such as Levitt and Sons, these new housing subdivisions located on the outskirts of towns and cities became known as suburbs. New houses at affordable prices was one reason that Americans moved to the new areas.

With affluent middle-class families moving to Levittown and other places, cities suffered. In particular, poor people in cities suffered as urban houses and infrastructures were not kept up. In other words, the housing changes and improvements did not reach everyone equally. Large sections of the United States as well as large sections of other countries such as India developed housing crises. Too many people did not have access to adequate shelter, let alone running water and electricity. Even by 2000, thousands in the United States, for example, were homeless. In India's rural areas, homes continued to be made in the traditional ways, even though modern construction methods and materials were known. Similarly, in India's vast urban areas, housing remained at a premium. In Japan, high urban land values made housing expensive but most Japanese by the end of the century lived in modern structures with square footages

A tenant farmer's cabin in Harmony, Georgia, ca. 1920s. © National Archives.

that compared to those of Europe. In the Inuit North, traditional building materials also gave way to more modern materials, although traditional structural forms keyed to the environment continued to be employed. In terms of daily life experience, housing does tell much about the haves and have-nots.

UNITED STATES, 1920–39

During the early part of the 20th century, homes in America changed significantly as electricity and other modern conveniences became commonplace and as the home itself became redesigned. Domestic use of electricity was for the most part at first devoted to lighting. Otherwise, applications inclined less to practical uses than to novel and ostentatious displays of wealth. In New York City, Mrs. Cornelius Vanderbilt, for example, would greet visitors to her home in a dress covered with tiny electric lights. Fortunately, electric doorbells to announce the arrival of visitors became much more common than electrified fashions. Electric lights on Christmas trees proved popular as early as 1882. By the 1890s, children's toys, such as electrically powered model trains for boys and lighted dollhouses for girls, were applying the new technology as well as defining gender roles. The gradual introduction of alternating current to replace direct current in the 1890s allowed the transmission of electricity over longer distances and thus a greater diversity of uses.

After lights, electric irons were usually the first acquisitions for newly wired homes. The electric iron became popular because it did not require its user to stand next to a hot stove; not only the ironer but also the entire home could be kept cooler in warm weather. For similar reasons, electric fans, using small Westinghouse-developed motors, also achieved early success. Early efforts of individual homeowners to attach small motors to foot treadles or hand cranks were supplanted in the 1910s by the introduction of one-piece electric sewing and washing machines. A fan was attached to a mechanical carpet sweeper to create the first electric vacuum cleaner, the only home appliance other than the iron to gain wide distribution before the end of World War I.

When the number of wired houses began to increase rapidly after 1918, the market for home appliances expanded just as quickly At that point General Electric bought several promising small appliance companies, including Hughes and Hotpoint, and began devoting its considerable technological skill and financial resources to the developing market. Improved design and mass production of washing machines, sewing machines, and vacuum cleaners reduced their cost and increased their sales. The attachment of small motors to eggbeaters and food grinders created highly popular kitchen products: electric mixers and blenders. Home appliances went from being expensive and unreliable toys for the rich to more moderately priced, dependable, and useful tools for a mass of middle-class Americans.

Though electric power enhanced various devices, it did not immediately turn them into the home appliances of the late 20th century. The electric washing machine, for instance, was at first a far simpler device than it would eventually become. A motor powered the agitation of water, detergent, and soiled items and drove the wringer, into which wet items had to be inserted by hand. The physical drudgery of hauling and heating water as well as scrubbing and wringing clothes was reduced, but time-consuming and somewhat strenuous human involvement in the laundry process continued. More modern washing machines, which could spin dry as well as agitate, did not appear until the end of the 1930s.

Early versions of some electrical home appliances existed by the 1920s but were far too expensive for widespread use. Electric refrigerators were both costly and undependable at first, leading most households to continue relying instead on either underground storage or iceboxes, insulated chests cooled by a block of ice. A 1921 survey of 1,300 electrified Philadelphia homes found that although most had irons and vacuum cleaners, and upper-class homes usually had an electric coffee percolator and washing machine, virtually none had an electric refrigerator. During the 1930s mass production and price cutting made electric refrigerators practical to a wide market for the first time; by the eve of World War II, half of all American homes possessed them. Electric ranges, dishwashers, and clothes dryers had similar histories but did not gain popularity until after the war.

Gas had earlier begun the reform of domestic lighting. Gas manufactured from coal, available since the first decade of the 19th century, had been supplanted after midcentury by petroleum-based kerosene and in the early 20th century by natural gas. Piped delivery became commonplace within cities. For quite some time gas and electric utility systems waged a direct and often fierce competition. Both electricity and natural gas were viewed as expensive and novel in the early 20th century, but their advantages over wood, coal, and kerosene were widely recognized. The relative inflexibility of gas pipes, the more limited applications of the fuel, and the dangers associated with leakage put natural gas at a disadvantage in the contest. As a result, the gas industry began concentrating its efforts on the improvement of gas cooking stoves, water heaters, and hot-air furnaces. Gas ranges with easy-to-clean enameled surfaces and effective thermostats were introduced with great success. By 1930, nearly half of all American homes cooked with gas, a quarter used coal or wood, a fifth used oil, and less than 3 percent employed electricity. Meanwhile, the percentage of gas used for illumination fell from 75 at the turn of the century to 21 by 1919.

Nationally standardized transmission of electric current (alternating current delivered to households at 120 volts) by 1910 and significant reductions in the price of electricity in the early 20th century further affected the competition. Standardization created a national market and encouraged the mass production of electrical products. In the decade before World War I, salesmen for electric utilities peddled electric irons, toasters, hair curlers, and other appliances based on the electric resistance heating coil to households already signed up for electric lighting. By the end of the war, electricity, the more versatile of the two commodities, had pulled ahead of gas. Except for water and home heating and cooking purposes, electric current would maintain its lead.

The introduction of home lighting substantially altered domestic life. Industry and street railway use of electricity peaked during the day, encouraging power suppliers to seek off-hours customers. Electric utilities naturally sought to encourage residential use of electricity. Meanwhile the spread of transmission lines for industrial and transportation purposes made residential connections less expensive. After 1910 falling prices helped home electrification to spread rapidly beyond the small proportion of homes, mainly residences of the urban wealthy class, that had enjoyed it for some time.

American home design was transformed as architects and builders came to appreciate the possibilities of electricity. Late-19th-century gas-equipped Victorian homes tended to be dark and divided into many rooms. Gas burned oxygen; produced odors and soot; and required gas jets that could ignite fires or, if snuffed out, release poisonous fumes and cause explosions. Gas-fueled houses were most functional, appealing, and safe if individual rooms could be shut off for airing out and minimizing drafts. Interiors decorated in deep reds, blues, greens, and browns were preferred for their capacity to conceal soot.

Around the turn of the century, a few architects, the best known of whom today is Frank Lloyd Wright, began to recognize the superior properties of electricity and take advantage of its adaptability and relative safety. They started designing houses with open interior plans in which living rooms, dining rooms, and kitchens flowed together. The only isolated and private spaces in these designs were bedrooms and bathrooms, the latter newly developed as piped water and sanitary waste disposal sewers made it practical and appealing to consolidate in one room sinks, toilets, and bathtubs previously placed in different locations inside and outside the house. Houses illuminated by electricity could have more numerous and flexible light sources, and thus more freedom in furniture arrangement. Also, because electric lights did not produce soot, electrified homes could also have lighter-colored carpets, walls, and ceilings, making their interiors much brighter than before.

Electric wiring, together with indoor plumbing, added substantially to the cost of house construction. To keep housing prices stable while adding these new technologies, builders proved eager to cut costs elsewhere by reducing the size and number of rooms. Early-20th-century house plans started to eliminate formal front parlors, merging them with the family sitting room to create a single living room, often opening directly into a dining room. Large entrance halls were reduced in size or even eliminated. As Gwendolyn Wright pointed out in *Building the Dream*, "By 1910 it was rare to have single-purpose rooms such as libraries, pantries, sewing rooms, and spare bedrooms, which had comprised the Victorians' sense of uniqueness and complex domestic life. In a moderately priced two-story house there were usually only three downstairs rooms: living room, dining room, and kitchen." Even kitchens began to shrink in size, allegedly to save housewives' steps but no doubt also to reduce construction costs.

The most widespread manifestation of the new minimalist approach to house design was the bungalow, which first appeared in California at the start of the 20th century and spread rapidly eastward. Small, simple, informal, efficient, and intended to be sparsely furnished, the bungalow was quickly proclaimed to be a new standard of sensible and thrifty family living. Between 1900 and 1920, nearly 7.5 million new

> *Electric lights produced no soot, so electrified homes could have lighter walls and carpets.*

urban dwellings were added to a turn-of-the-century total of 10 million. In the 1920s, another 5.7 million were occupied. Thus by 1930 a majority of urban homes had been built within the past 30 years. During that period changes in house design had the result of reducing the amount of privacy within homes and drawing residents into an increasingly electrified common realm (Kyvig, 46–52).

To read about housing in the United States in the 19th century, see the United States entries in the section "Housing" in chapter 5 ("Material Life") in volume 5 of this series.

FOR MORE INFORMATION

Kyvig, D. E. *Daily Life in the United States, 1920–1939: Decades of Promise and Pain.* Westport, Conn.: Greenwood Press, 2002.

Lower East Side Tenement Museum. <http://www.wnet.org/archive/tenement/>.

Patterson, J. T. *Grand Expectations: The United States, 1945–1974.* New York: Oxford University Press, 1996.

Wright, G. *Building the Dream: A Social History of Housing in America.* New York: Pantheon, 1981.

MATERIAL LIFE
|
HOUSING
|
United States,
1920-1939

United States,
1940-1959

United States,
1960-1990

India

Japan

Inuit

UNITED STATES, 1940–59

The demand for housing to fit new lives—to accommodate all the Americans who moved during the war or needed a place to put a new family—was again eased by financial help from the government. In 1949 congressional subsidies helped build low-income urban housing even as many universities built temporary housing for the huge number of new students the government was also sending to school. The GI Bill helped returning veterans get mortgages as well as educations. A great variety of developments in single-family homes appeared in the suburbs. Between 1945 and 1955 some 15 million housing units were constructed in the United States, leading to historic highs in home ownership. Before World War II would-be homeowners often had to offer down payments as high as 50 percent to buy a house, promising to pay the rest in periods of as short as 10 years. With the GI Bill some veterans put down nothing at all, and others offered a token one-dollar down payment with long-term mortgages.

After 1947 changes brought about by the Federal Housing Administration, working with the Veterans Administration, made available mortgages of up to 90 percent with interest rates as low as 4 percent—and with periods as long as 30 years to pay off the debt. By 1960, 60 percent of all Americans owned their own homes.

And by 1950 these two government agencies were also insuring 36 percent of all new nonfarm mortgages; by 1955 they handled 41 percent. The suburbs that grew out of governmental generosity became the market for the new consumerism, demonstrating once again the interdependence of public and private forces shaping the lives of every class. Taxes, withheld from salaries for the first time in 1943, continued to be deducted during the postwar period. People gladly maintained the New Deal tradition of tax-provided public services, such as twice-a-day mail deliveries and street cleaning.

The same technological and production skills that fired our defense efforts were turning 1950s America into a world of new things. Consumerism made it as easy to be distracted from the Russian menace as it was to ignore the one-third of the population that remained outside of the generally flourishing economy, the "other America" Michael Harrington clearly defined in 1962.

In the years between 1950 and 1970 the suburban population more than doubled, from 36 million to 74 million. People enjoyed living in the mortgage- and building-subsidized communities exemplified by Levittown. In the 1950s the typical American lived in suburbia. Everywhere groups of people established new roots with the help of money saved during the war from higher salaries and war bonds. If people shared no past experiences with new neighbors, they could still manage to focus on the future of the children most of them had in great numbers. Community efforts to build playgrounds, libraries, schools, swimming pools, and baseball diamonds brought many families together who did not know each other before the war.

The flight to the suburbs remained difficult for blacks. Although over a million African Americans managed to move away from the inner cities after 1950, by 1970 the suburban population still remained 95 percent white. Even though it was true that the American dream of family security embodied in home ownership was more possible than ever before, it was clearly not available to everyone. A gifted journalist, Thomas Hine, described the period between 1954 and 1964 in his book *Populuxe* (1986). Hine pointed out that the number of better-paying jobs running or maintaining new machinery was increasing faster than the number of low-paying jobs was declining. The average industrial wage for white men had doubled since pre-Depression days, allowing

Levittown, New York, was built in nine months. © National Archives.

many working-class people to see themselves as middle class. No longer made up of small proprietors, much of this new middle class, which even included service workers, was employed by large corporations. Because of the smaller number of Depression-born adults, more wealth was shared by fewer people.

When Vice President Richard Nixon challenged Soviet premier Nikita Khrushchev at a trade fair in Russia in 1959, he did not argue that Americans had little poverty, nor did he champion the civic freedoms that define American democracy. Instead he made a big issue of American consumer production for easier living. Later called the "kitchen debate" because the two men hovered about a model American kitchen set up in a model home for fair visitors, the confrontation gave Nixon a chance to bombard the Russians with statistics on American consumption. He boasted that 30 million American families owned their own homes and that 44 million families owned 56 million cars and 50 million television sets—awesome evidence, he asserted, of the success of democratic capitalism. The average working man, Nixon asserted, could easily buy the split-level house on display. He noted also that women bought an average of nine dresses and suits and 14 pairs of shoes a year, trivial statistics that made Khrushchev furiously retort that Americans were just interested in surfaces, in "gadgets" and obsolescent machines. Khrushchev did not pick up on the fact that our huge defense industry continued to subsidize many consumer goods. Were Americans just self-indulgent pleasure seekers? Karal Ann Marling, in her challenging book *As Seen on TV: The Visual Culture of Everyday Life in the 1950s*, depicts the kitchen as a symbol of the domestic culture of the 1950s. The model on display in Moscow appeared to be designed around new family values—even though such values reached deep into a past where oven, hearth, and warm food traditionally suggested security. Marling suggests that the several kitchen models sent to Moscow were more than just gadgetry, providing "a working demonstration of a culture that defined freedom as the capacity to change and to choose." By the end of 1959, women comprised over a third of the American workforce. Whether they worked to pay for new appliances or because new appliances gave them more time for self-fulfillment remains a middle-class issue. It has taken decades for Americans to acknowledge that many women have no choice about working outside the home. Their wages contribute to rent or mortgage payments and help pay for their children's basic needs.

The demand for informality and flexibility supported the invention of small portable appliances.

The escape into different levels of consumerism was real in postwar America for the great number of people with good jobs. Five years after the war was over the amount spent on household furnishings rose by 240 percent. Four years after the war 20 million refrigerators and 5.5 million stoves were bought. The icemen who once delivered large blocks of ice to put in wooden chests became part of American myth. To many the well-furnished domestic nest supplied stronger moral protection from the bomb than the official shelters a few continued to buy. In her carefully documented book *Homeward Bound: American Families in the Cold War Era* (1988), Elaine Tyler May uses the word "containment"—the same word government officials used to define our relationship with the Soviet Union—to define the lives locked into the domestic scene during the period from 1946 to 1960, when real income rose by 20 percent.

Most of the appliances created for the American home during these years—washing machines, blenders, toasters, electric razors, dishwashers, power mowers, even television sets—were simple in design to accord with a world in which people did their own household chores. Although wild colors came into the kitchen, and airplane models influenced some industrial architects, the basic domestic designs of this period reflected functional European modernism. In fact, certain classics of industrial design, like the sleek chairs fashioned by Charles and Ray Eames, became part of a rebirth of esthetic awareness emphasizing function and simplicity. Distinguished industrial architects and artists like Eero Saarinen and Raymond Loewy began to make their work available on a grand scale. Indeed, the most elegant of the period's new appliances remain in the collections of the Museum of Modern Art in New York City and in the Smithsonian collections in Washington, D.C.

The new emphasis on style in personal material surroundings also made choosing furnishings time-consuming and socially challenging. Taste started to be graded in popular magazines—fewer people wanted to be middlebrow when either highbrow or lowbrow items could suggest individuality and character. The ubiquitous picture window—sensibly created so that mothers could keep an eye on children from inside—also allowed neighbors to evaluate each other's home furnishings. If prewar furniture manufacturers could not always make the costly new styles available rapidly and cheaply, there was nevertheless no shortage of canvas butterfly chairs or curved boomerang coffee tables. As many as five million wrought-iron butterfly chairs were manufactured at the time, copied from the original basic Knoll chair designed to be an example of excellence in inexpensive furniture.

Easy portability as well as functional design was another mark of a period when many Americans moved as often as every year. Hine remarks that a feature of the "populuxe" age was that everything had handles or was easy to lift. The demand for informality and flexibility supported the invention of small portable appliances. Nothing stayed in its traditional place anymore: washing machines were in the kitchen; television sets ended up in the dining room. And many carried their entertainment to the beach or office. Portable radios—ancestors of the boom box—began to intrude on parks and even on public transportation.

By the end of the decade push-button products defined a new life. Even if a cook did not know the difference between "puree" and "liquefy," the blender appeared to take over all drudgery. Ads showed women talking on the phone as their wash whirled behind glass in a nearby machine, but they did not urge these women to learn new skills in their free time or offer them more stimulating lives. Too often "labor-saving" devices led simply to more labor in the home. No-iron fabrics and synthetic casual clothes made it easier for women to do all their own laundry. When market researchers discovered that women also wanted to feel useful, they urged producers to leave out essential ingredients in packaged mixes so that good wives could feel they were adding something of themselves to their family's lives when they baked a cake. Betty Friedan's 1963 classic *The Feminine Mystique* also helped women to recognize how extensively they were being manipulated to consume (Kaledin, 121–23).

To read about housing in the United States in the 19th century, see the United States entries in the section "Housing" in chapter 5 ("Material Life") in volume 5 of this series.

FOR MORE INFORMATION

Evans, S. *Born for Liberty: A History of Women in America*. New York: Free Press, 1989.

Harrington, M. *The Other America: Poverty in the United States*. New York: Macmillan, 1962.

Hine, T. *Populuxe*. New York: Knopf, 1986.

Kaledin, E. *Daily Life in the United States, 1940–1959: Shifting Worlds*. Westport, Conn.: Greenwood Press, 2000.

Marling, K. A. *As Seen on TV: The Visual Culture of Everyday Life in the 1950s*. Cambridge, Mass.: Harvard University Press, 1994.

May, E. T. *Homeward Bound: American Families in the Cold War Era*. New York: Basic Books, 1989.

Patterson, J. T. *Grand Expectations: The United States, 1945–1974*. New York: Oxford University Press, 1996.

Wright, G. *Building the Dream: A Social History of Housing in America*. New York: Pantheon, 1981.

UNITED STATES, 1960–90

Before long, changes in economic conditions, partly due to the drain caused by the war in Vietnam, meant the end of concerted efforts to eliminate poverty. But poverty persisted. A good way to comprehend the dilemmas involved in dealing with poverty is to consider a specific project that represented the hopes, failings, and ultimate destruction of a major effort supported by both parties to improve conditions for the poor. In St. Louis in 1958 the federal government constructed housing that, upon first impression, would seem to have answered the needs of families looking for a good place to live. Known as Pruitt-Igoe, this housing project consisted of 33 towers, each 11 stories high.

Pruitt-Igoe, and other projects like it, concentrated a large number of poor people in a small geographic area. That would have been bad enough, but design flaws made matters worse. Inadequate wiring made installation of window fans or window air conditioners impossible, causing the apartments to be miserably hot in the sweltering summers of St. Louis. Elevators stopped only on the 4th, 7th, and 10th floors. Residents on other floors had to walk up or down a level from the one on which the elevator stopped. Children were not always able to judge the time it would take to make a bathroom run from the playground to their apartments, and before long the elevators were filled with wretched odors and filth.

Perspectives of those who lived in Pruitt-Igoe differed from those who did not. To a resident, "A project ain't nothing but a slum with the kitchen furnished and an absentee landlord; except we know who the landlord is—it's the city and government." To an outsider, "Whether it is a pig pen or not isn't important. When people have done nothing to contribute to the society but make an application for welfare, a housing project is more than they deserve." Either way, Pruitt-Igoe had no future. Poor

In the 1970s, cities tried to improve the quality of available housing by destroying old, run-down apartment complexes. © CORBIS/Bettmann.

management, poor maintenance, too heavily concentrated living arrangements, and crime made the apartments uninhabitable within a decade. Judged to be beyond repair and too poorly conceived to justify salvage efforts, the buildings were imploded with dynamite in 1972 (Marty, 103–4).

To read about housing in the United States in the 19th century, see the United States entries in the section "Housing" in chapter 5 ("Material Life") in volume 5 of this series.

FOR MORE INFORMATION

Marty, M. A. *Daily Life in the United States, 1960–1990: Decades of Discord*. Westport, Conn.: Greenwood Press, 1997.

Patterson, J. T. *Grand Expectations: The United States, 1945–1974*. New York: Oxford University Press, 1996.

Wright, G. *Building the Dream: A Social History of Housing in America*. New York: Pantheon, 1981.

INDIA

Housing in India reflected the subcontinent's social, economic, and geographic diversity. Though the majority of the population has lived in rural areas, dominated by villages, recently there has been a shift toward urban centers.

India's diverse climate has affected the type of housing found in its villages. From the tropical southern states to the snowy mountains of the north, village homes were constructed from a wide range of materials. Broadly, they can be divided between temporary materials such as mud or bamboo and permanent materials such as brick or cement. The former were called *kachha* homes, the latter *pukka* homes.

For millennia, India has been a region composed of villages. Although every village was unique and specific to its region and inhabitants, some general features were found throughout. First, most villages had a core area where a cluster of homes and some businesses were found. These homes were usually of solid construction and were dominated by upper-caste members or wealthier members of the village. Along with the homes, there might have been a few shops, including a general store (called a *kirana* shop), along with a tea or coffee stall, a phone booth, and likely a bus or taxi stop.

Moving away from the village core, one might have found more temporary homes, dominated by members of lower castes. These homes were isolated on a plot of land or grouped together where several footpaths and plots of land met. If these communities grew, they might have become their own village. The caste system, an integral part of Hinduism—the way in which much of Hindu India was stratified—frequently required that members of the lower castes, or untouchables, live at some distance from the main village core.

Most villages had other features as well. A temple or mosque was in the village center, or sometimes at its periphery, depending on the community's wealth and

MATERIAL LIFE

HOUSING

United States, 1920-1939

United States, 1940-1959

United States, 1960-1990

India

Japan

Inuit

composition. A well, used for drinking water and other household needs, could usually be found at the village's edge, sometimes near the temple. Schools for village children may also have been at the village periphery. Finally, many villages had forests or jungle nearby for animal grazing and as a source of food and fuel.

Homes in a village were generally simple. They had few interior rooms—a bedroom and a general room that might have included a hearth for cooking as well as a kitchen area. One of the better homes in the southern region of Mysore was described: "The two main features of such houses were an inner, rectangular courtyard open to the sky, and a narrow, covered verandah (*jagali*) [which ran] almost the entire width of the house . . . " (Srinivas, 11). Families kept possessions on hooks on the walls or in large metal trunks that kept dust, insects, and rodents at bay. In the bedroom was a *charpoy*—a cot with a thin mattress over its webbed undergirding. Also, families preferred to store clothing in steel bureaus that could be locked to protect valuables. Most village homes did not have running water. Water was brought into the home by bucket to be used for cooking and cleaning. For a bathroom, some homes had outhouse-type structures, whereas others might have used a discreet plot for their daily needs.

Around the exterior of village homes there might have been a covered verandah, used both as a work space and for leisure. Many villagers maintained a small vegetable garden for their cooking needs and some flowers for decorative purposes.

As mentioned, many villagers moved to large urban areas to work. Urban areas frequently had an "old" city and a "new" city. In the old city, homes and shops lined tightly winding lanes crowded with humanity. A few major thoroughfares might have divided the old city into quadrants, frequently with a central temple, mosque, or fountain at the main juncture. Many old cities were at one time walled in for protection, and their walls and gates can still be seen.

The new cities were quite different. These areas often had broad, straight, tree-lined streets, with homes and shops arranged in a deliberate way. Many of the new cities were remnants of India's colonial past and were designed on a grid system. New Delhi, for example, had wide avenues with roundabouts at some intersections. The southern city of Pondicherry followed a strict grid system with streets that retained their original French names, such as Rue DeBussy. Many new cities had former cantonment areas. These areas were for housing European and Indian troops and were marked by their tidy lanes and similar housing styles. Remnants of this past linger on; for example, visitors to the Taj Mahal disembark from the train at the Agra Cant station, short for the Agra Cantonment.

Housing in new cities was increasingly in apartments or flats. These buildings were fast replacing smaller bungalows and other single-family homes. Apartments took a heavy toll on water resources and led to overcrowding with cars and scooters. Slums also existed, interspersed between blocks of apartments. These housed the unemployed, the lower castes, and untouchables, many of whom worked as servants in apartment homes nearby.

Modern apartment interiors were much like those in Europe or North America. Bedrooms, a kitchen, a living room, and a bathroom could all be found. Generally, most apartments had running water, although few had separate hot- and cold-water taps. Most homes had a small shelf or cabinet devoted to the family deity, and some homes even had a small prayer or *puja* room for this purpose. New homes were frequently designed according to *vasthu,* the arrangement of living space to promote health, wealth, and happiness.

Housing in India was as diverse as its populations. Caste and class, religion, and geography have all influenced home choices and design. The populous villages have dominated the housing pattern, largely influenced by a wide gulf between the rich and the poor. Nevertheless, more and more people settled in urban areas, replete with their own housing cultures, history, and challenges.

To read about housing in 19th-century India, see the India entry in the section "Housing" in chapter 5 ("Material Life") in volume 5 of this series.

~*Benjamin Cohen*

FOR MORE INFORMATION

Srinivas, M. N. *The Remembered Village*. Delhi: Oxford University Press, 1976.

JAPAN

A common misperception about housing in Japan is that people live cheek-to-jowl in tiny rabbit hutchlike structures, exorbitant in cost and flimsy in construction. The truth is that although the Japanese live in smaller houses than Americans, they occupy about the same floor space as the French, Germans, and British. The high cost of urban land makes Japanese housing very expensive, and of course the Japanese occupy lots smaller than those of their American counterparts, but not very much different from those in northern and western Europe.

Living floor space per house is only about 60 percent of that in American houses (89 square meters vs. 151 for the U.S.), but larger than in Britain (75.1) and Germany (79). The ratio of house cost to annual salary is slightly higher in Japan (440%) than in America (340%) but comparable to Germany (460%) and Britain (440%).

Most of Japan's freestanding private homes are new, relatively speaking. Approximately 40 percent of all buildings were destroyed in World War II bombing, and even greater damage was done to cities such as Tokyo, Ōsaka, Yokohama, and of course Hiroshima and Nagasaki. The high incidence of earthquakes has encouraged the Japanese to tear down dangerously old buildings in favor of earthquake-resistant structures. Also, the high urban density of the postwar period led Japan to build millions of apartment buildings for middle-income urban workers.

Companies often attract new workers by providing low-cost company-subsidized apartments *(danchi)*. These are very small (about 35 square meters), with communal laundry and recreation areas. Because they are meant to house young married couples with only one or two very small children, the space is modest at best. Commonly, couples later move out into their own condominiums, called "mansions" (certainly a marketing ploy), that are somewhat larger (60 square meters). About 65 percent of all housing in Tokyo is in multifamily buildings.

The Japanese have learned to make do with less furniture than in the West, employing ingenious space-saving multiuse furniture. Most modern Japanese now are comfortable sitting in chairs and at tables, but it is still quite common to sit cross-legged on plush straw carpeting (tatami). Tatami also serves as the foundation for beds, covered with thick quilts (futon) that are easily folded and stored in sliding-door closets and routinely aired and turned for efficient wear.

Most Japanese houses and apartments now employ glass windows and wooden or metal doors as in the West, but many Japanese still prefer the defused light that floods through rice paper windows and sliding screens (*shoji* and *fusuma*, respectively). The national government imposes very stringent construction standards. Most homes are made with many prefabricated modules that fit together snugly and safely. Prefab construction provides fewer model styles but lessens costs. Most homes are outfitted with tiny stoves, refrigerators, washing machines (dryers are more rare), and water heaters. Central air-conditioning and heating are rarer; most residents own small room appliances to take care of heating and cooling. Modern apartments are typically made of ferroconcrete.

To read about housing in early modern Japan, see the Japan entry in the section "Housing and Furnishings" in chapter 5 ("Material Life") in volume 4 of this series.

~*Louis G. Perez*

FOR MORE INFORMATION

Henshall, K. *A History of Japan: From Stone Age to Superpower*. New York: St. Martin's Press, 1999.

Waswo, A. *Housing in Postwar Japan: A Social History*. London: Curzon Press, 2002.

MATERIAL LIFE

|

HOUSING

|

United States, 1920-1939

United States, 1940-1959

United States, 1960-1990

India

Japan

Inuit

INUIT

In the popular imagination, Inuit are often associated with one of the most remarkable objects of material culture—the domed snow house or *iglu*. Contrary to popular belief, this type of traditional Inuit dwelling had a relatively limited distribution in the Inuit North and served primarily as a winter dwelling for the Inuit who lived in what is now the Central Canadian Arctic. Inuit in other regions used more permanent building materials and constructed their houses of stone, driftwood, or whalebone combined with sod. One common house form, known as a *qarmat*, combined the features of a tent and a sod house or *iglu*. The *qarmat*, which had solid walls and a skin or canvas roof, was used in springtime when warmer temperatures made both snow houses and sod houses damp and uncomfortable. In summer, Inuit often lived in tents and cooked outdoors.

Architectural style differed across the Inuit North, but vernacular architecture shared a number of common features. Most Inuit groups built semisubterranean houses that they entered through long, downward-sloping tunnels that served as cold traps. Houses usually consisted of single rooms divided into a raised sleeping area and an activity area. Storage porches were sometimes also constructed. Inuit throughout the North heated their homes with a stone lamp called a *qulliq*.

For the Inuit in the Central Arctic, the snow house proved to be an excellent form of shelter, and during midwinter, when families gathered to cooperate in seal hunting, they constructed large snow house communities on the ocean ice. The domed and somewhat spherical shape contributed to its ability to withstand intense winds. Its semisubterranean construction provided additional insulation.

During winter virtually all activities took place in the snow house. A snow house generally sheltered a single family, but two or more snow houses could be joined together with passageways. Quite frequently, if several families were gathered, they would also construct a large snow house for dances and religious ceremonies. Inuit in North Alaska used more permanent ceremonial buildings called *qarigit*. With the introduction of commercial fox trapping in the early 20th century

Before returning to his camp Lypa Pitsiulak, an Inuit living on an outpost camp in the Opingivik area of Nunavut, Canada, covers the opening of an igloo. © AP/Wide World Photos.

Canadian Inuit stopped using snow houses as their primary winter dwellings. Involvement in the fur trade not only provided access to other building materials but also took people away from winter seal-hunting communities.

Today, Inuit live in manufactured housing in planned communities, and in many northern communities, housing is provided by government. Single-family, multiroom homes tend to be the norm in smaller villages, whereas Inuit in large towns and cities often live in apartments. For the most part, Inuit residents have not been consulted about the layout or design of homes or about the way houses are sited. In the past, Inuit used their domestic space for processing game and repairing hunting tools. Many of these traditional activities have had to be reconfigured for modern houses. For example, high-rise apartments, such as those found in Nuuk, Greenland, are not well suited to butchering animals, drying skins, or repairing hunting equipment.

The reconfiguration of domestic space into multiroom homes has affected social interactions within the household. The existence of separate rooms for sleeping, eating, entertaining, and working has meant a reduction in the opportunities for close observation and interactions between adults and children. Some northern communities, however, have severe housing shortages, forcing two and three families to share a dwelling. In these cases, close interactions are impossible to avoid.

~*Pamela Stern*

FOR MORE INFORMATION

Lee, M., and G. A. Reinhardt. *Eskimo Architecture: Dwelling and Structure in the Early Historic Period.* Fairbanks: University of Alaska Press, 2003.

ISLAMIC WORLD

Housing styles are determined in part by climate, by available building materials, and by cultural tradition. Consequently, housing styles are remarkably stable across time, and this was particularly true in the Islamic World, which in the 19th century continued to be dominated by the empire of the Ottoman Turks. See the Ottoman Turks entry in the section "Houses and Furniture" in chapter 5 ("Material Life") in volume 3 of this series for a discussion of the housing that persisted throughout the 19th century and into the 20th.

LATIN AMERICA

See the Latin America entry in the section "Housing" in chapter 5 ("Material Life") in volume 5 of this series for a discussion of housing in the 19th century. In the 20th century, the pressure for urban housing escalated as people in the tens of thousands moved from the countryside to the cities. See the Latin America entries in the section "Urban and Rural Experience" in chapter 3 ("Economic Life") in this volume for a discussion of this shift in settlement, which put so much pressure on urban housing and created some of the worst urban slums in the world.

MATERIAL LIFE
|
TECHNOLOGY
|
Europe

United States,
1920-1939

United States,
1960-1990

Japan

Inuit

Technology

Near the end of his life, American intellectual luminary Henry Brooks Adams commented that the technological revolution that began in the 19th century and that accelerated in the 20th century was speeding humanity, if not the entire world, toward final cataclysmic destruction. Given the proliferation of weapons of mass destruction by the end of the century, Adams's horrific prediction may someday have some truth. However, for most people, particularly in the United States, the technological innovations of the 20th century radically altered and in many cases significantly improved daily life.

For Americans at the dawn of the 20th century, two technological advances changed the basic rhythms of life. The first was the automobile. The car as well as the highway systems that were built connected Americans in ways that were impossible to achieve in the 19th century. Moreover, the automobile energized the American economy. From fuel stations to auto body repair to sales, the car sparked tremendous job growth. Additionally, although cars polluted, they did seem to make urban areas less filthy. For instance, in 1900 in New York City, 15,000 horses died in the streets. Those that did not die deposited over 2.5 million pounds of manure and 60,000 gallons of urine on the streets every day. The other early-20th-century technological innovation that rapidly changed life was the electrification of cities, towns, and farms.

By the end of the 20th century, many more inventions changed how Americans lived and viewed themselves. As much as the 19th century had been the age of English technological superiority, the 20th century was America's century. The changes in daily life were big and small. Americans pioneered the use of nuclear energy and developed disposable diapers. Although initially behind the Soviet Union in the space race, they eventually landed on the moon first and created the world's first reusable space aircraft, the space shuttle. All of this came at a price. By the 1990s, the United States had spent hundreds of billions of dollars on its space program, outspending the Russians by billions. When the Americans discovered that their ball-point pens did not work in zero gravity, they spent thousands, if not millions, on a pen that would work in outer space. When the Soviets encountered the same problem, they decided to use a pencil.

American troops with a Maxim machine gun before the outbreak of World War I. The deadly effect of machine gun fire on attacking infantry contributed to trench warfare's static nature. © Library of Congress.

By the end of the century, Japan had become a leader in manufacturing new technology. For the Japanese, the idea of patents and copyrights is foreign. The individuals who develop technology for Japanese companies do expect to personally benefit from their work, which they believe should be made readily and cheaply available to society. In the Inuit North, the issue has been the preservation for and transmission of traditional technologies to new generations.

Not all technological advances served to improve daily life. Many of the most important 20th-century inventions were weapons, such as the modern machine gun and the atomic bomb. Advances in weaponry made the 20th century one of the most destructive periods in human history. Although one could draw on dozens of historical examples, World War I provides one of the most horrific. An entire generation of young men died on the battlefields of Europe. New weapons outstripped old military tactics. Even the use of trenches did not provide any security. New grenades, flamethrowers, gas attacks, and mortars specifically designed to kill troops hunkered in trench bunkers increased the death totals to catastrophic levels by 1919. Although Henry Adams did not live to see the end of World War I, one can see why he might have thought that the technological advances in the Western world were speeding life toward a terrible end.

MATERIAL LIFE
|
TECHNOLOGY
|
Europe

United States,
1920-1939

United States,
1960-1990

Japan

Inuit

EUROPE

All the countries involved in combat on the western front strained to provide the best fighting technology for their men. The expanded armies demanded extraordinary quantities of weapons. Moreover, the technical surprises of the war, including the stalemate on the battlefront, meant a search for new, more effective weapons. The American army of 127,000 men in April 1917 required thousands of modern artillery pieces and tens of thousands of machine guns and other automatic weapons, not to mention more than two million rifles over the next year and a half. Tents, shovels, and uniforms were needed as well on an unprecedented scale. Obtaining rations for millions of men, month after month, was an obligation no government dared ignore.

But in the common struggle to match and eventually to overwhelm the enemy, Germany's men in uniform had a severe disadvantage. With their country hindered by isolation and limited resources, the Germans found themselves barely making do, especially in food for the military.

The most common weapon to be found on the western front was the infantryman's rifle. Each army entered the war with a bolt-action weapon equipped to hold several cartridges. The standard British rifle was the short magazine Lee Enfield (SMLE). To load it, the rifleman pulled the bolt backward and inserted two five-round clips of cartridges from above, pressing them down into the weapon's boxlike magazine. The magazine (a receptacle for ammunition) was located under the barrel in front of the rifle's trigger. A spring in the magazine pushed the first cartridge upward toward the barrel as the bolt was closed. After loosing a round, the marksman needed only a short pull backward on the bolt to eject the previous round and to pull the next one into firing position. This efficient mechanism permitted a rapid rate of aimed fire for which the pre-1914 professional British soldier had been trained.

The German soldier on the western front was equipped with the five-round Mauser Gewehr 98 (G98) rifle. The standard American rifle at the time the United States entered the war was the five-round 1903 Springfield. Both had box-magazines like the Enfield. The French equivalent was the eight-millimeter Lebel designed in 1886 and modified in 1893 and thus designated the Lebel Model 86/93. It was longer and heavier than the standard British, German, and American weapons and used a tubular magazine holding eight cartridges and located below the rifle's barrel. Difficult to load quickly, it was the least effective of the rifles used by any of the belligerents on the western front.

The Mauser, Lebel, and Springfield all operated on the same principle as the British weapon. After firing a shot, the rifleman pulled the bolt backward to eject the spent cartridge, then moved the bolt forward. This pushed a new round into the firing chamber and cocked the weapon to fire once again. In all the belligerent countries, units in training and those on home guard duty had a low priority and often found themselves with older weapons.

The strains of producing large numbers of rifles fell with particular force on Germany and, later, the United States. An important solution for the German army was to depart from making the weapon from standardized parts. Marked with a star, the new "Stern Gewehr" indicated that it had been made from parts produced by different subcontractors. Whereas the original rifle was considered reliable, its parts could not be safely transferred to another weapon. The United States was unable to produce enough Springfields to equip its huge new army of 1917 and 1918, and only early arrivals in France got them. The solution was to use a modified version of the British Enfield available in large numbers in American and Canadian factories where British arms orders had already been placed. The minority of troops who got Springfields thought themselves lucky. "It was a great weapon," one Marine lieutenant recalled. "Not only was it accurate, but it rarely jammed," and "it seemed to be able to absorb the dirt—and we were always living in dirt—and still work."

The machine gun played an unexpectedly vital role in trench warfare. Prior to 1914, the weapon was considered to be the equivalent of a piece of light artillery, and many military leaders found it only marginally useful. At the start of the war, the future belligerents on the western front normally had only two machine guns for each battalion, although the Germans were in the process of increasing this to six per battalion. Unlike earlier, multishot weapons like the Gatling gun, the weapon invented by Hiram Maxim in the 1880s did not require a cranking apparatus to fire a stream of bullets at the enemy. Instead, it operated automatically when the gunner pulled the trigger or pressed a button to commence firing.

> *The machine gun played an unexpectedly vital role in trench warfare.*

In combination with barbed-wire obstacles, machine guns made it possible for a small number of soldiers to halt enemy offensives by inflicting massive casualties. Various estimates claimed that the firepower of one machine gun was the equivalent of 30, or perhaps as many as 60, individual riflemen. Placing the gun in a stationary position, the machine gun's crew could calculate in advance the area the weapon was able to cover. Even in the midst of a surprise attack, a trained machine gun crew could put the weapon into action within four seconds and deliver devastating fire. The machine gun itself presented only a tiny target for enemy counterfire.

British, French, and American troops all encountered the standard German machine gun, the MG 08. The German army employed some 72,000 of these deadly weapons on both the eastern and western fronts. The water-cooled MG 08 was fed by bullets held in a fabric belt and could fire around 450 rounds per minute. Weighing about 70 pounds, it had the disadvantage of being mounted on a heavy sledge, but lighter mounts were developed as the war proceeded. The British equivalent was the equally heavy Vickers .303.

Offensives on the western front impelled the belligerents to develop a lighter machine gun that could be carried forward by advancing troops. For Britain, the result was the air-cooled Lewis gun; weighing only 27 pounds, it was highly portable. This handy weapon dispensed with the bulky equipment needed by a water-cooled gun, and it used ammunition drums with 47 or 97 rounds instead of a heavy cloth belt. The Lewis gun replaced the Vickers .303 as the weapon carried by infantry battalions, the Vickers being transferred into special machine gun corps companies. The Germans and French followed suit. The German light machine gun, the MG 08/15, weighed 39 pounds. As its name indicated, it was a modified version of the army's standard machine gun: this lighter gun retained the original MG 08's water-cooled system and belt-fed ammunition.

The French had the least success in meeting the need for a light weapon with the firepower of a machine gun. Their eight-millimeter Model 1915 or Chauchat with its 20-round drum was notorious for jamming in the midst of battle, and the air-cooled weapon's light weight—barely 20 pounds—was little compensation for soldiers put in peril by its unreliability. Firing at a relatively slow rate of 250 rounds per minute served only to make it more unpopular, especially among American troops who were burdened with the weapon.

In 1914, artillery ranged from light field weapons designed to accompany advancing troops to heavy guns that had to be operated from fixed positions. Artillerymen in every army had two basic types of cannon at their disposal, "howitzers" and "guns." Howitzers, with relatively short barrels, fired shells into the air at a sharp angle—"high trajectory"—allowing them to strike even an entrenched enemy from above. Guns, with longer barrels than howitzers, fired shells directly at the enemy—"flat trajectory"—at a high velocity. Howitzers were limited, however, by their shorter range. Many cannon, especially those with larger calibers, came in both howitzer and gun models.

> *Shrapnel shells were designed to explode in flight over enemy troops.*

At first, artillerymen employed two varieties of shells. The high-explosive type contained a large charge intended to explode when the shell landed. Shrapnel shells contained anti-personnel devices like metal balls. They were designed to explode in flight over enemy troops. In 1914, most artillerymen still considered shrapnel rather than high-explosive shells the more useful in battle. A third type, shells carrying poison gas, appeared later in the conflict.

By 1914, the major belligerents on the western front had all developed artillery pieces based on the French 75-millimeter gun. That weapon, soon to be the most famous cannon in the world, was loaded from the rear and had a recoil that was absorbed by a hydraulic system. Such features permitted the gun to remain fixed on the ground, aimed in a given direction, and capable of firing at the unprecedented rate of 20 or more rounds per minute.

But some armies were better equipped for trench warfare than others. The French had planned for a mobile war in which their light 75-millimeter guns would move up with advancing infantry. These weapons proved invaluable in the first weeks of the war, firing more rapidly and striking from a greater distance than their German counterparts. But the French had neglected to build up a stock of heavier weapons. The Germans were best prepared for an artillery war in which both sides fired on the other's trenches. Their 77-millimeter gun approximated the characteristics of the French 75-millimeter. But they had taken pains in the decade before the war to build up their army's store of heavy guns (155-mm) as well as medium artillery pieces (the 105-mm howitzer). Thus, when the conflict bogged down, the Germans had a significant advantage. French infantrymen assaulting German defenses in the first years of the war found that their lightweight artillery offered them little support. Only in 1916 did the French begin to match the weight of German weapons.

The British army in 1914 was better prepared in its artillery for trench warfare than the French. The British Expeditionary Force that fought in the first months of the war had an equivalent to the French 75-millimeter in its 18-pound (3.3-inch) gun. It also had a supply of 4.5-inch howitzers that matched the German 105-

millimeter. The British possessed some heavier cannon like the 60-pound (120-mm) gun as well, but here they still had to catch up with the better-equipped Germans.

A basic problem for artillerymen was the shell shortage that afflicted all armies, particularly the British and French, by the winter of 1914–15. Remedying the situation by increased production created its own difficulties. Shrapnel shells were relatively easy and safe to produce quickly, and they were effective against soldiers exposed on bare ground. But trench warfare showed that pre-1914 expectations for artillery fire were mistaken. Armies needed massive quantities of high-explosive ammunition able to demolish enemy fortifications. Such shells required a higher level of skill to produce, given the danger they posed for armaments workers. The failure to solve the problem of quality control crippled operations. For example, the large number of "dud" shells British munitions factories produced weakened the crucial barrage that preceded the Battle of the Somme in July 1916.

Desperate to break through the enemy's lines, the various belligerents sought the biggest artillery pieces available. They built guns modeled on those carried by the era's battleships and borrowed those employed in coast artillery units. Such weapons weighed hundreds of tons and could be moved only on railroad cars. Some had to be operated by experienced naval gunners. Starting at the Battle of Verdun in 1916, both the Germans and the French employed such railway guns. The Americans brought a number of coast artillery cannon from the United States, along with army crews trained to fire such heavy weapons. Using the American weapons and other giant guns supplied by the French, coast artillerymen in the American Expeditionary Forces (AEF) struck at the German rear during the Meuse-Argonne offensive in 1918.

On the whole, the American army found itself so deficient in heavy weapons that most of its artillery had to come from the French and British. The AEF relied upon supplies of French 75-millimeter guns for lightweight field pieces. French 155-millimeter howitzers provided the bulk of the heavy firepower the Americans enjoyed. Most American artillerymen received their training from experienced French instructors.

Effective artillery operations required an elaborate system of support. Forward artillery observers and aerial spotters combined their efforts with those of an extensive entourage on the ground. One British artillery officer described his weapon as "a dignified old autocrat" with "a suite of servants and attendants." His artillery battery with four howitzers required a staff of at least six officers and 120 enlisted men to serve the cannon. Still more men were needed for the four heavy tractors and 15 three-ton trucks that moved the battery from place to place. After the first phase of the war, artillerymen on both sides operated from rear areas. Infantrymen in all armies expressed their hostility and jealousy toward gunners who seemed well away from the front. This apparent measure of safety was an illusion. Sophisticated techniques for locating and firing on enemy artillery emplacements ("counter-battery fire") made the gunners' lot a dangerous one.

The need to dislodge troops dug into trench fortifications gave mortars an important role in the war on the western front. Firing a shell high into the air, the mortar, like the much larger and heavier howitzer, made it possible to strike an entrenched enemy from overhead. The British Stokes mortar was little more than a lightweight tube with a spike at its base. A shell, containing a charge to propel it, was dropped down the tube, struck the spike, then flew toward the enemy. Its shells were color-coded with a green one set to go 300 yards and a red one 450, and a trained crew could fire a shell every three seconds. One German soldier, who had doubtless experienced enemy artillery and machine-gun fire, recorded his feeling that the trench mortar was the worst weapon he faced. "They fire noiselessly and a single one often kills as many as 30 men. One stands in the trench, and at any moment a thing like that may burst." Mortars also came in far larger forms. In trench operations, the standard German 170-millimeter mortar (Minenwerfer) contained more than 100 pounds of explosives and shards of metal. Shot high into the air, it was visible tumbling toward the enemy's lines.

The realities of trench warfare made the hand grenade a useful infantryman's tool. The British army had found no need for such a weapon in the mobile warfare that characterized colonial conflicts of the late 19th century. With no grenades available, British soldiers had to improvise in 1914 and early 1915, creating small explosive bombs from common trench items like tin cans. The Germans, by contrast, entered the war with an effective grenade as standard army equipment.

By the first anniversary of the war's beginning, the British troops were supplied with the effective Mills bomb. Containing a small quantity of explosives in a metal case, such a hand grenade could be thrown over barbed-wire barriers into the enemy's fortifications. Once released, it was timed to explode in a matter of seconds. Grenades could also be fired from rifles equipped with a special launching apparatus. One British soldier wrote home in May 1916 about the effectiveness of the device. "The Hun is very active and sends over coveys of rifle grenades at most inconvenient places and hours. . . . I hate their furking rifle grenades. They are more dangerous than shells and they have any number of them." As a portable, handheld bomb, the grenade more than other weapons endangered the soldier using it. It also imperiled those around him. Grenades were known to detonate instantly in the hand of the thrower, and a dropped grenade could injure scores of men in the immediate vicinity. Sometimes, the circumstances of battle made it impossible to release a grenade. A German soldier described combat with French troops in which one of his comrades "pulled the stopper out of the fuse, raised his bomb, and was just going to throw it" when the scene shifted. "At that very moment some German comrades came between him and his objective. He could not throw the bomb without hitting them; so he kept it in his hand, and in a few seconds it exploded, blowing him to pieces."

Both the flamethrower and the bayonet evoked special fear in potential victims. These weapons killed at close range, face-to-face in the case of the bayonet. The terror of being burned to death made the flamethrower a horror to the imagination. The Germans had developed a practical flamethrower in the years before the war and put it onto the battlefield in 1915, and soon all the other western front belligerents adopted the device. The German army became particularly adept in flamethrower attacks, assigning two-man flamethrower teams to pave the way for ground assault units. The weapon required that one man hold the pipe from which flame erupted while a second team member carried the reservoir containing the incendiary liquid and its gas propellant. The flamethrower attack was followed at once by an infantry advance.

The fire of a flamethrower frightened even those troops using it. To counteract this, the German General Staff sent instructions for assault troops specifying that "they have nothing to fear from the flames and smoke" because the tap on the flamethrower would be turned off before they moved into the enemy's trenches. Thus, "they can advance immediately after the cessation of the spray without danger, as small bursts of

> *Bayoneting an enemy soldier was like driving a knife into butter.*

flame on the ground . . . will burn out at once, and a little fire on the ground is at once extinguished when trodden upon." All armies had rifles equipped to hold bayonets below the barrel. The target of a bayonet attack had to defend himself against the frightening prospect of a cold steel blade penetrating his body. The French Lebel rifle carried an especially long metal blade. Menacing in appearance, it was prone to break in actual combat. The broad-bladed German "butcher bayonet" featuring saw teeth along part of one edge may have been designed specifically for its effect on the morale of those who faced it. Troops advancing with bayonets fixed presented a menacing picture to those on the other side of the battle line.

British and American military training emphasized bayonet attacks, as much to instill an aggressive attitude in troops as to prepare them for actual combat. Killing with the bayonet required close contact with the enemy, which occurred principally in surprise attacks and night assaults. British soldiers remembered what it felt like when bayoneting an enemy soldier: It was like driving a knife into butter. Because the victim's flesh and muscle tightened around the entry point, soldiers learned a three-step process: thrust with the bayonet, then twist the rifle to loosen it, then extract the blade.

With the exception of the French army, still dressed in the bright blue and red uniforms of the previous century, the combatants of World War I moved onto the battlefield in uniforms designed to conceal them from the enemy. After the slaughter of 1914, the French too accepted the fact that visibility to the enemy was less likely to terrify the foe than to offer him a wealth of attractive targets.

By contrast, from the first the German soldier wore a field gray (*feld-grau*) uniform with its camouflage aspects increased by a slight dull green tint. Calf-length boots, a 70-pound knapsack, and an ammunition belt rounded out his burden. The characteristic spiked helmet was covered with a camouflage shield. In trench warfare, a soldier's head was the most exposed part of his body, and spiked helmets made of leather and other soft headpieces proved too dangerous to wear. The familiar German metal helmet with its extensions on three sides to protect the ears and neck appeared at Verdun in 1916 and soon went into general use. The French adopted the less protective "Adrian" helmet and the British and then the Americans a simple flat model. The flat helmet mainly protected the top of the head. In general, helmets served best against flying shrapnel. As many combatants found out, a bullet traveling at high speed could penetrate a helmet with deadly results (Heyman, 27–35).

FOR MORE INFORMATION

Hallas, J. H. *Doughboy War: The American Expeditionary Force in World War I.* Boulder: Lynne
   Riener, 2000.
Heyman, N. M. *Daily Life During World War I.* Westport, Conn.: Greenwood Press, 2002.
Liddle, P. H. *The Soldier's War, 1914–1918.* London: Blandford Press, 1988.
Winter, D. *Death's Men: Soldiers of the Great War.* London: Penguin Books, 1978.

MATERIAL LIFE
|
TECHNOLOGY
|
Europe

United States,
1920-1939

United States,
1960-1990

Japan

Inuit

UNITED STATES, 1920–39

The technological innovations that shaped American daily life in the period 1920 to 1939 related significantly to the development of new forms of power. First, the gasoline-powered engine greatly shaped the way Americans lived and worked and moved around. Second, the use of electricity impacted the ways in which Americans built and used their homes.

Gasoline-powered, internal combustion engine–propelled vehicles had been around for more than a quarter century by the start of the 1920s, but not until that decade did they become a central factor in the everyday lives of ordinary Americans. Mass production, together with innovations in design, engineering, manufacture, and sales, brought a new or used car, truck, or tractor within the reach of most people. In 1920, barely 1 household in 3 possessed a car, though this represented a dramatic increase from 1 in 13 at the outset of World War I. Automobile ownership tripled during the 1920s, and by decade's end, four families out of five owned one. By 1929 almost 27 million cars were on the road; in the driveway or parking lot; at the gas station or repair shop; or, increasingly, stuck in traffic. Meanwhile truck and tractor registration tripled as well to 3,550,000 trucks and 840,000 farm tractors. Outside the impoverished South, car, truck, and tractor ownership was fairly widespread and evenly distributed. According to a 1927 survey, 54 percent of families in cities over 100,000 owned a car, while 60 percent did in towns under 1,000; farmers were even more likely to have a car or truck. In less than a decade, motor vehicle ownership had gone from being unusual to being commonplace, and American daily life was thereby transformed.

By the mid-1920s one of eight U.S. workers was somehow involved in the production, sales, service, and fueling of automobiles. The auto business, the biggest American industry, was reshaping the nature of employment and the economy. The automobile significantly changed the way people worked, conducted their business, shopped for necessities and desires, and spent leisure time. The automobile was undoubtedly the most notable of various new technologies that gained popularity in the 1920s. Radios and electrical home appliances such as vacuum cleaners and washing machines were others. The widespread adoption of the automobile and these other devices altered the manner in which people conducted their daily affairs; involved large numbers of people in their manufacture, sales, and maintenance; and established new assumptions about what individuals and families must possess and use to carry on a normal and satisfactory life.

The idea of self-propelled carriages had long fascinated American inventors, not to mention the carriage-using wealthy classes. Given the problems of highly polluting horse-drawn vehicles, especially in congested urban areas, a cleaner-running automobile had great appeal. In 1900 in New York City alone, 15,000 horses dropped dead on the streets, and those that lived deposited 2.5 million pounds of manure and 60,000 gallons of urine on the streets every day. The most obvious alternative transportation systems, above- or below-ground cable, steam, or electric-powered trolleys and trains, required large capital investments and could be envisioned only in densely populated areas.

At the outset, automobiles were not built with the masses in mind. As early as 1895, more than 300 individuals and companies were constructing experimental automobiles, mainly one-of-a-kind, large, expensive motorized buggies for wealthy hobbyists who could afford a chauffeur/mechanic. In 1901, Ransom Olds of Lansing, Michigan, began producing a car for the middle class, but even at a mere 40 percent of the average price of that year's automobiles, the $650 curved-dash Oldsmobile still cost more than an average American worker's annual income. In 1906, another Michigan automaker, Detroit's Henry Ford, began building a reliable four-cylinder, 15-horsepower, middle-class car, the $600 Model N. Ford was deluged with orders and was soon producing 100 Model Ns per day. Then in 1908 Ford announced the following:

A revolutionary device, the electric refrigerator, sits near its antiquated cousin, the icebox. © National Archives.

I will build a motor car for the great multitude. It will be large enough for the family but small enough for the individual to run and care for. It will be constructed of the best materials by the best men to be hired, after the simplest designs that modern engineering can devise. But it will be so low in price that no man making a good salary will be unable to own one—and enjoy with his family the blessings of hours of pleasure in God's great open spaces.

An unprecedented ten thousand of Ford's new car, the 20-horsepower Model T, sold in the next year at $825. To reach the mass audience he sought, Ford quickly began seeking ways to reduce the Model T's price.

Henry Ford sought to simplify and speed production to reduce prices and make the Model T affordable to more people. He announced in 1909 that customers could buy a Model T in any color they wanted, as long as they wanted black. By having only one color, Ford could reduce inventory and supply costs as well as cut production time and cost because black paint dried fastest.

Ford's greatest innovation was the replacement of individual construction crews with the moving assembly line. By subdividing the task of assembly, bringing parts to the assemblers, delivering them waist-high so as to reduce wasted motion, and speeding up the chain-driven line whenever possible, Ford dramatically reduced the time and cost of manufacturing. By 1914, the price of a Model T had fallen to $490.

The Model T's simplicity and sturdiness were major aspects of its appeal. Designed and built for durability as well as easy maintenance and repair by its owner, the Model T was reliable and comparatively inexpensive to operate. Once purchased, it would not involve significant additional expense, except for fuel, for a long time, and for nearly two decades its appearance changed but little. The Model T's hand-cranked starter and awkward planetary transmission were no more difficult to deal with than the mechanisms on most cars, at least in the 1910s. Its high axles and road clearance enabled it to travel the rough and rutted dirt roads that, outside main thoroughfares in major cities, had to be regularly traversed; and when, as often happened, a driver found himself stuck in mud, the lightweight Model T could be easily extracted. The popularity of Ford's "Tin Lizzie," as the Model T came to be called, helped to account for the jump in the number of automobiles from fewer than half a million in 1910 to 2.5 million in 1915 to 9 million by 1920.

At the same time that Henry Ford was promoting the Model T, another Detroit businessman, William C. Durant, was creating the General Motors Company. The impetuous if brilliant Durant, much more a speculator and salesman than an engineer like Ford, built or bought up numerous auto manufacturing companies, including Buick, Ransom Olds' Oldsmobile, Cadillac, and Chevrolet, as well as parts makers such as Fisher Body and Charles Kettering's electric starter and battery company. He also acquired numerous companies that soon proved worthless, such as firms making the two-cylinder Elmore and the Cartercar and, worst of all, the Heany Lamp Company, whose incandescent headlight patent turned out to be fraudulent. Durant fought a long battle for control of General Motors (GM) with the bankers who financed his acquisitions. He ultimately lost out to minority stockholders from the Dupont Company who used their enormous World War I munitions profits to buy a controlling 28 percent of GM common stock. By November 1920, when Durant was forced out of General Motors, he had nevertheless assembled a huge, sprawling company poised to take advantage of the rapidly growing market for automobiles.

By the 1920s, the automobile market was saturated with both new and used cars. This is a used-car lot in Lancaster, Ohio, in 1938. © Library of Congress.

As much as gasoline and the automobile reshaped American lives outside the home, electricity reshaped life inside the home. Electrified life not only had a different look than pre-electric life, but it also had a different rhythm, feel, and even aroma. Outside the domain of electricity, where natural sunlight, wood and coal fires, candles, and in recent decades kerosene and natural gas were the available light sources, there was, according to David E. Nye in *Electrifying America, 1880–1940*, "less light at night, and people tended to cluster around what little there was. The night outside was darker than the city's dark." Artificial light produced from wood, coal, candle, or petroleum was dim, smoky, sooty, and smelly. Its grime and odor permeated a home; even strenuous regular cleaning could not eliminate these residues. Light from fossil fuels was also expensive, therefore necessarily used sparingly. For the most part, people lived lives illuminated by the sun, with the rigid limitations and seasonal variations that it imposed.

The pre-electric environment lacked elements that subsequently have come to be taken so much for granted as to disappear from conscious notice. Nye calls attention to simple features of life without electricity: "The farmhouse had a lower noise level, and not just because there was no television; it had no humming refrigerator, no flushing toilet, no whirring appliance motors. Things did not make noises; the only sound came from people, animals, and natural forces, like the wind." Even before examining specific functions of electricity, one ought to consider the fundamentally different look, sound, and feel of the electric and electrified environment.

Bright light able to banish the night's darkness and lengthen the day was the earliest and in many ways most significant consequence of electrification, if scarcely its only result. Electric lighting enabled its possessors effectively and economically to make greater use of predawn, twilight, and evening hours. Thus it literally empowered them to redesign the basic schedule of their daily existence.

With electricity people could begin to arrange their days as they (or at least someone) chose. Electric lighting made it possible to live conveniently by the clock rather than constrained by the patterns of sunrise and sunset. By 1924 in Muncie, social investigators Robert and Helen Lynd found that middle- and upper-class business and professional men, the group with the greatest ability to determine their own schedules, did not begin their workday until 7:45 A.M., 8, 8:30, or even 9 A.M., but most commonly 8:30 A.M.. Their daily schedules stood in marked and deliberate contrast to the 70 percent of the labor force that belonged to the working class. The latter group normally started its workday between 6:15 and 7:30, chiefly at 7:00 A.M. Farmers who began their day's labor before 6:00 A.M. presented an even sharper contrast to the business and professional class.

By the 1920s, most families had a radio, and it connected them directly to the national culture. This couple sit in their living room in Scott's Run, West Virginia, listening to the evening programming in 1938. © Library of Congress.

Gender differences in daily schedules were also noticeable. In Muncie, working-class women began their day's labor even earlier than their husbands, with 40 percent up by 5 A.M., 75 percent by 5:30, and over 90 percent by 6 A.M. A majority of business-class housewives did not arise until 7 A.M. or after. In every case, electrification helped determine the day's routine.

The shift of daily schedules and the expansion of the productive hours of those with access to electricity were profoundly important. Growing industries and bureaucracies were able to manipulate their operations. Outside of the work environment, electrified society gained more opportunity to devote time to nonproductive, pleasurable pursuits. Nothing more rapidly and notably differentiated urban from rural life.

By 1920, electricity under human control had been available for more than 40 years, with Thomas Edison's invention of the incandescent light bulb in 1879 marking the beginning of its substantial practical usage. Edison and his laboratory assistants quickly thereafter developed lamp sockets, household wiring, and generators to make electric lighting systems functional, if at first very expensive. In 1882, Edison began offering home electric generators. In New York City in the same year, he also opened the first central generating station to provide power over utility lines. Within two years, 500 homes and several thousand businesses were using electric lights. Also during the 1880s direct current arc lamp streetlights began to compete with older coal gas-powered lighting systems in modernizing towns and cities. Electrically driven streetcars, industrial machinery, and elevators for new high-rise buildings started to appear as well.

The nature of work, particularly in the industrial sector, was dramatically affected by electricity. As late as 1905, less than 10 percent of all motive power nationally was electrical, but thereafter usage grew so rapidly that by 1930 the figure reached 80 percent. Electricity could drive small motors, reducing the need for elaborate systems of drive shafts, gears, and belts linking every factory mechanism to the central power source. Electric current could propel assembly lines for Henry Ford's automobiles and many other mass-produced goods. Electricity could coordinate a series of machines with automatic feeding devices and moving belts, and it could also regulate other systems of production with temperature gauges, flow meters, shut-off devices, and other control mechanisms.

The effects of electrification, from better lighted, cleaner, and safer factories, to increased output, to changes in the nature of work, could be momentous. For instance, Muncie's Ball Brothers Glass Manufacturing Company adopted electrical bottle-blowing machines to turn out as many glass jars with eight workers as could have previously been made by 210 skilled glassblowers and their assistants. Likewise, electric trucks, mixers, and cranes sharply reduced the need for unskilled heavy labor. Although electrification displaced many workers, it did not reduce employment. Instead it fostered new enterprises and created demand for different sorts of labor, for the most part semiskilled, clerical, or service work. Together with better organization of production in redesigned factories, electrification helped account for the great surge in productivity per American worker in the 1920s and 1930s (Kyvig, 21–24, 43–47).

To read about technology in the United States in the 19th century, see the United States entries in the section "Technology" in chapter 5 ("Material Life") in volume 5 of this series.

FOR MORE INFORMATION

Flink, J. J. *The Car Culture*. Cambridge: MIT Press, 1975.

Kyvig, D. E. *Daily Life in the United States, 1920–1939: Decades of Promise and Pain*. Westport, Conn.: Greenwood Press, 2002.

Nye, D. E. *Electrifying America: Social Meanings of a New Technology, 1880–1940*. Cambridge, Mass.: MIT Press, 1990.

Patterson, J. T. *Grand Expectations: The United States, 1945–1974*. New York: Oxford University Press, 1996.

UNITED STATES, 1960–90

Technology plays an important part in almost every aspect of American life: business and industry, farming, urban development, health care, law, politics, banking, courtship, marital relationships, child rearing, schooling, religion, housekeeping and home maintenance, cooking and dietetics, shopping, social interactions, the spending of leisure time, and more. But the benefits of technology often have a price. For example, our relentless quest for "the new" necessarily makes our present possessions obsolete. Determination to keep up with "the better" or "the different" imposes challenges on both bank balances and human emotions. Technology encourages uniformity and predictability, thereby erasing the distinctiveness of communities and cultures.

Technology's solutions to the problems of one generation often create new ones for the next. Disposable diapers, for instance: widespread usage did not begin until around 1970, when increasing numbers of mothers of infants and small children found employment outside the home. But since their introduction, there have been concerns about their effects on the environment. By the early 1990s, soiled diapers amounted to 1.4 percent of the bulk in landfills, according to a study conducted in Arizona. Was that too much? And whatever the quantity, should disposable diapers be banned for other environmental reasons—for seepage of waste into groundwater, for example? Not necessarily. Debates over comparative environmental costs and benefits of using disposable as opposed to laundered diapers typically end in a draw. Washing diapers consumes energy and puts both human waste and detergents—another technological advance with harmful environmental consequences—into sewer systems and larger bodies of water where the wastewater flows.

I'll Buy That!, published in 1986 by *Consumer Reports* magazine, identified and described "50 Small Wonders and Big Deals that Revolutionized the Lives of Consumers" during the magazine's 50-year history. The attention that the book's pictures and essays give to the automobile reveal the important role this technological wonder has played in American life. Through the years American-made cars grew bigger and more technologically complex. In the 1960s, automatic transmissions became standard on cars of all sizes. Power brakes, power steering, and air-conditioning came first in larger cars, then in cars of all sizes. In 1966, Oldsmobile introduced the Toronado, the first domestic car with front-wheel drive. Before long, this innovation, too, became a standard feature.

I'll Buy That! pointed to the 1965 Mustang as a symptom of change in Americans' buying habits. The editors describe the Mustang as neither a sports car nor a family car, but a "personal car." A 1962 version was a two-seater, but then, say the book's editors, there was a further corporate vision. "Put a young couple in something as

MATERIAL LIFE

TECHNOLOGY

Europe

United States, 1920-1939

United States, 1960-1990

Japan

Inuit

361

romantic as a Mustang and they might just be fruitful and multiply and three into two doesn't go." So the design was scrapped in favor of "two-plus-two"—that is, two seats in front, plus a small rear seat for two children. Of course, not by chance did the Mustang gain popularity. The Ford Motor Company launched it with a $10 million publicity campaign, calling it a "school bus," a "shopping cart," and a "dream boat." "Join the tide of history," one advertisement said, "with a car that scoots through traffic . . . hoards gas . . . and sports a low price tag." Creating the sense of need for the Mustang was just as important as creating the car itself.

The imported vehicle often served as a family's second car.

The Volkswagen Beetle, a tiny car with its engine in the rear, established its own popularity through unconventional advertising: "Think small" and "Ugly is only skin deep," for example. Despite the car's many inconveniences and crudities, VW owners drove their Beetles with immeasurable pride. Still, the Beetle was not a family car. The Toyota Corona, introduced in 1965, was. Its acceptance as an economical but comfortable car encouraged other Japanese manufacturers, particularly Honda and Nissan (known then as Datsun), to enter the American market; within a decade the three Japanese companies claimed about 20 percent of the U.S. market. This jeopardized the very existence of Chrysler Corporation and dented the prosperity of General Motors and Ford, the other two manufacturers in the Big Three. The popularity of smaller cars had implications for automobile safety, as tests showed that their drivers were more vulnerable to accidental injury or death than drivers of larger vehicles. Also affected by the increasing popularity of imported cars were the thousands of families whose breadwinners worked in manufacturing plants that now faced cutbacks caused by declining sales of American-made automobiles.

Ever since its invention, the automobile had played an important role in the development of America. By 1960, wrote historian Kenneth Jackson, "the best symbol of individual success and identity was a sleek, air-conditioned, high-powered personal statement on wheels." The presence of plain, low-powered, low-prestige foreign vehicles did not threaten that symbol. The imported vehicle often served as a family's second car, providing transportation rather than luxury. Nonetheless, it contributed to a phenomenon noted by Jackson: between 1950 and 1980 the American population increased by 50 percent, but the number of automobiles increased by 200 percent.

Americans' reliance on the automobile led President Eisenhower to propose and Congress to approve the Interstate Highway Act in 1956, providing for a 41,000-mile system of limited-access highways. Construction proceeded rapidly, with little regard for the farmland and urban neighborhoods that lay in the highways' paths or for the consequences of highway-spawned "sprawl." Connecting urban highways to the interstate system meant the construction of spaghettilike interchanges and resulted in the loss of more neighborhoods and the migration of more residents to suburbia. In the 1960s, factories, offices, and shopping centers also migrated to the suburbs, so that by 1970, according to Jackson, in 9 of the 15 largest metropolitan areas the suburbs were the principal sources of employment. In some cities, such as San Francisco, almost three-fourths of all trips to and from work were by people who did not live or work in the core city. Similar patterns in other cities explain why extensive public transportation systems were usually hopeless dreams.

Romance with the automobile helped create a "drive-through" culture. The "drive-in" culture restaurants, where carhops served patrons who ate in their cars, disappeared rather quickly as new technologies had customers shouting their orders into a loudspeaker and passing a window to pick up their orders. Drive-through banking was its counterpart, along with drive-through cleaners and drive-through pharmacies. Eventually there were even some drive-through funeral homes, where friends could pay their respects to the deceased without getting out of their cars. A drive-through bridal chapel was yet to come.

In 1970, although one family in five had no automobile, Americans' reliance on automobiles showed no signs of diminishing. Nor did the automobile industry escape numerous technological problems. One had to do with air pollution caused by automobile emissions. The California legislature, responding to complaints about the smog that was suffocating cities, became the pacesetter in setting emission control standards. It imposed limits on the amount of carbon monoxide and hydrocarbons permitted from automobile exhausts. The federal laws that followed permitted California to enforce stricter ones, as atmospheric conditions there differed from other parts of the country. Had mass transit—buses, subways, streetcars, and trains—held greater appeal, pollution problems might have been less severe, but mass transit could not compete with the convenience, power, and pride derived from automobiles. Nationwide between 1945 and 1967, mass transit rides fell from 23 billion to 8 billion.

More vexing for the American makers of big cars was consumers' growing preference for small ones, caused mainly by rising fuel costs resulting from the oil crisis. Japan's Datsun (known later as Nissan) and Toyota were serious about doing business when they entered the U.S. market. By 1968 they had been joined in the American market by other Japanese manufacturers (principally Honda, Mitsubishi, and Mazda), and Japan had passed Germany as the world's second-largest producer of motor vehicles.

In response, American makers marketed what were called captive imports. Mitsubishi made the Dodge Colt and Mazda made the Ford Courier pickup. General Motors owned 35 percent of Isuzu, maker of the LUV, marketed by GM. When imports reached 10 percent of all sales of passenger cars, the American automakers began producing their own subcompacts. The Ford Maverick and American Motors Hornet, introduced in 1969, and the Chevrolet Vega, Ford Pinto, and American Motors Gremlin in 1970 did not distinguish themselves as high-quality vehicles, but they positioned the American automobile industry to take on the greater challenges to come.

Those challenges arrived with the petroleum crisis that began in 1973, a crisis resulting from a situation President Nixon described in an address to Congress on June 29: "While we have 6 percent of the world's population, we consume one-third of the world's energy output. The supply of domestic energy resources available to us is not keeping pace with our ever growing demand." The demand for petroleum in the United States was 17 million barrels per day, but domestic output was little more than 11 million barrels per day.

The situation worsened in October 1973. The Yom Kippur War between Israel and its Arab neighbors prompted Middle Eastern oil-producing countries to impose an embargo on exports to countries regarded as sympathetic to Israel. Included were the United States, Canada, all of western Europe, and Japan. While the embargo was in effect, until the spring of 1974, panic buying caused long lines at gas stations. To keep their tanks full, drivers would fill up when they needed as little as three gallons. In January 1974, President Nixon signed into law a 55-mile-per-hour speed limit act, after having asked Congress to set the limit at 50 miles per hour. The reduced speed limit conserved an estimated 3.4 billion gallons per year, and highway fatalities in 1974 fell to 45,196 from 54,052 in the previous year. They soon climbed again as motorists flouted the unpopular law. Some states imposed limits on quantities of gas that could be purchased, causing drivers to go from station to station. Others restricted days on which cars with even- or odd-numbered license plates could fill up. Many communities organized carpools, and state highway departments provided lots to enable drivers to park their cars and share rides with others.

Anger over the problems the oil shortage caused was plentiful. After all, a way of life seemed in jeopardy. Those who suspected conspiracies believed that oil companies seeking to raise prices were responsible for the shortages. They claimed there were loaded tankers waiting offshore and supplies of gas hidden in the tanks of abandoned stations, all ready to be released when the price was right.

The gasoline energy crisis caused Americans to look to technological developments to decrease reliance on crude oil and seek other ways to power the nation. What could be done to guarantee that electricity, the lifeblood of America, would continue to flow without interruption? Government experts and utilities executives knew that demand for electrical power would increase dramatically in coming years. The threat of blackouts and "brownouts," which occurred when power had to be cut back because reserves had fallen too low, demanded answers. Electricity generated by nuclear power plants seemed to provide them. The Atomic Energy Commission estimated that by the year 2000 half the electrical power consumed in the United States would be generated by nuclear fuel. Building more nuclear-powered plants made sense.

Consequently, by 1966 half the new generators planned or being built were nuclear powered, even though serious but unpublicized accidents in nuclear reactors had occurred since testing first began on nuclear generators in 1949. In January 1966 the first nuclear-powered plant, the Enrico Fermi, located on Lake Erie between Detroit and Toledo, went into operation. The following October a malfunction caused the reactor to overheat. Safety devices and extraordinary efforts by plant workers averted a potentially enormous disaster. The Detroit police were able to call off their plans to evacuate the city, thus sparing something that would have been much more than a mere interruption in daily life. After being out of commission for several years, the Enrico Fermi reactor was eventually dismantled.

Thus nuclear power brought the American people a new environmental worry. Problems with other nuclear reactors—mainly accidents and difficulties in finding ways to store wastes that would remain radioactive for thousands of years—dashed hopes that nuclear power would be safe and relatively inexpensive. Nuclear power was not going to be the ultimate technological fix, the cure-all for energy shortages.

Finally, in the period 1960 to 1990 there were also technological developments in the home. In 1974 the Amana Refrigeration Company began to market small microwave ovens for home use. However, probably because meals cooked in them seemed less attractive and less tasty than those prepared in regular ovens, microwaves did not catch on for general use. Rather, they became "heat-things-up" devices, increasingly useful for families that found it impossible to gather around the dinner table at the same time. Also, as baby boomers headed off to their own apartments and as childless families became more numerous, microwaves proved useful for heating prepackaged dinners and leftovers. Another small but important technological device that was installed unobtrusively in many homes deserves mention: smoke detectors became household necessities after their introduction in 1970 (Marty, 57–61, 145, 149–51, 153–54, 222–23, 305–6).

To read about technology in the United States in the 19th century, see the United States entries in the section "Technology" in chapter 5 ("Material Life") in volume 5, of this series.

FOR MORE INFORMATION

Atomic Archive. <http://www.atomicarchive.com/>.

Consumer's Union. *I'll Buy That! 50 Small Wonders and Big Deals That Revolutionized the Lives of Consumers: A 50 Year Retrospective.* Mount Vernon, N.Y.: Consumer's Union, 1986.

Flink, J. J. *The Car Culture.* Cambridge: MIT Press, 1975.

History of Computing. <http://ei.cs.vt.edu/~history/>.

Kennan, E. *Mission to the Moon: A Critical Examination of NASA and the Space Program.* New York: Morrow, 1969.

Marty, M. A. *Daily Life in the United States, 1960–1990: Decades of Discord.* Westport, Conn.: Greenwood Press, 1997.

Patterson, J. T. *Grand Expectations: The United States, 1945–1974.* New York: Oxford University Press, 1996.

JAPAN

Japan has long been lionized for its excellent technologies. Unfortunately such praise often comes in negative comparison to its purported mediocre science. The premise is that Japan is adept at creatively adapting foreign "pure" research into technological development. The Japanese, it is argued, are great at miniaturization and refinement but weak in actual research.

As with all stereotypes, there is an element of truth to the statement. Japan has always valued workmanship and skill while dismissing the abstract ratiocination. Problem-solving and critical thinking skills have long been the Japanese forte. The application of concepts to reality is highly prized. Yankee ingenuity is less valuable to society than dogged perseverance.

MATERIAL LIFE

TECHNOLOGY

Europe

United States,
1920-1939

United States,
1960-1990

Japan

Inuit

None of this is to denigrate Japan's artistic, aesthetic, poetic, philosophical, or scientific accomplishments. Rather, the level of Japan's technologies reflects such obviously high standards that everything else seems to pale in comparison.

Not surprisingly then, the Japanese are not particularly interested in protection of intellectual property. They believe that society benefits when the workman and mechanic apply the innovations of scientists to the problem at hand. The Japanese are a little puzzled that Westerners are so intent on copyright and patent infringement. Certainly the inventor and scientist should be appropriately rewarded, but not at the expense of the consumer. Accordingly, Japanese who work in research and development sections of large companies do not expect to personally benefit financially from their innovations. Science in service to humanity might be Japan's watchword.

The transistor, the microchip, nuclear power, astrophysics, the internal combustion engine, jet propulsion, and quality control were all invented abroad, but the Japanese are the ones that refined and perfected ideas for real-life application. Small, inexpensive, and efficient electronics came to be produced in Japan, not because of cheap labor, but rather because its best minds were set to work to incorporate and refine products rather than to invent.

Japanese technology, then, is at the forefront of its productivity, but not just in the most obvious applications such as consumer goods. Its technology is at the forefront of its transportation, telecommunication, and financial networks. Similarly, Japanese architecture and engineering are famous worldwide, more for their practicality than for innovative aesthetic. Earthquake-proof high-rise buildings; prefabricated homes; bullet trains; super oil tankers; and safe, efficient nuclear power plants are its hallmarks.

Not surprisingly, Japan has devoted huge sums of financial support for development of technologies, founding a Science City around the University of Tsukuba. The National Institute of Advanced Industrial Science and Technology, an agency within the Ministry of Economy, Trade and Industry, maintains some 15 national laboratories, 8 of them in Tsukuba. The purpose is to integrate science and technology research for the benefit of the entire nation. Everyone benefits from this research because it is made available to private industry.

To read about technology in early modern Japan, see the Japan entry in the section "Science and Technology" in chapter 4 ("Intellectual Life") in volume 4 of this series.

~Louis G. Perez

FOR MORE INFORMATION

Callon, S. *Divided Sun: MITI and the Breakdown of Japanese High-Tech Industrial Policy, 1975–1993*. Stanford, Calif.: Stanford University Press, 1995.

Tatsuno, S. *The Technopolis Strategy: Japan, High Technology, and the Control of the Twenty-First Century*. New York: Prentice Hall Press, 1986.

INUIT

European explorers who encountered the Inuit in the 18th and 19th centuries almost uniformly remarked on their technologies. These industrial-era Europeans were frequently amazed that Inuit were able to survive in an environment that appeared to the Europeans to be so materially bleak. In fact, Inuit indigenous technologies were part of what enabled Inuit to live and prosper in the severe arctic climate. For the most part Inuit fashioned houses, clothing, tools, and ornaments with neither wood nor metal but were quick to adopt new materials and manufactured tools once they became available.

Today Inuit live in manufactured homes in modern towns and villages and are no longer forced to rely upon traditional technologies in order to survive physically. They work at wage-labor jobs, watch television, wear manufactured clothing, and purchase much of their food at stores. Rifles have replaced harpoons, kayaks are no longer used for hunting, and in many parts of the Inuit North dogsleds have been exchanged for snowmobiles. Nonetheless, for cultural and social reasons Inuit continue to use a number of traditional technologies.

Many, though not all, of the traditional technologies that remain in wide use are ones generally identified with women and women's activities. The *ulu*, or semilunar women's knife, continues to be widely used throughout the Inuit North. *Ulu* blades, which were usually fashioned from slate or cold hammered from copper, are now often made from commercial saw blades and hafted to bone or ivory handles. Many women own several *ulus* in different sizes for sewing, butchering, and other cutting tasks. *Ulus* are an item of technology that men make for women.

Sewing, however, is something that women do for men (as well as for children), and skillful sewing remains a valued practice in many Inuit communities. Despite the commercially manufactured parkas, boots, and mitts that are readily available, many Inuit prefer traditional-style outerwear. For the most part, cloth and other commercially available materials have replaced the skins that were traditionally used for clothing, and it is now common to find skins used for boots, mitts, and the decorative trim on parkas. Among the traditional-style clothing items still in wide use is the *amauti*, or women's parka. This parka is notable because it is specifically designed with a pouch at the back in which to carry a baby.

A number of traditional food-preparation techniques are also still in use. These include the methods for butchering animals as well as for preparing food to eat. In many parts of the Arctic it was not possible to cook foods year-round, and many Inuit traditional meat and fish dishes were eaten raw, frozen, dried, or fermented. These remain both delicacies and, in some cases, daily foodstuffs.

In the past, technologies were transmitted from one generation to the next in the same way that all cultural information was taught—informally, through observation, trial, and error. In the modern settlement this is not always possible, and many Inuit communities have made conscious efforts to teach traditional skills to children and young adults by establishing classes. Many Inuit communities also promote traditional technologies at annual cultural festivals, when they hold contests in snow house building, dogsled racing, or seal skinning.

~Pamela Stern

FOR MORE INFORMATION

Driscoll, B. *The Inuit Amautik: I Like My Hood to Be Full.* Winnipeg: Winnipeg Art Gallery, 1980.

Oakes, J., and R. Riewe. *Our Boots: An Inuit Women's Art.* New York: Thames and Hudson, 1996.

Zimmerly, D. *Qayaq, Kayaks of Siberia and Alaska.* Juneau: Alaska Division of State Museums, 2000 (originally published in 1986).

MATERIAL LIFE: WEB SITES

http://www.flex.com/~jai/articles/hinmeat.html
http://library.thinkquest.org/C005446/Food/English/russia.html
http://www.ifc.org/publications/pubs/impact/s8capitsp98/s8capitsp98.html
http://www.iath.virginia.edu/holocaust/infotech.html
http://www.pbs.org/wgbh/aso/databank/medhealth.html

6

POLITICAL LIFE

POLITICAL LIFE
|
GOVERNMENT
LAW & CRIME
REFORM
WAR

The ancient Greek philosopher Aristotle (384–322 B.C.E.) claimed that humans are by definition political animals, and by this he meant that an essential part of human life involves interacting in the public sphere with people who are not our intimate families. It is these relationships—along with their complex negotiations—that permit the development of cities, kingdoms, nations, and civilization itself. Throughout history different cultures have developed different political systems to organize their lives, and all political systems are in constant states of change as they accommodate the changing needs and interests of the populace. Political life involves two different spheres of influence: organizing the relationships among those within a political unit and negotiating the relations between different political entities (countries, tribes, or kingdoms). However, at its basic level, all politics is about power—finding out who has it and who does not.

People create a political system first of all to assure themselves of internal peace and security. As the political theorist Thomas Hobbes (1588–1679) noted, without a strong authority, people's incessant struggle for power would result in a life that is "nasty, brutish, and short." This is why we want our power structures clear. Our political systems also clarify and solidify our loyalties and allegiances—nationalism has served as a sentiment that can unify people with diverse interests and backgrounds.

As people interact in ever-widening circles, our political life must negotiate the often-difficult relations with other kingdoms, countries, or empires. Diplomacy is the tool of our political life that is to smooth these interactions, and war is the breakdown of these negotiations. In war—which has unfortunately dominated so much of human history—we can often see the noblest and worst expressions of our human spirit. In war we can also definitively see the struggle for power that marks our political life.

During the 20th century, several wars left indelible imprints upon daily life. World War I transformed the basic social structures not only in Europe and America but also in other areas of the globe such as the Middle East. For example, the war rearranged the politics of the Ottoman Empire, causing its ultimate downfall. In the vacuum, a new order appeared in Asia Minor. The war also caused Western governments to adopt more authoritarian control over life and labor. In the United States, for instance, the federal government moved toward the prohibition of alcohol as a wartime measure. Similarly, President Woodrow Wilson encouraged collective bargaining for organized labor as a means to keep the industrial peace while fighting a war in Europe. World War I also created international political and economic instability that contributed to the next two political crises of the 20th century, the worldwide Great Depression and World War II. Fighting economic and political chaos led to numerous reforms. President Franklin D. Roosevelt's New Deal embodied the spirit and legacy of these changes, which took place in many nations from Mexico to Great Britain. At the end of World War II, there was great hope that the political changes that occurred would create a lasting peace.

Despite the best efforts of a generation of politicians, peace remained elusive in the world. The final five decades of the 20th century were war-torn. A monumental conflict between the United States and the Soviet Union shaped all facets of daily life. Although the Americans and the Russians never met formally on the battlefield, their allies did in Korea and Vietnam. The death totals from these cold war conflicts is staggering. In Honduras alone, the "dirty war" between the right-wing government and suspected leftists led to the killing of 200,000 people. By 2000, a kind of disillusionment set in worldwide. After a century of political reform and wars to protect and expand democracy in the world, desperate poverty continued to be a common factor of daily life. Moreover, even with the creation of world governance bodies such as the United Nations, war, political murders, and diaspora were quite common. The political structures that had been fashioned during the early part of the century seemed outmoded by the century's end, unable to deal with basic problems such as health care, education, and security. Thus by the millennium, some political activists questioned the political structures of daily life, often calling for new political parties; new policies; and new ways of approaching the looming environmental, economic, and religious crises on the horizon.

POLITICAL LIFE

| GOVERNMENT |

United States,
1920-1939

United States,
1940-1959

United States,
1960-1990

Latin America

India

Islamic World

Soviet Union

Japan

Inuit

FOR MORE INFORMATION

Johnson, P. *Modern Times: The World from the Twenties to the Eighties*. New York: Harper and Row, 1983.

Van Evera, S. *Causes of War: Power and the Roots of Conflict*. Ithaca, N.Y.: Cornell University Press, 1999.

Government

The two major crises of the 20th century, the worldwide Great Depression and World War II, had an incalculable impact on all nations. One of the historical shifts sparked by these events related to governmental structures. In almost every Western country, the response to economic collapse and the rise of fascism was a reorganization of government. While building new public institutions, political leaders sought to become more responsive to the needs of their citizens. This became a hallmark of the 20th century.

The history of the United States clearly illustrates the change that the 1930s and 1940s brought. Before the great stock market crash of 1929, the U.S. government prided itself on how little it impacted the daily lives of its citizens. Although during the Progressive Era presidents Theodore Roosevelt and Woodrow Wilson had increased federal contact with average people, most of these actions were short-lived. For example, in 1921, the U.S. Congress passed the Sheppard-Towner Federal Maternity and Infancy Act, which appropriated over $1 million in federal money for mother and baby health care. Although successful, the program was eliminated in 1929.

Mass unemployment and social dislocation forced the federal government to transform its relationship with its people. During the presidential election of 1932, Democratic candidate Franklin D. Roosevelt promised a "new deal" for the American people. What he meant was that if elected, he would institute a program of bold and persistent experimentation. Once elected he made good on his promise and created dozens of new federal government bodies. These so-called alphabet agencies dramatically affected daily life. In fact, their names became household words and remain identifiable today. Everyone knew of the work of the Civilian Conservation Corps (CCC), National Labor Relations Board (NLRB), Tennessee Valley Authority (TVA), and Work Progress Administration (WPA). Moreover, these agencies touched the lives of millions. Roosevelt increased the influence of his administration during World War II.

Roosevelt was not alone in the world. Other world leaders such as Brazil's Getulio Vargas, Mexico's Lázaro Cárdenas, Argentina's Juan Perón, and the Soviet Union's Joseph Stalin were all charismatic leaders who sought to extend the national government (in reality or in appearance) to expand political participation and aid average people. In the United States and in Latin America, however, these reforms were challenged by both the far political right and the far political left. Conservative politicians such as Joe McCarthy believed the changes of the 1930s and 1940s had gone too far. Radicals such as Fidel Castro thought that the transformations were incomplete and had not done enough. But despite the criticism and political opposition, in most countries (excluding Cuba, of course), the governmental structures that flowed from the Great Depression and World War II were not jettisoned and remained central to the structure of political life in the 20th century.

In India, World War II was followed by independence from British rule and the traumatic division of British India into Muslim Pakistan and Hindu India. The 20th century witnessed both the birth and the death of the Soviet Union, which arose out of the collapse of Czarist Russia at the end of World War I and survived the attack of Nazi Germany during World War II. The Soviet Union fell in 1991 largely due to a bloated military establishment that left the government unable to meet the everyday economic needs of most of its people. Although still officially ruled by its emperor, Japan at the end of the century was a Western-style democracy that had moved further from where it had been politically in 1900 than any other country. The Inuit North, meanwhile, achieved political autonomy within Canada. In 2000, the nations of Latin America continued to strive for political stability and economic development and the states of the Islamic World continued to experience a rebirth of religious fundamentalism, which was born of anti-Western sentiment and which fueled the greatest political issue of the day—the rise of Islamic terrorism against Western interests.

UNITED STATES, 1920–39

Before the onset of what 1932 Democratic presidential candidate Franklin D. Roosevelt pledged would be "a new deal for the American people," most residents of the country seldom encountered the U.S. government in their daily lives. In the 19th century, the only federal service directly reaching people was the U.S. mail. Even in that instance, before the establishment of rural free delivery in the 1890s, contact with a federal postal worker required a trip to the post office, something not on most daily schedules. Noncitizens entering the country, inventors registering a patent, and currency counterfeiters were the only people almost certain to confront federal officials. Except during and just after the Civil War, the federal government imposed no direct taxes on individuals until 1913; thereafter it levied only a small graduated income tax on the wealthiest 10 percent of the population. Only times of war and military service created extensive contact with a federal government that was much expanded in the emergency situation. Every other year national elections raised issues for debate and drew a high percentage of adult white males to the polls, but election results seldom produced changes discernible at the grass roots. The addition of women to the electorate in 1920 and the simultaneous implementation of national alcohol prohibition increased the awareness and reality of the federal presence, but otherwise the U.S. government remained distant from their lives as people struggled with depression conditions.

By its various documentary efforts as well as its other attempts to measure the extent and impact of the depression, the New Deal made the lives of ordinary people more visible to the federal government. At the same time, the great variety of federal relief and recovery efforts that directly touched people at the grass roots made the nation's central government more immediately visible and meaningful to these same people. The specific actions of the New Deal to respond to the depression were unquestionably important in the 1930s. However, what may have been more profound and what was certainly longer lasting was the cultural shift pro-

The New Deal in action. Works Progress Administration (WPA) workers build a road while a WPA artist records the event, Michigan, 1939. © National Archives.

duced by the New Deal. Franklin Roosevelt's administration altered popular expectations so that for the first time in U.S. history, the federal government's response to the needs of ordinary individuals, not members of special groups such as veterans, slaves, immigrants, or elites, became the normal political expectation. In other words, the American political culture became more genuinely democratic than ever before (Kyvig, 195, 215).

To read about government in the United States in the 19th century, see the United States entries in the section "Government and Politics" in chapter 6 ("Political Life") in volume 5 of this series.

FOR MORE INFORMATION

Hicks, J. D. *Republican Ascendancy, 1921–1933*. New York: Harper Torchbooks, 1960.

Kennedy, D. M. *Freedom from Fear: The American People in Depression and War, 1929–1945*. New York: Oxford University Press, 1999.

Kyvig, D. E. *Daily Life in the United States, 1920–1939: Decades of Promise and Pain*. Westport, Conn.: Greenwood Press, 2002.

UNITED STATES, 1940–59

POLITICAL LIFE

GOVERNMENT

United States,
1920-1939

United States,
1940-1959

United States,
1960-1990

Latin America

India

Islamic World

Soviet Union

Japan

Inuit

From the 1940s to the 1960s, American political life was dominated by larger-than-life politicians such as Franklin D. Roosevelt and Joseph McCarthy. FDR's presence was a part of daily life. What the New Deal accomplished most successfully was the restoration of faith in the power of government to help individuals—those forgotten men and women who worked hard but could not manage to support their families. No manuscript collection is more moving than the file of letters collected in Eleanor Roosevelt's archives in the Roosevelt Library at Hyde Park from needy people asking for small loans of money until they could get on their feet again. Eleanor Roosevelt acted as Franklin's eyes and ears as she traveled all over the country to help the New Deal become synonymous with concern for human dignity. The creation of Social Security, workers' compensation, and higher income taxes for the rich, along with guarantees that workers could strike for fair wages, demonstrated respect for the American worker, even if a number of political promises fell short of fulfillment. Called "a traitor to his class," FDR made his commitments the source of loyalty for many blue-collar workers. The 31 "fireside chats" he gave on the radio made him a father figure to many who thought of the Roosevelts not as politicians but as moral leaders. Although people at the time never saw pictures of Roosevelt in a wheelchair or realized just how helpless he was (no one talked about disabilities), everyone knew about his bravery in reentering politics after surviving polio. His overpowering smile and his sense of humor won him admirers all over the world, and his aristocratic self-assurance—enriched by Eleanor's great social awareness—proved to be exactly what the country needed to inspire a national turn from provincial isolationism to global power.

In a prizewinning book, *No Ordinary Time: Franklin and Eleanor Roosevelt. The Home Front in World War II*, Doris Kearns Goodwin documents how amazingly popular FDR's radio speeches were. A May 1941 talk designed to alert the nation to the possibility of a national emergency got a 95 percent favorable response from the more than 65 million people in 20 million homes who listened. When popular comedians such as Bob Hope and Jack Benny were thrilled to have a listener rating of 30 to 35 percent, Roosevelt was getting radio audiences of over 70 percent. The only other broadcast that even approached FDR's for listeners was the audience for the Joe Louis–Max Schmeling world heavyweight boxing match in 1938—an encounter that seemed symbolic of battles to come.

Perhaps the most influential president of the 20th century, Franklin D. Roosevelt. © Library of Congress.

The paternalism of the New Deal made it easier for many to accept the new constraints on freedom that preparation for war demanded. Price controls and gasoline and food rationing, blackouts and air raid drills, limits on travel, censorship, and security clearances were all part of the war world that took over the New Deal in 1941. "Loose lips sink ships" declared a poster plastered in coastal towns, reminding ordinary people that everyone was involved in winning a war. Along both the East and West Coasts citizens prepared for attacks from enemy submarines or bombers. Communities set up first-aid stations, and even middle-school children trained with Red Cross manuals to learn simple survival techniques. Air raid drills in schools were conducted with buddy systems so that older children became responsible for smaller ones in reaching makeshift shelters or simply hiding under designated tables. Looking back on these moments as Dr. New Deal was replaced by Dr. Win the War, older Americans find it hard to reconstruct that reality of fear. More often they cherish the orderliness of the daily tasks that made them feel useful to the country as a whole. The New Deal raised America's self-confidence.

In 1944 Roosevelt's State of the Union message to Congress was broadcast as a fireside chat because so few newspapers would print the entire message. What FDR suggested then was to extend the original commitments of the New Deal into the country's wartime role in the world. A "basic essential to peace," he asserted, "is a decent standard of living for all individual men and women and children in all nations. Freedom from fear is eternally linked with freedom from want." As he went on to define America's role as one that would not repeat the tragic errors of isolationism, FDR made sure that people understood the need for firm inner discipline and well-organized government to control profiteering and social injustice.

In this speech FDR not only recommended a specific set of new laws to control the cost of living and equalize the burdens of taxation, but he also set up what he called a "second Bill of Rights," based on the belief that "true individual freedom cannot exist without economic security and independence." The rights he defined and connected with the war and with the needs of the entire world might not be as "self-evident" as FDR believed in the 1940s, but they will always be worthy of serious consideration. Roosevelt wanted "all" (in his introduction he did not say "all men," but rather "all—regardless of station or race or creed") to have the right to a useful and remunerative job, the right to a decent home and food and clothing, and the right to medical care and a good education. He also included protection for farmers and businessmen from monopolies and unfair competition abroad, and he articulated once again the concern to provide for the economic insecurities of old age. Always the main agenda of Eleanor Roosevelt's articles, lectures, press conferences, and columns, the bill of economic rights FDR wanted to guarantee—the nation understood—also remained his wife's first priority. Wanting to clarify the dreams of the New Deal for the rest of the world, FDR concluded this 1944 chat with a reminder that "unless there is security here at home, there cannot be lasting peace in the world."

Children who grew up in the midst of World War II gathered a sense of self-esteem from the many small roles they played to help win the peace. In Vermont, schools provided bags for gathering milkweed pods to replace the no longer available kapok fibers used for warmth and padding in jackets; in New York children collected fats to be used for making explosives. All over America young people saved tinfoil, flattened tin cans, and enjoyed squishing little yellow buttons of color in white margarine to make it look like rationed butter. Many children bought and sold 10-cent defense stamps, purchases that represented real sacrifice at the time, as 10 cents could also pay for an entire matinee at the movies, with short serials, cartoons, and two feature films included.

Mothers who had been convinced that being housewives was their only true profession often did both volunteer and paid work to contribute to the war effort. They labored in hospitals, knitted afghans, and helped plot and identify aircraft in undisclosed places all over American cities. Many women were proud to take jobs in defense plants doing "men's work" and to find themselves making higher wages than ever before. By the end of the war a rare group of intrepid women pilots were even flying huge bombers to destinations all over the world.

In one of his remarkable collections of interviews with Americans who lived through significant moments of American history, *"The Good War": An Oral History of World War II*, Studs Terkel recorded the impressions of a number of citizens who for the first time in their lives felt free of intense competition to survive. To a lesser extent this same experience became true on the home front: "It was the last time most Americans thought they were innocent and good without qualifications." One man noted, "It's a precious memory. . . . That great camaraderie of savin' tinfoil, toothpaste tubes, or tin cans, all that stuff made people part of somethin', that disappeared."

That sense of community also developed in parts of the army where people felt what it was like to work together for the same goals for the first time in their lives. One ex-soldier told Terkel they were in a tribal sort of situation where they helped each other without fear. The absence of economic competition and phony standards created for many men a real love for the army. Although the armed forces themselves at the time were a bastion of racism, as several of Terkel's black citizens reported, and many defense industries refused to give African Americans higher-paying jobs until Roosevelt issued an executive order mandating equality, people *had* to learn to work together. The dream of equal rights became part of the incentive for fighting a war against countries that made national ideals of inequality. Wartime belief in cooperation to win seemed more than simple propaganda. Another man Terkel interviewed remembered that the whole world seemed absolutely mad—people were in love with war.

Feeling they were "part of something" enhanced the lives of soldiers of all ages. One man recalled those moments of need when others were there to help him as the high point of his entire life. Civilians felt similar connections. A journalist whose patriotism led him at age 14 to lie about his age to get a job in an arms plant felt that he would have done anything for the president. When he was able to join the navy at 18, he told Studs Terkel, he was sure "there was right and there was wrong and I wore the white hat."

As much as Roosevelt dominated the years from the Great Depression through World War II, Joseph McCarthy, a senator from Wisconsin, seemed to dominate the years after Roosevelt's death. Politically, the period following World War II was different from the New Deal era as government solutions became suspect and as government itself sought to destroy Communists at home and abroad. The term McCarthyism, which now lives in the dictionary and is defined as "the political practice of publicizing accusations of disloyalty or subversion with insufficient regard for evidence" (*American Heritage Dictionary of the English Language*, 1969), was applied to that battle against leftists, including those who had helped the New Deal. In other words, Senator McCarthy made a political career of attacking the accomplishments of the Roosevelt years. McCarthy shared Richard Nixon's hostility to those who were running the State Department, which he claimed was infested with Communists. He boasted a list of 205 State Department spies, but when challenged to produce proof McCarthy changed his accusation to "bad risks" and lowered the number to 57. Later Senator Millard Tydings of Maryland offered McCarthy $25,000 to convict just one actual employee of the State Department. McCarthy never collected the money.

The country was looking for scapegoats to compensate for Russia's cold war aggression and for the "loss" of China to Communist ideology. McCarthy came up with Owen Lattimore, a Johns Hopkins professor and China scholar who would call his memoir *Ordeal by Slander*; Lattimore retired to England after being accused of spying for Russia. John Stuart Service, a State Department China desk expert in the 1940s who favored withdrawing U.S. support from Chiang Kai-shek, was fired in 1951 on trumped-up charges. The simple idea that ridding America of Communists at home would cure world tension and purify democracy appealed to many. By the end of 1950 Congress had also passed the Internal Security Act, also known as the McCarran Act, to register all Communists, strengthen espionage and immigration laws, and set up detention camps for spies and saboteurs in case of emergency. As early as 1947 the *American Legion* magazine boasted that the House Un-American Activities Committee had not summoned any farmer, workman, or "common man." Without exception, the legionnaires pointed out, the suspect people examined were college graduates, Ph.D.s, summa cum laudes, and Phi Beta Kappas from Harvard, Yale, Princeton, or other great colleges. Such dominant populist sentiments made it easy for Eisenhower to defeat the "egghead" Adlai Stevenson, who ran a sophisticated campaign against him in 1952. A professor at the University of Utah commented on Stevenson's defeat, "A whole era is ended, is totally repudiated, a whole era of brains and literacy and exciting thinking."

After the tremendous Eisenhower landslide in the presidential election of 1952, the Republican Senate made McCarthy head of his own committee on government operations. He himself had been elected by a margin of more than 140,000 votes. Immediately McCarthy sent two young assistants, Roy Cohn and G. David Schine, on a whirlwind tour of U.S. Information Services abroad that ended with the banning of "books, music, painting and the like" of any Communist or fellow traveler. Included were books by Henry David Thoreau and Foster Rhea Dulles, an anti-Communist professor who was a cousin of the secretary of state. Ordered to remove dangerous thinkers from libraries, some custodians actually burned books. Many librarians lost their jobs. Eisenhower openly criticized this outrage at a graduation speech in June 1952 at Dartmouth College. "We have got to fight Communism with something better," he declared, "not try to conceal the thinking of our own people." But the president did not countermand McCarthy's directive.

The infamous Senator Joe McCarthy waves papers in front of reporters, claiming that he has names of Communists within the U.S. federal government. © Library of Congress.

The Wisconsin senator was as out of control as a forest fire in a high wind. He made outrageous accusations and bullied innocent people to try to establish guilt by association or past connection. Such irresponsible behavior caused a fellow Republican, Margaret Chase Smith from Maine, to present to the Senate "A Declaration of Conscience," signed by six other brave Republicans. "I don't like the way the Senate has been made a rendezvous for vilification, for selfish political gain at the sacrifice of individual reputations and national unity," Smith proclaimed. "The American people are sick and tired of being afraid to speak their minds lest they be politically smeared as Communists." She concluded with a common sentiment: "I want to see our nation recapture the strength and unity it once had when we fought the enemy instead of ourselves." In 1952 Smith's name had been put in nomination for vice president by approving Republicans, although she did not receive the nomination.

Yet McCarthy seemed unable to stop. He did not even hesitate to accuse General George Marshall, wartime chief of staff and later secretary of state, of being a longtime Communist sympathizer, although it was Marshall's economic plan for rebuilding Europe that kept much of the West out of Communist control. Perhaps for party solidarity Eisenhower tolerated many of McCarthy's antics, but he responded to the attack on Marshall by declaring the general a distinguished patriot—"a man of real selflessness." He went on to assert, "I have no patience with anyone who can find in Marshall's record of service to this country cause for criticism." By 1951 many Americans began to agree with Harry Truman that Senator McCarthy was an asset to the Kremlin. Adlai Stevenson, twice the Democratic presidential nominee, commented that "perhaps this hysterical form of putrid slander . . . flourishes because it satisfies a deep craving to reduce the vast menace of world Communism to comprehensible and manageable proportions." Stevenson also noted the damage done to freedom: "We have all witnessed the stifling choking effect of McCarthyism, the paralysis of initiative, the discouragement and intimidation that follow in its wake and inhibit the bold, imaginative thought and discussion that is the anvil of policy."

> *The Rosenbergs' refusal to cooperate with the justice system they trusted was their undoing.*

When McCarthy took on the rest of the army, people speculated it was because his protégé G. David Schine had been denied special status when drafted, bringing his flashy political career to an end. Not only did McCarthy once again come up with no proven Communists in leadership positions in the U.S. army beyond one sympathizer dentist, but he also flaunted his bullying tactics on camera before the American people. The army–McCarthy hearings provided 35 days in 1954 of riveting television performances demonstrating the new medium as a strong force for exposing truth. No doubt remained about McCarthy's cruel character as he browbeat witnesses and lawyers alike. A documentary film, *Point of Order*, released in 1964 by Emile De Antonio, remains to show how offensive McCarthy's performances were. After eight years of destructive misuse of senatorial authority McCarthy was condemned by the Senate, 67 to 22, for misconduct in 1954. Through their representatives the American people made clear that they had had enough of profitless ranting. Three years later McCarthy would be dead of acute hepatitis. Yet the anxiety about Communism lingered in underlying fears of what the Russians might be up to in the postwar world. As late as 1958, 300 subscriptions were canceled when *Esquire* magazine published an anti-McCarthy article.

The final significant Communist trial of the McCarthy era, that of Julius and Ethel Rosenberg, reached beyond America. The whole world commented on the capital punishment meted out to these "atomic spies," who were also parents of two small boys. Their execution seized the literary mythic imagination and continues to haunt the definition of American justice. Even many who believed in capital punishment were appalled at the lack of moderation in the justice system that sent the Rosenbergs to their deaths with so little concrete evidence against them.

The British atomic physicist Klaus Fuchs had acknowledged in 1950 that he stole atomic bomb plans from Los Alamos. He served but 9 years of a 14-year sentence in a British prison. Yet in the United States anti-Communist fervor became so fierce that the Rosenbergs—whose messenger roles for an allegedly similar theft were much less certain—were executed. Later evidence made it clear that Ethel knew almost nothing about her husband's role. The government had arrested her as a bargaining chip to get more information from him. But the Rosenbergs' refusal to cooperate with the justice system they trusted was their undoing.

Years later, in March 1997, Alexander Feklisov, a retired KGB agent who had had frequent direct contact with the Rosenbergs, told the *New York Times* that the couple had given Russia no useful information at all about the atom bomb. Although Julius had given away some military secrets during 50 or so meetings between 1943 and 1946—when Russia was also our military ally—Feklisov claimed that Ethel was completely innocent. He thought she probably knew of her husband's activities, but added, "You don't kill people for that."

Convicted mainly on the testimony of Ethel's brother, David Greenglass, who had worked on the bomb, the Rosenbergs appeared to be an affront to the American myth of family solidarity. The press, instead of revealing the couple's affection for each other and their concern for their little boys, dehumanized them as robotlike Soviet ideologues. This practice continued even after the Rosenbergs' executions when their collected letters were edited to exclude homey details like their passion for baseball and music and the sustenance they found in their Judaism. To be sure, the Rosenbergs were unrealistically committed to Communism as a means to making a better world, but in 1942, a freer time, a *Fortune* magazine poll revealed that as many as 25 percent of all Americans considered themselves "socialists" and another 35 percent were open-minded about socialism. Just a few years earlier the dogmas the Rosenbergs accepted would never have brought about such extreme punishment. Yet the dogmas of the man who passed judgment upon them seemed equally distorted. Judge Irving R. Kaufman, perhaps afraid of being labeled soft toward fellow Jews, accused the couple of "a crime worse than murder" in putting the A-bomb into the hands of the Russians. When Eisenhower denied the Rosenbergs clemency, it was because he too believed they had increased the chances of atomic war and "exposed to danger literally millions of our citizens." He ignored the pleas of Pope Pius XII and the 40 members of the British Parliament who had joined the pope in urging leniency. Jean-Paul Sartre, a powerful French philosophic voice, called the executions "a legal lynching that covered a whole nation with blood."

Whether the Rosenbergs' deaths made Americans feel more secure or merely heightened their anxiety is worth debating. What is certain is the role that the Rosenbergs began—almost at once—to play in the literary imagination. They joined abolitionist John Brown, slave rebel Nat Turner, and anarchists Sacco and Vanzetti as characters in the mythology of American martyrs. As scapegoats, as government pawns, as intellectual outsiders, the Rosenbergs would find literary definition in such works as E. L. Doctorow's novel *The Book of Daniel* (1971) and Robert Coover's *The Public Burning* (1977) and in the poetry of Adrienne Rich and Sylvia Plath. The 1990s drama by Tony Kushner, *Angels in America,* would present a confrontation between Ethel Rosenberg and Roy Cohn, Senator McCarthy's aide, who boasted of getting her executed. "You could kill me," Ethel tells him, "but you couldn't ever defeat me."

Prominent liberal culture critics Leslie Fiedler and Robert Warshow reflected the general public's hostile approach to the doomed couple. Falling in with the consensus of cold war intellectuals, they made it clear that there could be little humanity in people who pursued the rigidity of Communist ideology.

In 1990, *Ethel: The Fictional Autobiography* by Tema Nason created a brave characterization. And a movie version of *The Book of Daniel* (1983) attempted to make her sympathetic—unfortunately, not by remembering Ethel as she was but by turning her into a compliant blonde. Tony Kushner's Ethel may well have captured her most essential traits. Students trying to evaluate this trial and what it meant for America must look into *Invitation to an Inquest: A New Look at the Rosenberg and Sobell Case* (1968) by Miriam and Walter Schneir (Kaledin, 5–8, 83–86).

To read about government in the United States in the 19th century, see the United States entries in the section "Government and Politics" in chapter 6 ("Political Life") in volume 5 of this series.

FOR MORE INFORMATION

American Memory. <http://lcweb2.loc.gov/ammem/>.

Coover, R. *The Public Burning*. New York: Viking Press, 1977.

Doctorow, E. L. *The Book of Daniel*. New York: Random House, 1971.

Goodwin, D. K. *No Ordinary Time: Franklin and Eleanor Roosevelt: The Homefront in World War II*. New York: Simon and Schuster, 1999.

Kaledin, E. *Daily Life in the United States, 1940–1959: Shifting Worlds*. Westport, Conn.: Greenwood Press, 2000.

Kennedy, D. M. *Freedom from Fear: The American People in Depression and War, 1929–1945*. New York: Oxford University Press, 1999.

Kushner, T. *Angels in America: A Gay Fantasia on National Themes*. New York: Theatre Communications Group, 1993.

Patterson, J. T. *Grand Expectations: The United States, 1945–1974*. New York: Oxford University Press, 1996.

Saville, P., dir. *Fellow Traveler*. 1989.

Terkel, S. *The Good War: An Oral History of World War Two*. New York: Pantheon Books, 1984.

POLITICAL LIFE

|

GOVERNMENT

|

United States,
1920-1939

United States,
1940-1959

United States,
1960-1990

Latin America

India

Islamic World

Soviet Union

Japan

Inuit

UNITED STATES, 1960–90

In the 1960s, much of what the federal government did became synonymous with the war on poverty. Attacking poverty first became a priority in the 1960s when Michael Harrington's book *The Other America* captured President John Kennedy's attention and stirred him and other national leaders to face the issues it raised. His administration was developing proposals for action when he was assassinated. Taking up more aggressively where Kennedy left off came naturally to Lyndon Johnson. His origins in rural Texas had included few of the material advantages that had been Kennedy's from childhood. On his first full day as president, Johnson asked his advisors to come forward with specific proposals, which reached him in time to permit him to declare "unconditional war on poverty in America" in his 1964 State of the Union address. "The richest Nation on earth," he said, "can win it. We cannot afford to lose it."

Circumstances were right in the mid-1960s for the nation to attack poverty through legislation and executive and other actions. The assassination of John F. Kennedy seemed to have inspired national leaders to believe that if they could not undo that wrong, they could at least right other ones. In President Lyndon Johnson, who had been majority leader in the Senate until he became vice president in 1961, they had someone who knew how to pull legislative strings and mobilize public sentiment more effectively than most presidents before him. Unrest stirred by the civil rights and student movements promoted the kind of introspection that leads nations as well as individuals to change what they can while they can do so on their own terms. The space race with the Soviet Union led schools across the country to insist that teachers teach better and students learn more and learn it faster. More extensive homework assignments and more demanding instruction, particularly in the sciences, were widespread, demonstrating a national mood to not let the Soviets win. This mood made it natural for education to be a weapon in the War on Poverty as well.

Besides, these were times of economic expansion, and with no military war being waged, a War on Poverty could be a war of choice. In August 1964, responding to Johnson's War on Poverty proposals, Congress enacted the comprehensive Equal Opportunity Act. Although conservatives in both parties opposed it (185 in the House and 34 in the Senate), the opponents were largely soft-spoken, fearful that opposition might be taken as indifference to poverty. The act was a noble effort, almost a heroic one, to solve the problems Harrington and others had identified. Each of its major parts held potential for changing the daily lives of countless Americans: It provided job training for the poor, programs to teach marketable skills to unemployed youths in inner cities, arrangements for recruiting middle-class volunteers to work in programs in poverty-stricken areas, funding for public works projects in poor areas, and structures for making loans to indigent farmers and small businesses. The Head Start program gave disadvantaged preschool children training in basic skills—more than 500,000 youngsters in 2,400 communities participated in 1965, the first year of operation. The 1965 Elementary and Secondary Education Act was designed to stimulate innovation in schools and make educating America's poor children a priority. Upward Bound helped youth from poor families attend college. The Office of Economic Opportunity served as the operational center in the War on Poverty, and the Community Action program encouraged grassroots involvement in program development. Its goal was to empower the poor to better look after their own interests.

Although this would seem to be a boon to cities, big-city politicians and state governors did not like the Community Action program at all. They resented what they took to be loss of control to tenant unions in public housing. They opposed organized voter registration drives and resisted other efforts by activists to give poor people the power to deal effectively with their own problems. The Community Action program therefore became the target of hostility and attacks. This in turn created fear that the War on Poverty would lead to class warfare, and it neutralized the effectiveness of other programs.

But troubles in the War on Poverty did not dampen President Johnson's enthusiasm for shaping what he called the Great Society. Proposals poured forth from the White House in 1965 and 1966, and Congress enacted laws on Capitol Hill at a pace not seen since the famous Hundred Days at the beginning of Franklin Roosevelt's first term in 1933 when Congress enacted 15 major laws between March 9 and June 16. Although the effectiveness of the legislation was mixed, the impact on daily lives of the intended beneficiaries and those who implemented the programs was considerable.

The Housing and Urban Development Act of 1965, for example, offered reduced interest rates to builders of housing for the poor and elderly, thus benefiting builders and construction workers as well as those who were to live in the units they built. It also provided funds for health programs, beautification of cities, recreation centers, and rent supplements for the poor. The new cabinet-level Department of Housing and Urban Development assumed responsibility for coordinating the creation of urban and regional planning agencies. The Urban Mass Transportation Act of 1966, establishing the cabinet-level Department of Transportation, provided funds and structures for development of mass-transit systems in urban areas. The Model Cities Act of 1966 provided over $1 billion for slum clearance and urban renewal.

The Elementary and Secondary Education Act, passed in 1965, designated more than $1 billion for educationally deprived children. However, because the funds were ultimately under the control of local school districts they were frequently diverted to other purposes. The Higher Education Act of 1965 established a scholarship and low-interest loan program for financially needy college students and library grants to colleges and universities. The Immigration Act of 1965 eliminated the discriminatory quotas designed to exclude certain national groups, or to admit them on a restricted basis, that had been in effect for 40 years and reaffirmed just 13 years earlier.

As life expectancy increased, resulting in growth of the elderly population that continues to the present day, provisions for caring for the elderly became more critical. Elderly persons worried about this, as did their children, whose houses and urban apartments did not have space for additional dwellers and whose incomes were typically not sufficient to provide for institutional care. After the Democratic landslide in the 1964 election, sentiment for new laws providing for medical care for the elderly enabled those who backed them to surmount the opposition, including that of the American Medical Association.

President Lyndon Johnson signs the 1965 Medicare Act into law while former President Harry Truman, a strong advocate of national health care programs, looks on, July 30, 1965. © Lyndon B. Johnson Library.

The Medicare program enacted by Congress in 1965 provided insurance to cover most hospital charges, diagnostic tests, home visits, and in some instances nursing home costs for the elderly. Participants in Medicare could volunteer to purchase supplementary coverage, subsidized by the government, to take care of other medical expenses, including visits to doctors' offices. Prescription drugs, eyeglasses, and hearing aids were not covered. At the end of Medicare's first year of operation, approximately 17.7 million elderly persons (93% of those eligible) enrolled in the voluntary medical insurance program. Also included in the Medicare bill were funds for nursing schools, medical schools, and medical student scholarships, all intended to train personnel to provide health care services.

The Social Security Act of 1935 was the first step toward providing the elderly with means to be cared for by others if they were unable to care for themselves. Sometimes the care was given in not-for-profit nursing homes. The more extensive benefits provided through Medicaid—a companion program to Medicare that provided funding to states to pay for medical care of the poor of all ages—quickly spawned a lucrative for-profit industry. Nursing homes, one observer noted, "changed from a family enterprise to big business. Major corporations, including several hotel/motel chains, purchased large numbers of facilities and nursing home issues became the hottest item on the stock exchange." Between 1960 and 1976, nursing homes increased in number from under 10,000 to 23,000; the number of residents more than tripled, to one million. The number of employees increased during this period from 100,000 to 650,000. Impressive though these numbers are, they do not compare in magnitude with the 2,000 percent increase in revenues received by the industry. Almost 60 percent of the more than $10 billion in revenues was paid by taxpayers through Medicare and Medicaid. While these numbers were all skyrocketing, the population of senior citizens increased by only 23 percent.

Who were the grandpas and grandmas in nursing homes? In the mid-1960s they were moving toward the profile that existed a decade later: more than 70 percent were over 70 years of age; women outnumbered men by 3 to 1; 63 percent were widowed, 22 percent had never married, 5 percent were divorced; only 1 in 10 had a living spouse. In fact, many residents were *not* grandpas and grandmas; more than 50 percent had no close relatives. More than 60 percent had no visitors at all. Fewer than 50 percent were able to walk. The average stay in nursing homes was 2.4 years, and only 20 percent of the residents ever returned to their homes. The vast majority died in the nursing homes, with a small number succumbing in hospitals.

Such a profile means that in addition to worries over health and finances and fear of being a burden to others, many elderly people lived in dread of having to move to a place other than their own home. "It is a time of no tomorrows," wrote former senator Frank Moss in 1977, "a time of no hope. Death lurks like a mugger in a dark alley. The elderly await the inevitable, when they are reduced to the simple act of breathing and eating—and less."

An initial appropriation of $6.5 billion got Medicare started, and increased Social Security payroll deductions were to provide for its long-term funding. However, Medicare and Medicaid planners underestimated the rate at which increases in doctors' fees and hospital charges, as well as the longer lives of the elderly, would create spiraling costs.

To celebrate the enactment of Medicare, President Johnson traveled to Independence, Missouri, where he signed the new bill into law in former president Truman's presence. Truman then became the first person to hold a Medicare card. What the two presidents celebrated, however, was a limited victory, for the American Medical Association had succeeded in restricting Medicare to bill-paying functions. The government had virtually no role in redesigning health care systems or controlling costs. By the 1990s, with expenditures for both Medicare and Medicaid having multiplied more than 10-fold, problems continued that might have been dealt with better when the programs were first created.

Programs in the War on Poverty had significant effects on the daily lives of millions of beneficiaries and benefit providers, even though they received only modest funding. The proportion of Americans recorded as being below the federal poverty line dropped from 20 to 13 percent between 1963 and 1968, and the ratio of African Americans living in poverty declined from 40 percent in 1960 to half that figure in 1968, but the problems of poverty remained daunting.

In attempting to account for the bursts of optimism that inspired the War on Poverty and public confidence in it, it is useful to reflect on the words of Lyndon Johnson, the war's mastermind. Speaking to Howard University students on June 4, 1965, Johnson laid out his vision for America, and particularly for the black students he was addressing. Members of their race were disproportionately represented among the poor, and he was sensitive to their circumstances. The breakdown of the family, President Johnson said, flowing from "the long years of degradation and discrimination, which have attacked [the Negro man's] dignity and assaulted his ability to produce for his family," was the main cause. So strengthening families was essential. To accomplish this and to solve all the other problems society faced, Johnson said, there was no single easy answer. Jobs were part of it, as were decent homes, welfare and social programs, and care for the sick. But another part of the answer is what moved President Johnson: "An understanding heart by all Americans" (Marty, 44–49).

To read about government in the United States in the 19th century, see the United States entries in the section "Government and Politics" in chapter 6 ("Political Life") in volume 5 of this series.

FOR MORE INFORMATION

American Memory. <http://lcweb2.loc.gov/ammem/>.

Marty, M. A. *Daily Life in the United States, 1960–1990: Decades of Discord.* Westport, Conn.: Greenwood Press, 1997.

Pakula, D., dir. *All the President's Men.* 1976.

Patterson, J. T. *Grand Expectations: The United States, 1945–1974.* New York: Oxford University Press, 1996.

POLITICAL LIFE
|
GOVERNMENT
|
United States,
1920-1939

United States,
1940-1959

United States,
1960-1990

Latin America

India

Islamic World

Soviet Union

Japan

Inuit

LATIN AMERICA

During the 20th century, extreme political tensions erupted throughout Latin America, as authoritarian legacies of previous centuries collided with creative attempts at change. The traditional political order began to ebb by the 1930s, at which time multiple new efforts developed, with various parties, movements, and political leadership styles appearing throughout the region. Regardless of the short-term results of individual endeavors, by the end of the century, state systems were much more complex, and more strata of Latin American societies participated in political life.

At the turn of the 20th century, the independent republics of Latin America embraced a liberal conception of the state and endorsed constitutional law. Yet the political system was highly exclusionary. Public power and authority emanated from nonstate sources such as land ownership, family lineage, and financial standing. Thus, a tiny elite of oligarchs and *caudillos* (military strongmen, often leaders of the landed elite) dictated as desired to the majority of the population and ensured that state apparatus functioned in accordance with their objectives.

By the 1930s, however, a variety of internal and external factors converged to significantly weaken the old exclusionary system. New groups emerged; proletarian classes, women, and students, for example, began pressuring elite politicians to expand privileges and rights. In some instances, elites conceded—as with women's suffrage. Yet, in general, elites showed themselves unable or unwilling to accommodate on broader scales or to address long-standing societal problems such as poverty. Frustrations mounted, and people lost faith in their traditional leaders and political systems. Multiple external factors simply exacerbated the sense of frustration, including the pressures of modernization, which increased as Latin America became more integrated into the world market system, and the Great Depression as well as other smaller shifts in international economic health. Also instructive was the revolution in Mexico (1910–17), followed by radical postwar reforms, and the Russian Revolution (1917) and the subsequent regimes of Lenin and Stalin.

The era from the 1930s to the 1950s introduced new political contenders ready to address old societal problems. In countries such as Argentina, Brazil, and Uruguay, radical groups including communists and anarchists pushed for revolutionary change and gained footholds among the most disenfranchised populations. More moderate groups sought nonrevolutionary reform and redistribution of wealth through democratic means. The Social Democrats and Christian Democrats, for example, succeeded in drawing support from wide cross-sections of Chilean, Venezuelan, and many Central American and Caribbean societies.

Populism also flourished during this period. New and highly charismatic leaders catered to national groups previously dismissed by politicians. With promises of democratic solutions to long-standing economic and social problems, populists such as Brazil's Getulio Vargas (1930–45), Mexico's Lázaro Cárdenas (1934–40), and Argentina's Juan Perón (1946–55) gained the support of large masses of urban working and middle-class constituents, took the presidential seats of their respective countries, and introduced nationwide reforms.

Through midcentury, then, as the old system disintegrated, newly developed political parties representing an expanded electorate enjoyed various successes. At the same time, Latin American states entered into a remarkable process of state organization and modernization. Administrations and bureaucracies grew, and previously distant regions became integrated into national territories. These stronger, more capable states often intervened directly in social and economic spheres, as when promoting industrialization, for example.

Rhetoric and aspirations outpaced concrete change, however, and the 1960s brought a major shift in direction. With the success of the Cuban Revolution in 1959 and the onset of the cold war, many Latin American leaders responded with

Latin America 1892

land over 1000 ft
land over 5000 ft

Caribbean Sea

PANAMA

Caracas

VENEZUELA
Llanos

BRITISH
GUIANA

DUTCH GUIANA
FRENCH GUIANA

Bogatá

UNITED STATES
OF COLOMBIA

Quito

EQUADOR

Negro

Belém

Manaus

Amazon

Fortaleza

A m a z o n i a

Natal

B R A Z I L

Recife

Xingu

Araguaia

PERU

San Francisco

Lima

A
n
d
e
s

La Paz

BOLIVIA

Mato Grosso

Salvador

Arica

G
r
a
n

C
h
a
c
o

Paraná

PARAGUAY

São Paulo

Rio de Janeiro

Asunción

Tropic of Capricorn

PACIFIC
OCEAN

P
a
m
p
a
s

ARGENTINA

CHILE

Porto Alegre

*Juan
Fernandez
(Chile)*

Santiago

Valparaiso

URAGUAY

Buenos Aires

Montevideo

La Plata

Bàhia Blaca

ATLANTIC
OCEAN

P
a
t
a
g
o
n
i
a

Falkland
Islands
(British)

Tierra
de Fuego

severity to the real and perceived threats posed by communism and other opposition movements. In the Southern Cone, for example, a chain of coups d'état occurred: Argentina in 1962, Brazil in 1964, Chile in 1973, Uruguay in 1974.

These and other coups ushered in long-term military dictatorships and bureaucratic authoritarian systems that resembled the authoritarian ways of times past. Regimes demanded strict order in all realms of society. Indeed, they adopted doctrines of "national security," enabling them to systematically repress any and all opposition within their countries. Often, they successfully neutralized internal dissent and disorder, but at the cost of tens of thousands of civilian lives.

Despite the harsh repression experienced by many Latin Americans, leftist revolutionary movements continued to expand throughout the latter half of the century and in some locations even came to power. Nicaragua's FSLN (Sandinista National Liberation Front) struggled through the 1970s and finally triumphed in 1979. (They continued in power until 1990, when they lost national elections.) Urban guerrilla groups appeared throughout Latin America, such as the Tupamaros in Uruguay and the Montoneros of Argentina. In Colombia, Guatemala, Peru, and El Salvador, civil wars raged between leftist politicomilitary organizations supported by broad civilian coalitions, and national militaries supported by right-wing paramilitaries and, in some instances, even death squads.

Many countries—including those of the Southern Cone—returned to civilian and democratic rule in the 1980s and 1990s. Throughout Latin America, as countries struggled for peaceful reconciliation, groups in opposition to one another signed peace accords and official truth commissions reported on human rights abuses committed during periods of repression.

Despite these efforts, the end of the century was not kind to most Latin American nations. Most countries suffered from extreme debt and inflation, worsened by economic recession. To service their debts, governments accepted assistance from international lending agencies, such as the International Monetary Fund and the World Bank. In so doing, however, governments were required to impose austerity measures, reversing many social welfare policies. At the same time that social spending fell to record lows, corruption soared in official circles. In fact, public anger about maladministration led to criminal charges against individual leaders or the ouster of whole governments in Brazil, Venezuela, Mexico, and Peru.

By the end of the century, Latin American governments faced multiple economic and social challenges, many of them related to the legacies of previous centuries. Despite shifts toward more democratic rule, governments continued to lack credibility among their populations. They still had not adequately addressed continuing problems of inequality and poverty, which meant that large sectors of the population continued to adopt desperate and sometimes violent measures in an effort to survive—as in Colombia, where a protracted civil war neared its fourth decade.

To read about government in 19th-century Latin America, see the Latin America entry in the section "Government and Politics" in chapter 6 ("Political Life") in volume 5 of this series.

~Molly Todd

FOR MORE INFORMATION

Argentina Comision Nacional sobre la Desaparicio de Personas. *Nunca Mas: The Report of the Argentine National Commission on the Disappeared with an Introduction by Ronald Dworkin.* New York: Farrar, Straus, Giroux, 1986.

Bazant, J. *A Concise History of Mexico from Hidalgo to Cárdenas, 1805–1940.* New York: Cambridge University Press, 1977.

Safford, F. *Colombia: Fragmented Land, Divided Society.* New York: Oxford University Press, 2002.

INDIA

For centuries, different kings and sultans governed India. These were autocratic monarchies where the majority of the people had little say in their government. Some venues existed, however, in which everyday people could approach the ruler and make a request, file a complaint, or otherwise be heard. For example, the Mughal rulers held daily meetings (*durbars*) during which locals could approach the emperor and state their cases. During India's colonial period, some of this informal intercourse continued, but under British rule, concepts of sovereignty and democracy were slowly introduced.

In 1885, a group of wealthy men, mostly lawyers and businessmen, formed the Indian National Congress. Indians convened this body to petition the British authorities for increased participation within the government. However, the Congress was more of a club for elites than a representative organization. This changed with the rise in national prominence of Mahatma Gandhi. Gandhi, who had been experimenting with different forms of political activism in South Africa, returned to India in 1919. From that time, he began to reform the Congress to make it a mass organization. He lowered the fee for joining, sent Congress members to speak in villages, and employed symbols and strategies that were appealing to more of the population. Gandhi, Jawaharlal Nehru, and the Congress led India's independence movement, and in August 1947, the country emerged from its colonial past as an independent, democratic, secular state.

Nehru became India's first prime minister. The Congress party had won the majority of votes in the heart of India, whereas the Muslim League had won a majority in the eastern and western wings of the subcontinent. Those areas became East and West Pakistan. In Nehru's first decade in office, he implemented an economic and social strategy whereby the government was the caretaker for the majority of the people. He implemented a series of five-year economic plans that focused on industrial development. Nehru felt that India could be lifted from poverty through state-controlled development. Where Gandhi envisioned an India governed by its villages and led by spirituality, Nehru saw India's dams and power plants as its "new temples."

In addition to economic initiatives, Nehru was deeply concerned with holding together India's multitude of ethnic groups. He faced his first serious challenge in the 1950s as several southern states lobbied for a redrawing of the political map along language lines. For example, Telugu speakers were divided between the old

Madras presidency and Hyderabad state. They wanted a state that was drawn along Telugu language lines. In 1956, Nehru agreed, and the map of India changed dramatically to reflect the wealth of language groups. Telugu speakers formed the state of Andhra Pradesh; Tamil speakers formed the state of Tamil Nadu, and so forth.

India surmounted the transition of power after Nehru's death in 1964, and after the administration of Lal Bahadur Shastri, Nehru's daughter Indira Gandhi was elected in 1966. Indira won the fifth general election in 1971, but a few years later her administration ran into trouble. Charges of vote tampering arose, and the legitimacy of her electoral victory came under scrutiny. Faced with losing power, Indira instituted India's only departure from democracy in 1975 when she declared a state of emergency. Under the emergency, the constitution was suspended, political opposition leaders were jailed without cause, and draconian social improvement schemes were enacted, including slum clearances and forced vasectomies. In 1977 the emergency was lifted, and Indira was voted out of office. She was followed by Morarji Desai and then reelected in 1980, serving until her assassination in 1984.

By the late 1970s and early 1980s, India faced a growing population problem that strained the government's ability to effectively administer the country. With a growing population, competition for jobs increased, leading to a growth in corruption. Because the government was a major employer for the country, corruption increasingly eroded its credibility. The bureaucracy grew bloated and inefficient. A government job was usually a permanent appointment, and thus inept employees were difficult to remove. Further, as the government limited competition, there was little or no incentive to operate efficiently.

Nowadays, the railway system in India is the country's largest employer. A position in the railway guarantees a regular salary, some benefits, and a pension. The railway and other government organizations also reserve a certain number of positions for India's traditionally oppressed castes and classes. This reservation system also applies to elected positions, whereby a certain number of seats are reserved for women and other recognized groups. These rights are embedded in India's constitution, drafted by Dr. B. R. Ambedkar (himself an untouchable, or *dalit*). Unlike America's constitution, which is short and difficult to amend, the Indian constitution is lengthy and easier to amend. Though it has served the diversity of the country quite well, its format has led to many changes and squabbles over new amendments, thus somewhat undermining India's stability at times.

By the 1990s India's claim to be a secular democracy was in trouble. Beginning with Indira Gandhi and extending to current political leaders, the combination of politics and religion has been used with deadly effectiveness. In 1992 the Hindu nationalist BJP (Bharatiya Janata Party) stirred emotions as they used symbols from India's epics (the *Ramayana* and *Mahabharata*) to make political gains. Some of the party's leaders dressed as gods and rode "chariots" that were really Toyota trucks. The climax came on December 6, 1992, when members of the BJP and other right-wing Hindu groups attacked and demolished a mosque as Congress leaders ineffectively protested. BJP leaders cheered on the riotous crowds. India's Muslims rightly felt threatened, and India's claim to being secular and protecting the interest of *all* its minority groups now rang hollow.

Although India has faced challenges to its democratic foundations, it has also remained remarkably resilient in the face of great challenges. Elections have regularly and peacefully occurred, and a myriad of political parties zealously enjoy the practice of politics. Throughout the country, late at night when groups of men huddle over small fires to keep warm, frequently they are not discussing women or gossip, but instead are debating politics. As long as this freedom remains, India's position as the world's largest democracy is in little jeopardy.

To read about government in ancient India, see the India entry in the section "Government" in chapter 6 ("Political Life") in volume 1 of this series.

~*Benjamin Cohen*

FOR MORE INFORMATION

Brass, P. R. *The Politics of India Since Independence*. 2d ed. Cambridge: Cambridge University Press, 1994.

Cohen, S. P. *India: Emerging Power*. Washington, D.C.: Brookings, 2001.

Khilnani, S. *The Idea of India*. New York: Farrar Straus Giroux, 1997.

Mistry, R. *A Fine Balance*. New York: Knopf, 2001.

POLITICAL LIFE

GOVERNMENT

United States,
1920-1939

United States,
1940-1959

United States,
1960-1990

Latin America

India

Islamic World

Soviet Union

Japan

Inuit

ISLAMIC WORLD

The Islamic world spans a vast amount of territory, from southeast Asia to northern Africa. After the collapse of the Ottoman Empire and the end of the European colonial mandate in the 20th century, many areas of the Islamic world faced the challenging task of building an entirely new social and political infrastructure. This monumental endeavor was further complicated by issues such as local ethnic rivalries and pressure from economically ambitious foreign governments.

One Islamic country that formulated a variety of responses to modernity is Iran. The Islamic Republic of Iran is located in southwest Asia, bordering the Persian Gulf. Iran is not an Arab country; it has a distinctive linguistic and cultural heritage that sets it apart from its neighbor Iraq. The official language of Iran is Persian, also know as Farsi, which is an Indo-European language. Whereas much of the Islamic world practices a form of Islam called Sunnism, most Iranians practice Shi'ite Islam. Shi'ite Islam began in the seventh century C.E. as the result of a dispute over who should lead the early Islamic community. Shi'ite Muslims give their allegiance to the family of the Prophet Muhammad and his relatives Ali, Fatima, and their sons Hassan and Husayn. Though Iran is a predominantly Muslim country, it also contains some religious minority groups such as Christian, Jews, and Zoroastrians.

At the beginning of World War II (1939–45), Iran was ruled by a dictatorial leader named Reza Shah Pahlavi (1877–1944). Reza Shah was a popular figure during his early tenure in Iran because he seized a large portion of Soviet-controlled Iranian land in a dramatic coup d'état in 1921. However, the Iranian people soon tired of his domineering leadership style. He employed repressive measures such as censorship of the press, autocratic reforms, and a series of Westernization campaigns that did not take into consideration the social and cultural traditions of his people.

In 1941 Great Britain and the Soviet Union invaded Iran, ostensibly because Reza Shah refused to expel a group of German nationals from the country. Many Iranian people suspected that the underlying motive for this invasion was colonial ambition on the part of England and the USSR. The two countries quickly defeated Reza Shah's army, arrested Reza Shah, and sent him into exile. After a brief period of military rule, they installed Reza Shah Pahlavi's son, Muhammad Reza Shah Pahlavi, as the new ruler of Iran. Many Iranian people accused Muhammad Reza Shah of being a puppet ruler. Muhammad Reza Shah dealt with his critics harshly. Many of his political enemies disappeared in the middle of the night, never to be seen again. His secret police force, SAVAK, was widely feared by the Iranian people.

Between 1963 and 1978, Muhammad Reza Shah continued his father's campaign of Westernization and industrialization in Iran. By modernizing Iran, the Pahlavi regime was attempting to gain greater control over the population. Sociologist M. Salehi points out that the Shah's government was trying to develop a political power structure wherein the Iranian people would not be able to exercise any form of resistance. "Political development in such a regime did not have the same meaning as it typically had for social scientists. From the point of view of the oppressors it meant the formation and articulation of machinery that could force people to act on demand. It included the anticipation that people would eventually develop the desired habits and adjust to the point where they would show no resistance" (Salehi, 27). Reza Shah attempted to control every aspect of people's everyday lives, even down to regulating what they should wear.

One of Muhammad Reza Shah's most controversial reforms was the abolition of the Iranian *chador* (a long black cloak for women that covered the whole body, including the hair). He told women that they had to adapt to Western modes of dress. Many traditional women, especially those from the older generation, refused to leave their homes because of this new law.

One of the main opponents of Muhammad Reza Shah's campaign of Westernization and modernization was the Shi'ite religious leader, Ruhollah Khomeini (1900?–89). Khomeini was a traditionally educated Ayatollah, a title reserved for respected scholars of Islamic jurisprudence. In addition to his credentials as a man of God, Ayatollah Ruhollah Khomeini had a reputation for political activism. He was an outspoken critic of Muhammad Reza Shah. Some of Khomeini's staunchest supporters were students. These students had grown up under Muhammad Reza Shah's repressive regime and were open to Khomeini's call for an Islamic revolution in Iran. Through a return to traditional Islamic values, these students hoped that they would be able to restore peace and prosperity to Iran.

Fearing that Khomeini would become a martyr if he was killed, the Shah of Iran deported him in 1964. From exile, Khomeini led an aggressive campaign to topple Muhammad Reza Shah from power and install an Islamic government in Iran. Enlisting the support of Iranian students, Khomeini was able to spread his revolutionary Islamic message throughout Iran. His words reached an even greater audience in 1971 when his radical pro-revolutionary treatise, *Velayat-e faqih*, was published. Khomeini used modern technology to launch one of his most successful propaganda campaigns. He recorded a number of sermons on audiotapes and released them to the Iranian public. This way, even illiterate people were able to hear his message.

In 1978 the Iranian revolution was touched off by a series of student demonstrations. Muhammad Reza Shah tried to suppress these demonstrations, and riots ensued. Sensing that he was rapidly losing control of his country, Muhammad Reza Shah left Iran for the United States in 1979. The same year, the Iranian people voted overwhelmingly for the establishment of the new Islamic Republic of Iran. Fearing for their lives, many supporters of the Shah—secularist, Westernized elites, intellectuals, and others—fled their homeland. Some who did not escape were executed. Now the supreme political and religious authority in Iran, Khomeini continued to engage in Islamist and anti-Western rhetoric. Khomeini's disdain for the West was manifested by the hostage crisis of 1979. A group of pro-Khomeini Iranian students stormed the American embassy in Tehran, captured 66 Americans, and held them as hostages. The students were protesting the fact that the United States granted asylum to Muhammad Reza Shah. The hostage crisis was a major diplomatic challenge for the United States; it took over 15 months of negotiations before the situation was finally resolved.

Many countries in the 20th century Islamic world struggled with challenges similar to those of Iran. Although some rulers such as Muhammad Reza Shah believed that Westernization was synonymous with progress, this idea was often at odds with traditional Islamic values. The message of leaders like the Ayatollah Ruhollah Khomeini appealed to people because it emphasized their religious and cultural heritage and gave them hope for the future.

To read about government in the Islamic Ottoman Empire in the 15th and 16th centuries, see the Ottoman Empire entry in the section "Government" in chapter 6 ("Political Life") in volume 3 of this series.

~*Molly Benjamin Patterson*

POLITICAL LIFE
|
GOVERNMENT
|

FOR MORE INFORMATION

Esposito, J., ed. *The Iranian Revolution: Its Global Impact.* Miami: University of Florida Press, 1990.

Farman-Farmaian, S. *Daughter of Persia: A Woman's Journey from Her Father's Harem Through the Islamic Revolution.* New York: Anchor Books/Doubleday, 1992.

Salehi, M. M. *Insurgency through Culture and Religion: The Islamic Revolution of Iran.* New York: Prager, 1988.

SOVIET UNION

The Communist Party created the Soviet government. One of Lenin's first actions after the Bolsheviks took power in 1917 was to set up a governing council of ministers, called commissars, of which he was chairman. All were Party members. This structure remained essentially unchanged during the history of the USSR. Top Party officials held top government positions. Important policies were handed down from the highest Party authorities: the Secretariat and its General Secretary, Politburo, and Central Committee. Thus a tiny group of men were the sole source of legislation, and state institutions existed to carry out their decisions. Moreover, very many regulations that directly affected people's lives were fashioned not by any legislative process but by decrees, put in place or withdrawn as the leaders willed.

USSR constitutions recognized freedom of speech, religion, the press, and assembly (as long as they served to "strengthen socialist reality") and proclaimed the inviolability of the home. Through its police powers, however, the regime dictated if, when, and to what extent people could enjoy their promised civil liberties. In May 1970, when police, without a warrant, forced their way into the home of biologist Zhores Medvedev, he reminded them that they were barging into "a private apartment," but the police sergeant retorted, "It belongs to the State. . . . and the police have the right to enter any apartment." Any activities the authorities interpreted as subversive of their own power were labeled seditious and the offenders punished, often harshly. Persecution of ordinary people was most severe in the Stalin era, but anyone at any time could be turned into a political criminal, because all crimes could be interpreted as crimes against the state: grand and petty theft, negligence in the workplace, arson, attempts to emigrate or publish abroad, and so on. Under Stalin, millions of people who had not committed any crimes were "repressed" and "liquidated." Against such injustices the public had no legal recourse because the Soviet constitution did not provide people adequate means to enforce constitutional rights through the courts. The secret police had wide authority to interrogate, torture, judge, and punish alleged criminals. Stalin's secret police (the NKVD) was the only governmental agency independent of the Party. All other Soviet organizations were subordinate to the Party, but the NKVD chief reported directly to Stalin.

After Stalin's death, the Party leadership decided to rein in the power of the secret police, though that agency remained a vigorous and useful means of control. Through its own apparatus as well as through its militia (ordinary police), subdivisions, and informants, the political police never ceased to watch, harass, and intrude on the private lives of Soviet citizens. The rest of the repressive process was left to a judicial system heavily weighted against defendants. Russian prosecutors could (and still can) overturn a court's decision.

The lowest court, which heard most trials, was called the people's court; it consisted of two lay assessors chosen from the general population and a professional judge. The judge and assessors listened to the prosecutor's and defense attorney's arguments during the trial, determined guilt or innocence, and pronounced sentence. Between the people's court at the bottom and the Supreme Court at the top were territorial, regional, and republic courts, which heard appeals from lower courts. Even though the Supreme Court was the highest court in the land, it had little real authority; it could not decide whether laws were constitutional, interpret laws, or throw laws out.

Most law enforcement and judicial workers, including militia, judges, procurators (assigned to oversee government agencies to make sure they acted within the law),

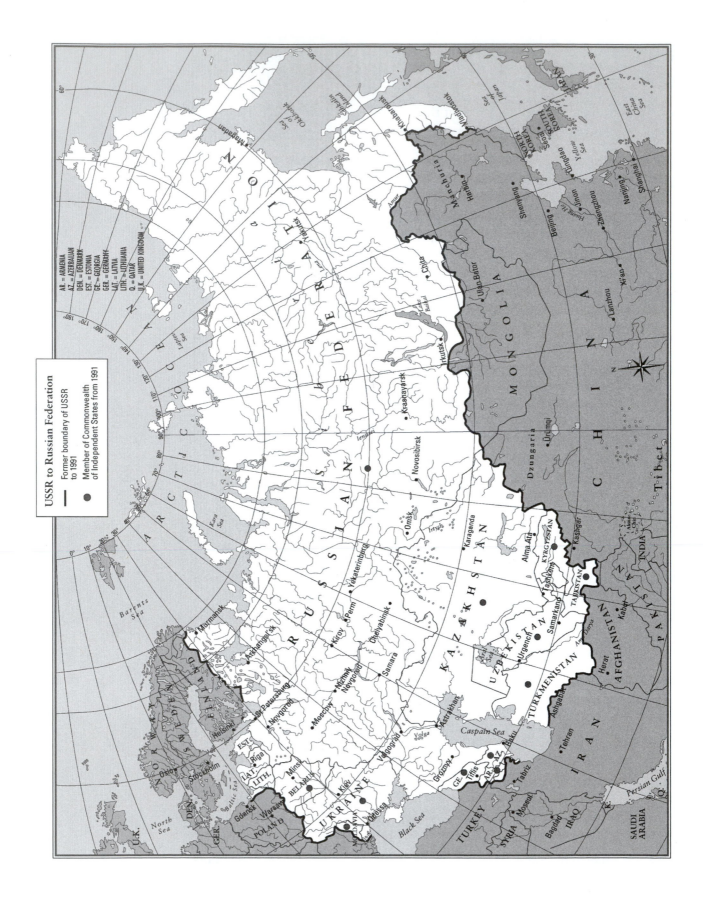

USSR to Russian Federation

Former boundary of USSR to 1991

Member of Commonwealth of Independent States from 1991

AR. = ARMENIA
AZ. = AZERBAIJAN
DEN. = DENMARK
EST. = ESTONIA
GE. = GEORGIA
GER. = GERMANY
LAT. = LATVIA
LITH. = LITHUANIA
Q. = QATAR
U.K. = UNITED KINGDOM

and detectives, were poorly paid and in the early years of the Union likely to be poorly educated, sometimes even illiterate. Professional training for these officials was gradually upgraded, but the best trained among them tended to be concentrated in the larger cities. Their low pay undoubtedly contributed to widespread unprofessional behavior, such as accepting bribes in money and consumer goods and public drunkenness.

Defense lawyers enjoyed a peculiar situation in Soviet life because they were not state employees and did not belong to a government-supported trade union. Instead, the union they were required to join was the relatively independent, self-supporting College of Advocates, about half of whose membership was women, which suggests the lowly status of the profession in the eyes of the government. The state could dictate the expulsion of a member for political reasons, and if that happened it was the end of an attorney's career. Although the government severely capped the fees that defense attorneys could charge clients, nearly all advocates accepted additional money under the table, especially in criminal cases. By accepting extra payments, a hardworking, talented lawyer could become prosperous. An ordinary criminal or client in a civil case was free to choose any defense lawyer from any part of the Soviet Union. Political prisoners, however, had to select from a list of attorneys approved by the secret police; non-Party lawyers were rarely allowed access to political prisoners. In a civil case, lawyers could assist clients from the beginning of a case to its end, but in a criminal matter, attorneys could not consult with clients until the state's preliminary investigation was finished. A client conferring with his attorney in a law office would most likely find himself in a shabby, airless, dimly lit, overcrowded room with no privacy. It was not until the late 1970s and early 1980s that the government began to allot Moscow lawyers more comfortable facilities and even private space for lawyer–client meetings. Under Stalin, defense counsel was not allowed for those accused of espionage, sabotage, or terrorism, and with the exception of show trials, such defendants were tried behind closed doors. To the end of the Soviet period, the outcome of trials of dissidents was determined by Party policy rather than evidence.

Comrades' courts, composed of workers, peasants, or both, were established on all farms, in factories, and in larger apartment complexes. Their main purpose was to control and prevent work-related misbehavior such as drunkenness on the job, lateness, or negligence by shaming the worker in front of family, friends, neighbors, and coworkers. Comrades' courts could also look into neighborhood and family problems. Punishments ranged from a small fine to a recommendation that the defendant be fired.

The Party was structured like a pyramid. At its base were the local cells, or PPOs (primary Party organizations) attached to workplaces. A PPO might have as few as three members, or (in the case of large industrial enterprises) hundreds. The PPO met once per month; its members were expected to recruit new members, carry out educational work, strive tirelessly for quality control in the workplace, and in general promote Party loyalty and uphold Party moral code. The next step up the pyramid was the city or county congress, composed of the local PPOs. That congress was subordinate to the provincial congress. The next level in the hierarchy was the Party congress for the individual republic. The peak of the pyramid was the All-Union Party Congress, which met annually until 1925. After that year it convened less regularly, with a 13-year gap between the 18th and 19th congresses (1939, 1952). After Stalin died, it met at least every five years; the most famous was the first post-Stalin 20th Congress (1956), in which the new Party chief, Nikita Khrushchev, in a "secret" speech vigorously condemned some of Stalin's crimes. The last All-Union Party Congress, the 28th, was held in 1990. The All-Union Party Congress had the appearance of representative government, but its main function was to rubber-stamp policies that had been fashioned at the highest levels.

Communist Party members were never more than about 10 percent of the population.

At each step up the pyramid, Party members elected representatives to the next higher level; those remaining below were expected to be subservient to orders from above. The most important local Party officials were not elected by representatives, however. They were directly appointed by the Central Committee. Delegates to the All-Union Party Congress chose members and candidate-members of the Central Committee. A candidate-member could not vote but might be selected as a full member when a place became vacant. The Central Committee was composed of Party leaders. In 1919, the Central Committee created out of itself three new committees: a Political Bureau, or Politburo (from 1952 to 1966 it was called the Presidium); an Organizational Bureau, or Orgburo (to 1952); and a Secretariat chosen by Politburo members.

The Politburo, the Party's highest policy-making and executive body, consisted of the most powerful members of the Party and was presided over by a secretary-general (called the First Secretary, 1953–85). Behind closed doors, it dealt with the nation's most pressing problems and created Party policies. The Orgburo met three times a week and reported to the Central Committee every two weeks. At first, it had as its responsibility the organizational and secretarial work of the Party. Stalin, the only one among the first Orgburo members to also be a member of the Politburo, made the Orgburo into his own power base. Through its powerful subcommittee of Records and Assignments the Secretariat directly and indirectly controlled all important Party appointments and supervised the whole Party network, a responsibility that Stalin, who was also on this committee, was able to assign to himself. Records and Assignments transmitted the Central Committee's orders to all lower Party organizations and determined whether those orders were carried out.

The number of Party members varied but was never more than about 10 percent of the population and consisted mostly of Russian male professionals. Not everyone who applied was accepted; not everyone wanted to belong. Party dues operated on a sliding scale depending on a member's income. Once admitted to the Party, members were expected to adhere to "Party discipline," which meant faithfully and unquestioningly carrying out directives handed down from above. From the 1920s to Stalin's death, members accused of defying Party policy faced expulsion from the Party, often followed by unemployment; arrest; imprisonment; and, during the Great Terror (1936–38), execution. Although the consequences of expulsion were not so dire after Stalin, being forced out of the Party could still result in the loss of important special privileges (travel, vacation, shopping, and health care), unemployment, and other deprivations. In any case, because the Party or its General Secretary controlled the police as well as all other aspects of government and law, everyone, member or not, submitted to Party dictates.

The 1924 constitution, the first constitution of the Soviet Union, proclaimed the sovereignty, equality, and independence of each constituent republic and, theoretically, gave republics the right to secede. In reality, Stalin was already moving quickly to stamp out any independence movements within the non-Russian republics. People who lived in the constituent republics were citizens of the Union rather than of individual republics. As in the pre-Soviet (RSFSR) constitution of July 1918, one worker's vote equaled five peasants' votes, whereas certain classes of citizens such as priests, nobles, and businesspeople, called exploiters, were denied the vote and civil rights altogether. The all-powerful Communist (Bolshevik) Party was not mentioned. Another omnipresent source of hardcore power not mentioned in the pre-Soviet constitution was the Vecheka—the secret police—but the 1924 constitution specifically provided for a centralized secret police agency (by that time known by its initials, OGPU). In addition to the secret police, the Union of Soviet Socialist Republics controlled defense, foreign relations, the economy, transportation, communications, education, public health, and the justice system. Everything else was left to the republics. There was no secret ballot. Direct elections occurred only locally—each next higher soviet (district, province, republic, union)—was elected by the level just below it. The constitution also guaranteed freedom of speech, a pleasure that nevertheless remained unknown in the Soviet Union.

Adoption of the constitution of 1936 (the Stalin Constitution), rich with declarations of universal voting rights and other basic liberties, coincided with one of the worst periods of terror in Soviet Union history. In June 1936, high Party officials who would soon be shot as traitors completed a draft of the new fundamental law. Its first chapter declared the USSR to be a "socialist state of workers and peasants" and that the land; its mineral wealth, waters, and forests; the factories and mines; rail, water, and air transport facilities; the banks; means of communication; large state-organized agricultural enterprises (state farms, machine and tractor stations, etc.); as well as municipal enterprises and the bulk of the dwelling houses in the cities and industrial localities were state property—that is, they belonged to the whole people.

Some land was designated as the permanent "socialist property" of collective and cooperative farms. This property included "livestock, buildings, implements, and output." Each peasant family could privately farm a small plot of land and possess a limited number of livestock and small tools. All citizens had the right to own and inherit "articles of household and . . . personal use and convenience" and a home.

The 1936 constitution also declared that all citizens had the right to education and gender equality, including equal pay for equal work and fully paid maternity leave (paternity leave was not mentioned); a "wide network of maternity homes, nurseries and kindergartens"; "rest and leisure"; employment; and financial support in old age and illness. As with civil liberties, these prerogatives in reality depended on the wishes and interests of Party authorities. Neither a republic nor an individual could challenge a law or the lack of an entitlement on the grounds that a constitutional right was being violated. Laws were often passed that conflicted with citizens' rights, or rights were trampled without any legal formalities. People with complaints could appeal to procurators or pursue other channels of appeal, and they might get satisfaction if the grievance did not conflict with Party policy. Although the constitution proclaimed an independent judiciary, all judges were in the Party's service. People caught in Stalin's net had no effective legal recourse. Some wrote letters of protest directly to him, the very perpetrator of their misery. Political prisoners were usually tried under special procedures designed to quickly process a predetermined sentence.

The Stalin constitution guaranteed a right of asylum for persecuted foreigners, but this too was an empty promise for hundreds of devoted communists and other European antifascists who fled to the Soviet Union only to be arrested as spies during Stalin's regime. Many of them were executed or died from the effects of their imprisonment. When she arrived at Moscow's Butyrki prison in 1939, Evgenia Ginzburg was thrown into a cell with women communists from Latvia, Germany, Italy, and China. One of the German women had been tortured by, and escaped from, the Gestapo, only to be arrested in Russia and tortured again.

The Brezhnev constitution of 1977 did not make any significant changes from the two previous Soviet constitutions. The dictatorship of the Party was reasserted. Citizens were guaranteed equality and basic human rights, with the proviso that they did not have the right to exercise their freedoms to the harm of other citizens or the state. The Party, this constitution declared, would be the only judge of whether such state and individual rights had been infringed.

Governmental structure paralleled that of the Party. Generally, the higher one's place in the Party, the higher one's place in the national government (USSR), and by the mid-1920s, only Party members held top jobs in the governments of individual republics.

The 1924 constitution allowed citizens to directly elect soviet members only on a local level, but after 1936, federal, republic, and local governments were composed of directly elected soviets. Nominations for office had to be approved by the Party, although not all nominees were members. The highest governmental body that people could vote for directly was the Supreme Soviet, which was divided into two chambers, the Soviet of the Union and the Soviet of Nationalities, each with around 600 deputies. Soviet Union deputies were elected directly by all voters, whereas deputies of the Soviet of Nationalities were elected by voters of the relevant nationalities. These two soviets, which met briefly twice a year, elected the standing committees and members of the Presidium of the Supreme Soviet (before 1936 called the Central Executive Committee). The Presidium made laws, issued decrees, and elected the Council of Ministers (from 1917 to 1946 called the Council of People's Commissars, or Sovnarkom), which was the main executive body of the Soviet government. A 1988 amendment to the 1977 constitution created the Congress of People's Deputies as the highest legislative and executive body. The Congress, whose members had been elected in the first multicandidate (but not multiparty) election in early Soviet times, first met in May 1989 and reorganized the Supreme Soviet.

The constitution of 1936 laid down election principles for the whole USSR. It provided for a secret ballot and universal one-person, one-vote suffrage. All Soviet citizens from age 18 were eligible to vote; any citizen 23 or over could be elected a deputy of the Supreme Soviet, since its members were elected directly, by secret ballot. After 1958 only the mentally ill were denied the vote, but from the 1960s, this group came to include political troublemakers who were identified as mentally ill and imprisoned in special psychiatric hospitals. Voting took place on a Sunday from six A.M. to midnight. Theoretically, Soviet voters were to follow a procedure familiar to U.S. voters. They were to be given a ballot with multiple candidates for each office, enter a booth, cross out names of all candidates except the ones they wanted to vote for, emerge from the booth, and drop their ballot into the ballot box. In fact, the ballot presented only one candidate for each office—there was nothing for Soviet voters to cross out and no particular reason to step inside a voting booth. All they were really expected to do was take a ballot and drop it into the box. If someone actually did go inside the booth, perhaps to cross out a name and write in another, a poll watcher would infer that the voter did not approve of the Party's choice. There could be serious repercussions. Despite the fact that election results were never in doubt, the voter turnout rate was usually close to 100 percent, a statistic Soviet leaders pointed to with pride as evidence of an enthusiastic, participatory grassroots democracy. In reality, just as local Party officials would observe who entered a voting booth, they would also know who did not show up at the polling place. It took courage to walk into a voting booth or stay at home on election day (Eaton).

FOR MORE INFORMATION

Eaton, K. B. *Daily Life in the Soviet Union*. Westport, Conn.: Greenwood Press. Forthcoming.
McClellan, W. *Russia: The Soviet Period and After*. 3d ed. Englewood Cliffs, N.J.: 1994.
Shapiro, L. *The Government and Politics of the Soviet Union*. London: Hutchinson University Library, 1965.

JAPAN

Japan's governmental systems are a curious creative adaptation and syncretism incorporating aspects of Western parliamentary democracy coupled with ancient traditional ideas of communalism and familism. The national government is familiar to Western political scientists because the structure was created by American social reformers who were part of the Allied Occupation of Japan (1945–52) after World War II. Indeed, those reformers wrote the early drafts of the 1947 constitution. Japan has maintained the structure and essence of that system but has tinkered with local forms of government.

Like the American system, Japan's is divided into executive, legislative, and judicial branches, but like the British, Japan's executive cabinet is elected from within the House of Representatives within the legislature (Diet). That house is composed

POLITICAL LIFE

GOVERNMENT

United States,
1920-1939

United States,
1940-1959

United States,
1960-1990

Latin America

India

Islamic World

Soviet Union

Japan

Inuit

of 500 members elected to four-year terms. In accordance with a recent reform, 300 are elected in single-member constituencies; the remaining 200 are elected in 11 multiple-member constituencies allocated by population. Members seldom serve their entire terms because elections can be called at any time by the prime minister so parties may take advantage of favorable political conditions.

The prime minister, who is commonly the president of the majority party or coalition of parties, appoints the cabinet. Half the members of the cabinet must be Diet members. The House initiates legislation. It can override a veto from the upper house by a two-thirds majority. In practice, however, such disagreements are routinely worked out in conferences before such an action becomes necessary. The bureaucracy writes most of the laws anyway, and in typical Japanese fashion, decisions are made long before any voting takes place.

"Super-ministries" such as the Ministry of Finance and the Ministry of Foreign Affairs dominate the cabinet. Until recently the Ministry of International Trade and Industry also wielded disproportional influence and power.

A 252-member House of Councilors operates as a check and balance to the House of Representatives, similar to the U.S. Senate and the British House of Lords. Members are elected for six-year terms by two different methods—152 are elected within prefectures based on population, and the remaining 100 members are elected in national general elections. The idea is to provide transcendent representation for a national constituency; in reality, many of these members are national figures, including movie and music stars who enjoy national fame and notoriety but have little political expertise or experience.

Despite its constitutional independence, the Supreme Court has never really exercised its right to rule on the constitutionality of laws. It therefore has never provided the checks-and-balances on the executive and legislative branches as envisioned by the drafters of the constitution. The court has been criticized for its timidity and the lengthy nature of its deliberations. Thorny issues typically can take decades and even then are not fully resolved. The expectation is that compromise and arbitration will solve most legal issues. Surprisingly, they usually do.

Critics claim that the bureaucracy is the real power in the government. Much smaller in size than its American and British counterparts, the top levels are the real decision makers of the country by virtue of a Byzantine system of extraconstitutional power and influence. Bureaucrats are routinely "lent" to various cabinet ministries, where they commonly draft bills that are ushered through the Diet without much discussion.

In addition, the educational backgrounds of politicians and bureaucrats as well as many employees in Japan's most prestigious private companies are remarkably similar. Most ministries and private companies hire the graduates from the top five or six most important universities. Because the graduates know each other from school, cooperation between and among the various governmental structures is natural.

A more disturbing link between the bureaucracy, the government, and the private sector, however, is called "to descend from heaven" (amaku-dari). This term refers to the common practice whereby high-ranking bureaucrats retire and are immediately hired into the very companies that their former ministries regulate. In America this would be considered influence peddling or even insider trading. In Japan few people seem to mind very much—at least not enough to outlaw the cozy relations between regulators and regulated.

Obviously very little can be done about the disturbing conflict of interest created when children of politicians and industry intermarry. But it happens in Japan to a remarkable degree, due in part to a perpetuation of arranged marriage in the country.

Prefectural assemblies are remarkably similar in structure to the Diet. The most important political parties commonly train young politicians out in the prefectures. Municipal governments are similar enough to facilitate cooperation. At local levels, however, traditional familial relations become more important than in the formalized upper structures. For instance, village and urban wards maintain traditional networks that help to ameliorate the strictures of formal political systems. Guilds, agricultural cooperatives, trade unions, political parties, and religious organizations also help to smooth out the process. Often traditional informal arbitration and compromise networks resolve disagreements without resorting to government. Regional family courts usually iron out personal and low-level wrinkles through arbitration.

Many social scientists have noted that Japan has astoundingly few personal lawsuits as well as an astoundingly high rate of criminal conviction. Both can be attributed in large part to lower-level governmental efforts. Potential lawsuits are avoided by arbitration; miscreants are socially pressured into admitting guilt and entering into some kind of mutually agreeable alternate form of justice.

Critics of Japanese government argue that the system is corrupted by inertia, rigidity, nepotism, cronyism, and a stunning irresponsibility at the top levels. The rank and file, however, pride themselves in their industry and honesty. The government is justly respected by the citizenry and can be said to be the reason the system works as well as it does. Virtually every level of government has a vested interest in maintaining the status quo. If it works, why fix it?

To read about government in early modern Japan, see the Japan entry in the section "Government" in chapter 6 ("Political Life") in volume 4 of this series.

~*Louis G. Perez*

FOR MORE INFORMATION

Foreign Press Center. *The Diet, Elections, and Political Parties.* Tokyo: Foreign Press Center, 1997.

Hitoshi, A., S. Muneyuki, and K. Sadafumi. *The Government and Politics of Japan.* Tokyo: University of Tokyo Press, 1994.

Junji, B. *The Establishment of the Japanese Constitutional System.* London: Routledge, 1992.

INUIT

Inuit lands lie within the current borders of Denmark (Greenland), Canada, and the United States (Alaska), and Inuit have been regarded as citizens of those nations since the middle of the 20th century. Governmental structures in the Inuit North

were, for the most part, created by non-Native administrators and follow forms in keeping with the political culture and governmental institutions of each nation. Nonetheless, in the modern era, Inuit have exercised their citizenship rights to adapt many of the imposed structures to suit their needs.

In the era prior to European and North American colonization of the North, Inuit communities were politically autonomous. Kinship was an important organizing institution. Though there were no formal leadership offices, there were community leaders, usually male heads of household, who made decisions for the group. A leader's authority stemmed from his personality and ability to command respect, but he could not compel others to accept his authority. Nonetheless, Inuit culture had many mechanisms that encouraged cooperation, especially within the extended family, and also enabled groups to fission temporarily or permanently as a way to reduce social stress.

The colonial powers in the North each governed differently, but invariably, colonial authorities sought to incorporate Inuit into the national political culture, and institutions and administrators often copied the practices in other parts of the North. Each of the colonial powers created village councils, sometimes called hunters' councils, as a first step in the development of modern local governments. In most cases, these village councils had little real authority.

It was only in the mid- to late 20th century that Inuit truly began to develop their own modern governmental institutions, but as noted earlier these were all within the parameters for governance established by the three nation states. In Canada and Alaska Inuit institutions of government grew out of the political efforts to secure land claims settlements and to protect their lands and livelihoods from encroachment by developers. In Greenland, the path to self-government was somewhat different.

Greenland became a Danish colony in 1721, but only in 1953 did Greenland become a county of the Danish Kingdom and Greenlanders become citizens of Denmark. This new political status altered the isolation that Denmark had maintained over Greenland and Greenlanders but did not actually result in the integration of Greenlanders into Danish society. Consequently, Greenlanders expressed increasing desire for either home rule as the Faeroese had, or independence from Denmark like Iceland, another former Danish colony. The proponents of home rule succeeded in their efforts, and since 1979, Greenland has controlled its domestic policies. Military defense and international relations remain with Denmark, although following a dispute about fishing rights in 1985, Greenland was permitted to withdraw from the European Economic Community. Greenlanders remain divided in their desires to be closer to or more independent from Denmark.

Canadian Inuit live in the provinces of Newfoundland, Labrador, and Quebec as well as in the Northwest and Nunavut Territories, and their contemporary political institutions tend to follow these political boundaries. Inuit in each of these regions have achieved some form of self-government largely through the land claims settlement process that began in the 1970s. Native corporations established through the land claims process have some quasi-governmental powers, but the creation of the

Nunavut Territory in 1999 is probably the most significant Canadian Inuit self-government achievement.

The Nunavut Territory, which was created through division of the existing Northwest Territories, has a population that is overwhelmingly Inuit. Several of the government structures were designed to reflect specifically Inuit values. In particular, the territorial government claims to govern in accordance with *Inuit Qaujimajatuqangit*, or the wisdom of the Inuit. Also, there are no political parties, and the Territorial Assembly makes decisions by consensus—an institution borrowed from the Northwest Territorial Assembly. Inuktitut, the Inuit language, is an official language along with English and French, and a government department is charged with promoting Inuit cultural values.

In Alaska, Inuit established state-chartered municipal governments. The two largest of these are the North Slope Borough and the Northwest Arctic Borough. The North Slope Borough, which encompasses all Alaskan lands north of the Brooks Range, is made up of eight separate villages. Inuit of that region formed the borough in 1972 in order to control zoning and to fund locally managed education and social services. In addition to traditional municipal activities, the North Slope Borough has departments concerned with wildlife management and with the preservation of Inuit heritage. The Prudhoe Bay oil fields lie within the North Slope Borough and are the primary source of tax revenues for the municipality. Contrary to popular expectation, the North Slope Borough as well as numerous Alaskan Inuit organizations are proponents of expanded hydrocarbon development in Alaska.

Nunavut, North Alaska, and Greenland all have nonethnic public governments. In each of these places, Inuit are able to govern in ways that they feel are compatible with their cultural values. This is the case, at least in part, because Inuit continue to be the majority ethnic group in these northern polities. This may change with demographic shifts that take more Inuit south and more non-Natives north. It is also reasonable to expect that as Inuit needs and values change, the government structures in the North will change in ways that are not always understood as specifically Inuit.

Numerous Inuit organizations are proponents of expanded hydrocarbon development.

The Inuit Circumpolar Conference, founded in 1977, is the only transnational Inuit body. It is a nongovernmental organization representing Inuit, Yupik, and Aleut peoples at the United Nations. It is also a permanent observer at the Arctic Council, a forum created by the eight circumpolar nations in 1996 to address the common environmental and political issues facing those nations. In both organizations, the Inuit Circumpolar Conference has taken the lead in international efforts to monitor and protect the arctic ecosystem.

~Pamela Stern

FOR MORE INFORMATION

Dahl, J., J. Hicks, and P. Jull, eds. *Nunavut: Inuit Regain Control of their Lands and their Lives*. Copenhagen: International Work Group for Indigenous Affairs, 2000.
Greenland Home Rule Government. <http://www.gh.gl/uk/govern/organiza.htm>.

McBeath, G. A., and T. A. Morehouse. *The Dynamics of Alaska Native Self-Government.* Washington, D.C.: University Press of America, 1980.

Paine, R., ed. *The White Arctic: Anthropological Essays on Tutelage and Ethnicity.* St. Johns: Memorial University of Newfoundland, 1977.

Simon, M. M. *Inuit: One Future—One Arctic.* Peterborough, Ont.: Cider Press, 1997.

POLITICAL LIFE
|
LAW & CRIME
|
Holocaust—
War Crimes

United States,
1920-1939

United States,
1960-1990

Latin America

Islamic World

Soviet Union

Japan

Africa

Law and Crime

Investigations into legal systems such as the ones presented here highlight basic social values and struggles for justice. Different groups have differing views on what is a legal authority; what constitutes a legitimate legal system; and, most importantly, what is fair. Thus, be sure to compare, for example, basic legal and ethical assumptions in the creation of legal systems. The differences are illuminating. In the Soviet Union, the law and its enforcement were a part of the larger system of social control and repression. In predominantly Muslim nations in the 20th century, the Qur'an remained the principal legal text. Along with the Sunna, the book provided the foundation for Islamic jurisprudence. Central to this system was the idea that religious and governmental authority were not separated. Hence, judges dispensed both civil and religious justice. Despite the power of this legal system, many Muslim nations in Africa and the Middle East experienced considerable discord over the proper place of Islamic law. By contrast, in the 20th century in the United States, Americans enjoyed a more secular legal system. And yet, religion remained an important aspect of court decisions, as can be seen in the Scopes "monkey trial" and the convictions of Sacco and Vanzetti. Thus, at the outset, be aware of the ways in which some of the common aspects of daily life such as religion impact legal systems.

The other issue at the heart of these entries is the quest for justice. In the United States, the legal system played a critical role in the fight for civil rights and liberties. Toward the end of the century, advances were made to safeguard suspects from unwarranted searches and seizures. It was decades, however, before the "third degree" was partially eliminated from police procedures. The rough handling of criminal suspects led to hundreds of false convictions and even some false executions. In part, the movement to remove bigotry and malfeasance in law enforcement stemmed from the experiences of World War II. Perhaps no episode demonstrated the horrors of an unequal legal system more than the Holocaust. Immediately after the war, people sought to reestablish the world's faith in legal systems. The United States was at the forefront of this movement. For example, against the opposition of the British and Russians, who believed the Nuremberg trials were unnecessary (they wanted execution without trial), the United States believed that impartial trials were essential to achieving justice. Inside the United States, the movement to reform and improve the legal system had significant results. The goal of the movement was to make equality under the law applicable to all people regardless of class, color, race, religion, or ethnicity. Although this goal ultimately remained elusive, by 2000 the American legal system was fairer and less capricious.

See also the entries that describe the development of legal and criminal justice systems in Japan, Latin America, Africa, and the Islamic World, where systems of justice both similar to and very different from Western systems were practiced.

HOLOCAUST—WAR CRIMES

The Holocaust was the touchstone event that led the international community to define war crimes and prosecute such barbaric acts. Before we describe the Nazi crimes themselves, it is necessary to take a broader look at the entire concentration camp system. In all, there were more than 9,000 concentration camps: transit camps, prisoner-of-war camps, slave-labor camps, camps for "work education," camps for political prisoners, camps for police detention, camps for children whose parents were inmates of labor camps, camps for medical experimentation, and camps for killing. Six of these camps were primarily killing centers: Chelmno, Sobibor, Belzec, Treblinka, Majdanek, and Auschwitz. Auschwitz was actually three camps: Auschwitz I, for political prisoners, such as resistance fighters; Buna, for slave laborers; and Birkenau, which housed the gas chambers, crematoria, barracks for the waiting victims, and medical laboratories.

Jews were not the only victims who suffered in camps. In fact, most of the inmates were not Jews, because Jews were usually sent to their death upon arrival (approximately three million Jews were sent to the death camps). Before the war there were three types of prisoners: political prisoners, asocials (criminals and sex offenders), and Jews. As soon as the war began, millions, in all sorts of categories, flooded the camps.

Inmates came from every country under the Nazi yoke: French resistance fighters, American prisoners of war (POWs), Polish slave laborers, Russian partisans, Italian Jews, and the Catholic priests who tried to save them. The number of prisoners in the political and labor camps grew from 21,400 in September 1939 to 160,000 in April 1943 to 524,286 by August 1, 1944.

Gypsies were housed in Auschwitz (20,000), and thousands more were imprisoned in Bergen-Belsen, Buchenwald, Dachau, Mauthausen, and Ravensbruck. Five thousand were sent first to Lodz and then to Chelmno to be gassed with carbon monoxide in mobile vans. Birkenau contained a special Gypsy camp for families whose children were used for medical experiments by the

War crimes: Nazi soldiers execute Soviet civilians near Kraigonev, 1941. © National Archives.

infamous Dr. Joseph Mengele. On July 31, 1944, all of these children were killed.

Ordinary Polish citizens were not held in much greater regard than the Gypsies and the Jews. Poles were also rounded up and sent to labor camps and concentration camps, where they were treated with brutality. In fact, proposals were made to limit marriages and births among the Polish people, and requests were made to eliminate Poles who were too ill to work.

Some were also assigned another category: ugly people. On November 16, 1944, after the transfer of asocials, a meeting was held by members of the German judiciary to discuss the "gallery of outwardly asocial prisoners" who "look like miscarriages of hell." It was proposed that they be photographed before being killed—reasoning that a picture was the only evidence needed to explain why they had been executed.

Soviet POWs made up another large proportion of the camp population. In all, 3.3 million Soviet soldiers died of starvation, exposure, brutality, or execution, most during their first year of imprisonment.

Communists, unionists, Social Democrats—in short, active members of groups that were regarded by the Nazis as a threat—were also sent to concentration camps. Even Jehovah's Witnesses who refused to stop their proselytizing, or would not recognize Nazi authority, were rounded up and sent to the camps. Although they were not deliberately exterminated, one-third of these Jehovah's Witnesses died in the camps. In addition, German homosexuals, seen as a threat to the master race, were sent to the camps.

The camps were run by a complex bureaucracy typical of German organization. Each camp had a commandant who was responsible for overall operations. Under him were a variety of administrators: first, the *Schutzhaftlagerführer*, who was responsible for inmate control; next, the administration chief, who was in charge of financial matters; below him, an array of deputies, engineers, doctors, and others; and finally, several hundred guards. At Auschwitz the guards were German SS (*Schutzstaffel*) troopers not considered good enough soldiers to be assigned to the battlefield. At Treblinka, Belzec, and Sobibor, the guards were Ukrainians.

War crimes: Jewish mothers and children assembled near Lubny in the Ukraine await execution by the Nazis, October 16, 1941. Courtesy of the USHMM Photo Archives.

A look at Auschwitz, the largest, most complex, and most infamous of the concentration camps, will provide a fairly complete picture of what life was like for the inmates of all three of the main types of camps: concentration camps, labor camps, and death camps or killing centers. As noted, Auschwitz was really three camps, each of which housed different categories of prisoners and each of which subjected the inmates to different types of treatment.

Rudolf Hoess, the commandant of Auschwitz, had been raised in a strict Catholic home. After he graduated from high school, at the age of 15, he volunteered to serve in World War I. Wounded three times, he also contracted malaria. He was decorated for his war activities. After the war, in 1921, Hoess was found guilty of murdering a French schoolteacher who had turned in a German comrade, during the period when France occupied the Ruhr. Hoess served five years in jail. In 1933 he joined the SS and, before assuming command at Auschwitz, he worked in another concentration camp.

Built on approximately 18 square miles of land that had been appropriated from Poland, the camp was "owned" by the Reich SS. In all, Auschwitz comprised three large camps and 45 satellite camps in Upper Silesia and southwestern Poland. It was guarded by 6,000 men in 12 companies of SS Death's Head Units. Auschwitz I, a concentration camp for political prisoners and non-Jews, contained two- and three-story brick buildings, some of which were barracks and others of which housed laboratories for some of the medical experiments conducted under the supervision of Mengele.

Auschwitz III, also known as Buna or Monowitz, was the labor camp. Here German companies, such as I. G. Farben, were able to solve the labor shortage created when Jews were expelled from their homes in the ghettos and were no longer available to work in factories. Well-known German companies, using monies from ordinary investments, simply relocated to Buna and other camps throughout the Reich and occupied territories. Decisions to run the factories right in the middle of the concentration camps were made by ordinary corporate executives eager to make a profit. These companies, some of which are familiar even today, included Daimler-Benz, Flick, Krupp, Messerschmitt, Siemens, Bayer, and BMW. Some 40,000 foreign workers, speaking nearly 20 different languages, were used as slaves for I. G. Farben at Auschwitz.

Each nationality had a different satellite camp: Ukrainian women, English POWs, French volunteers, and so on. These workers were intended to produce synthetic rubber for the war effort, but it took them four years just to build the plant, and ultimately, because of the poor treatment of the workers, and probably sabotage efforts as well, not a single pound of rubber was ever produced.

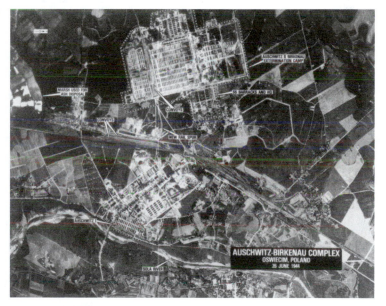

War crimes: Aerial reconnaissance photograph of Auschwitz concentration camp, June 26, 1944. © National Archives.

The workers lived in one of 60 wooden barracks, called blocks. Each, originally built to house 48 horses, held from 250 to 800 people who slept on bunks, fitted "like cells of a beehive." Each bunk held two men or women. With no pillows and only one blanket for two inmates, they slept on wooden planks, many layers high. In fact, the planks were so overloaded that they sometimes collapsed, crushing those below.

The bunks were divided by three corridors through which two people could barely pass. Only half the inmates could stand, while the others were forced to remain in bed, where even sitting up was impossible. Visiting someone else's section of the barrack, or another block, was out of the question, for there was no room. Some blocks had no lavatory or washbowl, only a bucket for washing and, at night, another for a latrine. Wooden latrines were shared by as many as eight blocks.

At one end of Buna were eight blocks that served as an infirmary and clinic. One block was for German political prisoners and criminals; another was for the *kapos* (the criminals who were put in charge of groups of workers). Another block served as the distribution center, and another was the quartermaster's office. Block 29 was a brothel that housed young Polish girls forced to serve as prostitutes for the SS.

Auschwitz II, also called Birkenau, was the death camp or killing center, or the Charitable Foundation for Institutional Care. The nine subunits that constituted Birkenau were surrounded by two barbed-wire fences, the inner one of which was electrified; chains of guard posts; and guard dogs two-thirds of the way out from the fences.

There were four gas chambers at Birkenau, each capable of killing 6,000 people per day. These were built in special combination units, which contained an underground dressing room, the gas chamber itself, and a crematorium in which to dispose of the bodies—immediately and efficiently.

The history of these buildings is worth noting because it reveals the cold, businesslike approach to the creation and the operation of the industry of murder. The earliest buildings were remodeled peasants' houses, but as the Germans began to put into operation Hitler's Final Solution, more resources were devoted to the killing centers. Private companies supplied the doors, windows, gas, and ovens. Carbon monoxide, rejected as an inefficient means of killing, was replaced with hydrogen cyanide—the commercial name for which was Zyklon B. Firms specializing in large-scale fumigation of buildings, barracks, and ships, ridding them of rodents and insects, were the primary suppliers of Zyklon B.

Each one of Birkenau's gas chambers could hold 2,000 people at a time. Two of the combination units had elevators that were used to bring the corpses from the gas chamber to the ovens. Inside each crematorium were five furnaces, each capable of incinerating from 45 to 75 bodies at once.

Not only was supplying the raw materials for this death industry a profit-making enterprise, but there were other ways to make money as well. Some businessmen earned contracts to receive goods taken from the bodies of the dead, such as gold teeth or women's hair. Dried by the heat of the crematoria, hair was made into felt and then thread, and, eventually, socks for submarine crews, stockings for railroad workers, cords for ships, cloth, ropes, the ignition mechanisms of bombs, and stuffing for mattresses. One kilo of hair went for $1.09.

One ambitious university student wrote his dissertation on "The Possibilities of Recycling Gold from the Mouths of the Dead." His ideas were later implemented by the Reichsbank, which received most of this gold. Ashes and bones were turned into fertilizer, and fat was used as fuel to operate the crematoria.

Among the designers and commanders of the six killing centers was fierce competition as to who ran the most efficient operation. Rudolf Hoess even bragged about his important contribution: substituting Zyklon B for carbon monoxide.

The invention of killing centers, and of this machinery of death, marked a turning point in the history of man's inhumanity to man. Throughout history, innocent people have been subjected to all manner of evil treatment, including genocide. During the Holocaust, those in the ghettos were starved to death or allowed to die of curable diseases, unnecessary exposure to the elements, or exhaustion. Others were subjected to random shootings, fatal beatings, and hanging. Outside the ghettos, the *Einsatzgruppen* were let loose upon unsuspecting victims, filling hastily dug mass graves with the populations of whole villages and towns.

Nevertheless, until the creation of the death camps, though thousands died, the methods used to kill them were generally haphazard, time-consuming, and inefficient, using little or no advanced technology. The newly constructed killing centers were streamlined, high-tech operations capable of killing and disposing of thousands upon thousands of people in a day.

The procedure for carrying out this mission was very simple. First, upon arrival at the camp, those selected for death were told that they were going to the bathhouses to be bathed and deloused. In an underground dressing room, approximately 107 feet by 25 feet by 9 feet, people were instructed to undress and leave their clothing neatly piled, and to remember where their clothes were placed so they could be retrieved after the showers.

> *The Nazi camps were high-tech operations capable of killing thousands a day.*

Second, signs stating "To the baths and disinfecting rooms," "Cleanliness brings freedom!," and "One louse can kill you" were posted on the walls, contributing to the illusion that all was well. (These signs were also posted in labor camps.)

Third, first the women and children, then the men, were ushered into the gas chambers that were disguised as showers. The SS guards remained in the chamber until the last minute to perpetuate the masquerade.

Fourth, as soon as the guards exited, the door was closed and screwed tightly shut, and the gas was discharged through ceiling vents. One-third of the people, those nearest the vents, died instantly. The rest screamed, staggered, and struggled for air. In 20 minutes all were dead.

Finally, the *Sonderkommando*, prisoners who were assigned to the task but who would soon be executed themselves, cleaned out the bodies, extracted any gold teeth (as much as 26.4 pounds per month), shaved off women's hair, and placed the corpses on elevators, 10 to 15 at a time, or carried them to the ovens, one floor up. The record for deaths per day probably belongs to Birkenau, which toward the end of the war was killing approximately 12,000 people a day.

Birkenau also housed the bulk of the so-called medical laboratories. Here the Nazis conducted thousands of experiments, mostly by people with little or no medical training, under the supervision of German doctors. Experiments were conducted for two different purposes. Some were more or less in the category of regular scientific experiments made to test a hypothesis; try a new serum; or solve a problem, particularly for the military.

For example, inmates were injected with diseases, such as tuberculosis, to test the effects of drug treatments. In other experiments, inmates were given typhus injections to preserve the bacteria for use in later experiments, given that typhus cannot live in an artificial culture. To find ways to help soldiers, half frozen on the battlefield, prisoners were submerged in ice water for hours. To learn how to treat injured soldiers, perfectly healthy people were subjected to "experiments" in which surgery was performed on flesh, muscles, and bones. All types of substances (poisons, gasoline, air, petroleum, chemicals) were injected into healthy people just to see what effects they produced.

What made these experiments especially horrifying was that no precautions were taken to protect the victim. No anesthetics or antiseptic techniques were used. All of these experiments were excruciatingly painful. Some people were so hungry they volunteered for experiments in exchange for food, but the rest were forced to participate, and even if they survived the "treatment" they were gassed when the experiment ended.

The second purpose for experimenting on inmates was even more sinister, and its effects, had Germany won the war, could have been far more long-range and destructive. The intention was no less than the complete subjugation of Europe.

These experiments involved the sterilization of both men and women deemed "unworthy" by the Nazi government. Groups targeted, in addition to Jewish people, were Poles, Gypsies, priests, and other so-called enemies. The plan was to sterilize people as quickly and as efficiently as possible, with the victim being unaware of what was happening. Some experiments focused on the introduction of a variety of chemicals into the bodies of unsuspecting women. The Bayer Company bought 150 Jewish women and forced them to participate in experiments with hormones. Men were exposed to high doses of X-rays while standing at a counter filling out forms. Eventually, these experiments proved to be impractical and much less reliable than surgery.

German universities took part in the experiments by collecting data, conducting autopsies, and making slides from amputated limbs and organs of healthy people who had been subjected to some type of experiment. Photographers took pictures of people in various stages of suffering, as well as of the dead, for record-keeping purposes. The Nazis, thinking they were doing a service to humankind, kept careful records of all these procedures. Doctors also worked on ways in which to increase the German population, including Mengele's work on twins. Mengele firmly believed that he would someday receive honors from the scientific community for his work.

On August 8, 1945, the Allies met in London to prepare for an international military tribunal and to develop a charter to establish the procedures for the trial of those responsible for the atrocities committed during the Nazi regime. The tribunal would consist of four judges and four teams of attorneys, representing France, Britain, the Soviet Union, and the United States. For the first time in history, the victors decided to prosecute their defeated enemies for alleged violations of criminal law. Secretary of War Henry L. Stimson, a friend and advisor to Supreme Court Justice Robert Jackson, was chosen to lead the American prosecution. On September 15, 1945, he announced that the objective of the trials was continued peace, not whether the United States should be soft or tough on the German people.

Not everyone was in favor of the painstaking trial. There were those among the Allies, especially among the British and the Soviets, who recommended summary executions without trials—the evidence was overwhelming. Robert Jackson strongly dissented. He spelled out the American view, upholding each man's right to a fair trial. What he meant by a fair trial he had previously addressed in a speech delivered to members of the American Society of International Law on April 13, 1945: "The ultimate principle is that you must put no man on trial under the form of judicial proceedings if you are not willing to see him freed if not proved guilty."

One of the most important and most controversial issues raised was the question of the criminal responsibility of the individual under international law. Does, in fact, international law apply to individuals as well as states? If so, for what acts may an individual be held criminally responsible? The international military tribunal's response was spelled out thus: "Crimes against international law are committed by men, not by abstract entities, and only by punishing individuals who commit such crimes, can the provisions of international law be enforced."

The site chosen for the trial was Nuremberg, then in total ruins but formerly the showplace for Nazi party pageants—demonstrating might, unity, and splendor. There the international judges and lawyers defined three kinds of crimes that were specified in the indictments of the charter: (1) crimes against peace, which focused on Germany's conspiracy to unleash total, aggressive war against its neighbors; (2) war crimes, which targeted violations of accepted international laws and customs of war (according to Article 46 of the Geneva Convention), including murder, ill treatment, and deportation of populations in the conquered territories; the killing of hostages and prisoners of war; the seizing of private property; and the wanton destruction of villages, towns, and cities;

Nazi defendants at the Nuremberg Trials, October 18, 1945. Courtesy of the USHMM Photo Archives.

and (3) crimes against humanity, which included murder, extermination, enslavement, deportations, and other inhumane acts committed against any civilian population before or during the war. All three counts of the indictments were interrelated by what is sometimes called the fourth indictment: the conspiracy—the carefully planned execution of all of these acts.

Every count in the indictments was backed up by the words, photographs, and films the Germans had meticulously put together with evident pride. Though witnesses might have had their own agendas as well as faulty memories and be therefore subject to dispute, the German documents not only presented the strongest possible irrefutable evidence but also supported the witnesses called to testify. These documents would also ensure a fair trial for the defendants.

The tribunal was scheduled to begin on November 20, 1945, after only eight months of preparation, arguably short for such a major trial and therefore a bone of some contention among some. There were 403 court sessions for which lawyers had gathered and studied more than 100,000 captured German documents. Piles of these documents were waiting to be filed in floor-to-ceiling racks. Help was desperately needed to stack and sort them. For this purpose, members of the Waffen SS were recruited from a nearby prisoner-of-war camp. They also built shelves, cleared away the rubble, and repaired the roof of the Palace of Justice.

Because there was only one guard for every 50 prisoners, they could easily have escaped, but none did. The American officer supervising them boasted that they were his troops now. If he told them to go out there and fight, they would, without asking who or where.

Hermann Goering, the only defendant permitted to take 12 days of court time to deny knowledge of events he ought to have known about, was found guilty on all counts and condemned to death by hanging. Major Airey Neave, a member of the British War Crimes Executive Team, had been chosen to act as legal advisor to the defendants and was therefore in a position to visit with them on many occasions. He was also responsible for amassing evidence on the treatment of slave laborers by the Krupp Works. On one of his visits to Goering in his cell Neave described seeing the photographs of Goering's wife and small daughter, Edda, on the table: "The photograph of Goering's daughter so like her father touched me. Then I felt suddenly angry. It was impossible to forget the Krupp guards who caught a prisoner trying to keep a snapshot of his parents. They seized it, tore it up and beat him till he bled."

Hans Frank was also condemned to death by hanging. His own diary, he admitted, bore witness against him. He referred to the tribunal judges and prosecuting attorneys as "such noble figures" sitting across from where he sat among such "repulsive characters as Streicher, Goering and Ribbentrop." He embraced his Roman Catholic religion and noted in his diary, "Religion is such a comfort now. I look forward to Christmas like a little child."

During most of the trial, Keitel was viewed as a pathetic instrument of crime.

Albert Speer, who had admitted that the ties between himself as armament minister and those in charge of slave labor were very strong, was given 20 years because of his apparent repentant attitude and his strenuous efforts to prevent Hitler's "scorched earth" policy, designed to annihilate what was left of Germany, from taking effect. On March 19, 1945, Speer had handed to Hitler the last of the memoranda he had written explaining that the war was lost and that what was important was to preserve Germany's infrastructure for the sake of the people. Hitler had responded that it was best to destroy even these things, that "the garbage left over will only be the inferiors because the good ones will be dead."

Julius Streicher, whose newspaper *Der Stürmer* was judged to incite murder, was sentenced to death by hanging. Streicher, upon hearing the verdict, was furious, and he stomped his feet all the way to the elevator.

For Wilhelm Keitel, the deliberations were the shortest among all the defendants. All the judges agreed that he was guilty on all four counts and sentenced him to death. During most of the trial, he was viewed as a pathetic instrument of crime. In the words of Francis Biddle, an American member of the tribunal, he was the "prototype of the criminally pliant general."

Eight other defendants were sentenced to death by hanging: Joachim von Ribbentropp, foreign minister; Ernst Kaltenbrunner, secret police chief; Wilhelm Frick, Minister of the Interior; Alfred Rosenberg, commissioner of the Occupied East-European Region; Fritz Sauckel, in charge of foreign workers from the occupied territories; Alfred Jodl, Keitel's immediate deputy; Dr. Arthur Seyss-Inquart, who was instrumental in policies governing areas of occupation; and Martin Bormann, private secretary to the Fuehrer, sentenced in absentia because he had not been captured.

Rudolf Hoess, deputy for party affairs and Hitler's confidant; Walter Funk, minister of economic affairs; and Admiral Erich Raeder, commander of the German navy, were sentenced to life imprisonment. Albert Speer; Constantin von Neurath, the first foreign minister and voice of "moderation"; Admiral Karl Doenitz, commander in chief of the navy; and Baldur von Schirach, leader of Hitler Youth, were given sentences ranging from 10 to 20 years. Franz von Papen, former ambassador to Austria; Hjalmar Schacht, financial advisor; and Hans Fritsche, a high official in the Propaganda Ministry, were acquitted.

The executions were scheduled to begin early in the morning of October 16, 1946, in the prison gymnasium. Goering escaped the gallows by swallowing a cyanide capsule during the night. The chaplains visited the condemned prior to the executions. They went to their deaths with relative calm, except for Streicher, who spat at Master Sergeant Woods, the executioner, and told him that the Bolsheviks would hang him one day, followed by the words "Heil Hitler." All of the corpses were photographed and then carried in trucks to a crematory in or near Munich. Some believe the destination was Dachau. It is believed that the ashes were emptied into the river Isar.

More trials took place at the conclusion of the military tribunals. Physicians were tried for their involvement in the selections, murders, and medical experiments; judges were tried for transforming German law into a new set of laws permitting mass murder; top executives of I. G. Farben were tried for manufacturing Zyklon B and constructing factories at Auschwitz; Alfred Krupp and other executives were tried for their use of slave labor.

The unfolding of the cold war between the United States and the Soviet Union shifted attention away from the trials and resulted in the sentences being reduced and pardons being granted. Germany became central to American economic and political interests.

The chief perpetrators—Hitler, Joseph Goebbels, and Heinrich Himmler—all committed suicide and escaped the trials. Many others took on new identities and escaped to South America or the Middle East; in addition, thousands entered the United States claiming to be anti-Communists fleeing from Soviet persecution. Hundreds of scientists, including war criminals, were brought to the United States to work for the military and the National Aeronautics and Space Administration—just as Jewish refugees such as Alfred Einstein had done before the war. Thousands of others who participated in the "crimes against humanity" were never tried.

For the very first time in history, individuals were held responsible for their particular crimes against humanity. Swearing allegiance, taking an oath, or taking orders were no longer acceptable reasons for their defense. Also, the masses of German recorded evidence presented at the tribunal will make it almost impossible for present and future revisionist historians to claim that these "crimes" did not occur or were exaggerated—"almost impossible," because there are always those who try to distort or deny the evidence. In the continuing struggle for freedom from persecution and unbridled hate, the Nuremberg trials played a significant role and as such must be remembered (Soumerai and Schulz, 179–86, 277–89).

FOR MORE INFORMATION

Conot, R. E. *Justice at Nuremberg*. New York: Harper and Row, 1983.

Dawidowicz, L. *The War Against the Jews, 1933–1945*. New York: Holt, Reinhart, and Winston, 1975.

Hilbert, P. *The Destruction of the European Jewry*. Chicago: Quandrangle Books, 1967.

The Holocaust History Project. <http://www.holocaust-history.org/>.

Pakula, A. J., dir. *Sophie's Choice*. 1982.

Soumerai, E. N., and C. D. Schulz. *Daily Life During the Holocaust*. Westport, Conn.: Greenwood Press, 1998.

UNITED STATES, 1920–39

Becoming the victim of a criminal act was a possibility, though a slight one, in the generally law-abiding society of the early-20th-century United States. Worry about crime, if not crime itself, became a more widespread aspect of daily life in the decades after World War I. In some respects, crime and the response to it simply reflected the social conflicts dividing the country. In others, it was yet another function of growing urbanization, changing technology, and increased awareness of what was happening outside the local community. But perhaps more than anything else, crime patterns measured changing standards of acceptable behavior.

The 1920s were barely under way when one crime took place that would epitomize the social conflicts of the era. In South Braintree, Massachusetts, in April 1920, two men shot a guard and the paymaster of the Slater and Merrill Shoe Company, then fled in an automobile with the company payroll. Police soon arrested two pistol-carrying Italian immigrants and charged them with robbery and murder. Nicola Sacco and Bartolomeo Vanzetti were interrogated for two days, mainly about their political beliefs, without being told the charges against them or their legal rights. Witnesses to the crime were asked to identify them standing alone, rather than pick them out of a lineup. None of these police procedures, declared by the U.S. Supreme Court decades later to be violations of constitutional rights to a fair trial, were uncommon at the time. Eleven years later, a federal report on law enforcement practices described "the third degree," or "the inflicting of pain, physical or mental, to extract confessions or statements" as "extensively practiced" by police across the country.

At the trial, Sacco and Vanzetti's political beliefs and their ethnic background appeared to carry more weight with the judge and jury than the weak case presented against them or the defense witnesses who placed Sacco miles away at the time of the robbery. The presiding judge, Webster Thayer, was heard to refer to the defendants as "those anarchist bastards." Once Sacco and Vanzetti were found guilty and sentenced to death, their lawyers failed repeatedly in efforts to persuade the prosecutor or judge to reopen the case on the basis of compelling new evidence. Even a confession to the crime by another death row inmate who bore a striking resemblance to Sacco failed to impress Judge Thayer.

The Sacco and Vanzetti case gained the attention of the immigrant community as well as many legal experts and intellectuals, both inside and outside the United States, who came to see it as a terrible example of ethnic prejudice and a blatant miscarriage of justice. Despite eight separate appeals, one to the U.S. Supreme Court, the convictions stood. Large crowds turned out to protest in Boston and New York

City. Nevertheless, Massachusetts put Sacco and Vanzetti to death in the Charles-town Prison electric chair in August 1927. The case fostered a sense of a harsh and socially uneven justice system, and the furor over the fate of Sacco and Vanzetti continued for years.

Despite a popular image of the 1920s as a lawless era, bank robbery, murder, and other serious felonies were comparatively rare occurrences, perhaps one reason why the Sacco and Vanzetti case received so much attention. The United States was in the midst of what many scholars agree was a long-term decline in serious crime that would not end until the 1960s. Although the total volume of illegal activity is by nature difficult to determine precisely, one measure of the crime rate, admittedly far from perfect, is the number of convicted criminals who were imprisoned. In 1926, the first year for which U.S. Census Bureau figures are available, 96,000 inmates resided in state and federal prisons. By comparison, at the end of the 20th century, over one and a quarter million prisoners were incarcerated. In proportion to popu-lation, the number of criminals imprisoned was over five times what it had been in the 1920s.

The rate at which crimes were committed did rise sharply during the 1920s, but only because an activity that earlier and later would be considered legal was for the moment labeled criminal. Prohibition law violations accounted for 65 percent of all cases in federal district courts during the era when the total liquor ban was being enforced. In 1921, federal officials prosecuted 29,114 prohibition cases, whereas by 1932, despite much diminished enthusiasm for the law, there were 65,960 such prosecutions. In the early 1920s, only 7 percent of commitments to federal prison were for liquor law violations, but by 1930, with stiffer penalties in place, 49 percent were so. State governments, which shared responsibility for prohibition enforcement but often displayed much less enthusiasm for doing so, also saw their caseload in-crease, though only at about half the rate of that of the federal justice system.

With a significant portion of the American people regarding prohibition as a mistake and not legitimately binding upon them, it is difficult to say whether sta-tistics so heavily dominated by liquor cases show a real increase in criminality. Fur-ther complicating the situation, small-scale prohibition violations, such as possession for personal use, usually either were not prosecuted or were plea-bargained down to a fine or suspended sentence. Prosecution focused, especially later in the period, on professional bootleggers and speakeasy operators. When even this tactic failed to stem the growing alcohol trade, it was clear that, particularly in urban America, drinking was not considered much more of a crime than jaywalking or illegal parking.

The image of a crime wave nevertheless existed. In large part this was caused by the volume and the particularly high visibility of prohibition violation. Sellers of bootleg liquor and operators of speakeasies had to make their presence known if they were to attract customers. Together with the many movies that, without dis-approval, depicted drinking and the activities of bootleggers, real-life evidence of prohibition violation certainly sent a mixed moral message to onlookers. Whatever citizens concluded about the wisdom of the alcohol ban or the morality of ignoring it, they no doubt acquired an impression that many people were breaking the law.

The activities of the Federal Bureau of Investigation (FBI) furthered the public sense of a crime wave. Reconstituted in 1924 under aggressive young director J. Edgar Hoover, the FBI strove to overcome a previous image of lethargy and corruption. Hoover sought to portray the FBI as an effective professional national crime-fighting force confronting a serious increase in criminal threats to society. The FBI began compiling national crime statistics in 1930 from local police reports of dubious reliability, raising consciousness and apprehension of criminal activity. Also the bureau began a campaign to collect the fingerprints of all Americans as a scientific means of solving crimes and protecting society from a variety of dangers. Hoover steadfastly avoided having the FBI take any part in prohibition enforcement, which he recognized as potentially threatening to the bureau's public image. Instead, he called attention to a series of small-town bank robbers such as John Dillinger, Bonnie Parker, and Clyde Barrow with whom the bureau could deal effectively, and he created the "Ten Most Wanted" list of criminals that brought more attention to FBI-targeted criminal activity. Hoover also worked closely with Hollywood filmmakers on their ever-popular crime dramas so that government agents, "G-men," would be portrayed as well-educated and trained, always proper and efficient, and inevitably successful at stopping crime. The director's tactics helped raise the FBI from obscurity to a well-known and respected federal agency by the end of the 1930s, yet at the same time stirred public concern about the threat of crime.

Law enforcement practices changed in the 1920s and 1930s. The scientific professionalism advocated by various crime commissions and demonstrated by the FBI began replacing the "third degree." Also the new technologies of the telephone and automobile started to alter basic police practices. Foot patrols continued in most cities, but more and more police took to automobiles to extend their range and speed of response. Summoned by telephone and dispatched by radio, they became more detached from the community's residents. This "mobilization" of police broke the everyday connection between the cop walking a beat and the neighborhood he patrolled.

Chicagoans celebrate the end of prohibition, 1933. © Library of Congress.

Efforts to deal with bootleggers who also equipped themselves with automobiles and telephones shaped law enforcement and affected public perceptions of it. Cars and trucks allowed bootleggers to move liquor quickly and evade detection by the police. At least this was the case until 1925 when the Supreme Court ruled in *Carroll v. U.S.* that police could not be expected to obtain a search warrant to examine a vehicle stopped on a Michigan highway, which they correctly suspected was transporting illegal alcohol. Drivers of all sorts were thereafter much more at the mercy of police who halted them on the road. Just as unsettling to the public, the Supreme Court ruled in 1927 that wiretapping of telephones was constitutionally permissible as long as it took place off the target's private property. According to *Olmstead v. U.S.*, evidence collected by listening in at phone company headquarters and then used to convict a Seattle bootlegger was akin to overhearing a conversation in a public place. Both the *Carroll* and *Olmstead* rulings, along with others allowing police in disguise to encourage and entrap people in prohibition violations, permitting both state and federal courts to punish the same offense, and sanctioning plea bargains instead of jury trials, caused worries that prohibition was undermining traditional justice standards. The liquor ban struck many as an infringement on their legitimate rights, allowing police to intrude too much into private life (Kyvig, 150–54).

To read about law and crime in the United States in the 19th century, see the United States entries in the section "Law and Crime" in chapter 6 ("Political Life") in volume 5 of this series.

FOR MORE INFORMATION

Carter, D. T. *Scottsboro: An American Tragedy.* Baton Rouge: Louisiana State University Press, 1969. Reprint 1979.

DePalma, B., dir. *Untouchables.* 1987.

Friedman, L. M. *Crime and Punishment in American History.* New York: Basic Books, 1993.

Kyvig, D. E. *Daily Life in the United States, 1920–1939: Decades of Promise and Pain.* Westport, Conn.: Greenwood Press, 2002.

Walker, S. A. *Popular Justice: A History of American Criminal Justice.* New York: Oxford University Press, 1980.

UNITED STATES, 1960–90

Reports of violent crimes, often sensationalized, filled the airwaves and newspapers, probably giving an exaggerated sense of the perils people faced in their daily routines. Increases in crime were nonetheless a legitimate concern. Between 1967 and 1974 crime grew rapidly, partly because of the bulge in the population profile of young men between the ages of 17 and 24, the years when some youths are most susceptible to committing crimes of violence and property. Among new reminders of the threat of crime was the increasingly common installation of burglar alarms. The routine screening of airline passengers to prevent hijacking, begun in 1973, was a reminder of a relatively new kind of crime.

As a candidate for president in 1968, Richard Nixon capitalized on people's fears by making "crime in the streets" an issue. His campaign theme of "law and order" seemed to be a transparent effort to take advantage of concerns generated by riots in African American areas of Los Angeles, Detroit, and other cities, but it worked. It fit well with his party's "southern strategy," aimed at wooing whites who disapproved of the policies on race pursued by the party to which they and their forebears had belonged for a century (the Democratic party).

The killing of African Americans by others of the same race accounted almost completely for the dramatic rise in urban homicide rates. The prevalence of such homicides puzzled scholars. Among their explanations, the most plausible is that African American populations in northern cities grew just as the industrial opportunities that had induced them to migrate there from the South all but disappeared. Consequently, they did not develop the customs and responsibilities shaped by reg-

POLITICAL LIFE

LAW & CRIME

Holocaust— War Crimes

United States, 1920-1939

United States, 1960-1990

Latin America

Islamic World

Soviet Union

Japan

Africa

ular employment that reduce inclinations to commit crimes. Poor schools and broken families contributed to a climate in which the commission of crimes lost much of its stigma.

In general, all Americans regardless of race or class witnessed increased crime rates every year since 1960. Crime rose or remained steady in most categories, with only occasional slight declines. Even though local reports of violent crimes alone were enough to make ordinary Americans worry about their security, high-visibility crimes made them aware that even the rich and famous were vulnerable.

Bribery, tax evasion, fraud, and other so-called white-collar crimes were probably more pervasive in American life than crimes against persons and property, and they affected the lives of others more widely. Higher prices, higher taxes, and insecure investments were among the harmful effects of white-collar crime. Perhaps more serious was the loss of confidence in government when federal, state, and local officials were involved—for example, in 1978, the former acting director of the Federal Bureau of Investigation (FBI) was indicted for having approved illegal break-ins and searches of the properties of a radical antiwar group. In the same year four U.S. congressmen were indicted on various charges; three of the four were subsequently reelected in their districts. Critics of the FBI wondered how many convictions of white-collar criminals there would have been if FBI agents devoted as much time and energy to making cases against them as they did to other crimes.

Crime rates began to drop only after the 1970s. According to the Federal Bureau of Justice Statistics, major crime dropped by 2 percent in 1981 and by another 5 percent during the first six months of 1982, compared with the same period in 1981. The unanticipated downward trend continued in 1983, but by the mid-1980s figures reported by the FBI showed the trend to have reversed again, suggesting that crime figures are cyclical. Most likely they are related to other cycles, such as those involving drug use. Between 1985 and 1990 the rate of crimes committed per 10,000 population again approached the level it had reached in 1980. In 1990 the overall crime rate was triple what it had been in 1960, and the rate of violent crimes had increased fivefold. Statistics gathered by the Federal Bureau of Justice Statistics support the inference of criminologists that the increases were partly due to a greater willingness by victims to report crimes.

Statistics tell only part of the story concerning crime in the United States. Events such as the attempted assassination of President Reagan in 1981 and the mass murders that occurred in Pennsylvania, Texas, Florida, and California in 1982, sensationalized by the mass media, heightened the nation's awareness of criminal occurrences. Incidents like the one in 1988 in which a man armed with an assault rifle killed five children and wounded the teacher and 29 others in a California schoolyard prompted local and state efforts to ban the sale and possession of such weapons. The federal government's ban on importation of semiautomatic assault weapons was largely a symbolic gesture, given that—according to the U.S. Bureau of Alcohol, Tobacco, and Firearms—imports represented only about 25 percent of such weapons available in the United States. The federal ban and actions taken at state and local levels opened intense debates over the rights of individuals to own firearms and of government to limit their sale and possession.

On September 29, 1982, four persons living in the Chicago area, three of them in the same family, died after taking Extra-Strength Tylenol capsules that had been laced with cyanide. The next day three more Chicagoans were poisoned in the same way, and a man in California suffered convulsions after taking Tylenol capsules. The manufacturer of this pain-relief medication immediately recalled Tylenol from counters across the United States, and law enforcement officials had a new kind of crime to deal with. In subsequent weeks there were more than 90 reports of "copycat" crimes involving tampering with foods and other consumer products. The Food and Drug Administration then required over-the-counter medicines to be carried in tamper-proof packages, a practice that soon spread to food products as well.

Another kind of crime, sexual abuse of children, became an urgent social issue in the mid-1980s. In October 1984, officials in the U.S. Department of Justice stated that as many as one out of four girls and 1 out of 10 boys might be sexually molested before the age of 18 and that perhaps only one-tenth of such molestations were being reported to law enforcement authorities. The year before, reports of hundreds of alleged incidents

> *Four persons died in Chicago after taking Extra-Strength Tylenol laced with cyanide.*

in a preschool in California led to indictments of seven persons on 115 counts of child molestation, with 93 more counts added later. The case resulted in the longest criminal trial in U.S. history and ended with the preschool director and her adult son found not guilty on 52 counts of child abuse and molestation. The director spent two years in prison as the case moved forward, her son was held for five years before being released on bail, and the state spent $15 million on the 30-month trial.

Although authorities did not know how extensive actual occurrences of molestation were, awareness of the potential for incidents increased. This was largely a result of accounts by persons claiming to have been the victims of sexual abuse in day-care programs and other places, including their own homes. They reported experiencing psychological pain and bewilderment, leading to shame and fear, and they seemed to speak for many more who were afraid or unwilling to reveal what had happened to them.

Parents naturally wondered whether their own children might have been the victims of sexual abuse, and they were urged to watch for signs of it. In addition to physical symptoms, there might be sleeplessness, fear of being in the presence of certain persons, or sexual conduct not appropriate for a given age. Parents warned their children against allowing anyone, including family members, to touch them in ways that made them feel uncomfortable. Warnings against getting into cars or going into rooms with persons they did not know or even speaking to such persons became common (Marty, 102, 198, 274–75).

To read about law and crime in the United States in the 19th century, see the United States entries in the section "Law and Crime" in chapter 6 ("Political Life") in volume 5 of this series.

FOR MORE INFORMATION

Friedman, L. M. *Crime and Punishment in American History*. New York: Basic Books, 1993.

Marty, M. A. *Daily Life in the United States, 1960–1990: Decades of Discord*. Westport, Conn.: Greenwood Press, 1997.

Nakano, D., dir. *White Man's Burden*. 1995.

Walker, S. A. *Popular Justice: A History of American Criminal Justice*. New York: Oxford University Press, 1980.

LATIN AMERICA

Violent crime and violations against human and civil rights rose significantly throughout Latin America during the 20th century, despite the existence of constitutional protections and complex justice systems. Multiple factors influenced this increase in crime, including population growth, extreme poverty, and the appearance of new forms of criminality (e.g., kidnapping, drug trafficking). Moreover, many countries suffered from systematic, even institutionalized criminal behavior on official and governmental levels, much of which remained unchallenged.

In many countries, crime statistics were closely linked to armed conflict, and violent behavior continued well beyond the silencing of guns or the signing of peace accords. Despite official programs for the decommissioning of weapons, many postwar societies remained highly armed, with a wide assortment of arms and ammunition available on black markets. And because former fighters on all sides of the conflicts often moved into other types of violent work—organized crime and common delinquency, for example—weapons continued to be in high demand.

Crime statistics were also linked to poverty and general marginalization. In Trinidad and Tobago, for example, unemployment rates for 15- to 25-year-old males reached some 30 percent in the latter part of the century; limited immediate opportunities and the lack of future prospects often made these individuals particularly susceptible to criminal activities, such as the lucrative drug trade (Ayres, 13). Here and elsewhere in Latin America, thousands of children and young adults, by choice or by force, ended up on the streets. According to one study, between 8 and 12 percent of children under the age of 18 made their home on the streets of Nicaragua and Honduras in the latter part of the century. Once on the street, many turned to crime to make ends meet. In 1969, in Sao Paulo, Brazil, nearly 2,000 people under the age of 17 were detained for infractions such as robbery and possession of drugs or weapons. Thousands of youth also affiliated themselves with gangs, such as the 13th and 18th Street *Salvatruchas* of El Salvador.

The poor and marginalized were not the only ones who committed crimes in 20th-century Latin America, however. Social and economic elites also committed a multitude of crimes: corruption; tax evasion, money laundering, and other financial scams; labor and child exploitation; and trafficking of drugs and arms.

A huge number of violations were committed by national militaries and security forces. At least 14 of the region's countries witnessed at least one military coup d'état during the course of the century; once in power, military juntas often instituted repressive laws intended to maintain power and control over the population. The Argentine regime, for example, established laws against terrorist and communist activities (1960, 1966); created war councils that expelled "undesirable foreigners" from the country (1969); and instituted the death penalty for political offenses

(1970). Furthermore, in 1971 the regime transferred the responsibility of judging "political subversives" to a newly created penal court. In the month of June 1972, this special tribunal pronounced sentences of 10 years to life in prison in 3,392 cases.

Military regimes in Brazil, Chile, Guatemala, El Salvador, and elsewhere passed similarly questionable laws and sentences, providing official sanction for systematic human rights violations. Despite the obvious nature of many crimes, official impunity reigned in much of Latin America. This pattern was encouraged by both authoritarian legislation and judicial systems that prosecuted crimes committed by the poor but left unchallenged those crimes committed by social and economic elites.

This discrepancy was largely based on the perception of the poor as a "dangerous class" that had to be closely monitored and controlled. One legal specialist from the region tellingly referred to the police and criminal justice systems of Latin America as "border guards" because they served to protect the elite from the poor. Indeed, throughout the century, examples abound of the military, police, and national security forces "maintaining order." For example, in 1932, powerful landowners in western El Salvador called in the *Guardia Nacional* (National Guard) to quell disturbances caused by agricultural laborers who had begun organizing to demand higher wages and better working conditions; within a few short weeks, some 30,000 mostly indigenous Salvadorans were killed. Similar strategies of labor control were used against Andean miners, and factory workers in Guatemala and elsewhere. In addition to summary execution, other systematic violations by security officials included arbitrary and prolonged detention, disappearances, and torture under interrogation.

Cases involving official use of extreme force rarely found their way to court. Brazil's Pastoral Land Commission reported that of 1,730 killings of peasants, rural workers, trade union leaders, religious workers, and lawyers committed between 1964 and 1992, only 30 cases went to trial by 1992, and just 18 resulted in convictions.

There were also frequent discrepancies between the numbers of detained nonelite suspects and cases presented in court. In 1967 in Chile, for example, only 3.76 percent of those detained ever made it into the courtroom. Sluggish justice systems often left many of the accused incarcerated for months or years before their trial or release. Prisons of the region were notoriously overcrowded and insufficiently staffed, offering deplorable sanitary and safety conditions for inmates.

Despite the apparently lawless nature of much of Latin America during the 20th century, the 1990s brought reason for hope. Many administrations established human rights commissions and appointed official ombudspersons to investigate complaints. Military and police forces returned to civilian control and received specialized instruction in human rights and international law. Perhaps most notably, however, international forces came into play in ending official impunity, as occurred with the 1998 arrest in London of the former dictator of Chile, General Augusto Pinochet.

~*Molly Todd*

FOR MORE INFORMATION

Ayres, R. L. *Crime and Violence as Development Issues in Latin America and the Caribbean.* Washington, D.C.: The World Bank, 1998.

Francini, P., prod., H. Babenco, dir. *Pixote*. Brazil: Embrafilme, 1981.

Meirelles, F., dir. *Cidade de Deus* [City of God]. Brazil: Globo Filmes, Miramax International, 2002.

Méndez, J. E., and P. S. Pinheiro, eds. *The (Un)Rule of Law and the Underprivileged in Latin America*. Notre Dame, Ind.: University of Notre Dame Press, 1999.

Rico, J. M. *Crimen y Justicia en América Latina*. 2d. ed. Mexico, Distrito Federal: Siglo 21 Editores, 1981.

Salvatore, R., C. Aguirre, and G. M. Joseph. *Crime and Punishment in Latin America: Law and Society Since Late Colonial Times*. Durham, N.C.: Duke University Press, 2001.

Scheper-Hughes, N. *Death without Weeping: Everyday Violence of Everyday Life in Brazil*. Berkeley: University of California Press, 1992.

ISLAMIC WORLD

The prophet Muhammad (570–632 C.E.) taught the early Muslim community to follow a code of laws called the sharia, a term that comes from the Arabic word meaning way or path. This set of rules governs most aspects of Muslim life, from personal etiquette to criminal law. Many features of modern Islamic law are based on the sharia system.

There are several different sources of legal authority in the sharia system. Muslims believe that God revealed the Qur'an to the prophet Muhammad using the archangel Gabriel as an intermediary. According to Islamic doctrine, the laws contained in the Qur'an are ordained by God and therefore irrefutable. Thus, the Qur'an is the highest source of legal understanding in Islam.

Another important source of legal authority is contained in the Sunna, meaning the customs of the prophet Muhammad and consisting of his sayings and actions as recorded by his companions and followers. Although Muhammad was not a legal expert, he passed down a number of important teachings to the Muslim community: "Like Moses, Muhammad was a political leader and judge as well as a spiritual guide and teacher" (Denny, 216). Early Muslim scholars detailed the Sunna of Prophet in hadith reports (written collections of his communications). For a jurist to use a piece of hadith in a legal proceeding, it must be verified by a using a precise method of authentication.

Although the Qur'an and the Sunna are two of the primary foundations of the sharia sytem, some experts in Islamic jurisprudence use other methods of reasoning, such as *ijma* (consensus) and *qiyâs* (analytical reasoning) to produce legal rulings that do not have a clear precedent elsewhere. The academic and theological discipline of interpreting Islamic law is called *fiqh*, a word that can also mean the entire corpus of laws contained within the sharia system (Hodgson, 514).

Beginning in the seventh century, Islamic jurists initiated a number of reform movements that served as the foundation of modern sharia practice. Compelled by the rapid expansion of the Islamic empire in the early period, specialists in the science of *fiqh* generated a comprehensive body of laws based on Islamic ethical, moral, and theological concepts (Lapidus, 103).

Some of the most eminent schools of Sunni Islamic law, such as the Hanafis, the Mâlikîs, the Shafiis, and the Hanbalis, began during the eighth and ninth centuries. Each one of these institutions bears the name of its founder and has its own distinctive form of legal reasoning. The first of these four schools, the Hanafis, was started by the liberal Iranian jurist Abu Hanifa (d. 767). The Hanafis are still active in Central Asia and India. In contrast, the conservative Hanbali school, founded by Ahmad ibn Hanbal (d. 855), focuses on traditional sources of legal understanding such as the Qur'an and hadith. There is very little room in the Hanbali school for legal ruling derived from interpretive reasoning. The Hanbali school of Islamic law is currently the prevalent school of legal thought in Saudi Arabia.

The different legal institutions within the Muslim world do not disagree about the veracity of the Qur'an, although there is some debate over which versions of hadith literature are correct. Most of the debate in legal circles revolves around the amount of liberty that jurists should take in the actual interpretation of Islamic law. For example, in most schools of Sunni law, analogy is a traditional method of reaching a legal decision. However, in the majority of Shi'ite courts, the use of analogy is not an accepted legal practice.

Most traditional sharia courts agree that there should not be a separation of church and state. The events of the 19th and 20th centuries challenged this notion. In the 19th century, colonial governments instituted European-style courts throughout much of the Islamic world. In an effort to Westernize their countries, certain leaders, such as Turkey's Mustafa Kemal Atatürk (1881–1938), made the controversial decision to abolish the traditional sharia system and establish courts modeled after European institutions. Many Muslims felt that the abolition of sharia interfered with their ability to practice Islam.

Among certain factions, this resentment ultimately led to political dissent and the formation of various resistance movements interested in reestablishing the mandate of *fiqh*. Other groups of Muslims wanted to reinterpret the entire sharia system to address the concerns of 20th-century life. Still others felt that sharia law had its place in religious institutions but not as part of government policy. This debate continues throughout much of the Muslim world.

Many modern Islamic countries have legal systems that rely to varying extents on sharia. However, some countries with majority Muslim populations have legal systems based on Western secular law. For example, Egypt has based its legal system largely on that of France. Organizations such as the Muslim Brotherhood are struggling to reintegrate sharia law into Egypt's constitution. The cause has a lot of popular support. Although secular countries in the Muslim world do not have government-sponsored sharia courts, pious Muslims are careful to follow sharia law anyway. Sharia governs many people's daily lives, especially in areas such as etiquette, devotional practice, and dietary and family law.

Although sharia is the universal law code in Islam, a wide variety of applications of sharia exist among scholars and government leaders in the Muslim world. Courts in countries such as Saudi Arabia base their judicial systems on the orthodox Hanbali understanding of sharia law. In other countries, such as Malaysia, Muslims are under the jurisdiction of sharia courts at the state level, but the federal government maintains an independent legal structure.

Under Islamic law, capital punishment is permissible in certain specific circumstances. This aspect of sharia engendered considerable controversy from human rights groups in the latter part of the 20th century. Specifically, countries such as Nigeria have notoriously poor human rights track records. All books of *fiqh* agree that acts such as fornication, apostasy, and murder are *harâm* (forbidden) and therefore punishable by death. It would be a mistake to assume that the death penalty is applied more often in Islamic countries than in non-Islamic countries.

The actual implementation of the death penalty for *harâm* crimes is variable not only by country, but also by the specific court's interpretation of sharia. Islamic law is not static; there are vastly different interpretations of Islamic law in the different regions of the modern Islamic world. This is true not only with regard to the death penalty, but to the entire range of civil and criminal law as well.

To read about law and crime in the early Islamic world, see the Islamic World entry in the section "Law" in chapter 6 ("Political Life") in volume 2 of this series.

~*Molly Benjamin Patterson*

FOR MORE INFORMATION

Denny, F. M. *An Introduction to Islam*. New York: Macmillan, 1985.

Hodgson, M.G.S. *The Venture of Islam: Conscience and History in a World Civilization: 1. The Classical Age of Islam*. Chicago: University of Chicago Press, 1977.

Judd, G., dir. "Muslims." *Frontline* (PBS). Program #2020. Original airdate: May 9, 2002.

Lapidus, I. *A History of Islamic Societies*. Cambridge: Cambridge University Press, 1988. [reprint]

School of Oriental and African Studies (the University of London), topic "Islamic Law." <http://www.soas.ac.uk/Centres/IslamicLaw/Materials.html>.

POLITICAL LIFE
|
LAW & CRIME
|
Holocaust—
War Crimes

United States,
1920-1939

United States,
1960-1990

Latin America

Islamic World

Soviet Union

Japan

Africa

SOVIET UNION

The Soviet version of ordinary law enforcement, as opposed to secret police, was the militia, founded in 1918. This police force was the state authority people came in contact with most often. Operating with the help of millions of unpaid volunteers, numerous informants, and military auxiliaries, the militia was subordinate to and fully cooperative with the secret police. Among their many duties, militiamen issued internal and foreign passports; registered citizens and foreigners; kept track, through their registration system, of where people lived and where they moved to; traced missing persons and draft evaders; located child support and alimony deadbeats; and supervised people sentenced to internal exile, certain categories of released jail and camp prisoners, juvenile delinquents, and orphans. The militia was also responsible for traffic control and other matters relating to the registration, inspection, and regulation of motor vehicles, including driver education and granting of drivers' licenses. Additionally, like police everywhere, the militia was expected to maintain order, for example, during parades and other public events.

In matters of public health, policemen were supposed to enforce health and sanitation codes and quarantine or track people with infectious diseases, including venereal diseases. They were expected to intervene in cases of family violence. Like their American counterparts, they often feared for their own safety when they had to wade into a family dispute. Because the USSR was poor in social service agencies, and because militiamen had such a wide mandate to maintain order, they were sometimes called "social workers with sticks."

Policemen were responsible for gun control. Private citizens and institutions could own hunting weapons if they had police permission and registered their guns at the local station house. The militia could confiscate weapons and ammunition from people who showed signs of dangerously irresponsible behavior. As with gun control laws in the United States and other countries, enforcement was not always successful. Toward the end of the Soviet era, many guns, stolen from the military, helped stock the armories of various ethnic guerrilla fighters and terrorists.

Not only firearms and cars were required to have licenses. Almost to the very last days of the Soviet Union, people were expected to register typewriters, printing presses, and photographic equipment with the militia. As information technology grew, so did the regime's efforts to stem the flow of news. Fax machines, computers, and copiers joined old-fashioned typewriters on the list of banned items and those who owned them were hunted down by police and, if found, arrested.

In addition, the militia granted residency permits and administered internal passports and the registration of hotel guests. When citizens wanted permission to travel abroad or emigrate, the secret police made the decisions and the militia did the necessary paperwork. These day-to-day cops on the beat were also empowered to carry weapons, make arrests, and enter and search homes.

Although its name changed several times, the basic functions of the Soviet secret, or political, police remained the same: to watch, monitor, arrest, and suppress by any means all suspected enemies of the regime. The Soviet secret police became the world's largest domestic and foreign intelligence service. Frequently its methods turned inward, devouring its own agents and even its own bosses: three of its chiefs, Genrikh Yagoda (1891–1938), Nikolai Yezhov (1895–1940), and Lavrenty Beria (1899–1953) were executed by the government they had bloodily served.

From the revolutionary era through the Stalin period, the domestic branch of the secret police also had wide powers to interrogate, try, convict, sentence, and execute. The first political police, called Cheka (short for Extraordinary Commission to Combat Counterrevolution, Sabotage, and Speculation), was formed in 1917. Originally intended as a temporary agency that would be disbanded when the Bolsheviks' power was secure, the Cheka specialized in terror against civilians and uncovering political opposition. From 1917 to 1921 it executed many thousands and sent thousands more to prisons and slave labor camps. As Bolshevik power encroached into new territories so did the power of the Cheka, with the result that local branches were established throughout the RSFSR (Soviet Russia). In 1922 the Cheka was replaced by the GPU (Soviet secret police).

Decrees issued in August and October 1922 gave the GPU the power to exile, imprison, and even execute certain kinds of criminals, including people the GPU judged to be counterrevolutionaries. In 1922, Lenin wrote, "The law should not abolish terror: to promise that would be self-delusion or deception." A law of November 15, 1923, set up a central Party agency, OGPU (Unified State Political Administration), to direct the work of GPU branches in the various Union republics. OGPU was given its own trial court, called the Judicial Collegium, which sentenced people accused of being counterrevolutionaries, spies, and terrorists.

OGPU took over the GPU's function as censor of printed matter, plays, and films. The system of slave labor camps, or Gulag (Central Camps Administration), which had existed since 1918, was brought under OGPU authority as people continued to be executed or sent to the camps for political reasons. The secret police constructed networks of unpaid local police helpers, called "rural executives" and "brigades for assisting the militia." It provided the police machinery for show trials and the massive repression and deportation of millions of peasants after the collectivization drive began in 1929. In 1934 all police agencies in the republics came under the direct control of the Moscow organization (then known as NKVD, People's Commissariat of Internal Affairs, which had absorbed OGPU). The NKVD became Stalin's direct instrument of repression and terror, answerable to no one but him. Under Stalin, the efficient machinery of repression was fine-tuned.

Torture of prisoners to produce confessions was usual under Stalin.

The NKVD and its successors (MGB and KGB, Ministry of State Security and Commissariat of State Security, respectively), besides administering spy and counterspy networks, prisons, and slave labor camps, at one time or another were in charge (directly or through various branches of the militia) of recording births, deaths, marriages, and divorces; administering the Fire and Forest Guards, highways and auto transport, weights and measures, railway construction, wartime rationing, and mass deportations of Soviet nationalities (1941–44); and arresting and executing Red Army soldiers who tried to retreat from front lines. Until the final days of the Soviet Union, the secret police had huge military forces at its disposal.

Torture of prisoners to produce confessions was usual under Stalin, and a conviction could be obtained solely on the basis of a confession if it was a political case. Helped by the vague, elastic wording of the criminal code, any action could be politicized as a crime against the state, including failure to bring in a good harvest. A law of August 7, 1932, made theft of public property, including collective farm property, subject to penalties ranging from 10 years' imprisonment to death. This law was aimed mainly at peasants, who could be prosecuted under it even for petty thefts of grain. Capital punishment was abolished a number of times but always quickly restored. It was done away with and restored in 1920, was abolished in 1947 but reinstated in 1950 for "traitors to the country, spies, and subversive-diversionists" because Stalin had a particular group of "enemies" he wanted shot. After Stalin, the death penalty remained and could be enforced not only for vaguely defined political crimes and violent crimes against people, but also, according to a decree of 1961, for various kinds of economic transgressions, such as large-scale theft and embezzlement, black marketeering, counterfeiting, and "speculation" (privately buying and reselling items for profit).

It was common for people who were to be arrested on political charges to be accused in the state-controlled media before any formal charges were brought. Especially under Stalin, the soon-to-be-arrested might first learn of his or her crime from reading the newspaper. The political show trials of the 1920s and 1930s, with their predetermined outcomes, were given widespread local and national press coverage, as were show trials for ordinary crimes. The latter kind of trial was held in factories and villages in order to teach the masses that crime does not pay. The practice of whipping up public sentiment against the accused was reformed somewhat after Stalin, but the media were still used in political cases to persuade the public that the defendant was guilty. For example, the writers Andrey Sinyavsky and Yuli Daniel were arrested in 1965 for having published their banned books outside the Soviet Union. In advance of their trial, Soviet radio announced that "their punishment would certainly have the backing of the Soviet public." Also before the trial began, Soviet readers unable to acquire the banned books could find out what they were missing by reading the negative, nearly hysterical newspaper descriptions of their content. In contrast, the media were not allowed to report on the preliminary investigation or trial of people suspected of ordinary (nonpolitical) crimes, even in sensational murder cases.

According to decrees issued in 1934 and 1936, people accused of "counterrevolutionary activities" could be barred from their own trials, were not entitled to a lawyer, and could not appeal a death sentence. These decrees were repealed in 1956. An amendment to the criminal code of 1934 stipulated that if a Soviet citizen was convicted of treason, espionage, or certain other "anti-Soviet activities," relatives who knew about the illegal activities but did not inform could be punished for the same offense. According to that law, even relatives who did not know about the accused's crime could be sent to Siberia for five years. Post-Stalin, there was no penalty for family members who were unaware of the crime, and if a political offender's property was confiscated, relatives were allowed to stay in the offender's house or apartment for a while.

During the Terror, the Military Collegium of the Supreme Court was one of the main bodies that tried and sentenced political prisoners after the accused had confessed. The trial and sentencing usually occurred within a few minutes. During the three years of the Terror, the Collegium processed tens of thousands of cases in this summary way; the majority of defendants were sentenced to death. The accused was required to be present at a trial before the Collegium, but not a defense attorney, a prosecutor, or witnesses.

Until Stalin's death, however, most political cases were not dealt with by courts, especially if evidence against the accused was flimsy or nonexistent. In such cases, it was especially convenient to bar the defendant, defense attorney, and witnesses from the proceedings, so in 1934, the Special Board of the NKVD was set up. The Special Board, which operated to the end of the Stalin era, consisted of high-ranking officials in the NKVD and the prosecutor-general of the USSR. After being tried in absentia, prisoners were informed of their sentences at a time and in a manner convenient to those running the prison. In addition, the Special Board could and usually did prolong the imprisonment of a convict who had served the original sentence. Because most prisoners not sentenced to death were sent to slave labor camps, this system provided the Soviet economy with a huge supply of cheap, easily replaceable workers for mines, construction, and land-clearing projects in the harsh climates of the far north and Central Asia. Court-sentenced prisoners, by comparison, had a better chance of being released after serving their time. Besides the charges of counterrevolution, espionage, and sabotage that became so common in the 1920s, 1930s, and 1940s, the Special Board frequently sent a "Member of the Family of a Traitor to the Fatherland" or a "Wife of a Traitor to the Fatherland" to the Gulag; these so-called crimes generally carried minimum sentences of 5 to 10 years, with the ever-present possibility of rearrest at any time after the sentence was served. Ilia Ehrenburg called the children of such convicts "special orphans."

In 1935 a new sentencing body emerged from the Special Board and coexisted with it. An order of the NKVD gave the powers of the Special Board to troiki (singular, troika), committees of three officials that included at least one NKVD officer. Troiki had the power to pass the same sentences as the Special Board. Even though court proceedings for political prisoners were formalities, with sentences usually determined before arrest, and Special Board proceedings were yet more summary, thousands of prisoners were shipped to concentration camps in Siberia or central Asia or otherwise uprooted from their homes for up to five years without being granted any kind of courtroom hearing. The troiki had only to affix the label "socially dangerous element" and the accused was en route to the Gulag. In 1937 Stalin handed down a special decree for a new kind of troika that was allowed to give death sentences, and that often consisted of two rather than three judges. These troiki were set up in all parts of the USSR. As with the Special Board, the defendant was not present at the "trial."

Executions could also be carried out by "special order" from Moscow, and during the period of the Great Terror, such orders were transmitted to secret police chiefs in various far-flung cities demanding the mass execution of tens of thousands of "enemies of the people." The authorities customarily covered up a victim's fate by withholding information, refusing to issue a death certificate, or by issuing a death certificate with false information about the date and cause of death. Lying to relatives about the sentence was common under Stalin and was done in a strangely ritualized manner: "ten years without the right of correspondence with confiscation of personal possessions" meant the victim had been executed. Under Stalin, the length of sentences imposed on political prisoners was related to the date of arrest. In the early 1930s, political offenders generally did not get more than 5 years. Under the secret police chief Yezhov, that sentence was increased to 10 years, and under his successor, Beria, it was more likely to be 20 to 25 years. The cruel boxcar journey to the Gulag, which could last a month, coupled with the extraordinarily harsh conditions of life in the camps, made it difficult for inmates to survive even 5 years, let alone 10 or 20. From 1937 to the end of 1938, at least 1.33 million people were arrested on political charges and sentenced to concentration camps or execution. Politicals whose imprisonments were almost over, or who had served their sentences and been released, might suddenly have the sentence lengthened or be arbitrarily rearrested. In 1937, Nadezhda Mandelstam and her convicted husband, the poet Osip Mandelstam, were afraid to allow themselves to be joyful when the time for his freedom approached. "We knew only too well that the length of your sentence was a matter of chance rather than of law—[it depended] on how your luck ran."

During the Stalin period, when an execution of a political prisoner was about to occur in one of the larger prisons, several wardens and a secret police officer appeared at the condemned person's cell to take him away. The condemned might have time to say good-bye to cellmates and give them personal property such as clothing. At Moscow's Lubyanka prison, the condemned person was taken to one of the rooms off the corridors in the basement, where he took off his clothes and put on white underwear. He was then brought to a special cell equipped with a tarpaulin rug to stand on, and shot in the back of the head. The tarpaulin was removed for cleaning. A doctor signed a death certificate, which was placed in the prisoner's file but usually not disclosed to relatives. The remains were carried off to burial in an unmarked mass grave. Mass repression subsided in the post-Stalin era, but political dissent and debate; freedom to emigrate, travel, and publish abroad; free economic enterprise; and free artistic expression remained strictly forbidden (Eaton).

FOR MORE INFORMATION

Eaton, K. B. *Daily Life in the Soviet Union*. Westport, Conn.: Greenwood Press. Forthcoming.

McClellan, W. *Russia: The Soviet Period and After*. 3d ed. Englewood Cliffs, N.J.: Prentice Hall, 1994.

Shapiro, L. *The Government and Politics of the Soviet Union*. London: Hutchinson University Library, 1965.

JAPAN

POLITICAL LIFE

LAW & CRIME

Holocaust—
War Crimes

United States,
1920-1939

United States,
1960-1990

Latin America

Islamic World

Soviet Union

Japan

Africa

Without doubt Japan has the lowest crime rate in the industrial world. Despite annual editorials in all the major Japanese newspapers trumpeting the alarming increase in crime, Japan has fewer incidents of violent crime throughout the entire nation than many large cities such as New York, Paris, Chicago, Los Angeles, Moscow, and London. In fact, in 2001 there were about 1,300 murders in all of Japan, almost identical to the combined total of just two American cities, Chicago and Los Angeles.

Major property crimes of theft and burglary occur at similar low rates. There are less than 1.5 robberies per 100,000 people, a rate that pales in comparison to those of the United States (over 200), Great Britain (about 65), and even Germany (less than 50). Similarly, Japan experiences about 1.2 murders per 100,000 people compared to 4 for Germany, 9 for Great Britain, and almost the same in the United States. Concomitantly, the Japanese legal system solves and clears about three-quarters of its property theft cases compared to less than half in Germany and only a quarter in the United States and Great Britain. Nearly 95 percent of all murders are solved in Japan. The United States and the other Western nations limp along at about 65 percent.

Various reasons for Japan's low crime rate have been suggested, including the high degree of racial, cultural, and economic homogeneity; stringent gun control; very low rates of illegal drug use; zealous neighborhood policing strategies; and Japan's high degree of social and familial interdependence at the expense of individuality.

Japanese police are credited with interacting with neighborhood residents, obviating a need for citizen surveillance such as neighborhood watch programs. Hundreds of neighborhood police "boxes" (koban) are sprinkled through most cities. In Tokyo, police brag that no resident must walk more than five blocks to the nearest koban. Critics note that police are very intrusive, visiting each home in the neighborhood twice annually to ask very private questions of residents. Foreign residents, including those of Korean ancestry who have lived in Japan for several generations, are required to register with police and are often under close surveillance wherever they go.

Japan has recently experienced a sharp surge in teenage crime, including a disturbing increase in crimes against the homeless. The most prevalent juvenile crime is schoolyard bullying (ijime), which all too often leads to suicide by the hapless victims. Recent national reform movements have had some success, as has resorting to economic sanctions against the parents of bullies. Illegal drug use is on the rise among youth, but again it pales in comparison to that in the United States, Great Britain, Germany, and France.

So-called white-collar economic crimes have increased significantly as well—tied, it is argued, to the country's decade-long economic malaise. Violent crime committed by the notorious organized crime syndicates (Yakuza) has recently increased, with almost weekly shoot-outs among rival urban gangs. Gambling, prostitution, sale of amphetamines, usury, and extortion are tightly controlled in Yakuza-run sections of the major cities. Yakuza support various right-wing political groups, a situation that makes law enforcement difficult. The some 3,000 shadowy gangs probably muster some 90,000 gangsters, a small percentage of the total population.

The Japanese legal system consists of an eclectic blend of Western influences. Much of civil and criminal law was highly influenced by 19th-century French (civil) and German (criminal) ideas. Before that, Japan followed Chinese models of procedural rather than codified laws.

A new national constitution was promulgated in 1947 during the American occupation after World War II. With it, new judicial systems were introduced, portions of which remain in force but are never practiced. For example, suspects are guaranteed trial by jury, but such a process has very rarely been practiced because that civil right was suspended in 1943. New juvenile codes were introduced, as were specific drug codes to conform to United Nations legal standards.

The apex of the legal system is the Supreme Court (Saiko Saibansho) of 15 justices, divided into three petty branches of five judges each. The full court concerns itself with the constitutionality of laws as well as judicial review. Justices are nominated by the national cabinet and then elected for life (retirement at age 70) by the lower house of the parliament.

The lower courts include nearly 600 summary courts that have jurisdiction over small claims and minor misdemeanors. There are some 50 family courts throughout the country that rule in matters of divorce, inheritance, and juvenile crimes. Another 50 district courts deal with major civil and criminal cases. Finally, eight high courts function as courts of appeal and have special jurisdiction over electoral issues. The Supreme Court can serve as the ultimate appeals court but commonly "rules by not ruling," that is, it usually upholds the lower courts' decisions.

The Japanese legal system leans toward arbitration and mediation at the local level. It has an astoundingly high rate of conviction. In 1988, for example, only 50 of 57,790 accused persons were acquitted (about 0.01%). Defense attorneys commonly do not dispute the guilt of the accused but rather argue mitigating circumstances. Defendants, however, are not allowed to plead guilty. The trial must proceed in order to determine extent of guilt. Judges then determine sentences on the basis of that guilt, of course, but also on the degree of remorse, attempts at reparation, and mediation.

Few convicted persons are actually imprisoned for anything but major crimes. There are fewer than 70,000 prisoners in a population of over 125 million, which is among the lowest incarceration rates in the developed world. The United States, with only about 2.3 times the population, has recently reported a prison population of over two million. Most prison terms are relatively short, though Japan still imposes the death penalty by hanging for particularly vicious murders. Recently some prisons came under criticism for alleged prisoner abuse.

The number of practicing attorneys in Japan is one of the lowest in the developed world. There are reputedly fewer Japanese lawyers (12,000) in the entire country than in New York City. Most practice corporate law; very few specialize in criminal law.

To read about law and crime in early modern Japan, see the Japan entry in the section "Law, Crime, and Punishment" in chapter 6 ("Political Life") in volume 4 of this series.

~Louis G. Perez

FOR MORE INFORMATION

Henderson, D. F. *Conciliation and Japanese Law.* 2 vols. Seattle: University of Washington Press, 1965.

Minear, R. H. *Japanese Traditions and Western Law.* Cambridge, Mass.: Harvard University Press, 1970.

Ramseyer, J. M., and M. Nakazato. *Japanese Law: An Economic Approach.* Chicago: University of Chicago Press, 1999.

AFRICA

During colonial rule in the first half of the 20th century, European nations often took a rather paternalistic approach when it came to their African subjects. Colonial rule was deemed as a way of introducing civility and order to savage Africa. European colonizers viewed the creation and enforcement of European-style laws as a para-

POLITICAL LIFE
|
LAW & CRIME
|
Holocaust—
War Crimes

United States,
1920-1939

United States,
1960-1990

Latin America

Islamic World

Soviet Union

Japan

Africa

mount concern in that it ensured that order would be maintained. Consequently, British, French, Belgian, and Portuguese colonial law and courts were installed in their respective colonies.

Before colonial rule, Europeans' depictions of Africans as lawless savages were inaccurate. Precolonial societies throughout the continent had already developed a very complex set of laws and courts. These systems were tested over centuries and, in general, served the people well. Though jails were rare, punishments were practical and harsh when necessary. Often these precolonial systems were based on a king, chief, or group of elders analyzing the nature of the disagreement and then determining the outcome.

The intentions of the colonial states were not noble, in that colonizers had self-serving interests. These laws and courts were designed to maintain order so that colonial governments could function and, more importantly, so the European countries could profit from African labor and natural resources. This self-serving nature was quite obvious; colonial law had a particular emphasis on property rights, labor, and credit, which were the main components of the colonial economic system. Colonial law had to justify European control of African land, enforce contracts, and punish debtors. Some colonies even sentenced debtors and those who broke labor contracts to forced labor camps, building railroads, working the fields, and the like.

Where it benefited the colonial state, indigenous laws were somewhat maintained. The British were particularly adept in incorporating customary laws into colonial law. British colonial rule employed indirect rule, which used already existing judicial and political institutions to govern the colony. Often African chiefs were kept in power (if they were loyal to the British) or even created. Colonialists believed that it was more natural for Africans to follow these indigenous laws.

Because colonial rule was unfair and harsh, some Africans committed acts that the colonial government deemed criminal. These ranged from minor acts such as violating zoning laws or petty theft to even murder or rebellions, though the latter were much more rare and infrequent. Stealing food for one's family, brewing illegal alcohol to pay for school fees, and simply running away from grueling work were common crimes. Arrests often came with fines, jail time, and forced labor. Due to the unjust nature of colonialism, many of these acts can now be looked back on as heroism or resisting imperial rule.

The duties of the police and military were to maintain colonial rule, enforce colonial laws, and arrest lawbreakers. These forces often consisted of white officers with African underlings. Because the jobs within these forces required harshness and brutality, they usually attracted those whose intentions were cruel or corrupt. Police were sent to arrest illegal workers, retrieve those who broke labor contracts, and remove illegal migrants from urban areas. As a result, these forces were detested by the African population in general and were often targets in times of violence.

Ironically, colonial courts offered Africans a medium within which to resist colonial rule. Africans could plead their cases and use reason to demonstrate the cruelties of colonial rule. The most extreme of these cases came from South Africa, where the African National Congress (ANC), the leading group in the antiapartheid movement and currently the country's ruling political party, used courts to petition for government reforms. In hopes of dismantling the ANC, the apartheid regime often arrested members, passed unjust laws against protesting, and even trumped up charges against the movement's leaders. The ANC took its cases to the courts and occasionally won. The best example came from the 1961 "treason trial," when Nelson Mandela and other leaders were charged with crimes against the state. The ANC won and the state's case was overturned, but many ANC members were later convicted of similar charges.

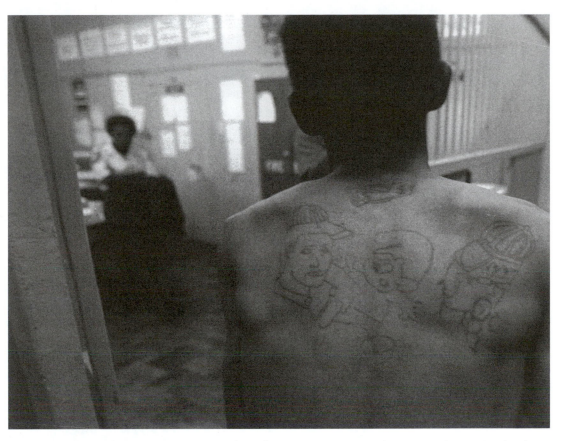

A gang member with prison tattoos sits at the police station in Mannenburg, Cape Town, South Africa. © AP/Wide World Photos.

After independence, judicial systems continued to be manipulated by the government, with the exception that these governments were run by African officials. The postcolonial period in Africa has been one of pain and problems. Overthrowing colonial rule was only part of the problem; developing the continent and overcoming the legacies of colonial rule have proven to be much harder. Leaders have failed to fulfill promises that have been made, which has led to popular discontent. As a result, many leaders and officials have used corrupt courts and police to maintain their positions of power.

Because colonial rulers and even independent governments wrongly manipulated laws to exploit Africans, many Africans feel justified in hating and disobeying the law. Unfortunately, this situation has led to contempt for police officers and judges who, in theory, are supposed to be protecting the people. These institutions have repeatedly neglected the needs of the people, so it is understandable that such sentiment has become widespread.

Islam has also shaped and influenced laws throughout the continent. Centuries before colonization, the Islamic faith and its sharia law were pillars of certain African societies. Sharia law is quite different from Western codes of law in that it calls for direct connection between religion and the judicial system. Many of its laws come directly from interpretations of the Qur'an. Aside from North Africa, which is almost completely Islamic, African nations such as Somalia, Mali, Senegal, Sudan, Nigeria, and Tanzania have sizable Muslim populations. Many of these countries have even formally adopted certain aspects of sharia law. As Islam becomes a more viable alternative to Western civilization, Islamic laws will most likely become more influential in Africa in the future.

At the end of the 20th century, law in Africa remained a complex system weaving together Islamic, Western, and indigenous judicial systems. As has been illustrated, law in Africa has been employed and manipulated unfairly by both foreign and domestic government officials. This cycle of corruption and manipulation of African judicial systems must be broken if Africans are to correct the ills of the past.

~Tyler Fleming

FOR MORE INFORMATION

Clayton, A., and D. Killingray. *Khaki and Blue: Military and Police in Colonial Africa*. Athens: Ohio University Center for International Studies, 1989.

Hills, A. *Policing Africa: Internal Security and the Limits of Liberalization*. Boulder, Colo.: Lynne Rienner, 2000.

Mann, Ki., and R. Roberts, eds. *Law in Colonial Africa*. Portsmouth, N.H.: Heinemann, 1991.

POLITICAL LIFE
|
REFORM
|
United States,
1920-1939

United States,
1940-1959

United States,
1960-1990

Islamic World

Japan

Reform

In the 19th century, the Western world engaged in various processes that scholars have collectively labeled (perhaps euphemistically) as modernization. From colonization of Africa, the Middle East, and Asia to the dramatic growth in corporate capitalism to the creation of large cities to the rise of international politics, few areas of daily life went untouched. People in the Western world and in fact most of the entire world became interdependent politically and economically. Japan, which had been isolated for centuries, began a process of rapid economic modernization in the late 19th century, eagerly adopting Western ideas and practices. Even socially and culturally, modernization forged new relationships among people thousands of miles apart. This interconnectedness created new possibilities for human understanding. At the same time, it created new vulnerabilities with horrific results.

One of the vulnerabilities of the modern world related to economics. Even at the dawn of the 20th century, much of the world economic structure was interwoven. Weakness or downturns in one area of the globe meant economic retrenchment in other areas. Such was the case with the worldwide Great Depression of the late 1920s and 1930s. Each nation affected by the devastating economic collapse had its own set of circumstances. Germany, for example, had struggled mightily in postwar Europe. By contrast, the United States had done well in the 1920s, although the growth was uneven and shaky. Blows such as a major stock market crash and banking fiascos put America down the path to economic ruin.

In the midst of the total disaster that the Great Depression brought, several reformers emerged in the Western world. These articles focus primarily on Franklin D. Roosevelt and his New Deal, which changed the political, economic, and social daily lives of all Americans. The entries nicely summarize how the New Deal stabilized the modern economy in the United States by providing stability, security, and relief. Many of the Rooseveltian changes are quite well known, such as banking reform and work projects. Also pay close attention, however, to those reforms that quietly but fundamentally changed daily life. Take rural electrification, for instance. When FDR took office in 1933 only 10 percent of American farms had electricity. When he died in 1945 only 10 percent did not.

The New Deal reforms were not universally successful. In fact, some groups in America were largely left behind as the United States moved past the Great Depression and World War II. Yet, from the 1950s through the 1970s, new reform movements appeared to deal with the habitual weaknesses of the "affluent society" (as John Kenneth Galbraith called it). Simply put, the problem was that the modern American economy failed to provide enough opportunities for everyone. In particular, African Americans were denied a chance to live without poverty and deprivation. As the great black labor leader A. Philip Randolph explained, the civil rights movement was about jobs *and* freedom.

Not all nations reacted to modernization with the same zeal to make it work for all members of society. In fact, some rejected the modern economy, which was based on capitalism; modern politics with its emphasis on democracy; and modern society, which utilized new technologies and new ideas. In the Muslim world, conservative reformers sought to return daily life to a point before Western modernization impacted the region. Many of these reformers adhered to the ideas of Ibn Abd al-Wahhab, an 18th-century Islamic jurist. Wahhabi ideology has influenced much of the Middle East, particularly Saudi Arabia and Afghanistan, where the Taliban movement ruled for years. In many ways, the contemporary clash between these Islamists and the rest of the modern world is a battle over reactions to modernization.

FOR MORE INFORMATION

Anderson, J. A. *Philip Randolph: A Biographical Portrait.* New York: Harcourt, Brace, Jovanovich, 1973.

Galbraith, J. K. *The Affluent Society.* Boston: Houghton Mifflin, 1958.

UNITED STATES, 1920–39

The New Deal era was the most innovative reform period in the 20th century. President Franklin D. Roosevelt promised that his administration would bring relief, reform, and recovery. The New Deal created a plethora of agencies designed to bring the United States out of the Great Depression. Despite the confusing and often overlapping nature of these "alphabet agencies," they dealt with two broad issues: reform in agriculture and reform in industry.

POLITICAL LIFE

REFORM

Among the first issues the New Deal addressed was the agricultural depression that had gripped the nation since the early 1920s and was being made worse in the 1930s by drought conditions. During the 1920s, over six million people abandoned farm country; although births exceeded deaths, America's rural population had fallen by 1.2 million. Various solutions to the farm problem had been put forth, but no plan for government intervention could be agreed upon, and no proposal for private action enlisted sustained voluntary compliance. With American farmers able to produce more crops, livestock, and dairy products than the market could absorb, inadequate prices for farm commodities were a central problem. Farmers often found they could not even recover their costs, much less gain a sufficient profit to be able to earn a living. By 1930, over a quarter of U.S. farms, home to over 7.5 million people, produced less than $600 of farm products a year. Schemes to use government facilities or private cooperative programs to hold farm commodities off the market to obtain higher prices failed repeatedly. By 1933, some groups of angry farmers in Iowa and elsewhere resorted to crop burning and milk dumping to achieve the same result, but with no more success. With their mortgaged land and equipment in jeopardy of foreclosure, a mob of desperate farmers in LaMars, Iowa, even threatened to lynch their local banker.

The New Deal responded with the Agricultural Adjustment Act (AAA), the first of many programs that would come to be known by their initials. Adopted by the Hundred Days Congress in May 1933, the AAA set up a federal administration, also called the AAA, to pay farmers who agreed to plant one-third fewer acres or raise one-third fewer animals so that they would suffer no decline in income when they cut production. The funds for the payments came from a tax on processed food. In essence, consumers would pay a small tax on their food to provide a subsidy to farmers for not producing a surplus and weakening the overall farm economy.

Charges that Roosevelt was a dangerous radical spread quickly among the wealthy.

Another provision of the AAA, insisted on by senators from farm states, sought to inflate the U.S. currency. Roosevelt had already taken a step in this direction weeks earlier by taking the United States off the gold standard, refusing to pledge, as in the past, to freely exchange dollars for a set amount of gold. The inflationary provision of the AAA moved the process much further. Inflated dollars would make it easier for debtors to repay mortgages and loans; thus, this measure benefited many indebted farmers, home owners, and small businesses. At the same time, however, planned inflation outraged lenders, who blamed Roosevelt for cheating them out of what was legitimately theirs. Hatred of Roosevelt and charges that he was a dangerous radical spread quickly among the wealthy.

Though the AAA was a sensible enough plan to raise commodity prices, allow farmers to earn a decent living, and insure a dependable national food supply, it was not without problems. The division it widened between the rich and the rest of the people was only the first of them. The AAA was approved by Congress after southern farmers had just planted their cotton and after spring litters of hogs had been born. To receive their AAA payments in 1933, farmers had to plow up 10 million acres of cotton fields and destroy six million baby pigs. At a time when hunger was a widespread problem, the "slaughter of little pigs," as critics called it, was hard for many Americans to understand.

The crop and pig destruction took place only in 1933; advance planning avoided the need to repeat the process thereafter. Still, in the same year, some moviegoers discerned a negative political message in Walt Disney's cartoon *The Three Little Pigs*. They equated the New Deal with the "big bad wolf" who destroyed helpless creatures. The cartoon itself was ambiguous. Others viewed the wolf as a symbol of the depression; the wise little pig who planned ahead, worked hard, and built a solid house as a role model; and the musical accompaniment, "Who's Afraid of the Big Bad Wolf?" as an upbeat New Deal anthem. In any interpretation of Disney's cartoon or popular understanding of the AAA, however, little pigs remained a central theme.

By paying landowners to take cotton fields out of production, the AAA unintentionally undermined many southern tenant farmers by eliminating their opportunity to produce a crop, earn a meager living, and remain on the land. In 1935, the New Deal set up a new agency, the Resettlement Administration, to help tenant farmers relocate, but fewer than 5,000 farm families actually benefited. In 1937, another new agency, the Farm Security Administration (FSA), started helping more tenant farmers to buy land. But neither of these programs was adequately funded or successful. A stream of former tenant farmers from Arkansas and Oklahoma continued to head for the vegetable fields and citrus groves of California. By the end of the decade, a million migrants made the trek west. Perhaps the FSA's greatest achievement was the slight improvement it was able to bring about in the cleanliness, order, and health conditions of migrant labor camps. Otherwise, the landless rural southern poor remained, at the end of the 1930s, the most wretched group of Americans.

In 1936, the Supreme Court ruled that the AAA was unconstitutional. The food-processing tax used to fund the program, a conservative-dominated Court decided, was not a legitimate use of federal power to levy taxes. Farm commodity prices immediately began to fall. The administration responded quickly by devising a new law, the Soil Conservation and Domestic Allotment Act, which paid farmers to plant soil-enriching grasses and legumes instead of soil-depleting crops such as cotton or corn. The basic plan of subsidizing farmers to restrict production and boost farm prices did not change, though the funding now came from the federal government's general budget rather than a special tax, and so the program was widely referred to as the Second AAA. Farm production, income, and life did not suffer a lasting setback from the Court's ruling, but it was not until World War II that the long agricultural depression was fully over.

The New Deal altered rural agricultural life significantly by bringing affordable electricity to many of the 9 out of 10 farms that lacked it. One of the important acts of the Hundred Days Congress was the establishment of the Tennessee Valley Authority (TVA). The TVA assumed control of hydroelectric dams and munitions factories built along the Tennessee River during World War I. These facilities were turned into providers of low-cost electricity and fertilizer for the river's watershed. By providing electricity at the cost of production, Roosevelt explained, the TVA would provide a "yardstick" to measure what power should cost, citing the four times higher per kilowatt hour price that private utility companies were charging at his rural Warm Springs, Georgia, cottage compared to the price charged at his Hyde Park, New York, home. The TVA boosted the economically backward eight-state Tennessee Valley region's agricultural productivity as well as gave its rural residents access to electric power. In so doing, the TVA established a model for regional power and economic development that the New Deal soon tried to copy along the Colorado, upper Missouri, Columbia, and other rivers.

The creation in May 1935 of the Rural Electrification Administration (REA) made government loans available to assist power companies and nonprofit cooperatives in erecting electric transmission lines in rural areas. Previously, that had not been commercially feasible because rural America had too few electric customers spread too far apart. Thus, many rural dwellers continued to make do with wood, coal, kerosene, and candles for heat and light. Some farmers used a gasoline-powered generator or an extra automobile battery to obtain a little electricity, whereas others did without. The isolation and sense of backwardness resulting from lack of access to the electricity that powered urban America evaporated as soon as the REA brought electric lines into the countryside. By 1940, a third of American farms had acquired electricity, and 10 years later, 90 percent had done so. The ability to switch on electric lights, motors, and appliances transformed rural life both technologically and psychologically.

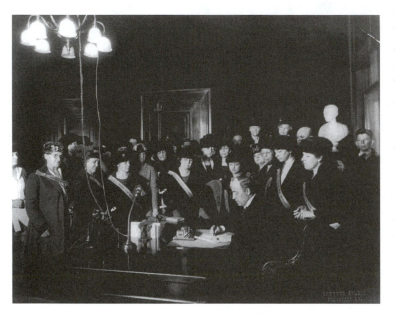

Women belonging to the suffrage movement watch the state's governor certify ratification of the 19th Amendment. © Library of Congress.

Putting people back to work and reviving American business was another of Roosevelt's prime objectives at the outset of the New Deal. Before the administration could put forth a plan to accomplish this, senators talked about adopting a law reducing the workweek to five 6-hour days. The 30-hour plan assumed that the American economy had reached a point where it could efficiently produce more goods and services than could be consumed. Thus, for everyone wanting a job to be able to have one, the available work needed to be spread out. Alabama Democratic senator Hugo Black, the 30-hour plan's chief sponsor, did not think incomes would shrink as much as working hours, but even if they did, the overall situation would be improved. Incomes might be smaller, but at least a significantly greater number of people could support themselves. Society and government then would not have to contend with a substantial portion of the population constantly out of work and a burden on others.

Rather than accept such an assessment, Roosevelt sought to stimulate a business rehabilitation that would link economic growth, job creation, and better treatment of workers. The National Industrial Recovery Act of June 1933 sought to modify traditional free enterprise's cutthroat competition, ruinous price-cutting, and harsh treatment of workers by allowing companies in the same industry to cooperate without being accused of monopolistic practices. Under the supervision of the government's National Recovery Administration (NRA), competing companies would agree on (1) minimum prices for their goods and services, (2) minimum wages and maximum hours for employees, and (3) fair working conditions and a reasonable code of business conduct. Companies participating in the NRA would also be obliged to bargain collectively with workers who chose to form labor unions. As he had done with banking reform, Roosevelt was striving with the NRA to rescue the private enterprise system by eliminating its worst excesses and requiring it to function under the supervision of government agencies that would seek to protect the public interest.

As the NRA started to function in the summer of 1933, many businesses hurried to agree on codes of fair competition. This allowed them to display the symbol of compliance, the NRA Blue Eagle, and gain the customer support that followed. Everywhere newspapers ads and store windows featured the NRA Blue Eagle and the slogan "We Do Our Part." In New York, a Fifth Avenue parade to demonstrate support for the NRA drew a quarter million marchers.

By October 1933, the 10 largest industries had all agreed to NRA codes, and many smaller industries soon followed suit. In return for their concessions (higher wages, acceptance of the principle of collective bargaining, and abolition of child labor in the cotton textile industry), the NRA allowed industries to set higher prices and limits on production. Not every business accepted its industry's code. Henry Ford, for instance, charged that the automobile code was a plot of his competitors to limit his success and refused to sign. Most businesses, however, went along with the NRA, and signs of renewed business confidence and recovery started to appear. The downward economic spiral ceased, wages and hours stabilized, and nearly two million jobs were created.

Criticism of the NRA did not take long to appear. Consumers soon complained about rising prices, businesses objected to government regulation and paperwork, and workers found that collective bargaining pledges went unfulfilled by business and unenforced by the government. The greatest complaint was that the NRA codes let the big companies in an industry set the competitive rules and put their smaller rivals at a disadvantage. Before long enthusiasm for the NRA was fading. By the time that the Supreme Court in 1935 found it to represent an unconstitutionally broad delegation of legislative power to an administrative agency, the NRA had already lost its effectiveness, done in by its reliance on voluntary cooperation with guidelines that the federal government helped to set but then did not enforce.

Abandoning efforts to secure business cooperation, in 1935 the New Deal moved in the direction of strengthening workers' ability to bargain collectively and effectively, presuming that this would lead to fair wages, hours, and working conditions. Competition, together with fair treatment of workers, would keep business functioning properly in an open market. The National Labor Relations Act, proposed by New York senator Robert Wagner and endorsed by FDR once it passed the Senate, had a dramatic effect on many workers. The Wagner Act, as it was frequently called, compelled employers to deal with the labor unions that employees—in elections supervised by the National Labor Relations Board (NLRB)—chose to represent them. The act also prohibited unfair labor practices such as discharging workers for union membership, favoring an employer-dominated company union, or refusing to negotiate in good faith with a union. All of these practices had long been common before the National Industrial Recovery Act and continued after its adoption. But now, with an independent federal agency overseeing labor relations, the weight of the federal government stood behind organized workers in their efforts to negotiate better terms of employment.

Two years later, the Supreme Court upheld the constitutionality of the Wagner Act, confirming a fundamental change in the relationship between no longer all-powerful employers and no longer helpless employees. From the adoption of the Wagner Act in 1935 until the Supreme Court's approval of it in 1937, the NLRB was asked to conduct 76 elections in which workers could choose whether to be represented by a union; from that point to the end of 1940, the NLRB supervised 3,310 such elections. The American Federation of Labor (AFL) or the Congress of Industrial Organizations (CIO) won over three-quarters of all such elections, labor unions became a workplace reality for over a third of American workers, and even nonunionized workers began to share in improved wages and working conditions.

Workers in some industries where treatment had been particularly brutal or compensation especially low moved most quickly to take advantage of the Wagner Act. The great manufacturing industries—automobiles, steel, and rubber—were among the first to undergo unionization campaigns. Employers found it hard to avoid NLRB elections to establish unions but found that as long as they agreed to keep talking to union representatives and appeared to be negotiating, they could easily resist agreeing to a contract. Such tactics frustrated workers in the rubber and auto industries who turned to sit-down strikes in which they simply took over a factory, refusing either to work or to leave, knowing it was unlikely that employers would remove them forcibly for fear of damage to valuable machinery. Workers in these and other industries formed picket lines to block companies that refused to settle with unions from doing business. Violence erupted on numerous occasions between security forces hired by stubborn employers and workers frustrated by failure to gain a satisfactory contract.

In 1938, the New Deal acknowledged that unions alone could not do everything for their members, much less those workers who remained unorganized. FDR obtained congressional approval of its last major measure for workers, the Fair Labor Standards Act. Adoption of this act, which set minimum wages and maximum working hours, was one mark of the relaxation, after 1937, of the Supreme Court's opposition to federal regulation of interstate commerce. The Fair Labor Standards Act granted many exceptions to its coverage, but nevertheless established a $.40 minimum wage and a higher rate for work in excess of 40 hours per week. These provisions improved wages and shortened the normal workweek for those who worked in the most depressed and labor-unfriendly industries.

By 1938 the New Deal had not ended the Great Depression in the United States, but it had reformed the structure of the economy, particularly in agriculture and industry, and allowed significant reforms to happen. These reforms improved the daily lives of Americans and laid the groundwork for future prosperity and economic security (Kyvig, 198–209).

To read about reform in the United States in the 19th century, see the United States entries in the section "Reform Movements" in chapter 6 ("Political Life") in volume 5 of this series.

FOR MORE INFORMATION

Badger, A. J. *The New Deal: The Depression Years, 1933–1940*. New York: Hill and Wang, 1989.

Kyvig, D. E. *Daily Life in the United States, 1920–1939: Decades of Promise and Pain*. Westport, Conn.: Greenwood Press, 2002.

The New Deal Network. <http://newdeal.feri.org/>.

Robbins, T., dir. *The Cradle Will Rock*.

UNITED STATES, 1940–59

Among the most important reform issues from the 1940s to the 1960s was civil rights. Because Jackie Robinson had broken the color line in major league baseball in 1947 and Harry Truman had desegregated the army in 1948, most Americans could see that moral progress toward equal opportunity was real. Few people noticed the tremendous number of African Americans, denied work in the South by new agricultural machines, who had flooded into most large cities. When the New Deal sought to help the one-third of the nation that was ill fed, ill housed, and ill clothed in the 1930s, Congress supported the president because so many Americans recognized these people as their neighbors. But a third of those excluded from postwar economic gains were black. Most white Americans ignored these African Americans. John Kenneth Galbraith's defining book on the 1950s, *The Affluent Society*, mentions race only once. Although *Black Metropolis* by St. Clair Drake and Horace Clayton described Chicago in 1945, it would not be until 1992, with Nicholas Lemann's broader national treatment, *The Promised Land: The Great Black Migration and How It Changed America*, that serious attention was given the greatest postwar social need.

That the best book written by a black intellectual during the 1950s should be called *Invisible Man* (1952) was entirely appropriate. Ralph Ellison's hero made it clear that he was invisible because people simply refused to see him. His story dramatized a number of American situations the black man found himself in: rural poverty, Negro colleges, Communist groups, religious fellowships, and race riots. The hero hiding in the sewer at the end of the novel was drawn to conclude that his invisibility had to be "covert preparation for a more overt action."

When in 1954 the Supreme Court, with the *Brown v. Board of Education of Topeka* decision, established that separate was not equal, the overt action began. During the second half of the 1950s black rights were tested in many ways. The period brought forth a number of dignified and courageous civil rights leaders and lawyers as well as many brave black individuals willing to put their lives on the line for justice. Some whites also worked behind the scenes with African Americans to help bring about successful school integration, to begin voter registration, and to extend the privileges of using facilities then denied blacks. Imagine that Jackie Robinson could not get a cup of coffee at a drugstore lunch counter or sleep in the same hotel with his teammates.

The event, modest though it seemed, that first turned everything upside down in the South was the 1955 refusal of Rosa Parks, a department store seamstress too tired after a long day's work, to give up her seat on an overcrowded bus in Montgomery, Alabama, so that a white man could sit down. After her arrest Parks urged fellow bus travelers to join her in a boycott aimed at getting fair treatment for blacks on all local buses. Parks was not the first person to protest the segregation of public transportation, but she was perfectly trained to make a trial case. Educated in the North and a former secretary of the National Association for the Advancement of Colored People (NAACP), Rosa Parks became a national heroine. Yet the store where she worked closed its alterations department, putting her out of work, and her husband was also fired from his job as a barber. Menacing telephone calls made their lives so miserable that they eventually had to move away from Montgomery. But the boycott, inspired by the eloquence of a young Martin Luther King Jr. and the know-how of Bayard Rustin, an experienced lawyer, was a success. After 381 days, during which many white women picked up their domestic help and many blacks walked for miles, the bus company acknowledged defeat. A national sense of fairness shaped attitudes—the entire country had begun to support the boycott. The United Auto Workers sent $35,000 to help run the carpool set up to drive black workers to faraway jobs. In 1991 actress Sissy Spacek helped dramatize the interracial nature of the protest on film in *The Long Walk Home*. Rosa Parks's defiance remains among the most productive acts of civil disobedience in American history.

When this moment pushed Martin Luther King Jr. onto the broad public screen as the head of the nonviolent Montgomery Improvement Association, people recognized a remarkable new leader. In the 1950s, as Taylor Branch's detailed book on the civil rights movement, *Parting the Waters: America in the King Years, 1954–1963*, reveals, a number of brave African American leaders such as Bayard Rustin, E. D. Nixon, Ralph Abernathy, and James Lawson were equal to the moment. King saw the black people at this time injecting new meaning into the veins of civilization with protest, not with guns. He was right. His eloquence was special; he made everyone feel that the great glory of American democracy is the right to protest for right, underlining the patriotism of his followers: "If we are wrong, the Constitution of the United States is wrong. . . . If we are wrong, justice is a lie." Under the guidance of King and the talented black lawyers Thurgood Marshall and Constance Baker Motley, the African American community asserted its demands for equal rights with considered dignity—in welcome contrast to the hysteria that had spread during the McCarthy period. The blacks' behavior in the civil rights struggles of the 1950s represented great courage, even as King's rhetorical skills seemed perfectly matched to every occasion. Aware of the risk to his life, King famously promised "to work and fight until justice runs down like water and righteousness like a mighty stream!"

The many photographs of people enjoying backyard barbecues and drive-in movies in 1958 belied the social complexity of the period. There were always some white people volunteering behind the scenes to make the society fairer—to demonstrate their commitment to making the new decision against segregation work. In 1957 as many as 10,000 students took part in a youth march for integration. Most Americans outside of the South believed integration would improve racial understanding.

But an unfortunate incident at Arkansas's Little Rock Central High School in 1957–58 may remain the most important historic measure of the integration mandate. When Orval Faubus, the governor of Arkansas, approved of local segregationists preventing nine black students from attending the all-white high school by using the state National Guard to keep them out, President Eisenhower called in federal troops to protect

Most Americans outside of the South believed integration would improve racial understanding.

the students and to enforce the law. In 1997 President Clinton returned to Little Rock to welcome back the then middle-aged students, noting that what happened in Little Rock changed the course of our country forever. Television news cameras in the 1950s caught the hatred of the menacing whites as well as the bravery of the well-starched blacks (eight were girls). Daisy Bates, the courageous president of the Arkansas NAACP, made herself the protector and counselor of the young people. It was she who demanded that Eisenhower call in the army. In spite of many threatening phone calls she did not lose her life, but, like Rosa Parks, Daisy Bates lost her livelihood when her fellow townspeople took all the advertising out of the newspaper she and her husband had run for 18 years. Later, Bates wrote a painful memoir of the crisis, *The Long Shadow of Little Rock*.

In 1997 President Clinton had to acknowledge that the law that reshaped Little Rock had failed to bring about equal educational achievement and the kind of social change that might enable blacks and whites to be close friends. By refusing to attend Clinton's 40th anniversary celebration of the Little Rock Nine, the NAACP underlined how much work remained to be done. Yet the years between 1957 and 1997 saw Central High become 60 percent black, and African Americans managed to get training for professional jobs as librarians, counselors, and information specialists. If too few blacks managed to fulfill their potential in terms of what was available to them, at least after 1957 a sense of possibility had replaced a sense of hopelessness. The black president of the Central High School Student Council in 1997 valued the motivation the students retained, saying that today's scholars had taken the torch from the Little Rock Nine and passed it from class to class.

During the 1950s, in a final effort to outwit the federal government, Orval Faubus temporarily closed all the public high schools. The remaining black students then had to get their diplomas through correspondence courses from the university (while whites created private academies so that they would not have to integrate their local schools). These extreme measures contented many older whites, who persuaded themselves that the pursuit of American justice for blacks was simply another Communist plot.

Such sentiment was displayed in the hardships faced by Autherine Lucy, a 26-year-old black woman who applied to the University of Alabama in 1956 to study library science. The first black student in 125 years, Lucy was threatened with violence. Mobs tried to kill her. Many suspected she was a Communist tool. For the

Voice of America, Lucy bravely broadcast an honest statement of her position: "I know very little about Communism," she declared. "I am an American. . . . In my struggle for recognition as an American student, I have approached it in the American spirit and without the help of any enemies of our country." Suspended from the school for her own safety and called before the Alabama House of Representatives for an investigation of Communist affiliations, Lucy continued to maintain her Christianity and her faith in democratic principles. The inspirational words of Martin Luther King Jr. helped many blacks to stand up for their beliefs in nonviolent confrontation: "Don't ever let anyone pull you so low as to hate them," he urged. "This is not a war between the white and the Negro but a conflict between justice and injustice."

Yet the roots of American racism run deep. In the 1950s television became a strong force in exposing many problems that the most idealistic Americans wanted to ignore. In 1956, when Emmett Till, a 14-year-old African American from Chicago, was brutally murdered in Mississippi for allegedly flirting with a white woman, the entire press corps was on the scene. His murderers were acquitted after the defense attorney, appealing to prejudice, asked that every Anglo-Saxon member of the jury have the "courage to free" the defendants—who then arrogantly sold the story of their crime. Thousands of people showed sympathy by visiting the black funeral home in Chicago where the young victim's mutilated body was on display. A sense of general outrage did not subside quickly.

David Halberstam, an important voice of 1950s journalism, speaking about the responsibility of the American press corps, noted that the *Brown v. Board of Education* decision had made a critical moral and social difference in the way the entire country viewed civil rights. When the Till case arrived there was a national agenda on civil rights in place, defining a crucial moment for the national media. Over the next decade, the *New York Times*, the American newspaper of historical record, would lead the way in making sure the nation as a whole became aware of the need to end the racial discrimination that prevented the fulfillment of American ideals among black citizens. Many responsible journalists helped make what was invisible become visible.

Still, in 1956, 19 southern senators and 82 representatives formulated a "southern manifesto," declaring that the Supreme Court had abused its judicial power in the *Brown* decision. All sorts of ruses, such as "pupil placement scores" and "private" public education, were inaugurated to make sure that opportunities for blacks remained unequal. Deeply institutionalized discrimination defined the civil rights struggle. When the Civil Rights Act of 1957 was so weakened by Congress as to be useless, Martin Luther King Jr. helped create the Southern Christian Leadership Conference (SCLC) to bring about political change. Thirty-five years after the *Brown* decision, it must be noted, 30 percent of all black children in the United States still went to public schools that were 90 percent nonwhite.

African Americans kneel on the sidewalk outside City Hall in Birmingham, Alabama, protesting racial segregation. © Library of Congress.

After World War II white middle-income Americans became more aware of their own prejudices. The movie *Crossfire* (1947) confronted anti-Semitism head-on, whereas *Gentleman's Agreement* (1947), based on a popular novel, made people realize that Americans also sanctioned unofficial quotas and subtle discrimination systems to keep Jews out of establishment schools as well as clubs and resorts. Although often reluctantly, American movies turned from disseminating wartime propaganda to becoming a source of education about social problems. *Pinky* (1949) was an extraordinary film about a black woman's "passing" as white. *The Defiant Ones* (1958) used the metaphor of the chain gang to show black and white linked together, and John Ford's 1956 classic Western *The Searchers* looked at racist attitudes toward Native Americans with new complexity. Edna Ferber's huge novel about Texas, *Giant* (converted into a box office success in 1956), dealt with prejudice against Mexicans in its Texas panorama. A distinguished drama, Carson McCullers's prizewinning *Member of the Wedding*, turned into a movie in 1953, made audiences consider how deeply black and white lives were intertwined. Such films also offered young people a chance to see themselves involved in social conflicts.

In May 1959, Irene Dobbs Jackson, sister to the distinguished Metropolitan Opera diva Mattiwilda Dobbs, offered to make herself a test case for getting blacks into the Carnegie Library in Atlanta. The trustees agreed at once to give this remarkable woman, who had six children and a doctorate from the University of Toulouse, a library card. From that moment on all the libraries in Atlanta were open to African Americans. An embarrassed white Atlantan wrote the local paper to acknowledge that he had never even realized that the libraries were segregated.

During the 1960s, labeled the civil rights decade, when many whites entered the South to help register black voters, some of the weaknesses of passive resistance would be revealed. But during the 1950s there was good reason to accept historian Howard Zinn's conclusion to Irene Dobbs Jackson's story: "The twentieth century may, eons from now, be viewed as the time when peaceful social change came into its own." The dignity of the civil rights movement, strongly begun in the 1950s, should remain a source of American pride (Kaledin, 93–98).

To read about reform in the United States in the 19th century, see the United States entries in the section "Reform Movements" in chapter 6 ("Political Life") in volume 5 of this series.

FOR MORE INFORMATION

Bates, D. *The Long Shadow of Little Rock: A Memoir.* New York: David and McKay Co., 1962.

Branch, T. *Parting the Waters: America in the King Years, 1954–1963.* New York: Simon and Schuster, 1988.

Eyes on the Prize. PBS Video. 1987.

Galbraith, J. K. *The Affluent Society.* Boston: Houghton Mifflin, 1958.

Garrow, D. J. *Bearing the Cross: Martin Luther King, Jr., and the Southern Christian Leadership Conference.* New York: Morrow, 1986.

Kaledin, E. *Daily Life in the United States, 1940–1959: Shifting Worlds.* Westport, Conn.: Greenwood Press, 2000.

Lemann, N. *The Promised Land: The Great Black Migration and How It Changed America*. New York: Knopf, 1991.

St. Claire, D. and H. Clayton. *Black Metropolis: A Study of Negro Life in a Northern City*. New York: Harper and Row, 1962.

Sitkoff, H. *The Struggle for Black Equality, 1945–1990*. New York: Hill and Wang, 1991.

POLITICAL LIFE

|

REFORM

|

United States,
1920-1939

United States,
1940-1959

United States,
1960-1990

Islamic World

Japan

UNITED STATES, 1960–90

Through the 1960s, civil rights remained a paramount reform issue in America. The daily lives of most Americans may not seem to have been directly affected by what came to be known as the unrest of the 1960s, but the changes wrought by protests in those years rippled across America. The most striking changes were the fruits of the civil rights movement, which in its modern form traced its origins at least as far back as World War II. At that time the cruel irony of asking African Americans to risk their lives for a country that denied them constitutionally guaranteed rights became glaringly obvious. Several Supreme Court decisions set precedents for the 1954 landmark case of *Brown v. Board of Education*. In *Brown* the Court ruled that schools designed to be "separate but equal" were inherently unequal and therefore unconstitutional.

Armed with the conviction that the Supreme Court's decision outlawing "separate but equal" schools extended to other aspects of their lives, and frustrated by resistance to calls for change, African American activists adopted a strategy that at first baffled those seeking to thwart them: they defied laws that denied them rights but refused to defend themselves against physical and verbal attacks. On February 1, 1960, four students at North Carolina A&T College in Greeensboro took the first nonviolent action of the 1960s. These students, the 66 who joined them the next day, the 100 the next, and the 1,000 by the end of the week, sat down at a "whites only" lunch counter in a Woolworth's store in Greensboro. The Greensboro "coffee party," which historian William Chafe says "takes its place alongside the Boston Tea Party as an event symbolizing a new revolutionary era," infuriated segregationists. Television cameras captured the segregationists' resistance and broadcast it nationwide, thereby creating support for blacks who were ready to take further direct actions.

The practice of holding sit-ins spread, and before the end of the year an estimated 70,000 activists put pressure on white business leaders by challenging segregation laws and practices in more than 150 cities. In 1961 came Freedom Rides, organized by James Farmer of the Congress on Racial Equality (CORE). The Freedom Riders, small interracial groups who traveled by public buses into the Deep South to test whether federal court orders on integration of bus depots were being honored, encountered hostile and often brutal treatment. Again, television cameras brought the bloody scenes into homes throughout America. More important, the spreading outrage provoked by those scenes forced the federal government to take sides, and there was clearly only one side it could take.

In 1962 the nation watched the violence that erupted when James Meredith, a black Mississippian, enrolled at his state's university under a court order to admit him. The next year federal marshals led black students past Governor George Wallace as he attempted to block the entrance to the University of Alabama. Television carried that, too, across the nation. With each such incident, awareness of the civil rights movement reached into the lives of viewers. Children, particularly, seemed to be impressed by what they saw. "They can do what they want to," a former principal of a southern black elementary school remarked, "but millions of little eyes are watching, and they're making plans."

Along with the Freedom Rides came protests and marches led by Martin Luther King Jr., and the Southern Christian Leadership Conference in Birmingham and other cities in the South. Stressing nonviolence as essential in the practice of civil disobedience, efforts led by King laid the groundwork for the now-famous March on Washington in 1963. At that event, King spoke from the steps of the Lincoln Memorial to a crowd of 250,000. Carried by television to millions more—perhaps the first civil rights demonstration to capture the attention of the entire nation—Dr. King departed from his prepared text to speak of his "dream." "I have a dream," he said, "that one day this nation will rise up and live out the true meaning of its creed: 'We hold these truths to be self-evident; that all men are created equal.'" Rhythmically he intoned the next seven sentences with "I have a dream." Two sentences said simply: "I have a dream today." With the audience stirred by his eloquence and passion, King urged the nation to "let freedom ring." Eight times he repeated that line, concluding with the following:

Surrounded by members of Congress with Dr. Martin Luther King Jr. in the background, President Lyndon Johnson signs the 1964 Civil Rights Act. © Library of Congress.

When we let freedom ring, when we let it ring from every village and every hamlet, from every state and every city, we will be able to speed up that day when all of God's children, black men and white men, Jews and Gentiles, Protestants and Catholics, will be able to join hands and sing in the words of the old Negro spiritual, "Free at last! Free at last! Thank God almighty, we are free at last!"

Just a month later, the Sunday-morning bombing of a church in Birmingham in which four black girls were killed was a sobering reminder that not everyone shared King's dream.

Despite the resistance that acts like the church bombing exemplified, modern America seemed ready for some of the changes demanded by civil rights leaders. In fact, the resistance helped build momentum for enactment of a civil rights law in 1964 that, among other things, prohibited racial discrimination in public accommodations in any business engaged in interstate commerce and in most employment situations. It soon became apparent that the Democratic Party's position on civil rights would cause it to lose its dominance in what had been known as the "solid South" since the Civil War. Indeed, when Lyndon Johnson signed the 1964 Civil Rights Act he remarked to an aide: "I think we just delivered the South to the

Republican Party for a long time to come." By the time of the presidential election that year, the phenomenon known as white backlash came into evidence not only in the South but in all quarters of America. Johnson's opponent, Senator Barry Goldwater of Arizona, had voted against the Civil Rights Act; although he lost the election, his followers adhered to his convictions on civil rights in rebuilding the Republican Party.

In 1965, responding to the leadership of President Johnson (himself a southerner), Congress passed the Voting Rights Act, aimed at removing barriers that had long kept African Americans out of polling places, particularly in the South. For decades thereafter the new voters generally supported the Democratic Party, although not in sufficient numbers to offset the loss of white voters. Through their actions on racial matters, both parties prompted ordinary citizens to ask themselves where they stood on matters of race, access to jobs, housing, and social opportunity. As voters answered these questions, both parties gained and lost supporters in regions outside the South as well as in it, although party affiliation continued to rest on much more than one's position on racial issues.

Laws and court decisions were not alone in pushing and pulling the American people one way or another on racial matters. Two other things came into play: violent behavior and increasingly militant language by blacks. The most extreme example of the former was the riot in Watts, a black ghetto in Los Angeles. On August 11, 1965, just five days after President Johnson signed the Voting Rights Act, a confrontation between white police and a black man stopped for a traffic violation sparked a six-day riot. When it was over, 34 people were dead, 900 were injured, 4,000 were under arrest, and property damage amounted to more than $30 million. Despite the presence of 1,500 police officers and 14,000 National Guardsmen, rioters destroyed entire city blocks. Seething black resentment of white police (in the 98% black Watts district, 200 of the 205 police officers were white) had set the stage for the riot, but the rioters lost whatever sympathies they might have inspired among whites, both in Watts and elsewhere, by chanting "Burn, baby, burn!" Riots in other cities, frequently sparked by confrontations between blacks and police, blurred the sense of progress that the court decisions and new laws had seemed to create.

The militant language of some black leaders dismayed many Americans, both white and black. Speeches by Malcolm X, a preacher formerly associated with the Nation of Islam, struck many as hateful and scornful of whites for the treatment of his people through the years. By stressing racial pride and dignity, he inspired his followers in ways whites had difficulty understanding. The assassination of Malcolm X by Black Muslims, followers of Elijah Muhammad, on February 21, 1965, did not silence his message.

Advocates of Black Power, led by Stokely Carmichael and the Student Non-violent Coordinating Committee (SNCC, known as Snick), used language just as harsh. Working closely with the powerless and disadvantaged victims of discrimination, they understood the daily suffering of members of their race. As were the followers of Malcolm X, the activists in SNCC were driven by deep cynicism about the honesty and good faith of America's white leaders and the entire country's white population.

The division between Stokely Carmichael and those who stood with him on one side, and Martin Luther King Jr. and his followers on the other, became starkly clear in June 1966. James Meredith was again a key figure in an event that once more drew Americans to their television sets. While he marched alone across Mississippi to give blacks the confidence to register and vote, a shotgun fired by an assassin from roadside bushes cut him down, planting 60 pellets in his body. With Meredith's consent, civil rights groups converged on the scene to complete the march.

At rallies along the way King continued to advocate nonviolence, but Carmichael spoke more militantly. Finally, in Canton, Mississippi, Carmichael exhorted: "The only way we are going to stop them from whuppin' us is to take over. We've been saying freedom for six years and we ain't got nothin'. . . . The time for running has come to an end. . . . Black Power. It's time we stand up and take over; move on over [Whitey] or we'll move on over you." "Black Power!" chanted the crowd. "Black Power! Black Power!" The call for Black Power shattered the facade of unity among civil rights leaders and their followers. Martin Luther King Jr. wanted yet to preserve a national coalition of blacks and whites committed to the cause of civil rights, but Stokely Carmichael refused to limit his efforts to stir black people to action.

By the late 1960s it was obvious that if enacting civil rights laws was difficult, changing practices was going to be even harder, especially by 1968. The assassination of Martin Luther King Jr. on April 4 led to more urban riots. Before the decade was over, riots occurred in more than 100 cities and resulted in at least 77 deaths. Thousands suffered injuries, and property destruction was incalculable. The well-publicized purpose of a civil rights law passed one week after King's death was to prohibit racial discrimination in housing policies and practices. However, a provision insisted on by Senator Strom Thurmond of South Carolina showed the ambivalence of white politicians toward militant blacks. This provision made it a crime to use the facilities of interstate commerce "to organize, promote, encourage, participate in, or carry on a riot; or to commit any act of violence in furtherance of a riot." Robert Weisbrot, a historian of the civil rights movement, has observed that the bill's priorities were clear: "modest federal involvement in black efforts to flee the ghetto, but overwhelming force to curb all restiveness within it."

Rachel Carson's *Silent Spring* helped forge a new environmentalist movement in the United States. © Library of Congress.

Before his death, Martin Luther King Jr. had planned a "Poor People's March on Washington" to shift the focus of the civil rights movement from racial to economic issues, believing that this might attract broader support. Leadership of the campaign fell to his successor in the SCLC, Ralph David Abernathy. Even under ideal conditions, the prospects of success were limited, but the weather in Washington at the time of the march was miserable. The political climate the campaigners faced was even worse, and their well-intentioned efforts seemed only to call attention to the powerlessness of poor blacks and their isolation from poor whites (Marty, 11–16, 87–89).

To read about reform in the United States in the 19th century, see the United States entries in the section "Reform Movements" in chapter 6 ("Political Life") in volume 5 of this series.

FOR MORE INFORMATION

Lee, S., dir. *Malcolm X*. 1992.

Marty, M. A. *Daily Life in the United States, 1960–1990: Decades of Discord*. Westport, Conn.: Greenwood Press, 1997.

Matusow, A. J. *The Unraveling of America: A History of American Liberalism in the 1960s*. New York: Harper and Row, 1984.

Sitkoff, H. *The Struggle for Black Equality, 1954–1992*. New York: Hill and Wang, 1993.

POLITICAL LIFE
|
REFORM
|
United States,
1920-1939

United States,
1940-1959

United States,
1960-1990

Islamic World

Japan

ISLAMIC WORLD

One of the most controversial issues in the modern Islamic world is the recent rise of fundamentalist reform. In the mid 1990s, one fundamentalist group, the Taliban, appeared in Afghanistan and went on to establish one of the most authoritarian Islamic regimes of the 20th century. This section provides a brief examination of the effects of modern Islamic fundamentalism on the rise of the Taliban movement in Afghanistan.

Many modern scholars of Islamic history and culture think that the term fundamentalism should not be associated with Islam. "It should be said that Muslims object to the use of the term 'fundamentalism,' pointing out quite correctly that it was coined by American Protestants as a badge of pride" (Armstrong, 168). Fundamentalism began in the United States in the late 18th and early 19th centuries. This conservative Protestant movement stressed the importance of traditional or fundamental Christian beliefs such as the literal interpretation of the Bible. In 1909 Orthodox Protestants published a series of 12 books called *The Fundamentals* that outlined a body of beliefs that serve as the doctrinal foundation of many modern conservative Christian movements. These beliefs include opposition to the Darwinian theory of evolution, a belief in the resurrection of the physical body after death, and the infallibility of the Christian Bible.

Many scholars feel that Islamism is a more appropriate term than fundamentalism to describe the essentially modern phenomenon of conservative political movements based on Islamic principles (Fuller and Lesser, 6). "Islamist movements now question some of the foundational principles of the postcolonial state, most notably that development is predicated on secularization and begins with accepting the qualitative superiority of western civilization values; thus, development must necessarily entail replacing some Islamic values in favor of western ones" (Esposito, 567). In the Islamist worldview, it is impossible to divorce religion and politics.

Much of the rhetoric used by modern Islamist groups such as the Taliban draws on the work of earlier Muslim intellectuals such as Ahmad B. Taymiya (1263–1328), a conservative Hanbali legal scholar (see the Islamic World entry in the section

"Law and Crime" earlier in this volume). Ibn Taymiya was born in Harran, Mesopotamia, and fled to Damascus after the Mongols invaded his homeland (Lapidus, 184). Ibn Taymiya believed that the *ulama,* or community of religious scholars, had an important role to play in Islamic statecraft. "Ibn Taymiya held that the 'ulamâ were responsible for upholding the law by giving religious advice to rulers, teaching true principle to the community of Muslims, and commanding good and forbidding evil' " (Lapidus, 194). The writings of Ibn Taymiya appealed to later Muslim reformers such as Ibn Abd al-Wahhab.

Ibn Abd al-Wahhab (1703–92) was an orthodox Jurist. Like Ibn Taymiya, he followed the strict Hanbali school of Islamic law, with its emphasis on a Qur'anic literalism and rejection of *ijma* (consensus). Appalled by the excesses of the Ottoman Empire, al-Wahhab advocated strict legislative reforms in the Islamic world. He opposed all forms of entertainment, including dancing, music, and gambling. Most of all, Ibn Abd al-Wahhab opposed the autonomy of the Ottoman Sultans. Many later Islamist leaders view Ibn Abd al-Wahhab as one of the earliest anticolonial activists in the Muslim world.

One of the most eminent converts to Wahhabism was Ibn Sa'udi, the chief of a tribal principality in central Arabia (Lapidus, 673). After his conversion to Wahhabism in 1745, Ibn Sa'udi waged war against his neighbors and successfully instituted a series of Wahhabi reforms on the Arabian peninsula. In 1803 the Wahhabis captured Mecca, the holiest city in the Islamic world. Even though they were expelled from Mecca in 1812 by Muhammad Ali of Egypt, Wahhabi ideology was not defeated. In fact, Saudi Arabia, as it is known today, remains a strict Wahhabi country. One aspect of Wahhabi Saudi law that has received a lot of international attention is the limitation placed on women's rights. For example, women in Saudi Arabia are not permitted to drive.

The Taliban has been heavily influenced by Wahhabi ideology. This Islamist group has gained notoriety in recent years for its support of Saudi-born Osama bin Laden and his radical anti-Western ideology. Many of the members of Afghanistan's Taliban movement received their education from *madrasas,* or Qur'an schools, located along the Afghan–Pakistan border during the 1970s and 1980s. Many of these *madrasas* were sponsored by pro-Wahhabi groups from within Saudi Arabia, or by other Islamist groups such as the Pakistani *Jam'iyyat-i Ulama-i Islam* (JUI, or Society of Islamic Scholars). "Since the start of the war in 1978, thousands of students, mostly Afghans but also Pakistani Pashtuns, have attended these schools. The schools are strongly influenced by the *Jam'iyyat-i Ulama-i Islam,* . . . a movement in Pakistan headed by Mawlana Fazlur Rahman" (Vogelsang, 329). These schools served young Afghan men, many of whom were refugees displaced by the Soviet invasion of Afghanistan (1979–89). These young men, disenfranchised and hopeless, readily accepted the revolutionary political rhetoric from the Islamist *madrasas* system. Many of the graduates from the Afghan–Pakistani *madrasas* concentrated their dissatisfaction on the political situation in their homeland. They believed that Afghanistan's problems were the result of colonial oppression and interference by foreign governments.

Students in Afghanistan expressed their frustration using rhetoric from both the Marxist and Islamist movements. Though these two doctrines may seem very different on the surface, both contain unifying themes such as liberation and class equality. Students called for social change through a return to traditional Islamic values. Many members of the Taliban movement in Afghanistan were influenced by the Egyptian Muslim Brother theorist Sayyid Qutb (d. 1966). Some of the more radical groups, inspired by Qutb's influential book, *Signs of the Road,* called for armed resistance against the state (Lapidus, 634). Students also used Marxist slogans to rally the people together under the banner of a new "Islamic revolution."

One of the most conflict-ridden policies of the Taliban's Islamic revolution is its treatment of women and girls. Many members of the international community have condemned the Taliban for forbidding girls and women to attend school. The Taliban says that it does not oppose education for females, only coed institutions, and they simply lack the resources to build schools for girls. Many members of the Taliban grew up in an environment where men and women lived entirely separate lives. As a result of being raised in either completely gender-segregated refugee camps or all-male boarding schools, members of the Taliban did not experience normal family life. Whereas many people were horrified by the Tabilan's treatment of women, these *madrasa*-educated young men did not see anything unusual in forbidding women to work, go to school, or even appear in public (Rashid, 33).

With over one billion adherents, Islam is one of the fastest-growing religions in the modern world. Islam is not a monolithic religion. It encompasses a tremendous range of theological, political, and social beliefs. Though Islamist groups receive a lot of attention from the world media because of their radical politics and willingness to engage in violence, the vast majority of Muslims are peaceful, law-abiding people who do not subscribe to Islamist views.

To read about reform in the Islamic World in the 19th century, see the Islamic World entry in the section "Reform Movements" in chapter 6 ("Political Life") in volume 5 of this series.

~*Molly Benjamin Patterson*

FOR MORE INFORMATION

Armstrong, K. *Islam: A Short History*. New York: Modern Library, 2000.

Esposito, J., ed. *The Oxford History of Islam*. New York: Oxford University Press, 1999.

Fuller, G. E., and I. O. Lesser. *A Sense of Siege: The Geopolitics of Islam and the West*. Boulder, Colo.: Westview Press, 1995.

Lapidus, I. M. A *History of Islamic Societies*. Cambridge: Cambridge University Press, 1988. Reprint 1998.

Rashid, A. *Taliban: Militant Islam, Oil and Fundamentalism in Central Asia*. New Haven: Yale University Press, 2001.

Vogelsang, W. *The Afghans*. Oxford: Blackwell, 2002.

POLITICAL LIFE

|

REFORM

|

United States, 1920-1939

United States, 1940-1959

United States, 1960-1990

Islamic World

Japan

JAPAN

Reform in Japan is more apparent than real. The nature of politics militates against much change. The Liberal Democratic Party (LDP), which has ruled Japan for most of the postwar years, much prefers the status quo. For instance, the 1947 constitution continues to be unamended because everyone is afraid of substantive change. The motto of Japan seems to be, "If it isn't broken, don't fix it."

The LDP leadership has been masterful, however, in the art of political compromise. They are particularly adept at co-opting popular causes, watering down proposed reforms, and then incorporating these watered-down reforms into their own political platform. Political realists might argue that this is the game of realpolitik. Nevertheless, the LDP has begrudgingly passed few reforms in the past few decades.

Salient among these reforms was a bill to reform the system of multicandidate election districts that had assured the LDP of the lion's share of elections in the major cities. Confronted by a grassroots movement against the system, the LDP seized the issue as if it were their own brainchild. The LDP then presented its own reform bill in the late 1990s whereby 300 representatives to the Lower House of the Diet were elected in single-member constituencies. The remaining 200 were elected in 11 multiple-member constituencies allocated by population.

Michio Ochi addresses a news conference at Prime Minister Keizo Obuchi's official residence in Tokyo. © AP/Wide World Photos.

When presented with a brief surge in discontent about sexual harassment and gender inequities in the workplace, the LDP appointed a few women to the cabinet as window dressing and dragged its feet for almost a decade before finally passing an embarrassingly weak equal employment opportunity law in 1986. The law was nearly toothless with regard to enforcement, calling for voluntary compliance.

Similarly, when a loose coalition of "green" nongovernmental organizations (NGOs) began to voice concerns about industrial pollution, the establishment enacted a piecemeal platform of environmental protection and conservation laws. Even when these laws were enforced, the miscreant industries managed to drag appeals through the courts system. The NGOs have accomplished more reform by forcing the issue through public demonstrations and letters to editors. The threat of public boycotts has often pressured business leaders to publicly apologize for harming the environment.

Other reforms have had similar histories. The irresponsible lending habits of major banks in the late 1980s and early 1990s brought the economy to a virtual standstill. Yet the LDP has steadfastly refused to go the way of the United States in forcing some savings and loans and banks to go bankrupt. Similarly, the very inefficient postal savings system continues to limp along, paying virtually no interest on savings, because no one within the establishment has a vested interest in reform.

As long as the LDP can manage to water down reform issues, and as long as the opposition political parties remain self-interestedly divided, very little reform will take place in Japan.

~Louis G. Perez

FOR MORE INFORMATION

McVeigh, B. J. *The Nature of the Japanese State: Rationality and Rituality*. London: Routledge, 1998.

Minoru, N. *The Policy-Making Process in Contemporary Japan*. New York: St. Martin's Press, 1997.

Takeo, Ya. "Who Has Obstructed Reform?" In *Unlocking the Bureaucrat's Kingdom: Deregulation and the Japanese Economy,* edited by Frank Gibney. Washington, D.C.: Brookings Institution Press, 1998, 91–115.

War

For many, war was daily life's constant companion in the 20th century. There were two cataclysmic world wars and a host of smaller, but not less bloody, conflicts such as the Russian Revolution. Although the death toll from these conflagrations is staggering, the political, economic, and social fallout was perhaps more influential. The entries in this section discuss the scope of the wars in the 20th century and provide details on how they impacted the lives of average people. Pay close attention to the ways in which wars changed daily life long after the fighting stopped.

Nearly all historians agree that World War I constitutes a watershed event in history. Simply put, life after the war was completely different. The war itself was horrific. It was so brutal that some have argued that the war ended in 1919 not because of any military victory but because there were no more men to fight. Literally, a generation of European men died on the battlefields. Universally, their tour of service was awful. Trench warfare was the worst situation imaginable. Soldiers fought in the midst of their own filth and next to their dead comrades. They had no pleasantries, no comforts, and no shelter from disease and death. Although the Allied forces won the war in 1919, the postwar political conditions did not foster an enduring peace. In fact, in the view of many, the war's end merely offered a long armistice in the war for global supremacy.

From the 1920s through the 1930s, various world powers jockeyed for position. Germany's quick rise in Europe is an oft-told tale. Notice, however, that in other areas of the globe, the fallout from World War I allowed other opportunistic politicians to appear. For example, in the Islamic world, the Ottoman Empire, which had backed the Central Powers, completely collapsed, allowing for a new Turkish state to form. Gathering war clouds finally brought their storm in the late 1930s. The second war in Europe was as bloody as the first, especially on the Eastern Front, where the Soviets suffered enormous casualties while stopping the German advance. Even worse, the Nazis perfected methods of ethnic cleansing, thus bringing new horrors to the modern world. In the Pacific, a militaristic Japan, which had fought a series of successful wars since the start of the century, finally over-extended itself by attacking the United States at Pearl Harbor and bringing on a war that ended with the first atomic bombs falling on Japanese cities.

By the time World War II ended, a third world war seemed quite possible. Whereas the first 50 years of the 20th century had been a fight with the radical right, the next 40 years was a fight with the radical left. Communism and capitalism were engaged in a death embrace. In theory, the war was between the United States and

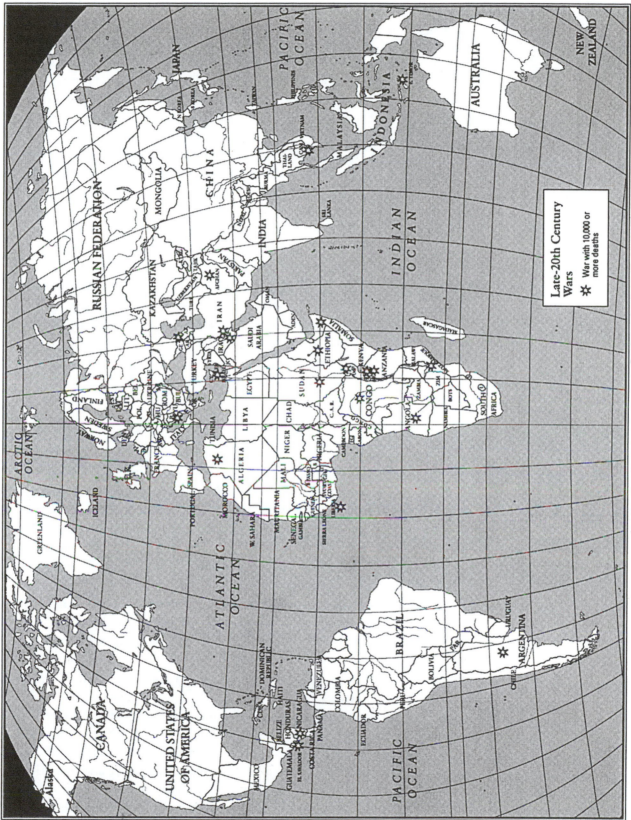

the Soviet Union. In practice, the war was fought by surrogates in Asia, Africa, Europe, and Latin America. When the so-called cold war broke out in fighting between leftist forces and forces allied with the United States, the results were eye-opening. In some cases, governments seeking to destroy the left-wing opposition killed tens of thousands of innocent civilians. These civil wars, known as the "Dirty Wars," in Latin America make up some of the darkest chapters in 20th century history.

By the 1960s, a new type of world conflict had appeared: the cold war between the United States and the Soviet Union. These two superpowers never met on the battlefield. Rather, they fought with surrogates in the Koreas, in Vietnam, and in Afghanistan. As the death toll began to mount in these conflicts, average people around the world began to reject war as a solution to global problems. Some even proclaimed that "military solutions" were an oxymoron. The peace movement had significant results in the United States by helping to end American involvement in the Vietnam conflict. Yet, the movement was not strong enough to wage peace in all areas. The Soviet Union became embroiled in Afghanistan in 1980. In Latin America, Argentina went to war with Great Britain in 1982 over the Falkland Islands. And in the Middle East, the decades-old conflict between Israel and the Islamic World continued. At the dawn of the 21st century, a lasting peace in the Middle East seems quite remote.

POLITICAL LIFE

|

WAR

|

Europe, 1914-1919

United States, 1939-1945

United States, 1945-1990

Latin America

Islamic World

Soviet Union

Japan

EUROPE, 1914–19

The quintessential experience of World War I was trench warfare. The trenches had their origins in the surprising turn the war took during its first few months. They were the products of failure: the unsuccessful French assault on Lorraine, the unsuccessful German drive southward to the Marne, the unsuccessful race northward by Anglo-French and German forces to outflank the enemy between Paris and the North Sea. Each of these efforts left large numbers of troops entrenched and facing their foes in what came to be a war of position.

The opposing lines stretched for over 450 miles from the Belgian coast to the Swiss border. In some areas, there were no trenches. In the extreme northern zone, the damp soil made it impossible to dig, and barricades provided soldiers with protection. In the Vosges, the mountain range at the southern part of the front, Germans faced Frenchmen in a series of village and rural strongpoints. But for most of the western front, soldiers dug into the earth, and as time went by, all armies built extensive trench lines.

The French faced an enemy on their own soil and committed themselves to driving him out as soon as possible. They constructed a line from which to launch attacks in the near future. As a result, French trenches were far less elaborate than those of the other belligerents. The British system was neater and more developed.

Unlike other armies, the German army had studied the lessons of the Boer War (1899–1902) and the Russo-Japanese War (1904–5) about the value of field fortifications. Elaborate trench systems were a part of German maneuvers since 1906.

Europe on the Eve of War 1914

Europe Post-WWI

Iceland (Danish)

Norwegian Sea

Faeroes (Danish)

Arctic Circle

FINLAND

Petrograd

Helsinki

Oslo

Stockholm

Tallinn

ESTONIA

Baltic Sea

Riga

LATVIA

North Sea

Glasgow • Edinburgh

DENMARK

LITHUANIA

USSR

Copenhagen

Danzig (free city under League of Nations)

Königsberg

Kaunas

UNITED

East Prussia

Hamburg

IRELAND

Dublin

Liverpool

KINGDOM

Amsterdam

NETHER-

Berlin

Warsaw

Brest Litovsk

Birmingham

GERMANY

POLAND

Bristol

London

Rhine

Kiev

Calais

Brussels

Frankfurt

Cracow

BELGIUM

LUX?

Prague

Lvov

SAAR (autonomous under League of Nations)

CZECHOSLOVAKIA

Paris

Vienna

ATLANTIC

Orléans

Budapest

OCEAN

Bern

AUSTRIA

HUNGARY

ROMANIA

FRANCE

SWITZ.

Lyon

Milan

Trieste

Bucharest

Bordeaux

Genoa

Venice

Belgrade

Danube

Zara

YUGOSLAVIA

BULGARIA

SAN MARINO

Adriatic Sea

MONACO

Marseille

ANDORRA

Sofia

Corsica

Rome

ITALY

ALBANIA

Barcelona

Naples

Aegean Sea

Madrid

Lisbon

PORTUGAL

SPAIN

Balearic Is.

Sardinia

GREECE

Cádiz

Gibraltar (British)

Almeria

Alicante

Mediterranean

Sicily

Athens

(Italian occupied)

Algiers

Tangier (International zone)

Tunis

Malta

Morocco (French)

Algeria (French)

Tunisia (French)

Sea

Libya (Italian)

Determined to hang on to the substantial portion of territory they held in Belgium and northeastern France, they also faced the burden of fighting on the eastern front against Russia. The Germans set up their first trench system by mid-September 1914, protecting the flanks of the city of Rheims. Their decision to stand on the defensive on the western front for much of the war led them to build the most extensive, even the most comfortable system. Over much of the fighting line, the Germans were able to choose the location of their defenses, avoiding difficult terrain such as areas prone to flooding in wet weather.

To serve on the western front meant entering a world most civilians could not imagine. A coal miner from the Ruhr or a farmhand from rural Scotland was probably less shocked by its hardships than someone from an urban, middle-class background. But nothing in prewar life, even for most professional soldiers, prepared them for the particular character of trench life on the western front.

Europe's means of long-range transportation at the start of the 20th century was the railroad. From the start of the war, the move to the front began with a train journey. Crowded into cattle cars—a sign on the standard French railroad car stated that it was suitable for eight horses or 40 men—soldiers of all the belligerents rode to the front, often at a snail's pace. Ammunition trains had priority, and the journey toward the fighting was likely to be an extended one with numerous delays. The discouraging sight of trains filled with wounded moving in the opposite direction was common. For British soldiers, and then for some Americans, the first leg of the journey was by Channel steamer to a port like Boulogne. They often encountered wounded British soldiers awaiting evacuation on the docks where they arrived.

Where rail transportation ceased, usually within 10 miles of the front, the soldier's feet took over. The initial fighting soon destroyed a wide belt of territory in northwestern Belgium and northeastern France. Soldiers marching to the front passed through villages or cities that had been the scene of fierce fighting during the mobile combat of 1914. A British enlisted man on his way to the front in Belgium in May 1915 encountered such a scene in the outskirts of Ypres: "Just over the canal bridge a timber wagon and two shattered horses came into view and we walked through the blood of these noble animals as we passed them on the road. We were now in the town proper—everywhere nothing but ruins could be seen—not a house but was either shattered by shells or gutted with fire."

Coming closer to the front, soldiers entered a zone of territory exposed to artillery fire from the enemy. Long before reaching a trench, a soldier could feel the dangerous potential of modern weapons. The young German soldier Ernst Jünger recalled reaching a village behind the lines when a series of shells struck at breakfast time. "A feeling of unreality oppressed me," he recalled, "as I stared at a figure streaming with blood whose limbs hung loose and who unceasingly gave a hoarse cry for help, as though death had him already by the throat." Soldiers normally entered the front lines at night via approach roads and communication trenches. Moving in the dark, along narrow and crowded sunken passageways, soldiers from all armies passed into this special world. One Englishman recalled what it felt like:

It was a two-mile trudge in the narrow ditches to the front line. No war correspondent has ever described such a march; it is not included in the official "horrors of war" but this is the kind of thing, more than battle or blood which harasses the spirit of the infantryman and composes his life. . . . He is only conscious of the dead weight of his load, and the braces of his pack biting into his shoulders, of his thirst and the sweat of his body, and the longing to lie down and sleep. When we halt men fall into a doze as they stand and curse pitifully when they are urged on from behind.

All trench systems consisted of several parallel lines of fortifications. A forward trench line was adjacent to "no-man's-land," the unoccupied ground separating the two sides, and had the greatest vulnerability to enemy attack. Here the enemy might enter and fire down the trench's entire length or an artillery shell might spread deadly metal fragments. To avoid such dangers, armies constructed "traverses," trenches built in zigzag patterns. Anyone moving down such a trench line had to make sharp turns into the next section.

Facing outward from the first trench, a soldier looked over several stretches of barbed wire protecting his position. One section, three feet high, was likely placed directly ahead in the outskirts of no-man's-land. Additional barbed-wire entanglements were normally placed another 50 yards or so into no-man's-land. Eventually, barbed-wire lines 50 yards thick were established, and sometimes a single or "international" barbed-wire system, maintained by both sides, separated the combatants.

All defensive systems had at least one additional trench line where troops could remain to support the front position. Here the various trench occupants constructed dugouts carved out of the forward wall of the trench. These offered additional shelter and some protection against shellfire. Officers' dugouts were often fairly spacious and, on the German side, even elaborate, whereas the French and the British dugouts were more like enlarged caves. The dugouts enlisted men constructed in the portions of the trench they occupied were more likely to be shallow diggings into the trench wall. In some cases rival trench lines ran through a single village, and sometimes a trench running through an individual house was occupied at one end by the troops of one belligerent, and occupied at the other by the soldiers of their enemy.

The German system featured deep shelters able to resist enemy artillery fire. Dugouts at the Battle of the Somme in 1916 were 30 feet below the ground. Digging in to stay, the Germans also put wooden walkways on the trench floor. Machine-gun posts constructed of concrete, iron, and wood supported the German trench lines. The German second line was often on the reverse slope of the hill on which they had placed their front position, thus making it even harder for the enemy to attack with artillery. By the middle of 1917, German positions in Flanders consisted of a mixture of trenches and supporting positions nine layers deep.

The French preferred a system in which mutually supporting strongpoints, connected by barbed wire, formed the front lines. A strong set of barbed-wire belts was to stretch across the entire front, and behind the front lines the bulk of French troops were concentrated in a second, reserve line. Such a policy was designed to reduce casualties in the front lines.

Few of the trenches of 1914 and 1915 survived unchanged until the end of the war. Rain and flooding made trench walls collapse. This necessitated constant repair and rebuilding. Moreover, although the shape of the western front remained static, trench lines were sometimes occupied permanently by the enemy. They then altered the trenches to their specifications.

The soldier in the trenches became enmeshed in an exhausting routine, one that reversed the normal patterns of daily living. Fighting on the eastern front, the Austrian concert violinist Fritz Kreisler wrote how the trenches brought men down to a more primitive level of existence than one could have imagined. Much of the work of the war—maintaining the trenches, repairing the barbed-wire barriers that separate your trenches from those of the enemy, bringing up supplies—had to be done at night.

A "stand-to" (or combat assembly) at dawn and at dusk, when enemy attacks were considered most likely, gave some form to the soldier's day. But otherwise, unless he was on sentry duty or assigned to a work detail, he slept as best he could during the daylight hours—then moved on to his nighttime activities. Arriving in Champagne in 1914, Jünger found a workday that began before dawn; the need to guard the trench and to continue constructing it gave each man only two hours' sleep at night. An enemy attack would deprive soldiers of any sleep.

The dead men from past battles were everywhere one turned. Bodies hanging on the barbed-wire entanglements of no-man's-land provided a grisly reminder of failed assaults. Decomposed corpses lying on the ground between the lines, in locations that made them too dangerous to remove, added to the grisly atmosphere. During an advance into no-man's-land in 1915, Ernst Jünger recalled: "My attention was caught by a sickly smell and a bundle hanging on the wire. . . . I found myself in front of a huddled-up corpse, a Frenchman. The putrid flesh, like the flesh of fishes, gleamed greenish-white through the rents in the uniform." The dead were buried near trenches or even interred in trench walls. As the soil shifted, a soldier might encounter a partially decomposed foot or hand sticking out from the side of a trench. An American corporal of the 27th Division recalled "an obstruction sticking out from the trench wall" that could not at first be identified in the dark. At daybreak, it was discovered to be "the foot and ankle of a French soldier who had been buried there by a shell" in a sector the French had evacuated more than a year before.

From the earliest stages of the war, soldiers encountered airplanes observing them from above. Their diaries recorded the sense of vulnerability that came from enemy

---

📷 *Snapshot*

Field Service Post Card (English) from World War I

When World War I soldiers were in action, they were not allowed to write letters home, given that any letters that fell into the hands of the enemy might give away troop dispositions or other vital military information. Instead, the troops were issued "field service post cards," like the one shown below, that told the family little more than that their loved one was still alive. The sender simply crossed out all information that did not apply.

NOTHING is to be written on this side except the date and signature of the sender. Sentences not required may be erased. If anything else is added the post card will be destroyed.

I am quite well.

I have been admitted into hospital

sick and am going on well.

wounded and hope to be discharged soon.

I have received your

letter dated _____
telegram "_____
parcel "_____

Letters follow at the first opportunity. I have received no letter from you

lately
for a long time

Signature only. Date:

(Fussell, 184)

---

flights over the trench lines. In the first years of the war, planes aided in directing artillery fire. Starting in 1916, soldiers on both sides of the battle line faced the threat of low-flying enemy planes conducting strafing attacks.

Troops confined in their trenches could watch aerial duels taking place above them. German artillery lieutenant Herbert Sulzbach recorded such an event in his diary. Sitting under cover with five of his comrades, he was soon able to "watch a number of dog-fights in the air and admire the way our new triplanes are operating. Nimble, lively, highly manoeuvreable and incredibly fast, they climb almost vertically to take on one enemy plane after the other. . . . The dog-fights go on in the afternoon; our squadron have knocked down five enemy planes in the course of today in our sector alone."

Each day soldiers on the western front faced the danger posed by enemy snipers. From the time the trench line took shape, individual riflemen sought targets among members of the enemy careless enough to expose themselves. As the war went on, sniping became the work of specially trained marksmen. Exposing the upper portion of the body, even for a split second, invited a fatal shot from a sniper in the enemy trench line or in no-man's-land. Ernst Jünger saw one of his men die that way in

November 1915. The German soldier "climbed on to a ledge in the top of the trench to shovel earth over the top. He was scarce up when a shot . . . got him in the skull and laid him dead on the floor of the trench." In certain instances, several enemy snipers fired on an exposed individual within a matter of seconds, and even senior officers on inspection tours died at the hands of these enemy marksmen. When snipers worked in teams—one as the spotter, one as the actual rifleman—their shots were especially accurate.

Snipers sometimes put their rifles in fixed positions, held by clamps, to cover an area that was certain to be frequented by the enemy: the entrance to a latrine, an exposed point in the trench line. This permitted them to fire even when there was no visible target in sight. Merely letting off a round at random from a fixed position gave a good chance of striking the enemy. At Aubers, a

Tanks returned some mobility to the static battlefield. Here a French tank assaults a German position. © Library of Congress.

German rifle was set up to fire every two minutes at the opposing British forces.

Although soldiers could exercise caution to protect themselves from enemy rifle fire, there was no effective defense against random artillery or mortar shells. Artillery shells that struck a trench or exploded overhead to send fragments of shrapnel downward could take an awful toll. One English sergeant recalled the shock of an artillery attack that broke the quiet of the morning in Flanders in May 1915:

Suddenly a tremendous explosion, a deathly stillness as if all were paralyzed, then fearful screams and groans and death gasps. . . . A high explosive German shell had fallen right into a wide part of the trench where many men had been. The sight of the wounded shedding their blood from gaping wounds and their agonized cries [followed]. . . . [T]his one shell bursting right in the trench accounted for a total of 25 men. The trench after the dead and wounded were removed presented a ghastly sight—it was red with blood like a room papered in crimson while equipment lay everywhere.

Firing a shell into the air at a sharp angle, a mortarman could place a round directly into the enemy line. Although the noise made by firing the piece gave some warning, no one could be sure of escaping when such shells struck the trench where they were located. The only certainty was that one's own mortars would retaliate.

Individual artillery and mortar rounds posed a sudden danger, but soldiers also faced prolonged shelling from masses of enemy heavy guns. Such an experience took a heavy psychological toll, and soldiers from both sides of the battle line described their feelings in surprisingly similar terms. Henri de Lécluse, a captain in the French army, experienced a 12-hour bombardment in the Vosges during the fall of 1915. He considered it his worst experience of the entire war, "an abominable day" that would haunt him for the rest of his life.

German shells, including some containing tear gas, pounded us without interruption. Many were large caliber, at least 105 mm. They fell right on top of us, sometimes they landed near us, in front or behind us. We were huddled next to the wall, silent, resigned to death, our faces hardened by anguish. Surrounded by the cries for help, the cries of pain from the wounded and by the groans of those mortally hit, we were being showered by fragments of stones and chunks of dirt thrown up by each projectile and blinded by the burning and suffocating smoke.

Facing this multitude of strains, no group of men could remain in the trenches indefinitely. All armies developed a system of rotation. While assigned to the front, parts of an infantry battalion spent several days in the first trench, but then left their position to others and took up a post in the reserve line. After an entire unit had been at the front for a given period, it was withdrawn to a zone several miles behind. The length of time in the trenches varied from one army to another. When not involved in a major battle, a soldier might expect to spend four to eight days in the front line and the support trench, followed by four days in a rear area.

Living in a ditch carved out of the ground meant that, even in the best of weather, a soldier was certain to become filthy. The onset of rain—and snow in colder weather—added to everyone's physical discomfort. The frequent rains of northwestern Europe turned trenches into muddy bogs. Laying wooden duckboards on the bottom of the trench provided only a partial solution, given that men often slipped off them as they moved about.

Mud in the trenches or out in the open made movement for men and draft animals difficult. Heavy clothing, instead of easing the burdens of trench warfare, added to it. A coat weighing 7 pounds could be transformed into a burden of more than 30 pounds when it was soaked with water and coated with mud. Standing in a waterlogged trench for days at a time put soldiers at risk for trench foot. A disease that resembled frostbite, it caused the feet to become numb and to turn red or blue. If it developed into gangrene, a sufferer might lose his toes or even his entire foot.

Exhausted or wounded soldiers sometimes drowned in the mud, something that happened to 16 members of a British division on the Somme in November 1916. A French soldier described "communication trenches [that] are no more than cesspools filled with a mixture of water and urine." In such an environment, trenches were "nothing more than a strip of water" and the soldiers themselves are transformed into "statues of clay, with mud even in one's very mouth." Jünger recalled fighting in Flanders in 1918 when "knowing that a wound would drown one for certainty in a mud-hole. A suffusion of blood on the surface of a shell-hole here and there showed that many a man had vanished thus."

To live in an unsterile outdoor environment brought an inevitable infestation of lice: chats and greybacks to the British, cooties to the Americans. The tiny insects lodged in men's clothing, especially in the seams, and despite sometimes elaborate efforts to remove them, they maintained a constant presence. Their bites caused unbearable itching as well as sores and scabs. Only pulling troops back from the trenches, letting the men bathe their bodies while their clothes were either washed or replaced, provided even temporary relief.

Even more horrible in the minds of those who served in the squalor of the trenches was the horde of rats to be found everywhere. Fattening on the corpses of the dead, they sometimes grew to the size of cats. As they grew accustomed to the presence of live humans, any fears of contact with people faded away. Soldiers sleeping in the trenches often found themselves awakened by rats crawling over their bodies—or even nibbling at their flesh.

A Red Cross orderly escorts a battered German prisoner to a field hospital for treatment. © Library of Congress.

Basic biological needs added to the squalor of trench life. No trench line was complete without some primitive form of toilet. In the British army, it was common to build a military toilet (or latrine) in an offshoot of a trench. Elaborately designed latrines existed on paper, but more often the reality was a small area off the main trench with receptacles like old food cans to hold feces. Special units had the task of removing the collected body wastes each night, and spreading chloride of lime as a disinfectant. For many soldiers who survived the western front, one of the most vivid memories was the smell of chloride of lime, a constant of trench life.

The area between the opposing trench lines was appropriately named no-man's-land, because it was too dangerous for any unit to be placed there. This space separating the belligerents was usually several hundred yards in width. In some circumstances, it might be as large as a thousand yards or, given the dictates of terrain, the trench lines might be separated only by a distance of 5 to 10 yards. Snipers operated from no-man's-land, and the area was a bone of contention for both sides seeking to exercise at least temporary control.

Although gigantic battles were rare but spectacular occurrences, small-scale combat for those in the trenches took place without letup. In the territory between the two trench lines, groups of soldiers met and fought on a daily basis. Both sides sought to dominate no-man's-land, because the ability to patrol up to the edge of enemy territory provided valuable information about his defenses as well as his intentions for the future. The clash of patrols, usually fewer than a dozen men in each, meant a constant clamor of gunfire at night—and a constant stream of fatalities and wounded.

Beyond the tangible benefits of aggressive patrolling, there was also the psychological impetus to send troops forward in this way. For senior British commanders such as generals in charge of divisions, aggressive patrolling promoted a fighting spirit in their frontline units. Precisely because large-scale encounters were relatively infrequent, instigating such miniature battles was seen as useful.

In addition to skirmishes that took place in no-man's-land, trench raids brought violent episodes into the life of a soldier at the front. In a trench raid, troops from one side penetrated the enemy's defenses and seized a portion of his trench line for at least a few minutes. These raids offered an opportunity to kill numbers of the enemy and to capture prisoners for interrogation. Initiated by the British, the practice caught on with the Germans and eventually the Americans. The French by contrast preferred to avoid such efforts as a waste of manpower.

Trench raids often involved groups of volunteers. The complex character of a trench raid dictated careful planning and even several dry runs against defenses built to simulate those of the enemy. A raid might begin with an artillery barrage aimed at isolating a portion of the enemy line from his reserve trenches, thus preventing the targeted area from being reinforced. Engineer units cut away barbed wire and other defensive impediments to permit the trench raiders through. Finally, the raiding force itself, with faces blackened and carrying special weapons such as clubs and hand grenades designed for close contact with the enemy, moved forward at the appropriate moment.

A classic example of the trench raid came in the fall of 1917 when German units struck at the first Americans to occupy a portion of the fighting front. In skilled fashion, the Germans used a brief barrage to cut off the troops from the First Division's 16th Infantry Regiment, located east of Verdun. Boxed in by the fire of 96 German guns, the novice American soldiers faced an assault by the experienced troops of the 7th Bavarian Landwehr Regiment. German combat troops moved rapidly across no-man's-land, entered the Doughboys' positions, and left within a few minutes.

Three dead American soldiers and 11 more carried off as prisoners of war attested to the way this smoothly coordinated maneuver had taken place. The Germans had acquired prisoners for interrogation, but equally important, they had made a potent effort to gain a psychological advantage over the newly arrived American troops (Heyman, 41–52).

FOR MORE INFORMATION

Ashworth, T. *Trench Warefare, 1914–1918: The Live and Let Live System.* London: Macmillan, 1980.

Brown, M. *Tommy Goes to War.* London: J. M. Dent, 1978.

Fussell, P. *The Great War and Modern Memory.* New York: Oxford University Press, 1975.

Heyman, N. M. *Daily Life During World War I.* Westport, Conn.: Greenwood Press, 2002.

Jünger, E. *The Storm of Steel: From the Diary of a German Storm-trooper Officer on the Western Front.* New York: H. Fertig, 1975.

Milestone, L., dir. *All Quiet on the Western Front.* 1930.

UNITED STATES, 1939–45

The storm clouds that gathered over Europe in August 1914 and that produced one of the world's most disastrous wars did not clear after the peace of 1919. Rather,

the clouds merely retreated and returned 20 years later. In the interim, the vanquished nations from World War I struggled to create stable political and economic systems. For many, the solution that they found was a violent form of government known as fascism. Fascist governments, both in Europe and in Asia, were willing to attack not only other countries but their own people as well. In Germany, Spain, and Italy, political civil wars broke out in the 1920s and early 1930s between factions often allied with communists or fascists.

The United States stayed clear of these developments in Europe and Asia. The guiding foreign policy of the period was known as neutrality, which had as a principle the idea that America should not enter into alliances with other nations, particularly belligerent ones. As the United States thus focused on its own interests during the 1920s and the 1930s, fascism slowly but forcibly took over many nations, including Germany, Italy, Spain, and Japan, and the world began to inch toward war.

As war clouds loomed again on the horizon, the American government began to take steps to ensure a semblance of security. Under President Herbert C. Hoover, the United States laid the groundwork for what became known as the "good neighbor" policy of goodwill and cooperation with Latin American countries. By 1940, President Franklin D. Roosevelt had brought the United States in close relationship with its friends to the south and negotiated defense agreements with all but one nation (Argentina).

President Roosevelt also began to put the United States on a war footing. The first order of business was to change the neutrality laws. After Italy, Germany, and Japan signed the Anti-Comintern (in other words, anticommunist) Pact in 1937, the neutrality laws were amended to allow "cash-and-carry" for allies of the United States. A nation that was attacked by a belligerent power could pay cash for arms and supplies and take them home on their own boats. This, of course, did not deter the Axis powers' war plans. On September 1, 1939, Hitler's armies invaded Poland, making the start of the war in Europe. When Roosevelt heard the news, he sighed and commented, "It's come at last. God help us all." By spring 1940, the Nazis had control of Denmark, Norway, and France.

By early 1940, FDR had abandoned neutrality and was actively supporting what was left of the Allies, namely Great Britain. He ordered that the United States begin to build a gigantic arsenal (later called the "arsenal of democracy") and in 1940 enacted the only peacetime draft. After the Battle of Britain (which the English won but at a high cost) in 1940, FDR began to give England outright support. He invented a policy known as lend-lease in which the United States would lend or lease war materials to the British and later other allies such as Russia who would promise to return them after the war. In a speech to the American people in support of this proposed policy, Roosevelt likened the idea to lending a hose to a neighbor whose house was on fire. Ohio's Republican senator Robert A. Taft (who led the opposition to American involvement before the Pearl Harbor attack in 1941) stated that the analogy was wrong. It was more like "lending" someone chewing gum. Once the person is done with it, you don't want it back.

With all eyes on the war across the Atlantic Ocean, it is somewhat ironic that the war came to the United States from the Pacific. The United States and Japan

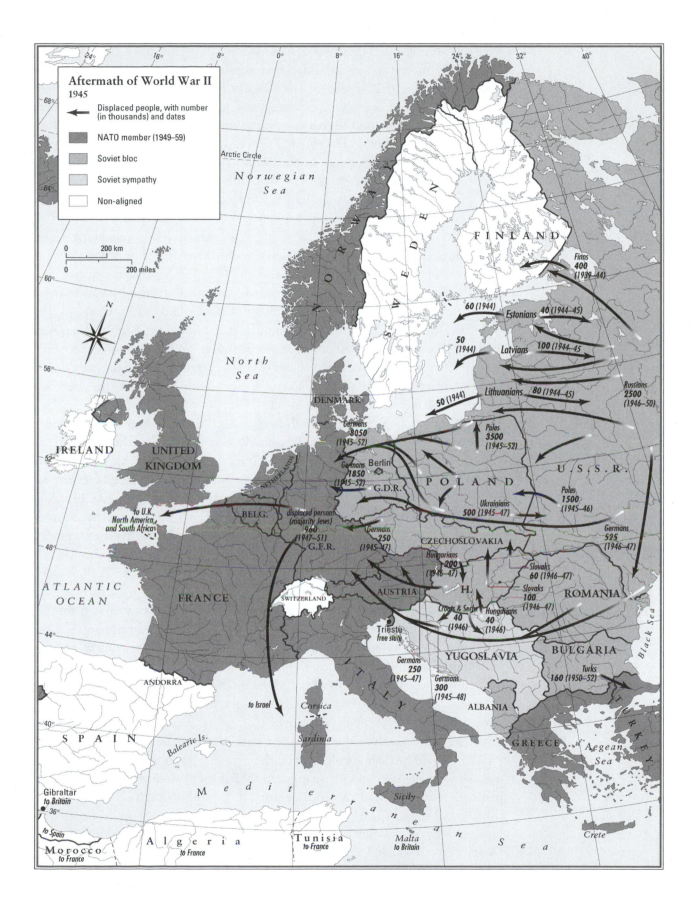

Aftermath of World War II
1945

← Displaced people, with number (in thousands) and dates

▨ NATO member (1949–59)

▨ Soviet bloc

▨ Soviet sympathy

□ Non-aligned

0   200 km
0   200 miles

Norwegian Sea

Arctic Circle

North Sea

FINLAND

Finns
400
(1939–44)

SWEDEN

NORWAY

60 *(1944)*

Estonians **40** *(1944–45)*

50
(1944)

Latvians **100** *(1944–45)*

Russians
2500
(1946–50)

DENMARK

50 *(1944)*

Lithuanians **80** *(1944–45)*

Germans
8050
(1945–52)

Poles
3500
(1945–52)

IRELAND

UNITED KINGDOM

NETHERLANDS

Germans
1850
(1945–52)

Berlin

G.D.R.

POLAND

U.S.S.R.

BELG.

to U.K.,
North America
and South Africa

displaced persons
(majority Jews)
960
(1947–51)
G.F.R.

Germans
250
(1945–47)

Ukrainians
500 *(1945–47)*

Poles
1500
(1945–46)

Germans
525
(1946–47)

ATLANTIC OCEAN

FRANCE

SWITZERLAND

AUSTRIA

CZECHOSLOVAKIA

Hungarians
200
(1946–47)

H.

Slovaks
60 *(1946–47)*

Slovaks
100
(1946–47)

ROMANIA

Croats & Serbs
40
(1946)

Hungarians
40
(1946)

Trieste
free state

Germans
250
(1945–47)

YUGOSLAVIA

BULGARIA

Black Sea

Turks
160 *(1950–52)*

TURKEY

to Israel

Corsica

Sardinia

ANDORRA

ITALY

Germans
300
(1945–48)

ALBANIA

GREECE

Aegean Sea

SPAIN

Balearic Is.

Gibraltar
to Britain

to Spain

Mediterranean Sea

Sicily

Malta
to Britain

Crete

Morocco
to France

Algeria
to France

Tunisia
to France

were not allies. In fact, they had serious, potentially deadly differences. In the 1930s, Japan grew more militaristic and began expansion into southeast Asia, trying to create an empire that it labeled the Greater East Asia Co-Prosperity Sphere. To secure their empire, the Japanese wanted to remove American power in the Pacific. For a few years they had been negotiating diplomatically. In fact, just before the attack on Pearl Harbor on December 7, 1941, the Americans and Japanese had been discussing ways to ensure peace in the Pacific. But the Japanese had other plans, and after General Hideki Tojo took over the civilian government in October 1941 war plans replaced any diplomatic solution. On December 8, 1941, President Roosevelt spoke before Congress and a stunned nation. "Yesterday, December 7, 1941," was "a date which will live in infamy." He then got what he needed—a declaration of war. Three days later Hitler and Italy declared war on the United States.

Although the Allies were in tough shape, they did have a few things on their side: the technological advances developed by the British, the human resources of the Soviet Union, and the industrial might of the United States. By the end of the war, the United States had manufactured 300,000 airplanes, 87,000 ships, 400,000 artillery pieces, 102,000 tanks and motorized guns, and 47 million tons of ammunition. War itself had two main theaters, one centered on the European continent and the other in and around the Pacific Ocean. Early in the war the focus was on Europe. The first victories came in late 1942 when British troops under General Bernard Montgomery broke through Nazi general Edwin Rommel's lines at El Alamein (near the Suez Canal) and began Operation Torch, which sought to cut through North Africa and attack Europe's underside. Nazi forces also suffered a major defeat at Stalingrad, where Soviet troops repulsed a better-equipped Germany army. After the Allies had stopped Nazi advances, they moved into Italy in 1943. All sides awaited the invasion of Germany. The question was not when but where. On June 6, 1944—D-Day—American, British, and other Allied forces invaded France. Although the battles on the beaches of France were extremely bloody, the Allies eventually secured a foothold and did not stop until they were at Berlin. Germany surrendered in May 1945.

While Nazi forces were retreating, the Americans began to focus on the Pacific. The strategy that they eventually adopted was called "island hopping." Instead of taking back every island occupied by the Japanese, the Americans were selective and jumped from one to another, making their way to the Japanese main islands. The turning point was the Battle of Midway when three American aircraft carriers, *Hornet*, *Enterprise*, and *Yorktown*, sank four enemy carriers, a cruiser, and three destroyers. Only the *Yorktown* was sunk. This led to very bloody invasions of other Japanese islands, such as the Solomon Islands and Guadalcanal.

While the American forces hopped their way to Japan, scientific and technological breakthroughs in atomic weaponry enabled the Americans to change their war plans. Since the turn of the 20th century, dreams of apocalyptic nuclear war were slowing becoming a real possibility. The American nuclear program benefited from Nazi social policy as Jewish scientists from Europe came to the United States to escape persecution and work on their ideas. By the late 1930s, an atomic bomb was in reach. FDR then decided that the United States should have atomic weapons in its arsenal. The Manhattan Project, which involved 100,000 scientists and engineers in the United States, Canada, and England, worked to create nuclear fuels and control their reaction. By 1945, they had a working prototype that detonated on July 16, 1945. There was little question that new president Harry S Truman would use the device to end the war. On August 6, 1945, the United States bombed Hiroshima, killing 80,000 people. Three days later the Americans dropped an atomic bomb on Nagasaki, killing 60,000 people. Japan immediately and unconditionally surrendered. World War II was over.

The war had an enormous effect on people's daily lives. The loss of life is staggering. Seventeen million soldiers and 18 million civilians died, including over six million Jews and others like Gypsies and homosexuals murdered during the Holocaust. Countless millions had their normal lives disrupted by war production, rationing, and the destruction of homes and businesses that war inevitably brings. Europe and Japan as well as other Asian nations were completely destroyed and had to be rebuilt after the war. Unfortunately the terrible conflict did not bring a lasting world peace in that the cold war began even as the Allies were celebrating their monumental victories over fascism in Europe and in Asia.

To read about war in the United States in the 19th century, see the United States entries in the section "War and Military" in chapter 6 ("Political Life") in volume 5 of this series.

~Andrew E. Kersten

FOR MORE INFORMATION

Blum, J. M. V Was for Victory: American Politics and Culture during World War II. New York: Harcourt, Brace, Jovanovich, 1976.

Keegan, J. The Second World War. New York: Viking, 1989.

Sherwin, M. A World Destroyed: The Atomic Bomb and the Grand Alliance. New York: Knopf, 1975.

Walker, J. S. Prompt and Utter Destruction: Truman and the Use of the Atomic Bombs Against Japan. Chapel Hill: University of North Carolina Press, 1997.

UNITED STATES, 1945–90

In this period, the United States engaged in several major shooting wars and in an ongoing ideological conflict with the Soviet Union known as the cold war. The cold war is the popular name applied to the deterioration of U.S.–Soviet relations after the end of World War II in 1945. The rivalry between the two nations was marked by a series of diplomatic and military incidents that frequently threatened but never actually led to open warfare. Each nation sought to limit the influence its rival exercised around the world. The United States sought to check the extension of Soviet power in central and eastern Europe, where Soviet-dominated communist governments came to power in the late 1940s, by economically, politically, and militarily rebuilding western Europe. Initiated in 1947 and lasting until 1951, the Marshall Plan sent more than $12 billion in economic assistance to help the coun-

POLITICAL LIFE
|
WAR
|
Europe, 1914-1919

United States, 1939-1945

United States, 1945-1990

Latin America

Islamic World

Soviet Union

Japan

tries of western Europe rebuild basic industries, increase trade, and raise basic standards of living. In Germany, which had been divided after the war into zones of occupation controlled by the Americans, French, British, and Soviets, the U.S. air force thwarted Soviet attempts to blockade the Allied sectors of Berlin, which were surrounded by the Soviet sector of Germany, by airlifting supplies into the city in 1948 and 1949.

The focus of the cold war shifted to Asia in 1950, where a shooting war commenced on the Korean Peninsula. The armies of Soviet-influenced North Korea invaded South Korea, a U.S. ally, on June 25. A U.S.-led coalition authorized by the United Nations came to the defense of South Korea, while China, which had become a communist state in 1949, eventually entered the war on the side of the North Koreans, who were also supplied by the Soviets. The war ended with a cease-fire in 1953, which left the peninsula divided between the communist North and the democratic South. Over 33,000 Americans died in the Korean War. At the start of the 21st century, U.S. forces were still stationed in South Korea.

The cold war continued until 1989–90, when the collapse of the Soviet Union and of the Soviet-controlled regimes of Eastern Europe left the United States without a significant rival as a world superpower. However, in the years since 1960, the United States had fought two other major wars. The first of these was the Vietnam conflict. The numbers of persons directly involved in the war in Vietnam provide a sense of the war's broad and powerful impact in America. Of the almost 27 million men of draft age during the war, 11 million were drafted or enlisted. The remaining 16 million who never served included some who enlisted in the National Guard or were granted conscientious objector status. Some were exempted for physical reasons. Others had educational, vocational, marital, or family hardship or other reasons for exemption. An estimated 250,000 men, many from urban ghettos, did not register at all. Fifty thousand evaded the draft or deserted the military by exiling themselves to Canada and other places.

Of the 2.7 million persons who served in Vietnam, 300,000 were wounded and 58,000 died. For their parents, spouses, siblings, and friends, the pain caused by the loss of loved ones was indescribable. Even though the flow of daily life in the United States seemed in some respects to be undisturbed, the loved ones of those who served and returned, those who evaded service, and even those who were exempted from it endured anxiety and heartache. For the rest, the daily reports on casualties, the commentaries on the war, and the protests the war inspired meant that happenings far away were affecting the lives of everyone.

U.S. Marine Corps flamethrower tank in action, Vietnam, 1966. © National Archives.

Protests against U.S. involvement in the war between North and South Vietnam began in the early 1960s. As troop levels went up, so did the numbers and vehemence of the protesters. On April 15, 1967, 125,000 Americans gathered in New York to rally against the war. More than 55,000 joined in a comparable event in San Francisco. Organized by a coalition known as the Spring Mobilization to End the War

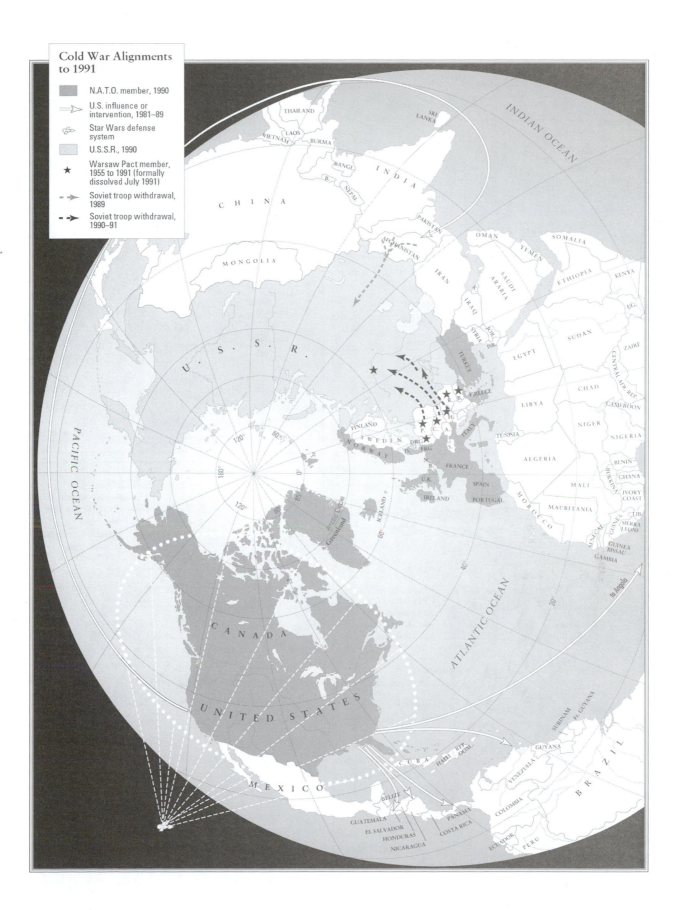

Cold War Alignments to 1991

- N.A.T.O. member, 1990
- U.S. influence or intervention, 1981–89
- Star Wars defense system
- U.S.S.R., 1990
- ★ Warsaw Pact member, 1955 to 1991 (formally dissolved July 1991)
- Soviet troop withdrawal, 1989
- Soviet troop withdrawal, 1990–91

INDIAN OCEAN

THAILAND
SRI LANKA
LAOS
VIETNAM
BURMA
BANGL.
INDIA
B.
NEPAL
CHINA
PAKISTAN
AFGHANISTAN
OMAN
YEMEN
SOMALIA
MONGOLIA
IRAN
IRAQ
K.
SAUDI ARABIA
ETHIOPIA
KENYA
UG.
SYRIA
JOR.
ISR.
EGYPT
SUDAN
ZAIRE
CENTRAL AFR. REP.
U. S. S. R.
TURKEY
GREECE
R. B.
CHAD
CAMEROON
LIBYA
NIGER
NIGERIA
FINLAND
D.
DRG
FRG
S.
H.
A.
P.
C.
TUNISIA
ALGERIA
MALI
BENIN
GHANA
BURKINA
IVORY COAST
SWEDEN
NORWAY
N. B.
ITALY
FRANCE
SPAIN
PORTUGAL
MOROCCO
MAURITANIA
GUINEA
SIERRA LEONE
CUB.
120°
60°
0°
40°
Arctic Circle
Greenland
ICELAND
U.K.
IRELAND
SENEGAL
GUINEA BISSAU
GAMBIA
180°
85°
60°
PACIFIC OCEAN
CANADA
ATLANTIC OCEAN
120°
20°
To Angola
UNITED STATES
SURINAM
Fr. GUYANA
GUYANA
BRAZIL
CUBA
HAITI
REP. DOM.
MEXICO
VENEZUELA
COLOMBIA
BELIZE
GUATEMALA
EL SALVADOR
HONDURAS
NICARAGUA
COSTA RICA
PANAMA
ECUADOR
PERU

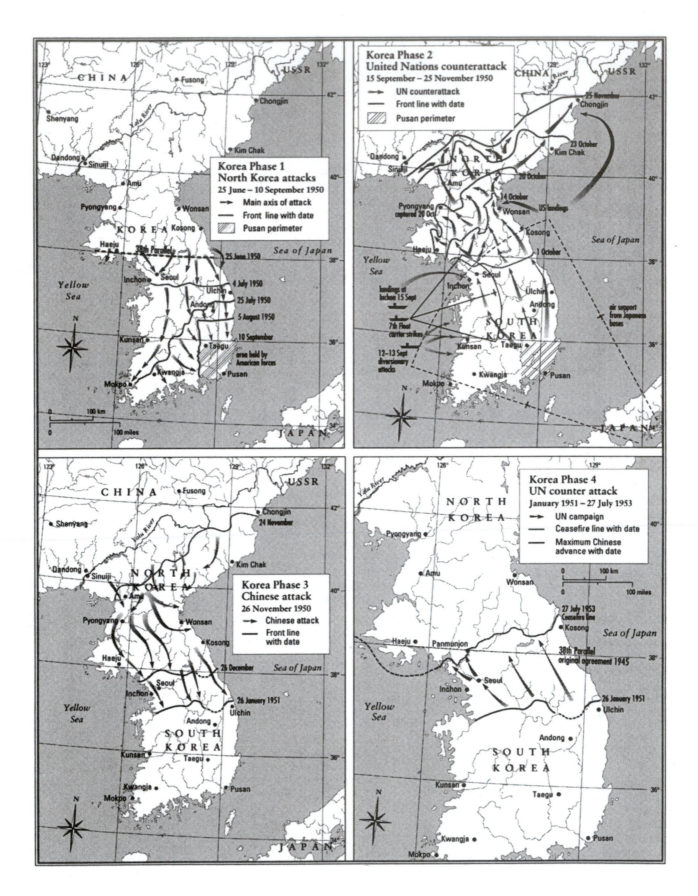

Korea Phase 1
North Korea attacks
25 June – 10 September 1950

→ Main axis of attack
— Front line with date
▨ Pusan perimeter

25 June 1950
4 July 1950
25 July 1950
5 August 1950
10 September
area held by American forces

Korea Phase 2
United Nations counterattack
15 September – 25 November 1950

→ UN counterattack
— Front line with date
▨ Pusan perimeter

25 November
23 October
20 October
14 October
US landings
1 October
air support from Japanese bases
landings at Inchon 15 Sept
7th Fleet carrier strikes
12–13 Sept diversionary attacks
Pyongyang captured 20 Oct

Korea Phase 3
Chinese attack
26 November 1950

→ Chinese attack
— Front line with date

24 November
26 December
26 January 1951

Korea Phase 4
UN counter attack
January 1951 – 27 July 1953

→ UN campaign
— Ceasefire line with date
— Maximum Chinese advance with date

27 July 1953 Ceasefire line
38th Parallel original agreement 1945
26 January 1951

in Vietnam, the demonstrations had the support of a broad range of groups and such prominent individuals as Martin Luther King Jr. and Dr. Benjamin Spock, whose book on baby and child care had been relied on by the parents of many of the protesters.

The efforts of antiwar protesters, most of them college-educated and middle-class, initially met with indifference. As the protesters became more insistent and more vocal, however, they increasingly alienated working-class people who knew that those fighting the war came primarily from their ranks. In December 1967 a Louis Harris poll reported that more than three-fourths of the population believed the protests encouraged the enemy to fight harder. Seventy percent of the respondents expressed the belief that antiwar demonstrations were "acts of disloyalty" to the soldiers fighting the war. A poll several weeks later showed that 58 percent favored continuing the war and stepping up military pressure on the Communists. Sixty-three percent opposed halting the bombing of North Vietnam as a tactic to see if the Communists would be willing to negotiate a peace settlement.

Leading the march against the Vietnamese conflict are Dr. Benjamin Spock, the tall, white haired man; and Dr. Martin Luther King Jr., third from right, in a parade on State Street in Chicago, March 25, 1967. © AP/Wide World Photos.

Yet the demonstrations showed that opposition to the war could not be taken lightly. The antiwar sentiment of some demonstrators sprang from moral outrage over the loss of American lives in what seemed to be a lost cause, of others from long-standing pacifist commitments. Still other demonstrators believed it made sense to cut losses in a war that was simply an imprudent endeavor.

Even though the antiwar movement failed to attract multitudes of followers, televised reports on marches and acts of civil disobedience created widespread uneasiness about the war. Critics of the news media, particularly Presidents Johnson and Nixon, were outraged by what they considered to be antiwar bias. Since then other critics have claimed (contrary to persuasive evidence) that the United States could have won the war if the media had reported more fully and accurately the U.S. military successes in Vietnam, rather than embracing the antiwar arguments.

Careful analyses show that most of the media, at least until 1968, held positions sympathetic to President Johnson's policies. Most continued to support the government's actions well into the Nixon presidency. On the other hand, the media's reports on antiwar activities tended to focus on violent or bizarre behavior by the protesters. *Time* magazine, for example, dismissed the April 1967 protests as a "gargantuan 'demo'" that was "as peaceful as its pacifist philosophy, as colorful as the kooky costumes and painted faces of its psychedelic 'pot left' participants, and about

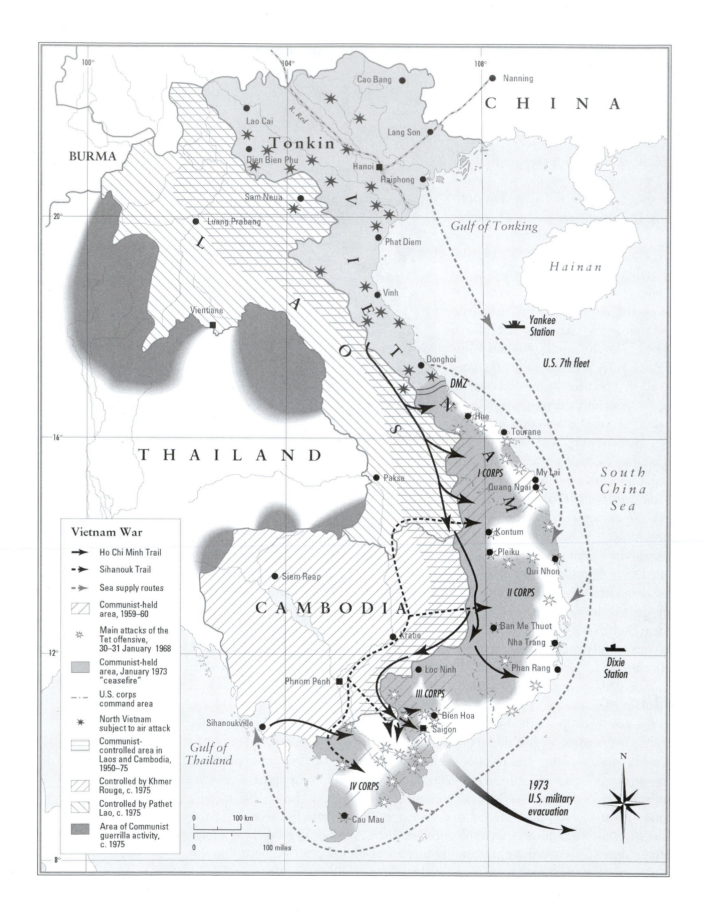

Vietnam War

→ Ho Chi Minh Trail

⇢ Sihanouk Trail

⇢ Sea supply routes

▨ Communist-held area, 1959–60

✳ Main attacks of the Tet offensive, 30–31 January 1968

▧ Communist-held area, January 1973 "ceasefire"

⋯ U.S. corps command area

✳ North Vietnam subject to air attack

▤ Communist-controlled area in Laos and Cambodia, 1950–75

▨ Controlled by Khmer Rouge, c. 1975

▨ Controlled by Pathet Lao, c. 1975

▨ Area of Communist guerrilla activity, c. 1975

CHINA

Nanning

Cao Bang

Lao Cai

Tonkin

Lang Son

Dien Bien Phu

Hanoi

Haiphong

Sam Neua

Luang Prabang

Gulf of Tonking

Hainan

Phat Diem

Vientiane

Vinh

Yankee Station

U.S. 7th fleet

BURMA

L A O S

Donghoi

DMZ

Hue

Tourane

THAILAND

Pakse

I CORPS

My Lai

Quang Ngai

South China Sea

Kontum

Pleiku

Siem Reap

Qui Nhon

II CORPS

CAMBODIA

Ban Me Thuot

Nha Trang

Kratie

Dixie Station

Loc Ninh

Phan Rang

Phnom Penh

III CORPS

Bien Hoa

Saigon

Sihanoukville

Gulf of Thailand

IV CORPS

1973 U.S. military evacuation

Cau Mau

N

0   100 km

0   100 miles

as damaging to the U.S. image throughout the world as a blow from the daffodils and roses that the marchers carried in gaudy abundance." By failing to give serious attention to the arguments advanced by the protesters—admittedly difficult to do in collages of short clips and sound bites—the media failed to give viewers and readers insights into the ideas and ideals of those who genuinely thought the war wrong.

The agony caused by an offensive launched by the North Vietnamese in January 1968 did more to turn sentiment against continuing U.S. involvement in Vietnam than anything the antiwar movement might have done. The media provided uncensored coverage of that offensive, named for Tet, the Vietnamese New Year. The North Vietnamese attacked at many points, but the focus of news coverage was on a siege at the combat base known as Khe Sanh. The siege lasted from January 21 until April 14 and included fierce battles, reported daily. At one extreme, television viewers saw hand-to-hand combat with knives, rifles, and grenades. At the other, they saw the dropping of 220 million tons of bombs by American planes in the area. By the time the siege ended, about 300 U.S. soldiers had been killed and 2,200 wounded, but estimates of enemy casualties ranged from 2,500 to 15,000.

Military and political leaders in the United States claimed that the Tet Offensive had failed. Nonetheless, as Nancy Zaroulis and Gerald Sullivan explain vividly in *Who Spoke Up?*, Tet was a turning point in the minds of many Americans who had previously supported the war effort or were neutral about it. Savagely fought contests struck raw nerves. Perhaps even more so did a photograph showing South Vietnam's police chief shooting a Viet Cong suspect in the head on a Saigon sidewalk. Or hearing a U.S. major say about the fighting at Ben Tre, a city of 35,000, "It became necessary to destroy the town to save it." When CBS anchorman Walter Cronkite, in his "Report from Vietnam" on February 27, 1968, expressed doubts about prospects for U.S. success, those doubts spread. They spread further when the Business Executives Move for Vietnam Peace, which claimed 1,600 members, said that "as businessmen we feel that when a policy hasn't proved productive after a reasonable trial it's sheer nonsense not to change it." Even the *Wall Street Journal*, always a spirited antagonist of the antiwar movement, published an editorial on February 23, 1968, stating that "everyone had better be prepared for the bitter taste of a defeat beyond America's power to prevent."

In subsequent months, more and more people expressed opposition to the war. They wrote letters to members of Congress and the president, placed advertisements in newspapers, signed petitions, and joined in vigils in public places, including military installations. They supported candidates who took antiwar positions, most notably presidential candidates Eugene McCarthy and Robert Kennedy in 1968 and George McGovern in 1972. A few refused to pay taxes, or to register for the draft, or to be inducted. A few burned draft cards and participated in strikes on campus and occasionally in workplaces. By engaging in nonviolent civil disobedience, they became subject to arrest, jailing, and court trials. More extreme actions included raids on offices of draft boards to destroy records by burning or pouring blood on them, as well as trashing, burning, or setting off bombs in buildings and, in several instances, committing suicide.

In the aftermath of the Tet Offensive and two weeks after a weak showing in the New Hampshire primary, President Lyndon Johnson announced on March 31 that he would not seek reelection. Vice President Hubert Humphrey, who hoped to be Johnson's successor, had been reluctant to question Johnson's policies, thus making himself the object of bitter and ferocious criticism by the war's opponents. The assassination of Robert F. Kennedy, Humphrey's leading rival for the nomination, added to the Democratic Party's turmoil. The Democratic National Convention in Chicago was a nasty affair. Protesters made the conventioneers angry, and Chicago police officers attacked the protesters, resulting in what came to be called a police riot.

As opposition to the U.S. role in Vietnam increased, Republican presidential candidate Richard Nixon claimed that he had a secret plan for ending the war. Humphrey gradually let his opposition to the war be known, and his strong campaign finish made the results of the election surprisingly close: Nixon received 43.4 percent of the popular vote, Humphrey 42.7 percent, and George Wallace 13.5 percent.

After the election, the antiwar movement lost whatever coherence it ever had and fell into general public disfavor. The Nixon administration's misleading statements of its intentions and its denunciations of the movement's leaders, along with divisions within the movement, were partly responsible. Probably more important were the excesses displayed by radical campus groups, such as the Weathermen, and the news media's willingness to be wooed by Nixon's foreign policy advisor, Henry Kissinger. Still, opponents of the war were able to mobilize for a Vietnam Moratorium Day on October 15, 1969. An organization of Republicans known as the Ripon Society, the liberal Americans for a Democratic Society, the United Auto Workers, and the Teamsters union, along with many political and religious leaders, endorsed the moratorium. A number of Vietnam War veterans were among the millions of participants in local protests across the nation.

Republican Richard Nixon claimed that he had a secret plan for ending the war.

Conflicts between supporters and opponents of the war continued into 1970, most notably on university campuses. During the academic year ending in the spring of 1970, there were nearly 250 bombings and about the same number of cases of arson, resulting in at least six deaths. The event that brought into sharp focus the conflict between those who opposed the war and those who defended U.S. policies and actions occurred on May 4, 1970. Five days earlier Nixon had shocked the nation by announcing that U.S. troops had invaded neutral Cambodia to wipe out enemy strongholds there. Ohio National Guardsmen, apparently in panic as they faced protesters of this action at Kent State University, fired 61 shots into a crowd of students, killing four and wounding nine. Students around the nation, reacting to what they had seen on television, threw their own campuses into turmoil, forcing some 400 colleges and universities to end the semester prematurely.

By mid-1970 the lines between opposing sides in the conflict over the war in Vietnam seemed fixed. While casualties mounted, protests continued. In April 1971, Vietnam War veterans marched in Washington, D.C., some on crutches. Others rode in wheelchairs. Thousands of veterans gathered at the U.S. Capitol, removed medals awarded them for bravery, and threw them away. But the demonstrations changed few minds. Nixon's policy of "Vietnamization"—that is, of turning the fighting of the war over to the Army of the Republic of Vietnam—meant that more U.S. troops returned home. The number of U.S. troops in Vietnam dropped from 536,000 in 1968 to 156,800 by the end of 1971. By March 1972 troop strength was down to 95,000, including only 6,000 combat troops. Those coming home made difficult reentries into the routines of everyday life, and the lives of those who remained in Vietnam changed: Estimates on drug use by troops in 1970 stood at about 50 percent. By March 1972 nearly 250 underground antiwar papers were circulating among U.S. troops. Reenlistment rates dropped sharply, and desertions spiraled upward, as did "combat refusal" incidents. Officers feared rebellion in their ranks, and some found their very lives in jeopardy.

Many Americans greeted with skepticism Secretary of State Henry Kissinger's announcement on October 26, 1972, that "peace is at hand." Even so, the nation was not ready to oust Richard Nixon from the presidency, and he easily defeated George McGovern in the presidential election the following week. The next month, peace talks made no progress, and again Nixon ordered bombing of North Vietnam. This prompted some who had not previously joined in protests to attend services of prayer and repentance, believing that as citizens they were party to morally indefensible actions. One such service, attended by persons of all ages, was led by Francis B. Sayre Jr., who had been dean of the Washington National Cathedral for 21 years. He was the son of a diplomat, the grandson of Woodrow Wilson, and the last person to have been born in the White House. After the service, most in attendance marched silently with Dean Sayre to the White House, where they were ignored.

Despite the strength of their feelings, protesters found it hard to sustain the momentum of protests against the war. When Richard Nixon was inaugurated for a second term on January 20, 1973, a counter-inaugural demonstration drew a crowd of more than 60,000 persons at the Washington monument. The mood there, write Nancy Zaroulis and Gerald Sullivan, was "one of witness. Most were there because they were unable not to be. They had come to manifest silent concern for a war in which, as Lincoln's [second inaugural address] had put it, 'Neither party expected . . . the magnitude or the duration which it had already attained.' " But "the stale rhetoric from the monument platform on a day when little remained to be spoken that had not already been said many times before could not hold the audience. Most wandered off in the direction of Pennsylvania Avenue to watch, unbelieving, the inaugural parade and its anticipatory bicentennial theme of 1776." (No one knew then, of course, that by 1976 both President Nixon and Vice President Spiro Agnew would have resigned in disgrace.)

Two days later Nixon announced in a televised statement that representatives of the United States and North Vietnam had initialed the Agreement on Ending the War and Restoring Peace in Vietnam. "Peace with honor," he declared, had at last been achieved. A cease-fire began several days later. Withdrawal of the remaining 23,700 troops was to be accomplished in 60 days, and all American prisoners of war were to be released. The agreement left South Vietnam, known as the Republic of Vietnam, at the mercy of North Vietnam. The South Vietnamese managed to continue their struggle for two more years, but as American aid dwindled, they saw their capital, Saigon, fall on April 30, 1975. It was left to President Gerald Ford to issue a proclamation stating that May 7, 1975, was the last day of the "Vietnam era."

Whether any actions on the part of war protesters through the years accomplished the results they sought was debatable then and remains so. Attempts then, as well as more recently, to portray those opposed to the war as irresponsible "anti-Americans" who committed treasonous acts under orders from communist leaders run contrary to facts. Like every mass movement, the one opposing the war in Vietnam included some radicals, and the radicals in this one engaged in bizarre, violent, destructive acts. But the movement was homegrown and eventually included persons of all ages from across the political spectrum. Leaders and followers in the movement, with rare exceptions, believed deeply in their American heritage as defined in the Constitution and built into their political traditions.

The second war was the liberation of Kuwait. In August 1990 the United States began a massive deployment of troops—230,000 from all branches of the military—in response to Iraq's invasion of Kuwait. For troops already on active duty, being sent to a possible combat zone in a desert in the Middle East was not exactly all in a day's work, but they were expected to be prepared for such a contingency. For the more than 125,000 reservists and members of the National Guard who were called to active duty by the Pentagon, readiness for war was another matter. Among them were men and women from all walks of now-disrupted lives. Not all were sent overseas, because some were needed to fill positions vacated by the full-time troops who had been deployed, but the abrupt changes in their lives and the lives of those they left behind were considerable.

The effects on most Americans of preparation for war had little to do with strategies or ethics, or even with disruption of their personal lives by calls to service. Rather, their concerns were with what it cost to fill the tanks of their cars with gasoline. Before Iraq's invasion of Kuwait on August 2, the price of gasoline in the United States averaged $1.09 per gallon. By mid-October it had risen to $1.40, even though only about 9 percent of imported oil had come from Kuwait. Various maneuvers by the government brought the price down again, but the episode brought three reminders: First, the reliance of Americans on automobiles was enormous. Second, the vulnerability of the nation's oil supply was something Americans would rather not think about. Third, oil and automobiles are so central to the American economy that anything threatening their place shakes the stock market badly. Worries about the war and its implications caused investors to be so jittery that the market lost 20 percent of its value from August to mid-October (Marty, 105–12, 265–66).

To read about war in the United States in the 19th century, see the United States entries in the section "War and the Military" in chapter 6 ("Political Life") in volume 5 of this series.

FOR MORE INFORMATION

Hering, G. C. *America's Longest War: The United States and Vietnam, 1950–1975*. New York: Wiley, 1979.

Jewison, N., dir. *In Country*. 1989.

Karnow, S. *Vietnam: A History*. New York: Viking, 1983.

Marty, M. A. *Daily Life in the United States, 1960–1990: Decades of Discord*. Westport, Conn.: Greenwood Press, 1997.

Military History Magazine. *Desert Storm*. Howell Press, 1991.

The Wars for Vietnam. <http://www.coursework.info/i/1411.html>.

Zaroulis, N. L. *Who Spoke Up? Americans Protest the War in Vietnam, 1963–1975*. Garden City, N.Y.: Doubleday, 1984.

Zwick, E., dir. *Courage Under Fire*. 1996.

LATIN AMERICA

Latin American soil witnessed few international wars during the 20th century, yet the region was rife with revolutions, civil wars, "dirty wars," and repeated foreign interventions. Much of the violence and bloodshed related to legacies of previous centuries: political and economic systems excluded the majority of the populations, and although poverty and inequality weighed heavily on societies, political leaders appeared unable or unwilling to combat such problems. Thus, continued exclusion and poverty drove many groups to hoist arms against ineffective political systems and leaders. Sometimes this brought success, as in Cuba and Nicaragua. In many cases, however, such action invited severe state-led repression.

Few wars of a truly international character occurred in Latin America during the century. Perhaps the most highlighted of these was the 1982 confrontation between Argentina and Great Britain for control over the Falkland Islands in the South Atlantic (known in Argentina as the Islas Malvinas). Border altercations between neighboring countries were much more frequent. In 1932, Bolivian and Paraguayan forces broke into war for control over the Chaco region. A cease-fire began in 1935 (with Paraguay decidedly the victor), and the two countries signed a peace treaty in 1938. The years of war, however, resulted in some 85,000 to 100,000 dead (Collier and Skidmore, 310). In Central America, long-standing tensions between El Salvador and Honduras erupted into several months of intense violence in 1969, leading to 2,000 deaths. Likewise, Peru and Ecuador struggled over their common border region, with violence exploding in the early 1940s and 1980s, and the late 1990s.

Twentieth-century Latin America witnessed a great number of strong revolutionary movements. Five of these movements succeeded, though for differing lengths of time. The first great upheaval occurred in Mexico. There, the revolution started in 1910 as a response to the *Porfiriato* (lengthy dictatorship of Porfirio Díaz, which began in 1876). The tenets of the Mexican Revolution, consolidated in the constitution of 1917, served as a model and inspiration for many future revolutionary movements in Latin America. And many leaders who emerged during the war, including Pancho Villa and Emiliano Zapata, attained legendary status.

Another successful revolution that changed the face of Latin America—and the world—was the Cuban Revolution. Similar to the case of Mexico, the Cuban Revolution began as a response to the harsh 25-year rule (direct as well as behind the

POLITICAL LIFE | WAR

Europe, 1914-1919
United States, 1939-1945
United States, 1945-1990
Latin America
Islamic World
Soviet Union
Japan

479

scenes) of strongman Fulgencio Batista. After years of organizing and several unsuccessful attempts, revolutionaries succeeded in forcing Batista's flight from office in 1959. Fidel Castro filled the political vacuum and responded rapidly to the desire for change among Cubans. As Castro and his colleagues consolidated the revolution, they made great advances in many social services, such as health care and education.

Revolution was also successful in Guatemala. The Guatemalan Revolution began in 1944 with the election of Juan José Arévalo Bermejo and grew stronger in 1950 with the election of Colonel Jacobo Arbenz Guzmán. These two presidents dedicated themselves to improving their country's economy and expanding public works. They also embarked on a massive land reform project. In 1954, however, a U.S.-sponsored coup d'état deposed Arbenz, terminating the revolution and sparking a civil war that did not officially end until 1996.

Other revolutions succeeded in Bolivia and Nicaragua. The Bolivian Revolution began in 1952, as the MNR (*Movimiento Nacional Revolucionario*, or National Revolutionary Movement) came to power. As with the Latin American revolutions that had come before, the new leadership pushed progressive changes in the economy, politics, and agriculture. Factional strife within the MNR ultimately led to its fragmentation, however, and an army takeover of the government in 1964 dealt the final blow to the revolution. Similar to the case of Bolivia, the Nicaraguan Revolution began in 1979 when, after nearly two decades of guerrilla warfare against the Somoza family dynasty, the FSLN (*Frente Sandinista de Liberación Nacional*, or Sandinista National Liberation Front) took control of the country's political reins. During their decade in power, the FSLN carried out an extensive agricultural reform program and vastly improved the system of education, reducing illiteracy from 52 percent to 12 percent. The revolution fizzled in 1990, when the FSLN lost national elections and stepped down peacefully from power.

Many revolutionary movements in Latin America were not successful, however. In other words, the revolutionaries did not succeed in taking over the political reins of their respective countries, and national institutions and systems were not significantly transformed. In such cases—from Uruguay and Paraguay in the Southern Cone to Colombia and El Salvador in the northern reaches of the region—political strife degenerated into protracted civil wars.

These revolutions and civil wars had many similarities. On a most basic level, they were fought between leftists and rightists, or liberals and conservatives. Coalitions of left-leaning political, military, and civil organizations sought to modify or eradicate the traditional exclusionary systems and, in so doing, increase mass participation in national government. Many movements adopted socialist and Marxist forms. Many shared the intention to educate the masses, as well as the desire to increase the economic and political independence of their nations.

Traditionally conservative leaders and economic elites interpreted the actions of leftist groups as threatening and, in many cases, adopted every imaginable tactic to counteract them. State-sponsored repression of opposition groups led to so-called "dirty wars" in many countries, including Guatemala and Honduras in Central America and throughout the Southern Cone. In such cases, governments and their armed forces—often with the support of the United States—waged all-out war on real and perceived subversives in an attempt to maintain order.

For example, the Chilean military, headed by General Augusto Pinochet, took power in a bloody coup in 1973. The regime dissolved Congress, declared political parties illegal, suspended the constitution, and imposed a state of siege on the Chilean people. Over the course of the next 15 years, the Pinochet regime responded to any and all opposition with massive repression, imprisonment, torture, disappearance, and assassination.

In Argentina, a similar dirty war occurred between 1976 and 1983. Also waged by a military regime, it resulted in more than 30,000 disappearances and deaths. In Guatemala, civil war combined with dirty war led to some 200,000 dead. A 1998 truth commission determined that because the vast majority of the victims were indigenous Maya, Guatemalan governments of the war period were guilty of genocide.

> *Pinochet responded to any and all opposition with massive repression.*

Many of the Latin American countries that fell into violence and war during the 20th century drew international attention and mediation. In most cases, negotiations led to cease-fires; peace accords; and, sometimes, broader representation within political systems. Many countries—including Argentina, Bolivia, Brazil, Chile, El Salvador, Guatemala, Haiti, and Paraguay—launched truth commissions that ultimately published their findings in wildly popular reports. Many victims pressed charges against perpetrators of human rights violations; some cases went to trial, though few defendants ever saw prison.

Despite many efforts at reconciliation, strong memories from 20th-century political violence and war continued to divide Latin American societies. At the end of the century, many of the base reasons for the violence—poverty and inequality—continued to exist, leading to new waves of violence in Peru, Mexico, and Colombia.

~Molly Todd

FOR MORE INFORMATION

Collier, S., and T. E. Skidmore. *The Cambridge Encyclopedia of Latin America and the Caribbean*. New York: Cambridge University Press, 1992.

The Disappeared. <http://www.desaparecidos.org>.

Feitlowitz, M. *Lexicon of Terror: Argentina and the Legacies of Torture*. Oxford: Oxford University Press, 1998.

Human Rights. <http://www.derechos.org>.

Memory of Silence. <http://www.hrdata.aaas.org>.

Montejo, V. *Testimony: Death of a Guatemalan Village*. Willimantic, Conn.: Curbstone Press, 1987.

Partnoy, A. *The Little School: Tales of Disappearance and Survival in Argentina*. Translated by Alicia Partnoy, Lois Athey, and Sandra Braunstein. Pittsburgh: Cleis Press, 1986.

Pierce Frost, M., and S. Keegan. *The Mexican Revolution*. San Diego: Lucent Books, 1997.

Skidmore, T. E., and P. H. Smith. *Modern Latin America*. 5th ed. New York: Oxford University Press, 2001.

Winn, P. *Americas: The Changing Face of Latin America and the Caribbean*. New York: Pantheon Books, 1992.

POLITICAL LIFE
|
WAR
|
Europe, 1914-1919

United States, 1939-1945

United States, 1945-1990

Latin America

Islamic World

Soviet Union

Japan

ISLAMIC WORLD

Long after truce was called in the European theaters, the aftershocks of World War I and World War II were felt as far away as the Gaza, Sinai, and the Hejaz. This article provides a brief description of how the world wars of the 20th century fractured the physical and cultural landscape of the modern Islamic world.

The Islamic world saw tremendous upheaval in the first two decades of the 20th century. During World War I (1914–18), the Ottoman Empire fought with the Central Powers (Austria-Hungary, Bulgaria, and Germany) against the Allies (a group of 28 countries including Great Britain and the United States). Established in the 13th century by a Muslim warrior named Osman, the Ottoman Empire once controlled Islamic lands ranging from the Balkans to North Africa. In the 20th century, however, the Ottoman Empire faced a period of decline:

The political structure within which most Arabs had lived for four centuries had disintegrated; the capital of the new Turkish (Ottoman) state was not Istanbul but Ankara in the Anatolian highlands, and the great city which had been the seat of power for so long had lost its attractive force; the dynasty which, whether or not its claims to the caliphate were accepted, had been regarded as the guardian of what was left of the power and independence of Sunni Islam had vanished into history. (Hourani, 316)

By joining with the Central Powers, the Ottomans hoped to regain control of some of their lost territory. They faced resistance not only from the European Allies, but also from local Arab nationalist forces that did not want to fall under the political and cultural domination of the Ottoman Empire. These Arab nationalists, aided by the British, systematically attacked Ottoman military bases throughout the Middle East. This series of attacks, known as the Arab Revolt (1916–18), is depicted in the 1962 Academy Award–winning film *Lawrence of Arabia*.

At the end of World War I, the Ottoman Empire was so severely weakened that it did not pose much of a threat to the Allied powers. Yet, the Allies had conflicting ideas about how to dispose of former Ottoman lands. In 1916 and 1917, the British made a promise to the Sharif of Mecca, Husein ibn Ali, that the Arabs would enjoy independence in return for their help in defeating the Ottomans. At the same time, the Allies had ratified the Sykes-Picot agreement (1916), a document that guaranteed former Ottoman territories to Britain, France, Italy, and Russia. In 1917, the issue was further complicated when the British announced their support for the Balfour Declaration, which called for the establishment of a Jewish state in Palestine.

After the end of World War II (1939–45), Jewish Holocaust survivors needed a safe place to rebuild their lives after the horrors they suffered under Hitler's racist Nazi regime. One place the Jewish people looked to was Palestine. Thousands of Jewish Holocaust survivors entered Palestine before the British relinquished their colonial mandate there in 1948.

The Jewish presence in Palestine and the subsequent formation of the state of Israel in 1948 comprise one of the most contentious issues in modern Middle East history. Zionists and their supporters argue that Israel is the rightful homeland of the Jewish people because such was decreed by God in the Torah (the Hebrew Bible). On the other hand, the Arab populations in this region denounce the Israelis for taking land that belonged to Arab families. They argue that the Holy Lands are of great religious and cultural significance to Muslims as well as Jews.

In the second half of the 20th century, the Israel/Palestine region faced some of its greatest challenges. Many Islamic countries joined the conflict after Israel took over the West Bank, the Gaza Strip, the Golan Heights, and the Sinai Peninsula during the Six-Day War of 1967. Even moderate Arab countries were reluctant to pull out of the region. For example, not until the Camp David Accords of 1978, when Israel agreed to return Sinai to Egypt, did Egypt withdraw from the Arab-Israeli conflict. Other Arab factions continued to struggle against what they felt was yet another form of colonial rule and oppression. Groups of Palestinians staged a series of riots in the Occupied Territories during the Intifada of 1987, striking out against Israeli control of the region.

The Arab-Israeli conflict is far from over and continues to be a destabilizing force in the Middle East. Although some Arab countries, such as Jordan, have moved toward peace with Israel, other elements have undermined the peace process. Suicide bombers routinely cause mayhem and panic in the streets of Israel. In 1995 an Israeli student delayed the peace process even further by assassinating Israeli prime minister Yitzhak Rabin. In Rabin's place, the right-wing Benjamin Netanyahu became prime minister, furthering divisiveness between the Israelis and their Arab neighbors.

Warfare in the modern Middle East has touched people of all religions and ethnicities. Jews and Muslims alike have instigated and been victimized by violence. A common misconception, stemming from the time of the Crusades, holds that warfare in the Middle East is always religiously motivated. Though some Middle Eastern groups use religious rhetoric when they talk about warfare, there are also political, economic, and social dimensions to many of the major conflicts in the modern Middle East.

Today, there are more than 50 independent Muslim states in the modern world (Esposito, 549). It is very difficult to make generalizations about their histories and their roles in the major wars of the 20th century. It is safe to say, however, that most modern Muslim countries were forced, either directly or indirectly, to formulate a response to colonialism. After the end of World War I, many Arabs resented the presence of European colonial governments in the former Ottoman territories. They felt that they had fought hard for their independence and that European colonial control was no better than Ottoman control. By the mid-1950s Arab countries such as Iraq, Syria, Transjordan, Lebanon, and Egypt were free from European colonial rule. Still others, such as the United Arab Emirates and Yemen, did not obtain fully independent status until the 1970s.

No discussion of warfare in the modern Islamic world would be complete without a few words about jihad. Certain factions that oppose the Israeli state often use the rhetoric of jihad to justify their attacks on civilians. It is important to realize that the word jihad has several different meanings. Although the concept of jihad has an important place in the social and political history of the Islamic world, it is not one of the core beliefs or "five pillars" of Islam. The prophet Muhammad taught the Muslim people that the greatest jihad is the struggle against the baser elements of the human condition. The act of physical warfare against an enemy is part of the lesser jihad. Attacks on unarmed civilians, women, and children are not justified in traditional Islamic law.

To read about warfare in the early Islamic world, see the Islamic World and Byzantium entries in the section "Warfare and Weapons" in chapter 6 ("Political Life") in volume 2 of this series.

~*Molly Benjamin Patterson*

FOR MORE INFORMATION

Esposito, J., ed. *The Oxford History of Islam*. New York: Oxford University Press, 1999.

Hourani, A. *A History of the Arab Peoples*. New York: Warner Books, 1991. Reprint 1992.

Lapidus, I. M. *A History of Islamic Societies*. Cambridge: Cambridge University Press, 1988. Reprint 1998.

Lapping, B., and N. Percy. *Fifty Years War: Israel and the Arabs*. PBS Home Video, 2000.

Lean, D., dir. *Lawrence of Arabia*. Columbia Tri-Star, 1962.

Rashid, A. *Jihad: The Rise of Militant Islam in Central Asia*. New Haven: Yale University Press, 2002.

POLITICAL LIFE

|

WAR

|

Europe, 1914-1919

United States, 1939-1945

United States, 1945-1990

Latin America

Islamic World

Soviet Union

Japan

SOVIET UNION

The Workers' and Peasants' Red Army, predecessor of the many-branched Soviet Armed Forces, was begun in March 1918 when Lenin assigned Leon Trotsky to form a tough new fighting force. With that army, the Bolsheviks aimed to maintain their one-party dictatorship and regain the territory of the Russian Empire. Opposed to the Reds in the Civil War of 1918–21 were the Whites, who represented an extraordinary range of political viewpoints, from monarchist to anarchist. Most White officers had served in the former Imperial Army during World War I and now commanded peasant soldiers, many of whom were also veterans of that war.

Despite their widespread discontent with army life, millions of peasants continued to be drafted into the Red Army, if only because there were far more peasants than any other group, and the urban workers favored by the Bolsheviks did not volunteer in great numbers. Prosperous peasants *(kulaks)*, however, were excluded from the privilege of serving, as were members of the merchant class (bourgeoisie) and former nobility, except when the army needed their expertise. For example, Trotsky established an officer corps that depended heavily on aristocratic former czarist commanders, though they were called military specialists rather than officers. Like conscripted peasants, former imperial officers were seldom willing to serve, but they feared arrest and what might happen to their families if they refused or deserted. Because the government did not trust these military specialists, it created a new kind of military official, the political officer (also called military commissar, or simply commissar), to keep an eye on the aristocrats. Among other duties, commissars carried out political indoctrination among the troops. In his satirical novel, *The Life and Extraordinary Adventures of Private Ivan Chonkin*, about Soviet life on the eve of World War II, Vladimir Voinovich depicts his peasant hero, Private Ivan Chonkin, at a political education meeting conducted by Yartsev, his unit's Senior Politruk (a *politruk* was a commissar who, among his other jobs, organized and led discussions). The subject is "The Moral Character of the Red Army Soldier."

"Who would like to go first [to summarize the material]? Chonkin?" [Yartsev] asked, amazed that Chonkin had raised his hand. . . . "I'm not prepared, Comrade Senior Politruk," Chonkin mumbled hesitantly, dropping his eyes. "So why did you raise your hand?" "I didn't raise my hand, Comrade Senior Politruk. I was getting a beetle out. Samushkin put a beetle down my back." (Eaton)

Later in the meeting, Chonkin's naive question, "Is it true that Stalin used to have two wives?" evokes a horrified, furious response from Yartsev, who pronounces the hapless private a "disgrace, not only to [the] unit and company, but to the entire Red Army as well." Voinovich's satire notwithstanding, many soldiers liked and admired their commissars for their ability to boost morale before a battle, or just for their friendship, as was the case with the World War II fighter pilot Igor Kaberov. Like the fictional Chonkin, Kaberov attended obligatory political meetings (often held under an airplane wing) that could turn nasty, as when comrades accused him of not carrying out his duty while on a mission and demanded his punishment. For young people about to risk their lives, a charismatic political officer's presence and pep talks must have been a psychological substitute for chaplains and other religious comforts banned in the armed forces.

In the late Soviet era, the military consisted of five main forces under the Ministry of Defense, as well as forces under the Ministry of Interior and secret police (KGB from 1954). The Ministry of Defense services were the strategic rocket forces, ground forces (army), troops of air defense, air forces, and navy. Other Ministry of Defense groups, such as the rear services of the armed forces, troops of civil defense, and (the least prestigious) construction troops, did not belong to any one service, but were sent where needed, as were the special troops of support personnel—engineering, chemical, signal, road building, railroad building, and automotive.

The KGB and Ministry of Interior (MVD) each had their own elite, highly trained, and well-equipped uniformed forces known collectively as security troops. During each semiannual draft call-up, agents from these government departments reviewed the new conscripts' files. Those assigned to one or another of the security troops were vetted for intelligence, physical fitness, and political dependability (demonstrated in part by membership and activity in the Party or Komsomol, the Young Communist League).

Internal troops, which were security troops subordinate to the Ministry of Interior, maintained political security and calm within the country's borders and guarded prisons and prison camps. Internal troops were stationed in every Soviet town over a certain size. Border troops, a branch of the KGB security troops, included air and naval units as well as ground forces. They were the first military units encountered by those entering the USSR, and probably the last those leaving would see. A human "iron curtain," border troops did whatever it took to ensure that illegal, unwanted, or suspect foreigners were turned back or arrested and that no one left the country without official permission. To keep their land closed and isolated, border troops used

hidden and open physical and electronic barriers . . . detection and alarm devices, explosives, trip wires, and observation posts. . . . aircraft . . . foot, horse-mounted and vehicular patrols . . . Specially trained . . . dogs . . . patrol boats . . . ambushes, trenches, ditches . . . searchlights, electronic and infrared devices, telescopes, mines, . . . fences, wire, ploughed areas . . . The entire 60,000 kilometers of border [was] patrolled on the ground, by water, or through the air around the clock, day in and day out. (Eaton)

Those entering or leaving the country were thoroughly checked by border troops, who looked for any kind of subversive literature, music, art, and the like, inspecting all means of transportation to make sure no one or nothing was being hidden inside. No one was allowed to live near, stroll, or drive around the immediate border area. Yet another branch of KGB security troops, signal troops, were responsible for installing, maintaining, monitoring, and overseeing security for communication facilities linking high government, Party, and military and secret service offices and bases throughout the USSR. There were also special KGB guard units for protecting the Kremlin and other important government office sites in Moscow and elsewhere.

> *Red Army soldiers often lacked bathhouses.*

The largest part of the Soviet military was the Red Army. Like most members of Soviet society, soldiers had to endure substandard housing plus shortages of food, clothing, and other basic necessities. They often had to live in tents for months, because the number of men being drafted always raced ahead of the government's ability or willingness to provide more substantial housing for them. Even brand-new barracks were likely to have been shoddily built, far from weatherproof with no indoor plumbing or electric lights. Soldiers often also lacked bathhouses. The degree to which conscripts ate well, or at least had enough food, depended on how concerned their officers were about their diet. As a result of the famine of 1932–33, the government ordered all units to grow their own food and raise their own livestock. Such military farms raised cows, pigs, bees, rabbits, wheat and other cereals, and fruit. Much time was diverted from military training while soldiers became field hands under officer farm managers, but they had to eat, and such agricultural enterprises were an integral part of major Soviet army units until the fall of the Soviet Union. Military farms usually had the same problems as nonmilitary ones: poor management, roads, housing, and equipment, and unwilling workers. When such farms did not produce enough, the soldiers' diet suffered. Besides being assigned to work on military farms, soldiers were often used as a source of free labor to work on civilian collective farms as well as in any other areas of the civilian economy. Even though soldiers got no reward for their extramilitary work, it is likely that people higher up the chain of command profited. It is also likely that the many hours spent in field hand work, railroad and apartment house building, and other kinds of heavy labor contributed to the army's chronic morale problems. There was generally no effective way to get grievances resolved. Soldiers wrote letters of complaint, sent them to the official channel (the Bureau of Red Army Men's Letters), and in most cases waited in vain for a response.

The USSR was drastically unprepared for the German invasion of Russia in 1941, in great part because Stalin had signed a nonaggression treaty with Hitler and because of the deadly purge of the Soviet military in 1937 and 1938. First came the arrests and executions of Marshal Mikhail Tukhachevsky and other high officers on grounds of treason. Suddenly it seemed that antigovernment conspiracies were everywhere in the military. By the time Stalin finished flushing out supposed armed forces traitors, some 40,000 officers had been discharged, many to be shot or sent to the gulag. The victims were mainly senior officers, including most of the marshals, army commanders, corps commanders, divisional commanders, and all but one navy fleet commander. When the purges were over, fewer than half of the senior Soviet officers were still alive. They had been convicted on false evidence, their confessions extracted under torture, but no one knows why Stalin went after them. When the "Winter War" with Finland (1939–40) showed how much the Red Army needed officers with military expertise, and war with Germany loomed or had already begun, more than one-fourth of the surviving arrested officers were freed, reinstated in their former ranks, and sent to war.

Naturally the purges degraded morale in the armed forces. Officers had to wonder whether any one of their orders might get them arrested, while soldiers and junior officers questioned how they could trust a senior officer's judgment, since so many had been convicted of treason. And who knew whether an arrested officer's replacement might not also turn out to be an "enemy of the people"? Officers' arrests may have contributed, in the late 1930s, to a decline in military discipline and a significant rise in accidents, suicides, and self-inflicted wounds among servicemen. And when war began, thousands of new, inexperienced officers paid with their lives for lack of training, as did millions of soldiers under their command. Even experienced officers, however, might be summarily executed for losing a battle. To save their own skins, officers sometimes denounced each other as traitors.

Even though millions of Soviet citizens supported the war effort, desertion remained a chronic, widespread problem throughout the conflict, as it had been during the civil war. Tens of thousands of soldiers assigned to defend border areas (Ukraine, Belorussia, Lithuania, Latvia, and Estonia) at the beginning of the war ran away or deserted to the German side because they hoped the Germans would bring their countries independence from the Soviet Union, or they sympathized with Nazi anti-Jewish policies. Many deserted because they had been alienated by Soviet terror.

The government tried to fix the problem by threatening soldiers with terrible reprisals if they retreated or fled, or (in the case of officers) did not prevent their men from doing so. A decree of August 1941 ordered officers'—including commissars'—families to be arrested if their men deserted. On September 12, 1941, Stalin decreed that special NKVD (secret police) detachments be sent to the front lines with orders to shoot any soldiers who tried to run away, a tactic that had also been used in the civil war. In 1942, Stalin decreed "not one step backward" for soldiers in battle, adding special regular army "blocking detachments" to the NKVD troops already assigned to shoot retreating soldiers. In addition, the order created penal battalions for disobedient or "cowardly" soldiers and their officers. These units were sent into battle ahead of regular troops, to attract enemy fire or become human minesweepers. Jokes or criticisms of military or government policies could land a soldier in a penal battalion and nearly certain death.

The Germans treated Soviet prisoners of war worse than they did other Allied prisoners because according to Nazi racism, Jews, Slavs, and Asians were the most inferior groups. Because the USSR was composed mainly of Jews, Slavs, and Asians, their German captors had no particular reason to treat them humanely, and didn't. Stalin considered his soldiers traitors for having been captured and readily abandoned them to their fate. The Red Cross was not allowed to deliver them food parcels from home or to try to protect them in any other way. As a result, Soviet POWs died by the hundreds of thousands in German prison camps, from starvation, disease, cold, and executions. When the other Allied POWs shared food packages with their Soviet comrades, starving Red Army prisoners "jumped on these gifts like a pack of dogs on a bone." The cheapness of their lives to the Germans is reflected in the fact that 600 were murdered in September 1941 in the first mass killing experimental use of Zyklon B poison gas at the Auschwitz death camp.

Those not captured also had only slim chances for surviving. Untrained or barely trained, ill-equipped replacements for wounded and killed soldiers were sent to the front lines and "shov[ed] . . . in front of the Germans." One such replacement, Gabriel Temkin, lived to write about his experiences as a raw recruit sent to combat with no weapons instruction and no weapons. When asked about preparation, a political officer told the men they would soon have on-the-job training. When he arrived at the front in May 1943, Temkin found weapons aplenty, left behind on the battlefield by hundreds of slain Red Army predecessors. He and his fellows simply picked up the guns and began shooting at the enemy, as best they could. The Germans "were not caught by surprise," he recalled. "Their heavy machine guns began to crackle and mowed down our soldiers." In the course of 10 days' savage fighting, Temkin's division lost about 200 men per day, losses regularly replenished by more new untaught recruits, though no territory was gained. In fact, at the beginning of World War II, the chances were that more than 60 of every 100 soldiers would be either dead or captured within six months. Nevertheless, many struggled courageously against the terrible odds.

The resistance by the garrison of the Brest fortress was heroic, despite the fact that the command had abandoned it. The fortress was besieged on all sides by the Germans but continued to resist for 28 days. The few survivors, after unprecedented suffering at the hands of the Germans, ended up in a Soviet prison camp in Siberia as "traitors to the homeland." They were not rehabilitated (i.e., freed, or their name cleared, or both) until many years after the war.

But the tide was turning. After the Germans were routed from Stalingrad, people knew the enemy would be defeated. By 1943 the devastation Germans had wrought on the USSR's heavy industries was being overcome. In 1944, Soviet military production was about four times greater than it had been in 1940, surpassing the Germans' war industry capabilities. By dint of working 55-hour weeks, Soviet engineers and laborers were each month pumping out thousands of airplanes, tanks, guns, mortars, and machine guns as good as, or better than, the Germans', as well as millions of bombs, shells, and mines. That same year saw the beginning of an American-British-Canadian program (lend-lease) that gave the Soviet war effort billions of dollars' worth of food, motor vehicles (Studebakers, Dodges, and Jeeps), clothing, gasoline, raw materials, weapons, ammunition, explosives, materials for heavy industry, railroad equipment, medicines, textiles, tanks, and planes. Not only regular armed forces troops benefited. After the Battle of Stalingrad, the government also allotted partisan bands more and better supplies of guns, food, and medicine, so that in 1943 and 1944 many more fighters joined the partisans. These developments may have buoyed troops' morale even though by war's end, Red Army dead and wounded far outnumbered casualties suffered by other Allied forces. Statistics vary, but probably around 20 to 30 million Soviet soldiers and civilians were killed in World War II. The number of German soldiers and civilians killed in the war amounted to about a third of the USSR's losses. In comparison, Great Britain and its Commonwealth countries lost 42 times fewer soldiers and civilians; the United States (whose losses did not ordinarily include civilians) lost 72 times fewer people. Soviet war dead included millions of civilians as well as combatants because much of the war was fought on their land for three and a half years, by an invader who succeeded in carrying out policies of mass murder against millions of Jewish residents and brutalities against millions of other Soviet ethnic groups. In addition, the USSR's war with Germany was a war of attrition: both sides ruthlessly used people as matériel, and the USSR had more people to expend. As late as 1944, when the land was cleared of the enemy, Soviet soldiers and officers were still being rushed into battle poorly trained, poorly equipped, and poorly supplied. When killed, they were still being quickly replaced by equally inexperienced, ill-trained recruits.

> *Red Army soldiers took revenge on the German people with rape being a prominent tactic.*

Besides the millions of soldiers who died in combat, hundreds of thousands of troops succumbed to infectious diseases like typhus and cholera, as well as from a lack of prompt, skilled emergency medical care, whether in the field or behind the lines. Hospitals behind the lines were shabby, unheated, and generally filthy, with few male orderlies who could restrain violent, battle-shocked patients. Inpatients fled if they could, even if it meant foregoing crucial surgery.

As victors, Red Army soldiers took revenge on the German population in a manner "both enormous in its scope and terrible in its fury," with rape being a prominent tactic. There were other injustices as well. At war's end, over two million Soviet citizens—POWs and others—were repatriated, often by force, from Germany and other European countries with the help of British and American authorities. Stalin presumed they were German collaborators, as thousands had been. For thousands of others, however, the only traitorous act was having been captured. The hapless returnees were automatically tarred with the same brush and dispatched to the same fate: execution or long prison camp sentences. Only 15 to 20 percent escaped such punishments after they arrived on Soviet soil.

Thanks to its new military might, the Soviet Union had leaped forward in world power and prestige, but remarkably, the daily life of soldiers after the war was not much different than it had been before the war. When Alexander Lebed arrived, in 1985, to command the garrison of the 331st Airborne Regiment, he saw that the whole base was "a trash heap without a single visible trash can or dumpster." Sanitary conditions were ghastly. All the garrison's soldiers were crowded into only two barracks; maybe that was the reason for the "total disregard for cleanliness." In the lavatory, "toilets and sinks were broken and three-fourths of the faucets were twisted off."

The walls were covered with slime and mildew. Everything was overflowing and leaking and smelled terrible. In the sleeping facilities, the side tables and stools were broken, and the entire hall had only two or three lightbulbs, which were coated with dust.

Such day-to-day existence in the midst of poverty and filth, bred in the soldiers, Lebed believed, "Boredom, hopelessness, and the desire to do something nasty, mean, and cruel to your neighbor." Lebed claimed that, with difficulty, he was able to set things right on the base.

In December 1979, the government sent troops into Afghanistan to defend the Soviet-backed government of the Democratic Republic of Afghanistan (DRA) against rebellious Islamic "holy warriors" (mujahideen). Altogether, some 642,000 Soviet soldiers served in Afghanistan from 1979 to 1989.

As in the past, soldiers usually had no leave during their stint. Mixing with the local population was forbidden and dangerous (though it did occur), and there were few or no opportunities for recreation. Soldiers were sent into the Afghan mountain and desert wildernesses, with their constant strong winds, extremes of hot and cold weather, and gun-clogging dust and sand, without sufficient water. Close to 15,000 *afgantsy* (soldiers of the war in Afghanistan) were killed by Afghan guerillas during the 10-year war. Thousands of survivors, men and women, came home wounded in body and mind. All the harshest aspects of Soviet military life—bullying, drug and alcohol abuse, mistreatment by officers, crime and corruption—continued and intensified in Afghanistan.

Afghanistan was a rich breeding ground for diseases such as jaundice, malaria, meningitis, dysentery, hepatitis, typhus, and skin diseases, which often were more life-threatening than the mujahideen. Besides having to shelter in ramshackle barracks with no heat, toilet, or washing facilities, *afgantsy* had to endure hunger—a regular feature of army life from the civil war on. The stingy rations were often so distasteful that soldiers spent their 10 rubles per month (the equivalent of just a few dollars) on food, or bought liquor and drugs when they could. Some committed suicide. Others stole government property and resold or bartered it to Afghans. Marketable items included gasoline, boots, uniforms, construction materials, automotive spare parts, rifles, and other weaponry, large and small. Kabul even had a special bazaar for the loot.

Dedovshchina (the practice of subjecting new army recruits to violence and cruelty) in Afghanistan added a new twist: recent arrivals were hazed even if they had already served their first six months and been the victims of dedovshchina. Only this time, the tormented sometimes found an opportunity to strike back. In the midst of a firefight with the enemy, officers or fellow soldiers who had tortured recruits might get picked off, dispatched by their erstwhile victims and not the Afghan enemy. Brutal officers had reason to be wary of their men in that there were cases of soldiers murdering officers while other soldiers simply stood by and watched.

Soviet soldiers committed atrocities on the mujahideen as well as on unarmed noncombatants, and the mujahideen in turn committed atrocities against Soviet soldiers and their Afghan allies, including women and children. One Red Army veteran described a horror he witnessed when four Afghans were "tied, laid on the road, and run over" with an armored personnel carrier. One Afghan "was a priest with a beard and they spared him." The next morning, however, when a soldier refused an officer's order to pour gasoline over the priest and burn him, the officer angrily slit the priest's throat. Elsewhere, a Soviet Army search party looking for their missing men found the burned bodies of three of their comrades lying near a campfire.

The fourth was put up above the fire like in a grill. Cut off tongues, ears, picked out eyes were spread around. I thought that my heart would never bear such a terror, that it would explode like a grenade. (Eaton)

Both sides generally killed prisoners. As in previous wars, most who returned physically or emotionally disabled did not get adequate help from either the military or civilian communities. What help they did get often came only after a determined struggle against bureaucratic indifference. Sometimes the paperwork needed to get veterans' benefits started was lost or filled out incorrectly. Although 3,000 veterans needing artificial legs had not received them by mid-1990, most would not have benefited anyway—more than half the veterans allotted Soviet-made artificial legs found them unusable. Disabled veterans of the Afghan war, like all other handicapped Soviet citizens, had to deal with social attitudes and official policies that stigmatized them as invalids and pariahs; assigned them low-level jobs and paltry pensions; and did nothing to make the outside world, including public transportation, accessible.

Workers in the former Soviet Republic of Georgia dismantle a Russian tank after the collapse of the Soviet Union in 1991. © AP/ Wide World Photos.

Increasingly as the country lurched toward the collapse of its government, resistance to military service grew stiffer, especially in the minority republics, where not serving became a matter of honor, abetted by sympathetic local officials. In 1990 and 1991, only 79 percent of those called up, countrywide, responded, and most of them were ethnic Russians. Of those who did answer the draft call, many subsequently deserted. Many officers became less enthusiastic about their career choice when, thanks to glasnost, they could compare their standard of living with that of officers in NATO armies.

Led by a cluster of ultraconservative generals, the Red Army's inglorious "last hurrah" was its failed attempt in August 1991 to unseat General Secretary Mikhail Gorbachev by force, undo the trend toward an open society that Gorbachev had set in motion, and keep the unraveling Soviet empire intact. Soldiers sent to the Kremlin in tanks were unwilling to attack their fellow citizens, as were many commanders. Prodemocracy civilians even clambered aboard tanks and posed for jubilant photos with the crews. Finally the Minister of Defense ordered the troops to leave; the attempted coup was history, as soon the Soviet Union would be.

In December 1991 the Red Army became the Russian army, a military that no longer had political workers as officers, but whose living conditions for common soldiers were still so hazardous that Russian mothers struggled to prevent their sons from serving, or traveled to Chechen battlegrounds to search for them and bring them home (Eaton).

FOR MORE INFORMATION

Beier, H. *Six Russian Men: Lives in Turmoil*. North Quincy, Mass.: Christopher, 1976.

Eaton, K. B. *Daily Life in the Soviet Union*. Westport, Conn.: Greenwood Press. Forthcoming.

Galeotti, M. *Afghanistan: The Soviet Union's Last War*. London: Frank Cass, 1995.

Goldhammer, H. *The Soviet Soldier: Soviet Military Management at the Troop Level*. New York: Crane, Russak, 1975.

Reese, R. *The Soviet Military Experience: A History of the Soviet Army, 1917–1991*. New York: Routledge, 2000.

Voinovich, V. *The Life and Extraordinary Adventures of Private Ivan Chonkin*. New York: Farrar, Straus, and Giroux, 1977.

POLITICAL LIFE

|

WAR

|

Europe, 1914-1919

United States, 1939-1945

United States, 1945-1990

Latin America

Islamic World

Soviet Union

Japan

JAPAN

Japan was involved in war for almost the first half of the century. Most of that time was spent in the acquisition of its colonial empire, later dubbed the Greater East Asia Co-Prosperity Sphere.

Late to the scramble for colonial empire building in the 19th and early 20th centuries, Japan believed Germany's Otto von Bismarck when he counseled in 1872 that in the game of global diplomacy, "might makes right." Within a generation of Japan's reopening by American Commodore Matthew C. Perry in 1854, the nation began an imperialist crusade in northeast Asia.

In short order Japan was involved in seven wars: the First Sino-Japanese War (1894–95), the Boxer Intervention (1900), the Russo-Japanese War (1904–5), World War I (1914–19), the Siberian Expedition (1918–19), the Manchurian Incident (1928–32), and what the Japanese call the Great Pacific War (1936–45). During that period it acquired a huge empire, including Taiwan (1895), Korea, ("liberated" in 1895 but part of its empire after 1910), Sakhalin and Kurile Islands (1895), Manchuria (1895, 1905, 1919, and again in 1932), and most of East Asia and the South Pacific. All of that territory was stripped away in 1945 as part of

Japan's unconditional surrender to the Allied powers. In addition, Japan lost sovereignty over the Ryukyu Islands (restored in 1972) as well.

Historians have argued that Japan's militarism can be traced back to its seven centuries of feudalism (1192–1868), but others maintain that for most of that period Japan was ruled by something even worse: armed bureaucracy. The governments of that period were staffed by warriors (samurai) who were highly educated in neo-Confucian civil and secular precepts.

Japan was ruled by largely civilian constitutional monarchist governments (1890–1945) that evolved into a British-style party cabinet system by 1918. But because war was endemic in Japan (as it was in the rest of the world) during this period, the military had considerable influence and power over the civilian government. Indeed, after about 1928 the military seemed to be determining Japan's foreign policy. The assassination of a client warlord in Manchuria (Zhang Zuolin) in that year set off a maelstrom of military adventurism on the Asian continent.

War, or the preparation for it, occupied much of Japanese efforts during the period. Squabbles between the army and the navy often rent the fabric of civilian government. Huge military appropriations prevented Japanese citizens from ever enjoying the fruits of the nation's miraculous industrialization and international trade. Some have argued that the military-industrial complex (to borrow a phrase from Dwight Eisenhower) was the very engine for that economy and industrialization. The acquisition of Japan's empire fed the war machine. Japan's economic cliques (zaibatsu) benefited from its military adventurism. The army and navy had to be supplied with the engines and supplies of war, and the acquisition of colonies abroad fed the nation and the zaibatsu with needed raw materials as well as markets for their products.

The frenzy for empire and war nearly destroyed Japan's developing representative form of government. A series of assassinations of civilian and financial leaders by militarist madmen in the 1930s cowed the surviving leaders into silence. National elections continued, but increasingly the military elbowed elected leaders aside. Indeed, by 1942 all political parties were abolished in favor of the umbrella fascist Imperial Rule Assistance Association. Women, who could not vote, were hustled into a similar association. Children spent each school day marching and practicing war-related exercises such as grenade throwing, rifle drill, and crawling under barbed wire. Special police (Kempeitai) monitored the population and many political activists were rounded up, imprisoned, and even secretly executed for the temerity of questioning the military's actions.

War was horrendous for the Japanese. Millions of young conscripts endured physical abuse from their officers. Estimates of combatant deaths range upward of 1.8 million, and perhaps an equal number of civilians were killed during Japan's wars. We may never know how expensive the war was in terms of bomb destruction. Some 300,000 people were killed during firebombing raids on Tokyo (March 1945) and atomic attacks on Hiroshima and Nagasaki (August 1945) alone. Some estimates suggest that 60 percent of Japan's industrial production and 40 percent of its residences were destroyed. Rice and other crops burned in the fields, and by early 1945 famine was widespread throughout the country. Japan did not equal its prewar trading totals until the late 1950s.

Even worse were Japan's atrocities committed abroad. The names Nanjing, Bataan, River Kwai, Manila, and hundreds of other sites of war crimes are etched indelibly into history. Perhaps 20 million Chinese died as a result of the 15 years of Japanese invasion. In one horrific campaign in 1942 (*Ichi-go*) Japanese troops cut a wide swath called "Three-All" (Loot All, Burn All, Kill All) of rapine and butchery. Thousands of women were forced into sexual slavery to feed vicious and brutal sexual appetites in Japanese military brothels. Hundreds of thousands of Koreans were pressed into slavery during the war; the total number of their deaths will never be known. All told, war was a bitter failure for Japan. It cost Japan tremendous ill will throughout the rest of the world. Even half a century later the nations victimized by Japan continued to chastise and criticize the Japanese for their wartime rapacity.

The Allied Occupation, run primarily by the United States under General Douglas MacArthur, forced the Japanese to reform on all levels. Women were given civil rights, including the right to vote, and workers were given the right to unionize. Progressive reform programs in the industrial, commercial, and agricultural sectors ensured that the country would maintain democratic social and political systems. The constitution of 1947 (aptly called the Peace Constitution) renounced war as an instrument of national foreign policy. Memories of the horrific war have kept the nation from revising that part of the constitution.

To read about war in early modern Japan, see the Japan entry in the section "Warfare" in chapter 6 ("Political Life") in volume 4 of this series.

~*Louis G. Perez*

FOR MORE INFORMATION

Dower, J. W. *Embracing Defeat: Japan in the Wake of World War II*. New York: W. W. Norton, 1999.

———. *War without Mercy: Race and Power in the Pacific War*. New York: Pantheon, 1986.

POLITICAL LIFE: WEB SITES

http://www.frontlineonnet.com/fl1805/18050800.htm
http://lanic.utexas.edu/la/region/government/
http://www.departments.bucknell.edu/russian/chrono3.html
http://www.warscholar.com/Timeline.html
http://www.time.com/time/newsfiles/organizedcrime/

7

RECREATIONAL LIFE

RECREATIONAL
LIFE

SPORTS

FILM

MUSIC

Play is serious business. All mammals play, but humans have cultivated recreation to a high art. After family and work, most of our energies and time are devoted to recreational activities, and as any modern sports enthusiast knows, we play with as much passion as we work. What are recreational activities? All forms of play share several characteristics. First, play is voluntary—one can't be forced to play. As such, it is in fact the very essence of freedom, and even slaves and prisoners treat themselves to games, music, or dance for the sheer voluntary quality of the activities. Second, recreation is also outside of workday life, limited in time, duration, and space. Thus, playtime by contrast almost defines work time; recess at school not only offers a break from study but also marks the serious times when one is to learn. Third, recreation has its own rules that are more rigorous and predictable than anything we can find in our more complex workday lives. The rules are clear, and at the end of the game—and there is a definitive end—there is a winner and a loser. Of course, cheating is always a possibility (archaeologists have even found loaded dice in Anglo-Saxon settlements), but even unsportsmanlike conduct is recognizable. It may be that we love games precisely for the clarity of the rules. Finally, recreational life builds a group identity among the players, and this is true even of individual sports such as archery or bicycling, for athletes in these sports see themselves as linked with others who share the pastime.

Although recreational activities throughout history share these general characteristics, the particular forms of play we choose shed light on who we are and what we value. In play, we prepare ourselves for the rest of our lives. For example, games ranging from Olympic events to chess hone our skills for war, whereas music and art stimulate our creativity. Violent sports from dogfights to boxing steel us to face violence in life, and team sports like American football prepare us to work together in an economy of separation of skills. In studying the games that people play, we can more fully understand the society they are creating.

During the 20th century, recreational life changed dramatically. In so doing, it changed Western culture. Entertainment became readily available with the invention and mass production of the television, the radio, and other leisure devices designed for the home such as the computer and computer games. Watching television became a passion for most Americans. As a result, a sort of national culture, if not an international one, was invented. Almost overnight, everyone who had a television began to experience the same cultural phenomena, such as Ed Sullivan, Elvis Presley, and Lucille Ball. By the 1950s, recreation was an essential part of any American's daily life. Americans played innumerable games, often in groups. For example, in the 1950s, bowling alleys and bowling leagues sprang up and spread quickly. Although some complained about being "clubbed to death," Americans were joiners until the late 1970s. They loved to participate, in Boy Scouts, church groups, and game clubs. This changed dramatically by 2000. In a very interesting sociological study, one scholar learned that in the late 1990s most Americans bowled alone. In fact, by the end of the century, recreational life was highly individualized. People participated in sports, but more often than not they exercised alone. They loved games but preferred to play on their home computers or home gaming systems. And, of course, watching television has never been a team activity. Yet, American recreation, no matter how individualized, had become a major cultural export to the world. Even Europe, China, and Russia enjoyed American pastimes such as basketball and watching the latest Hollywood movie.

During the 20th century, recreation also became more and more important to the economy. In fact, by century's end, a major share of the economy was related to either the tourism industry or the service industries that were tailored to those looking for fun. Most cities had very large entertainment districts. Cities developed shopping malls, theaters, fine dining, and professional sports to draw people's extra dollars. Cities often competed with each other for the same consumers. In this modern urban sweepstakes, the stakes were quite high. If a city did not attract enough shoppers, for example, it could become a ghost town. Having fun was big business and was taken seriously by all world leaders.

FOR MORE INFORMATION

Huizinga, J. *Homo Ludens: A Study of the Play Element in Culture*. Boston: Beacon Press, 1964.
Putnam, R. D. *Bowling Alone: The Collapse and Revival of American Community*. New York: Simon and Schuster, 2000.

RECREATIONAL
LIFE
|
SPORTS
|
Europe

United States,
1920-1939

United States,
1960-1990

Japan

Africa

Sports

As entertainment, as leisure, and as exercise, sport has always been a part of daily life. In the 20th century, however, it took on another dimension. It became big business, not just in the United States but across the world. In part, the growth of sport was an offshoot of the rise of the middle class in the Western world. These populations had not only the interest but also the means to support professional sports teams. The first sport to adopt a professional and corporate structure was baseball. Though the big leagues had their beginnings in the 19th century, the creation of the oligarchy of owners and their economic trust organization lie in the

20th century. This type of spoils system became the model for other sports such as basketball and football. The other hallmark of professional sports, paying athletes enormous sums of money, also originated in the early 1900s. In 1930, newspaper critics commented that Babe Ruth, the New York Yankees' incomparable slugger, made more money than the president of the United States, Herbert Hoover. In his defense, Ruth responded that he had had a better year.

As baseball slowly became the nation's pastime, other sports similarly modernized. Football, which had been extremely popular in high schools and colleges, now attracted a national following. Moreover, with the rise in widely circulated newspapers and the advent of radio, it was possible to follow one's favorite team and create a public interest in sporting contests. Only the Great Depression caused a momentary slowdown in the rise of professional sports in American daily life. And yet, some teams such as the Green Bay Packers thrived even in economic chaos. By the 1940s, sporting national championship games and series truly became national events, almost holidays.

The inclusion of national, professional sports into daily life grew stronger as the century drew to a close. Moreover, sport became wedded into the fabric of politics and economics. For example, in 1967, the heavyweight boxing champion, Muhammad Ali (born Cassius Clay), refused to be drafted in a protest of American foreign policy and military action in Southeast Asia. Ali was stripped of his championship belt, fined $10,000, and given a five-year prison sentence. Professional sports became a larger and larger part of the American economy. For example, in such places as Green Bay, Wisconsin, and Buffalo, New York, sports teams accounted for a lion's share of the tourism industry. Moreover, participating in sport became a major economic force. From bicycling to running to skateboards to fitness centers, Americans craved sport in their lives. When they were not watching or doing, they were reading about sports in magazines such as *Sports Illustrated* and books such as Jim Fixx's triumphantly successful *Complete Book of Running* (1978), which sold a staggering 620,000 copies. By the end of the century, these American trends in sport had become a major export in the world, particularly in Europe and Asia. American sports were also gaining popularity throughout the world, from baseball and golf in Japan, to basketball, boxing, and long-distance running in Africa. Spreading professional sports to all world markets was the untamed frontier and the unfinished business of sport moguls in the year 2000.

EUROPE

Europeans enjoyed, as both spectators and participants, a variety of sports during the 20th century. Many of the most popular sports, such as skating, skiing, and cycling, had evolved into competitive activities from purely recreational and utilitarian pastimes. Boxing, rugby, soccer, tennis, track and field, and wrestling, all competitive sports from their conception, remained so during the 20th century. With much zeal and enthusiasm, Europeans embraced the North American sports—baseball, basketball, football, hockey, and volleyball. The diffusion of sports from

RECREATIONAL
LIFE
|
SPORTS
|
Europe

United States,
1920-1939

United States,
1960-1990

Japan

Africa

North America to the continent transformed European sportive culture from provincial to international. The modern Olympic Games, established by Frenchman Pierre de Coubertin in 1896, promoted the international diffusion of sports during the 20th century. Throughout the century, many European capitals hosted both the summer and winter Olympic Games. In addition, other sportive spectacles, such as the Wimbledon tennis tournament and the Tour de France cycling race, attract huge international fields of spectators and participants while maintaining a particular European appeal. Despite the increasing cosmopolitan nature of some European sports, others, such as *boules* in France and bullfighting in Spain and Portugal, have preserved their provincial character.

Soccer developed in the mid-19th century in the English university system.

Many of Europe's most popular sports, in terms of recreational and competitive participants, originated as means of transportation. For centuries, Europeans have used skates and skis for transportation. In the 19th century, they used the bicycle and continued using it until the automobile replaced it in the early 20th century. The late 1800s witnessed the transformation of these activities into competitive sports. The development of lightweight, all-steel skates led to increased interest in speed and figure skating throughout Europe. Vienna hosted the first European speed and figure skating championships in 1892. Figure skating became an Olympic sport in 1908, as did speed skating in 1924. Although Europeans have dominated speed skating throughout the century, they have shared the limelight with Americans in figure skating. Competitive skiing increased in popularity during the early 1900s. Switzerland held the first organized slalom race in 1921, and the Olympic Games included the race in 1924. Cross-country skiing, long a means of winter transportation, became an Olympic sport in 1936. In the 1930s, the invention of ski lifts promoted recreational skiing and the proliferation of ski resorts throughout Europe's mountainous regions. After World War II, skiing gained global appeal, as Austrian Toni Sailer in the 1950s, Frenchman Jean-Claude Killy in the 1960s, Swede Ingemar Stenmark in the 1970s and the 1980s, and Italian Alberto Tomba in the 1990s became household names.

Two of the most popular sports, for both participants and spectators, are soccer and track and field. Europeans participate in soccer and track and field (or athletics) at various skill and competitive levels, from local clubs to national teams. Spectators fill soccer and athletics stadiums by the thousands to watch the events. Soccer developed in the mid-19th century in the English university system and spread throughout Europe and the British Empire during the late 19th century. The Fédération Internationale de Football Association (FIFA) formed to govern soccer in 1904. Today, major soccer leagues, each composed of 18 to 20 teams, exist in Germany, Italy, Spain, Netherlands, England, Portugal, Poland, and France among others. Track and field, another English sport transplanted to the continent in the late 19th century, consists of running, jumping, and weight-throwing events. During the 1920s and 1930s, Finnish athletes dominated the long-distance running and weight-throwing events. After World War II, the Soviet Union and its Warsaw Pact allies provided generous financial support to their track and field teams, thereby ending England's and America's hegemony over the sport. With the end of the cold war, track and field competition lost its political significance, and the emblems of athletic shoe companies replaced national flags on athletic uniforms.

During the 20th century, Europeans enthusiastically embraced the North American sports of basketball, football, and hockey. Invented in 1891 by Dr. James Naismith in Springfield, Massachusetts, basketball quickly gained popularity in Europe before World War II, becoming an Olympic sport in 1936. After the war, it became the continent's most popular indoor sport. By century's end, professional basketball had grown to 124 teams across 45 nations. Currently, the best European players often play in America's National Basketball Association. Europeans adopted Canadian ice hockey early in the century, with it becoming an Olympic sport 1920. Today, scores of hockey teams dot Europe, with many of the best players eventually playing in North America's National Hockey League. In 1991, the National Football League sponsored the World League of American Football, an international professional league, consisting of three European teams, one Canadian team, and six American teams. Renamed NFL Europe in 1998, the league was reorganized around six European teams. The season extends from April to June and consists of 10 games and a championship final, the World Bowl.

More than any single sport or event, the Olympic Games have made sport part of Europeans' everyday lives. With the games held every four years, participants and spectators, whose hometown might host the event, look forward with much anticipation for the sport spectacle. European cities have hosted 16 of the 27 Summer Olympic Games since 1896 and 12 of the 19 Winter Olympic Games since 1924. A true international event, the Olympic Games have exposed Europeans to the world's best athletes. Despite the goodwill fostered by the Olympic Games, they have been manipulated and marred by politics, as in Munich in 1976 when Palestinian terrorists kidnapped and murdered members of the Israeli Olympic team. During the cold war, tensions between the East and West played themselves out in Olympic stadiums, culminating in the boycotts of Moscow in 1980 and Los Angeles in 1984. Originally an amateur movement, by century's end the Olympic Games had fully recognized and accepted professional athletes.

As a sport spectacle, the Olympic Games are rivaled only by the Tour de France, a cycling race that lasts 23 days and covers about 2,500 miles. Though most of the race occurs in France, the course ventures into Spain, Italy, Switzerland, and Belgium. First held in 1903, the Tour de France is restricted to male cyclists, although a women's race was held from 1984 to 1989. Europeans dominated the race until Greg LeMond became the first American to win the tour in 1986. He claimed the title again in 1989 and 1990. Another American, Lance Armstrong, won the race from 1999 to 2003.

~Adam Hornbuckle

FOR MORE INFORMATION

Baker, W. J. *Sports in the Western World*. Rev. ed. Urbana: University of Illinois Press, 1988.

Guttman, A. *The Olympics: A History of the Modern Games*. 2d ed. Urbana: University of Illinois Press, 2002.

Mandell, R. D. *Sport: A Cultural History.* New York: Columbia University Press, 1984.

Young, D. C. *The Modern Olympics: A Struggle for Revival.* Baltimore: Johns Hopkins University Press, 1996.

UNITED STATES, 1920–39

Sporting contests had long been occasions for socializing, wagering, and admiring the performance of racehorses, hunting dogs, and skilled athletes. World War I military experience had exposed many men to baseball, boxing, and track and field. American Legion programs kept many veterans engaged in these sports, as both players and coaches of younger participants. Middle-class involvement in hunting and fishing increased. Vastly more expensive elite sports such as golf and tennis gained popularity as well. However, the most notable growth in sports during the 1920s was in the size of the audience. Not only the number of spectators at sporting events but the radio audience for them as well propelled sports forward as leisure activity.

Baseball drew the largest audience. The "big leagues" of professional baseball were confined to the northeast quarter of the country where the proximity of urban centers and the convenience of rail transportation made two eight-team leagues possible. The American League had been around since the turn of the century, the National League considerably longer, and their only direct competition with each other, the World Series, since 1903. Professional baseball was damaged by the scandal that swirled around the 1919 Chicago White Sox, eight of whose players were convicted of taking bribes from gamblers to lose the World Series to the Cincinnati Reds. Establishment of a baseball commissioner to police owners and players restored faith that the games were

Girls against boys. Children in Irwin, Iowa, play baseball in the local schoolyard. © National Archives.

fair contests. A tighter, harder, "lively" ball was introduced along with new rules to assure frequent replacement of the ball so that it could not be softened up. These changes aided hitters, increased the possibility of home runs, and attracted more fans than ever before. Larger crowds, not to mention stadiums built in the 1920s to hold them, marked the growing popularity of what fans already called "the national pastime."

Radio and newspapers carried accounts of big league baseball far beyond the 10 cities where it was played (New York had three teams; Boston, Chicago, Philadelphia, and St. Louis two each; and Cincinnati, Cleveland, Detroit, Pittsburgh, and Washington were the others). Minor league professional teams existed in smaller cities and towns of the South, Midwest, and Pacific coast. Additional legions of semiprofessional and amateur baseball teams made it difficult for Americans to remain entirely unfamiliar with the game. Star players became celebrities whose exploits were widely known and admired. The most famous of all, home run slugger Babe Ruth of the New York Yankees, answered criticism that his 1930 salary was higher than President Herbert Hoover's by saying, "I had a better year." Most agreed.

Since the 1890s, football had become extremely popular at high schools and colleges with the playing fields and resources to support it. As enrollments grew and physical education became part of curricular and extracurricular activity, football increased its following. Whereas standard teams put 11 players on the field, low-enrollment schools often adapted the rules to permit games with 5 or 6 on a side. Not only did students and alumni flock to games, but so too did people whose only connection to a school was an enthusiasm for its teams. Recognizing a potential publicity and financial bonanza, universities built stadiums seating several times their enrolled student bodies and began hiring talented players with "athletic scholarships." Excellent teams and outstanding players or even the opportunity to have a good time watching a losing effort drew huge crowds, unprecedented throngs of 60,000 to 80,000 and even more, to college campuses on fall Saturday afternoons. By the end of the 1920s, college football brought in an estimated $21.5 million,

> ### 📷 *Snapshot*
>
> **"Take Me Out to the Ballgame" (1908)**
>
> The words for "Take Me Out to the Ballgame" were written in 1908 by Jack Norworth, who at the time had never been to a baseball game. One day, while riding a New York City subway train, Norworth saw a sign that read, "Ballgame Today at the Polo Grounds." The sign inspired Norworth to write a series of baseball-related lyrics that were later set to music by Albert Von Tilzer and thereby became the beloved baseball song "Take Me Out to the Ballgame." The song is today one of the best-known and most widely sung songs in the United States.
>
> Katie Casey was baseball mad,
> Had the fever and had it bad;
> Just to root for the home town crew, ev'ry sou Katie blew
> On a Saturday, her young beau
> Called to see if she'd like to go,
> To see a show but Miss Katie said, "No,
> I'll tell you what you can do":
> Take me out to the ball game,
> Take me out with the crowd
> Buy me some peanuts and crackerjack
> I don't care if I never get back,
> Let me root, root, root for the home team,
> If they don't win it's a shame
> For it's one, two, three strikes you're out,
> At the old ball game. . . .
> (Bruun and Crosby, 514)

$4.5 million more than professional baseball during the same year. Professional football, employing ex-college stars, began attracting large crowds in the same cities that supported major league baseball but generally remained a sidelight to the enormously popular college game.

During the winter months between fall football and spring and summer baseball, school and college gymnasiums housed a sport invented only in the 1890s. Basketball had almost instantly become popular with both males and females throughout the country. Rules differed for five-member men's teams and six-member women's teams, and, except in a few Midwestern states, women's basketball did not become the spectator sport that the men's game did. Men's basketball drew fans to high school and college games and even to industrial leagues. Businesses hoping to advertise themselves and build employee morale would recruit and reward workers who were talented ballplayers. For basketball players and fans alike, this was the extent of professionalism in the 1920s and 1930s.

The development of women's collegiate athletics such as basketball was a direct result of a federal law. Here U.S. women's basketball player Katrina McClain, center, is overwhelmed by members of the Women's Unified Basketball Team in Barcelona, Spain, August 6, 1992. © AP/Wide World Photos.

Except for boxing, baseball, horse racing, and football—professionalized sports that attracted crowds of spectators and quickly gained radio audiences as well—most sports remained predominantly kids' games. Large numbers of children and younger adults played baseball; bicycled; swam; ran; and, in northern regions, ice-skated and skied. But these sorts of leisure-time activities tapered off rapidly after high school, the Lynds noted in *Middletown*, a victim, they surmised, of the popularity of the automobile.

One notable exception to the general pattern of reduced adult sport activity was the rise in the popularity of golf in the 1920s. The game was restricted to the wealthy because of equipment costs, the time required to play a round, and the expense of maintaining a large and carefully groomed grass course. Media reports of the triumphs of Atlanta attorney Bobby Jones, an amateur who regularly defeated professional competitors, together with the opening of more private and even public courses, boosted interest in golf. By the end of the decade, an estimated three million players could be found on some four thousand courses nationwide.

The depression caused enthusiasm for golf to sag but gave rise to an alternative—miniature golf, invented in the late 1920s. It required much less exertion, skill, and time to play; was far less expensive; and thus was accessible to more people as a leisure-time activity. A wide public took up miniature golf. So popular did it quickly become that by 1930 there were an estimated 30,000 courses in operation across the United States. Among other things, miniature golf's popularity suggests that many people looked more for relaxation and amusement in their daily lives than for strenuous exercise (Kyvig, 135–37).

To read about sport in the United States in the 19th century, see the United States entry the section "Sports" in chapter 7 ("Recreational Life") in volume 5 of this series.

FOR MORE INFORMATION

Bruun, E., and J. Crosby. *Our Nation's Archive: The History of the United States in Documents.* New York: Black Dog, 1999.

Burns, K., dir. *Baseball.* PBS Video, 1994.

Lynd, R. S., and H. M. Lynd. *Middletown: A Study in Modern American Culture*. New York: Harcourt, Brace, and World, 1929.

Rader, B. G. *American Sports: From the Age of Folk Games to the Age of Televised Sports*. Englewood Cliffs, N.J.: Prentice Hall, 1995.

Sayles, J., dir. *Eight Men Out*. 1988.

UNITED STATES, 1960–90

In keeping with his image as a young and vigorous president, John F. Kennedy urged the American people to get out of their armchairs and do something to get in shape. In fact, he charged the President's Council on Youth Fitness with developing a program to improve the physical condition of the nation's schoolchildren. The council proposed standards for measuring fitness and urged schools to provide children with at least 15 minutes of vigorous activity daily. Running became a popular activity, even an obsession, for many people, and the commercial world encouraged a running craze. German shoes imported to meet new demands included Adidas, designed by Adi Dassler, and Puma, the product of his brother Rudi. From Japan came Tiger Marathons. New Balance, a Boston manufacturer of orthopedic footwear, designed a new type of shoe for runners. Before long other companies produced their own versions. Reports on testing and rating of shoes appeared as regular features in magazines on running, and shoes became status symbols.

Other sports such as tennis and golf also flourished, as did spectator sports. Major league baseball gained fans in cities through the expansion or relocation of franchises. In the process, other fans were left behind or left out. The process began in 1953 when the Boston Braves moved to Milwaukee; the St. Louis Browns to Baltimore in 1954, becoming the Orioles; and the Philadelphia Athletics to Kansas City in 1955. The bigger news came in 1958 when the Brooklyn Dodgers moved to Los Angeles and the New York Giants to San Francisco, reflecting the westward shift of the population in general. Over the next dozen years, a fan-boggling shuffling of franchises occurred. Three more existing franchises moved: the Kansas City As to Oakland, the Milwaukee Braves to Atlanta, and the Washington Senators to Minneapolis–St. Paul, becoming the Minnesota Twins. Eight new ones were created: the Los Angeles/Anaheim Angels; the Washington Senators, becoming the Rangers when the team moved to Dallas–Fort Worth; the Houston Astros; the New York Mets; the Montreal Expos; the San Diego Padres; the Kansas City Royals; and the Seattle Pilots, which became the Milwaukee Brewers. The expansion prompted the American and National Leagues to form two divisions each in 1969, with league playoffs determining competitors in the World Series.

Baseball fans had new records to talk about during these years: Roger Maris hit 61 home runs in 1961, breaking Babe Ruth's 34-year-old record. The fact that his teammate, Mickey Mantle, was close on his heels made the race for the record all the more exciting. The next year Maury Wills stole 104 bases for the Los Angeles Dodgers, breaking Ty Cobb's previous record of 96. His teammate, Sandy Koufax, struck out 18 batters in a nine-inning game. In 1965 Koufax struck out a record 382 in the season and pitched a perfect game, his third no-hitter. Television's coverage of such feats made them nationally celebrated events.

Developments in football made it possible for that sport to challenge baseball's dominance as the national pastime. The National Football League (NFL) and the American Football League (AFL) merged in 1966 and agreed to a playoff game between the leagues. Thus in 1967 the Super Bowl was born. At first the NFL dominated, with the Green Bay Packers winning the first two Super Bowls, but in 1969 Joe Namath, the charismatic quarterback of the New York Jets, led his AFL team to victory over the Baltimore Colts.

These were interesting years in boxing, too, as much outside the ring as inside it. A young athlete from Louisville gained fame by his actions in the ring and infamy by his words outside of it. Cassius Marcellus Clay, the 1960 light-heavyweight gold medal winner in the Olympics, came into his heavyweight title match with Sonny Liston four years later as an 8 to 1 underdog, but he won. Then he announced that he had joined the Nation of Islam, renounced his "slave name," and, following the lead of another black Muslim, assumed the name of Cassius X. A few weeks later he said that henceforth he would be known as Muhammad Ali, adding another dimension to controversies about him. More than any other heavyweight champion, except possibly Joe Louis in the 1940s, Ali became the subject of conversations across the land, and controversies involving him would become more intense later in the decade.

Despite Kennedy's push for fitness and the importance of professional sporting evenings in the daily lives of many Americans, it is hardly accurate to say the nation was immersed in a fitness craze by the late 1960s. Many Americans continued to lead sedentary lives. Still, running claimed the interest and time of millions of Americans. Many runners became insatiable consumers of running gear, causing rapid growth of new companies. Nike, a company founded in 1972, soon gained a dominant role in many sports.

Bicycling reached new levels of popularity in the early 1970s, when for the first time since 1897 Americans purchased more bicycles annually than automobiles; 60 percent of the bicycles were purchased by adults. Other nonteam sports such as golf and tennis held their appeal, and multitudes were hooked on team sports made for the occasional athlete, such as slow-pitch softball.

Spectator sports, however, particularly as they were carried into homes on television, consumed far more of the ordinary American's time. Regular-season games drew substantial audiences, but playoff games hooked viewers to a much greater extent. The playoffs that gained enormous popularity in the 1960s and 1970s were the NCAA men's basketball tournaments played each March and April. The astonishing success of the UCLA teams, coached by John Wooden, was particularly intriguing. After winning the championships in 1964 and 1965, UCLA missed the next year, but then for seven consecutive years, 1967 to 1974, they were the big winners.

Other records, especially those established over long periods, gripped sports fans—especially if they contained an element of controversy. When Hank Aaron broke Babe Ruth's career home run record by hitting his 715th on April 8, 1974, some wondered if he could have done it if he had not played about 25 additional games as a result of the lengthening of the major league baseball season from 154 games to 162 in 1962. Denny McLain's 31-victory season for the Detroit Tigers in 1968 was made more interesting by McLain's reckless lifestyle, which ultimately cut short his career and landed him in jail. Other events in sports proved controversial, such as the decision of the American League to install a gimmick advocated by the unconventional owner of the Oakland Athletics, Charles Finley: the designated hitter, known as the DH, became the regular pinch hitter for pitchers in 1973. The National League refused to use the DH, creating odd situations when teams from the two leagues met annually in the World Series and All-Star games.

Most controversial among sports fans was heavyweight champion Muhammad Ali, whose request for conscientious objector status on the basis of his adherence to Muslim teachings was denied. For refusing to be inducted into the military, Ali was arrested on April 28, 1967, given a five-year prison sentence, and fined $10,000. Boxing authorities had earlier stripped him of his title. An outrage, said some. Just what he deserved, said others.

For refusing induction into the military, Ali received a five-year prison sentence.

Ali, always a fountain of words on any subject, had his own say: "The power structure seems to want to starve me out. I mean, the punishment, five years in jail, ten-thousand-dollar fine, ain't enough. They want to stop me from working. Not only in this country but out of it. Not even a license to fight for charity. And that's in this twentieth century. You read about these things in dictatorship countries where a man don't go along with this or that and he is completely not allowed to work or to earn a decent living."

By the 1970s and early 1980s, physical fitness had taken a more important place in American lives. In particular, running continued to be a popular activity, so much so that Jim Fixx's *The Complete Book of Running* found 620,000 buyers in 1978. Health clubs, with their elaborate exercise equipment, prospered by attracting men and women who spent their days behind desks. Stock-car racing, widely regarded as a blue-collar sport, attracted many participants and fans, particularly in the South.

Around home, skateboarding gained in popularity, particularly among teenagers. Sometimes skateboards were used for stunts, sometimes simply as a sporting way to get to school. Before long skateboarding became competitive, with cash prizes awarded in regional events. Parents who held their breath or turned away as their offspring performed daring stunts must have been surprised when a study by the Consumer Product Safety Commission in 1975 showed that skateboarding ranked 25th in danger among activities measured, whereas bicycling was rated the most dangerous. An alternative to skateboards made a quiet arrival in 1980 when Rollerblade, Inc., a Minneapolis firm founded by a 20-year-old Canadian hockey player, perfected the design for in-line roller skates with "blades" of polyurethane wheels and molded boots like those worn by skiers.

Sporting events, such as Muhammad Ali's regaining the heavyweight title by beating Joe Frazier in 1975 and losing it to Leon Spinks three years later, gave sports fans something to talk about, even if these matches were carried only on closed-circuit television. Other subjects of conversation were the skyrocketing salaries of athletes made possible when they gained free agency rights. Fans began to get a taste of things to come when O. J. Simpson agreed to a three-year, $2.9 million deal to complete his football career with the Buffalo Bills and when baseball player Jim "Catfish" Hunter left the Oakland As to sign a contract with the New York Yankees in 1975 for $2.85 million. Hunter led the Yankees to championships in 1977 and 1978.

A different kind of conversation began at the 1976 Super Bowl, when television cameras panning the sidelines focused on the Dallas Cowboys cheerleaders. Dressed in tight-fitting, low-cut, skimpy outfits, they drew oohs and ahhs from male television viewers and complaints from those who considered this another instance of sexual exploitation for commercial purposes. But then, everything done in professional sports—and much of what occurred in college sports, too—was designed to have consumer appeal. Highly paid stars in professional sports played the same role as did the stars in the movie industry: their success at the box office mattered more than their success on the field, although the two were usually inseparable.

Major league baseball tested its place in the hearts of many Americans when a seven-week players' strike interrupted the 1981 season. The strike caused the middle third of the schedule to be canceled, resulting in the major leagues' first split season. The origins of the discord between players and management lay in legal actions taken by players in the mid-1970s to gain the right for veteran players to sign with other teams as free agents. When the owners' absolute power over players was broken, they established a system that required the loss of a free agent to be compensated in the form of a player from the team with which the free agent had signed. In the impasse that followed, fans were caught in the middle and left with a gameless midsummer.

In 1982 the National Football League (NFL) faced a similar situation. No games were played during a 57-day strike. In 1987, though, when the season was interrupted by a 24-day strike by players over rules surrounding free agency, management canceled games on the first weekend but then fielded teams made up of replacement players and regulars who drifted back. When the players decided to go back to work, the owners told them they could not play immediately and would not be paid. The National Labor Relations Board ruled in the players' favor and ordered the NFL to pay striking players more than $20 million in lost wages and incentive bonuses for the game they had missed. As with baseball, the fans were on the sidelines—mostly disgusted with both players and management.

The United States hosted the 1984 Summer Olympics in Los Angeles. Broadcast by ABC, the event's 168 hours on the air drew ratings higher than expected, and it produced several heroes: Carl Lewis won gold medals in the 100-meter dash, the 200-meter dash, the 400-meter relay, and the long jump, duplicating what Jesse Owens had done in 1936 in Berlin. In contrast to earlier times, the rules of the Olympics allowed Lewis to earn about $1 million yearly and still compete as an amateur. Another hero was the Olympics' real crowd-pleaser, Mary Lou Retton, a 16-year-old whose five medals included a gold in all-around gymnastics. Her feat gained her many commercial endorsements.

By 1988 the Olympics were greeted as welcome television fare by millions of viewers. To accommodate their interests, the Winter Games, held in Calgary, Canada, were extended to 16 days. But ratings were disappointing, partly because the United States won only 2 of the 46 gold medals, in addition to a silver and three bronzes. The Summer Games, held in Seoul, Korea, also lasted 16 days. Although the competition provided enjoyable viewing, much of the attention went to controversies concerning the use of drugs that had been banned—particularly anabolic steroids. Taking steroids makes athletes stronger and enables them to train harder, putting them at a competitive advantage, but it also has harmful side effects. Altogether, 18 athletes were disqualified before or during the games, including Canada's Ben Johnson, who had defeated Carl Lewis in the 100-meter dash.

The popularity of bicycling increased tremendously during the 20th century. Here bike riders take part in an event in Leicester, Massachusetts. © AP/Wide World Photos.

Physical fitness participants in this decade wanted to look good; feel good; lose weight; have fun; make friends; develop personal discipline; and, above all, stay well. Avid runners claimed that running gave them more daily energy, sharpened their mental edge, kept them in good physical condition, and increased their resistance to illness. Tennis players were just as avid about their sport, although they made fewer claims for its benefits. Bowlers, golfers, skiers, bikers, and participants in other sports were avid, too, but their fitness claims were less audible. Many of them considered their participation as recreational rather than fitness-driven.

Private health clubs eagerly exploited the fitness interests of many Americans. The number of clubs increased from 7,500 in 1980 (not including YMCAs or golf, tennis, and other sport-specific clubs) to more than 20,000 by the end of the decade. Membership in health and fitness clubs reached about 40 million before the end of the decade. The quest for fitness could be satisfied in one's home, too, as the popularity of *Jane Fonda's Workout Book* (1981) bears witness. In addition to providing an exercise regimen, this book by an actress turned political activist and now fitness promoter included dietary advice and musings on ways for women to maintain good health. A best seller, it opened the way for Fonda's further commercial ventures— exercise studios, cassette tapes with music to accompany workouts, and an exercise video. Other exercise promoters, such as Richard Simmons, also produced videos for use at home, and sales of home exercise equipment by Nordic Track, Nautilus, and other companies boomed. So did sales of improved equipment for outdoor sports (Marty, 38–40, 123–25, 213–14, 286–89).

To read about sports in the United States in the 19th century, see the United States entry in the section "Sports" in chapter 7 ("Recreational Life") in volume 5 of this series.

FOR MORE INFORMATION

Deardorff, D. L. *Sports: A Reference Guide and Critical Commentary, 1980–1999.* Westport, Conn.: Greenwood Press, 2000.

Marty, M. A. *Daily Life in the United States, 1960–1990: Decades of Discord*. Westport, Conn.: Greenwood Press, 1997.

Rader, B. C. *American Sports: From the Age of Folk Games to the Age of Spectators*. Englewood Cliff, N.J.: Prentice-Hall, 1983.

JAPAN

As in many other areas of Japanese material culture, sports are a rich eclectic mixture of the native and the imported. Virtually every new sport becomes a temporary mania called *boom* and engenders an instant fan base, yet traditional sports maintain their loyal supporters. High school sport club members earnestly practice to master the intricacies of their chosen sport. Supporters turn out in droves to cheer their heroes on to victory.

Golf is by far the most popular participatory sport. Although it is very expensive by Western standards owing to the high cost of land, more people in Japan shell out huge sums of money for clubs, lessons, equipment, and greens fees than anywhere else in the world.

Membership in prestigious clubs can cost $1 million and have been traded, sold, or split like stock on the common market. In addition to the numerous courses, virtually every medium-sized town has two or three micro driving ranges ensconced on building roofs and tiny corners of land.

Tennis is popular among the young, particularly women who often take to the courts while their husbands prowl the golf links. Skiing is popular among college students who pay enormous sums for equipment, clothing, and travel to mountain slopes.

Baseball is a widely popular spectator sport. Most large cities have a franchise that competes in one of two leagues. Tokyo has several teams. Teams are limited in the number of foreign players who may be employed and several Japanese players, notably Hideo Nomo and Ichiro Suzuki, have gone on to play in the American major leagues. The annual high school championship held in Tokyo draws thousands of spectators and occupies enormous chunks of television time.

Soccer has recently become very popular as a result of the 2002 World Cup, which Japan hosted jointly with South Korea. American football and basketball have also prospered.

The chief native sport is sumo, though some claim that the recent domination of American (Akebono and Mushimaru became *yokozuna* grand champions) and Mongolian (Asashoryu) wrestlers have dulled popularity of the traditional sport. Sumo combines courage, brute strength, complex strategies, and great agility with ancient traditions and rituals to present a colorful grand show in five annual tournaments across the country.

Judo and jujitsu maintain their ancient martial arts traditions, as does karate, kendo, andaikido. There are elements of sports competition in all of them, but they are more properly categorized as hobbies than sport.

Bowling was briefly popular in Japan, especially in the 1950s and 1960s, but the popularity has waned. Kite fighting is still practiced on the club level, as are various forms of archery (including a ritualized mounted form) and swordplay. Badminton and boxing have large followings—the former as participation, and the latter as a spectator sport.

To read about sports and games in early modern Japan, see the Japan entry in the section "Games" in chapter 7 ("Recreational Life") in volume 4 of this series.

~*Louis G. Perez*

FOR MORE INFORMATION

Powers, R. G., and K. Hidetoshi. *Handbook of Japanese Popular Culture.* New York: Greenwood Press, 1989.

Whiting, R. *The Chrysanthemum and the Bat: Baseball Samurai Style.* New York: Dodd, Mead, 1977.

INDIA

Although India achieved political independence during the 20th century, some traditions and pastimes established during the 19th century continued, and popular sports fell into this category. See the India entry in the section "Sports" in chapter 7 ("Recreational Life") in volume 5 of this series for a description of the popular sports that continued into the 20th century.

AFRICA

RECREATIONAL
LIFE
|
SPORTS
|
Europe

United States,
1920–1939

United States,
1960–1990

Japan

Africa

Sport in 20th-century Africa can be seen in terms of the increasing incorporation of the continent into the international sporting community. Because the 20th century represents both the colonial and postcolonial periods in Africa's history, it is not surprising that significant changes in the continent's sporting characteristics have occurred over this time.

As with all institutions, Africa had its own indigenous sports before the institution of colonial rule. Wrestling, for instance, was an important activity in many African societies. Wrestling in most communities, however, represented more than good exercise. Wrestling matches were a necessary ritual that tested the physical prowess of the community's males and provided one way to help determine the political hierarchy of the community. The strongest males would be the best at both arduous agricultural labor and community defense, and so were best equipped to support the society. Youngsters in many African societies also engaged in similar sorts of hand-to-hand combat; stick fighting; archery; and, perhaps most importantly, dance.

These precolonial forms of sport persisted throughout the 20th century, but after the inception of colonial rule, their social significance eroded. Colonial administrators believed that most forms of indigenous African sport were puerile and violent and did not contribute to the proper socialization of Africans into the colonial system. Obviously, European colonizers felt that European sports were more appropriate, and over the first half of the 20th century, they introduced and popularized team sports such as hockey, cricket, and football (soccer). The idea behind the introduction of team sports was to instill the concepts of teamwork, fair play, and obedience to rules into African populations that colonial officials considered uncivilized. Despite that all of these socializing aspects of sport were present in precolonial sports such as wrestling and stick fighting, colonial policies rapidly and oppressively undermined traditional sporting activities in favor of European ones.

European sports became quite popular in Africa during the colonial era. Football quickly became the most popular sporting activity for young African men. Local teams and leagues of African players popped up all over the continent; it was not uncommon for teams to travel considerable distances to play a match in neighboring towns, or even neighboring colonies. Furthermore, in the colonial era it was not necessarily uncommon to find teams of African players matching up against teams of colonial Europeans. Frustrations against the colonial system could be played out on the football field and served to prove that Africans could compete with and sometimes defeat their European rulers in sport. The combination of confidence and communal solidarity that football provided often spilled over into the political arena as Africans, united by means of a particular football club, began to develop strong nationalist sentiments. Indeed, it has been written that in colonial Zanzibar the local football clubs were the direct predecessors of the nationalist organizations that eventually took power from the British.

The national pride generated by sports teams has certainly continued throughout the postcolonial era. As African countries gained their political independence, mostly in the 1950s and 1960s, they also became eligible to compete in international sporting competitions such as the football World Cup and the Olympic Games. Most African countries have had difficulty achieving the distinction they deserve in the international sporting arena over the last 40 years, due partly to Eurocentric attitudes held by the decision-making bodies of the various international sporting organizations and partly to a lack of sports funding in African countries. Most African countries are extremely underdeveloped, and so most national funds are allocated to projects that either meet the current survival needs of the population or will help to make the country more self-sufficient and prosperous in the future. Sports are usually not considered in either of these categories and, as such, remain underfunded by national governments.

Nonetheless, Africa has made great strides in the international sporting community. Though Africa was able to qualify for only one bid to the final round of the 1970 World Cup, through decades of political maneuvering and apt performance on the field, in 1998 five African teams qualified for the final round of the World Cup, held in France. East Africans, especially Kenyans, have gained a reputation as the world's finest long-distance runners. Likewise, some of the most successful professional basketball players in the United States since the early 1980s have been Africans, including Manute Bol, Dikembe Mutombo, and Hakeem Olajuwon. The African presence in international sports is certainly on the rise.

Indeed, the political power of Africa in the international sporting scene has had significant impact on one African country in particular. While black South Africans were suffering under the egregious injustices of the apartheid system of racial segregation in that country, other African countries were forging political alliances with countries worldwide to isolate the South African government politically, economically, and socially. Through various sanctions designed to cripple the South African economy, the international community hoped to force South Africa to end its apartheid policies. International sports became a high-profile media through which to isolate South Africa. By the 1970s, through the efforts of African nations working together with European, Asian, North American, and South American countries, South Africa had been banned from competing in the World Cup, international cricket, and the Olympics. In 1977, the United Nations adopted a resolution disallowing any member nation from engaging in international sport with South Africa.

The apartheid regime in South Africa fell in the early 1990s, and South Africa was reinstated to the international sporting family. Because Africa had never hosted a World Cup, many, including the president of the Fédération Internationale de Football Association (FIFA), felt that South Africa would be the perfect place to host the tournament in 2006. In 2000, South Africa lost its bid to Germany in the final vote due to the abstention of one voter, illustrating the Eurocentric power balance still extant in international sports. Thus, for all the progress that Africa has made in the 20th century, there is still much to be accomplished in the 21st.

~Matthew Heaton

FOR MORE INFORMATION

Baker, W. J., and J. A. Mangan, eds. *Sport in Africa: Essays in Social History.* New York: Africana, 1987.

Darby, P. *Africa, Football and FIFA.* London: Frank Cass, 2002.

Film

Though Thomas Edison and his team invented the necessary technology in the 19th century, it was not until the 20th century that the motion picture industry was created. Movies reshaped daily life in a profound and fundamental way. Virtually overnight, this new cultural medium brought vivid new experiences to average people. By far it made more of an impact than the introduction of radio. In 1923, the United States had 15,000 movie theaters with an average seating capacity of 500 and a weekly attendance of 50 million people. The small town of Muncie, Indiana, alone had nine movie theaters and sold 31,000 tickets each week. The town's weekly church attendance was only 20,600.

Regardless of the decade, in the 20th century there were several consistent themes in films. One was the relationship between men and women. The portrayal of women reflected conflict over gender roles. Many films sought to hem in women's social,

RECREATIONAL
LIFE

FILM

Europe

United States,
1920–1939

United States,
1940–1959

United States,
1960–1990

India

Soviet Union

Japan

economic, and political positions. Take, for example, Clara Bow's *It* (1927) or Sharon Stone's *Basic Instinct* (1992), both of which had female characters who went beyond the bounds of appropriate behavior only to be brought back to society's norms by men. Another major theme was sex. Today's moviegoers might be surprised at how sexually explicit early movies were. Rudolph Valentino's *The Sheik* (1926) created quite a stir. Film comedies were also popular at the beginning and at the end of the century. The comedians of the early 1920s such as Charlie Chaplin, Buster Keaton, and Harold Lloyd remain household names. In 2000, the major comedians had not achieved the same stature or notoriety, yet they earned millions of dollars for the movie companies. Violent films were as popular in the 1920s as they were in the 1990s. In fact, by the end of the century, many of the great action films, such as *King Kong* (1933 and 1977), were remade. Romances, too, sold lots of tickets. One of the most successful was *Why Change Your Wife?* (1920), directed by Cecil B. DeMille. DeMille also pioneered the last category, political films. DeMille's tour de force was *Birth of a Nation* (1915), a racist, pro-Klan portrayal of the Reconstruction period of American history.

The movie industry had enormous cultural influence in America and elsewhere during the 20th century. Film itself became an international medium. Some of the greatest filmmakers, such as Grigory Chukhrai and Andrey Tarkovsky, came from Russia, and filmmaking continued to thrive in the Soviet Union despite decades of repression and censorship. Japan and India both developed internationally recognized film industries in the late 20th century with Japanese films becoming the basis for later American pictures and the vibrant film community in Bombay becoming known as "Bollywood." Throughout the world, film stars were viewed as major celebrities, and their lives were followed passionately by adoring fans. Moreover, actors used their fame to influence politics, especially from the 1930s through the 1990s. In the 1950s, many actors were accused of being Communist and lost their jobs in the political climate of McCarthyism. Perhaps no other artists were as powerful as those in the movie industry. Take note of the actors discussed in these sections and investigate their political lives (Helen Gahagan Douglas and Alec Baldwin are of particular interest).

RECREATIONAL
LIFE
|
FILM
|
Europe

United States,
1920-1939

United States,
1940-1959

United States,
1960-1990

India

Soviet Union

Japan

EUROPE

The origins of both the art and technology of film are to be found not primarily in North America but rather with painters, photographers, and animal physiologists in Europe. The French painter Louis-Jacques-Mandé Daguerre patented a photographic process, daguerreotype, that, in combination with the twirling images on the drums and disks of parlor toys of the early 1800s, began paving the way for the invention of live-action pictures. The British photographer Eadweard Muybridge, who was challenged by a California racehorse breeder to prove that galloping horses intermittently have all four hooves off the ground at the same time, was the first to capture this otherwise imperceptible movement on film, an accomplishment the French physiologist Etienne-Jules Marey replicated in 1882 with his chronophotographic gun designed to film birds in flight. The unwieldy first motion-picture machines, developed in France and Britain by Louis Le Prince and William Friese-Greene, were followed by Thomas Alva Edison's incandescent kinetoscope projector (1894), popular in Europe. After seeing one at the famous world exhibition in Paris, the French Lumière Brothers developed a lighter-weight hand-cranked model, the cinematograph (1895), which freed European filmmakers to film outdoors and made Europe the heart of the film industry in the early decades of the 1900s.

Most early European films were not longer than a few minutes. Typically within a lineup of vaudeville attractions, along with circus and animal acts, shadow shows, comedy routines, and cabaret sketches, screenings originally took place at fairgrounds, in storefronts, or at variety theaters and were typically advertised not by title, but by the type of projection machine. Essentially documentary shorts, these films portrayed moving subjects with little narrative content—workers leaving a factory, a child being fed, a picnic alongside a river, or the arrival of a train in a station. It was not until Georges Méliès, a popular French magician and illusionist, incorporated literary narratives into longer "trick" films that "living photographs" actually became visual stories. Méliès's amazing *Le Voyage dans la lune* (A Trip to the Moon) (1902), adapted from a futuristic tale by Jules Verne, brought the magic of special effects to nickelodeon audiences. Permanent movie houses, which existed in Europe 10 years before their American counterparts, were eventually superseded by elaborate "dream palaces" with luxurious interiors, a style adopted later by the lavish studio and star systems of Hollywood.

World War I, however, brought European cinema to a near standstill, in part because the chemicals used for developing celluloid were needed for gunpowder. And by the end of the war, almost all films shown in Africa, North and South America, Asia, and Europe were American productions. Germany, which prohibited American imports in order to curb anti-German propaganda, was for a time the only exception. The state-subsidized film company, UFA, which quickly became the largest studio in Europe, ushered in Germany's golden age of cinema with world-famous Expressionist directors, such as Ernst Lubitsch, F. W. Murnau (*Nosferatu*), Fritz Lang, and Robert Wiene (*Das Kabinett des Dr. Caligari*). However, the Dawes Plan, while providing reparations, also completely devastated German film production by flooding the country, Hollywood's only rival, with American films, buying up UFA, and putting virtually all of Germany's filmmakers on American payrolls. Though many directors eventually returned to Germany, they left an indelible imprint of their considerable artistic talents and chiaroscuro style on Hollywood.

Sound technology in the late 1920s and early 1930s further curtailed the European film industry's reach. Suddenly, voice quality and foreign accents were a potential liability for European actors, such as Emil Jannings, Lya de Putti, and Pola Negri, and many silent stars were replaced by stage actors. The language issue also delayed the conversion to sound film in Europe, although dubbing technology and new multilingual studios, such as Paramount's in the Parisian suburb of Joinville, eventually overcame this obstacle and facilitated Hollywood's domination of European markets, despite local quota laws. France was particularly vulnerable to the popularity of sound and the influx of American and German film companies. Nevertheless, because of its investment in independent studios and the success of the French avant-garde movement led by Germaine Dulac and Fernand Léger, French directors, such as the famous Jean Renoir (*La Grande Illusion*, 1937), gained international recognition and won France the second largest film audience in the world by 1940.

Still reeling from crippling inflation, German cinema in the early 1930s explored questions of poverty and social morality in such films as Pabst's adaptation of Bertolt Brecht's *Die Dreigroschenoper*; *Der blaue Engel* (1930); and Fritz Lang's *M* (1931), starring Peter Lorre as a child murderer. The social themes of the early 1930s in Germany, influenced to some extent by Sergei Eisenstein's dialectical montage and socialist revolutionary cinema, yielded abruptly to the rise of National Socialism when Germany's entire film industry fell under the control of Goebbel's Propaganda Ministry. During Hitler's reign, filmmakers were obliged to create either propaganda films supporting the Third Reich, such as Leni Riefenstahl's *Triumph des Willens* (1935) and *Olympische Spiele 1936* (1938), or nonpolitical escapist entertainment films. Germany's Jewish directors and producers were banned from the industry and emigrated to Hollywood, the "New Weimar," to escape deportation. Other fascist regimes, particularly Mussolini's Italy and Franco's Spain, created similar intolerable environments of artistic repression and persecution for filmmakers such as Spain's Luis Buñel (*Un Chien Andalou*), who was forced out of his homeland by the Spanish fascists.

European cinema was all but decimated during World War II, and only Italy, because of its early surrender, retained many of its studios intact. Not surprisingly, the Italian Neorealists, such as Roberto Rossellini (*Germania, anno zero*, 1947), Luchino Visconti (*Ossessione*, 1942), and Vittorio De Sica (*Ladri di biciclette*, 1948), embraced a Socialist aesthetic and provided alternatives to Hollywood's narrative genres. French film of the Occupation and postwar era is dominated by literary adaptations by such well-known directors as Jean Cocteau (*La Belle et la bête*) and a number of new documentary directors, such as Alain Resnais (*Nuit et brouillard*, 1956), who, along with the theorist and founder of the influential journal *Cahier du Cinéma*, André Bazin, prefigured the evolution of the *nouvelle vague*—the French New Wave movement in 1959. François Truffaut (*Quatre cents coups*); the radical Jean-Luc Goddard (*A bout de souffle*); Claude Chabrol, whose work is a tribute to Hitchcock; and Eric Rohmer's ironic ethical conundrums (*Pauline à la plage*), rejected Eisenstein's montage in favor of mise-en-scène, a technique that used camera placement and long takes, as in Ingmar Bergman's *Persona* (1966), to work against conventional continuity. Films such as Alain Resnais's *Hiroshima Mon Amour* and the postmodern film *L'Année dernière à Marienbad* were emblematic of the movement's success, which would add such impressive new directors as Agnes Varda, Jacques Demy, and Louis Malle to the list of directors bringing European cinema into the 1970s and even into the 1990s.

After years of repression, postwar filmmakers were further set back by Europe's radical physical and political partitioning at the outset of the cold war. For much of the 1950s West Germany produced popular yet innocuous and politically conservative *Heimatfilme*, depicting sunny images of healthy Germans in alpine landscapes in stark contrast to the Socialist images in the East. In 1962 a group of young German filmmakers, among them Alexander Kluge, Rainer Werner Fassbinder, Völker Schlöndorff, Werner Herzog, and Wim Wenders, signed a manifesto in Oberhausen to replace the lack of artistic innovation in German filmmaking with *das neue deutsche Kino*, a New German cinema. Fassbinder's dark social consciousness films explored characters' troubled interiors (*Die Ehe der Maria Braun*, 1979), Herzog's films such as *Aguirre, der Zorn Gottes* (1972) and *Jeder für sich Gott gegen Alle* (1974) confronted audiences' idealism with society's barbarism, and Wim Wender displayed truly postmodern expressions of alienation and existential dislocation (*Die Angst des Tormanns beim Elfmeter*, 1971). Although many of these directors, including Margarethe von Trotta, continued working into the 1980s and 1990s, another new cadre of filmmakers emerged after unification, calling for a new New German cinema— films that combine the intellectual appeal of European cinema with the positive emotional appeal of Hollywood features. This group, led by contemporary directors such as Tom Tykwer (*Lola rennt*), produced upbeat, more commercially viable films, even "New German comedies" such as Dorris Dörrie's *Männer* and her more recent *Erleuchtung garantiert*, filmed in video verité style. Spain's Pedro Almodovar enjoyed similar international success with such well-known postmodern films as *Mujeres al borde de un ataque de nervios* (1988) and *Todo sobre mi madre* (1999).

Eastern European cinema remained decidedly political and nationalized until 1989, having rather quickly established state film schools that remained under restrictive Socialist measures enforced by the Soviet Union. Occasionally political intolerance allowed for experimentation, as with the Czech New Wave in the 1960s that was only to be banned later after the Soviet invasion in 1968. The courage of the Polish directors Jerzy Kawalerowicz, Andrzej Wajda, and Roman Polanski (*Knife in the Water*, 1962) in the 1960s and 1970s and Solidarity filmmakers in the 1980s, including the well-known Agnieszka Holland, should not be overlooked. Romania, Bulgaria, and Yugoslavia, which eventually became well known for animation films, were similarly restricted to Socialist content until the collapse of the Soviet Union in 1992, when funding became an urgent obstacle. Despite economic challenges and political transitions, European cinema has played a pivotal role in the development of filmmaking worldwide and continues in our increasingly global economy to gain in notoriety.

~*Jennifer Ham*

FOR MORE INFORMATION

Cook, D. *A History of Narrative Film.* New York: W. W. Norton, 1996.
Gianetti, L. *A Brief History of Film.* Englewood Cliffs, N.J.: Prentice Hall, 2001.
Vincendeau, G., ed. *The Encyclopedia of European Cinema.* New York: Facts on File, 1995.

UNITED STATES, 1920–39

Unlike radio broadcasting, another important means of communication was not altogether new in the 1920s. Motion pictures did change fundamentally during the decade, however. The addition of sound to on-screen images transformed the movie-going experience. With 95 million movie tickets being sold each week by the end of the decade and movie attendance remaining very popular during the depression years that followed, cinema, like radio, had an enormous impact on American daily life. The combination of visual and aural images provided vivid multidimensional experiences that could be shared by a scattered mass audience. Movies, as much as or more than radio, served to break down provincialism, increase awareness of the unfamiliar, and create a national community with a specific set of shared experiences.

Picture palaces appealed to a middle-class audience willing to pay 30 cents to see a movie.

By the early 1920s, feature-length as well as shorter silent films, often accompanied by live vaudeville acts, had become a popular form of cheap entertainment in large and medium-sized cities. In January 1923, the United States had 15,000 silent movie theaters, with an average capacity of 507 and a weekly attendance of 50 million, leading one historian to conclude that going to the movies had developed into a normal feature of life for every segment of society. One region represented a clear exception to this generalization: the South. The highly conservative, mostly rural, and deeply impoverished region had few theaters outside of its larger towns and cities. As late as 1930, for instance, Georgia had only one-third as many movie theater seats per thousand population as any state outside the region. Rural southerners with little cash as well as few automobiles to get to a theater in town were, whether black or white, for the most part left out of the growing national film audience until after World War II. Racial segregation further inhibited African Americans from going to the movies, except in cities (northern as well as southern) large enough to support theaters catering particularly to them; in those circumstances movies became highly popular among African Americans as the least oppressive white-dominated form of entertainment. Because only a relatively few "race movies" reflected their own culture, African Americans, as well as Hispanics and Asians in the Far West, saw mainly mainstream American films if they saw anything at all.

Approximately 1,000 American theaters were "picture palaces"—large, elegantly decorated, air-conditioned auditoriums located in urban centers. Picture palaces generally seated 1,500 or more and appealed to a middle-class audience willing to pay 30 cents or more to see a movie and, usually, live vaudeville acts—singers, dancers, comedians, acrobats, jugglers, or magicians—in extraordinary surroundings. Many came equipped with a "mighty Wurlitzer" organ to accompany the motion picture as well as provide independent entertainment. Even grander picture palaces termed "atmospherics" were built later in the decade, with expansive lobbies; thick carpeting; statuary and paintings; exotic Spanish, Moroccan, or Byzantine styling; and ceilings that seemed to resemble open skies with moving clouds or twinkling stars. Smaller, less elaborate versions of picture palaces in smaller cities likewise sought to make the experience of going to the movies a departure from ordinary life, yet the motion picture itself accomplished this feat even in the plainest theaters that were the norm in urban neighborhoods and small towns.

Movie audiences continued to grow. Muncie, Indiana's, nine movie theaters sold 31,000 tickets each week in 1924, while church attendance averaged 20,600, helping to explain religious hostility to motion pictures already seen as frequently immoral and decadent. Sunday, in fact, was the biggest day of the week for Muncie's theaters. By 1928, 65 million tickets were being sold nationally each week to a population slightly less than twice that number. With many theaters changing their presentation two or more times a week and urban areas having many theaters, some people were buying tickets more often than once a week. Other people seldom if ever went to the movies during the 1920s or afterward, but moviegoing was becoming very much a commonplace aspect of American life.

Wherever there was a significant minority population, either African American or Hispanic, theaters generally segregated the seats. Minority patrons were required to sit in a separate area, usually a balcony. In some cases, minorities were simply excluded. No wonder that separate theaters catering exclusively to minority audiences, offering opportunities to go to the movies without discomfort, cropped up in places with sizable African American or Hispanic populations. The Asian population was too small to sustain much of a movie culture of its own, although a few Japanese theaters, importing films from Japan and employing *bench* (film explainers who performed beside the screen), struggled along in southern California.

By the early 1920s, the vast majority of silent films had settled into a few subject categories: the crime story, the Western, the historical costume drama, the contemporary domestic melodrama, the romance. As the audience shifted from nearly all working class to increasingly middle and upper class, so too did the settings of the stories. Increasingly, films pictured a society where, in the words of cinema historian Robert Sklar, "nearly everyone (who was not a cowboy or a cross-eyed comedian) dressed in evening clothes, lived in an elegant home, and passed the time in cabarets." Films of this sort encouraged audiences to think of material opulence as widespread. This ideal of consumption was reinforced by the increasingly popular movie magazines. Fan magazines called attention to the extravagant homes and lifestyles of the Hollywood community as well as to the biographies of movie stars who had risen from modest circumstances to achieve positions that, the implication was clear, were to be envied.

The portrayal of women in 1920s films reflected what moviemakers thought audiences would find acceptable in the years immediately following the adoption of woman suffrage. Films with contemporary urban settings were especially likely to feature restless young women, single or married, eager to escape the home and obtain a status equal with men. Positions of superiority over men were shown as a waste of women's true talents. At the same time women should not be *Manhandled* (the title of a 1922 film) and lose their virtue; maintaining virtue was vital to a successful marriage. Even a free-spirited and apparently sexually liberated female such as Clara Bow in *The Plastic Age* (1925) or *It* (1927) must demonstrate chaste goodness underneath her naughty behavior to win her man. The triumph of conventional virtue, often after some audience-attracting misconduct, proved to be a constant theme.

Many of the most popular and memorable silent films of the early 1920s did have strong sexual themes. Between 1921 when he appeared in *The Sheik* and 1926 when he died suddenly at age 31, Rudolph Valentino was the most popular screen actor, playing role after role in which his character's aggressive sexuality was explained by his Latin or Arab or European background. Swedish-born Greta Garbo became the silent screen's female equivalent of Valentino in films such as *The Temptress* (1926) and *Flesh and the Devil* (1927). The films of Garbo, Valentino, and others conveyed to the large audience eager to watch them that non-Americans were more free and open in their sexual behavior. Even the hugely popular silent film comedians of the early 1920s, Charlie Chaplin, Buster Keaton, and Harold Lloyd, earned many of their laughs through inept and ludicrous efforts at courtship. Yet at the same time, a couple of sex scandals within the California film community caused a nervous industry to start a program of self-censorship that sharply curtailed the sexual content of most films and inaugurated a 40-year period in which most sexual messages were subtle, indirect, and modest.

Still, in the 1920s a growing national audience received a great deal of information about sexual matters through film, information not previously available. For a pioneering study of the influence of movies, young people testified over and over that they learned a great deal about how to act from what they saw on the screen. One young woman reported that she imitated movie actresses who closed their eyes while kissing. A young man reported, "It was directly through the movies that I learned to kiss a girl on her ears, neck, and cheeks, as well as on the mouth." And the rapid pace of silent movie romances convinced other young people that romance occurred quickly; they reported that kissing and necking were happening earlier than before in their relationship. "I know love pictures have made me more receptive to lovemaking," said one 16-year-old high school sophomore; "I always thought it rather silly until these pictures, where there is always so much love and everything turns out all right in the end, and I kiss and pet much more than I would otherwise."

Not all films offered uncomplicated endorsements of romance between attractive males and compliant females. In the ambiguously titled 1920 silent film *Why Change Your Wife?* director Cecil B. DeMille presented the beautiful Gloria Swanson as a frumpy housewife who is losing her husband to a glamorous, well-made-up, and well-dressed interloper. The wife responds by acquiring a wardrobe of sexy, sleeveless, backless dresses of gold lamé and feathers, and, of course, she wins back her husband. On one level the film conveyed the message that married as well as single women needed to pay attention to their appearance. At the same time, viewers were at least as likely to carry away Swanson's memorable observation, "The more I see of men, the better I like dogs."

Another theme in 1920s films helped shape perceptions as to how people beyond the audience's personal experience were dealing with national prohibition. Although few films in the early 1920s depicted drinking or bootlegging, by middecade a wave of films about contemporary urban jazz-age "flapper" society did so. "No such picture would be considered properly finished," observed one New York film reviewer, "without a number of scenes depicting the shaking up and drinking down of cocktails and their resulting effect on those who partake of them." In a representative sample of 115 films from 1930, liquor was referred to in 78 percent and drinking depicted in 66 percent. Further analysis of 40 of those films reveals that whereas only 13 percent of male villains and 8 percent of female villains could be seen consuming alcohol, no less than 43 percent of heroes and 23 percent of heroines were shown doing so.

Moviegoers could hardly avoid the impression that drinking was widespread and that prohibition violation was socially respectable.

Attending a movie seldom involved sitting in complete silence, in part because most theaters presented silent pictures accompanied by a piano player, an organist, or even an orchestra. Shortly after middecade, however, thanks in part to the technological advances made with radio, films with their own synchronized sound accompaniment began to appear. In 1926, Warner Brothers premiered its Vitaphone sound system in short, predominantly musical films. In October 1927, they brought out the first feature-length "talking picture," *The Jazz Singer*, starring vaudeville performer Al Jolson in a story, appropriately enough, about a young man caught in a cultural conflict between his traditionalist family and his own modern tastes and opportunities. An immediate sensation, *The Jazz Singer* drew audiences as fast as movie theaters could be equipped to show it.

With the instant popularity of talking pictures, most theaters found they could drop the practice of interspersing vaudeville acts and live music with silent motion pictures. The grand picture palace, which had the upper hand as long as theaters presented a combination of film and live entertainment, lost its economic advantage as full programs of sound motion pictures became available. A few vaudeville troupes, such as the Three Stooges and the Marx Brothers, were able to transfer their style of entertainment to film, but for the most part vaudeville faded. Warner Brothers and other studios (e.g., Fox, Metro-Goldwyn-Mayer, and Paramount), quick to seize the opportunity to make "talkies," soon gained dominance in a movie industry transformed during the late 1920s. These studios profited spectacularly as well as gained control over much of what the millions of moviegoers throughout the country would thereafter be able to see.

It was considered acceptable for silent movie audiences to react out loud to the film.

The rapid switch from silent to sound motion pictures altered the behavior of moviegoers, historian Robert Sklar points out. It was considered quite acceptable for silent movie audiences to react out loud to what they saw on the screen. An ongoing series of comments could create a bond among members of an audience sitting in the dark, furthering a sense of community among those in a neighborhood or small-town theater or even creating one temporarily in an urban picture palace. Talking by viewers made going to silent movies a shared experience and rendered each screening a unique and personal event. With talking pictures, however, audience conversation served to distract from the film dialogue, and audience members who spoke aloud were promptly hushed by ushers or fellow patrons. As Sklar observed, "The talking audience for silent pictures became a silent audience for talking pictures." As a result, moviegoing soon became a much more private and passive experience even in a crowded theater.

The addition of sound offered filmmakers new ways to attract and excite audiences. The very fact that films could make their points with sound as well as visual messages allowed them to become much more fast paced and complex, and thus inherently more compelling. By 1930, the year the Census Bureau counted 123 million Americans, the weekly sale of movie tickets, stimulated by the popularity of talkies, reached three-fourths that number. Despite the severe economic problems of the 1930s, movie attendance, while slipping somewhat, remained strong throughout the decade.

The sounds of shooting and screams as well as the noise of galloping horses, creaking doors, and thunderous explosions seemed guaranteed to generate thrills and sell tickets. Stories set in wartime became far more popular than they had been in the silent era, especially after a film set in World War I became the biggest hit of 1930. Ironically, *All Quiet on the Western Front* was based on a German novel stressing the universal destruction and tragedy of war. Horror films, such as *Dracula, Frankenstein,* and *King Kong,* likewise attracted crowds. *King Kong* proved particularly popular. The story revolved around a clash between modern science and a powerful force of primitive nature. The filmmakers shrewdly kept the contest even until the last scene, when warplanes finally destroy the giant ape as he climbs to the top of New York's newest and tallest skyscraper, the Empire State Building. The sounds of shooting and pounding horses' hooves helped Westerns, which had been slipping in popularity but were relatively inexpensive to produce, regain an important position in Hollywood's output.

Contemporary crime dramas offered other opportunities to exploit sound using gunfire, breaking glass, squealing tires, and wailing sirens. Although crime stories had long been a staple of motion pictures, the films of the silent era tended to focus on solitary murders. At the outset of the sound era, gangster movies took over. Fables of big-city bootlegging, films such as *Little Caesar, The Public Enemy,* and *Scarface,* offered more opportunity for violence—and noise. These films tended to present gang leaders as principled, even noble characters, ambitious young men striving to succeed in a chaotic and violent social environment. The motion picture industry's self-imposed morality, reinforced after 1934 by the Roman Catholic Church's firm insistence that Hollywood measure up to its standards or face a ban on its worshippers' attendance, required that wrongdoing be punished in the end. Nevertheless, gangster films often left audiences with the impression that prohibition laws, not the bootleggers themselves, were ultimately at fault.

Sound made possible films with subtle sexual double meanings that could escape censorship.

Sound also made possible films that depended on shocking or clever fast-paced dialogue, often with subtle sexual double meanings that could titillate audiences but escape censorship. The comedies of the Marx Brothers and Mae West in the early 1930s first exploited the humorous possibilities of sound. Increasingly as the decade wore on and as the industry put in effect a 1934 self-censorship production code, filmmakers turned away from overt sexuality and toward much more subtle, so-called "screwball" comedies. Films such as *It Happened One Night, My Man Godfrey,* and *His Girl Friday* combined wacky situations, witty talk, and romance.

Films that featured singing and dancing offered additional opportunities to exploit sound. Some of the most popular films of the decade, from *Gold Diggers of 1933* to *The Wizard of Oz* in 1939, involved song and dance. Even gangster movies often took the opportunity to show a nightclub chorus line, although they were not just intending to provide musical entertainment as cameras lingered leeringly over long-legged, scantily clad female dancers.

The Great Depression and the public's perceived attitude about it shaped 1930s films a great deal. In the early 1930s, films tended to portray contemporary societies thrown into chaos, whether because of the emergence of gangsters, the presence of zany figures such as Groucho Marx, or the arrival in New York of King Kong. As the political and economic situation appeared to improve after Franklin Roosevelt's election as president, films began to take on a more optimistic tone. A large number of historically or literary-based films, from *David Copperfield* in 1935 to *Gone with the Wind* in 1939, offered images of people coping successfully with other and even worse circumstances. Screwball comedies always concluded happily in marriage. Even Frank Capra's popular political melodramas such as *Mr. Deeds Goes to Town* (1936) and *Mr. Smith Goes to Washington* (1939) ended with the triumph of traditional morality. A new form of film, the animated cartoon pioneered by Walt Disney, offered perhaps the most resolutely optimistic storylines of all. The triumph of the most industrious of the *Three Little Pigs* conveyed this confident message in a short 1933 film whose theme song, "Who's Afraid of the Big Bad Wolf?" became an early New Deal anthem. In 1937, Disney offered essentially the same message, though this time using human outcasts living in a forest rather than barnyard animals, in the hugely popular first feature-length animated film, *Snow White and the Seven Dwarfs*.

Escape from the reality outside the theater became another commonplace in 1930s movies. Many films portrayed contemporary drama or romance that could easily have been played out against any background. Significantly, they were most often set in upper-class environments with glamorous women in evening gowns, relaxed and confident men in tuxedos, expensive automobiles, and even more luxurious homes. Whether this was done to cheer up audiences, inspire consumption, or simply reflect the Hollywood lifestyle remains unclear.

Other forms of cinematic escapism were likewise popular. Busby Berkeley produced a series of elaborately choreographed and imaginatively photographed musicals that also involved upper-class lifestyles but achieved their effect as much from their dancers' complete departure from the conventions of real life. Meanwhile, child actress Shirley Temple starred in a series of films that showed her singing, dancing, and cheerfully triumphing over adversity, often in exotic settings and usually assisted only by some elderly male companion. The plump preteen-age girl with curly hair, deep dimples, and an ever-present sunny smile became so popular that mothers all over the country rushed to dress their daughters in Shirley Temple outfits and give them Shirley Temple hairdos.

Perhaps the most escapist film of the decade was the 1939 hit *The Wizard of Oz*, which transported a young girl from depressed black-and-white Kansas to the vivid color (new to film) of Oz, a land populated by talking scarecrows, lions, tin men, wicked witches, and other fantastic creatures. The film contained the populist message of L. Frank Baum's novel on which it was based that simple human virtues of honesty, courage, sensible thought, mutual support, and affection were more to be relied on in times of difficulty than hocus-pocus in the capital city. Most audiences, however, no doubt left the theater caught up more in the dazzling color, music, and fantasy than in the subtle political message.

Gone with the Wind, another huge 1939 hit, also provided an escape from reality, particularly for Southerners still mired in the worst poverty in the nation, a condition that could be traced back to the outcome of the Civil War. *Gone with the Wind*, based on an immensely popular 1937 novel by Margaret Mitchell of Atlanta, was a timeless story of fickle romance. Set in Georgia, the story portrayed an antebellum South that never was, a gracious society of considerate masters and happy, loyal slaves. In the film's reconstruction of the past, the Civil War destroyed property and lives but not the Southern spirit. Fantasy it was, especially in its positive treatment of race relations and opportunities for strong, independent women in Southern society, but far less inflammatory than the previous Civil War epic, *Birth of a Nation*, with its myth of a heroic Ku Klux Klan. In part because of the reputations of its stars, Clark Gable and Vivien Leigh, and in part because it was among the first all-color feature films, *Gone with the Wind* became an enormous success.

Not only did the economic depression affect what was on the screen, it also influenced what went on in the theater. Ticket sales fell 25 percent between 1930 and 1933, and though they began to recover the following year, all of the industry's ingenuity was required to avoid economic disaster. The silent-era practice returned of showing serials—short, intensely thrilling films that invariably left Flash Gordon or another central character suspended in a perilous situation until the next episode a week later would produce an escape followed by entrapment in yet another predicament. Bank nights, which involved the drawing of lucky ticket stubs for cash prizes, became similarly popular, as did giveaways of cheap glassware and china, one piece a week so that only regular customers could build a set.

Theater operators struggling to hold onto their audiences not only continued the practice of changing what they were showing one, two, or more times a week, but they also began offering double features—two full-length films for the price of one. Producers and distributors disliked this latter practice but were powerless to stop it. By the mid-1930s half the theaters in the United States were showing double features. Also, theaters that once disdained selling popcorn and candy because it seemed cheap and undignified now discovered that candy returned a 45 percent profit and popcorn three or four times its cost. In many theaters the sale of food and drink represented the difference between profit and loss, and snacking while watching a movie became commonplace.

Another innovation was the drive-in movie theater, which made its first appearance in New Jersey in 1933. Intended to take advantage of the American enthusiasm for automobiles, drive-ins allowed customers to park on a carefully designed incline and watch a movie without ever getting out of their cars. Providing sound in sizable, open-air theaters was a problem (and a nuisance to those nearby but not in the drive-in) until the development of the individual car speaker in 1941. Nevertheless, many large urban areas had at least one drive-in movie by the end of the 1930s, though the brief boom time for such theaters would not occur until the 1950s.

Going to the movies, despite a small decline caused by the economic hard times, remained the most widespread form of commercial entertainment during the 1930s.

Along with listening to the radio, watching movies became a routine way of learning about the world beyond one's own immediate view. The image of life beyond the neighborhood, small town, or farm might not be accurate, but it was far more vivid and detailed than any earlier available impression. Thus film, together with radio, had a profound influence in connecting people's daily lives to a larger national culture.

The end of the 1930s brought color films and FM radio broadcasting. At the 1939 New York World's Fair, RCA engineers unveiled their new technology of television, although they would not be able to make it commercially viable until after World War II. Thus, important technological improvements were occurring that would soon have consequences for mass communication of sight and sound. However, the fundamental shift in the daily lives of ordinary people from a relatively isolated existence to easy participation in a centrally defined mass culture had already taken place. Information about appropriate behavior; taste; fashion; and, above all, what was going on in the world beyond one's immediate experience was available as never before (Kyvig, 77–89).

FOR MORE INFORMATION

Fleming, V., dir. *The Wizard of Oz*. 1939.

Jowett, G., and J. M. Linton. *Movies as Mass Communications*. Beverly Hills, Calif.: Sage, 1980.

Kyvig, D. E. *Daily Life in the United States, 1920–1939: Decades of Promise and Pain*. Westport, Conn.: Greenwood Press, 2002.

Sklar, R. *Movie-Made America*. Rev. ed. New York: Vintage, 1994.

UNITED STATES, 1940–59

During the 1940s sales of movie tickets soared to 3.5 billion a year. By then movies would be the "things" that embodied American ideas—not just for Americans, but for the whole world. Entertaining, informative, and relatively cheap, films reinforced the values this country wanted to honor, the ideas people would be willing to make sacrifices for. A 1940s classic, *Mrs. Miniver*, created to glorify the bravery and ingenuity of our British ally—personified by the charming Greer Garson—could be seen in New York along with the famous Rockettes's precision dancing stage show at the elegant Radio City Music Hall for 75 cents. The film broke all attendance records for the time, grossing over a million dollars.

One anthropologist, Hortense Powdermaker, referred to Hollywood as a "dream factory," while Robert Sklar, an historian, defined the whole country as "movie-made America." The power of the motion picture industry to influence how Americans saw themselves, to turn myths into live traditions, would become more and more apparent. When we elected our first movie star president, critics remarked that Ronald Reagan sometimes seemed to confuse his World War II movie roles with what actually happened. In the 1940s the social and cultural makeup of the movie

industry reflected the values of an America concerned with helping people recognize what was worth fighting for.

Hollywood's representation of the American dream has been definitively described by the television movie critic Neal Gabler in a social history of the film industry, *An Empire of Their Own: How the Jews Invented Hollywood*. Examining the lives of Hollywood tycoons as symbolic American successes, Gabler reveals the anxieties of the movie moguls' world as suggestive of the values of most new Americans. In articulating on film their own immigrant dreams of the good life available in America, the filmmakers helped influence how other Americans defined their identities. Most convincingly, Gabler records the intense and often uncritical patriotism that shaped the moviemakers' attitudes toward foreign ideologies, like the Nazism so many in the industry had fled and the Communism that others believed was a threat to American life. In the 1940s the movie empire demonstrated unquestioning patriotism—a wholehearted commitment to the war effort that would help both to educate soldiers and to stir up civilian support for the war. Films such as *This Is the Army* (1943), *Yankee Doodle Dandy* (1942), *The Fighting 69th* (1940), and *Lifeboat* (1944) attempted to revitalize the American myths of ethnic success and integrated culture. All groups needed to believe that individuals could do well working together in a pluralistic society for a common goal.

> *In the 1940s the movie empire demonstrated unquestioning patriotism.*

During the war years attendance at local theaters mounted to over 90 million viewers a week. Commitment to the war effort by the film industry extended to many different levels. Movie houses—palaces of imagination in the 1930s—were used in the 1940s as community centers. In their spacious lobbies people gathered to buy and sell war bonds and to collect flattened tin cans and aluminum pots as well as surplus fats for making munitions. Even youngsters worked at selling defense stamps at small tables set up near the ticket takers to remind people of their civic responsibilities. When movie stars joined in the sale of government bonds at American theaters everywhere they sold over $350 billion worth. People did not hesitate to lend their savings to the government.

Teenagers also collected money in movie lobbies to boost the canteens of the United Service Organizations. Many young soldiers stationed all over America in army training camps far from their homes needed "wholesome" places for entertainment on weekend leaves. Members of the film industry worked with local volunteers to make these Stage Door Canteens represent homey refuges of warmth and hospitality for young strangers. Even though the armed forces were racially segregated during World War II, the canteens for relaxation often made a point of being integrated. Actress Bette Davis, one anecdote records, threatened to sever connection with her local canteen when some officious volunteers questioned the interracial dancing that took place there. Although most of the elegant theaters where such community activities could happen were torn down in the 1960s when television became a more socially isolating way to view movies, a film called *Stagedoor Canteen* (1943) remains a tribute to the idea of innocent entertainment and welcome for out-of-towners under supervision of the movie industry. The Hollywood Canteen, sponsored by 42 craft guilds including both white and African American musicians' locals, fed thousands of meals to eager soldiers and sailors during its first two years. Yet it is the movies themselves—the "things" that embody the ideas of the 1940s— that students will continue to consider the most important social artifacts of the war. Almost every film made during the war years reveals some social aspect of wartime America.

On the most obvious level Hollywood filmmakers offered the government their resources to create training films for the army—telling soldiers about our allies and introducing our enemies. The public would be offered similar fare. Propagandistic work like *A Yank in the R.A.F.* (1944) and *Journey for Margaret* (1942), about an evacuated English child, were meant to demonstrate our deep connection with the British. Ideological films like *Hitler's Children* (1943) or Charlie Chaplin's *The Great Dictator* (1940) made it easier to dislike Germans. Exaggerated features of treacherous Japanese film characters helped Americans accept the necessity to incarcerate patriotic fellow Americans. Not until after the war, when Japan had become an American friend, was a film made to expose the injustice of the internment camps. Made out of Jeanne Wakatsuki Houston's memoir, the film *Farewell to Manzanar* in 1976 captures one Japanese American's story of the humiliations of displacement. Other movies created during wartime to familiarize the American people with our new allies, the Russians—like *Mission to Moscow* (1944)—would haunt their Hollywood producers and writers after the war when the relationship with Russia disintegrated and a blacklist labeled the creators of such sympathetic scripts Communist sympathizers.

That distinguished writers like John Steinbeck joined the war effort with *The Moon Is Down* (1943) and *Lifeboat* (1944) suggests the extent of involvement of serious writers and artists in wartime propaganda. A list of Hollywood producers, writers, directors, technicians, and stars who put personal preferences aside to do what was most helpful for their country in fighting the war would fill a small book. Two favorites—the witty movie star Carole Lombard and the bandleader Glenn Miller, who traveled as an enlisted army officer entertaining troops—lost their lives in military air crashes. No one in the movie community criticized the government or questioned the need to get behind the war. A rare pacifist, star Lew Ayres, emphasized his opposition to killing by joining the medical corps. Newsreels—shown in Translux theaters for short subjects—were also included with feature films, recording ugly realities just as TV news did during the Vietnam War. There were honest journalists like Ernie Pyle who described what continuous fighting did to people, but there was also protective censorship. People on the home front complained if too much brutality was exposed. Movies were constructed to show the enemy—not American young men—being blown to bits. Students might consider how much such attitudes shift in different decades by looking at the 1998 film *Saving Private Ryan*, an effort to depict the invasion of Europe with utmost accuracy.

Glorification of the war experience became essential while the war was being fought. Although films such as *The Story of G.I. Joe* (1943), *A Walk in the Sun* (1945), and *Pride of the Marines* (1945) stressed a wholesome distaste for war as human activity, they made a point of demonstrating the surprising courage of the ordinary individual in the multicultural foxhole. Critics tend to make fun of the Hollywood melting-pot group: black-white, Catholic-Jew, slum kid–stockbroker dependent on each other in submarine or fighter plane; but the need to nourish the myth of equality for those willing to die for it brought about a more realistic exploration of American prejudice in films after the war. A 1939 movie like *Gone with the Wind* could get away with showing blacks to be dully loyal or simply silly. In the name of the national unity forged out of the Civil War, this famous classic praised only the individual spunk of whites enduring social disaster—slavery was not an issue in the film. After World War II African Americans would be taken more seriously in films, and American prejudice would be discussed in the open. Such movies as *Crossfire* and *Gentleman's Agreement* (both 1947) would also help to alert many to the reality of American anti-Semitism. *Intruder in the Dust* (1949) allowed viewers to appreciate the intelligence of a black hero. In 1948, acknowledging the need for equality of opportunity in an important section of American life, Harry Truman integrated the army. In 1945, during Roosevelt's brief fourth term, the government repealed the 1882 Chinese Exclusion Act, which set quotas on Chinese immigration and denied citizenship to the Chinese.

The 1940s film industry's contribution to pure entertainment to help people escape the tensions of war and the problems of reshaping postwar life also included such classic musicals as *State Fair* (1945) and *The Harvey Girls* (1945). Film noir masterpieces such as *The Maltese Falcon* (1941), *Laura* (1944), *Double Indemnity* (1945), *The Postman Always Rings Twice* (1946), and *Spellbound* (1945) made distraction exciting. Westerns like *The Ox-Bow Incident* (1943) and *My Darling Clementine* (1946) extended the mythology of the West with greater compassion.

Through the 1950s, movies continued to have a link with larger national political issues. The House Un-American Activities Committee (HUAC), designed to ferret out Communists in labor unions in the 1930s, became an invigorated source of terror under the control of Congressman J. Parnell Thomas. In 1947 a group of Hollywood screenwriters and directors summoned before the committee to account for past Communist beliefs were considered especially dangerous because of their power to influence American opinion through the movies. Called "unfriendly witnesses" because they took the Fifth Amendment to keep from having to name friends, the "Hollywood Ten" were all indicted for contempt of Congress. Although even film star Ronald Reagan testified at the time that he did not believe Communists had ever been able to use motion pictures to spread their ideology, the Supreme Court upheld the indictment. These people were fined a thousand dollars each and sent to jail for a year. Richard Nixon, who would become the most prominent committee member during the 1950 Alger Hiss trial, demanded that new movies be made to spell out "the methods and evils of totalitarian Communism." But the only examples J. Parnell Thomas could find of dangerous old movies were those made during the war, like *Mission to Moscow* and *Song of Russia*—corny propaganda films created to help wartime allies appear sympathetic. Ironically, Chairman Thomas, accused of stealing from the government he had been protecting from Communists, would soon find himself in the same prison where he had sent one of the Hollywood Ten, Ring Lardner Jr. As a result of this arrest Lardner, a particularly talented writer, would not see his name on any list of screen credits for 17 years. But by 1970 his gifts would be valued again; he won an Oscar for work on M*A*S*H.

After this trial the atmosphere of fright was so great that a national blacklist was set up not only to deny future employment to the Hollywood Ten but also to keep anyone with questionable political allegiances from working in the media. Loyalty oaths became a part of the American scene, and many less talented and less influential people lost government and teaching jobs—also considered positions of influence. Fortunately for the history of freedom of speech, a panoramic array of gifted writers has recorded many versions of this period of anxiety, labeled "scoundrel time" by playwright Lillian Hellman in her book of the same name. In the future when scholars and critics collect all such memoirs and compare them, careful research may reveal how much prejudice may have been involved in accusations against intellectuals and New Deal civil servants and whether, indeed, 1930s writers connected with the Communist party continued to support the Soviet Union.

Although a number of films tried to capture the mood of this decade, two remain classical comments on the emotions of the time. "Friendly witnesses" (the label for those who believed it a patriotic duty to name all the Communists they knew) Elia Kazan and Budd Schulberg collaborated on the 1954 prize-winning movie *On the Waterfront*. Awarded eight Oscars, it examined the dilemmas involved in becoming an

> *Loyalty oaths became a part of the American scene.*

informer. Kazan acknowledged using his own story in the film to justify his testimony before the House Un-American Activities Committee. In the movie the informer, whose moral choices are relatively simple, becomes a hero.

A film offering a different viewpoint could be made only at a much later time. In 1976, once-blacklisted artists Walter Bernstein and Martin Ritt wrote and directed the Woody Allen production *The Front*, re-creating the lives of a writer and comedian barred from work during the 1950s. Although there is humor in the delicatessen cashier character who "fronts" for the talented writer denied his livelihood, the themes of humiliation and loss of self-esteem involved in being blacklisted dominate the film. The comedian, brilliantly played by Zero Mostel, who had himself been a victim of the blacklist, commits suicide. Such despair was real for artists at this moment because their survival demanded audiences. "The Great Fear," as British scholar David Caute termed the fear of Communism in a long book on anti-Communist purges under Truman and Eisenhower, touched almost every kind of contemporary activity.

To be sure, by the 1990s, when Russian spy files were opened to reveal the Venona documents of deciphered codes passed by the Russian Secret Service, the KGB, to its American agents, there could be no doubt that the American Communist Party had been controlled by the Kremlin. And there was evidence for espionage where many believed none had existed. But the number of actual subversives remained small. In an eloquent 1950 book, *The Loyalty of Free Men*, Alan Barth, a journalist for the *Washington Post*, pointed out that the number of Communist Party members equaled about 1/30th of 1 percent of the population—yet the general hysteria of the late 1940s and early 1950s appeared extreme. In 1954 a famous critic of American civilization, Lewis Mumford, echoed the concerns of liberals: "In the name of freedom we are rapidly creating a police state; and in the name of democracy we have succumbed not to creeping socialism but to galloping Fascism" (Kaledin, 76–78).

FOR MORE INFORMATION

Caute, D. *The Great Fear: The Anti-Communist Purge under Truman and Eisenhower.* New York: Simon and Schuster, 1978.

Chaplin, C., dir. *The Great Dictator.* 1940.

Jowett, G., and J. M. Linton. *Movies as Mass Communications.* Beverly Hills, Calif.: Sage, 1980.

Kaledin, E. *Daily Life in the United States, 1940–1959: Shifting Worlds.* Westport, Conn.: Greenwood Press, 2000.

Sklar, R. *Movie-Made America.* Rev. ed. New York: Vintage, 1994.

Whitfield, S. J. *The Culture of the Cold War.* Baltimore: Johns Hopkins University Press, 1991.

UNITED STATES, 1960–90

Television did not bring about the demise of the motion picture industry, as some had predicted years earlier that it would. The industry held its own partly by producing made-for-television films and selling broadcast and videotaping rights of movies after they had run in theaters. Sales in foreign countries also helped. Most of the industry's revenue, however, poured in through box offices, as going to movies remained a popular social activity. People were still willing to pay more to see a film on a big screen. In 1975, box-office revenue broke the record set the previous year. Higher admission prices accounted for part of the increase, but the average weekly attendance of 21 million, up 10 percent from the previous year, was the main reason. These figures are notable mainly because they represent a reversal of the 25-year downward spiral from the average attendance of 80 million in pretelevision days.

Blockbuster films brought in much of the industry's revenue. In 1975, Steven Spielberg's spine-tingling *Jaws* was the big moneymaker. The violence and terror wrought by a huge man-eating white shark in a resort community evidently appealed to the tastes of vast numbers of the reading and moviegoing public. Like other popular films, it was based on a novel; when the film was released, there were 5.5 million copies of Peter Benchley's novel in print. Another film based on a novel, *One Flew over the Cuckoo's Nest,* did very well at the box office and achieved critical acclaim with its portrayal of life and medical treatment in mental institutions. In 1977 came another blockbuster: *Star Wars,* a movie saturated with special visual and sound effects. Some of this film's appeal lay in its depiction of the romance of fighting a "just" war; some lay in the drama of science fiction.

The diverse tastes of producers and audiences were evident in the variety of films winning honors each year. In 1982, for example, *Gandhi,* the story of the man who led India's struggle for independence, won an Oscar for best picture. Several years later the Oscar went to *Amadeus,* which treated the life of the great composer Wolfgang Amadeus Mozart. Then came *Out of Africa* and *The Last Emperor,* the latter the story of a bygone China. Named best picture in 1988 was *Rain Man*, starring Dustin Hoffman, who was named best actor for his performance; this film introduced audiences to autism, a baffling mental disorder. It was followed by *Driving Miss Daisy*, with Jessica Tandy playing the role of an eccentric but lovable elderly woman and winning best actress for it. Then came *Dances with Wolves*, directed by and featuring Kevin Costner (best director) in a romanticized story of the Lakota Sioux nation.

Award-winning films were often bested at the box office by those featuring daring themes or techniques. That explains the success of the 1981 blockbuster *Raiders of the Lost Ark,* and another in 1982, *E.T.—The Extra-Terrestrial,* the story of love between an Earth boy, lonely in suburbia, and a stranded alien from space. Both were directed by Steven Spielberg. *E.T.* grossed $228 million at the box office and demonstrated the commercial success that lay in embedding a film's vocabulary ("Elliot," "ouch," and "phone home") into the language of everyday life and in marketing a film's images on such things as lunch boxes, bicycles, and even underwear. Another blockbuster success was Tim Burton's *Batman* in 1989. Although it did not match the revenue produced by *E.T.*, the "Batmania" it inspired paid dividends to marketers of products bearing the image or logo of the Batman.

Sylvester Stallone's *Rambo: First Blood, Part II* is a good example of a popular film featuring violence. Stallone played the role of a Vietnam veteran who freed prisoners of war, thereby exposing the alleged indifference of the U.S. government. The film's prowar perspective drew complaints from those who thought it tried to revise truths about the war, but the complaints did not keep Rambo from becoming a folk hero or Rambo guns and knives from becoming popular children's toys.

In 1984 the Motion Picture Association of America (MPAA) added a new rating, PG-13, the first change since the introduction of the rating system 16 years earlier. The new rating placed films between PG (parental guidance suggested) and R (restricted). It was "advisory" in that it did not exclude viewers under age 14, but it informed parents that violence or other content in the film might not be suitable for their children. In 1990 the MPAA replaced the controversial X rating, which had come to be regarded as synonymous with pornography, with NC-17. The new rating was intended for movies that despite depictions of explicit sex or extreme violence, such as *Henry & June*, were regarded as serious artistic efforts (Marty, 209–10, 281–82).

FOR MORE INFORMATION

Jowett, G., and J. M. Linton. *Movies as Mass Communications.* Beverly Hills, Calif.: Sage, 1980.

Kubrick, S., dir. *Dr. Strangelove.* 1964.

Marty, M. A. *Daily Life in the United States, 1960–1990: Decades of Discord.* Westport, Conn.: Greenwood Press, 1997.

Parker, A., dir. *Mississippi Burning.* 1988.

Ritt, M., dir. *Norma Rae.* 1979.

Sklar, R. *Movie-Made America.* Rev. ed. New York: Vintage, 1994.

Whitfield, S. J. *The Culture of the Cold War*. Baltimore: Johns Hopkins University Press, 1991.

INDIA

The film industry in India is very large, and from tea vendors to diplomats, everyone relishes seeing films. Popular actors and actresses are carefully followed in the media, and gossip about their personal lives is a frequent topic of conversation.

India's introduction to the motion picture came through the British presence in the subcontinent. On July 7, 1896, at the Watson Hotel in Bombay, the Lumière Brothers' Cinematographe ran several short soundless films. India produced its first indigenous film in 1913—*Raja Harishchandra* by Dhundiraj Govind Phalke, shown in Bombay, with both Hindi and English titles. The first Indian "talkie," *Alam Ara*, appeared in 1931, directed by Ardershir Irani and produced by the Imperial film company. An industry was born, and India went on to develop one of the world's largest and most vibrant film cultures.

India's most famous filmmaker was Satyajit Ray. Ray was born in Calcutta in the state of West Bengal in 1921. He was deeply influenced by Bengal's great literary figure, Rabindranath Tagore, whose college he attended. Ray first gained national and international fame for his film *Pather Panchali* (1955), which won the Grand Prix at the Cannes Film festival. In this work, Ray began to follow the life of an everyday Bengali named Apu. He continued to tell Apu's story in subsequent films, *Aparajito* (1956) and *The World of Apu* (1959), to form a trilogy. Later in his career, he set to film one of Tagore's best-known works, *At Home and the World* (1984). In 1992, Ray received an Academy Award for lifetime achievement. He died the same year.

Seeing a film in India can provide an insight into the country and its people. There are movie theaters throughout the country, in cities and in small towns. In villages, movies are often shown against a large white sheet hung from the side of a building or between two trees. In urban areas, theaters are usually large, holding between 500 and 2,000 people. They frequently have balconies where couples on a date might find privacy during a film. In many theaters, the seats are divided into different ranks. People line up outside the theater to buy the appropriate ticket. Movie houses sometimes assign seats. The least expensive seats are usually immediately in front of the screen. Here, those who cannot afford a better seat will sit on the floor. Behind them and in the balconies are the better seats, perhaps more cushioned or with a clearer view. Because Indian films are long, there is usually an intermission. Vendors walk through the aisles selling soft drinks and other snacks. Viewers in India frequently call out to the characters on the screen, warning them of impending danger, scolding a villain, or cheering the hero.

India's major film center is in Bombay (Mumbai), and most films produced there are in the Hindi language. However, because India has 14 official languages and thousands of dialects, the films are dubbed into other regional languages and can attain national appeal. Its thriving film industry has earned Bombay the nickname

"Bollywood." Bollywood produces an impressive number of films each year—more than 240 films in the year 2000. However, Bombay is not the only center of film production. The southern states of Andhra Pradesh and Tamil Nadu combined to produce more than 500 films in 2000. This southern film industry is called "Tollywood," playing on the word *tali*, a large tray on which South Indian dishes are traditionally served.

Most films in India include several common tropes. Though this formula pleases the producers and much of the audience, it does make for somewhat limited achievement in artistic terms. Films usually revolve around a love story. Included in the mix will be a wicked mother-in-law, a buffoonlike servant or cohort, a sassy Westernized woman (usually appearing in a miniskirt), a thug, a birth, a death, and a marriage. Sadly, most films also include a rape scene. In addition, Indian films have become known for their lavish musical scenes whereby the characters break into song and the setting shifts from India to the Swiss Alps, New York City, Paris, or some other exotic setting, only to return to India when the song and dance are complete. Films usually end on an upbeat note with the lovers united. Indian films are carefully censored, and most do not show much beyond simple kissing. However, through dance gyrations and longing looks between lovers, it is not difficult to imagine the characters' feelings.

In recent years, Indian films have begun to appear in major European and North American movie rental stores. This not only acknowledges the large number of South Asians living outside of the subcontinent, but also demonstrates a new respect for the Indian film industry by Hollywood and Western markets. One popular recent film is *Lagaan: Once Upon a Time in India* (2001). Other films include *Such A Long Journey* (1998), *Fire* (1997), and *Kama Sutra: A Tale of Love* (1997).

Indian filmmakers also produce documentaries, covering a range of topics from social issues to politics. Among India's best-known documentary filmmakers is Anand Patwardhan. His works have included *In the Name of God* (1993), which examined the political chaos and religious frenzy that led to the destruction of the Babri mosque in 1992. In addition, in the wake of India and Pakistan's nuclear tests (1998), Patwardhan directed *War and Peace* (2002), a film that examines the environmental damage caused by the nuclear programs and the misconceptions that everyday citizens in India and Pakistan have concerning each other.

India has a rich tradition of filmmaking. Even during its colonial period, Indians took an active interest in making and viewing films. Since independence in 1947, the film industry in India has grown to be the largest in the world, releasing more than a film per day. Love stories, action adventures, art films, and documentaries all add to a rich mosaic of filmmaking that extends from village India to the nearest American movie rental shop.

~*Benjamin Cohen*

FOR MORE INFORMATION

Rajadhyaksha, A., and Paul Willemen, eds. *Encyclopedia of the Indian Cinema*. London: Fitzroy Dearborn, 1999.

SOVIET UNION

As with nearly all those who worked in the arts during the Soviet era, filmmakers were subjected to repression and censorship. Film censorship began even before writers were hired, because scripts had to conform to official demands for certain themes, such as village life, Lenin's (and earlier, Stalin's) life, Soviet industry, and various national occasions and celebrations. After a writer was hired and the script was written, it had to pass through some 17 to 20 "editorial" (censorship) committees. When "editors" were finished with a script, the work emerged radically pruned of politically incorrect material. Soviet screenwriters had a joke to describe their situation: "What is a telephone pole?" "A telephone pole is an edited pine tree." After the censorship boards had done their work, the film was carried off to private showings for higher-level civilian and military censors. If a film passed this scrutiny, it was returned, with a panoply of certifications and stamps, to its director. The government determined how many copies of the movie were to be made and where it could be shown. As with painters and photographers, filmmakers could not point their cameras anywhere they pleased. It was forbidden to film tall landmarks, military personnel, landscapes near a military base or weapons factory, or scenes of everyday life that showed Soviet reality in a bad light. In one of his movies, Andrei Kuznetsov recalled, censors discarded a scene in which the hero meditated about life and death. The censor's rationale was that "Soviet people are too positive to dwell upon death!" For some mysterious reason, calendars showing the actual date of filming were also off-limits. After Khrushchev's denunciation of the "cult of personality," all previous Soviet films with Stalin portraits had to be doctored to eliminate the offending pictures.

Sergei Eisenstein's fruitless struggle in the 1930s to produce a politically acceptable *Bezhin Meadow* and Andrey Tarkovsky's later, ultimately successful, battle to show his *Andrey Rublev* in the Soviet Union illustrate the relative but still very constricted liberalization after Stalin. *Bezhin Meadow* was made and remade for the censors but never allowed to be shown, even though the director was a world-famous filmmaker. In 1935, when *Bezhin Meadow* was about 60 percent finished, Boris Shumyatsky, the head of the Central Administration of Cinematography, stole it away to view it himself and show it to other leading members of the Soviet film industry, as well as to Party elite. These viewings resulted in such heavy criticism of the work that the director had to start over practically from scratch, hiring a new screenwriter (the famous Isaac Babel, soon to be arrested and shot) and new actors. But in March 1937, Shumyatsky once again decreed that work on the film had to stop. It was attacked in the press; meetings were organized specifically for condemning the unfinished movie that very few had been allowed to see. Many film workers (including Eisenstein himself) were called on to speak at those meetings. A few brave souls defended Eisenstein and the film, spoke ambiguously, or called in sick. Eisenstein was allowed to continue in his profession, but Shumyatsky was arrested and executed in 1938. Because of a 1941 bombing raid, only a few stills remain of *Bezhin Meadow*. This was not to be Eisenstein's last brush with the censor, however. He had planned a trilogy on the life of Tsar Ivan the Terrible. Part one, completed in 1944, won a Stalin Prize for its portrayal of Ivan's dynamic leadership. Perhaps Stalin saw his own portrait therein. He may also have recognized himself in part two, which shows Ivan's advancing paranoia and extraordinary violence. Whatever the reasons, part two was banned and not shown until 1958, 10 years after Eisenstein's death. Part three was never made.

Andrey Tarkovsky's renowned film *Andrei Rublev,* set in the early 15th century, is about Russia's most famous icon painter. The work had its premiere in 1967 but was banned from further screening. Censors objected to it in part because it showed Russians in a light as bad as—or worse than—their enemies, the Turks. Maybe that was the reason Soviet authorities considered the film "too depressing" for USSR audiences. The authorities eventually approved its distribution abroad, and it was unofficially entered in the Cannes Film Festival, receiving the International Critics Prize. The internal ban on *Andrei Rublev* was lifted in 1971, when it was allowed showings in Moscow's suburbs, albeit with only word-of-mouth publicity. The movie theaters showing the film were packed. Tarkovsky was fortunate to be able to present all five of his feature-length movies, a success won at the cost of an ongoing struggle against censorship.

In other cases as well, diplomatic compromises with censors sometimes ended in the production and domestic distribution of worthwhile films, including Grigory Chukhrai's masterpieces, "Ballad of a Soldier" (1959) and "The Clear Sky" (1961). Chukhrai well knew how to delicately balance social criticism with praise for his country's accomplishments. Nevertheless, his movies about vulnerable human beings struggling to survive in an often cruel society brought him into conflict with authorities who threatened to expel him from the Party. Once when Khrushchev fell asleep during a screening of the Italian film *8 1/2,* Chukhrai was ordered not to award it the Moscow Film Festival's grand prize. His refusal to cave in, Chukhrai said, resulted in his being refused permission to travel abroad for several years. The struggle against censorship was a struggle many filmmakers (and their potential audiences) often lost. Worthwhile movies were shelved, or so compromised by censorship that they were no longer artistically significant. At the Fifth Congress of the Union of Soviet Cinematographers, in May 1986, union members, emboldened by Gorbachev's glasnost, voted out their repressive First Secretary, as well as the union's entire secretariat, and elected a leader more in tune with the liberalizing times (Eaton).

FOR MORE INFORMATION

Dewhirst, M., and R. Farrell, eds. *The Soviet Censorship.* Metuchen, N.J.: Scarecrow Press, 1973.

Eaton, K. B. *Daily Life in the Soviet Union.* Westport, Conn.: Greenwood Press. Forthcoming.

JAPAN

Except for the realm of literature (where Japan has won two Nobel Prizes), Japan's cinema is arguably its single most important contribution to world culture in the

20th century. One would be hard-pressed to discover some remote portion of the world where the inhabitants were not familiar with the works of Kurosawa, Mizuguchi, Itami, Gosho, Ozu, Naruse, Kinoshita, and scores more.

It was in cinema that Japan first began to break out of the oft-bruited stereotype that the Japanese were little more than emulators and refiners of the creative arts. Almost from its faltering first steps Japanese film received plaudits from abroad. If imitation is the sincerest form of flattery, then Japanese cinema is much admired by foreign directors. Indeed, the films of the exceptional directors named in the last paragraph were often copied and emulated by directors around the world. Most cinema buffs know about how *The Magnificent Seven* (and even *Three Amigos*) was adapted from Kurosawa Akira's *Seven Samurai*. Many more know that *Sanjuro* and *Yojimbo* became *Fistful of Dollars* and *Last Man Standing*, respectively, and that *Hidden Fortress* was the precursor of *Star Wars*.

Without question the films of Kurosawa are best known to the outside world. His lifetime collaboration with Mifune Toshiro includes his most influential works, *Roshomon*, *Throne of Blood*, and *Ran*, and the previously mentioned *Seven Samurai*, *Sanjuro*, and *Yojimbo*. His grand epics stunned the film world and highly influenced many Japanese as well as American directors. Yet his best works were small films such as *Ikiru*, *Drunken Angel*, and *Stray Dog*.

If Kurosawa is best known outside Japan, the films of Mizuguchi Kenji are more beloved in Japan itself. His chilling ghost stories, most notably *Ugetsu*, as well as his "woman" films, *Story of O-haru*, *Princess Yang*, *Sisters of Gion*, and *Osaka Elegy* (the latter two starring the luminescent Yamada Usuzu), are famous for giving voice to women. He is also famous for the "long-shot" technique that gave his films the literal wide vision later emulated by many other directors.

Ozu Yasujiro has been characterized as the "most Japanese" of the famous directors. He began his career in silent movies and is one of only a handful who managed to bridge the old and new technologies. His famous films are characterized as deeply human, almost claustrophobic in their intensity despite the fact that he perfected the social comedy genre. His most famous films, *Tokyo Story* and *Late Spring*, examine families in crisis. His films are also famous for their "low-shot" style where the viewer is usually at ground level, staring up into the faces of the protagonists,

His contemporary Gosho Heinosuke is less well known outside of Japan but has the distinction of being the most literary among the directors. He introduced Japanese literature to the world in *An Inn at Osaka*, *Where Chimneys Are Seen*, and *Growing Up*.

Similarly, Naruse Mikio used Japanese literature in many of his dark, brooding films. He introduced the works of Nobel Prize winner Kawabata Yasunari to Western film buffs in *Three Sisters with Maiden Hearts* and turned Hayashi Fumiko's novel into *Repast*.

Kawabata's most famous novel, *Snow Country*, was filmed by Toyoda Shiro, who specialized in psychological dramas, including *Grass Whistle* and *Marital Relations*.

Many of Japan's most famous directors are renowned for their work in the dark film noir genre, which is characterized by slow, intense dramatic dialogue. Only a few directors are justly famous for their humorous satire. Kinoshita Keisuke made several charming films, including *Carmen Comes Home* and *Carmen's Pure Love*, both about a naïve reformed stripper. Even his serious films such as *Twenty-four Eyes* and *A Japanese Tragedy* convey a rare humor and sense of the absurd.

More noted for his humor is Itami Juzo, who is best known to the West as the creator of the first "noodle Western," *Tampopo*. His other well-known films, *A Taxing Woman*, *A Taxing Woman Returns*, *The Funeral*, and *The Gentle Art of Japanese Extortion* (which nearly cost him his life at the hands of a would-be Yakuza assassin), employed an ensemble cast of actors that included his former wife, Miyamoto Nobuko. His suicide in 1997 is still the source of great mystery.

The most versatile of the famous directors is Yoshimura Kimisaburo. He is famous for finishing *An Osaka Story* in the style of the director Mizoguchi, who died before the film could be finished. Yoshimura is also noted for completing the only successful Kabuki film, *The Beauty and the Dragon*.

Clearly the most political of Japan's famous directors is Imai Tadashi, who specialized in leftist topics even before becoming a member of the Communist Party of Japan. His attack on the militarism of World War II in *The Enemy of the People* counterbalanced his wartime propaganda film, *The Numazo Military Academy*, and he then found his stride in *Darkness at Noon*, *And Yet We Live*, and *Here Is a Spring*.

If he had never made another film, Ichikawa Kon would be justly celebrated for his antiwar classic, *Harp of Burma*. Happily, he made others, but perhaps his best is *A Girl at Dojo Temple*, which was banned by the World War II militarist government. Ichikawa thought he could slip the film past government censors by using puppets in the style of Bunraku theater. Only a few badly faded copies survived.

Cinema historian Donald Keene estimates that 90 percent of all of Japan's films did not survive into modern times. Many perished in the Great Kanto Earthquake of 1923, and many more burned during the firebombing of Tokyo in 1945.

~Louis G. Perez

FOR MORE INFORMATION

Davis, D. W. *Picturing Japaneseness: Monumental Style, National Identity, Japanese Film*. New York: Columbia University Press, 1996.

Richie, D. *A Hundred Years of Japanese Film: A Concise History, with a Selective Guide to Videos and DVDs*. Tokyo: Kodansha International, 2001.

Schilling, M. *Contemporary Japanese Film*. New York: Weatherhill, 1999.

Music

For most people, music is a central part of daily life. We listen to and make music for entertainment, for solace, for worship, and for remembrance. Social historians who investigate the nature of daily life have long considered music a unique window into a society's values, taboos, fears, hopes, and conflicts. By studying music, one can learn not only about a culture's aesthetics but also about a society's structure

RECREATIONAL LIFE

MUSIC

United States, 1920-1939

United States, 1940-1959

United States, 1960-1990

Soviet Union

Japan

Inuit

and history. Thus, the entries in this section give an accurate representation of people's tastes and their daily concerns. This historical aspect of music is most true in open societies such as that of the United States. However, in closed and controlled societies, like the Soviet Union's, understanding music is a more complex exercise. As in other Western nations, Soviet music reflected trends in realism and formalism. However, by the 1960s, the Communist Party censored many artists and altered their works. In the United States, musicians and composers faced fewer censors. And, as the century progressed, music became more important in daily life.

Although it is perhaps easy to stretch the meanings in music, several major shifts in popular music are clearly visible during the 20th century. The obvious change was the ascent of rock and roll as a musical and cultural force and the subsequent marginalization of so-called classical music. The transformation began during the 1940s when big bands conducted by Tommy Dorsey, Benny Goodman, and Glenn Miller became enormously popular. They performed songs that resonated with the younger generation such as "Praise the Lord and Pass the Ammunition" and "Boogie Woogie Bugle Boy." This new music also carried significant legitimacy in the white and black communities because it drew on musical roots common to both, and it laid the groundwork for the most important musical icon of the 20th century, Elvis Presley. Presley offered something to everyone who listened. He was a working-class hero, a sex symbol, a better-than-average crooner who created opportunities for black and white musicians. Elvis also ignited entire generations of rock musicians to seek their fortune in the industry.

The musicians who followed Elvis, such as Bob Dylan, Joan Baez, and the Beatles, were more politically conscious. Moreover, it was not just the records themselves that made statements. The rock concerts, like the massive Monterey International Pop Festival (1967) and the Woodstock Music and Art Fair (1969), also had politics on center stage. And yet, rock and roll remained fundamentally about sex and drugs. In other words, the most significant music of the 20th century was about the counterculture. Or, perhaps better put, the music of the young generation dealt with the alienation, disappointments, and horrors of the modern world and the ways to break out of the tight regimentation created by the generations of older people.

This generational conflict died down in the 1970s and 1980s as the music industry homogenized rock and roll for all audiences. And as pop music lost its edge, sales slipped. In 1979 alone, 40 percent fewer records were sold than in 1978. This slump occurred not just in rock and roll. Classical music was quickly disappearing as a mainstream cultural phenomenon. Nevertheless, artists from the African American community revitalized music in America. Rap music put the edge back on popular music. The record industry moguls quickly turned controversy into sales. By the end of the century, rap and various related forms like hip-hop dominated the airwaves, the television, and the youth culture generally. As with Elvis, some cultural critics saw this development as the debasement of American culture, whereas others reveled in the new music, seeking to find out what in fact it meant about the United States at the dawn of the new millennium.

In other cultures, such as those of the Japanese and Inuit peoples, Western musical traditions and practices existed side-by-side with traditional musical forms and instruments. The Japanese acquired an appreciation of Western music in the late 19th century and by the late 20th century had embraced most of the major trends in American popular music. The Inuit, although open to Western musical influences, were careful to retain traditional musical forms as an important way to preserve their culture and pass it on to new generations.

UNITED STATES, 1920–39

Music underwent a notable evolution during this era, 1920–39. Largely because of the phonograph and radio, specialized forms of music entered the cultural main-stream. Classical music acquired a much expanded audience, though because of its well-established repertoire it was less influenced than other musical genres by the new technologies. A few new concert music composers did emerge, including Americans Aaron Copland, George Gershwin, and Roy Harris, and Russian émigré Sergei Rachmaninoff. Only short pieces or excerpts could be presented uninterrupted on 78 rpm records, but radio networks allowed full-length performances of symphonic music and opera to reach audiences far beyond the urban centers to which they had previously been largely confined. When Saturday-afternoon broadcasts of the Metropolitan Opera of New York allowed a small-town Iowa homemaker to indulge a taste for opera along with a wealthy Manhattan matron, a national high-art culture was indeed emerging.

The music of various ethnic groups served as a cultural bond for groups that were themselves scattering geographically. In some cases the music also introduced that culture into the mainstream. Phonograph recordings of the music of recent European immigrant groups emerged first. Such music became a staple of the recording industry early in the 20th century, but sales of "foreign" music, already dwindling as immigration restriction and cultural assimilation took effect, declined sharply when the Great Depression arrived.

Some record companies became interested in African American music in the early 1920s. Reflecting the social segregation of the era, companies such as Okeh, Paramount, Brunswick, and Columbia began producing separate lines of "race records." African American musicians found themselves confined to recording blues, jazz, and gospel music but nevertheless made available a great deal of both traditional and innovative African American music. More than 5,000 blues and 1,000 gospel records by 1,200 artists appeared during the 1920s and 1930s. Generally excluded from the radio, African American music thrived with the phonograph. The music served to connect the majority of African Americans who remained in the South and the increasing number who migrated north. A 1927 survey of African American homes in two Georgia counties found that none owned a radio but nearly one in five possessed a phonograph. Nationally, five to six million "race records" were sold annually by middecade.

Phonograph records helped spread the sounds of African American jazz, which music broadcasters at first considered inappropriate for radio. White youth such as Jimmy McPartland of suburban Chicago and Leon "Bix" Beiderbecke of Davenport,

RECREATIONAL
LIFE
|
MUSIC
|
United States,
1920-1939

United States,
1940-1959

United States,
1960-1990

Soviet Union

Japan

Inuit

Iowa, listened excitedly and repeatedly to blues and jazz recorded by African American musicians. Because the 78 rpm records of the day could hold only one or two tunes per side, they would play the same record over and over until every note and phrase became familiar. They learned to play jazz by imitation and soon began performing at school dances. While few young men (and fewer women) would follow McPartland and Beiderbecke into careers as jazz musicians, many more would collect, play, and dance to the new sounds of jazz.

The music of rural white southerners developed quite separately, not intertwining substantially with black music until the post–World War II era merger of "rhythm and blues" (the new recording industry label for what had previously been called race music) and "hillbilly" music. Radio broadcasts of the *Grand Ole Opry* and the *National Barn Dance* did a great deal to popularize southern white folk music. At the same time, efforts by early entrepreneurs such as the Carter family and Jimmie Rogers to collect, record, and copyright their own versions of traditional tunes helped establish a more common approach to "country music," modifying the highly localized original styles. Even a culture based on tradition underwent standardization.

When the depression reduced markets for ethnic, country, and race records to a trickle, hard-pressed record companies took the lead in stimulating the development of a more homogenized popular music. Creative producers such as Jack Kapp of Decca Records and John Hammond of Columbia Records used newly developed recording technologies to improve sound quality. Kapp also opted for a smaller inventory of highly promoted releases and reduced the price of a record by half to 35 cents. Such business strategies helped create music widely embraced by the public.

Kapp worked to develop hit records by blending elements of various musical genres. He encouraged the orchestras of Guy Lombardo and Tommy Dorsey to emphasize clear, simple melodies as well as light, steady rhythms that would be good for dancing. He also promoted singers with soft, pleasant voices such as Bing Crosby and the four Mills Brothers. Decca's generally upbeat style of music appealed to many Americans in the depression decade, and its more affordable prices helped shape a popular mass-market music business that would explode within a few years.

John Hammond, Kapp's main rival, likewise produced records that softened the styles of jazz and blues. He played an important role in creating new dance music that by the mid-1930s was beginning to be called "swing." Hammond helped clarinetist Benny Goodman increase his band's already considerable appeal by adding flamboyant drummer Gene Krupa and rhythmically steady piano player Jess Stacy. Hammond also brought African American musicians such as bandleader Count Basie and singer Billie Holiday to national attention. He was far more aggressive than Kapp in bringing African American music and artists into the cultural mainstream, a step that foreshadowed and helped prepare the way for subsequent social and political developments.

The early 1930s' creation of the coin-operated automatic phonograph placed popular music in restaurants, dance halls, night clubs, soda fountains, and the taverns opening up after the repeal of prohibition. The 150,000 machines produced between 1933 and 1937, soon to be labeled jukeboxes, each held 50 records. Not only did the jukebox help revive the record business, but it also focused industry and audience attention on music of the greatest popularity. Jukebox owners naturally wanted the jukeboxes filled with the records most likely to attract customers' nickels. By 1939, with 60 percent of all records sold going into Wurlitzer, Seeburg, and other jukeboxes, a once quite diversified music industry was moving itself and the nation's culture toward greater uniformity.

The jukebox boosted the popularity of dancing, an already notable element of mass American culture. Various forms of dancing had long been a part of American life, of course, but the rise of the phonograph expanded opportunities for many, especially young working- and middle-class people, to engage in social dancing. Throughout the United States, in small communities as well as urban centers, dancing became highly popular. As a phonograph industry trade journal pointed out, "Not everyone can have a five-piece band waiting to play for them" (Kyvig, 170–74).

To read about music in the United States in the 19th century, see the United States entry in the section "Music" in chapter 7 ("Recreational Life") in volume 5 of this series.

FOR MORE INFORMATION

Chakhnazarov, K., dir. *Jazzman*. 1984.

Any music by Woody Guthrie.

Kenney, W. H. *Recorded Music in American Life: The Phonograph and Popular Memory, 1890–1945*. New York: Oxford University Press, 1999.

Kyvig, D. E. *Daily Life in the United States, 1920–1939: Decades of Promise and Pain*. Westport, Conn.: Greenwood Press, 2002.

UNITED STATES, 1940–59

The music of the 1940s and 1950s was quite significant in shaping the rest of the 20th century. The special music of the war years became popular for dancing on 78 rpm platters even when the leaders of the big bands—such as Tommy Dorsey, Benny Goodman, and Glenn Miller—were either in uniform or entertaining troops. Middle-class teenagers often held weekend dances with records in neighborhood homes as well as in high school gymnasiums. Some coastal towns inaugurated curfews. Although not every community had complete blackouts, walking about at night in streets with dimmed lights was unwise. Older high schoolers, imitating many movie stars and draftees, might smoke a cigarette or two at such record parties. Often their parents gave consent to smoking. But drinking and drugs were not fashionable. Soft drinks and nonalcoholic cider prevailed. Potato chips, pretzels, and popcorn were the only junk food available.

Everyone could sing along with wartime favorites like "Don't Sit Under the Apple Tree with Anyone Else but Me," "Praise the Lord and Pass the Ammunition," and the Andrews Sisters' sensational "Boogie Woogie Bugle Boy." "Rosie the Riveter" became a particular swing favorite on the home front. Young people—themselves often lonely at home—enjoyed the yearning in sad songs of separation like "I'll Walk Alone" and "Saturday Night Is the Loneliest Night in the Week."

The 1950s may have been the richest decade in American history for African American music. All the great classical jazz musicians and singers, including Louis Armstrong, Duke Ellington, Billie Holiday, and Ella Fitzgerald, performed during this decade. As the LP brought back the early sounds of King Oliver, Ma Rainey, and Bessie Smith, the new Motown sound began to shape itself in Detroit. Marian Anderson in 1955 became the first black woman to sing at the Metropolitan Opera, opening the stage for a great parade of superb African American singers. And although Paul Robeson—because of his Communist sympathies—had his request for a passport denied along with opportunities to sing and act, many recordings of his rich, deep voice remained to be transferred to the new vinyl LP recordings.

Despite the popularity of the music from Motown and from the Met, the decade of the 1950s was the decade of Elvis. It was entertainer Steve Allen who first focused discussion on Elvis Presley's pelvic gyrations by making him stand still as he serenaded a tethered hound dog. But Jackie Gleason deserves credit for pushing Presley's talents on the 1956 *Tommy and Jimmy Dorsey Stage Show* in spite of the Dorsey brothers' protests. Gleason rightly recognized Elvis as another hero of working-class culture, labeling him a guitar-playing Marlon Brando who had "sensuous, sweaty, T-shirt and jeans animal magnetism." Elvis managed to step forward—in between the quaint clowns and trained animal acts—to send rock-and-roll music into affluent suburban America. Although Dick Clark was on *American Bandstand* every afternoon in Philadelphia with well-groomed youngsters and modest songs, Elvis's ability to attract huge audiences suddenly put him in great demand. Milton Berle even hired him to inject life into his dying show—at what was then the outrageously high salary of $50,000 a week.

Like the rebel James Dean portrayed in 1950s movies and the exposer of phonies Holden Caulfield represented in the 1951 classic *Catcher in the Rye*, Elvis Presley became a symbol of youthful independence. By the singer's third appearance in 1957 on America's most popular variety show, *The Toast of the Town*, host Ed Sullivan defended Elvis as "a real decent, fine boy." The press began to stress his patriotism and how good he was to his mother. Estimates are that over 82 percent of the American viewing audience saw Elvis on the Ed Sullivan show—54 million people watched as the cameras shot him only from the waist up.

Fifty years later Elvis Presley would be esteemed by music critics not for his sensationalism but for the agility of his voice and for the variety and range of his ballads. The accusation that he borrowed much from African American gospel music and from black blues had to be understood in the same way that blending of cultural currents must always be explained in a country made up of complex energies. Elvis's rock and roll and rockabilly represented in music the integration of black and white folk cultures that the law attempted to bring about on the social level. Greil Marcus in his classic *Mystery Train: Images of America in Rock 'n' Roll Music* attributes Elvis's great popularity to the self-respect he offered people who were only on the edge of the new affluence. Marcus believes Presley managed to stabilize country music even as he pulled away from it. The power of his music stems from tensions. Although

Elvis was a rebel, he made it clear how impossible it was to break away from his roots.

If Elvis remained "king" after the 50 intervening years since appearing with Ed Sullivan, it may be because the tensions he communicated are still part of an upwardly mobile society. The country music Elvis Presley offered America in his own extreme forms continued to celebrate traditions people were losing in the decade after the war. To many, Elvis suggested how much Americans remained trapped by fate. Often his message seemed to be simply that his music passed on lost values from many different roots. Greil Marcus's belief that Elvis embodied "the bigness, the intensity, and the unpredictability of America itself" may well be true. Although many black musicians complained that Elvis stole their material, his African American audience endured.

It is easy to make fun of "amateur hours" like Ed Sullivan's. Fred Allen, a witty radio comedian who did not survive on television, said that Sullivan would stay on the air as long as other people had talent. But there was talent—a prodigious amount. In the 1950s Sullivan offered the public artists as varied as the violin prodigy Itzhak Perlman and the great black musical performers Ella Fitzgerald, Duke Ellington, and Lena Horne. At a time when black singer Nat King Cole could not get a sponsor for a television series because of his race, Sullivan made a vast audience aware that talent had nothing to do with race or ethnicity. As the nation's leading TV impresario for 23 years, Ed Sullivan shaped American values and taste. Money spent for music lessons and musical instruments soared from $86 million in 1950 to $149 million in 1960. During these early "golden years" Sullivan's Sunday night show brought families and neighbors together in living rooms to watch and discuss new talents.

Conservatives considered Elvis Presley's hips the most dangerous and subversive part of his rock 'n' roll act. Elvis "The Pelvis" was considered by some to be an example of social decline. Millions of others flocked to his shows and bought his records. His music helped to transform modern America. © Library of Congress.

How much television influenced national values remains a chicken-and-egg dilemma. The new medium allowed many Americans to appreciate for the first time the best of the national pastime as big-league baseball appeared on the screen. TV also exhibited cultures and countries never thought about in isolationist pre–World War II America. The video screen revealed aspects of nature never imagined before and expanded viewers' visions of what the global village contained. Such images could dispel fear (Kaledin, 18, 138–39, 165).

To read about music in the United States in the 19th century, see the United States entry in the section "Music" in chapter 7 ("Recreational Life") in volume 5 of this series.

FOR MORE INFORMATION

DeCurtis, A., and J. Henke, eds. *The Rolling Stone Illustrated History of Rock & Roll: The Definitive History of the Most Important Artists and Their Music*. New York: Random House, 1992.

Kaledin, E. *Daily Life in the United States, 1940–1959: Shifting Worlds.* Westport, Conn.: Greenwood Press, 2000.

Kenney, W. H. *Recorded Music in American Life: The Phonograph and Popular Memory, 1890–1945.* New York: Oxford University Press, 1999.

Marcus, Greil. *Mystery Train: Images of America in Rock 'n' Roll Music.* New York: E. P. Dutton, 1982.

Presley, Elvis. *30 No. 1 Hits.* CD, 2002.

UNITED STATES, 1960–90

Changes in sexual mores and practices were just one part of the interwoven forces that created an American culture quite different from that of a generation earlier. Rock music, with its increasingly explicit sexual themes, was another. Herbert London contends that "like the inscriptions on the Rosetta stone that solved the mystery of hieroglyphics, rock music provides a key record of the Second American Revolution that may unlock its inner logic." Not wishing to overstate the case, he adds that "rock is a spectator at the cultural storm, not its ruler. It may rekindle the ashes with a spark, but it cannot make the original fire."

Historians trace the origins of rock music to several sources. One was the rock–and-roll craze of the 1950s, featuring black musicians like Chuck Berry and Little Richard as well as white ones, including Elvis Presley, Jerry Lee Lewis, and Buddy Holly. The new phenomenon, writes historian Edward P. Morgan, "represented a merging of such traditional strains as black blues, jazz, gospel, and white country music." A second source, Morgan says, lay in "traditional folk music—protest songs from the labor movement, antiwar tradition, ballads, and folk-blues." By the mid-1960s, a gentler phase of folk music, with Bob Dylan, Joan Baez, and Peter, Paul, and Mary as leading artists, yielded to more critical variations. These variations reflected the alienated perspectives of the Beat movement characterized by the poetry of Allen Ginsberg and Jack Kerouac and the countercultural lifestyle of the 1950s that was called Beatnik.

As rock music evolved with its merged traditions, much of it expressed the political sensitivities of the civil rights movement and antipathy to the arms race with the Soviet Union. Performers also attacked what they regarded as repressive social mores. In other words, like music of earlier eras, it reflected the times. Although the majority of the population regarded the lifestyles of the rock musicians and their most devoted followers as countercultural, the ingredients of rock music gradually infiltrated the larger culture. That may explain why it became the subject of so much scholarly analysis such as that provided by James Haskins and Kathleen Benson, who, in *The 60s Reader,* outline three distinctive characteristics of rock music.

First, rock's sexually explicit lyrics revealed society's new sexual permissiveness. Those who found it offensive contended that its sexual themes also fed this permissiveness, something those who "dug it" could hardly deny. Second, not only did rock music belong to the youth culture, but the youth's elders could scarcely tolerate it. To them it seemed raucous and incoherent, its lyrics unintelligible. Television shows like *Hit Parade*, starring Rosemary Clooney and appealing to audiences across generation lines, disappeared. Third, rock broke down the barriers between white musicians and their black counterparts. By the 1960s, the new music, aimed at both blacks and whites, was well established, and a distinctive, affluent teenage market wanted more.

A "generation gap," encouraged if not created by the sound, lyrics, and staging of rock music, soon became a matter of concern to older generations. Indeed, Haskins and Benson say that "nowhere did that gap present itself more clearly than in the controversy over rock 'n' roll and over its most popular purveyor at the turn of the decade, Elvis Presley. He rode in a gold Cadillac, he dressed in gold lamé suits, he gyrated his hips so sensuously that when he appeared on television the cameras never showed him below the waist. Parents were enraged; young people were delighted. A generational tug-of-war resulted." Attempts at censoring rock music on the radio and banning rock stage shows failed to reduce its seemingly inevitable appeal to the younger generation.

Three developments of the 1960s proved wrong any thoughts that American performers would be unable to sustain enthusiasm for rock 'n' roll or that the appeal of its performers might wear thin. One was the enduring strength and adaptability of folk music. Continuing the tradition of Woody Guthrie and Pete Seeger (whose music had been inspired by social conditions of the 1930s and 1940s), Joan Baez, Bob Dylan, Judy Collins, and others, as well as groups like the Kingston Trio and Peter, Paul, and Mary, now appealed to millions with their songs of alienation and protest.

Poster for the Supremes, Motown legends, 1965. © Library of Congress.

The second was the arrival of groups from England, particularly the Beatles in 1964 and the Rolling Stones a year later, to be followed by others such as the Who. These performers, Morgan says, bypassed "the more tepid rock and roll imitations" and "reached back to the blues roots of rock and roll and figures like Chuck Berry. Together with a kind of working-class stance and each group's distinctive signature—the Beatles's path-breaking chord combinations and harmonies, the Rolling Stones's swaggering alienation—resulted in a burst of new energy in popular music." David Chalmers describes the appearance of the Beatles on *The Ed Sullivan Show* in 1964 as "electrifying." "Their well-scrubbed look, their Teddy Boy dress and the hair down over their ears, their wit, their ensemble performance that did not submerge the individual personalities, their compelling but not overwhelming acoustical beat, and their lyrics of love and holding hands created a powerful personal chemistry. They came across as real." The very power of the Beatles, Jeff Greenfield observed later, "guarantees that an excursion into analysis cannot fully succeed." Even so, he writes, "they helped make rock music a battering ram for the youth culture's assault on the mainstream, and that assault in turn changed our culture permanently."

The third was the success of Motown Productions, a Detroit-based music empire closely tied to the civil rights movement of the mid-1960s. Its success lay in grooming, packaging, marketing, and selling the music of black performers, such as the Supremes, to masses of white Americans. Using methods practiced by the Detroit automobile factories in which he had worked, its founder, Berry Gordy, according to David P. Szatmary, "ensured the success of the Supremes by assembling the parts of a hit-making machine that included standardized songwriting, an in-house rhythm section, a quality-control process, selective promotion, and a family atmosphere reminiscent of the camaraderie fostered by Henry Ford in his auto plant during the early twentieth century." The Temptations and other groups assembled later were all part of the Motown machine. The machine itself enjoyed success from 1964 until things came apart in 1967, but the sounds and the stars it got started continued.

The sudden burst in popularity of rock music should not obscure the fact that other forms of popular music—jazz, country, and traditional folk music, for example—also thrived.

As rock 'n' roll evolved in the later 1960s, many groups of performers sprang up, some of them attracting huge followings. Listing and describing these groups in any detail is unnecessary, but several happenings in the world of rock music demonstrate what an important part the performers played in the cultural transitions of the late 1960s and early 1970s.

Among the most striking was that a number of rock 'n' roll superstars—leaders of protests against "the establishment"—became big moneymakers. According to *Forbes* magazine, in 1973 at least 50 superstars earned an estimated $2 million to $6 million annually. Overlooked in this report, of course, are the sums earned by mainstream American businesses through production and sale of the superstars' records and promotion of their concerts. By the early 1970s seven corporations accounted for 80 percent of all sales, and those sales were enormous. In 1950, record companies' sales totaled $189 million. Five years later they reached $277 million. By 1971, sales of records and tapes amounted to $1.7 billion in the United States alone. In two more years sales stood at $2 billion (compared with $1 billion in network television and $1.3 billion in the film industry). That was only part of the story: In 1973 sales of records and tapes reached $555 million in Japan, $454 million in West Germany, $441 million in the Soviet Union, and $384 million in the United Kingdom.

The stars and superstars paid a high price for the money and adulation they enjoyed. Heavy performance and recording schedules and frenetic lifestyles, saturated with drugs and alcohol, sometimes ruined them. Janis Joplin, whose intense performances were laced with obscenities, died of an overdose of heroin in 1970. Jimi Hendrix, known as the most extreme acid-rock guitarist, was the victim of an overdose of sleeping pills in the same year. And Jim Morrison, whose dialogues with the audience were filled with raw sexuality, died of a heart attack in 1971, his body ravaged by the excesses of his lifestyle. Joplin, Hendrix, and Morrison were all 27 years old when they died. Elvis Presley died at age 42 in 1977, the victim of a dissipated life.

As rock music gained wider acceptance, not by moving closer to mainstream America but by drawing mainstream America closer to it, some performers gained critical acceptance with their distinctive styles and sounds. The lyrics of Bob Dylan, set to folk melodies, were ambiguous enough to express the protests of almost anyone. Mostly, though, the performances of his touring group, the Band, reflected the outlook of his own baby-boom generation. Some consider Dylan's style as marking the beginning of the use of the term *rock* instead of *rock and roll*.

Other performers helped extend the influence of rock music. As young people played the record albums of Simon and Garfunkel, for example, their parents picked up both the lyrics and the tunes. Perhaps they shared the performers' concern over the "sounds of silence," of "people talking without listening"; or perhaps they too hoped to find a "bridge over troubled waters." The Beatles had caught on quickly with youth in the United States, and they attracted older listeners by experimenting with exotic instruments, melodies from classical music, and sophisticated recording techniques, creating something called studio rock. Although the Beatles disbanded in 1970, their records continued to gain in popularity. Until the death of John Lennon in 1980, and even thereafter, rumors of a comeback persisted.

The wider acceptance gained by Bob Dylan, Simon and Garfunkel, and the Beatles, among others, displayed the adaptability of rock music and the swiftness with which it changed. The folk-based performers' style came to be known as soft rock. Some groups, such as the Rolling Stones, drew fans with a blues-based, hard rock style. In the late 1960s, as experimentation with drugs moved through the counterculture and permeated the youth culture, acid rock gained popularity with its dissonant, glass-shattering sounds. Jefferson Airplane and the Grateful Dead were the two best-known acid-rock groups. Also gaining fans in these years were groups modeled on Led Zeppelin, whose loud, blues-based music combined with a macho stage show was called heavy metal.

> *The Woodstock Music Festival and Art Fair was a well-calculated business venture.*

Consciousness-raising, a popular term in the late 1960s, was applied to almost anything that enabled people to see things in different ways. Rock music's main consciousness-raising events were the festivals staged by promoters in various parts of the country. Although those who attended—perhaps as many as 2.5 million fans between 1967 and 1969—often displayed boundless enthusiasm, media coverage of the biggest festivals attracted much unfavorable attention to the music, the performers, and the fans.

The Monterey International Pop Festival in 1967 was the first large gathering of rock bands and superstars. The event that let the whole nation know that a new phenomenon had arrived, however, was the Woodstock Music and Art Fair. Held in a large pasture in the Catskill Mountains at Bethel, New York, for four days in August 1969, it appeared to be an event of young people simply coming together for a good time. But it was not a spontaneous happening. Rather, like other rock festivals, it was a well-calculated business venture. It was planned by John Roberts, a young millionaire who had graduated from the University of Pennsylvania, and his partner, Joel Rosenman, a Yale Law School graduate. Working with Michael Lang and others who gave the event stronger connections with the counterculture, they intended to make money from the performances by rock stars but also from the sale of food and souvenirs (such as posters of the late Che Guevera, the revolutionary ally of Cuba's Fidel Castro who had been killed in 1967). They also sold movie and recording rights to the festival. One of the promoters observed that although those who came "fancied themselves as street people and flower children," he and his partners were in fact "a New York corporation capitalized at $500,000 and accounted for by Brout Issacs and Company, tenth largest body of CPAs in New York City."

Despite careful planning, events at Woodstock were so chaotic that no one was certain how many were there. Estimates ranged between 300,000 and 460,000. They came from all over America to hear acid guitarist Jimi Hendrix, folksinger Joan Baez, Jefferson Airplane, the Who, the Grateful Dead, and other rock stars and groups. Traffic jams were horrendous. Torrential rains accompanied by intense heat made mud bathing and nude parading a natural pastime. Shortages of food, water, and medical facilities contributed further to making Woodstock a mess. In the midst of the mess, loving and sharing went on everywhere, and everywhere folks were using marijuana, LSD, barbiturates, and amphetamines. Yet round-the-clock entertainment helped maintain a measure of orderliness—and even peacefulness. Supporters of Woodstock hailed it as an example of the better world to come. There were no signs of violence. Looking at it from a distance, mainstream America could not imagine a place for such things in their everyday lives. The generation of youth that thrived on such events wore the term *Woodstock* proudly. Others regarded it with contempt.

The Woodstock Music Festival and Art Fair had about 450,000 participants in August 1969. © AP/ Wide World Photos.

Four months after Woodstock, a rock festival at a stock-car race-track near Altamont, California, was the climax to an American tour by the Rolling Stones. With about 300,000 in attendance, promoters hired members of a motorcycle gang known as Hell's Angels to keep order. From the outset the crowd was rough and rude. When a naked, obese man climbed on the stage and began to dance, the cyclists triggered a melee by beating him to the ground. By the end of the festival an 18-year-old black youth had been stabbed to death, and three others died from accidents, drug overdoses, and beatings. If this, too, was the wave of the future, a sign of cultural transitions in the making, it was an unsettling one.

Nonetheless, the back-to-nature notions of rock music conveyed by the festivals continued to strike a responsive chord in urban youth. At the same time, a brief turn to a gentler, more reflective style enabled rock music to continue its progress across generational lines and into the American mainstream. The evolution of rock was not over, however, as blendings with folk, blues, and country music continued.

The big names in rock music in the mid-1970s included Elton John (the first performer to fill Dodger Stadium in Los Angeles since the Beatles had done so in 1966); Billy Joel; and Stevie Wonder, to whom Motown Records offered contracts guaranteeing $13 million over seven years. New performers occasionally hit it big. Critics compared one of them, Bruce Springsteen, to Bob Dylan, Elvis Presley, and Buddy Holly, claiming that his style demonstrated the power that had characterized rock music in the 1960s. Springsteen's appearance on the cover of both *Time* and *Newsweek* showed the mainstreaming of rock music. So did the sale of two million Elvis Presley records within a day of Presley's death in 1977.

The evolution of rock continued, with blues-based hard rock and heavy metal increasing in popularity. Punk rockers, most notably the Sex Pistols, took things in another direction, emphasizing rebellion and featuring such things as screaming obscenities and hair dyed orange. Pop rock offered a softer sound that was more appealing to middle-of-the-road audiences. Art rock attempted to mix classical sounds with rock and jazz.

Disco was another music phenomenon of these years. Regarded initially as dance music by black singers, it captured attention with *Saturday Night Fever*, a 1978 movie starring John Travolta. The Bee Gees's album of its soundtrack sold 30 million copies worldwide. Disco blended pop, rock, and black styles, accompanied by repetitive rhythms and dance beats. Discotheques attracted dancing revelers of all ages. Disco garb, including skintight Lycra jeans and dresses slit thigh-high, appeared everywhere. The disco beat filled the airwaves. Disco record sales zoomed upward. *Newsweek* described disco as "rhythm without blues; a body trip, not a head trip. It is relentlessly upbeat and unabashedly embraces the consumer society's latest trendy goods." Disco's popularity soon faded, but for a time it was all the rage.

Popular music—rock, jazz, soul, traditional pop, country, and disco—was big business getting bigger. In 23 countries, sales of recordings totaled $8.6 billion in 1977; the U.S. share, $3.5 billion, was 28 percent higher than the previous year. Sales increased by 18 percent in the next year. Revenues surpassed the receipts of movies, the theater, and professional sports, sometimes several times over. In 1979, however, sales spiraled downward by as much as 40 percent. One reason, the Recording Industry Association of America complained, was radio's growing practice of playing record albums without commercial breaks; this encouraged listeners to tape-record new releases on their units at home.

Contemporary music accounted for nearly two-thirds of the records sold. Who bought them? Not just teenagers, as some might have thought. Teenagers from earlier times had grown up and kept on buying. Three studies reported that in the late 1970s about 40 percent of the buyers were in their 30s and another 36 percent in their 20s; teenagers accounted for less than 25 percent of sales. Buyers of records spent large sums attending concerts, too, as big-name performers drew large, enthusiastic, and often boisterous crowds. The Rolling Stones, for example, grossed $13 million on their 1975 tour.

Stressing the moneymaking aspects of popular music obscures the fact that there were bands across the country playing in clubs and bars, and sometimes just for themselves, simply because they liked the music and they liked to play. Their musical energy found a good partner in the energy of the music.

Classical music offered another creative leisure activity, and concertgoing was popular, at least among older persons. Most symphony orchestras and opera companies, however, faced annual deficits, caused not by poor attendance but by high labor and production costs. In their 1976–77 season, the 200 largest performing arts organizations had deficits totaling an estimated $125 million. Some, such as the New York City Opera Association, were threatened with bankruptcy. After failing to reach agreements with its various unions, the association canceled its 1980–81 season, but two months of mediation and compromise made it possible to salvage part of the season. Similar problems shortened the seasons for the North Carolina, New Jersey, Denver, and Kansas City symphonies. Because admission receipts covered only a small part of arts organizations' costs, the more performances they gave, the greater their losses. These woes extended to the lives of individual artists, for whom chronically low pay alternated with unemployment. As performers sought to better their individual lots by demanding higher wages, they put in jeopardy the organizations with whom they performed.

By the 1980s, the rock music young people had found so appealing and their elders so appalling in earlier decades enjoyed a large measure of acceptance in mainstream America. Indeed, it became a standard feature of mainstream advertising. One reason is that the teenagers of the 1960s did not forsake their earlier tastes in music when they reached their 30s. Another reason is that rock music lost much of its shock quality. A third is that the varieties of rock music were so plentiful that persons who did not like one variety had plenty of other choices. The same was true of performing groups. Fans could love one and detest another. Consequently, variations of rock music thrived alongside country music; surf music; jazz; disco; and a new arrival, Jamaican reggae.

Music continued to be big business. Bruce Springsteen's *Born in the USA* sold more than 13 million copies within 18 months of its 1984 production, and his concert tour, lasting from July 1984 to October 1985, attracted some five million fans. Respondents to a *Rolling Stone* poll placed him first in six categories, and one of his singles, "Dancing in the Dark," earned him American Music Awards and Grammys. He was not alone among rock stars, as many others also enjoyed large followings.

On occasion, rock music became more than big business. Or, rather, it joined the big business of fund-raising. In the mid-1980s, Live Aid concerts featuring many of the most prominent stars and bands were broadcast by satellite to raise money through "telethons" in some 30 nations. People in need around the world benefited from millions of dollars raised by these events. In the United States, some Live Aid concerts were held for the benefit of farmers facing hard times.

British pop singers Phil Collins, left, and Sting are shown onstage during the Live Aid concert held at London's Wembley Stadium, England, July 13, 1985. © AP/Wide World Photos.

Rock music's lyrics, with themes of sex and violence, worried many. The National PTA and the Parents' Music Resource Center (a group based in Washington, D.C.) urged the Recording Industry Association of America to rate its records in a system similar to the one used for motion pictures. The association refused to do so, but it recommended that its members label some of their records "Explicit Lyrics—Parental Advisory." Such measures did not appease rock music's harshest critics. Allan Bloom, a professor at the University of Chicago, seemed to reflect their sentiments in his attack on rock music in his best-selling *The Closing of the American Mind*. He contended that rock music "has one appeal only, a barbaric appeal, to sexual desire—not love, not *eros*, but sexual desire undeveloped and untutored. . . . Rock gives children, on a silver platter, with all the public authority of the entertainment industry, everything parents always used to tell them they had to wait for until they grew up and would understand later."

Those who worried about rock music had more to worry about when rap became popular in the late 1980s. Initially rappers mixed bits of songs, repeated passages, and added rhythmic scratching sounds as background for recited lyrics, or raps. At first rap was a street phenomenon accompanied by acrobatic displays in break dancing and a hip-hop look featuring, among other things, fancy sneakers, caps turned backward, and heavy gold jewelry. Soon it made its way into recording studios, and by the 1980s it gained considerable popularity for its protests (typically as insults) against poverty, violence, and racism. Sales surveys found that the biggest market for rap was among suburban white youth.

Before the end of the decade the lyrics of several rap groups, such as Slick Rick and 2 Live Crew, drew sharp criticism for their explicit description of sexual organs and activities and for seeming to encourage violence against women. To many, the lyrics were offensive or unintelligible. When a sheriff in Florida brought an obscenity complaint against a store owner for selling records of 2 Live Crew, a U.S. District judge convicted the owner after months of hearings. The leader of 2 Live Crew and two band members were arrested and brought to trial, too, but a jury found them not guilty of obscenity charges. The jury foreman acknowledged that members of the jury found it difficult to understand the key piece of evidence, a tape recording of the performance that had led to the defendants' arrest.

The difficulties faced by symphony orchestras, opera companies, and composers suggested that classical music was no longer a central feature of American culture. Operating deficits were common. Listening audiences had never been diverse, but in the words of an anonymous administrator quoted by the *New York Times*, they were now "white, rich, and almost dead." Portions of their audiences were tired of the standby classical pieces by great composers of the past; other portions had no use for the avant-garde works of contemporary composers. Imitations of classical forms by contemporary composers did not work either.

Moreover, as younger generations matured they generally failed to replace their popular tastes, which were so different from those of previous generations of youth, with classical ones. Linda Sanders explained it this way in *Civilization*: "It was one thing for educated adults to tell hormone-crazed teenagers back in the 1950s that 'Blue Suede Shoes' was worthless trash. It was quite another for educated adults to try to tell other educated adults in the 1980s that blues, reggae, and minimalism (or, for that matter, the Beatles, Bruce Springsteen, and Prince) were either musically or spiritually inferior to Bach and Beethoven." Add to this the maturing generations' opinion that classical music was for the intellectual and social elite, and it is easy to see why classical music was losing its appeal and its audiences.

Technology also caused problems for performers of classical music. The intensity and spontaneity of live performances were unmatched, but if precision and purity were what mattered, these could be found by listening to compact disks through high-quality sound systems. For the price of a ticket, a music lover could purchase a couple of choice compact discs and listen to them repeatedly, without the hassle of attending a concert.

Performing groups therefore had to change their programming, the staging of performances, promotion methods, and general understandings of themselves. They had to find the balance between perpetuating a sacred classical canon and being a community center for the enjoyment of music and advancement of musical knowledge (Marty, 67–70, 120–21, 210–12, 283–86).

To read about music in the United States in the 19th century, see the United States entry in the section "Music" in chapter 7 ("Recreational Life") in volume 5 of this series.

FOR MORE INFORMATION

DeCurtis, A., and J. Henke, eds. *The Rolling Stone Illustrated History of Rock & Roll: The Definitive History of the Most Important Artists and Their Music.* New York: Random House, 1992.

Greenfield, J. "They Changed Rock, Which Changed the Culture, Which Changed the US," in J. Podell, ed., *Rock Music in America.* New York: H.W. Wilson, 1987.

Haskins, J., and K. Benson. *The 60s Reader.* New York: Viking Kestrel, 1988.

Kenney, W. H. *Recorded Music in American Life: The Phonograph and Popular Memory, 1890–1945.* New York: Oxford University Press, 1999.

London, H. *Closing the Circle: A Cultural History of the Rock Revolution.* Chicago: Nelson-Hall, 1984.

Marcus, G. *Mystery Train: Images of America in Rock 'n' Roll Music.* New York: E. P. Dutton, 1982.

Marty, M. A. *Daily Life in the United States, 1960–1990: Decades of Discord.* Westport, Conn.: Greenwood Press, 1997.

Morgan, E. P. *The 60s Experience: Hard Lessons about Modern America.* Philadelphia: Temple University Press, 1991.

Russell, K., dir. *Tommy.* 1975.

Sanders, L. "Facing the Music." *Civilization* (May/June, 1996): 38–39.

Szatmary, D. P. *Rockin' in Time: A Social History of Rock and Roll.* 2d ed. Engelwood Cliffs, N.J.: Prentice Hall, 1991.

SOVIET UNION

To begin to understand Soviet music, one must first learn about realism. The concept of socialist realism, first proposed by Stalin in 1932, was publicly introduced as the officially preferred artistic style at the First Congress of Soviet Writers in Moscow (August 17 to September 1, 1934). The idea was presented in a speech by Stalin's spokesman, Andrey Zhdanov, and was soon used as a wide net to snare all arts, including painting, sculpture, film, theater, and music. As interpreted by Stalin's regime and after, socialist realism demanded a "realistic," easily understood, unambiguous picture of life and human nature coupled with an unflagging optimism that Soviet humanity in all circumstances and historical periods was headed toward a Communist dawn with fingertips of rose. Socialist realism was only secondarily an artistic style; primarily it was a means of control, and therefore an opposing artistic movement emerged—formalism.

Formalism was originally a literary movement that began about 1914–15 in Moscow and St. Petersburg. Formalists studied art for art's sake; they were not generally interested in using the arts for political purposes. But after its appropriation as an official damnation in the early 1930s, the term was lavishly applied to avant-garde work in all the arts as well as in science and teaching.

During World War II, writers and other creative artists were expected to produce works radiating patriotism and hostility to the enemy. After the war had been won, the censorial emphasis returned to repressing those works and artists who diverged from socialist realism and other aspects of Party policy. Zhdanov led vicious attacks against artists perceived as subversive, denouncing such national treasures as Mikhail Zoshchenko, Anna Akhmatova, and Boris Pasternak. These and other writers Zhdanov labeled "anti-Soviet, underminers of socialist realism, and unduly pessimistic." Sergey Eisenstein and the composers Sergey Prokofiev and Dmitry Shostakovich were accused of "neglect of ideology and subservience to Western influence." Although Zhdanov died in 1948, the cultural purges he spearheaded continued until Stalin's death in 1953.

By the beginning of 1936, the young composer Shostakovich was a highly regarded artist whose groundbreaking opera, *Lady Macbeth of the Mtsensk District* (premiered 1934), was popular and critically successful both at home and abroad. But on the morning of January 28 Shostakovich officially became a "formalist"—a social and artistic outcast. The opening shots occurred via two *Pravda* articles; the first, "Muddle Instead of Music" (January 28), savaged his *Lady Macbeth* and accused it of "effete" formalism and other political crimes. Equally guilty of political-artistic blunders, according to the article, were all other avant-garde composers as well as music critics who praised their work. For Shostakovich's friend and mentor, Vsevolod Meyerhold, the article took an especially ominous turn by equating formalism with "Meyerholdism." *Lady Macbeth* was quickly pulled from the repertoire and did not reappear until after Stalin's death. Shostakovich withdrew his *Fourth Symphony* (1935–36) from a planned performance in case authorities might object to it also, but even that precaution did not satisfy Stalin's wrath against Shostakovich's music (of "quacks, grunts, and growls"), other avant-garde composers, and music critics who approved their work. Soon there appeared yet another *Pravda* offensive, "Falsehood in Ballet" (February 6), this one aimed at Shostakovich's music for the ballet *The Bright Stream* (1934), which was hastily canceled. Finally, as if to prove that formalist dissonance was everywhere, *Pravda* published "Cacophony in Architecture." Meetings organized for the purpose of denouncing targeted colleagues were part of a ritual that often preceded arrest. After the *Pravda* articles, the Moscow Union of Composers sponsored three days of denunciations of Shostakovich. Many arrests of composers and music critics followed, though Shostakovich himself was not among them.

By the 1960s, according to the Communist Party, there were essentially two kinds of music: "relevant" and "irrelevant." Relevant works were those with officially acceptable accompanying words, so that anyone could know the correct ideas the music was supposed to express. Contemporary Soviet music with no text, such as a sonata or a symphony, was irrelevant, and even when a piece was not banned, serious obstacles were set up that made it difficult, if not impossible, to get it performed. When music was performed without words, it was the reviewer's job to inform readers about the work's political implications. Given that the only way for any Soviet artist to earn a living and be allotted special privileges was to get commissions from the state, composers wrote music for government-approved words. Music with politically incorrect text would have to be tailored and adjusted. There were instances in which music was changed to accommodate new words, or chunks of music with offending words were simply amputated. Sometimes it was enough just to change the title of a work, as when Rimsky-Korsakov's *Easter Overture* became *Radiant Holiday*. If the offending words remained, they could be a serious obstacle to performance within the Soviet Union. Shostakovich's *Thirteenth Symphony*, which includes a choral rendition of Yevtushenko's poem "Babi Yar" (about a massacre of Kiev Jews during World War II), was unofficially banned in the Soviet Union for many years.

> *Soviet music with politically incorrect text would have to be tailored and adjusted.*

Although a certain degree of creative freedom was allowed to a few famous Soviet composers, such as Shostakovich, Khachaturian, and Kabalevsky, most younger Soviet composers were forced to write their cutting-edge compositions "for the drawer," circulating printed copies of their so-called irrelevant works, or performing them only among a select group of trusted friends and colleagues. Sometimes, to impress the rest of the world, the government sent outstanding music by young Soviet composers to international music festivals, even while performance of those same compositions was not allowed within Soviet borders.

Works by contemporary foreign composers might be performed if the composer had demonstrated a pro-Soviet bias, but those who left the Party or otherwise showed hostility to Soviet policies were classified as "bad" composers and their works were not performed. Soviet conservatories emphasized the classics and did not encourage an interest in experimental modern music. Upon graduation, each musician was given an "artist's certificate" good until the date stamped, which listed the works he or she was allowed to perform.

Music censors were often accomplished musicians with a conservatory degree. Besides censoring compositions, they also scrutinized lectures about music. Anyone who planned such a lecture had to first prepare a copy for the censors, who reviewed it and informed the author how it had to be revised. Lecturers planning to talk about Tchaikovsky, for example, might be advised to mention that Lenin heard the composer's *Sixth Symphony* in London, and liked it. Just as plays had censors in the audience to check the actual performance, those who spoke in public about music knew that censors would be listening to ensure that the talk conformed to the one the censors had approved. Every concert organization also had its "music editor" whose function was to meet with musicians ahead of a concert to ensure that the program would be ideologically acceptable, and that the musicians had permission to perform it.

The official path through the censorship bureaucracy was labyrinthine and slow, but, as in all other areas of Soviet life, there were alternate routes via personal connections. A patron with clout could ignore the decisions of underlings, give permission to get a new composition performed, and secure a favorite pianist a dacha, superior medical care, or an apartment with space for a piano. Top Party bosses who liked to patronize the arts and artists expected something worthwhile in return—the reflected glory of celebrity and the ability to get their own children, however untalented, into a conservatory. Maya Plisetskaya's relatives were honored Soviet artists; their prestige could not save her father, but it did rescue her mother from the gulag and exile in a dusty Kazakh town (Eaton).

Nonetheless, despite all the restrictions imposed by the Soviet government, radio and recordings allowed music lovers in the Soviet Union to stay abreast of developments in music elsewhere in the world. Since the end of the 1950s, foreigners had been bringing Western pop music, newspapers, and magazines into the USSR and these found their way into the black market, mainly in major cities like Moscow, Leningrad, Tallin, Riga, and Lvov. By the early 1960s, the demand for Western pop music was so high and so outstripped supplies of equipment for making records and tapes that fans ingeniously made crude copies of records with used X-ray film (bought cheaply from hospitals and clinics). A small hole was cut in the center of the film, the edges were rounded off with scissors, and, using special equipment, the grooves were cut. Music fans called such copies "ribs" after the images on the film.

In the late 1960s, the Beatles became both musical and spiritual gurus for many young Soviets, and by 1969 there were several thousand amateur rock bands in Moscow alone. At first, authorities made little effort to control amateur rock shows, though the government was not enthusiastic about such performances. But after some Leningrad fans rioted at a 1967 concert, Leningrad amateur guitar-vocal groups had to get authorization before appearing in public. In 1969, the state tried to co-opt such groups by inviting them to become, in effect, government employees whose performances had to be government approved. With their superior state-supplied equipment and numerous gigs, particularly in smaller towns and cities where they had no competition, these official rock bands enjoyed much popular success. There were notable holdouts, however. Boris Grebenshchikov, leader and songwriter of the nonofficial rock band Aquarium, became a kind of cult figure for many Soviet youth, and his Leningrad home became a place of pilgrimage. Staircase walls leading up to his eighth-floor communal apartment were covered with pilgrims' graffiti, such as "Boris you are life" and "We cannot survive without you." Signatures beneath the graffiti revealed the writers' hometowns—thousands of miles away from Leningrad. Youngsters waited patiently just to touch Grebenshchikov's hand.

As Western contacts, even before the advent of *glasnost* policy of the 1980s, punched more and larger holes in the iron curtain that had surrounded Soviet culture, more Western youth fads poured through—besides rock there was Zen, heavy metal, and break dancing. In the 1970s and 1980s, as Western technologies became ever more accessible, young people liked to gather in a friend's apartment or room to watch and swap music videos.

By the beginning of the 1980s, it became possible to turn a room or apartment into a workshop for creating tape cassettes. This process allowed the music of famous groups to be more easily distributed around the country, even though under Leonid

Brezhnev's regime (1964–82) most forms of rock were officially banned. Official intolerance intensified under Yuri Andropov, who became First Secretary in 1982 and who personally hated and mistrusted rock. The effect of the crusade was to energize the radical rock community. Over the next few years the prospects for freer expression seemed to grow. By 1985, Andropov and his successor, Konstantin Chernenko, were dead and Mikhail Gorbachev, the new Party leader, was about to introduce greater openness (glasnost) to outside influences. But popular culture never became truly free. The government always feared that rock groups and their fans would easily get out of control, so although the militia and KGB (secret police) allowed the rock community to exist, it was always being watched, regulated, and suppressed. Musicians and fans were subject to arbitrary arrests; concerts were broken up and equipment was confiscated.

KGB men were not the only threats to rockers and other Western-oriented youth (or the only stalkers with thin ties, for that matter). *Lyubery* were a gang of teenage hoodlums from Lyubertsy, a working-class suburb 12 miles southwest of Moscow, who from the early 1970s had been preying on their victims. Anyone with "chains or foreign badges . . . dyed hair or [who] brings shame on our country . . . anyone who looks or acts as a protester" was fair game for *Lyubery* violence, according to one 16-year-old gang member. Or as another gang member declared, "We come [into Moscow every night] to beat up punks, hippies, heavy metal and break dance fans." *Lyubery* stayed away from drugs, alcohol, and nicotine; practiced bodybuilding, boxing, martial arts, and weight training and dressed in a unique costume: white shirts, thin black ties, and baggy checkered trousers. Thus dressed, they liked to stalk city streets with their hands behind their backs. In many cases these gangs seemed to have the tacit approval and even the protection of police. There were similar lower-class suburban gangs in other Soviet cities, sometimes directed by embittered *Afgantsy* (Afghanistan war veterans) and sometimes by professional thieves who commuted into cities to terrorize and rob. The media reported on their transgressions or did not, depending on orders from above.

~*Joyce E. Salisbury*

RECREATIONAL
LIFE
|
MUSIC
|
United States,
1920-1939

United States,
1940-1959

United States,
1960-1990

Soviet Union

Japan

Inuit

FOR MORE INFORMATION

Dewhirst, M., and R. Farrell, eds. *The Soviet Censorship*. Metuchen, N.J.: Scarecrow Press, 1973.

Eaton, K. B. *Daily Life in the Soviet Union*. Westport, Conn.: Greenwood Press. Forthcoming.

Maltby, R., ed. *Passing Parade: A History of Popular Culture in the 20th Century*. New York: New Oxford Press, 1989.

Robinson, H. *Sergei Prokofiev: A Biography*. New York: Viking, 1987.

JAPAN

At the dawn of the 20th century, Japan's musical culture had only recently been refashioned in conformity with European aesthetics and performance standards. Impressed by the British military's use of music in the 1863 Battle of Kagoshima, the leaders of the Meiji government mandated the wholesale importation of Western instruments and music as part of its overall aim of achieving cultural parity with Western countries. Military leaders and education reformers emphasized the practical utility of Western music, rather than its aesthetic qualities, for realizing national objectives enshrined in the slogan *fukoku kyouhei* (rich country, strong military). Indigenous elite and folk music forms seemed ill suited to such purposes and were consequently dismissed as "barbaric," "unscientific," and "unmelodic," though they did in fact manage to survive.

At the end of the 20th century, Japan boasted a truly heterogeneous musical soundscape. Virtually every kind of ethnic, classical, folk, or popular music form had found an audience in Japan. Moreover, in contrast to the situation a century earlier, indigenous genres were thriving due to government support, foreign interest, a revised educational curriculum, and an experimental climate in which musicians working in diverse fields appropriated and incorporated elements from native musical systems into their music. Japan today is one of the most prosperous and inclusive music markets in the world.

Twentieth-century Japanese music is typically divided into three categories: *yougaku* (Western music), referring primarily to European art music; popular music, drawing on a variety of imported and native traditions; and *hougaku*, a catchall category invented in the Meiji era to designate all the elite and folk forms commonly identified as purely Japanese. But a great deal of cross-pollination has occurred across categorical boundaries: Takemitsu Touru (1930–96), best known as a composer of *yougaku* and film scores, frequently incorporated indigenous instruments in his compositions; Yamamoto Houzan (b. 1937), master of the *shakuhachi* (bamboo flute), has recorded several jazz albums; and Misora Hibari (1937–89) moaned her maudlin *enka* ballads (which many contend express the singular soul of Japan) over guitar and saxophone accompaniment. So, although in many tangible ways musicians in each of the three genres inhabit different worlds, there has also been considerable transgression of their boundaries, making for an eclectic musical climate.

The introduction of recorded sound technology early in the century and of radio broadcasting in 1926 made a musical smorgasbord available to Japanese audiences quite early in the 20th century. By the 1920s, consumers could choose from opera (Italian or Beijing), French *chanson*, Argentine tango, American jazz, Hawaiian hula, Russian ballads (e.g., "Katusha's Song" from the 1915 Japanese production of Tolstoy's *Resurrection*), Cuban rumba, or *naniwa bushi* (Ōsaka narrative ballads), to name a few. Even the Korean folk song "Arirang" was a hit record at the height of Japan's colonial occupation of Korea. Though many of these genres were actively suppressed as "frivolous" or "enemy music" during the war years (1937–45), no revival of *hougaku* ensued. *Gunka* (military songs) dominated the airwaves during this period, but the government also enjoined musicians to craft a new national music (*kokumin ongaku*) that would captivate a war-weary populace and inspire greater sacrifice for the war effort.

Predictably, the influence of American music (particularly jazz, country and western, and rock 'n' roll) predominated in the realm of postwar popular music, though

Latin American and Hawaiian music maintained sizable followings. Many musicians, in fact, made their living performing for U.S. troops stationed in Japan during the Occupation and the Korean War.

In 1950, at the height of this influx of foreign music, the government established the Living National Treasure system, granting special recognition to bearers of skills and techniques associated with "intangible cultural properties" such as music, dance, and acting. Musicians thus recognized include Yamamoto Houzan and Hayashi percussionist Katada Kisaku. Oral transmission of native vocal and instrumental traditions also continues via the time-honored *iemoto* (lineage-school) system, through which housewives and hobbyists can learn to play *koto* (harp) or *biwa* (lute). Recent curricular reforms expose elementary school students to indigenous music traditions as well.

Since the 1960s, popular music has become increasingly diversified, while the theoretically distinct realms of *yougaku* and *hougaku* have entered into sustained dialogue. Beatles-based "group sounds" were all the rage in the 1960s, but in the 1970s the more confessional singer-songwriter style known as "new music" (e.g., Chage and Aska) became popular. The phenomenon known as "idol singers," which made huge stars of rosy-cheeked if meagerly talented teenagers "discovered" in shopping mall talent shows, dominated the music industry in the 1980s, becoming one of Japan's most influential cultural exports to mainland Asia. Though its following continues to shrink, *enka* maintains cultural capital as the "song of Japan," elegizing rural hometowns, lost love, and strong drink.

Stereotypes suggest that the Japanese are technically adept but soulless musicians. Yet a number of Japanese artists—including conductor Seiji Ozawa, jazz artists Toshiko Akiyoshi, Sadao Watanabe, and Keiko Matsui, New Age keyboardist Kitaro, the Bluegrass 5, electronica composer Ryuichi Sakamoto, heavy metal's Loudness, composer and marimbist Abe Keiko, Branson fiddler Shoji Tabuchi, and girl punkers Shounen Knife—have refuted this image and earned international acclaim. Although reservations about authenticity torment Japanese enthusiasts of reggae and hip-hop, the motto of the Japanese salsa band Orqesta de la Luz—"Salsa no tiene frontera" (Salsa has no boundaries)—affirms the globalized, borderless nature of contemporary music making.

Music remains an essential element of everyday life in Japan, integral to religious festivals, socialization of children, commerce, and even crosswalk signals. Perhaps nowhere is the importance of music more obvious than in the modern ritual of karaoke, in which friends and coworkers take turns singing into a microphone over recorded accompaniment. Though some aspire to karaoke greatness, it is essentially noncompetitive and intended to facilitate amity and trust between participants. Greasing the wheels of commerce and fostering intimacy, communal singing has become an important vehicle for cementing social relationships, proving the enduring relevance of music to modern Japanese life.

~E. Taylor Atkins

FOR MORE INFORMATION

Atkins, E. T. *Blue Nippon: Authenticating Jazz in Japan*. Durham, N.C.: Duke University Press, 2001.

McClure, S. *Nippon Pop*. Tokyo: Tuttle, 1998.

Yano, C. *Tears of Longing: Nostalgia and the Nation in Japanese Popular Song*. Cambridge, Mass.: Harvard University Press, 2002.

INUIT

Music has a prominent place in Inuit culture, and traditional forms and styles exist alongside newer introductions. In the contemporary period, there are many different genres of Inuit music, and many of these tend to be regionally specific.

Traditionally Inuit music was vocal and the only accompaniment, if any, was a drum. The music had a particular cadence and rhythm, but the lyrics were the central feature of traditional songs. Inuit culture places great value on emotional restraint, and clever song lyrics, which were coded or satirical, provided an opportunity to express emotions and opinions that could not be stated outright. Historically, drum songs, often accompanied by dances, were found throughout the Inuit North, although in the early 20th century in many parts of the Inuit North, missionaries attempted to suppress Inuit traditional music as an expression of pagan belief. Recently, however, traditional drum songs and dancing have experienced a bit of a revival as a traditional Inuit folk art, and Inuit drummers and dancers have been invited to perform at folk festivals and at several international events.

Less widely distributed was traditional throat singing. Similar to a form of musical expression from Central Asia, Inuit throat singing was usually performed by women who used each other's mouths as sound boxes to resonate tones. Like drum dancing and singing, throat singing is also receiving institutional support and wider attention as a folk art. In 2002 a young throat singer from Nunavut, Tanya Tagaq Gillis, toured with the Icelandic pop star Bjork.

Contemporary Inuit music takes its inspiration from many different sources and may be classified into a variety of genres. These include hymns and other Christian-themed music, dance music, and political songs.

Missionaries were extremely successful in converting Inuit, and today most Inuit regard themselves as Christian. Greenlanders, especially, have been noted for writing hymns. For example, Rasmus Berthelsen (1827–1901) composed "Guuterput quisinnermiu" (Our Lord in Heaven), which is a Christmas standard in Greenland. Other Greenlandic hymn writers included Jonathan Petersen (1881–1965), Henrik Lund (1875–1948), and Pavia Petersen (1904–43). Several Canadian Inuit should also be regarded as hymnists.

Inuit adopted Scottish reels and jigs along with the fiddle and the accordion from the commercial whalers who fished in Arctic waters in the mid- to late 19th and early 20th centuries. This imported dance music, with its old-fashioned quality, is often treated as indigenous Inuit music and is still performed and danced to at community celebrations and festivals in the Canadian North. Viagat music, from Greenland, is another type of contemporary dance music. It was especially popular in the 1950s and 1960s and takes its inspiration from American country-and-western and dance band music that Greenlanders first heard during World War II.

Country-and-western music is extremely popular in the Canadian North, and several Inuit musicians there compose and perform in the country-and-western style. Their lyrics frequently address the experience of living in the contemporary North as well as social and political issues. Charlie Paninoniak (b. 1954), who has been called both the Inuit Bob Dylan and the Elvis Presley of the North, is a popular singer/songwriter. One of his songs, "I.T.C.," is about the founding of the Canadian Inuit political organization Inuit Tapirisat of Canada. Recently, Canadian Susan Argaluk has had commercial success both in and outside the North.

Greenlandic musicians since the 1970s have taken their direction from rock music trends. The Greenlandic rock band SUME released its first album, "Sumut" (Where To?), in 1973. The songs on it and subsequent albums by the same band expressed the aspirations of young Greenlanders for greater independence from Denmark. SUME and other bands of that period were part of the political movement that culminated in home rule for Greenland in 1979.

Guitarist Rasmus Lyberth (b. 1952) is one of the best known contemporary Greenlandic musicians. Many of the tunes of this self-taught musician seem to be based on traditional drum songs. He is a troubadour and solo performer whose lyrics include both political and romantic themes.

Since the 1990s Greenlandic music, especially, has become more internationalized. The song "Zoo inuillu" (Zoo and the People), by North Greenlander Ole Kristiansen (b. 1965), tells the story of a young man lost in a city and unable to escape. Greenlandic versions of techno and hip-hop have also found a following in Greenland.

~Pamela Stern

FOR MORE INFORMATION

Hauser, M. *Traditional Greenlandic Music*. Copenhagen: Forlaget Kragen and Ulo, 1992.
Roberts, H. H., and D. Jenness. *Eskimo Songs: Songs of the Copper Eskimos. Report of the Canadian Arctic Expedition, 1913–18*. Vol. 14. Ottawa: F. A. Acland, 1925.

RECREATIONAL LIFE: WEB SITES

European Basketball Web site: http://www.eurobasket.com
European Hockey Web site: http://www.eurohockey.net
International Association of Athletic Federations Web page: http://www.iaaf.org/
International Olympic Movement Web site: http://www.olympic.org/
International Soccer Federation Web site: http://www.fifa.com/index.html
NFL Europe Web site: http://www.nfleurope.com
Tour de France Web site: http://www.letour.fr
http://www.coe.ufl.edu/courses/EdTech/Vault/Folk/1900–1950s.htm
http://www.vor.ru/century/music.html
http://www.besmark.com/ww1b.html
http://www.ibf-uba-boxing.com/
http://www.filmsite.org/maltin.html
http://www.exencer.com/World/

8

RELIGIOUS LIFE

The human world is made up of more than the material and social environments that surround us. Throughout history, people have left records of their recognition of and longing for something larger than themselves, and this desire to transcend daily life forms the basis for people's religious faith. Religions have two intertwined components—belief and rituals, and the second derives from and preserves the first. Thus, through careful enactment of rituals, the faithful believe they can rise above the mundane realities of day-to-day life, and historians find that the study of religious practices offers a window into people's spiritual beliefs.

Religious beliefs have served to help people make sense of the natural world, from its beauties to its disasters. For example, an ancient Egyptian pharaoh (Akhenaton) and a medieval Christian saint (Francis) both wrote magnificent poetry praising the blessings of this world. In addition, the Buddha and the Hebrew scriptures' Book of Job both talk about the deep sufferings of this life. In these ways, religion has always helped people make sense of the world that surrounds them.

At the same time, religious rituals serve the needs of society. The faithful reinforce their social ties by worshiping together, and sociologists of religion argue that religion is the symbolic worship of society itself. Sacred songs, dances, and feasts have always served to bind communities closer together, and in these ways the religious and secular lives of the people mingle. This intimate relationship between religious beliefs, rituals, and societies makes the study of religious life a fruitful one. The complex nature of societies also yields complexities in religious beliefs and practices. Throughout history, we can follow the reforms and, indeed, the revolutions in religious ideas that have profoundly shaped our past.

Through the study of religious life, we can thus learn about how people viewed the natural and supernatural, how rituals organize people's daily lives, and how beliefs brought out the best (and the worst) in people. At the same time, we can glimpse the deep longing in the human souls that has generated some of people's noblest thought. In the 20th century, all religions shared an abiding concern about the present and future state of human affairs. However, for most of the century, rather than working together to find common solutions, people of different religions often fought. Given recent world events, this statement appears self-evident. In the Middle

RELIGIOUS LIFE

MORALITY

RELIGION

East and in other regions of the world, religious conflict was a common aspect of daily life. Yet religious fights have also been common within nations including India, the Soviet Union, and the United States. Americans tend to take pride in pointing out their ecumenism and their struggle for religious tolerance. Still, it is true that John F. Kennedy was not the first American Catholic to become president; he has been the only Catholic to be president. Old religious prejudices die hard.

Despite the conflagrations within religions and between religions, religion was critically important in the 20th century. It provided a basic structure to daily life. Prayers and rituals such as weddings and funerals gave a semblance of order in an increasingly disordered world. Religion also gave people access to ethical ideas. During the 20th century, so much of daily life changed that people's notions of what was right and what was wrong often were left behind. For example, by the end of the century, medical science and technology enabled people to live through terrible illnesses. And yet, often the quality of life for those who survived life-changing and life-debilitating diseases was inadequate. For some, the solution was euthanasia. But was this murder or mercy killing? How can an individual decide? Answers did not come easily. In fact, an investigation into 20th-century morality shows just how fluid and flexible ethical ideas were. Nevertheless, by the end of the century, human rights and natural rights were gaining increasing prominence. The difficulty, as always, was putting those moral ideals into practice for everyone regardless of race, creed, color, or religion.

FOR MORE INFORMATION

Esposito, J. *The Oxford History of Islam.* New York: Oxford University Press, 1999.
Ludden, D., ed. *Making India Hindu.* Delhi: Oxford University Press, 1996.
Marty, M. E., and R. S. Appleby. *The Glory and the Power: The Fundamentalist Challenge to the Modern World.* Boston: Beacon Press, 1992.

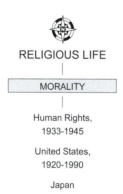

RELIGIOUS LIFE
|
MORALITY
|
Human Rights,
1933-1945

United States,
1920-1990

Japan

Morality

Defining and deciding what is right and what is wrong sounds easy enough. Most certainly, murder, stealing, adultery, and cheating are wrong in any culture. And yet morality is more complex than that. Reflecting on World War II, Walter Mondale, former vice president of the United States, remarked that the United States had failed the test of humanity by not offering more aid and comfort to the victims of the Holocaust. In short, the Americans were morally wrong in their *inactions*. The entry on the Holocaust provides two examples of this: the damned voyage of the luxury ship *St. Louis* and the Evian Conference. The former is more clear-cut than the latter. The Americans ought to have allowed the passengers of the *St. Louis* to disembark. Their fears and prejudice cost the lives of nearly 500 men, women, and children. Analyzing the Evian Conference is a more difficult task. Should Roosevelt have pushed more? What were the options? What were the political pitfalls? We can judge FDR in hindsight, but how accurate was his foresight? These questions point to the difficulty in deciding what was historically right and what was wrong.

Despite the errors in judgment and the terrible, perhaps unforgivable ethical mistakes, people in the 20th century struggled to maintain a moral life. What makes this century different from others were the new technological devices used in ethical causes. Some used radio and television to make an impact. For example, in the 1950s, Senator Joseph McCarthy used every means at his disposal to discredit and destroy the lives of people that he thought were Communists or Communist sympathizers. Among those who stood against McCarthy was Edward R. Murrow, who used his television news broadcasts to defend the innocent. He even managed to secure the reinstatement of an air force captain who had lost his commission when it was found out that members of his family belonged to the political Left. Television was also the medium of choice for certain "televangelists." Their weekly broadcasts drew millions to the faith and drew millions of dollars to their ministries. Despite the scandals of the 1990s in which certain ministers were caught cheating on their churches and discovered to have engaged in sexual affairs, television remained a major force for practicing Christians. Television also affected the moral sense of Americans by showing them events in the world and giving them more information with which to make judgments. Many have said that the Vietnam War was lost on American television sets before it was lost on the battlefields of Southeast Asia. Seeing the fighting as well as the body bags had a profound impact on the ways in which Americans thought about the war. In the end, most Americans decided that it was not a just war and agreed with their president, Richard M. Nixon, that a way out ("peace with honor," Nixon called it) had to be found. The television and other electronic media (such as the internet) did not change the fundamental moral questions of the 20th century, but they did make the ethical decisions more difficult in that they made both sides of the story available to anyone. Compare the entries on American and Japanese notions of moral behavior to how universal and how culture-specific ideas of morality can be.

HUMAN RIGHTS, 1933–45

Walter Mondale, vice president of the United States, once said that America in the 1930s had failed the test of humanity by not doing more to stop Hitler's war on European Jews. In other words, the United States (and the world) had not acted morally when presented with opportunities to stop the massacre and to fight for human rights. Two episodes demonstrate this clearly: the Evian Conference and the voyage of the *St. Louis*.

By 1938, it was abundantly clear to the Jews in Germany, as well as in the annexed Austria, that war, and worse, was in store for them and that they had to leave the two countries. Where they should go became the central question. In July, mounting pressure in the United States coerced President Franklin D. Roosevelt to call for a conference at Evian, an idyllic spot by the Lake of Geneva in France. Representatives from 32 nations met to determine what they could do to help the persecuted Jews.

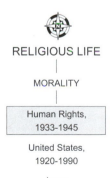

RELIGIOUS LIFE

MORALITY

Human Rights,
1933-1945

United States,
1920-1990

Japan

Both German and Austrian Jews had obtained permission to send delegates to present a grand plan for systematic emigration. President Roosevelt, who had called for the conference, did not assert pressure on the international community to receive refugees beyond their already existing plans. He was well aware of the anti-immigrant sentiment in the United States. The Great Depression, he reasoned, deserved his complete attention because it affected almost one-third of the population of the United States. Hitler, accurately sensing the lack of willingness for serious intervention by the delegates, issued a statement expressing the hope that "the other world" would aid the "criminals." He would do his part and put the Jews on "luxury ships to wherever." To underline his point, Hitler ordered the synagogues of Munich, Nuremberg, and Dortmund destroyed shortly before the conference convened. He was right. There were very few offers of assistance. Holland and Denmark were willing to extend temporary asylum to a few refugees, and the Dominican Republic made a generous offer to receive 100,000 Jews, but very few were able to take advantage of the offer.

Hitler expressed great satisfaction that the countries represented seemed in no way anxious to take in any Jews. Hitler was now convinced that the rest of the world hated the Jews as much as he did.

On May 13, 1939, 937 mostly Jewish passengers considered themselves most fortunate. They had booked passage on the luxury liner *St. Louis* destined for Cuba and freedom. They had been able to obtain American quota designations promising them eventual entry into the United States. In the interim, special permits had been issued to permit them temporary residence in Cuba while their American visas were being processed. A day before departure, however, the president of Cuba invalidated the landing permits, unbeknownst to the passengers and Gustav Schröder, the captain of the German luxury liner, who was a decent individual who did everything in his power to make his passengers comfortable. He removed a picture of the Fuehrer from the social hall of the boat and permitted religious services to take place, much to the consternation of some National Socialist crew members. When the liner arrived and docked in Havana, the passengers gathered on the decks and joyfully greeted relatives below. Soon, however, they and the captain were advised that they would not be able to set foot on Cuban soil unless they came up with an unexpected million dollars, a sum impossible to raise in spite of furious negotiations between the Cuban government and members of the American Joint Distribution Committee in the United States.

In desperation, the passengers sent a telegram to President Roosevelt, asking him personally for help. Captain Schröder also appealed to the U.S. government on behalf of his passengers. An editorial appearing in the *New York Times* expressed the sentiments shared by many: "We can only hope that some hearts will soften and some refuge will be found. The cruise of the *St. Louis* cries to high heaven of man's inhumanity to man." All to no avail. The decision to bar the refugees from entering the United States reflected widespread feelings against immigrants, something that was difficult for the passengers to understand. Did they not have the necessary quota designations?

On the return journey to Europe, the passengers could clearly see the lights of Miami. They also noticed a U.S. Coast Guard ship patrolling the waters. The passengers at first believed it was there to assist them, but instead it was making sure none of them jumped overboard to freedom. Captain Schröder did what he could; he even devised a plan, if all else failed, to run the *St. Louis* close to the Sussex coast of England, set the ship on fire, and evacuate the passengers ashore. In the meantime, negotiators from the American Joint Distribution Committee had worked around the clock to make arrangements for the passengers to enter Belgium, Holland, France, and England—a miracle of sorts, given the tensions of the approaching war. Propaganda Minister Goebbels was upset. How could anyone accept Jews?

On Tuesday, June 13, 1939, the world learned that the "wandering refugees" would not be returning to Germany. In Berlin, Goebbels ordered that the British and French governments be heavily criticized in the German press for "selling out to the Jews."

Only the 288 passengers able to disembark in England survived the war; almost all the others ended up in Hitler's death camps after the Germans invaded their respective countries. Captain Schröder, who had been so helpful, tried to make a living as a writer after the war. He used parts of his diary of the voyage in his writings. Some of the surviving passengers helped him by sending him food and clothing. They also spoke up on his behalf and helped to acquit him when he was put on trial under the de-Nazification process. In 1957, two years before his death, the West German government honored him for his important role in saving the passengers of the *St. Louis* on their ill-fated trip to Cuba (Soumerai and Schulz, 60–64).

FOR MORE INFORMATION

The Holocaust History Project. <http://www.holocaust-history.org/>.

Rosenbert, S., dir. *Voyage of the Damned*. 1976.

Soumerai, E. N., and C. D. Schulz. *Daily Life During the Holocaust*. Westport, Conn.: Greenwood Press, 1998.

Thomas, G., and M. M. Witts. *Voyage of the Damned*. New York: Stein and Day, 1974.

UNITED STATES, 1920–90

Moral philosophy in 20th-century America was the product of a complex movement both away from and toward the set of ethics developed in the 17th and 18th centuries. Thus, to understand morality in the 20th century, it is helpful to know a little about its origins. Initially, Americans, specifically in the British North American colonies, were quite hostile to moral philosophy. The Puritans had no use for it; they had the Bible and asked for no more. Moral philosophy was taught at Harvard with the aid of European textbooks. But the knowledge was distrusted. Writing in 1726, the leading Puritan, Cotton Mather, stated that "there are some very unwise Things done [presently]. One is the employing of so much Time upon Ethicks in our Colleges."

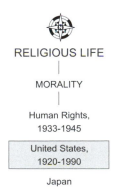

RELIGIOUS LIFE

MORALITY

Human Rights, 1933-1945

United States, 1920-1990

Japan

The 18th century saw a dramatic change in American moral thought. Influenced by English and French deists and freethinkers, Revolutionary leaders like Ethan Allan, Benjamin Franklin, Thomas Paine, and Thomas Jefferson adopted a kind of utilitarianism combined with the doctrine of natural rights. As Jefferson wrote, "Nature has constituted *utility* to man, the standard and the test of virtue." In other words, natural rights such as life, liberty, and particularly the pursuit of happiness provided the greatest good to the greatest number. The Founding Fathers were never quite clear in their moral philosophy and never resolved or fully recognized the tension within their ethics. They did not answer the question whether an act is right because God commanded it or whether God commanded it because it is right. In other words, do we have rights because God says so or does God say so because we have rights?

In the early 19th century, partly because of a religious revival, Americans began to reject the moral philosophy of the revolutionary generation and moved back toward a religious conception. The transcendentalists and other like-minded thinkers believed that moral truths or principles were not found through reason but by "intuitions of the mind," as James McCosh said. Following the Civil War, two new sets of ideas came to influence American moral philosophy: evolutionary ethics and idealism. Influenced by German philosophers such as Kant and Schopenhauer, idealism was the successor to transcendentalism. Such thinkers as Josiah Royce believed that what was right led to self-realization or the development of the individual's own good. Thus the idealist position was more egotistical than the utilitarians' view of good, which emphasized the idea that what was good made the greatest number happy. Countering idealism was a more empirical moral philosophy based on Charles Darwin. Thinkers such as John Fiske and Herbert Spencer, who were quite popular in the United States, argued that evolution in the human world promoted the greatest general happiness.

Social Darwinism and other evolutionary ethics as well as idealism were severely attacked in the 20th century as two other philosophies became important. The first was pragmatism, which defined good as the thing that satisfied desire and frustrated the least in the world. Pragmatists such as William James were challenged by noncognitive theorists such as George Santayana who further individualized morality. Good to these thinkers was in essence in the eye of the beholder. Ethical judgments were, in this view, expressions of preference that could be sincere or insincere, well-founded or ill-founded, and neither true nor false in the way that other judgments were. For example, a noncognitive ethicist would argue that the statement "killing is wrong" is only an expression of feelings and cannot be proven true. One can convince others of this sentiment, but in the end it remains a preference and not a moral absolute. Reactions against both pragmatism and noncognitive theory were strong especially after World War II, when moral relativism was shunned and challenged by the return of Christian morality. Protestants such as Paul Tillich and Reinhold Niebuhr, both of whom influenced civil rights leaders such as Martin Luther King Jr., blended Christian theology and natural rights. In essence they revived the kind of ethics that the Founding Fathers espoused but with a sharp focus on Protestantism. They defended natural rights, social justices, and democracy as

Antiabortion protestor Bob White of Attleboro, Massachusetts, right, shouts slogans at pro-choice demonstrators as the two groups of demonstrators converge in Boston, Sunday, October 3, 1999. © AP/Wide World Photos.

Jefferson and Paine had done, but these religious leaders added a Biblical urgency and justification. Thus when Martin Luther King Jr. spoke for civil rights he used Biblical imagery. In his final major speech, King described a "promised land" in which everyone regardless of color enjoyed their natural rights.

Martin Luther King Jr. and the new civil rights movement were not the only things that challenged America's moral sensibilities. Beginning in the 1950s, other developments such as the widespread introduction of the television reshaped American ethics. The presence of Edward R. Murrow on TV from 1951 to 1958 redeemed the medium from general accusations of narrow-mindedness. To his credit Murrow represented decency in an uneasy political world. He not only extended the vision of his audience, but he also managed to get one air force officer who had been dismissed for the beliefs of his father and sister reinstated. Guilt by association was acceptable to McCarthy. But Ed Murrow shared Marya Mannes's fear that television was not fulfilling its potential for good. He saw the medium being used "to distract, delude, amuse and insulate us" instead of opening and educating American minds.

Another effort to establish television as a source of moral education focused on the introduction of a variety of religious leaders. Big-time televangelism got its start in the 1950s. Billy Graham, Norman Vincent Peale, and Fulton J. Sheen all had their own programs. In contrast to 1940, when less than half the population belonged to institutionalized churches, in the late 1950s the 73 percent of Americans who identified themselves as church members welcomed religious television. In 1954, the same year that "under God" was added to the Pledge of Allegiance, a religious boom took place. On television the Catholic Monsignor Sheen, "sponsored by God," was so popular that he won a 1952 Emmy Award as TV's most outstanding personality. With a live audience of over a thousand, Sheen's show *Life Is Worth Living* reached another 25 million over the air to surpass Uncle Miltie for two years. At one point Sheen almost beat out *I Love Lucy* in the ratings game.

Televangelism—like most news broadcasts at the time—was designed to harmonize with broad institutional complacency. Television preachers focused on individual salvation, not on social action. The personal conversion they celebrated could ignore the poor that Michael Harrington wrote about and Dorothy Day served. Nor did the TV evangelists involve themselves in discussions of civil rights or nuclear disarmament. At a time when theologians such as Paul Tillich and Reinhold Niebuhr were struggling to articulate what the good life should be and how the skeptic could come to terms with fundamentalism, the televangelists of the 1950s offered easier paths away from Godless Communism. They did not challenge contemporary institutions. A 1954 survey revealed that 9 out of 10 Americans believed in the divinity of Christ and 2 in 3 accepted the existence of the devil. Pollsters reported that 46 percent of their respondents believed that the clergy were the nation's most useful citizens. The church seemed to be the one institution people trusted. Voters shared Dwight Eisenhower's belief that the American people would not follow anyone who was not a member of a church (Kaledin, 142–43).

To read about morality in the United States in the 19th century, see the United States entry in the section "Morality" in chapter 8 ("Religious Life") in volume 5 of this series.

~*Andrew E. Kersten*

FOR MORE INFORMATION

Commanger, H. S. *The American Mind: An Interpretation of American Thought and Character Since the 1880s*. New Haven: Yale University Press, 1950.

Frankena, W. K. *Ethics*. Englewood Cliffs, N.J.: Prentice-Hall, 1963.

Kaledin, E. *Daily Life in the United States, 1940–1959: Shifting Worlds*. Westport, Conn.: Greenwood Press, 2000.

Miller, P. *The New England Mind: The Seventeenth Century*. New York: Macmillan, 1939.

Redford, R., dir. *Quiz Show*. 1994.

Whitfield, S. J. *The Culture of the Cold War*. Baltimore: Johns Hopkins University Press, 1991.

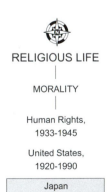

RELIGIOUS LIFE

|

MORALITY

|

Human Rights,
1933-1945

United States,
1920-1990

Japan

JAPAN

The ethical system of any nation is an amalgam of its philosophical and religious history. Because Japan's religious tradition is a creative adaptation of external influences, so is its morality. Korean Buddhist missionaries brought Confucianism to

Japan in the fifth century. It was inextricably intertwined with its cultural partner, Buddhism. The ensuing syncretism in the next several centuries added native Shintōist taboos and Daoist geomancy brought by Japanese pilgrims who journeyed to China in search of enlightenment.

A new layer of morality was added some eight centuries later by neo-Confucianism, which reformed the basic premises of Confucianism: cosmic and natural law governing universal human secular society. Humans were perfectible by educational development and fulfillment. The goals were social order and harmony, accomplished by adhering to natural laws of hierarchy tempered by benevolence and filial piety. What was good for society was ultimately good for the individual.

Neo-Confucians believed that laws were superfluous if leaders were moral and upright in the treatment of the people. Law codes were therefore rare, the leaders preferring to rule according to situation and communal needs. Rectification and rehabilitation were preferable to punishment. Miscreants were to learn and society was to benefit by resolution of every dispute. Justice was served when society restored harmony and order. Revenge and retribution hindered the recovery of harmony. Obviously reality mandated that feudal governments provide some order to the country, so regional "house codes" were issued specifying appropriate justice according to precedent. No national codes existed, however.

In the Meiji era (1868–1912) Japan experimented with Western morality, partially because of Western criticism inherent in the Unequal Treaties foisted on Japan in the early part of the era (1854–78). Japan codified its laws in hopes of revising those treaties.

A constitution (1890) was followed by a civil code (1898), and together with various commercial and criminal codes; they formed the basis of national morality. As the nation turned increasingly inward at the end of the 19th century in reaction to Western cultural imperialism, Japan's morality similarly shifted back toward traditional ethics. The government supplemented legal codes with imperial edicts that enjoined the people to practice neo-Confucian filial piety in personal relations.

After World War II, a new constitution in 1947 fundamentally altered the legal system, but the Japanese continued to behave communally and socially. Western social scientists have argued that Japanese fear the social shame that is imputed to them and their families more than any personal guilt for religious sin.

Obviously Japan is mindful of Western morality in its relations with foreigners, and many Japanese have been educated abroad. Judeo-Christian ideas have crept into Japanese ethical thinking, but the society maintains much of its traditional social and moral precepts.

~Louis G. Perez

FOR MORE INFORMATION

Davis, W. *Japanese Religion and Society: Paradigms of Structure and Change*. Albany: State University of New York Press, 1992.

Lebra, T. S. *Japanese Patterns of Behavior*. Honolulu: University of Hawaii Press, 1976.

ISLAMIC WORLD

One characteristic of Islamic life is its attempt to carefully preserve the moral traditions outlined in the Qur'an (or Koran, the Muslim Holy Book). See the Islamic World entry in the section "Religious Beliefs" in chapter 8 ("Religious Life) in volume 2 of this series for the origins of these traditions. Follow the traditions of morality into the 19th century in the Islamic World entry in the section "Religion" in chapter 8 ("Religious Life") in volume 5 of this series.

Religion

As a major facet of daily life, religion cannot be overlooked or underestimated. In a recent poll of Americans, over 95 percent stated that they were affiliated with or identified with a specific religion. Had that poll been taken in other areas of the world, the percentage no doubt would have been higher. Despite repressive governments that have tried to eliminate religious practice in places like the Soviet Union, people's need to believe in something higher seems to be a commonality without borders. The entries that follow explore several religions in a handful of regions. Take special note of the cross-cultural similarities and differences. In particular, focus on the ways in which religions impact individual daily life as well as society in general.

One thing that all religions have in common is that they help structure an individual's daily life. In the United States, during the 20th century, most Christians followed a similar practice. Although prayers were commonly performed before meals and before bedtime, Sunday was the day set aside for worship. This did not change significantly despite the growing competition from professional and amateur sports as well as family time. Most churches had similar kinds of liturgies and practices. Nevertheless, the differences among Christian sects were extremely important during the first half of the century. In particular, major fights broke out among Protestants over women's rights, the prohibition of alcohol, and civil rights. These fights died down from the 1960s onward as ecumenism (i.e., the promotion of religious unity among Christians) became more common. In the Middle East and Asia as well, religion provided a basic structure of daily life. For example, Muslims share basic fundamentals. They adhere to five pillars of faith and like many other religions, Islam has a common book and common prayers. Even in 20th-century India, where Hinduism was a major yet extremely diverse religion, there was basic commonality among all adherents. In fact, one could argue that these religions share similar ideas about devotion and daily practice as well as a deep concern for the spiritual present and future of the world.

In addition to bringing some basic frameworks to daily life, religion also impacts other aspects of society. In these entries, pay particular attention to the ways in which religion influences politics. Both in the Middle East and in India, religion plays an enormous role in political decisions and in government itself. During the 20th century, Islamic groups took control of various countries, including Iran and Afghanistan. Moreover, because of their demographic importance in large sections of the Middle East and Europe, Muslim citizens dramatically influenced government policy. The United States often appeared to be an exception to this trend, but in reality religion has always played a key role in its politics, too. This was especially true in the decades following World War II. Religious groups were intimately involved not only in elections such as the 1980 presidential campaigns but also in the creation of a wide range of policies that concerned civil rights, abortion, and school prayer. Perhaps at no other time was religion as influential during the century as it was in its last decade.

See also the entries on Latin America, Japan, the Soviet Union, India, and the Inuit peoples to understand the different ways that very different religions (or, as in the case of the Soviet Union, the official lack of religion) shaped and influenced societies across the globe in the late 20th century.

UNITED STATES, 1920–39

Religion played a role in most American lives in the 1920s and 1930s, but for the most part it was a limited one. Throughout the country, most people belonged to a church, almost always a Christian church and usually a Protestant one. The social investigators Robert and Helen Lynd observed, however, that membership vastly exceeded the number of individuals who attended services on a weekly basis or provided financial support. In turn, churches contributed little to community charities, far less than they spent on foreign missionary work. Questioning of dominant Christian beliefs was rare, but at the same time there was much, in the Lynds' words, "outwardly conforming indifference."

While church membership was taken for granted, choice of creed varied. Christian denominations prevailed overwhelmingly, with Jews the only statistically significant exception. The Roman Catholic Church, drawing primarily on the large 19th-century Irish immigrant population as well as more recent arrivals from southern and Eastern Europe and Hispanics in the Southwest, was the largest Christian denomination. A sizable Orthodox community existed as well among recent Eastern European immigrants. Two-thirds of Christians, however, affiliated with one or another of the Protestant sects. Baptists were especially prominent in the South, Lutherans in the upper Midwest and Northwest, and Mormons in the intermountain West. The largest denominations, the Methodists, Congregationalists, Episcopalians, and Presbyterians, could be found almost everywhere, though often not as the largest group in one location. The Protestant community was further fragmented by north–south divisions within the Baptists and Methodists and by the existence of numerous smaller churches that had declared independence because of some theological or other dispute. By the 1920s, Middletown, Indiana, a typical example, had 42 churches catering to 28 different Christian denominations (and one Jewish congre-

gation) for a city with fewer than 40,000 residents. People tended to stay with the church into which they were born and almost never switched to a different faith.

Despite doctrinal differences, religious practice shared many common features. Homes, more often than not, contained religious decorations, pictures, or artifacts such as crosses, crucifixes, or menorahs. Most families routinely paused before meals for a brief prayer asking that they and their food be blessed. Otherwise, religious matters were normally centered in the church. Clergymen reported that they visited homes at times of bereavement, when called upon to provide counsel, and often simply to stay in social contact with their members. Conducting prayer services in the home, however, was increasingly a thing of the past.

Sunday was the day most given over to religious activities. Religious education programs had developed over the previous half century; graded curriculums were patterned after secular education but centered on Bible study and were conducted by church volunteers. "Sunday schools" had shifted the focus of religious training from the home to the church. By the 1920s parents more often sent their children to Sunday school than attended services themselves, and male involvement on Sunday morning, though not uncommon, was proportionally least frequent of all. Two-thirds of the adults in Middletown's churches on a normal Sunday, the Lynds noted, were female.

Christian churches held services on Sunday mornings and, with declining frequency, on Sunday and Wednesday evenings as well. The extent of formal ritual varied, but congregational singing as a part of the service was nearly universal. Especially in Protestant churches, the minister's sermon was the centerpiece of the service. Ministers acknowledged that they devoted a great deal of their time to preparing their sermons, which for the most part dealt with the need for faith and conduct according to principles linked to the Bible. They tended to avoid comments on current affairs with which their congregation might disagree.

A Lutheran church service in Irwin, Iowa, in the 1920s. © National Archives.

Controversy within a congregation might be unusual, but differences among denominations and even within them were more common. The issue of alcohol divided Baptists, Methodists, and other firm prohibitionists from most Catholics, some Lutherans, and others who, largely because of ethnic background, were not opposed to drinking. Liquor, religion, and politics intertwined in 1928. Southern Methodists and Baptists became unusually outspoken in their hostility to Democratic presidential candidate Alfred E. Smith, a Catholic governor of New York, son of immigrants, and open opponent of national prohibition; these normally Democratic southerners threw their support to Smith's presidential rival, the prohibition-supporting Quaker Republican, Herbert Hoover. Northern urban Catholic voters responded by rallying around Smith. Religious tension and mutual distrust became a central factor in the contest that Hoover eventually won by a comfortable margin.

Race created other religious divisions throughout the period. Largely white Protestant denominations, principally the Methodists and Baptists, could count half a million African American members by 1940. However, 99 percent of them worshipped only with other African Americans in segregated congregations. Most African Americans, 15 times as many, in fact, belonged to their own entirely separate churches. Most of these were small churches in the rural South, but the largest Protestant congregation in the nation was Harlem's 14,000-member Abyssinian Baptist Church. Harlem was also home to the flamboyant mystic George Baker, who called himself Father Divine. He preached a strict code of conduct and attracted a large following among poor blacks (and some whites) who considered him God in the flesh.

Father Divine was not the only charismatic religious figure of the time. Evangelists who preached with extraordinary emotional fervor were popular, especially at the revival meetings that some churches held annually. Most evangelists were best-known within their own denominations, but a few developed national followings with the help of radio and large urban revival meetings. Ex-Chicago White Stockings outfielder Billy Sunday, perhaps the most famous, held revivals in, among other places, New York City's Madison Square Garden. Aimee Semple McPherson created her own Church of the Four Square Gospel in Los Angeles. In the 1930s, Detroit's Catholic Father Charles Coughlin gained a radio audience in the millions for broadcasts highly critical of the New Deal from his "Shrine of the Little Flower."

Among more conventional churches, the most noticeable distinction was whether they embraced a view of society conditioned by modern science or clung to older traditions of belief. The latter stance was coming by the 1920s to be called fundamentalism after a 1910 religious tract, "The Fundamentals." This widely distributed pamphlet advocated a literal interpretation of the Bible, including the creation story, the virgin birth and resurrection of Jesus, and the Second Coming. Fundamentalism was embraced by various theological seminaries as well as by a number of highly successful evangelists, including Billy Sunday and former presidential candidate William Jennings Bryan. It gained a large following particularly, but not exclusively, in the South and Midwest and other more rural and conservative parts of the country.

The most spectacular head-on clash of fundamentalism and modernism took place in Dayton, Tennessee, in 1925, after the Tennessee legislature, sympathetic to the fundamentalist viewpoint, adopted a law banning the teaching of Charles Darwin's scientific theory of evolution in public schools. A challenge to the law by the American Civil Liberties Union through Dayton teacher John Thomas Scopes led to a courtroom battle in which civil libertarian Clarence Darrow defended Scopes and the unrestrained teaching of science. William Jennings Bryan, defending the anti-evolution law and the fundamentalist views on which it was based, found himself called to testify as an expert on the Bible. Darrow got Bryan to express some uncertainty about the literal truth of biblical stories such as the creation of the universe in six Earth days and the swallowing of Jonah by a whale. As a result, fundamentalism came in for much ridicule in more modern circles. Scopes, however, was convicted, the Tennessee law remained in place, and fundamentalist views held firm in more conservative areas of the country. The highly publicized *Tennessee v. Scopes* trial deepened the rift between modernists and fundamentalists, leaving each side thinking the other not merely thoroughly mistaken but actively hostile to the truth.

For most Americans, however, religion did not involve such intense disputes over theology and civil liberty. Instead, it consisted of a general approval of things as they were, with success explained as a reward for virtue and difficulty as a test of character. The contented pro-business views of dominant Protestantism were reflected in Bruce Barton's 1925 book, *The Man Nobody Knows*, which quickly became one of the decade's best sellers. Barton depicted Jesus as a dynamic leader "who picked up twelve men from the bottom ranks of business and forged them into an organization that conquered the world," a swell guy anyone would enjoy knowing and following.

Townspeople leave a church service in El Cerrito, New Mexico, ca. 1920s. © National Archives.

Dominant American Christianity involved learning Bible stories and memorizing verses of Scripture as a child; holding some general but not deeply examined religious beliefs; and participating in church rituals of baptism, marriage, and death. Not only were Sunday schools and "vacation Bible schools" common, but public schools routinely conducted brief prayers and hosted activities by the YMCA and other religious groups. No wonder that when the Lynds surveyed high school juniors and seniors in Middletown they found that 83 percent of boys and 92 percent of girls agreed that Christianity was the one true religion; of the balance, as many expressed uncertainty as rejected this view. Perhaps a better measure of the depth of these beliefs was that 58 percent of males and 68 percent of females agreed that the Bible was a sufficient guide to all the problems of modern life, whereas only 26 percent of boys and 20 percent of girls disagreed; the balance of respondents were uncertain (Kyvig, 128–32).

To read about religion in the United States in the 19th century, see the United States entry in the section "Religion" in chapter 8 ("Religious Life") in volume 5 of this series.

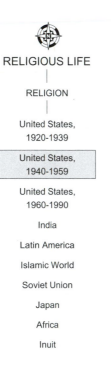

RELIGIOUS LIFE

RELIGION

United States, 1920-1939

United States, 1940-1959

United States, 1960-1990

India

Latin America

Islamic World

Soviet Union

Japan

Africa

Inuit

FOR MORE INFORMATION

Barton, B. *The Man Nobody Knows*. Indianapolis: Bobbs-Merrill, 1925.

Kyvig, D. E. *Daily Life in the United States, 1920–1939: Decades of Promise and Pain*. Westport, Conn.: Greenwood Press, 2002.

Lynd, R. S., and H. M. Lynd. *Middletown: A Study in Modern American Culture*. New York: Harcourt, Brace, and World, 1929.

Marty, M. E. *Pilgrims in Their Own Land: 500 Years of Religion in America*. Boston: Little, Brown, 1984.

Marty, M. E., and R. S. Appleby. *The Glory and the Power: The Fundamentalist Challenge to the Modern World*. Boston: Beacon Press, 1992.

UNITED STATES, 1940–59

Notable institutional changes took place within the religious establishments in the years 1940 to 1950. Americans felt the need to protect their children from "Godless Communism." It was a time when atheists and agnostics were fired from jobs with the same gusto that earlier inspired anti-Communists to take work away from liberals. An American skeptic, Elinor Goulding Smith, published an article in *Harper's* magazine in 1956 titled "Won't Somebody Tolerate Me?" Smith could not believe the extent of hostility she experienced as an agnostic in the cold war. She felt it her duty to champion respect for diversity of opinion.

The rise in church membership during the 1950s astonished those who identified America with the Enlightenment spirit that defined the Founding Fathers. During his administration Eisenhower even had himself baptized in the White House. In 1954, inspired by Eisenhower's minister, Congress added the words "under God" to the Pledge of Allegiance to the United States. And, beginning in 1955, "In God We Trust" was engraved on all U.S. currency. Statistics revealed that although only 49 percent of Americans were church members in 1940, just before the war, membership rose to 55 percent in 1950. And by 1959 an all-time high of 69 percent of polled Americans acknowledged church membership. The generalized breakdown was 66 percent Protestant, 26 percent Catholic, and 3 percent Jewish No other Western culture was so religious.

In 1952 the Revised Standard Version of the Bible sold 26.5 million copies in its first year of publication. For two years in a row—1953 and 1954—it was on the bestseller list. The religious enthusiasm of the 1950s, unlike that in other periods of American history, involved every class and economic division. A 1954 survey revealed that four out of five people would not vote for an atheist for president, and 60 percent would not permit a book by an atheist to remain in a public library.

Will Herberg's popular book *Protestant-Catholic-Jew: An Essay in American Religious Sociology (1955–1960)* characterized the spiritual mood as "religiousness without religion." He saw the new affiliations not as a way of reorienting life to God but as a way to sociability. Churches provided social communities for a nation of uprooted individuals. What might be more disillusioning about the 1950s was the degree to which American religion—committed to fighting the materialism of Communism—was also involved with marketing itself. In 1957 Billy Graham, an enormously popular evangelical preacher, reported a $1.3 million budget, a tremendous amount for the time.

Television provided a new arena for evangelism. Billy Graham, Fulton J. Sheen, and Oral Roberts became important leaders in the religious cold war. Norman Vincent Peale sold over two million copies of *The Power of Positive Thinking* by 1955; Joshua Loth Liebman's *Peace of Mind* found thousands of readers beyond his own Jewish community. In California a drive-in church—"pews from Detroit"—matched the excitement of drive-in movies and fast foods. A dial-a-prayer service offered solace for those who could not get out. Religious movies such as *The Robe* (1953), *The Silver Chalice* (1954), and *The Ten Commandments* (1956) dramatized Christian struggles in terms easily translated into cold war images. Spiritual biographies such as Catherine Marshall's *A Man Called Peter* (1952) and Jim Bishop's *The Day Christ Died* (1957) provided personal inspiration.

J. Edgar Hoover's minister preached that Communism was really just secularism on the march. Detective fiction writer Mickey Spillane quit writing corpse-strewn best sellers to become a Jehovah's Witness. The well-endowed actress Jane Russell called the Lord a "livin' doll," Elvis Presley offered up a special Christmas record, and the notorious gangster Mickey Cohen joined Billy Graham's crusade for Christ. Commitment did not have to be associated with any special religion. Nor did religious choice necessarily involve social action. The focus, as in all else during the decade, was on the individual family—the personal, not the civic. A popular slogan claimed that "the family that prays together stays together." Both Billy Graham and Norman Vincent Peale discouraged social activism, too readily identified with socialism.

Socially committed groups like the Catholic Worker people and the Quakers called attention to the needy. And the black civil rights workers depended on African American churches and ministers as much as on lawyers to back their efforts toward change. For many, peace of soul and mind still centered around ideas of patriotism and community.

In the Levittown Herbert Gans described, 13 houses of worship—including two synagogues—sprang up during the first two years. Controlled by outside organizations, these religious establishments met local social needs by providing nursery schools, couples' clubs, and associations to bring about political changes. Gans saw no social hierarchies among churches. A Levittowner described the most common attitude: "Religious differences aren't important as long as everyone practices what he preaches."

Memories of the Depression and World War II and nightmares of the Holocaust and the H-bomb made the turn to religion often more than just social or material. The great power of the African American churches during this decade demands ongoing respect and study. In his recent detailed work on the civil rights movement, *The Children*, David Halberstam pays special homage to James Lawson, admitted to Vanderbilt Divinity School in 1959 in a token gesture. Along with John Lewis and James Bevel, Lawson helped connect religious faith—as Martin Luther King had—with social justice. He taught his followers to move beyond the passivity of their elders, yet to remain nonviolent as they became the next decade's "freedom riders." Black preachers spread their deep religion among people risking their lives for a better society, not for easy salvation. But they too were often invisible at the time.

Women denied access to power through careers and institutions also began to play a greater policy-making role in organized religion. Their great enrollment as church members demanded attention on other levels. As early as 1951 the first woman Methodist minister was ordained. And women deacons were encouraged by Southern Presbyterians to help in the fight against Communism. Mary Lyman, ordained a Congregational minister in 1950, became the first woman to hold a faculty chair at Union Theological Seminary. Before her retirement as dean of women students in 1955 she played a vigorous advocacy role for other women in the ministry. She also wrote about women's concerns for international accords through the World Council of Churches in a 1956 book, *Into All the World*. In 1957 New York City boasted its first woman Presbyterian minister, and also its first Episcopalian "vestry person."

On the West Coast, Georgia Harkness of the Pacific School of Religion published three books during the 1950s emphasizing Christianity's need to create greater meaning for the people in the pews, a belief designed to make better use of women's social gifts. Edith Lowry—an example of such outreach as a Protestant minister to migrant workers—in 1950 took over the directorship of the Home Mission for the National Council of Churches. "Golden Rule Christians" emerged in many church organizations to guide members toward ethics—lived religion—in everyday life (Kaledin, 111–13).

To read about religion in the United States in the 19th century, see the United States entry in the section "Religion" in chapter 8 ("Religious Life") in volume 5 of this series.

FOR MORE INFORMATION

Barton, B. *The Man Nobody Knows*. Indianapolis: Bobbs-Merrill, 1925.

Herberg, W. *Protestant-Catholic-Jew: An Essay in American Religious Sociology*. Garden City, N.Y.: Doubleday, 1955.

Kaledin, E. *Daily Life in the United States, 1940–1959: Shifting Worlds*. Westport, Conn.: Greenwood Press, 2000.

Marty, M. E. *Pilgrims in Their Own Land: 500 Years of Religion in America*. Boston: Little, Brown, 1984.

UNITED STATES, 1960–90

A revival of interest in religion as the 1960s approached was another sign that many had come to regard religion as a commodity to be chosen or disregarded according to the needs of their daily lives. Church membership and participation were less likely than in the past to be traditions continued from generation to generation. In the later 1950s, church membership increased at a rate slightly higher than the growth of the population, reaching an all-time high in 1960. Nearly two-thirds of the population claimed to be church members.

Did increases in membership mean that church-related activities were a part of the daily life of large numbers of Americans? Polls taken in the 1960s revealed a relatively high measure of participation, but the picture was mixed. A Louis Harris poll in 1965, for example, showed that roughly half the U.S. population claimed to attend church weekly. The numbers for Protestants were substantially lower than for Catholics. Another poll reported that regular weekly church attendance declined from 49 percent in 1958 to 45 percent in 1965. A third poll indicated that in 1957, 69 percent of those polled believed the influence of religion was growing, but that figure dropped to 33 percent in 1965. In fact, 45 percent thought religion's influence was declining.

Numbers aside, religious ferment in these years was noteworthy. A spirit of ecumenism, that is, of promoting unity among religions, became evident. At the very least, interdenominational rivalries cooled. The editor of a Lutheran periodical probably spoke for many when he wrote near the end of 1963 that "some of the expressions Protestants have long been using about Roman Catholics will necessarily and in all fairness have to be drastically qualified. Wince though we might at first, we

RELIGIOUS LIFE

RELIGION

Members of the Christian group called "Children of God" sing before sitting down for lunch at their headquarters in Los Angeles. © AP/Wide World Photos.

won't be able to escape thinking and speaking of Romans in much more deliberate and 'defrosted' tones."

Nonetheless, although desires for unity led to discussion of mergers and collaborative efforts, church denominations maintained their identities and distinctive practices. Individual members did not witness sweeping changes in their own places of worship. To a greater extent than their churches' leaders, they had probably always been more open to acceptance of religious pluralism—that is, to the sense that rivalries between denominations were self-defeating. Supporters of pluralism believed that allowing the free practice of religion and avoiding the concentration of power and authority in one church was in accord with American ideals and preserved the freedom of all.

Sometimes powerful forces caused church members to ignore denominational lines. Protestants, no matter what their formal affiliations were or their views on evangelist Billy Graham's methods or message, could not ignore him or the movement he represented. In the years following his huge rally in Madison Square Garden in New York in 1957, Graham intertwined his message of the Christian Gospel with expressions of faith in American progress. The fact that he became a favorite of presidents and the news media helped to establish him as an important public figure. At the same time, his rallies broadcast over television brought him into the private lives of millions of Americans. Other evangelists built followings by emulating Graham. Going further, adapting their preaching styles to the settings of show business, these "televangelists" carried on lucrative ministries.

The work of Father John Courtney Murray, the principal figure in leading American Catholics to understand the meaning of religious freedom, prepared them for the changes in Church practices that were to come from the Second Vatican Council. The council, held in Rome in four sessions between 1962 and 1965, was convened by Pope John XXIII to reassess the role of the Church in the modern world. Continued by his successor, Pope Paul VI, the council issued a number of documents, the most important for American Catholics being the Declaration of Religious Liberty. This document asserted one's right not to be coerced by individuals or society into acting contrary to one's conscience or into not following one's conscience in religious matters. By this time, the election of a Roman Catholic to the presidency of the United States and the conduct in office by John F. Kennedy had persuaded many Americans that Catholicism was no threat to American democracy.

As Pope John XXIII intended, the council "threw open the windows" of the Church. Changes in practices among American Catholics resulting from the council were striking. Regular attendance at Mass remained an integral part of life for many Catholics, but after November 29, 1964, priests offered the liturgy in English rather than Latin. Removal of restrictions in everyday life, such as one prohibiting the eating of meat on Fridays, gave Catholics a greater sense of being in mainstream America. So did the Church's softened opposition to easing civil divorce laws. At the same time, the Church's official opposition to the use of contraceptives of any kind—affirmed formally by Pope Paul VI in 1968 in the encyclical *Humanae Vitae*—kept it at odds with Catholics and non-Catholics who accepted birth control as morally right. Also at odds with the Church were those who advocated birth control because of fears that a "population bomb" would explode if growth was not kept under control.

The Vatican Council's Declaration on the Church's Relations with Non-Christian Religions had considerable significance for Jews as well as Catholics. It condemned displays of anti-Semitism and denounced all prejudice and discrimination on the basis of race, religion, nationality, or tribe. Will Herberg, author of *Protestant-Catholic-Jew*, helped Jews come to understand and strengthen their place in the religious scene in America. At the same time, their assimilation into the cultural mainstream posed a threat to their distinctive identity, as wartime and postwar Jewish immigrants established themselves in America and joined migrations to suburbs, leaving behind their enclaves in the city. So too did the growing frequency of interfaith marriages. Jewish leaders recognized that even though the practice of religion among Jews as measured by synagogue attendance and religious observances in their homes was minimal, their identity was inherently associated with religion. Consequently they encouraged establishment of Hebrew day schools and after-school religious studies programs. Nearly two-thirds of the nation's one million Jewish children engaged in formal study of religion. Jewish leaders also supported efforts to increase the number of programs in Jewish studies in American colleges and universities. The number of such programs increased from 10 to 70 in the 20 years preceding 1965.

Jewish leaders also participated in interfaith conferences aimed at combating prejudice and implementing the Vatican Council's Declaration on the Church's Relations with Non-Christian Religions. These conferences affirmed the acceptance of Jews in the trio of faiths Herberg had described in *Protestant-Catholic-Jew*. Mainstream Protestants began to purge their Sunday school materials of portions that seemed to justify anti-Semitism. As Protestants, Catholics, and Jews gradually felt more secure in the pluralistic religious scene, they were more ready to accept into it believers in Islam, Buddhism, and other religions.

Perhaps religious denominations lowered their voices in speaking of one another because they recognized the need to work together against forces in American life that ran contrary to beliefs they shared. The leadership that black churches in the South provided in civil rights struggles compelled their white counterparts to examine their own teachings and practices. Such self-examination almost always led to formal and informal support of those seeking an end to racial segregation.

Some church members believed that decisions of the U.S. Supreme Court in 1962 (*Engel v. Vitale*) and 1963 (*School District of Abington Township v. Schemp*) finding school-sponsored prayer and devotional Bible reading in public schools to be unconstitutional were signs of the power of antireligious forces. In the first case (involving the recitation of a prayer composed by the New York Board of Regents) Justice Hugo Black, writing the opinion for the majority, observed that the daily classroom invocation of God's blessings as prescribed in the prayer was a religious activity. The opinion stated the following:

[W]e think that the Constitutional prohibition against laws respecting an establishment of religion must at least mean that in this country it is no part of the business of the government to compose official prayers for any group of the American people to recite as a part of a religious program carried on by government. . . . When the power, prestige and financial support of government is placed behind a particular religious belief, the indirect coercive pressure upon religious minorities to conform to the prevailing officially approved religion is plain.

So intense in some quarters was the reaction that U.S. Congress held hearings on a proposed amendment to the Constitution that would permit such religious activities. In these hearings and in additional statements by church leaders, it became clear that there were good reasons for drawing a line between private and public devotional practices. Mainly, it protected children from having imposed on them teachings that were at odds with their own beliefs. Besides, the greater forces in the secularization of America were found in the commercial and entertainment worlds, and they were not likely to be turned back by reinstatement of school-sponsored prayers and devotional Bible readings in the schools.

Matters of faith and practice cannot be ignored if we wish to understand everyday life in the late 1960s and early 1970s. Jewish children had bar mitzvahs and bat mitzvahs, Christian children celebrated first communion and confirmation, and Muslims learned early in life the place of prayer in their daily routines. Hundreds of religious bodies flourished. Leaders continued to strive for church unity, even though their efforts had few discernible effects on individual lives. Similarly, they advocated positions on social issues of war and peace, racial and civil strife, economic justice, and world hunger, but except for activists in their midst, church members often failed to support or even accept those positions.

Many Americans found inspiration, guidance, and fellowship in their churches, synagogues, mosques, and meetinghouses, but because these were human institutions, they were also places for contests over doctrine and practice and disputes over budgets, programs, personnel, and facilities. Many longtime church members could recount strife with fellow members in their congregations, and official and unofficial schisms within denominations were common. That may explain why many who claimed to have religious convictions had no formal religious affiliations and why polling data on church membership and attendance fluctuated.

In 1967, Gallup polls showed that 98 out of every 100 Americans had a preference for some church. About two-thirds called themselves Protestants and one-fourth said they were Catholics. Jews accounted for 3 percent, and "all others" the same. The slight changes in the next eight years might lead one to believe that not much changed in the world of religion, in that the total expressing some preference dropped by only

> *There were other signs of an uncertain future for religion.*

four percentage points. The numbers claiming to be Protestant or Jewish declined slightly, and Catholic and "all other" preferences showed slight increases.

But as early as 1968, evidence was beginning to grow that the American people were pessimistic about the state of religion and morality. A Gallup poll that year showed that 50 percent of those polled believed life was "worse" as far as religion was concerned, and 78 percent said morals were declining. A series of five polls conducted over a period of 11 years showed a decided increase in the number of persons who saw religion's influence as waning. The 67 percent in the polling sample who believed religious influence was diminishing matches almost exactly the 69 percent in 1957 who saw it as increasing. Between 1968 and 1970 the respondents believing religious influence was being lost increased from 67 to 75 percent. However, by 1974 that figure had dropped all the way down to 56 percent, confirming notions that these were years of real uncertainty about the status of religion.

There were other signs of an uncertain future for religion. Total attendance in churches and synagogues declined, reaching the point where only 4 in 10 claimed to be regular churchgoers. Whereas regular church attendance reported by Protestants declined from 39 to 37 percent during these years, among Catholics the decline was from 66 to 55 percent. Financial contributions also declined, and, measured in constant dollars, money spent on church construction decreased in five years by more than one-third from the $1 billion spent on it in 1970. Yet another worrisome matter was a sharp decline in the numbers of persons studying in seminaries to be pastors and priests.

One explanation for the uncertain state of church membership lies in changes in the age distribution within the population. The disproportionately youthful population apparently felt less need for religious affiliations, or perhaps they believed churches failed to serve their needs. Changes in family structures and commitments and increased demands on family time also had affected involvement in religious activities. Some individuals probably became dropouts to protest against their churches and denominations for positions taken on social issues, whether too liberal or too conservative.

Perceptions of decline must also take into account the search by many for alternatives to the religions they had come to question. In almost all denominations there were "underground" movements of individuals who believed that traditional places of worship had become stagnant and unresponsive. They sought to create a different kind of worshipping community, simpler in structure and free of trappings and traditions. Often these communities were simply groups of men and women who gathered in the homes of their members. Few lasted more than a year or two.

The Jesus movement sprang up in California in the late 1960s.

Some who sought alternatives to traditional forms of religious practice found it in the Jesus movement that sprang up in California in the late 1960s. The first ones in the movement were known to the bemused public as "Jesus freaks," young persons claiming to be "born again." Their lives had lost meaning and purpose, they said, and finding it neither in drugs nor in the counterculture, they responded emotionally to calls to focus everything on Jesus. Their ecstatic version of faith resembled that displayed in earlier Christian revivals. For many, it was the "ultimate trip." The apparent innocence, simplicity, and spirit of community displayed by the Jesus people helped the movement to spread rapidly, often through campus networks. In 1971 the Religious News Writers Association called the Jesus movement the news event of the year in religion.

The most radical members in the Jesus movement formed highly disciplined "families" and repudiated everything they regarded as "establishment." Typically living communally, sharing everything, they required their members to renounce their biological families and the churches in which they had been raised. Distraught parents, believing their offspring to be the victims of mind control, sometimes tried to retrieve them with the aid of "deprogrammers." In less radical ways, the Jesus movement broadened its boundaries. The emotions of the movement drew favorable responses from persons in established Christian churches who would not have considered joining it in its informal communal or coffeehouse days. Just as effects of the counterculture had seeped into the lives of people in mainstream America at the very time when it was itself vanishing from the scene, so it happened with the Jesus movement. Its effects, particularly its "born again" themes, continued after the movement itself was gone.

The continuation resulted in part from the work of musicians such as Pat Boone and Johnny Cash, who fused Christian lyrics with rock music to reach vast numbers with the Jesus movement's message of sin and salvation. Families playing the musicians' tapes learned the words and tunes without connecting them to their origins. Church youth groups that went to see *Godspell*, which opened a long run on May 17, 1971, had by then no reason to connect the lyrics to the movement that inspired it. Nor, as moms and dads sang along with their records of Andrew Lloyd Webber's popular musical *Jesus Christ Superstar*, which opened on October 10 of the same year, did they think about the emotion-filled movement that had popularized the message it carried.

The spirit and practice of the Jesus movement had counterparts among Pentecostalists, who believed they were restoring and maintaining practices neglected since Christianity's early days. Prophesying, interpreting prophecy, speaking in tongues, and performing miraculous acts of healing played an important part in Pentecostal ministries. Their distinctiveness did not prevent Pentecostalists from finding a place in the American religious scene, alongside the growing evangelical and fundamentalist churches. Regarded as either evangelical or fundamentalist or both were Baptists, Assemblies of God, Seventh-Day Adventists, Nazarenes, and various churches known simply as "Christian." At the same time, mainline Protestant churches suffered declining membership, among them the Methodist, Lutheran, Presbyterian, and Episcopalian churches; the Disciples of Christ; and the United Church of Christ.

Although people identifying themselves as fundamentalists and evangelicals have much in common (indeed, many claim to be both), it is useful to draw distinctions. Fundamentalists stress a belief in the inerrancy of the Bible, meaning that the Bible is free of error. They regard the Bible as the absolute authority on religious matters. Many fundamentalists apply biblical authority to secular matters as well. Evangelicals stress their "born-again" conversions, their acceptance of Jesus as their personal Savior and the Bible as the authority for all doctrine, and their obligation to spread the faith through personal witness and by supporting missionaries. Billy Graham, the best known of the evangelicals, embodied these convictions. Graham's eloquence as an evangelist and the efficiency of his organization enabled him to maintain national prominence and respect throughout the 1960s and 1970s and into the 1980s and 1990s.

During these years, the Roman Catholic Church maintained its vitality as its members adapted to changes initiated by the Second Vatican Council. The aggressive mission practices of the Church of Jesus Christ of Latter-day Saints (Mormons) resulted in its rapid growth. The astonishingly swift triumph of Israel in the Six-Day War with Arab States in 1967 revitalized Jewish communities in the United States, but problems resulting from assimilation and dispersal of Jewish people in America continued to threaten Jewish identities.

Also during these years, groups sometimes described as cults claimed a share of public attention. Hare Krishna followers, for example, handed out literature, tried to sell books, and begged for contributions in major airports. The Unification Church of the Reverend Sun Myung Moon was an aggressive recruiter of new members (known as "Moonies" for their absolute subservience to the leader). Various Eastern religions, transcendental meditation, and quasi-religious "technologies of the spirit" also attracted followers, but they represented such minute slivers of the population that their impact was negligible on mainstream America.

Religious bodies also found themselves in unsettled circumstances. Although the Jesus movement described earlier faded away rather quickly, a new one just as quickly succeeded it. Focusing on a new birth through faith in Jesus, those swept up in the born-again movement sought to convert others to beliefs in personal salvation. "I found it!"—a catchy phrase displayed on bumper stickers and billboards—provided a theme for sermons, particularly by televangelists, as well as for pamphlets and person-to-person testimonies. Christians critical of the "I found it!" theme claimed that those using it got it wrong. The message, they said, should be, "He found me"; in other words, it was God who did the finding. Such criticism did not slow the movement. The aggressive bearers of the born-again message, particularly those in the Campus Crusade organization led by evangelist Bill Bright, gained many converts. Complaints that the movement used high-pressure tactics did not faze its followers.

The born-again movement represented a part of the upsurge of evangelicalism in the 1970s. Between 1963 and 1978, the percentage of Americans claiming to have been "born again" and having personally experienced salvation rose from 24 to 40. By the end of the 1970s, more than 50 million Americans claimed to be evangelicals. Local congregations played a part in evangelicalism's growing strength, as did church-related colleges, publishing firms, and the denominations sponsoring or supporting them. Evangelicals regarded their Gospel-centered emphasis and clear-cut moral codes, along with their belief in conversion experiences, as standing in sharp contrast to what they perceived to be the consequences of "secular humanism." Evangelicals and fundamentalists, who were more rigid in their Biblical literalism than other Christians and harsher in their criticisms of societal changes, blamed secular humanism for increases in teenage sexual activity, alcohol and drug abuse, and discipline problems in public schools.

Catholics around the world mourned the death in 1978 of Pope Paul VI, who had had the task of dealing with the changes brought by the Second Vatican Council called by Pope John XXIII. Those changes affected Church members in many ways. Liturgical practices continued to evolve, moving farther away from the rituals of the traditional Latin Mass. Traditionalists regretted the abandonment of the distinctive black habits nuns had worn and objected to seeing priests without clerical collars. More disturbing to Catholic parishioners was the departure in unprecedented numbers of priests, brothers, and sisters who sought dispensation from their sacred vows and left their religious orders or diocesan positions. Men and women entering the orders were far too few in number to replace them. Perhaps more serious for the Church's future, the Catholic parochial schools that had long been an important instrument in carrying out the Church's mission faced cutbacks and closings. For the hierarchy, managing Church affairs became more difficult. Although the pope remained supreme and bishops wielded considerable authority, grassroots assertiveness meant that power was decentralized. In other words, the people in the Church had greater influence in Church matters than ever before.

Upon the death of Paul VI, his successor honored the two preceding popes by taking the names of both, becoming Pope John Paul I. However, he died just 34 days after his election. His successor, Karol Cardinal Wojtyla from Poland, took the name John Paul II. When the new pope traveled to the United States in October 1979 he was greeted by huge, enthusiastic crowds in New York City, Philadelphia, Des Moines, Chicago, and Washington, D.C. His warm and gentle manner pleased the throngs who came to see and hear him. The pope's pilgrimage had more than creating goodwill as its purpose, however, for he used the occasion to stress human rights and speak on behalf of the poor. If this meant opposing abortion and criticizing the consumerist culture of the United States, the pope was not reluctant to be candid. One effect of his visit was to give a boost to the claims of religion to a legitimate place in American life.

Certain changes in organized religion begun in the 1960s, such as allowing the ordination of women into the ministry in Protestant churches, proved to be deeply divisive. Although women were ordained with little or no controversy in some denominations, the ordination of 15 women in the Episcopal church created fierce controversy among Episcopalians. Because the church officially opposed the ordination of women, those who participated in ordination ceremonies were censured or admonished and sometimes subjected to formal canonical trials. Some Episcopal priests and members of that denomination were so antagonistic to allowing women to be ordained that they led their local parishes into a separate, conservative Episcopal body. Opposition to changes in emphasis and language, along with alternative versions of central rites in the updated version of the *Book of Common Prayer,* added to the resentments of dissenters and gave them another reason for separation.

The Roman Catholic Church continued to take strong positions against the ordination of women, with Pope Paul VI and Pope John Paul II speaking forcefully against it. Nonetheless, stirrings for change were evident among lay Catholics and some clergy, who claimed that there were no substantial theological reasons to deny women ordination. The role of women also became a point of controversy in the three strands of Judaism. Several were ordained as rabbis in Reform Judaism, and one became a presiding rabbi in Pennsylvania in 1979. A survey among Conservative rabbis showed that a majority favored ordination of women. Orthodox Jews called for expanded roles for women, but only in keeping with their understandings of religious law.

> *Homosexuality was potentially the single most divisive issue facing churches since slavery.*

The fact that churches could no longer ignore or evade questions of homosexuality is not surprising, for homosexuals would not allow them to do so. Most of the major denominations experienced turmoil as they grappled with the issue of homosexuals in their churches. Some sought ways to minister to them without condoning homosexuality, but militant conservatives, who regarded them as blatant sinners, opposed openness and efforts to support them. Whether gay men and lesbians could be ordained into the ministry, even in churches less antagonistic toward them, was a particular source of discord. Indeed, homosexuality was potentially the single most divisive issue facing churches since the time of slavery.

A decade earlier, religious conservatives had criticized the political actions of mainstream religious leaders on behalf of civil rights or against the Vietnam War. Now, reacting to changes in society that they found objectionable, they became politically active themselves. Besides opposing protection of rights and opportunities for homosexuals, they called for legislation against pornography, worked to defeat the Equal Rights Amendment, and demanded laws to counter the effects of the 1973 Supreme Court decision allowing abortion.

A large part of evangelicals' and fundamentalists' success in political action resulted from their use of television to raise money for promoting their causes. Evangelist Oral Roberts, broadcasting from Tulsa, Oklahoma, showed that it was possible to build an expansive television ministry by combining evangelical preaching with faith healing—healing by placing the healer's hands on the believer and praying fervently. Based in Louisiana, Jimmy Swaggart reached huge audiences, as did Jim and Tammy Bakker's PTL (Praise the Lord; later People That Love) broadcast from South Carolina. Pat Robertson's *700 Club*, featuring interviews with evangelical leaders and carried on the Christian Broadcasting Network (CBN) he founded in 1961, became a powerful force in conservative political causes.

Jerry Falwell aimed to register millions of new conservative voters for the 1980 election.

In 1979, televangelist Jerry Falwell used his *Old Time Gospel Hour*, broadcast on more than 300 television stations, to launch an explicit political movement, the Moral Majority. Falwell, pastor of the Thomas Road Baptist Church in Lynchburg, Virginia, claimed that the moral ills of society—reflected in such things as sex education in the schools, the Equal Rights Amendment, and abortion—could be corrected through the political mobilization of moral people. Joining forces with other well-funded conservative organizations, he aimed to register millions of new conservative voters for the 1980 election. Success gave him reason to say, "We have enough votes to run the country. And when the people say, 'We've had enough,' we are going to take over."

Conflict within denominations also affected church members. The Southern Baptist Convention, the largest Protestant body in the United States, came under the control of organized conservative forces in 1979. Much the same thing had happened in the two-million-member Lutheran Church–Missouri Synod a decade earlier, resulting in strife and schisms. The principal issue dividing Baptists was inerrancy, the teaching that the Bible was without error in all respects. Conservatives claimed that students in Baptist seminaries were taught that the Bible may not be completely accurate in scientific, historical, and geographical details. Further, they charged, this doubting of scriptural inerrancy had made its way into pulpits in Baptist churches and was threatening the purity of Baptist teachings. Their opponents held diverse views of biblical authority. Although they also regarded the Bible as the inspired Word of God, they were willing to apply scholarly interpretive methods to discover its meaning. The division over this and other issues continued throughout the 1980s and into the 1990s.

A phenomenon that worried members of all mainline, evangelical, and fundamentalist churches was the appearance of religious groups labeled "cults" by their critics and the media. Typically, these groups sprang up around leaders who based their teachings on claims of revelation beyond traditional religious teachings and scriptures. They guaranteed salvation and satisfying lives to all who submitted to their absolute authority and severed all ties with families, jobs, schools, and friends. While the leaders often lived in royal splendor, they assigned demeaning tasks to their followers. Indoctrination and repetitive rituals, some of them emotionally and physically dangerous, played important parts in the leaders' tactics.

Willingness of the groups' followers to surrender unquestioningly to their leaders was demonstrated most dramatically in November 1978, when the People's Temple, founded in California by Jim Jones, came to a tragic end. By then Jones had led his followers to Jonestown, Guyana, where they engaged in a mass murder and suicide. The deaths of more than 900 People's Temple members made headline news as television networks carried the story into homes across the nation.

Although members of such groups claimed to belong to them voluntarily, many former members contended that they had been converted by deception and subsequently compelled to endure treatment designed to destroy their egos. In addition to indoctrination, tactics included limiting members' sleep, changing their diet, controlling all conversations, and doing other things to disorient them and make their alienation from society complete. Although the number of people who joined groups with such practices was small, the lives affected by them—the members and the families of members—were affected profoundly. Consequently, discussions were widespread about ways of protecting particularly the young from such groups' advances.

Polls showed that the religious involvement of the American people remained relatively constant throughout the 1980s. About 92 percent of the American people had a religious preference, 68 percent said they were members of a church or synagogue, 40 percent said they attended church or synagogue in a given week, and 56 percent claimed religion to be very important in their lives. Mainstream denominations suffered general declines in membership, however, whereas more conservative ones held their own or gained.

Alongside traditional religious commitments, something described loosely as New Age gave expression to spiritual sentiments. Its basic doctrine, according to *Time* magazine, was, "you can be whatever you want to be." Defining New Age, though, is difficult. It includes, says *Time*, "a whole cornucopia of beliefs, fads, rituals; some subscribe to some parts, some to others. . . . All in all, the New Age does express a cloudy sort of religion, claiming vague connections with both Christianity and the major faiths of the East, plus an occasional dab of pantheism and sorcery. The underlying faith is a lack of faith in the orthodoxies of rationalism, high technology, routine living, spiritual law and order." It is not surprising that in the postmodern 1980s there were organizations, publications, radio stations, and some 2,500 bookstores to serve the growing number of persons attracted to the sort of spirituality New Age offered.

Conflict was common within religious denominations. In some instances, as in the Southern Baptist Convention, conservatives faced off with moderates over interpretation of the Bible. Year after year the conservatives consolidated their power and began to place limits on what seminary professors could teach. Some whose teaching did not meet their standards were removed. Here and there, and from time to time, moderates made modest gains in efforts to keep the conservatives from controlling everything in the church body, but before the decade ended it was apparent that moderates would soon have no power.

In other denominations—the United Presbyterian Church in the United States, for example, and the Episcopal Church—differences over policies and practices created discord. As earlier, ordination of women and the churches' positions on homosexuality were at the center of prominent disputes. Ordination of women as rabbis was a troubling question in Judaism. The Church of Jesus Christ of Latter-day Saints (LDS), whose members are known as Mormons, found itself at sharper-than-usual odds with the Reorganized Church of Jesus Christ of Latter Day Saints (RLDS) over a document purporting to show that Joseph Smith, founder of the LDS, had wanted his son to be his successor. Joseph Smith III had led his followers to Missouri and formed the RLDS, whereas Brigham Young had persuaded many Mormons to go with him to Utah and establish a new kingdom there. The document, "discovered" by an accomplished forger, did nothing to keep the LDS from being the fastest-growing denomination in the United States.

Despite long-standing opposition by Protestant denominations to diplomatic recognition of the Vatican, President Reagan appointed an ambassador to that political state and ecclesiastical entity in 1984. A coalition of Protestant groups responded by filing a lawsuit to nullify the new relationship, claiming it violated guarantees of separation of church and state.

Discord existed within the Roman Catholic Church, too, providing further evidence that the Church once run with unquestioned authority now had to cope with dissent and disobedience. In 1986 the Vatican ordered Father Charles E. Curran, who taught moral theology at the Catholic University of America, to retract his statements on the moral authority of the Church on such matters as birth control, abortion, homosexuality, premarital sex, and divorce. When Curran said that "for reasons of conscience" he could not change his positions, the Vatican withdrew his credentials for teaching as a Catholic theologian. Around the same time, the Vatican reassigned some of the authority of Seattle's Archbishop Raymond G. Hunthausen. It considered his teachings on birth control, homosexuality, and nuclear arms to be too liberal.

Though the discord in these instances involved a scholar and an archbishop, there is little doubt that the views of Curran and Hunthausen were shared widely among Catholic laity. Perhaps that is why the Vatican felt it necessary to crack down on them, hoping its action would keep discord from spreading. To reinforce the Church's position on its authority—as well as on such matters as birth control, medical procedures using artificial means in human reproduction (in vitro fertilization), and abortion—Pope John Paul II undertook a highly publicized tour of the United States in September 1987. His reception was favorable in the nine cities he visited.

Around the same time, charges of sexual misconduct made against prominent members of the clergy brought Catholicism unfavorable attention. Most prominent among those charged was the archbishop of Atlanta; revelations of his "intimate relationship" with a woman led him to resign. Accusations against parish priests known well in their own communities caused greater concern. Accusations of misconduct gained credibility by reports of a 25-year celibacy study done by a former priest, now a psychotherapist, that reported significant degrees of sexual and homosexual involvement among priests. Church officials claimed that because the study was based on interviews with persons who were in treatment for sexual misconduct or who had been touched by such misconduct, it was distorted.

For television evangelists, 1987 was a bad year. It started when Oral Roberts, one of the best known among them, announced that God would call him "home" unless his followers contributed $8 million to a medical fund he had started. The money came in, but Roberts's fellow evangelists thought his announcement had tarnished fund-raising practices for all of them. They all depended on contributions from viewers and could not afford to have their lifelines jeopardized.

The more widely publicized scandal occurred in 1987 when other televangelists accused Jim Bakker, the leading public figure in an organization known as PTL (Praise the Lord, or People That Love), of an extramarital sexual encounter. In addition, they claimed, Bakker had paid more than $250,000 to silence the person with whom it occurred. One of the accusers, the Reverend Jimmy Swaggart, remarked that "the gospel of Jesus Christ has never sunk to such a level as it has today." When the scandal forced Bakker to resign, PTL leaders asked televangelist Jerry Falwell to rescue the organization. Despite strenuous fund-raising efforts, PTL soon declared bankruptcy. The entire scandal placed under further scrutiny the practices televangelists used to raise funds and called into question their high incomes and lavish lifestyles. Eventually Bakker was convicted of 24 counts of fraud, sentenced to a prison term of 45 years, and fined $500,000. In the next year, Jimmy Swaggart himself was forced to confess to his Baton Rouge, Louisiana, congregation that he had committed a "sin," later reported as involving sexual misconduct. His denomination, the Assemblies of God, suspended him from preaching for a year, and when he refused to comply, it removed him from the ministry. Before long he was preaching again as an independent minister.

> *The practices televangelists used to raise funds called into question their high incomes.*

Attempts continued by what came to be known as the New Christian Right to change American institutions. For example, it sought to have public schools teach theories concerning the origins of the universe and humankind based on a literal interpretation of the Bible. Advocating what it called scientific creationism, the New Christian Right argued that schools taught theories of evolution as though they were a religion and that their own theories merited equal time. Laws in Arkansas and Louisiana requiring schools to teach "creation science" were ruled unconstitutional in both instances, but that did not deter leaders of the New Christian Right from trying to find new ways to accomplish their goals—ways that usually met the same fate in the courts.

The New Christian Right also pushed for a constitutional amendment that would have allowed voluntary individual or group prayer in public schools, overturning the 1962 Supreme Court decision it judged to be so objectionable. President Reagan sent a proposed amendment to Congress in 1982, but it died in committee. The intensity of the Christian Right's commitment to an amendment increased when a Supreme Court ruling in 1985 seemed to put more mortar in the wall of separation between church and state by invalidating an Alabama law that permitted a one-minute period of silence daily "for meditation or voluntary prayer" in public schools (Marty, 52–56, 169–73, 230–34, 317–20).

To read about religion in the United States in the 19th century, see the United States entry in the section "Religion" in chapter 8 ("Religious Life") in volume 5 of this series.

FOR MORE INFORMATION

Herberg, W. *Protestant-Catholic-Jew: An Essay in American Religious Sociology.* Garden City, N.Y.: Anchor Books, 1960.

Marty, M. A. *Daily Life in the United States, 1960–1990: Decades of Discord.* Westport, Conn.: Greenwood Press, 1997.

Marty, M. E. *Pilgrims in Their Own Land: 500 Years of Religion in America.* Boston: Little, Brown, 1984.

Marty, M. E., and R. Scott Appleby. *The Glory and the Power: The Fundamentalist Challenge to the Modern World.* Boston: Beacon Press, 1992.

Whitfield, S. J. *The Culture of the Cold War.* Baltimore: Johns Hopkins University Press, 1991.

INDIA

India was home to some of the world's great religions. From its soil sprang Hinduism, Buddhism, and Jainism, and it was home to the world's majority of Muslims. In addition, people practiced other faiths within India, including Sikhism along with Christianity, Judaism, and Zoroastrianism. India's tribal population practiced a form of animism that was likely the subcontinent's oldest type of spiritual or religious practice.

Although the majority of the population of India practiced Hinduism, it was not easily defined by any one text, sect, practice, or belief. For example, within Hinduism, when a person died, the family cremated the body, and the ashes were usually spread in a river or lake. Yet among some Hindus, in addition to these rituals a grave or marker stone was also constructed to honor the departed. Among lower castes, with a few exceptions, the deceased were buried.

Hinduism can generally be divided into two major bodies, with countless others subdividing or straddling the two. Followers of the god Vishnu were called Vaishnavas. These followers worshiped in Vaishnaivite temples as well as the avatars of Vishnu, Ram, and Krishna, and were generally found in the northern and central regions of India. The second group, called Saivas, were those who worshiped the god Shiva. Saivites were generally found in southern India, where they formed a majority, but also in the far north of the country. A third branch of Hinduism, Shaktism, was found in Bengal in the east. Here, the mother goddess was worshipped along with her feminine power or Shakti.

Before the 19th century, almost no average Indian would identify himself or herself as "Hindu." The term had not yet become widely used. The term seems to have come from the Sanskrit word *Sindhu,* which refers to the Indus River located in the Sind region in northwest India. Thus, the term Hindu referred to *all* of the people living beyond the Indus River, not to any particular faith (Frykenberg, 30). Further, a distinction must be made between the words Hindu and Hindi. A Hindu was a person who practiced some form of the faith, whereas Hindi referred to the language spoken in much of India, but did not imply a particular religious affiliation. Many people from a variety of faiths spoke Hindi, but not all of them were Hindus. Although Hindi has been one of the two official languages of India besides English, there are 18 other national languages.

Daily religious worship in India followed a myriad of practices. The great majority of Hindus attended a temple that contained an emblem of the god they worshiped. This might be a carved stone statue, a wooden piece, or some other form. The deity was in an inner room of the temple, and viewing was limited to certain times of day or restricted numbers of worshipers. Upon approaching the deity, people might have prostrated themselves, put their hands together in prayer, or shown some other sign of reverence. Most temples had at least one priest, usually a member of the Brahman caste, who alone had the accessibility to the sanctum sanctorum of the shine. Temple visitors might have made a financial contribution to the temple's upkeep and an offering of food, often a coconut. The coconut was broken in the temple as a symbolic offer to the god. In return, after the offer had been accepted, the priest offered pieces of the coconut meat to the temple visitors to be eaten as a return offer of the deity. At other times, visitors might have been offered some water, either a small amount in their palms to drink, or some to be sprinkled over their heads. This would be holy water used in some way to cleanse or otherwise worship the deity. Finally, temple visitors might receive a mark on their foreheads that showed their devotion to and presence at the temple.

Temples and places of worship followed a variety of forms. Many temples were made of stone or marble and dated back hundreds of years. Their inner courtyard stone floors were worn smooth by countless pairs of bare feet. Other religious locations were much different—such as a small shrine on the edge of a lane or in a field where a passerby can stop, pray, and make some small offering. Locals who served that particular deity usually maintained these mini shrines.

Most Hindus also maintained some small shrine or small religious items in their homes for personal worship. Many had a small room or space devoted to worship. The family might have kept a picture of the deity surrounded by incense or flowers. Also, worshipers sprinkled certain powders extracted from auspicious sources on the image while chanting a prayer or mantra.

For many people, daily rituals began in the predawn light. Though some laborers might have begun work immediately, for others—if there was time—the first minutes of the day were spent exercising. Men and women left their homes—even in the dark—and took a long and vigorous walk through their neighborhoods. It was not uncommon in larger cities to see people carrying hand weights and swinging their arms vigorously while they walked. After the walk, people frequently practiced some form of yoga and stretching. Not only did this practice add to physical health, but also the peace achieved through meditation was connected with spiritual well-being. Using the bathroom for morning ablutions followed exercise. This, along with a bath and the cleaning of one's body, were basic and critical elements of morning rituals. The bath was in the form of a shower, or a bucket filled with water and poured with a cup over oneself. People who did not have easy access to water might swim or bathe in a nearby pond, stream, or river.

After bathing and donning clean clothes, many people spent some time in prayer, perhaps lighting incense or a candle and placing auspicious colored powder on the deity, and then on the devotee—usually a red mark on the forehead, or sometimes three white stripes representing different sects of faith Vaishnava and Shiva. While doing this, the devotee might chant mantras or sing songs. In addition, many people rang small bells while reciting certain prayers. After morning prayer, whether a short prayer or a longer ritual, breakfast was taken and the day began in earnest.

Daily rituals in India were punctuated by other events centered on the family. Families considered marriage and childbirth important, both to carry on the family name and to ensure labor to help with the family occupation. Most marriages began with the bride's and groom's parents arranging for the marriage. Families performed an engagement ceremony replete with a meal, a priest, and much pomp. Before the wedding, depending on the family, their caste, and their income, the bride and groom might have visited with each other and each other's friends and families. Much teasing occurred as the couple was made to promise to be good to each other, along with more lighthearted promises. Then a priest performed the marriage, with the couple carrying out certain traditional rituals specific to their families and faith. In some marriages among lower castes and untouchables, a Brahmin priest did not officiate; marriages were conducted in the presence of the families' community leaders, with no brahminical ceremonies. But in all Hindu marriages, the groom placed an ornate necklace, called a *mangle sutra*, around the bride's neck to symbolize their union.

After marriage, the birth of a new child had its own rituals. When the mother was sufficiently along in her pregnancy, she would return to her own family home to deliver the child. Once the child was born, after a few days the family performed a naming ceremony, a joyful event to which friends and family were invited. A priest performed the ceremony to give the child his or her proper name, and sweets and a meal were usually prepared and offered to the guests.

Just as in marriage and birth, in death there were also certain frequently observed rituals. Generally, after a person died, the family cremated the body within 24 hours. At the cremation—by means of a pyre of wood built outside and in a special location—the body was burnt. For men, the oldest son would crack the skull, in accordance with a Hindu belief that the soul resides in the skull, and for the deceased to become reincarnated, a tenet of Hinduism, the soul must be released. After the fire, the son spread the ashes in a river and set the soul free. Some among the non-Brahmin castes buried the deceased.

Generally, religious faith and its accoutrements were more common and more frequently propitiated in India than in Europe or North America. Temples, shrines, mosques, and other places of worship dotted the landscape. Although India's Muslim and Christian communities have separate traditions, due to their long association with the Hindu majority, their birth, marriage, and death ceremonies have been influenced by Hinduism. Further, people worship in their homes throughout the days and weeks of the year. Those sites have their own rituals and occasions, adding to India's colorful spiritual and religious milieu.

To read about religion in ancient India, see the India entry in the section "Religious Beliefs" in chapter 8 ("Religious Life") in volume 1 of this series; for 19th-century India, see the India entry in the section "Religion" in chapter 8 ("Religious Life") in volume 5 of this series.

~Benjamin Cohen

FOR MORE INFORMATION

Dubois, A. *Hindu Manners, Customs and Ceremonies*. 3d ed. Translated by Henry Beauchamp. Oxford: Clarendon Press, 1906.

Frykenberg, R. E. "The Emergence of Modern 'Hinduism' as a Concept and as an Institution: A Reappraisal with Special Reference to South India (1)." In *Hinduism Reconsidered* edited by G. Sontheime and H. Kulke. New Delhi: Manohar, 1989, 29–49.

Ludden, D., ed. *Making India Hindu*. Delhi: Oxford University Press, 1996.

LATIN AMERICA

Since the times of conquest and colonization, the Roman Catholic Church has played a highly influential role in Latin American society and politics. Although traditionally conservative and authoritarian, the Church in Latin America underwent a revolution of its own during the 20th century. Elements within the Church adopted much more progressive and liberal ideals and increasingly supported the poor and dispossessed. At the same time, alternate religious and spiritual beliefs and practices existed, including Protestantism and spiritism.

For most of its history in the Americas, the Roman Catholic Church supported the conservative status quo. Bishops were members of the social, cultural, and economic elite and enjoyed relatively easy access to government and military structures and individuals.

During the first half of the 20th century, however, a variety of factors converged to weaken the influence of conservative elements of the Church. Anticlerical sentiments rose in some groups, particularly with proletarian, Marxist, and socialist organizations. At the same time, Protestantism began making inroads into other sectors of the population. Furthermore, many foreign-born priests had begun working in Latin American missions, particularly in poverty-stricken urban neighborhoods. There, they witnessed firsthand the dangers of daily life for people on the fringes of society. As such experiences heightened their social consciousness, they pressed the Church hierarchy to more appropriately address Latin American realities.

The late 1950s and 1960s brought grand reforms as the Catholic Church reassessed its relation to Latin American society. Religious services became more accessible to broader strata of society as local vernacular replaced Latin. Priests and nuns gained greater authority and became increasingly active in the community. During this period, religious workers began establishing *comunidades eclesiásticas de base* (CEBs),

or base ecclesiastic communities, in particularly poor areas of both rural and urban zones. With the CEBs, Church workers joined themselves with the poor, providing opportunities for worship and undertaking practical tasks to improve life conditions within the community. For example, many CEBs established agricultural cooperatives, acquired basic health care services, and constructed houses and communal buildings. Church workers in the CEBs also endeavored to form leaders of community members, for both Bible study and non-religious community functions.

Priests and nuns involved in these efforts found more official support from the Church hierarchy following the Second Vatican Council (1962–65). This meeting solidified the Church's dedication to social justice and human rights. The 1968 general conference of Latin American Bishops at Medellín, Colombia, further strengthened this new mission. At Medellín, the bishops redefined the Catholic concepts of sin and salvation as collective rather than individual matters. They posited that not only individuals but also systems and structures of power and wealth exploited the poor. They declared the Church's "preferential option for the poor"; as clergy identified with the everyday life of the poor, they committed themselves to radical social change.

Following Vatican II and the meeting at Medellín, social activism among church workers exploded. Priests and nuns urged nonviolent protest and resistance against systems of oppression. Some workers, like renowned Colombian priest Camilo Torres, even offered their support to armed revolutionary movements. Clergy adopted and passed on a "theology of liberation" that became both a religious doctrine and a political phenomenon through much of Latin America. In response to the structural sources of injustice and repression, this liberation theology mobilized the poor and less-powerful populations to work toward liberating social change.

Throughout the 1970s and 1980s, the Catholic Church consistently drew international attention to the grave inequalities and repression in many Latin American countries. For example, National Conferences of Bishops in Brazil, Colombia, Chile, Peru, and Bolivia pressed their governments for land reforms. The Ecuadoran Church went one step further when it announced in 1971 that it would turn over tens of thousands of acres of the Church's arable land to 2,000 landless families. As military dictatorships in Chile, Argentina, El Salvador, Guatemala, and elsewhere adopted brutal methods of maintaining order, Church workers advocated human rights. Such activism frequently led to direct confrontations between the Church and the military governments that subordinated human and civil rights to national security doctrines. Militaries often targeted church workers—clergy and laity alike—as "subversives." In El Salvador, for example, 1980 brought the murder of four U.S. churchwomen and Archbishop Oscar Arnulfo Romero at the hands of state security forces. And in 1989, the Atlacatl batallion of the Salvadoran army assassinated six Jesuit priests who had long been outspoken opponents of the repressive government.

Social activism also contributed to continuing tensions within the Church itself. Indeed, many churches appeared divided between the older, more conservative hierarchy and the younger, more progressive (even radical) clergy. In Argentina, for example, the traditionally conservative Church hierarchy opposed neither the military coup of 1973 nor the subsequent regime headed by General Augusto Pinochet. In fact, the Church supported the regime by arguing in favor of the repression of guerrilla movements. At the same time, however, sectors of the Church became highly involved in peace and justice movements, supporting nonviolent resistance groups such as the Mothers of the Plaza de Mayo and their vigils for the detained–disappeared. These more progressive sectors of the Church also ultimately adopted crucial roles in peace negotiations and national truth and reconciliation commissions.

By the end of the century, and particularly following the wave of democratization during the late 1980s and 1990s, the Roman Catholic Church in Latin America had arrived at an ambiguous political and social position. Backlash by conservative elements severely dampened the progress of more progressive and social justice–focused sectors.

Although the Roman Catholic Church has long been the most influential of Latin American organized religions, it is important to note that it has always existed alongside a variety of other religious practices, including spiritism. Forms of Aztec, Mayan, Incan, and other indigenous religious traditions persisted in the 20th century throughout Mexico, Central America, and the Andean region. Other traditions developed in regions of Latin America

> ### 📷 Snapshot
>
> **Mexico's Virgin of Guadalupe**
>
> In 1523, just a few years after Hernán Cortés and his armies had conquered the Aztec Empire, Catholic missionaries arrived to convert the American Indians to Christianity. Among their first converts was an Indian whose baptized name was Juan Diego. In 1531, Juan Diego was walking to Mass when he was struck by a blinding light. A beautiful, dark-skinned Indian woman appeared to him and told him that she was the Virgin Mary and requested that he build a church on the hill of Tepeyac on which they were standing. After another visitation, Juan Diego was supposedly able to convince the Church authorities of his vision by gathering roses that the Virgin had caused to bloom in winter, and by the image of the Virgin that miraculously appeared on the mantle in which Juan Diego had carried the flowers. As a result, a church was built on Tepeyac on the site of an ancient Aztec temple to the goddess Tonatzin. The church was rebuilt in 1709. In 1745, the Vatican officially recognized the miracle of Guadalupe. New additions were built on the church in 1906 and 1976. On December 12, the day Juan Diego is said to have picked his roses, Mexicans celebrate their Aztec and Christian heritage by honoring the Virgin of Guadalupe. In August 2002, Pope John Paul II canonized Juan Diego. (http://www.sancta.org/)

where Africans arrived as slaves during the 17th through 19th centuries. Such traditions include *umbanda* and *candomblé* in Brazil, *santería* in Cuba, and *voudou* in Haiti.

In addition, Protestantism—present since early in the century—grew exponentially throughout Latin America during the final two or three decades of the 20th century. By the 1990s, some 10 percent of Latin Americans identified with Protestant denominations, nearly half of them baptized or converted since 1980.

In conclusion, although a variety of religious or spiritual beliefs and practices existed alongside one another through the 20th century, Roman Catholicism continued to dominate in Latin American society. Each denomination operated on different levels, but all had at least one struggle in common: they attempted to provide explanations for and solutions to problems of inequality and poverty that continued to pervade Latin American society.

To read about religion in 19th-century Latin America, see the Latin America entry in the section "Religion" in chapter 8 ("Religious Life") in volume 5 of this series.

FOR MORE INFORMATION

Berryman, P. *Liberation Theology: Essential Facts About the Revolutionary Movement in Latin America—and Beyond.* Philadelphia: Temple University Press, 1987.

Foley, E. *El Salvador.* New York: Marshall Cavendish, 1995.

Garciagodoy, J. *Digging the Days of the Dead: A Reading of Mexico's Dias de Muertos.* Niwot: University Press of Colorado, 1998.

Garrard-Burnett, V., ed. *On Earth as It Is in Heaven: Religion in Modern Latin America.* Wilmington, Del.: Scholarly Resources, 2000.

Romero. Los Angeles: Vidmark Entertainment, 1989. This film tells the story of the "awakening" of Salvadoran Archbishop Oscar Romero, following him from his conservative beginnings through his "education" by poor peasants and progressive colleagues, to his unfailing efforts to bring social justice and peace to wartime El Salvador.

Smith, C., and J. Prokopy, eds. *Latin American Religion in Motion.* New York: Routledge, 1999.

ISLAMIC WORLD

More than one billion Muslims live in the world today, spread across five continents. Islam is an ever-growing and ever-evolving world faith. Muslims are an ethnically, linguistically, and politically diverse group of people. Like most major world religions, Islam is facing many challenges as it looks to the future. "The history of Islam in the contemporary world, as through much of history, continues to be one of dynamic change. Muslim societies have experienced the effects of rapid change, and with it the challenges in religious, political and economic development. Muslims continue to grapple with the relationship of the present and future to the past" (Esposito, 690). Despite the challenges of modernity, Islamic religious beliefs and practices have remained remarkably consistent over time.

Muslims follow the religion of Islam, which they believe God revealed to the Prophet Muhammad in the seventh century c.e. These revelations are contained in the Qur'an, the holy book of Islam. Islam is a strongly monotheistic faith. The word Islam means "submission," specifically "submission to God." Although there is a tremendous amount of diversity in 20th-century Islamic practice, Muslims all share a core set of beliefs that guide their daily lives. Much of modern Islamic practice is governed by the traditions and the teachings of the Prophet Muhammad.

The primary doctrine of Islamic practice is the belief in the unity of God. Muslims also acknowledge the existence of angels. One of the most important angels in Islamic cosmology is the Archangel Jibril (known in the West as Gabriel), who served as an intermediary between God and the Prophet Muhammad. According to the Qur'an, there were 25 Prophets, beginning with Adam and ending with Muhammad, the last or seal of Prophets (Denny, 93–94). Another central tenet of Islam is the belief in a final time of judgment, when all people living and dead will be called forth by God to answer for their deeds on earth. The Qur'an says that the righteous will live in eternal paradise and the sinners will suffer the torments of hell. Finally, Muslims believe in the idea of predestination, the concept that all the events of life on Earth are guided by the will of God.

Though the outward manifestations of Islamic practice may vary by region or sect, Muslims worldwide believe in the primary doctrines of Islam. This Islamic path is guided by acts of faith called the five pillars of Islam. The first pillar of Islam is the *shahadah*, or profession of faith. When Muslims say the *shahadah*, they are testifying in Arabic that "there is no God but God and Muhammad is the Prophet of God." The *shahadah* is a central part of Muslim daily prayer. When people convert to Islam, they recite the *shahadah* as part of their conversion process. Religionist Frederick Denny explains that the *shahadah* is such an integral part of the religion of Islam that it is "a matter of orthodoxy [and] 'doctrinal correctness,' whereas the remaining four pillars are chiefly concerned with orthopraxy" (Denny, 93–94).

The remaining four pillars of Islam are acts that pious Muslims strive to follow as part of their devotional lives. The second pillar of Islam is called *salat*, or prayer. Muslims are required to perform five prayers, facing Mecca, every day at fixed times. There are now special computer programs designed to help Muslims gauge the correct time and direction for prayer. *Zakat*, or poor tax, is the third pillar of Islam. *Zakat* is usually calculated at 2.5 percent of wealth in excess of a specified minimum (Denny, 122). In Muslim countries, the government has traditionally regulated the giving and receiving of *zakat*. Muslims living in non-Muslim countries often give *zakat* to Islamic charities or to their local mosques. During the month of Ramadan, Muslims participate in the fourth pillar of Islam, *sawam* (an Arabic word meaning fasting). Muslims all over the world participate in this fast. They go without food or drink from sunrise until sunset for an entire month. One of the purposes of fasting during the month of Ramadan is for Muslim people to become closer to the poorer members of the Muslim community who might not have enough to eat and drink year-round. No Muslim is obligated to perform a devotional act that would cause undue hardship. For example, pregnant women are not permitted to fast during the month of Ramadan. A person with a health concern such as diabetes is also released from the obligation of fasting.

The last pillar of Islam is the *hajj,* or annual pilgrimage to Mecca. All Muslims who are physically and financially able try to make the *hajj* at least once in their lifetime. During the *hajj*, Muslims of many different cultural and ethnic backgrounds travel to the city of Mecca to perform a series of devotional acts. The American political activist Malcolm X wrote that his experiences on the *hajj* changed his life. He realized that all people, of every race and nationality, could worship together in peace. As the result of making the pilgrimage to Mecca, Malcolm X renounced his allegiance to the Nation of Islam and converted to Sunni Islam. In recent years, however, the *hajj* has sometimes become a forum for voicing political dissent. After the 1987 *Hajj* ended in violence between Sunni and Shi'ite factions, Iranian president Ali Khamenei charged the world press with pitting Shiism against Sunni Islam. The Saudi government, which is in charge of organizing the *hajj* each year, has taken measures to ensure that this type of political hostility will not occur in Mecca, the holy city of the Prophet Muhammad.

Islam, the youngest of the major Abrahamic world religions, shares a great deal with both Judaism and Christianity. All of these religions are trying to develop a way of expressing their faith that is relevant in the modern world. One way that

Muslims have been able to maintain a strong sense of community is by adhering to a core system of beliefs and rituals that transcend political and cultural boundaries.

To read about religion in the early Islamic World, see the Islamic World entry in the section "Religious Beliefs" in chapter 8 ("Religious Life") in volume 2 of this series; for the Ottoman Empire, see the Sufism (Ottoman Empire) entry in the section "Deities and Doctrines" in chapter 8 ("Religious Life") in volume 3 of this series; for 19th-century England, see the Islamic World entries in the sections "Morality" and "Religion" in chapter 8 ("Religious Life") in volume 5 of this series.

~*Molly Benjamin Patterson*

FOR MORE INFORMATION

Denny, F. M. *An Introduction to Islam*. New York: Macmillan, 1985.

Esposito, J. *The Oxford History of Islam*. New York: Oxford University Press, 1999.

X, Malcolm, with the assistance of Alex Haley. *The Autobiography of Malcolm X*. New York: Grove Press, 1966.

RELIGIOUS LIFE

RELIGION

United States,
1920-1939

United States,
1940-1959

United States,
1960-1990

India

Latin America

Islamic World

Soviet Union

Japan

Africa

Inuit

SOVIET UNION

The Soviet Union was the first modern state to promote atheism as official policy. Article 52 of the 1977 Soviet constitution guaranteed freedom of religion and conscience and separation of church and state, but it also reaffirmed the right of atheists to promote their views—a right not granted to religious groups. That omission gave the state a free hand to ban such groups from publicizing their activities. Also, since Party and government were entwined, and the Party was openly antireligious, constitutional promises of freedom of worship had no force. Criminal laws also blocked religious freedom. For example, it was a crime to involve minor children or anyone else in religious ceremonies or activities that might be harmful to their health. These were handy laws that could be applied whenever the state wanted to prevent fasting, baptism, Sunday school classes, bar mitzvah ceremonies, circumcisions, and so on. Being openly religious blocked people's chances for career advancement in that believers were barred from Party membership. All denominations had to get official permission for such things as opening or closing churches, repairing church buildings, resolving problems with local authorities, and organizing religious conferences. Repressions waxed and waned; although the state never forbade religion, worshippers were always aware of their government's hostility.

For example, on March 19, 1922, Lenin personally ordered a campaign of terror against Russian Orthodox clergy and supporters who were trying to prevent the government from confiscating valuable objects from churches. In that letter, Lenin urged that Russian Orthodox priests and their "bourgeois" followers be smashed "with utmost haste and ruthlessness." During the first five years after the revolution the Bolsheviks executed 28 Russian Orthodox bishops and more than 1,200 Russian Orthodox priests. Many others—clergy and parishioners—were imprisoned, exiled, or both. Besides the lives lost, seminaries were closed and church publications banned. In 1927, Metropolitan Sergii (the church's de facto leader) tried to save his church by declaring it subservient to the government, a tactic that earned him many bitter enemies, inspired the growth of an underground church movement, and failed to restrain the Party's ferocious attacks against it. By 1933, only 100 Moscow churches, out of 600 in the early 1920s, remained open. By 1941, only 500 of about 54,000 churches active in the country before World War I were still open. Several thousand Orthodox had been executed by the late 1930s.

Despite decades of repression, many Soviets continued to regard themselves as followers of one or another of the empire's array of religious traditions. Christianity and Islam had the most followers. Christians belonged to a variety of denominations, of which the Russian Orthodox Church, Russia's pre-revolutionary state church, had the most followers. There were also significant numbers of Roman Catholics, Baptists, and other Protestant sects, especially Evangelical Christians. About 90 percent of Soviet Muslims belonged to the Sunni denomination that supported an elected caliph. The rest, mostly Azerbaijanis, were Shias who supported an hereditary caliph as their leader. Judaism also had many believers. Other religions with a smaller number of faithful included Buddhism, Lamaism, and shamanism.

Many old Russian Orthodox churches, including Leningrad's St. Isaac's and Kazan cathedrals and churches within Moscow's Kremlin, were turned into museums, including "museums of atheism" where people could go to see the terrible things religion had done. Valuable church property was carted away to state museums, was sold abroad for hard cash, or simply vanished. Sometimes church assets were recycled for new functions, as when bells were used to summon peasants to work rather than worship or were melted down for industrial use. Moscow's Cathedral of Christ the Savior was dynamited in 1931 in order to build in its place a palatial government facility, meant to be the world's largest building, topped by "the world's largest Lenin . . . pointing the way to the future, with the world's largest index finger, 15 feet long." But in what some believers regarded as a sign from God, the ground beneath the church was too soft to support such a huge structure. The site remained a ditch until the 1960s, when Khrushchev had it made into the world's largest outdoor public swimming pool. Clouds of vapor arising in winter from the heated water proved, to some at least, the pool's hellish origin. But for some secret Baptists, it furnished a place for new converts to be discreetly baptized. As unsuspecting Muscovites swam, the Baptists "prayed and dunked." Similarly, St. Petersburg's (Leningrad's) Church of Sts. Peter and Paul, first built by Peter the Great for Lutherans of that city, was closed by government decree as a place of worship in the 1930s, used as a warehouse, and in the 1960s converted to an indoor city swimming pool, a purpose it served for 30 years. In 1926 the visiting German writer Walter Benjamin described in his diary Moscow's Our Lady of Kazan Cathedral, with its "gloomy" anteroom just right for hatching "the shadiest deals, even pogroms, should the occasion arise." He went on to describe "the actual place of worship."

It has a few small stairs in the background that lead up to the narrow, low platform on which one advances past the pictures of saints. Altar upon altar follows in close succession, each one indicated by the glimmer of a small red lamp. . . . Those portions of the wall . . . not hidden by [very large] pictures are covered in luminous gold. A crystal chandelier hangs from the cloying, painted ceiling.

Benjamin observed how worshippers approached an icon (painting of a saint or deity), crossed themselves, kneeled, touched their foreheads to the ground, crossed themselves again, and proceeded to the next icon. When worshippers approached smaller, glass-covered icons on stands, they bowed and kissed the picture instead of crossing themselves. Benjamin was disconcerted to find that some stands held invaluable antique icons side-by-side with cheap mass-produced pictures.

When the state introduced a continuous workweek, eliminating Sunday as a day of worship and rest, many believers met for Sunday-evening services after work. The government countered such efforts by substituting secular rituals and holidays for religious rites, including those that mark life's transitions: birth, marriage, death. The secular version of infant baptism was a naming ceremony: the baby, flanked by two family friends, received a certificate and the friends promised to be the child's "moral guardians." An official objection to church baptism was that it was unhealthy to bring an infant into a drafty church and sprinkle cold water on its bald little head. Civil weddings, which were the norm, were sterile affairs done in assembly-line style. Couples who wanted something more memorable might arrange for a church wedding, though many kept such weddings secret to protect their careers.

Christmas and (especially) Easter remained important holidays for Soviet Christians, whether or not they were particularly religious. At Easter, bakeries stocked kulich, a traditional yeast-risen coffee cake, and paskha, an unbaked cheesecake filled with candied fruit and nuts, eaten along with the kulich. The kulich, which is supposed to be tall, even towering, is sliced horizontally in rounds, and then (if necessary) in halves and quarters, with the top round being saved as a kind of lid to put atop leftover cake. Slices are placed on a platter along with slices of paskha, or the paskha may be placed on top of the kulich. Paskha, which means Easter, was officially called "spring cake" in order to erase its religious associations. People who wanted to prepare their own paskha and kulich struggled to find the ingredients. Also at Easter, people dyed eggs reddish brown by boiling them with onion skins. Elderly women, the mainstay of Russian Orthodox Church worshippers, brought homemade bread and cakes to church to be blessed. It was also customary to visit family graves before Easter. Relatives of the departed went to the graves to "tidy up": paint the railings that customarily encircle each grave, clip grass, pull weeds, and clean the stone crosses with their inset photos of the deceased. On the actual memorial day, families put flowers, Easter eggs, and sometimes even small glasses of vodka on the graves (Eaton).

FOR MORE INFORMATION

Benjamin, W. *Moscow Diary*. Edited by Gary Smith, translated by Richard Sieburth. Cambridge: MIT Press, 1986.

Binyon, M. *Life in Russia*. New York: Pantheon, 1983.

Eaton, K. B. *Daily Life in the Soviet Union*. Westport, Conn.: Greenwood Press. Forthcoming.

Smith, H. *The Russians*. New York: Ballantine, 1977.

JAPAN

Although predominantly Buddhist in orientation, Japan's population is eclectic in its approach to religion. Newspaper surveys annually report that the total number of people who claim adherence to one of the myriad sects of Buddhism or to Shintō, its other main religion, total more than the population. In other words, some people report that they are Buddhist as well as believers in Shintō.

The indigenous religion Shintō is a loose amalgam of pantheist and animist beliefs that came to congeal into something of a unified dogma only in the late 19th century. Its principal tenets are of a common ancestry descendant from various now anthropomorphic spirits called *kami* who must be propitiated with annual rituals called *matsuri*. Almost totally without sacred canon or moral system, the chief idea is that all things are interrelated by common essence, and the existence and placement of everything is determined by function and propriety.

During the Meiji era (1868–1912) Shintō was nationalized by means of the creation of a priestly caste and systems for worship at national and local shrines. After World War II the religion regenerated into thousands of independent rustic local shrines and a score of traditional national ones (notably Ise, Izumo, Atsuta, and Yasukuni). Meiji-era funeral and wedding rituals and ceremonies continue to be popular. The most popular shrines are those of the fox, *kami Inari*, which is tied to magic and to symbols of human and agricultural fertility. Newlyweds flock to these shrines to pray for healthy children. Amulets and wooden prayer fetishes are popular, particularly among high school students about to sit for college entrance exams.

Picturesque shrines dot the rural countryside and are also prominent at the entrance of virtually every Buddhist temple. Curiously, the native *kami* are said to help protect the Buddhas within the temples. Religious historians note that the two religions came together in the medieval feudal period in a syncretism called *Ryobu* (Both Ways) Shintō. Some religious leaders taught that the *kami* were local incarnations (avatars) of the Buddhas. The two religious establishments coexist today without much sectarian enmity. Patrons visiting Buddhist temples unconsciously perform Shintō ablution rituals (rinsing hands and the mouth) before entering the temple. Symbolic offerings of food, drink, incense, and money are often made at the outer shrine as well as in the inner temple.

Buddhism, which came to Japan from northern India through China and Korea beginning in the fifth century, has evolved into a plethora of semiautonomous sects. Originally a renunciation of esoteric religion that denied the existence of phenomena, it has mutated and regenerated into hundreds of paths to enlightenment. The original Indian Buddhism was in many ways an engine of social and moral reform. It taught that desire is the origin of pain. The simplistic remedy was to rid oneself of the chimera of existence through meditation on the nothingness that is reality. Obviously this complex philosophical conundrum begged for rational explanation. Rational thinking, however, was defined as part of the problem because if one does not exist, then thinking is illusion as well.

The major schools of thought (*Tendai, Shingon, Kegon*) that came from China and flourished for five centuries or so were superseded by two main streams of thought

in the early feudal period. *Zen* (*Chan* in Chinese) emphasized renunciation and meditation in remote rustic hideaways, and the so-called Pureland sects appealed to divine intercession. Zen itself split into two main subsects (*Rinzai* and *Soto*), emphasizing meditating and "shocking" the mind by contemplation of antirational (*koan*) puzzles. Pureland adherents argued that salvation and enlightenment by rational means and through good works are impossible. Enlightenment can only be accomplished through intercession of the merciful Buddha *Amida* (by merely chanting his name) or of the name of holy canons such as the *Lotus Sutra*.

Virtually all of the sects of Buddhism continue to prosper in Japan today. Most eke out a living (and some thrive) by performing various social functions for the surrounding neighborhoods. Chief among these functions are various rituals for the dead. Virtually every Japanese deceased person is cremated after a Buddhist funeral, and families gather at prescribed times (49 days after death is most common) for ceremonial meals and rituals. Suitable donations to the priest and temple are expected. The temples typically perform charitable acts, including appropriate rituals for dead animals and even for discarded tools. Annual ceremonies are held, for example, wherein used needles are stuck into blocks of tofu. The idea is that after a hard life, the needles deserve to rest in something soft.

In the two decades bracketing either side of World War II an explosion of "New Religions" gained acolytes and adherents. Centered on charismatic shamanlike figures, these offshoots of Shintō and Buddhism (and even a few of Christianity) grew in popularity. The wartime government tried to squelch these upstarts on the premise that they were inimical to the nation and to public decency. A handful survived to become very popular in modern times. Chief among them is *Tenri-kyo*, which boasts its own internationally known university (*Tenri-dai*), and *Soka Gakkai* (Value-Creating Society). The latter sprouted its own political party, *Komeito* (Clean Government Party), which was briefly influential in the 1970s and 1980s. Somewhat diminished by scandal, the party has disassociated itself from *Soka Gakkai* and continues to wield considerable power in coalition-building politics.

Other minor religions flourish in modern Japan, protected by a liberal 1947 constitution. Christianity is the chief among the lesser religions, with about 1 percent of the population belonging to both Roman Catholic and Protestant churches. *Aum Shinrikyo*, a virulent form of Buddhism, arose in the mid-1990s when the crazed acolytes of a madman killed about a dozen people by assassination and by releasing poison gas at Tokyo subway stations.

To read about religion in early modern Japan, see the Japan entries in the sections "Religious Beliefs" and "Religious Practices" in chapter 8 ("Religious Life") in volume 4 of this series.

~*Louis G. Perez*

FOR MORE INFORMATION

Earhart, H. B. *Japanese Religion: Unity and Diversity*. Belmont, Calif.: Wadsworth, 1982.
Kitagawa, J. M. *Religion in Japanese History*. New York: Columbia University Press, 1966.

Mullins, M., S. Susumu, and P. L. Swanson, eds. *Religion and Society in Modern Japan: Selected Readings*. Berkeley, Calif.: Asian Humanities Press, 1993.

AFRICA

The issue of religion in Africa in the 20th century requires a far more extensive examination of the different African lifestyles and cultures than can be covered here. Followers of every major world religion reside in Africa, but many of them only in small numbers or localized communities. Two main religions, Islam and Christianity, dominate the African continent, accompanied by the millions of Africans who continue to practice traditional, indigenous religions. Through an examination of these three main religious groups and the interactions between them, a general understanding of some of the issues of religious life in Africa in the 20th century can be garnered.

Islam has been a formidable cultural force in Africa since the seventh century C.E., first brought to the continent by Muslim Arabs just a few decades after the death of the Prophet Muhammad. Islam has continued to spread throughout the continent until the present day. In the 20th century, Islam was the dominant religion throughout North Africa from Egypt to Morocco, as well as along the Swahili Coast of East Africa from Somalia to Mozambique, and had made inroads into the African interior in most of West Africa and in other parts of the continent, such as Sudan and Uganda.

Christianity exists in Africa in two forms. Ancient Christianity came to Africa within decades after the crucifixion of Jesus, and a community of Christians was established in Egypt in the first century C.E. Remnants of this community still exist, known today as the Coptic Church in Egypt. Likewise, Christianity traveled to Ethiopia and had become the state religion by the fourth century C.E. Ethiopia has thus been a Christian state for over 1,500 years and continues to be so today. This kind of long-standing Christianity is different in many ways from the Christianity brought much later by European missionaries because it has had many centuries to develop to suit an African lifestyle and meet the needs of an African community.

The other form of Christianity evident in Africa is European Christianity, first brought by Portuguese explorers and missionaries in the 15th century. Over the course of the next 400 years, missionaries from many other European countries sent proselytizers to Africa. Missionary activity became a central component of the "civilizing" mission of European colonial governments in Africa in the 19th and first half of the 20th centuries.

As Islam and Christianity spread across Africa, they encountered preexistent African religious beliefs and practices. Although both Christian and Muslim clerics attempted to suppress indigenous beliefs and bring converts into their folds, both religions were unable to do so entirely. Millions of Africans practice their traditional religions to this day, often in conjunction with Islam or Christianity. Most African religions actually bear much in common with other world religions, including Christianity and Islam. African religions all recognize a God, a spiritual

entity that created humans and the universe, just as do Christianity and Islam. Likewise, African religions require proper ritualistic behavior and stress the social need for humans to treat each other well, lest dire consequences occur, as do Christianity and Islam. Because of such similarities, accompanied by the general pluralistic nature of African religions, many Africans did not see it as problematic to accept the teachings of Islam and Christianity and simply incorporate them into traditional African beliefs. Islamic and Christian missionaries usually saw things differently and focused on African beliefs in witchcraft, sorcery, and worship of inanimate objects as proof of the "barbaric" nature of African religions.

In the colonial period, African Christians in particular began to bridle at such derogatory suggestions and increasingly came to see the Christian church in Africa as an extension of the colonial apparatus designed to suppress African culture and exploit African labor. This realization resulted in the development of several African independent churches, meant to provide a form of Christianity that would be compassionate and beneficial to Africans. These movements were swiftly and often violently suppressed by the colonial governments.

Colonial governments not only found themselves dealing with indigenous African religions, but several colonies also presided over regions with substantial Muslim populations. Colonial governments did not take the heavy-handed approach with Muslim populations that they did with populations practicing traditional religions. Often colonial governments allowed preexisting Islamic social, juridical, and educational institutions to continue functioning on a local level, with little interference from colonial governments. However, colonial governments often did favor Christian institutions over Muslim ones whenever a conflict or allocation of funds occurred, breeding resentment in many Muslim communities. Thus, Islamic identity became a basis for nationalistic sentiment in the mid-20th century, as African populations all over the continent organized and demanded an end to the colonial occupation of Africa and the institution of a proper Islamic government.

With the eventual success of nationalist movements throughout Africa, mostly in the 1950s and 1960s, African countries entered a new era of political independence. The role of religion in politics has been a serious issue in many countries in Africa in the postcolonial era, particularly in countries that have large populations of both Christians and Muslims. In Nigeria, for example, the northern population is predominantly Muslim, whereas the southern population is predominantly Christian or followers of traditional religions. Over the past 40 years, violence has exploded between Muslims and Christians in Nigeria on multiple occasions and has resulted in the deaths of thousands of Nigerians on both sides of these altercations. The same has been the case in Sudan, where warring armies of Muslims and non-Muslims have thrown the country into turmoil for much of the country's independent era. These conflicts often revolve around whether Christians or Muslims will control the political and legislative processes of the country. Each side is fearful of the measures that the other would take to restrict their freedoms should they gain ultimate power. Thus, at the end of the 20th century, despite the religious pluralism prevalent throughout the continent, religious conflict still persists in many places, and it will be the challenge of the 21st century to dissipate these tensions.

To read about religion in Africa in the 17th and 18th centuries, see the Africa entry in the sections "Religious Beliefs" and "Religious Practices" in chapter 8 ("Religious Life") in volume 4 of this series.

~Matthew Heaton

FOR MORE INFORMATION

King, N. Q. *African Cosmos: An Introduction to Religion in Africa*. Belmont, Calif.: Wadsworth, 1986.

Levtzion, N., and R. L. Pouwels, eds. *The History of Islam in Africa*. Athens: Ohio University Press, 2000.

Mbiti, J. S. *Introduction to African Religion*. 2d ed. Oxford: Heinemann International, 1991.

Mugambi, J. N. K. *Christianity and African Culture*. Nairobi: Action, 2002.

INUIT

Christian missionaries were at the forefront of European, American, and Canadian colonization of the Inuit North, and today most Inuit are at least nominally Christian. In fact, the flag for the newly created Nunavut Territory in Canada is dominated by a traditional Inuit monument known as an *inukshuk* in the shape of a crucifix.

Many different Christian denominations worked to convert Inuit. Moravians converted the Inuit of Labrador, and Lutherans and some Moravians ministered to Greenlanders. In Alaska, individual territories were allocated to various denominations, while in Canada Catholic Oblate missionaries competed with Anglicans for Inuit souls. Today, Inuit in all three countries are both ordained ministers and lay leaders in their churches.

Christian missionaries played quite an important role in the colonization and development of the Inuit North. Though most worked very hard to stamp out any activity, such as drum dancing, that might possibly be regarded as a traditional Inuit religious practice, they also were responsible for developing some of the first and most comprehensive dictionaries and grammars for Inuktitut, the Inuit language. Missionaries also developed writing systems for Inuktitut, and many missionaries recorded information about traditional Inuit spirituality that otherwise would have been lost. In many parts of the Inuit North, missionaries provided health care and schools and introduced new economic activities. Only in the mid- to late 20th century were these activities taken over by governments.

In the pre-Christian era, religion and cosmological beliefs were remarkably similar throughout Inuit North. This was undoubtedly due to the relatively recent (since 1000 c.e.) dispersal of Inuit through the North American Arctic. Numerous spirits or *torngait* who could assist humans or could cause trouble dominated the Inuit cosmological world. The *torngait* would cause illness or hunting misfortune, especially if humans violated any of a large number of taboos. When this happened, it usually fell to a shaman to diagnose the cause of the trouble. But far from being benevolent religious practitioners, shamans often used their spiritual skills to extract sexual or other favors.

Inuit believed, and some still believe, that animals and many natural objects have a soul or life force that may take human form and interact with humans from time

Mariano Ajpilaajuk, an elder from Rankin Inlet in Nunavut, speaks about the land and sea during a ceremony in Iqaluit, Nunavut, Canada, 1999. © AP/Wide World Photos.

to time. When an animal dies, the soul is reborn in another animal. Because animals are said to give themselves to hunters who show them respect, it behooves hunters to be generous with their catch and to act in ways that do not give offense to either humans or animals.

In recent years, Inuit have established social movements that combine values associated with Christianity and traditional Inuit culture in order to improve the social well-being of their communities. *Inupiat Ilitqusiat*, which means "wisdom and lessons of the Inupiat people," is one of the most successful of these movements. Inupiat is the ethnonym of the Inuit of North and Northwest Alaska. The principles of Inupiat Ilitqusiat, which include sharing, respect for others, cooperation, hard work, conflict avoidance, humor, responsibility, and trust in a higher power, were first articulated by Inuit political leader Willie Hensley in 1980. Hensley, along with leaders of the Friends Church and other political leaders, set about creating Inupiat Ilitqusiat as a formal spiritual movement that could address the sense of moral and spiritual void that was afflicting Inuit communities in Alaska. In particular, these leaders were concerned about the diminishing importance of traditional subsistence hunting and the social relations that it entailed as well as the loss of Inuit values and growing problems with substance abuse. Overall the movement has been quite successful, and many of the local institutions in Northwest Alaska have worked to integrate the principles of Inupiat Ilitqusiat into the conduct of their activities.

~Pamela Stern

FOR MORE INFORMATION

Lowenstein, T. *Ancient Land: Sacred Whale, The Inuit Hunt and Its Rituals*. New York: Farrar, Straus and Giroux, 1993.

Merkur, D. *Powers Which We Do Not Know: The Gods and Spirits of the Inuit*. Moscow: University of Idaho Press, 1991.

Turner, E. *The Hands Feel It: Healing and Spirit Presence among a Northern Alaskan People*. DeKalb: Northern Illinois University Press, 1996.

EUROPE

In the 20th century, Europe was considered a highly secular continent in which most of the political (and other) decisions were made without obvious regard for religious considerations. Yet, at the same time, Europeans did have strong religious traditions and controversies. See the Catholicism and Protestantism entries in the section "Deities and Doctrines" in chapter 8 ("Religious Life") in volume 3 of this series for the major branches of Christianity that grew up on European soil. Furthermore, in the 20th century, Europe's population became increasingly diverse, and many residents embraced Islam. See the Islamic World entry in the section "Religion" in this chapter of this volume.

RELIGIOUS LIFE: WEB SITES

http://www.hindunet.org/festivals/
http://comedition.com
http://www.risu.org.ua/content.php?page_id=126&l=en
http://www.1upinfo.com/country-guide-study/soviet-union/soviet-union119.html
http://www.nhc.rtp.nc.us/

PRIMARY SOURCES

ACCOUNT OF A MASS EXECUTION OF HOLOCAUST VICTIMS, 1942

Viewed as one of the most horrific events of the modern world, the Holocaust led to the deaths of millions. Working for a construction company, Hermann Friedrich Graebe witnessed the systematic execution of Jewish people and later recorded his experience in the graphic account given below.

I, the undersigned, Hermann Friedrich Graebe, make the following declaration under oath:

From September 1941 to January 1944 I was director and chief engineer of the Sdolbunow branch of the Josef Jung Construction Company of Solingen. In this capacity I had, among my other duties, to visit the firm's projects. Under the terms of a contract with the army construction services, the company was to build grain warehouses on the old Dubno airfield in the Ukraine.

On October 5, 1942, at the time of my visit to the construction offices in Dubno, my foreman, Hubert Moennikes, living at 21 Aussenmuhlenweg, Hamburg Haarburg, told me that some Dubno Jews had been shot near the building in three huge ditches about 30 metres long and 3 metres deep. The number of people killed daily was about 1,500. The 5,000 Jews who had lived in Dubno before the Pogrom were all marked for liquidation. Since the executions took place in the presence of my employee, he was painfully impressed by them.

Accompanied by Moennikes, I then went to the work area. I saw great mounds of earth abut 30 metres long and 2 high. Several trucks were parked nearby. Armed Ukrainian militia were making people get out, under the surveillance of SS soldiers. The same militia men were responsible for guard duty and driving the trucks. The people in the trucks wore the regulation yellow pieces of cloth that identified them as Jews on the front and back of their clothing.

Moennikes and I went straight toward the ditches without being stopped. When we neared the mound, I heard a series of rifle shots close by. The people from the trucks—men, women and children—were forced to undress under the supervision of an SS soldier with a whip in his hand. They were obliged to put their effects in certain spots: shoes, clothing, and underwear separately. I saw a pile of shoes, about 800,000 pairs, great heaps of underwear and clothing. Without weeping or crying out, these people undressed. During the fifteen minutes I stayed there, I did not hear a single complaint, or plea for mercy. I watched a family of about eight: a man and woman about fifty years old, surrounded by their children of about one, eight, and ten, and two big girls about twenty and twenty-four. An old lady, her hair completely white, held the baby in her arms, rocking it, and singing it a song. The infant was crying aloud with delight. The parents watched the groups with tears in their eyes. The father held the ten-year-old boy by the hand, speaking softly to him: the child struggled to hold back the tears. Then the father pointed a finger to the sky, and, stroking the child's head, seemed to be explaining something. At this moment, the SS near the ditch called something to his comrade. The latter counted off some twenty people and ordered them behind the mound. The family of which I have just spoken was in the group. I still remember the young girl, slender and dark, who, passing near me, pointed at herself, saying, "Twenty-three." I walked around the mound and faced a frightful common grave. Tightly packed corpses were heaped so close together that only the heads showed. Most were wounded in the head and the blood flowed over the shoulders. Some still moved. Others raised their hands and turned their heads to show that they were still alive. The ditch was two-thirds full. I estimate that it held a thousand bodies. I turned my eyes toward the man who had carried out the execution. He was an SS man; he was seated, legs swinging, on the narrow edge of the ditch; an automatic rifle rested on his knees and he was smoking a cigarette. The people, completely naked, climbed down a few steps cut in the clay wall and stopped at the spot indicated by the SS man. Facing the dead and wounded, they spoke softly to them. Then I heard a series of rifle shots. I looked in the ditch and saw their bodies contorting, their heads, already inert, sinking on the corpses beneath. The blood flowed from the nape of their necks. I was astonished not to be ordered away, but I noticed two or three uniformed postmen nearby. A new batch of victims approached the place. They climbed down into the ditch, lined up in front of the previous victims, and were shot. . . .

Graebe, Hermann Friedrich: "Account of Holocaust Mass Shooting, 1942." In Modern History Sourcebook at http://www.fordham.edu.

PRESIDENTIAL ORDER RACIALLY INTEGRATING THE ARMED FORCES OF THE UNITED STATES, 1948

On July 26, 1948, President Harry S Truman issued Executive Order 9981, which formally ended segregation in the military forces of the United States. The order called for complete equality of opportunity for all members of the armed services, regardless of race, religion, or national origin.

WHEREAS it is essential that there be maintained in the armed services of the United States the highest standards of democracy, with equality of treatment and opportunity for all those who serve in our country's defense:

NOW THEREFORE, by virtue of the authority vested in me as President of the United States, by the Constitution and the statutes of the United States, and as Commander in Chief of the armed services, it is hereby ordered as follows:

1. It is hereby declared to be the policy of the President that there shall be equality of treatment and opportunity for all persons in the armed services without regard to race, color, religion or national origin. This policy shall be put into effect as rapidly as possible, having due regard to the time required to effectuate any necessary changes without impairing efficiency or morale.

2. There shall be created in the National Military Establishment an advisory committee to be known as the President's Committee on Equality of Treatment and Opportunity in the Armed Services, which shall be composed of seven members to be designated by the President.

3. The Committee is authorized on behalf of the President to examine into the rules, procedures and practices of the Armed Services in order to determine in what respect such rules, procedures and practices may be altered or improved with a view to carrying out the policy of this order. The Committee shall confer and advise the Secretary of Defense, the Secretary of the Army, the Secretary of the Navy, and the Secretary of the Air Force, and shall make such recommendations to the President and to said Secretaries as in the judgment of the Committee will effectuate the policy hereof.

4. All executive departments and agencies of the Federal Government are authorized and directed to cooperate with the Committee in its work, and to furnish the Committee such information or the services of such persons as the Committee may require in the performance of its duties.

5. When requested by the Committee to do so, persons in the armed services or in any of the executive departments and agencies of the Federal Government shall testify before the Committee and shall make available for use of the Committee such documents and other information as the Committee may require.

6. The Committee shall continue to exist until such time as the President shall terminate its existence by Executive order.

Harry Truman
The White House
July 26, 1948
Executive Order 9981 at www.trumanlibrary.org.

EXCERPT FROM *TO THE LIGHTHOUSE* BY VIRGINIA WOOLF, 1927

Virginia Woolf led a life filled with mental instability and the deaths of many people close to her. Her writings reflect the tragic situations in her life and introduced a form of writing referred to as stream of consciousness. Woolf published a number of books that illustrate this new technique, including *To the Lighthouse*, first published in 1927.

"But it may be fine—I expect it will be fine," said Mrs. Ramsay, making some little twist of the reddish brown stocking she was knitting, impatiently. If she finished it tonight, if they did go to the Lighthouse after all, it was to be given to the Lighthouse keeper for his little boy, who was threatened with a tuberculous hip; together with a pile of old magazines, and some tobacco, indeed, whatever she could find lying about, not really wanted, but only littering the room, to give those poor fellows, who must be bored to death sitting all day with nothing to do but polish the lamp and trim the wick and rake about on their scrap of garden, something to amuse them. For how would you like to be shut up for a whole month at a time, and possibly more in stormy weather, upon a rock the size of a tennis lawn? she would ask; and to have no letters or newspapers, and to see nobody; if you were married, not to see your wife, not to know how your children were,—if they were ill, if they had fallen down and broken their legs or arms; to see the same dreary waves breaking week after week, and then a dreadful storm coming, and the windows covered with spray, and birds dashed against the lamp, and the whole place rocking, and not be able to put your nose out of doors for fear of being swept into the sea? How would you like that? she asked, addressing herself particularly to her daughters. So she added, rather differently, one must take them whatever comforts one can. . . .

Woolf, Virginia. *To the Lighthouse*. New York: Harcourt, Brace. 1955.

WORLD WAR II RATION BOOK, 1944

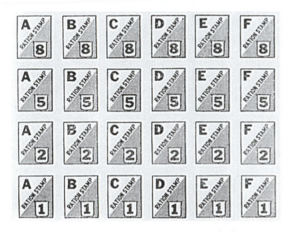

War Ration Book No. 3, a World War II coupon ration book. © Library of Congress.

Pictured here with a contemporary description is a ration coupon book, a common feature of life in the United States during World War II. In May 1942, the Office of Price Administration required civilians to register for ration books like this one to purchase sugar. Later such other commodities as coffee, coal, oil, and gas were also rationed.

War ration book no. 3. This new ration book, replacement for present books when their stamps are used up, will be distributed during the early summer. It contains four pages of "point" stamps, similar to the point stamps in war ration book 2, though slightly different in design and printed in brown ink. It also contains four pages of "unit" stamps for the type of rationing now used for sugar, coffee, and shoes. Each page of 48 stamps bears the design of a different war machine, including guns, tanks, aircraft carriers and planes.

Library of Congress/LC-USE6-D-010120: memory.loc.gov.

MOHANDAS GANDHI ON THE PROBLEMS AND FUTURE OF INDIAN WOMEN

The embodiment of passive resistance, Mohandas Gandhi (1869–1948) worked to bring an end to the violence that plagued India in the 20th century. To encourage an end to uprisings, Gandhi fasted until the fighting ceased and wrote volumes on numerous social issues.

I am firmly of opinion that India's salvation depends on the sacrifice and enlightenment of her women. . . .

I had flattered myself that my contribution to the women's case definitely began with the discovery of satyagraha. But the writer of the letter is of opinion that the fair sex requires treatment different from men. It is so, I do not think any man will find the correct solution. No matter how much he tries, he must fail because nature has made him different from woman. Only the toad under the harrow knows where it pinches him. Therefore ultimately woman will have to determine with authority what she needs. My own opinion is that, just as fundamentally man and woman are one, their problem must be one in essence. The soul in both is the same. The two live the same life, have the same feelings. Each is a complement of the other. The one cannot live without the other's active help.

But somehow or other man has dominated woman from ages past, and so woman has developed an inferiority complex. She has believed in the truth of man's interested teaching that she is inferior to him. But the seers among men have recognized her equal status.

Nevertheless there is no doubt that at some point there is bifurcation. Whilst both are fundamentally one, it is also equally true that in the form there is a vital difference between the two. Hence the vocations of the two must also be different. The duty of motherhood, which the vast majority of women will always undertake, requires qualities which man need not possess. She is passive, he is active. She is essentially mistress of the house. He is the breadwinner. She is the keeper and distributor of the bread. She is the care-taker in every sense of the term. The art of bringing up the infants of the race is her special and sole prerogative. Without her care the race must become extinct. . . .

As I have watched millions of peasants in their natural surroundings and as I watch them daily in little Segaon, the natural division of spheres of work has forced itself on my attention. There are no women black-smiths and carpenters. But men and women work on the fields, the heaviest work being done by the males. The women keep and manage the homes. They supplement the meager resources of the family, but man remains the breadwinner.

The divisions of the spheres of work being recognized, the general qualities and culture required are practically the same for both the sexes.

My contribution to the great problem lies in my presenting for acceptance truth and ahimsa in every walk of life, whether for individuals or nations. I have hugged the hope that in this woman will be the unquestioned leader and having thus found her place in human evolution, she will shed her inferiority complex. If she is able to do this successfully, she must resolutely refuse to believe in the modern teaching that everything is determined and regulated by the sex impulse. I fear I have put the proposition rather clumsily. But I hope my meaning is clear. I do not know that the millions of men who are taking an active part in the war are obsessed by the sex specter. Nor are the peasants working together in their fields worried or dominated by it. This is not to say or suggest that they are free from the instinct implanted in man and woman. But it most certainly does not dominate their lives as it seems to dominate the lives of those who are saturated with the modern sex literature. Neither man nor woman has time for such things when he or she is faced with the hard fact of living life in its grim reality.

I have suggested in these columns that woman is the incarnation of ahimsa. Ahimsa means infinite love, which again means infinite capacity for suffering. Who but woman, the mother of man, shows this capacity in the largest measure? She shows it as she carries the infant and feeds it during nine months and derives joy in the suffering involved. What can beat the suffering caused by the pangs of labour? But she forgets them in the joy of creation. Who again suffers daily so that her babe may wax from day to day? Let her transfer that love to the whole of humanity, let her forget that she ever was or can be the object of man's lust. And she will occupy her proud position by the side of man as his mother, maker and silent leader. It is given to her to teach the art of peace to the warring world thirsting for that nectar. . . .

My good nurse in the Sassoon Hospital, Poona, as I was lying on a sick bed years ago, told me the story of a woman who refused to take chloroform because she would not risk the life of the babe she was carrying. She had to undergo a painful operation. The only anesthetic she had was her love for the babe, to save whom no suffering was too great. Let not women, who can count many such heroines among them, ever despise their sex or deplore that they were not born men. The contemplation of that heroine often makes me envy woman the status that is hers, if she only knew. There is as much reason for man to wish that he was born a woman as for woman to do otherwise. But the wish is fruitless. Let us be happy in the state to which we are born and do the duty for which nature has destined us.

Gandhi, Mohandas K. "Women's Problems: Women and India's Future." http://www. mkgandhi.org/sfgbook/eighteenth.htm.

EXCERPT FROM THE SUPREME COURT'S DECISION ON ABORTION RIGHTS IN *ROE V. WADE,* 1973

On January 22, 1973, the U.S. Supreme Court rendered its decision in the case of *Roe v. Wade,* thereby liberalizing access to abortion for American women and politicizing the abortion issue. By a 7-2 vote, the Court struck down a Texas criminal abortion statute, and all similar state statutes, for violating the constitutional right to privacy, especially as it pertained to a woman's decision, in consultation with her doctor, to terminate a pregnancy. However, the majority opinion, written by Justice Harry Blackmun, also noted that the right to privacy was not absolute and recognized the ability of the state to regulate or even prohibit abortions for pregnancies that had developed past the first trimester.

In view of all this, we do not agree that, by adopting one theory of life, Texas may override the rights of the pregnant woman that are at stake. We repeat, however, that the State does have an important and legitimate interest in preserving and protecting the health of the pregnant woman, whether she be a resident of the State or a nonresident who seeks medical consultation and treatment there, and that it has still *another* important and legitimate interest in protecting the potentiality of human life. These interests are separate and distinct. Each grows in substantiality as the woman approaches term and, at a point during pregnancy, each becomes "compelling."

With respect to the State's important and legitimate interest in the health of the mother, the "compelling" point, in the light of present medical knowledge, is at approximately the end of the first trimester. This is so because of the now-established medical fact, referred to above at 149, that until the end of the first trimester mortality in abortion may be less than mortality in normal childbirth. It follows that, from and after this point, a State may regulate the abortion procedure to the extent that the regulation reasonably relates to the preservation and protection of maternal health. Examples of permissible state regulation in this area are requirements as to the qualifications of the person who is to perform the abortion; as to the licensure of that person; as to the facility in which the procedure is to be performed, that is, whether it must be a hospital or may be a clinic or some other place of less-than-hospital status; as to the licensing of the facility; and the like.

This means, on the other hand, that, for the period of pregnancy prior to this "compelling" point, the attending physician, in consultation with his patient, is free to determine, without regulation by the State, that, in his medical judgment, the patient's pregnancy should be terminated. If that decision is reached, the judgment may be effectuated by an abortion free of interference by the State.

With respect to the State's important and legitimate interest in potential life, the "compelling" point is at viability. This is so because the fetus then presumably has the capability of meaningful life outside the mother's womb. State regulation protective of fetal life after viability thus has both logical and biological justifications. If the State is interested in protecting fetal life after viability, it may go so far as to proscribe abortion during that period, except when it is necessary to preserve the life or health of the mother.

Measured against these standards, Art. 1196 of the Texas Penal Code, in restricting legal abortions to those "procured or attempted by medical advice for the purpose of saving the life of the mother," sweeps too broadly. The statute makes no distinction between abortions performed early in pregnancy and those performed later, and it limits to a single reason, "saving" the mother's life, the legal justification for the procedure. The statute, therefore, cannot survive the constitutional attack made upon it here.

Roe v. Wade at www.tourolaw.edu.

EXCERPT FROM *DOCTOR ZHIVAGO* BY BORIS PASTERNAK, 1957

Boris Leonidovich Pasternak (1890–1960) is well known as both a poet and novelist. Born in Moscow, the child of an artist and a concert pianist of Jewish descent, Pasternak studied music and philosophy before devoting himself to poetry and literature in 1913. During the 1930s, because he was persecuted by Stalin's regime and publication of his work was restricted, Pasternak began translating literature from other languages, including Shakespeare's plays. *Doctor Zhivago,* generally considered his masterpiece, was published in 1957 in Italy but was denied publication in the USSR. Pasternak won the Nobel Prize for literature in 1958 but was denounced by the Soviet government and forced to renounce the award. He thereafter persuaded the government to allow him to remain in Russia and lived in virtual exile in an artists' colony outside Moscow until his death in 1960.

One day in the summer of 1903, Yura was driving across fields in a two-horse open carriage with his Uncle Nikolai. They were on their way to see Ivan Ivanovich Voskoboinikov, a teacher and author of popular textbooks, who lived at Duplyanka, the estate of Kologrivov, a silk manufacturer, and a great patron of the arts.

It was the Feast of the Virgin of Kazan. The harvest was in full swing but, whether because of the feast or because of the midday break, there was not a soul in sight. The half-reaped fields under the glaring sun looked like the half-shorn heads of convicts. Birds were circling overhead. In the hot stillness the heavy-eared wheat stood straight. Neat sheaves rose above the stubble in the distance; if you stared at them long enough they seemed to move, walking along on the horizon like land surveyors taking notes.

"Whose fields are these?" Nikolai Nikolaievich asked Pavel, the publisher's odd-job man who sat sideways on the box, shoulders hunched and legs crossed to show that driving was not his regular job. "The landlords or the peasants'?"

"These are the master's." Pavel, who was smoking, after a long silence jabbed with the end of his whip in another direction: "And those are the peasants'!—Get along," he shouted at the horses, keeping an eye on their tails and haunches like an engineer watching his pressure gauge. The horses were like horses the world over: the shaft horse pulled with the innate honesty of a simple soul while the off horse arched its neck like a swan and seemed to the uninitiated to be an inveterate idler who thought only of prancing in time to the jangling bells.

Nikolai Nikolaievich had with him the proofs of Voskoboinikov's book on the land question; the publisher had asked the author to revise it in view of the increasingly strict censorship.

"The people are getting out of hand here," he told Pavel. "A merchant in a nearby village had his throat slit and the county stud farm has been burned down. What do you make of it? Any talk of it in your village?"

But evidently Pavel took an even gloomier view than the censor who urged Voskoboinikov to moderate his passionate views on the agrarian problem.

"Talk of it? The peasants have been spoiled—treated too well. That's no good for the likes of us. Give the peasants rope and God knows we'll all be at each other's throats in no time.—Get along, there!" . . .

In a second-class compartment of the train sat Misha Gordon, who was traveling with his father, a lawyer from Orenburg. Misha was a boy of eleven with a thoughtful face and big dark eyes; he was in his second year of gymnasium. His father, Grigory Osipovich Gordon, was being transferred to a new post in Moscow. His mother and sisters had gone on some time before to get their apartment ready.

Father and son had been traveling for three days.

Russia, with its fields, steppes, villages, and towns, bleached lime-white by the sun, flew past them wrapped in hot clouds of dust. Lines of carts rolled along the highways, occasionally lumbering off the road to cross the tracks; from the furiously speeding train it seemed that the carts stood still and the horses were marking time.

At big stations passengers jumped out and ran to the buffet; the sun setting behind the station garden lit their feet and shone under the wheels of the train.

Every motion in the world taken separately was calculated and purposeful, but, taken together, they were spontaneously intoxicated with the general stream of life which united them all. People worked and struggled, each set in motion by the mechanism of his own cares. But the mechanisms would not have worked properly had they not been regulated and governed by a higher sense of an ultimate freedom from care. This freedom came from the feeling that all human lives were interrelated, a certainty that they flowed into each other—a happy feeling that all events took place not only on the earth, in which the dead are buried, but also in some other region which some called the Kingdom of God, others history, and still others by some other name.

To this general rule Misha was an unhappy, bitter exception. A feeling of care remained his ultimate mainspring and was not relieved and ennobled by a sense of security. He knew this hereditary trait in himself and watched morbidly and self-consciously for symptoms of it in himself. It distressed him. Its presence humiliated him.

For as long as he could remember he had never ceased to wonder why, having arms and legs like everyone else, and a language and way of life common to all, one could be different from the others, liked only by few, and moreover, loved by no one. He could not understand a situation in which if you were worse than other people you could not make an effort to improve yourself. What did it mean to be a Jew? What was the purpose of it? What was the reward or the justification of this impotent challenge, which brought nothing but grief?

When Misha took the problem to his father he was told that his premises were absurd, and that such reasonings were wrong, but he was offered no solution deep enough to attract him or to make him bow silently to the inevitable.

And making an exception only for his parents, he gradually became contemptuous of all grownups who made this mess and were unable to clear it up. He was sure that when he was big he would straighten it all out.

Pasternak, Boris. *Doctor Zhivago*. Translated by Max Hayward and Manya Harari. New York: Pantheon Books, 1958.

EXCERPT FROM A REPORT CRITICIZING THE FAILURE OF THE U.S. GOVERNMENT TO HELP RESCUE JEWS FROM THE NAZI HOLOCAUST, 1944

The magnitude of the Germans' war on European Jews from the 1930s through the end of World War II is nearly unimaginable. And yet, the Holocaust was known to many Allied governments, including that of the United States. But what did the United States do to stop the mass murder? Could the United States in fact have done more to help Europe's Jews? In this 1944 report to President Franklin D. Roosevelt, the American Secretary of the Treasury, Henry J. Morgenthau, outlines American acquiescence during the Holocaust while suggesting possible actions that the government could take.

"Report to the Secretary on the Acquiescence of This Government in the Murder of the Jews, January 13, 1944"

One of the greatest crimes in history, the slaughter of the Jewish people in Europe, is continuing unabated.

This Government has for a long time maintained that its policy is to work out programs to save those Jews of Europe who could be saved.

I am convinced on the basis of the information which is available to me that certain officials in our State Department, which is charged with carrying out this policy, have been guilty not only of gross procrastination and willful failure to act, but even willful attempts to prevent action from being taken to rescue Jews from Hitler.

I fully recognize the graveness of this statement and I make it only after having most carefully weighed the shocking facts which have come to my attention during the last several months.

Unless remedial steps of a drastic nature are taken, and taken immediately, I am certain that no effective action will be taken by this Government to prevent the complete extermination of the Jews in German controlled Europe, and that this Government will have to share for all time responsibility for this extermination.

The tragic history of this Government's handling of this matter reveals that certain State Department officials are guilty of the following:

(1) They have not only failed to use the *Governmental machinery* at their disposal to rescue Jews from Hitler, but have even gone so far as to use this Government machinery to prevent the rescue of these Jews.

(2) They have not only failed to cooperate with *private organizations* in the efforts of these organizations to work out programs of their own, but have taken steps designed to prevent these programs from being put into effect.

(3) They not only have failed to facilitate the obtaining of information concerning Hitler's plans to exterminate the Jews of Europe but in their official capacity have gone so far as to surreptitiously attempt to stop the obtaining of information concerning the murder of the Jewish population of Europe.

(4) They have tried to cover up their guilt by:

    (a) concealment and misrepresentation;

    (b) the giving of false and misleading explanations for their failures to act and their attempts to prevent action; and

    (c) the issuance of false and misleading statements concerning the "action" which they have taken to date . . .

One of the best summaries of the whole situation is contained in one sentence of a report submitted on December 20, 1943, by the Committee on Foreign Relations of the Senate, recommending the passage of a Resolution (S.R. 203) favoring the appointment of a commission to formulate plans to save the Jews of Europe from extinction by Nazi Germany. The Committee stated:

"We have talked; we have sympathized; we have expressed our horror; the time to act is long past due."

The Senate Resolution had been introduced by Senator Guy M. Gillette on behalf of himself and eleven colleagues, Senators Taft, Thomas, Radcliffe, Murray, Johnson, Guffey, Ferguson, Clark, Van Nuys, Downey, and Ellender.

The House Resolutions (H.R.s 350 and 352), identical with the Senate Resolutions, were introduced by Representatives Baldwin and Rogers.

The most glaring example of the use of the machinery of this Government to *actually prevent the rescue of Jews* is the administrative restrictions which have been placed upon the granting of visas to the United States. In the note which the State Department sent to the British on February 25, 1943, it was stated:

"Since the entry of the United States into the war there have been no new restrictions placed by the Government of the United States upon the number of aliens of any nationality permitted to proceed to this country under existing laws, *except for the more intensive examination of aliens required for security reasons*." (Underscoring supplied)

The exception "for security reasons" mentioned in this note is the joker. Under the pretext of security reasons so many difficulties have been placed in the way of refugees obtaining visas that it is no wonder that the admission of refugees to this country does not come anywhere near the quota, despite [State Department official] Beckenridge Long's statement designed to create the impression to the contrary. The following *administrative* restrictions which have been applied to the issuance of visas since the beginning of the war are typical.

(a) Many applications for visas have been denied on the grounds that the applications have close relatives in Axis controlled Europe. The theory of this is that the enemy would be able to put pressure on the applicant as a result of the fact that the enemy has the power of life or death over his immediate family.

(b) Another restriction greatly increases the red tape and delay involved in getting the visas and requires among other things two affidavits of support and sponsorship to be furnished with each application for a visa. To each affidavit of support and sponsorship there must be attached two letters of reference from two reputable American citizens.

If anyone were to attempt to work out a set of restrictions specifically designed to prevent Jewish refugees from entering this country it is difficult to conceive of how more effective restrictions could have been imposed than have already been imposed on grounds of "security."

It is obvious of course that these restrictions are not essential for security reasons. Thus refugees upon arriving in this country could be placed in internment camps similar to those used for the Japanese on the West Coast and released only after a satisfactory investigation. Furthermore, even if we took these refugees and treated them as prisoners of war it would be better than letting them die. . . .

David S. Wymann. *America and the Holocaust: A Thirteen-Volume Set Documenting the Editor's Book: The Abandonment of the Jews*. Vol. 6. Amherst: University of Massachusetts Press, 1989. 238–55.

EXCERPT FROM TITLE IX OF THE EDUCATION AMENDMENTS OF 1972

The most visible result of Title IX of the Education Amendments of 1972, which prohibits sex discrimination in any educational program or activity that receives federal funds, is the expansion, over the last 30 years, of athletic programs for women. Despite the long list of exceptions given below, the act forced most colleges and universities to increase funding for women's athletics, add women's sports teams, increase the number and amount of athletic scholarships for women, and provide women with better athletic equipment and training.

Section 1681. Sex

(a) **Prohibition against discrimination; exceptions.** No person in the United States shall, on the basis of sex, be excluded from participation in, be denied the benefits of, or be subjected to discrimination under any education program or activity receiving Federal financial assistance, except that:

(1) Classes of educational institutions subject to prohibition
in regard to admissions to educational institutions, this section shall apply only to institutions of vocational education, professional education, and graduate higher education, and to public institutions of undergraduate higher education;

(2) Educational institutions commencing planned change in admissions
in regard to admissions to educational institutions, this section shall not apply (A) for one year from June 23, 1972, nor for six years after June 23, 1972, in the case of an educational institution which has begun the process of changing from being an institution which admits only students of one sex to being an institution which admits students of both sexes, but only if it is carrying out a plan for such a change which is approved by the Secretary of Education or (B) for seven years from the date an educational institution begins the process of changing from being an institution which admits only students of one sex to being an institution which admits students of both sexes, but only if it is carrying out a plan for such a change which is approved by the Secretary of Education, whichever is the later;

(3) Educational institutions of religious organizations with contrary religious tenets this section shall not apply to any educational institution which is controlled by a religious

organization if the application of this subsection would not be consistent with the religious tenets of such organization;

(4) Educational institutions training individuals for military services or merchant marine

this section shall not apply to an educational institution whose primary purpose is the training of individuals for the military services of the United States, or the merchant marine;

(5) Public educational institutions with traditional and continuing admissions policy

in regard to admissions this section shall not apply to any public institution of undergraduate higher education which is an institution that traditionally and continually from its establishment has had a policy of admitting only students of one sex;

(6) Social fraternities or sororities; voluntary youth service organizations

this section shall not apply to membership practices—

(A) of a social fraternity or social sorority which is exempt from taxation under section 501(a) of Title 26, the active membership of which consists primarily of students in attendance at an institution of higher education, or

(B) of the Young Men's Christian Association, Young Women's Christian Association; Girl Scouts, Boy Scouts, Camp Fire Girls, and voluntary youth service organizations which are so exempt, the membership of which has traditionally been limited to persons of one sex and principally to persons of less than nineteen years of age;

(7) Boy or Girl conferences

this section shall not apply to—

(A) any program or activity of the American Legion undertaken in connection with the organization or operation of any Boys State conference, Boys Nation conference, Girls State conference, or Girls Nation conference; or

(B) any program or activity of any secondary school or educational institution specifically for—

(i) the promotion of any Boys State conference, Boys Nation conference, Girls State conference, or Girls Nation conference; or

(ii) the selection of students to attend any such conference;

(8) Father-son or mother-daughter activities at educational institutions

this section shall not preclude father-son or mother-daughter activities at an educational institution, but if such activities are provided for students of one sex, opportunities for reasonably comparable activities shall be provided for students of the other sex; and

(9) Institutions of higher education scholarship awards in "beauty" pageants

this section shall not apply with respect to any scholarship or other financial assistance awarded by an institution of higher education to any individual because such individual has received such award in any pageant in which the attainment of such award is based upon a combination of factors related to the personal appearance, poise, and talent of such individual and in which participation is limited to individuals of one sex only, so long as such pageant is in compliance with other nondiscrimination provisions of Federal law.

"Title IX of the Education Amendments of 1972" at www.dol.gov.

PREAMBLE OF THE INDUSTRIAL WORKERS OF THE WORLD (IWW), 1905

The International Workers of the World—otherwise known as the Wobblies—was one of the most radical labor organizations in American history. Its membership, which included lumberjacks, miners, and farmhands, was dedicated not only to the improvement of the working class but also to the elimination of capitalism. This excerpt from the IWW's preamble outlines the group's basic beliefs.

The working class and the employing class have nothing in common. There can be no peace so long as hunger and want are found among millions of working people and the few, who make up the employing class, have all the good things of life.

Between these two classes a struggle must go on until workers of the world organize as a class, take possession of the earth and the machinery of production and abolish the wage system.

We find that centering of the management of industries into fewer and fewer hands makes the trade unions unable to cope with the ever growing power of the employing class. The trade unions foster a state of affairs which allows one set of workers to be pitted against another set of workers in the same industry, thereby helping defeat one another in wage wars. Moreover the trade unions aid the employing class to mislead the workers into the belief that the working class have interests in common with their employers.

These conditions can be changed and the interest of the working class upheld only by an organization formed in such a way that all its members in any one industry, or in all industries if necessary, cease work whenever a strike or lockout is on in any department thereof, thus making an injury to one an injury to all.

Instead of the conservative motto, "A fair day's wage for a fair day's work," we must inscribe on our banner the revolutionary watchword, "Abolition of the wage system." It is the historic mission of the working class to do away with capitalism. The arm of production must be organized not only for the everyday struggle with capitals, but also to carry on production when capitalism shall have been overthrown. By organizing industrially we are forming the structure of the new society within the shell of the old.

"Preamble of the Industrial Workers of the World." In Erik Bruun and Jay Crosby, *Our Nation's Archive: The History of the United States in Documents.* New York: Black Dog, 1999. 547–48.

EXCERPTS FROM THE PREAMBLE AND GENERAL CLAUSES OF THE NUNAVUT LAND CLAIMS AGREEMENT, 1993

On May 25, 1993, the Canadian government, the government of the Northwest Territories, and the Tungavik Federation of Nunavut signed an agreement calling for the creation of the new territory of Nunavut, an autonomous Inuit region that would have its own government and legislative assembly. For the first time, the accord allowed the Inuit peoples of Arctic Canada to control their own local affairs.

An Agreement

BETWEEN:

The Inuit of the Nunavut Settlement Area as represented by the Tungavik Federation of Nunavut

AND:

Her Majesty The Queen in Right of Canada.

WHEREAS the Inuit represented by the Tungavik Federation of Nunavut assert an aboriginal title to the Nunavut Settlement Area, more particularly described in Article 3, based on their traditional and current use and occupation of the lands, waters and land-fast ice therein in accordance with their own customs and usages;

AND WHEREAS the *Constitution Act, 1982* recognizes and affirms the existing aboriginal and treaty rights of the aboriginal peoples of Canada, and treaty rights includes rights that may be acquired by way of land claims agreements;

AND WHEREAS the Parties agree on the desirability of negotiating a land claims agreement through which Inuit shall receive defined rights and benefits in exchange for surrender of any claims, rights, title and interests based on their assertion of an aboriginal title;

AND WHEREAS the Parties have negotiated this land claims Agreement based on and reflecting the following objectives:

to provide for certainty and clarity of rights to ownership and use of lands and resources, and of rights for Inuit to participate in decision-making concerning the use, management and conservation of land, water and resources, including the offshore;

to provide Inuit with wildlife harvesting rights and rights to participate in decision-making concerning wildlife harvesting;

to provide Inuit with financial compensation and means of participating in economic opportunities;

to encourage self-reliance and the cultural and social well-being of Inuit;

AND WHEREAS the Inuit, in a vote held on November 3 to 6, 1992, approved the Agreement and authorized it to be signed by the duly appointed officers of the Tungavik Federation of Nunavut;

AND WHEREAS following the Inuit ratification vote the Parties completed the text of Article 40 and certain other parts of the Agreement and finalized the text for purposes of clarity, all pursuant to their authority under the Agreement as approved by the Inuit ratification vote;

AND WHEREAS

Cabinet authorized the Minister to sign the Agreement;

AND IN RECOGNITION of the contributions of Inuit to Canada's history, identity and sovereignty in the Arctic;

NOW, THEREFORE, THE PARTIES AGREE AS FOLLOWS:

PART 1: GENERAL

4.1.1 The Government of Canada will recommend to Parliament, as a government measure, legislation to establish, within a defined period of time, a new Nunavut Territory, with its own Legislative Assembly and public government, separate from the Government of the remainder of the Northwest Territories.

4.1.2 Therefore, Canada and the Territorial Government and Tungavik Federation of Nunavut shall negotiate a political accord to deal with the establishment of Nunavut. The political accord shall establish a precise date for recommending to Parliament legislation necessary to establish the Nunavut Territory and the Nunavut Government, and a transitional process. It is the intention of the Parties that the date shall coincide with recommending ratification legislation to Parliament unless the Tungavik Federation of Nunavut agrees otherwise. The political accord shall also provide for the types of powers of the Nunavut Government, certain principles relating to the financing of the Nunavut Government, and the time limits for the coming into existence and operation of the Nunavut Territorial Government. The political accord shall be finalized before the Inuit ratification vote. It is the intention of the Parties to complete the Political Accord by no later than April 1, 1992.

Nunavut Land Claims Agreement, Indian and Northern Affairs Canada Web site at www. ainc—inac.gc.ca.

EXCERPTS FROM A SPEECH BY SOVIET LEADER JOSEF STALIN, 1924

Born under the name Dzhugashvili, the man who propelled Russia into the global world changed his name to Josef Stalin, which means Man of Steel. To meet his goals, Stalin used whatever means he deemed necessary, including countless imprisonments and executions. In the speech below, delivered on November 26, 1924, Stalin explains the events surrounding the October 1917 uprising that led to the Communist seizure of power.

The Facts about the October Uprising

First of all about the October uprising. Rumours are being vigorously spread among members of the Party that the Central Committee as a whole was opposed to an uprising in October 1917. The usual story is that on October 10, when the Central Committee adopted the decision to organise the uprising, the majority of the Central Committee at first spoke against an uprising, but, so the story runs, at that moment a worker burst in on the meeting of the Central Committee and said:

"You are deciding against an uprising, but I tell you that there will be an uprising all the same, in spite of everything." And so, after that threat, the story runs, the Central Committee, which is alleged to have become frightened, raised the question of an uprising afresh and adopted a decision to organise it. This is not merely a rumour, comrades. It is related by the well-known John Reed in his book *Ten Days*. Reed was remote from our Party and, of course, could not know the history of our secret meeting on October 10, and, consequently, he was taken in by the gossip spread by people like Sukhanov. This story was later passed round and repeated in a number of pamphlets written by Trotskyites, including one of the latest pamphlets on October written by Syrkin. These rumours have been strongly supported in Trotsky's latest literary pronouncements.

It scarcely needs proof that all these and similar "Arabian Nights" fairy tales are not in accordance with the truth, that in fact nothing of the kind happened, nor could have happened, at the meeting of the Central Committee. Consequently, we could ignore these absurd rumours; after all, lots of rumours are fabricated in the office rooms of the oppositionists or those who are remote from the Party. Indeed, we have ignored them till now; for example, we paid no attention to John Reed's mistakes and did not take the trouble to rectify them. After Trotsky's latest pronouncements, however, it is no longer possible to ignore such legends, for attempts are being made now to bring up our young people on them and, unfortunately, some results have already been achieved in this respect. In view of this, I must counter these absurd rumours with the actual facts.

I take the minutes of the meeting of the Central Committee of our Party on October 10 (23), 1917. . . . The question of the current situation and the uprising was discussed. After the discussion, Comrade Lenin's resolution on the uprising was put to the vote. The resolution was adopted by a majority of 10 against 2. Clear, one would think: by a majority of 10 against 2, the Central Committee decided to proceed with the immediate, practical work of organising the uprising. At this very same meeting the Central Committee elected a *political* centre to direct the uprising; this centre, called the Political Bureau, consisted of Lenin, Zinoviev, Stalin, Kamenev, Trotsky, Sokolnikov and Bubnov.

Such are the facts.

These minutes at one stroke destroy several legends. They destroy the legend that the majority on the Central Committee are opposed to an uprising. They also destroy the legend that on the question of the uprising the Central Committee was on the verge of a split. It is clear from the minutes that the opponents of an immediate uprising—Kamenev and Zinoiev—were elected to the body that was to exercise political direction of the uprising on a par with those who were in favour of an uprising. There was no question of a split, nor could there be. . . .

This, of course, does not mean that the October uprising did not have its inspirer. It did have its inspirer and leader, but this was Lenin, and none other than Lenin, that same Lenin whose resolutions the Central Committee adopted when deciding the question of the uprising, that same Lenin who, in spite of what Trotsky says, was not prevented by being in hiding from being the actual inspirer of the uprising. It is foolish and ridiculous to attempt now, by gossip about Lenin having been in hiding, to obscure the indubitable fact that the inspirer of the uprising was the leader of the party, V.I. Lenin. . . .

The proletarian struggle is not, however, an uninterrupted advance, an unbroken chain of victories. The proletarian struggle also has its trials, its defeats. The genuine revolutionary is not one who displays courage in the period of a victorious uprising, but one who, while fighting well during the victorious advance of the revolution, also displays courage when the revolution is in retreat, when the proletariat suffers defeat; who does not lose his head and does not funk when the revolution suffers reverses, when the enemy achieves success; who does not become panic-stricken or give way to despair when the revolution is in a period of retreat. . . .

In Trotsky's opinion, the principal lesson of the proletarian revolution is "not to funk" during October. That is wrong, for Trotsky's assertion contains only a *particle* of the truth about the lessons of the revolution. The *whole* truth about the lessons of the proletarian revolution is "not to funk" not only when the revolution is advancing, but also when it is in retreat, when the enemy is gaining the upper hand and the revolution is suffering reverses. The revolution did not end with October. October was only the beginning of the proletarian revolution. It is bad to funk when the tide of insurrection is rising; but it is worse to funk when the revolution is passing through severe trials after power has been captured.

Stalin, Joseph V. "Trotskyism or Leninism?" Speech delivered November 26, 1924. http://www.marxists.org/reference/archive/stalin/works/1924/11_19.htm#s1

EXCERPTS FROM THE 1936 SOVIET CONSTITUTION

The constitution adopted in December 1936 was the second constitution of the USSR. To American eyes, it seems like an enlightened document seeking to create a kind of utopian existence in which all people shared equally in the wealth of the nation, in which gender equality, old age security, civil liberties, and education were guaranteed. And yet, the issuing of this constitution coincided with the Great Terror in which Stalin loyalists executed countless Russians. The 1936 constitution outlined the aspirations of a nation whose reality was controlled by the leadership of the Communist Party.

Chapter I

The Organization of Soviet Society

ARTICLE 1. The Union of Soviet Socialist Republics is a socialist state of workers and peasants.

ARTICLE 2. The Soviets of Working People's Deputies, which grew and attained strength as a result of the overthrow of the landlords and capitalists and the achievement of the dictatorship of the proletariat, constitute the political foundation of the USSR.

ARTICLE 3. In the USSR all power belongs to the working people of town and country as represented by the Soviets of Working People's Deputies.

ARTICLE 4. The socialist system of economy and the socialist ownership of the means and instruments of production firmly established as a result of the abolition of the capitalist system of economy, the abrogation of private ownership of the means and instruments of production and the abolition of the exploitation of man by man, constitute the economic foundation of the USSR.

ARTICLE 5. Socialist property in the USSR exists either in the form of state property (the possession of the whole people), or in the form of cooperative and collective-farm property (property of a collective farm or property of a cooperative association).

ARTICLE 6. The land, its natural deposits, waters, forests, mills, factories, mines, rail, water and air transport, banks, post, telegraph and telephones, large state-organized agricultural enterprises (state farms, machine and tractor stations and the like) as well as municipal enterprises and the bulk of the dwelling houses in the cities and industrial localities, are state property, that is, belong to the whole people.

ARTICLE 7. Public enterprises in collective farms and cooperative organizations, with their livestock and implements, the products of the collective farms and co-operative organizations, as well as their common buildings, constitute the common socialist property of the collective farms and cooperative organizations. In addition to its basic income from the public collective-farm enterprise, every household in a collective farm has for its personal use a small plot of land attached to the dwelling and, as its personal property, a subsidiary establishment on the plot, a dwelling house, livestock, poultry and minor agricultural implements in accordance with the statutes of the agricultural cartel.

ARTICLE 8. The land occupied by collective farms is secured to them for their use free of charge and for an unlimited time, that is, in perpetuity.

ARTICLE 9. Alongside the socialist system of economy, which is the predominant form of economy in the USSR, the law permits the small private economy of individual peasants and handicraftsmen based on their personal labor and precluding the exploitation of the labor of others.

ARTICLE 10. The right of citizens to personal ownership of their incomes from work and of their savings, of their dwelling houses and subsidiary household economy, their household furniture and utensils and articles of personal use and convenience, as well as the right of inheritance of personal property of citizens, is protected by law.

ARTICLE 11. The economic life of the USSR is determined and directed by the state national economic plan with the aim of increasing the public wealth, of steadily improving the material conditions of the working people and raising their cultural level, of consolidating the independence of the USSR and strengthening its defensive capacity.

ARTICLE 12. In the USSR work is a duty and a matter of honor for every able-bodied citizen, in accordance with the principle: "He who does not work, neither shall he eat."

The principle applied in the USSR is that of socialism: "From each according to his ability, to each according to his work."

Robert Beard, "1936 Constitution," <http://www.departments.bucknell.edu/russian/const/36cons01.html>, Bucknell University.

EXCERPTS FROM THE GI BILL, 1944

Signed into law by President Franklin Roosevelt on June 22, 1944, the Service-men's Readjustment Act (popularly known as the GI Bill of Rights) provided for payment for the hospitalization of veterans, for home and business loans to veterans, for job counseling and employment placement services for veterans, and for unemployment benefits for veterans. However, perhaps the most important provisions of the bill were found in Title II, which provided veterans with education and training at government expense. By 1952, almost eight million servicemen, nearly half of those who had served in World War II, had received some education or training under the GI Bill.

Title II

Chapter IV—Education of Veterans

1. Any person who served in the active military or naval service on or after September 16, 1940, and prior to the termination of the present war, and who shall have been discharged or released therefrom under conditions other than dishonorable, and whose education or training was impeded, delayed, interrupted, or interfered with by reason of his entrance into the service, or who desires a refresher or retraining course, . . . shall be eligible for and entitled to receive education or training under this part: Provided, that such course shall be initiated not later than two years after either the date of his discharge or the termination of the present war, whichever is the later: Provided further, that no such education or training shall be afforded beyond seven years after the termination of the present war: And provided further, that any such person who was not over 25 years of age at the time he entered service shall be deemed to have had his education or training impeded, delayed, interrupted, or interfered with.

2. Any such eligible person shall be entitled to education or training, or a refresher course or retraining course, at an approved educational or training institution, for a period of one year . . . Upon satisfactory completion of such course of education or training . . . such person shall be entitled to an additional period or periods of education or training, not to exceed the time such person was in the active service on or after September 16, 1940, and before the termination of the war . . . but in no event shall the total period of education or training exceed four years.

3. Such person shall be eligible for and entitled to such course of education or training as he may elect, and at any approved educational or training institution at which he chooses to enroll, whether or not located in the State in which he resides, which will accept or retain him as a student or trainee in any field or branch of knowledge which such institution finds him qualified to undertake or pursue. . . .

5. The Administrator shall pay to the educational or training institution, for each person enrolled in full time or part time course of education or training, the customary cost of tuition, and such laboratory, library, health, infirmary, and other similar fees as are customarily charged, and may pay for books, supplies, equipment, and other necessary expenses, exclusive of board, lodging, other living expenses, and travel, as are generally required for the successful pursuit and completion of the course by other students in the institution: *Provided,* That in no event shall such payments, with respect to any person, exceed $500 for an ordinary school year. . . .

6. While enrolled in and pursuing a course under this part, such person, upon application to the Administrator, shall be paid a subsistence allowance of $50 per

month, if without a dependent or dependents, or $75 per month, if he has a dependent or dependents. . . .

11. As used in this part, the term "education or training institutions" shall include all public and private elementary, secondary, and other schools furnishing education for adults, business schools and colleges, scientific and technical institutions, colleges, vocational schools, universities, and other educational institutions, and shall also include business or other establishments providing apprentice or other training on the job. . . .

United States Statutes at Large, 1944. Vol. 58, part 1. Washington, D.C.: Government Printing Office, 1945. 288–94.

CUMULATIVE INDEX

Boldface numbers refer to volume numbers. A key appears on all verso pages.

Banquets: China (Tang Dynasty), **2:**60, 83; Greece (ancient), **1:**253; India (20th Century), **6:**316; Islamic World (Middle Ages), **2:**85; Mesopotamia, **1:**343; Rome (ancient), **1:**256–57, 430; Soviet Union, **6:**318; Vikings, **2:**397–98

Bansuni, **5:**424

Baptism: Catholicism (Spain, Italy, England), **3:**380–81; Christianity (England, Spain, Italy), **3:**31, 396; England (15th & 16th Centuries), **3:**32, 74; Europe (Middle Ages), **2:**79, 410; Italy (15th & 16th Centuries), **3:**37–38, 79; Kongo (17th & 18th Centuries), **4:**485; Latin America (19th Century), **5:**471; Latin America (20th Century), **6:**43; Protestantism (England), **3:**365, 382; Soviet Union, **6:**598; Spain (15th & 16th Centuries), **3:**34, 76–77

Baptists: England (17th & 18th Centuries), **4:**491–92; Soviet Union, **6:**597; United States (Civil War era), **5:**456, 457, 458, 459; United States (1920–39), **6:**569, 570. *See also* Southern Baptist Convention

Baraka, **4:**467

Barbarians. *See* Foreigners, treatment of

Barbary Coast, **3:**18

Barbers: Europe (Middle Ages), **2:**182; Mesopotamia, **1:**360; Spain (15th & 16th Centuries), **3:**192

Barbettes, **2:**239, 259

Barbour, Emma Sargent, **5:**163, 164, 165

Barca, Calderón de la, **3:**212

Barcelona, **3:**287

Bardi family, **3:**8

Barges, **2:**139. *See also* Shipping; Ships and vessels

Barkesdale, William, **5:**314–15

Barkova, Anna, **6:**233

Bark painting, **1:**241

Barley: Byzantium, **2:**208; China (Tang Dynasty), **2:**204; England (15th & 16th Centuries), **3:**92, 241; Europe (15th & 16th Centuries), **3:**236; Vikings, **2:**126, 203

Barley break game, **3:**58, 317

Barnard, Christiaan, **6:**277

Barnett, Margaret, **6:**303

Barnitz, Albert, **5:**367, 370

Baronets, **5:**113

Barons and baronesses, **3:**271

Baroque art, **4:**453

Barracks. *See* Camps, military

Barranda, Joaquín, **5:**179

Barreda, Gabino, **5:**179

Barros Arana, Diego, **5:**19

Barrow, Bonnie and Clyde, **6:**416

Bars. *See* Taverns

Barter: Africa (17th & 18th Centuries), **4:**135; Aztec, **3:**122; Latin America (19th Century), **5:**246; 17th & 18th Centuries, **4:**132–33

Barth, Alan, **6:**527

Barton, Bruce, **6:**572

Baseball: Japan (20th Century), **6:**508; players' strike (1981), **6:**506; United States (Civil War era), **5:**429; United States (19th Century), **5:**397, 399–400; United States (1920–39), **6:**500–501; United States (1960–90), **6:**503, 504–5

Basements and cellars, **5:**262

Bashir II (Lebanon), **5:**354

Bashir III (Lebanon), **5:**354

Basilica churches, **2:**447

Basketball: Africa (20th Century), **6:**510; Europe (20th Century), **6:**499; invention of, **6:**499, 502; United States (1920–39), **6:**502; United States (1960–90), **6:**504

Basmati rice, **5:**243

Basque language, **3:**161

Bas-reliefs, **1:**230–31

Bassa dansa, **3:**347

Bastet, **1:**476

Batab, **3:**296, 311

Batabob, **3:**295

Bates, Daisy, **6:**443

Bathhouses: Byzantium, **2:**403–4; Islamic World (Middle Ages), **2:**232; Rome (ancient), **1:**100, 414

Bathing: Europe (Middle Ages), **2:**181; Greece (ancient), **1:**278; India (ancient), **1:**301, 336, 449; India (19th Century), **5:**265; India (20th Century), **6:**589–90; Rome (ancient), **1:**85; United States (1920–39), **6:**272; Vikings, **2:**261. *See also* Bathing rooms

Bathing rooms: India (ancient), **1:**301; Mesopotamia, **1:**271; Rome (ancient), **1:**414

Bathrooms: India (19th Century), **5:**265; India (20th Century), **6:**344. *See also* Bathing rooms; Latrines; Toilet facilities

Baths: Aztec, **3:**234; England (17th & 18th Centuries), **4:**226; Japan (17th & 18th Centuries), **4:**229

Batista, Fulgencio, **6:**480

Batman (film), **6:**529

Battering rams: Byzantium, **2:**361; Mesopotamia, **1:**372

Battle casualties: Greece (ancient), **1:**295, 378, 379, 381–82; Japan (20th Century), **6:**493; Korean War, **6:**370, 470; Latin America (20th Century), **6:**44, 479; Mesopotamia, **1:**287, 370, 372, 373; Rome (ancient), **1:**369; Soviet Union in World War II, **6:**488, 489; Vietnam conflict, **6:**370, 470; World War I, **6:**63, 261–62, 267–68, 349

Battle of. *See specific battle*

Batu Khan, **2:**220

Bauer, Brian, **3:**403

Bayezit I, **3:**10

Bayezit II, **3:**12, 19, 292

Bayle, Pierre, **4:**475

Bayonets, **6:**354–55

Bay Psalm Book, The, **4:**214

Bazalgette, Joseph, **5:**141

Bazin, André, **6:**514

Beans: Aztec, **3:**248; Civil War soldiers, **5:**222; Inca, **3:**2; Japan (17th & 18th Centuries), **4:**248; Latin America (19th Century), **5:**246; Maya, **3:**101, 246; United States (Civil War era), **5:**222; United States (Western Frontier), **5:**228, 230

Bear: Europe (Middle Ages), **2:**378; Inuit, **6:**321

Bear baiting: England (15th & 16th Centuries), **3:**330; Europe (Middle Ages), **2:**371; Middle Ages, **2:**369

Beards: Europe (Middle Ages), **2:**257, 260; Greece (ancient), **1:**325; Mesopotamia, **1:**317; Vikings, **2:**260

Beardsley, Aubrey, **5:**10

Beat generation, **6:**225, 542

Beatings. *See* Corporal punishment; Domestic violence; Punishment

Beatles, **6:**543, 545, 553

Beat to Quarters (Forester), **4:**218

Beavers, **5:**48–49, 119, 122, 228

Becker, Nubia, **6:**77

Bede, venerable, **2:**169

Bedouin. See Nomads

Bedrooms: England (15th & 16th Centuries), **3:**254; England (Victorian era), **5:**262–63, 264; Europe (Middle Ages), **2:**131; India (19th Century), **5:**265; Italy (15th & 16th Centuries), **3:**258; Middle Ages, **2:**301; Rome (ancient), **1:**280

Beds: Australian Aboriginals, **1:**281; China (Tang Dynasty), **2:**272; Civil War military, **5:**256; England (Victorian era), **5:**264; Europe (Middle Ages), **2:**267, 268–69; Islamic World (Middle Ages), **2:**273; Italy (15th & 16th Centuries), **3:**258–59; Japanese (Middle Ages), **2:**267; Mesopotamia, **1:**273; Middle Ages, **2:**267; North American colonial frontier, **4:**274; Vikings, **2:**228, 267, 270

Bedu masks, **4:**446

Beecher, Henry Ward, **5:**382

Beedle, Irwin P., **5:**187

Beef. *See* Meat

Beer: Africa (20th Century), **6:**331; England (15th & 16th Centuries), **3:**238–39; England (17th & 18th Centuries), **4:**262; England (Victorian era), **5:**239, 241; Europe (Middle Ages), **2:**214; Greece (ancient), **1:**266; Japan (20th Century), **6:**330; Latin America (19th Century), **5:**245; Mesopotamia, **1:**263, 286; Middle Ages, **2:**213; New England, colonial, **4:**265; North American colonial frontier, **4:**259–60; Nubia, **1:**259; Rome (ancient), **1:**269; United States (1920–39), **6:**307; United States (Western Frontier), **5:**409

Bees: Maya, **3:**247; Mesopotamia, **1:**78; Rome (ancient), **1:**85. *See also* Honey

Beetle. *See* Scarab beetle

Beeton, Isabella, **5:**237

Beeton, Samuel, **5:**191

Beggars: China (Tang Dynasty), **2:**325; England (15th & 16th Centuries), **3:**272; India (20th Century), **6:**58; Latin America (19th Century), **5:**97; Spain (15th & 16th Centuries), **3:**275

Beggar's Opera, The (Gay), **4:**450

Belgium: asylum offered to Jews, **6:**563; food in 15th & 16th Centuries, **3:**235; Holy Roman Empire, part of, **3:**283, 287

Belize: language, **3:**166; sculptures, **3:**351

Belknap, Keturah Penton, **5:**278

Bell, John, **5:**312–13, 316

Bello, Andrés, **5:**19

Bells: Europe (Middle Ages), **2:**387; Middle Ages, **2:**407

Belts: Europe (Middle Ages), **2:**238; Latin America (19th Century), **5:**289; Mongols, **2:**245, 246; Native Americans (colonial frontier of North America), **4:**304; United States (Civil War era), **5:**273; Vikings, **2:**240, 241

Bembo, Pietro, **3:**213

Benedictine monks (Middle Ages), **2:**435, 436

Benedict of Nursia, **2:**435, 436

Benjamin, Judah P., **5:**317

Benjamin, Walter, **6:**597–98

Benjamin, the Jew of Granada (Maturin), **5:**183

Bentinck, William, **5:**67

Benton, Thomas Hart, **5:**6

Beowulf, **2:**169

Berdan's Sharpshooters, **5:**291

Berenguer, Ramón, **3:**287

Berggolts, Olga, **6:**234

Beria, Lavrenty, **6:**425

Bering land bridge, **3:**2

Berke Khan, **2:**429

Coal: England (17th & 18th Centuries), 4:176; England (Victorian era), 5:75, 135, 141. *See also* Mining

Coalition of Labor Union Women, 6:131

Coatecoalli, 3:298

Coatlicue, 3:355

Coats: China (Tang Dynasty), 2:243; England (Victorian era), 5:281, 282; Europe (Middle Ages), 2:238; United States (Civil War era), 5:274; Vikings, 2:240

Coba, 3:120

Cobo, Bernabé, 3:249, 392

Coca: Inca, 3:105, 248–49, 390; Latin America (19th Century), 5:246

Coca-Cola, 6:329

Cochise, 5:366

Cochuah, 3:420

Cocidos, 3:240

Cockcrow, 3:128

Cockfighting: China (Tang Dynasty), 2:376; England (15th & 16th Centuries), 3:330; England (17th & 18th Centuries), 4:421; Europe (Middle Ages), 2:371; Middle Ages, 2:369; United States (19th Century), 5:398

Cocoa: Aztec, 3:122; England (Victorian era), 5:238; introduction to Europe, 3:222; Latin America (20th Century), 6:314. *See also* Chocolate

Cocom, 3:46

Coconut milk, 5:252

Coconuts: Hindu religious offering of, 6:589; Polynesia, 2:211

Cod, 2:202–3

Code of Hammurabi. *See* Laws of Hammurabi

Codex Borbonicus, 3:217

Codex Borgia, 3:374

Codex Fejérváry-Mayer, 3:217

Codex Justinianus, 2:340

Codex Mendoza: astronomy, 3:185; child care, 3:48, 84; child labor, 3:184; information contained in, 3:217; punishment, 3:73, 86, 183; Tenochtitlan, 3:123; warrior outfits, 3:233

Cod fishing (17th & 18th Centuries), 4:131–32

Codices: Aztec, 3:217; Maya, 3:214

Codpieces, 3:225–26

Cody, William, 5:87

Coemptio marriage in Roman Empire, 1:48–49

Coffee: Civil War soldiers, 5:221, 248, 249–50; England (17th & 18th Centuries), 4:260; England (Victorian era), 5:238; Germany (1914–18), 6:304; India (19th Century), 5:248–49, 251–52; India (20th Century), 6:301, 316; Islamic World (Middle Ages), 2:219; Latin America (19th Century), 5:19, 97, 132–33, 245, 246, 325; Latin America (20th Century), 6:314; Ottoman Empire, 3:244–45, 261; United States (Civil War era), 5:220, 221, 222; United States (1920–39), 6:307; United States (Western Frontier), 5:230, 232, 248, 251

Coffeehouses, 4:143

Coffee wagons in Civil War, 5:250

Coffin Texts, 1:512

Cognatic lineage systems, 4:368

Cognomen, 1:27

Cohabitation and Australian convicts, 4:32–33

Cohn, Roy, 6:377

Coif, 2:239

Coins. *See* Gold coins; Money

Coke, Edward, 3:252

Colbert, Jean-Louis Baptiste, 4:356

Colden, Cadwallader, 4:435

"Cold Food Festival," 2:455

Cold Harbor, Battle of, 5:42, 44

Cold War, 6:40; education and, 6:204; film and, 6:514; historical overview, 6:454, 456, 469; Olympic Games during, 6:499; space race and, 6:187; United States (1940–59), 6:376–77; United States (1945–90), 6:469–70

Colegio Nacional, 5:179

Colhuacan urban life, 3:124

Colitis, 6:271

Collars: Spain (15th & 16th Centuries), 3:227–28; United States (Civil War era), 5:270–71, 275

Collasuyu, 3:300

Collecting as Victorian England activity, 5:439

Collectivism of agriculture (Soviet Union), 6:174–75, 318

Colleges. *See* Universities

Collegia, 1:118, 129

Colleone, Bartolomeo, 3:40

Collins, Wilkie, 5:191

Collinson, Frank, 5:88

Colloquial literature of China, 5:193–94

Colombia: coffee, 5:97; gold, 5:132. *See also* Latin America *entries*

Colonial America. *See* British colonies in North America; New England, colonial; North American colonial frontier

Colonial Australia. *See* Australia, colonial

Colonial rule: Arab world, 6:230, 483; Britain, 5:349–52; 6:9, 25, 155, 230; France, 6:25, 230; Inuit, 6:402; Islamic World (19th Century), 5:16–17, 352–53, 455; Italy, 6:230; Latin America (19th Century), 5:340; Roman Empire, 1:98; Spain, 6:230; United States (Civil War era), 5:345; women under, 6:85. *See also* British colonies in North America; New France (17th & 18th Centuries)

Colonial rule of Africa: division of ethnic groups, 6:25; drink, 6:331–32; economic life, 6:86, 124; education, 6:86, 212–13; health and medicine, 6:294; historical overview, 6:25–26; law and crime, 6:431–33; religion, 6:601–2; science and technology, 6:193; sports, 6:509–10; taxes, 6:331–32; urban and rural life, 6:177; women, 6:86

Colonial rule of India: cities, 6:344; communication methods, 6:254; government, 6:388; historical overview, 6:9; medicine, 6:286; military, 6:9; 19th Century, 5:14; revolts against, 6:9

Colonization of New France, 4:9–10

Colors: Australian Aboriginals, 1:314, 315; Byzantium, 2:248; China (Tang Dynasty), 2:254, 262; Europe (Middle Ages), 2:250; Greece (ancient), 1:309, 311; Mesopotamia, 1:232, 234, 271, 303–4; Middle Ages, 2:248; United States (Civil War era), 5:272. *See also* Purple color

Colosseum, 1:107

Colt, Miriam Davis, 5:62, 105, 206, 279

Columbaria, 1:522

Columbia disaster, 6:189–90

Columbus, Christopher, 3:1, 10; 5:122

Combs: China (Tang Dynasty), 2:263; Europe (Middle Ages), 2:260

Comintern, 6:257

Comitia centuriata, 1:351

Comitia tributa, 1:351

Commerce. *See* Merchants; Retail sales; Trade

Committee of Union and Progress, 5:391–92

Common Book of Prayer, 3:367

Commoners: Aztec, 3:280–81; England (15th & 16th Centuries), 3:271–72; England (Victorian era), 5:109; Maya, 3:279; Spain (15th & 16th Centuries), 3:274–75

Common law: England (17th & 18th Centuries), 4:391–94; England (Victorian era), 5:335; Italy (15th & 16th Centuries), 3:306

Common law marriages in Latin America, 6:43–44

Common Sense Teachings for the Japanese Children (Ekken), 4:512–15

Communal property in Spain (15th & 16th Centuries), 3:95

Communes, 2:320

Communication: India (20th Century), 6:253–55; Japan (20th Century), 6:258–59; Mongols' system, 2:363; signals, naval, 4:218; smoke signals (Australian Aboriginals), 1:181; Soviet Union, 6:255–58; 20th Century, 6:241–59; United States (1920–39), 6:242–46; United States (1940–59), 6:246–49; United States (1960–90), 6:242, 249–53. *See also specific methods (e.g., telephones)*

Communism: demise of, 6:371; Soviet Union, 6:392–99. *See also* Cold War

Communist Party, Soviet: membership of, 6:396; structure of, 6:395–96, 398

Community Action program, 6:381

Community colleges, 6:204, 205–6

Compadrazgo, 6:44

Company of One Hundred Associates, 4:10, 351, 372

Compasses: China (19th Century), 5:156; China (Tang Dynasty), 2:281; ocean navigation (17th & 18th Centuries), 4:180–81

Competition: Europe (Middle Ages), 2:97; Vikings, 2:398

Complete Book of Running (Fixx), 6:497, 505

Compurgation (Middle Ages), 2:326, 327, 330

Computers: India (20th Century), 6:254; United States (1940–59), 6:119; United States (1960–90), 6:250–51. *See also* Personal computers (PCs)

Computer virus, 6:253

Comte, Auguste, 5:179

Conan Doyle, Arthur, 5:191

Concentration camps. *See* Holocaust

Concilia plebis, 1:351

Concrete, 1:227

Concubines: China (Tang Dynasty), 2:46, 60; Islamic World (Middle Ages), 2:48; Mesopotamia, 1:65, 110; Middle Ages, 2:40; Ottoman Empire, 3:260, 267. *See also* Polygamy

Conestoga wagons, 4:318

Confederate Army (U.S. Civil War), 5:42–44, 71–72. *See also* Civil War (United States)

Confederate Bible Society, 5:189

Confederate Conscription Act, 5:99–101

Confederate Constitution, 5:490–92

Confederate Subsistence Department, 5:222

Confession: Catholicism (Spain, Italy, England), 3:380, 382; Europe (Middle Ages), 2:459; Maya, 3:419–20

Confessions (Rousseau), 4:210

Confirmation: Catholicism (Spain, Italy, England), 3:380–81; Christianity (England, Spain, Italy), 3:31; England (Victorian era), 5:463; Spain (15th & 16th Centuries), 3:34

Conflict of the Orders, 1:337

Confucianism: China (19th Century), 5:322, 447, 451–52, 463, 464; China (Tang Dynasty),

Centuries), 3:241; United States (Western Frontier), 5:234

Deus ex machina, 1:427

Devi, Phoolan, 6:79–80

Devil in Catholicism, 3:363

DeVoto, Bernard, 5:46–48, 231

Devshirme, 2:318; 3:349

Dewey, John, 5:177, 452; 6:199, 200, 204

Dharma, 1:206, 352–53, 466; 5:466

Dhotis, 5:286

Dial-a-prayer, 6:573

Dialects: Europe (Middle Ages), 2:168; Greece (ancient), 1:176, 334; India (ancient), 1:431; Italy (15th & 16th Centuries), 3:163; Japan (17th & 18th Centuries), 4:212; Rome (ancient), 1:189; Spain (15th & 16th Centuries), 3:161–62; Sumerian, 1:194. *See also* Language

Diamonds in Latin America, 5:132

Diapers: life at sea (17th & 18th Centuries), 4:79; United States (1960–90), 6:361

Diarrhea, 5:199, 204

Díaz, Porfirio, 5:159, 179

Dice: England (15th & 16th Centuries), 3:318; Europe (Middle Ages), 2:367, 369, 372; India (ancient), 1:449; Italy (15th & 16th Centuries), 3:323; Mesopotamia, 1:406; Rome (ancient), 1:415–16; Spain (15th & 16th Centuries), 3:315, 321; United States (Civil War era), 5:429; Vikings, 2:375

Dickens, Charles: Christmas, writings on, 5:406; Lao She, influence on, 5:195; magazines, stories published in, 5:189–90; popularity in U.S., 5:181, 184–85; white collar workers, writings on, 5:83, 110

Dickstein, Morris, 6:222

Dictators of ancient Rome, 1:351

Diderot, Denis, 4:210

Diet: Africa (17th & 18th Centuries), 4:240–42, 430; Australia, colonial, 4:49, 51, 242–43; Australian Aboriginals, 1:260, 261; Aztec, 3:248; Byzantium, 2:190, 197, 208–10; changes after European conquest of Americas, 3:221–22, 236; China (19th Century), 5:248; China (Tang Dynasty), 2:128, 187, 197, 204–6, 455; Civil War soldiers, 5:219–27; as cure (Middle Ages), 2:179; England (15th & 16th Centuries), 3:238–39; England (1914–18), 6:303; England (17th & 18th Centuries), 4:140, 245–48; England (Victorian era), 5:218, 237–42; Europe (Middle Ages), 2:124, 197, 198–201, 277; France (1914–18), 6:303; Germany (1914–18), 6:303, 304; Greece (ancient), 1:256; Inca, 3:105, 106; India (19th Century), 5:219, 242–44; India (20th Century), 6:315–17; Inuit, 6:320–21; Islamic World (Middle Ages), 2:282; Islamic World (19th Century), 5:247, 468–69; Italy (15th & 16th Centuries), 3:242; Japan (17th & 18th Centuries), 4:114, 146, 229, 248–50; Japan (20th Century), 6:319–20; Latin America (19th Century), 5:219, 244–47; Latin America (20th Century), 6:314–15; Maya, 3:246–47; Mesopotamia, 1:246, 263; Native Americans (colonial New England), 4:250–51; Native Americans (New England, colonial), 4:61–62; New England, colonial, 4:117–18, 250–53; 19th Century, 5:218–48;

North American colonial frontier, 4:244–45; Nubia, 1:259; Ottoman, 3:244–45; Polynesia, 2:210–12; Rome (ancient), 1:256; seamen, 4:253–55; 17th & 18th Centuries, 4:238–55; United States (1920–39), 6:306–9; United States (Western Frontier), 5:218, 227–37; Vikings, 2:202–3. *See also* Food; *specific types of food and drink*

Diet (Japan governmental body), 6:399–400

Diet plans, 6:280, 302, 310

Digest of Roman Law, 1:365

Dillinger, John, 6:416

Dining rooms in Victorian England, 5:263

Dinner: England (15th & 16th Centuries), 3:237; England (17th & 18th Centuries), 4:247; England (Victorian era), 5:219, 238, 240–42; Europe (Middle Ages), 2:201; Latin America (20th Century), 6:315; life at sea (17th & 18th Centuries), 4:254; New England, colonial, 4:252; North American colonial frontier, 4:244; Ottoman Empire, 3:244; 17th & 18th Centuries, 4:239; United States (Western Frontier), 5:234. *See also* Meals

Dinner parties. *See* Banquets

Diocletian, 1:389

Dionysius, 1:480, 492

Dioscorides, 2:181, 188

Diphtheria: England (Victorian era), 5:209; Spain (15th & 16th Centuries), 3:194

Diplomats (Mesopotamia), 1:139, 155, 343

"Dirty wars" (Latin America 20th Century): deaths in, 6:8, 33, 44; historical overview of, 6:480–81; Honduras, 6:370; women's role in protests, 6:61, 77

Disciples of Christ, 5:458

Disco, 6:547

Discovery, 6:189

Discovery and Conquest of Mexico, The (Castillo), 3:421–22

Discrimination: Africa (20th Century), 6:193; Catholic Church condemnation of, 6:577; China (Tang Dynasty), 2:324; England (17th & 18th Centuries), 4:492–93; India (20th Century), 6:110, 140, 154–56; Inuit, 6:161; Japan (20th Century), 6:140, 159–61; Jews (17th & 18th Centuries), 4:483; Latin America (20th Century), 6:134; Title IX of Education Amendments of 1972, 6:618–19; 20th Century, 6:139–61; United States (1920–39), 6:145–49, 516; United States (1940–59), 6:16, 150–51, 375–76; United States (1960–90), 6:110, 129, 151–54. *See also* Anti-Semitism; Civil rights movement

Diseases: Africa (17th & 18th Centuries), 4:220–21; Africa (20th Century), 6:293–95; China (Tang Dynasty), 2:185–86, 192; England (17th & 18th Centuries), 4:224; England (Victorian era), 5:451; Europe (Middle Ages), 2:181; 15th & 16th Centuries, 3:188–90, 194, 196, 199; Greece (ancient), 1:294–98; India (ancient), 1:301–2; Inuit, 6:295–96; Japan (20th Century), 6:291; Mesopotamia, 1:284–88; Native Americans (colonial New England), 4:88, 231; 19th Century working-class people, 5:217; North American colonial frontier, 4:223; Paris (Middle Ages), 2:114–15; Puritans, religious doctrine, 4:233; Rome (ancient), 1:298–301; Soviet Union, 6:288; Spain (15th & 16th Centuries), 3:194; United States (Civil War era), 5:137; United States (1960–90), 6:278; Vikings, 2:164. *See also specific diseases*

Disney, Walt, 6:98, 521

Disneyland, 6:98–99

Dispensaries, 4:225

Disraeli, Benjamin, 5:10

Dissection: Greece (ancient), 1:296; Mesopotamia, 1:287; Rome (ancient), 1:301

Dissenters, 4:471–73, 491–92

Distilleries in colonial New England, 4:265–66

Ditches, 4:333

Divination: Inca, 3:392–93; Japan (17th & 18th Centuries), 4:423

Divine Comedy (Dante), 2:461; 3:396

Divine right of kings, 3:284

Divine River judgments in Mesopotamia, 1:359, 362, 526

Diviners: Greece (ancient), 1:379; Mesopotamia, 1:370, 527; Rome (ancient), 1:495, 496. *See also* Entrails, reading of

Divorce: ancient world, 1:39–40; Byzantium, 2:63; Catholic Church views on (1960–90), 6:577; China (Tang Dynasty), 2:41, 46–47; England (17th & 18th Centuries), 4:37–38; Europe (Middle Ages), 2:41, 42; Greece (ancient), 1:45, 47, 68; India (19th Century), 5:41; Islamic World (Middle Ages), 2:40, 49; Islamic World (19th Century), 5:38; Japan (17th & 18th Centuries), 4:40; Jesus Christ on, 3:381; Maya, 3:46; Mesopotamia, 1:39, 41, 42; New England, colonial, 4:42; Polynesia, 2:68; Rome (ancient), 1:37, 50; 17th & 18th Centuries, 4:29; Spain (15th & 16th Centuries), 3:35, 59; 20th Century, 6:33; United States (1920–39), 6:35–36; United States (1940–59), 6:38; United States (1960–90), 6:42; United States (Western Frontier), 5:60; Vikings, 2:44–45, 57

Diwali, 5:396, 406, 414–15

Dix, Dorothea, 5:199

Dixie Primer for Little Folks, 5:160, 167

Dixie Speller, 5:160, 167

Dixon, James, 4:487

Dixon, Thomas, 6:140, 146

Dobiwallas, 5:52

Doblado, Leucadio, 3:227

Dockers (China), 5:94, 115

Doctoral, E.L., 6:379

Doctors. *See* Healers and healing; Physicians

Doctors' Plot (Soviet Union), 6:158

Doctor Zhivago (Pasternak), 6:614–16

Dodge, Richard I., 5:280, 369

Doenitz, Karl, 6:412

Doges: Italy (15th & 16th Centuries), 3:276; Venice, 3:277

Dogfighting: 15th & 16th Centuries, 3:313; Middle Ages, 2:369

Dogs: England (Victorian era), 5:440; Mesopotamia, 1:78, 93; Paris (Middle Ages), 2:114; Polynesia, 2:212; United States (Western Frontier), 5:229; Vikings, 2:462. *See also* Hunting dogs

Dog shooting, 4:424

Dog tents, 5:254, 258

Dokia Makrembolitissa, 2:63

Dolabra, 1:386

Dom Casmurro (Machado de Assis), 5:197

Domestic life: ancient world, 1:19–72; defined, 1:19; 2:29; 6:31; 15th & 16th Centuries, 3:29–88; Middle Ages, 2:29–92; 19th Century, 5:25–79; 17th & 18th Centuries, 4:27–100; 20th Century, 6:31–108. *See also* Children; Family life; Marriage; Sexuality

Domestic Revolutions (Mintz & Kellogg), 6:39

Domestic violence: Africa (17th & 18th Centuries), 4:47; China (Tang Dynasty), 2:333; Europe (Middle Ages), 2:43; Islamic World (Middle Ages), 2:48; Latin America (20th Century),

Lend-lease policy of U.S.

New England, colonial, **4:**62; 19th Century, **5:**41–54; North American colonial frontier, **4:**53; 17th & 18th Centuries, **4:**45–65; Soviet Union, **6:**82; support of family (colonial frontier of North America), **4:**35; 20th Century, **6:**52–60; United States (Civil War era), **5:**42–46, 448; United States (20th Century), **6:**34, 53–55; United States (Western Frontier), **5:**46–50

Menarche, **6:**273

Men-at-arms in Middle Ages, **2:**346–47

Mencius, **5:**464

Mendieta, Salvador, **5:**158

Menelaus, **1:**520

Menes. *See* Narmer

Menestras, **5:**246

Mengele, Joseph, **6:**405, 410

Men of Tomorrow, **6:**54

Men's clothing: Australia, colonial, **4:**285–87; China (Tang Dynasty), **2:**242–43; England (17th & 18th Centuries), **4:**290–92; England (Victorian era), **5:**269, 281–82; Europe (Middle Ages), **2:**237–38, 239; France (17th & 18th Centuries), **4:**292–94; Greece (ancient), **1:**310–12; India (19th Century), **5:**286; Japan (17th & 18th Centuries), **4:**294–96; Latin America (19th Century), **5:**288–89; Middle Ages, **2:**236; Mongols, **2:**245; Native Americans (colonial frontier of North America), **4:**287–89; Native Americans (colonial New England), **4:**296–97; New England, colonial, **4:**296–98; North American colonial frontier, **4:**287–90; Nubia, **1:**312–13; Polynesia, **2:**255, 394; Puritans, **4:**297, 298; seamen, **4:**298–300; 17th & 18th Centuries, **4:**284–300; United States (Civil War era), **5:**274–76; United States (Western Frontier), **5:**277–78; Vikings, **2:**240. *See also* Suits; Uniforms; *specific items (e.g., shirts, trousers, underwear)*

Men's liberation movement in United States, **6:**55

Menstruation: Aristotle on, **1:**297; *Causes and Cures* (Hildgard of Bingen), **2:**477–78; India (ancient), **1:**38; India (20th Century), **6:**104; Mesopotamia, **1:**64; Muslims, **2:**423; Polynesia, **2:**67; United States (1920–39), **6:**273–74

Mental illness and treatment: Greece (ancient), **1:**297; India (19th Century), **5:**211; Mesopotamia, **1:**286; United States (1940–59), **6:**276; United States (1960–90), **6:**130–31, 280–81

Menteshe, **3:**292

Mercenaries (ancient Greece), **1:**380–81

Mercenarii, **1:**129

Merchants: Africa (17th & 18th Centuries), **4:**331; Aztec, **3:**122, 281; China (Tang Dynasty), **2:**229, 321, 324; England (Victorian era), **5:**111; European class in 15th & 16th Centuries, **3:**269; Europe (Middle Ages), **2:**226, 290, 322; 15th & 16th Centuries, **3:**89; Islamic World (Middle Ages), **2:**321; Japan (17th & 18th Centuries), **4:**75, 145–46; Latin America (19th Century), **5:**117; Maya, **3:**200, 278, 372; Ottoman Empire, **3:**118–19; Spain (15th & 16th Centuries), **3:**114, 274; Vikings, **2:**240, 294. *See also* Trade

Merchant vessels (17th & 18th Centuries): clothing, **4:**299; food, **4:**253; government, **4:**362–63; idlers, **4:**363; punishment, **4:**385, 399; seamen, **4:**363; second mates, **4:**363; shipmasters, **4:**362. *See also* Life at sea

Mercury: Inuit, **6:**302; United States (1960–90), **6:**312

Meredith, James, **6:**447, 449

Mergers, **6:**132

Meritocracy (China), **2:**296, 306

Meroitic Empire, **1:**14. *See also* Nubia

Merovingian dynasty, **2:**2

Merry Mount, **4:**441

Mesoamerica. *See* Aztec; Inca; Latin America *entries*; Maya

Mesopotamia: abandonment by spouse, **1:**42–43; abandonment of children, **1:**52, 64; abortion, **1:**52; accounting, **1:**171–72, 174, 184, 196–97; adoption, **1:**42, 53; adoption of slaves, **1:**53, 110; adultery, **1:**42; algebra, **1:**219; amulets, **1:**51, 318, 524, 528, 529, 530; animals, **1:**272; appeals, **1:**359, 360; appearance, **1:**317–19; apprenticeships, **1:**54; architecture, **1:**271; art, **1:**230–32; astrology, **1:**219, 526, 528–29; astronomy, **1:**209, 219, 221, 528–29; banquets, **1:**343; barbers, **1:**360; bas-reliefs, **1:**230–31; bathing rooms, **1:**271; battering rams, **1:**372; battle casualties, **1:**287, 370, 372, 373; beards, **1:**317; beds, **1:**273; beer, **1:**263, 286; bees, **1:**78; birds, **1:**220, 527; board games, **1:**406; boat building, **1:**157; bows and arrows, **1:**393–94; boxing, **1:**405; brain surgery, **1:**286; branding of slaves, **1:**489; bread, **1:**246; bricks, **1:**270; bride-price, **1:**40–41; bronze, **1:**232, 272, 318; calendar and time, **1:**208–9, 528; camels, **1:**78, 156; canoes, **1:**158; captives as slaves, **1:**109, 373; caravans, **1:**78, 141, 156, 157, 158; carpentry, **1:**120; cartography, **1:**221; castration, **1:**62, 64, 286; cataloguing and classifying, **1:**219–20, 220; cattle, **1:**77; chairs, **1:**272; chariots, **1:**391, 392; cheese, **1:**246, 263; childbirth, **1:**51–52, 285, 287; childless couples, **1:**42; children, **1:**21–23, 51–55; clans, **1:**119; clay tablets, **1:**173–75, 183–84; clothing, **1:**303–5; colors, **1:**232, 234, 271, 303–4; concubines, **1:**65, 110; construction industry, **1:**121; contraception, **1:**64, 66; contracts, **1:**142; cooking methods, **1:**247–48; **2:**246–47; corpses, care of, **1:**506; correspondence, **1:**196; cosmetics, **1:**317–19, 318; counterfeit money, **1:**132; courts and judges, **1:**359–60; craftsmen, **1:**119–22, 330; creation stories, **1:**453–54, 507; crowns, **1:**318; cuneiform, **1:**1, 172–74, 218–19; curses, **1:**525; dance, **1:**420–22; daughters, **1:**22, 52; death, burial, and the afterlife, **1:**456, 507–11; death penalty, **1:**361; debt slavery, **1:**109, 133; decimal system, **1:**218; deities, **1:**119, 455–56, 471–74, 486–87; deportation, **1:**330, 371; dice, **1:**406; diet, **1:**246, 263; diplomats and ambassadors, **1:**139, 155, 343; diseases, **1:**284–88; dissection, **1:**287; diviners, **1:**370, 527; divorce, **1:**39, 41, 42; dogs, **1:**78, 93; donkeys, **1:**77–78, 156, 158; doors, **1:**271; dowry, **1:**40–41, 110; dreams and dream interpretation, **1:**455; drink, **1:**263; drinking water, **1:**92; drugs, **1:**220, 283, 285–86; dyes, **1:**121, 303; eating habits, **1:**247; economic life, **1:**74; education, **1:**54, 183–86; eldercare, **1:**53, 110; engineering, **1:**392; entrails, reading of, **1:**527; envelopes, **1:**174; epics, **1:**194–96; equinoxes, **1:**209, 219; estates and

inheritances, **1:**53–54, 110; ethnicity, **1:**330; eunuchs, **1:**65; exorcists, **1:**283, 284, 285, 527, 528; eye doctors, **1:**283; family life, **1:**21–23; famine and starvation, **1:**287, 501; fasting, **1:**341, 509, 528; fathers' role, **1:**21–22; fertility plays and festivals, **1:**437; fireplaces, **1:**271; fish, **1:**247; floods, **1:**76; floorplans, **1:**271; floors and floor coverings, **1:**121, 273; food, **1:**246–49; footwear, **1:**304; foreigners, treatment of, **1:**330, 344; fortifications, **1:**369–70; fowl, **1:**247–48; fruit, **1:**246–47; furnishings and goods, **1:**272, 273; games, **1:**405–8; geometry, **1:**219; ghosts, **1:**509–10, 529; glass, **1:**121; gold coins, **1:**131, 132; gold jewelry, **1:**317, 318; government, **1:**339, 340–44; grains, **1:**246; guilds, **1:**119; hairstyles, **1:**317–19; harems, **1:**286, 347; headdresses, **1:**317; health and medicine, **1:**283–88; helmets, military, **1:**392; heralds, **1:**360; herbs and spices, **1:**247–48; hieroglyphics, **1:**172; historical overview, **1:**1–3; history of, **1:**1–3; holidays, festivals, and spectacles, **1:**435–37; homosexuality, **1:**64; honey, **1:**247; horses, **1:**78, 140; hours, calculation of, **1:**209; housing, **1:**270–73; human sacrifices, **1:**486; human waste disposal, **1:**92, 272; hunting, **1:**392, 405–8; hygiene, **1:**248; hymns, **1:**194–95; ideograms, **1:**172; incest, **1:**65; infant mortality, **1:**52; intercalary month, **1:**209; irrigation, **1:**75, 78, 79; ivory, **1:**273; javelins, **1:**394; jewelry, **1:**317–19; kings, **1:**340–44, 370, 372; lamentation-priests, **1:**487; landowners, **1:**330, 371; language and writing, **1:**1, 171–75, 183, 184, 196, 197, 343; latrines, **1:**92, 271; law, **1:**359–62; leather, **1:**122, 303; lesbianism, **1:**65; lexical lists, **1:**220; life expectancy, **1:**287; lighting, **1:**271; linen, **1:**303; literature, **1:**184, 193–97; locusts, **1:**76, 287; looting of conquered nations, **1:**317, 370–71, 372–73; lunar calendar, **1:**208–9; lunar festivals, **1:**436; luxury items, trade in, **1:**140; magic and superstition, **1:**283, 284, 524, 525–31; map of, **1:**2; marketplaces, **1:**91; marriage, **1:**21, 22, 40–43; marriage of slaves, **1:**110, 489; mathematics, **1:**218–19; meat, **1:**246–47; medical fees, **1:**283–84; medical malpractice, **1:**287; medical texts, **1:**285–86; menstruating women, **1:**64; mental illness, **1:**286; metal artwork, **1:**232; metalworkers, **1:**122; midwives, **1:**52, 283; military draft, **1:**371; milk and dairy products, **1:**246, 263; money, **1:**76, 130, 131–33; mourning rights, **1:**508–9; mud huts, **1:**271; music, **1:**347, 420–22, 487; musical instruments, **1:**421; mustaches, **1:**317; mythology, **1:**194–96, 436, 453–54, 455, 509; names, **1:**22, 52, 119, 453; natural disasters, **1:**287; new year's celebration, **1:**435–37; nomads, **1:**79–80; numbers, **1:**173, 218; obelisks, **1:**231; old age, **1:**287; omens, **1:**272, 285, 436, 526–28; onions, **1:**246; oracles, **1:**530; ovens, **1:**247; paint, **1:**232; paintings and drawings, **1:**231, 232; palaces, **1:**90, 92, 342; parents, care of, **1:**53, 110; paternity issues, **1:**54; perfume, **1:**319; perjury, **1:**359; physicians, **1:**283–84; pictographs, **1:**1, 172, 174; picture carvers, **1:**231; plague, **1:**287; plays, **1:**435, 436; poetry, **1:**196; polo, **1:**406; polygamy, **1:**42; pornography, **1:**63; pottery, **1:**120; prayers, **1:**194, 486–87, 525, 530; pregnancy, **1:**285, 287; prescriptions, **1:**286; priests and religious ritual, **1:**65, 407, 437, 454, 484, 485–89, 526–27; prisoners of war,

Mining: Africa (17th & 18th Centuries), **4:**120; Africa (20th Century), **6:**125; England (17th & 18th Centuries), **4:**176; England (Victorian era), **5:**93, 109; Greece (ancient), **1:**113, 144; Latin America (19th Century), **5:**17; Latin America (20th Century), **6:**56, 103, 134; Rome (ancient), **1:**366; 17th & 18th Centuries, **4:**119

Mining (United States [Western Frontier]): entertainment and relaxation, **5:**435–36; food, **5:**231, 331–32; labor of, **5:**83, 87, 90–92, 99, 102–3; technology, **5:**290, 296–99

Minka, **4:**277

Minks, **5:**119, 122

Mintz, Steven, **6:**39

Minuets (Latin America), **5:**426

Miracle plays, **2:**396

Mirandola, Giovanni Pico della, **3:**8

Mirrors, **2:**259

Misdemeanors: England (15th & 16th Centuries), **3:**303; England (Victorian era), **5:**335. *See also* Crimes

Miserere, **3:**132

Miso, **4:**249

Misora Hibari, **6:**555

Missionaries: Africa (19th Century), **6:**601; Africa (17th & 18th Centuries), **4:**184; Africa (20th Century), **6:**601; China (19th Century), **5:**156; Inuit, **6:**603; Maya, Aztec, and Inca, **3:**23, 156, 419–21; North American colonial frontier, **4:**489–90

Mississippi River trade, **5:**125

Miss Ravenel's Conversion from Secession to Loyalty (DeForest), **5:**188

Mistral, Gabriela, **6:**77

Mistry, Rohinton, **6:**229

M'ita, **3:**72, 107, 204

Mitchell, John, Jr., **5:**407

Mitchell, Sally, **5:**419

Miti chimalli, **3:**85

Mitimas, **3:**125, 282–83

Mitnal, **3:**398

Moats, **2:**285

Mobile telephones (Japan), **6:**259

Moby Dick (Melville), **4:**218

Moccasins, **4:**288, 304–5

Moche culture, **3:**3–5, 357

Model Cities Act of 1966, **6:**382

Model T, **6:**115, 116, 357–58

Modern Cookery for Private Families (Acton), **5:**237

Modernism, **6:**220

Mohammed Ali, **5:**17, 353–54; **6:**11

Mohawk River, **4:**317

Molly Hootch case, **6:**214

Monasteries: Buddhism, **2:**432, 441, 444; Byzantium, **2:**64, 432; China (Tang Dynasty), **2:**432, 437–40; Europe (Middle Ages), **2:**180, 432, 433–36; London (Middle Ages), **2:**111; Middle Ages, **2:**407, 432–40; Vikings, **2:**437

Monastic schools: Europe (Middle Ages), **2:**148–49; Vikings, **2:**152

Mondale, Walter, **6:**560, 561

Monday as holiday in England, **4:**436

Money: Africa (17th & 18th Centuries), **4:**132, 135; ancient world, **1:**130–38; Aztec, **3:**122; China (Tang Dynasty), **2:**103, 281; coins, ancient Greek art on, **1:**238; counterfeit, Mesopotamia, **1:**132; England (15th & 16th Centuries), **3:**110–11; England (17th & 18th

Centuries), **4:**139; Greece (ancient), **1:**130, 134–35; India (ancient), **1:**131, 137–38; invention of coinage, **1:**131; Islamic World (Middle Ages), **2:**132; Japan (17th & 18th Centuries), **4:**144–45; Maya, **3:**101; Mesopotamia, **1:**76, 130, 131–33; Polynesia, **2:**256; Rome (ancient), **1:**135–37; 17th & 18th Centuries, **4:**132–33; Vikings, **2:**136–37; wampum, **4:**138

Moneychangers: Greece (ancient), **1:**135; Islamic World (Middle Ages), **2:**104–5

Mongols: adultery, **2:**343; bows and arrows, **2:**362; children, **2:**384; Christianity and, **2:**429; clans and tribes, **2:**31, 37; clothing, **2:**66, 245–47; communication system, **2:**363, 385; cosmetics, **2:**258; crimes, **2:**343; death penalty, **2:**326, 343; deities, **2:**428; drink, **2:**219–22; drunkenness, **2:**220, 221; estates and inheritance, **2:**38; fermentation, **2:**213, 220; footwear, **2:**245; hair, **2:**265; headdresses, **2:**245–46; health and medicine, **2:**178, 179, 190–94; historical overview, **2:**20–23; hunting, **2:**363, 377, 384–86; Islam and, **2:**429; kinship, **2:**37–39; law, **2:**326, 341–44; leather, **2:**51, 66, 245, 362; military service, **2:**362; milk and dairy products, **2:**66, 220; personal appearance, **2:**257, 264–67; physicians, **2:**190–91; polygamy, **2:**37, 40; prophecy, **2:**428–29; punishment, **2:**384; religious beliefs, **2:**427–29; shamans, **2:**190–91, 427–28; sheep and goats, **2:**66; shields, **2:**362; silk, **2:**362; taboos, **2:**428; taxes, **2:**343, 427; trade, **2:**140; treason, **2:**343; trousers, **2:**245; underwear, **2:**362; warfare and weapons, **2:**361–63; wine, **2:**221; women, **2:**30, 64–67, 245

Monjas, **3:**352

Monks: Buddhism, **2:**417, 432, 433, 438–40; Europe (Middle Ages), **2:**258, 433, 434–35

Monk's Confession, A (Guibert of Nogent), **2:**475–77

Monogamy: China (Tang Dynasty), **2:**46; Maya, **3:**46. *See also* Marriage

Monopolies: 17th & 18th Centuries, **4:**133–34; trading companies (17th & 18th Centuries), **4:**149–50

Monosodium glutamate (MSG), **6:**312

Monotheism: defined, **3:**361; Islam, **5:**456, 468; **6:**594; Jews and Christians, **6:**141; Middle Ages, **2:**408, 409; 17th & 18th Centuries, **4:**464–65

Monrovia, founding of, **5:**343

Montaigne, **3:**133, 135

Montana roundups, **5:**89

Monte delle Doti, **3:**38, 81

Monterey International Pop Festival, **6:**545

Montezuma, the Last of the Aztecs (Maturin), **5:**183

Montgomery, Bernard, **6:**468

Months, names of: Rome (ancient), **1:**214; Vikings, **2:**163. *See also* Calendars

Montiel, Tiburcio, **5:**341

Montreal fur trade, **4:**137

Moon: Cult of Moon among Incas, **3:**55, 71, 143; day of week named for, **3:**128; health associated with in 15th & 16th Centuries, **3:**188, 193; Inca time based on, **3:**141, 142, 152, 205; Maya, **3:**136, 201, 202; Spain (15th & 16th Centuries), **3:**95. *See also* Astronomy

Moon, Sun Myung, **6:**581

Moon Festival, **2:**456

"Moonies," **6:**581

Moon landing, **6:**188

Moore, Marinda Branson, **5:**167

Moors, **3:**305

Morality: China (19th Century), **5:**451–53; England (Victorian era), **5:**446, 449–51; Europe (Middle Ages), **2:**159; France (17th & 18th Centuries), **4:**475; human rights (1933–45), **6:**561–63; Islamic World (19th Century), **5:**453–55; Islamic World (20th Century), **6:**568; Japan (17th & 18th Centuries), **4:**456; Japan (20th Century), **6:**566–67; 19th Century, **5:**446–55; Quakers (17th & 18th Centuries), **4:**490; 20th Century, **6:**560–68; United States (Civil War era), **5:**447–48; United States (1920–90), **6:**563–66

Morelos, José María, **5:**470

Morgan, Edward P., **6:**542, 543

Morgan, Marabel, **6:**73

Morgan, Sarah, **5:**272

Morgenthau, Henry, **6:**16, 150, 616–18

Morisco, **3:**274

Mormons: United States (Civil War era), **5:**458; United States (1920–39), **6:**569; United States (1960–90), **6:**581, 586; United States (Western Frontier), **5:**348

Morning dress, **5:**284

Morocco: colonial power over, **6:**230; as part of Ottoman Empire, **3:**21. *See also* Islamic World *entries*

Morrill Act (Civil War era), **5:**167

Morrison, Jim, **6:**544

Morrison, Toni, **6:**227

Morsico, **3:**413

Mortality, infant. *See* Infant mortality

Mortality in battles. *See* Battle casualties

Mortality rate. *See* Life expectancy

Mortars (World War I), **6:**353–54

Morte d'Arthur (Marlowe), **3:**206, 209

Mortgages. *See* Housing

Morton, Thomas, **4:**441

Morua, Martin de, **3:**235

Mosaics: Greece (ancient), **1:**267, 277; Rome (ancient), **1:**239, 279

Moscow class structure, **6:**138–39

Moses Maimonides, **2:**156

Mosques: Baghdad (Middle Ages), **2:**117, 118; India (20th Century), **6:**343; Islamic World (Middle Ages), **2:**104, 445–46; Islamic World (19th Century), **5:**469; Muslim, **2:**421, 441

Mosquitoes: Australian Aboriginals, **1:**281; United States (Western Frontier), **5:**105, 203

Moss, Frank, **6:**382

Motecuhzoma I, **3:**310

Motecuhzoma Ilhuicamina, **3:**248

Motecuhzoma Xocoyotzin, **3:**20–21, 168, 297, 341, 356, 421–22

Motepatasca, **3:**249

Mothers Against Drunk Driving (MADD), **6:**323, 329

Mother's Book, The (Child), **5:**161

Motion pictures. *See* Film

Motley, Baker, **6:**442

Motown, **6:**543–44

Moulton, Gary, **5:**202

"Mountain men," **5:**46–47, 230–31

Mount Olympus, **1:**478, 479, 483

Mourning rites: China (Tang Dynasty), **2:**465–66; Greece (ancient), **1:**518; Mesopotamia, **1:**508–9; Polynesia, **2:**469; Rome (ancient), **1:**523

Movement for the Emancipation of Chilean Women, **6:**76

Movies. *See* Film

Moxa, **4:**229–30

Moxibustion therapy, **2:**186

Moyano, María Elena, **6:**76

Mrs. Miniver (film), **6:**523

356, 387–89; wild animals, hunting of, 1:259, 405, 416; wine, 1:87, 259; women's clothing, 1:312–13

Nuclear energy: Japan, 6:192; United States (1960–90), 6:364–65

Nuclear family, defined, 1:21

Nuclear threat, 6:40, 183. *See also* Cold War

Nuclear weapons: invention of, 6:183, 184; United States (1939–45), 6:468–69, 493

Nudity: 15th & 16th Centuries, 3:223; Greek art, 1:237–38. *See also* Sexuality

Nullification crisis (United States), 5:313–14, 316

Numbers: Arabic numerals, 2:165; Aztec, 3:85, 140, 151; England (15th & 16th Centuries), 3:160; Maya, 3:136–37, 200–202; Mesopotamia, 1:173, 218; Roman numerals, 2:165

Numina, 1:454–55

Nun, 1:475

Nunavut Territory: creation and government of, 6:403; land claims agreement (1993), 6:620–22

Nuncheon, 2:201

Núñez, Rafael, 5:341

Nuns: Buddhism, 2:432; Civil War hospitals, 5:201; convents (Byzantium), 2:64; Europe (Middle Ages), 2:53–54, 258, 434–35; Latin America (20th Century), 6:591–92; Middle Ages, 2:51

Nur al-Din, 2:359

Nuremberg Trials, 6:404, 410–12

Nurses: England (Victorian era), 5:110; Soviet Union, 6:290; World War I, 6:61–62

Nursing homes, 6:383

Nut (Egyptian goddess), 1:475, 476

Nutrition: development of field of, 6:302–3; United States (1920–39), 6:307–8; United States (1960–90), 6:310–11, 312

Nuts: Africa (17th & 18th Centuries), 4:240; Byzantium, 2:209; China (Tang Dynasty), 2:204, 206; Greece (ancient), 1:255; India (19th Century), 5:53–54, 244; Vikings, 2:203

Nuzi: women's role, 1:30–31. *See also* Mesopotamia

Nyamakala, 4:154

Nye, David E., 6:358–59

Oath of the Horatii, The (David), 4:454

Oaxaca, Valley of, 3:3

Oaxacan Civilization, 3:3

Obelisks (Mesopotamia), 1:231

Observation and experimentation: Australian Aboriginals, 1:229; China (Tang Dynasty), 2:164; Europe in Middle ages, 2:161; Holocaust victims, 6:409, 410; Islamic World (Middle Ages), 2:167

Obstetrics. *See* Childbirth

Oca, 3:105

Occupations. *See* Professions and occupations

Oceanic exploration and travel: England (17th & 18th Centuries), 4:7–9; map (17th Century), 4:8; 17th & 18th Centuries, 4:1–2, 7, 315

Ocelotl, 3:233

Ochpaniztli, 3:69, 186

O'Connor, Flannery, 6:221

O'Connor, Sandra Day, 6:74

Ocopa, 5:245

Octavian, 1:10. *See also* Augustus Caesar

Odin, 2:399, 412, 413–14

Odoric of Pordenone, Friar, 2:266

Odyssey: on death, burial, and the afterlife, 1:520; educational role of, 1:188; on magic, 1:533; on money, 1:134; on slavery, 1:111, 112; stories of, 1:200, 481; on travel and transportation, 1:161; on women, 1:33–34

Oedipus the King (Sophocles), 1:200

Office of Economic Opportunity, 6:381

Officers. *See* Military officers; Naval officers

Office work, 6:117

Ogden, Peter Skene, 5:47, 49

Oghul Qaimish, 2:65, 246

Ögödei, 2:221, 246, 343, 363, 428

OGPU (Unified State Political Administration), 6:426

Oil: Japan (17th & 18th Centuries), 4:249; lighting in Spain (15th & 16th Centuries), 3:256; Nubia, 1:259. *See also* Olive trees and olive oil

Okitsuga, Tanuma, 4:18

Olaf Sigurdson (Viking king), 2:7

Olaf Skotkonung (Viking king), 2:137, 415

Olaf Tryggvason (Viking king), 2:137, 279, 374, 397, 415

Old age: China (Tang Dynasty), 2:87, 90–92; England (17th & 18th Centuries), 4:84; Europe (Middle Ages), 2:87, 88–89, 183; Greece (ancient), 1:297; India (20th Century), 6:47, 58; Inuit, 6:51; Japan (17th & 18th Centuries), 4:86, 359; Japan (20th Century), 6:292; life at sea (17th & 18th Centuries), 4:89–92; medical care (United States 1960–90), 6:382–83; Mesopotamia, 1:287; Middle Ages, 2:86–92; New England, colonial, 4:88–89; North American colonial frontier, 4:82–83; Rome (ancient), 1:297; 17th & 18th Centuries, 4:80–92; Vikings, 2:87, 89–90

Old Bailey, 5:336

Old English, 3:159

Old Jules (Sandoz), 5:31–32

Oligarchy in India, 1:353

Oliphant, Margaret, 5:191

Oliver Twist (Dickens), 5:181, 185, 190

Olive trees and olive oil: Byzantium, 2:130, 208, 284; Greece (ancient), 1:83, 144, 255, 440; Islamic World (Middle Ages), 2:206; Italy (15th & 16th Centuries), 3:243; Rome (ancient), 1:85, 99, 256

Ollamaliztli, 3:315–16, 326

Ollo podrida, 3:241

Olluca, 5:246

Olmec Civilization, 3:3

Olmstead, Frederick Law, 5:421

Olmstead v. U.S. (1927), 6:416

Olympic Games: Africa (20th Century), 6:510; England (Victorian era), 5:402–3; Europe (20th Century), 6:499; Greece (ancient), 1:6, 63, 66, 211, 381, 411–13, 479; reinitiated in 1896, 6:498; South Africa ban, 6:511; 20th Century, 6:498; United States (1960–90), 6:506–7

Omecihuatl, 3:373

Omens: ancient world, 1:524–25; Aztec, 3:218, 354; China (Tang Dynasty), 2:164; Greece (ancient), 1:379; Inca, 3:393; Mesopotamia, 1:272, 285, 436, 526–28; Polynesia, 2:364, 365. *See also* Diviners; Entrails, reading of

Ometecuhtli, 3:373

Ometeotl, 3:341, 354, 373–74

Omeyocan, 3:139, 373

Onam, 5:415

"On Being Brought from Africa to America" (Wheatley), 4:215

One Day in the Life of Ivan Denisovich (Solzhenitsyn), 6:234

One Flew over the Cuckoo's Nest (film), 6:281, 528

One Hundred Days of Reform of 1898 (China), 5:324

Ongghot, 2:428

Only Yesterday (Lewis), 6:12

Onsen, 4:229

On the Origin of Species by Means of Natural Selection (Darwin), 5:154

Opera: Latin America (19th Century), 5:426; New York Opera Association, 6:547

Opium: China (19th Century), 5:131, 375–76; England (Victorian era), 5:207; India (19th Century), 5:54, 442; Latin America (19th Century), 5:246

Opium War: causes of, 5:375; Chinese defeat in, 5:323; effects of, 5:130; foreign influence resulting from, 5:176; historical overview, 5:13; start of, 5:132, 355; Taiping Rebellion resulting from, 5:452

Oppenheimer, J. Robert, 6:184, 185–86

Oracle of Pachacamac, 3:392

Oracles: ancient world, 1:485; Greece (ancient), 1:493–94; Mesopotamia, 1:530

Oral tradition: Australian Aboriginals, 1:192; Europe (Middle Ages), 2:169; Middle Ages, 2:145–46, 167; Polynesia, 2:23, 25, 176; Vikings, 2:172

Oratory (ancient Rome), 1:191, 203, 205

Orchestras: Latin America (19th Century), 5:427; United States (1920–39), 6:245

Ordeal by Slander (Lattimore), 6:376

Ordeals to determine innocence/guilt: Europe (Middle Ages), 2:327; Vikings, 2:330

Order of Santo Stefano, 3:276

Ordinary seamen on merchant vessels (17th & 18th Centuries), 4:363

Oregon Trail, 5:6, 487–88

Oresme, Nicole, 2:161

Oresteia, 1:200–201

Orfeo, 3:213

Organically grown food, 6:312

Organized crime (Soviet Union), 6:430

Organized labor: Latin America (19th Century), 5:326. *See also* Labor unions

Organ transplants, 6:277

Orhan, 3:180

Origen, 2:70, 76

Orisha, 4:466

Orlando furioso (Ariosto), 3:206, 213

Orlando innamorato (Boiardo), 3:206, 213

Orphanages (England), 5:35, 389

Orphics, 1:520

Ortaoyuno, 3:350

Ortega, Aniceto, 5:426

Ortenberg, David, 6:158

Orthodox Church. *See* Greek Orthodox Church; Russian Orthodox Church

Osaka (17th & 18th Centuries), 4:144–45, 337

Osamu, Dazai, 6:237

Oshogatsu, 4:438

Osiris: death of, 1:289; description of, 1:476; family of, 1:475; as god of the dead, 1:476, 507, 512; Set's feud with, 1:471

Osman, 3:10

Ostia, 1:147–48

Ostraka, 1:178–79, 188

Ostrogothic kingdom, 2:2

Other America, The (Harrington), 6:120, 129, 380

Otogi-zoshi, 4:213

Otomies, 3:5

Otranto, 3:12

Pipa, **2:**390

Pipe organs (Byzantium), **2:**286

Pipes: England (15th & 16th Centuries), **3:**343; Mesopotamia, **1:**421; panpipes, **3:**357. *See also* Bagpipes

Pirates: ancient trade, **1:**138; Australian Aboriginals, **1:**154; England (Victorian era), **5:**333; Greece (ancient), **1:**111, 161; Rome (ancient), **1:**163–64; 17th & 18th Centuries, **4:**400; women as, **4:**65

Pistols: United States (Civil War era), **5:**292. *See also* Guns

Pitch pot, **2:**376

Pitti, Buonaccorso, **3:**323

Pius V (Pope), **3:**332

Pius IX (Pope), **5:**471

Pius XII (Pope), **6:**379

Piva, **3:**347

Pizarro, Francisco, **3:**22–23

Pizza, **3:**242

Placer mining, **5:**296–97

Plague: Byzantium, **2:**189–90; Europe (Middle Ages), **2:**311; Greece (ancient), **1:**296; Islamic World (Middle Ages), **2:**85; Mesopotamia, **1:**287; Paris (Middle Ages), **2:**114–15. *See also* Bubonic plague

Planets. *See* Astronomy

Plantations: Latin America (19th Century), **5:**17, 118, 146, 267, 326, 379; United States (Civil War era), **5:**84, 86, 118–20, 137

Plantlife. *See* Botany

Plaster: England (15th & 16th Centuries), **3:**252, 254; United States (Western Frontier), **5:**254

Plate armor, **2:**348–49

Plato, **1:**44, 67, 266, 411, 424, 521

Platter, Thomas, **3:**58

Plautus, **1:**203

Play. *See* Recreational life; *specific type (e.g., Art, Dance, Entertainment, etc.)*

Playing cards. *See* Cards

Plays. *See* Theater

Plebeians, **1:**337, 351

Pledge of Allegiance, **6:**573

Pleiades constellation, **3:**204

Pliny the Elder, **2:**169

Pliny the Younger, **1:**116, 205, 441

Plows: Australia, colonial, **4:**106; Byzantium, **2:**284; China (Tang Dynasty), **2:**126–27; India (19th Century), **5:**302; Vikings, **2:**126. *See also* Horse collars

Plumbing: India (19th Century), **5:**265. *See also* Bathing; Bathrooms

Plunder. *See* Looting of conquered nations

Plutarch, **1:**533

Plymouth Plantation, **4:**251

Pneumonia: United States (1940–59), **6:**275; United States (Western Frontier), **5:**107

Poaching, **5:**334, 335

Pocket boroughs (England), **4:**354

Pocket watches, **5:**2–3

Podesta, **3:**291

Poe, Edgar Allen, **5:**182, 186, 315

Poema de mio Cid, **3:**161

Poetry: Africa (17th & 18th Centuries), **4:**203; Aztec, **3:**354; China (Tang Dynasty), **2:**153, 173–74; England (15th & 16th Centuries), **3:**208–9; Europe (Middle Ages), **2:**169, 170; Europe (20th Century), **6:**217, 218; Greece (ancient), **1:**424, 427; India (ancient), **1:**207; Inuit, **6:**239; Islamic World (Middle Ages), **2:**402; Islamic World (19th & 20th Century), **6:**231; Japan (20th Century), **6:**238–39; Mesopotamia, **1:**196; Middle Ages, **2:**146, 168; New England, colonial, **4:**215; Rome

(ancient), **1:**203, 430; Soviet Union, **6:**233, 234–35; Spain (15th & 16th Centuries), **3:**345; United States (1940–59), **6:**222, 224–25; Vikings, **2:**172, 399. *See also* Love poetry

Pogroms against Jews, **6:**23, 143

Point of Order (De Antonio), **6:**378

Poison gas: World War I, **6:**4; Zyklon B, **6:**408, 413, 488

Poisoning: China (Tang Dynasty), **2:**205; Inuit, **6:**302; Islamic World (Middle Ages), **2:**192; Rome (ancient), **1:**69

Poitiers, Battle of, **2:**472–73

Poland: Holocaust, **6:**405; Jews in, pre-World War II, **6:**144, 270; Ottoman Empire, war against, **3:**12. *See also* Europe *entries*

Polanski, Roman, **6:**515

Polar bears, **6:**321

Police. *See* Law enforcement

Polio, **6:**19

Polio vaccines, **6:**275

Polis. *See* City-states

Politburo, **6:**396

Political life: Africa (17th & 18th Centuries), **4:**330–31; Africa (20th Century), **6:**178; ancient world, **1:**327–401; China (19th Century), **5:**322–24; England (17th & 18th Centuries), **4:**56; England (Victorian era), **5:**318–22; Europe (Middle Ages), **2:**159, 311; holidays and festivals (17th & 18th Centuries), **4:**429; India (20th Century), **6:**10, 78; Islamic World (19th Century), **5:**327; Latin America (19th Century), **5:**324–27; Middle Ages, **2:**287–366; 19th Century, **5:**305–94; purposes, generally, **4:**343; Rome (ancient), **1:**127; 17th & 18th Centuries, **4:**343–415; 20th Century, **6:**369–494; United States (Civil War era), **5:**308–18; urban social structure, **2:**320–25. *See also* Government; Law; Social structure

Political parties: England (17th & 18th Centuries), **4:**352; England (Victorian era) **5:**320. *See also specific parties*

Political statements in art: Greece (ancient), **1:**238; Rome (ancient), **1:**239

Poliziano, Angelo, **3:**213

Polk, Leonidas, **5:**460

Polkas, **5:**426

Pollution: automobile as cause of, **6:**363; England (Victorian era), **5:**135, 141, 210; Greece (ancient), **1:**518; India (ancient), **1:**338; Inuit, **6:**296, 321–22. *See also* Environment

Polo: Byzantium, **2:**403; China (Tang Dynasty), **2:**369, 375; Islamic World (Middle Ages), **2:**402; Mesopotamia, **1:**406

Polybius, **1:**555–57

Polychrome decoration, **3:**352–53

Polygamy: Africa (17th & 18th Centuries), **4:**30; Australian Aboriginals, **1:**28; Greece (ancient), **1:**47; Inca, **3:**52, 142–43; Islamic World (Middle Ages), **2:**40, 48; Islamic World (19th Century), **5:**37, 447, 454; Maya, **3:**46; Mesopotamia, **1:**42; Middle Ages, **2:**40; Mongols, **2:**37, 40; Native Americans (colonial frontier of North America), **4:**34

Polynesia: animism, **2:**408, 430; aristocracy, **2:**299, 308–9; breakfast, **2:**210; brother-sister marriage, **2:**301, 308; chants, **2:**176–77; childbirth, **2:**431; children, **2:**86, 299; clothing, **2:**235, 236, 247, 254–56; coconuts, **2:**211; cooking methods, **2:**211–12; creation stories, **2:**430; dance, **2:**364, 386, 393–94; death, burial, and the afterlife, **2:**431, 459, 469–70; deities, **2:**408, 430; divorce, **2:**68; drink, **2:**213; education, **2:**177; education of

priests, **2:**431; fish, **2:**212; floors and floor coverings, **2:**234, 235; food, **2:**210–12; fortifications, **2:**365; fruits, **2:**211–12; health and medicine, **2:**178; helmets, **2:**365; heroes, **2:**176, 177–78; historical overview, **2:**23–25; housing, **2:**233–35; human sacrifices, **2:**364, 365, 366; infanticide, **2:**68; landowners, **2:**300; language, **2:**167, 175–78; middle class, **2:**300; money, **2:**256; mourning rites, **2:**469; music, **2:**386, 392–94; musical instruments, **2:**387, 392–93; mythology, **2:**176, 177, 430; omens, **2:**364, 365; oral tradition, **2:**23, 25, 176; ovens, **2:**211; population, **2:**308; poultry, **2:**212; priests, **2:**409, 430–31; primogeniture, **2:**67, 308; prisoners of war, **2:**366; religious beliefs, **2:**408, 429–32; religious ceremonies and festivals, **2:**386, 392, 393, 431; roofing, **2:**233, 234; slaves, **2:**300, 469; social structure, **2:**290, 299–300; sweet potatoes, **2:**211–12; taboos, **2:**210–11, 234, 290, 300, 409, 469; tea, **2:**213; temples, **2:**431, 440; treaties, **2:**366; vegetables, **2:**211–12; warfare and weapons, **2:**68, 288, 364–66; weaving, **2:**254; women, **2:**30, 67–69, 364, 394; writing, **2:**176; yams, **2:**211–12

Polytheism: ancient world, **1:**453, 470; China (Tang Dynasty), **2:**408; 15th & 16th Centuries, **3:**361; Greece (ancient), **1:**462; Hinduism, **5:**456; India (19th Century), **5:**456, 466; Middle Ages, **2:**408; Polynesia, **2:**408, 430; Vikings, **2:**408–9, 412. *See also* Deities

Pō, **2:**460

Pomare I, **2:**309

de Pompadour, Madame, **4:**58

Pompey, **1:**69, 164

Pongal, **5:**415

Pontifex Maximus, **1:**495

Pontifical Catholic University of Chile, **5:**180

Poor Law Amendment (England), **5:**35, 321, 381, 388–90

Poor Law "settlements," **4:**84

Poor persons: Catholic Church and, **6:**592; China (Tang Dynasty), **2:**325; Church care of, Europe (Middle Ages), **2:**89; England (15th & 16th Centuries), **3:**272; England (17th & 18th Centuries), **4:**188–89, 274–75, 375–76, 407, 472–73; England (Victorian era), **5:**282, 387–90, 476; Europe (Middle Ages), **2:**323; France (17th & 18th Centuries), **4:**293, 308; India (20th Century), **6:**388; Italy (15th & 16th Centuries), **3:**98–99; Jews as, **6:**142; Latin America (20th Century), **6:**172, 388, 421; seamen's families (17th & 18th Centuries), **4:**44; United States (Civil War era), **5:**137, 139, 383–85; United States (1929–59), **6:**128; United States (1960–90), **6:**128–29, 380–84; Vikings, **2:**295

Poor Richard's Almanac (Franklin), **4:**173–74

Popes: age of, **3:**40; Catholicism (Spain, Italy, England), **3:**15, 135, 362, 364, 366; legal jurisdiction (Middle Ages), **2:**328–29; power established, **2:**411, 425. *See also* Catholic Church

Popinae, **1:**129

Popol Vuh, **3:**104, 214–15, 397–98, 416–19

Popol Vuh: The Mayan Book of the Dawn of Life (Tedlock), **3:**416–19

Poppies, **5:**131

Poppo, **2:**415

Population: Changan (Tang Dynasty), **2:**117; China (19th Century), **5:**144; China (Tang Dynasty), **2:**127, 323; cities during 20th Century, **6:**162, 163; city dwellers in Europe

Roads

Vaishnavas

ABOUT THE CONTRIBUTORS

General Editor

Joyce E. Salisbury is Frankenthal Professor of History at University of Wisconsin–Green Bay. She has a doctorate in medieval history from Rutgers University. Professor Salisbury is an award-winning teacher: she was named CASE (Council for Advancement and Support of Education) Professor of the Year for Wisconsin in 1991 and has brought her concern for pedagogy to this encyclopedia. Professor Salisbury has written or edited more than 10 books, including the award-winning *Perpetua's Passion: Death and Memory of a Young Roman Woman*, *The Beast Within: Animals in the Middle Ages*, and *The West in the World*, a textbook on western civilization.

Volume Editor

Andrew E. Kersten received his B.A. in History at the University of Wisconsin–Madison and his M.A. and Ph.D. at University of Cincinnati. Since 1997, he has taught in the History Department at the University of Wisconsin–Green Bay. Kersten has been published in the *Queen City Heritage*, *The Michigan Historical Review*, and *The Missouri Historical Review* and has contributed to several anthologies and encyclopedias, and is the author of *Race, Jobs, and the War: The FEPC in the Midwest, 1941–1946* (2000) and the co-editor of *Politics and Progress: The State and American Society since 1865* (2001). Currently, he is writing a history of the American Federation of Labor during World War II.

Additional Contributors

E. Taylor Atkins, Northern Illinois University
Benjamin Cohen, University of Utah
Katherine B. Eaton, Independent Scholar
Tyler Fleming, University of Texas at Austin
Jennifer Ham, University of Wisconsin–Green Bay
Roy S. Hanashiro, University of Michigan–Flint

Waïl S. Hassan, Illinois State University
Matthew Heaton, University of Texas at Austin
Adam Hornbuckle, Independent Scholar
Bruce E. Johansen, University of Nebraska at Omaha
Susan Orpett Long, John Carroll University
Molly Benjamin Patterson, University of Wisconsin–Madison
Louis G. Perez, Illinois State University
Paula Rentmeester, University of Wisconsin–Green Bay
James Stanlaw, Illinois State University
Pamela Stern, University of Waterloo
Roger K. Thomas, Illinois State University
Molly Todd, University of Wisconsin–Madison

We also acknowledge the following authors of Greenwood Publishing's "Daily Life through History" series, whose books contributed much to entries in the current volume:

Katherine B. Eaton, *Daily Life in the Soviet Union*. Forthcoming.
Neil M. Heyman, *Daily Life During World War I*, 2002.
Eugenia Kaledin, *Daily Life in the United States, 1940–1959: Shifting Worlds*, 2000.
David E. Kyvig, *Daily Life in the United States, 1920–1939: Decades of Promise and Pain*, 2002.
Myron A. Marty, *Daily Life in the United States, 1960–1990: Decades of Discord*, 1997.
Eve Nussbaum Soumerai and Carol D. Schulz, *Daily Life During the Holocaust*, 1998.